THE
CHURCHILL
DOCUMENTS

BOOKS BY MARTIN GILBERT

THE CHURCHILL BIOGRAPHY

Volume III: The Challenge of War, 1914–1916
Document Volume III* (in two parts)
Volume IV: World in Torment, 1917–1922
Document Volume IV* (in three parts)
Volume V: Prophet of Truth, 1922–1939
Document Volume V*: The Exchequer Years, 1922–1929
Document Volume V*: The Wilderness Years, 1929–1935
Document Volume V*: The Coming of War, 1936–1939
Volume VI: Finest Hour, 1939–1941
Churchill War Papers I*: At the Admiralty, September 1939–May 1940
Churchill War Papers II*: Never Surrender, May–December 1940
Churchill War Papers III*: The Ever-Widening War, 1941
Volume VII: Road to Victory, 1941–1945
Volume VIII: Never Despair, 1945–1965
Churchill: A Photographic Portrait
Churchill: A Life

*The document volumes are also being published by Hillsdale College Press as *The Churchill Documents*

OTHER BOOKS

The Appeasers (with Richard Gott)
The European Powers, 1900–1945
The Roots of Appeasement
Children's Illustrated Bible Atlas
Atlas of British Charities
Atlas of American History
Atlas of the Arab-Israeli Conflict
Atlas of British History
Atlas of the First World War
Atlas of the Second World War
Atlas of the Holocaust
Atlas of Jewish History
Atlas of Russian History
The Jews of Russia: Their History in Maps
Jerusalem Illustrated History Atlas
Sir Horace Rumbold: Portrait of a Diplomat
Jerusalem: Rebirth of a City, 1800–1900
Jerusalem in the Twentieth Century
Exile and Return: The Struggle for
Jewish Statehood
Auschwitz and the Allies
The Jews of Hope:
The Plight of Soviet Jewry Today
Shcharansky: Hero of Our Time

The Holocaust: The Jewish Tragedy
The Boys: Triumph over Adversity
The First World War
The Battle of the Somme
The Second World War
D-Day
The Day the War Ended
In Search of Churchill
A History of the Twentieth Century,
1900–1933: Empires in Conflict
A History of the Twentieth Century,
1934–1951: Descent into Barbarism
A History of the Twentieth Century,
1952–1999: Challenge to Civilization
Never Again: A History of the Holocaust
The Jews in the Twentieth Century
Letters to Auntie Fori: The 5,000-Year
History of the Jewish People
Israel: A History
The Righteous: The Unsung Christian
Heroes of the Holocaust
Kristallnacht: Prelude to Destruction
Churchill and America
Churchill and the Jews

EDITIONS OF DOCUMENTS

Britain and Germany Between the Wars
Plough My Own Furrow: The Life of Lord Allen of Hurtwood
Servant of India: Diaries of the Viceroy's Private Secretary, 1905–1910

THE
CHURCHILL
DOCUMENTS
Martin Gilbert

Volume 11
The Exchequer Years
1922–1929

Hillsdale College Press, Hillsdale, Michigan

Hillsdale College Press
33 East College Street
Hillsdale, Michigan 49242
www.hillsdale.edu

Originally published in 1979 by William Heinemann Ltd. in Great Britain and in 1981 by Houghton Mifflin in the United States.

Printed in the United States of America

Printed and bound by Edwards Brothers, Ann Arbor, Michigan

Cover design by Hesseltine & DeMason, Ann Arbor, Michigan

THE CHURCHILL DOCUMENTS
Volume 11: *The Exchequer Years, 1922–1929*

Library of Congress Control Number: 2006934101

ISBN: 978-0-916308-24-7

First printing 2009

Contents

Note
to the New Edition

W inston Churchill's personal papers are among the most comprehensive ever assembled relating to the life and times of one man. They are so extensive that it was only possible to include in the narrative volumes of his biography a part of the relevant documents.

The Companion Volumes, now titled *The Churchill Documents*, were planned to run parallel with the narrative volumes, and with them to form a whole. When an extract or quotation appears in a narrative volume, the complete document appears in an accompanying volume of *The Churchill Documents*. Where space prevented the inclusion of a contemporary letter in the narrative volume, it is included in the document volume.

In these three volumes of *The Churchill Documents*—Volume 11: *The Exchequer Years, 1922–1929*, Volume 12: *The Wilderness Years, 1929–1935*, and Volume 13: *The Coming of War, 1936–1939*—are set out all the documents relevant to *Winston S. Churchill*, Volume V: *The Prophet of Truth, 1922–1939*. Mention in these texts of the "Main Volume" refers to this fifth volume of the biography.

Preface

THIS IS THE fifth set of document—or companion—volumes published since the Churchill biography was begun under Randolph Churchill's authorship nineteen years ago; and the third set of documents prepared and published since his death. Like each of its predecessors, this volume is based primarily on the Churchill papers themselves, one of the fullest and richest private archives of twentieth-century British history.

Since Randolph Churchill's death ten years ago, many new archives have been made available to research, including substantial Cabinet, Ministerial and private archives; and I have therefore incorporated in this volume—as in Companion Volumes III and IV—several hundred original documents bearing directly on Churchill's career from other archival sources.

Given the size of this volume, 1,475 pages of documents, as compared to less than 330 pages in the equivalent section of Main Volume V, it has been possible here to present a comprehensive picture of Churchill's work and thought between October 1922 and June 1929, making full use of many different types of document, including diary extracts, transcripts of meetings, official telegrams and private letters, a substantial number of which are published here for the first time.

In taking Churchill's story forward another six and a half years, this volume provides material for his last year as a Liberal, for his return to the Conservatives, and for his four and a half years as Chancellor of the Exchequer in a Conservative Cabinet. In order to give a rounded picture, I have chosen documents which span every aspect of Churchill's life at that time, from the most personal and reflective, to the political and the administrative, the literary and financial, the national and

the international. The 'Exchequer Years' were, for Churchill,
a period of great controversy, and of great creativity; of ideas
and achievements which enhanced his career; of skilful negotiations; of insight and of vision.

Throughout 1923 Churchill was seen by many observers as
one of the principal instruments for a revived Liberal Party.
During 1924, when the Liberal Party, led by Asquith, decided
to support Ramsay MacDonald's first minority Labour Government, Churchill turned away from the Liberal Party of which
he had been so central a figure for twenty years. The letter
which he intended to send to Asquith's daughter, Violet
Bonham Carter, on 28 December 1923 (printed in full in this
volume on pages 89–90), and the letter which he actually sent,
on 8 January 1924 (pages 92–4) show the reasons for his
opposition to the course chosen by the Liberal leadership. So
too does his letter to *The Times* of 17 January 1924 (pages 94–
7).

Churchill's move from the Liberal to the Conservative Party
during 1924 is charted here in detail, as are his two unsuccessful
attempts to return to Parliament in 1923 and 1924: the only
period he was out of Parliament during a political career of
fifty-five years. Then, for more than four and a half years,
between November 1924 and June 1929, Churchill served as
Chancellor of the Exchequer in Stanley Baldwin's Conservative
Cabinet. During this period he absorbed himself in the intrica-
cies, and the challenges, of national finance.

In this volume are documents which deal, not only with the
preparation of each of Churchill's five budgets and their reception, but with the many other aspects of the economy with
which he was concerned. His desire to revive the British
economy after the war, and to reduce unemployment, can be
followed in his hesitations about Britain's return to the Gold
Standard, expressed in his letter to some of his senior advisers
on 22 February 1925 (pages 411–12); in his continual searches
for a reduction of Government expenditure in order to reduce
income tax and stimulate production; in his strong preference
for armoured units as opposed to cavalry; in his persistent
efforts to reduce naval expenditure; in his opposition to airships;

in his support for a system of Premium Bonds; in his determination to tax the motorist more severely; in his search for an increased revenue from the taxation of luxury goods; and in his work in trying to come to a settlement of the vexed question of the Allied war debts.

Churchill's continuing concern for promoting social reform; his successful efforts to introduce pensions for both widows and orphans; his desire to extend the existing system of state-aided national insurance, are all documented in these pages; so too is his strenuous attempt to relieve British industry of the burden of Rates, an attempt that dominated much of his work in 1928, the reasons for which were fully set out in his Cabinet memoranda of 12 December 1927 (pages 1128–37) and of 20 January 1928 (pages 1187–94). Criticisms of the derating scheme are also printed, together with a friend's warning, on 6 March 1928 (pages 1219–21), about the nature and strength of that criticism. As his friend wrote:

Altogether the Dardanelles situation seems to be re-creating itself. Everybody loves the idea, everybody but you is frightened at its boldness & magnitude. Everybody therefore stands looking on idly—perfectly ready to be pleased if it succeeds & equally ready to say 'I told you so' if it doesn't & to kick you downstairs.

Following this warning, Churchill wrote directly to Neville Chamberlain: both his letter and Chamberlain's reply are printed in full (pages 1227–9).

In these pages the attitude of Churchill's critics is represented with each change in his fortunes: from the Liberals who were distressed at his return to Conservatism, to the Conservatives who resented his position of growing strength within their Party, and to the Socialists, from whom his sharp criticisms often provoked extreme anger. The extent of Labour hostility to Churchill, the reasons for it, and his different methods of dealing with it, can be followed in the letters which Stanley Baldwin sent to King George V, reporting on Parliamentary business. The first of these letters printed here is dated 11 December 1924 (page 299). These letters, of which 21 are printed in this volume, give a vivid and often humorous account of Churchill's success as a Parliamentarian, and of his oratorical prowess.

Critical assessments, not always untinged with malice, are provided at regular intervals through the private comments of Lord Beaverbrook, Sir Samuel Hoare, L. S. Amery, J. C. C. Davidson, C. P. Scott and others. Churchill's own relationship with Beaverbrook can be traced, in all its moods, in their 'Exchequer Years' correspondence, which is printed here in full. So too can the essentially incompatible natures of Churchill and Neville Chamberlain, whose correspondence between 1924 and 1929 is often acerbic; as are also Chamberlain's private comments on Churchill, seen in his letter to Baldwin on 30 August 1925 (pages 533–4), and his further comments, in letters to Lord Irwin on 27 August 1927 (pages 1046–7), on 25 December 1927 (pages 1154–5), and on 12 August 1928 (pages 1327–9).

The letters to and from Churchill's friends are a noted feature of his archive. A letter from Alfred Duff Cooper, of 20 March 1924 (pages 126–7), shows an early stage of what was quickly to become a close friendship. So too does Churchill's correspondence with Brendan Bracken, Professor Lindemann, Robert Boothby, Desmond Morton and Harold Macmillan. To Macmillan he wrote, on 5 January 1928 (pages 1172–3): 'It is always pleasant to find someone whose mind grasps the essentials of a large plan'. Many of Churchill's friends from the earlier years were also in regular correspondence at this time, and, as his exchanges with A. J. Balfour, Austen Chamberlain, Sir Roger Keyes and T. E. Lawrence show, praise and criticism could often march side by side, with no breach in friendship.

During the six and a half years covered by this volume, Churchill and his wife were often apart, both because of the dictates of public life, and of Clementine Churchill's uncertain health. As a result, he sent her more than sixty letters, each of which is printed in this volume. Through these letters one can trace Churchill's political views and moods, his reflections on men and events, his comments on contemporary life, his forecasts for the future and his own personal philosophy.

Among the personal documents for this period of Churchill's life are a series of long descriptive letters which he wrote to his wife from Chartwell—his 'Chartwell Bulletins' he called them—in which, as well as accounts of the political scene, he focused on Chartwell itself, the house and farmyard news, the building of dams and lakes, disputes with the architect, the construction of cottages, the planning of gardens, bricklaying, painting and the entertaining of friends. The first of these Chartwell Bulletins is dated 20 February 1924 (pages 108–10).

Churchill constantly sought to put his wife's mind at rest; 'it was essential', he wrote to her on 22 October 1927 (pages 1068–9), 'to avoid fretting about troubles which will never come to pass'. And in a letter of 4 April 1928 (pages 1245–6) he wrote again: 'Don't let external things fret your mind.' Five months later he advised her (pages 1349–50):

Mind you rest & do not worry about household matters. Let them crash if they will. All will be well. Servants exist to save one trouble, & shd never be allowed to disturb one's inner peace. There will always be food to eat, & sleep will come even if the beds are not made. Nothing is worse than worrying about trifles. The big things do not chafe as much: & if they are rightly settled the rest will fall in its place.

Each of Churchill's letters to his wife gives eloquent testimony to the love he bore her. 'I think so often & so tenderly of you,' he wrote on 8 April 1928 (pages 1253–4), '& of the glory and comfort you have been to me in my life & of your sweet nature which I love so much, & your unchanging beauty which is my delight.' Yet Churchill was always conscious of his own short-comings: on 26 September 1927 he had written to her (pages 1055–6): 'You know how much you mean to me, & what I owe you. I will try & be more of a help to you'; and in his letter of 4 April 1928 he wrote (pages 1245–6): 'I am afraid that very often my business & my toys have made me a poor companion.'

In this volume can also be traced the growing relationship between Churchill and his son: his correspondence with his son's schoolmasters, his ambitions for Randolph, their holidays together, a father's advice, and the manifold problems of their relationship. Another noted feature of these letters is Churchill's devotion to his three daughters, Diana, Sarah and Mary, as is his loyalty to those members of his family, and close friends, who had fallen on hard times, or who found themselves in dispute with him politically.

In his letters to his wife, and in his other personal correspon-

dence, Churchill's observations of people and events are shown
in all their aspects: serious, severe, reflective, tolerant, cynical
and humorous. Watching his six-year-old daughter Mary in the
company of the Conservative Prime Minister, Stanley Baldwin,
he wrote (page 1056): 'How women admire power!' and seeing
for the first time the future Queen Elizabeth II, then aged two,
he remarked (page 1349): 'This last is a character. She has an
air of authority & reflectiveness astonishing in an infant.'

Churchill's financial affairs are also detailed in this volume,
both in his letters to his wife, and in those which he wrote to
his brother Jack, a partner in the stockbroking firm of Vickers
da Costa, through which Churchill transacted many of his
investments. Churchill's literary work can be followed in his
correspondence with his publishers, with those experts to whom
he sent his books for criticism before publication, and with those
friends and colleagues to whom he sent the finished works.

During the years covered by this volume, Churchill was
active both as an author, and as a journalist. Indeed, his
historical work led to protests in Parliament, and prompted him
to write a strong defence of his writings in a letter to the then
Prime Minister, Andrew Bonar Law, on 3 March 1923 (pages
32–6).

Although many of Chuchill's contemporaries regarded him
as a man of war, as did one of the reviewers of *The World Crisis*
in March 1929 (page 1443, note 2), nevertheless, Churchill's
four and a half years as Chancellor of the Exchequer were one
of the happiest and most productive periods of his career. Thus
one senior Conservative politician wrote to another, on 6 June
1927 (pages 1005–6):

The remarkable thing about him is the way in which he has suddenly
acquired, quite late in his Parliamentary life, an immense kind of tact,
patience, good humour and banter on almost all occasions; no one used
to 'suffer fools ungladly' more fully than Winston, now he is friendly
and accessible to everyone, both in the House, and in the lobbies, with
the result that he has become what he never was before the war, very
popular in the House generally—a great accretion to his already
formidable parliamentary powers.

Churchill's Parliamentary and constitutional interests can be seen in many of the documents published here, as, for example, his attitudes to Trade Union power as expressed in his letter to E. L. Spears on 27 May 1927 (pages 999–1003), and in his various criticisms of Soviet communism. 'Nearly everyone who has anything to do with the Bolsheviks,' he wrote in a private letter on 9 February 1928 (pages 1203–4), '. . . has come off soiled, or disillusioned, or poorer.' Also printed here are his reflections on electoral and franchise reform, as in his memorandum of 8 March 1927 (pages 958–66), and many documents and letters bearing on his administrative and departmental work at the Treasury, and on his contributions to the work of the Cabinet. Indeed, Churchill's achievements as a Conservative Cabinet Minister were noted with approval by many of his contemporaries. 'You seem to me,' one Conservative colleague, formerly an implacable opponent, wrote to him on 14 April 1927 (page 988), 'to have decidedly increased in brilliancy since you returned from riotous living with the Liberal harlots to your own Spiritual Home.'

While he was Chancellor of the Exchequer, Churchill was made Chairman of several important Cabinet Committees, and was given by Baldwin the responsibility for a number of intricate negotiations. Printed here are full transcripts of his negotiations on the Irish Boundary with the leaders of both North and South in December 1925 (pages 603–17), and his protracted efforts in 1926 to persuade the Mine Owners to adopt a more moderate policy towards the Miners, and to find a formula which the Miners could accept as a fair basis for a return to work: see the transcript of his remarks to the Miners' leaders on 26 August 1926 (pages 749–59), his discussion with the same leaders on 3 September 1926 (pages 768–72), and his discussion with the Mine Owners' representatives on 6 September 1926 (pages 781–807); as well as the Committee, and Cabinet, discussions arising out of these meetings, and his dispute with his cousin Lord Londonderry, who was himself a Mine Owner (pages 778–80, 829, 833–4 and 864–7).

On imperial matters, Churchill held strong views about Egypt, the Sudan, Iraq and India, all of which are expressed in his memoranda, in Cabinet discussions, and also in his

correspondence with individual colleagues. He expressed his
views on British policy in Egypt in a Cabinet memorandum of
30 December 1924 (pages 317–21) and in a letter to Austen
Chamberlain on 21 May 1926 (page 724). I have also printed
in full Churchill's discussions on world affairs with the French
President on 11 January 1925 (pages 338–40); and his opposition to a continuing British defence of Iraq, expressed in his
notes for a Cabinet meeting of 19 September 1925 (pages 544–
6), in his letter to Austen Chamberlain of 14 May 1926 (pages
722–3) and in his record of a conversation with King Feisal of
28 November 1927 (pages 1117–19).

Among Churchill's most frequently and forcefully expressed
views was his belief that another European war was inevitable,
unless France and Germany could be reconciled. To achieve
this reconciliation, he was prepared to use all Britain's power
and influence, for he feared greatly the appearance of what he
described to A. J. Balfour as 'Armageddon No 2'. He set out his
views, his fear and forecasts, at a meeting of the Committee of
Imperial Defence on 13 February 1925 (pages 393–7); in a
Treasury minute of 14 September 1928 (pages 1337–9); and in
several reflections on Anglo-American relations, including a
Cabinet memorandum of 19 November 1928 (pages 1380–2).

Churchill often reflected on the interaction of military weakness and foreign policy, and on the implications of this interaction for the future security of Britain. In a letter to Baldwin
on 22 January 1927 (printed in full on pages 917–18) he set out
his philosophy in this regard:

Short of being actually conquered, there is no evil worse than submitting to wrong and violence for fear of war. Once you take the position
of not being able in any circumstances to defend your rights against the
aggression of some particular set of people, there is no end to the
demands that will be made or to the humiliations that must be accepted.

Fifteen months later, reflecting on his plans for the de-rating
of industry, at a time when those plans were being circumscribed
and curtailed, Churchill wrote again to Baldwin (pages 1250–1):

To act by half-measures with a lack of conviction miscalled 'caution',
is to run the greatest risks and lose the prize. No, let us be audacious.

One does not want to live forever. We have the power: let us take the best measures.

Printed here for the first time are the documents of Churchill's editorship of the *British Gazette* in May 1926, during the General Strike: both his own activities and the points of view of his critics are fully documented (pages 692–722), together with the text of each of the articles he himself wrote for the newspaper. Churchill's proposals for the Reform of the House of Lords are set out in a Cabinet memorandum of 17 November 1925 (pages 577–87). So also is his philosophy of government (page 705): 'Ample force to preserve the laws and life of the nation is at the disposal of the State. But force is not an instrument on which a British Government should rely. We rely on reason, on public opinion and on the will of the people.'

A noted feature of the years 1924 to 1929 was Churchill's growing intimacy with Stanley Baldwin. In this volume I have printed sixty letters which Churchill sent to Baldwin during these years, and twenty letters from Baldwin to Churchill. Many of these are personal, amusing and affectionate. I have also tried to document Churchill's friendship with, and support for one of his senior Treasury officials, P. J. Grigg; and his estrangement from the head of the Civil Service, Sir Warren Fisher, to whom he addressed several critical minutes, including one on 1 December 1925 (pages 600–3), and another on 30 April 1926 (pages 689–90). 'I must beg you,' Churchill wrote to Warren Fisher in a further note on 17 December 1927 (pages 1140–2), 'to inscribe hope, and confidence in the growing strength of the country, upon all your memoranda.'

This volume also traces Churchill's relationship with Epping, his first Conservative constituency since he had crossed the floor of the House of Commons in 1904, and follows his life at Chartwell, as it was described by those who were his guests, including Sir Samuel Hoare, Thomas Jones, Victor Cazalet and James Scrymgeour-Wedderburn. Also documented here are the secret meetings at Chartwell, and in London, between Churchill and Ramsay MacDonald during the Coal crisis of 1926 (pages 764–5 and 768–71).

Churchill's correspondence between 1923 and 1929 reveals

many aspects of his character, of his constructive work, and of his aspirations. In a letter to Lord Beaverbrook on 28 December 1926 (printed in full on pages 905–6), Churchill expressed his innermost convictions about the future, setting them in the context of his observations on Beaverbrook's career, but clearly applicable equally to his own. As Churchill wrote to his friend of twenty years:

> You have had wonderful success in yr eventful life while still quite young, & everything you have touched has prospered. All yr direct & finite ambitions have been attained. What lies before you now, properly understood holds I believe greater possibilities & deeper satisfactions than any you have known—even in the fierce battle-days of youth.
> The best part of life lies before you: & the hardest & fiercest work. Splendid opportunities will reward the earlier risks & toils. Personally I have so far enjoyed life more every year. But I do not think that wd continue if I felt that the future was closed or cabined. I do not feel that it is—either in my own case or in yours.
> There are vy great things to be done by those who reach a certain scale of comprehension & of power in their early prime. As long as health & life are ours, we must try to do them,—not to be content except with the best & truest solutions.

A year and a half later, in another letter to Beaverbrook on 21 May 1928 (printed in full on pages 1290–1), Churchill set out his philosophy of history—'the slowly emerging truth', as he called it—and he continued:

> But what a tale! Think of all those people—decent, educated, the story of the past laid out before them—What to avoid—what to do etc patriotic, loyal, clean—trying their utmost—What a ghastly muddle they made of it!
> *Unteachable from infancy to tomb*—There is the first & main characteristic of mankind.

At the bottom of this letter Churchill noted: 'No more war.' This was to be the theme of all his arguments and activities both in this decade, and in the decade that lay ahead.

Acknowledgements
to the New Edition

The following foundations and individuals gave generous support for the publication of *Winston S. Churchill*, Volume V: *The Prophet of Truth, 1922–1939*, and volumes 11, 12, and 13 of *The Churchill Documents*: the Lynde and Harry Bradley Foundation, Milwaukee, Wisconsin; the Earhart Foundation, Ann Arbor, Michigan; the late George B. Ferguson, Peoria, Arizona; Mr. and Mrs. Thomas N. Jordan, Jr., Healdsburg, California; Mr. and Mrs. Tim M. Roudebush, Lenexa, Kansas; Mr. and Mrs. Emil A. Voelz, Jr., Akron, Ohio; and the Saul N. Silbert Charitable Trust, Sun City, Arizona.

Acknowledgements

AS WITH EACH of the earlier volumes of this biography, I am grateful to Her Majesty the Queen, who graciously gave permission for me to have access to the Royal Archives; for help in answering my various queries relating to the Royal Family, I should like to thank Sir Robin Mackworth Young, Librarian, Windsor Castle, and Miss Jane Langton, Registrar.

I am also particularly grateful to Dr Christopher Dowling, Keeper of the Department of Education and Publications, Imperial War Museum, for the time and energy which he has given to the Churchill Biography for more than a decade, on all matters relating to military personnel; to Miss Grace Hamblin, for guiding me so effectively on all questions concerning Churchill's life at Chartwell; and to Gordon Phillips, Archivist and Researcher of *The Times*, for answering so patiently my many queries.

As well as the Churchill papers in the possession of the Chartwell Trust, I have included documents from forty-seven other collections and archives, and should like to thank the owners, custodians and copyright holders of the following sets of papers: the Cabinet papers and the Treasury papers, at the Public Record Office, Kew; the archive of *The Times*; and the archives and private papers of the following individuals, L. S. Amery; Earl Baldwin; Earl Balfour; Lord Beaverbrook; Lord Boothby; Lord Bracken; Lord Carson; Viscount Cecil of Chelwood; Sir Austen Chamberlain; Neville Chamberlain; Lord Cherwell; Randolph Churchill; W. P. Crozier; Viscount Davidson; the 17th Earl of Derby; the 11th Earl of Dundee; Viscount French of Ypres; Sir James Grigg; Earl Haig; Sir James Hawkey; Lady Blanche Hozier; Lord Irwin (later Earl of Halifax); Dr Thomas Jones; Lord Keyes; Andrew Bonar Law; T. E. Lawrence; Sir

Shane Leslie; Louis Loucheur; the 9th Duke of Marlborough; Sir Edward Marsh; Lord Melchett; the Marquess of Reading; Cecil Roberts; the 5th Earl of Rosebery; the 5th Marquess of Salisbury; C. P. Scott; R. C. Sherriff; Brigadier-General Sir E. L. Spears; Baroness Clementine Spencer-Churchill; Viscount Swinton; Viscount Templewood (Sir Samuel Hoare). I should also like to thank all those archivists, librarians and individuals who provided me with access to their archives, and who also helped me to trace materials, or gave me materials for the compilation of the notes. Without this help, I could not have completed many of the exchanges of letters between Churchill and his friends, colleagues and critics; nor could I have carried out my intention to include a brief biographical note for every person mentioned in the text and to give short explanations to many of the historical and personal allusions. I am grateful for this help to Guy Acloque, Archivist, the Grosvenor Office, London; Catherine Alicot, Editions Payot, Paris; Julian Amery, MP; the Marquess of Bath; B. S. Benedikz, Head of Special Collections, University Library, the University of Birmingham; A. O. Bennett, Registrar, the Institute of Chartered Accountants in England and Wales; J. K. Bishop, County Archivist, Lancashire County Council; Patricia Bradford, Archivist, Churchill College, Cambridge; Lord Boothby; Dr David Butler; H. A. Cahn; Eric Ceadel, Librarian, Cambridge University Library; the Central Statistical Office, London; Sybil, Marchioness of Cholmondeley; Margaret Clay, Enquiries Librarian, Home Office, London; the 11th Earl of Dundee; Dr Michael Dunnill; G. P. Dyer, Librarian and Curator, Royal Mint; Nina Elkins; Donald L. Forbes; Major Steuart Fothringham; Antoine Gaujal, Directeur du Service, Service des Archives, Assemblée Nationale, Paris; Professor Richard Gombrich; John Grigg; Lady Mary Grosvenor; Robert P. Hastings; W. R. Hearst Jr; Geoffrey Heywood; Dr Roger Highfield; H. Hodgson, Secretary, the National Association of Bookmakers, Ltd; Ann Hoffman; J. W. Hunt, Librarian, the Royal Military Academy, Sandhurst; the India Office Library and Records; Robert Rhodes James, MP; Gwyn Jenkins, Research Assistant, Department of Manuscripts and Records, the

National Library of Wales; Tristan Jones; Andrew G. Lajer, Great Britain Specialist and Rare Stamp Department, Stanley Gibbons Limited; Charles Lysaght; J. A. McCracken; the 11th Duke of Marlborough; Miss J. Monks, the Institute of Chartered Accountants in Ireland; Robert Newman, Public Relations Manager, Pirelli Limited, London; Peter Olney; A. E. B. Owen, Manuscript Department, University Library, Cambridge; N. J. Page, Secretary-General, Institute of Actuaries, London; G. W. Pardy; A. H. Peachy, Building Centre Group; H. C. R. Pearson; W. J. Reader; James Ritchie, Keeper, National Library of Scotland, Department of Manuscripts; Kenneth Rose; Martin Russell; Michael M. Sacher; Dr Robert Shackleton, Bodley's Librarian, Oxford; T. G. Smith, Librarian and Archivist, HM Customs and Excise; the Hon. Lady Soames; Antonio Spallone, Librarian, Istituto Italiano di Cultura, London; Patrick Strong, Keeper of College Library and Collections, Eton College; Dr Charles Stuart; Mrs Renée Taylor, Public Relations, Chanel Limited; Mrs G. Thomson, Administrative Assistant, the Institute of Chartered Accountants of Scotland; Maggie Tong, Assistant to the Archivist, Churchill College, Cambridge; Dr Philip Waller; Lady White; G. J. Windsor, Treasury Chambers, London; Yvonne Woodbridge, Deputy Departmental Record Officer, Treasury Chambers, London; and Woodrow Wyatt, Chairman of the Horserace Totalisator Board.

I have published here, for the first time, several letters written by Churchill which are now in private collections. I should like to thank the owners of these collections for their kindness in sending me this material: Robert P. Hastings; David Satinoff; Randolph U. Stambaugh; and Godspeeds' Bookshop, Boston, USA.

I am also grateful to the authors, editors and publishers of the following books, for permission to print individual documents from: Lord Citrine, *Men and Work: An Autobiography* (Hutchinson, London, 1964); William Albert Samuel Hewins, *The Apologia of an Imperialist: Forty Years of Imperial Policy* (Constable, London, 1929); Robert Rhodes James, *Victor Cazalet, a Portrait* (Hamish Hamilton, London, 1976); Sir Frederick William

Leith-Ross, *Money Talks, Fifty Years of International Finance* (Hutchinson, London, 1968); Desmond MacCarthy (editor), *H.H.A.: Letters of the Earl of Oxford and Asquith to a Friend*, second series, 1922–1927 (Geoffrey Bles, London, 1934); Lord Reith, *Into the Wind* (Hodder and Stoughton, London, 1949); and Lord Riddell, *Lord Riddell's Intimate Diary of the Peace Conference and After* (Victor Gollancz, London, 1933).

For preparing the cartoon printed on page 335, I should like to thank Gerry Moeran, of Studio Edmark, Oxford. For help in typing both notes and documents since work on this volume began more than four years ago, I am grateful to Mrs Wendy Rioch, Mrs Judy Holdsworth, Miss Sue Townshend, and Miss Penny Houghton. I should also like to thank Taffy Sassoon and Lloyd L. Thomas for their help in proof-reading.

For help for more than a year, in collecting material from a wide range of sources, including newspapers and libraries, I should like to thank Larry P. Arnn, of Arkansas and California, whose efforts have been persistent and valuable. I am particularly grateful to the Winston S. Churchill Association of the United States, and its President, Professor Harry V. Jaffa, for having made Mr Arnn's services available, and for help in other ways.

Both in collecting important extra material from the Public Record Office, first at Chancery Lane and then at Kew, and in scrutinizing the work at every stage, I must once again thank my wife, whose archival help and personal encouragement have been indispensable.

Merton College   Martin Gilbert
Oxford
26 July 1978

PROLOGUE

Return to Conservatism
1922—1924

November–December
1922

Winston S. Churchill to Louis Spears[1]

(*Spears papers*)

18 November 1922   2 Sussex Square
Private

My dear Louis,

I am greatly touched by the extreme kindness of yr offer & the willing sacrifice that it involves.[2] It is a splendid proof of yr friendship. I cd not accept it from you. I want you to enjoy yr seat in Parliament & I shall like to feel I have one or two friends there. I am off to Rome for the winter; & meanwhile if I or my work are assailed in the House I shall rely upon you & Archie[3] to defend me. The Whips will find me a seat if I wanted one; but what I want now is a rest.

Come round and see me before I go. I shall be here all next week. My

---

[1] Edward Louis Spears, 1886–1974. Joined the Kildare Militia, 1903. Captain, 11th Hussars, 1914. Four times wounded, 1914–15 (Military Cross). Liaison officer with French 10th Army, 1915–16. Head of the British Military Mission to Paris, 1917–20. Brigadier-General, 1918. National Liberal MP for Loughborough, 1922–4; Conservative MP for Carlisle, 1931–45. Churchill's Personal Representative with the French Prime Minister, May–June 1940. Head of British Mission to de Gaulle, 1940. Head of Mission to Syria and the Lebanon, 1941. First Minister to Syria and the Lebanon, 1942–4. Knighted, 1942; created Baronet, 1953.

[2] Churchill having lost his Parliamentary seat at the 1922 General Election, Spears, who had just been elected to Parliament for the first time, had offered to give up his own seat and let Churchill stand in his place.

[3] Archibald Henry Macdonald Sinclair, 1890–1970. Educated at Eton and Sandhurst. Entered Army, 1910. 4th Baronet, 1912. Captain, 1915. 2nd in Command of the 6th Royal Scots Fusiliers, while Churchill was in command, January–May 1916. Squadron-Commander, 2nd Life Guards, 1916–18. Elected to the Other Club, 1917. Major, Guards Machine Gun Regiment, 1918. Private Secretary to Churchill, Ministry of Munitions, 1918–19. Churchill's personal Military Secretary, War Office, 1919–21. Churchill's Private Secretary, Colonial Office, 1921–2. Liberal MP for Caithness and Sutherland, 1922–45. Secretary of State for Scotland, 1931–3. Leader of the Parliamentary Liberal Party, 1935–45. Secretary of State for Air in Churchill's wartime Coalition, 1940–5. Created Viscount Thurso, 1952.

kindest regards to yr wife. Will you both come and lunch one day. Let me
know.

Yours ever my dear friend
Winston S.C.

Sir Eustace Tennyson d'Eyncourt[1] *to Winston S. Churchill*

(*Churchill papers: 8/41*)

1 December 1922

Dear Churchill,

Thank you very much for your letter of the 28th November, enclosing
proofs of a chapter of your first volume on Admiralty Administration.

I have been carefully through the proof, and if you will allow me to say so,
I think you have made the subject very clear and comprehensible to the
ordinary reader. It gave me the greatest pleasure to read it and to recall
those strenuous early days of the War when you and Lord Fisher[2] kept us
all up to concert pitch. His opinion of Lord Jellicoe[3] absolutely changed after
Jutland from that expressed in the letters you quote.

There are one or two small points which perhaps might be corrected, if
you think it worth while.

On the first page at the bottom you say the 15″ gun had a 2,000 lb pro-
jectile: the actual weight is really 1,920 lbs.

At the bottom of the 4th page, the Tribal Class Destroyers are given as
having 31 knots speed. They were actually designed for 33 knots, although
31 was probably about their limit at sea.

In the middle of the 5th page, the experimental Destroyer 'SWIFT' is

---

[1] Eustace Henry William Tennyson d'Eyncourt, 1868–1951. A naval architect, 1898–
1912. Director of Naval Construction and Chief Technical Adviser at the Admiralty, 1912–
23. President of the Landships Committee of the Admiralty, 1915–16. Knighted, 1917.
Vice-President of the Tank Board, 1918. Managing Director of Armstrong Whitworth's
shipyards at Newcastle, 1924–8. Director of the Parsons Marine Steam Turbine Company,
1928–48. Created Baronet, 1930. One of the principal inventors of the Tank.

[2] John Arbuthnot Fisher, 1841–1920. Known as both 'Jackie' and, because of his somewhat oriental appearance, 'the old Malay'. Entered Navy, 1854. First Sea Lord, 1904–10.
Admiral of the Fleet, 1905. Created Baron, 1909. Retired, 1911. Head of the Royal Commission on Fuel and Engines, 1912–14. Reappointed First Sea Lord, October 1914; resigned
May 1915. Chairman of the Admiralty Inventions Board, 1915–16.

[3] John Rushworth Jellicoe, 1859–1935. Entered Navy, 1872. Captain, 1897. Knighted,
1907. Vice-Admiral, 1910. Second Sea Lord, 1912–14. Commander-in-Chief of the Grand
Fleet, 1914–16. Admiral, 1915. First Sea Lord, 1916–17. Chief of the Naval Staff, 1917.
Created Viscount, 1918. Admiral of the Fleet, 1919. Governor-General of New Zealand,
1920–4. Created Earl, 1925.

given a speed of 40 knots: really she never got more than about 36. Just below that, on the same page, you say the Scouts had a litter of 12-pdr guns. When built, these were 4″ guns.

At the top of that page the 'BLONDE' is mentioned as having 2,500 tons displacement: this was actually 3,350.

I do not know if you would care to make the point, but the importance of speed in Light Cruisers was, I think, enormously brought out in the War by this fact, that not one of the Light Cruisers, either the 'ARETHUSAS', the C Class or the D Class, although frequently engaged with the enemy, was ever sunk by gunfire. I have continually used this argument when I have been asked to add more armour and general protection to this Class, the added weight of which would of course militate against their speed.

I hope you are now feeling quite strong again after your operation.[1]

With kind regards,
Yours very sincerely,
Eustace H. T. d'Eyncourt

Lord Beatty[2] *to Winston S. Churchill*

(*Churchill papers: 8/41*)

9 December 1922

My dear Churchill,

I have read the pages dealing with The Heligoland Bight Action of 28th Aug 1914.

You state in it that 'The Heligoland Batteries were not able to come into action——' This is not quite correct. They did come into action opening fire on our Light Craft, which, though not effective as far as hits were concerned, was effectual in warning them as to how close they were to the Enemy Batteries. You also state that 'The German Battle Ships and Battle Cruisers could not cross the Bar of the outer Jade till 11 pm'. I assume that the fact that the German Battle Ships and Battle Cruisers were in the Jade and in this predicament came to your knowledge after the event or I should have been informed of it. I certainly was not aware of it and expected to meet a

---

[1] In October 1922, at the start of the General Election campaign, Churchill had been taken ill with appendicitis. As a result, he had been able to go to his constituency only at the end of the campaign.

[2] David Beatty, 1871–1936. Entered Navy, 1884. Rear-Admiral, 1910. Churchill's Naval Secretary, 1912. Commander of the 1st Battle Cruiser Squadron, 1913–16. Knighted, 1914. Vice-Admiral, 1915. Commander-in-Chief of the Grand Fleet, 1916–18. First Sea Lord, 1919–27. Created Earl, 1919. Admiral of the Fleet, 1919.

superior Force at any moment. In fact Enemy Battle Cruisers were reported as being sighted in the misty weather which prevailed on several occasions. I think if it remains in some reference should be made to the fact that I was not aware that I should not be engaged by a superior Force. Obviously it would have made a great deal of difference to my dispositions, and to my action in going to Tyrwhitt's[1] support—and would certainly have lessened very considerably my anxieties. Or was it another instance of the failure of Admiralty Staff Work. At the bottom of the sheet under proof there is a slip The *Nore* being named instead of presumably The *Nab*.

There has been another storm about the 2 new Battleships and I now think it is alright and we shall get them. If there is any further trouble I'll let you know and you can write to House of Lords.

The poor old Admiralty is not being well treated in this respect and I never would have thought it possible that we should have such a struggle to maintain our meagre position as a Sea Power of reduced relative values.

I envy you in the Sunshine and the warmth of the South and I am sure it will do you great good.[2]

Please my respects and good wishes to Mrs Churchill.

Yours v sincerely
Beatty

Sir Hugh Trenchard[3] *to Winston S. Churchill*

(*Churchill papers: 8/41*)

12 December 1922   Air Ministry

My dear Mr Churchill,

I have read through your chapter, and the following are my remarks:

[1] Reginald Yorke Tyrwhitt, 1870–1951. Entered Navy, 1883. Commodore, commanding the Destroyer Flotilla of the First Fleet, 1913–16. Knighted, 1917. Created Baronet, 1919. Commanded the Third Light Squadron, Mediterranean, 1921–2. Commanding officer, coast of Scotland, 1923–5. Commander-in-Chief, China Station, 1927–9. Admiral, 1929. Commander-in-Chief, the Nore, 1930–3. Admiral of the Fleet, 1934.

[2] On 2 December 1922 Churchill had gone to the South of France, to the Villa Rêve d'Or, near Cannes, which he had rented for six months.

[3] Hugh Montague Trenchard, 1873–1956. Entered Army, 1893. Active service, South Africa, 1899–1902 (dangerously wounded). Major, 1902. Assistant Commandant, Central Flying School, 1913–14. Lieutenant-Colonel, 1915. General Officer Commanding the Royal Flying Corps in the Field, 1915–17. Major-General, 1916. Knighted, 1918. Chief of the Air Staff, 1918–29. Air-Marshal, 1919. Created Baronet, 1919. Air Chief Marshal, 1922. Marshal of the Royal Air Force, 1927. Created Baron, 1930. Commissioner, Metropolitan Police, 1931–5. Created Viscount, 1936. Trustee of the Imperial War Museum, 1937–45. His elder son, and both his stepsons, were killed in action in the Second World War.

Page 1. (where marked A.)

The correct answer is: 22 aeroplanes and 26 seaplanes ready, and there were 17 more aeroplanes and 26 more seaplanes being got ready and unserviceable.

Page 2. (where marked B.)

The correct statement is: £40 millions were used in building British Zeppelins *and airship stations.* (It was not all used on the airships.)

Page 2. (where marked B.1)

I should not have said that the policy of flying aeroplanes off warships and carriers was hopelessly neglected. It was not so much neglected as action in that respect was appallingly dilatory as regards experimental work and providing necessary material.

Page 2. (where marked C.)

It is correct to say that 6 Zeppelins were destroyed in the air or in the sheds, but it is not correct to say that no others were destroyed except by accident, as several were *crashed* after being damaged by gunfire.

In this connection, if it is of any use to you, I forward you some notes on aircraft questions that you may like to read. These we had drawn up by our Historical Section for Sir Walter Raleigh.[1]

I thoroughly agree with the policy stated in your chapter, especially the point that as we had no aircraft to get to their height the proper way was to attack the German airships in their sheds. The offensive policy is the only policy, as you say.

I hope you are well and getting a good rest and enjoying yourself. It seems to me that we have more work and a harder time here than ever, and we are reviewing all the old questions again.

My wife asks to be remembered to you and Mrs Churchill.

Yours very sincerely,

H. Trenchard

[1] Walter Raleigh, 1861–1922. Professor of English Literature, Oxford, from 1904 until his death. Knighted, 1911. Shortly after his death, in 1922 the Oxford University Press published his book *The War in the Air: Being the Story of the Part Played in the Great War by the Royal Air Force*, volume one. The remaining five volumes were written by others.

Winston S. Churchill to Clementine Churchill
(*Spencer-Churchill papers*)

18 December 1922   2 Sussex Square,
                                                   London

My darling Clemmie,

This is certainly a most delectable house, & in spite of the Riviera sunshine, it is a pleasure to return to it. Mrs Cowie[1] is at her best & I have had a few people everyday to lunch and dinner. I have also dined with Venetia,[2] & with Goonie.[3] I have sketched out the following plans for visitors for yr consideration. Goonie & Jack[4] think they cd come about Feb 22 for a fortnight (Jack probably less). On Mar 7 the Laverys[5] wd leave England & Goonie & I wd meet them at Avignon for about a weeks painting there. John has never seen it. I dont expect you want to see that region again. Then I wd bring John & Hazel on to us for a fortnight ie from Mar 14 to Mar 28.

Charlie[6] came to see me yesterday—vy mellow and affectionate. He is sending for the Plates today & will give me a cheque for £829. He is going to give us cuttings from his vines. There is a peculiarly long black grape with a vy good flavour. He & Edie[7] are lunching tomorrow. He was much attracted at the idea of coming to Cannes: He has to go back to Ireland now where he is to be Ulster Prime Minister for a month while Sir James Craig[8] recuperates at Cannes! Then he wd like to come to us for ten days at the end of January.

Eddie[9] who also has published a new work of Georgian poets wd like to

[1] Churchill's housekeeper at 2 Sussex Square.

[2] Beatrice Venetia Stanley, 1887–1948. Clementine Churchill's cousin. On 26 July 1915 she married Edwin Montagu. Of some of Asquith's letters, Churchill wrote in *Great Contemporaries*: 'They were addressed to brighter eyes than peer through politicians' spectacles'; hers were the eyes to which he was referring.

[3] Lady Gwendeline Bertie, 1885–1941. Known as 'Goonie'. Daughter of the 7th Earl of Abingdon. She married Churchill's brother Jack in 1908.

[4] John Strange Spencer Churchill, 1880–1947. Churchill's younger brother, known as Jack. Educated at Harrow. A stockbroker. Major, Queen's Own Oxfordshire Hussars, 1914–18. Served at Dunkirk, 1914; on Sir John French's staff, 1914–15; on Sir Ian Hamilton's staff, 1915; on General Birdwood's staff, 1916–18.

[5] Sir John and Hazel Lavery (see page 19, note 2).

[6] The Marquess of Londonderry (see page 14, note 2).

[7] The Marchioness of Londonderry (see page 133, note 1).

[8] James Craig, 1871–1940. A Protestant. Born in Dublin, the son of a wealthy distiller. A stockbroker by profession. Served in the South African War, 1899–1902. Unionist MP, 1906–21. A leading opponent of Irish Home Rule before 1914. On active service against the Germans in South-west Africa, 1914–15. Created Baronet, 1918. Parliamentary Secretary, Ministry of Pensions, 1919–20. Financial Secretary, Admiralty, 1920–1. First Prime Minister of Northern Ireland (under the Government of Ireland Act), from June 1921 until his death. Created Viscount Craigavon, 1927.

[9] Edward Howard Marsh, 1872–1953. Known as 'Eddie'. Educated at Westminster and Trinity College, Cambridge. Entered the Colonial Office as a 2nd Class Clerk, 1896. Private Secretary to Churchill, December 1905–November 1915. Assistant Private Secretary to

come for ten days at the beginning of Jan. He wd fit in vy well with Victor L[1]—who I hear is much looking forward to coming.

That is all I have committed you even tentatively to. But darling telegraph to me on receipt of this whether I shall *clinch* these plans or not. They seem to me vy nice & variegated. Sarah Wilson[2] has just written me a line asking me to dinner. I shall find out what her plans are & will let you know.

Poor Annaly & Old Marcus Beresford slipped off vy suddenly.[3] They were genial figures for many years.

I am leaving all business out of this letter because it takes too long to write; & Beckenham[4] does not come till too late to catch the post. I will dictate to him as soon as he comes a long account of Chartwell, of the let, of the packing up—& as soon as I hear from Cork of the children's journey. I am having gt difficulty in getting places before Christmas.

The franc has gone a little the wrong way: but on the other hand those London & Rhodesian shares I bought from Abe[5] for £1,000 a month ago are worth nearly £1,500 today.

Asquith, November 1915–December 1916. Private Secretary to Churchill, 1917–22 and 1924–9. Private Secretary to successive Secretaries of State for the Colonies, 1929–36. Elected to the Other Club, 1932. Knighted, 1937.

[1] Victor Alexander George Robert Lytton, 1876–1947. Educated at Eton and Trinity College, Cambridge. Succeeded his father as 2nd Earl of Lytton, 1891. Civil Lord of the Admiralty, 1916; Additional Parliamentary Secretary, Admiralty, 1917; British Commissioner for Propaganda in France, 1918; Civil Lord of the Admiralty, 1919–20. Under-Secretary of State for India, 1920–2. Governor of Bengal, 1922–7. Acting Viceroy of India, April–August 1925. Head of the League of Nations' Mission to Manchuria, 1932. Chairman of Palestine Potash Ltd; Central London Electricity Ltd; the London Power Company, and the Hampstead Garden Suburb Trust Ltd. His elder son was killed in a flying accident in 1933 and his younger son was killed in action in 1942.

[2] Lady Sarah Isabella Augusta Spencer-Churchill, 1864–1929. Eleventh and youngest child of the 7th Duke of Marlborough. Churchill's aunt. In 1891 she married Lieutenant-Colonel Gordon Chesney Wilson, Royal Horse Guards. In 1899 she was taken prisoner by the Boers in South Africa but later exchanged for a Boer prisoner, and sent to Mafeking, then under siege. She published her *South African Memories* in 1909. Her husband was killed in action in France on 6 November 1914.

[3] Luke White, 3rd Baron Annaly, a former Captain in the Scots Guards and Master of the Pytchley foxhounds from 1902 to 1914, had died on 15 December 1922, aged 65. Lord Marcus de la Poer Beresford, a former Manager of the Royal Thoroughbreds, had died on 16 December 1922, aged 73. Both had been friends of Churchill's parents, and of Churchill himself.

[4] Henry Anstead Beckenham, 1890–1937. Entered Admiralty, 1910. Assistant Private Secretary to Churchill, 1912–15; to Sir W. Graham Greene, 1916; to Jellicoe when First Sea Lord, 1917; to Wemyss when First Sea Lord, 1918; to Churchill, 1918–22. Secretary to the British Empire Exhibition, Wembley, 1923–5.

[5] Abe Bailey, 1863–1940. One of the principal mine-owners of the Transvaal. Knighted, 1911, for his services in promoting South African Union. Served as a Major on the staff of the South African forces which attacked German South-West Africa, 1915. Created Baronet, 1919. His son John married Churchill's eldest daughter, Diana, in 1932 (divorced, 1935).

Darling one I have worked abt 10 hours a day at my book. The Times man[1] has been here each day & we are going through his selections page by page. I am going to leave the Times part finished before I come to you. It will take me up till Saturday. There are so many points of detail to check. Admiral Jackson[2] came up to day & I have plenty for him to do. I am going to see Beatty at 11.30. There are abt two hundred minor points to be checked.

Curtis Brown[3] has greatly improved upon the London Magazine offer. He has now firm offers from Pearson's Monthly & from 'Good Housekeeping' in the United States of £400 & £320 respectively for each of 4 & possibly 6 articles—ie 720 an article: whereas I only was to get 3 to 400 from the London. The articles are to be on contemporary international questions. They want one on Czecho-Slovakia. You wd not mind a flying visit to Prag. It wd be rather fun. Any how I shd like to go. I shall close with these offers if I can get 6 articles guaranteed. That wd give me 4,300 less 430 commission = 3,870. We ought to be content with that in addition to our income.

My darling I ought to have caught yesterday's post but I was so entangled in one of my chapters I missed it. But this shd reach you at least on Wednesday & I hope tomorrow. It carries to you now as ever my tender love & devotion.

My sweet one
Always yr ever loving
W

PS. Yr Mama[4] is here. She wanted to go: but I made her stay on.
The baby[5] is blooming & sweet. The others are vy good.

[1] William Lints Smith (see page 148, note 3).

[2] Thomas Jackson, 1868–1945. Entered the Navy, 1881. Captain, 1905. Director of the Intelligence Division of the Naval War Staff, 1912–13. Director of the Operations Division, Admiralty, 1915–17. Commanded the Egyptian and Red Sea Division of the Mediterranean Squadron, 1917–19. Vice-Admiral, 1920. Knighted, 1923. Admiral, retired list, 1923.

[3] Adam Curtis Brown, 1866–1945. Educated in the United States. Editorial Staff, *Buffalo Express*, 1884–94. Sunday Editor, *New York Press*, 1894–8; London correspondent, 1898–1910. Established the International Publishing Bureau, London, 1900; Managing Director, 1900–16. Managing Director, Curtis Brown Ltd, Literary Agents, 1916–45.

[4] Lady Henrietta Blanche Ogilvy, 1852–1925. Daughter of the 7th Earl of Airlie. In 1873 she married Sir Henry Hozier (who died in 1907). Mother of Clementine, Nellie and William.

[5] Mary Churchill, 1922– . Churchill's fifth and youngest child. Served with the Auxiliary Territorial Service, 1940–5; accompanied her father on several of his wartime journeys. In 1947 she married Captain (later Lord) Christopher Soames. They have five children.

Lord Beatty to Winston S. Churchill

(*Churchill papers: 8/41*)

20 December 1922

My dear Churchill,

Many thanks for the proof which I return. I certainly have nothing to complain of indeed you are very kind and I feel proud to have earned such comments from an ex First Lord. There is one small point marked with green pencil which might be misunderstood ie 'Fifth, that there had been some trouble in a ship which he had commanded'—

This would be read to mean that there had been trouble with officers or men which was not true (as you probably don't remember that the trouble was connected with an Engine Room defect which was caused by hot bearings during a Full Speed Trial which necessitated Docking and Repairs).[1]

Good luck to you for 1923 and I hope you will have a Happy Christmas.

Yours sincerely
Beatty

[1] In volume one of *The World Crisis*, page 87, Churchill wrote about Beatty: 'A few weeks after my arrival at the Admiralty I was told that among several officers of Flag rank who wished to see me was Rear-Admiral Beatty. I had never met him before, but I had the following impressions about him. First, that he was the youngest Flag Officer in the Fleet. Second, that he had commanded the white gunboat which had come up the Nile as close as possible to support the 21st Lancers when we made the charge at Omdurman. Third, that he had seen a lot of fighting on land with the army, and that consequently he had military as well as naval experience. Fourth, that he came of a hard-riding stock; his father had been in my own regiment, the 4th Hussars, and I had often heard him talked of when I first joined. The Admiral, I knew, was a very fine horseman, with what is called "an eye for country". Fifth, that there was much talk in naval circles of his having been pushed on too fast. Such were the impressions aroused in my mind by the name of this officer, and I record them with minuteness because the decisions which I had the honour of taking in regard to him were most serviceable to the Royal Navy and to the British arms.'

1923

Winston S. Churchill to Jack Churchill
(*Churchill papers: 28/152*)

4 January 1923   Villa Rêve d'Or
                                                                                      Cannes

My dear Jack,

Letter herewith. Courtaulds have done vy well. You are still holding the
London & Rhodesians I suppose. I see they are about 5/6. I leave it entirely
to yr judgement. If you can get more do. I have paid £829 from Londonderry
for plate into the bank—so they don't want any more money.

The Franc has dipped a bit. If it makes a sudden drop of 4 or 5 points
don't hesitate to close the deal. We can sell again if it rises. Neither Paris or
Lausanne look vy healthy. And how are the French going to improve their
finances!

I won here 25,000 francs playing quite low—& hope to keep some of it.
It dropped £20 over night on the Exchange—but I console myself by reflecting on the other side of that question.[1]

Weather has been rather cloudy: but it will be lovely when you & Goonie
come. All is well with us for the moment.

With best love to you both & all

Yrs

W

PS. I have been slaving like a nigger at the book.
We begin in Times Feb 9 & publish Mar 1.
The cigars are delicious.

---

[1] Before the fall in the Exchange, 25,000 francs were worth £321.

Victor Cazalet:[1] *diary*

(*Robert Rhodes James: 'Victor Cazalet, A Portrait'*)

5 January 1923

It is lovely here at Cannes. The time passes with great rapidity and one appears to do nothing. We play tennis, lunch, dine out, and go to the Casino. I only play when Clemmie wants to. I fear it does not interest or amuse me very much as I am not a gambler. I hate losing, and I get too excited when I win, and feel I'm wasting time while I'm there.

Winston has taken to gambling with terrible earnestness. He plays twice daily and is now 20,000 francs up after a month's play. He does not play very high. He works very hard all day, either at his book or painting. I had a very long talk with him one night, from 11 pm to 1 am. I roused him on Free Trade. We had discussed Lloyd George[2] and his last Cabinet. LG, he said, had made one howler after another during the past 18 months, especially in foreign policy. He (Winston) had disagreed with him on all.

Apropos of the Versailles Treaty, Winston told me he said at the time to LG that he would not put his name to it for £1,000. It was cruel and relentless and spelt chaos. But he still maintains that we could not have got through the four critical years after the war except under a Coalition. The year 1919 when there was nearly a revolution was, he thought, the danger year.

As to FE[3] he confessed that the ex-Lord Chancellor had been brutal to his subordinates. The majority of men are fools, said Winston, and when you yourself see the right thing to do, you can't influence them to do it. It was, however, no use FE damning all Conservatives as fools, because whatever he said they would still remain in the Conservative Party.

Winston also told me that he himself was not nearly so ready to see

[1] Victor Alexander Cazalet, 1896–1943. Educated at Eton and Christ Church, Oxford. Oxford half blue for tennis, racquets and squash, 1915. Served on the western front, 1915–18, when he won the Military Cross. A member of General Knox's Staff in Siberia, 1918–19. Conservative MP for Chippenham from 1924 until his death. Parliamentary Secretary, Board of Trade, 1924–6. Political Liaison Officer to General Sikorski, 1941–3. Killed in the air crash in which Sikorski died.

[2] David Lloyd George, 1863–1945. Educated at a Welsh Church school. Solicitor, 1884. Liberal MP for Caernarvon, 1890–1931. President of the Board of Trade, 1905–8. Privy Councillor, 1905. Chancellor of the Exchequer, 1908–15. Minister of Munitions, May 1915–July 1916. Secretary of State for War, July–December 1916. Prime Minister, December 1916–October 1922. Independent Liberal MP, 1931–45. Created Earl, 1945.

[3] Frederick Edwin Smith, 1872–1930. Known as 'FE'. Conservative MP, 1906–19. With Churchill, he founded the Other Club in 1911. Head of the Press Bureau, August 1914; resigned, October 1914. Lieutenant-Colonel, attached to the Indian Corps in France, 1914–15. Solicitor-General, May 1915. Knighted, 1915. Attorney-General, November 1915–19. Created Baron Birkenhead, 1919. Lord Chancellor, 1920–2. Created Viscount, 1921. Created Earl, 1922. Secretary of State for India, 1924–8.

people and be easy of access as LG had always been. I agreed, but added,
'LG never listened if he did not want to hear, and one never felt one could
trust him on any matter. Now *you*, Winston if you want to, as you showed
at Oxford, *you* can win over any young man as you did; only you don't
usually try.'[1] 'No,' he confessed, 'I don't like new people.'

Then I touched on the problem of the unemployed, and suggested that
a policy of Free Trade might possibly be responsible for some of it. He rose
at once, almost furious—'Well Victor, I'm not going to discuss *this* matter
with you.' But he did for over an hour. I told him that extensive travels in
tariff countries had made me think the matter over. In those countries
unemployment did not exist; why were we always subject to it? At this he
gave me the clearest exposition on the necessity of Free Trade for the
country I've ever heard. In that respect he is still a Liberal. 'Otherwise,'
he admitted, 'I'm a Tory.' I accused him of changing views on his life.
He stoutly denied it. After the age of twenty-five, when once he had made
up his mind on a subject he had never changed it, and challenged anyone
to produce a single instance to the contrary.

Then I asked him about the future of the Tory Party. I hoped they
would take up emigration and housing and slums. He said *not* because it
meant expense. He went on talking as he went upstairs, and as he undressed.
He is the most unselfconscious individual I have ever met, once he is
interested in a subject. I have read two chapters of his book. It is very fine.
He is taking enormous trouble with it. If he can keep quiet for another
six months and bring out this great work the future still holds unlimited
scope for his genius.

---

[1] On 18 November 1920 Churchill had spoken on the Coalition Government, and on
Russia, at Oxford University. That same morning, at the end of a Cabinet meeting in
London, he had asked if it might be recorded in the Cabinet Minutes that no Cabinet
Minister would be 'fettered' as regards making anti-Bolshevik speeches. His request granted,
he had gone to Oxford, where he had spoken at the Oxford Union. It was his view, he had
declared, 'that all the harm and misery in Russia has arisen out of the wickedness and
folly of the Bolshevists, and that there will be no recovery of any kind in Russia or in eastern
Europe while these wicked men, this vile group of cosmopolitan fanatics, hold the Russian
nation by the hair of its head and tyrannizes over its great population'. He had continued:
'The policy I will always advocate is the overthrow and destruction of that criminal regime.'

Winston S. Churchill to Jack Churchill

(*Churchill papers: 28/152*)

10 January 1923   Cannes

My dear Jack,

I will write to you early next week about dividing the fund. I shall have Beckenham with me then & can explain my view fully. I have no doubt we can agree.

I want to pay about £500 of bills for building work at 2 Sussex Square & I may require to sell some stock. If so Coats seems to me to be the one. But if you think Fines better take some of them. I am telling Bernau[1] to ask you for what he wants.

I am wondering whether you have got rid of the London & Rhod. There seems to be a good many transactions in them at 5/10½. Do exactly what you think fit. 6/- is better than 5/10. If you want me to pay for the stock sell some more Fines or Coats. Why has Rezende jumped so much? A whole pound in a month? I have about 380 shares. There is a good profit on the original investment wh was under £1,000. They must now be worth over £1,500.

What about Courtaulds. I thought perhaps you wd have nipped out at 66/-. But I suppose having caught hold you couldn't let go. Now they have recessed again.[2]

The franc business goes vy well. Here again I leave it entirely to you. If there is a steady gradual fall I shd hold on. It may go to 75 easily. If there is a sudden drop of four or five points it might be well to get out and come in again in the recovery. If there is a slow recovery I shd hope you could get out at not worse than 68. I am strongly of opinion that the Ruhr business will turn out ill for France.[3]

---

[1] William Henry Bernau, 1870–1937. Started work at Cox & Co, bankers, 1889; in charge of the Insurance Department, 1910–35; retired, 1935. Churchill's insurance broker.

[2] The main shares held by Churchill at this time were 'Coats', J. & P. Coats, Patons & Baldwins Limited (manufacturers and merchants of threads, yarns and knitting wools); 'Fines', Fine Spinners & Doublers Limited (later a Courtaulds subsidiary); Courtaulds Limited (manufacturers of artificial silk); 'London and Rhodesian', the London and Rhodesian Mining and Land Company limited (later Lonrho, of which Sir Abe Bailey was then the principal shareholder); Rezende Mines Limited (a Rhodesian gold mine of which Sir Abe Bailey was Chairman); 'City Lights', the City of London Electric Lighting Company Limited; 'Imps', the Imperial Tobacco Company (of Great Britain & Ireland) Limited; Peruvian Government Bonds; Brazilian Government Bonds; and 'Mexican Eagles', the Mexican Eagle Oil Company Limited (founded in 1908, voluntary liquidation, 1963).

[3] Using the argument that Germany was in *voluntary* default in its reparations deliveries of coal, the French Government had ordered both French and French Colonial troops to occupy the Ruhr—the German industrial area *east* of the river Rhine. The occupation itself took place on 11 January 1923, with Belgian troops also taking part. As Churchill forecast, the Germans responded by a general strike and passive resistance.

The armies & the whole community will offer evy kind of passive resistance. I believe the general value of the franc—apart from fluctuations will fall a good deal further. There will be no comfort in Lausanne, & may be further evil.

I have now accumulated about 27,000 francs profit by gambling. I have had to work vy hard as I have not played any large coups. I deposited the fruits in sterling here & they have appreciated accordingly.

The weather is pleasant but cloudy. I am still in the throes of my book. Beckenham starts on Sunday to help me over the finale of proof correcting.

With best love,
Yours always
W

Winston S. Churchill to Edward Marsh
(*Marsh papers*)

18 January 1923   Cannes

My dear Eddie,

I have noted down a few quotations which I thought might go in at the top of the chapters. You very kindly said you could get them verified for me without much trouble, and if so I should be very much obliged. I shall be home on the 24th and will be very grateful if you can think of any more.

Can you find out for me what exactly Prince Louis' percentage was? I have referred to his German origin. I think he was a Hessian. Others say he was of Austrian extraction.[1]

Lord Londonderry[2] to Winston S. Churchill
(*Churchill papers: 2/126*)

19 January 1923   Mountstewart
                                                        Co. Down

My dear Winston,

I have tried to get a place in the train 'bleu' but I understand every place is booked for days and weeks ahead. I am doubtful also of being able to get

---

[1] Marsh noted on the bottom of Churchill's letter: 'P. Louis was the son of Prince Alexander of Hesse and of the Rhine, by his morganatic wife Countess Julie von Hanke.'

[2] Charles Stewart Henry Vane-Tempest-Stewart, Viscount Castlereagh, 1878–1949. Educated at Eton and Sandhurst. Conservative MP for Maidstone, 1906–15. Succeeded his father as 7th Marquess of Londonderry, 1915. Served briefly on the western front as 2nd in Command, Royal Horse Guards, 1915. Under-Secretary of State for Air, 1920–1. Minister of Education and Leader of the Senate, Government of Northern Ireland, 1921–6. Returned to Westminster as First Commissioner of Works, 1928–9 and 1931; and as Secretary of State for Air and Lord Privy Seal, 1931–5. Churchill's second cousin.

away. There is a heritage of difficulty here and as one question is disposed of another crops up immediately. I have always loved your optimism and your encouragement and also your assistance when you were responsible for us, but I feel very gloomy now and I really do not see a break of any kind in the clouds.

The Free State is an impossible proposition and no one can make a success of the idea embodied in that title, and it is merely a question of whether at some stage of the descent of Ireland to anarchy and chaos the British Government will step in, and tan Ireland like a large nanny which has mutinied against a long suffering nurse. If Ireland is to be left to its own devices, it is an ugly sore and in the end may poison the whole body of the Empire.

All the analogies of a dominion are faulty. There is really no inbetwixts and betweens. I see that so clearly here. You must be independent or dependent, you can't be one day one thing and the next day another. Either your government governs or it does not govern. I won't weary you on your well-earned holiday with grumbles, but I feel very depressed from a source of impotence and inability to do anything to save the disaster.

I believe that when a country is burdened with taxation and when Finance is obtrusively the governing factor, that nothing else develops at all, and our role, and it is a d—d unattractive one is just to hold on while the atrophying influence is operating. This influence will see us out and probably the next generation too, so I more than ever long for a bout of complete irresponsibility which must be delightfully refreshing.

You are feeling it I know far more than I ever could, because your continuous and gigantic responsibility for practically seventeen years must contribute to the reaction of leisure which no one knows better than yourself how best to employ. Thank you so much for asking; I should have loved to have come and basked in the sunshine at Cannes and it would have been a real pleasure to have seen you in an atmosphere other than that of hurried visits connected with this eternal and in many ways silly problem of Ireland: but I feel it is not to be this year and God knows where we will all be next year. However I am expecting you here for Whitsuntide and I hope we shall have some sunsets which will satisfy your passion for colour. My best love to Mrs W.

Yrs affectionately
Charley

Winston S. Churchill to Clementine Churchill

(*Spencer-Churchill papers*)

27 January 1923   Ritz Hotel, London

My darling,

We arrived after a quite easy and comfortable journey, and Randolph[1] was not a bit overtired. The next day I took him and Pebbin[2] down to Chartwell, where Tilden[3] met us. I went most carefully into the whole question of the new wing at the back of the house. It practically corresponds to the staircase tower in the front angle and gives a good pantry between the kitchen and the dining room on the same level, a cook's sitting room above it 12' by 15', your maid's room the same size above that, and an additional bedroom or servant's room on top. All these rooms have full sized windows not shut in in any way. A hanging gallery passes from your maid's room to your private staircase. It looks very attractive on the plan. The cost of this addition will be between £400 and £600 according to the extent to which the old material can be used. I think it is well worth doing. It permits the following other alterations to be made.

First. As you enter the front door on the right is the downstairs library and on the left a hall which we had intended to use for a pantry and lavatory. The library ceiling is now exposed and is really a very fine oak roofed ceiling like Blois. The hall ceiling is the same, and it is a pity to waste this room in the old part of the house upon pantry and lavatory. It can therefore be made into an additional reception room with an oak ceiling, in the direct line of the drawing room and the boudoir. When the doors are opened all through the length of these three rooms will be over 80 feet. Tilden is very keen on this. It undoubtedly makes a very fine sweep. The lavatory and cloak room on

---

[1] Randolph Frederick Edward Spencer Churchill, 1911–68. Churchill's only son. His godfathers were F. E. Smith and Sir Edward Grey. Educated at Eton and Christ Church, Oxford. On leaving Oxford in 1932, without taking his degree, he worked briefly for the Imperial Chemical Industries as assistant editor of their house magazine. Joined the staff of the *Sunday Graphic*, 1932; wrote subsequently for many newspapers, including the *Evening Standard* (1937–9). Reported during Hitler's election campaign of 1932, the Chaco War of 1935 and the Spanish Civil War. Unsuccessful Parliamentary candidate, 1935 (twice), 1936, 1945, 1950 and 1951. Conservative MP for Preston, 1940–5. On active service, North Africa and Italy, 1941–3. Major, British mission to the Yugoslav Army of National Liberation, 1943–4 (MBE, 1944). Historian; author of the first two volumes of this biography.

[2] Henry Winston Spencer Churchill, 1913– . Known as Peregrine and 'Pebbin'. Jack Churchill's younger son. Inventor and Company Director.

[3] Philip Armstrong Tilden, 1887–1956. Architect, and decorator in murals. Among the houses on which he worked were Sir Philip Sassoon's houses, Port Lympne, and 25 Park Lane; and Lloyd George's house at Churt in Surrey. He also exhibited black-and-white drawings at the Royal Academy, and designed bookplates. A Governor of the Old Vic Theatre, and of Sadlers Wells. Author of a novel, *Noah* (1932), and a volume of memoirs, *True Remembrances* (1954).

this plan move into the old cook's sitting room (where we now have lunch), and the pantry, as I have said, goes into the ground floor of the new tower or wing. The arrangement of the kitchen, pantry and the dining room all adjoining and on one level, is, according to Tilden the best.

Another result is that the dirty dark bedroom on the top floor but one, will now be cut off entirely from the windows and will become a box-room, linen room, housemaids' cupboard, etc. It will be lighted from a skylight. This again renders possible a movement at the bottom of the children's wing. Their lower room takes in the office room on its immediate left. A very large window has been made here and the room is now a very large one. Though oddly shaped, it is quite attractive, the two rooms having been thrown into one.

The room with the funny trefoil pattern windows will become the new office, a long row of windows opening below the terrace. None of these changes involve any alteration in the work. They certainly greatly improve the house, though on the balance they neither add to nor diminish our bed-room accommodation. However every room becomes a good room, and every window a proper window giving full light and air. The new reception room will also be a very great addition.

I will get everything forward into a condition in which we can discuss the whole question as soon as I come out, and then let Tilden go ahead on a tele-gram. Goonie and Jack are coming down with me to see it tomorrow. The moving of the earth is not yet completed but in another ten days it will all be finished. All the work on the garden is going forward steadily.

I have been working continuously at the book and there are many things I can settle here which it is quite impossible to do by correspondence. I think it will be finally off my hands by the time I leave on Sunday week.

We have had a blow over the American serial rights. Owing to the irrita-tion over the Lloyd George episode[1] and the fiasco of the Kaiser's Memoirs, I cannot get a bid of any kind. We have been hoping to make two or three thousand from this source, and it is a great disappointment that it should have dried up so inopportunely. The Scandinavian rights have been sold for £100, which is not bad.[2]

I dined with Goonie the night I arrived. On Thursday, with Venetia—

[1] While Lloyd George was still Prime Minister he had accepted a proposal from the literary agent, Curtis Brown, to write his War memoirs on his 'retirement'. After his defeat in the General Election of 1922 he had postponed writing them, on the grounds that nobody could be certain whether his current 'retirement' would be permanent or not. They were eventually published in 1933, followed in 1938 by his memoirs of the Peace Conference.

[2] On 29 January 1923 Clementine Churchill wrote to her husband from Cannes: 'I am so sorry about the American Serial Rights. Perhaps however when the Book comes out the Yanks will come forward again. Mr Baldwin does not seem to have been able to charm the bird out of the Bush and Bonar is almost as much hated here in France as Ll G, only they don't say so' (*Spencer-Churchill papers*).

very pleasant. Last night Archie and I dined at the Turf. He starts for Cannes tomorrow and they are both staying for ten days at the Carlton. I am dining with Jack Wodehouse[1] on Monday night and with Haldane[2] on Tuesday. Grey[3] and Garvin[4] lunched with me yesterday and we had a long interesting talk. They are very pessimistic about the state of Europe and seem to think that some awful thing is going to happen quite soon. I do not believe it. I think the awful thing has happened.

I went to see Sir Hugh Fraser,[5] the counsel whom my solicitors recommended, about the 'Evening News' libel. There is no doubt it is a gross libel unprotected by privilege. I am therefore issuing a writ in the course of the next few days against the 'Evening News' and am scrutinising other papers which repeated the offence.[6]

I have also undertaken to join the Artillery which is replacing the old Oxfordshire Hussars.

Such is my report.

Tender love my darling one to you & to yr kittens. Randolph was sad at going back, but bore up bravely.

I am longing to get back again to the sunshine.

I have vy good rooms here—quite moderate charges.

Your ever loving
W

[1] John Wodehouse, 1883–1941. Liberal MP for mid-Norfolk, 1906–10. Captain, 16th Lancers; served in France, 1914–17, and in Italy, 1918 (wounded, awarded the Military Cross). Churchill's personal political Secretary, 1922–5. Succeeded his father as 3rd Earl of Kimberley, 1932. Owner of over 11,000 acres in Norfolk. Killed in a German air raid. His brother Edward had been killed in action in 1918.

[2] Richard Burdon Haldane, 1856–1928. Liberal MP, 1885–1911. Secretary of State for War, 1905–12. Created Viscount, 1911. Lord Chancellor, first under Asquith, 1912–15; then under Ramsay MacDonald, 1924.

[3] Edward Grey, 1862–1933. 3rd Baronet, 1882. Educated at Winchester and Balliol College, Oxford. Liberal MP for Berwick-on-Tweed, 1885–1916. Foreign Secretary, 1905–16. Created Viscount Grey of Fallodon, 1916. Ambassador on a special mission to the USA, 1919.

[4] James Louis Garvin, 1868–1947. Editor, The Observer, 1908–42. An original member of the Other Club, 1911. Editor, Pall Mall Gazette, 1912–15. Editor-in-Chief, Encyclopaedia Britannica, 1926–9. His only son was killed in action in 1916 on the western front.

[5] Hugh Fraser,   –1927. Called to the Bar, 1886. Reader and Examiner in Common Law at the Inns of Court, 1897–1924. Knighted, 1917. Arbitrator, Building Trades Dispute, 1923. Editor of the 6th edition of the Law of Libel and Slander. Judge of the King's Bench Division of the High Court of Justice from 1924 until his death.

[6] More than a year later, on 14 March 1924, the Bolton Evening News published an article entitled 'Mrs Winston Churchill'. In the article, Churchill and his father were said to have been 'hell' to their wives. On April 10 Churchill's solicitors submitted a Statement of Claim to Tillotsons Newspapers Ltd, owners of the paper. On May 31 the Churchills received apologies from Fred L. Tillotson, Director of Tillotsons Newspapers Ltd, and from A. C. Fox-Davies, the writer of the paragraph.

Geoffrey Dawson[1] *to Winston S. Churchill*

(*Churchill papers: 2/126*)

28 January 1923

My dear Churchill,

By an odd coincidence I had just been reading the proofs of your chapter when your letter came & was thinking I should like to see you while you are in England. But I can't lunch tomorrow, I'm afraid. What I could do is to come to the Ritz just before or after—12 or 3—if that is any good to you—Thank you so much for congratulations, though I'm not sure that its really an occasion for them, either from my point of view or from that of 'The Times'!

Will you telephone a time that suits? 6600 Holborn will always reach me, either here or at the Office.

Yours sincerely
Geoffrey Dawson

Winston S. Churchill to Sir John Lavery[2]

(*Churchill papers: 1/165*)

29 January 1923   Ritz Hotel

My wife and I were truly grieved that you and Hazel were not able to get away as we had arranged. We have had moderate weather. It is very cold, but still the sun shines nearly every day for most of the day.

I have not made much headway in painting and should greatly have valued the stimulus of your presence and example. My pictures take me much longer now, and I have been four or five days trying to do some pretty reflections of bright coloured ships in the clear water of the harbour. I should have liked to have seen you splash them on.

---

[1] George Geoffrey Robinson, 1874–1944. Educated at Eton and Magdalen College, Oxford. Fellow of All Souls, 1898. Private Secretary to Milner in South Africa, 1901–5. Editor of the *Johannesburg Star*, 1905–10. Editor of *The Times*, 1912–19 and 1923–41. Took the surname of Dawson, 1917.

[2] John Lavery, 1856–1931. Painter. Born in Belfast. A Roman Catholic. Exhibited his first oil painting at Glasgow, 1879. Vice-President of the International Society of Sculptors, Painters and Gravers, 1897. Knighted, 1918. President of the Royal Society of Portrait Painters from 1932 until his death. Some of Churchill's earliest paintings had been done in Lavery's London studio. Lavery married Hazel Martyn, as his second wife, in 1910.

Winston S. Churchill to Lord Londonderry
(*Churchill papers: 2/126*)

29 January 1923   Ritz Hotel

Thank you so much for your letter. We are most grieved that you cannot come to us, but I know how intimate and insistent are your Irish ties. I am up to my neck in work, as usual, about the publication of my book. I shall look forward to sending you a copy about the first week in March, when it is to see the light.

Ireland has indeed to go through a long and cruel apprenticeship. But human societies would never have been erected out of anarchy or maintained against its perpetual assaults unless there was inherent in tribes and peoples that deep desire for self-preservation on which laws and civilisation are maintained. I do not believe for a moment that the Irish are an exception to the common run of mankind, although I know it is the fashion for many Irishmen to say so. I believe they are going to come through all right, but I can quite understand the worry it is to you during this long period of disorder, uncertainty and expense.

Winston S. Churchill to Clementine Churchill
(*Spencer-Churchill papers*)

29 January 1923   Ritz Hotel

My Darling,

I send this by Archie, who is just starting for Cannes. I have no news beyond what I wrote you two days ago. I have been working steadily at the book and there is practically nothing now to do except to read the final page proofs. All the outstanding points are settled. All the maps, tables, appendices, preface, are complete. It has been a tremendous hustle. My old Admiral worked very well at the end. We are still in doubt about the title, which is to be settled finally on Tuesday. 'The World Crisis', 'The Meteor Flat' and 'Within the Storm' are the best suggestions we have up to date. They are none of them very satisfactory.

Freddie[1] has returned from America and we are dining together tonight.

[1] Frederick Edward Guest, 1875–1937. The third son of 1st Baron Wimborne. Churchill's cousin. Served in the South African War as a Captain, Life Guards, 1899–1902. Private Secretary to Churchill, 1906. An original member of the Other Club, 1911. Treasurer, HM Household, 1912–15. ADC to Sir John French, 1914–16. On active service in East Africa, 1916–17. Patronage Secretary, Treasury (Chief Whip), May 1917–April 1921. Privy Councillor, 1920. Secretary of State for Air, April 1921–October 1922. Liberal MP, 1923–9. Joined the Consevative Party, 1930. Conservative MP, 1931–7.

Sarah[1] came to see me yesterday. She goes to America on Wednesday. She was full of information: said the Government were divided on the evacuation of Cologne. Baldwin[2] has returned empty handed from America. There is no doubt they are finding the problem no more easy to settle than we did.

I am just off to Chartwell again with Jack and Goonie. We picnic there. Tilden comes too.

I am lunching with Frances Horner[3] on Wednesday and am going to the Grigg wedding.[4] I telegraphed to you this morning to know if you had sent a present. If not, I will send one.

Jack and I went to a play together last night. Tomorrow I dine with the Wodehouses; Tuesday with Haldane. Garvin is reading my proofs now and comes to lunch on Tuesday to tell me his impression. It will be very interesting to learn if he is pleased.

Tender love my sweet—a vy nice photo in the Times yesterday of your hitting a back hander.

I am much looking forward to coming out again

Your loving devoted
W

Winston S. Churchill to Clementine Churchill

(*Spencer-Churchill papers*)

30 January 1923   Ritz Hotel

My darling one,

The week is passing very rapidly away and I am so busy that I hardly ever leave the Ritz except for meals.

Lots of people have been to see me or have wished to make pleasant plans. I lunched with Edie[5] yesterday. Millie[6] was there, and I saw also old Harry

[1] Lady Sarah Wilson (see page 9, note 2).

[2] Stanley Baldwin, 1867–1947. Educated at Harrow and Trinity College, Cambridge. Conservative MP for Bewdley, 1908–37. Financial Secretary to the Treasury, 1917–21. President of the Board of Trade, 1921–2. Chancellor of the Exchequer, 1922–3. Prime Minister, 1923–4 and 1924–9. Lord President of the Council, 1931–5. Prime Minister (for the third time), 1935–7. Created Earl, and Knight of the Garter, 1937.

[3] Frances Graham, 1858–1940. She married Sir John Horner in 1883. Their home at Mells in Somerset was a centre of social entertainment. Their eldest son Edward was killed in action in 1917.

[4] On 31 January 1923 Edward Grigg (see page 113, note 2) married Joan Alice Katherine Dickson-Poynder, the daughter of Lord and Lady Islington.

[5] Lady Londonderry (see page 133, note 1).

[6] Millicent Fanny, 1867–1955. Daughter of the 4th Earl of Rosslyn. In 1884 she married the 4th Duke of Sutherland (who died in 1913). In 1914 she married Brigadier-General

Chaplin[1]—marvellous fellow, 82 and resolved to hunt again in spite of tubes and every kind of horror: Lord Derby[2] sends him *every day* a hare which he eats roast for luncheon. I went to the Co-Optimists with Jack Wodehouse and his wife last night. Tonight I am dining with Haldane. Tomorrow I lunch at New Court to do business in the city.[3] I am going to visit Jack's office for the first time. On Thursday the Prince[4] is lunching with me at Buck's Club with Freddie Guest and Jack Wodehouse to talk polo and politics. In the evening I am dining with Maud.[5] Austen[6] is bidden and also Sir George Younger.[7] On Friday I dine again with Venetia.

On Saturday I am going to pay another visit to Chartwell. I shall have extensive plans to put before you for dealing with the back entrance problem and also with the drive up to the front entrance and the pathway to the tennis court. Nothing will be done, however, till you agree.

Percy Desmond FitzGerald (who died in 1933) and in 1919 she married Lieutenant-Colonel George Ernest Hawes. Churchill was a lifelong friend of her and her two sons, and in 1921 (when Colonial Secretary) he appointed her elder son, the 5th Duke of Sutherland, as his Under-Secretary of State.

[1] Henry Chaplin, 1840–1923. Educated at Harrow and Christ Church. Conservative MP, 1868–1906 and 1907–16. Chancellor of the Duchy of Lancaster, 1885–6. President of the Board of Agriculture, 1886–92; of the Local Government Board, 1895–1900. Created Viscount, 1916. A keen sportsman, famed for his prowess in the hunting field; nicknamed the Squire. In 1876 he married Florence, elder daughter of the 3rd Duke of Sutherland. She died in 1881; he died on 29 May 1923.

[2] Edward George Villiers Stanley, 1865–1948. Educated at Wellington College. Lieutenant, Grenadier Guards, 1885–95. Conservative MP for West Houghton, 1892–1906. Postmaster General, 1903–5. 17th Earl of Derby, 1908. Director-General of Recruiting, October 1915. Under-Secretary of State at the War Office, July–December 1916. Secretary of State for War, December 1916–18. Ambassador to France, 1918–20. Secretary of State for War, 1922–4. Member of the Joint Select Committee on the Indian Constitution, 1933–4.

[3] New Court, St Swithin's Lane, EC4, in the City of London, was the head office of N. M. Rothschild & Sons Ltd, bankers.

[4] Edward Albert Christian George Andrew Patrick David, 1894–1972. Entered Royal Navy as a Cadet, 1907. Prince of Wales, 1910–36. 2nd Lieutenant, Grenadier Guards, August 1914. Attached to Sir John French's Staff, November 1914. Served in France and Italy, 1914–18. Major, 1918. Succeeded his father as King, January 1936. Abdicated, December 1936. Duke of Windsor, 1936.

[5] Maud Burke. Born in New York. In 1895 she married Sir Bache Edward Cunard, 3rd Baronet (who died in 1925). She died in 1948.

[6] Joseph Austen Chamberlain, 1863–1937. Educated at Rugby and Trinity College, Cambridge. Conservative MP, 1892–1937. Chancellor of the Exchequer, 1903–5. Unsuccessful candidate for the leadership of the Conservative Party, 1911. Secretary of State for India, 1915–17. Minister without Portfolio, 1918–19. Chancellor of the Exchequer, 1919–21. Lord Privy Seal, 1921–2. Foreign Secretary, 1924–9. Knight of the Garter, 1925. First Lord of the Admiralty, 1931.

[7] George Younger, 1851–1929. Educated at the Edinburgh Academy, the son of a successful brewer. President of the National Union of Conservative Associations in Scotland, 1904. Conservative MP for Ayr Burghs, 1906–22. Created Baronet, 1911. Chairman of the Conservative Party Organization, 1916–23. Treasurer of the Conservative Party, 1923–9. Created Viscount, 1923. Chairman, George Younger & Sons, Brewers, Ltd.

The 'Evening News', confronted with the writ, have sent round wishing to apologise and protesting that they never meant any harm. I find many of the other papers issued even worse libels, and my idea is to deal with them altogether and make them all come up in court and tender their apologies. The 'Evening News' has offered to pay all expenses. This is, of course, without prejudice. I have not quite decided what course to take.

The Franc has continued to topple down and now stands at 76.60 tonight! 77.40 this morning.

I am settling up a lot of business here and am reconsidering most of my investments. There is a considerable slump on the bad news from the Ruhr, from Turkey and from America, in none of which spheres have our new rulers managed to achieve any useful result.

Commander Hilton Young,[1] the new Chief Whip of the Lloyd George Liberals, asked to come to see me. He seems very anxious to find me another seat. He will no doubt look about, but it is what Asquith[2] called 'A dark and difficult adventure'.

I am practically through the book now and have nothing more to do except to read finally through the page proofs and alter commas and odd words. We have reached the moment when one must say 'As the tree falls, so shall it lie'.

Geoffrey Dawson, the new Editor of the 'Times', came to see me yesterday and suggested himself the title of 'The Great Amphibian', but I cannot get either Butterworth[3] or Scribner[4] the American publishers to fancy it. They want 'The World Crisis' or possibly 'Sea Power and the World Crisis' or

---

[1] Edward Hilton Young, 1879–1960. Barrister, 1904. Assistant Editor, The *Economist*, 1909–10. City Editor, the *Morning Post*, 1910–14. Naval Mission to Serbia, 1915. Severely wounded at Zeebrugge, 1918, and promoted to Lieutenant-Commander; commanded the British armoured train at Archangel, 1919 (DSO). Liberal MP for Norwich, 1915–23 and 1924–9. Financial Secretary to the Treasury, 1921–2, and Chief Whip of the Lloyd George Liberals, 1922. Married the widow of 'Scott of the Antarctic', 1922. Joined the Conservative Party, 1926. Knighted, 1927. Conservative MP for Sevenoaks, 1929–35. Secretary, Department of Overseas Trade, 1931. Minister of Health, 1931–5. Created Baron Kennet, 1935.

[2] Herbert Henry Asquith, 1852–1928. Educated at the City of London School and Balliol College, Oxford. Liberal MP, 1886–1918 and 1920–4. Home Secretary, 1892–1905. Chancellor of the Exchequer, 1905–8. Prime Minister, 1908–16. Created Earl of Oxford and Asquith, 1925. His eldest son, Raymond, was killed in action in 1916.

[3] Thornton Butterworth, Churchill's publisher from 1919 to 1939. He published all five volumes of Churchill's *The World Crisis* (the first in 1923, the fifth in 1931), as well as the single volume abridged and revised edition (1931) and the Sandhurst edition (1933). He also published Churchill's *My Early Life* (1930); *India* (1931); *Thoughts and Adventures* (1932); *Great Contemporaries* (1937) and its enlarged edition (1938); and *Step by Step* (1939).

[4] Charles Scribner, 1890–1952. Joined his father's publishing house, Charles Scribner's Sons Ltd, 1913; Secretary, 1918–26; Vice-President, 1926–32; President, 1932–52. On active service as a 1st Lieutenant, France, 1917–18 (US Remount Service). After publishing *The World Crisis* he published Churchill's *Marlborough* in six volumes, but declined to publish *A History of the English-Speaking Peoples*.

'Sea Power in the World Crisis'. We have to settle tomorrow for certain. The 'Times' is very friendly and helpful. They have turned some of their best men on to try to find mottoes for the chapter headings I have been unable to fill. Garvin has read it all through and is absolutely satisfied with it. He is going to write a tremendous review in the 'Observer' when the time comes.

I see in my press cuttings very nice photographs of Sarah[1] and Diana[2] in the Battle of Flowers; also one of you and Oliver[3] bombarding some unlucky wight.

Tyrrell[4] has just been to see me, back from Lausanne. Evidently he had a terrible time with the All-Highest,[5] but of course he was very discreet.

Muriel Beckett[6] was at dinner last night and, as usual, laid it on with a trowel.

I am much looking forward to getting away again. I do hope we are going to have some pleasant sunshine in which I can paint to my heart's content.

Au revoir my darling
Tender love for all
Your devoted
W

[1] Sarah Millicent Hermione Spencer Churchill. Born while her father was returning from the siege of Antwerp, 7 October 1914. Edward Marsh was her godfather. An actress, she published *The Empty Spaces* (poems) in 1966, and *A Thread in the Tapestry* (recollections) in 1967.

[2] Diana Churchill, 1906–1963. Churchill's eldest child. In 1932 she married the eldest son of Sir Abe Bailey, John Milner Bailey (from whom she obtained a divorce in 1935). In 1935 she married Duncan Sandys MP.

[3] Oliver Locker-Lampson (see page 120, note 1).

[4] William George Tyrrell, 1866–1947. Educated at Balliol College, Oxford. Entered the Foreign Service, 1889. Private Secretary to Sir Edward Grey, 1907–15. Knighted, 1913. Assistant Under-Secretary of State at the Foreign Office, 1919–25; Permanent Under-Secretary, 1925–8. Privy Councillor, 1928. Ambassador in Paris, 1928–34. Created Baron, 1929. President of the British Board of Film Censors, 1935–47. His younger son, Hugo, died of wounds received in action, February 1915; his elder son, Francis, was killed in action in February 1918.

[5] George Nathaniel Curzon, 1859–1925. Educated at Eton and Balliol College, Oxford. President of the Oxford Union, 1880. Conservative MP, 1886–98. Under-Secretary of State for India, 1891–2; for Foreign Affairs, 1895–8. Created Baron, 1898. Viceroy of India, 1898–1905. Created Earl, 1911. Lord Privy Seal, May 1915–December 1916. President of the Air Board, 1916. Member of the War Cabinet, 1916–19. Secretary of State for Foreign Affairs, 1919–24. Created Marquess, 1921. Lord President of the Council, 1924–5. In 1923 he negotiated, at Lausanne, a Treaty of Peace between Britain and Turkey.

[6] Muriel Helen Florence Paget, 1878–1941. Daughter of Lord Berkeley Charles Sidney Paget, 4th son of the 2nd Marquess of Anglesey. In 1896 she married Rupert Evelyn Beckett (1870–1955), third son of the 1st Baron Grimthorpe. A friend of Churchill since 1900.

Winston S. Churchill to Jack Churchill

(*Churchill papers: 28/152*)

am   Cannes

10 February 1923

My dear Jack,

Many thanks for yr letter.

I shd like you to sell the Coats and buy me another 1,000 City Lights. For this purpose you might take the balance from the February franc money wh perhaps you can discount for me, as Vickers[1] suggested.

Sale of Coats	1,625
Balance	144
Feb Franc deal	720
	£2,489
1,000 City Lights @ 47	£2,450
	(about)

Wd you advise my getting another 500 Mexican Eagles? If so sell enough of the Imps (there is a good profit on them) to cover the purchase.

The weather is unsettled. I am going to play polo this afternoon for the first time!

Best love
Yours
W

Winston S. Churchill to Jack Churchill

(*Churchill papers: 28/152*)

16 February 1923   Cannes

My dear Jack,

I am delighted at the good news about yr 14%. It is a well-won tribute to yr sagacity, influence, industry & long acquired reputation. It shd make a considerable difference.

---

[1] Horace Cecil Vickers, 1882–1944. Apprenticed to a firm of stockbrokers as a clerk at the age of 12. Member of the London Stock Exchange, 1904. Founded the firm of Vickers, da Costa, of which he became the Senior Partner, 1917 (his son Ralph Cecil Vickers, MC, became its Chairman in 1972; his daughter, Joan Vickers, was created Baroness in 1974, having been a Conservative MP, 1955–74). Churchill's stockbroker.

I am much interested in all you say about the book. I get 10/- on every copy—& receive £5,000 on account for the first volume. After 10,000 have been sold therefore my 10/- revives. We might conceivably sell 15,000. Do let me know anything else you hear.
Business.

1. I agree that the American money shd come home. Take the necessary steps & let us have a good scheme of investment. The sooner the better.
2. I noticed the Peruvian rise. It wd only have amounted to £100 & we have more profit on the alternatives.
3. Have we got the 7½% Brazilians or the 8%. The 7½ are worth more than the 8%. I hope we have got the right ones.
4. *Cox.* It makes me shiver to think what we may have escaped. Fancy if they had impounded or embezzled my overdraft! I don't see how they could have made away with the shares in their hands. Surely that was not a danger. But it is disconcerting to see how uncertain the ground is under one's feet.

It will be quite easy to pay off the loans if they want them. But surely it is not difficult to borrow £10,000 at 5% on £30,000 of securities. We will wait & see what happens. With vy best love

Yrs always
W

PS. What about selling a bear in marks. How can they keep this up long. It is a pure manoeuvre. France has got them by the balls. Although she gets no pleasure out of it, neither do they. Write me a proposition; or if it is urgent sell £2,000 for the end of April. Act as you think fit.
PPS. Just played 6 chuckers of Polo successfully.

Winston S. Churchill to W. H. Bernau

(*Churchill papers 28/144*)

17 February 1923   Cannes
Private

Dear Mr Bernau,
   I was vy much startled & surprised to read the news that Cox's had been taken over by Lloyds. It is the end of a long story & closes an enterprise & business wh played so prominent a part in the life of the Army that one can hardly adjust ones mind to the change. I know you will feel vy much the

changes in the control & management of the gt firm you have served so long.[1]

With regard to my account, my pass book just received shows that the excess overdraft is about £864. I am giving the architect a cheque for £500 and there are about £200 of other cheques besides—total say 1,5 or 1,600£ excess. Mr J Churchill is paying in about £330 wh is in his hands, & at the end of the first week in March he will send you about £700 more which is a profit already made & to be paid to me then. This will leave the account almost £500 beyond the overdraft figures. But I am expecting almost immediately to receive from Messrs Scribners N York the new instalments on account of book, wh will be about £1,000 and this will be put at once into my current account. I shd hope therefore that it will not be necessary to sell any stock; but if you prefer it, I can tell Mr Churchill to send you another 6 or 700£. He will do whatever you wish & I am instructing him accordingly.

The weather here has been indifferent, but I am getting much better in myself.

Yours truly
Winston S. Churchill

[1] On February 24 Bernau replied: 'Beyond the sentiment of Cox's having disappeared as a separate Bank, there is nothing to be said against it. The small earthen vessel cannot travel down the stream of modern enterprise in company with the large brass pots, better inside one of them. In 10 years time there will be no private Banks. . . . As far as our customers are concerned, the only difference there will be is the further security of Lloyds enormous funds. The same men will attend to them and the same facilities will be given to them. You can always write to me and look to me to carry on exactly as in the past.'

Winston S. Churchill to Sir James Masterton-Smith: [1] *telegram*

(*Bonar Law papers*)

21 February 1923
Urgent

If further questions,[2] grateful if you would point out to PM[3] that practically all Admiralty matters have already been fully dealt with by official historian. Winston.

Sir James Masterton-Smith to Patrick Gower [4]

(*Bonar Law papers*)

21 February 1923
Personal

Dear Gower,

You should see at once the enclosed telegram which Mr Churchill has just sent me from Cannes. Mr Churchill, of course, is referring to the two volumes of the Official History of the War entitled 'Naval Operations' which were

---

[1] James Edward Masterton-Smith, 1878–1938. Educated at Harrow and Hertford College, Oxford. Entered Admiralty, 1901. Private Secretary to five First Lords: McKenna, 1910–11; Churchill, 1911–15; Balfour, 1915–16; Carson, 1916–17; Sir E. Geddes, 1917. Assistant Secretary to Churchill, Ministry of Munitions, 1917–19; War Office, 1919–20. Knighted, 1919. Permanent Under-Secretary of State, Colonial Office, 1921–4.

[2] At question time on 19 February 1923 several Labour MPs, including Josiah Wedgwood, George Lansbury, J. H. Thomas and Oswald Mosley, had criticized Churchill's publication of Admiralty telegrams in *The Times* serial of his new book, *The World Crisis*. Four days earlier, on February 15, Bonar Law had been asked in the House of Commons on whose authority Churchill was publishing these Admiralty telegrams. He replied: 'I am informed that Mr Churchill was given copies of some of his own official minutes and of the Admiralty orders or telegrams based on or leading up to those minutes by the authority of the First Lord of the Admiralty. It is of course an obligation upon Ministers and officials not to disclose confidential State or official papers or information without the previous approval of His Majesty's Government for the time being, or in the case of Cabinet information without the consent of His Majesty.'

[3] Andrew Bonar Law, 1858–1923. Born in Canada. Brought to Scotland at the age of twelve. Conservative MP, 1900–10 and 1911–23. Parliamentary Secretary, Board of Trade, 1902–5. Leader of the Conservatives in the House of Commons, 1911. Secretary of State for the Colonies, May 1915–December 1916. Chancellor of the Exchequer, 1916–19. Lord Privy Seal, 1919–21. Prime Minister, 1922–3. Two of his three sons were killed in action.

[4] Robert Patrick Malcolm Gower, 1887–1964. Educated at Marlborough and Emmanuel College, Cambridge. Entered the Inland Revenue, 1910. Transferred to the Treasury, 1919; Assistant Private Secretary to Bonar Law, 1917–18. Private Secretary to Austen Chamberlain, 1919–22. Private Secretary to successive Prime Ministers (Bonar Law, MacDonald and Baldwin), 1922–8. Knighted, 1924. Chief Publicity Officer, Conservative Central Office, 1929–39.

written and published by the late Sir Julian Corbett.[1] These two volumes, as is stated on their title page, were part of a 'History of the Great War based on official documents by direction of the Historical Section of the Committee of Imperial Defence'. Further in each volume the following note appears 'The Lord Commissioners of the Admiralty have given the author access to official documents in the preparation of this work, but they are in no way responsible for his reading or presentation of the facts as stated'.

Yours sincerely,
J. E. Masterton-Smith

PS. Mr Churchill's point is that on the naval side of the period dealt with in his book all the facts—in one form or another—have already appeared in the official History.

Patrick Gower to Sir James Masterton-Smith

(*Bonar Law papers*)

26 February 1923

My dear Masterton Smith,

I showed the Prime Minister your letter of the 21st instant and the telegram which you had received from Mr Churchill in regard to the publication of official documents in his 'Times' Articles. The Prime Minister hardly thinks that the telegram really deals with the criticisms that are being made in the House of Commons and elsewhere.

Yours sincerely
Patrick Gower

[1] Julian Stafford Corbett, 1854–1922. Naval Historian. Barrister, 1877–82. Special Correspondent, *Pall Mall Gazette*, Dongola Expedition, 1896. Lecturer in History, Royal Naval War College, 1903. Admiralty representative, Historical Committee of the Committee of Imperial Defence; on 27 August 1915 he agreed to undertake an official naval history, and began work on 17 March 1916. Knighted, 1917. Author of the first three volumes of *Naval Operations*, part of the Official History of the Great War, published in 1920, 1922 and 1923 (posthumously); the 4th and 5th volumes were written by Sir Henry Newbolt, and published in 1928 and 1931.

Winston S. Churchill to Andrew Bonar Law

(*Bonar Law papers*)

3 March 1923
Private and Personal

Dear Prime Minister,

I have read in the newspapers the Questions and Answers in the House of Commons on the subject of the use of official documents in war memoirs, and in case the Government are considering the subject, I think it right that the following points should be borne in mind.

The question of what should be disclosed cannot be decided without reference to what has already been disclosed with the acquiescence of the Government. Lord Kitchener's biographer,[1] dealing with matters in which I am concerned, has made the freest use of official documents of all kinds, including a prolonged extract from one of my Cabinet memoranda in 1915. I raised this matter in the Cabinet at the time, you yourself being present, and the matter was dismissed as wholly unimportant.

Lord Jellicoe has written two volumes on the naval war. The first of these deals exclusively with my period and was the foundation of widespread criticisms in the press upon the administration of the then Boards of Admiralty. Lord Jellicoe gives an account of confidential conferences on board his Flagship in 1914, in which he attributes to me, in perfect good faith and courtesy, opinions which I do not accept.

Lord Fisher has published two volumes full of confidential matter largely related to the period with which I am concerned. He prints various important memoranda which he wrote as First Sea Lord or for the Committee of Imperial Defence. In his book entitled 'Memories' he has printed six or seven pages of practically verbatim extracts from Colonel Hankey's[2] minutes of the War Council discussions of 1914 and 1915. These explain fully his position in regard to the very controversial issues connected with the Dardanelles.

---

[1] George Compton Archibald Arthur, 1860–1946. 3rd Baronet, 1878. Entered Army, 1880. Private Secretary to Lord Kitchener, 1914–16. Assistant to the Director of Military Operations, War Office, 1916–18. On several missions to France; he acted as interpreter between Sir Douglas Haig and General Nivelle before the battle of Arras, March 1917. His publications included *Life of Lord Kitchener* (3 vols, 1920) and *Concerning Winston Spencer Churchill* (1940).

[2] Maurice Pascal Alers Hankey, 1877–1963. Entered Royal Marine Artillery, 1895. Captain, 1899. Retired, 1912. Secretary to the Committee of Imperial Defence, 1912–38. Lieutenant-Colonel, Royal Marines, 1914. Knighted, February 1916. Secretary to the War Cabinet, 1916–18; to the Cabinet, 1919–38. Created Baron, 1939. Minister without Portfolio, September 1939–May 1940. Chancellor of the Duchy of Lancaster, 1940–1. Paymaster-General, 1941–2. His brother Hugh was killed in action in South Africa in March 1900. His brother Donald was killed in action on the western front in October 1916.

Sir Ian Hamilton,[1] in his two volumes 'Gallipoli Diary', quotes quite freely and where necessary verbatim from the official telegrams which he sent and which he received and discloses through his diaries every phase and detail known to him of the Dardanelles operations. Not the slightest comment has been made in any of these cases, and no complaint or action was evoked from the Cabinet of the day.

Also, the Official Naval History, in two volumes comprising a thousand pages, covers the whole of this period, adduces almost every essential fact, and cites or quotes all the important telegrams. For the whole of these operations I bore the prime responsibility, and have always been held accountable by the public. All these telegrams were approved in writing by me and the bulk of them are my own drafts. Anyone who chooses to read the late Sir Julian Corbett's text and compare the lengthy summaries of the telegrams with the actual text, will see how extremely unsatisfactory and how unintentionally unfair this method of citation is.

The 'Official History of Australia in the War', a volume of over 600 pages, also deals of course fully and freely with all the Admiralty matters that concerned Australia, and in particular with the genesis of the Dardanelles Operation. The writer[2] has not hesitated to quote textually some private letters of mine to Sir John French[3] which have come into his possession, and of course he makes use of secret and official information to a very large extent. Verbatim extracts from telegrams sent by me from the Admiralty are freely quoted when required to build up the argument, which argument I need scarcely say is to assign the whole of the blame for the enterprise and its failure to me. (See particularly pages 171–201.)

On the military side, Lord Haig's Staff have recently published in two volumes the most secret matters connected with the campaigns of 1916, 1917

[1] Ian Standish Monteith Hamilton, 1853–1947. Entered Army, 1872. Major-General, 1900. Knighted, 1900. Chief of Staff to Lord Kitchener, 1901–2. General, 1914. Commander of the Central Force, responsible for the defence of England in the event of invasion, August 1914–March 1915. Commanded the Mediterranean Expeditionary Force at Gallipoli, March–October 1915, after which he received no further military command.

[2] Charles Edwin Woodrow Bean, 1879–1968. Became a schoolmaster in Australia, 1903. Barrister, 1904. Journalist on the *Sydney Morning Herald*, 1908; London correspondent, 1910–13; leader-writer, 1914; correspondent with the Australian Force, 1914–18. Head of the Australian Historical Mission to Gallipoli, 1919. Official Historian of the First World War for the Australian Government, 1919–42. Chairman of the Australian War Archives Committee, 1942–6. His first volume of the *Official History of Australia in the War* was published in 1922, and subsequent volumes in 1925, 1929, 1933, 1937 and 1942.

[3] John Denton Pinkstone French, 1852–1925. Entered Navy, 1866. Transferred to Army, 1874. Lieutenant-General, commanding the Cavalry in South Africa, 1899–1902. Knighted, 1900. Chief of the Imperial General Staff, 1912–14. Field-Marshal, 1913. Commander-in-Chief of the British Expeditionary Force in France, August 1914–December 1915. Commander-in-Chief, Home Forces, 1915–18. Created Viscount, 1916. Lord Lieutenant of Ireland, 1918–21. Created Earl of Ypres, 1922.

and 1918, and have reflected severely upon the late Prime Minister and the Government of the day. Lord French, while not actually a member of the Cabinet in which we both sat, dealt freely with every aspect of his command, using secret information to the utmost and referring freely to War Council meetings. Sir William Robertson[1] and General Callwell[2] (Director of Military Operations at the War Office during the first year of the war) have also written books dealing controversially with the confidential matters with which they were concerned.

Thus it may be said that practically every important naval and military authority and actor in these events had already told his story to the public, and in doing so has freely used confidential information and quoted from official documents, both departmental and Cabinet; and that in no case has the slightest objection been taken by the Government of the day.

Passing from the important authorities who have freely stated their case or had it stated for them and from the Official History, to writers of less responsibility, you should note that Mr Filson Young,[3] in his account 'With the Battle Cruisers', prints the actual text of the Admiralty orders relating to the Action of the Dogger Bank. No comment of any sort or kind was made on this nor any action taken by the Government. Yet strong criticism of the Admiralty is made by Mr Filson Young in his book and sustained in important particulars by these confidential documents. These instances can be multiplied almost indefinitely.

[1] William Robert Robertson, 1860–1933. Entered Army as a Private, 1877. 2nd Lieutenant, 1888. Intelligence Department, War Office, 1900–7. Brigadier-General, 1907. Major-General, 1910. Commandant of the Staff College, 1910–13. Director of Military Training, War Office, 1913–14. Knighted, 1913. Quarter-Master-General, British Expeditionary Force, 1914–15. Chief of Staff, British Expeditionary Force, 1915. Chief of the Imperial General Staff, 1915–18. Commander-in-Chief, Home Forces, 1918–19. Commander-in-Chief, British Army of Occupation on the Rhine, 1919–20. Created Baronet, 1919. Field-Marshal, 1920. He published his memoirs, *From Private to Field Marshal*, in October 1921.

[2] Charles Edward Callwell, 1859–1928. Entered Army, 1878. Intelligence Branch, War Office, 1887–92. Attached to the Greek Army during the Graeco-Turkish War, 1897. Colonel, 1904. Angered because several of his contemporaries were appointed to General Officer over his head, he retired from the Army in 1909. Satirized Army procedure and War Office routine in *Service Yarns and Memories*, published in 1912. Recalled to the active list, 1914. Acting Major-General, August 1914. Director of Military Operations and Intelligence at the War Office, 1914–16. Special Mission to Russia, 1916. Adviser on ammunition supply, Ministry of Munitions, 1916–18. Major-General, 1917. Knighted, 1917. Military historian: in November 1919 he published *The Dardanelles Campaigns and Their Reasons*.

[3] Alexander Bell Filson Young, 1876–1938. *Manchester Guardian* Correspondent, South African War, 1899–1900. Literary Editor, *Daily Mail*, 1903–4. Lieutenant, Royal Naval Volunteer Force, 1914. On Sir David Beatty's Staff, 1914–15. War Correspondent, western front, 1916–17. Special Correspondent of *The Times*, Spain and Portugal, 1917–19. Editor, *Saturday Review*, 1921–4. Adviser on Programmes to BBC, 1926–38. Author of twenty-five books, mostly on naval matters: his book, *With the Battle Cruisers*, was published in March 1921.

On this basis and in the light of these facts I have considered myself entitled to publish the text of the telegrams for which I was responsible or which I wrote myself, the substance of which has already been partially or fully disclosed. It would appear unfair and unreasonable that a Minister should be the only person debarred from stating his own case in regard to war matters in which he has been held responsible, after every naval or military personage concerned has had the fullest latitude conceded to him. In view of the precedents which have been created, for good or for ill, in regard to these war matters, and of the disclosures which have already been made, a former Minister ought, subject to the public interest in regard to any particular topic, to be authorised to exercise a similar freedom.

With regard to the question of references to Cabinet proceedings and the Privy Councillor's oath, I regret that the full text of what I have written was not before you at the time you made your comment. Had this been so and you had been able to consider the work as a whole, you would perhaps have seen that there are no invidious and controversial disclosures, or any which affect in the least current State interests. The very general and descriptive references which are made to Cabinet proceedings, particularly those on the outbreak of war, disclose no facts which have not for years been public property, the most detailed accounts having been published in the newspapers of the opinions of individual Ministers with much hostile comment. My work as a whole is, as would have been seen from the full text, a reasoned explanation and defence of the attitude of this country before the war and on its outbreak and of the action of the Administration of which I was a member.

I claim that in principle I have in no way trespassed beyond the limits which have frequently been used by Ministers in defending, on the platform or in the country, themselves, their departments or the Government to which they belonged. The fact that these matters could not be discussed at the time on account of war interests should make it all the more necessary that after the lapse of so many years a reasonable latitude of discretion should be conceded to responsible persons.

I may add that of course I consulted the Prime Minister of the day (Mr Asquith) in regard to every reference, however general, which I made to Cabinet proceedings, and that I consulted my principal colleagues of those days on every reference to important matters in which they were concerned, and received from them their written assent and even warm approval to what I proposed to say.

I cannot feel that in regard to these bygone matters, separated from us by eight years and by an epoch of events, handled in the way they were and within the limits which I have explained, that it was necessary for me to ask you to make a formal submission to the King. Had any question of practical and immediate significance been involved, I should certainly have done so, in spite of any difficulty I might have felt in corresponding on such a subject with an Administration with some of whose members I have recently been in personal and political dispute.

Yours faithfully
Winston S. Churchill

PS. I re-open this letter in consequence of the remarks made by the Home Secretary at Cambridge last week.[1] The contracts on which my book is based were made before a word of it was written and leave me entirely free as to what is published. There is no obligation on me to publish any official document, and I derive no financial advantage from doing so. Whether the book succeeds or fails and whatever its contents, I am equally secured. It is only by publishing certain documents and telegrams which I have written myself and for which I bear the prime responsibility, that I can deal with the lies and fictions which have ruled for so long and which I have borne all these years without making any reply, while every other version has been put before the public.

Winston S. Churchill to Edward Marsh

(*Marsh papers*)

5 March 1923 Cannes

Would you kindly look at page 171 of the 'Official History of Australia in the War'? Here is a quotation from one of my most private letters to French. I cannot conceive how the author procured it. Could you ascertain from Australia House the whereabouts of the author, Mr Bean. Is he in England or in Australia? I propose to address him on the subject.

Yours ever,
W

[1] Speaking on the evening of 2 March 1923, to the Cambridge University Conservative Association, the Home Secretary, William Bridgeman, told the undergraduates present: 'He hoped that nobody would go into politics with the object of making money by it. It was very unfortunate when they saw, as they did sometimes now, politicians who took to literature in the form of being able to use, for the purpose of making money by their publications, information which they acquired overtly and confidentially. What was so bad about it was that it was impossible he thought, for a man who had access to private and confidential State papers to avoid publicity which might seem unfair to people, or the friends of people, who had not got the same opportunity of referring to those secret documents which the author had.'

Sir Maurice Hankey to Andrew Bonar Law

(*Bonar Law papers*)

8 March 1923

Prime Minister,

In order to check the arguments in Mr Churchill's letter of the 3rd March in detail, it would be necessary to make a searching examination of the various books which he cites as having been based on official information. I do not suppose that at this stage and in the present pressure of work you would wish me to undertake this. It happens, however, that I have read several of the books he mentions, and broadly speaking, subject to some exaggeration and subject to the remarks which follow, I think the statements in the early part of his letter are justified.

A number of persons who have held official positions have undoubtedly used secret information to which they had access, usually in order to defend their own conduct. The subject has several times been considered by the War Cabinet and by the Cabinet, who have always felt that they could not interfere. I do not think there has been any case where it could be shown that these revelations have been detrimental to the public interest, except so far as cumulatively, the revelation of the methods of conducting official business, is detrimental as tending to cause mistrust in the confidential nature of official relations.

I disagree totally in Mr Churchill's remarks on the Official Naval History. Sir Julian Corbett's work is not, like Mr Churchill's, an *ex parte* statement based on such official material as supports his own case. On the contrary, it is based on the whole of the information—telegrams and their replies, despatches, logs of ships, proceedings of Committees, Reports from the Allies and from the enemy, in fact, on every available source of information. Moreover, the Official Histories had in all cases been carefully overhauled by the Government Departments concerned, before publication and the proofs were sent to the principal actors, including Mr Churchill himself. I do not think any impartial person could say that Mr Churchill's reputation has suffered in any way from the Official Histories. I know nothing of the Official History of Australia in the War, to which he refers, and have never seen the book, but the Historical Section tells me that the allusions therein to War Council proceedings are taken from the published Report of the Dardanelles Commission.

There is some exaggeration in his statement 'that practically every important naval and military authority and actor in these events has already told his story to the public, and in doing so has freely used confidential information and quoted from official documents both Departmental and Cabinet'.

Lord Haig,[1] I understand, wholly disassociates himself from the recent work in which a member of his staff co-operated. There are some who did not live long enough to give their own version; for instance, Admiral Cradock, Lord Kitchener, Sir Arthur Wilson, or Prince Louis of Battenburg. There are others who have never done so, such as Admiral Sir Henry Jackson, Admiral Carden, Admiral de Roebeck and Admiral Oliver;[2] Mr Asquith (whose book I understand is to deal only with pre-War matters), Lord Grey, and others. Nevertheless, his statement is true within limits. For instance, his remarks on Mr Filson-Young's book, 'With the Battle Cruisers' are, I think, broadly speaking correct.

In any case, the fact that so many revelations have been made, and by so many writers, appears to be all the more justification for an enquiry with the object of investigating if there is an abuse and checking it, and laying down some standard by which writers should be guided. As suggested above, it has been difficult to say that any particular work was detrimental to the public interest and yet the cumulative effect of so many revelations may be detrimental.

Mr Churchill's statement that he consulted Mr Asquith in regard to references to Cabinet proceedings, and his principal colleagues on every reference to important matters in which they were concerned, is a new factor of great interest which should certainly be communicated to the Cabinet Committee.

Although the Cabinet Enquiry was brought on by the publication of Mr Churchill's book, I understand that it is intended as a general enquiry rather than an investigation into Mr Churchill's book in particular, and the enquiry is at present being conducted on broad lines.

[1] Douglas Haig, 1861–1928. Entered the Army, 1885. Knighted, 1909. Chief of Staff, India, 1909–11. Lieutenant-General, 1910. Commander of the 1st Army Corps, 1914–15. His successful defence of Ypres, 19 October–22 November 1914, made him a national figure. Commanded the 1st Army at Loos, November 1915. Succeeded Sir John French as Commander-in-Chief, British Expeditionary Force, 19 December 1915. Field-Marshal, January 1917. Created Earl, 1919.

[2] During the early months of the Great War, while Churchill was First Lord, Lord Kitchener was Secretary of State for War (drowned while on his way to Russia in 1916); Sir Christopher Cradock was Commander of the North American and West Indies Station (drowned at the Battle of Coronel); Admiral of the Fleet, Sir A. K. Wilson, was recalled from retirement at the age of 72 to be a naval adviser to the First Lord; Prince Louis of Battenberg was First Sea Lord until replaced by Lord Fisher in October 1914; Admiral Sir Henry Jackson was one of the senior Admiralty planning officers at the time of the Dardanelles campaign, succeeding Lord Fisher as First Sea Lord in May 1915; Vice-Admiral Carden was in command of the Anglo-French squadrons at the Dardanelles, September 1914 to March 1915, when ill-health forced him to retire; Vice-Admiral de Robeck was Carden's second-in-command, and succeeded him as Vice-Admiral commanding the Dardanelles naval forces in March 1915; and Vice-Admiral Oliver was Chief of the Admiralty War Staff from 1914–17.

Mr Churchill's letter appears to me to be a real contribution to the subject as setting forth a point of view which ought to be taken into account, and I would suggest that Mr Churchill's permission should be obtained to circulate his letter as a secret document to the members of the Committee.

Winston S. Churchill to Cornelia Lady Wimborne[1]

(Spencer-Churchill papers)

13 March 1923
Private

My dear Aunt Cornelia,

Thank you vy much for yr letter & for all you say.

I did not change at all in regard to Ivor[2] after the war. But his position changed in two important ways. First when the Government ceased to be Liberal & became Coalition, all the Tory peers were available for office, & were pushed strongly by their party wh greatly predominated in influence & numbers. This vastly increased the competition wh a peer like Ivor has to face in the House of Lords. Secondly after making a speech in more or less the Lansdowne[3] sense in the Lords, he took for some time practically no part in politics and led a pleasant life dropping his political connexions & remaining completely inactive in a public sense. It is idle in these circumstances to expect kinship or friendship to supply the elements of political success. A man must make & keep a political position & circle for himself. Then he becomes a factor large or small & is taken into everyones consideration, & then a friend may help, when the issue is evenly balanced, to turn the scale in a favourable way. But to blame me for not succeeding in securing office for him, while he remained as I have said quite out of the battle, is unreasonable.

[1] Lady Cornelia Henrietta Maria Spencer-Churchill, 1847–1927. Churchill's aunt; eldest daughter of the 7th Duke of Marlborough. She married in 1868 Ivor Bertie Guest (1835–1914), who was created 1st Baron Wimborne in 1880.

[2] Ivor Churchill Guest, 1873–1939. Churchill's cousin; a grandson of the 7th Duke of Marlborough. Educated at Eton and Trinity College, Cambridge. Liberal MP for Plymouth, 1900–6; Cardiff, 1906–10. Created Baron Ashby St Legers, 1910. Privy Councillor, 1910. Paymaster-General, 1910–12. Succeeded his father as 2nd Baron Wimborne, 1914. Lord Lieutenant of Ireland, 1915–18. Created Viscount, 1918.

[3] In July 1918 the 5th Marquess of Lansdowne, a former Viceroy of India and Secretary of State for War, had publicly advocated a negotiated peace with Germany. Earlier, from May to November 1915, he had served as a colleague of Churchill's in the War Cabinet, at which time he was Minister without Portfolio (a post he held until Lloyd George became Prime Minister in December 1916). On 30 October 1914 his second son, Lord Charles Mercer Nairne, had been killed in action in France.

Nevertheless after our talks I sought out Lloyd George, then Prime Minister, & pressed Ivor's wish & services upon him. It was he who used the argument that Freddie had filled the place, & that there was not room for two, & that we shd be accused of family intrigue etc. But I must admit I was impressed with what he said, & so I am sure would the outside public have been.

I write you this in all frankness not because I seek any action on yr part or on Ivor's. But because I felt rather hurt that at the time of my illness, he shd have been almost my only old friend who never gave a sign of life; & because I have heard what is the reason of his estrangement. I have therefore troubled you by these letters setting out exactly what my action has been towards him: & it is I am sure characterised by uniform friendship & goodwill, though no doubt with unequal success in meeting his wishes.

Now that a new situation has supervened Ivor, if he takes the trouble, will I daresay soon & easily build up for himself a good & interesting political position. No one will be more pleased than I to watch any success he may achieve.

With my best love & good wishes
Believe me your affectionate nephew
Winston S. Churchill

Sir James Stevenson[1] *to Winston S. Churchill*

(*Churchill papers: 2/126*)

14 March 1923

My Dear Mr Churchill,

It was characteristic of you to send me such a kindly letter. Believe me I value your opinion higher, (and I am sure you will not misunderstand) than that of any Minister past or present of the Crown in my lifetime. My greatest satisfaction has been derived from my association with your wonderful energy, high ideals and work for the State.

Dont worry about Beckenham. I will see to him all right.[2]

---

[1] James Stevenson, 1873–1926. Managing Director of John Walker & Sons, Distillers. Director of Area Organization, Ministry of Munitions, 1915–17. Vice-Chairman, Ministry of Munitions Committee, 1917. Created Baronet, 1917. Ordnance Member of the Munitions Council, 1918. Surveyor-General of Supply, War Office, 1919–21. Member of the Army Council, 1919. Member of the Air Council, 1919–21. Personal Commercial Adviser to Churchill at the Colonial Office, 1921–2. Created Baron, 1924.

[2] Henry Beckenham, who had ceased to work for Churchill at the beginning of 1923, served as Stevenson's secretary in 1924 and 1925, when Stevenson was Chairman of the Standing Committee of the British Empire Exhibition at Wembley.

Confidential

Dont lie low too long. Things are in the 'melting pot'. LG is playing what *looks* like a good game but it isnt. Nobody trusts him. They are sick of Simon[1] and Asquith. They want a leader all right and if you would only formulate a programme and cast it on the breeze I am sure it would draw. There can only be *two* parties. That is the line of country to ride. There are hundreds of thousands who wont vote at all at present. They have *no* party. But they are anti labour. Dont overlook the fact that they are *learning* to govern. The passivity of the present Govt is beyond belief. They *settle* nothing. Baldwin is scared of the Treasury officials. Bonar is relying on Lloyd Greame,[2] only he is sadly lacking in experience, Belgium is getting 'fed up' with France, the Yank is lying low. . . .

Dont forget if at any time I can assist you I am yours to command. So far as I am concerned you have only made *one* mistake. You dont take me into your confidences *politically*. Give me a trial. That is all I ask.

I see photos from time to time of Mrs Churchill playing tennis, and conclude she is well. . . .

Good luck, and again many thanks,
Ever yours
James Stevenson

[1] John Allsebrook Simon, 1873–1954. Educated at Fettes and Wadham College, Oxford. Fellow of All Souls. Liberal MP for Walthamstow, 1906–18; for Spen Valley, 1922–31. Solicitor-General, 1910–13. Knighted, 1910. Attorney-General, with a seat in the Cabinet, 1913–15. Home Secretary, 1915–16, when he resigned in opposition to conscription. Major, Royal Air Force, serving in France, 1917–18. Liberal National MP for Spen Valley, 1931–40. Secretary of State for Foreign Affairs, 1931–5. Home Secretary, 1935–7. Chancellor of the Exchequer, 1937–40. Created Viscount, 1940. Lord Chancellor, 1940–5.

[2] Philip Lloyd-Greame, 1884–1972. Educated at Winchester and University College, Oxford. On active service, 1914–17 (Military Cross). Joint Secretary, Ministry of National Service, 1917–18. Conservative MP for Hendon, 1918–35. Parliamentary Secretary, Board of Trade, 1920–1. Knighted, 1920. Secretary of the Overseas Trade Department, 1921–2. President of the Board of Trade, 1922–3, 1924–9 and 1931. Assumed the name Cunliffe-Lister, 1924. Created Viscount Swinton, 1935. Secretary of State for the Colonies, 1931–5; for Air, 1935–8. Cabinet Minister Resident in West Africa, 1942–4. Minister of Civil Aviation, 1944–5. Minister of Materials, 1951–2. Secretary of State for Commonwealth Relations, 1952–5. His elder son died of wounds received in action in 1943.

Sir Maurice Hankey to Andrew Bonar Law

(*Bonar Law papers*)

15 March 1923   Offices of the Cabinet

Prime Minister

If you intend to speak on the Air Estimates or the Army Estimates, I suggest it is worth your while to glance through Mr Churchill's speech in the House of Commons on March 21, 1922. [Hansard vol 152, c 131].[1]

It was a very valuable contribution to the question of the Navy–Air controversy and to the question of a Ministry of National Defence. While favouring the Ministry of National Defence as an ultimate goal, he clearly explained why the question could not be rushed. He stated that the questions of a Joint Staff College and 'Amalgamation' must be considered first, and that the latter inquiry would last a year.

M. P. A. Hankey

Winston S. Churchill to the Duke of Marlborough[2]

(*Marlborough papers*)

7 April 1923   Cannes

My dear Sunny,

I send you herewith a copy of my new book wh I hope you will find interesting.

It has been vy pleasant out here, & such a relief after all these years not to have a score of big anxieties & puzzles on one's shoulders. The Government

---

[1] During the debate on the Air Estimates for 1922–3, Churchill had advocated a separate Air Service, linked with the other Services under a Ministry of Defence. 'Let us just consider what the future holds for us,' he had said. 'We are no longer an island. When once the navigation of the air has been brought to a high degree of Perfection as it must undoubtedly be in the generation ahead of us, we have lost to a very considerable extent that distinctive insular position on which our safety and our greatness have hitherto depended.' Later in his speech, he had declared: 'No solution of a harmonious or symmetrical character will be achieved in the coordination of the services except through the agency of a Ministry of Defence. . . .'

[2] Charles Richard John Spencer-Churchill, 1871–1934. Churchill's cousin. Known as 'Sunny'. Succeeded his father as 9th Duke of Marlborough, 1892. Paymaster-General of the Forces, 1899–1902. Staff Captain and ADC to General Hamilton during the South African War, 1900. Under-Secretary of State for the Colonies, 1903–5. Lieutenant-Colonel, Queen's Own Oxfordshire Hussars, 1910. An original member of the Other Club, 1911. Employed at the War Office as a Special Messenger, 1914–15. Joint Parliamentary Secretary, Board of Agriculture and Fisheries, 1917–18.

moulders placidly away. But I must confess myself more interested in the past than the present.

I return at the end of the month.

Yours affectionately,
W

Winston S. Churchill to Lord Carson[1]

(*Carson Papers*)

7 April 1923   Cannes

My dear Carson,

I venture to send you a copy of my new book about the first phase of the Naval War. It deals with many topics in which we have both had a share, & I hope that it may be of interest to you.

What days we have lived through! I am more interested in the past than in the present.

Yrs sincerely
Winston S. Churchill

Edward, Prince of Wales to Winston S. Churchill

(*Churchill papers: 8/46*)

12 April 1923   St James' Palace

My dear Winston,

Thank you ever so much for your letter & for sending me a copy of your new book which we've all been looking forward to for some time. I've been seeing Freddie in hospital & we've been talking about you, & the book, which I've already started reading. I'm so glad you've had a lot of polo & are fit enough again to enjoy it. Its great news to hear you are playing in London this coming season & I hope we'll get lots of games together. I shant have time to play seriously so shall only compete in 'station games' such as we had two years ago. I've had a lot of fun race riding & its very sad that it

---

[1] Edward Henry Carson, 1854–1935. Educated at Trinity College, Dublin. Barrister. Conservative MP, 1892–1921. Knighted, 1900. Solicitor-General, 1900–6. Leader of the Ulster Unionists in the House of Commons, 1910–21. Attorney-General, May–October 1915. First Lord of the Admiralty, December 1916–July 1917. Minister without Portfolio in the War Cabinet, July 1917–January 1918. Created Baron, 1921. A Lord of Appeal in Ordinary, 1921–9.

& the hunting is all over. The govt are going through a tricky time arn't they? & seem somewhat rocky & the house is becoming a very exciting & noisy place.

Thanking you again, Believe me,

Yours sincerely,

Edward P

H. H. Asquith to a friend

(*Asquith papers*)

26 April 1923

... I sat in the stalls with a curious little knot of neighbours: Ramsay MacDonald[1] and Clynes[2] (who were in black frock-coats), Buckmaster,[3] Simon and Winston Churchill!

The ennui of the long waits was relieved for me by being next to Winston, who was in his best form and really amusing. Between two fugues (or whatever they are called) on the organ, he expounded to me his housing policy: 'Build the house round the wife and mother: let her always have water on the boil: make her the central factor, the dominating condition, of the situation', etc, etc,—in his most rhetorical vein.

Out of the proceeds of his book he has bought a modest country house and 80 acres of land in Kent, and is busy rebuilding and developing. I suggested that he should call it (after the title of his book) 'The World Crisis'. He has sold 10,000 copies of his first volume at 30s and hopes to reap a second harvest by a cheap edition at 10s.

[1] James Ramsay MacDonald, 1866–1937. Labour MP for Leicester, 1906–18, for Aberavon, 1922–9, and for Seaham, 1929–31. Leader of the Labour Party, 1911–14. Prime Minister and Secretary of State for Foreign Affairs, January to November 1924. Prime Minister, 1929–35. National Labour MP, 1931–5. Lord President of the Council, 1935–7.

[2] John Robert Clynes, 1869–1949. Labour MP, Manchester Platting, 1906–31; 1935–45. President, National Union of General and Municipal Workers. Parliamentary Secretary, Ministry of Food, 1917–18. Privy Councillor, 1918. Food Controller, 1918–19. Chairman, Parliamentary Labour Party, 1921–2. Lord Privy Seal, 1924. Home Secretary, 1929–31.

[3] Stanley Owen Buckmaster, 1861–1934. Liberal MP, 1906–10 and 1911–14. Lord Chancellor, 1915–16. Created Baron, 1915. Chairman of the Political Honours Review Committee, 1924 and 1929. Created Viscount, 1933.

Winston S. Churchill to Louis Loucheur[1]
(*Loucheur papers*)

30 April 1923   2 Sussex Square
Private

My dear Loucheur,

I sent you on Friday a copy of my book.

I am speaking next Friday in London, and will try to make a helpful reference to Anglo-Franco-German affairs. In case there is any decisive change in the position as we discussed it in Paris, perhaps you will drop me a line.[2]

With all good wishes,
Believe me,
Yours sincerely,
Winston S. Churchill

The Duke of Devonshire[3] *to Winston S. Churchill*
(*Churchill papers: 2/126*)

2 May 1923
Private

My dear Winston,

You have taken so much interest in the affairs of the Middle East, and have played so prominent a part in connection with them, that I should like

[1] Louis Loucheur, 1872–1931. Engineer, contractor and munitions manufacturer. One of the first French businessmen to receive political office during the war. Under-Secretary of State at the Ministry of Munitions, December 1916–April 1917. Minister of Munitions, 1917–20. Elected to the Chamber of Deputies, 1919. Helped in the drafting of the economic section of the Treaty of Versailles, 1919. Minister for the Liberated Areas, 1921; Minister of Trade, 1924; Minister of Finance (for seventeen days), 1925; Minister of Trade, 1926; Minister of Labour, 1928. Author of the 'Loucheur Law' of 1928 to help deal with housing crises by building low-priced houses with the help of public funds.

[2] Speaking at the Aldwych Club on the evening of May 4, Churchill declared: 'The whole solution of European difficulties lies in a reconciliation between France and Germany. The only possible policy for Britain, and, I will add, for Italy, is to promote, to hasten, to press, as far as they possibly can to insist upon that reconciliation. We must not lose patience, still less must we despair, because we are temporarily baffled. We must not allow any one particular phase of French policy to estrange us from the great French nation. We must not turn our backs on our friends or on our past. We must persevere along the main line of conduct. There is a growing opinion on both sides of the Rhine that nothing but ruin and misery lies ahead in the confusion of this intense and unlimited rivalry, and I cannot see why at this juncture there is any reason for a disastrous reversal or change in the course along which we have been advancing.'

[3] Victor Christian William Cavendish, 1868–1938. Liberal Unionist MP, 1891–1908. Financial Secretary to the Treasury, 1903–5. Succeeded his uncle as 9th Duke of Devonshire, 1908. A Civil Lord of the Admiralty, 1915–16. Governor-General of Canada, 1916–21. Secretary of State of the Colonies, October 1922–January 1924.

to let you know the latest developments before they become public property. I accordingly enclose an advance copy of an announcement that is to be published tomorrow both here and in Baghdad. The publication here will take the form of a statement in both Houses of Parliament.

The upshot is to reduce the term of the Treaty of October 1922, and consequently of our mandatory responsibility for Iraq, to a maximum period of four years as from the date of the ratification of peace with Turkey. After that period we shall spend no more money on Iraq and shall not be responsible for its defence.

The new policy has the full concurrence of Feisal[1] and the Iraq Government, in consultation with whom the proposed announcement was drawn up.

Yours sincerely,
Devonshire

Margot Asquith[2] to Winston S. Churchill
(*Churchill papers: 8/46*)

4 May 1923   44 Bedford Square

Dear Winston,

I have known you many years—nor can I forget your kindness & consideration to me when I was very ill on your Yacht in our wonderful tour to Athens etc.[3] I hope you will not think it presumption on my part if I write to tell you what I think of yr book. . . .

I am not a famous writer or person like these are but I am a severe critic & I think your book a great masterpiece, written with a warmth of words, an economy of personal laudation, swiftness of current, selection, lucidity, & drama unexcelled by Macaulay. I started & finished it in a night & having closed it determined to write this one line, one further word from an old friend & someone who is alas! no longer young.

[1] Feisal Ibn Hussein, 1885–1933. Third son of Hussein, Sherif of Mecca. Accompanied his father as an exile to Constantinople, 1891. A Member of the Turkish Parliament, 1913. Leader of the Arab revolt against the Turks, 1916–18. Proclaimed himself King of Syria and Palestine, 10 March 1920. Deposed by the French, and fled from Damascus, 25 July 1920. Elected to the throne of Mesopotamia (Iraq), 1921, where he ruled until his death.

[2] Emma Alice Margaret Tennant, 1864–1945. Known as Margot. She married H. H. Asquith (as his second wife) in 1894, and published four separate volumes of memoirs, including *The Autobiography of Margot Asquith* in 1921.

[3] In May and June 1912 Churchill and H. H. Asquith had sailed on board the Admiralty Yacht *Enchantress* to the Mediterranean, visiting Lord Fisher at Naples and Lord Kitchener at Malta. Among those on board the yacht during its cruise were Clementine Churchill, Margot Asquith and Violet Asquith (who kept an account of the voyage in her diary, extracts from which she published in 1965 in her book *Winston Churchill As I Knew Him*).

Lie low; do nothing in politics, go on writing all the time & painting; do not join yr former colleagues who are making prodigious asses of themselves in every possible manner: Keep friends in every port—lose *no* one. Pirate Ships are no use in times of Peace.

Your man of war is for the moment out of action but if you have the patience of Disraeli with your fine temper glowing mind & real kind unvindictive nature you cd still command a great future.[1]

Yours affectionately
Margot Asquith

Winston S. Churchill to the Duke of Devonshire
(*Churchill papers: 2/126*)

7 May 1923   2 Sussex Square

Many thanks for sending me an advance copy of your announcement about Iraq. It seems to have been well received generally in this country, and it certainly constitutes an honourable fulfilment of our obligations. It seems to me, however, that we are rather letting ourselves in for all the work and costs, and excluding ourselves from any chance of return. If things go well, there ought to be some returns both indirect and direct in four years; and I certainly feel that in these circumstances we should have a special interest in the country secured to us. However, I dare say it will be possible to provide for this later. It would certainly be a pity faithfully to receive all the kicks and to reject any of the halfpence when at last they arrive. I know how great your difficulties have been. I presume the words, 'Nothing in this Protocol shall prevent a fresh agreement from being concluded, etc' are intended to provide for the contingency I have noted.

---

[1] In a speech on 24 May 1923 Churchill said: 'After seventeen rough years of official work I can assure you that there are many worse things than private life. To see so many things being done, or left undone, for which one cannot possibly be blamed oneself, has afforded me great refreshment. . . . I can assure you that I am in no hurry to give up my seat in the stadium and join the pleasant throng of crowd, players and police upon the football ground. But I do hope in the interval before the match actually begins that I shall have now and again an opportunity of expressing my opinions' (*Churchill papers: 9/67*).

Lord Riddell:[1] *diary*

(*'Lord Riddell's Intimate Diary of the Peace Conference and After'*)

30 May 1923

. Horne[2] suggested to Baldwin that he would be wise to invite Winston to join the Government, as he would thus secure a powerful colleague and an excellent debater. Baldwin was evidently impressed by the idea, but doubtful of giving effect to it. Horne had lunch with Winston the other day and asked him where he stood politically. He replied, 'I am what I have always been—a Tory Democrat. Force of circumstance has compelled me to serve with another party, but my views have never changed, and I should be glad to give effect to them by rejoining the Conservatives.'

Winston S. Churchill to John Rees[3]

(*Churchill papers: 2/126*)

9 June 1923   2 Sussex Square

My dear Sir,

I appreciate the honour you have done me in inviting me to submit my name as a candidate to the Caerphilly Liberal Association. I need scarcely say that my sympathies are wholly with you in your endeavours to present a constructive progressive Liberal alternative to the blighting doctrines of

[1] George Allardice Riddell, 1865–1934. Began work in London as a boy clerk in a solicitor's office. Solicitor, 1888. Chairman of the *News of the World*, 1903. Knighted, 1909. An original member of the Other Club, 1911. Liaison officer between the Government and the Press, 1914–18. Created Baronet, 1918. Created Baron, 1920. President of the Royal Free Hospital, 1925. Among his charitable bequests were £100,000 each to the Royal Free Hospital and the Eastman Dental Clinic. In his will he also left £1,000 to Churchill.

[2] Robert Stevenson Horne, 1871–1940. Lecturer in Philosophy, University College of North Wales, 1895. Examiner in Philosophy, Aberdeen University, 1896. Active at the Scottish Bar, 1900–14. Assistant Inspector-General of Transportation, with the rank of Lieutenant-Colonel, 1917. Director of Department of Materials and Priority, Admiralty, 1917. Director, Admiralty Labour Department, 1918. Third Civil Lord of Admiralty, 1918–19. Knighted, 1918. Conservative MP, 1918–37. Minister of Labour, 1919. President of the Board of Trade, 1920–1. Chancellor of the Exchequer, 1921–2. Declined office under Bonar Law and turned to the City for employment, where he became Chairman of the Great Western Railway Company, the Burma Corporation and several other companies. Created Viscount Horne of Slamannan, 1937.

[3] John Rees, Secretary of the Caerphilly Division Liberal Association. In the 1922 election, in a straight contest between Labour and Conservative, Caerphilly had elected a Labour MP, Morgan Jones, a former imprisoned Conscientious Objector, who continued to represent the Division until his death in 1939, when he was succeeded by another Labour candidate, Ness Edwards, who had worked in the coal mines from the age of 13. A Liberal who contested the seat in 1923 came bottom of the poll, with 18 per cent of the vote.

Socialism. I have not, however, since the General Election, addressed my mind to the question of attempting to re-enter the House of Commons, and I do not yet feel the time has come when I should do so.

With many thanks, therefore, for your courtesy,

Charles Scribner, Junior to Winston S. Churchill
(*Churchill papers: 8/49*)

22 June 1923   New York

Dear Mr Churchill,

I should have written before had there been any encouraging developments in the sale of 'The World Crisis'. The last weeks however have been more hopeful and reorders are coming in steadily but the quantities ordered are very small. The sales total about 2,500 and I shall be very disappointed if they do not mount up to between 4,000 and 5,000 before the next volume appears. Of course this is absurdly small numbers, considering the interest and quality of your book which is admitted by all who have read it. Everyone I have met who has done so has been enthusiastic, but unfortunately this has not yet proved contagious, and it is now hot enough here to weaken any burst of enthusiasm. There are undoubtedly many things that we might have done to help matters, which we did not think of, but on the other hand we have spent over $5,000 in newspaper publicity and have mailed about 30,000 circulars with letters to lists of selected book buyers; the latter is now showing fair results.

Enclosed are some reviews. . . . Had I known that you had not seen any I should have sent them earlier, but in some way I got the impression from London that you had arranged personally with some agency to have all clippings sent. As you will see, they are all complimentary as unusual; perhaps the best thing that could happen would be for some one to start a little controversy by 'knocking' what you say. We have been trying to get some notices from such men as Franklin Roosevelt,[1] Admiral Sims,[2] and Frank H.

[1] Franklin Delano Roosevelt, 1882–1945. United States Assistant Secretary of the Navy, 1913–20 (he first met Churchill in this capacity, in 1918). Taken ill with poliomyelitis, 1921: convalescing, 1922–4. Manager of Al Smith's campaign for the Democratic Presidential nomination, 1924. Governor of New York State, 1929–33. Thirty-second President of the United States (in succession to Herbert Hoover), 1933–45.

[2] William Snowden Sims, 1858–1936. Naval cadet, 1876. Inspector of Target Practice, 1902–8, and Naval Aide to the President (Theodore Roosevelt), 1907–8. Captain, 1911. A staunch advocate of Anglo-American solidarity, and a fierce critic of naval inefficiency. Commander of the Atlantic Destroyer Flotilla, 1915–17. Rear-Admiral, 1917. Head of the

Simmonds,[1] that would command more attention than the average reviewer, and we hope to succeed when your next volume appears, if not before. . . .

I was glad to hear from your letter how well the edition in England was selling; it should relieve Butterworth's blood pressure. The papers here a week or two ago were full of a rumor that you might be the next British Ambassador[2] but I doubted if such a post would attract you. It would have been fine, as I should have had to call on you in Washington and have a drink of ambassadorial whisky—not that there is any lack of quantity or consumption here, but you never know how poisonous it may prove.

Very sincerely yours,
Charles Scribner Jr

Winston S. Churchill to Philip Tilden
(Randolph U. Stambaugh Collection)

20 July 1923   2 Sussex Square

Dear Mr Tilden,

The staircase in its new form raises several vy difficult questions. The bottom is much too near the wall. I only asked for the windows at the cross landings. We really must discuss the matter. Can you come round here tomorrow morning before you go to the country. The matter is both urgent & serious.

Yours sincerely,
Winston S. Churchill

Naval Liaison Mission to Britain, April 1917, he was a forceful advocate of the convoy system. He also persuaded the United States Government to despatch an anti-submarine force overseas. President of the Naval War College, 1917–18. Vice-Admiral, May 1918. Commander of the United States Forces Operating in European Waters, June–December 1918. Admiral, December 1918. Honorary knighthood, 1918. Retired from the Navy, 1928.

[1] Frank Herbert Simmonds, 1878–1936. Journalist and historian. Educated at Harvard. Associate editor of *New York Tribune*, 1915–18, and a noted war correspondent. Pulitzer Prize, 1916, for the 'ablest editorial'. From 1917 to 1920 he wrote a five-volume *History of the World War*. Syndicated columnist for McClure Syndicates, 1918–36, covering international affairs. In 1935 he published his best-known book, *The Great Powers in World Politics*.

[2] On 2 February 1923 Sir Esmé Howard had succeeded Sir Auckland Geddes as British Ambassador to the United States. In March 1930 he was himself succeeded by Sir Ronald Lindsay.

Lord Alfred Douglas[1] to Winston S. Churchill
(*Churchill papers: 2/127*)

4 August 1923

Sir,

You went into the witness box the other day after having succeeded in getting an assurance from my counsel (who betrayed me) that you would not be cross-examined. Well I have another case, raising again all the same issues, against the *Jewish Guardian*.

There will be no council to be cajoled or frightened this time for I shall take the case myself, & I challenge you to show your face in the witness box & answer the questions which I shall put to you. The enclosed refers to a meeting which took place last night when a resolution calling on the Government to institute an immediate enquiry into the matters specified was carried unanimously by a crowded audience who received me with the greatest enthusiasm.[2]

Yours with the utmost contempt
Alfred Douglas

Sir Douglas Hogg[3] to Winston S. Churchill
(*Churchill papers: 2/127*)

10 August 1923
Private & Confidential

Dear Churchill,

. . . I think you stated my objection to a prosecution very fairly, but I dont quite agree with your forecast of the defence. No doubt he [Lord Alfred

---

[1] Alfred Bruce Douglas, 1870–1945. Son of the 8th Marquess of Queensbury. Poet, and friend of Oscar Wilde. Received into the Catholic Church, 1911.

[2] On 3 August 1923, at a lecture in London entitled 'Who Murdered Lord Kitchener and the Truth about Jutland', Lord Alfred Douglas repeated his allegation that Churchill had been involved in a conspiracy with Jewish bankers in 1916. Douglas stated that the first, official, Jutland communiqué issued from the Admiralty had been deliberately pessimistic, in order to depress the New York stock market, and that Churchill had then issued a second, more hopeful communiqué, so that stock and share values would rise: and that this was part of a deliberate Jewish-organized conspiracy to make money out of the war—a conspiracy which Churchill had joined for financial gain.

[3] Douglas McGarel Hogg, 1872–1950. Educated at Eton. A West India merchant. On active service in South Africa, 1900. Called to the Bar, 1902. King's Counsel, 1917. Attorney-General to the Prince of Wales, 1920–2. Knighted, 1922. Conservative MP, St Marylebone, 1922–8. Attorney-General, 1922–4 and 1924–8. Privy Councillor, 1922. Lord Chancellor, 1928–9. Acting Prime Minister, August–September 1928. Created Baron Hailsham, 1928; Viscount, 1929. Secretary of State for War, 1931–5. Lord Chancellor, 1935–8. His brother Ian (a friend of Churchill at Sandhurst) died of wounds received in action in France on 2 September 1914. Both his brothers-in-law also died on the western front, one in action in 1915, the other of illness in 1918.

Douglas] would renew his charges in the most extreme form. But he would mix up with that renewal the staleness of the charge & would use it at once as a proof that his charges were not unfounded, & as an injustice to himself & evidence that the object of the prosecution was to stifle his Jewish Guardian action & prevent a fair trial there. We can't say that we are giving him an opportunity to substantiate his 'charges in open Court'; he will retort that he provided himself with that opportunity by the Jewish Guardian action, & that it is because we fear the exposure of that action that we seek to place him at the disadvantage of fighting the issue as an accused criminal instead of as an injured Plaintiff. In truth there is no such disadvantage, but that is not what a jury will think.

That he is trying to goad you into taking some such step is I think fairly clear from his two letters to you. He is a dangerous & unbalanced man, brilliantly clever, quite unscrupulous, & with a craving for notoriety, which such a prosecution would bring him far more than a new edition of the Morning Post action. If he republishes his charges in pamphlet form, as the 'publicity committee' indicates he may, I would willingly take the action you desire, whether he does it before or after his Jewish Guardian trial, but I really think there would be risk of a disagreement if we prosecute at present & that would be disastrous for all concerned.

I am hoping not to be in London for some time, but we expect to be back at my Sussex home about the 20th & if you thought it worth while to run down there we should be very pleased to see you & give you a meal or put you up for the night as best suited your convenience. The address is in the reference books, Carter's Corner Place, Hailsham, telephone 19 Hurstmonceux. I fear you will think me unsympathetic to your point of view, but indeed I realise how odious & horrible it is to have such charges made, although perhaps as an outsider I can see more plainly than is possible to the injured party, how absolutely ridiculous & fantastic every one knows them to be, & at the same time a lawyer cant help seeing more plainly than a layman the dangers of a criminal libel prosecution. I think I told you that I had a long talk with Bodkin,[1] & that he shared my view.

Yours sincerely,
Douglas McGarel Hogg

[1] Archibald Henry Bodkin, 1862–1957. Educated at Highgate School, London. Called to the Bar, 1885. Recorder of Dover, 1901–20 and 1931–47. Knighted, 1917. Director of Public Prosecutions, 1920–30.

Winston S. Churchill to Clementine Churchill

(*Spencer-Churchill papers*)

13 August 1923   2 Sussex Square

My darling Clemmie,

I have been toiling for three hours at proofs so that I hope you will excuse typescript.

We had a pleasant Sunday at Philip's.[1] Blandford[2] was there, & Mrs Lionel Tennyson,[3] and on the Sunday evening H. G. Wells[4] turned up or rather down from an aeroplane.

I worked nearly all day.

I took Fowler[5] with me on Saturday in the little car, and drove all the way there. I sent him back by train to get the big car in order. This morning I drove the car back myself alone. It is exactly 50 miles, and we did it in an hour and 55 minutes, in spite of the fact that we met all the race traffic going to Folkestone. I can drive the car quite easily now, which will be a great help in our arrangements. It goes vy nicely at 35 miles ph & will do 40 easily.

I enclose you two letters about the Douglas case. One from Evans[6] (who was at Lympne) and one from the Attorney General, you will see they both tend to the same conclusion, which no doubt I shall have to accept.

[1] Philip Albert Gustave Sassoon, 1888–1939. Educated at Eton and Christ Church, Oxford. Succeeded his father as 3rd Baronet, 1912. Conservative MP for Hythe, 1912–39. Private Secretary to Sir Douglas Haig, 1914–18. Parliamentary Private Secretary to Lloyd George, 1920–2. Trustee of the National Gallery, 1921–39. Under-Secretary of State for Air, 1924–9 and 1931–7. Privy Councillor, 1929. First Commissioner of Works, 1937–9.

[2] John Albert Edward William Spencer-Churchill, 1897–1972. Marquess of Blandford. Captain, 1st Life Guards, 1916. 10th Duke of Marlborough, 1934. Mayor of Woodstock, 1937–8; 1938–9. Lieutenant-Colonel, Liaison officer with the United States Forces, 1942–5.

[3] Clarissa Madeline Georgiana Felicité Tennant, a daughter of Baron Glenconner and a niece of Margot Asquith. Her brother Edward was killed in action on the western front on 22 September 1916. In 1915 she married Captain William Bethell, 2nd Life Guards (marriage dissolved in 1918). In 1918 she married a descendant of the poet Tennyson, Major the Hon Lionel Hallam Tennyson, who succeeded his father as 3rd Baron Tennyson in 1928, and from whom she obtained a divorce in that same year. In 1928 she married James Beck.

[4] Herbert George Wells, 1866–1946. Author and novelist. Among his earliest works were *The Time Machine* (1895), *The War of the Worlds* (1898) and *The First Men in the Moon* (1901). On his return from a visit to Russia in 1920 he published *Russia in the Shadows*. He parodied Churchill in his novel *Men Like Gods* (1923), where he wrote, of 'Rupert Catskill', that 'his wild imaginings have led to the deaths of thousands of people'.

[5] Churchill's chauffeur. He and Churchill had driven to Sassoon's country house at Lympne, on the Channel coast. On 3 September 1923 Clementine Churchill wrote to her husband: 'Fowler took the big car to the works to have a window put in after you separated & it is still there—not done! The little car leaks like an old Tub & is scratched all over! We *must* get a hard-working competent chauffeur.'

[6] Lewis Noel Vincent Evans, 1886–1967. Solicitor, 1911; joined the Department of the Director of Public Prosecution, 1913. On active service in France, 1915–18; wounded. Subsequently Deputy Director of Public Prosecutions.

Max[1] rang up last night to tell me the points of the Government note to France. I told him I was in general agreement with it. It is a very strong note, and will produce serious internal reactions in the Conservative Party. I think when the Government deliberately take a step of this kind towards a foreign country no one should try to weaken its effect.

I am to see Baldwin at 3 o'clock tomorrow, so I shall go up and work at Sussex Square tomorrow morning.

I will send the proofs tomorrow.

Tender love my darling one, I am just going to Chartwell, having finished my toil, in order to examine the progress. Masterton arrives this evening.

With many many kisses, from me & Mary
Your ever loving husband
W

Winston S. Churchill to Clementine Churchill
(Spencer-Churchill papers)

15 August 1923   2 Sussex Square
Secret

My darling Clemmie,

My interview with the PM was most agreeable. He professed unbounded leisure & recd me with the utmost cordiality. We talked Ruhr, Oil,[2] Admiralty & Air, Reparations, the American Debt & general politics. I found him thoroughly in favour of the Oil Settlement on the lines proposed. Indeed he might have been Waley Cohen[3] from the way he talked. I am sure it will come off. The only thing I am puzzled about is my own affair. However I am to see Cohen on Friday. It is a question of how to arrange it so as to

[1] William Maxwell Aitken, 1879–1964. A Canadian financier. Conservative MP, 1910–16. Knighted, 1911. Elected to the Other Club, 1912; resigned, 1920. Canadian Eye-Witness in France, May–August 1915; Canadian Representative at the Front, September 1915–16. Newspaper proprietor: bought the *Daily Express*, his largest circulation newspaper, in December 1916. Created Baron Beaverbrook, 1917. Chancellor of the Duchy of Lancaster and Minister of Information, 1918. Minister of Aircraft Production, 1940–1. Minister of State, 1941. Minister of Supply, 1941–2. Lord Privy Seal, 1943–5. Known as 'Max'.

[2] At the beginning of August Churchill had been offered £5,000 by two oil companies, Royal Dutch Shell and Burmah, to represent them in their application for a merger with the Anglo-Persian Oil Company, in which the Government held a majority share. For the outcome of Churchill's work, see his memorandum of 20 November 1923 printed on pages 68–9 of this volume.

[3] Robert Waley Cohen, 1877–1952. Educated at Clifton and Emmanuel College, Cambridge. Joined the Shell Company, 1901; subsequently Managing Director of the Shell Transport and Trading Co Ltd, and of United British Oilfields of Trinidad Ltd. Petroleum Adviser to the Army Council. Knighted, 1920. President of the United Synagogue. Vice-Chairman, University College, London.

leave no just ground of criticism. My talk with the PM was quite general & I did not raise the personal aspect at all at this preliminary & non-committal stage. Masterton in whom I confided was vy shy of it on large political grounds. However I shall proceed further before making up my mind.

I entered Downing Street by the Treasury entrance to avoid comment. This much amused Baldwin. However Max rang up this morning to say he hoped I had had a pleasant interview, & that I had greatly heartened the PM about the Ruhr! He is a little ferret. He has to go to Scotland tonight so I am going to dine at the Vineyard instead of his coming here.

Keyes[1] came down last night & we had long jolly talks about the war & what they killed each other for. I purchased in London two delicious young lady grouses wh were the feature of dinner. This morning we rode. The rides on the common are lovely—but vy little grass.

However there is beautiful park in wh we trespassed, but wh we can easily get permission to use. The work progresses quite well. I have just returned from a 3 hours inspection, wood sawing etc. The water flows. There will be lots for you to see when you return.

I did a further deal in the franc, realizing to date in all about £150 profit. I have 8 articles to write as soon as the book is finished £500, 400, & 200 = 1,100. We shall not starve.

I do hope you are enjoying yrself my beloved & not tiring yrself out. The happy mean. With tender & fondest love

Your ever devoted
W

Winston S. Churchill to Clementine Churchill

(*Spencer-Churchill papers*)

16 August 1923   2 Sussex Square
Secret

My darling,

Tilden has sent the enclosed plans which are a variation upon the original. I think they are an improvement, as they get over the difficulty of the end

---

[1] Roger John Brownlow Keyes, 1872–1945. Entered Navy, 1885. Naval Attaché, Athens and Constantinople, 1905–7. Commodore in charge of submarines, North Sea and adjacent waters, August 1914–February 1915. Chief of Staff, Eastern Mediterranean Squadron (Dardanelles), 1915. Director of Plans, Admiralty, 1917. Vice-Admiral in command of the Dover Patrol (and Zeebrugge raid), 1918. Knighted, 1918. Created Baronet, 1919. Deputy Chief of the Naval Staff, 1921–5. Commander-in-Chief, Mediterranean, 1925–8; Portsmouth, 1929–31. Admiral of the Fleet, 1930. National Conservative MP, 1934–43. Director of Combined Operations, 1940–1. Created Baron, 1943. Churchill wrote the foreword to his memoirs, *Adventures Ashore & Afloat* (1939). His elder son was killed in action in Libya, leading a raid on General Rommel's headquarters, 18 November 1941.

window being choked by the yew tree and also give a better facade towards the roadway. On the other hand it is on a very small scale, and I am going to try to get them to mock up some poles and tarpaulins that one may see what the size will be. We shall have to take a final decision Tuesday at the latest. Meanwhile I am agreeing to everything up to the eaves.

The progress is really quite good. The plasterers work till 7 every night— $10\frac{1}{2}$ hours every day—and the north tower will be completely plastered by your return. The staircase is making great progress and I dare say will reach the upper storey next week. The water will be connected in a few days with the cisterns, and all the baths, taps, kitchens, etc, all over the house will flow. The time is getting ripe for another visit by Ebner's men; there will be three or four floors for them to do.

I dined with Max last night. After much beating about the bush the mystery of his learning of my visit to Baldwin was explained. He had visited him afterwards at B's request, and found him delighted. Max says he is bound to go down now, as the Tory party will never support him in what is undoubtedly intended to be a German orientation. You should not mention to your host[1] any of the facts narrated here.

The children come back tomorrow, and I have had a delightful letter from Diana. I am going to amuse them on Saturday and Sunday by making them an aerial house in the lime tree. You may be sure I will take the greatest precautions to guard against them tumbling down. The undergrowth of the tree is so thick it will be perfectly safe, and I will not let them go up except under my personal charge.

Your ever loving devoted
W

PS. All the morning work. Good progress.

Winston S. Churchill to Clementine Churchill

(*Spencer-Churchill papers*)

2 September 1923   Flying Cloud[2]

My darling,

This is a most attractive yacht. Imagine a large four-masted cargo boat, fitted up in carved oak like a little country house, with front doors, staircases

---

[1] Oliver Locker-Lampson (see page 120, note 1).
[2] The Duke of Westminster's yacht. The Duke's nearest residence to Bayonne was the Woolsack, Mimizan, Landes.

& lovely pictures. She can sail 12 knots & motor 8, & accommodates 16 guests—at present only the two Drummonds[1] & me.

We lie in the harbour of Bayonne, today under bright skies, & awaiting my brush & paint box from the poop. Benny[2] must get back by the 12th at latest; & the plan is thereafter to rendezvous here and at Mimizan by Oct 1 for polo & tennis, in regard to the latter of wh you are earnestly desired to contribute. We will motor down with both cars comfortably from Havre— taking 2 or 3 days as fancy serves, & stay during October. Benny very charming & Violet[3] too. They are vy glad to have me; but wd much like you. It is absolute quiet & peace. One need not do anything or see anybody. The polo ground is reported excellent & the first game is today. There are numerous frogs who do not play too well, Ivor W is coming with his cracks, & Alfonso the Toreador.[4] We have got quite a good team, bearing in mind the handicap.

I have warned Bendor that perhaps I may be kept in England by important business (oleaginous); & it is entirely as we like. He has no party. I do hope I shall be able to get away.

The fares for the ponies from Boulogne to Bayonne are only £6 each and this by special arrangement includes the return journey. I shall make them walk to Folkestone so it is not vy expensive.

I had a long talk with Southborough[5] who takes the high line about oil.

[1] Sir Eric and Lady Drummond. Sir Eric, later 16th Earl of Perth, was Secretary-General to the League of Nations from 1919 to 1933. On 3 September 1923 Clementine Churchill wrote to her husband: 'The poor League of Nations is on its trial. I hope it prevails & is not made a laughing stock of—I couldn't bear that overbearing devil Mussolini to have it all his own way. But how can the L of N accomplish anything without a Navy & an Army behind it.' Mussolini had just invaded and occupied the Greek island of Corfu.

[2] Hugh Richard Arthur Grosvenor, 1879–1953. Known also as 'Bendor'. Educated at Eton. Succeeded his grandfather as 2nd Duke of Westminster, 1899. ADC to Lord Roberts, South Africa, 1900–2. Commanded an armoured car detachment, Royal Naval Division, 1914–15. Personal Assistant to the Controller, Mechanical Department, Ministry of Munitions, 1917. His uncle, Lord Hugh Grosvenor, a Captain in the Household Cavalry, was killed in action in November 1914.

[3] Violet Mary Nelson, who had married the 2nd Duke of Westminster in November 1920. She had previously been married to George Rowley, Coldstream Guards. In 1926 she obtained a divorce from the Duke of Westminster, and a year later she married, as her third husband, Frederick Cripps, brother of Sir Stafford Cripps.

[4] Leon Fernando Maria Jaime Isidoro Pascual Antonio, 1886–1941. Posthumous son of King Alfonso XII of Spain, he was proclaimed King at birth (as Alfonso XIII). He married Victoria Eugénie, a granddaughter of Queen Victoria, in 1906. He was outlawed, and fled the country, following the Republican majority in the 1931 elections. He died in exile in Rome.

[5] Francis John Stephens Hopwood, 1860–1947. Assistant Solicitor, Board of Trade, 1885. Knighted, 1901. Permanent Secretary, Board of Trade, 1901–7. Member of the Transvaal and Orange River Constitutional Enquiry, 1906. Permanent Under-Secretary of State for the Colonies, 1907–11. Privy Councillor, 1912. Additional Civil Lord of Admiralty, 1912–17. Created Baron Southborough, 1917. Secretary to the Irish Convention, 1917–18. President of the Commission to India on Reform, 1918–19. President of the China Association.

He considers it my duty & in every way appropriate. He thinks it may be possible to secure an invitation from the Anglo Persian as well. Thus I should represent all three gt corporations whose differences alone prevented this vy important public advantage from being secured last year. If the Government are agreeable, I think I shall have no doubts about going forward. But this will be a sad bar to our delightful October plans.

My beloved, I do beg you not to worry about money, or to feel insecure. On the contrary the policy we are pursuing aims above all at *stability*. (like Bonar Law!) Chartwell is to be our *home*. It will have cost us £20,000 and will be worth at least £15,000 apart from a fancy price. We must endeavour to live there for many years & hand it on to Randolph afterwards.[1] We must make it in every way charming & as far as possible economically self contained. It will be cheaper than London.

Eventually—though there is no hurry—we must sell Sussex & find a small flat for you & me or a house no bigger than [?].

Then with the motor we shall be well equipped for business or pleasure. If we go into office we will live in Downing Street!

The estate at the moment is at least as large as it was when I succeeded, but part is invested in Chartwell instead of in shares.

You must think of it in this light. I expect in the next six months to increase it by at least £5,000 apart from the oil possibilities, which I do not count. The second volume £5,000 is now at hand & will finish Chartwell finally & keep us going for six or seven months with the surplus + our income. I have already planned out the third volume & anticipate no difficulty in completing it by April. It is really quite reasonable to count on £6,000 from this—perhaps £8,000.

Out of this I shall increase & replenish our capital. The cheaper we can live, of course, the better. But I am budgetting to spend about £10,000 pa apart from the capital expenditure on Chartwell, or the payment of bills wh have been so greatly reduced. I am sure we can make a good plan on these lines.

The three articles = £1,200 & anything that can be got in America—at least $600 are a makeweight for contingencies.

Add to this my darling yr courage & good will and I am certain that we can make ourselves a permanent resting place, so far as the money side of this uncertain & transitory world is concerned. But if you set yourself against Chartwell, or lose heart, or bite your bread & butter & yr pig then it only means further instability, recasting of plans & further expense & worry.

---

[1] Churchill continued to live at Chartwell until his death in 1965, when the house and gardens were opened to the public, under the administration of the National Trust. At the time of Churchill's death, his son Randolph was living at Stour, East Bergholt, Suffolk; and it was there that he died in the early summer of 1968.

I look forward much to coming back & seeing the progress made. The achievement is not so far off as it seems. When we return from Mimizan & Bayonne we shall I trust be clear of Tilden, Browne, Mott & Jeff & Co for ever.[1] And the spring of 1924 will cover with its verdure the stains & blemishes with wh they have disfigured our gardens. You must push ahead with the plans for there—modest but complete; so that we can discuss them on my return. Meanwhile I will prepare the sinews of war with three or four hours writing a day.

I have finished or shall have by tomorrow all the proofs—and Vol II will be out of & off my hands forever.

My darling one—my heart is full of love for you & your dear kittens, & my keenest wish is to see you happy & prosperous & safe. For this I will indeed work my utmost and amid imprudence of all kinds.

Do write & tell me yr news & also telegraph each day.

Your devoted
W

PS. I have had a long morning writing & now I am going to paint.

Winston S. Churchill to Clementine Churchill

(Spencer-Churchill papers)

5 September 1923   Flying Cloud

My darling,

We have been vy successful at the tables. Benny with persistent luck & without playing vy high has won over half a million francs. I pursing a most small & conservative game am nearly 30,000 to the good. We are now off by sea to San Sebastian. The weather has turned vy dull today & it is raining hard. But tomorrow perhaps the sun will let me paint again. There was an extraordinary accident at the Bull fight at Bayonne on Sunday. The Bull infuriated tossed the sword out of his neck, it whirled through the air and pierced the heart of a young spaniard in the third tier of the audience.

Mrs Taylor[2] of Cannes & the British Embassy Paris has turned up here!

[1] Clementine Churchill shared her husband's vexation with their architect. Two days later, in commenting on the Japanese earthquake, in which more than 100,000 people had been killed, she added: 'What fun the Japenese Tildens (if there are any left) will have putting all the Pagodas up again. I shall suggest to our Tilden that he hurries up with Chartwell & then emigrates to Tokio.'

[2] Evelyn, daughter of Admiral Sir Charles Fane, and wife of John Taylor, British Vice-Consul at Cannes from 1921 until 1940, and owner of John Taylor and Son, estate agents, of Cannes and Nice.

She has got all her service stripes back and seems thoroughly replenished. Lots of Cannes visitors are to be seen—including Pulitzer[1] (& men) & Mrs Norton.[2] That foolish Pulitzer lost 2 millions at Deauville and is now condemned to play a vy humble game till his next year's income arrives.

It continues to be vy pleasant here. I write & work in bed all the morning as usual. If the sun shines I paint. I thereafter go down to the 'Office'. This seance usually lasts till about 3.30 am: but last night we got to bed at 4!

I am looking forward greatly to coming back and seeing you all again. I hope the progress of Chartwell continues under yr supervision to be rapid—or comparatively rapid.

What a swine this Mussolini[3] is. I see Rothermere[4] is supporting him! I am all for the League of Nations. Poor devil it is life or death for it now.

The more I think over oil, the more I feel it right. I shall certainly take the next step—wh after all is not irrevocable.

Tender love my dearest. No letter has reached me yet from you; but I suppose they will overtake me soon. In a few days I will turn homewards.

We are just leaving the river for the sea & I send this back by the pilot.

Your devoted & ever loving
W

[1] Ralph Pulitzer, 1879–1939. Entered his father's newspaper empire in 1900, as a business clerk for the New York *World*. Vice-President of his father's Press Publishing Company, 1906; President, 1911 and Editor of the *World*. Under his control, the newspaper gained a reputation for impartiality, employing distinguished journalists such as Walter Lippman and Herbert Swope. But financial success eluded him, and the *World* closed down a year after his death. He was married to Frederica Vanderbilt Webb, a granddaughter of William H. Vanderbilt and Consuelo Balsan's niece. He divorced his wife in 1924, in Paris.

[2] Jean Mary Kinloch, daughter of Brigadier-General Sir David Alexander Kinloch. In 1919 she married Richard Henry Norton, second son of the 5th Baron Grantly. A friend of Lord Beaverbrook, during the General Strike, she manned the switchboard at the *Daily Express*. In 1929 she accompanied Beaverbrook on his visit to Russia. In the Second World War she worked first in a mobile canteen, then in a shell factory. She died in 1945. Churchill, on learning while in Cabinet that Mrs Norton was dying, told his colleagues: 'The Cabinet can do no more business today,' and suspended the meeting.

[3] Benito Mussolini, 1883–1945. Socialist journalist and agitator before 1914; editor of *Avanti*. Founded the patriotic *Il Popolo d'Italia*, 1914. Served on the Austrian front, 1917. Founded the Fascist Party at the end of the war. President of the Council of Ministers, 1922–6. Minister for Foreign Affairs, 1924–9 and 1932–6. Prime Minister, 1926–43. Minister of War, 1926–9 and 1933–43. Fled from Rome, 1943. Head of the German-controlled Government of Northern Italy, 1944–5. Murdered by Italian anti-Fascists.

[4] Harold Sidney Harmsworth, 1868–1940. Younger brother of Lord Northcliffe, with whom he had helped to establish the *Daily Mail* and *Evening News*. Created Baronet, 1910. Proprietor of the *Daily Mirror*, 1914. Created Baron Rothermere, 1914. Launched the *Sunday Pictorial*, 1915. Director-General of the Royal Army Clothing Factory, 1916. President of the Air Council, 1917–18. Created Viscount, 1919. Two of his three sons were killed in action in the First World War, one in November 1916, the other in February 1918.

Winston S. Churchill to Louis Spears

(*Spears papers*)

20 September 1923   2 Sussex Square

My dear Louis,

I am afraid I have been neglectful in replying so tardily to yr vy kind letter and invitation.

I have been at Bayonne and am just about to return thither to play a month's polo with Westminster. Here I have been gripped by my second volume wh is now finished & will be published in October. I shall be back in England in November & will look forward to seeing you then.

Politics continue to mark time and will do so for a while. I am very content to have for the first time in my life a little rest, & leisure to look after my own affairs, build my house & cultivate my garden. It is nice for you and Archie being in Parliament & you shd take every opportunity of making good speeches. Then someday when I rejoin that assembly—if ever—I shall be able to back you up.

Please remember me to yr wife & give her my vy best regards in wh my wife joins.

I remain my dear Louis,

Yours vy sincerely
Winston S. Churchill

Winston S. Churchill to Edward Marsh

(*Marsh papers*)

27 September 1923   2 Sussex Square

My dear Eddie,

You are always so kind in looking over my stuff and I have such confidence in your English and punctuation, that I should be very grateful to you if you would look through the proof of one or two articles I have written lately. The first is about my escape from the Boers which I have written for the 'Strand Magazine'. I will send you the second portion of it in a few days, if you will let me. I have also written an article answering Wells and giving him one or two wipes in the eye. I particularly want you to look through this for me, and I think you will like it in view of the impudent references to you in his book.[1]

Yours ever,
W

[1] In the chapter entitled 'The Wonderful Road', of *Men Like Gods*, H. G. Wells wrote of 'Freddy Mush' that he wore an eyeglass and spoke in an 'impotent falsetto'. He was also

J. L. Garvin to Winston S. Churchill
(*Churchill papers: 8/45*)

Sunday
midnight

My dear Winston,

I have been at the proofs all day, sombrely enthralled, and just finished, cannot well express my admiration for the stern massiveness and grandeur of the Second Volume. There's nothing to suggest—nothing: its all too close and sound as it appears to me; but of course having been with you heart and soul from beginning to end of the 'Great Attempt' I am not so exempt perhaps from bias as one should be. Still I'm certain history will vindicate this Volume and you; and hope to write in due time another full page review in The Observer which will influence ordinary minds. Mind you true tragedy, supreme tragedy are not the worst in life, far from it: the squalid morass of unattempting impotence is the stifling of the soul and hope of man. Its wonderful how you've done it: again the technical part so sober, the imaginative part so throbbing.

I never was less happy about politics: our Country ignored, ordered, helpless, submissive. Baldwin no genius but trying to put his teeth in where he should: English enough for me who have no party now & few friends. Shall I keep these proofs in confidence—would like to—or send back.

Ever yours
JLG

Winston S. Churchill to Lord Balfour[1]
(*Churchill papers: 2/127*)

26 October 1923

First of all let me say with what pleasure I heard last night from Robert Horne of the very great improvement in your health, that you are able to

---

described as being 'awfully clever at finding out young poets and all that sort of literary thing. If ever there is a literary academy, they say, he is certain to be in it. He's dreadfully clever and sarcastic.' In addition, Mush was said to be deeply enamoured of food, and given to speaking with his mouth full.

[1] Arthur James Balfour, 1848–1930. Educated at Eton and Trinity College, Cambridge. Conservative MP, 1874–85; 1885–1906; 1906–22 (City of London). Prime Minister, 1902–5. First Lord of the Admiralty, 1915–16. Foreign Secretary, 1916–19. Lord President to the Council, 1919–22 and 1925–9. Created Earl, 1922.

walk considerable distances and have indeed been enormously refreshed in mind and body by your long enforced rest.

My second point is of a distasteful character, and I can assure you I am deeply grieved you should have to be troubled and bored with it. The enclosed leaflet is being sold at various places in London, and is presumably traceable to Lord Alfred Douglas. I have long been anxious to obtain a further assertion of his insolent charges in a form which would enable a process of criminal libel to be instituted. Subject to certain evidence which the police are taking identifying him with the publication, there can be no doubt that this pamphlet revives and renews in an explicit form the charge that I fabricated the first Jutland despatch as part of a conspiracy to bring off a financial coup in America to the advantage of Sir Ernest Cassel[1] by whom I was paid a large sum of money as a reward.

I do not intend to let this rest, and failing any other alternative I shall myself institute proceedings for criminal libel. The Attorney-General[2] and the Director of Public Prosecutions,[3] without having yet reached a final decision, are strongly inclined to institute a State prosecution; and I have strongly pressed them to do so. This has many advantages over the private prosecution, not the least being that it will save me from paying what is in effect a heavy pecuniary fine in legal expenses. I think it highly probable that a decision will be come to in a positive sense in the next few days. In the event of a prosecution it will be necessary for you to give evidence. This, however, will probably be inevitable whatever course is now taken. Douglas's action against the 'Jewish Guardian' is still pending, and the solicitors of the 'Jewish Guardian' have told my solicitors that they will require to go over again the whole Admiralty Jutland evidence, calling all the witnesses concerned. I feel very strongly that this would be a most unsatisfactory process. Douglas would not be risking his liberty and has neither money nor reputation to lose. He would simply have another opportunity without the slightest personal inconvenience or hazard of proclaiming his charges through the columns of every newspaper in the world, and in the end the jury would take a decision not on the truth or falsehood of these charges but on the technical

[1] Ernest Joseph Cassel, 1852–1921. Born in Germany of Jewish parents. Educated in Cologne. Settled in England, 1870, and engaged in banking. Naturalized as a British subject, 1878. A close personal friend of the Prince of Wales (later Edward VII). Among his achievements were the reorganization of the finances of Uruguay; the issuing of three Mexican loans; the purchase of the Royal Swedish Railway; the financing of the Central London underground railway; and the founding of the National Bank of Egypt. He was also instrumental in acquiring (for Vickers) the Barrow Naval and Shipbuilding Construction Company, and the Maxim Gun Company. Knighted, 1899. Privy Councillor, 1902. In 1909 the National Bank of Turkey was created under his auspices. Churchill's financial adviser, 1900–17.

[2] Sir Douglas Hogg (see page 51, note 3).

[3] Sir Archibald Bodkin (see page 52, note 1).

question of the meaning of the word 'invent' or the significance of the words 'a paying proposition'. On the other hand in a criminal action the issue is perfectly clear and simple, the trouble and inconvenience to us is no more, and the punishment of this creature in the opinion of Archibald Bodkin almost certain. It is possible Bodkin may already have communicated with you, and I only write this to explain the position more fully.

I am sending you herewith an advance copy of my second volume which is to be published on Tuesday next. I do hope you will feel in reading it that I have stated my own case and my own views without needless offence.

Hoping to see you when you return to London, believe me

Andrew Dewar Gibb[1] to Winston S. Churchill
(*Churchill papers: 2/126*)

28 October 1923

My dear Colonel Churchill,

I have come to the conclusion that I should like, if I were satisfied on one or two points, to strike a blow for the Labour Party. Should I be asking the impossible if I asked you to give me an introduction to one of the saner spirits in that party, if you know some of them, in order that I might have as influential an introduction as could be into those circles.

If I am wrong in imagining that the great ones in politics know the leading men of all parties, then I hope you will attribute my request to ignorance & forget about it. If not, I should be most grateful for your help.

Yours sincerely
A. D. Gibb

Winston S. Churchill to Andrew Dewar Gibb
(*Churchill papers: 2/126*)

29 October 1923

It would be difficult for me to assist you on the path to which you are inclined. I could not do so without insincerity, seeing how opposed my con-

---

[1] Andrew Dewar Gibb, 1888–1974. Called to the Bar, 1914. Served under Churchill, as Officer commanding D Company, 6th Royal Scots Fusiliers, 1915–16; Captain and Adjutant, 1916. He published *With Winston Churchill at the Front* in 1924. Regius Professor of Law, Glasgow University, 1934–58. Unsuccessful Conservative Candidate at Lanarkshire Hamilton in 1924 and at Greenock in 1929. Unsuccessful Scottish National Party candidate for the combined Scottish Universities, 1935, 1936 and 1938. Chairman of the Scottish National Party, 1936–40.

victions are to the doctrines of Socialism. Moreover, I expect an introduction or recommendation from me, however politely received, would lead to your being viewed with natural suspicion by those with whom you desire to work.

Lord Balfour to Winston S. Churchill

(Churchill papers: 2/127)

29 October 1923
Private

My dear Winston,

1. Very many thanks for your second volume.[1] I shall always value it as coming from yourself; and if I get half as much pleasure out of it as I did out of the first I am to be congratulated indeed.

2. I am very sorry that you should be tormented again by that miserable gad-fly Lord Alfred Douglas. I will of course do what I can to help in the matter.

As regards the course to be pursued, I feel too ignorant of matters legal to offer advice that is worth having. There is no doubt that nothing short of a criminal prosecution will secure justice. But I suppose there is always *some* danger of a jury illegitimately acquitting in a criminal case, though a verdict of a different tenor would certainly be given if the case were a civil one. On this matter, however, you have the best advice at your disposal, and cannot be wrong in following it.

Surely the last trial must have cost Lord Alfred, as no doubt it did the Morning Post, a considerable sum. If he had to pay it, I am surprised at his desiring to repeat the operation; if he didn't pay it, how will he get either solicitors or Counsel to enter into a new case with no prospect of remuneration? There is no doubt that he is not merely very spiteful, but also a little mad.

I expect to be in London before the meeting of Parliament.

With kindest regards to your wife,

I am, yrs ever
AJB

---

[1] Volume Two of *The World Crisis* was published on 30 October 1923. It dealt principally with the story of the Dardanelles. It had a first printing of 7,500 copies, and a further 5,000 copies were sold by 1933. Churchill received a £5,000 advance on a royalty of 33⅓ per cent of the published price (30 shillings) of every copy sold.

Austen Chamberlain to Winston S. Churchill

(*Churchill papers: 8/47*)

31 October 1923

My dear Winston,

Thank you much for your book.[1] I have this time deliberately refrained from reading the Times extracts, so that I might have the full & unmixed enjoyment of the whole. I look forward to a rich feast of interest.

'Well, & what do you think of it all?' as Rosebery[1] once asked 20 years ago. If Baldwin means business I must be on his side & I fear that you must be on the other, & so our ways will part again. I am really sorry, for I have enjoyed *working* with you as you know I have always enjoyed your friendship & your company. We will keep up this friendship at any rate whatever happens in politics. I expect that your course is simplified tho' not in the way or on the lines that we both hoped.

Yours very sincerely
Austen Chamberlain

Stanley Baldwin to Winston S. Churchill

(*Churchill papers: 8/47*)

1 November 1923   10 Downing Street

My dear Churchill,

I have for many years made a practice of buying every book written by a friend, and thinking I might include you in this category I was an early purchaser of your first volume.

And now, before I had time to secure the second, comes your delightful present!

Believe me I am grateful and shall value it as the gift of the author.

If I could write as you do, I should never bother about making speeches!

Yours sincerely
Stanley Baldwin

---

[1] Archibald Philip Primrose, 1847–1929. Succeeded his grandfather as 5th Earl of Rosebery, 1868. Lord Privy Seal, 1885. Secretary of State for Foreign Affairs, 1886 and 1892–4. Prime Minister, 1894–5. In 1906 he published a short memorial volume, *Lord Randolph Churchill*. His younger son Neil Primrose was killed in action in Palestine on 18 November 1917.

Lord Rothermere to Winston S. Churchill: telegram

(*Churchill papers: 2/126*)

14 November 1923   Cap Martin

Very interested to read you are standing for Manchester.[1] Although leaning towards tariff reform shall instruct all my newspapers daily and Sunday in that area to urge your return as in the best interests of Manchester itself. Shall do same with Asquith, Maclean[2] and Simon in their constituencies. LG requires no help.

Rothermere

Lord Beaverbook to Lord Rothermere: telegram

(*Beaverbrook papers*)

14 November 1923

Although I have taken very active part for week past, ill health has interfered with full enjoyment of ridiculous side to political development. George, Churchill, Chamberlain, Birkenhead spent weekend with me. Conclusion of Conference was unanimous advice to Chamberlain and Birkenhead to join Baldwin's Government.

At Monday's meeting Baldwin tried donkey and carrots scheme. Chamberlain and Birkenhead refused. Last evening Baldwin tried to persuade Birkenhead along honest man lines. Failed again. Derby wrote Baldwin last evening giving notice of resignation unless Birkenhead included in Government and persuaded to speak from Lancashire platform throughout election.

As to prospects of Government at election I think Baldwin will be defeated and George will be strengthened if political tactics adopted. I see no prospect of anybody taking sufficient interest unless you come home and take charge.

Max

[1] On 13 November 1924 the Liberal Association of Manchester Exchange had asked Churchill to stand as its candidate in the forthcoming General Election, and it was reported in the Press that he had agreed to do so. But this was a false rumour, and he declined the offer. A Conservative held the seat in 1922, it was won by the Liberals in 1923, but held again by the Conservatives from 1924 to 1945. On November 14 Churchill was asked to stand for West Salford by the local Liberal Association. On November 15 a further invitation came from the Liberal Association of Manchester Mossley, and on November 16 from the Aberavon Liberal Association. He declined these three offers.

[2] Donald Maclean, 1864–1932. Solicitor. Liberal MP for Bath, 1906–10; for Peebles and Selkirk, 1910–18; for Peebles and South Midlothian, 1918–22; for North Cornwall, 1929–32. Deputy Chairman of Committees, House of Commons, 1911–18. Chairman, London Appeal Tribunal, 1916–18. Knighted, 1917. Chairman of the Liberal Parliamentary Party, 1919–22. President of the Board of Education (in MacDonald's National Government), 1931–2.

Sir Robert Waley Cohen to Winston S. Churchill

(*Churchill papers: 2/128*)

15 November 1923

My dear Churchill,

I write to confirm our conversation yesterday in which you informed me that in consequence of the unexpected political developments you now feel bound to re-enter public life, and that you therefore find it necessary to withdraw from the work upon which we have been engaged together.

You have always made it clear that with you the public interest would count first and would outweigh every other consideration, and my colleagues and I in the Shell Company, as well as the Directors of the Burmah Company, have been more than content to receive your co-operation on that basis. We shall lose it now with the deepest possible regret, but with a full understanding and appreciation of your sentiment in the matter.

Yours sincerely,
R. Waley Cohen

Winston S. Churchill: memorandum

(*Churchill papers: 2/128*)

20 November 1923

During the summer I was invited by the Burmah & Shell Oil Companies to adjust their relations with the Anglo Persian Oil company & to effecting an Amalgamation of the three Companies under British management. It was proposed that I shd become a Director of the Burmah Company & shd thus have a direct & public & personal interest in it. At this time I was of course out of Parliament & expecting to remain so for a number of years.

Before coming to any decision I thought it right to consult the Prime Minister & at the beginning of August I had an interview with him & learned from him that he was disquieted at the position of the Anglo-Persian company & at the impending decline in the value of the Government holding. He was also on general grounds averse from the continued participation of the British Government in the Oil business. He expressed the opinion that a sum of twenty millions would be a vy good price for the Government to obtain for their shares. On this I went further into the matter with all the companies concerned, & at the end of August I had a second interview with the Prime Minister. I told him that I believed that a scheme could be framed wh wd satisfy the various requirements he had in mind & that subject to his approval I was willing to take part in formulating such a scheme. I made it clear of course to Mr Baldwin that I should have a personal interest. The Prime Minister expressed his entire approval, & informed me that he thought it desirable the questions shd be re-examined.

During the month of September the outline of a scheme was prepared by the companies under my guidance & submitted to the Government for their consideration.

This scheme can be published & I believe that it will be found to be of advantage both to the State & to the special interests of the Admiralty. That however is a matter of opinion.

Before this scheme could be examined by the different Departments concerned, the political situation suddenly changed. The Prime Minister made his declaration in favour of Protection & I felt it my duty to re-enter public life in order to oppose the Government and publicly to criticise & attack this policy. I therefore felt it impossible to continue the work I had undertaken, and as I did not wish to be hampered in my full freedom of opposition to the Government by association with any special interests however legitimate or respectable, I informed the companies at the beginning of November before making my speech at Manchester[1] that I must withdraw from the negotiation & renounce any personal interest.

Winston S. Churchill to Lord Beaverbrook: telegram

(*Beaverbrook papers*)

22 November 1923   Leicester

Head of column two front page Daily Express today. This point is most misleading. British exports boots last ten months over three times as large, in spite hostile tariff, as foreign import boots under free trade. Will give brief special interview in answer if you will send your man for insertion tomorrow's issue. Winston

---

[1] On 16 November 1923 Churchill spoke in the Free Trade Hall, Manchester, when he made a fierce and sustained attack against Protection. Baldwin's decision to 'assassinate' Free Trade, he declared, was a 'Party verdict, obtained by Party politicians, and exploited for Party purposes', not a measure of statecraft, but 'an act of faction'. It was quite untrue that foreign imports caused domestic unemployment, as Baldwin had stated at Plymouth. 'I have studied the trade of Britain,' Churchill said, 'for more than 20 years, and I have never heard such a doctrine seriously propounded by any high and responsible authority before.' Churchill went on to point out that one of Baldwin's Ministers, Neville Chamberlain, had said that price rises resulting from the tariff on foreign goods could be offset by higher wages. This was a very 'reckless' argument, he warned: 'Surely they had had enough of this mad race between a rise in wages and a rise in cost of living?'

Sarah Churchill to Winston S. Churchill

(*Churchill papers: 1/172*)

29 November 1923   Chartwell

Darling Papa,

Many happy returns of your Birthday,[1] and I hope you may have many more. I wish you could have been down here for it.

I looked at our Christmas dinners to-day (the chickens) and they are very plump. It did not rain here to-day but there was a cold East wind. One of the sheep got out into the rose garden and had to be chased back with much vigour by Cousin Moppet.[2] But it did no damage.

Please give my love to Mummie. Mary sends a Birthday hug and kiss.

Much love, and many kisses from

x x x x x x x Sarah x x x x x x x x

Winston S. Churchill to Sir George Barstow[3]

(*Churchill papers: 6/1*)

30 November 1923

I wonder if you could give me a few points against the Capital Levy. I have undertaken to make a speech on Tuesday next to the business men of Leicester in refutation of Mr Pethick Lawrence's[4] policy. I am sure there would be no objection on political grounds to your assisting me, as both the Government and the Liberal Party are equally fighting this principle and the Chancellor has himself repeatedly denounced the measure.

Among the points I am anxious to get cleared up are these.

[1] Churchill celebrated his forty-ninth birthday on 30 November 1923.

[2] Maryott Whyte, Clementine Churchill's first cousin. A 'Norland' nanny. She lived at Chartwell between the wars, and was Mary Churchill's nanny, as well as looking after Chartwell when Mrs Churchill was in London. During the Second World War, when Chartwell was closed, she lived in a cottage on the estate to supervise the outdoor staff.

[3] George Lewis Barstow, 1874–1966. Entered Local Government Board, 1896; Treasury, 1898. A Principal Clerk, Treasury, 1909. Controller of Supply Services, Treasury, 1919–27. Knighted, 1920. Government Director, Anglo-Iranian Oil Company, 1927–46. Chairman, Prudential Assurance Co, 1941–53. One of his two sons was killed on active service in 1941.

[4] Frederick William Pethick-Lawrence, 1871–1961. Educated at Eton and Trinity College, Cambridge. Barrister and Economist. Editor of *The Echo*, 1902–5; the *Labour Record and Review*, 1905–7. Joint-editor, *Votes for Women*, 1907–14; imprisoned for nine months in 1912 for conspiring in connection with militant suffragette demonstrations. Urged a negotiated peace with Germany, 1917. Labour MP for West Leicester, 1923–31; for Edinburgh East, 1935–45. Financial Secretary to the Treasury, 1929–31. Member of the India Round-Table Conference, 1931. Privy Council, 1937. Created Baron, 1945. Secretary of State for India and Burma, 1945–7. He published his memoirs, *Fate Has Been Kind*, in 1943.

First, capital consists of land, mines, houses, plants, railways and other forms of real estate. But these do not stand by themselves. There is in addition liquid capital and credit, both of which are required to make the wheels of production go round. This liquid capital is represented by balances in the banks, which balances depend upon the market value of shares in Companies of all kinds. A sudden attempt to take three thousand millions of capital (the proposal) to extinguish an equal amount of the National Debt would force an enormous depreciation in every class of security. Perhaps it might be a 50% depreciation. The land, houses, plants, etc, would remain as they were, but owing to the general fall in values, half our power would be gone to set them in motion. What in your view is there beyond the real estate and apart from mere credit? Surely there is value, the basis of credit. How do you think this is best expressed.

A second section of my argument would deal with the flight of capital in the advent of a Levy. The return of the Labour Party, for instance, would surely mean that foreign capital in this country would immediately be transferred to the United States or elsewhere, thus aggravating the fall in British securities. How much is this foreign capital estimated at? Surely it must be at least a thousand millions. Every foreigner who had a British security would wish to get rid of it before the fall. Similarly, British investors would in large numbers sell their stocks and invest the proceeds abroad. The Labour Party argue that you cannot move capital out of the country. That is true so far as real estate is concerned; but a great deal of the credit can be transferred in a flash from British to American enterprises, ie foreigners would buy up the depreciated British stocks very cheaply and use the additional credit so obtained to foster their own business in competition with ours. The deposits would be withdrawn from the banks where they now form a fund of money available for enterprises of all kinds, and they would be transferred to foreign banks long before any measure could be taken by the new Government to prevent it. As for the interest and capital, ie where the plant is actually abroad, none of this would of course be brought over here by its owners. It would be left to accumulate in foreign countries until better times. How much can this be estimated at?

Thirdly, there would be an enormous depreciation in exchanges. Take America alone for instance. We have to make our purchases of cotton and wheat and pay our indemnity. What is the estimated total of all payments we have to make to America in a year—if you like, the last completed year? Suppose the exchange were altered by a dollar to our disadvantage, that would involve a payment of how much more per annum by us?

I must explain that Mr Pethick Lawrence says quite clearly that if he took three thousand millions by Capital Levy and extinguished the debt, he would save about 135 millions at 4½%, but that he would lose on this three thousand millions Income Tax, Super Tax and Death Duties, which he estimates at about ninety millions. Therefore he does not claim to save more than forty-five or fifty millions. It should be easy to show that the depreciation of securities and the loss on exchanges would impose such a great additional burden on the British nation that this fifty million of saving in interest would be wiped out many times over. I wish you could give me one or two broad figures to sustain this argument.

Lastly, I am asked when the Debt will be paid off, how it will be paid off, and what we are doing to pay it off. I am told that the Napoleonic debt is still running, and asked if we are to go on for hundreds of years bearing this burden. I answer that at the close of the war the interest was over 6% on seven thousand millions, ie 420 millions a year; and that it is now 4½%, ie 315 millions a year. By persisting in a sound financial policy we may expect it to come down to 3% or even 2½%, ie 210 millions a year, or even about 18 millions. Further, it must be remembered that in regard to internal debt Income Tax, Super Tax and Death Duties are collected. What do you consider these average out at? Income Tax is 4/6. How much ought we to allow on the corpus of seven thousand millions as Super Tax and Death Duties? Surely a flat rate of 7/6 would be a good basis of calculation. If so, the State would really be paying one and three-quarter percent, less than the nominal rate of interest on the Debt, ie when the interest on the Debt was scaled down to 2½% it would really only be one and a quarter per cent or about 100 millions a year. Apart from all this, there are the sinking funds which, though suspended temporarily, will work to reduce the capital of the Debt. A 1% sinking fund will extinguish the Debt in how many years?

I am so sorry to bother you with all this, but the argument I am going to deliver to the business men will be keenly studied.

PS. In case you find a difficulty in writing to me on this, pray let me know by telegraph, as in that case I must endeavour to get my facts checked elsewhere. I shall be at the Grand Hotel, Leicester, until tomorrow evening.

Sir George Barstow to Winston S. Churchill
(*Churchill papers: 6/1*)

Undated

Dear Mr Churchill,

I enclose you some notes on Capital Levy which I hope may be of use to you, though the subject is rather out of my beat.

I suppose a Capital Levy if *successfully worked*, would be a deflationary measure tending therefore to send up the £ in relation to the dollar. It is necessary therefore to stress the panic argument, & the flight from sterling which would follow. I think it is undoubted that the violence of the 'remedy' is its essential vice: & that in order to mitigate it, & to make it possible to raise 3,000 million, any Govt that proposed it would be driven to some inflationary measure.

With best wishes for Thursday in Leicester.

Yours sincerely
G. L. Barstow

I am sorry I have not been able to get the notes typed: or to supply all the figures.

Lord Londonderry to Winston S. Churchill

(*Churchill papers: 2/126*)

2 December 1923 Stockton-on-Tees

My dear Winston,

One line to wish you well. The topsy-turveydom of politics bewilders me and I wonder when we shall fight under the same banner instead of maintaining a delightful friendship while being in opposing Camps.

FE came here last night and I was particularly pleased because we have both always clung to you, but been as far apart at intervals as the poles. However when the opportunity came I naturally jumped at it and sent him a wire to come here after his Newcastle speech and he replied in exactly the same spirit. Very characteristic.

Again the best of health. I wish I could do something for you.

Yours affectionately
Charley

Sir William Beveridge[1] to Winston S. Churchill

(Churchill papers: 2/126)

7 December 1923

Dear Mr Churchill,

May I send you a line to say how extremely sorry I was to see the Leicester result?[2]

It looks to me like a piece of horrible ingratitude and wrong judgment in respect of what you did for the country in the war.

Yours sincerely,
W. H. Beveridge

Sir William Tyrrell to Winston S. Churchill

(Churchill papers: 2/126)

7 December 1923   Foreign Office
Personal

My dear Churchill,

Your defeat stamps this election & covers Leicester with shame, but I rejoice to see you stick to your platform of opposition to extremes on either side of politics.

Taking a long view & as one wishing for your success in public life I cannot help thinking that you are well out of this Parliament which has nothing but an inglorious future—luckily a short one before it.

From all sides I hear you made one of the best fights ever put up. You will have but a short breather before you are at it again.

Please dont think me a beastly nuisance for writing such a 'reasonable' letter when you must still be feeling very sore.

Yours ever
W. Tyrrell

[1] William Henry Beveridge, 1879–1963. Educated at Charterhouse and Balliol College, Oxford. Civil servant at the Board of Trade, 1908–16; Ministry of Munitions, 1915–16; Ministry of Food, 1917–18 (Permanent Secretary, 1919). A pioneer of state insurance. Knighted, 1919. Director of the London School of Economics and Political Science, 1919–37. Member of the Royal Commission on the Coal Industry, 1925. Master of University College, Oxford, 1937–45. Chairman, Interdepartmental Committee on Social Insurance, 1941–2. Liberal MP, 1944–5. Baron, 1946. Author of more than twenty books on politics and political science.

[2] The election was held on December 6. Churchill was defeated, the result being: Pethick-Lawrence (Labour) 13,634; Churchill (Liberal) 9,236; Instone (Conservative) 7,696. In his memoirs Pethick-Lawrence recalled how: 'When the figures were announced Churchill came up to me and, congratulating me, said: "Well, anyhow, it is a victory for Free Trade." '

George Lambert¹ to Winston S. Churchill
(*Churchill papers: 2/126*)

[7] December 1923

My dear Winston,

I am very very sorry. Your speeches were the finest in the Campaign—something to bite at—they were not pap or slosh.

Yours sincerely
George Lambert

Lord Inchcape² to Winston S. Churchill
(*Churchill papers: 2/126*)

7 December 1923

My dear Winston,

It was like yourself to decide to fight a very doubtful seat when you could have gained an easy victory in many another. I regret immensely your defeat but of course another seat must be found for you, & that speedily. It is too early yet to count ones chickens but it looks as if Free Trade was safe. Poor Baldwin how miserable he must feel and how he must be cursing his advisers.

Yours sincerely
Inchcape

The Marquis of Dufferin and Ava³ to Winston S. Churchill
(*Churchill papers: 2/126*)

7 December 1923   Carlton Club

Dear Churchill,

Please let me tell you how very sorry I am that you were beaten at Leicester. I know that most of us Northern Ireland people hoped you would

¹ George Lambert, 1866–1958. Liberal MP for South Molton, 1891–1924; 1929–31. Civil Lord of Admiralty, 1905–15. Privy Councillor, 1912. Chairman of the Liberal Parliamentary Party, 1919–21; Liberal National MP, 1931–45. Created Viscount, 1945.

² James Lyle Mackay, 1852–1932. In India, 1874–93. Knighted, 1894. Member of the Council of India, London, 1897–1911. Created Baron Inchcape, 1911. Shipowner. Chairman of the Government's Port and Transit Committee, 1915, and several other shipping Committees, 1915–19. In charge of the disposal of the Government's surplus shipping and all enemy shipping, 1919–21. Member of the National Economy (Geddes) Committee, 1921–2. Chairman of the Indian Retrenchment Committee, 1922–3. Created Viscount, 1924; Earl of Inchcape, 1929. Director of many companies, including several connected with coal.

³ Frederick Temple Blackwood, 3rd Marquess of Dufferin and Ava, 1875–1930. Succeeded his brother as Marquess, 1918. Formerly Captain, Grenadier Guards and 9th Lancers: on active service both in South Africa (when he was severely wounded) and on the western front 1914–18 (when he was again wounded). Speaker of the Senate of Northern Ireland from 1921 until his death.

be successful, as, though we hated the Treaty business, you have been a very good friend to us, ever since.

Yours sincerely,
Freddy Dufferin

Lord Weir[1] to Winston S. Churchill

(*Churchill papers: 2/126*)

7 December 1923
Personal

My dear Churchill,

Just a line to let you know how sincerely I regret yesterday's performance, and how much I sympathise with you. In business we respect and value the man who does things. Apparently the opposite is true in politics, but the devil is that, while in normal times we can go ahead and prosper without much statesmanship, to-day there is nothing but creative work in front of statesmen.

I am not wise enough to forecast the happenings of the next few weeks, but if you get thoroughly tired of politics let us have a talk together soon. Out of it may come a real opportunity of doing useful work.

With kindest regards to Mrs Churchill and yourself,

I am
Yours sincerely,
Weir

Alexander Shaw[2] to Winston S. Churchill

(*Churchill papers: 2/126*)

7 December 1923

Dear Mr Churchill,

May I send a line of very hearty congratulation on the splendid fight which you put up at Leicester? The effect throughout the country of your close and

---

[1] William Douglas Weir, 1877–1959. Shipping contractor; his family won its first Royal Navy contract in 1896. A pioneer motor car manufacturer. Majority shareholder in G. & J. Weir Ltd, manufacturers of machinery for steamships. Scottish Director of Munitions, July 1915–January 1917. Controller of Aeronautical Supplies, and Member of the Air Board, 1917. Knighted, 1917. Director-General of Aircraft Production, Ministry of Munitions, 1917–18. Created Baron, 1918. Secretary of State for Air, April–December 1918. Adviser, Air Ministry, 1935–9. Created Viscount, 1938. Director-General of Explosives, Ministry of Supply, 1939. Chairman of the Tank Board, 1942.

[2] Alexander Shaw, 1883–1944. President of the Oxford Union, 1905. Barrister, 1908. Liberal MP, 1915–18; Coalition Liberal, 1918–23. Parliamentary Private Secretary to Sir John Simon, 1915. On active service on the western front, 1916. Chairman of the Special Arbitration Tribunal on Women's Wages, 1917–18. A Director of the Bank of England, 1923–43. President of the United Kingdom Chamber of Shipping, 1927. Member of the Imperial Shipping Committee, 1931. Succeeded his father as 2nd Baron Craigmyle, 1937.

damaging examination of Protection was great and noticeable. Many of us felt very sorry that you had consented to fight a forlorn hope, but the fact that you did so, and tackled your self imposed task so magnificently has given you a higher place than ever in the esteem of Free Traders all over the country. Now that there is such urgent need for you in the House of Commons all your admirers will hope that you may be there again within a very short time.

Believe me,
With all respect,
Sincerely yours,
Alexander Shaw

Lady Sarah Wilson to Winston S. Churchill
(Churchill papers: 2/126)

8 December 1923

Dear Winston,

I cannot tell you how sad I am abt Leicester. It is a great loss to the House of Commons.

Why oh! Why did you not stick to Manchester. Gordon & I lived near Leicester (at Brooksby) for 10 years & we always thought they were beastly people.

I was at the Carlton Club that foggy Election night & when your poll was announced, there was grim silence, & stodgy Lord Midleton,[1] who was sitting next to me—said—'Well, I am genuinely sorry. We wanted Winston in the House of Commons.'

Cornelia Lady Wimborne to Winston S. Churchill
(Churchill papers: 2/126)

9 December 1923

Dearest Winston,

I am so sorry for the disappointment to you & Clemmie in this election. It does seem hard. But you have contributed more than anyone to the defeat of Protection & it cannot be long, before you return to the political arena.

How Baldwin has smashed the Tory party.

Yours affectionately
CW

[1] St John Brodrick, 1856–1942. Educated at Eton and Balliol College, Oxford. Conservative MP, 1880–5 and 1885–1906. Privy Councillor, 1897. Secretary of State for War, 1900–3; for India, 1903–5. Succeeded his father as 9th Viscount Midleton, 1907; created Earl, 1920. He published his memoirs, *Record and Reactions 1856–1939*, in 1939. In 1901 Churchill had attacked his military policy in a series of speeches published with the title *Mr Brodrick's Army*.

Lord Haldane to Winston S. Churchill

(*Churchill papers: 2/126*)

9 December 1923

My dear Churchill,

You have always been a most loyal friend to me. But quite apart from that I was concerned to see that you had not been returned to our Parliament.

Of course you ought to have been, on public grounds but you are not the first to be despitefully used by our people.

Anyhow I do not think that this incident in the least affects your real position in the public eye, a position which unique gifts of expression and of energy have given to you.

Patience, everything comes to him who knows how to wait. It may not be for long but you will have to wait.

We see the surface too near to judge what is the current beneath it.

Yours most sincerely
Haldane

H. A. L. Fisher[1] to Winston S. Churchill

(*Churchill papers: 2/126*)

9 December 1923

My dear Winston,

Your brilliant fight for Liberalism and Free Trade resounded through the country even though it failed to counter balance the deplorable lack of preliminary organization which appears to have existed at Leicester. I reproach myself that I didn't lend a hand for I might have been of some use with the teachers and writers and with those whom they influence but from the first I put myself at the disposal of the Central Office who sent me round the country speaking for candidates who were considered to have doubtful chances of success. I understand that you were pretty certain to win.

The moral is that the Liberals must join together to work to create a machine. There must be complete concentration at headquarters otherwise

---

[1] Herbert Albert Laurens Fisher, 1865–1940. Historian. He published his first book, *The Medieval Empire*, in 1898, and a further seven works by 1914. Member of the Royal Commission on the Public Services of India, 1912–15, and of the Government Committee on alleged German outrages, 1915. Liberal MP, 1916–18 and 1918–26. President of the Board of Education, 1916–22. A British delegate to the League of Nations Assembly, 1920–2. Warden of New College, Oxford, from 1925 until his death. He published his *History of Europe* in 3 volumes in 1935. Governor of the BBC, 1935–9.

I do not see how we can hope to gain ground during the limited period which must elapse before another election. That the country is Free Trade and Anti-Socialist is demonstrated beyond possibility of cavil.

With much admiration and sympathy,

Yours sincerely

Herbert Fisher

Winston S. Churchill: statement to the Court, Old Bailey

(Churchill papers: 2/127)

10 December 1923

No false report was issued from the Admiralty about the Battle of Jutland. I was not a Cabinet Minister at the time. I had left the Cabinet in November, and the Admiralty in May, of the previous year, 1915. I was never consulted in any way about the 'first official report' or any other official report issued by the Admiralty about the Battle of Jutland. I never drafted or suggested a single word of it. I never saw it until I read it in the newspapers the day after it was issued.

The 'first official report' of the Battle of Jutland was issued by the Admiralty through the Press Bureau on June 2, at 7 pm. It was drawn up by the Chief of the Staff, Vice Admiral Sir Henry Oliver,[1] and was carefully revised and finally approved by Mr Balfour, the First Lord. It was of course strictly in accordance with the information possessed by the Admiralty at that time. The actual draft of this report exists and will be produced. The corrections are in Mr Balfour's handwriting. Mr Balfour will, I have no doubt, confirm these statements; and further corroboration can be obtained from Vice Admiral Sir Henry Oliver, from Sir H. Jackson,[2] from Sir Graham Greene,[3]

[1] Henry Francis Oliver, 1865–1965. Entered Navy, 1878. Naval Assistant to Sir John Fisher, 1908–10. Rear-Admiral, 1913. Director of the Intelligence Division of the Admiralty, 1913–14. Churchill's Naval Secretary, October 1914. Acting Vice-Admiral and Chief of the Admiralty War Staff, November 1914 to 1917. Knighted, 1916. Commanded 1st Battle Cruiser Squadron, 1918. Commanded the Home Fleet, 1919; the Reserve Fleet, 1919–20. Second Sea Lord, 1920–4. Admiral, 1923. Commander-in-Chief, Atlantic Fleet, 1924–7. Admiral of the Fleet, 1928.

[2] Henry Bradwardine Jackson, 1855–1929. Entered Navy, 1868. A pioneer of wireless telegraphy. Knighted, 1906. Chief of the Admiralty War Staff, 1912–14. Admiral, 1914. In August 1914 he was put in charge of planning the seizure of German colonies. First Sea Lord, May 1915–December 1916. President of the Royal Naval College, Greenwich, 1916–19. Admiral of the Fleet, 1919.

[3] William Graham Greene, 1857–1950. Entered Admiralty, 1881. Private Secretary to successive First Lords of the Admiralty, 1887–1902. Principal Clerk, Admiralty, 1902–7. Assistant Secretary, Admiralty, 1907–11. Knighted, 1911. Permanent Secretary, Admiralty, 1911–17. Secretary, Ministry of Munitions, 1917–20.

Secretary to the Admiralty, and from Sir James Masterton Smith, Private Secretary to Mr Balfour. . . .

So much for the 'first official report' of the Battle of Jutland.

At a later period, however, I made a statement of my own on the Battle of Jutland. This statement was issued by the Admiralty through the Press Bureau at 10.20 pm on June 3, twenty-seven hours after the issue of the 'first official report', and it appeared in the newspapers of June 4.

This statement of mine originated in the following way:

On learning that a battle had been fought in the North Sea I went round, on the morning of June 3, to the First Lord's office at the Admiralty to ask for full information, which I was sure would be readily afforded to me seeing that I was the late First Lord. I went into the room of Mr Balfour's private secretaries, and was there shown the telegrams from the Fleet and told such details as were known about the battle.

There were in the room at that time Sir James Masterton Smith, principal private secretary to Mr Balfour, and Sir Douglas Brownrigg,[1] the Admiralty's Chief Censor. . . . As I took a fairly cheerful view of what had occurred, it was suggested to me that I might make a statement of a reassuring character to the public on my authority as the ex-First Lord. In reply to this suggestion I said that I could only make a statement on the battle if I were directly invited to do so by the First Lord. Mr Balfour then asked me into his room and told me that he thought it would be very helpful if I made a statement of a reassuring character. I thought it my duty to comply with this request. I returned to the private secretaries' room, and dictated to an Admiralty stenographer a statement which I will presently read.

In order to be quite sure that my statement was based on sound lines, I went round to see Lord Fisher, at Berkeley Square, and showed the statement to him. I found he was in general agreement with my estimate of the situation. I thereupon telephoned to the Admiralty authorising them, if they chose, to publish the statement. They did so, and it appeared in the newspapers of June 4. . . .

It follows from the evidence which I have given on this first allegation that there is no truth in the rest of the story. I was not concerned in any 'financial plot' to issue 'false news of the battle', as no plot existed and there was no false news of the battle. I was not a 'tool in the hands' of any 'Jewish friends'; and I rendered no services to any 'Jewish taskmasters'. I received no reward,

---

[1] Douglas Egremont Robert Brownrigg, 1867–1939. Entered Navy, 1881. Succeeded his father as 4th Baronet, 1900. Captain, 1907. Naval Attaché, Tokyo and Peking, 1910–12. Retired from the active list as a Captain, 1913. Recalled as Chief Censor, Admiralty, 1914–19. Rear-Admiral, 1919. He published his wartime memoirs, *Indiscretions of a Naval Censor*, in 1920.

consideration or bribe from any 'Jewish taskmasters' or 'Jewish friends', or from any other person.

There is only one point in these malicious inventions which has the slightest connection with truth. The statement that 'After the Jutland business his (Mr Churchill's) house was furnished for him by Sir Ernest Cassel' is untrue. It is true, however, that ten years before the Battle of Jutland—not after it— Sir Ernest Cassel furnished for me a room in my house at 10, Bolton Street. Sir Ernest Cassel was a great friend of mine, and a great friend of my father's before me. I first got to know him well about the year 1897. At the end of the year 1905, when for the first time I took a small house of my own in Bolton Street, he asked my mother whether he might furnish my sitting room for me. I accepted this gift from him as an act of spontaneous friendship. That is the sole foundation of truth which exists for these libels; and, as I have stated, it occurred ten years before the Battle of Jutland, and not after it.

I did not spend the week-end with Sir Ernest Cassel before the Battle of Jutland occurred. It is only a detail, but it is as untrue as the rest. I never at any time discussed any matter connected with the Battle of Jutland with him until after these libels had appeared, when I naturally drew his attention to them. He then in the last year of his life, although very ill, immediately offered to come forward and join in any prosecution which it might be thought right or necessary to institute. On these points, however, evidence will be given by those who have the task and the duty of defending his memory.

Finally, let me explain why it was that I did not institute a prosecution for libel, or why the late Government, of which I was a member, did not file a criminal information against Lord Alfred Douglas when these articles in 'Plain English' first appeared at the beginning of 1921. As soon as they were brought to my notice I sent them to the Law officers of the Crown and expressed my desire to institute proceedings. The Attorney-General, now the present Lord Chief Justice, Lord Hewart,[1] advised that the publication, 'Plain English', and its author, Lord Alfred Douglas, were of such a character as to render proceedings unnecessary. He advised that the articles should be treated with contempt, as their probable object was to procure an advertisement for a publication otherwise insignificant and obscure. He advised that no action should be taken unless these libels were repeated in some reputable or responsible quarter. He assured me that if at any time it was decided to take action, or if these matters obtained publicity in any other way, he would repeat and justify his advice in public: and this he is ready to do now.

[1] Gordon Hewart, 1870–1943. Called to the Bar, Inner Temple, 1902. Liberal MP, 1913–22. Solicitor-General, 1916–19. Knighted, 1916. Attorney-General, 1919–22. A member of the Cabinet from November 1921 to October 1922. One of the British signatories of the Irish Treaty, December 1921. Created Baron, 1922. Lord Chief Justice, 1922–40. Created Viscount, 1940.

Sir William Graham Greene to Winston S. Churchill

(*Churchill papers 2/127*)

14 December 1923

Dear Mr Churchill,

Now that the trial of Lord A. Douglas is over, I must send you my hearty congratulations on the result. In all my life, & my memory is not so defective as that miserable Counsel would have liked to make out, I cannot recall the case of any public man who has suffered such abuse & misrepresentation. It is not possible to hope that your enemies will cease to deprecate your actions and motives, but at any rate this particular outrageous falsehood cannot be publicly repeated.

It is largely due to such unjustifiable attacks that you lost your seat at Dundee and failed at Leicester, though I confess that I thought that you made a mistake in preferring a Leicester Division to a Manchester one. Your opening speech at Manchester was the best that was delivered on the Free Trade policy & I hoped that you would have been able to speak in many parts of the country in the same manner. However, it cannot be long before another opportunity of returning to the House will come to you & then your success should be certain. If Labour be called upon to form a govt it will take all their time to prove that you were wrong in what you said of them.

After reading your last volume, which I did with great interest, I feel that I have no suggestion to make. You have made the case as complete as it could be made.

With kindest regards to Mrs Churchill,
I am, yours sincerely
W. Graham Greene

Sir Arthur Conan Doyle[1] to Winston Churchill

(*Churchill papers: 1/165*)

14 December 1923

My dear Churchill,

May I say how much I sympathise with the monstrous persecution you have endured. The sentence was far too light—a restcure in a quiet retreat without a bill to pay.[2]

---

[1] Arthur Conan Doyle, 1859–1930. Historian and novelist. Inventor of Sherlock Holmes. During the First World War he was gathering material for his six-volume history *The British Campaign in France and Flanders*, published at intervals between 1915 and 1920.

[2] Lord Alfred Douglas was sentenced to six months in prison.

This fellow Douglas wrote me an abusive letter once over my psychic work. I answered 'It is only your approval which could shock me'. I have heard no more.

I wish you would yourself look into this psychic question. It is far the most important thing upon earth & we want leaders of energy.

Yours sincerely
A. Conan Doyle

Austen Chamberlain to Winston S. Churchill

(*Churchill papers: 2/127*)

14 December 1923

My dear Winston,

My wife & I would like to say to you & Mrs Churchill with what close sympathy we have followed the outrageous ordeal to which you have been subjected & how much we rejoice at your complete vindication, only marvelling at the leniency of the sentence inflicted by the Judge.[1]

It seems almost insulting to congratulate you & yet the ways of the law are so strange to a layman & the license allowed in attacks on public men so extreme, that it is matter for congratulation to us all when one of our member vindicates public honour even from such vile & groundless charges.

I am very sorry that you are still out of Parlt. I could not on this occasion offer you public support nor would you have wished it, but I should like you to know that I declined on grounds of private friendship & our very recent association in govt to send your opponent a letter wishing him success.

All good wishes to you & yours for the X'mas season & New Year.

Yrs very sincerely
Austen Chamberlain

[1] Horace Edmund Avory, 1851–1935. Barrister, Inner Temple, 1875. Senior Counsel to the Treasury at the Central Criminal Court, 1899. Knighted, 1910; King's Counsel, 1910. Judge, King's Bench Division, High Court, from 1910 until his death. Privy Councillor, 1932.

Charles Masterman[1] to Winston S. Churchill

(*Churchill papers: 2/126*)

Undated
Private

My dear Winston,

I have delayed writing, partly through fatigue, which has kept me in bed, & partly to await the result of this accursed crew which have rendered your life a burden just when you ought to be taking a rest. A thousand congratulations on your complete victory over them. I wish to heaven you had won Leicester, your loss was one of the great disappointments of the campaign. But you must get back at the very first opportunity & if I can be of any use to you in however humble a fashion, please command my services.

Lucy & I both send good wishes to Clemmy & yourself. Take a good rest for Xmas.

Ever yours,
Charles F. G. Masterman

Frederick Kellaway[2] to Winston S. Churchill

(*Churchill papers: 2/127*)

14 December 1923

Dear Churchill,

May I congratulate you on the result of the Douglas trial? Whilst it is true that no one who knew you would attach the slightest importance to Douglas' ravings, and I imagine that nobody who knew Douglas attached any importance to them either, it was high time it should be demonstrated that the libelling of public men can be punished by process of law. In a less sophisticated state of society than ours there would have been more suitable

[1] Charles Frederick Gurney Masterman, 1874–1927. Liberal MP, 1906–14. Under-Secretary to Churchill, Home Office, 1909–12. Financial Secretary to the Treasury, 1912–14. Chancellor of the Duchy of Lancaster, 1914–15. Forced to leave the Government after nine months of being unable to find a parliamentary constituency after being defeated at a by-election in February 1914. Liberal MP, 1923–4.

[2] Frederick George Kellaway, 1870–1933. Began work as a journalist in Lewisham, 1898. Liberal MP for Bedford, 1910–22. Joint Parliamentary Secretary, Ministry of Munitions. 1916–18. Deputy Minister of Munitions, 1918–19. Secretary, Department of Overseas Trade, 1920–1. Postmaster-General, 1921–2. Chairman and Managing Director, Marconi Inter-, national Marine Communication Co, 1924–33. Vice-Chairman and Managing Director, Marconi's Wireless Telegraph Company. Deputy Governor, Cables and Wireless Ltd.

methods of dealing with this class of reptile. Now that an example has been made of one of the worst offenders, similarly minded persons will be more careful. You have done a public service, and I send you my hearty congratulations.

I was sorry you did not succeed at Leicester. You must get back to the House. The outlook is dark and troubled; the country will need your energy and vision.

Yours faithfully,
F. Kellaway

Lord Balfour to Winston S. Churchill

(*Churchill papers: 2/127*)

17 December 1923
Private

My dear Winston,

I think you have been *most* ill-used in this affair of Alfred Douglas; and I don't the least wonder at your feeling intense disgust at being dragged into this sordid conflict. But you came out of it with flying colours; and I hope we need neither of us give it another moment's thought. As for my own share in the business, I wish I could think you owed me any special debt of gratitude; but I cannot lay that flattering unction to my soul. There was a plain tale to tell, and all I could do was to tell it plainly.

I am not happy about politics; and I fear that Baldwin's astounding performance may injure causes even more important than the interests of the Party which he leads.

Yours
AJB

T. E. Lawrence[1] *to Winston S. Churchill*

(*Churchill papers: 8/47*)

23 December 1923

Dear Mr Churchill,

I hope you won't continue to want a copy of my book.[2] It's very dear (30 guineas): it won't be ready for at least a year: and it's not at all the sort of thing you will like: much too hesitant: hysterical sometimes, long-winded, & quite unpleasant in parts. It has no political interest, & does not slang any prominent people: in fact only the apparent secrecy of its production gives it any attraction at all, and it's only coming out shyly because it's so horrible a give-away of my own essential smallness!

There, isn't that enough to put you off? I've been reading your second volume lately: its moderation of statement upon the Dardanelles pleased me very much, but there is not enough of your power in it. The opening pages of the first volume were the most tremendous thing. People poke fingers at rhetoric, but that's because most of it is bad. Do let yourself rip before the end of things, once, completely. It's far & away the best war-book I've yet read in any language.

T. E. Lawrence

[1] Thomas Edward Lawrence, 1888–1935. Born in North Wales. Educated at Oxford. Travelled in Syria and Palestine while still an undergraduate. Obtained a first-class degree in history, 1910. On archaeological work at Carchemish, 1911–14. Explored, with Leonard Woolley, the Negev desert south of Beersheba, 1914. Served in the Geographical Section, General Staff, War Office, 1914–15; military intelligence, Egypt, 1915–16. Accompanied Ronald Storrs to Jedda, 1916, at the inauguration of the Arab revolt against the Turks. Liaison officer and adviser to the Emir Feisal, 1917–18. Took part in the capture of Akaba from the Turks, July 1917, and the capture of Damascus, October 1918. Accompanied Feisal to the Paris Peace Conference, 1919. Elected a Fellow of All Souls, Oxford, 1919. Joined the Middle East Department of the Colonial Office, January 1921; resigned, 1922. Enlisted in the Royal Air Force (as J. H. Ross), 1922, and again (as T. E. Shaw), 1923. Served in India, 1926–8. Retired from the RAF, 1935. Killed in a motor-cycle accident.

[2] The privately printed edition of *Seven Pillars of Wisdom*.

Violet Bonham Carter[1] *to Winston S. Churchill*

(*Churchill papers: 2/126*)

26 December 1923
Boxing Day

My dear Winston,

Thank you so much for writing—I showed your letter to Father (which I was sure you would not mind)—he & I had a long talk this morning. I think what you say about the possible Tory reaction which may result for the apparition of a Labour Govt a very *real* danger—

But there is another—(& to my mind a greater one) we must not lose sight of—ie the reaction *towards Labour* which wd follow inevitably & immediately from any part or alliance at this moment between ourselves & the Tories. As you truly said our Party has been re-inforced from the Left in the last Election—& I believe many Libs wd secede to Labour if they thought anything of the kind were contemplated now. They may feel differently about it after Labour has been in for a time. Everything of course depends on how they behave in office.

I think you tend to underrate a little the *immense* domestic difficulties & complications with which the Labour Party will be faced *in office.* They never had any inner unity or even any pretence at outward discipline or civility to their leaders in Opposition. And I think that in office these chasms will be widened rather than bridged. If Ramsay MacDonald tries to proceed on the mild Liberal lines we expect, he will certainly be faced with trouble from his wild men—& be driven to look to us for protection—

If he rides for a fall & goes forward with a Fire-Eaters' programme we turn him out—the King refuses a Dissolution—& we come in with a better chance surely than we should have now, though not—I agree—a good one.

The question of the Dissolution is of course a moot point. Father asks me to say that there are an immense number of Dominion precedents for refusing one under such conditions—(Beauchamp[2] did it once in Australia himself). What Father feels above all is that it wd be disastrous for almost any Party

---

[1] Helen Violet Asquith, 1887–1969. Elder daughter of H. H. Asquith. Educated in Dresden and Paris. Married, 1915, Sir Maurice Bonham Carter (who died in 1960). President of the Women's Liberal Federation, 1923–5 and 1939–45; President of the Liberal Party Organization, 1945–7. A Governor of the BBC, 1941–6. Member of the Royal Commission on the Press, 1947–9. Unsuccessful Liberal candidate, 1945 and 1951. DBE, 1953; created Baroness Asquith of Yarnbury, 1964. Published *Winston Churchill as I Knew Him*, 1965.

[2] William Lygon Beauchamp, 1872–1938. Succeeded his father as 7th Earl, 1891. Governor and Commander-in-Chief of New South Wales, 1899–1901. First Commissioner of Works in Asquith's Government, 1910–14. Lord President of the Council. 1910 and 1914. His wife was a sister of the 2nd Duke of Westminster.

in their *own* interests to come in now—& tackle this Devil's cauldron—(not of our own brewing) which seethes & bubbles on all sides—

Let Labour have a try—& find out for themselves & show their followers & the country what the difficulties are—

I thought Ramsay's last speech—as reported in the *Times*—was couched in a milder & more timid vein—

I am bound to say that I am a little influenced by the knowledge that what Labour themselves want *more than anything else* at this moment is to see us shepherded into the same pen with the Tories—whether as leaders or camp-followers, & I feel it *must* be bad strategy to do what your opponents most passionately want. I *do* share your feelings about the rocks ahead if Labour is refused a Dissolution on a popular largesse-scattering Budget—which *we* oppose—It is a *great* risk—& it is only because I think the alternative risk an even greater one that I feel we must face it—

I honestly think it quite *possible* that differences within the Lab Party itself may destroy them & prevent Ramsay MacDonald from stage-ing their fall as it suits him best—

Father sends his love & asks me whether the quotation in your letter is 'He who *Kills* not when he may'?—That, he says has the real Winstonian ring & there is a great deal to be said for it—

We know nothing of what the Labour amendt to the Address is to be—They probably dont know themselves as yet—I imagine they will have to extend 'feelers' nearer the time if they want us to vote for it.

Propose yourself here for a night if you want to see Father at anytime—it is always a delight to him to talk to you—

Forgive this endless letter—give all my love to Clemmie & tell her I shall LOVE to bring the children[1] on the 15th Jan—

A glorious New Year to you dear Winston—& a successful one to all our united fortunes—Bless you—

Ever yours,
Violet

PS. I dreamt all Xmas Eve that I was discussing with you the rival merits of Second Ballot—PR & Alternative Vote—& woke up exhausted! & convinced that *all* wd result in our ruin.

---

[1] Lady Violet and Sir Maurice Bonham Carter had four children, one of whom, Laura Miranda, married in 1938 Jo Grimond, later Leader of the Parliamentary Liberal Party.

Winston S. Churchill to Violet Bonham Carter: unsent letter[1]

(Churchill papers: 2/126)

28 December 1923   2 Sussex Square
Private

My dear Violet,

I have been thinking over all you say in your letter, but it does not in any way remove my apprehensions. You know how sincerely I should like to see your father, for old time's sake and many other reasons, once more at the head of an Administration; but I very much fear that the course which is going to be taken will be injurious to this prospect and generally to the prospects of the Liberal Party.

The installation of a Socialist Government in power will be a deep shock to the country; the effect of this shock will be a formidable Tory reaction. If in two or three months the Socialist Government is dismissed from Office after they have staged some popular programme they will certainly demand a dissolution. I do not believe that the King will face the storm of refusing this dissolution, particularly when he will be told he is jeopardising his Crown by taking sides against one section of his subjects and standing between the whole mass and the benefits offered to them. Moreover, by that time the Conservative Party will be in a much stronger position than at present. The Election returns show on what a narrow margin a hundred seats have changed hands. With Protection out of the way and an actual living Socialist target to fire at they will certainly feel great hopes of improving their position. The Liberals will be held to have taken an enormous responsibility in putting the Socialists in power; the blame for any mis-government and disturbance which may arise will be thrown upon them. They will be accused of having committed an act of faction without regard to the general interest of the country, which was tranquillity and steady recuperation. Many people in our fluctuating electorate will be unable to look upon them as any real defence against Socialism and manifestly their numbers prevent them from offering any independent alternative to it.

I think should these circumstances arise, the Conservative Party will not encourage the Crown to resist the Socialist demand for dissolution and will not give any measure of support to a Liberal Administration. They will say: 'No; the hour is past for that: we believe we can win fifty or sixty seats back by a new appeal. We are certainly not going to act as bottle holders to those

---

[1] After this letter had been dictated and typed, Churchill wrote on it, in his own handwriting: 'My dear Violet' and: 'Yours ever W'. But he then decided not to send it, and his secretary, Miss Fisher, noted on the top: 'Not to be sent.'

who kicked us into the street three months ago and deliberately erected this Socialist monstrosity.'

It seems to me that the course of events may well lead us to another early General Election in which the efforts of both Tories and Socialists will again be directed to wiping out the Liberals. If the Socialist Party play their cards well—and think what cards have been put in their hands—I see no reason why they should not get the support of many Liberals, while others will be crushed out or fall back upon local arrangements with the Conservative.

I hope the far-reaching significance of the act of the Liberal Party in installing a Socialist Government in power without a majority will not be under-rated. It is a most tremendous step, measureless from many points of view and certainly fraught with deep injury to our prosperity and national reputation. At present all public opinion blames the Tories for their criminal folly and partisanship at the Election, but on the morrow of the vote which I fear will be given before next month is over these censures will have an entirely different direction. The Liberal Party, acting on purely Party lines, will have taken a step of a very decisive character, for the consequences of which, whatever they may be, they will be held lastingly responsible.

I would not write all this without indicating an alternative course. It is this: We should find out, as can easily be done without our committing ourselves, whether the Baldwin Government will drop Protection and will state that they consider that issue settled by the vote of the electors. If they say this, as I believe they will, I do not think they ought to be turned out by a deliberate vote simply for the purpose of putting the Socialists in power. They might fall in the course of a few weeks or months through general weakness, but before that happens a situation more favourable to the Liberal Party may be reached, and at any rate we should not be liable to be saddled with the direct responsibility of having brought about what I am sure will be considered by the overwhelming majority of the Nation a very unfortunate and unpleasant result. It is quite possible that in such a breathing space definite offers of support might be made by the Conservatives which would enable a Liberal Government to take Office under good conditions and for a period long enough to rectify our existing unfair electoral machinery.

Forgive me for boring you with all this.

Yours ever

W

Clementine S. Churchill to Professor Lindemann[1]

(Cherwell papers)

30 December 1923

My dear Professor Lindemann,

Your charming Christmas letter gave both my husband and myself great pleasure.

The political horizon is indeed murky.

If Mr Asquith does not think better of it it seems to me he will ruin his party (to say nothing of damaging the country). I should think the result would be that half the liberals would eventually go labour & the other half would join the Tories.

---

[1] Frederick Alexander Lindemann, 1886–1957. Born at Baden Baden (where his mother was taking the cure); son of an Alsatian father who had emigrated to Britain in the early 1870s, and an American mother. Educated at Blair Lodge, Scotland, Darmstadt, 1902–5, and Berlin University, 1906–10. Doctor of Philosophy, Berlin, 1910. Studied physical chemistry in Paris, 1912–14. Worked at the Physical Laboratory, RAF, 1915–18, when he helped to organize the kite balloon barrage. Learned to fly, 1916. Personally investigated the aerodynamic effects of aircraft spin. Professor of Experimental Philosophy (physics), Oxford, 1919–56. Student of Christ Church (where he subsequently resided), 1921. Elected to the Other Club, 1927. Published his *Physical Significance of the Quantum Theory*, 1932. Member of the Expert Committee on Air Defence Research, Committee of Imperial Defence, 1935–9. Unsuccessful by-election candidate at Oxford, 1937. Personal Assistant to the Prime Minister (Churchill), 1940–1; in 1953 Churchill's Private Secretary, John Martin, wrote to him: 'Those without experience in the inner circle will never know the size of Winston's debt to you and how much stimulus and inspiration of ideas flowed from your office.' Created Baron Cherwell, 1941. Paymaster-General, 1942–5 and 1951–3. Privy Councillor, 1943. Viscount, 1956.

January–July
1924

3 January 1924

Dear Mr Cecil Roberts,

I have not until now found an opportunity to thank you for the energetic and cordial support which you gave me during the recent election. We had every disadvantage to contend with: no local press; no organisation; universally interrupted meetings. In these circumstances, the special efforts of the *Nottingham Journal* were invaluable, but I have to thank you in addition for your own personal assistance and encouragement, of which I am most sensible.

Yours very truly,
Winston S. Churchill

Winston S. Churchill to Lady Violet Bonham Carter

(Churchill papers: 2/132)

8 January 1924

I have thought a good deal over your letter and in the interval I feel clearer in my mind as to the future course of events and my own part, such as it is, in them. I can quite see after your father's speech, and in view of the existing circumstances, that there is no possibility of averting the great mis-

---

[1] Cecil Edric Mornington Roberts, 1892–1977. Educated at Mundella Grammar School. Poet and novelist, he published his first book in 1912. Literary Editor, *Liverpool Post*, 1915–18, and naval correspondent with the Grand Fleet and Dover Patrol. Assistant Director of Munitions Overseas Transport, 1918. Editor *Nottingham Journal*, 1920–5. Unsuccessful Liberal candidate, 1922. Author of more than thirty books, novels and plays between 1922 and his death.

fortune of a Socialist Government being formed. It is to what is to happen thereafter that I am directing my thoughts.

Let us assume, then, that on the 17th or 18th the Government moves that a humble address be presented, etc, that an amendment be carried against it to the following effect 'We have no confidence in Ministers who have declared protection is the sole remedy for unemployment', or some similar formula. Let us assume that the great bulk of the Liberal Party vote for this amendment; the House is adjourned and Macdonald is sent for and forms his Government; the House reassembles early in February; what is the result? Unless there is a new King's Speech and a new Address, the question is still that a humble address be presented to His Majesty etc, to which has been added an amendment condemning the Protectionist Administration. The debate on the Address is then resumed. The Order paper will of course be covered with the usual litter of amendments: to them will certainly be added an amendment in the following sense 'And further, we have no confidence in an Administration composed exclusively of Ministers who are declared Socialists and whose policy of a Capital Levy has been decisively rejected by the majority of the electorate.' Now here is the crux, and perhaps a parting of the ways. I am sure Lloyd George will want to vote against this motion on the grounds of 'give the Socialist kid a chance', but what will the Liberal Party do? Do you think it can really be carried into the Lobby to support a Socialist Government against its declared principles? If so, I can hardly believe that all will vote; in fact I know of some at any rate who will not. I think it possible that, if the Conservative Party have by then dropped Baldwin and developed a policy of offering co-operation in the Constituencies, there may even be an appreciable number who will refuse to make themselves the prop of a Socialist Government. I had a talk with Grey the other night and certainly did not think that he was very keen on keeping the Socialists in. Runciman[1] clearly has views in the same direction. I am making no concealment of mine, though after all I do not delude myself by supposing that I count in any way in the situation.

It seems to me well worthy of consideration whether the Liberal Party should not be led directly into the Lobby against the Socialist Government; it would thus be terminated in a single day, before it could do any mischief or undermine the commercial and business activities of the country. Even if

[1] Walter Runciman, 1870–1949. Educated at Trinity College, Cambridge. Liberal MP, 1899–1900; 1902–18. Shipowner. President of the Board of Education, 1908–11. President of the Board of Agriculture and Fisheries, 1911–14. President of the Board of Trade, 1914–16. Liberal MP, 1924–9; 1929–31. Liberal National MP, 1931–7. President of the Board of Trade, 1931–7. 2nd Baron, 1937. Created Viscount Runciman of Doxford, 1937. Head of Mission to Czechoslovakia, 1938. Lord President of the Council, October 1938–September 1939.

Lloyd George and the more Socialistly-minded wing went into the Lobby with the Socialists, the only result could be a Liberal Administration, with a very great measure of freedom of action and the tacit support of the Conservative Party.

I believe this is the only chance of such a happy result. I am sure that if the Liberals keep the Socialists in office by their votes and regular attendance through the Session, a minority—maybe a small minority—of them will certainly co-operate with the Conservatives. I believe, further, that the Conservative Party will gradually gain in strength by the reaction caused in the country at the apparition of this Socialist monstrosity, and when eventually the Socialists are turned out the Conservatives will be as anxious to go to the country as Ramsay Macdonald. They will be quite sure they can win sixty or seventy seats, and all chance of procuring their acquiescence in a Liberal Government will have passed away.

My counsel, therefore, is that the Liberal Party should be independent and impartial; that it should not take sides with Socialism any more than with Protection and that it should vote on the merits of each proposition set down on the Order paper without regard to the immediate consequences to the Government of the day.

Perhaps you will let me know, dear Violet, what you think of this: certainly show it to your father if you think it would not bore him. I should like him to know how my mind is moving, because I think that is always the right relation, and I do not believe in surprises amongst friends.

I am sorry to say that Randolph has the measles, so that we have had to put off the children's party for the 15th. Will you let me know when you are coming to London, and let me give you lunch.

Winston S. Churchill to a correspondent[1]

(*'The Times'*: *18 January 1924*)

17 January 1924   2 Sussex Square

Sir,—The currents of party warfare are carrying us all into dangerous waters. The enthronement in office of a Socialist Government will be a serious national misfortune such as has usually befallen great States only on the morrow of defeat in war. It will delay the return of prosperity: it will check

[1] This letter was published in full by *The Times* under the triple headline:

THE DANGERS OF SOCIALISM
MR CHURCHILL'S WARNING
DUTY OF HOUSE OF COMMONS

enterprise and impair credit; it will open a period of increasing political confusion and disturbance; it will place both the Liberal and Labour parties in a thoroughly false position. The Liberal Party will be led into supporting Socialists whom they have just been fighting in hundreds of constituencies throughout the country, and who will still be attacking them and undermining them in these constituencies with ceaseless activity.

The Socialist Party will be called upon to conduct and administer the business of this immense community, without the reality of power which springs from the will of the majority or the sense of responsibility which arises from the reality of power. They will be invited to cure the distresses of the time on the express condition that they use none of the remedies which they have advocated, in which they believe, and under the threat that if they have recourse to these remedies they will be immediately dismissed. They will be invited to continue in office on sufferance in order that, if they are violent, they may be defeated, and if they are moderate, they may become divided. And this is called 'giving a fair chance to Labour'. It is no fair chance to Labour; it is no fair chance to Britain; it is a fair chance only to faction and manoeuvre.

It is impossible that the Socialist Party should be so foolish as to be unaware of this position. If they are willing, and indeed eager, to form a Government, it cannot be with any hopes of carrying forward a fruitful and efficacious policy according to their lights with reasonable continuity. It can only be because they see in the prestige of office, and in the assumption of administrative power, the means of preparing and shaping the issues in the near future for a far greater political convulsion than we have yet experienced.

To expect that the Crown will refuse a dissolution to Socialist Ministers who, after two or three months of office, seek to present a far-reaching programme to the nation, is to lay too heavy and too invidious a burden on the august function of the Constitution embodied in the person of the Sovereign. A General Election fought on issues fundamental to the existing state of society and presided over by a Socialist Government actually holding the reins of power and the sole guarantee of law and order will be a formidable event. It is not one from which British citizens secure in their constitutional rights should shrink, if it is inevitable. But it is an event which while it impends will cast a dark and blighting shadow on every form of national life and confidence and on every prospect of trade revival. This is, however, the conclusion and climax towards which at the present time the officials of all parties are obstinately marching.

It is astonishing that we should be committed to such dangerous prospects with so little real cause. Although party antagonisms are so active and feverish, there never was a moment in our modern history when there was a greater body of general agreement upon what should be immediately done or attempted in domestic and foreign policy. The great central mass of the nation earnestly desires to see foreign affairs and social reform dealt with by the new Parliament on their merits, without rancour or prejudice and in a sincere spirit of good will. All such prospects will be destroyed by the accession to office of a minority party innately pledged to the fundamental subversion of the existing social and economic civilization and organized for that purpose and for that purpose alone. Strife and tumult, deepening and darkening, can be the only consequence of minority Socialist rule.

It ought not, however, to be supposed that the procedure of the House of Commons or the character of the British Constitution renders such disastrous developments and contingencies inevitable. Lord Grey wisely said in the House of Lords yesterday that the best way of escaping from the party and constitutional difficulties in which the country is now involved was by following the simplest and most obvious course which is open to Parliament.

What, then, is the simplest and most obvious course? It is surely for the House of Commons to send an Address to the Crown in reply to the Gracious Speech, which Address shall be a sincere and complete expression of its opinion. A newly-elected House of Commons is the supreme tribunal of the nation's affairs. It is the duty of the House of Commons, representing the will of the people newly recorded at the election, to express its whole mind. It is its duty to relieve the Crown by every means and to the utmost possible extent from difficulty or controversy. The House of Commons will fail in its duty if it tenders to the Crown an incomplete, partial, or misleading Address. The House is entire master of its procedure in this matter, and can readily give effect to its wishes, whatever they may be.

If and when Mr Clynes's amendment[1] has been carried, it is for the House of Commons to say whether it will present the Address to the Crown in that form or whether it will add any further expression of its views. After the passage of Mr Clynes's amendment, it will be open to the House, after any adjournment that may be proposed, to continue the debate upon any other amendment and to continue it irrespective of whether a new Government has or has not at that moment assumed office. There is nothing to prevent the House of Commons, if it chooses, sending to the Crown an Address in reply to the Gracious Speech which, if it expresses want of confidence in his Majesty's present Ministers, also records its repudiation of Socialism and its distrust of those whose policy of a capital levy and of the nationalization of the

---

[1] Parliament had first met, following the General Election, on January 8, the balance of seats being Conservative 258, Labour 191 and Liberal 159. A Labour opposition amendment to the King's Speech was moved by J. R. Clynes on January 17, the day on which Churchill sent this letter to *The Times*.

means of production, distribution, and exchange have been so signally defeated at the polls. Such an Address would truthfully express the general mind of the House and the decision of the electors, and would reduce and limit to normal constitutional dimensions the burden placed upon the Crown.

Watching the long series of disastrous and purposeless party follies which have marked and are still marking the progressive degeneration of our affairs, I feel bound to place on record a warning of the dangers into which we are drifting, and to point to a means whereby, in accordance with the wish of the great majority of the electors and in full harmony with the spirit of the Constitution, these dangers can even at the eleventh hour be avoided. Our difficulties, no doubt, will not be ended by any single step; but I am sure that by recording a simple, straightforward, and complete expression of the collective national wish the new Parliament will at the outset of its life have established itself on a basis from which the solution of these difficulties will be rendered far easier.

Yours faithfully,
Winston S. Churchill

Lady Violet Bonham Carter to Winston S. Churchill

(*Churchill papers: 2/137*)

18 January 1924

My dear Winston,

I was on the point of answering your letter when I recd your Manifesto in the paper—& now I feel there is no more to be said. I am very sorry you should have published it because it is a public definition of your difference of opinion with the rest of the Party—& I rather hoped that the difference might have been bridged & reconciled by events before it was known to the world at large.

But of course I recognize & respect the strength & the sincerity of your conviction—though I cannot share it.

To turn the Labour Party out a week after putting them in appears to me as a purely frivolous 'wrecking' action—We can—& clearly have—quite clearly defined our view of Capital Levy & Socialism—& they know that if they attempt either they will be turned out—It may be unwise for them to carry on on these lines, with their teeth drawn, but that is not our business.

Father's speech on Thursday was masterly—as fine a thing as I have ever heard him do. Wise—generous—courageous—& extremely dexterous & witty—The Labour men were genuinely & deeply moved—One of the

Clydeside tigers said to Simon 'Well—we've got no men in our party as big as that'—Snowden[1] was typical—Ramsay I thought looked a little sea-sick when Father said turning to him 'Nothing but an *iron* sense of public duty could possibly have induced my right hon friend to take office under *such conditions as these*'—

I dont think that more than 5 of our men will vote against the Amendment —possibly not so many (& they are mostly either Welsh or Tory at heart).

I think the Labour Govt will suffer for the timidity & inefficiency of its members not for their violence. I am infinitely sorry to think that you are not with us over this—

Ever yours
Violet

Brigadier-General E. S. D'Ewes Coke[2] to Winston S. Churchill
(*Churchill papers: 2/137*)

18 January 1924

Dear Mr Churchill,

My only excuse for writing is that we were Cadets together at Sandhurst: but I am anxious to let you know how very welcome your letter in The Times to-day is.

The ordinary educated man like myself has been greatly puzzled by recent events, and I have found a pretty general agreement among clubmen and others that the decent elements in England should express their determination that Socialists shall not govern this Country until they can command a real majority of votes. I think that many of us feel that there is a real danger of England following the example of Russia, to the apathy of whose 'middle-class' was due the success of the Revolutionaries.

But, when Mr Asquith and others seem to see no danger, what are we, who are comparatively in the dark, to think?

We need a leader who can stir up the loyal and steady citizens, who still are largely in the majority. Thanking you for your very timely 'Warning'.

Yours truly,
E. S. D'Ewes Coke

[1] Philip Snowden, 1864–1937. Educated at Board School. Entered the Civil Service, 1886; retired, 1893. Chairman, Independent Labour Party, 1903–6 and 1917–20. Socialist MP for Blackburn, 1906–18; for Colne Valley, 1922–31. Privy Councillor, 1924. Chancellor of the Exchequer, 1924 and 1929–31. Created Viscount, 1931. Lord Privy Seal, 1931–2.

[2] Edward Sacheverell D'Ewes Coke, 1872–1941. 2nd Lieutenant, King's Own Scottish Borderers, 1894. On active service at Chitral, 1895 (when he was severely wounded), and on the North West Frontier of India, 1897–8. Major, 1913. Served on the western front, 1914–18. CMG, 1915; Brigadier-General, 1916; DSO, 1918. Retired from the army, 1922.

Albert G. Cooke[1] to Winston S. Churchill

(*Churchill papers: 2/137*)

20 January 1924

Dear Sir,

You will no doubt remember that some time ago I wrote you asking you to consider your position & come out boldly on behalf of the Conservative cause & principles, knowing full well that your sympathies were more or less in accordance with our views than with those of the Lloyd George or Asquith party.

Now I venture again to once more make an appeal to you Sir, viz; (a) After having read your published letter of last week, I am more firmly convinced that you are the man who can save the present situation, especially in conjunction with Lord Birkenhead, who is just as brilliant as yourself from a political point of view, both splendid & powerful orators & politicians —Both of you are really & at heart Conservatives.

When I was a boy 40 years ago, I used to swear by your late esteemed & respected parent 'The only Randolph', how I remember his plucky courageous uphill fights in B'ham & the Midlands, he was a gem to listen to.

Now granted that everyone makes mistakes & 'Stanley Baldwin' has made his insomuch that he never ought to have had the late rushed Election. But still it is over now & he has been defeated on an error of tactics & I suppose will pay the penalty of such error in the Division Lobby tomorrow night in the House of Commons.

But I appeal to you Sir & to such men as Lord Birkenhead to waive aside personal feelings & consideration & rally to the Conservative & True patriotic cause as the only Saviour of this grand old Empire of ours from destruction. Tomorrow night should Asquith & L. George carry out their intentions of placing the Labour & Socialist Party in Office (against the will of the People) they mark the death knell of the Liberal Party, which destruction will be swift & sure whenever the People get a voice in the matter. (b) What I would venture to suggest Sir is this, that you & Birkenhead throw your whole weight in with Stanley Baldwin, the most honest, truest & straightest gentleman that ever aspired to be Premier of this grand old Country of ours. A brief few years under his guidance as Premier, would be beneficial to all, both Capital & Labour & I urge you Sir to throw in your lot with his for the better & greater advancement of the workers of this Country of ours & for the honour of our Grand Old Empire. Support him

[1] Albert G. Cook, Secretary of the St Mary's Ward Conservative Committee, Kidderminster. From 1922 until 1945 Kidderminster was represented by J. S. Wardlaw-Milne. In 1945 the seat was won by the Labour candidate, L. Tolley (who had come bottom of the Poll in the 1923 election).

Sir, he lacks that fire & devilment which alone can defeat the Socialists & the Wait & See Liberals. But to his honesty of purpose, his Integrity, & to his whole hearted endeavour to do his best to uplift & better the lot & comfort of the Workers of this Country, there can be no doubt whatever.

You Sir & Lord Birkenhead can help him & assist us, as no other 2 men breathing can, to obtain this end, & then will come your reward before long, in attaining the highest offices of the realm, & more than ever that, the appreciation of a great & noble People, who will ever feel grateful to you both for the services rendered to a great & noble cause, placing National Interest before that of Party, & above all using your great & noble Gifts in the cause of 'The People, Humanity, & the British Empire'.

Now Sir, Come along, help us & 'Stanley' to do justice to old England & the British race—& your reward will be both 'Swift sure & grateful'.

Believe me to be
Yours very faithfully
Albert G. Cooke

PS. Good old Winston, shew this to Lord B & come over & help us. The Conservatives Want *you both.*

FOLLOWING A THREE-DAY debate, the Labour amendment was finally carried late on the evening of January 21, by 328 votes to 256. Only ten Liberals voted in support of the Conservative Government, and a further six Liberals abstained: but 137 Liberal MPs, led by Asquith, voted with the Labour Opposition. On the day after this vote, Stanley Baldwin resigned as Prime Minister, and Ramsay MacDonald formed Britain's first Labour Government, dependent upon Liberal support for its survival.

Ramsay MacDonald to Winston S. Churchill

(*Churchill papers: 2/132*)

27 January 1924
Private

My Dear Churchill,

No letter received by me at this time has given me more pleasure than yours.[1] I wish we did not disagree so much!—but there it is. In any event

---

[1] Ramsay MacDonald had become Prime Minister on 22 January 1924, at the head of Britain's first Labour Government. The Labour Party having won 191 seats, and the Con-

I hope your feelings are like mine. I have always held you personally in much esteem, & I hope, whatever fortune may have in store for us, that personal relationship will never be broken. Perhaps I may come across you occasionally.

Yours very sincerely
J. Ramsay MacDonald

Winston S. Churchill to Louis Loucheur
(*Loucheur papers*)

28 January 1924   2 Sussex Square

My dear Loucheur,

My wife and I are coming to Paris on the 6th and will be staying there for rather more than a week. I have no engagements at present, and I shall be grateful if you will let me know which night you will come and dine with me to meet Lord Crewe.[1] When I hear from you, I will write to him.

I am looking forward also to meeting Jean de Pierrefeu,[2] with whom you promised to put me in touch. My object in coming to Paris is to verify certain facts and figures about the late war for the purposes of my third volume on which I am now engaged. This volume will deal much more with the land fighting than the previous volumes, and I am deep in the study of the enormous & brilliant French literature which has come into being on the subject. I have been much interested in Mermeix's[3] books on the various 'Crises du Commandement', and perhaps you could introduce me to him or let me know whether he is an authority of high repute.

---

servatives 258, MacDonald's Government was dependent for its survival upon the support of the 159 Liberal MPs. Churchill's letter to MacDonald has not been found in MacDonald's own papers, nor does there appear to be a copy of it in Churchill's papers.

[1] Robert Offley Ashburton Crewe-Milnes, 1858–1945. Lord-Lieutenant of Ireland, 1892–5. Secretary of State for India, 1910–15. Created Marquess of Crewe, 1911. Lord President of the Council, 1915–16. President of the Board of Education, 1916. Ambassador to Paris, 1922–8. Secretary of State for War, 1931.

[2] Jean de Pierrefeu. Served in the French infantry, 1914–18. Sergeant-major, 1914; 2nd Lieutenant, 1915; member of the Information Section of the French General Staff, where he printed and circulated the daily official communiqué, 1915–18. In 1920 he published an account of his war work, *Trois Ans au Grand Quartier Général*. The English edition, entitled *French Headquarters, 1915–18*, was published in London in July 1924.

[3] Gabriel Terrail, French author, who wrote under the pseudonym Mermeix. His books on the First World War included *Joffre: La Première Crise du Commandement*, 1919; *Nivelle et Painlevé: La Deuxième Crise du Commandement*, 1919; *La Commandement Unique*, 1920; *Foch et les Armées d'Occident*, 1920; *Sarrail et les Armées d'Orient*, 1920, and *Les Négociations Secrètes et les Quatres Armistices*, 1921.

Literature apart, I want to have a good talk with you about the new situation. . . .

Lord Darling[1] to Winston S. Churchill
(Churchill papers: 2/132)

30 January 1924

My dear Winston,

Not one of the many letters I have had touches me so much as yours.[2]

Your friendship I have valued long, & highly—& if it colours somewhat your estimate of me, I like to feel that it is not entirely unmerited.

As to the Press, I confess that I am astonished at their cordiality.

Now in regard to yourself—I can't help feeling very anxious as to how you may come through this troublesome time—no one—to my thinking, has so much power to bring low these grotesque figures, now perched so high, as you have—& I feel sure that your chance will come—& that you will know how to seize it—May this be soon. . . .

Please remember me to Mrs Churchill.

Ever yours sincerely
Darling

H. G. Tanner[3] to Winston S. Churchill
(Churchill papers: 2/132)

4 February 1924

Dear Sir,

BRISTOL WEST LIBERAL ASSOCIATION

It is generally believed here that Col Gibbs,[4] the present Member, is to receive a Peerage in Mr Baldwin's list of Resignation Honours. This would

---

[1] Charles John Darling, 1849–1936. Barrister, 1874. Queen's Counsel, 1887. Conservative MP for Deptford, 1888–97. Knighted, 1897. Judge of the Queen's Bench Division of the High Court of Justice, 1897–1923. An original member of the Other Club, 1911. Chairman of the Committee on Courts Martial, 1919. Created Baron, 1924.

[2] Sir Charles Darling had been created Baron on 12 January 1924.

[3] Chairman of the Bristol West Liberal Association.

[4] George Abraham Gibbs, 1873–1931. On active service in the South African war, and (with Churchill) present at the capture of Pretoria, June 1900. Conservative MP for West Bristol, 1906–28. On active service, 1914–17. Conservative Whip in the House of Commons, 1917–24 and 1924–8. Created Baron Wraxall, 1928.

create a vacancy, which we consider provides us with an excellent opportunity of returning a Liberal Member.[1]

West Bristol's long Tory record is rather misleading, as at the last redistribution the entire character of the constituency was changed, and it now includes parts of the former Thornbury division of Gloucester and of Bristol North.

The only time it was fought since the changed conditions was in 1922, when Mr Raffety,[2] who now represents Bath, received rather more than 11,000 votes. The conditions at that time were very unfavourable, as the Liberal Party was divided and the most influential leaders of Liberalism in Bristol were identified with the National Liberal Wing. Re-union has now become a reality, and we believe that with a front rank Candidate, the Seat can be won.

Col Gibbs is a near neighbour, and has long associations with the constituency, advantages which are not likely to be enjoyed by the new Conservative Candidate, as there are rumours of one of the defeated Ex-Ministers coming down to fight the Seat.

I write to know whether you would be willing that I should propose your name to the committee which has been appointed to secure a Candidate.

I very much hope you will consent, as I not only believe that you could win the Seat, but that your presence as a Member for Bristol would be a great advantage to the Party in the whole of the West of England.

Yours faithfully,
H. G. Tanner

PS. As time is short a telegraphed reply would be appreciated.

Winston S. Churchill to H. G. Tanner

(*Churchill papers: 2/132*)

5 February 1924
Private and Confidential

My dear Mr Tanner,

I am very much obliged to you for your letter of the 4th instant, and am honoured by the fact that you should have thought of me in connection with

[1] As Colonel Gibbs did not receive his peerage until 1928, his re-election in 1924 was such a certainty that no Liberal candidate stood against him, and the Labour candidate received only 21 per cent of the vote. In the 1928 by-election another Conservative, C. T. Culverwell, won the seat, which he held until 1945, when it was again won by a Conservative, Oliver Stanley.

[2] Frank Walter Raffety, 1875–1945. A barrister. Liberal MP for Bath, 1923–4. He was an unsuccessful Parliamentary candidate not only in 1922, but also in 1921, 1924, 1929 and 1935.

the possible vacancy in West Bristol. The position, however, is not free from difficulty.

In the first place, West Bristol is a Conservative stronghold, and I am sure it could not be won at the present time in the face of Conservative opposition.

Secondly, I am, as you no doubt know, strongly opposed to Socialist Minority Government, which I think will prove eventually detrimental both to Liberal and National interests. I should not, therefore, be prepared to embark upon a by-electoral contest against the Conservatives, particularly in a seat where the result would be almost certainly adverse.

I have, however, received a copy of the 'Bristol Guardian' of February 4, which contains several references to myself remarkable in a Conservative newspaper. Of course if it were possible for me to stand on a Liberal, Free Trade and Anti-Socialist platform without Conservative opposition, or as an Independent Liberal pledged against Protection and Socialism, and un-opposed by the Conservatives, I should feel it very difficult to refuse; and I believe that I could render useful service to the general interests of the country in this critical and peculiar situation. If on this basis your Association cared to tender me an invitation, I would give it my most earnest attention.

I am going to Paris tomorrow for a fortnight, but of course I could return at any time if circumstances rendered it necessary.

H. G. Tanner to Winston S. Churchill

(*Churchill papers: 2/132*)

6 February 1924

Dear Mr Churchill,

Thank you for your letter of the 5th inst.

I am sorry that you should be of opinion that West Bristol is a Conservative stronghold which could not be won at the present time in the face of Con-servative opposition.

With you as Candidate, I think we should have excellent chances of success. As mentioned in my former letter, the character of the constituency has entirely changed in recent years.

The 'Bristol Guardian' to which you refer has a very small circulation and less influence in Bristol, and I think the Conservatives are certainly bound to fight the Seat. It is rumoured that there will be a Labour Candidate, which would, I think, improve our chances.

I think I may state that my Association is opposed equally to the Con-servative and Labour Parties, and that it approves of Mr Asquith's policy

in supporting Liberal measures by whatever Government they are introduced.

There is in West Bristol particularly a very large number of electors who
are not ordinarily associated with the Liberal Party, who would certainly
vote for you, owing to the admiration they feel for the great services you
have rendered to the State in the past, and because they realise that if
Parliament is to be representative, you certainly should be a Member.

Your recent book has made many friends for you, and would bring you
many votes which would ordinarily be cast on the other side.

If you could see your way to reconsider your decision, we should go into
the fight with high hopes of success.

Yours faithfully,
H. G. Tanner

Winston S. Churchill to Clementine Churchill

(*Spencer-Churchill papers*)

17 February 1924

The Woolsack
Mimizan
Landes

My darling,

We had two good hunts, but no pig. Four hours galloping made me
tired, stiff & well. We shall try again tomorrow.

Yesterday we motored to Biarritz & raided the Casino. Play was meagre,
but after some vicissitudes I collected five milles & levanted with them.

The sun has been shining brilliantly upon a biting cold atmosphere. How
one misses central heating. Nothing can make a house comfortable without
it. We are so accustomed to this great luxury that one shivers at its momentary
absence.

The young persons have proved quite harmless & show themselves vy
anxious to please in every way. Old Bacon[1] comes in daily & recriminates
about the English & the Franc. I rebuke him & his Poincaré[2] with statesmanlike austerity—& much verbiage. He is I think a little chastened.

Asquith seems to have been precipitate in playing the Dictator about

[1] The Mayor of Mimizan.
[2] Raymond Poincaré, 1860–1934. Minister of Public Instruction, 1893 and 1895; of
Finance, 1894 and 1906. Prime Minister, 1911–13. President of the French Republic,
January 1913–February 1920. Prime Minister and Minister of Foreign Affairs, January
1922–June 1924. Minister of Finance, 1926–8. Prime Minister, 1926–9.

Poplar;[1] & I don't think he will be able to Cat & Mouse the Government he has just installed as he & his tea-party wd no doubt like. I want *time* to work. A few months anyhow. Freddie wired me urging early return on account of the critical situation; & I think I had better get back tomorrow. It is impossible for me to chuck the dinner to Frank Kellogg[2]—or the Press Club fixture. Then there are—the 4 articles for the Sunday Chronicle & the next monthly for Ray Long[3] = £1,500. I must gather this for Tilden who is pressing anew.

Lastly there is Chartwell, wh I am sure will need the eye of the master, in the absence of the mistress in the next few weeks. So important to get it *finished*, and get the grass & greenery growing. 'Finish'—that is the vital thing. I will however keep open the plan of coming out to join you after the 23rd & will wire you from London. We cd easily stay together at a hotel. But I am inclined to think that once back, I shall stay put.

My sweet one—I am so glad you are in such a downy basket. Do not over

[1] The Board of Guardians was the body responsible for administering the Poor Law. In 1922 Sir Alfred Mond, then Home Secretary, had ruled that the Board of Guardians in Poplar had paid wage and relief scales that were too high, beyond even the scale of union wages, and that they had also been lavish in other ways, in their administration. Mond had prescribed lower scales for them to follow, later known as the 'Mond scales'. In January 1924, after the election, John Wheatley replaced Sir Alfred Mond at the Home Office. The Poplar Board immediately petitioned the new Home Secretary to rescind the Mond scales. He complied. An outcry from ratepayers ensued, led by the Poplar Ratepayers Association. On 13 February 1924, Asquith issued his first challenge to his partners in the Liberal–Labour truce, reminding the Labour Party that the Liberal Party was 'the arbiter of their destiny', and calling upon them to rescind Wheatley's administrative act. On February 27 the House of Commons debated a Liberal motion of censure against Wheatley's action. Wheatley gave assurances that no general change of Poor Law policy was intended, that Poplar would remain under the same controls as all the other Boards, and that this would ensure economy. No division was taken on the Liberal motion.

[2] On 22 February 1924 Churchill had presided over the George Washington Birthday dinner of the English Speaking Union. Frank Kellogg, the United States Ambassador to Britain, was the guest of honour. In its report of the speech on the following day, the *Continental Daily Mail* quoted Churchill as saying: 'Although we disagree profoundly, and I expect and even hope, will have long and sustained quarrels in future years—(laughter)—I am very glad on this occasion, for this all-commanding object of welcoming Mr Kellogg, that we are united in Empire accord. (Hear, Hear.)' Churchill added: 'Mr Kellogg lands in England to find a domestic situation which may puzzle him, because the oldest residents here do not understand it themselves.' During his speech Churchill described the future co-operation of Britain, France and Germany as 'not a visonary ideal, but sober, practical politics which we should all endeavour to advance, and in which, I am sure, so far as reasonable considerations admit, the Ambassador and the great country he represents over here will be willing to lend a friendly hand'.

[3] Ray Long, 1878–1954. Born in Indiana. Managing Editor of the *Cincinnati Post*, 1905–8; of the *Cleveland Press*, 1908–10. Editor of the *Hampton Columbian*, 1911–12; of *The Red Book Magazine* and *The Green Book Magazine*, 1912–18. Editor-in-Chief and Vice-President of International Magazine Company (*Cosmopolitan, Hearst's, Good Housekeeping, Harper's Bazaar*), 1919–31. Subsequently Chairman of the Board of Ray Long and Richard Smith, Inc, publishers.

exert yrself at tennis. Doubles not Singles *please*. I have undertaken to encounter Mr Stanley Baldwin on Mar 11 at the Cambridge Union on the question—'That this House has the highest regard for rhetoric' which the undergraduates are proposing. I shall try my best *pro* the motion.[1]

The oil scandals in USA seem to be broadening into absurdity & universal suspicion & discredit.[2] How glad I am we have nothing like this in our country. The oil of Britain like Caesar's wife must be above suspicion.

Poodle I love you. I feel quite lonely & sometimes frightened without you to give me a kiss or a hug.

I will visit Chartwell on Wed (DV) & will report to you at length the progress of the toil.

Tender love my sweet Clemmie—

Your own ever devoted
W

[sketch of pig]

PS. Yr letter just recd. It must be jolly there.[3] Sunshine & Peace. Alas we do not get too much of them.

W

[1] On the evening of 11 March 1924 the Cambridge Union debated the motion 'That this House has the highest regard for rhetoric'. Although Churchill had agreed to defend the motion, he was unable to do so on account of his unexpected candidacy at the Westminster Abbey by-election. Baldwin, in opposing the motion, began by saying that he had accepted the invitation to debate because 'it had been arranged for Winston Churchill to precede me. Under those circumstances all I would have had to do was to stand up for one brief moment and say—"There, gentlemen, is my case." ' (Laughter.) Baldwin went on to argue, as *The Times* reported, that rhetoric was 'one of the greatest dangers to our civilization'; it had been 'responsible for more bloodshed on this earth than all the guns and explosives that were ever invented. Rousseau, Robespierre and Danton had caused the French Revolution with rhetoric, and Kerensky had filled the Russian people with rhetoric until they had come to their present chaos. Rarely would they find that men of wisdom and constructive ability had the gift of rhetoric. St Paul was no orator, but his speeches and teachings had lasted a very long time. If they went back 2,000 years he would back St Paul against Lord Beaverbrook in preaching Christianity every Sunday.' At the end of the debate the vote was 297 for, and 297 against the motion: the Chairman cast his vote in favour, to carry the motion.

[2] Beginning in 1921 valuable oil lands belonging to the American Navy had been transferred from the Navy Department to the Department of the Interior, and then leased to an oil-magnate, E. L. Doheney. In addition, further oil lands, the 'Teapot Dome' lands in Wyoming, had been sold to another oil-man, H. F. Sinclair. In January 1924 a Senate Committee discovered that a former Secretary of the Interior, A. D. Fall, had received 'loans' of $100,000 from Doheney and $25,000 from Sinclair, while W. G. McAdoo, a former Secretary of Treasury, had received 'fees' of more than $150,000 from Doheney for legal services rendered after he had retired from the Government. No scandal was so profoundly to upset American opinion until the 'Watergate' affair more than fifty years later.

[3] Clementine Churchill was staying in the South of France, at Consuelo Balsan's villa, Lou Sueil, at Eze.

Winston S. Churchill to Clementine Churchill
(*Spencer-Churchill papers*)

20 February 1924   2 Sussex Square

I have just come back from Chartwell. There is considerable progress all along the line. The drawing room has two coats of plaster, and the cornice is up. The dining room has one coat of plaster, and all the French windows are in with their glass. They are lovely and add enormously to the appearance of the wing. The pantry dresser and cupboards are nearly finished. The red tiles are rapidly going down in the passage from the school-room to the kitchen. The light, water and heating are complete in the kitchen wing. The steps from the road down into the kitchen wing are finished. The new chimney stack to help the boilers is finished and is quite unobjectionable. A complete test was made by Benhams yesterday of the water arrangements which they now pronounce quite satisfactory.

Out of doors. The roadway wall is finished with the exception of the outer curves, and so are the palings. The grass has been laid behind the wall to within a foot of it, where a little border has been left for planting. Tilden pointed out that a row of fruit trees along that wall might easily grow ten to twelve pounds worth of fruit a year, which would pay the interest on the money spent in building the wall. I think this is a point to be considered. After all it is a kitchen garden wall to all intents and purposes.

The steps by the nursery summer house are half done, and the brick curves on each side of the summer house are finished. We shall get to the end of this job before you return. At last the tiles are going up on the blister. They are already up as high as the first floor windows, and you could not tell that they were not real bricks.

The circular steps to the lower terrace are all finished. The effect is very fine. They do not take up much room on the terrace, and they are very easy to walk up and down.

The first bay of the embankment wall is complete and looks very fine from below. It is of course much the best built of the whole wall. The brick pier on which the girder is to rest is also finished, and the girder goes up tomorrow. I am now busy filling in the earth behind the wall, and we shall soon see what our resources are. I am taking the bit of wall near the yew hedge near the summer house steps, as we need the stone. This was in accordance with your wishes.

The question has arisen whether you want leaded lights in the apertures round your bathroom, or whether ordinary twisted glass will suit you. Will you let me know what you decide? The leaded lights will cost about £3 more.

The pigs, ponies and cows are doing well. The new pig is getting very near her time, and I hope soon to report a large family. Twenty-four new chickens have been hatched, and more are expected shortly.

I am investigating the bull problem further and hope to make a plan which will work. That, I think, is all my Chartwell news. I am going down again tomorrow after lunch in order to push things forward.

I found the children very well, with the exception of Mary who, as you know, has had slight influenza. She is getting on all right, and Moppet is quite contented with her progress. Influenza has also broken out at Sandroyd, and Randolph is a victim. Mr Hornby[1] told me on the telephone that the attack was a mild one and that Randolph was very difficult to keep quiet on account of his spirits. His temperature is only 99. Today it is normal. This, however, knocks on the head my plan for bringing him to Chartwell on Sunday. I shall try to go down and see him as soon as he is approachable, and will keep you informed of his progress.

My affairs have not gone badly here in my absence. The South Africans have had a good rise, which more than makes up the temporary set back in Shells, wh too are recovering. Jack got me some of the Japanese loan, on which there is also a small profit.

Everything political seems quite quiet and generally proceeding in the direction which I desire. The Burnley election will be most interesting, as the Liberal Party left without any guidance is supporting both sides. I hear, however, that Henderson[2] will be elected.[3]

Tomorrow I shall have to do my second article, (done), and on Friday and Saturday I have two short speeches to prepare; but I shall hope to get to Chartwell in the afternoons all the same.

We had a very good hunt the last day at Mimizan. There were no less than eleven pigs *embarrois de choix*. I saw seven all together, including one quite big one, and two others separately galloping through the woods. After a long chase we finally slew a sow. She ran for twenty minutes as fast as the horses could gallop. The two young persons did not make a particularly

[1] William Meysey Hornby, 1870–1955. One of the founders of Sandroyd, he was headmaster from 1898 to 1931.

[2] Arthur Henderson, 1863–1935. Apprenticed as a moulder; later active in the Trade Union movement. Labour MP, 1903–18; 1919–22; 1923; 1924–31. Chairman, Parliamentary Labour Party, 1908–10. Chief Whip, Labour Party, 1914; 1921–4; 1925–7. President of the Board of Education, May 1915–August 1916. Paymaster-General, August–December 1916. Member of Lloyd George's War Cabinet, December 1916–August 1917. Government Mission to Russia, 1917. Home Secretary in the first Labour Government, 1924. Secretary of State for Foreign Affairs, 1929–31. President of the World Disarmament Conference, 1932–3.

[3] The Burnley by-election, caused by the death of the Labour MP, was not contested by the Liberals, but only by Labour and the Conservatives. Henderson, the Labour candidate, received 24,571 votes, as against 17,534 cast for the Conservatives.

good impression, and I think Benny had quite enough of them before they departed.

I enjoyed myself so much at Mimizan. I wished indeed that I had been able to finish the week there and come across to you. I shall not be through my work till Monday or Tuesday, the 25th or 26th. These articles are so important and must be delivered exactly to the hour. I continue to read a great deal about the war, consuming on the average a book a day. I think I shall stay here till you come back, as I am pretty full now of ideas which should be set down.

Winston S. Churchill to Clementine Churchill

(*Spencer-Churchill papers*)

21 February 1924

My dearest one,

Enclosed you will find some account of our affairs.

I have been busy all the morning dictating my article, & am now off to Chartwell. I wrote to Consuelo[1] to thank her for her invitation.

I telegraphed to you about Randolph & the baby. All is going well.

Last night I dined at the Vineyard.[2] Max, LG, Rothermere—you will exclaim 'Lampost'. Still it was pleasant—& we had a most amusing film.

Tender love, my darling

Your devoted

W

Clementine Churchill to Winston S. Churchill

(*Spencer-Churchill papers*)

24 February 1924   Lou Sueil
                                                     Eze

My Darling—

Your telegram about the Abbey Division excited me a good deal.[3] I hope all may happen as you wish—I notice in today's Continental Daily

---

[1] Consuelo Vanderbilt, 1877–1964. Born in New York. She married Churchill's cousin the 9th Duke of Marlborough in 1895, at the age of 18, and obtained a divorce in 1921 (after which she married Lieutenant-Colonel Jacques Balsan, CMG). Mother of the 10th Duke of Marlborough and Lord Ivor Charles Spencer-Churchill. In the 1920s and 1930s Churchill was a frequent visitor at her château, St Georges Motel, near Dreux (some 50 miles to the north of Paris). In 1935 she published her memoirs, *The Glitter and the Gold*.

[2] Lord Beaverbrook's house in Fulham.

[3] Churchill had decided to stand at the by-election for the Abbey Division of Westminster, as an Independent candidate, if possible with both Liberal and Conservative support.

Mail a 'one inch long' report of your Shirley Kellogg speech in which you widen the existing breach between yourself & official Liberalism.[1]

Do not however let the Tories get you too cheap. They have treated you so badly in the past & they ought to be made to pay. I must wait for Times for complete report.

The advance at Chartwell seems considerable & I am longing to see it.

I am distressed that after her measles Mary should have influenza & our poor little Randolph too in his chilly school. . . .

Give the children much love from me. I hope Moppett is not exhausted from nursing measles & influenza in such quick succession.

In the French *non* political world Poincaré is still an idol—They love him & venerate him & I cannot find any reflection (among the ordinary French people who came here) of the Loucheur view which was so prevalent among the 'politicos' we met in Paris 10 days ago.

The Times of Saturday has just come—I see they carefully leave out your political remarks & only print your polite greetings to Mrs Kellogg—In the Political Notes I see the Times impartially advocates the Abbey Division being given to Sir George Lloyd,[2] Pretyman[3] & Jack Hills.[4] What fools the people who direct the Times are to imagine that any of these men can

[1] During his speech on 22 February 1924 (see page 106, note 2), Churchill said, with reference to domestic politics: 'I welcome the presence here of Mr J. H. Thomas. I have not concealed, or at least I have not been successful in concealing, the fact that I am an uncompromising opponent of the Government of which he is a member. If I had my way it would never have been born, and if I could still have my way its tenure would be fleeting and precarious.' Churchill added: 'But if I am an opponent I am sure he will admit I am a frank, outspoken, straightforward opponent, and not one of those who would promise him every assurance of fair play and then try to stab him and his colleagues in the back when they are doing their best in the essential naval defence of the country.'

[2] George Ambrose Lloyd, 1879–1941. Educated at Eton and Cambridge. Travelled widely in the East as a young man. Honorary Attaché, Constantinople Embassy, 1905. Special Trade Commissioner to Turkey, including Mesopotamia, 1907. Conservative MP for West Staffordshire, 1910–18. A director of Lloyds Bank, 1911–18. Captain, 1914. On active service in Gallipoli, Mesopotamia and the Hedjaz; he accompanied T. E. Lawrence on one of his desert raids. Present at the capture of Gaza, 1917. Knighted, 1918. Governor of Bombay, 1918–23. Conservative MP for Eastbourne, 1924–5. Privy Councillor, 1924. Created Baron, 1925. High Commissioner for Egypt and the Sudan, 1925–9. Chairman British Council, 1936.

[3] Ernest George Pretyman, 1860–1931. Educated at Eton. Served in the Royal Artillery, 1880–9. Conservative MP for Woodbridge, 1895–1906; for Chelmsford, 1908–23. Civil Lord of Admiralty, 1900–3. Secretary to the Admiralty, 1903–6. Parliamentary Secretary, Board of Trade, 1915–16. Civil Lord of Admiralty, 1916–19. Privy Councillor, 1917.

[4] John Waller Hills, 1867–1938. Solicitor. Conservative MP, 1906–18, 1918–22 and 1925–38. A Director of the Midland Railway Company, 1910–22. Captain, 4th Battalion, Durham Light Infantry, 1914; Major, 1915. Acting Lieutenant-Colonel, commanding the 20th Battalion, Durham Light Infantry, July 1916. Wounded, 30 September 1916, and returned to his Parliamentary duties. Chairman of the West Midland Commission on Industrial Unrest, 1917. Financial Secretary to the Treasury, 1922–3. Privy Councillor, 1929.

help the Tory Party out of the quagmire of inefficiency & stupidity in which they are up to their necks.

My Darling do not stand unless you are reasonably sure of getting in— The movement inside the Tory Party to try & get you back is only just born & requires nursing & nourishing & educating to bring it to full strength. And there are of course counter influences as none of the Tory Leaders want you back as they see you would leap over their heads—The Times I feel sure is against you at present or at any rate not helping—Couldn't we cultivate John Astor[1] gradually?

I feel that though no genius he would be quite as much help as Beaverbrook. The Times can really do more than the Daily Express. I hope I shall get a letter as so far I have only your telegram about the Abbey Division.

I feel very anxious about it all—I am sure with patience all will come right; but these silly Tories are probably now so pleased with Ramsay over the 5 Cruisers that they will not yet feel the need of your help in fighting Labour.[2]

Perhaps your hour will come only after Labour has a big independent Majority & shews itself in its true colours. I fear these ruminations may not seem very intelligent as I am cut off from knowing what really is going on.

Tender love
Clemmie

Winston S. Churchill to Clementine Churchill

(*Spencer-Churchill papers*)

24 February 1924   2 Sussex Square

My Darling,

This Westminster Abbey by-election swooped down upon me like a thunderstorm. Rothermere & Max offered the full support of their press; & it was necessary for me to let it be known straight away that my cap was in the ring.

---

[1] John Jacob Astor, 1886–1971. Educated at Eton and New College, Oxford. 2nd Lieutenant, 1st Life Guards, 1908. ADC to the Viceroy of India, 1911–14. On active service, 1914–18 (severely wounded); Major, 1920. Conservative MP for Dover, 1922–45. Chief Proprietor of *The Times*. President of the Press Club, the Newspaper Press Fund and the Commonwealth Press Union. Chairman of the Middlesex Hospital, 1938–62. Lieutenant-Colonel, 5th Battalion City of London Home Guard, 1940–4. Created Baron Astor of Hever, 1956.

[2] On 21 February 1924 the Parliamentary Secretary for the Admiralty, C. G. Ammon, in answer to questions, told the House of Commons that the Government had decided, in view of the serious unemployment, which was especially marked in the shipbuilding industry, to proceed with the earlier Conservative programme to lay down five new cruisers.

It is an amazing constituency comprising—Eccleston Squ, Victoria Station, Smith Sq, Westminster Abbey, Whitehall, Pall Mall, Carlton House Terrace—part of Soho, the south side of Oxford Street, Drury Lane theatre & Covent garden! It is of course one of the choicest preserves of the Tory Party. I have had an interview with Colonel Jackson[1] their head whip wh was entirely satisfactory. He & Younger are working tooth & nail to secure me the support of the official Unionist Assn, tho I made it clear I intended to stand as an Independent candidate with Liberal as well as Conservative supporters.

There must be at least a hundred MP resident voters in the division, & I shall have no difficulty in securing a vy fine & representative platform. Grigg,[2] L. Spears & other Liberal MP's will fight for me, & it is possible E. Grey (a resident)[3] will give me his support. McKenna[4] too—I think. Then I hope to get a letter from AJB also a resident—altogether it is an exceedingly promising opportunity, & if it comes off I will hold the seat for a long time.

There are 30 Liberals in the House & at least another 30 candidates who wish to act with the Conservatives, & who the Cons are anxious to win as allies.

The idea is that by making the gesture of giving me this seat, the whole of this movement will be focused around me. However we have had so many ups & downs that I will not speculate upon the remarkable possibilities wh wd be opened by success.

At Baldwin's suggestion I had a long talk with him yesterday of the friendliest character. He evidently wants vy much to secure my return &

[1] Francis Stanley Jackson, 1870–1947. Educated at Harrow and Trinity College, Cambridge. On active service in South Africa, 1900–2. Conservative MP for Howdenshire, 1915–26. Financial Secretary, War Office, 1922–3. Chairman of the Conservative Party, 1923–6. Privy Councillor, 1926. Knighted, 1927. Governor of Bengal, 1927–32.

[2] Edward William Macleay Grigg, 1879–1955. Educated at Winchester and New College, Oxford. Editorial staff of *The Times*, 1903–5; 1908–13. Served in the Grenadier Guards, 1914–18 (Churchill shared his frontline dugout in November 1915). Military Secretary to the Prince of Wales, 1919. Knighted, 1920. Private Secretary to Lloyd George, 1921–2. National Liberal MP for Oldham, 1922–5. Governor of Kenya, 1925–31. Elected to the Other Club, 1932. National Conservative MP, 1933–45. Parliamentary Secretary, Ministry of Information, 1939–40. Financial Secretary, War Office, 1940. Joint Parliamentary Under-Secretary of State for War, 1940–4. Minister Resident in the Middle East, 1944–5. Created Baron Altrincham, 1945. Editor of the *National Review*, 1948–55.

[3] Lord Grey of Fallodon, although living mostly in Scotland, owned 33 Eccleston Square, a house which he had rented to Churchill and his wife immediately after their marriage in 1908, and in which the Churchills had lived until moving to Admiralty House in 1912. It was subsequently the headquarters of the Labour Party.

[4] Reginald McKenna, 1863–1943. Liberal MP, 1895–1918. President of the Board of Education, 1907–8. First Lord of the Admiralty, 1908–11. Home Secretary, 1911–15. Chancellor of the Exchequer, May 1915–December 1916. Chairman, Midland Bank, 1919–43.

co-operation. Their eyes are fully open to the dangers that lie ahead. MacDonald is making a gt impression on the country, & there is no doubt that he is gaining numerous adherents—mostly at the expense of the Liberals.

I informed LG of my resolves. He said I was only acting in accordance with my convictions & made no reproaches of any kind. I enclose you Younger's letter as it shows how vy sensible the Cons have become under the pressure of events.

Of course if I stood as a Cons it wd almost certainly be a walk over. But I cannot do this, & it is far better for all the interests we are safeguarding that I shd carry with me moderate Liberals.

I do not think there is any need for you to alter yr plans. If you are here by the third or fourth of March you will be in time for the fight—if there is one.

Randolph is to come home for a few days to recuperate. The other boys are doing this, & Hornby quite approves. Mary is practically well. Tender love my sweet cat—Enjoy yourself & get fit for the fray.

Your devoted
W

PS. I must read Mrs Spears[1] book wh impressed you so much.

In Bernard Shaw's Methusalah Adam after being 1,000 years in Heaven wanted to come back to earth for a spell. He asked St Peter for the necessary pass. 'Certainly' said St Peter, 'I suppose you want to take Eve with you.' 'No' said Adam 'I am going to turn over a new leaf!'

Austen Chamberlain to Lord Birkenhead

(*Austen Chamberlain papers*)

26 February 1924
Confidential

My dear FE,

Baldwin surprised me by proposing to drive down to see me on Sunday,[2] when he lunched with me at my cottage. The object of his visit was to consult

---

[1] Mary Borden, born in the United States, had married Louis Spears in 1918. In 1924 she published *Three Pilgrims and a Tinker*, the second of twenty novels which she was to write, the last in 1956. She died in 1968.

[2] Sunday, February 24.

me as to Winston's candidature for the Abbey Division, and he surprised me by the friendly way in which he talked of Winston and by the sense which he expressed of the advantage of getting Winston over. I, of course, took the same view, and Baldwin undertook to make further enquiries.

I have seen him again to-day. Briefly the position is this—that it is too early for Winston to come out as a Conservative with credit to himself. On the other hand, the Abbey Conservatives would be unwilling to adopt him as an Independent anti-Socialist candidate. I do not know whether the Central Office could force him upon them—probably not—but in any case this would involve a split and would not be in Winston's interest. Both the Liberal and Labour parties, for what they are worth, in the Division, would back an out-and-out Conservative against Winston. This being so, no friend of Winston would wish him to stand.

Baldwin proposes to see Winston again and to explain the position to him. We want to get him and his friends over, and though we cannot give him the Abbey seat, Baldwin will undertake to find him a good seat later on when he will have been able to develop naturally his new line and make his entry into our ranks much easier than it would be to-day.

Our only fear is lest Winston should try and rush the fence. I am sure you will agree with me that this would be a mistake and I want you to send this letter on to Winston, adding your appeal to mine that he should not destroy these happy chances by any rash attempt on Abbey.

Yours ever
Austen Chamberlain

Austen Chamberlain to Winston S. Churchill

(*Churchill papers: 6/2*)

3 March 1924

My dear Winston,

I lunched with Philip Sassoon today who told me that you were angry with me, briefly because Baldwin would have got you the Westminster seat & that I had made difficulties & discouraged him.

Don't let the sun go down upon your wrath, for this is not true. I found Baldwin much more friendly to you than I had expected & inclined to get you the seat *if he could*, & all I said was in agreement with his view, ie that SB couldn't *force* you on the Association, but that if he could persuade the Asstn to take you, that would be the best thing possible for our party—quite apart from my personal feelings which would lead me to wish you back in any case.

My advice to you through FE not to fight *against* the Conservative Asstn may be right or wrong. For the chances of the constituency I am dependant on the reports of other men, & they were that you would be beaten. But believe me, I beg you, I have acted throughout as a friend, &, tho' you might think my judgement wrong, you would not question the friendship if you had heard every word that I have said on the subject.

Yrs sincerely
Austen Chamberlain

Sir Philip Sassoon to Winston S. Churchill

(*Churchill papers: 6/2*)

4 March 1924

My dear Winston,

I am *so* glad you are standing. You are BOUND to get in. Let me know how I can help you. I shd like to help in every way possible.

Best of luck
from Philip

H. A. Gwynne[1] to Stanley Baldwin

(*Baldwin papers*)

7 March 1924   Carlton Club
Confidential

My dear Baldwin,

There will be no opportunity for a talk so I inflict on you a letter.

This *Abbey Division* affair is going to be your 'Jena or Austerlitz'. Make no mistake. If you survive it, you are safe as the Conservative party is safe but if the other side win, you will go and with you all that is fine in our party will disappear and LG, Birkenhead, Beaverbrook, Rothermere & Co will form their Constitutional party and give the country over to socialism.

---

[1] Howell Arthur Gwynne, 1865–1950. Reuter's chief war correspondent in South Africa, 1899–1902. Editor of the *Standard*, 1904–11. Editor of the *Morning Post*, 1911–37. One of Churchill's most outspoken public critics at the time of the siege of Antwerp in October 1914.

This is the test of your leadership. I am told that it has been notified to Nicholson[1] that no ex-Cabinet members are to speak. The reason given for this is that Austen & Horne have threatened to speak for Winston—if ex-Cabinet ministers speak for Nicholson.

Now, believe me, both as a friend and as one who believes that you have a mission to put England right, if you yield to this threat you are done. A leader must lead and exact obedience or he is no leader. If I were in your place, I should call for Horne & Austen and forbid them to speak for Winston. If they refuse, then it is open war but it would be a short war and you will win. If they obey you are the undoubted leader, to be feared and respected.

I know your difficulties and your sensitiveness. But at times, a man has got to be brutal if he is to persist and then, it seems wise, in *the* crisis of your political life. Be strong and ruthless, if necessary. Please don't yield in this case, for I know the forces against you and I know how much they are relying on Westminster to kill you.[2]

Yours sincerely,
H. A. Gwynne

Please don't trouble to answer.

[1] Otho William Nicholson, 1891–1978. Educated at Harrow and Magdalene College, Cambridge. Lieutenant, Royal Engineers, 1914–18. Mayor of Finsbury, 1923–4. Conservative MP for Westminster, Abbey, 1924–32. Brigadier commanding the 40th Anti-Aircraft Group, 1938–41; the 54th AA Brigade, 1941–2. Assistant Commandant, School of AA Artillery, 1942. Director of J. & W. Nicholson & Company, Distillers.

[2] On 5 March 1924 Lord Rothermere's *Daily Mail* had come out in support of Churchill's candidature, telling its readers: 'Mr Churchill has immense knowledge, moral courage, singular experience, oratorical power, and Parliamentary skill, which are urgently needed by the Conservative Party. If Socialism is to be beaten—*and the real tug has yet to come and will be severe enough when it does come*—leaders such as he will be required to beat it.' But on the following day *The Times* declared: 'Mr Churchill, in fact—not for the first time in his career—has mistimed an important decision and shown himself an essentially disruptive force.'

Austin Hopkinson,[1] *Esmond Harmsworth*[2] *and Murray Sueter*[3] *to Stanley Baldwin*

(*Baldwin papers*)

7 March 1924   House of Commons
Private

Dear Mr Baldwin,

The undersigned members of your party are greatly perplexed and disturbed by the issues which have arisen in the Westminster Abbey Election. We feel that it would be an advantage to our party in the present and impending conflict with Socialism if we could gain the adherence of a body of Liberals in the House and in the country who while preserving their own identity would work loyally and effectively with us on main issues. We feel that Mr Churchill's candidature whatever may be said against it might carry us a long step further towards this result. You have yourself appealed for the co-operation of Liberals on the broad lines of the policy which you have now declared. In these circumstances we would ask that the whole question of the official attitude of the party towards the contest in Westminster may be very carefully reviewed by you and your colleagues. Apart from these general grounds we have been informed that considerable irregularities are alleged against the character and procedure of the meeting of the Westminster Abbey Constitutional Association which nominated Mr Nicholson. We mention only one of these. The refusal to hear Major Hills, a duly nominated candidate. In this matter also we would respectfully ask

[1] Austin Hopkinson, 1879–1962. On active service in South Africa, 1900. 2nd Lieutenant, The Royal Dragoons, 1914–16; Private, 1918. Independent MP for Mossley, 1918–29 and 1931–45; a frequent speaker on air matters. Lieutenant, Fleet Air Arm, 1940.

[2] Esmond Cecil Harmsworth, 1898–1978. Only surviving son of the 1st Baron (later Viscount) Rothermere (whose other two sons were both killed in action on the western front). Served in the Royal Marine Artillery, 1917–18. ADC to Lloyd George at the Paris Peace Conference, 1919. Conservative MP for the Isle of Thanet, 1920–9. Supported Churchill at the Abbey by-election, 1924. Elected to the Other Club, 1928. Chairman of Associated Newpapers Ltd, 1932–71. Chairman of the Newspaper Proprietors' Association, 1934–61. Member of the Advisory Council, Ministry of Information, 1939. Succeeded his father as 2nd Viscount Rothermere, 1940. Chairman of the Daily Mail and General Trust Ltd.

[3] Murray Fraser Sueter, 1872–1960. Entered Navy, 1886. Assistant Director of Naval Ordnance at the Admiralty, 1903–5. Member, Advisory Committee in Aeronautics, 1908–17. Captain, 1909. Director of the Air Division at the Admiralty, 1911–15. Superintendent of Aircraft Construction, 1915–17. Commanded Royal Naval Air Service units, Southern Italy, 1917–18. Rear-Admiral, 1920. Conservative MP, 1921–45. Knighted, 1934.

that before the endorsement of the Conservative Party is finally given you and your colleagues should satisfy yourselves of these facts.[1]

Yours truly,
Austin Hopkinson
Esmond Harmsworth
Murray F. Sueter

Winston S. Churchill to Stanley Baldwin

(*Baldwin papers*)

7 March 1924   2 Sussex Square
Private

My dear Baldwin,

You will receive today authoritative evidence of the irregularities wh vitiated the Selection meeting of the Abbey Constl Assn. This presents the opportunity for securing a gt advantage for the cause we have at heart. Mr Nicholson's withdrawal or even the non-interference of the Central Office in the fight, wd result in a resounding victory for Conservative and Imperial interests & for anti-Socialism. It will also lead directly to the creation of a Liberal wing working with Cons party in the coming struggle.

I am sure you do not wish to be compelled by technicalities to fire upon the reinforcements I am bringing to yr aid. Act now with decision, & we shall be able to work together in the national interest. I have no other thought but to unite & rally the strongest combination of forces against the oncoming attack.

Do not let this opportunity slip away, & all of us be weakened thereby.

I can come to see you if you wish at any time to-day.

Yours sincerely
Winston S. Churchill

[1] An identical letter was sent to Baldwin on the same day signed by eight more Conservative MPs, including Henry Warden Chilcott, Sir Martin Conway, J. S. Rankin, Oliver Locker-Lampson, Sir Burton Chadwick and Sir Philip Sassoon. On 8 March 1924 Sir Burton Chadwick was reported in the *Sunday Times* as saying: 'It is admitted by every member of Parliament to whom I have spoken that Mr Churchill would be a great asset to Parliament.'

Stanley Baldwin to Oliver Locker-Lampson[1]

(Baldwin papers)

10 March 1924   House of Commons
Private

Dear Locker-Lampson,

I gave the most careful attention to the points raised in the two letters you were good enough to send me.

Colonel Jackson has had a thorough investigation made of the proceedings of the meeting at which the candidate was chosen and he has had an interview with the Chairman.

From his report, I cannot find any reason to refrain from doing what a party leader is bound to do, that is, from supporting the choice of the local association.

Any other course would tend to bring the Central Office into direct conflict with the local Associations which would be disastrous.

Yours sincerely,
Stanley Baldwin

Austen Chamberlain to his wife

(Austen Chamberlain papers)

12 March 1924

Everyone here is agog about the Westminster Election. If I can vote, I shall vote quietly for Winston saying nothing about it but it is amazing how unpopular he is. . . .

His Drury Lane meeting was noisy. I scarcely think that he will win & Ll G expects that the socialists will creep in between him & Nicholson. It will be terrible for him if he is beaten again & I shall be very sorry.

---

[1] Oliver Stillingfleet Locker-Lampson, 1881–1954. Educated at Eton and Trinity College, Cambridge. Editor of *Granta*, 1900. Called to the Bar, 1907. Conservative MP, 1910–45. Lieutenant-Commander, Royal Naval Air Service, December 1914; Commander, July 1915. Commanded the British Armoured Car detachment in Russia, 1916–17. Parliamentary Private Secretary to Austen Chamberlain, 1919–21. Churchill's Private Secretary, 1926.

Brendan Bracken[1] to his mother

(*Bracken papers*)

12 March 1924

My Dearest Mama,

We are deep in an awful fight at Westminster and I think we are going to win. At any rate I am of opinion that we will pull it off.

We are fighting all the three great parties in the State & only Winston could pull it off.

A good deal of attention here is directed to the Irish vote which may pull the fat out of the fire—it will I hope be given in Winston's favour.

I hope you are all well & I am looking forward to your visit to London.

Much love
Brendan

Lord Beaverbrook to Arthur Brisbane[2]

(*Beaverbrook papers*)

13 March 1924

The Abbey Division of Westminster, which Churchill is contesting against an official Tory, has been another terrible hash-up on the part of the Conservatives. Most of the leaders of Conservatism wanted him back, but they had not the nerve, or the power, to thrust him on the Local Conservative Association, which is supposed to choose the candidate.

Now, whatever happens, there will be bad trouble. If Churchill gets in, he will return 'savaged' against the Conservatives. If he is beaten there will

[1] Brendan Bracken, 1901–58. Educated in Australia and at Sedbergh School. Journalist and financier. Conservative MP for North Paddington, 1929–45; for Bournemouth, 1950–1. Elected to the Other Club, 1932. Chairman of the *Financial News*. Managing Director of the *Economist*. Chairman of the *Financial Times*. Parliamentary Private Secretary to the Prime Minister (Churchill), 1940–1. Privy Councillor, 1940. Minister of Information, 1941–5. First Lord of the Admiralty, 1945. Created Viscount, 1952. One of Churchill's closest friends and political colleagues during the 1920s, 1930s, 1940s and 1950s, he first visited Chartwell as an overnight guest on 22 December 1924.

[2] Arthur Brisbane, 1864–1936. Of Scottish ancestry, his family were among the earliest settlers in upper New York State. Educated in France and Germany. Joined the New York *Sun* as a reporter (at $15 a week), 1893. Editor of the New York *Sunday World*, 1896. Editor of William Randolph Hearst's *New York Journal*, 1897 (at $150 per week, and an additional dollar for every 1,000 increase in circulation); by sensational reporting he stirred up a strong public demand for war with Spain, and was a leading supporter of the Spanish–American War of 1898. He continued to work for Hearst newspapers until his death: his column 'Today' was syndicated throughout the United States, gaining him the largest readership of any American journalist of his time.

be all kinds of accusations of 'betrayal' against the Tory leaders, echoed by all the members of Parliament and Privy Councillors who openly or secretly have been supporting Churchill.

The third possibility is, that the Socialist will slip in between the Official and the Independent Conservative Candidates. In that event the blame for the disaster will be placed upon Baldwin—and justly too. The Ex-Prime Minister is a very well-meaning man, but utterly unfit mentally for high command. He really ought never to have committed himself to Churchill, seeing that his own entourage and followers were quite of the contrary opinion.

The funny side of the position is, that after Baldwin had privately endorsed Churchill's candidature, he went down into the country to secure Austen Chamberlain's help and approval.

Chamberlain has, of course, been 'coalescing' with Winston Churchill and Birkenhead for years—so Baldwin naturally counted on his warm approval. Instead of which Chamberlain was very frigid and said he could not support Churchill for Westminster until he repented in sackcloth and ashes for his Liberal past, and joined the Tories openly as a penitent convert. The Tory right was, of course, delighted with Austen Chamberlain's attitude and have re-instated him in favour—and *they* count most for the moment. On the other hand Sir Robert Horne, who was supposed to be more favoured than Chamberlain for the reversion of the Tory leadership by the orthodox, came out openly in favour of Churchill, and so lost caste, and goes down one peg below Chamberlain. All this is humorous enough, though it has its serious side.

Lord Balfour to Stanley Baldwin

(*Baldwin papers*)

14 March 1924
Private

My dear Baldwin,

I am much worried by the Westminster Election, and greatly fear that if Winston is beaten a Socialist will win; with disastrous results to the Party all through the country.

Do you see any objection to my sending the enclosed letter to Winston for purposes of publication? If you felt it in any way disloyal to yourself; if you thought it would weaken your position, or tie your hands, I should not for a moment think of sending it. But IF you see no objection, a good many persons, who conceive themselves to know something about electoral opinion in the constituency, think that it would be of material assistance to Winston. Will you let me know your views?

I leave tomorrow morning for Cannes: & I dine tonight with Midleton at 34 Portland Place.

Yours ever
Balfour

Lord Balfour to Winston S. Churchill

(*Churchill papers: 6/2*)

14 March 1924

My dear Winston,

You have expressed a wish that I should give public expression to my views on the contested Election now going on in the Abbey Division of Westminster. I have few qualifications for the task; I know nothing at first hand of local conditions; I have no special title to intervene in local affairs; and I am not the Leader of the Party, or of any section of the Party.

This may indeed enable me to approach the subject from a detached point of view. I can speak as a private individual untrammelled by the administrative rules which, when dealing with Party Organisations, every Party Leader must unswervingly follow, and which I should certainly follow myself were I in Mr Baldwin's place. I may freely express the personal hopes and wishes with which I watch the contest in which you are engaged.

These are inevitably, and I think rightly, influenced by my strong desire to see you once more in the House of Commons—once more able to use your brilliant gifts in the public discussion of the vital problems with which the country is evidently confronted. On these you, and many others who are associated with you, think as we do; and, where matters of great moment are in debate, those who think alike should act together. Your absence from the House of Commons at such a time is greatly to be deplored; and since, as I believe, your convictions on fundamental questions—whether imperial or social—are shared by a majority of the electors in the Abbey Division, your return for that historic seat would be warmly welcomed by men of moderate opinion throughout the country—and by no one more than

Yours very sincerely,
Balfour

Lord Balfour to Stanley Baldwin
(*Baldwin papers*)

15 March 1924
Private

My dear Baldwin,

As I promised you last night, I do not propose to send my draft letter to Churchill for publication. But I am rather startled this morning to see that Amery[1] has made a public appeal to the Party in the Abbey Division, begging them in the interests of unity to vote against Winston. This hardly seems to me to be fair play; and I leave it to you to consider whether, in the circumstances, you think any change of policy is, as regards my letter in the public interests, either possible or advisable. If you think so, you might send on the letter to Winston, who has not yet seen it.

Yours ever
AJB

I am just off.

Winston S. Churchill to Lord Balfour
(*Balfour papers*)

15 March 1924   2 Sussex Square

My dear Arthur,

I was delighted to hear of yr action yesterday.

A letter from you will in my judgement turn the scale. Thousands of conservatives are supporting me, & other thousands hanging in the balance.

There was a sort of understanding that shadow cabinet ministers shd not intervene on one side or the other; & as you know Austen told Neville[2] that if he (N) spoke on Nicholson's platform Austen wd speak on mine.

[1] Leopold Charles Maurice Stennett Amery, 1873–1955. A contemporary of Churchill's at Harrow. Fellow of All Souls College, Oxford, 1897. *Manchester Guardian* correspondent in the Balkans and Turkey, 1897–9. Served on the editorial staff of *The Times*, 1899–1909. Conservative MP, 1911–45. Intelligence Officer in the Balkan and eastern Mediterranean, 1915–16. Assistant Secretary, War Cabinet Secretariat, 1917–18. Parliamentary Under-Secretary, Colonial Office, 1919–21. First Lord of the Admiralty, 1922–4. Colonial Secretary, 1924–9. Secretary of State for India and Burma, 1940–5. Known as 'Leo'.

[2] Arthur Neville Chamberlain, 1869–1940. Son of Joseph Chamberlain, his mother died in childbirth in 1875. Educated at Rugby and Mason College, Birmingham. In business in the Bahamas, 1890–7. Lord Mayor of Birmingham, 1915–16. Director-General of National Service, 1916–17 (when his cousin Norman, to whom he was devoted, was killed in action on the western front). Conservative MP for Ladywood, 1918–29; for Edgbaston, 1929–40. Postmaster-General, 1922–3. Paymaster-General, 1923. Minister of Health, 1923, 1924–9 and 1931. Chancellor of the Exchequer, 1923–4 and 1931–7. Prime Minister, 1937–40. Lord President of the Council, May–November 1940.

This sort of mutual abstention policy, has now been departed from by Amery who in the enclosed letter has definitely taken public action against me.[1]

In these circumstances surely your letter would be permissible.

I do hope you will feel yrself able to send it to me or to the Press. The whole Sunday press—*without exception*—will support me tomorrow & if your letter could be issued today I am confident the result will be decisive.

All good wishes for yr holiday.

Believe me
Yours very sincerely,
Winston S. Churchill

Lord Derby to Lord Rawlinson[2]

(*Derby papers*)

19 March 1924
Private

I have not been long enough back to hear much political news but I am rather disturbed at what I have heard that we seem to be very broken as a Party and Winston Churchill's candidature for Westminster has made a cleavage between ourselves and the Liberals much greater than it was, in addition to which the fear is that he may so split our vote that the Socialist will get in, in which case he is done as far as any reconciliation with our Party is concerned. This is a pity because he is a fine fighting force in the House and would be of great assistance. I think the majority of our Party want to see him elected but there are a certain number of die-hards, headed by Amery, who are prepared to go to any steps to prevent this happening.

[1] Concerned though he was on political grounds by Amery's intervention, Churchill responded to a friendly personal letter from Amery by writing to him, on March 20: 'My dear Amery, I never bear a grudge for conscientious opposition, & I was sure that your action was inspired by no personal ill-will. On the contrary I believe it was against yr personal feelings that you took the course you did. I can therefore in all sincerity thank you for yr letter' (*Amery papers*).

[2] Henry Seymour Rawlinson, 1864–1925. Entered Army, 1884. On Kitchener's staff in the Sudan, 1898. Brigadier-General, 1903. Major-General commanding the 4th Division, September 1914; the 7th Division & 3rd Cavalry Division, October 1914; the IV Corps, December 1914–December 1915. Knighted, 1914. Lieutenant-General commanding the Fourth Army, 1916–18. General, 1917. Created Baron, 1919. Commanded the forces in North Russia, 1919. Commander-in-Chief, India, 1920–5.

Thomas Jones: [1] *diary*

(*Jones papers*)

20 March 1924

Luncheon at Bellomo's with Lord Astor [2] and Garvin. Garvin told us that Churchill was in for Westminster, but between Astor's house and the restaurant a messenger caught us with the figures of the recount, which put Churchill out by 43 votes. [3] We were all sorry.

The Dardanelles pursues Churchill most unfairly, for it was one of the big conceptions of the war, and if put through with vigour might have shortened the war by a couple of years.

Alfred Duff Cooper [4] *to Winston S. Churchill*

(*Churchill papers: 6/2*)

20 March 1924   Foreign Office

My dear Winston,

I saw the first news on the tape this morning and sent you a telegram before the heart breaking correction appeared. I know you have the lion's courage which will enable you to make light of this cruel blow but it may possibly help you a little to know that there are a great number of young and eager Conservatives whose enthusiastic support you command and who

[1] Thomas Jones, 1870–1955. Lecturer in Economics, Glasgow University, 1899–1909. Joined the Independent Labour Party, 1895. Special Investigator, Poor Law Commission, 1906–9. Professor in Economics, Belfast, 1909–10. Secretary, National Health Insurance Commissioners (Wales), 1912–16. Deputy-Secretary to the Cabinet, 1916–30. Companion of Honour, 1929. Member of the Unemployment Assistance Board, 1934–40.

[2] Waldorf Astor, 1879–1952. Conservative MP for Plymouth, 1910–19. Chairman of the Directors of the *Observer* newspaper from 1911 until his death. Created Baron, 1916. Succeeded his father as 2nd Viscount, 1917. Parliamentary Secretary to Lloyd George, 1918; to the Ministry of Food, 1918; to the Ministry of Health, 1919–21. Chairman of the Royal Institute of International Affairs, 1935–49. In 1906 he married Nancy Witcher: they lived at Cliveden, in Buckinghamshire, and at 35 Hill Street, Mayfair.

[3] The final result was: Nicholson (Conservative), 8,187; Churchill (Independent and Anti-Socialist), 8,144; Brockway (Labour), 6,156; Scott Duckers (Liberal), 291.

[4] Alfred Duff Cooper, 1890–1954. Educated at Eton and New College, Oxford. On active service, Grenadier Guards, 1914–18 (DSO, despatches). Conservative MP for Oldham (Churchill's first constituency), 1924–9. Financial Secretary, War Office, 1928–9 and 1931–4. MP for St George's, Westminster, 1931–45. Financial Secretary, Treasury, 1934–5. Privy Councillor, 1935. Secretary of State for War, 1935–7. First Lord of the Admiralty, 1937–8. Minister of Information, 1940–1. British Representative, Singapore, 1941. Chancellor of the Duchy of Lancaster, 1941–3. British Representative, French Committee of National Liberation, 1943–4. Ambassador to France, 1944–7. Knighted, 1948. Created Viscount Norwich, 1952. In 1919 he married Lady Diana Manners.

while deploring this wretched misadventure have confidence that it is only an incident in what must be the most brilliant career of our time. They look forward to the time which cannot be far distant when you will be their inspired and inspiring leader. Then they will be able to say 'Nil disperandum Winston duce et auspice Winston's'. And at present you can say to them some other lines from the same poem which if I remember them rightly go—

> 'O fortes, pejoraque passi,
> Mecum saepe viri
> Nunc vino pellite curas
> Cras ingens iterabimus aequor'[1]

The *ingens aequor* is the General Election which cannot fail to carry you to triumph. I apologise for such a long letter and such an improper one as coming from a Civil Servant.

Yours
Duff Cooper

Winston S. Churchill to Lord Balfour
(*Balfour papers*)

20 March 1924   2 Sussex Square

My dear Arthur,

Yr letter had a tremendous influence & the result is really remarkable. I am quite satisfied—tho of course the few missing votes are provoking—that the contest did good & has greatly advanced the policy of Union & cooperation.

I have been careful to handle the situation in such a way as to leave no needless soreness.

I am personally most grateful to you for yr courageous support and I feel deeply honoured that after all the vicissitudes of my life I shd have obtained it on a great public occasion like this.

I do hope you are having sunshine. We are both looking Southward though still irresolute.

Yours always
W

---

[1] 'O mighty heroes, who have shared with me many a hardship, now drive away your cares with wine; tomorrow we shall journey over the vast ocean.' Horace Odes, I, 7.

General Spears to Winston S. Churchill

(*Churchill papers: 6/2*)

Thursday

Dear Winston,

It was the finest fight there ever was & shows what you can do. To have so deeply moved in so short a time this stodgy Division is almost unbelievable —but it is bitterly disappointing too—I wd have given my right hand to get you in. I could not bear to hear you speak so went away. The awful thought is that altho' we did our best just a little more effort, a little more strain would have done it—that is the dismal thing.

But anyway the bad spell is broken, the unpopularity is a thing of the past & the next time is a certainty.

Yours ever
Louis

Lord Knollys[1] to Winston S. Churchill

(*Churchill papers: 6/2*)

20 March 1924   St James's Palace

My dear Churchill,

A very few lines as an old friend to say how greatly disappointed & sorry I am at the result of the Election, though you made a most gallant fight.

Everybody whom I have met told me that they intended to vote for you as they regarded you as being the best & most efficient public man to defend the country against Socialism.

My son[2] came all the way from his Sanatorium in the north of Norfolk,

[1] Francis Knollys, 1837–1924. Gentleman Usher to Queen Victoria, 1868–1901. Private Secretary to Edward VII when Prince of Wales and King, 1870–1910. Knighted, 1886. Created Baron, 1902. Private Secretary to George V, 1910–13. Created Viscount, 1911. He died on 15 August 1924.

[2] Edward George William Tyrwhitt Knollys, 1895–1966. Page of Honour to King Edward VII, 1904–10; to King George V, 1910–11. On active service, 1914–18: London Regiment and Royal Air Force; MBE, DFC. Succeeded his father as 2nd Viscount, 1924. Cape Town Director of Barclay's Bank, 1929–34. Managing Director of the Employers' Liability Assurance Corporation Ltd, 1933–41 and 1948–54. Deputy Commissioner, South Eastern Civil Defence Region, 1939–41. Governor and Commander-in-Chief, Bermuda, 1941–3. Chairman, British Overseas Airways Corporation, 1943–7. Chairman of Vickers Ltd, 1956–62; of the English Steel Corporation, 1956–62.

for one night, in order to vote for you & Probyn[1] came from Sandringham though he is over 91, for the same purpose.

Pray do not think of taking any notice of this letter as I know you must be almost overwhelmed by your correspondence.

Yours very sincerely,
Knollys

Sir Martin Conway[2] to Winston S. Churchill

(*Churchill papers: 6/2*)

20 March 1924   House of Commons

Dear Churchill,

I could not attend the count this morning to my regret. I was overjoyed to read the message that you were elected & plunged into the depths when the news of a recount, & finally of your failure by so narrow a margin came to my ears. Well! we did the best we could & your work was entirely first-rate. I doubt whether the 'machine' is pleased with itself. For a third time the party-dunderheads have had their way & plunged us deeper into the mire. One comfort there is: you have not lost but gained prestige. I refuse to analyse any 'might-have-beens' except the many 'might-have-been-worse's' which you so ably escaped. You deserved to win. You were never more wanted in the House than now. The election being over every MP I have thus far met has expressed to me regret at the result—a set of—well I won't call them names. Better luck next time and may it be soon!

Please give my condolences to Mrs Churchill, who proved herself so valuable a help to us all.

Yours very sincerely
Martin Conway

---

[1] Dighton Macnaghten Probyn, 1833–1924. Entered the Army, 1849. On active service, winning the Victoria Cross during the Indian Mutiny of 1857. Knighted, 1876. Comptroller and Treasurer to the Prince of Wales, 1877–91. General, 1888. Keeper of the Privy Purse, 1901–10. Extra Equerry to King George V, 1910–24. He died on 20 June 1924.

[2] William Martin Conway, 1856–1937. Educated at Repton and Trinity College, Cambridge. Art Historian. Alpine, Latin-American, Himalayan and Arctic explorer. Unsuccessful Liberal candidate, 1895. Chairman of the Society of Authors, 1895, 1898 and 1899. Knighted, 1895. Professor of Fine Arts, Cambridge, 1901–4. Trustee of the Wallace Collection, 1916–24. Director-General of the Imperial War Museum, 1917. Conservative MP, Combined English Universities, 1918–31. Created Baron, 1931.

Lord George Hamilton[1] to Winston S. Churchill

(*Churchill papers: 6/2*)

21 March 1924
Private

My dear Winston,

Let me heartily congratulate you upon the magnificent fight you put up. You only just missed achieving a victory which would have marked a real epoch in British politics.

I have abstained from taking any part in politics during the past 20 years, but I am quite convinced that, until the Die-Hards are put into their proper place, there is no prospect of a return to power, place or control of national affairs by the Conservatives.

I warned Chamberlain[2] twenty years ago that if he and his organisation chose to raise the question of food, I care not in what shape, his Party would be smashed; but I did not think that our leaders would behave as idiotically as they have done during the past three or four years.

Wishing you all success, and hoping that you will persevere in your effort to establish a National Party,

Believe me,
Yours very truly,
George Hamilton

Lord Cecil of Chelwood[3] to Winston S. Churchill

(*Churchill papers: 6/2*)

21 March 1924

My dear Winston,

Forgive me for adding one more to the many letters which you must be receiving. You will know I hope that on personal grounds I am very sorry

[1] Lord George Francis Hamilton, 1845–1927. 3rd son of the 1st Duke of Abercorn. Under-Secretary of State for India, 1874–8. First Lord of the Admiralty, 1885–6 and 1886–92. Secretary of State for India, 1895–1903. Chairman of the Royal Commission on the Poor Law and Unemployment, 1905–9. Chairman of the Mesopotamia Commission, 1916–17. He had been present with Lord Randolph Churchill on the eve of Lord Randolph's resignation in 1886.

[2] Joseph Chamberlain, 1836–1914. President of the Board of Trade under Gladstone, 1880–5. Secretary of State for the Colonies, 1895–1903, when he left the Conservative Party in order to campaign for Imperial Preference. Father of Austen and Neville.

[3] Lord Edgar Algernon Robert Cecil, 1864–1958. Third son of the 3rd Marquess of Salisbury. Educated at Eton and University College, Oxford. Conservative MP for East Marylebone, 1906–10. Independent Conservative MP for Hitchin, 1911–23. Under-Secretary of State Foreign Affairs, 1915–18. Minister of Blockade, 1916–18. Assistant Secretary of State for Foreign Affairs, 1918. Created Viscount Cecil of Chelwood, 1923. Lord Privy Seal, 1923–4. President of the League of Nations Union, 1923–45. Chancellor of the Duchy of Lancaster, 1924–7. Nobel Peace Prize, 1937.

for the result in the Abbey Division. There can be no question that you
ought to be in the House of Commons if that body is to be truly representative
of the country. May I say how delighted I was with what you said about
the League.[1]

Hoping that we may soon meet,

Yours ever,
Cecil

Winston S. Churchill to Lord Cecil of Chelwood

(*Chelwood papers*)

23 March 1924   2 Sussex Square
Private

My dear Bob,

During many of my meetings I saw among my supporters yr friend
Weigall;[2] & my mind went back to the days when we all travelled to
Birmingham together to try & fend the Conservative host off the Protectionist back. Who shall say what share in the awful events of the last 20
years, the Chamberlain movement may not have unwittingly to bear. I have
tried my best to keep the Free Trade flag flying & on the same issue being
presented I shd do the same again.

It is absolutely necessary now that a 'Conservative & Liberal Union' shd
come into being to provide a sound basis for National Government; & on
the whole my belief is that what is necessary in England is in the end always
done somehow. I am quite loyal to yr League of Nations & will help in any

[1] During the Abbey by-election campaign, Churchill, while sharing a platform with the
other three candidates at Essex Hall on March 17, said of the League of Nations: 'Another
great war would shatter the structure of our civilization. It might lead to a destruction of
the human race on such a scale that the world would be cast back thousands of years in its
progress.' At this point Churchill was interrupted, and a man in the crowd was ejected from
the hall. Then he continued: 'There should be a complete disclosure of armaments to an
international body. In order that the League should secure its full strength it was necessary
that the defeated nations should be admitted. He made no exceptions. He would open the
door and encourage all nations to come in.' During the speech Churchill continued to be
interrupted many times. At one point he resumed his seat and refused to go on, at which
point Lord Phillimore, the Chairman, jumped to his feet and exclaimed: 'It is no good
asking for peace among the nations if you do not have peace at home, and you will not
have peace at home as long as you allow your disorderly minds to give play to disorderly
tongues.'

[2] William Ernest George Archibald Weigall, 1874–1952. Conservative MP for Horncastle,
1911–20. Inspector of Quarter Master General Services, Northern Command, 1914–17.
Chairman of the Food Survey Board, Ministry of Food. Knighted, 1920. Governor of South
Australia, 1920–2. Chairman of the Royal Empire Society, 1932–8. Created Baronet, 1938.

way I can. But the foundation must be a settlement between Germany &
France in wh Britain helps.

Thank you vy much for writing,
Yours vy sincerely,
Winston S. Churchill

PS. I shd like to have a talk soon.

James Monteith Erskine[1] to Stanley Baldwin

(*Baldwin papers*)

24 March 1924

Dear Mr Baldwin,

I don't want you to think that there is any change in my expressed loyalty
to you personally as Leader of the Party.

My conviction was & is that Winston Churchill would have done more
to strengthen the Conservative Party than would his opponent. It seems a
pity that the best interests of the country should often be at the mercy of a
local association divided in its own counsels & in no way representative of
local opinion.

The 25 or 30 MP's who came out in the open for Winston in no way
measure the actual feeling in the House. Any number told me they wanted
him to win & were quietly working for his return.

So far as I am concerned, &, as I said on the Platform, I hold no particular
brief for him.

In fact my acquaintanceship with him was nil.

What influenced me was the attitude, not one of himself, but, of a large
number of the best Liberals willing to come over to help us *not* as a Coalition
or Centre Party, but purely as a left wing—and solely with the view of
stemming the Socialist tide. If then we slam the door in their faces we must
take the consequence.

---

[1] James Malcolm Monteith Erskine, 1863–1944. Educated at Wellington College. Conservative MP for Westminster St Georges, 1921–9. Knighted, 1929.

Lady Londonderry[1] *to Winston S. Churchill*

(*Churchill papers: 2/132*)

25 March 1924

My dear Winston,

So many thanks for your letter. I admire your spirit immensely and I hope the luck may be yours the next time—but I still say—that it would have been yours this time had you read the future as I did—much as I love you, I should fight my vy hardest to prevent the 'near future' as you call it, becoming what you would like it to—Did you read Friday's Times?[2] I only saw it yesterday, as we have just returned from our tour of the Border—I thought the article gave the absolutely correct view of the political situation concerning yourself—Please Winston reflect—a half way house is no use to anyone, least of all to you—Remember what my Mother-in-Law[3] always said—There are only two lobbies etc.

I return to L House on the 1st. I hope you will still be in London.

My best love—
from yours affectionately,
Edie

[1] Edith Helen Chaplin, 1879–1959. A daughter of the 1st Viscount Chaplin, and a granddaughter of the third Duke of Sutherland. She married Lord Londonderry (then Viscount Castlereagh) in 1899. Founder and Director of the Women's Legion, 1915–19. Colonel-in-Chief, Women's Volunteer Reserve, 1914–15. Created Dame Commander of the British Empire, 1917 (the first woman to be so appointed). A close personal friend of the first Labour Prime Minister, Ramsay MacDonald.

[2] The Abbey by-election result was announced in *The Times* on Friday, 21 March 1924. *The Times* leader described Churchill's candidature as a 'blunder', and continued: 'That it was so nearly successful is proof indeed of the vigour and skill with which he fought his campaign; but success, from his own point of view, was the one justification for embarking on it at all.' The leader concluded its comments on Churchill by stating: 'No one beyond a small embittered few desires to exclude his brilliance and his driving power from the House of Commons, and no one will regard his defeat in this neck and neck contest as anything but a temporary rebuff. The features of the late campaign that attracted legitimate criticism were his ill-timed insistence on sheer anti-socialism as the paramount claim on the voters at this moment and the impulse which drove him, holding these views, to jeopardize a seat which without him was at least anti-socialist. It is no new thing after all, to discover that judgement is not the most conspicuous of Mr Churchill's remarkable gifts.'

[3] Lady Theresa Susey Helen Chetwynd-Talbot, eldest daughter of the 19th Earl of Shrewsbury. In 1875 she married the 6th Marquess of Londonderry. She died in 1919.

Sir Albert Lindsay Parkinson[1] to Winston S. Churchill

(*Churchill papers: 2/132*)

26 March 1924
Confidential

Dear Sir,

I was much interested in your bye-election and the close result and I should much have liked you to have won.

Would you care to consider standing as our Candidate at the coming General Election? Blackpool has always been Conservative until the last election, when, like many other places, it went wrong over 'Protection', but we shall win it back again.

Your father, the late Lord Randolph Churchill made his famous speech here, 'Chips, Chips, Chips',[2] and you also have addressed a meeting at Blackpool.[3]

If you are prepared to consider this constituency, and I hope you will, I will, with great pleasure place your name before the Executive, and I have no doubt about your adoption and subsequent election.

Yours very truly,
A. Lindsay Parkinson

[1] Albert Lindsay Parkinson, 1870–1936. Builder and Government Contractor. Mayor of Blackpool, 1918–22. Knighted, 1922. Chairman of the Conservative and Unionist Association of the Blackpool Parliamentary Borough.

[2] On 24 January 1884 Lord Randolph Churchill, after describing how a deputation to Gladstone of working men had been given a few chips as souvenirs of Gladstone's wood-cutting exploits, continued: 'Is not this, I thought to myself as I read the narrative, a perfect type and emblem of Mr Gladstone's government of the Empire? The working classes of this country in 1880 sought Mr Gladstone. He told them that he would give them and all other subjects of the Queen much legislation, great prosperity, and universal peace; and he has given them nothing but chips. Chips to the faithful allies in Afghanistan, chips to the trusting native races of South Africa, chips to the Egyptian fellah, chips to the British farmer, chips to the manufacturer and the artisan, chips to the agricultural labourer, chips to the House of Commons itself. To all who leaned upon Mr Gladstone, who trusted in him, and who hoped for something from him—chips, nothing but chips—hard, dry, unnourishing, indigestible chips. . . .'

[3] Churchill had spoken at Blackpool on 9 January 1902, when he had praised Lord Rosebery's call for a negotiated settlement of the Boer War. Churchill declared: 'I welcome Lord Rosebery's speech because I think it shows the beginning of an Opposition which can provide an alternative Government. I do not believe in Oppositions which are so thoroughly disreputable that no one can trust them to govern the country. I welcome the criticism of Lord Rosebery as that of the only man able to put a responsible criticism before the country. It is not of an anti-national character. He possesses the three requirements which an English Prime Minister must have. He must have a great position in Parliament; he must have popularity in the country, and he must have rank and prestige in the great circle of European diplomacy; and I know of no other man than Lord Rosebery on the Opposition side who possesses those three qualifications.'

Lord Birkenhead to Lord Derby

(*Derby papers*)

28 March 1924
Secret

My dear Eddy,

. . . There will be a shadow cabinet early next week to decide whether without Coalition we shall accept the half of a Liberal wing under Winston. Probably about 30 Liberals could be got. The idea is that they should come as Jo came still calling themselves Liberal something. Do come if you can: you will see how much it means in Lancashire or elsewhere.

Yours ever,
FE

PS. If you can't come write to me or Baldwin.

Winston S. Churchill to Albert Thomas[1]

(*Churchill papers: 6/2*)

31 March 1924

It is very kind of you to write to me. The Election, of which you saw the first beginnings, proved the most interesting in which I have ever been concerned. I found myself opposed by the organisations of all three great Parties, and nevertheless succeeded in coming within fifty votes of victory. Although the result was not achieved, I am quite content with the manifestations of public and popular support which I obtained.

I am much interested in the changes which have taken place in France, but I do not know at present how to interpret them. It seems to me that Poincaré has obtained a new lease of life,[2] and therefore I fear the lid will be screwed tighter upon the European purgatory. However, before I form any judgment I must have a talk with our friend, Loucheur, who has, I have no doubt, received important assurances as to policy.

Once more thanking you for your letter, believe me

---

[1] Albert Thomas, 1878–1932. A leading French Trade Unionist. Elected as a Socialist Deputy in 1910. Put in charge of railway organization, September 1914. Under-Secretary for Armaments, May 1915–December 1916. Minister of Munitions, December 1916–September 1917. During a mission to Russia in 1917 he persuaded Kerensky to undertake a further military offensive. Director of the International Labour Organization, Geneva, from 1919 until his death.

[2] Not so; Poincaré's Government fell on 8 June 1924, and he did not become Prime Minister again until 23 July 1926 (when he held office for three years).

Winston Churchill to Stanley Baldwin
(*Churchill papers: 2/132*)

1 April 1924

Martin Conway told me of his talk yesterday with you and others. While I quite agree that there is no need to make any sweeping declaration of policy at the present time, it is necessary to face the fact that an arrangement about seats is urgent and lies at the root of the matter. Unless assurances cannot be given in a considerable number of individual cases to sitting Liberals that, if they act generally with the Conservative Opposition against the Socialist Government, the movement which is on foot will be discouraged, checked and perhaps frustrated. I recognise that this process could not be effected by a general declaration, but only individually.

It would be sufficient at the present time, in my opinion, if the Conservative Whips were told as a definite decision of policy to encourage sitting Liberals to act consistently with the Opposition against the Government by giving them assurances of immunity from Conservative attack to the greatest extent which may be honestly found possible in the next few weeks or months.

A decision to do less than this seems to me to be a decision adverse to the tendencies and movement which we have discussed, and amid the many uncertainties of the political situation the opportunity which is now open may pass. You are at liberty to quote this part of my letter to your colleagues, if you think it worth while.

I also send you for your own personal information a copy of the letter written in February 1922, of which I spoke to you. I shall be obliged if you will kindly treat it as completely confidential and send it me back after reading it yourself. I am sure you will feel that a fair and generous offer was made at that time to the leaders of the Conservative Party, and one which if it had been taken would have avoided many of the difficulties which have since arisen. As a National Liberal who shared in the responsibility for making this offer, I of course feel that our subsequent treatment by those with whom we were working was, to say the least of it, hard. But I have not at any time allowed personal feelings to complicate the situation.

Winston S. Churchill to Sir Archibald Salvidge[1]

(Churchill papers: 2/132)

1 April 1924

My dear Salvidge,

I shall be very glad if you will dine with me at 8.30 on Monday evening, and I am keeping myself free until I hear from you. Should we do better alone, or shall I ask FE? Needless to say I shall not discuss the proposed Liverpool demonstration[2] with anyone. There are two or three people who know about it already, but they are all in our confidential circle.

I am looking forward very much to a talk with you.

Winston S. Churchill to Sir Lindsay Parkinson

(Churchill papers: 2/132)

2 April 1924

My dear Sir,

I am greatly honoured by your letter and the invitation which it conveys. I am not yet in a position to come to any decision upon the next General Election. I think the next few weeks will clarify the situation and enable us to see our immediate steps more plainly. In the meantime perhaps you will allow me to mention your suggestion in conversation confidentially to Colonel Jackson. You realise, I presume, that I could only stand on the platform which I adopted at Westminster, ie of a Liberal in effective co-operation with the Conservative Party against Socialism.

Yours very faithfully,

[1] Archibald Tutton James Salvidge, 1863–1928. Chairman, Liverpool Conservative Workingmen's Association, 1892. Alderman, Liverpool City Council, 1898. Chairman of Council, National Union of Conservative and Unionist Associations, 1913–14. Chairman, Liverpool Advisory Committee on Recruiting, 1914–16. Knighted, 1916. Chairman of the Liverpool Constitutional Association.

[2] Churchill's proposed speech to a Conservative audience, planned for 7 May 1924 at the Sun Hall, Liverpool (see page 152).

Winston S. Churchill to Lord Granville: [1] *unsent draft*

(*Churchill papers: 2/132*)

[3] April 1924

Dear Granville,

The question of finding a candidate to be adopted by the Conservative Association, holding broad views on the necessity for cooperation with a Liberal Wing, lies outside my province.

I am anxious to retain and organise a distinctly Liberal block, ready to cooperate with the Conservative Party, and am therefore only in touch with the Liberal side of this movement. I could, of course, oblige you with names of such Liberals, but that I gather is not what you are seeking. I have, therefore, handed over your letter to some Conservative friends of mine who believe in working on the lines indicated in your letter and who may possibly be able to advance the matter.

I think it of great importance that the Conservative and Liberal wings in this matter should develop separately and with a clear determination to cooperate against a common foe when the time comes.

Winston S. Churchill to Lord Balfour

(*Churchill papers: 2/132*)

3 April 1924

You will be interested to know how things are moving here. I carefully abstained from the slightest recrimination about the Westminster Election and took occasion to renew within two or three days friendly relations with the Central Office and with Baldwin. Sir Martin Conway has formed a group of about twenty Conservative Members of Parliament, who have the sympathetic acquiescence of a great many more, for the purpose of furthering those ideas of union and co-operation which the Westminster Election represented. He has been very actively interviewing the various Conservative authorities, and is pleased with his reception. I have had a talk with Jackson and arranged that Freddie Guest, on behalf of the Anti-Socialist Liberals,

---

[1] Granville George Leveson Gower, Viscount Granville, 1872–1939. Succeeded his father as 3rd Earl Granville, 1891. Entered the Diplomatic Service, 1893. Councillor of Embassy, Berlin, 1911–13; Paris, 1913–17. Diplomatic Agent, Salonica, 1917. British Minister in Athens, 1917–21; in Copenhagen, 1921–6; at the Hague, 1926–8. Ambassador in Brussels, 1928–33.

should go into the question of seats with Eyres-Monsell,[1] a Conservative Whip. We have over thirty sitting Liberal Members who, if they receive reasonable assurances about their seats, will increasingly act in general harmony with the Conservative opposition to the general Government. In addition there are at least twenty seats in the country now held by Socialists, which could be won by Liberals, and only by Liberals, if these enjoyed the tacit support of the local Conservative Associations. You will see what a vital factor a block of fifty like this, counting double on a division, might be in maintaining a stable Government in the next House of Commons. I had a very friendly talk with Baldwin on these lines, and following thereupon, at the request of the Conservative Whips, he assembled the Shadow Cabinet which yesterday gave a fairly satisfactory general decision encouraging co-operation as much as possible by dealing with the question of seats individually and on their merits. I think this must just be allowed to work for a few weeks. Appetite may come in eating. On the whole, therefore, I am content with the movement of affairs.

So far as I am concerned, I am sure it was a good thing to contest the Abbey. I have already had half a dozen invitations from Conservative Associations to stand, two of which invitations carried with them also the support of the local Liberal Party. The epidemic of strikes, the increasing industrial unrest, and the precarious condition of the Government are all working powerfully to undo the folly of the Carlton Club in 1922. I am sure that even if Headquarters were unfavourable instead of being favourable, arrangements would be come to in a great many Constituencies. I do not think there will be much 'cut-throating' at the next General Election. As you once observed, 'This is a singularly ill-contrived world, but not so ill-contrived as that.' Salvidge of Liverpool, whom you know, expects to be able shortly to tender me an invitation to address as a Liberal the Liverpool Conservative Working Men's Association. This would be a significant incident. I have had a long talk with LG. He has greatly altered his point of view, and seems inclined to lean towards those National Liberal elements which he somewhat precipitately dispersed after the last General Election. I think that if things are steered and driven in the right direction, he might well be a buttress of a future 'Conservative and Liberal Union' Administration in which the colleagues who stood by him in 1922 were influential. He

[1] Bolton Meredith Monsell, 1881–1969. Known as 'Bobby'. Entered HMS *Britannia*, 1894; midshipman, 1896. Torpedo Lieutenant, 1903. Assumed the additional surname of Eyres, 1904. Conservative MP for South Worcestershire, 1910–35. A Conservative Whip, 1911. An original member of the Other Club, 1911. Returned to the Navy, 1914; on active service in Egypt, 1915; Commander, 1917. Treasurer of the Royal Household, 1919. Civil Lord of Admiralty, 1921; Financial Secretary, Admiralty, 1922–3. Privy Councillor, 1923. Chief Conservative Whip, 1923–31. Parliamentary Secretary, Treasury, 1923–4, 1924–9 and 1931. Created Viscount Monsell, 1935. Government Director, Board of British Airways, 1937.

has not shown the slightest resentment at the open lobbying which Freddie Guest and others have been doing to recreate the National Liberal wing. In short, the movement towards the reconstruction of a strong instrument of government with an adequate majority, and with a proper subordination of Party and personal interests, is making steady headway.

Your letter about Westminster played a very great part in that Election. Jackson told me that in his view it had turned 1,500 votes. It did much more than that. It created a preponderance of power on our side of the argument which, with two or three more days, would have given a very considerable victory, and without which I ran a great risk of a fiasco. I do not think the episode has left any scars behind.

I trust you are having pleasant weather. It is glacial here, and the worst cold than in the winter. You are well out of it. Don't bother to answer this letter, which is only sent to give you my report.

Winston S. Churchill to Professor Lindemann
(Cherwell papers)

3 April 1924

My dear Lindemann,

I have undertaken to write on the future possibilities of war and how frightful it will be for the human race. On this subject I have a good many ideas, but I should very much like to have another talk with you following on the most interesting one we had when you last lunched here. Do let me know when you are likely to be in London in the next few weeks, so that we can fix a lunch together.

Thank you so much for the letter you wrote my wife about the Election. It was exciting but provoking.

Yours sincerely,
Winston S. Churchill

Robert J. Prew[1] *to Brendan Bracken*

(*Churchill papers: 8/198*)

8 April 1924

Dear Mr Bracken,

I have duly forwarded to New York the last of Mr Churchill's series of articles, 'The Socialist Fraud'.

I have done so with some misgivings as, frankly, I do not like the article. Of the four articles which Mr Churchill has written, three of them are either direct or indirect attacks on Socialism. I do not for a moment think it would be the policy of our newspapers to open our columns to any writer— even so brilliant a one as Mr Churchill—for the purpose of engaging in a damaging campaign against any British political party. Mr Churchill's first article seems to me to have quite adequately expressed his views on Socialism.[2]

Yours faithfully,
Robert J. Prew

Sir Archibald Salvidge to Winston S. Churchill

(*Churchill papers: 2/132*)

11 April 1924   Liverpool

Dear Mr Churchill,

At a joint meeting of the Central Committee of the Liverpool Working-men's Conservative Association, representing 23 Branches in the 11 Parliamentary Divisions, and the Executive Committee of the Women's Unionist Federation held today, it was unanimously resolved to invite you to address

---

[1] Robert J. Prew, 1887–1952. Sub-editor of the *Continental Daily Mail*, 1906; Deputy-editor, 1907. On active service with the Inns of Court Regiment, 1914–19. Chief London correspondent of Hearst newspapers, 1919–29. Literary Editor of the *Daily Mail*, 1929–32; Assistant Editor, 1932–8; Editor, 1938–40. Joined Board of Reuters, 1941; retired, 1944. Chairman of Fine Technical Publications, Ltd, 1949.

[2] The only articles published by Churchill in the United States during 1924 were personal recollections, most of them later reprinted in *Thoughts and Adventures*. These were: 'The Battle of Sidney Street', 'Memoirs of the House of Commons', 'Plugstreet', 'Adventures in the Air', 'Perils in the Air', 'My Dramatic Days with the Kaiser', 'When I Risked Court Martial in Search of War', 'A Difference with Kitchener' and 'A Hand-to-Hand Fight with Desert Fanatics', all of which appeared in *Cosmopolitan*. He also published 'Shall we All Commit Suicide' in the *Nation*, on 3 December 1924. In England, Bracken had published Churchill's article entitled 'Liberalism' in the January 1924 issue of *English Life*, and a further article, 'The Party Game', in the April 1924 issue. *English Life* was a magazine then owned by Bracken. The disputed Hearst article was most probably 'Socialism and Sham', which had been published in England in the *Sunday Chronicle* on 6 April 1924.

a Mass Meeting in Liverpool at an early date on the 'Present Dangers of the Socialist Movement'. The Committee feel that the time has come when all classes of the people, irrespective of attachment to any political party, who are opposed to Socialism should unite in resistance to its growing menace. We gladly recognise that the exposition of your views is in harmony with our own on this subject, and indeed after careful perusal of your recent speeches on the political situation we find little, if any, divergence between us.

Under these circumstances we feel that in asking you to accept our invitation to address a meeting under our auspices we are in no way departing from the fundamental principles of the Party to which we are firmly attached. On the other hand, the same feeling will doubtless animate you should you find yourself able to accept this invitation.

Yours faithfully,
Archibald Salvidge

Winston S. Churchill to Sir Archibald Salvidge

(*Churchill papers: 2/132*)

12 April 1924

Dear Sir Archibald Salvidge,

I have received your letter of the 11th instant, and have carefully considered the invitation which you have been good enough to send me on behalf of the Liverpool Workingmen's Conservative Association and the Women's Unionist Federation.

Whatever differences may exist at the present time between us are differences only of method or of degree. They are not comparable to the gulf which separates the convictions of those who care about the greatness of Britain and the social progress of the people from the subversive and ruinous aims and retrograde character of the Socialist movement. In these circumstances and having particular regard to the terms of your letter, I feel it my duty to comply with your invitation and will hold the 6th or 7th May at your disposal as may be found convenient.

Yours faithfully,
Winston S. Churchill

Winston S. Churchill to Lord Derby

(*Derby papers*)

13 April 1924   Paris
Private

My dear Eddie,

We have been so comfortable here & have had a most interesting & delightful week thanks to yr excellent hospitality. I have seen most of the principal people outside the Government, and am now off to pay a visit of ceremony to the Tiger.[1]

I find a gt improvement in Opinion, a strong reaction against the Poincaré policy even amongst those who have supported it hitherto, a realization of the vital need to work with England and to reach an accommodation with Germany. What a pity these possibilities shd fall as an inheritance to AM.[2] You or we might have had them. However the main thing is an advance towards a settlement—never mind through which agency.

I was vy glad to see the firm decision of yr Lancashire meeting—I am in accord with yr policy as expressed at the party meeting by those present.[3] The urgent need is to afford a broad rallying ground for those forces. We who work for the greatness of Britain & the Cons Party have an Imperial duty to perform in this respect far superior to ordinary party hobbies. I am vy glad to see my friends restored to the councils of the party. You will be all the stronger for having them with you. *Experience* is vital to political sagacity.

[1] Georges Clemenceau, 1841–1929. Mayor of Montmartre, 1870. Member of the Chamber of Deputies, 1876–93 and 1902–29. Radical journalist; editor of *Justice*. Minister of the Interior, 1906. Prime Minister, 1906–8. Prime Minister and Minister of War, November 1917–January 1920. In *Great Contemporaries* (1937) Churchill wrote: 'Happy the nation which when its fate quivers in the balance can find such a tyrant and such a champion.'

[2] Alexandre Millerand, 1859–1943. Elected to the French Chamber of Deputies as a Radical Socialist, 1885. Minister of War, January 1912–January 1913; and again from January 1914 to October 1915. He resigned following accusations that he had failed to find sufficient heavy artillery. Commissar-General for Alsace and Lorraine, 1919–20. Minister for Foreign Affairs, January 1920. Prime Minister, 1920. President of the Republic, 1920–4.

[3] On 9 February 1924, at a meeting in Manchester of the Lancashire and Cheshire Division of the Conservative and Unionist Party, Sir Archibald Salvidge had moved a resolution, at Lord Derby's suggestion, stating 'that it is undesirable that Protection should be included in the programme of the Conservative Party at this juncture'. Although the resolution was opposed by Colonel Jackson, the Chairman of the Conservative Party, it was adopted unanimously. Two days earlier, at a meeting of ex-Cabinet Ministers, only L. S. Amery had spoken in favour of Protection, its principal critics being Austen Chamberlain and Lord Curzon. Following this discussion, and the so-called 'Lancashire Plot', Baldwin had told a Conservative Party meeting in London on 11 February 1923: 'I do not feel justified in advising the Party again to submit the proposal for a general tariff to the country, except on the clear evidence that on this matter public opinion is disposed to reconsider its judgement of two months ago.'

Painlevé[1] lunched with me and asked me to send you the inscribed copy of his book wh accompanies this note. You will no doubt write him a line.

Once more vy many thanks for yr kindness wh Clemmie & I have greatly appreciated.

Believe me
Yours sincerely,
Winston S. Churchill

Winston S. Churchill to Clementine Churchill
(*Spencer-Churchill papers*)

17 April 1924   Chartwell

My Darling,

This is the first letter I have ever written from this place, & it is right that it shd be to you.[2] I am in bed in your bedroom (wh I have annexed temporarily) & wh is sparsely but comfortably furnished with the pick of yr two van loads. We have had two glorious days. The children have worked like blacks; & Sergeant Thompson,[3] Aley,[4] Waterhouse,[5] one gardener & 6 men have formed a powerful labour corps. The weather has been delicious,

[1] Paul Painlevé, 1863–1933. Mathematician; Professor in the Faculty of Sciences at Lille, 1886; at the Sorbonne, 1891. Elected to the Chamber of Deputies, 1906, as an independent Socialist. Minister of Public Instruction and Inventions, October 1915–December 1916. Minister of War, March 1917–September 1917. Prime Minister, and Minister of War, 12 September–13 November 1917 (when he was succeeded as Prime Minister by Clemenceau). President of the Chamber, 1924. Prime Minister for the second time from April to November 1925. Minister of War, 1925–6. Minister of Air, 1930–1 and 1932–3.

[2] Churchill and his wife were to continue to live at Chartwell until Churchill's death fifty years later. On 18 August 1924 his cousin Frederick Guest wrote to him: 'I loved seeing your home & I think it is a triumph' (*Churchill papers: 2/134*). Among the overnight guests during 1924 were Lloyd George (August 18), Sir Roger Keyes (August 19), Sir Archibald and Lady Sinclair (August 30), Oliver Locker-Lampson (December 7) and Brendan Bracken (December 22).

[3] Walter H. Thompson. Detective Constable, Special Branch, Scotland Yard, 1913. Bodyguard to Lloyd George, 1917–20. Bodyguard to Churchill, 1920–32. Accompanied Churchill to Palestine, 1921, and to the United States, 1931–2. Retired from the police force with the rank of Detective Inspector, 1936. Worked as a grocer, 1936–9. Recalled to the police force, 1939, and served as Churchill's personal bodyguard from September 1939 until May 1945, accompanying him on all his war-time journeys.

[4] The chauffeur who had succeeded Fowler. Later, Aley became chauffeur to Brendan Bracken, and on Bracken's death in 1958 he burnt, at Bracken's explicit request, all Bracken's letters and private papers.

[5] Waterhouse had been gardener to the previous owner of Chartwell, William Erskine Campbell-Colquhoun. From 1922 to 1924, after the Churchills had bought Chartwell, but while the house was still empty, Waterhouse remained in a cottage on the estate, and earned his living by tilling the land and by selling the produce of the kitchen garden.

& we are out all day toiling in dirty clothes & only bathing before dinner. I have just had my bath in your de luxe bathroom. I hope you have no *amour propre* about it! The household consists of the nursery party reinforced by Lily—the Kn maid. I drink champagne at all meals & buckets of claret & soda in between, & the *cuisine* tho' simple is excellent. In the evenings we play the gramophone (of wh we have deprived Mary) & Mah Jongg with yr gimcrack set.

All yesterday & today we have been turfing & levelling the plateau. The motor mower acts as a roller and we have done everything now except from the yew tree to the Kn garden end. Here as you know there is more levelling & also the pathway made by the carts to make good. I hope to finish tomorrow.

Your steps are nearly made in the centre of the bank. The front basement windows go on apace. I expect I shall end by facing the intervening spaces as well. There is only a foot or two left!

You will be pleased with the effect. It is majestic. The drawing room floor is finished & half planed.

Lastly we have ¾ turfed the great bank below the plateau.

Everything is budding now that this gleam of deferred genial weather has come.

> Only one thing lack these banks of green—
> The Pussy Cat who is their Queen.

I do hope my darling that you are all enjoying yourselves & that you are really recuperating. How I wish you were here. It wd be quite easy. I shd simply move back into Henry VIII. But the disadvantages of no morning sun make me resolute to use the studio eventually. You cannot imagine the size of these rooms till you put furniture into them. This bedroom of yours is a magnificent aerial bower. Come as soon as you feel[1] well enough to share it. Don't go to London. I will send the motor to meet you at Newhaven & if you telegraph one day in advance everything will be ready for you.

I had a satisfactory conversation with Jackson. He is going to try to fix up St Georges for me.[1] The Liberal Party is in a stew. They are disgusted with the position into wh they have been led & then left without leading. There is an intensely bitter feeling agst Labour, wh everywhere is cutting Liberal throats in the constituencies. How often I find myself called wrong, for warning people of follies in time. Perhaps you have the same experience in the domestic sphere!

[1] Westminster, St George's, the neighbouring constituency to Westminster, Abbey. Its MP from 1921 to 1929 was James Monteith Erskine (see page 132, note 1) who had been returned unopposed in both 1923 and 1924. In 1929 the seat was won by Sir Laming Worthington-Evans with a majority of over 16,000. In the 1945 election it was also held by a Conservative.

Tender love my sweet Clemmie. Please keep wiring, & think sometimes of yr devoted

paterfamilias porcus
Yr ever loving
W

PS. I thought the Wells book quite good.[1]

Sir Leslie Wilson[2] *to Winston S. Churchill*

(*Churchill papers: 2/147*)

19 April 1924   Government House, Mahableshwar
Personal

My dear Churchill,

You may be surprised to get a letter from me as we haven't always seen eye to eye—I am not quite sure that statement is correct—for owing to your most unfortunate illness after the excellent dinner you gave me at your home before the Carlton Club meeting, I am still a little doubtful as to what your real feelings were at that most important period in the political history of the country.

My real object in writing is to tell you that I am honestly & sincerely sorry you were not successful for the Abbey Division & if I had been in England, I should, whatever my position in the Conservative party had been, supported to the best of my ability your Candidature. I believe the appropriate word in the American language is 'pep' but that is at any rate as it appears to me from a distance, what the opposition to the present government wants, and you could, as I know well, have given it. The Press, the Liberal Party, & my own party seem to be all in agreement on the wonderful moderation of the Labour Govt! Let the Labour Govt get a majority over both Parties & where will that moderation be then? The Labour

---

[1] H. G. Wells' novel *The Dream*, published by Jonathan Cape in April 1924.

[2] Leslie Orme Wilson, 1876–1955. 2nd Lieutenant, Royal Marine Light Infantry, 1895; Captain, 1901. Severely wounded during the war in South Africa, 1899–1901. Conservative MP for Reading, 1913–22; for South Portsmouth, 1922–3. Lieutenant-Colonel Commanding the Hawke Battalion, Royal Naval Division, at Gallipoli, 1915; in France, 1916. Severely wounded in France, 1916. Parliamentary Assistant Secretary to the War Cabinet, 1918. Chairman of the National Maritime Board, 1919. Parliamentary Secretary, Ministry of Shipping, 1919. Chief Unionist Whip (Parliamentary Secretary to the Treasury), 1921–3. Knighted, 1923. Governor of Bombay, 1923–8; of Queensland, 1932–46. His younger son was killed in North Africa in December 1941.

Party will get that majority unless the programme which they will enforce with a clear majority is properly exposed and the people have no idea of the power of Government with an unchallengable majority in the House of Commons.

I am, temporarily, at any rate out of politics but am responsible for the welfare of a great Presidency with over 20 million people, 92% of whom are illiterate & who only want to continue their lives without grave internal strife—The vast majority are absolutely loyal to the British Raj & the self seeking minority—who in no way represent the people of India—will have their way if a Labour Govt comes into power with a clear majority. I needn't tell you what that will mean to India & the Empire.

I hope sincerely you will get into the House soon and, when there, you will as no one else can, espouse the cause of India & its *loyal* millions. The Vox Populi of India is not *yet* the Vox Delhi—*Far* from it.

Yours vy sincerely,
Leslie Wilson

On reading this over I am doubtful, if in my present position I should have written it, knowing no politics now but, as it really expresses what I feel, I send it, knowing that you will regard it as it is marked Personal.[1]

Clementine Churchill to Winston S. Churchill

(*Spencer-Churchill papers*)

19 April 1924   Dieppe

. . . I suppose that if there were a real Liberal move to the right Baldwin would not be in a hurry to provide you with a safe Tory Seat such as St George's? He would probably suggest that you stand as a Liberal for a Liberal Seat with no Tory opposition. This would suit his book better as the minute you become a Conservative his Leadership is endangered—both by you & FE whom you would bring back with you as a possible Leader.

---

[1] For Churchill's reply, nearly two years later, see page 659.

Winston S. Churchill to Professor Lindemann

(*Cherwell papers*)

21 April 1924

Dear Professor Lindemann,

Thank you so much for your letter and for the copy of 'Daedalus' which has safely reached me. I shall certainly read it with much curiosity.[1]

I wish you would make enquiries about the man who is said to have discovered a ray which will kill at a certain distance. I have met people who say that it can actually be seen to kill mice etc. It may be all a hoax, but my experience has been not to take 'NO' for an answer.[2]

Winston S. Churchill to Thornton Butterworth

(*Churchill papers: 8/199*)

23 April 1924

Dear Mr Butterworth,

Although I have made and am making good progress with Volume III, politics have proved a very disturbing influence on my calculation. The Westminster Election, for instance, took a whole month, and it is quite possible that a General Election may be upon us in July, taking another month. In these circumstances I may find it necessary to postpone publication from October 1924 to March 1925. I have already communicated with Mr Lints Smith[3] of 'The Times', and they are quite agreeable to such a

---

[1] In November 1923 the scientist J. B. S. Haldane had published *Daedalus: or Science and the Future*. Originally a paper read to the Heretics, at Cambridge, it argued that the emphasis in science was moving from physics to biology, and predicted the production of 'ectogenic children', conceived, nurtured and born outside the womb. Once this process were developed, Haldane argued, man would have power to regulate populations both as to quantity and quality. He predicted, in addition, the elimination of disease, and life-spans regulated by man rather than nature. Developments such as these, he warned, would demean the family and raise political questions beyond the present capacity of mankind to resolve them. But he viewed scientific progress as salutary as well as inevitable, and wrote that: 'Moral progress is so difficult that I think any developments are to be welcomed which present it as the naked alternative to destruction, no matter how horrible may be the stimulus which is necessary before man will take the moral step in question.'

[2] On 10 May 1924 Churchill wrote again to Lindemann: 'There is an article in "John Bull" of May 3 which deals with the subject of the deadly ray, which it might be worth your while to look at, if only to despise it.'

[3] William Lints Smith, 1876–1944. Joined the *Aberdeen Journal* as a journalist at the age of 17. Became editor of the *Crosby Herald* at the age of 20. Later served in the news department of the *St James Gazette*. One of the most successful news-gatherers of his day, he served as Editor and Manager of *Sporting Life*, 1911–14, before joining *The Times* in 1914. Manager of *The Times* from 1920 until his retirement in 1937.

postponement, which in that case would mean that the serial would be running in their columns in February next.

It is not necessary to come to any final decision for another two months, and it is quite possible that I may make such progress as to be able to keep to my original plan. But I send you this early intimation of a possible alteration.

Winston S. Churchill to Dr Percy Edmunds[1]

(*Churchill papers: 6/2*)

25 April 1924

Dear Dr Edmunds,

I am extremely grateful to you for your most kind letter of April 16, which conveys to me the views and wishes of so many friends in the Soho Wards of the Abbey Division. I need scarcely say that these matters to which you refer are causing me the deepest possible consideration at the present time. My own inclinations run very strongly in the direction of continuing my association with such a splendid set of enthusiastic supporters and patriotic citizens. The complication and difficulty which presents itself arises solely from what I will venture to call the 'national aspect' of politics. It might be injurious to the cause I have at heart if I were to find myself in violent opposition to the Conservative Party in one Constituency while doing my utmost to promote unity of action throughout the country. I am sure you will appreciate this difficulty and bear with me if I take some time to solve it satisfactorily.

Will you kindly treat this letter as confidential, showing it only to the officers of the Soho Wards Committee who have signed the letter you have been good enough to send me.

Yours very faithfully,

[1] Percy James Edmunds, born 1862. Honorary Physician, Church Beneficence Society. Fellow of the Royal Society of Medicine. Surgeon, Central Division of the Metropolitan Police. Surgical Assistant and Ophthalmic Assistant, University College Hospital. His practice was at 5 Great Marlborough Street, London W1. Chairman of the Soho Wards Committee of the Abbey Division of Westminster.

Captain Edward Altham[1] to Winston S. Churchill

(Churchill papers: 2/132)

28 April 1924   United Service Club

Dear Mr Churchill,

On the strength of my association with you in a humble capacity during the war, which you were good enough to recall after the recent Navy League Meeting, I am writing to ask for your assistance in my first political effort. As a member of the Committee of the newly formed Conservative Training Association I have to speak at a Debate which is taking place at the Central Offices on Wednesday (30th) for the edification of our younger members. The subject is: 'That this meeting approves the decision of the Electors of the Abbey Division at the recent bye-election in Westminster'.

I have been deputed to *oppose* the motion, which I am very willing to do. The subject in itself is perhaps rather a stale one but it serves as a title for much wider issues and it is with the object of doing justice to these that I am appealing to you for some 'high explosive'.

As I see it the result of the Abbey election was a colourless repetition of a semi-moribund form of Conservatism which is powerless and futile against the live opposition of the forces which are menacing the State in the present day. Leaving personalities out of the question.

Your election would have marked a new era in which men who, realising the ever growing peril to the Empire of a Socialist Government in this country, would fall in under the same flag and line up to oppose a common enemy. The Abbey election replaced a worthy member of the rank and file of the Conservative Party. It did not bring the powerful re-inforcements to the Anti-Socialist cause which your election would have produced.

These are the broad lines on which I hope to carry my opposition to the motion on Wednesday.

The Conservative Training Association has been inaugurated with the blessing of the Party Leaders and it is our hope to create an organisation which will help young men to fit themselves for the political conflict of the future. The young Conservative, however, will not be content to follow blindly the old party shibboleths and to listen to conventional platitudes. He is looking for a live policy and a virile leadership. He entirely fails to see why men, whose political creeds appear to be divided only by the control of Party Funds, should be held bound in opposing camps.

I feel therefore that I have a great opportunity to present to them the

[1] Edward Altham, 1882–1950. Lieutenant, 1902: served in the second Battle Squadron, 1911–14. Commanded *Wildfire* in the bombardment of the German army's right wing off the Belgian Coast, October 1914. Commanded the monitor *General Craufurd* off the Belgian coast, August–November 1915. CB, 1919.

advantages of an alliance with moderate Liberals (if the latter still wish to serve under that flag) and of the views and aims which you have urged and will, I hope, urge again on the Electorate, in giving a lead to such an alliance . . .

Winston S. Churchill to Captain Edward Altham

(*Churchill papers: 2/132*)

29 April 1924

I am much interested in your letter and in the debate in which you are going to take part. I think the point which you intend to make is the true one, and you express it in terms which naturally I regard as extremely effective. There are, however, two other aspects of the argument on which it might be worth your while to dwell.

The first is: is there any reason to believe that the Conservative Party will by itself and alone be able to command a majority of the electors in this country or to secure an effective governing majority even of the Members of Parliament in the immediate future? If not, we should be condemned to the confusion and intrigue of a Three Party system and government by minority unless a body of Liberals co-operated on broad lines with the Conservatives in a manner similar to that of Mr Chamberlain and Lord Hartington in 1886. The good of the country requires a strong and broad foundation for government.

The other point is a local one. It will certainly do great injury to the Conservative Party if great Constituencies like Westminster are treated as if they were pocket boroughs and passed from father to son and uncle to nephew as in the bad old days. It is surely lamentable that 'The Times' should in a leading article openly describe this historic seat as a 'kept' Constituency.

With good wishes, believe me

Winston S. Churchill to Lord Birkenhead

(*Churchill papers: 2/132*)

30 April 1924

I am so glad to see by the papers that you are better. I tried to get hold of you yesterday morning, but in vain. I shall be in London from Sunday night until I go to Liverpool on Wednesday, and I want to see you in order to discuss two points of considerable difficulty: the McKenna duties[1] and the Ulster boundary situation.[2]

Have you got a copy of your letter which reassured Arthur Balfour on this? I think I shall find it necessary to say that we consulted the highest legal authorities at the time and that, while the decision rests under the treaty with the Commissioners, we were led to believe that no reasonable Commission could make other than minor adjustments of the boundary. Further, what is your view about the need of fresh legislation in the event of Ulster refusing to appoint a representative? We really ought to have a talk about these matters which if not handled satisfactorily may prove great stumbling blocks.

The Budget is very good and shows real political comprehension. It makes one feel what fools the Tories (and Liberals) have been to pass this great opportunity of distributing a surplus accumulated by the sacrifices of the direct tax-payers. Mad Baldwin!

I am free Tuesday night, if you could dine.

Colonel Jackson to Winston S. Churchill
(*Churchill papers: 2/133*)

8 May 1924

My dear Churchill,

May I be allowed to offer my congratulations upon your brilliant speech at Liverpool—I read it with great pleasure—I hope you were satisfied with your visit there.[3]

Yours ever
F. Stanley Jackson

[1] A set of tariffs on luxury articles which had been introduced by the Conservative Government in 1923. These duties, which included a tax on foreign cars, clocks and watches, brought in £2½ million a year to the Exchequer. The Labour Government had said that it would repeal them (as a means of retaining Liberal support).

[2] On 24 April 1924 a Conference on the Boundary Provisions of the Irish Treaty had broken down in London. For some months pressure had been growing in the Irish Free State for a revision of the boundary between the Free State and Ulster. This boundary had been fixed while Churchill was Secretary of State for the Colonies, responsible for Irish affairs, and had been approved by both Belfast and Dublin on 30 March 1922. During 1924 the Conservative Party strongly opposed any substantial change in the boundary to the detriment of Ulster.

[3] On 7 May 1924 Churchill spoke to more than five thousand Liverpool Conservatives at the Sun Hall, Liverpool. It was the first Conservative meeting at which he had spoken for twenty years. There was no longer any place, Churchill declared, for an independent Liberal Party. Only the Conservatives offered a strong enough base 'for the successful defeat of Socialism'. Liberals like himself must be prepared to support the Conservatives at the Polls, and to be supported by them, sustained by a 'broad progressive platform'. Churchill repeated these arguments at a luncheon given by the Liverpool Conservative Club on the following day.

Lord Halifax[1] to Winston S. Churchill

(*Churchill papers: 2/133*)

8 May 1924
Private

Dear Mr Winston Churchill,

Nothing that I can think or say could be of much importance to you, but I must, for my own sake, take the opportunity of telling you of the extreme pleasure with which I have read your speech in the Yorkshire Post this morning, and of my entire agreement with, and admiration of it. I am the more encouraged to do this by the desire I have had for some time to tell you how completely I think you have made out your case in regard to the Dardanelles and the war generally. It is a real refreshment to see someone possessed of your courage and ability. It has seemed to me that whatever the incidental advantages might be from the fact of such a Government as the present being in power, they are as nothing in comparison with the disadvantages arising from the fact of such a Government being accepted at all. The risks of such a Government and the consequences to be drawn from it having existed seem to me decisive on this point.

You will forgive me for writing, but, after all, public men are public property, and when one feels all the approval that I do, it is pleasant to express it.

I am,
Yours truly,
Halifax

Winston S. Churchill to Lord Halifax

(*Churchill papers: 2/133*)

9 May 1924

I am very grateful to you for the kindness of your letter which I greatly value. I am much encouraged by the fact that you consider, after studying the documents in my book, that I have made out a good case for the war policy that I advocated. I suffered very much at the time from popular misconceptions about Antwerp and the Dardanelles, which it was impossible to

---

[1] Charles Lindley Wood, 1839–1934. Groom of the Bedchamber to the Prince of Wales, 1863–77. Succeeded his father as 2nd Viscount Halifax, 1885. Ecclesiastical Commissioner for England, 1886. President of the English Church Union, 1869–1919 and 1931–4. Father of Edward Wood (Churchill's Parliamentary Under-Secretary at the Colonial Office, 1921–2; subsequently Viceroy of India as Lord Irwin, and Foreign Secretary as Lord Halifax).

correct during the war. Now that the facts are becoming known there is a great change in educated public opinion, and only the Socialists continue to excite prejudice for purely political reasons.

I am also very glad that you feel as I do about the dangers to which the country is exposed through the perfectly needless stimulus which has been so greatly given to Socialist power and prestige.

Though I do not think we have corresponded before, it was a great pleasure to have your son with me at the Colonial Office in his first Ministerial appointment.

Sir Samuel Hoare[1] to Winston S. Churchill

(Churchill papers: 2/133)

9 May 1924
Private and Personal

Dear Winston,

I must write this line to congratulate you upon the success of your two Liverpool speeches. If I may say so, they have both greatly strengthened your position with the Conservative Party. Your Conservative friends are now looking with keen anticipation to the debate upon the McKenna duties, when they much hope that your friends in the House will follow your excellent lead. I was very glad that you had so satisfactory a talk with Baldwin and Chamberlain.

Please do not trouble to answer this.

Yours sincerely,
Samuel Hoare

[1] Samuel John Gurney Hoare, 1880–1959. Educated at Harrow and New College, Oxford. Conservative MP for Chelsea, 1910–44. Succeeded his father as 2nd Baronet, 1915. Lieutenant-Colonel, British Military Mission to Russia, 1916–17, and to Italy, 1917–18. Deputy High Commissioner, League of Nations, for care of Russian refugees, 1921. Secretary of State for Air, October 1922–January 1924 and 1924–9. Secretary of State for India, 1931–5; for Foreign Affairs, 1935. First Lord of the Admiralty, 1936–7; Home Secretary, 1937–9; Lord Privy Seal, 1939–40; Secretary of State for Air, April–May 1940. Ambassador to Spain, 1940–4. Created Viscount Templewood, 1944.

Winston S. Churchill to Colonel Jackson

(*Churchill papers: 6/2*)

10 May 1924   2 Sussex Square
Private and Confidential

You will perhaps read in the Daily Telegraph an account of my meeting in Westminster last night.[1] They were of course bitterly disappointed at my refusal to give them a decided answer. I could easily form a 'Westminster Conservative and Liberal Union' which would comprise at least 2,000 members, seven-eighths of whom would be Conservative. Such an Association would include many of the strongest business and professional elements in the Constituency, and would be representative not merely of the poorer quarters but of all the Wards. I have received promises which make it clear that such an Association would be largely, if not wholly, self-supporting, and I am sure it would soon compare very favourably in power and repute with the existing body. I have not, however, decided to take such a step, because I hope that matters may be adjusted in a different and smoother way.

You will receive in the next ten days an extensively signed Memorial. Three hundred active and influential Conservatives and a certain number of Liberals are taking round the papers for signature. The greatest care will be taken not to include any names not on the Register. When this Memorial is presented, you will be able to judge for yourself what its weight and value is. I shall take no decision until I know what you think about it. It seems to me that, if you take the line of saying that you are bound by the decision of the local Association, it follows that you are also responsible, in the event of a local difference of a serious character or of the representative quality of that Association being impugned, to make it clear that it must be put on a sound basis if your action is to be dictated by it.

It may be that some compromise could be arrived at by procedure on these lines. At any rate I hope that you will weigh the issue very carefully, and will not hesitate to come to see me if you think any discussion between us would be useful.

---

[1] The *Daily Telegraph* of 10 May 1924 had reported Churchill's meeting on the previous evening with friends and workers who had supported him in the Abbey by-election. During the meeting, a resolution had been passed inviting Churchill to stand for the seat in the next election. He replied: 'I am not going to pronounce finally upon such an issue tonight. I earnestly hope at the next General Election to be able to use my whole strength in the main battle all over the country. I must, above all things, consider what is most likely to conduce to my general usefulness.'

Winston S. Churchill to Stanley Baldwin

(*Churchill papers: 2/133*)

10 May 1924   2 Sussex Square
Private and Confidential

I have been making enquiries among my Liberal friends in the House about the McKenna Motion. Guest, Seely[1] and Grigg will vote with you, and Guest tells me that he finds quite a lot of support among those with whom he usually acts. He seemed to think that as many as twenty (and perhaps more) might go into the Lobby. On the other hand there are other issues on which a better vote could be obtained. Several Liberals, for instance, have told me they must vote for the repeal of the McKenna duties in consequence of the line they took in the elections when challenged on this subject; whereas on Imperial Preference they would feel much more free on grounds not of economics but of keeping faith with the Dominions.

On the McKenna duties it has occurred to me that it would be wise for one of my friends to put a question to the Government, asking them whether in view of the dislocation and the hard times, etc, they will not consent to abolish the McKenna duties in three steps spread over three years. The Government of course would say 'No', and well-disposed Liberals would feel that they were voting not against the abolition of the duties but against inadequate notice to the trades and against needless dislocation. Thus no question of principle would arise. It seems to me that this is much better than any sort of amendment such as I see is proposed.

I am glad you liked my line at Liverpool, and am much obliged to you for your friendly reference to it.

Show this letter to Austen if you wish, as it will explain the position.

[1] John Edward Bernard Seely, 1868–1947. Educated at Harrow and Trinity College, Cambridge. Liberal MP, 1900–2; 1923–4. Under-Secretary of State for the Colonies, 1908–11. Secretary of State for War, 1912–14. Resigned in March 1914, following the Curragh incident. Commanded the Canadian Cavalry Brigade, 1915–18. Gassed, 1918, and retired from Army with rank of Major-General. Under-Secretary of State to Churchill, Ministry of Munitions, and Deputy Minister of Munitions, 1918. Under-Secretary of State for Air, 1919. Created Baron Mottistone, 1933. Chairman of the National Savings Committee, 1926–43. His son Frank was killed leading his company at the battle of Arras, 1917.

Winston S. Churchill to Lord Derby

(*Derby papers*)

10 May 1924   2 Sussex Square
Private and Confidential

My dear Eddie,

It is really very kind of you to write to me. I have been so grieved to hear of your very serious illness which for some days caused all your friends so much anxiety. I did not know how ill you had been until the worst was over. I do hope and trust you will continue to make steady progress and will not worry about politics or affairs until you are completely restored.

Yes, I had a magnificent meeting at Liverpool, and great sympathy was shown. I was a little tied up by my notes at Sun Hall, as I was so anxious to make a declaration to the country; but at the Conservative Club I let myself go, and I think they were all quite pleased. Salvidge made an important statement against general tariffs which was quite well accepted by the whole company. I feel time may be very short now before the fight comes. I hope you will use all your influence to make sure that seats are not thrown away to the Socialists by splitting votes in cases where a friendly Liberal has an unmistakeably better chance of winning than a Conservative candidate. There must be thirty or forty seats which will turn on such a policy this time. And this may well make a difference between victory and defeat.

Yours v sincerely,
Winston S.C.

Lord Derby to Winston S. Churchill

(*Churchill papers: 2/133*)

12 May 1924
Private & Confidential

Dear Winston,

You may be quite sure that I shall act up to what you suggest as being the proper course of action, and that is support Liberals who seem to have better chances of winning than Conservatives. It is what I did in the 1922 Election with the National Liberals, and as you know it came off, and I think would do so again, but there is no doubt whatever, for reasons which I will tell you when I see you, that one's influence has, to a certain extent, gone in Lancashire, and it will take a certain amount of regaining.

This is confidential. The Conservative Chairman in one constituency where Labour is in did have a try to work with the Liberals even to the extent of approaching the Liberals with a view to settling who the candidate should be, whether a Liberal or Conservative, but the Liberals would not have it, and until you have some arrangement working, of the old Liberal–Unionist type, we shall have these difficulties. Once you get that started I believe a good many of our difficulties would be solved. Of course there are a great many people who want the Liberal Party to drop out. I am dead against that. I am perfectly certain that the mere name of Liberal carries a great many people with it, and if you do not keep it you will not find that members of that Party go to the Conservatives. I believe they would go one-third to Conservatives and two-thirds to Labour.

I wish you were back in Parliament. We want some real hard fighters there, and I do not know anybody better than you. You must let me know if you are thinking of a Lancashire seat, and let me see if I could prepare the ground for you. Of course it is difficult to know what seat to recommend until I know what Liberals are likely to join what I will call the Liberal–Conservative Party. I am sure there are seats which a man like you could win.[1]

I shall be in London some of next week & will try to see you.

Yours ever,
Derby

Winston S. Churchill to James Erskine
(*Churchill papers: 2/133*)

13 May 1924   2 Sussex Square

I am very much obliged to you for your letter, and am glad to hear your news. My plans are still unsettled, as I am waiting to see what the result will be of the Memorial which will be presented to the Central Office.

I regret very much to hear that you have been involved in difficulties on account of having supported me. If there is any way in which I can assist you in their removal, do not fail to let me know. My position is rather stronger now than it was with the leaders of your Party, and I should have

[1] That same day, 12 May 1924, Churchill declined an invitation to stand as Conservative candidate for the Lancashire constituency of Royton. On the following day he declined a similar invitation from the Kettering Conservative Association. Royton had returned a Liberal in the 1923 election, but was to return a Conservative in the 1924 election. Kettering had returned a Labour-Cooperative in 1923, but was to return a Conservative in 1924. (In 1940 it was represented by John Profumo, one of the Conservative MPs who voted against Neville Chamberlain on 8 May 1940.) On 3 July 1924 Churchill was asked to stand as Conservative candidate for North Hackney, but declined. On July 12 he was asked to stand as the official Conservative candidate for Barnstaple, but again declined.

thought that the change which has taken place among important people in the Abbey Division, of which you write, would also have relieved the situation as far as you are concerned.

I should greatly like to have a talk with you in the near future. Could you, for instance, lunch here at one o'clock on Monday? Alternately, I am free on Saturday morning, if that would be more convenient to you.

Winston S. Churchill to Brendan Bracken
(Churchill papers: 8/198)

15 May 1924

My dear Bracken,

Many thanks for your letter which I have just received. I think it would be rather a nuisance to get into a lawsuit with these people, with whose other branches I have so very much more important business. I think a letter of protest should be written, and I enclose one for you to forward.

The MacDonald article will be ready on Thursday or Friday of next week and will appear on Sunday week. It is not a diatribe, but a critical appreciation. Will you let me know in the next few days what you are able to do about this article? I have only sold the English serial rights to the 'Weekly Dispatch'. I think we ought to get £100 for the American rights. Would it be a good thing for me to let Curtis Brown have a shot as well, or would this queer your pitch?

Yours sincerely,

Winston S. Churchill: draft letter for Brendan Bracken to send to Robert J. Prew
(Churchill papers: 8/198)

15 May 1924

Dear Sir,

I have consulted Mr Churchill on the question of the four articles. He desires me to say he is surprised at the position your firm have adopted. The four articles were purchased as a series, and no suggestion or stipulation was made as to the exclusion of any particular topics. Mr Churchill understood that he had perfect freedom to write on the subjects he selected and that you would purchase the whole four articles as they appeared in the (English) 'Sunday Chronicle'. But for the fact that the two articles which you decided not to print had been reserved for you under your agreement, he could certainly have sold them elsewhere.

In these circumstances Mr Churchill is advised that he has a lawful claim against you for the fulfilment of the agreement. Before deciding, however, on any further steps, Mr Churchill would like to know whether the facts have been brought to the notice of the higher authorities in your firm, as he is reluctant to believe that they would not wish to settle the case in an equitable manner.

Yours faithfully,
BB

R. A. Butler[1] *to Winston S. Churchill*

(*Churchill papers: 2/133*)

16 May 1924   The Union Society
                                                        Cambridge

Dear Sir,

I write on behalf of the Cambridge Union to invite you to take part in our final Debate of the Year on *June 10th* Tuesday. Merging as it does into the Festive Season and owing to the lateness of the end of term it promises to be a particularly large Debate and your presence would lend an added distinction to the occasion.

We were very disappointed that you were unable to come last term but we can not help feeling, perhaps somewhat selfishly that the result of the Westminster Bye Election will have at least one slight merit in that it will leave you free to undertake this visit which we most heartily propose to you.

I personally would take this opportunity of extending to you the warmest of welcomes on the part of the Society, were you able to come, and offering you our hospitality for that evening.

As regards subject, I would prefer to leave that to you. A motion on Socialism would be very welcome.

Hoping very much that you will be able to pay us the honour of a visit which long awaited as it is will be all the more appreciated.

Yours sincerely
R. A. Butler
President

[1] Richard Austen Butler, 1902–   . Educated at Marlborough and Pembroke College, Cambridge. President of the Union Society, 1924. Conservative MP for Saffron Walden, 1929–65. Under-Secretary of State, India Office, 1932–7. Parliamentary Secretary, Ministry of Labour, 1937–8. Under-Secretary of State for Foreign Affairs, 1938–41. Privy Councillor, 1939. Minister of Education, 1941–5. Minister of Labour, 1945. Chancellor of the Exchequer, 1951–5. Lord Privy Seal, 1955–61. Home Secretary, 1957–62. Deputy Prime Minister, 1962–3. Secretary of State for Foreign Affairs, 1963–4. Created Baron Butler of Saffron Walden, 1965. Master of Trinity College, Cambridge, 1965–78.

Winston S. Churchill to R. A. Butler

(*Churchill papers: 2/133*)

19 May 1924

I thank you most cordially for your letter asking me to take part in your final Debate on June 10th, and much appreciate the honour done me by this invitation. I regret however that, as explained in my telegram last week, I must again ask you to excuse me. The Westminster Election threw my literary and other work so much in arrears that I fear it is quite impossible for me to add to my public engagements for the next few months. I am sure you will understand my position and will, I trust, give me an opportunity of visiting the Union at some other time.

Stanley Baldwin to Winston S. Churchill

(*Churchill papers: 2/133*)

20 May 1924
Private

My dear Churchill,

I hope you will treat the article in the 'People' with the contempt it deserves and accept my assurances that the offensive remarks were never uttered by me.[1] I am looking forward to dining with you on Thursday and hope that our meeting may be productive of useful results.

There will probably be a very important division at 8.15 and we shall come post haste after it is taken.

Yours sincerely,
Stanley Baldwin

[1] On Sunday, May 17, the *People* had published an interview with Baldwin, in which the Conservative leader was said to have spoken disparagingly of 'this Churchill plotting'. He was also said to have stated that he had spoken at the Carlton Club in opposition to the Coalition in 1922 'because I was determined that never again should the cynical and sinister combination of the chief three for Coalition—Mr Lloyd George, Mr Churchill, and Lord Birkenhead—come together again.'

Sir John Lister-Kaye[1] to Winston S. Churchill

(*Churchill papers: 2/133*)

27 May 1924

Dear Winston,

Thank you very much for having written your letter to the 'Weekly Despatch' of Sunday May 25th, which I have read many times with the greatest interest.

What I particularly liked was your admirable restraint. Your clear recording of facts which are now historical could not be surpassed as the greatest possible indictment against Socialism.

One of the facts recorded in your letter will, I hope, sink deeply into the minds of all Conservatives and Liberals in Great Britain. Your words are:—

'It needed the double folly of the Conservative and Liberal failures to 'convert the Socialist minority, less than a third of the Chamber, into 'the Government of the country, and to carry in one wide sweep the chief 'opponent of Britain in her hour of need to the supreme direction of her 'Imperial affairs.'

This sentence of yours should be the keynote of your endeavour to overcome the double folly of the Conservatives and the Liberals and might be the foundation of a Union at least of determination on the part of those two great Parties together to fight and defeat Socialism in Great Britain and to destroy the Socialist hopes of forcing at a later date upon Great Britain the two measures lately brought forward by the Socialists—'Nationalisation of Mines', by which they propose to place the basic industry of Great Britain in the hands, and under the complete control of the Miners' Federation, representing say 1,200,000 miners—and, further, the proposal from the Minister of Health[2] to construct 2,500,000 houses at a cost to the already overburdened Income Tax Rate payer of Great Britain, of £600,000,000 destroying also the hope of ownership of their homes by the householder, so strong and noble an instinct to work, in the heart of every true Briton.

Two thirds of the voters at the last General Election voted Conservative and Liberal, and one third voted Socialist.

Would it not be possible to arrange that each of those Conservative and Liberal two thirds of the voters of Great Britain should receive a copy of

[1] John Pepys Lister-Kaye, 1853–1924. Succeeded his father as 3rd Baronet, 1871. Groom-in-Waiting to King Edward VII, 1908–10. His wife, Natica Yznaga del Valle, of New York, Louisiana and Cuba, was a close friend of Churchill's mother.

[2] John Wheatley, 1869–1930. The son of an Irish labourer, he worked as a miner from boyhood, and later, for ten years, served on the Glasgow Corporation. Labour MP for the Shettleston Division of Glasgow, 1922–30. Minister of Health, 1924.

your letter to the 'Weekly Despatch' dated May 25th 1924. Should this be carried out and if it were followed by Conservative and Liberal Propaganda would it not give those millions of voters, who have already recorded their votes against Socialism the opportunity of insisting that 'Conservative' or 'Liberal' their next vote must and shall be 'Anti-Socialist'.

My sincerest good wishes to you in your great endeavour,

Yours ever,[1]

Winston S. Churchill to Stanley Baldwin

(Churchill papers: 6/2)

30 May 1924
Private and Confidential

In view of the need of co-operation and of marshalling all available forces for the coming fight, and my own strong desire to assist in this work, I feel I ought to write to you about the situation at Westminster and my responsibilities towards it. There is no doubt in my mind that, had the electors been allowed a free choice at the recent Election, I should have been returned not only by a large majority of votes but by a substantial majority of Conservative votes; and if these votes were weighed as well as counted, the preponderance would have been more decisive. At least 7,000 Conservatives, including a great preponderance of the professional and business classes, gave me active and enthusiastic support. The existing Constitutional Association is not representative of the Conservative forces in the Division, but draws its strength almost entirely from two Wards, St Margaret's and St John's, and to a very large extent from the weaker elements in these Wards.

I do not here go into the complaints made about the manner in which the official Conservative candidate was chosen by the Association. But, as you know, it has led to the resignation of many of the principal officers of the Association, including the Chairman. As it now exists the Constitutional Association has no representative basis, and consists almost entirely of 'shilling a year' members of whom, I am informed, a large majority are women. It seems to me a very serious thing that the fortunes of this great

---

[1] This letter was sent to Churchill by F. E. Jones, Sir John Lister-Kaye's private secretary, who wrote in his covering note: 'The enclosed letter was dictated to me yesterday by Sir John Lister Kaye Bart. I took it to Sir John for his signature this morning but I am grieved to tell you that Sir John passed away quite suddenly this morning. He was practically quite well yesterday but the heart failed suddenly at 11 oc this morning. I thought you would like to have the letter as Sir John took great pleasure in writing it to you.'

and famous Constituency at the very heart of the Empire should be determined by a body which cannot honestly be said to be generally representative of the elements of Conservative strength which exist in the Division. I conceive that there is a very large public case which could be deployed upon this subject.

Since the Election great pressure has been exerted by my supporters to induce me to stand again for the Constituency at the General Election. Strong Committees have been formed in every Ward, representative of every class and comprising many leading citizens of both sexes. A Memorial, which will shortly be presented to the Central Office, has been signed by over 1,500 electors, a number sufficient to form an Association which would be far stronger in authority, influence and, I believe, numbers than the existing Constitutional Association. I am assured on all sides now that the electors are sure there would be no danger of the Socialists winning by splitting the vote, that I have only to form my own Organisation and set to work in the Constituency to secure my return to Parliament at the General Election whatever line the Central Office may be directed to take. I share this view; and it would be very agreeable to me to throw myself into the work of preparation, and so gratify the many friends and helpers who urge me to this course: and if I were thinking only of my own inclinations and of the local situation, I should not hesitate to do so. My only reason for troubling you in the matter is my desire, if possible, to avoid: (a) a conflict with the official Conservative Party whose victory at the polls I desire to help by every means; and (b) the absorption of my personal energies in a hard-fought local contest, when I might render more useful service generally throughout the country and particularly in London.

But if these considerations weigh with me and complicate my decision, they ought surely to have some value in your mind and in those of your friends. It is because I believe this is so that I write to ask you to consider whether you can suggest any course which will prevent the discord and dissipation of effort which otherwise seems to be inevitable. Is it not, for instance, possible for the Central Office, in view of all the circumstances, to insist upon the Westminster Constitutional Association being placed upon a basis properly representative of the Conservative strength in the Division, before promising or giving its support to the choice of that Association? There is of course the precedent of the English Universities Election a few years ago when, owing to a division of opinion and a rival Association being formed, your predecessor, Mr Bonar Law, declared that the Central Office could take no part and must remain neutral, and when in consequence Sir Martin Conway was elected. I should be quite content with this, and I believe that in such circumstances the contest would be so much in my favour that I could give a great deal of help in other Constituencies. More-over, if a really representative Association were formed, I should be perfectly ready to abide by its decision, provided Mr Nicholson kept a similar engagement. The decision of such a representative body would release me from my obligations to my friends and supporters. Either of these alternatives seem to me worthy of your consideration. There may be others which may suggest themselves to you. Anyhow after talking the matter over with several of your colleagues, I thought it would be a good thing to lay the issue frankly before you, in order that you may see what can be done to use all available forces to the best possible advantage. I am treating this as a private letter, but I am showing it confidentially to a few friends, and you are of course at liberty to use a similar discretion.

PS. The enclosures may interest you. There is no doubt that the journalist who behaved in such a treacherous and improper manner to my Election Agent is the same man at whose hands you suffered so unfairly in a recent interview. Captain Gillmore is at your service, if you should require any confirmation of the facts adduced.

Stanley Baldwin to Winston S. Churchill

(*Churchill papers: 2/133*)

2 June 1924

My dear Churchill,
     Your letter of the 30th only reached me this morning, as I left London early on Saturday for Worcester and I stayed in the country over Sunday.
     I will consider it very carefully in consultation with a few of my friends.

Yours sincerely,
Stanley Baldwin

Sir Samuel Hoare to Winston S. Churchill

(*Churchill papers: 2/133*)

17 June 1924
Private & Personal

Dear Winston,
     I made a point of seeing both Stanley Baldwin and Stanley Jackson yesterday with reference to your letter and Freddie Guest's letter. From my

talk with them it appears to be certain that there will be great trouble in Westminster if you stand there. I put it to them that if you stood down, we ought to find you some other constituency without any further delay. They both told me privately that they have a constituency in view, and I understand that Jackson has already asked you to see him on the subject. If I may make a suggestion, I would say that it will be better if you can carry on the negotiations yourself direct with Jackson and Baldwin. I am inclined to guess that Oliver Locker-Lampson's deputation did not assist the progress of a settlement.

As to Freddie Guest's letter I understand that in the majority of the seats which it mentions, no Conservative candidate has been adopted. The difficulty on our side is that in certain cases we have no pledge for the future. Would it not be possible for Guest to draw out some general undertaking rather on the lines of your own recent speeches. I am sure that this course would greatly expedite matters.

I need not say that I am always ready to discuss both these questions with you or Guest at any time, and that I am most anxious to assist in a satisfactory settlement.

Yours sincerely,
Samuel Hoare

Winston S. Churchill to Sir Samuel Hoare

(*Churchill papers: 2/133*)

18 June 1924   Chartwell Manor,[1]
Private & Personal   Westerham, Kent

My dear Hoare,

Many thanks for your letter. I am to see Jackson tomorrow (Thursday) and, of course, I shall be most anxious to find a way in which we can work together. I have, however, a distinct position in Westminster and a strong following which with a few months' work could, I am sure, be developed into a successful independent candidature and I cannot cut myself off from this for good reasons, both public and personal.

With regard to what you say about Freddie Guest's letter, I will, if you

---

[1] From 1924 to 1930 Churchill's 'Chartwell' notepaper was headed:

CHARTWELL MANOR

After 1930 the name of the house was given on his notepaper by the name it had come to be known, simply:

CHARTWELL

think it advisable, draw up on my return from Birmingham during the week
end, an outline of the arrangement which I think should be come to in the
Constituencies in question or such others as may subsequently be added to
the list. This will define the platform on which such candidates should stand.
What do you think of the name Liberal-Conservative? It is novel in England
but Sir John MacDonald[1] held power in Canada at the head of a Liberal-
Conservative party, and such a party name is now, I understand, in wide
use in Spain (a doubtful precedent!).

When I have made my draft perhaps you can arrange a meeting or lunch
where Guest and I and possibly Seely and Grigg (though this I must arrange
later) could meet three or four of your friends and discuss the draft in
committee. It would not take long.

Time is passing and though the sea is calm and the ship's company
lethargic we know that very dirty weather is approaching certainly soon.

Winston S. Churchill to Claude Lowther[2]

(*Churchill papers: 2/133*)

22 June 1924   Chartwell Manor

My dear Claude,

It was very kind indeed of you to have thought of me in connection with
the vacancy at Lewes. I am not at all anxious to fight any by-election now,
expense and worry of so many by-elections are perfectly intolerable.

The Central Office are, however, behaving in an extremely friendly
manner to me and I dare say something will be arranged in the future so
far as the General Election is concerned which will be agreeable both to me
and to my friends who, like you, have given me such warm-hearted support.

I should love to come some day to Hurstmonceux and paint your borders,
but at the present time I am completely absorbed in the toil and throes of
getting into this small house which we have been re-building with infinite
labour.

---

[1] Sir John MacDonald, Prime Minister of Canada from 1869 to 1872 and from 1878 until
his death in 1891 (his Party remained in power until 1896).

[2] Claude Lowther, 1872–1929. Conservative MP, 1900–6; 1910–18. Served with the
Imperial Yeomanry in South Africa, 1900. In August 1914, he raised a battalion of Sussex-
men, known as Lowther's Lambs, whom he commanded in France. In 1915 he raised three
more battalions. He lived at Hurstmonceux Castle, near Lewes, in Sussex; in August 1915
Churchill painted one of his earliest paintings at the castle, within sound of the artillery fire
on the western front.

Colonel Jackson to Winston S. Churchill
(*Churchill papers: 2/133*)

24 June 1924
Private

My dear Churchill,

I have just received the memorandum, for which many thanks. I will discuss your proposals with Baldwin & one or two others.

I am quite hopeful that we shall shortly devise a working arrangement, which *will work*—tho' the difficulties in the way are *not* small.

Yours ever,
F. Stanley Jackson

Brendan Bracken to Messrs Spearn and Rubens[1]
(*Churchill papers: 8/198*)

1 July 1924   Eyre and Spottiswoode Ltd

Dear Sirs,

The Montreal Standard on 14th June contained an article written by Mr Winston Churchill and reprinted without his permission. I enclose the cutting for your information.

Mr Churchill instructs me to ask you if you will proceed on his behalf against the Montreal Standard to recover damages for this gross literary piracy. He attaches great importance to this matter as it is impossible for him to arrange for the sale of his articles in America if his contracts are nullified by unscrupulous newspapers. I suggest that you should claim 1,000 dollars damages against the Montreal Standard and that they should be obliged to print a full apology in a prominent position in their newspaper.

This letter may be taken as official instructions from Mr Churchill.

Yours faithfully,

---

[1] New York attorneys, of 149 Broadway.

Gideon Murray[1] to Winston S. Churchill

(*Churchill papers: 2/134*)

2 July 1924
Private

My dear Churchill,

I read your article on Lloyd George in the Weekly Despatch and it has left me with much misgiving as the inference I draw, however erroneous it may be, is that you would be prepared to see him associated with you & with us in the future reassortment of parties.[2] I hope you will forgive the liberty I take in asking you whether I am right or not because personally I am not prepared at this or at any time in the future to support Lloyd George and there are many Unionists I know who think like myself and also will say so *without qualification* if the issue arises.

Many of us wish to see you definitely with us and when the time comes you can have our support if you want it; but if Lloyd George is with you anything may happen & it will create a discord which will most certainly affect your own position.

This is what I wanted to talk to you about.

My congratulations on your speech last night and your neat turning of the tables on Thomas![3]

Yours truly,
Gideon Murray

[1] Gideon Murray, 1877–1951. British Administrator, St Vincent, 1909–15; St Lucia, 1915–17. Unionist MP for St Rollox, Glasgow, 1918–22. Member of the Speaker's Parliamentary Devolution Conference, 1919–20. Succeeded his father as 2nd Viscount Elibank, 1927. President of the West India Committee, 1930–7.

[2] In his article, 'The Future of Lloyd George', published in the *Weekly Dispatch* on 29 June 1924, Churchill speculated on whether Lloyd George would lead the Liberal Party 'to the Right or to the Left?' The Liberal Party, he wrote, might be forced, as a result of Socialist policies, 'to make common cause with the Conservative Party in defence of the liberties and prosperity of Britain'. In such an event, he wrote, especially if there were 'a crisis of the first magnitude', then 'the British people would surely turn for help, whether against external or internal foes, to the dauntless, tireless, resourceful, and commanding statesman to whom they resorted in the terrible times of war; and we may be sure that in the future as in the past they would not turn for help in vain'.

[3] Churchill and J. H. Thomas had each spoken at a Dominion Day banquet on the evening of 1 July 1924. Thomas had spoken of his pride in the Empire, but went on to express his sorrow that the Empire was so often a tool of party politics. The Labour Government, he said, was trying to stop this practice. Churchill, speaking after Thomas, had agreed that the Empire was greater than Party, although both the Liberal and Conservative Parties were 'far astray' in their ideas of Empire. 'The Tories,' he said, 'had nearly lost the Empire in trying to keep it; and the Liberals had kept it in trying to throw it away.' As for the Labour Party, Churchill said, there was not yet sufficient material to judge them. But 'so long as they endeavoured to keep together the general mass interest of the Empire and safeguard its lasting value, they would deserve the respect of all his Majesty's subjects'.

Winston S. Churchill to Gideon Murray
(*Churchill papers: 2/134*)

3 July 1924   Chartwell Manor

My dear Murray,

You need not draw any inferences of the kind you apprehend from my article. Perhaps we may have the chance of a talk later.

Stanley Baldwin to Austen Chamberlain
(*Austen Chamberlain papers*)

21 July 1924

My dear Austen,

I got your letter just as I was leaving for the country on Friday night and was distressed to learn the impression that my Lowestoft speech had made upon you. Do read again carefully the last three paragraphs but one as reported in the Times.[1]

I followed exactly the line I indicated to Winston after dinner at Sam Hoare's. I purposely put it shortly as I wanted no doubt to exist as to the meaning.

I made our own policy—Imperial and Safeguarding—clear and indicated that that was the dividing line, and that those who agreed with us on these important questions could not be happy in their present environment.

For men with such views, our party offered the only home.

And I ended by inviting them on to our platform.

That invitation should now be accepted. Winston, in private, accepts our policy. It is up to him now to address a meeting and say so.

I cannot see any difference between us. Donald Maclean who spoke on Friday saw my meaning clearly enough.

The only papers which pretend to discover a difference are Beaverbrook's. I don't know what his game is but he is always trying to drive a wedge in between you and me, and so far as I am concerned, he will never succeed.

Yours very sincerely,
Stanley Baldwin

[1] Speaking at a mass meeting of the East Anglian Conservatives at Lowestoft, Baldwin contrasted the Conservative 'happy family' with Liberal disunity. Even Liberal supporters, he said, 'see in our party the largest united body of men and women in the country animated by as keen a desire as they have to improve the social conditions of our people, but sharing with them such aspirations as they have for the prosperity of our own trade. Up and down the country those men and women will come to us and they will be welcomed when they come.' Baldwin added: 'All those who feel that they can unconditionally adopt our policy and work loyally with us we will welcome as comrades-in-arms in the great fight that lies before us, and if any man is prepared to adopt our platform, let him come forward and say so like a man.'

August 1924

(*Churchill papers: 2/134*)

2 August 1924   The Durdans
Confidential   Epsom

My dear Winston,

I have been daily meaning to write to you for months, beginning with
the Westminster election, when I was in a fever of anxiety for your return:
I who have not taken the faintest interest in anything political for so many
years. You stood as an Independent Anti-Socialist, and in both capacities
you enlisted my warmest sympathy.

I am equally interested in you now. In fact it is the only point on which
I can feel interest. It is extraordinary that parties do not rally to the anti-
socialist cry, which I should have thought would be predominant in this
old country. But as things are, they seem to me to be allowed an easy course,
which will probably lead them to success.

Yours ever,
AR

Brendan Bracken to Winston S. Churchill
(*Churchill papers: 8/198*)

3 August 1924

Dear Churchill,

I enclose a cheque for £100. I have some more accounts to collect from
the Dominions which amount to about £50. Your article about Snowden
arrived in New York yesterday and the article about FE arrives there in ten
days. These will fetch 200 dollars each.

I want to remind you that the cheque I am now sending includes 200
dollars for the article on Ramsay MacDonald. Do you remember that you
told me at Sussex Square you felt you had been let down by McLures

Syndicate who declined to purchase the article after prolonged negotiations?
You said it was impossible to sell it & you gave quite a lot of abuse to
American newspaper representatives whom you described as 'men of straw'.
I told you I believed it could be sold but you were rather discouraging.

Our man in New York has now established a good little connection which
enables him to sell your articles for 200 to 250 dollars each after they had
been published in England weeks before. If you intend to write 52 articles
for the Weekly Dispatch in 1925 you will receive over £3,000 for the
American rights and an additional £500 for the British Empire syndications.

I have written this long letter to remind you of Clough's poem which you
quoted so much at Leicester but which you forget in this affair.[1]

Yours ever
Brendan Bracken

Dont answer this note.

Sir Harry Goschen[2] to Winston S. Churchill

(<i>Churchill papers: 7/1</i>)

5 August 1924

Dear Mr Winston Churchill,

Our Member for this, the West Essex Division, Sir L. Lyle[3] has intimated
to me that it is not his intention to stand for Parliament at the next Election—

---

[1] Arthur Hugh Clough's poem, 'Say Not the Struggle Naught Availeth'. One of Churchill's
favourite poems (he quoted it in a broadcast on 27 April 1941), it read:

Say not the struggle naught availeth,
  The labour and the wounds are vain,
The enemy faints not, nor faileth,
  And as things have been they remain.

For while the tired waves, vainly breaking,
  Seem here no painful inch to gain,
Far back, through creeks and inlets making,
  Comes silent, flooding in, the main.

If hopes were dupes, fears may be liars;
  It may be, in yon smoke conceal'd,
Your comrades chase e'en now the fliers,
  And, but for you, possess the field.

And not by eastern windows only,
  When daylight comes, comes in the light;
In front the sun climbs slow, how slowly!
  But westward, look, the land is bright!

[2] Harry William Henry Neville Goschen, 1865–1945. Educated at Eton. A Director of the
Agriculture Mortgage Co-operative Ltd and of the Atlas Assurance Company. OBE, 1918.
Prime Warden of the Goldsmiths Company, 1919–20. Chairman of the National Provincial
Bank. Knighted, 1920. Created Baronet, 1927.

[3] Charles Ernest Leonard Lyle, 1882–1954. Educated at Harrow and Trinity Hall,
Cambridge. Chairman, later President, of Tate & Lyle Ltd, Sugar Refiners. Vice-President
of the Lawn Tennis Association (having represented England at Lawn Tennis). Conservative
MP for Stratford, East Ham, 1918–22; for Epping, 1923–4. Parliamentary Private Secretary
to the Food Controller, 1920–1. Knighted, 1923. Created Baronet, 1932. Subsequently
Chairman of the East Dorset Conservative Association, and Conservative MP for Bournemouth, 1940–5. Created Baron, 1945.

& under these circumstances I should be very glad to recommend your name to the Executive Committee of this Conserv & Unionist Association, of which I happen to be Chairman, as their Candidate at the next Election.

Should this idea appeal to you, I presume I might tell them that you would stand as a supporter of the Conservative Party, their leaders & Policy, & especially as regards Ireland the Policy they have outlined in a publication called 'Looking Ahead' which has just been issued.

This constituency has returned a Conservative Member for many years & if my suggestion coincides in any way with your views I shall be pleased to send you any further particulars with regard to the constituency.

I remain, yours truly
W. H. Goschen

Winston S. Churchill to Lord Balfour

(*Churchill papers: 2/134*)

7 August 1924 Chartwell Manor

I have several times mentioned to you the letter which FE wrote you on your return from Washington in the first half of 1922, for the purpose of reassuring you upon the question of the interpretation to be placed on Article XII of the Irish Treaty. I do not know whether you have had any search made among your papers, and if so, with what result. The letter now becomes of very considerable importance. I remember it well. It set forth massively the argument that the Article could only mean minor readjustments of boundary and not redistribution of territory. It would therefore show exactly what was in the minds of the British Ministers at the time. I do not need to point out the use of such a document in the discussions to which we are now condemned. I have sent for my Colonial Office papers of 1922, and it is possible that I have a copy of this letter among them. It might well be in my dossier for the conduct of the Bill in the House of Commons. Could you at the same time (if you have not already done so) ask your private secretary to search your archives of that time? It would be within a month of your return from Washington.

Winston S. Churchill to Sir Harry Goschen

(*Churchill papers: 7/1*)

11 August 1924   Chartwell Manor
Strictly confidential

It is very kind of you to write to me with such a fine offer. I do not think there would be any difficulty so far as policy is concerned. I intend to do my utmost to secure a victory for the Conservative and Anti-Socialist forces at the General Election, and the programme now declared by the leaders of the Conservative Party has my full concurrence.

I have not read the publication 'Looking Forward', so I do not know what particular reference is made to Ireland in it. I think it will be necessary to be very prudent and careful in dealing with this boundary question. There are so many enemies at work at the present time, and the powers of evil are so strong that great wariness is required, especially in choosing the battle ground for the next election. We certainly do not want to make the Socialists and Anti-Imperialist Radicals a present of such a cry as a breach of the Irish Treaty. My position is similar to that of Mr Austen Chamberlain and Lord Birkenhead in that I am a signatory of the Treaty, and naturally I could not do anything which would be a breach of solemn undertakings entered into.

There is of course no question but that the intention of the British signatories of the Treaty, clearly and publicly made known at the time to the Irish signatories, was that the Boundary Commission should deal, as its name implies, with a readjustment of boundaries and not with a wholesale redistribution of territory. I am advised on high authority that that is the only natural reading of the Article. Considering that a majority of the Commission decides and that two out of the three members would be nominated either by the Imperial Government or by the Imperial Government and the Northern Government, I cannot believe there is very great risk of a wrong view being taken by the Commission. However, it is of the utmost consequence to reassure Ulster, and it is in that direction that a solution must be sought. Of course far better than any Commission would be an arrangement between Craig and Cosgrave,[1] such as was definitely provided for by the agreement entered into by Craig and Collins[2] while I was at the Colonial

---

[1] William Thomas Cosgrave, 1880–1965. Member of the Dublin Corporation, 1909–22; Alderman, 1920–2. Imprisoned after the Easter rising, 1916. Treasurer of Sinn Fein. Sinn Fein MP, 1917–22. Minister of Local Government in the Dail Cabinet, 1919–21. Chairman of the Provisional Government, 1921–2. President of the Irish Free State, 1922–32. Also Minister of Finance, 1922–3, and Minister of Defence, 1934.

[2] Michael Collins, 1890–1922. Born in County Cork, the son of a Catholic farmer. Worked first as a Post Office employee, then as a bank clerk in London, 1906–16. Took part in the

Office early in 1922. I am not without hopes that something like this may be arranged. The difficulty is that while Cosgrave could take anything however unfavourable to the Free State from a Commission set up under the Treaty, he would be violently attacked even if he got a more favourable settlement if that were arrived at on his personal responsibility.

I can hardly conceive that this question will be a cause of a General Election in Great Britain, and I trust that the interval which has now happily been secured may enable some arrangement to be arrived at. It is so important to all the interests of the British Empire that a decisive victory should be won over the Socialists at the next appeal, that the greatest care and thought ought to be given in choosing the issues and marshalling the forces.

On the question of my contesting the West Essex Division, I should like to have an opportunity of communicating with Colonel Jackson. He has one or two seats in view in or close to London, and has promised to bring matters to a head as soon as possible. I am anxious to take a Constituency near the Metropolis, because if I had a fairly safe seat there, I could throw myself into the fight against the Socialists throughout London and help in the general campaign. I expect Colonel Jackson will take a little holiday now, but if you will allow me to communicate with him and then write to you again when I have his reply, I shall be very grateful.

With many thanks for your most kind and complimentary proposal, believe me

Yours very truly,
Winston S. Churchill

Winston S. Churchill to Colonel Jackson
(*Churchill papers: 2/134*)

14 August 1924   Chartwell Manor

I send you a letter I have received from Goschen. You mentioned this Constituency and Goschen's favourable attitude to me when we last talked. I expect you have been taking a short and well-earned holiday, but I hope when it is over you will let me know what progress you have made in your Richmond plan. Time is slipping away, and nothing is settled. I thought the

---

Easter rebellion in Dublin, 1916. Imprisoned for eight months, 1916. Adjutant-General of the Irish Republican Army, 1917–18. Imprisoned for a second time, 1918. Minister of Home Affairs, and Finance Minister, in the Sinn Fein Government, 1919–21. One of the Delegates who negotiated the Irish Treaty with Britain, 1921–2. Chairman of the Provisional Free State Government, and Minister of Finance, 1922. Commanded the Irish Free State army.

action of the Government in signing this farcical Russian Treaty the first
definite indication I have seen of their expectation of an early Election.
Obviously they meant to rally their own crowd and not be stultified by
charges that they had abandoned their Russian policy under which they
made so much last year. The fight may well be upon us in October or
November. I trust we shall not be out-manoeuvred over the Irish question.
I think your remarks on the subject both sensible and courageous.[1] It would
be a disastrous issue.

Winston S. Churchill to Sir Harry Goschen

(Churchill papers: 7/1)

15 August 1924   Chartwell Manor

My dear Sir Harry Goschen,

I have written to Jackson, and will let you know what his answer is.

On the Irish question I am glad to tell you that I have succeeded in
running to earth a letter which Birkenhead wrote to Lord Balfour in
February 1922, which shows quite clearly the views of the signatories of the
Treaty—that article 12 dealt with a mere readjustment of boundary and not
in any way with a wholesale redistribution of territory. This letter, I hope,
will be published in the next week or so, and I trust it may afford a basis
upon which British public opinion may take a decided stand. I feel bound
to carry out strictly, so far as I am concerned, what we meant at the time,
and what we said we meant at the time. But I certainly do not feel bound
to take such steps to facilitate the obtrusion of a policy which goes far beyond
what we settled with the Irish people. The whole matter, however, requires
the most prudent handling. Anything more disastrous than to have an
Election where the Conservative Party would be accused of Treaty breaking,
tearing up scraps of paper, etc, cannot be imagined. We should be playing
into the hands of the foes of the British Empire all along the line. These are
not the times when the Constitutional forces can afford to make a mistake.

Perhaps you will wait until the letter to Lord Balfour is published before
communicating with Baldwin. I am on quite good terms with him, and
think of writing to him myself upon the Irish question.

[1] Speaking at Hull on 7 August 1924, Colonel Jackson had advocated the settlement of the
Irish Boundary question by judicial tribunal, rather than by political conflict at the General
Election, and he expressed his belief that both North and South would accept the findings of
such a tribunal.

Colonel Jackson to Winston S. Churchill

(*Churchill papers: 7/1*)

19 August 1924   Scotland
Private & Confidential

My dear Churchill,

Your letter of the 14th, enclosing one you have received from Sir Harry Goschen, has just reached me here—Goschen consulted us as regards asking you to stand for Epping & I said, tho' I doubted your accepting, I hoped he would put the invitation forward—we look upon the seat as a good one & I should think *you* would have no difficulty there—I believe you would prefer to be nearer London. As regards Richmond, I approached the sitting member—Becker[1]—& I am sorry to say, I found him very obstinate—he is a difficult, & I fear, unreliable fellow. They want to be rid of him & have told him so, & this has made him worse.

I am not now very hopeful of Richmond for you.

Have you done anything further with Erskine? I wish we could fix this seat up for you—but I am afraid E's price is prohibitive! I realise that time is slipping by & we cannot afford to wait much longer.

I shall be up here until Sept 6 but I will keep in touch with you by letter.

You do not say in your letter if Epping appeals to you.

When I was in London last week I was speaking to the Principal Agent[2] about fixing *you* up, & I am expecting to hear from him—when I do so, I will send you any suggestions I may have to make. You may depend on me to 'push on' as well as I can.

I am glad to think that you approved of what I said in Hull on the Irish situation. I *do* hope we shall find a way out by agreement.

I expect to hear from Baldwin tomorrow what was the result of his visit to James C.

Yours sincerely
F. Stanley Jackson

[1] H. T. A. Becker, Independent Conservative MP for Richmond, 1922–3; Conservative MP, 1923–4. In 1922 Becker was supported by the Anti-Waste League. At the General Election of 1924 Richmond was held by another Conservative, Sir N. J. Moore.

[2] Herbert Edwin Blain, 1870–1942. Principal Traffic Assistant, Liverpool Corporation Tramways, 1903. President of the Municipal Tramways Association, 1910–11. Operating Manager, London Underground Railways. Member of Council, Institute of Transport. Awarded the CBE, 1920, for war work, having helped in providing War Motor Transport and Personnel, in training drivers for the Army Services Corps, and in providing Air Raid Shelter facilities. Principal Agent, Unionist Central Office, 1924–7. Knighted, 1925.

Winston S. Churchill to Clementine Churchill

(*Spencer-Churchill papers*)

19 August 1924   Chartwell Manor

My darling,

You know my idle habits punctuated by toil at articles and book. Your delightful letter received this morning makes me ashamed not to have written.

Since you left we have had visitors, to wit, Freddie Guest, LG and Keyes. Each has stayed one night in Henry VIII. I had a long and very satisfactory talk with LG, and we were closer together politically than we have been since he took part in putting in the Socialists. I am in active correspondence with the Unionist leaders on the subject of the FE letter. LG was all for its being published. I think it will make a very considerable difference, and I very much hope this difficulty is not going to become too gravely embarrassing.

My lunch with Rosebery was delightful. We had two hours, to me most pleasant conversation, and evidently he found it agreeable too for I got a letter from him the next day begging me to go back again one day this week. I am proposing to him to let me take Randolph too. He is thoroughly *au fait*, and in very much better health than he was two years ago. He wants us to stay with him for the Edinburgh meeting (at Dalmeny), and perhaps on the whole it would be as well to have a Liberal headquarters, especially as it is Liberal Imperialist.

Everyone is working frantically at your room. The whitewashers, the oakstainers, the carpenters and the plasterers are hard at work from morn till night. I hope that all will be to your liking when you return. They are allowing nothing to stand in the way of this.

Work on the dam is progressing. Owing to the fact that the months have got mixed and apparently we are having April instead of August, the water has been rising steadily. We have this evening seven feet. It will be completely finished by next Tuesday, or eight weeks from its initiation. I am at it all day long and every day. You will see a great transformation when you come back.

Meanwhile the old lake is practically dry. There is an average of a foot of mud, and I am going to go at it hard with my railway to clear it out. Thompson and I have been wallowing in the most filthy black mud you ever saw, with the vilest odour, getting the beastly stuff to drain away. The moor hens and dab chicks have migrated in a body to the new lake and taken up their quarters in the bushes at the upper end. There are about eleven of them there now.

Archie has returned to London with Marigold.[1] Her arm is broken quite

[1] Marigold Forbes, daughter of Colonel J. S. Forbes. She married Sir Archibald Sinclair in 1918.

near the shoulder joint, and it will be practically impossible to make a complete cure. Luckily it is the left arm, which will be always a little stiff. It will not be necessary to operate. Archie is coming down here to spend Thursday night.

A formal offer has arrived from Mr Blain, the head Conservative Agent, of the West Essex Division. I am getting him down here to lunch. Sir Roger Keyes lived in that division, and tells me that there is a very favourable disposition among the Conservative notables. It looks one of the safest seats in the country. But you can never tell.

Rosie turned up one afternoon to spy out the land, and we are all bidden to her palace any time we like to go. It will take a great deal to get me away from Chartwell.

Rosebery has just wired saying that he will be delighted to 'welcome the fourth generation'.

I have arranged with Lord Stevenson that we all visit Wembley on Wedy 27. The children are vy keen.

Have you heard from Lady Carson.[1] It occurs to me she may have written to *you*, as I agreed to Thursday night for our visit to them, but have heard nothing more.

My beloved—it will be jolly having you back on Monday. The house seems vy empty without you. With tender love,

Your devoted,
W

PS. The 9 elder swine are sold for £31. They have eaten less than £1 a week for 18 weeks of life—so there is a profit of £13. Not bad on so small a capital. WSC

Winston S. Churchill to Clementine Churchill
(Spencer-Churchill papers)

22 August 1924 Chartwell Manor

My darling,

I took Randolph over to the Durdans, and we had another very pleasant lunch with Lord Rosebery. He took the trouble to find in his library a most

---

[1] Ruby Frewen, daughter of Colonel Stephen Frewen. She married Lord Carson (as his second wife) in 1914. They lived at 5 Eaton Place, London, and Cleve Court, Minster-in-Thanet, near Ramsgate, Kent, only a short drive from Chartwell. Carson died in 1935, as did his wife.

interesting book called 'Paradoxes and Puzzles' by Paget, published some forty-five years ago, in which there is the most effective vindication of the Duke of Marlborough in regard to the Brest Expedition charge that I have yet seen. Paget ridicules the accuracy of Macaulay, and convicts him repeatedly not merely of mistakes but of deliberate misrepresentations of facts etc. This has turned my mind very seriously to the great literary project which so many people are inclined to saddle me with.

I am sorry to say that poor Bateman, the groom, has become very seriously ill. It is probable that he has sleeping sickness. He has been removed to the Isolation Hospital at Hever, and is not expected to live. The origin and character of this new disease are obscure, but Dr Ward, Junior,[1] who is dealing with the case, tells me that it occurs scattered about at considerable intervals and that there is no question of contagion or of any known principle of infection though it is classified as infectious. None of us have been in contact with Bateman, except in the open air riding or mounting the ponies. It is almost certain that he could not have contracted it or originated it in this area, for he only came here a fortnight ago from Roehampton. I have been doing all that was necessary and possible for his wife and household.— 23rd. Bateman is dead. The cause is sleeping sickness. It may be an abscess in the brain following the one he had on the lungs. But this is not vy likely. The Doctor says there are no preventatives wh need or can be taken.

Everything is progressing in your room; and the little room with the hot chimney is also papered and finished. The oak stainers are busy all over the house, and have finished the roof of the hall. They are fixing the new mantelpiece. I do not know whether it will be ready by Monday.

There are 7 feet 6 inches of water in the dam, and it is rising steadily two or three inches each twenty-four hours. However, I regret to say that two or three leaks have made their appearance and will require some additional concrete in the shape of buttresses. They do not amount to much.

We are having a great deal of rain in showers, but sunshine in between.

Archie spent last night here and made himself agreeable. He and Marigold would like to come here Sunday week, that is to say the weekend after your return. How does this fit in with Jack and Goonie? If they will not be with us then, it would be nice to entertain the others. Send me a telegram on receipt of this.

We are all looking forward much to your return on Monday.

[1] Kenneth Langhorne Stanley Ward, son of Dr Stanley Edward Ward. Dr Ward junior had received his medical degree at Edinburgh in 1917. A former Surgeon Royal Navy, he was Medical Officer at the Infant Welfare Centre, Sandridge, near St Albans, and Assistant Medical Officer at the Edenbridge Cottage Hospital, four miles from Chartwell. Earlier he had been Resident Medical Officer at St Mary's Hospital for Women and Children at Plaistow.

My dearest—it will be a comfort to have you back again. I do hope you have enjoyed yourself. My fondest love—Your devoted

W

[sketch of pig]

Stanley Baldwin to Winston S. Churchill
(*Churchill papers: 2/134*)

22 August 1924

My dear Churchill,

Thank you for sending me a copy of that exceedingly interesting letter: I think its publication would be opportune.

I have been putting in a fortnight working round my constituency (including a visit to Belfast!) and am off to Aix tomorrow. I want a rest.

I hope you like your new home: I was staying in your neighbourhood in the summer, at Chevening and at Squerryes.[1]

Yours very sincerely
Stanley Baldwin

Brendan Bracken to Winston S. Churchill
(*Churchill papers: 8/198*)

25 August 1924   Eyre and Spottiswoode Ltd

Dear Churchill,

I heard from our lawyers in New York while I was in Scotland that the Montreal Standard have offered to apologise very humbly for their action in pirating your article. An apology from a pirate is not worth much, so I have told our lawyers to go hard for damages. I suggested 2,000 dollars as appropriate compensation to you. If the Montreal Standard compromise by offering half I shall accept if you approve. They might pay the sum we claim but I do not think they would do so unless we brought them into court.

The following sums are owing to you. £100 for American rights of the articles sold up to the present. £14 from Le Petit Parisien. £30 from the

[1] Chevening, the home of the 7th Earl of Stanhope; and Squerryes, the home of Lieutenant-Colonel Charles Warde, Lord of the Manor of Westerham, and patron of the livings of Westerham and Crockham Hill.

Times of India. I expect the American account to be paid this week. £1 has just been received from Malay. There are one or two other small sales in far away places of which I have not yet had particulars.

Yours ever,
Brendan Bracken

Winston S. Churchill to Sir Roger Keyes

(*Keyes papers*)

25 August 1924   Chartwell Manor
Private

My dear Keyes,

I am deeply grateful to you for the books. I sat up till half past one devouring them.

This is the first time I have ever read the story of the Battle of Jutland. I had only the vaguest idea of what had taken place. The Staff Book is admirable in its lucidity and is written with great and restrained power. The published report, which I also have, suffered very much from its Bowdlerisation, but nevertheless, as you said, 'It is all there.' The article in the Naval Magazine is obviously by the same pen or one of the same pens, and is also a most powerful commentary.

I don't think much of Major Alexander, OBE.[1] A Major with the OBE would also *prima facie* excite my suspicions. But this fellow's work reeks of spiteful ignorance, and I notice that his judgment leads him to condemn both your two 'Hoods' and Gallipoli.

I am shaken in my view as to the small consequences which would have resulted from a complete victory at Jutland. I think there is no doubt we could have entered the Baltic with consequences on Russia which no man can measure at the end of 1916 and in 1917. The series of diagrams really tell the tale. One feels as one studies them that a shrinking hand and anxious doubting spirit guided the British Fleet that melancholy day and night. The *gravamen* was the night!

Would you mind very kindly looking at the file on Jellicoe's letter of October 1914 to the Admiralty, and letting me know what Minutes it contains? My recollection is that I simply affixed my initials to the draft prepared under the direction of the First Sea Lord with the advice of

---

[1] Arthur Charles Bridgeman Alexander, born 1873. 2nd Lieutenant, 1898; Captain, 1899; invalided and retired on pension, 1912. General Staff Officer, Bermuda Command, 1915–19. Retired, 1919. In September 1923 he published *Jutland: A Plea for a Naval General Staff.*

AKW.[1] There would be no objection to my seeing the file, as it comes in my own period of office and the Admiralty have already furnished me with a copy of everything in which I was concerned. So if this is any trouble, I can write to Murray[2] about it.

It was very nice seeing you here. We must foregather again when you come South. You will find me then with a perfectly clear view on all the issues great and small involved in Jutland.

I saw the Zeebrugge show at Wembley today. It was stirring. Randolph was thrilled.

With all good wishes,
yours vy sincerely,
Winston S. Churchill

Winston S. Churchill to Sir Harry Goschen

(*Churchill papers: 7/1*)

28 August 1924   Chartwell Manor
Private and Confidential

My dear Goschen,

You may be quite sure that I would not have kept you so long without an answer if I was not considering most seriously the exceedingly important and complimentary proposal which you have made to me. My difficulty is that everybody whom I should consult is away on holidays. Jackson will not be back for nearly a fortnight. Blain has just gone away. And although I have communicated with both of them, I have not been able to have that personal talk which is indispensable before I take a final decision. There has been another project in hand on which Jackson has been very keen, but which now must be brought to a head one way or the other in the course of the next ten days. I could undertake to give you a definite answer not later than September 10 or 12, if you could keep the position open for so long.

The Irish issue continues to occupy my thoughts. I am sure that it would be possible to expel the Socialists from power during October on the Russian

---

[1] Arthur Knyvet Wilson, 1842–1921. Entered Navy, 1855. Fought in the Crimean War. Awarded the VC in 1884 during the Sudan Campaign. Commander-in-Chief of the Home and Channel Fleets, 1901–7. Knighted, 1902. Admiral of the Fleet, 1907. First Sea Lord, 1910–11. Worked at the Admiralty without any formal post, October 1914–June 1918. He declined a peerage on his retirement.

[2] Oswyn Alexander Ruthven Murray, 1873–1936. Entered the Admiralty (Secretary's Department), 1897. Assistant Secretary, 1911–17. Knighted, 1917. Permanent Secretary from 1917 until his death.

Treaty, and that quite an important number of Liberals would be with us on that question in the fight that would ensue. This would be an excellent issue on which to marshal the Constitutional forces for what we must all realise may be a very critical Election for the British Empire. I am so anxious that the break should come on that, and not on some question where we shall be accused of trying to wriggle out of a Treaty obligation.

I am just off to stay with Lord Carson, and Balfour is coming there tomorrow in order to discuss the publication of the letter about which I wrote you, and generally to take stock of the future.

Could you not come to see me here before you go on your holiday? I am only an hour from London in a motor car, and I should so much like to give you lunch or dinner on Saturday, Sunday or Monday. There are a number of things that can be discussed in conversation, which take too long to put in a letter.

Pray excuse my not signing this letter myself, as I have to leave immediately.

Yours sincerely,

Winston S. Churchill to Lord Carson

(*Churchill papers: 2/134*)

30 August 1924   Chartwell Manor

I spoke to LG on the telephone and arranged to go and dine with him at Churt tomorrow (Sunday) night.

He told me that he does not speak until the 10th, so that our letter published on the 8th will be most opportune. He reiterated his intention to endorse every word of it in the strongest terms. He also spoke to me about the Russian Treaty, hoping that any move from the Unionist Benches will be couched in terms, and entrusted to someone not obnoxious to the Liberal view. They are officially opposing the Treaty.

The 'Daily News' had a very important criticism both in its Leader and in its City article of yesterday.[1] I really think this issue might be made decisive if handled with skilful vigour.

[1] Both articles dealt with the Russian treaty. The leading article maintained that: 'It is no business of ours either to support or to oppose communism in Russia; we have no intention—or we ought to have no intention—of imposing our economic beliefs upon the Soviets. But we have still less intention of allowing the Soviets to impose their creed upon us, and if this is the irreducible condition of agreement, it is clear for the time being agreement is not possible.' The city article was headlined 'A One-sided Treaty' and declared: 'A constructive agreement with Russia is needed. But these documents would simply enable the bankrupt Communist rulers of the country to cover up their universal failure in the economic sphere.'

We enjoyed ourselves so much during our visit to you, and I hope and believe our talk may bear fruit.

Winston S. Churchill to Sir Robert Horne
(*Churchill papers: 2/134*)

30 August 1924   Chartwell Manor

I see in the press cuttings a good deal of comment about our meeting and I am sure there will be a great deal of interest in it when the time comes.

I went to stay with Carson a few days ago and met AJB there. He is quite willing to take the Chair. As I had not received any invitation from him to stay at Whittingehame I accepted an invitation to stay with Rosebery for the night of the meeting. I shall probably travel North the night before. My wife will be with me and I will go on to stay with AJB the night after the meeting. I hope you will still be there.

I have succeeded in getting a very important letter from FE to AJB unearthed. This letter shows very clearly our views at the time of the Irish Treaty of the interpretation of Clause 12. Carson and Craig were delighted with it. So was LG. It is to be published on September 8 and LG is going to associate himself with it in his speech on the 10th.

I am really hopeful after all I have heard that we may succeed in preventing the Irish Treaty from becoming an issue at the election. It would only divide friends and unite enemies. The Russian issue is the one, and with good handling might well be decisive.

Do not, I pray you, stress unnecessarily the Irish question in any speeches you may have to make before we meet. I have every hope all will go well.

Winston S. Churchill to Sir Raymond Greene[1]
(*Churchill papers: 2/134*)

30 August 1924   Chartwell Manor

I promised to let you know about North Hackney. I feel I cannot any longer overcloud your plans. Other propositions have been made to me which obviate the necessity of my fighting a *sitting* Liberal, and other prospects which are equally good.[2]

[1] Walter Raymond Greene, 1869–1947. Conservative MP for Chesterton, 1895–1906. On active service in South Africa, 1899–1900, and on the western front, 1914–18. Lieutenant-Colonel, 1915. DSO, 1916. Conservative MP for North Hackney, 1910–23. Succeeded his father as 2nd Baronet, 1920.

[2] During August 1924 Churchill also turned down an invitation to stand as official Conservative candidate for East Islington (which had been won by the Liberals in 1923).

Will you please convey to your Committee and their Secretary my most sincere thanks for their kindness in thinking of me in this connection, and assure them how warmly I appreciate their thought.[1]

Lionel Curtis[2] to Winston S. Churchill

(*Churchill papers: 2/134*)

31 August 1924

My dear Winston,

Many thanks for your letter of the 26th. When I saw the announcement that you were to speak on the same platform as Horne, I mournfully inferred that you had accepted his views on the Boundary question which will I believe hang like a millstone round the neck of the Conservative Party. I am somewhat relieved to hear that you have no present intention of committing yourself on this particular subject to his views. But I should be still more relieved if you were prepared to commit yourself to the view which I am sure you would have taken if you had remained in office and responsible for Irish Policy at this time.

In making up your mind I ask you to take no other criterion than this 'what do British interests demand'. Unless the Commission is constituted the world at large including an overwhelming mass of opinion in the Dominions will say that we have failed to give effect to the spirit of the Treaty. We cannot evade this by taking advantage of a slip in draughtsmanship, described as a slip by the Judicial Committee. The Republicans have taken their stand on the forecast that England as in the Treaty of Limerick and as in the Act of Union evaded the compact. At one blow we shall destroy all the work for which you more than anyone were responsible in creating the Free State. The breakdown of the Treaty means for sure and certain war with Ireland, if that breakdown is really attributable to a failure of faith on our part. It will be a war which cannot be terminated by another Treaty

---

[1] J. H. Harris, the Liberal MP for North Hackney, had defeated Sir Raymond Greene at the 1923 Election. Harris was himself defeated by the Conservative candidate in the election of 1924, after which the seat was held by the Conservatives until won by Labour in 1945.

[2] Lionel George Curtis, 1872–1955. Served in the South African War as a Private, 1899. Secretary to Sir Alfred Milner in South Africa, 1900. Town Clerk, Johannesburg, 1902–3. Assistant Colonial Secretary, Transvaal, 1903–9. Editor of the *Round Table*, 1909. Professor of Colonial History at Oxford, 1912. Member of the British League of Nations Section at the Paris Peace Conference, 1919. Secretary to the British Delegation at the Irish Conference in London, 1921. Colonial Office Adviser on Irish Affairs, 1921–4. Author of several books and numerous pamphlets on Commonwealth affairs and theory. Companion of Honour, 1949.

because no one in Ireland will ever trust us again. It is a war which can only end by conquest followed by armed occupation which every year will become not less but more difficult to relax. British faith in this matter to be of any use must be like the honour to Caesar's wife, beyond question. I beg you to think out the practical consequences of the policy voiced by Horne. They lead straight over a precipice from the bottom of which there is no return. If the Conservatives return to power on that policy God help them for they will return with an endless Irish war on their hands with the humiliating alternative advocated by the N Whig and the Morning Post of acknowledging an Irish Republic.

Of course you only got the Bill through by refusing to alter a comma but I don't think you dispute the reason I gave in my last letter. At that moment to have re-opened negotiations on the Treaty, would have re-opened negotiations on the Oath, and have thrown the game into De Valera's[1] hands. The fact remains that when the Free State were at open war with the Republicans we did get them to agree to alter the Treaty in the matter of the Council of Ireland on the ground openly stated by you that the effect of this provision had not been fully foreseen—was in fact what the Judicial Committee have since called a casus improvisus. The interpretation of the reference to the Commission was foreseen and was deliberately left to the Commission for their own interpretation.

I am sure that if the oversight had been pointed out in Parliament you would have resisted amendment. But I am equally sure that if it had been pointed out in the Irish Conference all the British Delegates would have agreed to make the necessary provision against it.

When you talk about coercing Ulster, is it not going rather far to apply coercion to a revision of the boundary by arbitration? Consider the case of many thousands of Protestant Conventers in Donegal Cavan and Monaghan, who were placed in Southern Ireland against their expressed will and at the dictate of those who had signed the Covenant with them in the six counties? It is one of the most significant features of the Irish situation that no course is possible, inaction as well as action which does not expose its authors to a charge of violating pledges. In these circumstances the only possible principle is to select the clearest and most binding pledges and beyond question these

[1] Eamon De Valera, 1882–1975. A leading figure in the Easter Rebellion, Dublin, 1916. Sentenced to death; sentence commuted to life penal servitude on account of his American birth. Released under the general amnesty, June 1917. President of the Sinn Fein, 1917–26. Elected to Parliament as a Sinn Fein MP, 1918. Imprisoned, 1918; escaped from Lincoln Jail, February 1919. 'President' of the Irish Republic, 1919–22. Rejected the Irish Treaty and fought against the Free State Army, 1922–3. Leader of the Opposition in the Free State Parliament, 1927–32. Minister of External Affairs, 1932–48. Head of the Government of Eire (Taoiseach), 1937–48, 1941–4 and 1957–9. President of the Republic of Ireland, 1959–73.

are contained in a Treaty most fully discussed and thrice ratified by Parliament.

But if the revision of the Boundary by Arbitration is coercion, it is too late for you at any rate to condemn it on that ground. LG's letter (misdated 5th Dec 1921) written on behalf of all the British Signatories to Craig, and printed and laid before Parliament with the Treaty must be held in mind. After setting out the two alternatives for N Ireland under the Treaty, LG says, that if she opts out, 'we should feel unable to defend the existing boundary, which *must be subject to revision* on one side and the other by a Boundary Commission under the terms of the Instrument'. Clearly it had never crossed your minds that owing to a flaw in the terms of the Instrument there might be no boundary commission if N Ireland opted out.

I will do my best to get you copies of the Hansard Debates, and will indeed undertake to do so, because in the public interest it is vital that one in your position should be able to refresh his memory. But I am experiencing some difficulty in being allowed to have a copy myself to take to Oxford to study during December. . . .

Bear with me for troubling you with such voluminous letters. The two finest pages in your career are those at the Admiralty which saved the country in the late war, and after it at the Colonial Office where you surmounted, as hardly any one else could have done the incredible difficulties of carrying the Treaty into effect. For you of all men to forget what you had done and turn to smashing your own handiwork would break my heart.

Yours very sincerely,
L. Curtis

September 1924

Winston S. Churchill to Lord Balfour

(Balfour papers)

1 September 1924   Chartwell Manor
Private & Confidential

My dear Arthur,

I send you a note, a duplicate of which I am sending to Carson, of my discussion with LG. If there is anything further that occurs to you that I can do, please let me know.

I propose to get into touch, and keep in touch, with everybody concerned from the middle of September onwards. Everything must be kept as confidential as possible. But the situation is so obviously critical that Sunday newspaper forecasts have already appeared, stating that the Conservatives are looking forward to defeating the Government on the Russian issue. I think the significance of this matter is of course realised in all quarters. It will be impossible to avoid public discussion, and I do not think that it will do any harm.

Would you very kindly tell your servants at Carlton Gardens that my secretary, Miss Fisher,[1] is coming there on Sunday morning at about nine o'clock to distribute to the Press Association and the Central News certain correspondence which you are sending to the Press. They might otherwise not understand her visit and action.

I altered the hour & day as the result of a talk with Geoffrey Dawson.

Yours always
Winston S. Churchill

---

[1] Lettice Fisher. Churchill's secretary and stenographer, 1923–9. She remained with Churchill while he was Chancellor of the Exchequer, holding the rank of Junior Administrative Assistant at the Treasury, 1924–9.

Winston S. Churchill to Lord Balfour and Lord Carson

(*Balfour papers*)

1 September 1924
Secret

I visited LG at Churt on Sunday. I informed him of the upshot of our talk, carefully avoiding compromising Craig. But I made it clear that in your view everything should be done to prevent the Ulster issue disturbing the general marshalling of forces for the Election. I mentioned the possibility that Carson might conceivably act for Ulster in the event of Craig finally deciding that a new situation was created by the publication of the FE–Balfour letter. LG was very much pleased at all this. He stated that when he speaks on the 10th he will most strongly endorse the FE–Balfour letter and declare that that, and that only, was what he and his Government intended, and that that is what they believed is the law. He offered to show me beforehand the kind of terms in which he would deal with this point, but I really do not think this is necessary in view of the complete agreement which exists.

We then passed to the general situation, and particularly Russia. He is quite ready to try to turn the Government out on the Russian Treaty, and to bring matters to a head as soon as Parliament reassembles. He does not expect that all Liberals will agree, but Asquith, Simon and Runciman have either committed themselves against or are opposed to the Treaty. LG observed that it would only take forty or fifty Liberal votes to decide the matter. He was extremely anxious that this issue should be handled with skill and tact, so as to make it not only easy for Liberals to vote against the Treaty but almost impossible for the bulk of them not to do so. When he first attacked the Treaty, the 'Daily News', the 'Star' and the 'Westminster Gazette' were all against him, as well as the 'Manchester Guardian'. Now all have come round except the 'Manchester Guardian'. He therefore feels in a stronger position, as a considerable proportion of the Party seem inclined to make this a real cause of quarrel with the Government. He thought the situation would be upset if an amendment were couched in terms wider than was necessary to inflict the censure. For instance, Kingsley Wood's[1] motion published in the Sunday papers gives several reasons for

[1] Kingsley Wood, 1881–1943. Member of the London County Council, 1911–19. Chairman, London Insurance Committee, 1917–18. Conservative MP for Woolwich West, 1918–43. Knighted, 1918. Parliamentary Private Secretary to the Minister of Health, 1919–22. Parliamentary Secretary, Ministry of Health, 1924–9 (when Neville Chamberlain was Minister); Board of Education, 1931. Privy Councillor, 1928. Chairman, Executive Committee of the National Conservative and Unionist Association, 1930–2. Postmaster-General, 1931–5. Minister of Health, 1935–8. Secretary of State for Air, 1938–40. Lord Privy Seal, April–May 1940. Chancellor of the Exchequer from May 1940 until his death.

rejecting the Treaty, about which there would certainly be strong differences of opinion, eg the treatment by the Bolshevist Government of its own subjects. He urged that the issue should be concentrated mainly, and if possible entirely, on the British guarantee. We had no right to lend British money in such circumstances and on such security, when domestic and Imperial needs were so pressing. I asked him to let me have his own terms for a motion. This he is going to do after consulting Masterman, whom he is very anxious to carry along with him, and who is also against the Treaty. I undertook to see that these terms were put before the Conservative leaders in ample time.

Another point was the personality of the mover and seconder. Having regard to the fact that we want to get the largest number of Liberals to vote, it is no use putting up anyone with whom they are accustomed to find themselves in marked disagreement. Apart from the terms of Kingsley Wood's Motion, Kingsley Wood himself would do very well. Another Conservative who would be very suitable is Wise,[1] the Member for Ilford. He may think of some others later on. The important thing is to have a Motion moved in terms and by speakers who will produce the best division.

LG fully contemplated that an Election would follow the defeat of the Government, and the vote would be given with that prospect clearly in view. He said that the moment they had committed themselves to guarantee this loan, they had put their fingers in the cog-wheels and would be drawn to their ruin. Of course you will both realise what a bleak prospect an Election offers to many Liberals at the present time, attacked as they are from both sides and without any second ballot, etc. He did not think anything like an arrangement, bargain or deal about seats was possible. The knowledge of any such formal deal would only lead to desertions from Liberal to Labour. There ought, however, to be as much tacit arrangement and good management as possible. In most cases the presence of a Liberal candidate in the field in a three-cornered contest would help the Conservative rather than the Labour. But there were a number of cases in which the Conservatives had no chance anyhow of winning the seats, but could ensure the return of the Liberals by not pressing their candidature. These cases ought to be talked over before the end of the month.

With regard to the larger aspects of the future, he fully confirmed what I told you of his own personal wishes. He would like to be able, with those Liberals who supported him—and they might be the larger portion of the Party—to give support in the next Parliament to a broad Unionist Adminis-

[1] Frederic Wise, 1871–1928. A stockbroker. Director of the *Daily Express*. Reported on the Financial Position of Germany for the Paris Peace Conference, 1919. Conservative MP for Ilford from 1920 until his death. Knighted, 1924.

tration, not because of a share of the offices, but for the sake of certain main issues of policy. Agreements between leading men or old Parties to share offices and obstruct progress would always end in discredit, but agreement on practical measures of policy would explain and justify themselves. He spoke of the great influence which Hartington and Joe had had on Lord Salisbury's Government from '86 to '92, and the general satisfaction that that Government gave to the broad mass of the nation for a long time. This is the sort of situation he foresees and is not discontented with, at any rate for the next year or two.

LG desired me particularly to remind Carson that he (LG) had always pointed out that Ulster had considerable counterclaims against the Free State in the matter of population and areas. For instance, in Monaghan & Donegal there are definite patches of Protestants. These counterclaims should all be brought forward if the Commission sits, not because they are counterclaims which in themselves could easily be acceded to, but because they would be make-weights to enable the Commission to give satisfactory decisions on the disputable points. He hoped this side of the case is being very carefully studied.

I suggested that he and Carson should meet at a dinner that I would arrange when he returns from Wales after September 15, and this proposal attracted him. He spoke with real cordiality about both of you. I have not the slightest doubt that his heart is with those who handled the Great War situations in his Government, and particularly the Unionist ex-Ministers who stood by him at the downfall of the Coalition. On the other hand he is well aware that a false step on his part might lose him much of the main Liberal support which, in circumstances of extraordinary difficulty, he is utilising against the Socialists' action.

I think it is of the greatest importance that Carson should take a hand, not only in the Irish part of this business, but in its general aspect. If he were willing during the latter part of September to get into touch with the younger Unionist Ministers, for instance Sam Hoare, Walter Guinness,[1] Edward Wood,[2] as well as keeping control of his own representatives of the

[1] Walter Edward Guinness, 1880–1944. 3rd son of the 1st Earl of Iveagh. Educated at Eton. Wounded while on active service in South Africa, 1900–1. Conservative MP for Bury St Edmunds, 1907–31. On active service, 1914–18 (despatches thrice). Under Secretary of State for War, 1922–3. Financial Secretary, Treasury, 1923–4 and 1924–5. Minister of Agriculture and Fisheries, 1925–9. Created Baron Moyne, 1932. A director of Arthur Guinness, Son, and Company, brewers. Elected to the Other Club, 1934. Secretary of State for the Colonies, 1941–2. Minister Resident, Cairo, 1944 (where he was murdered by Jewish terrorists).

[2] Edward Frederick Lindley Wood, 1881–1959. Educated at Eton and Christ Church, Oxford. Conservative MP for Ripon, 1910–34. Parliamentary Under-Secretary of State for the Colonies, 1921–2. President of the Board of Education, 1922–4. Minister of Agriculture,

extreme Right, that would be far and away the best chance of making sure that a wise and far-seeing policy is pursued by the official leadership in the present delicate and critical circumstances.

I hope that you will feel that the situation, though full of difficulty, is certainly not without its practical and hopeful side.

Colonel House[1] *to Winston S. Churchill*

(*Churchill papers: 8/196*)

2 September 1924

Dear Mr Churchill,

I want to congratulate you and felicitate with you over your admirable article in the current number of 'Nash' Magazine, entitled 'Shall We All Commit Suicide'.

I hope you will not object to its wide publication throughout America, for I am taking steps to get the Peace Societies to distribute it by the thousands. In my opinion, nothing has been written on the subject of peace and the necessity for the League of Nations that is more illuminating or more trenchant.[2]

Sincerely yours,
L. M. House

1924–5. Created Baron Irwin, 1925. Viceroy of India, 1926–31. President of the Board of Education, 1931–4. Succeeded his father as 3rd Viscount Halifax, 1934. Secretary of State for War, 1935. Lord President of the Council, 1937–8. Foreign Secretary, 1938–40. Ambassador in Washington, 1941–6. Order of Merit, 1946. One of his three sons was killed in action in Egypt in October 1942.

[1] Edward Mandell House, 1858–1938. Born in Houston, Texas. Personal Representative of President Wilson to the European Governments, 1914, 1915 and 1916. Special Representative of the United States at the Inter-Allied Conference, Paris, 29 November 1917; at the Supreme War Council, Versailles, 1 December 1917; and during the Armistice negotiations, 1918. United States Peace Commissioner, Paris, 1919. Member of the Mandates Commission, 1919.

[2] On 14 November 1924 a New York attorney, Raymond B. Fosdick, wrote to Churchill that his article constituted the 'most forceful and vivid picture that I have ever seen of war as the outstanding peril of the world'. Fosdick continued: 'The article was brought to my attention by Colonel House, and it seemed to me that it ought to be given the widest possible circulation here in the United States. Colonel House told me that you would have no objection to its reproduction, and I, therefore, put it in pamphlet form, copies of which I am enclosing herewith. So far about two hundred and fifty thousand of these copies have been distributed to a selected mailing list, including the chief manufacturers, judges, lawyers, engineers, politicians and educators of the United States. The demand for the pamphlet is rapidly increasing, and I am now placing an order with the printer for a larger edition. The response that has come from this distribution is really quite amazing. My office in the last few days has been literally flooded with letters from all parts of the country, and the expressions of

William Coote[1] to Winston S. Churchill

(*Churchill papers: 2/134*)

4 September 1924   County Tyrone

Dear Mr Churchill

The County Tyrone loyalists are organising a monster Demonstration of all the forces within their County to be held at Omagh on 24th inst to protest against the contemplated legislation of the present Government to coerce Ulster on the Boundary question.

Our Committee are anxious to secure the services of a leading British Politician to address this first meeting of protest to be held over Ulster, it will, therefore, be a most important meeting.

It occurred to me you are the man who could focus this question in the minds of the British people, and at the same time be a great opportunity for you to obtain that effective entrance into the public leadership of all the constitutional forces of the United Kingdom, anxiously calling for some great leader to overcome their petty jealousies and marshal them for victory, and I am hoping you will consent to be our chief speaker on the occasion.

Pardon my saying so, but I believe you are the coming leader of the Constitutional or Conservative Party, and if God spares you health the future Prime Minister of Britain, but you have a lot of prejudice to overcome, and your intervention on behalf of Ulster is an opportunity of a lifetime.

I could not agree with some parts of your political past—I however admire your honesty in protecting Ulster since the Free State Treaty came into the area of actualities. . . .

I realised only yesterday you are engaged to speak at Edinburgh on the 25th, and will shift our date either to the 22nd or 23rd or to the 26th to suit you, but we are determined if we can to hold our meeting before Parliament resumes.

I feel, however, I should again impress upon you the importance of this meeting to *you* as to *us*.

---

appreciation and approval in regard to your article have been most enthusiastic. We are now making arrangements to have the article given out by radio, so that it will reach an even larger audience. Perhaps you will allow me to express my humble opinion that in the preparation of this paper, you have rendered a great public service—far wider, doubtless, than you had any idea of when you first prepared it. It has made you a host of friends in the United States, and we shall follow eagerly your new work for international liberalism as you enter upon the new duties and responsibilities, which have so recently opened before you.'

[1] William Coote, 1863–1924. Auctioneer, stock-owner and manufacturer of woollen yarns. Conservative MP for South Tyrone, 1916–22. A Protestant. Grand Master of the Orangemen of England. A Member of the Ulster Parliament for Tyrone and Fermanagh. He died on 14 December 1924.

By one dramatic sweep you can brush all the Party mediocrities aside and through Ulster be the modern Carson of British politics, and fighting Tyrone will open for you this new vista in your future life.

If you will consent to come please wire me 'Coote, Clogher, Tyrone' an ambiguous telegram, such as 'agreed', and, giving date, I will then see my Committee privately, and arrange for a public invitation. Meantime, the whole matter will be kept by me a dead secret even from my Committee until I hear from you.

I am,
Faithfully yours,
Wm Coote

Winston S. Churchill to William Coote

(*Churchill papers: 2/134*)

5 September 1924   Chartwell Manor
Private and Confidential

Dear Mr Coote,

I am honoured by the invitation which you have sent me, but as I am a signatory of the Treaty, it is impossible for me to comply with your request. I do not at all approve of the way in which the present Government has handled the situation. It ought never to have been allowed to reach this particular point. If Article 12 is to be rigidly enforced, why is Article 5 allowed to remain a dead letter?[1] Surely these two Articles ought to be dealt with together. And if they were so dealt with, we should certainly get much nearer to that settlement by agreement which Sir James Craig and Michael Collins both signed in 1922 an undertaking to effect.

A very important letter from Lord Birkenhead to Lord Balfour, written at the time the Treaty was being passed, will be published in the papers of Monday next. This letter shows most clearly that the British signatories of the Treaty intended and believed that Article 12 should only deal with a readjustment of boundaries and not with a redistribution of territory. We then received the highest legal advice to the effect that no impartial Commissioner could take any other view. We have every reason to believe at the present time that the highest legal authorities would be of the same opinion as those who advised us. If this belief is correct, I cannot myself see that you

[1] Under Article 5 of the Irish Treaty, signed on 6 December 1921, the Provisional Government of Southern Ireland had agreed to pay compensation to the British Government for the Irish Free State's 'share' of the British National Debt. The British claim was for a minimum of £155¾ million. For the resolution of this issue, and Churchill's leading part in it, see the negotiations of 1–3 December 1925 (pages 603–617).

would be running any risk at the hands of a Tribunal constituted as is proposed. I quite understand your deep anxiety, however, in view of so much that has happened in the past. I shall certainly do anything that is in my power to bring this matter to a settlement by agreement. I am sure I should destroy any influence I possess if I were to take the course which you have been good enough to suggest to me. Believe me I greatly appreciate what you say of the manner in which I endeavoured to handle Irish matters while they were in my charge.

Needless to say, I shall treat the whole of this matter as strictly confidential.

Winston S. Churchill to Lord Rosebery

(Churchill papers: 2/134)

10 September 1924   Chartwell Manor

Politics are, I hope, moving towards a crisis. The major part of the Liberal Members in the House of Commons is opposed to the Russian Treaty. Lloyd George means to vote against it with all the support he can get. Simon and Runciman have both declared against it, and Asquith is known to be opposed. The division on the Russian Treaty may well dismiss the Government from power. At any rate I should hope that if they were defeated on this, those who had combined against them would be willing to go a step further and say they no longer possessed the authority to conduct the foreign relations of Britain. It will be far better to force an election on this issue, if possible, than to fight over a Socialist electioneering budget or a sheaf of promises in the new King's Speech next year. The key to the position is therefore the division on the Russian Treaty.

In order to give the best possible chance for a concentration to the Right, it is essential that the Irish issue should be got out of the way. If the Conservative Party were led into opposing the execution of the Irish settlement, and still more into influencing the House of Lords to reject the Amending Bill, many Liberals would be thrown with Labour and both would be presented with an admirable issue on which to fight.

I have been labouring constantly since I saw you to get this Irish business adjusted. I luckily remembered the letter written by FE to Balfour. I got it unearthed and published. I hope that it may afford some ground for Ulster to appoint a Commissioner. Carson, whom I have seen, is not at all ill disposed to such a solution. Once a Commissioner is appointed by Ulster, the whole business will stand over for five or six months while the Commission is at work; and before that time we may have—if all goes well—a friendly Government in power. There are of course many slips between cup and lip; but I do believe as a result of many interviews I have had with people of consequence, that there are good chances of success both in the House of Commons and at the polls.

The meeting Horne and I are going to address in Edinburgh under Balfour's Presidency is intended to emphasise the vital need of all the Constitutional and Imperial forces in the country working together in this juncture, not looking for minor causes of disagreement but on the contrary dwelling on all that great body of doctrine and interest which they have in common. It is very important to me to emphasise as much as possible my Liberal connection. Several Liberal Members of Parliament are coming on the platform, and we hope a number of local Liberals of importance will attend. I am very glad to be staying with you for the occasion, as the fact will undoubtedly be taken to indicate your approval of what we are trying to do in the national interest.

Winston S. Churchill to Sir Harry Goschen

(Churchill papers: 7/1)

11 September 1924   Chartwell Manor

Dear Sir Harry Goschen,

I have carefully considered the suggestions you and Mr Hawkey[1] have made to me that I should contest the West Essex Division at the next General Election, as Constitutional Candidate with the support of the Unionist Association. I have received a letter from Colonel Jackson urging me to take this course and offering me the full support of the Central Office. In those circumstances, and if you find there is a general wish among the Unionists of the Division that I should come forward, it would, I think, be my duty to comply with their request. A most grave and critical General Election is swiftly approaching, and every effort must be made to win a decisive victory for the Constitutional and Imperial cause and to lay the foundations of a period of stable and orderly progress.

---

[1] Alfred James Hawkey, 1877–1952. Educated at Woodford Collegiate School. A baker; Chairman of Clark's Bread Company; Vice-Chairman, Aerated Bread Company. Elected to the Woodford Urban District Council, 1909; Chairman, 1916–34. Chairman of the Wanstead and Woodford UDC, 1934–7. Organized Food Control in Woodford, 1914–18. Deputy Chairman of the Epping Conservative Association, 1922–6; Chairman, 1927–52. Knighted, 1926. Mayor of Wanstead and Woodford, 1937–8 and 1943–5; responsible for emergency feeding and information services in the Borough during the blitz, 1940–1. Member of the Essex County Council. Created Baronet, 1945. In his war memoirs Churchill described Hawkey as 'my ever faithful and tireless champion'.

Diana Churchill to Winston S. Churchill
(*Churchill papers: 1/172*)

Saturday   St Michaels,
                                                           Holland Park

My darling Papa,

I see from the newspapers that you are going to stand for West Essex in the next General Election. Sarah and I are both very well indeed. I am now in the upper fifth and at the end of the year we take the 'Oxford School Certificate'. I have just had a letter from Mummy & she has told me all about Randolph going back to Eton.

I am going out this afternoon & this evening we are going to have a small party & dancing.

I hope you are quite well, very much Love from your loving

Gold-Cream-Kitten

Sir Archibald Sinclair to Winston S. Churchill
(*Churchill papers: 2/134*)

23 September 1924

My dear Winston,

. . . I am sorry to see that Craig does not appear to be likely to appoint a commissioner. Surely it was very foolish of JH[1] to go off to South Africa at this crisis. With JH on the ocean, and Ramsay immersed in foreign affairs, and involved in personal explanations of his financial transactions,[2] nobody seems to be making any attempt to handle the Irish question.

[1] James Henry Thomas, 1874–1949. Began work as an errand boy at the age of nine; subsequently an engine-cleaner, fireman and engine-driver. Labour MP for Derby, 1910–31; National Labour MP, 1931–6. General Secretary, National Union of Railwaymen, 1918–24 and 1924–31. President of the International Federation of Trade Unions, 1920–4. Vice-Chairman of the Parliamentary Labour Party, 1921. Secretary of State for the Colonies in the first Labour Government, 1924. Elected to the Other Club, 1925, but resigned in 1930. Minister of Employment and Lord Privy Seal, 1929–30. Secretary of State for the Dominions, 1930–5; for the Colonies, 1935–6.

[2] In the summer of 1924 the *Daily Mail* had publicized the story that an enquirer into the share transfer lists at Somerset House had discovered that Alexander Grant had made Ramsay MacDonald a gift of 30,000 shares in his prospering biscuit manufacturing firm of McVitie and Price. Grant's father and MacDonald's uncle had been friends: both working at one time as guards on the Highland Railway. In the 1924 Honours List, announced in June, Grant had received a baronetcy, adding fuel to the cry of corruption. MacDonald had received not only shares, it appeared, but also a Daimler car. On one occasion, while MacDonald was making a speech, a cry from the audience of 'biscuits!' killed the speech. One of those most active in the campaign against MacDonald was the Conservative MP Sir Kingsley Wood.

With regard to Russia, I wish LG had not been quite so downright. Of course I am delighted that Asquith and Grey have come up to his support, but a good many of the rank and file seem to think he has been trying to snatch the lead, and would be inclined to resort to any expedient to avoid a general election, with which they think that LG is threatening them. I am beginning to be doubtful whether we shall get the election on the Russian Treaty after all, but if not we shall at any rate have produced a very uncomfortable situation for the Labour Party. . . .

We were so grateful to you for our most happy visit to Westerham. I hope all is going well with the dam, and that your work on the lower lake is now finished.

The Scotch papers feature your adoption for Epping as the most prominent news of the day. Best of wishes for your Edinburgh meeting.

Yours ever,
Archie

Sir George Lloyd to Winston S. Churchill
(Churchill papers: 7/1)

24 September 1924

My dear Churchill,
    The news which I have just read of your standing for Epping as a Unionist is the best bit of news for our party that I have heard for a long time and I write this brief line to tell you how glad I am.

Yours
George Lloyd

Sir Almeric Fitzroy[1] to Winston S. Churchill
(Churchill papers: 7/1)

27 September 1924   Scotland

My dear Winston,
    I must send you one line to express to you my own deep satisfaction that you have got an almost certain safe seat and that you are once more back with us.

---

[1] Almeric William Fitzroy, 1851–1935. Entered the Educational Department of the Privy Council Office, 1876. Clerk of the Privy Council, 1898–1923. Chairman of the Departmental Committee on Physical Deterioration, 1903-4. Knighted, 1911. Member of the Royal Commission on Venereal Diseases, 1913–16; and of the Dentist's Act Committee, 1918–19.

It is a feeling which will be widely felt in the Party and which will continue to grow.

Am here with Inchcape who sends you his *warmest regards* and tomorrow I go to George Younger's and with him to Newcastle. Midleton who is also here shares my feeling.

All best wishes ever,

Yours
Almeric

General *Colvin*[1] *to Winston S. Churchill*

(*Churchill papers: 7/1*)

28 September 1924   Scotland

My dear Mr Churchill,

I am so glad you have accepted the invitation of the W Essex Unionist Assosn to represent them at the next Election and I can only say how pleased I shall be to do all I can to help you. There are probably a few 'Die Hards' who will be rather obstinate but I think we shall be able to win them over in the end especially after your convincing speeches at Edinburgh.[2] I have no fears as to the result of the Election. The Liberal candidate G. Sharp[3] is the son of a Wesleyan minister and was born in S Africa. At Oxford he was I think President of their Debating Society. He has fought in elections & made some headway but he has had the assistance of the Labour Vote and now I am glad to see there is to be a Labour candidate who will probably poll easily as many votes as Sharp.

Sharp poses as the champion of the League of Nations, there are numerous

[1] Richard Beale Colvin, 1856–1936. Lieutenant, 1881. On active service in South Africa, 1900–1. Colonel, Territorial Force, 1902. Colonel Commanding the 2nd London Mounted Brigade, 1915 (mentioned in despatches). Area Commandant, France, 1917. Brigadier-General, 1917. Conservative MP for Epping, 1917–23. Lord Lieutenant of Essex from 1924 until his death. Knighted, 1934.

[2] On the evening of 25 September 1925 Churchill had spoken at the Usher Hall, Edinburgh, to an enthusiastic meeting of Scottish Conservatives. There was now 'no gulf of principle', he said, between Conservatives and Liberals; but the Labour Party was the enemy of both, and they must combine to defeat it. He was particularly critical of the Labour Government's Treaty with Soviet Russia (see Volume V of this biography, pages 48–9).

[3] Gilbert Granville Sharp, 1894–1968. On active service, 1915–16 (wounded at the Battle of the Somme). Special Instructor of Signals, 1917. President of the *Cambridge* Union, 1921. Unsuccessful Liberal candidate for Epping in 1922, 1923, 1924, 1929 and 1935. Member of Council of the Liberal Party Organization, 1941. Recorder of King's Lynn, 1943–57. Chief of the Legal and Advice Branch, British Section, Austrian Control Commission, 1944–5. QC, 1948. Unsuccessful Liberal candidate for Falmouth and Camborne, 1950. Justice of Appeal of the Supreme Court of Ghana, 1957–62. A Commissioner in the Crown Court, Manchester, 1963–7.

branches in the constituency, the majority of its members are pacifists but there are also Unionists and I used to attend their meetings to counteract any opponent.

I am very sorry that there are no large halls in the division. 600 or 700 is about as many as can be accommodated in the largest buildings which makes the work of electioneering harder.

I thought perhaps you would be glad of a little local information and my wife and I hope that you & Mrs Churchill will make every use of our house when you visit the constituency.

I shall be returning home in about a fortnight.

Believe me,

Yours sincerely,
R. B. Colvin

Lady Blanche Hozier to a friend

(Blanche Hozier papers)

30 September 1924   Dieppe

So Winston is on the war path again—after a prolonged holiday that he has enjoyed. His last ploy has been helping to build a couple of cottages on his small property; Chartwell Manor is not far from Sevenoaks. He also helped to make a swimming lake there. Beginning and ending this manual labour with the daylight.

October 1924

Winston S. Churchill to General Colvin

(Churchill papers: 7/1)

1 October 1924   Chartwell Manor

Dear General Colvin,

I am very much obliged to you for your letter and for the offer of your invaluable support. I was so glad to hear from Sir Roger Keyes some time ago that you were favourable to the idea of my standing for West Essex. I intend to make a complete tour of the Constituency before the Election, unless it comes upon us with startling suddenness. Mr Hawkey has made a plan which covers the ground in about thirty meetings. I do trust that everything will be done to set me free as much as possible, when the Election comes, for the national fight. It is for this reason I must particularly rely upon those who are convinced of the gravity of the issues of the next Election. I feel that I can do a good service to our cause generally in London, if I am supported in Epping. I am going, therefore, to ask for special efforts, and possibly the formation of special Committees.

I shall of course concentrate upon Epping to the exclusion of everything else unless, and until, I know that we are absolutely safe there. If a Socialist stands, the prospects seem to me very good. But you never know that the malice which the Socialists bear me may not lead to their withdrawing their candidate at the last moment, and throwing all their votes to the Liberals.

I shall hope to see you when you return from Scotland. Thank you very much for your offer of hospitality, which I will avail myself of in the near future.

Winston S. Churchill to Rear-Admiral Arthur Smith-Dorrien[1]

(Churchill papers: 2/135)

2 October 1924   Chartwell Manor
Private and Confidential

Dear Admiral Smith-Dorrien,

I am much obliged to you for your letter, and will reflect on all you say. As a matter of fact I have been a Home Ruler ever since the South African Constitution of 1906. I have been a Free Trader—though not a pedantic one—ever since I can remember. I have opposed Socialist candidates at nearly every Election I have fought in the last twenty-four years. Meanwhile I have seen the Conservative Party change its views on almost every great question, including Home Rule; and I remember their declarations of about seven different policies in regard to Tariff Reform. The present platform is very little removed from that adopted by Lord Balfour in 1904. I would have supported this, if it had not been mixed up with the general question of Protection. That general question of Protection is now formally excluded from the Conservative programme. I do not see where the complaints against me for want of stability find their justification.[2]

Winston S. Churchill to Lord Balfour

(Churchill papers: 2/135)

2 October 1924   Chartwell Manor

My dear Arthur,

As you have no doubt heard, matters have come to a head. The Liberals have, I believe, definitely made up their minds to take the fight with all its disadvantages for them upon the Russian Treaty with the Campbell Prosecu-

[1] Arthur Hale Smith-Dorrien, 1856–1933. Served with the Naval Brigade in Zululand, 1879. Lieutenant of the *Eclipse* during the Egyptian War, 1882. Rear Admiral, retired list, 1909. Chairman of the Westminster Constitutionalist Association, 1924 (it was he who had suggested to Churchill that he stand as a 'Constitutionalist' candidate). Brother of General Sir Horace Smith-Dorrien.

[2] Admiral Smith-Dorrien had written to Churchill on 28 September 1924 to congratulate him on his Edinburgh speech. His letter had continued: 'It seems to me you have a great opportunity before you, now that you have opened up *your umbrella*—your patriotism & courage are undoubted, also your capability, but I do not think the country has sufficient confidence in you because of your apparent *lack* of stability in the past, & this is very natural, for I myself have been among that number. I *now* say to myself, surely by *this time* Mr Winston Churchill must have learnt by experience & I see that he is heavily supported by Earl Balfour—as you say in your speech, there can only be two parties in the future' (*Churchill papers: 2/134*).

tion[1] thrown in, and not wait for a Socialist Budget. Horne spoke to Asquith in the sense of our conversation, and it may well be that this factor also weighed in the decision. I do not think we could ever get a more favourable issue than the Campbell Prosecution case solemnly censured by Parliament, plus the Russian Treaty also on the board. These two issues could be rammed in by speakers of every grade and class all over the country. On both issues the Liberals will be at grips with the Socialists, and the general prospect seems to me to be full of hope.

On the other hand it is probable from all I hear that the Government, if defeated on either issue, will resign and not dissolve. This will necessitate a new Government being formed, I presume by the Conservatives, *before the* Election; and the character, quality, composition, *etc*, of that Government will no doubt play no small part in the success of our appeal. The significance of all this will be apparent to you and to many others.

It was quite evident as soon as I got up to London that the Irish question was not going to be any trouble. It now seems likely that Carson will be appointed by the Government to represent Ulster, and I am sure that this matter which might have been a stumbling block will now pass out of the sphere of immediate action.

How opportune our Meeting has been for Scotland! I hear from many quarters of the good it has done. It may easily decide the fortunes in our favour of a dozen at least of Conservatives or friendly Liberals.

I was so glad to find you so strong and well, and thoroughly fit for a crisis in which your influence may be incalculable. I greatly enjoyed my stay at Whittingehame. It was very kind of you to ask us there.

Will you give my regards to Miss Alice.[2] I have ordered the Ant and Butterfly books. But how shall I have time to read them now!

---

[1] J. R. Campbell, the Communist editor of the *Workers' Weekly*, had published an article calling on soldiers not to obey the orders of their officers. In September 1924, Ramsay MacDonald had agreed to drop the Government's prosecution of Campbell. On 8 October 1924 the House of Commons debated the Campbell case. Asquith, who demanded a Select Committee, was supported by Baldwin, and the Labour Government was defeated by 364 votes to 198. MacDonald at once called for a General Election, which was fixed for October 29.

[2] Alice Balfour, 1850–1936. Balfour's sister. Acted as controller of Balfour's household. Like her brother, she never married.

Winston S. Churchill to Colonel Jackson

(Churchill papers: 2/135)

2 October 1924   Chartwell Manor

My dear Jackson,

The enclosed card has been sent to me anonymously. It strikes me as an extremely good piece of propaganda. Possibly the reference to Germany requires attention, in view of our general attitude of acquiescence in the Dawes Report. The message is so pithy and direct that it would, I am sure, make an appeal. These sort of cards ought to be in the possession of keen supporters, who could send them themselves to others they wished to stir up. If the Central Office had a stock, they might be distributed through the Agents in the various Constituencies, the cost of the cards being included of course in the local Election expenses. The distribution, however, would be a matter for individuals, who certainly are entitled to write a letter or send a post card if they choose.

If the Government were dismissed on the Campbell Prosecution, I should prefer this even to the Russian Treaty, though that of course will be on the board at the same time. I do trust the Liberals will stand firm; and I am sure that, knowing as you do the great issues at stake, nothing will be neglected on your part that is practical to encourage them to do so.

Epping looks all right. They seem to be quite certain that the Labour man is going to stand, and the quarrel between Liberals and Labour should make this still more certain. I shall be very active from now on, and hope that by the time the Election comes I may be strong enough to give you help in the national sphere.

There are a certain number of seats that I must talk to you about. It really is no use turning would-be friends into enemies, unless you are sure you can get your own man in. Take Sinclair for example in Caithness. He will get in whatever happens. But if he is opposed by a Conservative, he will be quite independent and potentially hostile. Whereas if he is not opposed, I am sure I can bring him along. He has voted right in nearly all the critical divisions, including the Five Cruisers, Singapore and Imperial Preference, and can of course be counted on in the Russian issue.[1]

---

[1] Sir Archibald Sinclair had been elected unopposed in 1923, and was again unopposed in 1924 and 1931. In 1929 he defeated both a Conservative and an Independent Labour candidate, and in 1935 he defeated a National Government candidate. In 1945 he was himself defeated, coming third (with 5,503 votes) to an Independent Conservative (who polled 5,564 votes) and a Labour candidate (who polled 5,558 votes).

Winston S. Churchill to Sir Robert Horne

(Churchill papers: 2/135)

2 October 1924   Chartwell Manor

My dear Horne,

Nothing could be better than that the issue should come on the Campbell Prosecution. There will be a general feeling in this country that the Government has behaved in an improper manner. They will be forced more and more to fall back on their Left wing and become increasingly discredited in the process. It will be better than the Russian Treaty, though that of course will be on the board as well. I am so glad you talked to the old man. I am sure it helped in the decision.

I see much talk in the papers that the Government if defeated on either issue will resign instead of dissolving. This will throw the onus of forming a Government upon the Conservative Party *before the Election*. It would become of the utmost importance to marshal the greatest strength. I am sure after our talk the other night this will be in your mind.

I shall be much obliged if you will look into the Caithness situation and see whether anything can be done. Sinclair has voted with us in nearly all the critical divisions, including the Five Cruisers, Singapore and Imperial Preference. He is very hot against the Bolshevist Treaty, and has supported Lloyd George vigorously within the Liberal Party. He is very strong in Caithness, where he owns fifty thousand acres, and is at the same time most popular. He thinks he can get in no matter what happens, and I believe this is true. I do not, however, want a Conservative to oppose him. It will only make him entirely independent and hostile. Whereas if he is not opposed, I am pretty sure I can bring him along into my group. He has considerable abilities, and is just the sort of man who should be in Parliament. Some time ago Atholl[1] wrote him a letter in a rather hectoring spirit, offering to bargain for Conservative support. This drew from Sinclair a rough answer. (They were both in the Household Cavalry together.) In consequence the Atholls seem to have been able to work up opposition, and a Conservative candidate is either in the field or about to come into the field. I am most anxious this should be prevented, for the reasons I have set out above. I am sure you will do your best. Do not imagine that Sinclair is asking it. On the contrary he professes satisfaction at Conservative opposition. Will you let me know if it

---

[1] John George Stewart-Murray, Marquess of Tullibardine, 1871–1942. Educated at Eton. Entered the Army, 1890. On active service in Egypt and the Sudan, 1898: a friend of Churchill's, they were together at the Battle of Omdurman. On active service in South Africa, 1899–1902, and at Gallipoli, 1915. Conservative MP, 1910–17. Succeeded his father as 8th Duke of Atholl, 1917. Lord Chamberlain, 1922. Known as 'Bardie'.

would be a good thing for me to write to the Duchess of Atholl?[1] I believe she is the one who manages that establishment.

Winston S. Churchill to Sir Robert Horne

(Churchill papers: 2/135)

2 October 1924   Chartwell Manor

My dear Horne,

We were so interrupted on the telephone that it was impossible to continue. Frankly I should be very sorry if the Campbell Prosecution did not bring matters to a head. I think the Government would be frightfully damaged if they were hailed before the country for a definite misdemeanour and gross breach of honourable tradition. A large part of their energy, usually expended in attacking our criminal civilisation, would be occupied in defending themselves from the charge that they had twisted the course of justice because they were incapable of prosecuting a man who tried to stir up mutiny in the armed forces. The Communists would bite at them savagely all the time from the other flank. I think that if the Government were beaten on this narrow issue, they might find it difficult to demand a dissolution. One can hardly ask for a dissolution if one is found with one's hand in the till. If there were no dissolution, a Government would have to be formed by the Conservatives before the Election. It would probably be a much better Government than one formed when an Election was not in view. Therefore if one had a free choice in regard to these two events, I would rather (a) see them turned out on the Campbell Prosecution and (b) see them resign instead of dissolve. The Russian Treaty of course would be on the board in either case.

I am apprehensive that if the Government survives the Campbell Prosecution, they may wriggle out of Russia. They can always pick a quarrel with the Bolsheviks about Georgia. It would be quite easy to pen a despatch from the Foreign Office tomorrow which the Labour Party would not dissent from in principle, but to which Moscow would return so rough an answer that MacDonald could easily say he could not continue negotiations in the face

---

[1] Katharine Marjory Ramsay, 1874–1960. Educated at Wimbledon High School and the Royal College of Music. Married the 8th Duke of Atholl in 1899 (he died in 1942). Commandant, Blair Castle Auxiliary Hospital, 1917–19. DBE, 1918. A leading Scottish educationalist. Conservative MP for Kinross and West Perth, 1923–38. Parliamentary Secretary, Board of Education, 1924–9. Member of the Royal Commission on the Civil Service, 1929–31. Among her publications were *Searchlight on Spain* (1938) and *The Tragedy of Warsaw* (1945). Her husband fought with Churchill at Omdurman in 1898. Her elder brother was killed in action in South Africa in 1899.

of such treatment. Also there are many slips between cup and lip, and there is nothing like seizing the opportunity when it flashes up.

It may be too late to do anything, but I beg you to consider these thoughts which are of course only put down by one who is watching events without the latest and closest information.

Sir Robert Horne to Winston S. Churchill

(*Churchill papers: 2/135*)

3 October 1924
Private

My dear Winston,

I have your two letters and I entirely agree with most of what you say. The Liberals however, as you will see from this morning's paper, have taken their own line. Lloyd George, whom I have not seen again but with whom Austen Chamberlain and others had a talk yesterday, was very emphatic in his view that it would be a mistake to get to the country before the discussion on the Russian Treaty had taken place in the House of Commons. The result you will see in the motion which they have tabled. It weakens our vote of censure because it undoubtedly implies that in putting forward our motion we are proceeding on inadequate evidence. However, it cannot be helped now and we must proceed with our motion and see what emerges. We shall be compelled, in the end I suppose, to vote for the Liberal motion, otherwise the Government would escape defeat.

As to Caithness-shire, I think it would be quite a useful thing if you wrote to the Duchess of Atholl saying what you know of Sinclair and the prospects which you hold out of bringing him along with you. You could use as a 'card of entry' the fact that she came to your platform in Edinburgh and presumably, therefore, is interested in getting as many Liberal Members on our side as possible. I shall have a talk with Jack Gilmour[1] about it.

Ever yours,
R. S. Horne

[1] John Gilmour, 1876–1940. Educated at Edinburgh University and Trinity Hall, Cambridge. Conservative MP for East Renfrewshire, 1910–18; for Glasgow Pollock, 1918–40. On active service in South Africa, 1900–1 (despatches twice), and in France, 1914–18 (despatches, DSO). Scottish Unionist Whip, 1919–22 and 1924. Succeeded his father as 2nd Baronet, 1920. Privy Councillor, 1922. Secretary of State for Scotland, 1926–9. Minister of Agriculture and Fisheries, 1931–2. Home Secretary, 1932–5. Minister of Shipping, 1939–40.

Winston S. Churchill to Sir Robert Horne

(*Churchill papers: 2/135*)

6 October 1924   Chartwell Manor

My dear Horne,

Many thanks for your letter. The moment I saw the Liberal Amendment demanding an enquiry, I felt that this would destroy the Government, and I therefore spoke in that sense at Epping. I presume there will be no difficulty in getting your people to vote for the Amendment, if they are not able to carry the direct censure. I think the Enquiry is a deadly move on the part of the Liberals. If MacDonald refuses it, it will look as if he has something to conceal; if he accepts it, he is humiliated beyond measure.

I do not think that it is much use speculating as to whether a break on Wednesday or a break a month later on the Russian Treaty would be most beneficial. Anyway there is not much in it. But broadly speaking in these matters I always feel it is very dangerous indeed to lose an opportunity. One never knows what may happen before it comes back again. I do trust therefore that nothing will stand in the way of carrying the Liberal Amendment for an enquiry, and I should be relieved to know that that is your view too.

I think it would be fatal for the Conservatives to take office for the purpose of immediately dissolving. For them to take office and have their Ministers re-elected and to try to carry on in the present House of Commons with a measure of Liberal support would mean that this favourable opportunity of taking the Socialists by the throat might be lost forever. While you were dependent upon Asquithian support, you would not be able to deal with Imperial Preference, to provide for the defence of Singapore, or in any way to safeguard threatened industries. This would dishearten and irritate your own Party and lead to quarrels with your Asquithian supporters. In six months or so the position would become impossible, and an Election would have to take place. But this time the Labour Party would have escaped from the position in which they now stand and would be rolling forward in general attack on all our institutions and affairs. I am strongly of opinion that if the moment is seized now, Labour will be much disappointed with the result. They are of course a numerical upgrade in the country as they gradually absorb the Radical Party. But this is the first time they will ever have been confronted with the real hostility of the two great Parties, neither of whom are quarrelling on any question of principle. You will never get such a good issue as the Russian Treaty issue again, nor shall we have a moment when the leader of the Socialist Party is himself so personally hampered by his conduct in accepting the McVitie fortune. I am sure strong and vigorous leadership now will produce a very favourable situation, and a much better Parliament than the present one.

Winston S. Churchill to the Duchess of Atholl

(*Churchill papers: 2/135*)

6 October 1924   Chartwell Manor

As you were on our platform at Edinburgh the other night and also sent me friendly messages at the time of the Westminster Election, I feel that you are probably in favour of the general principle of co-operation against the Socialists at the present juncture. This being so, I feel entitled to write to you about the Conservative opposition which is being started in Caithness to Archie Sinclair. He is a great friend of mine, as you know, and I think a young Member of exceptional ability. His position in Caithness is so strong that he is confident (and I think with reason) that he can hold the seat whatever happens. In these circumstances you cannot expect him to enter into bargains. The mere fact that such a bargain had been made would, if it leaked out, do him great injury with his supporters. On the other hand his votes in the last Parliament on almost every critical occasion have been very satisfactory. On Imperial Preference, on the Five Cruisers, on Singapore, and now on the Ulster Amendment he has voted with the Conservative Opposition. While doing this he has in no way lost his influence in the main body of the Liberal Party. I am afraid lest this Conservative candidature, which I am told you and Bardie have been fostering, will antagonise him. If he is opposed and gets back in spite of Conservative opposition, he will undoubtedly be perfectly independent and somewhat estranged. Whereas if he is not opposed by the Conservatives, who have not the slightest chance of returning their man, I am pretty sure he will increasingly gravitate towards us. You must understand that Sinclair has in no way approached me on this subject. In fact I think he would rather resent it than otherwise, as he considers his own position so strong. But I am looking at the future, and from that point of view I think he is just the sort of candidate who can hold Caithness firmly for the main causes we care about.

I trust you will consider these arguments very carefully; and perhaps you will be good enough to let me know what are your views. Sir Robert Horne advised me to write to you on the subject. He has himself spoken to Gilmour in the sense which I advise.

Believe me
Yours very sincerely,

Randolph S. Churchill to Winston S. Churchill

(*Churchill papers: 1/165*)

6 October 1924   Eton College

My Dear Papa

I think it is such fun here being allowed such liberty. I am now quite settled down. Last Sunday I went to breakfast with Doctor Alington.[1] There were three other boys there. Long leave is from Saturday November 15th till the following Monday. I don't start fagging till to-morrow as new boys are always given a fortnight to settle down in. I am learning to play fives and the Eton game of football, which is great fun. I don't think though that it is as much fun as soccer which we used to play at Sandroyd.

Best love
Randolph

Sir Henry Rider Haggard[2] to Winston S. Churchill

(*Churchill papers: 2/135*)

6 October 1924
Private

Dear Mr Winston Churchill,

I have been talking with our mutual friend Martin Conway, &, in agreement with him, I write this to you, though perhaps you will think that I, who am not a politician, indeed merely a lover of his country, Conservative but, (in the *wider* sense) Free Trade principles, have little right to express opinions on such a matter.

To be brief: Nobody wants a General Election at this moment. Yet if the Labour Govt falls there is no one (for various reasons, familiar to you,) who could form a new Govt in the *existing* House. I need not detail them.

But, I, or rather we, think that *you* might do so. You are of no party but just an anti-socialist. That is a broad base to stand on at the present time—at least many moderate people will think so. Why not put yourself forward?

---

[1] Cyril Argentine Alington, 1872–1955. Fellow of All Souls. Headmaster of Shrewsbury School, 1908–16; of Eton College, 1921–33. Dean of Durham, 1933–51. A theologian of high repute, and author of many volumes of scholarship and philosophy.

[2] Henry Rider Haggard, 1856–1925. Novelist: author of more than fifty volumes. Three of his best known romances were *King Solomon's Mines*, published in 1885, *She* (1887) and *Allan Quartermain* (1887). He was knighted in 1912. On 7 January 1897 Churchill had written to his mother of how Rider Haggard was among those authors who 'are all losing or have already lost their prowess'. He himself, as a boy of eleven, had written to congratulate Rider Haggard on *King Solomon's Mines*.

I know that you are not in the House at the moment, but that is easily remedied.

Verbum sap: Forgive me for instrusion in such a matter but out of the mouths of political babes & sucklings possibly may come wisdom! At any rate we have been acquainted since you were a boy & that must be my excuse.

Conway has seen this note.

Sincerely yours
H. Rider Haggard

Winston S. Churchill to A. J. Hawkey

(*Churchill papers: 7/1*)

6 October 1924   Chartwell Manor

My dear Mr Hawkey,

I am provisionally setting aside for you Friday, the 10th, as well as Thursday, the 9th, Tuesday and Wednesday, the 14th and 15th, Wednesday, Thursday and Friday, the 22nd, 23rd and 24th, and Tuesday, the 28th till Friday the 31st. I do not want to do more than is necessary, but you are at liberty to fix two or three meetings on any of those nights. Please let me have a programme accordingly at your convenience. I do this on the assumption that the Election is coming almost immediately. By the time your programme is made out, we shall be able to see.

I got back in an hour and twenty minutes the other night through the Blackwall Tunnel, and I hope to be able to do a great deal from here at any rate until the Election begins in earnest. I am staying with General Lloyd[1] for the Woodford Meeting. I shall come over to him in time for dinner before the Meeting on Thursday, and perhaps we could have a talk then.[2]

I was very pleased with my reception at the Club. What a fine Club it is! Surely we ought to have a Women's Meeting fairly early in the programme. I would arrange for Mrs Churchill to address them after me.

Yours sincerely,

[1] Francis Lloyd, 1853–1926. Entered the Army, 1874. Served in the Sudan campaigns of 1885 and 1898, and in South Africa, 1900–2, where he was severely wounded. Brigadier-General Commanding the 1st Guards Brigade, 1904–8. Major-General, 1909. Knighted, 1911. Commanded London District, 1913–19. Lieutenant-General, 1917.
[2] General Lloyd lived at Rolls Park, Chigwell, Essex.

Lord Londonderry to Winston S. Churchill

(Churchill papers: 2/135)

7 October 1924

My dear Winston,

I am sorry to be the last as I shall no doubt be of your many friends to say how delighted I am that we shall have the full value of your powerful support. As you know it is what I have always hoped and yet the bridge seemed impossible to build. I have always felt in complete sympathy with all your ideas and yet I never could see how in normal times we should ever be on the same side.

I do hope I shall see you soon and hear all your plans and ideas.

Yours affectionately
Charlie

Winston S. Churchill: public statement[1]

(Churchill papers: 2/135)

7 October 1924

There is a very great deal to be said for the Motion which the Liberal Party have officially placed upon the paper, demanding a full Parliamentary enquiry into this scandalous affair. Such an enquiry would enable the whole matter to be probed in a far more searching manner than would be possible in any Debate however prolonged. The Committee of Enquiry would be able to examine individual Ministers at length and in detail. It would be able to examine the Director of Public Prosecutions and the Treasury Counsel concerned. It would be able to inspect the file of documents and evidence upon which the Attorney-General[2] arrived at his original decision to authorise the Prosecution. We should then see exactly what evidence was before him at that time. Those who know how carefully the Director of Public Prosecutions prepares cases submitted for the decision of the Law Officers, will at once realise how very instructive the inspection of such a file of papers will be. The Committee would be able to examine the Police authorities upon the ante-

---

[1] Churchill gave this statement to the Press Association, which circulated it to all newspapers.

[2] Patrick Hastings, 1880–1952. A mining engineer, 1898–9. On active service in South Africa, 1900–1. A journalist, 1902–3. Called to the Bar, Middle Temple, 1904. Labour MP for Wallsend, 1922–6. Attorney-General, 1924. Knighted, 1924. A leading barrister; author of three plays, and *The Autobiography of Sir Patrick Hastings* (published in 1948).

cedents of Mr Campbell,[1] and upon his various activities. They would be able to examine the Treasury Counsel, Mr Travers Humphreys,[2] as to the exact circumstances in which he was led to make the statement which he did in announcing the withdrawal of the Prosecution, how the decision was conveyed to him, and what he meant by using the expression, 'It has been represented.' The Committee would be able to examine the Private Secretaries of the Law Officers or other persons in their immediate circle, so as to ascertain whether any representations were made to them which they in turn communicated to their Chiefs. They would be able to examine the group of Socialist Members who, it is alleged, met together to bring pressure upon the Government to drop the Prosecution. Lastly they would be able to examine the Communists themselves who have made, and still make, the most serious charges against the Government. In this way the whole matter would be cleared up, and the Attorney-General would have every opportunity of being fairly judged by the House of Commons upon a matter which undoubtedly touches both his personal and his professional reputation. If the Government have got nothing to conceal and nothing that they are ashamed of, they would have nothing to fear from such an Enquiry; and there is no doubt that it is a very business-like way of proceeding in a case of this kind.

However, I do not entertain for a moment the belief that the Government will agree to a Motion for Enquiry. After the very sweeping denials of the Attorney-General, such a Motion, if carried against the Government, would clearly imply that the House of Commons did not believe what he said and did not accept his word or the word of the Government. Such a Motion, however it may be phrased, is a vote of want of confidence couched in a singularly damaging and wounding form. [Ministers would have to be very anxious to cling to office who would submit to being thus treated by the House of Commons; and apart from any exposures which the Enquiry might bring to light, the Government would have to recognise and submit to the fact that their good faith was impugned by a majority of the House of Commons. The Government accused in such a way have really no choice as to their action. They can in my opinion only say 'Either you believe what we have solemnly stated or you disbelieve it. If you believe it, there is no need for

---

[1] John Ross Campbell, 1894–1969. Educated at elementary school, Paisley. Joined the British Socialist Party, 1912. On active service, 1914–18 (Military Medal, 1917). Editor of the *Glasgow Worker*, 1921–4; acting editor of the *Workers' Weekly*, 1924–6. Member of the Executive Committee of the British Communist Party, 1923–64, and of the Communist International, 1925–35. Served six months in prison for 'seditious conspiracy', 1925–6. Editor of the *Daily Worker*, 1949–59.

[2] Travers Humphreys, 1867–1956. Called to the Bar, 1889. Junior Counsel to Crown at the Central Criminal Court, 1908; Senior Counsel, 1916. Knighted, 1925. Recorder of Cambridge, 1926–8. Judge of the King's Bench Division, 1928–51. Privy Councillor, 1946.

an Enquiry. If you disbelieve it, then that is a vote of want of confidence, and a vote of want of confidence not only in a particular Minister but of want of confidence in the Government as a whole.' I do not rate the Labour Ministers so poorly as to suppose they would put up with that.][1] I therefore regard the political situation as critical in the last degree. An Enquiry seems to be the very least that the House of Commons can demand; and yet I cannot believe that the Government will be able to accept it.

An appeal to the country on the grave issues of this dropped Prosecution would in my judgment be very serious for Ministers. [It would be perfectly apparent that for all their fine words they are incapable of prosecuting to conviction persons who deliberately endeavour to stir up mutiny in the Armed forces of the Crown and to provoke Civil war.] They would find themselves haled before the Tribunal of the nation, charged with gross misdemeanour in the conduct of high affairs. It is the kind of question on which the average elector, the plain member of the public, would find it easy to make up their minds which side they were on. The prominence of such a question would in no way diminish the importance of the Russian Treaty. On the contrary there is in my opinion a very close connection between the conduct of the Government in stopping the Prosecution of this Communist Editor, and their surrender against their better judgment to the extremists of their Party and to the dictation of Moscow in the matter of the guaranteed loan to the Russian Bolsheviks. In both cases you see His Majesty's Socialist Ministers forced to go back upon their better judgment in consequence of subterranean, and possibly external, pressure. In both cases they knew what was the right course to take. The Prime Minister refused to allow a guaranteed loan to Russia. The Attorney-General set out to do his duty in prosecuting the Communist Editor for sedition. In both cases they recoiled from the clear, plain path of duty; and in both cases their recoil is acclaimed in Moscow as the result of the influence exerted upon a British Cabinet and British Ministers by a foreign organisation and by the friends of that foreign organisation in London. There are in the ranks of the Socialist Government many men of high reputation, men who stood by their country in the war, men who have lived their lives in the public eye and in the House of Commons for a whole generation. The position of these men is pathetic. They have been unable to keep their feet upon the slippery slopes on which they tried to stand. Well was it said of the French Revolutionary: 'No one knows how far he will go when he tries to work with men who are ready to go to all lengths.'

But what are we to do? Our course is clear. We ought to stand together. We have got to show that somewhere in this nation there are strong, con-

---

[1] Churchill deleted the sentences in square brackets before issuing this statement to the Press Association.

vinced, resolute, resisting forces taking up their stand on broad grounds of principle and determined to defend to the best of their powers the peace, the freedom and the prosperity of the nation.

Winston S. Churchill to Lord Newborough[1]

(Churchill papers: 2/135)

7 October 1924

Dear Lord Newborough,

The Socialists have been given every chance. They have had strictly fair play under the British Constitution which works evenly for all. Instead of doing their duty by the country, they have fawned upon their disreputable friends in Russia. Instead of following their own judgment, they have submitted to the dictation of a handful of foreign-minded and foreign-inspired extremists at home. They have shown themselves bankrupt in ideas. They have utterly failed to deal with Unemployment. They have mis-managed the Housing Problem. They have dissipated the surplus which the Conservative Government had accumulated. They have flouted the Dominions. They have deprived the British Navy of the power of defending Australia and New Zealand. They have tampered with the clean and impartial administration of justice. It is upon this record they are forcing an Election on the country.

A great opportunity will be presented to the nation of freeing itself from the period of political confusion into which we have been plunged, and of securing a stable Government national in its character and progressive in its spirit. Such a Government will give an interlude of peace and order which will enable our trade and industry to revive and will restore the influence of Britain abroad. The Mother Country will once again become a rallying point for the Empire; and by joining hands with our kith and kin across the oceans, we may consolidate the foundations of national strength and future prosperity.[2]

[1] Thomas John Wynn, 1878–1957. Succeeded his brother as 5th Baron Newborough, 1916. Lieutenant, Royal Naval Reserve. A Justice of the Peace for Merioneth.

[2] On 8 October 1924 Lord Newborough read this letter to a Mass Meeting at Blaenau Festiniog, in North Wales. 'It was listened to,' he wrote to Churchill on the following day, 'with attention & interest, which was all the more remarkable seeing that, out of an audience of eight or nine hundred, 50% were socialists or had socialistic tendencies.' The letter would, he added, 'do an immense amount of good to us, in this constituency'. But at the General Election, the Liberal MP was returned, Labour came second, and the Conservative bottom of the Poll.

Bernard M. Baruch[1] to Winston S. Churchill

(*Churchill papers: 2/135*)

10 October 1924

My dear Friend:

I am in receipt of a reprint from NASH'S PALL MALL MAGAZINE of September 24, 1924, of an article by you entitled 'Shall We Commit Suicide?' I want to thank you for it and to tell you how proud I am of having a friend who can think and say things the way you do. Would you object to my reprinting the article and sending it out here in America?

I see that the labor government is gone. It appears to me that the Mc-Donald government achieved a very interesting position over here. Although the impressions about him are rather widely scattered, the general feeling is that he is a man of peace. People here seem to overlook everything else. They think that his attitude in the London Conference gives him a high position among those who have striven for better international relations and international understanding. The fall of his government has rather stressed that feeling here. People raise that point and overlook any other point of criticism that might be leveled at him. I thought this might interest you, and am sending it along only for whatever value it may be to you for your guidance.

Your picture has also appeared here accompanied by a statement that you will probably be one of the leaders in the new House to be elected.

Please present my compliments to your very charming wife.

As always, and with best wishes for the attainment of what your heart desires,

Sincerely yours,
Baruch

Winston S. Churchill to Lord Balfour

(*Churchill papers: 7/1*)

11 October 1924   Chartwell Manor

I should be very much obliged to you if you felt it at all possible to write me a letter on my candidature at Epping.

There has been a great deal of enthusiasm in the Unionist Party there at

[1] Bernard Mannes Baruch, 1870–1965. Of Jewish parentage; born in New York. Financier. Chairman, Allied Purchasing Commission, 1917. Commissioner in Charge of Raw Materials, War Industries Board, 1917–18. Chairman of the War Industries Board, 1918–19. Economic Adviser to the American Peace Commission, 1919. Member of the President's Agricultural Conference, 1922. American Representative on the Atomic Energy Commission, 1946.

my adoption. Of course, there is a certain amount of Die-hard dissent and a certain number of resignations from the local Committees have taken place and perhaps 100 individuals have declared their abhorrence at the prospect of my representing them. On the other hand, nearly 400 new members have joined the Unionist Association in the last few days and all the meetings I have had, even at this early stage in the contest, have been wonderful.

There is a very powerful Unionist organisation working with great enthusiasm on my side. I was invited by them to stand as a 'Constitutional' candidate.

In reply to questions I have said: 'I am a Liberal, opposed to the official Liberal leaders on account of their putting the Socialists into power. I am a Liberal working shoulder to shoulder with the Conservatives in a national emergency in the same way (pardon the presumption) as Joe and Hartington and others threw in their lot with the Conservatives in 1886 and rendered the long reign of Lord Salisbury possible.'

In short, I am standing exactly on my Westminster platform, with the difference that I have the official support of the Unionist Party, both local and national.

A letter from you at this juncture would be of very great service and it occurs to me that you might make it the occasion of an expression of your view on the present situation.

How quickly events have moved, and how far they have moved in our direction!

The Unionist Central Office have just told me that they hope to arrange 25 or 27 candidatures for my class of Liberals. Most of these will get in and be an important factor in a stable majority.

In addition, a whole series of arrangements are being made between the Unionist Central Office and Abingdon Street. These arrangements take the form of avoiding losses to Labour by mutual concessions in triangular contests. Asquith, Simon and LG will probably, according to Jackson, not be opposed by the Unionist Party.[1] Thus, with infinite pains and toil, the folly of the Carlton Club is being repaired!

A letter which reached me about Thursday would be particularly timely.

---

[1] At Paisley, H. H. Asquith was unopposed by the Conservatives (but was defeated by the Labour candidate). At Spen Valley, Sir John Simon was unopposed by the Conservatives (and defeated his Labour challenger). At Caernarvon Boroughs Lloyd George was likewise unopposed by the Conservatives (and defeated his Labour challenger).

Winston S. Churchill to Lord Carson

(*Churchill papers: 7/1*)

11 October 1924   Chartwell Manor

Events have moved very swiftly since we last had a talk and I am sure you will feel that on the whole we have much to be thankful for. I am very hopeful that Socialism will receive a decided check and that we shall get a stable working majority.

I hope to have with me about 25 Members who will occupy the same position as the Liberal Unionists in the '86 crisis.

It occurs to me that you might perhaps care to write me a short letter in support of my candidature in Epping. I have the full support of the official Unionist Party, both local and national. They have invited me to stand as a 'Constitutional' candidate.

In answer to questions I have said: 'I am a Liberal who is working with the Conservatives in the same way as Joe, Hartington, yourself and others in '86.' This is quite acceptable to the overwhelming majority of the Conservative Party and, of course, I also receive a certain amount of Liberal support. There is an element of opposition from the extreme Conservative people. About 100 individuals have protested against my selection.

On the other hand, over 400 new members have joined the Unionist Association since it took place.

If you feel inclined to write me a letter, I am sure it would have a beneficial effect on the dissentients.

I should not dream of asking you to do this if I thought that it would be in any way counter to your feelings; and anyhow, if for any reason you think it undesirable, I shall perfectly understand.

You told me of your own case when you stood for Trinity College and how you insisted on retaining the word 'Liberal', in spite of the pressure put upon you to stand as a Conservative. This is the sort of point that would be particularly useful to me.

Winston S. Churchill to Colonel Jackson

(*Churchill papers: 2/135*)

12 October 1924   Chartwell Manor

LG has just rung me up and asked me to bring the following matter to your notice—

He has received a letter from Sir Hugh Vincent[1], Chairman of the Conservative-Unionist Association of Carnarvon Borough, asking him, in effect, to give a pledge to support any Conservative Government which may be formed as a result of the Election.

It is quite impossible for him to answer this letter either way without doing great harm to general interests. If he says 'Yes' he will be repudiated by the Liberals; if he says 'No' he will offend the Conservatives.

Considering the scale on which events are moving it is very injudicious to force issues in this crude way. Hundreds and thousands of Liberal votes might easily go over to the Socialists if matters are clumsily handled.

LG suggests that you should ask Sir Hugh Vincent by telegram to come up and see you in London and the matter could then be discussed verbally tomorrow or next day.

It is quite impossible to ask Party Leaders to give undertakings of this kind in order to facilitate their own personal election.

I saw Derby last night. He is going to try to fix Dudley Ward[2] and Waring[3] in some Lancashire seats which are still open. I presume this is not disagreeable to your general policy.

Yours very sincerely,

Hugo Baring[4] to Winston S. Churchill
(Churchill papers: 2/135)

13 October 1924   Paris

My dear Winston,

This is just a line to tell you that though I live so much in France now I follow your fortunes with the greatest interest, & I rejoice to think you are in

[1] Hugh Corbet Vincent, 1863–1931. Admitted a solicitor, 1886. Three times Mayor of Bangor. Unsuccessful Conservative Candidate for Caernarvon District, January 1910. Knighted, 1924.

[2] William Dudley Ward, 1877–1946. Liberal MP for Southampton, 1906–18; Coalition Liberal, 1918–22. Treasurer of His Majesty's Household, 1909–12. Vice-Chamberlain, 1917–22. Privy Councillor, 1922. In 1913 he married Winifred Birkin (Freda Dudley Ward). He was not re-elected to Parliament after his defeat in the General Election of 1922.

[3] Walter Waring, 1876–1930. Educated at Eton. Joined the 1st Life Guards, 1897. On active service in South Africa, 1899–1900. Captain, 1904. Liberal MP for Banffshire, 1907–18. On active service in France and Macedonia, 1915–17. Coalition Liberal MP for Blaydon, 1918–22. Parliamentary Private Secretary to the Secretary of State for War, 1919–22. National Liberal MP for East Lothian and Berwickshire, 1922–3. Unsuccessful Conservative Candidate for Wallsend, 1929.

[4] Hugo Baring, 1876–1949. Sixth son of the 1st Baron Revelstoke, and brother of Maurice Baring. Educated at Eton. Lieutenant, 4th Hussars; on active service (with Churchill) in the Tirah Campaign, 1897. Severely wounded in South Africa, 1900. Captain, 10th Hussars, 1914; wounded at Ypres, November 1914. Served with the British Mission to Siberia, 1918–19. A Director of Parr's Bank, 1911–18; the Westminster Bank, 1918–45; Resident Director, Westminster Bank, Paris, 1920–39.

the forefront of this struggle on which so much depends. May all good luck attend you & may you soon take your place—right at the top.

Don't bother to answer this but let us meet one day when peace reigns again at Eton where our sons are under the same roof.[1]

Yrs affectionately
Hugo Baring

Esmond Harmsworth to Winston S. Churchill

(Churchill papers: 7/1)

14 October 1924

Dear Mr Churchill,

This is to wish you every success. I am sure however that this time it will be yours.

I don't in the least regret the Abbey Election. For I feel certain that it helped you enormously to the position you have now taken up.

Looking forward to seeing you once again thump the familiar box in the House of Commons.

Yours v sincerely
Esmond Harmsworth

Lord Carson to Winston S. Churchill

(Churchill papers: 7/1)

14 October 1924

My dear Churchill,

As you know I am out of Politics but it wd be hypocritical to pretend that I did not feel deeply interested in the present conflict which is National rather than Party. You & I have had many differences but this is the time to forget them & I hope you will have the undivided & hearty support of all my old party in the Epping Division. I am not enamoured of coalitions but I remember how well the old Liberal Unionists (of whom I was one myself) were able to help the Conservative party in the controversies which first

---

[1] Hugo Baring's only son, Francis Anthony Baring, had been born in 1909, two years before Randolph. Educated at Eton and Magdalene College, Cambridge, and a passionate lover of music, in 1933 he married Lady Rose McDonnel, elder daughter of the 6th Earl of Antrim. He was commissioned as a 2nd Lieutenant in the Royal Artillery in April 1939, and was killed in action in France in June 1940 (leaving two sons, aged 6 and 4, and a daughter aged 18 months). From 1953 to 1973 his widow was Woman of the Bedchamber to Queen Elizabeth II.

brought me into Public & Parliamentary life & I feel we must rely on some such arrangement now if we are to have a stable & progressive Govt which can alone restore confidence & thus solve many of the difficult problems that are urgent. With best wishes for your success.

Yours sincerely
Carson

Lord Balfour to Winston S. Churchill
(*Churchill papers: 7/1*)

14 October 1924   Scotland

My dear Winston,

You are engaged in a great fight, and, speaking as a lifelong Conservative and Unionist, I heartily wish you a triumphant victory. Nor do I doubt that you will obtain one. Our organisation in Epping has given a clear lead; our Central Office strongly supports its decision; and I feel sure that all members of our Party in the constituency will enthusiastically respond to the call.

My hopes indeed go further than this. There must be many in Epping, as elsewhere, who realise that new problems must be looked at in a new perspective. The controversies of the past they treat as matter for the historian; the controversies of the future they abandon to the prophets. As practical men their business is with the present; and in the present they can discover no controversies seriously dividing men of moderate opinions.

In these circumstances, it is surely the plain duty of all who may be thus described to work strenuously for those with whom they agree, lest those from whom they differ should be given the opportunity of doing irreparable mischief to the country. The danger is a real one; and the electors of Epping are to be congratulated on having secured a candidate so eminently qualified by his eloquence and vigour to expose its true character to the country. In the performance of this great task I am certain that you will deserve success, and very confident that you will obtain it.

Yours sincerely
Balfour

Colonel Jackson to Winston S. Churchill
(*Churchill papers: 2/135*)

15 October 1924
Private and Confidential

My dear Churchill,

I find that there is a good deal of feeling amongst some of our Associations as to the desirability of obtaining a definite undertaking from candidates who are expecting the support of the Conservative Party, but who are not calling themselves Conservatives, and are actually in some places standing as Liberals. I think we ought, if possible, to appease this anxiety by having some undertaking from these candidates. Do you see any objection to a letter such as the enclosed being sent to the Chairman of the Association in the Constituency where these candidates are standing? Will you let me know by return.[1]

Yours sincerely,
F. Stanley Jackson

Winston S. Churchill to Lord Beaverbrook: telegram
(Beaverbrook papers)

15 October 1924   Westerham

The 27 rabbits[2] had better lie in Bramble patch for present with their ears neatly folded. Winston

Winston S. Churchill to Major Kenyon-Slaney[3]
(Churchill papers: 2/135)

20 October 1924   Chartwell Manor

Dear Major Kenyon-Slaney,

Tavistock was a seat which in 1918 pronounced decidedly in favour of a national, as against a Party, policy. Its Electors realised then that the strong forces which, acting together, had carried us through the perils of the war, ought to continue in comradeship until the difficult years which follow every great war had been successfully surmounted. The position is the same today. We cannot afford to let our politics remain in their present confusion. Four Prime Ministers and three General Elections in two years spell the futility of Britain in the world and the negation of social progress at home. The supreme need is a sound and stable Government, with a proper majority

[1] A note at the foot of this letter states: 'Churchill strongly opposed to any such letter going out.'

[2] The twenty-seven Liberal MPs who were standing, like Churchill, on an anti-socialist platform, in co-operation with the Conservatives, and without any Conservative candidate to oppose them.

[3] Philip Percy Kenyon-Slaney, 1896–1928. On active service, 1914–21 (Military Cross). Conservative MP for Tavistock from 1924 until his death.

behind it and real responsibility for its public acts. The existing chaos and uncertainty ought to be brought to an end. It can only be brought to an end in present circumstances by a Government pledged against reaction in any form, not only by its words but by the composition and character of its supporters. Such an administration must be fairly founded upon the Unionist Party. The Unionist Party have prepared themselves for this duty by laying aside special and narrow Party views, and by adopting a broad national platform. In scores of Constituencies all over the country Liberals are supporting Unionist candidates. The Unionist Party have withdrawn their candidates against Mr Asquith, Sir John Simon and Mr Lloyd George, in order that these Statesmen may have a straight fight with their Socialist opponents, and also in order that the new House of Commons may be truly representative of the political ability and experience of the whole nation. This is the moment for the Tavistock Division of Devonshire to range itself upon the side of a movement larger than ordinary Party groupings. We cannot afford faction for faction's sake. A strong effort by the Tavistock Electors at this juncture—Liberals as well as Conservatives—should send you to Westminster to stand as a bulwark against Socialist designs and help to secure for the nation that breathing space which after all its struggles and exertions it rightly deserves.

> With all good wishes, believe me

Sir Ian Hamilton to Winston S. Churchill
(*Churchill papers: 7/1*)

25 October 1924

My dear Winston,

Moved by some anxiety I pulled out my little Wolseley & ran down to Epping this afternoon. Round about I know a farmer or two, a cowman or two and a couple of big wigs. As I went as a proclaimed non politician it may interest you to hear that the result of my touting was that I came back fairly comfortable in my mind. You may take it from me that your two last speeches, the one in the open air & the last one, turned the scale. As you must know your danger (like that of Dizzy) lies in the hard upper crust of the Diehards. All best fortune to you—personally.

> Yours ever
> Ian Hamilton

Winston S. Churchill to a constituent

(*Churchill papers: 2/135*)

26 October 1924
Unionist Central Committee Rooms,
South Woodford

Dear Sir,

Fifty-two millions of British money (not one hundred millions) was spent as part of the war expenditure to make good the promises this country had made to the Russian Loyalists after the Bolsheviks deserted the Allied cause. The Labour Party were officially represented in the Government which made these promises, though not in the Government which had to carry them out.

THE GENERAL ELECTION was held on Wednesday 29 October 1924, and the results were announced two days later. Churchill was elected for Epping with 19,843 votes (as against 10,080 votes cast for the Liberal Candidate, and 3,768 for the Labour Candidate). The result of the election gave the Conservatives 419 seats (8,039,598 votes,) Labour 151 seats (5,489,077 votes), the Liberals 40 seats (2,928,747) and the Communists one seat (55,346 votes). Ramsay MacDonald resigned on 4 November 1924 and Britain's first Labour Government was at an end.

Lord Hindlip[1] to Winston S. Churchill

(*Churchill papers: 2/130*)

31 October 1924

My dear Churchill,

May I congratulate you. I hope you will be a Blister on the Bolshie's back! Agatha sends her best wishes.

Yours ever
Hindlip

[1] Charles Allsopp, 1877–1931. Succeeded his father as 3rd Baron Hindlip, 1897. Owner of 3,500 acres. On active service in South Africa, 1900. Married, in 1904, Agatha Lilian Thynne, a great-granddaughter of the 2nd Marquess of Bath. A Junior Conservative Whip in the House of Lords, 1907–14. Captain, War Office Staff, 1914–19.

Sir Reginald Barnes[1] *to Winston S. Churchill*

(*Churchill papers: 7/1*)

31 October 1924

My dear old Winston,

I am *so* glad, & so is everyone else—barring the Bolshies. Well done old Friend, it is a comfort to think that anyhow there is someone in the House who has the guts to stick up for the old Flag. Make me one of your private secretaries when you are PM will you!

Best love, & I hope to see you again soon. Don't bother to answer this if you are too busy.

Your old pal,
Reggie

T. E. Lawrence to Winston S. Churchill

(*Churchill papers: 7/1*)

31 October 1924

This isn't congratulation, it's just the hiss of my excess delight rushing out. You've done it gloriously—all the conditions to your credit; two bye-elections, two books, to whet the public appetite, and then this smashing success. Tactically, it seems to me, the ground is all in your favour now: only let's hope there will be enemy enough to provide you with exercise. Probably there will be, since some of the very shell-back Tories will want cracking occasionally: and their own chiefs are mild.

However this isn't my affair. Thank you for providing the jolliest bit of news for months.

T. E. Lawrence

[1] Reginald Walter Ralph Barnes, 1871–1946. Entered Army, 1890. Lieutenant, 4th Hussars, 1894. Went with Churchill to Cuba, 1895. Captain, 1901. Brigadier-General, commanding the 116th Infantry Brigade, and the 14th Infantry Brigade, 1915–16. Commanded the 32nd Division, 1916–17, and the 57th Division, 1917–19. Major-General, 1918. Knighted, 1919.

The Exchequer Years
1924–1929

November 1924

---

1 November 1924   Foreign Office
Private & Secret

Philip Sassoon's guests on Thursday[1] at the Dinner I mentioned to you yesterday, were,—Birkenhead, Churchill, Beaverbrook, Sam Hoare, and Lloyd Graeme, and the conversation ran on the following lines.

'FE to Winston—"I suppose you expect to get Office?"'

'Winston replies—"that will depend very much on what I am offered."'

' "No." said FE—"You have been hungering and thirsting for Office for two years and you will take anything they offer you." '

On Winston showing resentment, FE proceeded to give the company a sketch of all the tricks and subterfuges he and Winston on occasions had resorted to in order to obtain office. Beaverbrook attempted to interrupt him and by that time FE was carrying more than was good for him. He thereupon turned on Beaverbook and said: 'Well, Max you stepped fairly into the gutter in order to get Office; you would have given your eyes at one time for the Board of Trade, but you preferred a peerage.'

After that there was general mudslinging, but my informant was very much struck by the outward deference paid to you and their acceptance of you as dispenser of patronage.

Beaverbrook showed very plainly, his disappointment at the size of the majority which he thinks has robbed him of his power, but he expressed a hope that the lesson you would learn from this Election, was the power of the Press . . . and he also expressed the conviction that you would be bound to give Office to Winston sooner than see him become the nucleus of dissatisfaction in your own party.

My impression is that you have so many fools in your party wedded to the

---

[1] Thursday, 30 October 1924. The election had been held on October 29, and the first Ministerial Offices (including Churchill's) were announced on November 6.

slogan that anybody as brilliant as Winston must be given Office, that it would be worth while to silence them.

If therefore, you decide to include Winston and FE I do trust that your offer to them will be on the lines of 'take it or leave it'.

Forgive this effusion which is due to my intense desire to help in any way, however modest, to ensure your success.

Yrs always sincerely,
W. Tyrrell

Lord Darling to Winston S. Churchill
(*Churchill papers: 2/138*)

1 November 1924

My dear Winston,

You hardly need a letter from me to realise with what pleasure I can again put MP on the envelope I address to you.

I hope soon to see you holding again a great Office in the State—& Mrs Churchill aiding you as she too well can.

Ever yours sincerely
Darling

Lionel Curtis to Winston S. Churchill
(*Churchill papers: 2/138*)

1 November 1924   Oxford

Dear Winston,

A line to send you my heartfelt congratulations on your election. The continued exclusion from the House of Commons of its greatest living speaker was a reflection on our institutions. I have never been there for the last two years without feeling how you were missed.

A majority like this wants a stronger leader to control it than the Conservatives have got. Baldwin has not got the engine power to give him steerage way.

The reports which reach me about Masterton are not vy cheering, & suggest little hope that he will be able to return to the Colonial office this year. I am vy much afraid that his place will not be kept open for him for more than a year after his sick leave began. Its a real tragedy.[1]

Yours sincerely
L. Curtis

[1] Masterton-Smith did not return to the Colonial Office, and his illness, a form of severe melancholia, grew increasingly worse (see page 527). He died in 1938.

Pamela Lytton[1] to Winston S. Churchill

(Churchill papers: 2/138)

1 November 1924   Government House
                                         Darjeeling

Dear Winston,

I send you our congratulations from the wilds of the Himalayas. The Reuters arrived up here last night, after dark. They came by rider, to the sound of a horn—all sufficiently dramatic and picturesque for their contents! —a Conservative victory at the Polls.

It is glorious your being back in Parliament again, and also 'of the' Conservatives once more. I am so glad your victory was mentioned, and that I knew your triumph quickly. I rejoice for you, and for Clemmie—please tell her.

The Revolution in Bengal is crushed. This has been Victor's great work for four months. With infinite patience, firmness and tact, he won the Government of India, and persuaded Lord Reading[2] to agree to policy, and to support him entirely. Hence the Labour Cabinet's decision, and hence the Viceroy's ordinance.

Tegart[3] and his police have been magnificent, and Victor's 'Coup' was brought off in perfect secrecy, almost before day light. Seventy arrests!

We are now able to take a holiday, before going to Calcutta for the winter. We are climbing the mountains with strings of ponies, and tents and domestics—and gazing at the most gorgeous scenery—but I hate India!

With love and many good wishes from
Pamela

[1] Pamela Frances Audrey Plowden, 1874–1971. Daughter of Sir Trevor Chichele-Plowden. On 4 November 1896 Churchill wrote to his mother: 'I must say that she is the most beautiful girl I have ever seen.' In 1902 she married Victor Lytton, later 2nd Earl of Lytton. Their elder son, Edward, Viscount Knebworth, died in 1933 as a result of an aeroplane accident; their younger son, Alexander, Viscount Knebworth, was killed in action at El Alamein in 1942.

[2] Rufus Daniel Isaacs, 1860–1935. Liberal MP, 1904–13. Knighted, 1910. Solicitor-General, 1910. Attorney-General, 1910–13. Entered Cabinet, 1912. Lord Chief Justice, 1913–21. Created Baron Reading, 1914; Viscount, 1916; Earl 1917. Special Ambassador to the USA, 1918. Viceroy of India, 1921–6. Created Marquess, 1926. Secretary of State for Foreign Affairs, 1931.

[3] Charles Augustus Tegart, 1881–1946. Educated at Trinity College, Dublin. Joined the Indian Police, 1901. On active service in France (artillery officer), 1918. Chief of Police, Bombay (retired, 1931). Knighted, 1926. Member of the Council of India, London, 1932–6. Government Adviser on Police Organization, Palestine, 1937, where he established the system of strategic fortified police posts known as the 'Tegart Fortresses'. Served with the Ministry of Food, London, 1942–5.

Lord Wimborne to Winston S. Churchill

(*Churchill papers: 7/1*)

[1] November 1924

Dear Winston,

Just a line to offer you my heartiest congratulations on your very decisive victory & to tell you how delighted I am that you are once again in public life. I hope to goodness the Tories will have the good sense to offer you high office. It will be reassuring to think of a progressive mind among their counsels, as a majority such as theirs is hardly conducive to a programme of social reforms. It will be very interesting to see the immediate effect in the party of your co-operation. To the popular mind I should imagine you are more than anyone else the symbol of anti-socialism & as such have the strongest claims as the result of the election fought largely on this issue.

I hope, indeed, I shall see you Chancellor (or fulfilling the very interesting experiment of Viceroy of India)[1] but apart from these speculations, I hope you get whatever you want & you will have as always my very best wishes.

Yr affectionate cousin
Ivor

Lord Rosebery to Winston S. Churchill

(*Churchill papers: 2/138*)

4 November 1924   Edinburgh

My dear Winston,

My congratulations are not the less warm because they are tardy. I am quite delighted with your victory, and hope you will take a leading part in the new parliament. I also trust that the victorious Party will not be inebriated by their triumph and commit follies. That is my chief fear.

Your election was very great. But the greatest triumph was in this little County, where an anarchist called Shinwell[2] with a majority of over 5,000 saw the majority disappear and replaced by a minority of 642.

[1] In April 1926 Lord Reading was succeeded as Viceroy of India by Lord Irwin. There was further speculation about Churchill becoming Viceroy of India in 1929 (but Irwin was succeeded by the Earl of Willingdon in 1931).

[2] Emmanuel Shinwell, 1884– . Unsuccessful Labour candidate for Linlithgowshire, 1918; elected, 1922; re-elected, 1923. Defeated, 1924; re-elected at a by-election in April 1928 and again at the general election of 1929. Defeated in 1931. Parliamentary Secretary, Mines Department, 1924 and 1931. Financial Secretary, War Office, 1929–30. Labour MP for Linlithgow, 1928–31; for Seaham, 1935–50; for Easington, 1950–70. Minister of Fuel and Power, 1945–7. Secretary of State for War, 1947–50. Minister of Defence, 1950–1. Chairman of the Parliamentary Labour Party, 1964–7. Created Baron (Life Peer), 1970.

By the by, I was impressed, after your speech at Edinburgh, by the silence of 'The Times', which gave you a bad report, and no article at all. To what was this due: do you know?

Yours ever,
AR

Winston S. Churchill to Sir Alan Burgoyne[1]
(*Churchill papers: 2/136*)

4 November 1924

Thank you very much indeed for your most kind letter.[2] I think it very likely that I shall not be invited to join the Government, as owing to the size of the majority it will probably be composed only of impeccable Conservatives. Should, however, the contrary prove the case, there is one man to whom I should in the first instance be bound. He might obtain an Under-Secretaryship or, alternatively, he might not wish to come to me. Apart from this there is nothing I should like better than the suggestion with which you have complimented me. I have never forgotten the magnificent work you did for the Navy before the war.

Winston S. Churchill to Andrew Dewar Gibb
(*Churchill papers: 2/136*)

5 November 1924

My dear Gibb,

I am very sorry you did not succeed.[3] Fighting an Election is, however, a most valuable educational experience; and once one has one's foot on the political ladder, there is a chance of progress. I think the Conservative Party

---

[1] Alan Hughes Burgoyne, 1880–1929. Unsuccessful Conservative candidate, 1906. Treasurer of the Navy League, 1909–13. MP for Kensington North, 1910–22. Member of the Admiralty Committee on the Restriction of Enemy Trade, 1914–15. On active service in France, Italy and Palestine, 1915–18; Lieutenant-Colonel, 1918. Secretary of the Parliamentary Air Committee, 1916–18; Treasurer, 1919–20. Controller of the Priority Department, Ministry of Munitions, 1918–19. Knighted, 1922. Unsuccessful candidate at the 1923 election. Conservative MP for Aylesbury from 1924 until his death.

[2] Burgoyne had written on November 1 that he was certain Churchill would be a member of the next Government, and offering his services 'as a Parliamentary Secretary'.

[3] Andrew Dewar Gibb had stood as a Conservative for the Hamilton Division of Lanarkshire, where he received 8,372 votes, as against 13,003 cast for the Labour candidate. He was again unsuccessful as a Conservative in 1929, and as a Scottish Nationalist candidate in both 1935 and 1936.

ought to get some young fellows like you with good war records to settle down as Candidates in some of those seats where there has been so much rowdyism, and put them in a position to break it up by two or three years' intensive treatment. However, perhaps this is a very Spartan course to recommend.

Let me hear from you later.

Leopold Amery: diary

(Amery papers)

5 November 1924

Met Winston looking very cheerful, and no wonder getting, as we learnt afterwards, in the shape of fatted calf what he had failed to get while sojourning with his former depraved associates.[1]

Winston S. Churchill to Stanley Baldwin

(Baldwin papers)

[5] November 1924   Chartwell Manor

My dear Prime Minister,

Forgive me for returning to AJB. I am sure it will add to the éclat of yr Government if he were formally associated with it. His reputation is august. Wd it not be possible to appoint him a Minister without portfolio for purposes connected with the League of Nations & (or) the CID? I hazard this suggestion of course without knowing yr general plan.[2]

May I make one other. Esmond Harmsworth wd be a valuable addition to the Government for reasons on wh I do not need to dilate, but also because of his own abilities & character. No doubt you have this already in yr mind.[3]

I have been reflecting deeply upon the vy great duties you have entrusted to me.

Yours vy sincerely,
Winston S. Churchill

Of course no answer.

[1] Baldwin had appointed Churchill to be Chancellor of the Exchequer. Amery had been appointed Secretary of State for the Colonies.

[2] Balfour entered the Government on 27 April 1925 as Lord President of the Council (in succession to Lord Curzon). But as a Member of the Committee of Imperial Defence he attended several important meetings of the CID between November 1924 and April 1925.

[3] Esmond Harmsworth received no Government appointment between 1924 and 1929.

J. C. C. Davidson[1] *to Stanley Baldwin*

(*Baldwin papers*)

6 November 1924

Winston's appointment is genius—you have hamstrung him—so that his hairy heels are paralysed. He will do all right.

Sir Robert Horne to Winston S. Churchill

(*Churchill papers: 2/138*)

6 November 1924

My dear Winston,

I send you my warmest congratulations on your appointment to the Exchequer. It realises in 1924 what I urged LG to do in 1922. Thus belatedly do the Fates perform their ca' canny job!

I am sure you will make a great success of it. Baldwin has probably treated me as badly as any public man has ever treated a colleague who has supported him in difficult times without much reason for loyalty: but it will be *your* duty to prove that he was right in doing so. I am sure that you will not fail. In fact for the sake of the country you *must* succeed.

And this, in the ironical scheme of things, while Baldwin as my enemy gives me a slash across the face it will only remain for you as my friend to give me the 'coup de grace'. 'Moriturus te saluto.' Good luck to you and my best wishes.

Ever yours
R. S. Horne

[1] John Colin Campbell Davidson, 1889–1970. Educated at Westminster and Pembroke College, Cambridge. Private Secretary to successive Colonial Secretaries (Crewe, Harcourt, Bonar Law), 1910–15. Private Secretary to Bonar Law, 1916–20. Conservative MP for Hemel Hempstead, 1920–3 and 1924–7. Parliamentary Private Secretary to Stanley Baldwin, 1921–2; to Bonar Law, 1922–3. Parliamentary Secretary, Admiralty, 1924–7. Chairman of the Conservative Party, 1927–30. Chancellor of the Duchy of Lancaster, 1931–7. Chairman of the Indian States Enquiry Committee, 1932. Created Viscount, 1937.

George Lambert to Winston S. Churchill
(*Churchill papers: 2/138*)

6 November 1924

My dear Winston,

I congratulate you but I congratulate the Country still more.

You are in my judgment the fittest man in all England to be Ch: of the Excheq:, and I am certain that your fine instinct for economic fact will make you in most critical times a worthy successor of Great Liberal Chancellors. Had LG made you Ch: of Ex: a year or two ago, he would not now have been niggling with the remnant of a party that Asquith & he have destroyed.

Winston my boy, I have got a fair instinct for politics. I think I shall live to see you Prime Minister.[1]

May good luck go with you!

Yours sincerely
George Lambert

Winston S. Churchill to William Lints Smith
(*Churchill papers: 8/198*)

6 November 1924

Dear Mr Lints Smith,

The announcement which you will probably have read in this morning's papers makes it impossible for me to publish my third volume in February as I had hoped; and I cannot yet see how and when it is to see the light of day. More than two-thirds of it are finished, and but for this over-riding event I should have been punctual to my engagement. Perhaps you will let me know whether you still wish to keep the contract alive or whether you would rather be completely free. I am very sorry to disappoint you; the more so as I had taken a great deal of trouble, and the general scope and plan of the work gave me a certain amount of confidence.

Winston S. Churchill to Thornton Butterworth
(*Churchill papers: 8/199*)

6 November 1924

Dear Mr Butterworth,

I am sorry to say that it will be impossible for me to complete the third volume of my book and publish it in February as I had hoped. My whole

[1] Lambert lived until 1958.

time will be taken up by my new work, and this book must just remain in its box till the skies are clearer. I have taken a great deal of trouble with it, and more than two-thirds are in a very advanced condition. Some day perhaps we can talk of it again.

Will you kindly let me know how the other two volumes are selling and what sums there are to my credit on their account.

Austen Chamberlain to Stanley Baldwin

(*Austen Chamberlain papers*)

6 November 1924
Secret and Personal

I am alarmed at the news that you have made Winston Chancellor, not because I do not wish Winston well but because I fear that this particular appointment will be a great shock to the Party. If FE or I could help you, we are at your service. . . .

You will remember that the first reason you gave me for not offering Horne the Treasury was that you wanted Neville there. I told you that H would accept the Treasury and that I did not think that he would take Labour, whilst N would gladly go to Health if H went to the Exchequer. . . .[1]

Neville Chamberlain to Stanley Baldwin

(*Baldwin papers*)

7 November 1924

I rather felt my breath go when I heard that Winston and Steel-Maitland[2] had been actually appointed. I didn't know you were going to be as quick as that! but I don't go back on my views as to the wisdom of your choice in either case, though they don't seem too popular.[3]

[1] On the following day Austen Chamberlain wrote to his wife: 'Beloved: SB is mad! FE is as much disturbed as I am & feels that W's appointment in place of H will rouse great antagonism & is not good for W. But H rang me up again this morning & forebade me to do anything. "I am a proud man and I will not be forced on someone who made it clear that he did not want me".' (*Austen Chamberlain papers*).

[2] Arthur Herbert Drummond Ramsay Steel-Maitland, 1876–1935. Educated at Rugby and Balliol College, Oxford. President of the Oxford Union Society, 1899. Fellow of All Souls College, Oxford, 1900. Conservative MP, 1910–18 and 1918–29. An original member of the Other Club, 1911. Parliamentary Under-Secretary, Colonial Office, 1915–17. Created Baronet, 1917. Head of the Department of Overseas Trade (Development and Intelligence), 1917–19. Minister of Labour, 1924–9.

[3] Not all commentators were hostile to Churchill's appointment to the Exchequer. On November 7, the same day as this letter, Herbert Sidebotham wrote in the *Daily Despatch*:

David Lloyd George to Winston S. Churchill: telegram
(*Churchill papers: 2/138*)

7 November 1924

Warm congratulations on your appointment to a great office. Best wishes.
Lloyd George

Randolph Churchill to Winston S. Churchill
(*Churchill papers: 2/138*)

7 November 1924   Eton College

Dear Papa—
   I am so glad to see that you are Chancellor of the Exchequer. Everyone
here is very pleased about it. On Wednesday we had a Scout Field day. We
went in lorries about seven miles. When we got there we had different Scout-
ing games which were rather fun. I am looking forward very much to long
leave. I do hope you are well.

Much Love From
Randolph

Consuelo Balsan to Winston S. Churchill
(*Churchill papers: 2/138*)

7 November 1924   South of France

My dear Winston,
   We are delighted to see your appointment. I know that it has always been
your ambition to succeed your Father in this office and it is a curious trick
of Fate that you should have returned to the Conservative Party before
doing so. It is not a long step from the Treasury to PM and I can see no
serious rivals, so mind you move with circumspection and care. What tremendous opportunities for years of useful work lie ahead of the Conservative
Party unless they succumb to the sleeping sickness of security. The Liberal
Party must be reconstructed & kept going, it is too dangerous for the only
alternative to the present Government to be a Socialist one.
   Will you please make an end of the Socialist Sunday Schools—for they

---

'Mr Churchill is not only by common consent the ablest commoner in the Conservative
Party, but there is good reason to think that the Chancellor of the Exchequer is the post
that will best suit his abilities. . . . Finance in the hands of a real orator will become, as
Gladstone made it in the old days, a glowing enthusiasm.'

are the most subversive movement of all the Communist activities. The Labour Party has added one million votes to its strength during the last years & if these SSS are allowed to continue their teaching against God's law & man's indiscriminately, no appeal to Patriotism &—righteousness will influence the next generation of electors. The law protects a minor against the evil of alcohol & the contamination of vice. Is it not an equally serious offence to corrupt a child's mind so that he is no longer able to distinguish good from evil? That is what the SSS have been doing for the last 15 years since I started fighting them in West Ham yet the authorities & the Church have done nothing! It is time they did.

Forgive such a long letter and dont trouble to answer. I am so pleased you have joined the forces of law & order—carry them down the stream of social reform & dont let them feel too secure! The best of luck & may God prosper you—Love to Clemmie,

affectionately
Consuelo

L. S. Amery: diary

(*Amery papers*)

7 November 1924

The new cabinet duly announced in the Press and no little surprise and some annoyance at Winston's preferment. If he means to play the game about Empire development and Preference no one could be better. If he doesn't he may make my position very difficult.

Winston S. Churchill to Lord Rosebery

(*Rosebery papers*)

8 November 1924   Chartwell Manor

My dear Lord Rosebery,

Thank you so much for yr letter of congratulation. The plan of campaign wh I outlined to you in my typed note of early October has worked out vy exactly; & we have today a great & good chance. I think everyone wishes to be worthy of it. Five years of steady sensible liberal (with a small 'l' of course) Government will improve our affairs appreciably.

I am vy glad to go to the Exchequer, & on Wednesday next I propose to wear at the pricking of the Sheriffs, those robes wh have slumbered in their tin box since January 1886.[1]

The Times has been none too friendly, but as they are sun worshippers this ought not to matter in the immediate future.[2]

Let me come and lunch with you again please when you come south.

With every good wish,
Believe me Yours vy sincerely
Winston S. Churchill

Sir James Barrie[3] to Winston S. Churchill

(*Churchill papers: 2/138*)

9 November 1924

My Dear Churchill,

It was a great pleasure to me to read of your appointment to the Chancellorship of the Exchequer. As you know, I dont see eye to eye with you about the Labour party, but with the outlook that you have I think your joining with the Conservatives was your proper and honourable and straightforward course, and as for the appointment itself I look upon it as not only the most

---

[1] On 13 November 1924 the *Oldham Standard* reported that, at Churchill's first official function as Chancellor of the Exchequer, 'the robes he wore were those which his father, Lord Randolph Churchill on leaving the Treasury, refused to hand over to his successor. He declared that he had paid for them and meant to keep them.'

[2] On 4 November 1924, three days before Baldwin announced his new Cabinet to the public, *The Times* had criticized what it considered a campaign to place Churchill in the Cabinet, calling it unfortunate that 'Mr Churchill should be publicly paraded at this moment, as he was paraded last night by Sir William Bull and others, as a kind of special hero of the elections. That demonstration was at least ill-timed. In spite of its prudent inclusion of a telegram of loyalty to Mr Baldwin, it will revive suspicions, however ill-founded, of an old familiar intrigue which was more obvious in the election of 1923 than it has been in the last few weeks.' But in the same article *The Times* had itself suggested that Churchill should be included in the Cabinet for his 'wit, imagination, and driving power'. On November 7, after the new Cabinet had been announced, *The Times* leader called his appointment 'the most daring appointment, from the public point of view'. They added: 'Mr Churchill's administrative ability, which is not questioned, will be tested to the uttermost in an office which, more than any other falls under the constant test of vigilant expert criticism. He has an immense opportunity of showing, what the public have often doubted, that he is capable not merely of brilliant imagination, but of taking the best advice and of forming a sober judgement upon it. In any case his fitness for the post will be determined solely henceforth by his achievements at the Treasury, and not by any more discursive political activity.'

[3] James Matthew Barrie, 1860–1937. Playwright and novelist, he published his first book in 1887, and his most famous work, *Peter Pan*, in 1904. Created Baronet, 1913. Order of Merit, 1922. President of the Society of Authors from 1928 until his death.

interesting of all, but as the one most likely to redound to the glory of our country.

Yours sincerely
J. M. Barrie

L. S. Amery to Winston S. Churchill
(*Churchill papers: 2/136*)

9 November 1924

My dear Winston,

I meant to try & get hold of you over the week end for a talk, but have been seedy. There are several matters we ought to settle between ourselves at once, like Wembley, and a much wider range of matters on which we can, I believe, achieve really great results in cooperation. You have a wonderful opportunity for creative finance &, happily, know enough about the Treasury to go there as master & not as mouthpiece. If you have any time for a talk tomorrow afternoon I could come across to the Treasury any time before 5 pm.

There are certain things like Singapore & the Economic Conference Resolutions, which I feel we ought to announce with the least possible delay. The same I think also applies to the Geneva Protocol which I don't believe we can possibly accept, even if the Dominions accepted it, which is extremely improbable.

Yours very sincerely
L. S. Amery

Winston S. Churchill to L. S. Amery
(*Churchill papers: 18/2*)

9 November 1924   Treasury Chambers

I am told that action about Wembley is urgent. I have not yet formally examined the financial aspects with the Treasury. I have, however, heard from Barstow that he does not think that any additional loss will be incurred by re-opening next year, and even possibly some recovery of the deficit may be achieved. If this basis is sustained on further examination, I should personally be quite ready to advocate the re-opening and continuance of the Exhibition, because the indirect advantage to inter-Imperial trade and the educative value, from an Imperial point of view, are of high consequence.

I am writing to the Prime Minister in the sense of this letter and I am suggesting to him that if the facts are found to be as I believe them, he might announce our intention to keep the Exhibition open next year in his speech at the Guildhall and, at the same time, add an appeal to the industrial community to come in and do their best to support the Exhibition. It would, of course, be necessary to make it clear that we would not come forward ourselves unless supported by similar efforts on the part of the other guarantors and parties concerned.

Of course I write this in ignorance of the Prime Minister's views, but I shall know tomorrow. Meanwhile I suggest to you that we should meet at the Treasury tomorrow morning at 12.30 and see if a workable plan can be hammered out, and a suitable passage drafted for the Prime Minister. Perhaps you will get hold of Stevenson and bring him with you as I know he has the whole matter at his finger ends.

Winston S. Churchill to Stanley Baldwin

(*Churchill papers: 18/2*)

9 November 1924   Chartwell Manor

What are your views about Wembley? Personally I have been very keen to see it re-open, but of course without knowing the finances. I found in my preliminary talk with Barstow that he did not think any further loss would be incurred by our running it a second year, on the contrary he thought that we might get some of the money back for ourselves and the guarantors. It is like having a second brew of tea out of the same pot. As long as we can be sure we don't lose any more I think we should be justified in going on because of the indirect advantages to Inter-Imperial trade and of the great educative value from an Imperial point of view. I have a little band of workmen here with whom I have been constructing my dam for the last three months; almost every one of them has had his day at Wembley and from the talk I have heard among them there is no doubt that it has left a profound impression on their minds. It brings the British Empire home to them in a way which nothing else can do.

On the other hand we could of course only come forward ourselves provided the other guarantors and the Dominions jointly played up and this will require a little negotiation.

I am seeing Lord Stevenson to-day on the finance and shall be glad to talk to you with more knowledge tomorrow.[1]

---

[1] The Wembley Exhibition did reopen for a further season in 1925.

Sir Philip Chetwode[1] *to Winston S. Churchill*

(*Churchill papers: 2/138*)

10 November 1924

My dear Churchill,

Will you allow your one time Military Secretary to congratulate you and wish you all success on your new high office.

I can clearly describe the feeling of relief in the army at getting a Government which is likely to govern, and will have an Imperial outlook. It is in no small way due to your persistent Campaign Against the Reds and all those who prefer any flag but their own.

Don't be too ferocious with the poor army—we are just beginning to get back to 1914 standards—in fact better in some respects—but I am sure you know well our difficulties.

I hope it may not be long before I have to congratulate you on being PM.

Yours sincerely,
Philip W. Chetwode

Winston S. Churchill to Lord Beatty

(*Beatty papers*)

11 November 1924   Treasury Chambers

My dear Beatty,

I am so grateful to you for your kind letter of congratulations.

I am one of your greatest admirers, and I never cease to proclaim you as an inheritor of the grand tradition of Nelson.

How I wish I could have guided events a little better and a little longer. Jutland would have had a different ring if the plans already formed in my mind after the Dogger Bank for securing you the chief command had grown to their natural fruition.

I live a good deal in those tremendous past days.

Once more my sincere thanks,
Yours ever,
Winston S.C.

[1] Philip Walhouse Chetwode, 1869–1950. Entered Army, 1889. Succeeded his father as 7th Baronet, 1905. Brigadier-General, 1914; Major-General, 1916; Commanded the 5th Cavalry Brigade, 1914–15; the 2nd Cavalry Division, 1915–16; the Desert Corps, Egypt, 1916–17; the 20th Army Corps, 1917–18. Took part in the capture of Jerusalem, 1917. Lieutenant-General, 1919. Military Secretary, War Office, 1919–20. Deputy Chief of the Imperial General Staff, 1920–2. Commander-in-Chief, Aldershot, 1923–7. Commander-in-Chief, India, 1930–5. Field-Marshal, 1933. Order of Merit, 1936. Created Baron, 1945.

Winston S. Churchill to Austen Chamberlain
(*Austen Chamberlain papers*)

11 November 1924   Treasury Chambers
Personal

My dear Austen,

I was a little chilled—I admit—because I wanted to rejoice with you on
the restoration to power of several old friends. Also I am indeed sorry that
Horne is not with us. I hope that is only temporary. I am sure you will try
yr utmost—& so will I.

Yr vy kind letter quite warms me again.

With all good wishes,
Believe me
Yours vy sincerely
Winston S. Churchill

Winston S. Churchill to Austen Chamberlain
(*Austen Chamberlain papers*)

14 November 1924   Treasury Chambers
Private

My dear Austen,

I cannot help feeling that the decision about Russia involves a very critical
issue for the Government. When millions have been so excited on the subject
during the Election, it would be most dangerous to disappoint their reasonable expectations and to lead them to suppose that now we are all in office
we have receded from the views we expressed during the campaign. Failure
on the part of a Government to respond to the mandate given them by the
Electors would immediately cause widespread dissatisfaction. The Labour
Party would be swift to point the moral, ie that we had only used the Russian
bogey to frighten the Electors into giving us their votes, and that the moment
we were ourselves responsible we made very little change in the policy of our
predecessors. Such an impression would affect the prestige of the Government from the very outset.

Moreover we shall in all probability have to proclaim in a few days' time
that we believe the Zinoviev letter[1] to be authentic, and that it is only part

[1] A letter, signed Grigory Zinoviev, Chairman of the Third Communist International (the
Comintern), and by Arthur MacManus, the British member of the Comintern Presidium,
urging the British Communist Party 'to stir up the masses of the British proletariat', to create

and parcel of the general policy of propaganda unceasingly pursued by the Soviets. If we say this, it follows that we believe the Bolsheviks have broken their solemn engagements under which they were admitted to this country both in the days of the Krassin Mission[1] and in those of Rakovsky.[2] If they have thus broken their engagements, and have attempted to stir up rebellion in our midst, what grounds are there that can justify our proceeding to allow them to remain here?

The representatives of no other country would be permitted to remain if convicted, in our opinion, of similar offences. I am certain that no mere Note or answer will by itself be sufficient to satisfy either justice or public opinion. It is essential that *action* should follow a declaration of the authenticity of the Zinoviev letter. The question is what action.

The more I reflect on the matter, the more sure I am that we should revoke the recognition of the Soviet Government which was decided on by MacDonald. This would not mean that we should lose touch with Russia. It would still be possible to revert to the arrangement instituted under the Coalition Government between Horne and Krassin. A Trade Delegation could remain, and no needless obstacle would be put in the way of trade with Russia. We should not be depriving ourselves or the Russians of any material or practical advantage so far as commerce is concerned. We should strip a Power which had violated its engagements of the diplomatic status it had sought and received at our hands. This would, I am sure, be everywhere accepted as a strong and sensible act giving full expression to the national mandate. It would not of course be an irrevocable act, because if after a few years of probation it was found that the Soviet Government had desisted

---

communist cells among soldiers, sailors and munition workers, and to beware of Ramsay MacDonald and the 'bourgeois' Labour Party. The letter was first published in the *Daily Mail*. The Labour Party declared it to be a forgery, but during the election campaign Baldwin had told an audience at Southend: 'It makes my blood boil to read of the way in which Mr Zinoviev is speaking of the Prime Minister today. Though one time there went up a cry of "Hands off Russia!" I think it is time somebody said to Russia: "Hands off England!"'' On 10 December 1924 Baldwin told the House of Commons that the letter was genuine. Later it was shown to be a forgery, although the Conservative Party Managers, believing it to be genuine, had paid £5,000 to one of the men who had 'discovered' it.

[1] A Mission, led by the Soviet Commissar for Foreign Trade, Leonid Krassin, which in May 1920 negotiated with the Lloyd George Government, and secured the opening of Soviet trade relations with Britain. Churchill, who was then Secretary of State for War, strenuously opposed the negotiations (see Volume 4 of this biography, pages 391–2, 398–400 and 412–30).

[2] Christian Georgievich Rakovsky, 1873–1941. Born in Bulgaria. A social-democrat leader in the Balkans before 1914. Negotiator for the Bolsheviks in the Ukraine, 1918. Effective ruler of the Ukraine, 1919–22. One of the Soviet negotiators at Genoa, 1922. Soviet Chargé d'Affaires in London, 1923–5. (Ambassador, 1925); Ambassador in Paris, 1925–7. Recalled by Stalin to the Soviet Union, 1927. In exile, 1927–36 (as a supporter of Trotsky). Tried during the Stalin purges, and sentenced to imprisonment for life. He died in prison in 1941.

from propaganda in the British Empire, recognition could again be extended. I am sending a similar letter to the Prime Minister.[1]

Yrs vy sincerely,
Winston S. Churchill

Winston S. Churchill to Sir Warren Fisher[2]
(*Churchill papers: 18/3*)

16 November 1924   Chartwell Manor

1. Will you kindly tell me why the financial year dates from March 31st and the income tax year from April 5th instead of from a common date for the two, or instead of running concurrently with the calendar year? Would it not be a great convenience and simplification if all years were concurrent and expressed simply by the date of the year instead of by such expressions as—1924/25? I am well aware of the inconvenience of anything which interrupts the statistical continuity.

2. In regard to Admiralty finance and to a less extent in regard to the War Office and the Air Ministry finance I am sure that the absence of any capital account due to the domination of March 31st constitutes a serious weakness in Treasury control. I have repeatedly seen the Treasury urging the Admiralty to spend more money before the 31st March in order to lighten the burden on the following year, or to take advantage of a surplus accruing in the currency. The power, possessed by the Admiralty in particular, of throwing the March payments to contractors on one side or the other of the 31st gives them a margin which before the War often amounted to several millions by which their whole presentation of their finances to Parliament may be clouded.

In my opinion this power of manipulation ought not to be possessed by a spending department which should be confined to rigid figures. The whole of this elasticity should be in the hands of the Treasury. For instance when a ship is laid down, or a dock yard like Singapore commenced, Parliament

---

[1] British Diplomatic relations with Soviet Russia were not severed by the Conservative Government until 1927. They were re-established by the Labour Government in 1929.

[2] Norman Fenwick Warren Fisher, 1879–1948. Educated at Winchester and Hertford College, Oxford. Entered the Inland Revenue Department, 1903. Seconded to the National Health Insurance Commission, 1912–13. Deputy Chairman, Board of Inland Revenue, 1914–18; Chairman, 1918–19. Knighted, 1919. Permanent Secretary of the Treasury, and Official Head of the Civil Service, 1919–39. Member of the Committee on Ministers' Powers, 1929–32. Subsequently a Director of several companies, including the Anglo-Iranian Oil Co.

should be informed not only of the total cost but of the annual instalments over the whole period of construction. If Parliament agrees to the building of a ship or yard the whole amount should be credited as a book entry to the Admiralty and the inevitable fluctuations in the financing of this irrevocable capital charge should be kept entirely distinct from the ordinary administrative and annual expenditure.

Unprotected by the mystifying veil of fluctuation in capital expenditure sanctioned by Parliament, the growth of establishment and maintenance charges would be nakedly presented to the House of Commons. If the First Lord of the Admiralty says to Parliament 'I have effected the reduction of a million in the naval estimates', the House would reply 'Not at all, you have merely delayed paying for a portion of capital expenditure to which we are already committed which will fall upon us in succeeding years and in the meanwhile your establishment charges have in fact advanced by half a million. You have therefore no credit for your economy, on the contrary are guilty of an increase.'

On the other hand the Treasury ought to be able to say to the Admiralty 'It is convenient for us to vary the annual instalments for the building of this ship within the following limits. If it suits us to accelerate the discharge of our capital liability we shall invite you to expedite your construction as far as practicable. If under-spending occurs we will carry this sum forward to your credit as a book entry for the next year. Once we have agreed to the total for a ship and to the date of completion we shall not argue with you about that portion of the expenditure, nor will you yourselves be allowed to hide behind any diminution of it.'

Following this train of thought I should like to see naval estimates presented in two parts, viz The Current and Capital Expenditure. This would prevent the lax growth of normal charges from being obscured by slothfulness in working off irrevocable capital liabilities. The precious power of *viremont* [1] should be as far as possible reserved to the Exchequer and as little as possible enjoyed by the spending department.

Pray let me know what is involved in this change in accounting.

---

[1] *Viremont:* a banking term, meaning the transfer of funds from one branch of Government financing to another.

Winston S. Churchill to Sir George Barstow

(*Churchill papers: 18/2*)

16 November 1924   Chartwell Manor

WAR PENSIONS

I wish to be supplied with very complete statistical information on this subject and if necessary some extra expense may be incurred.

Let actuarial calculations be made showing the estimated expense of this charge up to the year 1968 ie 50 years after the conclusion of the War. The estimated number of pensioners, male and female should also be shown year by year over this period. The ordinary table of mortality adopted by the great insurance companies may be accepted. The standard of administration might be take nas the average of the last three years, which comprise as your tables show both severe economy and liberal relaxation. It is probable that the lives of many of the disabled men will be much shorter than the average longevity through their war injuries; but against this fact must be set the continuous pressure of Parliament to a more compassionate administration. Balancing the two I think the last three years' average and the ordinary table of mortality would make a very fair basis. However I am quite ready to consider alternatives.

As soon as the above calculations have been made let a scheme be worked out for spreading the whole of this war pension charge evenly over the 44 years up to the year 1968. Explain to me how the finance of such a scheme would work (this need not wait for precise figures, rough typical figures can be taken).

I presume that a fund would be formed under War Pensions Commissioners and that the Treasury would issue each year so much pension stock as was necessary to defray the difference between the average charge over the 44 years and the actual charge for the year. I presume that these issues would be so dated as to expire year by year in increasing quantities during the period when the actual cost of the pensions fell below the average figure.

Let me see these figures. Show the amount it would be necessary to borrow in each year until the parity is reached and the subsequent burdens thrown on the Exchequer after parity has been passed.

Show me any better way that occurs to you of achieving the purpose I have in hand.

I may add that this matter should not be handled except in such a way that it would hardly be worth while handling it again.

Let me know the estimated capital liability of the State for pensions at the close of the War and the estimated capital liability to-day. For the purpose of the former figure you are of course entitled to use retrospective knowledge.

Meanwhile I think a letter should be prepared to the Pensions Ministry drawing their attention to the rapid increase of expenditure which has followed upon the relaxation of control by the late Government.

Winston S. Churchill to Sir Horace Hamilton[1]

(*Churchill papers: 18/7*)

16 November 1924   Chartwell Manor

I have studied these Tables.

1. Will you explain to me why the McKenna Duties produced five and a half millions in 1920–21 and only two and a half millions in 1923–24?[2]

2. Table 3 presents an extraordinary picture of greatly increased consuming power in all commodities except beer and spirits in spite of greatly increased taxation. It proves that the mass of the population has vastly improved its scale of living and diminished its consumption of alcohol. It is indeed an impressive and encouraging picture.

The question which arises is the one I posed to you last week—Has this great increase in the consuming power been accompanied by a proportionate increase in the producing power, or even possibly by a diminution in the producing power?[3] Has it been gained at the expense of the Direct tax

[1] Horace Perkins Hamilton, 1880–1971. Educated Tonbridge School and Hertford College, Oxford. Entered the Inland Revenue Department, 1904; transferred to the Treasury, 1911; Private Secretary to successive Chancellors of the Exchequer, 1912–18. Deputy Chairman, Board of Inland Revenue, 1918–19. Chairman, Board of Customs and Excise, 1919–27. Knighted, 1921. Permanent Secretary, Board of Trade, 1927–37. Permanent Under-Secretary of State for Scotland, 1937–46. Adviser to the Syrian Government on taxation, 1946–7. United Kingdom Member of the Commonwealth Economic Committee, 1947–61.

[2] Sir Horace Hamilton replied on November 18: 'the revenue from the McKenna duties in 1920/21 amounted to £5,481,000, nearly £4,000,000 of which came from motor cars, their parts and accessories. The post-war boom was then over, and in the autumn of 1920 one of the severest trade depressions on record began to develop. The result on the yield from the McKenna duties was a heavy fall to £1,698,000 in 1921/22. This was followed by a subsequent recovery to £2,357,000 in 1922/23 and £2,590,000 in 1923/24 (the last two figures relate only to Great Britain and Northern Ireland, the earlier figures including the Irish Free State). Finally, the gradual fall in prices in recent years must have had some effect in reducing the yield of the ad valorem duties on imports' (*Churchill papers: 18/7*).

[3] On November 21 Sir Horace Hamilton, in a second letter to Churchill, wrote that 'you may care to have one or two notes on Table 3 which go to modify in some degree the favourable view of the consuming power of the population which the figures taken by themselves present. For instance, the increased consumption of tea and cocoa is no doubt largely due to the fact that they are the cheapest drinks apart from water, and denotes little more than that people can no longer afford to drink beer and spirits in the same quantities as heretofore.'

payer? Is it true for instance that the capital reserves of individuals and of businesses have been and are being depleted? Are we living on our hump? This grave question should engage your most searching attention.

3. A transference of wealth from the few to the many which produces a smaller expenditure on articles of luxury and a greater expenditure upon commodities of general consumption would not in itself excite any anxiety; and no doubt this factor is powerfully at work. But if the process of saving and the accumulation of capital has been seriously checked the consequential reactions would be none the less serious through being deferred. Are these reactions not already manifested in the growth of unemployment? If this were so the pleasing picture of the Customs and Excise would undergo a melancholy transformation. It would portray a great increase of indulgence by the mass of the consumers without any increase of production, obtained at the expense of the saving power of the community and by the depletion of its capital resources manifesting itself already in the decay of enterprise, the growth of unemployment and the pauperization of a large proportion of the people.

We must get to the root of this matter if wise decisions are to be taken.

4. Please now let me have your best possible forecast for 1925/26. I shall quite understand that such estimates are at this stage largely speculative.

5. Will you also endeavour tentatively to forecast the next three years of Customs & Excise on the present basis of taxation. Give me your own forecast and what you think is safe. Of course it will be purely speculative. Give me also this forecast on the basis of a 10% expansion in national well-being expressed in trade and consumption fully operative at the end of the third year. Do this also on a 15% basis. You are entitled to give these figures under all reserve.

Winston S. Churchill to Philip Snowden

(*Churchill papers: 18/1*)

17 November 1924   Treasury Chambers

My dear Snowden,

Now that I am entering on my new appointment I feel that it would be a great advantage to myself and of benefit to the public interest if you would give me an opportunity of a conversation with you about the more important outstanding points. If this suggestion commends itself to you I could be at your disposal at any time on Friday next, and I need not say that I shd greatly value the meeting.

Yours sincerely

Sir Philip Sassoon to Winston S. Churchill

(*Churchill papers: 2/136*)

17 November 1924   Air Ministry

My dear Winston,

Thank you ten thousand times for your most charming letter which has given me enormous pleasure. Thank you also for all you did on my behalf. It was very very kind of you & I am certain that I owe my job a great deal to your efforts on my behalf.[1] You know that I am grateful. Nothing could suit me better than being here—as I love the work & consider myself Extremely Lucky to be working under such a nice fellow as I am. It is marvellous that you should be at the Exchequer & that we shd be all together—It is a jolly Troupe; & I hope will prove a successful one—I am looking forward to having Clemmie to stay with me this week.

á bientot, Winston, & again thank you for *everything*. What a good friend you have been to me all my life. I am so happy.

Alfred Duff Cooper to Winston S. Churchill

(*Churchill papers: 1/172*)

20 November 1924

My dear Winston,

I have been thinking over all the advice you were kind enough to give me the other morning and I feel convinced that you are right and that as usual the bolder way is also the wiser.[2]

It was wonderfully kind of you in the midst of all your heavy work to find time to talk to me and to give thought to my future. Someone who was recently urging me to try to get the job in question used as an argument your well known loyalty to your friends, saying that if once I had served you I could always rely on your assistance. But that I feel sure that I can do in any case and I believe that in this instance you have shown yourself a better and more thoughtful friend to me by dissuading me from taking the job than you could have in any other way.

Yrs ever
Duff Cooper

[1] Sir Philip Sassoon had been appointed Under-Secretary of State for Air.
[2] On November 11 Duff Cooper had gone to see Churchill at the Treasury, hoping to become his Parliamentary Private Secretary. In his diary Duff Cooper noted: 'He said he was very flattered at my wanting the job and that he was prepared to give it to me, but that he strongly dissuaded me from taking it. He said that I ought to get on by making speeches and that having a job of that sort could only hinder me' (*Old Men Forget*, page 137).

Winston S. Churchill to Austen Chamberlain

(*Austen Chamberlain papers*)

21 November 1924   Treasury Chambers
Secret

My dear Austen,

I hope you will allow me to see the Intercepts as they emerge. I have as
you know always studied them from their earliest beginnings, for which I
was to some extent responsible, in the autumn of 1914. They are bound to
come to the knowledge of the First Lord & the S of S for War, & also I
believe to that of the S of S for India. In these circumstances it wd not be
right for the Chancellor of the Exchequer to be left in ignorance of this all
important class of information.

In MacDonald's time he was himself long kept in ignorance of them by
the Foreign Office, & this ignorance was shared by Snowden. But I have
ascertained that Horne as Ch of the Exchequer was accustomed to see them
when we were last colleagues together.

Yours vy sincerely
Winston S. Churchill

Austen Chamberlain to Winston S. Churchill

(*Churchill papers: 18/1*)

21 November 1924   Foreign Office

My dear Winston,

I will speak to you about the directions that I have given in regard to the
class of secret papers of which you speak. I have stopped all circulation except
necessary communications with opposite numbers in other offices. These
papers no longer go to any minister. But I must give you my reasons verbally.
I do not wish to put them in writing as you will understand when I tell them
to you.

Yrs sincerely
Austen C.

Winston S. Churchill to Austen Chamberlain

(*Austen Chamberlain papers*)

21 November 1924   Treasury Chambers
Secret

My dear Austen,

Many thanks for your note. Oddly enough since I wrote to you this morning an incident has occurred illustrating my point of view. The First Lord[1] & Beatty came by appointment to discuss Singapore, which as you know is a big matter for me. The First Lord immediately quoted from the intercept of the Japanese Ambassador's[2] account to his Govt of his conversation with you on Singapore—how you 'appeared embarrassed' etc—Obviously a discussion between the Treasury & a spending Department where the latter has superior secret information not in possession of the Chancellor is bound to be conducted on very uneven terms. On the other hand, knowing the subject from end to end, I do not see how the First Ld & the S of S for War cd be denied information necessarily in the possession of their subordinates in the respective Intelligence branches.

I am sure you will bear all this in mind.

Yours vy sincerely
Winston S. Churchill

Austen Chamberlain to Winston S. Churchill

(*Churchill papers: 18/1*)

21 November 1924   Foreign Office

My dear Winston,

This illustrates one of the difficulties.

Both you & the First Lord have had my account of my conversation with

[1] William Clive Bridgeman, 1864–1935. Educated at Eton and Trinity College, Cambridge. Conservative MP for Oswestry, 1906–29. A junior Opposition Whip, 1911. A Lord Commissioner of the Treasury, 1915–16. Assistant Director, War Trade Department, 1916. Parliamentary Secretary Ministry of Labour, 1916–19; Board of Trade, 1920–2. Home Secretary, 1922–4. First Lord of the Admiralty, 1924–9. Created Viscount, 1929. A Governor of the BBC, 1933–5, and its Chairman, 1935.

[2] Gonsuke Hayashi, 1861–1939. Son of General Hayashi, military commander of the Edo period. Graduated in law at Tokyo University, 1887, and joined the Japanese Diplomatic Service. 1st Secretary, London, 1896. In January 1902 he negotiated the Anglo-Japanese treaty with Lord Lansdowne. Created Baron, 1907. Ambassador to Italy, 1908–19. Governor-General of Kwantung, 1919–20. Ambassador to Britain, 1921–6: GCVO, 1921; GCMG, 1926. Appointed Grand Master of Ceremonies, Tokyo, and Baronet, 1929. Privy Councillor 1934.

the Japanese Ambassador in your hands since the 18th. It is more accurate than the Ambassador's. Why or for what purpose the First Lord chose to quote the intercept I don't know, but so unimportant is that intercept that I did not see it myself till you directed my attention to it.

It ought never to have gone to the Admiralty.

I am 'embarrassed' by your request & still more embarrassed by the First Lord's use of the intercept, but was it of any consequence to either of you to know that the Ambassador reported (untruly) that I was 'embarrassed' with him. I think not, tho' it may have given you a slightly malicious joy!

Yrs
Austen C.

Winston S. Churchill to Austen Chamberlain

(*Austen Chamberlain papers*)

22 November 1924   Treasury Chambers
Secret

My dear Austen,

I am sorry to find from your answers that you contemplate making such serious changes in the system which was in vogue when we last were colleagues. Knowing this system and its origins as I do, I do not believe that in practice it will be possible to deprive the Admiralty and the War Office of the special information they have hitherto enjoyed and which but for the Admiralty would never have been at the disposal of the Foreign Office.

I do not see how information which is necessarily at the disposal of the Directors of Naval and Military Intelligence can be withheld from their responsible political chiefs; and if these Ministers are to receive this information, it follows that the Chancellor of the Exchequer should not be denied it. I do not know of course what directions you propose to give, but I should not be prepared myself to acquiesce in any exclusion from these vital matters except upon the decision of the Prime Minister. Would it not be well before you reach any final conclusion in your mind for us to have a talk with the Prime Minister, at which talk perhaps the First Lord of the Admiralty and the Secretary of State for War might be present. Both these heads of departments have been privy in the past to these matters & I feel sure that you will agree that so great a change in the relations of colleagues and in the whole principle of the conduct of Foreign Affairs as we have known it for so many years ought not to be lightly adopted.

As far as my recollection goes the India Office were also privy to this special information & have a separate source for interception & deciphering under the Government of India.

On the general question I can only say that I have studied this information over a longer period and more attentively than probably any other Minister has done. All the years I have been in office since it began in the autumn of 1914 I have read every one of these flimsies and I attach more importance to them as a means of forming a true judgment of public policy in these spheres than to any other source of knowledge at the disposal of the State.

Yours vy sincerely
Winston S. Churchill

Winston S. Churchill to Austen Chamberlain

(Austen Chamberlain papers)

22 November 1924   Turf Club
Private   Piccadilly

My dear Austen,

I cannot refrain from writing you a line to tell you how much I sympathise with you in the evil chance & wrong conduct wh has upset yr well & carefully conceived plan & policy.[1]

I hope however that you will be able to retrieve the situation in the course of the next week or so from an international point of view.

I think foreigners will be fairly lenient in their judgments, because no doubt every foreign colony in Egypt is in gt anxiety & sheltering behind Allenby[2] & the British authority.

Yours vy sincerely
Winston S. Churchill

PS. As one who differed on the Russian show, may I add unstinted congratulations on the reception of yr notes by the Press & public.

W

---

[1] On 20 November 1924 Major-General Sir Lee Stack—the Governor-General of the Sudan and Sirdar of the Egyptian Army—was murdered in Cairo by Egyptian extremists (see page 257, note 1, and page 275 note 1).

[2] Edmund Henry Hynman Allenby, 1861–1936. Entered Army, 1882. Major-General, 1909. Commanded 1st Cavalry Division, British Expeditionary Force, 1914. Commanded the Cavalry Corps, 1914–15. Commanded 5th Army Corps, 1915. Knighted, 1915. Commanded 3rd Army, 1915–17. Lieutenant-General, 1916. General, 1917. Commander-in-Chief, Egyptian Expeditionary Force, 1917–19. Received the surrender of Jerusalem, 11 December 1917. Created Viscount Allenby of Megiddo, 1919. Field-Marshal, 1919. High Commissioner for Egypt and the Sudan, 1919–25. His only son was killed in action in France in 1917.

Winston S. Churchill to Lord Birkenhead[1]

(*Churchill papers: 18/1*)

23 November 1924   Treasury Chambers
Secret & Personal

My dear Fred,

I send you the enclosed correspondence which raises an issue wh I think
is most important. There is no reason why Austen shd adopt an attitude of
exclusiveness & secrecy in Foreign affairs which is quite different from the
position taken by all his predecessors in any Govt in wh we have been colleagues. The matter affects Bridgeman, Worthy,[2] myself, and you; & I trust
you will act with me in the matter. Please let me have these papers back, &
burn this letter.

Yrs ever
W

Austen Chamberlain to Winston S. Churchill

(*Churchill papers: 18/1*)

23 November 1924   Foreign Office
Secret & Personal

My dear Winston,

I shall welcome a talk with you & the PM if necessary, even a Cabinet
decision on the subject on which we differ.

Meanwhile you will have clearly in mind that my ban is not directed
against *you* but against circulation. I have always expected that someone—if
not you, then another—would demand an explanation in Cabinet. I did
explain my reasons to the Zinovieff letter Comttee because they arose out of
what I learned in that connection.

The amazing Allenby has not yet thought it necessary to inform me of
what passed at his interview with Zaghlul[3] or since!

---

[1] Lord Birkenhead had been appointed Secretary of State for India in the new Government.

[2] Laming Evans, 1868–1931. Admitted solicitor, 1890; retired, 1910. Conservative MP
for Colchester, 1910–18, 1918–29, and for Westminster St Georges, 1929–31. Inspector of
Administrative Services, War Office, 1914–15. Controller, Foreign Trade Department,
Foreign Office, 1916. Assumed the prefix surname of Worthington, 1916, and known as
'Worthy'. Created Baronet, 1916. Parliamentary Secretary, Ministry of Munitions, 1916–18.
Minister of Blockade, 1918. Minister of Pensions, 1919–20. Minister without Portfolio,
1920–1. Secretary of State for War, 1921–2 and 1924–9.

[3] Saad Zaghlul, 1860–1927. A leading Egyptian nationalist, he participated in Arabi
Pasha's revolt of 1882. Detained by the British, 1882–4. Councillor of the Native Court of
Appeal, 1892. Appointed Minister of Education by Lord Cromer, 1906. Vice-President of

The more I consider it, the better I am satisfied that the course you advocated at our second Cabinet was right.[1]

Yrs
Austen C.

Winston S. Churchill to Austen Chamberlain
(*Austen Chamberlain papers*)

23 November 1924
Private

Chartwell Manor

My dear Austen,

I think you must be relieved at the way in which the Allenby excursion has been received by the Press, and even the French I see are not unfavourable. I expect every foreign Consul in Cairo has been telegraphing to his Government supporting the action which the British have at last taken to discharge their responsibilities to Europe in the maintenance of order. The only thing which occurs to me is in connection with the fine of £500,000. Would it not be well to issue tonight for Monday's Press a brief statement on the lines of that which you showed us at the Cabinet yesterday morning, viz that 'the British Government did not intend to benefit themselves in any way from the money but would devote it exclusively to philanthropic institutions in the Sudan in memory of Sir Lee Stack's[2] lifelong work for the Sudanese people'.

I think myself that this would round the whole thing off safely and it would, I am sure, be so much in accord with the Cabinet's view that you would have no need to wait for their formal approval.

Forgive me for making this suggestion. I daresay it has already occurred to you.

Yours vy sincerely
Winston S. Churchill

---

the Legislative Assembly, 1914. Urged Egyptian autonomy, 1918; arrested, March 1919 and deported to Malta. Negotiated in London with Lord Milner and Adly Pasha, 1921. Returned to Egypt, 1921. Deported, first to Aden, then to the Seychelles, then to Gibraltar, 1921–3. Released, April 1923. Prime Minister of Egypt, January 1924; forced to resign after the murder of Sir Lee Stack, November 1924. President of the Chamber of Deputies, 1925–7.

[1] Zaghlul resigned on 24 November 1924, and was succeeded as Prime Minister by Ahmad Ziwar Pasha, the President of the Senate, who at once accepted, in full, Lord Allenby's ultimatum (see also page 275, note 1).

[2] Lee Oliver Fitzmaurice Stack, 1868–1924. Entered the Army, 1888. Served in Crete, 1899. Joined the Egyptian Army, 1899. On active service in the Sudan, 1902. Sudan Agent, 1908. Civil Secretary, Sudan Government, 1913–16. Sirdar of the Egyptian Army, 1917–24. Acting Governor-General of the Sudan, 1917–19; Governor-General, 1919–24. Knighted, 1918.

Brendan Bracken to his mother

(*Bracken papers*)

23 November 1924

Dearest Mama,

I shall never be so happy as I was last week. Dear Winston became Chancellor after two years of enforced absence from Parliament and after a campaign of misrepresentation & abuse that seemed to blight his hopes & chances for a very long time.

Winston S. Churchill to Lady Keyes[1]

(*Keyes papers*)

24 November 1924   Treasury Chambers
Private

I have not till now had a moment to thank you for all your work in the Election. I was greatly influenced in deciding to come to Epping by the fact that you and Roger were entrenched there. Certainly the result has from every point of view far exceeded my hopes. There is however no rose without its thorn, & I feel that my duties as Chancellor of the Exchequer will leave me on the other side of the table to the Admiralty, at any rate during the unhealthy Estimate season. I hope that before you repent of your exertions you will come & have it out with me at luncheon at No. 11, where we shall be installed in the New Year.

Once more thanking you,

Believe me, yours sincerely,
Winston S. Churchill

Thomas Jones: diary

(*Jones papers*)

24 November 1924

At 3.15 pm I saw the Prime Minister.

. . . we talked of Beaverbrook, whose spectre is never very far from SB's mind. Beaverbrook had come back from Edwin Montagu's[2] funeral in the

---

[1] Eva Mary Salvin Bowlby, 1832–1973. She married Sir Roger Keyes in 1906.

[2] Edwin Montagu, 1879–1924. Liberal MP, 1906–22. Financial Secretary to the Treasury, February 1914–February 1915; May 1915–July 1916. Chancellor of the Duchy of Lancaster, February–May 1915; January–June 1916. Minister of Munitions, July–December 1916. Secretary of State for India, June 1917–March 1922. Montagu died on 15 November 1924. A month later Venetia Montagu wrote to Churchill: 'Edwin had such love and admiration for you. The last event of public interest of which he showed any realisation was when you were made Chancellor of the Exchequer and he was so thrilled and delighted' (*Churchill papers: 1/199*).

same coach as Winston. Winston was much moved at the loss of an old friend and colleague, but Beaverbrook was utterly callous and could only retail sordid gossip of old intrigues.

Winston S. Churchill to Sir Horace Hamilton

(*Churchill papers: 18/7*)

24 November 1924

You certainly dim the startling brilliancy of the figures I studied.

1. I suppose the quality of the beer has also diminished as well as the quantity.

2. What about money spent on entertainment, cinemas & the like.

3. What is yr general view of the consuming power of the people, compared to pre war.

WSC

Winston S. Churchill to Sir Warren Fisher

(*Churchill papers: 18/3*)

25 November 1924

We might at any rate get rid of the clumsy expression '1924-5' which conveys so little to the mind, and call each financial year after the calendar year in which nine out of its twelve months fall, ie the present year would be 1924 and next year, 1925. What do you think of this?

Winston S. Churchill to Sir Otto Niemeyer[1]

(*Churchill papers: 18/3*)

25 November 1924

WAR DEBTS

This situation has been transformed by the Dawes scheme and by the ability and readiness of Germany to pay Reparations of which our share will

[1] Otto Ernst Niemeyer, 1883–1971. Educated at St Paul's and Balliol College, Oxford. Entered the Treasury, 1906; Controller of Finance, 1922–7. Member of the Financial Committee of the League of Nations, 1922–37. Knighted, 1924. A Director of the Bank for International Settlements, 1931–65, and of the Bank of England, 1938–52. Chairman of the Governors, London School of Economics, 1941–57.

rise in four or five years to 25 millions p.a.[1] In the pessimism which prevailed when Mr Chamberlain was Chancellor of the Exchequer the Cabinet was urged to blot out as a friendly gesture all European war debts while immediately funding our debt to the United States. Happily this counsel was rejected as far as European debts were concerned.

The Balfour Note reflected the first attempt of the Cabinet to secure something from Europe to relieve us of our annual payments to the United States. With the principle of this Note I was at the time in hearty accord. I would have closed gladly on a European offer of 32 millions pa reparations and repayments, thus leaving us neither gainers nor losers on the balance.

But the advantage of delay has been very great. 25 millions a year from Germany is actually in sight. This would have been thought utterly impossible only two years ago. The fact is that a few years of peace is bound to lead to the economic and financial recovery of all these great European nations (except Russia excluded by Communism). I believe the British claims on France and Italy may well prove to be of very great value. These countries will not be able, as their prosperity revives, to remain indifferent to the honourable discharge of their obligations.

Sooner or later we shall get proposals from them to compound the debts; and if we are not too precipitate or too sentimental, we ought to be able to receive much more than the minimum of 8 millions p.a. which would result from a present day adoption of the principle of the Balfour Note.

I consider that we should therefore state that all our previous offers have lapsed. Balfour, Bonar Law, Curzon—all are swept away. They were not accepted, the conditions have changed, and they no longer exist. The field is perfectly clear. We are paying in full our obligations to the United States. We preserve unabated in any respect our claims against our Ally debtors. If this situation is to be altered, it is for them to make proposals for a settlement. And we shall add that, failing such proposals, we shall have to invite them at no distant date to take steps to fund the debts and place them on a business footing.

These are my general views of the attitude we should adopt at the present time, and I think that we should quite soon bring the whole question of French and Italian debts forward into the European arena.

Talk to me about this.

---

[1] On 9 April 1924 two private American citizens, Charles G. Dawes of Chicago and Owen D. Young of Boston, at the request of the Reparations Committee, had issued a report which reassessed Germany's reparation payments at a lower figure than before, and suggested a scheme whereby these payments would be distributed among the Allied and Associated Powers. During 1924 the United States Government gave Germany a loan of $110 million to enable her to rebuild her industry, and thus repay the outstanding reparation payments.

Cabinet minutes

(Cabinet papers: 23/49)

26 November 1924

The Chancellor of the Exchequer gave the Cabinet a review of the present financial situation. After setting forth in some detail the prospects of the present financial year and the date at present available regarding the Budget for 1925–6, he appealed to his colleagues to assist him to the utmost, by careful financial administration in their respective departments, to make the necessary financial provision without involving excessive taxation. In particular, he urged that the Government should concentrate on a few great issues in the social sphere, such as the solutions of the housing problem and an 'all-in' insurance scheme, rather than fritter away our resources on a variety of services which, though possibly good in themselves, were not of vital national importance.

In regard to armaments, the Chancellor of the Exchequer recognised that some increase in the Royal Air Force must be faced in order to secure the safety of the Country, and that there was little, if any, room for reduction in the size of the Army, though he appealed to the Secretary of State for War to keep carefully in view the possibility of any administrative measures for the reduction of expenditure. In view of the probable necessity for the development of a naval base at Singapore and the Admiralty desire for an increase in the Cruiser Programme, he indicated that some investigation was required as to the rate at which these projects could be undertaken consistently with our financial situation and the desirability from a political point of view of avoiding any increase in expenditure on armaments in the forthcoming financial year.

Winston S. Churchill to Sir Warren Fisher and Colonel Guinness

(Churchill papers: 18/3)

26 November 1924

THE ANDERSON REPORT[1]

I presume this scheme in its entirety would be called 'All-in Insurance' and would cover all forms of State Insurance, except of course Unemployment Insurance, which would remain separate.

[1] The Anderson Committee on national insurance had been set up in 1923 by Stanley Baldwin—then Chancellor of the Exchequer. The Anderson Committee report, which was completed early in 1924, had urged a substantial extension of contributory, and compulsory insurance, to which the Government would be the principal contributor.

Pray let me have the existing payments of contributions by employers and workpeople and the contribution of the State both to Unemployment and Health Insurance. Let me also have the present total expenditure by the State on non-contributory Old Age Pensions from the beginning of the Old Age Pensions scheme to the present time. Let me also know what is the future actuarial estimate of the expenses of the non-contributory Old Age Pensions up to 1950 presuming no new contributory schemes are adopted.

Nothing is said in this Report about the effects of the new contributory schemes upon the existing structure of voluntary insurance. What would be the attitude of the existing Insurance Companies and interests to the adoption of these schemes? Would they be content to carry on all their work on the basis that the benefits of their subscribers would be additional to the basic State scheme? If so this would be very satisfactory and would undoubtedly enable every class to make a special provision for its old age—provision on a compulsory State basis and everyone else improving upon this through the voluntary societies to any extent they were able.

The contribution of 1/- a week in addition to the Health Insurance and Unemployment contribution seems to be a very serious factor. The Committee do not attempt to prescribe how it shall be shared between employers and employed. I presume half and half. If so an additional 6d a week in respect of these new schemes would be a very heavy burden on employers. I should like some figures about this. Can you give me a few typical cases of large and small employers showing what the additional 6d a week would mean compared to their total weekly wage bill. The acceptance of such a scheme by the employers would be rendered more easy if it were accompanied at the same time by a reduction in direct taxation. Surely the Inland Revenue could take one or two specimen firms employing 50, 1,000 or 5,000 people and see what the annual burden for the new insurance would be at 6d a week compared with the relief which would be afforded by a reduction of 6d in the standard rate of Income Tax.

It seems to be desirable that if the State commits itself to these new schemes with their heavy increasing liabilities ultimately attaining £35,000,000 a year and mortgaging the future to that extent it would be essential that the schemes themselves should contain certain powers of easement. For instance if the rate of real wages in any lustrum[1] has advanced there should be power to increase the contributions of the employed themselves in some recognised proportion. Or again, if the prosperity of the country undergoes a general decline there should be power to reduce benefits from,

---

[1] A period of five years. The word derives from the purificatory sacrifice made in Roman times by the censors for the people once in five years, after the census had been taken. In Latin, the term was also sometimes used for a period of *four* years.

say, 10/- to 8/-. I see great difficulties in this but yet great need for it if we are not to bind the future almost beyond what our title warrants.

What is the position about the removal of the thrift disqualification. I was under the impression that this had already been done by the late Government but I am now assured that no action had been taken. What was the estimated cost of removing the thrift disqualification if done as an isolated act of policy. It would clearly be comprised within the ambit of these new schemes, and as we are committed to it anyhow it is an additional argument for its adoption.

I am deeply interested in all these projects and I should like to meet the Committee one day next week or as many of them as are available. 'Security for 6d' is an impressive motto.

The whole of this subject and its examination are to be kept at this stage secret.

Neville Chamberlain: diary

(*Neville Chamberlain papers*)

26 November 1924

This afternoon I saw Winston Churchill at his room in the Treasury about pensions for widows & old age. The interview arose out of a discussion in Cabinet in the morning. I first gave him the history of the investigations which had been made by the Com^{ee} under my chairmanship with the assistance of the actuary Duncan Fraser[1] & he then expounded to me the picture which he said he had made for himself of his next budget. He was anxious to reduce direct taxation in order to relieve industry and he thought if the Depts played the game & didn't fritter away surpluses on minor refunds he might be able to take 6^d off income tax & reduce super tax possibly making it apply to net instead of gross income though this might necessitate transferring part of the burden to the medium sized estates paying death duties.

[1] Duncan Cumming Fraser, 1864–1952. A leading Actuary, and life-long Liberal of the strongest convictions. 18th Wrangler at Cambridge, 1885. Joined the Royal Insurance Company at its Liverpool Head Office, 1886; appointed Actuary of the company in 1888, a position which he held until his retirement in 1926. A Member of the Departmental Committee on Railway Superannuation Funds, 1910. Contributed substantially to the Seamen's clauses of the National Insurance Act, 1911. Honorary Actuary of the *Titanic* Relief Fund, 1912. Member of the Actuarial Advisory Committee, 1912–15. Honorary Actuary of the *Lusitania* Relief Fund, 1915. Adviser, first to the Conservative Party, and then to the Conservative Government, on widows, orphans and old age pensions, 1924. Honorary Actuary to the National Disasters Relief Fund until 1938. In 1941 he lost, by enemy action, almost the whole of his comprehensive mathematical and actuarial archive and library, at both his home and at his office: he himself was rescued unhurt from beneath the ruins of his Merseyside home. His wife, however, died shortly after this bombing raid.

But he would have to balance the benefits by doing something for the working classes & for this he looked to pensions. He had examined the Anderson[1] report & found it very hopeful for it was not expensive in the earlier years & in later years he would have better trade, German Reparation & Inter Allied Debts to help him. He wished to set the subject free from personalities (I gathered that he meant he wasn't going to claim *all* the credit for himself) it would have to be my bill but he would have to find the money and the question was would I stand in with him, would I enter partnership & work the plan with him *keeping everything secret*. It might be that in 3 month's time he wd find it impossible to jump the fence this year; in that case it must be postponed but if he could manage it for next Budget he wd like to do so & he wd then scratch & scrape & claw up everything he could in the way of money to help. I said I liked his idea & would consider it favourably, that personalities didn't enter into the question so far as I was concerned & I would communicate with him again. It was curious how all through he observed how he was thinking of personal credit & it seemed plain to me that he regretted still that he was not Minister of Health. He spoke of the position, '*You* are in the van. *You* can raise a monument. *You* can have a name in history' etc and went on to orate about housing. He felt sure that in 4 years we could have 7 to 800,000 houses built if the Weir scheme[2] came off. He cordially approved my idea about demonstration by offering specimen Weir houses at reduced rates and volunteered at once to find £50,000 for the purpose. A man of tremendous drive and vivid imagination but obsessed with the glory of doing something spectacular which should erect monuments to him.[3]

[1] John Anderson, 1882–1958. Educated at Edinburgh and Leipzig Universities. Entered the Colonial Office, 1905; Secretary, Northern Nigeria Lands Committee, 1909. Secretary to the Insurance Commissioners, London, 1913. Secretary, Ministry of Shipping, 1917–19. Knighted, 1919. Chairman of the Board of Inland Revenue, 1919–22. Joint Under-Secretary of State to the Viceroy of Ireland, 1920. Permanent Under-Secretary of State, Home Office, 1922–32. Governor of Bengal, 1932–7. MP for the Scottish Universities, 1928–50. Lord Privy Seal, 1938–9. Home Secretary and Minister of Home Security, 1939–40. Lord President of the Council, 1940–3. Chancellor of the Exchequer, 1943–5. Chairman of the Port of London Authority, 1946–58. Created Viscount Waverley, 1952. Order of Merit, 1957. Member of the BBC General Advisory Council.

[2] In the summer of 1923, Lord Weir had commissioned the design of the 'Weir House', the first house manufactured in a factory and assembled on the construction site. Speaking at the Albert Hall on 5 December 1924, Stanley Baldwin had pledged a vigorous Conservative policy to deal with slums, adding: 'I have no doubt in my own mind that the emergency buildings designed by Lord Weir and other pioneers will play their part in helping to find the solution.'

[3] For Churchill's account of this discussion, see his letter to Baldwin of 28 November 1924 (quoted on page 271). For Chamberlain's own further reflections on his meeting with Churchill, see his diary entry for 1 December 1924 (quoted on page 278).

Winston S. Churchill: departmental note[1]

(*Churchill papers: 18/3*)

26 November 1924

GERMAN COMMERCIAL TREATY

I do not see my way at present clearly through this fog. The President of the Board of Trade[2] says that safeguarding of industries can only be effectuated by duties imposed not against particular countries but imposed generally against all. He therefore does not mind according most favoured nation treatment to Germany in the Commercial Treaty; and if he accords such treatment we shall be debarred from safeguarding any particular industry against any particular attack by dumping, low wages or unfair competition (pardon these theoretical terms) from any particular foreign country. Free traders have always held themselves at liberty to deal with exceptional emergencies by licences or prohibition operative against particular countries. If we surrender this right to Germany in the Commercial Treaty we shall be compelled to put on general duties against all countries whenever unfair conditions arise in any one country. I therefore view the proposed departure with some disquietude. It looks as if the safeguarding of industries policy could only be achieved through the establishment of a partial general tariff. But this is barred by the Prime Minister's explicit pledges against using safeguarding of industries as a wedge to set up a general tariff. Are we not therefore moving on this road towards a complete deadlock? Will the policy of the President of the Board of Trade, taken in conjunction with the Prime Minister's pledges, be more likely to kill safeguarding of industries or to kill Free Trade? I would like to discuss this.

Sir William Joynson-Hicks[3] *to Winston S. Churchill*

(*Churchill papers: 22/19*)

26 November 1924   Home Office

My dear Churchill,

I have made enquiry of Scotland Yard as to the question of looking after Egyptians in London on which you sent me a note at the Cabinet this morn-

---

[1] Sent to P. J. Grigg, Sir Warren Fisher, Sir Horace Hamilton and Sir Otto Niemeyer.

[2] Sir Philip Lloyd-Greame, who assumed by Royal Warrant the surname Cunliffe-Lister on 27 November 1924, under the will of his wife's aunt.

[3] William Joynson-Hicks, 1865–1932. Known as 'Jix'. Solicitor. Conservative MP, 1906–29. Created Baronet, 1919. Parliamentary Secretary, Department of Overseas Trade, 1922–3. Postmaster-General and Paymaster-General, 1923. Entered the Cabinet as Financial Secretary to the Treasury, 1923. Minister of Health, 1923–4. Home Secretary, 1924–9. Created Viscount Brentford, 1929. Chairman of the Automobile Association. Vice-President of the Safety First Council and the Institute of Transport. President of the National Church League. Member of the Joint Select Committee on Indian Affairs, 1931–2.

ing. I am told that we have a pretty good eye on the Egyptian student groups and Scotland Yard have no reason to anticipate any drastic action by them, unless it were some isolated fanatic; and of course it is practically impossible to discover in advance what such an individual has in his mind. All we can do at the moment is to give the best possible protection to anyone whom we think such a person might attack.

Yours very sincerely,
W. Joynson-Hicks

Winston S. Churchill to Lord Birkenhead

(*Churchill papers: 22/19*)

27 November 1924
Private

PROVISION OF ARTILLERY FOR INDIAN NATIVE TROOPS

I have always been against this. If a mutiny or rising took place in India, the Europeans could fortify themselves in strong houses or hastily constructed defences. They could maintain themselves against an enemy not provided with artillery. The moment guns pass into the possession of the rebels, all these refuges could be destroyed quite easily and their inhabitants massacred. A history of the Mutiny shows most clearly how great was the danger of letting artillery pass into native hands, and the rules instituted thereafter are in my opinion still necessary. Chelmsford's[1] remark about the Native States being 'trusted entirely or not at all' reads oddly in connection with the precautions which the Committee immediately recommended.

Winston S. Churchill to Sir George Barstow

(*Churchill papers: 18/3*)

27 November 1924

The most practical line is to have a new page in the Navy Estimates which would repeat in a different form facts already contained in the rest of the

[1] Frederic John Napier Thesiger, 1868–1933. Elder son of 2nd Baron Chelmsford. Fellow of All Souls, Oxford, 1892. Barrister, 1893. He married Churchill's cousin, Frances Guest, daughter of the 1st Baron Wimborne, 1894. Captain, Dorset Regiment, 1902–14. Succeeded his father as 3rd Baron, 1905. Governor of Queensland, 1905–9; of New South Wales, 1909–13. Viceroy of India, 1916–21. Created Viscount, 1921. First Lord of the Admiralty, 1924. Agent-General for New South Wales, 1926–8. Warden of All Souls, 1932–3.

Estimates. This page would show the outstanding cost of the capital commitments of the Navy and the progress made in diminishing or increasing it by the programmes of ships and works sanctioned in any year. Take the five cruisers for instance. We put down 10 millions in Capital Account. Add six more 1925 cruisers: 12 millions. Add Singapore (Navy votes): 11 millions. Total: 33 millions. Diminution during the year 1925, say, 4 millions. Increased commitment during the year: 23 millions. Outstanding commitment March 31, 1926, (estimate): 21 millions.

I have not made up my mind about this. But I think the publication of such a table would be a great deterrent. Parliament would keep on saying, 'Look at all this we have got to push ahead of us. The outstanding commitment is steadily growing. The rate at which our liabilities are being worked off is very small. True, the Navy have made a reduction in their ordinary current charges and the total of Navy votes this year is less than it was last year. But then look how the Capital Account is mounting up.' This would be a line of criticism very hard to meet. I do not think the Admiralty would like it at all. Only a very real case of public danger would be required to sustain these rapid increases. We might try a return in this form for the Cabinet in the first instance, assuming a naval construction of 5, 6, 5, 5 and 5 cruisers, plus Singapore, plus the rest of the construction programme now in progress, and showing in each of the yearly periods up to 1930 what our capital commitment will be.

In the Navy Estimates, as I see them, there would of course also be a table showing the agreed rate at which the different capital schemes sanctioned would normally be worked off, so that Parliament would see for years ahead what our expenditure on Singapore, for instance, was going to be and what the effect on Navy votes would be of assenting to five cruisers a year, each costing as much as a 1912 Dreadnought.

I think such a return in the Naval Estimates, as I have indicated, would be so formidable a deterrent that I am even wondering whether it might not make it too difficult to do what is necessary to maintain our naval defence. I am sure the Admiralty would fight it like tigers. Yet they have no case for refusing this disclosure in an intelligible form to Parliament of facts already buried in the Estimates.

Let me have a sketch of these pages in more or less accordance with actual facts and possibilities as now known to us. I am not coming to any decision one way or another for a while.

Winston S. Churchill to Sir Richard Hopkins[1]

(*Churchill papers: 18/3*)

28 November 1924
Secret

My mind is moving on the following lines, but of course I am forming no conclusions at present.

(1) The treatment of the Super Tax and of the Estate Duties would be simultaneous and connected. The wealthy direct taxpayer could bear his burden easier and enterprise would be less hampered in the form of Death Duties than of the existing high rate of Super Tax. The proposal therefore is primarily a transference of burdens from one form of tax to another among a particular class of taxpayers. But it is proposed that this class shall derive a substantial net benefit from the transference, the amount of which would be stated to Parliament.

(2) We have to consider the principles appropriate to a period of diminishing taxation, ie the degree and order of relief to various classes of taxpayers. I do not desire sensibly to diminish the Super Tax burdens resting upon the greatest fortunes, nor on the other hand to increase the burden of Death Duties upon them. On many grounds this class may well be left to stand where they do. I wish to relieve chiefly the lower and medium classes of Super Tax payers, giving the greatest measure of relief to the lowest class comprising professional men, small merchants and business men—superior brain workers of every kind. Where these classes possess accumulated capital in addition to their incomes, the increase of Death Duties operating over the same area will reclaim a substantial portion of the relief afforded by the reform of the Super Tax. The doctor, engineer and lawyer earning 3 or 4 thousand a year and with no capital will get the greatest relief; the possessor of unearned income derived from a capital estate of 2 or 3 hundred thousand pounds, the smallest relief; while the millionaire will remain substantially liable to the existing scales of high taxation.

(3) From this point of view the treatment of the Super Tax on a net basis, rather than through the agency of a uniform 20 or 25% reduction, is far more suitable. As the tide of taxation recedes, it leaves the millionaires stranded on the peaks of taxation to which they have been carried by the flood. The smaller class of Super Tax payers gets progressive relief not only

---

[1] Richard Valentine Nind Hopkins, 1880–1955. Educated at King's Edward School, Birmingham, and Emmanuel College, Cambridge. Member of the Board of Inland Revenue, 1916; Chairman, 1922–7. Knighted, 1920. Controller of Finance and Supply Services, Treasury, 1927–32; Second Secretary, Treasury, 1932–42; Permanent Secretary, 1942–5. Member of the Imperial War Graves Commission. Chairman of the Central Board of Finance of the Church Assembly.

in volume but in rate of tax. The existing scales of Super Tax remaining unaltered would automatically give this relief progressively, as the scale is descended in almost exactly the proportions most conducive to the public interest. On the other hand the re-grading of the Estate Duties emphasizes in this class the distinction between the capitalist and the high income earner; and the millionaire whose relief from Super Tax, as you observe, is relatively unappreciable is not asked to bear any additional burden of Death Duties. In fact the combination of the net Super Tax with the retrogression of the Death Duties on the lower, and especially the medium, estates seems to fulfil almost exactly the purpose I have in mind.

(4) Moreover, I hope that the net relief to every class of taxpayer affected will be such as to enable all but the very old, if they prefer it, to cover the increased Estate Duties by insurance obtained by a reduction of the Super Tax. This principle would at any rate be operative over a large proportion of the taxpayers affected. Thus everything fits closely together on the net Super Tax principle, while my objects would not in any way be obtained by a fixed percentage reduction.

(5) Following further the idea of a receding tide of taxation, it is evident that creating the Super Tax on the net basis increases the yield of the Super Tax in proportion as the standard rate of Income Tax is lowered. Just as we have seen the millionaire left close to the high water mark and the ordinary Super Tax payer draw cheerfully away from him, so in their turn the whole class of Super Tax payers will be left behind on the beach in proportion as the great mass of the Income Tax payers subside into the refreshing waters of the sea. The harmonious and natural character of the process is graceful and pleasing in the last extreme. The longer and the further such a process were carried, the more it would conform to sensible public opinion on these matters.

(6) I am not convinced that it is necessary to complicate this process by the adding back to the Super Tax returns of the repayments of Income Tax paid with regard to personal allowances and relief. These personal allowances and relief form only a small proportion of the tax liability of the classes with which we are dealing; and I do not see why they should not be ranked with Super Tax in respect of repayments of Income Tax on this head. With regard to the other difficulties which you mention of certain classes of taxpayers making their Super Tax returns, experience shows that they would much rather be 'spared' the tax than the 'embarrassment'. You must also remember that a diminution in the pressure of Super Tax would probably relieve quite a large class of Super Tax payers from the strain now put upon their ingenuity in making sure they do not pay a larger amount of taxation than the law actually requires. I think there is no doubt that on the whole

their mental stress will be lessened rather than aggravated by the changes I have in mind.

(7) I do not attach much importance to the argument that it is unreasonable to collect Super Tax on incomes already destroyed by Income Tax. It certainly appears an anomalous and clumsy system, and this aspect should be considered for what it is worth. But of course any system of taxation is arbitrary, and an anomalous or illogical method of collecting burdens loses itself in the final important fact—What has each person got to pay?

(8) It is quite true that whereas placing the Super Tax on the net basis commits us to a fixed reduction unrelated to the sums of money abatable for relief, a percentage reduction can be precisely adjusted. The combination of the treatment of the Death Duties with the reduction of Super Tax enables this process of adjustment to be regulated with equal exactness from this external source.

(9) The whole of the foregoing notes must also be considered in relation to the actual financial problem of 1925. If a reduction of Super Tax (and Income tax, though that is not what I am now discussing) is to be achieved, the cost involved, even after allowing for the yield of increased Estate Duty, is so substantial that we could not afford it unless we drew largely upon the existing outstanding arrears of Income Tax and Super Tax. In view of the directions which have been given not to press the collection this year, a reserve of 10 or 12 millions will perhaps be available from this source. This will be required to balance our Budget at its turning point. Here again the argument closes like the breech of a gun. Our justification for pressing the collection of arrears will be the relief we are affording this class of taxpayers. The whole class will be in a good humour, will make their best efforts to discharge their liabilities, and public opinion will support the pressure applied to delinquents.

Let me have a table showing the amount and percentage of relief secured by every grade of Super Tax payer from the placing of the Super Tax on a net basis. For the purposes of this table you may ignore the complications of subsequently reclaimed personal reliefs and allowances of Income Tax.

You have shown me tables for re-grading the Estate Duties to produce 7 and 15 millions respectively. I should like an intermediate table yielding about 10 millions. We shall then be able to compare the relative Super Tax relief and Estate Duty burden on every class of taxpayer affected. I recognise of course that the coincidence is not exact and you cannot actually rank an income of £5,000 a year in the same category as an estate of £100,000 yielding £5,000 a year. But for the purposes of judging broadly the appropriate scale of Estate Duty which at each grade should collect the Super Tax relief I have in mind, a comparison of these tables would be useful.

All the above set of arguments are interdependent and self-contained. They form a group by themselves in the Budget problem. It is not relevant to your special work to look beyond this group. But you should know that I am bearing in mind the relation of the group as a whole to the general scheme of the Budget; and in this connection I contemplate an additional burden placed upon employers for the purposes of widows' and earlier old age insurance. The net relief of direct taxation would in my general statement be related to this additional burden to be assumed by the employing class for the benefit of the mass of the people. Even when this is considered, however, it would be my wish to show a net relief to that class in the interests of a revival of enterprise.

These notes should enable you to carry our discussion a stage further.

Winston S. Churchill to Stanley Baldwin
(*Churchill papers: 18/7*)

28 November 1924
Most Secret

My dear Prime Minister,

I had a long and agreeable talk with Neville Chamberlain on Wednesday, of which I will give you the gist.

I explained to him that while widows' and old age insurance fell in his Department and that he would be primarily responsible for the preparation and conduct of the measure, the expense was nevertheless such a serious factor in the whole financial future of the country that the policy ought to play its part in the Budget scheme. If I should be successful in my treatment of the new Estimates, and if the Revenue showed expansion, I might be able to deal in an effective manner with the direct taxpayers' burdens in 1925. This would stimulate enterprise and afford the employing classes a relief from which they could defray their share of the new insurance contributions. But it would be difficult to give a relief to the direct taxpayer, unless the relief was balanced to some extent by the additional burden arising from the new insurance, and unless also from the standpoint of social and political justice a relief to the direct taxpayer should be accompanied by a benefit to the mass of the public. To give a further relief of indirect taxation would exhaust any funds I am likely to have available. But the assumption by the State of the very large capital liabilities involved in the new insurance for the benefit of the mass of the people might well be taken as an equipoise in the general scheme of the Budget, and an equipoise moreover which involves no additional loss to the Revenue in the next few years.

I also pointed out to Chamberlain the part the War Pensions played in our future finance. If there were no claims of insurance in the way, I should feel very tempted to spread the War Pensions evenly over, say, a period of fifty years. This would enable me to make remissions not only of direct but also of indirect taxation, if all went well. But if the insurance policy was to be financed, then it seems to me essential to link the increased charges for insurance reaching, say, 35 millions as a maximum in 1950 with the even more rapid diminution of the War Pension charges petering out steadily through the death of the pensioners. Thus we could not be accused of compromising the future of our finances for the sake of an immediate advantage, and our whole policy would hold together. For these reasons I asked that he should consult me in the preparation of his scheme, and that if action were decided upon, he should allow his Insurance Bill to form an integral part of the general financial arrangement. Chamberlain seemed to think that this was reasonable, and I hope you will think so too.

We then discussed the time for action. I told him that I did not know whether the Budget this year would be 'Hope' or 'Humdrum'. If the expenditure of the Departments increased and other factors were adverse, it would be no use trying to make petty remissions of taxation, and it would be better to wait until 1926 when a respectable surplus might be available. I told him that by February I should be able to let him know for certain whether we could act in 1925 or 1926. I hope myself greatly that 1925 will be possible, because the relief to the direct taxpayer will stimulate trade revival, and the beginning of the Pensions scheme will make a profound impression on the social life of the country and particularly on the position of women. I suggested that no mention should be made in the King's Speech of insurance, but that you would take some opportunity, perhaps at the Albert Hall, of holding up Housing and Insurance as the two greatest social achievements for which we hope this Parliament will be remembered.

We talked a good deal about the scheme which you had explored in Opposition on insurance, and the need of considering its results in conjunction with the interdepartmental scheme which is now ready. We agreed that he should immediately form a strong secret group or Committee of the best experts to assemble all the knowledge on the subject and thrash out all its actuarial possibilities and the various methods. I promised to supply any funds that may be needed for the expenses of such a thorough examination.

We then talked about Housing and found ourselves in the most complete accord. We should leave to the building trade the existing profitable building, and devote our energies to the development of alternative methods of construction for the housing of the classes who cannot afford to pay at the existing prices. He wished to set up specimen Weir steel houses for the local authorities to inspect in different parts of the country. With your approval I will place a sum up to £50,000 at his disposal for the purpose of demonstration in steel and other alternative methods.

I should propose to make with the Secretary of State for Scotland[1] arrangements for exhibitions on a somewhat larger scale. Weir is very keen to feed up whole *blocks* of houses to them and begin to make a definite inroad upon the Scottish housing shortage. In this case the Treasury will assist by a certain guarantee to Weir for a portion of the risk of his enterprise. This will enable him to offer his houses to the Scottish local authorities at rates which more nearly approach the cheapness of mass production than otherwise would be possible.

Yours vy sincerely
WSC

Thomas Jones: diary

(*Jones papers*)

28 November 1924

The Chancellor of the Exchequer sent for me about 6 o'clock. I saw him alone. He was drinking some whisky-and-soda, and he got some tea for me. He was very confidential. 'I understand you talk a lot with the PM and that you give him advice—good advice, I have no doubt. Well, I want this Government not to fritter away its energies on all sorts of small schemes; I want them to concentrate on one or two things which will be big landmarks in the history of this Parliament, and if you are doing anything for a speech at the Albert Hall I would like you to fix on two things and make them stand out—Housing and Pensions. I think I see my way to help both of these if I can stop the Departments spending in other directions. I was all for the Liberal measures of social reform in the old days, and I want to push the same sort of measures now. Of course I shall have to give some relief to the taxpayers to balance these measures of reform. If trade improves I can do that, but we cannot have a lot of silly little cruisers, which would be of no use anyway. I had some talk with the PM and Neville Chamberlain along these lines, and in order to avoid any mistake I put down my impressions of the talk in a letter to the PM. Here is a copy; you had better read it.' This I did, and told him I was very grateful for his guidance, but I was sure the Prime Minister's heart was in the right place on all these matters.

[1] Sir John Gilmour (see page 208, note 1).

Lord Beaverbrook to Lord Rothermere
(*Beaverbrook papers*)

28 November 1924

I get very amusing accounts of the Cabinet proceedings. It appears that Churchill and Chamberlain do not always agree. Amery is at odds with the new group. Neville Chamberlain is not always on amicable terms with his brother. Baldwin sits silent, except when he announces the next speaker in the Cabinet debates. . . .

I have Churchill and Birkenhead dining with me to-night. They are both showing just a touch of the 'beggar on horseback' disposition; but that is natural.

Lord Rosebery to Winston S. Churchill
(*Churchill papers: 8/196*)

29 November 1924

My dear Winston,

I am afraid my little granddaughter rather disturbed the intimacy of our conversation yesterday, and put out of my mind a burning question, which is, have you done with Paget?[1] If so I would be glad if you would return it to me, because of course a Chancellor of the Exchequer's budget may swallow up anything. Anyhow, I hope it has put you on good terms with your immortal ancestor.

Yours ever,
AR

PS. If you really have done with Paget, please send him to The Durdans.

[1] John Paget's book, *The New 'Examen'*, first published in 1861, a defence of John, Duke of Marlborough, against the accusations of Macaulay. Churchill was much influenced by Paget in embarking on his own biography of the Duke. He also wrote a special introduction to a reissue of *The New 'Examen'*, published in 1934. In the course of this introduction Churchill noted, of Paget: 'For seventy years his work was out of print, and scarcely mentioned even in the catalogues of the libraries. Only here and there some laborious scholar, or some great book-lover like Lord Rosebery, cast his eye upon these powerful writings, often merely to dismiss them with a shrug or with a sigh. It is a measure of the increasing interest in history which distinguishes the present generation, that they should have been rescued from oblivion and presented once again to the public, and this time to a more instructed public.'

Winston S. Churchill to Sir Laming Worthington-Evans: not sent

(*Churchill papers: 18/2*)

29 November 1924

My dear Worthy,

I do not think we have enough troops in the Sudan or in Egypt and it may well be that time is vital and that days, and possibly hours, have their value. Would it not be wise to make the Navy land 1,500 men for Alexandria and Cairo and shove two more battalions into the Sudan, relieving the Navy with troops from home or elsewhere as soon as possible? Is there not a cavalry regiment in Palestine which could be spared?

Winston S. Churchill to Lord Birkenhead: not sent

(*Churchill papers: 18/2*)

29 November 1924

My dear Fred,

Just read the enclosed and send it on to Austen. I think he has sent exactly the wrong answer and as usual is making the heaviest weather over the personal point.[1] I am quite sure Allenby will come round if he is given a chance. Perhaps you will think my phrase about 'recall' is rather stiff. Personally it is what I would say in all the circumstances, but of course it is very dangerous to interpolate a personal touch in somebody else's correspondence.

All this for your private eye.

[1] On 20 November 1924 Major-General Sir Lee Stack, Governor-General of the Sudan and Sirdar of the Egyptian Army, had been murdered in Cairo by Egyptian extremists. On the day of Sir Lee Stack's funeral, the High Commissioner in Egypt, Lord Allenby, had sent an ultimatum to the Egyptian Government, without waiting for instructions from the Foreign Office in London. Austen Chamberlain had strongly disapproved of Allenby's action in acting without authorization. Among the terms of the ultimatum was a fine of £500,000, and the withdrawal of all Egyptian officers from the Sudan within twenty-four hours. Half an hour after the Egyptian Government had hesitated over certain o f the points, British troops occupied the Customs at Alexandria. As a result of Austen Chamberlain's disapproval, Allenby had threatened to resign, telegraphing to this effect, but then telegraphing again, offering to postpone the issue.

Winston S. Churchill to Austen Chamberlain: not sent

(*Churchill papers: 18/2*)

29 November 1924

My dear Austen,

I have just read Allenby's reply to your telegram of yesterday. I think the point to hook on to is that contained in his sentence 'I do not wish to obtrude the question of my resignation at this moment'. That after all is exactly what we want.

I read this telegram as marking a better spirit on his part and as a withdrawal from an untenable position under the heavy fire of our artillery. The salient facts are that he is not going to resign now, that he is going to treat Henderson[1] with consideration and do his utmost to maintain absolute unity and loyal and helpful co-operation. That, after all, is exactly what we want. We have never asked him to stay on for ever, nor have we undertaken to keep him there for ever. I should therefore feel inclined to view his telegram in a favourable sense and treat the personal crisis as settled for the time being. Thus we shall get round the corner.

As for the future, do not let us judge it yet. I think that Allenby is doing very well, that we are going to succeed in Egypt, that Europe is going to behave properly, and that Parliament is going to be ardent in your support. I think we ought to let this go on. Whenever a success is achieved, everybody gets into a good temper and every personal problem becomes easier.

As you have been kind enough to court suggestion from colleagues on the Egypt Committee, I have put down the sort of message I should send him on Monday if I were unlucky enough to have to bear your burden.

After all Henderson was sent to help keep him straight on the larger issues, and it is quite natural he should be irritated about this. The more I meditate on his telegram, the more sure I am that he wants to patch it up.

Winston S. Churchill: draft telegram to Lord Allenby

(*Churchill papers: 18/2*)

30 November 1924

Your unnumbered of the 29th. We have feelings not only of confidence but of admiration for your broad handling of the Egyptian crisis in itself. But we

---

[1] Nevile Meyrick Henderson, 1882–1942. Educated at Eton. Entered the Diplomatic Service, 1905. Counsellor, Constantinople, 1921–2; Acting High Commissioner, 1922–4. Minister Plenipotentiary, Cairo, 1924; Paris, 1928–9; Belgrade, 1929–35. Knighted, 1932. British Ambassador to the Argentine, 1935–7; to Germany, 1937–9. Privy Councillor, 1937.

have also to consider French opinion, American opinion, and, not the least important, possible action by the League of Nations. Moreover, we have to justify our policy to Parliament. You ought also to have some confidence in us and not attribute hesitation or infirmity of purpose where none exists.

We fear that any rumours or talk of your resignation in the present crisis will aid the enemies of Britain and encourage mutinies in the Sudan and murders in Cairo. His Majesty's Government cannot tolerate this. We are therefore very glad to learn that you do not wish to obtrude the question of your resignation at this moment. As soon as the crisis has been surmounted and there will be no danger to Imperial interests or to the lives of Europeans in Egypt it will be open to you to renew a request for relief or for His Majesty's Government to send you orders of recall. Such events can be considered in their proper time. Meanwhile, we accept with cordiality your undertaking to use Mr Henderson's help and maintain absolute unity with His Majesty's Government in loyal and helpful co-operation, and we for our part will do our utmost to convince you we are not lacking in this spirit.[1]

[1] Allenby's irritation with the 'imposition' of Nevile Henderson could not be overcome and Allenby resigned as High Commissioner in June 1925. Aged 63, he held no further official appointments. The military historian Cyril Falls noted: 'Allenby's worst foe was his violent temper,' and he added: 'although he never apologised for fits of unjustified anger, he often made amends for them' (*Dictionary of National Biography 1931–1940*, page 12).

December 1924

Neville Chamberlain: diary

(*Neville Chamberlain papers*)

1 December 1924

Thinking over this interview[1] I was a good deal puzzled as to what WC meant by some of his expressions about 'secrecy' & 'working together'. 'You and I can command everything if we work together' was one of his sentences. I wondered how far the PM knew of his plans, so I went to see the latter in Downing St next day (Thursday Nov 27) at 5. It soon appeared that WC had told him everything and also given him an account of our interview. SB's explanation of the phrase about 'personalities' was that WC desired to make the final announcement about pensions in his Budget speech & wished to disarm any jealousy on any part by intimating that I should have the conduct of the Bill and any credit that that might bring.

Winston S. Churchill to William Bridgeman

(*Churchill papers: 18/2*)

1 December 1924

My dear First Lord,

I have now had a comparative table made out upon the existing pay of the three Services having regard to age and rank. It seems to show that the Naval Officer receives more pay and allowances without marriage allowance than either the Army or Air Force Officer of equivalent age and rank receives with such allowance. If this is so, I doubt whether it would be in the interests of the Navy to re-open the whole question of pay co-ordination. Such an issue ought certainly not to be re-opened only on the question of marriage allowances. I should not be indisposed to consider favourably the appointment of a Pay Co-ordination Committee which would deal with the whole

---

[1] Chamberlain's discussion with Churchill on the afternoon of November 26 (see page 263).

question of the rates of pay and allowances now enjoyed by the Fighting Services, including, of course, the question of the reduction of the pay of new entrants which is an urgent question of great importance. But I am entirely opposed to dealing with one single item.

If after considering the table which I enclose you wish to circulate your memorandum to the Cabinet I will prepare a statement in reply and when both have been circulated we can ask for a decision.

I am sorry that it should be my duty to be so contentious in these matters

Winston S. Churchill to Austen Chamberlain

(*Austen Chamberlain papers*)

1 December 1924   Treasury Chambers
Private and Personal

My dear Austen,

Yours of the 28th. This particular question is, I understand, being explored further with a view to settlement. I thought that a pack of small nations, most of them in leash to France, would increase the chorus against us; and then there is also the risk of offending the Dominions if they are not asked and the small nations come. But I quite see there may be other arguments which outweigh these.

Your letter raises larger issues on which I should like to say a word. I expect to be rather a heavy burden to you in your diplomacy. It will be my duty to claim on behalf of the British taxpayer substantial repayments of debt from France, from Italy and from other Powers; and to resist the repeated attempts which they and the United States will make to gain advantages at our expense. This will cause a certain amount of friction, and every kind of pressure from threats to wheedling and from abuse to flattery will be employed by them. All the same it seems to me that the interests of the taxpayer are a legitimate and necessary part of the load the Foreign Office has to bear. These interests may have to be sacrificed here and there in order to procure some other advantage or because we are not strong enough to secure equitable treatment for ourselves. I shall certainly have to ask in the next few months for a definite move to assert our claims for debt repayment against France and Italy. They will be furious, and if they think they can avoid their legal obligations by bluster there is no resource they will not try. We can avoid all this trouble by throwing up the sponge, by sitting still and putting up with being fleeced. Then there will be lots of compliments about the good feeling which we have established in Europe and about what a very agreeable and friendly nation we are. But I think this is a pretty thin diet to give to the taxpayers of this country in their present circumstances.

The situation about debts has vastly altered since we were last in office together. Europe is recovering. France and Italy as they become richer will become increasingly desirous for financial respectability. The same sort of influence that made us settle the American debt will be operative upon them about our debt. I do not see why we should not get a substantial annual payment from both France and Italy if we use to the full the great advantages of our position.

The whole of this process will mean worry for you—sulky instead of smiling Ambassadors, etc. But my reason for writing to you at this length is to beg you to take this debt reclamation policy upon your shoulders as one of the leading objectives of British foreign policy and only to abandon it if some even greater interest is seriously in danger.

Yours vy sincerely
Winston S. Churchill

Winston S. Churchill: Cabinet memorandum[1]

(Churchill papers: 22/21)

1 December 1924   Treasury Chambers
Secret

AMERICAN CLAIM TO REPARATION[2]

1. The United States Government, which did not sign the Treaty of Versailles, is putting forward a claim in respect of damages to United States citizens in the war (both before and after America became belligerent) against the Dawes annuities to be paid by Germany to meet charges arising under the Treaty of Versailles. The amount of that claim is unknown. It is popularly reported that applications have been received for about 1,100 million dollars, but that the American–German Tribunal of Assessment may reduce this total to under 500 million dollars. Whatever the amount, if the American claim were allowed, it would reduce the sum available to the signatories of the Treaty of Versailles for their Treaty charges, including reparations.

2. We are advised that legally America has no claim. She cannot benefit

---

[1] Circulated to the Cabinet as Cabinet paper 516 of 1924.

[2] On 26 November 1924, at an Allied Conference in Paris, the American representative, Colonel A. J. Logan, had put forward a claim by the United States for a share in the Dawes payments, in respect of the cost of the American army of occupation in Europe, and of material losses suffered by American nationals throughout the war.

under a Treaty whose obligations she has not assumed. Moreover, the Treaty of Versailles gives the Reparation Commission a first charge on all the assets and revenues of Germany, and any subsequent agreement by Germany with America could only give a claim ranking after that first charge.

3. The United States urge that the Dawes Report speaks of claims by the 'Allied and Associated Governments' and that these words were inserted specially to cover the present American claim. But the Dawes Committee were appointed by the Reparation Commission under the Treaty of Versailles to consider how the German Budget could be balanced and implicitly how it could meet the Treaty of Versailles charges on Germany. The Committee were private individuals who, neither by their terms of reference nor by their actual knowledge, were in a position to decide on claims outside the Treaty. They never in fact discussed the matter; the Treaty phrase 'Allied and Associated Governments' was merely inserted in order not to debar any claim which might be a good one under the Treaty. There was good reason to insert it because America had in fact a perfectly good claim for her armies of occupation. But in no circumstances could the Dawes Committee have pronounced on a large international issue, such as the present American claim.

4. But the case does not depend on mere legal arguments. All other countries which signed the Treaty of Versailles had their claims to reparation valued by the Reparation Commission and, in most cases, very considerably cut down. The United States never put in such a claim and indeed disavowed any intention of claiming reparations. America has not had her claims valued by the Reparation Commission, but by a private American–German Tribunal. The Germans, if their total payment is fixed by the Dawes annuity, have no particular interest in cutting down claims.

Moreover, the Reparation Commission would only admit claims for damage during the period when the claimant was a belligerent. The American claim is known to include claims for damage *pre* the entry of America into the war.

5. Other countries, signatories of the Treaty of Versailles, have to account to the Reparation Pool for the assets which they hold. America is believed to hold about 300 million dollars of German private property, of which she has returned, under the Winslow Act, 20 million to 30 million dollars to the owners. In so far as she does not use this asset for pre-war claims, then she ought to make it available for the general Reparation Pool. Further, when in 1920 the Allied countries received compensation for the tonnage lost in the war, America retained the whole of the tonnage seized in American ports (about 164 per cent of her actual tonnage lost), and the understanding with President Wilson was that she should pay for the excess *in cash* to the Repara-

tion Pool. She has never done so. The amount is believed to be about 7 millions sterling, less expenditure on repairs.

7. In our view, if, on grounds of international courtesy, we are to admit this claim, we must first be told to what figure it amounts in order that we may consider the price of our courtesy. In the second place, if the Americans wish now to share in the benefits of the Treaty of Versailles, they ought, if not to undertake all the obligations of the Treaty, at any rate to admit that they must have their claim valued, and account for their assets, in the same way as the Allies. In other words, they must set off their assets against the claim; they must allow the Reparation Commission to consider the basis of the claim, and they must accept a method of payment which will ensure their ranking equally with the Allies both in benefits and responsibilities.

WSC

Winston S. Churchill: draft Cabinet memorandum
(Churchill papers: 18/21)

1 December 1924

I wish to prepare my colleagues for the new position which our debt claims against France and Italy and our reparation claims against Germany are approaching. I cannot do better than reprint the Note which I circulated to the Cabinet of 1922.

These questions have passed through various stages. In the first phase we were to pay everything and be paid by nobody. We were to fund the American debt on terms less good than we subsequently obtained, and to forgive France, Italy, etc, all they owed to us. The second phase was represented by the Balfour Note, where we contemplated asking as much of Europe as the United States asked of us and no more. This offer found no response either in the New World or in the Old and I consider it has definitely lapsed. The third phase was the American debt settlement. Here we decided that the main foundation of our world-wide credit required whatever happened elsewhere the strict and punctual fulfilment of our bond to the United States. Having discharged our own obligations we remained entirely free to deal with our debtors as might best serve our interests. Since that time there have been two proposals which the British Government has made in a tentative and conditional form to their European debtors. There have been the Bonar Law proposals designed to prevent the French from going into the Ruhr, and Lord Curzon's proposals of the 11th August 1923. Neither of these suggestions have met with any acceptance from Europe. I therefore consider that the field today is completely clear and that we stand in respect of the United States upon our settlement and in respect of Europe upon our full legal rights.

Meanwhile, the condition of the world has been improving. The healing process of the frightful injuries of war, though inappreciable at any given moment, has been continuous. The despair of 1921 of receiving any reparation from Germany has given place to the fact that we are actually receiving about £10,000,000 a year at the present time, and to the prospect that in four or five years to come we shall be receiving under the Dawes Agreement and Spa percentages £25,000,000 a year. France and Italy are also reviving. Whatever may be the unsoundness of the national finances of France, whatever weaknesses may appear in the governing structure of Italy, there is no doubt that both these great economic entities are bound during the continuance of peace to accumulate wealth. In proportion as they accumulate wealth and reach through peace a stable condition they will need and seek financial respectability. The same forces and arguments which, much against the grain, led us to settle with the United States will be operative upon the Governments of France and Italy in proportion as they pass from the war atmosphere to that of peace, in proportion as they gain commercial and economic strength. We already see signs of the wish of these countries to escape from an indecent repudiation of their just liabilities provided that it does not cost too much. I see no reason why we should not if we handle this matter firmly and patiently achieve a result which will be better even than the Balfour Note position. Possibly even we may reach the £50,000,000 from all debt and reparation sources mentioned in my memorandum of August 1922. But it might indeed be possible to make an arrangement in the near future which after the lapse of a number of years would yield us a still larger annual receipt.

I submit this issue to my colleagues as one of high public consequence. I am well aware of the difficulties in which it lies and of the burdens which it must necessarily impose on our diplomacy. Surely it would be inopportune to make financial demands on France and Italy in a period when we ourselves are to some extent dependent on their good-will in regard to the Egyptian imbroglio. I believe also that the passage of time, though not too much time, will be favourable to us, and will make them more anxious to acquire a certificate of financial solvency than they are at present. I should therefore propose at the forthcoming Conference of Finance Ministers not to raise in any formal manner the question of debt repayment. On the other hand in the private conversations which I shall probably have with the other Finance Ministers I should make it quite clear that we stand on our full rights, that we expect them to make proposals to us individually, and that failing such proposals we should not indefinitely remain inactive.

It is much too soon to make up our mind as to the moment or the terms of settlement. It would clearly be in our interests as in the interests of all countries to scale down these debts, reduce the interest and if necessary defer the immediate annual instalments in order to strike a bargain. In making such a bargain we should be bound to consider what the United States have never considered, namely, shot and shell expended in the common cause. But all this we may leave till the proper season, which may well be the spring or summer of 1925.

My object in circulating this paper is to apprise the Cabinet of the large issues towards which events in many courses are simultaneously moving.

Winston S. Churchill: Cabinet note[1]

(*Churchill papers: 22/21*)

2 December 1924   Treasury Chambers
Secret

INTER-ALLIED DEBTS

I venture to reprint for the information of my colleagues a copy of a note relating to inter-Allied debts which I circulated to the then Cabinet in August 1922. This question is bound to loom very largely in the next six or twelve months, and my note will, I think, provide a useful starting point for our deliberations on the matter.

WSC

MEMORANDUM BY THE SECRETARY OF STATE FOR THE COLONIES: 3 AUGUST 1922

The financial effects hoped for from the Balfour note cannot possibly be produced unless that note remains for two or three years the unaltered policy of Great Britain. We have suffered hitherto by foreign countries thinking that we have no will of our own in these matters. The United States has a will of its own, very clearly and obstinately expressed, namely, to exact payment from Great Britain. France has a will of her own, equally clearly expressed, namely, to pay nobody. If Great Britain remains a sort of spongy, squeezable mass, on which these two conflicting wills may imprint their stamp, our fundamental interests will suffer. If, however, we show over a considerable period of time that, having declared our policy, we are prepared to stand by it firmly and calmly, no matter what foreign countries do or their backers in

[1] Circulated to the Cabinet as Cabinet paper 518 of 1924.

the British press say, other nations will be forced to take our will into consideration. It will become a factor in world affairs, and play its proper part in the general account.

There is not the slightest doubt that the debts and reparations due to us, at their lowest valuation, will be worth 50 millions a year. Let European countries once feel that whatever they do or say, or whatever happens to their credit or currency, we are going to maintain a continuous demand for payment to this extent from them, and they will accommodate themselves to the idea. If the United States, while exacting payment from us, chooses to be lenient to our European debtors, our security in respect of these debtors is directly improved. I do not see why we should not next year endeavour to make arrangements with our European debtors by which their debts to us are scaled down to the 50 million annual limit. At any rate, a discussion on these lines should not be excluded from study. But the vital need appears to be that we should stand utterly unmoved in the position we have deliberately taken up.

WSC

Winston S. Churchill to Sir George Barstow
(*Churchill papers: 18/3*)

2 December 1924

I have often been struck by the enormous length and number of telegrams from Persia. Every day pages and pages are sent about obscure matters which only very rarely eventuate in action of any kind. I should like the volume and cost of these telegrams to be the subject of examination. It would be interesting to know how much the Exchequer has had to pay in the present year for telegrams between the Foreign Office and its representatives in Persia.[1] What is the rate per word with Persia? What is the total expenditure of the Foreign Office on telegrams? What proportion of this expenditure arises from Persia and the Persian Gulf?[2]

---

[1] In 1924 the British Minister in Teheran was Sir Percy Loraine, later Ambassador in Ankara (1933–9) and in Rome (1939–40).

[2] After Barstow had defended the cost of the telegrams from Persia, Churchill replied, on 9 December 1924: 'I still think that the Foreign Office representatives in Persia are unnecessarily verbose in their telegrams, and that more trifling matters are sent at these expensive rates from this part of the world than from any other.'

Winston S. Churchill to Sir Maurice Hankey

(*Churchill papers: 18/3*)

2 December 1924
Private

Have the Admiralty got some scheme for working up the submarines stationed at Hong Kong to an ultimate total of 21? Do you know anything about this? Are there any papers before the CID on the subject? If so, I should be glad to see them. I should have thought it was very provocative to build up a large submarine base in close proximity to the Japanese coast. Suppose the Japanese owned the Isle of Man and started putting 21 submarines there! My information about this was private, but it came from a well-instructed quarter.[1]

Committee of Imperial Defence: minutes

(*Churchill papers: 22/31*)

4 December 1924

MR CHURCHILL stated that he had never considered that the League of Nations, in view of the present state of the world, was in a position to preserve peace. He was of the opinion that the preservation of peace could only be attained by the maintenance of good understandings between various groups of Powers, possibly arrived at under the auspices of the League of Nations. He did not consider that people would undertake obligations of an unlimited character which it was impossible to define.

He suggested that the proper method to be adopted was to work in stages by means of regional agreements under the League of Nations to protect special points of danger, and by making definite tracts of country demilitarised zones, which would be kept free from all troops and military works. In the first instance, such a zone might be drawn up between France and Germany, and various Powers might be induced to guarantee the sanctity of such a zone. Whichever of the two Powers, France or Germany, was the first to violate this zone, that Power would then become 'the aggressor', and

---

[1] On 11 December 1924 Churchill minuted for Sir George Barstow: 'We must certainly break into this plan of imminent preparations for a gigantic naval war in the Far East. It will be well, however, to await the Naval Estimates' (*Churchill papers: 18/3*). On 13 December 1924 Hankey replied to Churchill that the cost of the Singapore defences would be approximately £2,500,000 'but something will have to be added for anti-aircraft defence and something more for local seaward defence (Naval)', reaching a probable total of no less than £3,000,000. (*Treasury papers: T172/1440*).

would be dealt with as such by the Powers who were signatories to the regional agreement.

As a second stage he suggested that the same scheme could be applied to the Polish side and a demilitarised zone laid down there. He pointed out that all the Powers who were signatories to one agreement might not necessarily be signatories to another. Such schemes might eventually be applied to all points of danger in the world, and he suggested that it was desirable to go from one practical step to another. If these schemes were worked out under the ægis of the League of Nations, the authority of the League would be vastly strengthened. With regard to the present Protocol, he was in agreement with the suggestions put forward by Lord Balfour as to the reasons for its rejection. He considered that such a statement would eventually act on the conscience of the United States and thereby induce them to become a Member of the League.

Winston S. Churchill to L. S. Amery

(*Churchill papers: 18/2*)

4 December 1924
Private

My dear Amery,

I trust you will give further consideration to your proposal to change the present system by which the military and air forces' expenditure on Iraq and Palestine are borne on the Colonial Office vote. It was only after most disastrous expense that this reform was effected by me. The War Office declared themselves the sole judge of the military forces required. They blindly quartered battalions of troops all over the country, and in presenting their bill to Parliament indicated that they had no choice but to carry out the policy of the Government in maintaining Iraq. In order to evict them from control, it was necessary that the Colonial Office should have plenary power; it was necessary to overrule or disregard the warnings of the General Staff, and to use the Air arm as a new and unprecedented instrument in maintaining internal order. This position can only be maintained if the Colonial Secretary is master not only over the Civil but over the Military expenditure in Iraq and Palestine, just as he is in Nigeria and East Africa. He can only be master if he holds the purse strings and if he is responsible for obtaining from Parliament the necessary funds.

I am quite sure that the moment this position is altered the War Office will wish to place more Regular troops both in Palestine and in Mesopotamia, partly because they want to put the troops somewhere rather than retrench them, partly because the General Staff will always be raising the scales of defence which are required. If countries like Iraq and Palestine are to be kept within the British Dominions, it can only be by adopting the same kind of cheap methods which the Colonial Office has shown itself capable of devising in East and West Africa. Knowing this subject as I do, I should feel bound to resist a reversion to what I know would be an enlargement of expenditure to dimensions swiftly fatal both to Iraq and Palestine.

I recognise of course that the Turkish incursion into Mosul makes the expense in Iraq at the present time very difficult. But I had certainly hoped, as the forecasts made by me will show, that the cost would have fallen by now below the ————[1] millions of this year and the ————[1] millions of the estimate for next. It may be that before the end of the present financial year the Turkish situation will be relieved, and in that case I hope that at least a million can be got off the Iraq estimate for 1925–26.[2]

Winston S. Churchill to Stanley Baldwin
(Churchill papers: 18/2)

4 December 1924   Treasury Chambers

My dear Prime Minister,

There is very great force in Lloyd-Greame's suggestion which you adopted, that we should without delay make up our minds exactly what we mean to do about Imperial Preference. Whether we announce the exact decisions next week or leave them till the Budget, is to my mind a minor matter. Unless we have decided how we are going to settle the two or three outstanding points which new facts have created, we shall never be able to sing in tune. Amery will be trying to force the pace, and I at the other end, trying to put the brake on. (Excuse the mixture of metaphors. I have always held that this

---

[1] Left blank in Churchill's copy of this letter.

[2] The British Government's expenditure in Iraq between 1920 and 1926 totalled more than £78 million. This figure was made up as follows:

1920–1	£32,000,000
1921–2	£23,000,000
1922–3	£8,000,000
1923–4	£6,993,000
1924–5	£4,750,000
1925–6	£4,000,000

The principal reduction between 1920 and 1923 had been as a result of Churchill's own decision, when Secretary of State for the Colonies, to transfer the control of Iraq from the Army to the Royal Air Force.

is quite legitimate if it conveys the meaning, and Shakespeare agrees with me!)

What are the outstanding points?

(1) Are we entitled, in view of your Election declarations, to impose a new duty for Preferential purposes on an article like tinned salmon, etc, which is consumed by quite large numbers of people? In this connection I think you will find an appreciable number of your followers have definitely stated after your Gravesend speech that they will not support a duty on tinned salmon, while others have defined their support of Imperial Preference as limited by rebates from existing duties.[1] Only yesterday Amery's private secretary, Wallace,[2] whom I met by chance, told me that he had given pledges in this sense, and so had a good many others of his acquaintance. Then you will remember what Derby said of the statement he was going to make in public. If this is so, it would surely be worth our while not to have a wrangle about whether a pledge is being kept or broken; and if the tinned salmon is really a vital matter in your mind, to deal with it by bounty. I am having a plan prepared for this, and will be ready with it on Monday. It will not be very popular with anybody, but it will reconcile our duty to the Dominions with the most generous recognition of any undertakings we have given to the electors.

(2) *Apples*. Here no bounty is possible because of the anger which would be excited among our farmers. We might say that we do not consider apples food in any real sense, within the meaning of any pledges that we gave.

(3) The dried fruit position has been altered by the reduction of one-third in the duty. So far as these fruits are preserved in sugar, I can meet this difficulty by an additional rebate on the sugar.

(4) The impending renewal of an Anglo-Greek treaty is sure to affect currants, and the Conference proposals must be re-cast to cover these new facts.

(5) Honey is a very small matter, and perhaps it should be dealt with by bounty rather than by duty. I am looking into this.

(6) Lastly there is the sugar preference. It is very tiresome losing

[1] During an election address at Gravesend on the evening of 23 October 1924, Stanley Baldwin declared: 'I pledge myself here, as I have pledged myself before, that there will be no taxation of food if the Unionist Party is returned to power.'

[2] David Euan Wallace, 1892–1941. Educated at Harrow (as were both Churchill and Amery). Joined the Army, 1911. On active service in France, 1915–18 (wounded, despatches four times, Military Cross). Assistant Military Attaché, Washington, 1919. Conservative MP from 1922 until his death. Parliamentary Private Secretary to L. S. Amery, 1924–8. An Assistant Government Whip, 1928–9. Civil Lord of the Admiralty, 1931–5. Secretary, Department of Overseas Trade, 1935–7. Parliamentary Secretary, Board of Trade, 1937–8. Financial Secretary to the Treasury, 1938–9. Minister of Transport, 1939–40. Senior Regional Commissioner for Civil Defence in London, 1940.

£1,200,000 of revenue when nobody foresaw such an immediate consequence of the arrangements at the Conference. Still of course if the ten
years' guarantee of the halfpenny preference was what you all meant at the
time, this loss will have to be faced.

If we could meet on Monday afternoon, you will find me ready with all
the various alternatives which are open, and with a full budget of all the
various undertakings which have been given. So far as I myself am concerned, I carefully avoided both in the Westminster and the Epping Elections saying anything inconsistent with carrying out the whole of the Conference proposals literally (so far as physically possible) on the ground that
a promise is a promise and that this is an act of high Imperial diplomacy.
Do not therefore suppose that I am raising these questions because they
create any personal difficulties for me. I am only raising them because I
want to see the best solutions adopted in the interests of the Government.

I expect that the Opposition will try to draw me into this debate at some
point or another; and once we have reached definite conclusions, I shall be
quite prepared to intervene and defend the policy we have decided upon.

I am very grateful to you for the word 'exceptional' which, it seems to me,
safeguards entirely the position you adopted at this Election against a general
tariff. I believe this word will have the effect of robbing our opponents of a
dearly coveted grievance.

> Yours very sincerely,
> Winston S. Churchill

Winston S. Churchill to Lord Rosebery
(*Churchill papers: 8/196*)

4 December 1924

I now return to you The Durdans[1] Paget's 'Examen'. I am so glad you did
not remember its absence when I lunched with you the other day. I had a
guilty conscience on the subject, as I am afraid I have kept it a very long
time. I have now obtained another copy of my own by advertising, and I
am very glad indeed to possess such a little known and deeply interesting
book. It certainly has cleared away some of the difficulties that I had felt to
eventually undertaking to write about 'Duke John'. (That would be rather
a good title, wouldn't it?)

[1] Lord Rosebery's home near Epsom. He also lived at Dalmeny Park, near Edinburgh,
and at Mentmore, in Buckinghamshire, which his wife Hannah had inherited from her
parents. From 1887 he lived, while in London, at 38 Berkeley Square, and in 1897 he bought
the Villa Delahante, at Posilipo near Naples.

You were speaking to me about Frank Harris[1] the other day. Oddly enough I have just received a long and friendly letter from him. I am in some doubt how to answer it.

Winston S. Churchill to Sir George Barstow

(*Churchill papers: 18/3*)

4 December 1924

I have looked through this file. We must wait until the Air Ministry estimates are presented, as they will be, I have no doubt, in the course of the next ten days. Will you ask them in sending the estimates to give, with all necessary reserve, a forecast of the increase that is expected in the next four or five years through the working of the present expansion scheme. I think there is no doubt that this has got to go forward, at any rate for the present. But here, as in the case of Singapore and the cruisers, I think our line should be to slow down the rate of expansion.

If, for instance, 1932 were taken instead of 1925, it would no doubt afford a very great measure of relief. I do not feel, however, that this present year is opportune for raising the question. Next year or the year after, when we have perhaps arrived at a debt settlement with France, it will be possible to re-examine the rate of expansion. Moreover, the expense in the earlier years is not so formidable as it becomes later on. I expect Trenchard is pretty good in getting value for money, but of course I should be willing to agree to your pressing the Air Ministry for some system of cross-checking the very heavy vote items. I think we might try to push one or two of the new aerodromes over into next year, not as a matter of principle but as part of the haggling on the general estimate.

[1] Frank Harris, 1856–1931. Author and playwright, he published his first book in 1894. Editor of the *Fortnightly Review*, the *Saturday Review* and *Vanity Fair*. In 1906 he acted as Churchill's literary agent for *Lord Randolph Churchill*, securing for Churchill a substantial advance on the original sum of money offered for the book. In 1922 he published *My Life and Loves*, which contained so-called 'revelations' about the sex life of, among others, Lord Randolph Churchill.

Winston S. Churchill to Sir Otto Niemeyer

(*Churchill papers: 18/3*)

5 December 1924

There will be a debate in the House of Commons on Inter-Allied Indebtedness, probably on Wednesday next.[1] Mr Lloyd George will raise the matter and there will be strong expressions of opinion from all sides of the House in favour of our putting pressure on France and Italy to pay us, and also no doubt many reflections, veiled or open, upon American extortion. Let me have a brief by Saturday morning. The argument and policy which I wish to sustain will be as follows:

(1) The greatness of the British contribution to the War. This should comprise the relative rates of taxation paid in England, America, France and Germany by persons possessing £5,000, £10,000, £15,000, etc. Such taxation would comprise the average pressure of death duties as well as that of income tax and super-tax. My object in reciting these facts will be to show that we have taxed ourselves far more heavily than any other country, and I shall indicate a possible connection between this exceptional rate and the unemployment which has attended its operation.

(2) The burden thrown upon us, and which we alone are bearing. Do not fail to include our loss by the securities we had to sell to America.

(3) I propose to state quite concisely and accurately the exact position of the French and Italians relatively to ourselves and the United States, and our relation to both. This arises from a history of the debt. Bradbury's letter covers this ground. Please check it and let me have your views upon it at each point.

(4) I shall ask the Cabinet for authority to proclaim that we adhere to the policy of the Balfour Note as our guide and that we shall steadfastly use every endeavour to procure from our European debtors and from Germany sums sufficient to cover the payments we have contracted to make to the United States. I shall make it clear that we in no way waive our full legal rights at the present time.

(5) I shall assert the principle of *pari passu* payments in the strongest possible terms. I have abandoned priority in consequence of Bradbury's[2] letter.

(6) Give me a note on the American debt settlement. My line in dealing

---

[1] Wednesday, 10 December 1924. For the reception and content of Churchill's speech, see Stanley Baldwin's letter of December 11 to King George V, quoted on page 299 of this volume.

[2] John Stanwick Bradbury, 1872–1950. Educated at Manchester Grammar and Brasenose College, Oxford. An Insurance Commissioner, 1911–13. Knighted, 1913. Joint Permanent Secretary, Treasury, 1913–19. Principal British Delegate, Reparations Commission, Paris, 1919–25. Created Baron, 1925. Chairman of the National Food Council, 1925–9. President, British Bankers' Association, 1929–30 and 1935–6. The first treasury pound notes were known as 'Bradburys'.

with this will be that whatever views may be held as to the terms and as to the opportuneness of this settlement it has placed us in a very strong position. We can look every man in the face, etc. We have no need to ask favours from anybody, nor are we under any obligation to give concessions. I shall frankly say I differ from the settlement. After all that is public property and has been often quoted. But I shall point out the weight of expert opinion behind it and the favourable results which followed for our credit.

Let me also have a statement showing how much it costs to pay the Americans money each year with the dollar at 4·30, 4·40 or at parity. Surely we are saving a good deal in this repayment.

Winston S. Churchill to Stanley Baldwin

(*Churchill papers: 18/2*)

6 December 1924
Personal

My dear Prime Minister,

I have prepared the enclosed note which I thought of circulating to those who are to come to your Committee on Monday afternoon. As however it hangs so much on your Gravesend speech I send it to you in the first instance and would like to know your wishes before showing it to anyone else. There is no doubt that we have the power to do whatever we choose in this matter so far as votes in the House of Commons are concerned and personally I will, if you so decide, propose the duty even on tinned salmon, etc. But I am sure that we shall be involved, for the sake of very small objects, in an altogether disproportionate amount of worry and labour, and of all sorts of lengthy explanations. These will become almost metaphysical in dealing with the relation of one pledge to the other, of what is meant by 'increasing taxation on food' etc.

On the other hand the Board of Trade proposal, which I presume has Lloyd-Greame's assent, cuts the Gordian knot at a stroke. I can picture the consternation of Simon & Co if it were adopted. I believe also that it would be of much more practical use to Dominion trade. I hope at any rate you feel yourself free to consider it.

The German Treaty seems to have gone very well. I knew the Liberals would like it, but I thought there would be a certain amount of Conservative complaint. However there is overwhelming approval.[1]

[1] Following negotiations throughout October and November 1924, on November 29 an agreement had been reached in London between Britain and Germany for an Anglo-German

I am so sorry to bother you with all this on a Saturday. It is only my wishes for the success of your Administration that prompt me.

Yours sincerely,
Winston S. Churchill

Winston S. Churchill to L. S. Amery

(*Churchill papers: 18/2*)

7 December 1924
Private

My dear Leo,

I have been thinking over the plans for the alterations in the Colonial Office which you talked to me about; and before I received the Memorandum you have written for the Prime Minister, I had written the enclosed note with the exception of the last paragraph which I have added after reading yours.

I have, as you know, a very long experience of the Colonial Office, having been there as Under Secretary for two years and a half from 1905, and as Secretary of State for nearly two years from 1921. I speak therefore with first hand knowledge of the work in all its branches. The key of the whole situation is the determination of the Dominions' Premiers to deal direct with the British Prime Minister. During the War Conferences, as well as afterwards, their wishes and the force of events gravitated irresistibly to a meeting of Prime Ministers, and I am sure that this remains the foundation they value most of all. Once this is recognised, I do not think that they will object to a great deal of preparatory and routine work being done by the Colonial Secretary and his Department.

And as an old Colonial Secretary, I should greatly regret to see that Office shorn of a sphere of business which, although not onerous, adds vastly to its dignity and rank in the Government hierarchy. I have, however, long felt that the title of Secretary of State for the Colonies ought to be changed. I proposed myself when appointed in 1921 that it should be altered to Secretary of State for Imperial Affairs; and I am still prepared to support you in

Commercial Treaty. The Germans undertook to grant Britain most-favoured nation status, and to guarantee no further discriminatory treatment against British imports. The British undertook to introduce a Bill in Parliament removing all restrictions upon persons of German birth residing in Great Britain, thus abolishing their legal status as 'ex-enemy aliens'. The question as to whether Britain would remove a 26 per cent reparations levy on German imports was left open.

pressing for such an alteration. A variant of this might well be to make the office a double Secretaryship of State, as your last paragraph appears to suggest. You would then be Secretary of State for Colonial Affairs and Secretary of State for Dominion Affairs, and separate Letters of Patent might be prepared accordingly.

I am quite sure, however, that having regard to the position of the Prime Minister in inter-Imperial relations, there is no sufficient case for the creation of a separate additional Secretaryship of State. Such an appointment would not be popular in the Dominions, because it would be held to prejudice the relation of Prime Minister with Prime Minister. It would certainly be greatly criticised in the House of Commons as an unnecessary multiplication of Ministerial posts.

Again, I think that the creation of two permanent Under Secretaries at £3,000 a year each would be criticised as unwarrantable. The permanent Secretary for the Dominions would not in practice have work to do comparable in volume to that of other permanent Secretaries of the first class. This is a not a matter of opinion but of fact. As for an additional Parliamentary Under Secretary, I am of course in the hands of the Prime Minister. If he appoints a Minister, it will be my duty to provide the salary. I am sure, however, that the Bill will encounter a great deal of opposition by those who know the actual facts of Colonial Office work. Ormsby-Gore[1] will, it seems to me, have a real grievance at this further inroad upon his now restricted duties.

I do hope you will weigh all these matters. Believe me it distresses me very much to have to differ from you on points to which I know you attach so much sentimental importance. I am very glad to think it is not me but the Prime Minister and the Cabinet who will have to decide them. I shall certainly accept their view, having stated my own. We can have a further talk about all this when I dine with you on Friday.

[1] William George Arthur Ormsby-Gore, 1885–1965. Educated at Eton and New College, Oxford. Conservative MP, 1910–38. Intelligence Officer, Arab Bureau, Cairo, 1916. Assistant Secretary, War Cabinet, 1917–18. Member of the British Delegation (Middle East Section) to the Paris Peace Conference, 1919. British Official Representative on the Permanent Mandates Commission of the League of Nations, 1920. Under-Secretary of State for the Colonies, 1922–4 and 1924–9. Privy Councillor, 1927. First Commissioner of Works, 1932–6. Secretary of State for the Colonies, 1936–8. Succeeded his father as 4th Baron Harlech, 1938. High Commissioner, South Africa, 1941–4. Chairman of both the Midland Bank, and the Bank of West Africa. A Trustee of both the Tate and National Galleries.

Victor Cazalet: diary

(*Robert Rhodes James: 'Victor Cazalet, A Portrait'*)

7 December 1924

To Winston—where I spent a very wonderful and interesting day. Winston was in very good form; he had earned (from his writings) £500 that day. He gets 6/- a word in the USA. He talked to me of the coming Budget, Baldwin, Balfour and the Cabinet. It was superb. He has no idea why Baldwin chose him as Chancellor of the Exchequer and would have taken the Ministry of Health. He is simply absorbed in his work, and is well on with schemes for pensions etc. He is very sorry about Horne; otherwise he is very well pleased with the Cabinet.

He told me he was now Baldwin's man, prepared to fight all his battles. He told me everything, and even sometimes said, 'What do you think?' We agreed that Balfour was the greatest master of manners the world had ever known. Winston became quite boyish in his desire to hear what Balfour had said of him. He loves Balfour, and said the tragedy had been that Balfour had never bothered to get hold of him when he was a young Conservative MP and Balfour was Prime Minister; if he had he would probably have gone down with him. He longed to have served under him, and thought him the most fluent and easy speaker in the world. But F. E. Smith was probably the greatest on any kind of platform. He knew that FE *spoke* better than he did.

Ramsay MacDonald, vain and bitter, had frittered all Snowden's good work away. Snowden, very able and independent, had been to see him. He had been an excellent Chancellor in the Labour Government, and had practically said to all Socialists, 'Abandon hope all ye who enter here.'

Winston S. Churchill: Cabinet memorandum[1]

(*Churchill papers: 22/22*)

9 December 1924   Treasury Chambers
Secret

FUTURE STATUS OF THE EGYPTIAN ARMY

I trust we shall not relinquish the practice of having a British Sirdar for the Egyptian Army, and of having British officers and instructors employed therein. It would be a great mistake for us to depart from well established custom in this matter, and the demand of Egypt for European instructors of

[1] Circulated to the Cabinet as Cabinet paper 533 of 1924.

other nationalities could scarcely be resisted if we declined to help in the organisation of their forces.

WSC

Winston S. Churchill to Lord Salisbury[1]

(*Churchill papers: 18/2*)

9 December 1924   Treasury Chambers

. . . I think that the statement 'property without service cannot be defended' requires qualification by such words as 'in theory' or 'as an abstract moral principle'.

Practically it is capable, I think, of effective defence on the grounds that the existing capitalist system is the foundation of civilisation and the only means by which great modern populations can be supplied with vital necessaries. If this is so, an attempt to hunt down 'the idle rich', whoever they are, wherever they may be found, might be attended with so much friction and injury to the general system of capital and to the freedom arising under a capitalist system that it would be more trouble than it was worth. The existing system of death duties is a certain corrective against the development of a race of idle rich. If they are idle they will cease in a few generations to be rich. Further than that it is not desirable for the legislature to go.

The christian or the moralist alone can pursue an inquisition into what is 'service' and what is 'idleness'. A dilettante philanthropist wasting money on ill-judged schemes may be a poorer asset to the State than a man who having, say, £10,000 a year spends £5,000 selfishly and allows the rest to accumulate at compound interest increasing funds available for enterprise and employment. Again, a man may be a most admirable citizen, spend his whole life in public and philanthropic service, and yet be accustomed to be maintained on such a scale and in such a state that a very large number of persons are kept in unproductive employment serving him.

My maturer views of life lead me to deprecate the personal inquisition, except when self-instituted, into actions which are within the law. I think the rich, whether idle or not, are already taxed in this country to the very highest point compatible with the accumulation of capital for future production. An increasing distinction between earned and unearned income might however

[1] James Edward Hubert Gascoyne-Cecil, Viscount Cranborne, 1861–1947. Educated at Eton and University College, Oxford. Conservative MP, 1885–92 and 1893–1903. Succeeded his father (the former Prime Minister) as 4th Marquess of Salisbury, 1903. President of the Board of Trade, 1905. Lord President of the Council, October 1922–January 1924. Lord Privy Seal, 1924–9. Leader of the House of Lords, 1925–9.

be profitably pursued. The question of the relation of Super-Tax as opposed to Death Duties in regard to enterprise and industry is also a very interesting topic. In the case of the largest estates the toll of Death Duties has already in my opinion required the full limit of taxable capacity, and any advance beyond the present point could not be attended by an increase of revenue.

Winston S. Churchill to Sir Richard Hopkins

(*Churchill papers: 18/3*)

10 December 1924

I am writing the enclosed letter to Sir Ernest Moon[1] whom I have known for a great many years as the Speaker's Counsel. Pray check it for me.

There is no doubt that the present high level of the Super-tax is keenly resented by the class of taxpayers subjected to it. It is probable that a diminution in the rate would be attended by better returns and a better public sentiment in the class affected. If I should be able to proceed on the lines I have discussed with you I should certainly couple the relief with an extension of the process of inquiry which you have now set on foot. The results which have been obtained are certainly remarkable. Can you give me a calculation showing on this basis what might be expected to be the extra yield of the Super-tax if strict collection can be made. This might give me the power to make the reduction which I have in mind.

Will you explain to me how it is this difficulty arises only on the Super-tax. I thought the Super-tax was levied on the income assessed for taxation the year before. Therefore surely these 'errors' which you have detected have been committed in the Income Tax returns and not in the Super-tax returns which follow automatically upon them.

Meanwhile I shall certainly support your Department in its proceedings. I think some assurance should be given to taxpayers that these forms will not be required at intervals of less than, say, five years. I think also these important taxpayers should be handled with courtesy and not summarily ordered to attend at the tax collector's office with their share certificates, etc. After all, they are your most important clients and deserve a certain amount of ceremony.

I presume you are bearing in mind the instructions I have given not to press the collection of the revenue unduly in the present financial year.

[1] Ernest Robert Moon, 1854–1930. Barrister. King's Counsel, 1902. Counsel to the Speaker, 1908–29. Chairman of the Enemy Trading Committee, 1916–19. Chairman of the Foreign Office Committee on Claims Against the Russian Government, 1918.

Stanley Baldwin to King George V

(*Baldwin papers*)

11 December 1924

The debate gave Mr Winston Churchill the opportunity of making his first important declaration as Chancellor of the Exchequer. It would be almost superfluous to say that he achieved an immediate success. The most noticeable feature of his speech was the fact that the Treasury has already succeeded in exercising its sobering influence. There was a conscious restraint and absence of gesture which showed that Mr Churchill was speaking with a grave sense of responsibility and with due regard to his brief. This did not, however, prevent him from revealing his consummate skill in exposition and debate. In the course of his speech which was obviously intended for international consumption and was not addressed to the House of Commons alone, he made it clear that the Government's policy in regard to Allied debts followed in the main the lines of the Balfour Note; that the British Government were prepared to cancel all inter-allied debts, but if that was impossible that they would ask from Europe as much and no more than the United States might find it necessary to require from this country; and that any payments made by our debtors in Europe to their creditors in the United States should be accompanied simultaneously and pari passu by proportionate payments to this country.

The policy apparently met with the warm approval of all Parties in the House including the Labour Party whose spokesman, Mr Philip Snowden, made an admirable speech in the course of which he gave the Chancellor of the Exchequer his blessing subject to minor qualifications.[1]

---

[1] During the course of his speech on Inter-Allied Debts on 10 December 1924, Churchill told the House of Commons: 'The British burdens in the war were not inferior to those borne by any other Allied nation. It is not right to use boasting words or to draw invidious comparisons, but when the duration of the effort, the loss of life and treasure, the influence exerted and I may add the achievements gained by land and sea—when the whole of these are computed, weighed and measured, and justly weighed and measured, we are, I think, entitled to respect from every quarter. But if this was our share in the struggle, our financial burdens since the War have been incomparably greater than those of any other victorious Power. We paid all our own expenses in the War. We have discharged and are discharging all our liabilities punctually. We have not hitherto pressed any Allied debtor to meet its obligations and this policy has imposed the greatest sacrifices upon the British taxpayer. No other victorious nation is making similar or equal sacrifices. The taxation of all classes is high, direct and indirect, but the rate of direct taxation in this country is higher than in any other country. And in this country we not only impose high taxes, but those taxes are paid by the taxpaying public.'

Winston S. Churchill to Sir Samuel Hoare

(*Churchill papers: 18/2*)

12 December 1924
Private and Personal

Although we are committed to the principle of Singapore, we have yet to decide the rate and stages by which it shall be executed and the methods of defence. I understand that the present plan is to defend the Base against the landing of a besieging army, by powerful submarine flotillas. But surely submarines are not the way to prevent the landing of such an army. A few submarines might no doubt do good work upon the transports as they approached; but the Base defence even now—and how much more in ten years' time—against a landing would be by aeroplanes.

Surely the aeroplane side of this problem requires re-examination. There ought to be a large economy in using air power instead of submarines for this purpose. Further, I am by no means sure that heavy bombing machines might not be a substitute for the two great batteries of guns it is proposed to mount. If so, how much better to have this cost represented in mobile air squadrons rather than tied up forever to one spot in two heavy batteries. . . .

I am going to press for a new and detailed examination of methods, stages and rate of construction at Singapore. It seems to me that if this work were completed in fifteen or twenty years, the air should play a far larger part in it than is now contemplated. We ought to arrive at a time table showing exactly what will be done each year in the fifteen or twenty years, and at what period each of the successive methods of defence will come into operation. I should be very glad if you would talk this over with Trenchard, and perhaps we can then discuss it together.

Winston S. Churchill to Sir Richard Hopkins

(*Treasury papers: T171/239*)

14 December 1924

. . . what I am aiming at is a substantial diminution in annual burden on the direct taxpayer. I believe that this burden is at the present time a grave discouragement to enterprise and thrift and a potent factor in the tendency of high profits. I want to make a real impression upon this. For this purpose I am anxious to supplement my modest resources of relief by a direct transfer of the burdens from current taxation to Death Duties. I am sure this is in accordance with modern thought and my instinct is that the change will be welcomed by the classes affected.

Moreover the imposition of the increased Death duties and the friction that will arise thereupon will assist us in the general presentation of the treatment of the higher classes of direct taxpayers. It harmonises with the plan of emphasising the distinction between earned and unearned income in the lower ranges. It is intended to be an encouragement to people to bestir themselves and make more money while they are alive and bring up their heirs to do the same. The process of the creation of new wealth is beneficial to the whole community. The process of squatting on old wealth though valuable is a far less lively agent. The great bulk of the wealth of the world is created and consumed every year. We shall never shake ourselves clear from the debts of the war and break into a definitely larger period except by the energetic creation of new wealth. A premium on effort is my aim and a penalty on inertia may well be its companion.

On the other hand it would be well to work out a minor alternative with the further possibility that we may have to knock a penny or two off the standard rate of taxation in each case.

I am anxious to introduce the penny postage from the end of October at a cost of $2\frac{3}{4}$ millions in that year and slightly over £5 millions in the next year. Will you bear this in mind in considering ways and means?[1]

WSC

Sir Samuel Hoare to Winston S. Churchill

(*Treasury papers: T172/1440*)

15 December 1924

I have had a preliminary talk with Trenchard and, broadly speaking, we are both in entire agreement with your views and believe that the substitution of torpedo and bombing squadrons for submarines and heavy guns—the latter in any case requiring aircraft to 'spot' for them—should result in substantial economy and enhanced efficiency. Further I personally feel that, in view of the year which must elapse before the docks and other works can be completed, it is premature at the present time to attempt to take any final decision as to what the precise strength of the defending force should be.

---

[1] The Penny Post was first introduced on 10 January 1840. On 3 June 1918 the rate was raised to 1½d (for the first four ounces) and on 1 June 1920 it was raised again to 2d (for the first three ounces). A reduction was made on 29 May 1922 to 1½d (for the first one ounce, raised to two ounces on 14 May 1923). No further reduction was ever made, and on 1 May 1940 the rate was raised to 2½d (for the first two ounces). In July 1978 the rate stood at the equivalent of 1/9½d.

I am going into the matter further with Trenchard and later on would welcome an opportunity of discussing it with you.

Austen Chamberlain to Winston S. Churchill

(Austen Chamberlain papers)

15 December 1924
Private and Confidential

My dear Chancellor,

I refrained from discussing inter-allied debts with anyone while abroad, permitting myself to observe in a phrase which I hope you will pardon me for using, that we had an English proverb which indicated that it was unnecessary to bark oneself when one kept a dog; but Clémentel[1] insisted on accompanying me round the Ceinture at Paris. All that I would say to him or to others was that, whilst we should not grudge France the most favourable treatment that she could obtain from America, we could not contemplate with equanimity the idea that France should repay America in advance of us. Clémentel at once accepted this view. He suggested that, after you had disposed of the business for which the meeting of Finance Ministers is called, you might have a Conference of all the debtor and creditor Powers to consider inter-allied debts. I asked him whether he did not think it might be well that he and you should exchange ideas before you called in the rest of the world and he said that he would be very glad to do so.

He handed me the enclosed letter, which I undertook to deliver to you. You will see that the point on which he desired to insist is that the loan which he seeks in London is to repay a London obligation falling due next year, and he stated that not one penny of it will be taken out of England, his only object being to meet his obligation without destroying the value of the franc. In so far as this is true and the whole truth it would meet, I think, the objection felt by the Treasury and the Governor of the Bank[2] to a French flotation, but I am in no position to judge whether he has in fact disclosed his whole

---

[1] Etienne Clémentel, 1862–1936. Deputy, Puy-de-Dôme, 1898. Occupied several Ministerial posts between 1898 and 1924, including Minister of Colonies, 1898, and Minister of Commerce, 1916–20. Instrumental in establishing the Inter-Allied Wheat Executive, 1916, and the Inter-Allied Maritime Transport Council, 1917. Senator, 1918. President and founder of the International Chamber of Commerce, 1919. Minister of Finance, 1924–5.

[2] Montagu Collet Norman, 1871–1950. Educated at Eton and King's College, Cambridge. On active service in South Africa, 1900–1 (despatches). A Director of the Bank of England, 1907–19. Governor of the Bank of England, 1920–44. Privy Councillor, 1923. Created Baron, 1944.

hand. Consider me therefore merely as a postman who transmits to you a request and an explanation for your consideration.

May I add that I was delighted to see from the papers what an outstanding success your first appearance in the House of Commons as Chancellor of the Exchequer had been? I have never doubted that you will greatly enhance your reputation in this post, which will give you an opportunity of showing to the country your possession of just those powers which perhaps hitherto have been recognised only by your personal friends.

Austen Chamberlain

Winston S. Churchill to Austen Chamberlain
(Churchill papers: 18/2)

15 December 1924   Treasury Chambers

I send you a copy of a letter which I am sending very confidentially to the Prime Minister. The letter speaks for itself, so I will not repeat its contents. I thought perhaps if you were so inclined, that I might ask for the subject of Japan to be raised at the next Cabinet after Wednesday's. What I seek is a declaration to the Cabinet by you, ruling out a war with Japan from among the reasonable possibilities to be taken into acount in the next 10, 15 or 20 years. Subsequently I hope that the Cabinet will give an instruction in this sense to the Committee of Imperial Defence.

Winston S. Churchill to Stanley Baldwin
(Churchill papers: 18/2)

15 December 1924
Secret & Personal

My dear Prime Minister,

I told you last week of my anxiety about the Navy Estimates and of the preliminary forecast of a rise of £10 millions which had reached me. In our present position with prospects of three or four years of government ahead I am bound to try and deal with the finances on at least a three years' basis as this is the only way of getting a settled policy and avoiding the awful waste by chopping and changing which has marked the last three years. Moreover, as you well know, everything at the Exchequer depends on the effects in successive years of any remissions of taxes.

It is no use my trying to take off taxes this year in order to have to put them back the next year. Therefore the prospects of expenditure in the next three years are a vital part of my calculations. I therefore asked the Admiralty a few weeks ago for the forecast of their new construction programme over the next four years. It reached me on Saturday in the form of this simple graph. You will see that it involves an increase on new construction alone of £17¼ millions in the next three years. New construction is always an index and such a development of new construction must carry with it an increase on other Votes. For instance, this coming year the Estimates are to be £10 millions up, of which only £4 millions is new construction. The growth on other Votes is therefore about £6 millions. Singapore will be running through the Estimates at the same time.

I have no hesitation in saying that on the new construction programme outlined the total increase over the present year in 1927/8 would be not £17¼ millions but at least £25, and probably more. The present Estimates are £55 millions, therefore in three years' time we shall be confronted with Navy Estimates of £80 millions. There is also an inevitable increase on the Air in that period of probably another £5 millions.

I should therefore have a minimum of £35 millions increase to face on armaments expenditure. This of course renders impossible any relief of taxation and blots out any social schemes. I get, as you know, about £4 millions saving on debt redemption and conversion and another two or three on war pensions decline, say £7 millions a year. If taxation could be reduced there would also be a certain increase in the Inland Revenue and Customs. This increase has however first of all to overcome the lag of the Snowden remissions.

I had hoped to stimulate trade by a remission of Income Tax and possibly a regrading of the Super-tax in a favourable sense. As there could be no question of this or of any remission to encourage trade, we cannot speak with much confidence about the expansion of the revenue. Still, I daresay that I might count on another £15 millions in three years' time. Add this to the three instalments of 7 already mentioned and you have approximately £36 millions to meet the increased expenditure of 30 millions on armaments and any expansion on education, existing pensions, etc. There is nothing in it on this basis. To accept these armament increases is to sterilize and paralyse the whole policy of the Government. There will be nothing for the taxpayer and nothing for social reform. We shall be a Naval Parliament busily preparing our Navy for some great imminent shock. Voilà tout!

Borrowing is no use at this juncture, as your own knowledge of the Treasury will remind you. We have to face a whole series of Conversion operations leading up to the great Conversion climax of 1929. To borrow on the one hand while paying your £50 milllions sinking fund on the other, would only stultify the new borrowing, and the reduction of the sinking fund would equally destroy all the economies of conversion and probably lose us in four or five years £15 or £16 millions of saving. The Governor of the Bank will, I hope, have told you this weekend about the imminence of our attempt to re-establish the gold standard, in connection with which he is now going to America. It will be easy to attain the gold standard, and indeed almost impossible to avoid taking the decision, but to keep it will require a most strict policy of debt repayment and a high standard of credit. To reach it and have to abandon it, would be disastrous. Therefore I repeat there is nothing for it, if we accept the armament policy, but to put out of our mind all idea of reduction of taxation and practically all plans of social reform during the whole lifetime of the present Parliament.

I feel sure that such a policy will not only bring the Government into ruin but might well affect the safety of the State. The vast growth of the Navy Votes will be challenged not only by the Socialists and Liberals, who will increasingly make common cause against it, but also by all that formidable body of opinion on our own side which was marshalled so effectively by Rothermere in the last year of the Coalition and did so much to make it unpopular. We should come up to the Election with these enormous Navy Estimates and nothing else to show. Besides this, we should be accused of starting up the whole armament race all over the world and setting the pace towards a new vast war. I cannot conceive any course more certain to result in a Socialist victory. If the Socialists win in a tremendous economy wave, they will cut down and blot out all these Naval preparations so that in the end the Admiralty will not get the Navy programme for the sake of which your Government will have broken itself.

I am sure you have no intention of allowing our policy to follow such a foolish course and I know you will be supported by the Cabinet, by the House of Commons and by the nation itself in a wise and far-reaching restraint. I daresay the Admiralty themselves are to a certain extent merely trying it on. It seems to me however that this very great danger must be grappled with from the outset, and I have asked myself what is the best way.

You know I do not write about these naval matters without experience. It seems to me that the Admiralty imagine themselves confronted with the same sort of situation in regard to Japan as we faced against Germany in the ten years before the war. They have a wonderful staff of keen, able officers, whose minds are filled with war impressions. The whole of this great thinking body is preparing the Navy for the impending struggle. Hong Kong is to become a strong base for submarines, twelve and possibly up to 21 being provocatively stationed there in time of peace right under the very noses of the Japanese. Singapore is to be developed as fast as possible. The new construction programme is to be pushed forward. All the reserves of stores and ammunition are to be rapidly completed on lavish scales. One hundred merchantmen are to be armed with six inch guns. Every technical service is to be brought to the highest perfection. For what? A war with Japan! But why should there be a war with Japan? I do not believe there is the slightest chance of it in our lifetime. The Japanese are our allies. The Pacific is dominated by the Washington Agreement. America is far more likely to have a quarrel with Japan than we are. What question is pending between England and Japan? To what diplomatic combination do either of us belong which could involve us against each other?

There is absolutely no resemblance between our relations with Japan and those we had with Germany before the war. Then we were joined with France by a military agreement begun in 1906. France was set against Germany by the terrible quarrels of the past. England, France and Russia formed the counterpoise to the Triple Alliance. Europe was divided into two armed camps. Germany made a bold bid for naval supremacy, and we had to face this mighty power across the narrow North Sea with every feeling that our whole national existence was at stake.

Japan is at the other end of the world. She cannot menace our vital security in any way. She has no reason whatever to come into collision with us. She has every reason to avoid such a collision. The only sufficient cause which could draw us into a war with Japan would be if she invaded Australia. Does anybody imagine she is going to do so? Would she not be mad to do so. How could she put an army into Australia, over 5,000 miles across the ocean and maintain it at war with the Australians and the whole British Empire. Nothing less than half a million Japanese would be any good, and these would have to be continually supplied and maintained. It is an absolute absurdity. Even if America stood inactive Japan would be ruined. She would never attempt it.

On the other hand suppose we had a dispute with Japan about something in China and we declared war upon her, what would happen? We should have to move the best part of our Fleet to Singapore. Hong Kong would of course be taken by Japan in the early days. What should we do then? We should have to send large armies (how we should raise them I do not know) to go and attack Japan in her home waters. The war would last for years. It would cost Japan very little. It would reduce us to bankruptcy. All the time it was on we should be at the mercy at home of every unfriendly power or force hostile to the British Empire. We could never do it. It would never be worth our while to do it. The only war it would be worth our while to fight with Japan would be to prevent an invasion of Australia, and that I am certain will never happen in any period, even the most remote, which we or our children need foresee. I am therefore convinced that war with Japan is not a possibility which any reasonable Government need take into account.

I think the Foreign Secretary ought to be asked to advise the Cabinet and the CID on this point. If he so advises, the Admiralty ought to be told that they are not expected to be in a position to encounter Japan in the Pacific Ocean and they are not to prepare for such a contingency. The CID or the Cabinet should relieve them definitely of such a responsibility. They should be made to recast all their plans and scales and standards on the basis that no naval war against a first class Navy is likely to take place in the next twenty years. They should be told that the lives of all their ships are to be prolonged; that the replacements contained in the attached programme are to be spread over at least three times the period specified; that the extra cost involved by these replacements is to be met to the extent of at least one-half by savings on the existing basis of other Navy Votes. On this basis they would be required to confine themselves to approximately £55 millions in 1925/26 and not to exceed £60 millions by 1928/29. We should also seek a further Naval Conference at Washington or here to regulate the construction of vessels other than battleships and the rate of replacements.

This will lead to very hard fighting and possibly some casualties. If it were achieved and we manage our other affairs as successfully as we have begun, we may be able to secure a second term of power. In which case by a steady yet moderate maintenance of our armaments the Empire will be in a far stronger position militarily, navally, financially and socially than by any other method.

Yours vy sincerely
Winston S. Churchill

Winston S. Churchill to William Bridgeman
(*Churchill papers: 18/2*)

15 December 1924   Treasury Chambers

My dear First Lord,

I am much obliged to you for sending me a graph showing the proposed naval programme for the next few years. I am sure you will be well aware of the cardinal issues which the great increases of the Navy Estimates must raise. Expenditure on this scale would, if sanctioned by the Cabinet, (a) prevent any appreciable relief of taxation during the lifetime of the present Parliament, (b) exclude any form of social legislation which involved finance, and (c) present naval estimates of about 80 millions in 1928–29 as the main issue for the consideration of the electorate. I believe that if this were the course of events, we should have taken the most effective step to secure the return of the Socialist Administration, and the naval programme for which everything would have been sacrificed would thus have been broken up before it had been completed. I hope you will consider these possibilities, as they would seem to be rather disagreeable from every point of view. It is surely worth considering whether a more moderate policy, if persevered in not for four years but for eight or nine, might not leave us in a stronger naval position.

I am of course aware that a certain proportion of replacements are a necessity to the Admiralty, and our differences (wide though they be) are differences of degree rather than of principle. The scale of the expenditure you contemplate is, however, so enormous, and its consequences, if persisted in, would be, as I judge, so injurious to the country, that I must endeavour to examine in detail the Admiralty policy which it expresses. I am therefore asking the Treasury to send forward a number of requests for information under various heads. I am sorry to cause your Department so much trouble, but it has always been customary for the Admiralty to supply the Chancellor of the Exchequer with the fullest information in regard to the Navy Estimates. I remember in 1913 supplying every detail that was sought by the Treasury. I trust therefore that you will give directions in accordance with these precedents.

Believe me
Yours very sincerely,
Winston S. Churchill

Winston S. Churchill to Austen Chamberlain

(*Austen Chamberlain papers*)

16 December 1924   Treasury Chambers
Private

My dear Austen,

I return Clémentel's note of which I have kept a copy. I fear I cannot act in the way he wants. In the first place it is not a matter which rests with me but with the City: and in the second I clearly could not favour an arrangement which would be a precedent for anyone who owed money here (say by getting an overdraft at a Bank in the first place) to claim that he should be allowed to issue a loan which would not involve 'any transfer of funds'. Of course the distinction Clémentel tries to make is quite artificial and would be no use in warding off other foreign loans, of which I know there are several only too eager to come. After all the French have recently obtained large credits to support the franc and they should use them. If we are ever going to get the French to pay interest on their debts we must not let them think this can be done by borrowing from us.

I suggest that you should reply to Clémentel by saying that you have discussed his letter with me: that it is the established practice of the Treasury not to intervene either for or against market loans, but to leave them as has been done in this case to the judgment of the market: and that I regret that it is quite impossible for me to depart from this policy in the present case.

Yours vy sincerely
Winston S. Churchill

Cabinet minutes

(*Cabinet papers: 23/49*)

17 December 1924

The Chancellor of the Exchequer insisted, as a condition of his consent to the proposals of the Unemployment Committee that the Trade Facilities committee should scrutinise each individual application with the greatest care with a view to avoiding the stimulation of concerns of mushroom growth and anything which could be represented as a subsidy to German ship-owners who were competing with British enterprise.

Sir Otto Niemeyer to Winston S. Churchill

(*Treasury papers: T171/247*)

18 December 1924

The main advantage of a non-contributory system is I think social and moral and to some extent administrative. . . .

The social advantages are so great that I think that we should be well advised not to limit ourselves to Widows' Pensions but to include in any pension legislation the Anderson Committee's recommendations on contributory old age pensions at 65. I believe this is our one chance of avoiding in the long run having to make this change on a non contributory basis.

Stanley Baldwin to King George V

(*Baldwin papers*)

18 December 1924   House of Commons

The Prime Minister with his humble duty to Your Majesty.

Four or five years ago a prophet would have been totally bereft of honour, not only in his own country, if he had foretold that in December 1924 the House would see Mr Lloyd George, in unholy alliance with Captain Wedgwood Benn,[1] leading a vigorous attack on the principles of the Safeguarding of Industries Act, and on the other side Mr Winston Churchill appearing as a doughty champion in its defence. But mercurial temperaments such as these must always be anathema to a prophetic soul. . . .

Towards the close of the proceedings Mr Runciman further developed the attack, but it is doubtful whether he could have made a more eloquent and vigorous appeal to the House if the proposals of the Government had in fact constituted full-blooded protection. 'Men are wrought by cunning, by importunity, and by vehemence,' and the Opposition had made use of all these means. But they found their match in Mr Winston Churchill whose winding up speech was one of the best which he has delivered in the House. For the first ten minutes he kept the House rocking with laughter while he taunted and gibed at Mr Runciman, Mr Lloyd George, Sir Alfred Mond,[2] and Captain Wedgwood Benn. Then, turning to the more serious aspect of the question, he successfully shattered the hypotheses which they had manufactured for the purposes of their attack, and finally brought delight to his supporters by a most astute and clever attack on Mr Snowden. It was a wanton act, he said, on the part of the late Chancellor to deprive the State of the revenue derived from the McKenna duties. Here were duties which nobody objected to: taxation on luxuries, taxation paid by the rich, and taxation which yielded £2½ millions of revenue—half the cost of the penny post, and all this sacrifice merely in order to gratify a theory.

---

[1] William Wedgwood Benn, 1877–1960. Liberal MP, 1906–27. A Junior Lord of the Treasury in Asquith's Government, 1910–15. On active service, 1915–19 (Royal Flying Corps, despatches twice). Joined the Labour Party, 1927. Labour MP, 1928–31 and 1937–42. Secretary of State for India in Ramsay MacDonald's second Government, 1929–31. Created Viscount Stansgate, 1941. Secretary of State for Air in Clement Attlee's Government, 1945–6. One of his three sons was killed in action in 1944; another, Anthony Wedgwood Benn, disclaimed his father's title, and was a member of the Labour Governments of 1964 and 1974.

[2] Alfred Moritz Mond, 1868–1930. A Director of Brunner, Mond & Co, 1895. Created, by 1926, the Imperial Chemical Industries (ICI), with a capital of £95,000,000. Liberal MP 1906–10, 1910–23 and 1924–8. Created Baronet, 1910. First Commissioner of Works, 1916–21. Minister of Health, 1921–2. Joined the Conservative Party, 1926. Created Baron Melchett, 1928.

The whole house was enthralled by his speech. It was Mr Churchill at his best, full of confidence and fight, crushing yet good humoured in the scorn which he heaped upon his opponents, never at a loss for a word and full of eloquence and power which cannot be surpassed by any Member sitting in the House of Commons.

Lord Derby to Winston S. Churchill

(*Churchill papers: 18/1*)

18 December 1924
Confidential

My dear Winston,

One line of hearty congratulation on your speech of last night. It was a great personal triumph & I as an old friend of yours, am delighted.

I strongly approve of your policy. The pledge is kept—and yet here is a chance of some real Imperial preference, but don't let Amery have too much to do with the spending of the £1,000,000. I distrust him very much. Don't spend too many millions—think of us poor income taxpayers—I wish you could consider only imposing a super tax on our real income ie allow us to deduct the amount we pay in income tax & only impose supertax on what is left. I am afraid it may be too costly a plan.

Yours ever
Derby

Winston S. Churchill to Sir Richard Hopkins

(*Treasury papers: T171/239*)

20 December 1924

1. Can you suggest a method of helping more the class between £1,000 & 2,000.
2. The Estate duty seems to fall in rather heavy percentage on the £2,000.
3. Wd it be possible to spare or relieve *unearned* income under £500 pa when enjoyed by persons over (say) 60 or 65 years of age. What wd be the adm cost of a workable plan. This wd meet your point about 'the attack on living'.

WSC

Victor Cazalet: diary

(*Robert Rhodes James: 'Victor Cazalet, A Portrait'*)

21 December 1924

Peter[1] and I spent the day at Winston's. We were quite alone except for a Mr Bracken, Australian Editor of *English Life*. I can't say how kind, nice, pleasant and interesting Winston was. It was a wonderful day. We talked for hours, chiefly on the question of the Safeguarding of Industries Act, which he fears may be a pitfall unless carefully handled. His powers of speech and language, his wonderful comprehension, and *now* his geniality and willingness to listen to others, are quite extraordinary.

Winston S. Churchill to H. C. Osborne[2]

(*Churchill papers: 1/174*)

22 December 1924

Dear Mr Osborne,

You are aware that no provision has been made for my youngest daughter, Mary, in the Children's Trust. I must at a later date consider her case. All I can see my way to doing at present is to settle on her the Royalties of various books of mine which are still extant. Of these the 'Life of Lord Randolph Churchill' and 'The World Crisis' Volumes I and II are the only two publications from which any appreciable revenue need be expected. There are, however, very small sums (a few pounds or even shillings a year) collected by Mr A. P. Watt[3] for my earlier books, and these may as well be brought in too. Both 'Lord Randolph Churchill' and 'The World Crisis' have yet to be published in their cheap editions, and it is possible that there will be some effective yield from this.

[1] Peter Victor Ferdinand Cazalet, 1907–73. Educated at Eton and Christ Church. Brother of Victor Cazalet. Amateur rider, 1930–8; he rode in the Grand National in 1935. National Hunt trainer from 1939; subsequently National Hunt trainer to Queen Elizabeth (the Queen Mother). Before the age of sixty he saddled his 1,000th winner. Served in the Royal Artillery, 1939–40; in the 2nd (Armoured) Battalion, Welsh Guards, 1939–45.

[2] Henry C. Osborne, 1869–1950. Joined the staff of Nicholl Manisty & Co, Solicitors, in 1883, and remained with that firm for the rest of his life. As Managing Clerk, he handled Churchill's legal and financial affairs during the inter-war years. In 1941–2, when his health failed, this aspect of his work was taken over by G. W. Pardy, who acted for Churchill until 1951–2, when Nicholl Manisty & Co was taken over by Messrs Fladgate & Co.

[3] Alexander Pollock Watt, 1837–1914. Literary Agent, of Norfolk House, Norfolk Street, Strand. A. J. Balfour's literary agent in the 1890s (Balfour called Watt his publishing 'broker'). Introduced by Balfour to Churchill in December 1897, when Churchill was looking for a publisher for the *Malakand Field Force*. Worked as Churchill's literary agent from 1898 to 1905.

Will you draw up a Deed, assigning to Mary the net proceeds of all the Royalties accruing to me after February 1, 1925, on all publications of mine published before that date; and vest these proceeds in the Trust, either as a separate or as a part of the general Trust, and on broadly the same conditions *mutatis mutandis*. I should thus retain the power to arrange with the publisher for any new cheap editions, but would derive no benefit therefrom myself. The Trust would of course be irrevocable.

Perhaps you will write to me about this.

Winston S. Churchill to P. J. Grigg[1]

(*Churchill papers: 18/2*)

22 December 1924

My dear Grigg,

If you will look in the Prime Minister's room in the House of Commons, you will see two very nice electric light shades made of large discs of imitation alabaster. These give a very pleasant light. Will you send for someone from the Office of Works, and find out whether (a) they can put a similar shade in my room at the House of Commons, and (b) what they think about putting one in the Treasury Board Room. I cannot think that the present iron structure can have any real association with the room, as it is plainly the worst form of Victorianism. I do not like the naked light. I don't believe the disc would be any more anachronistic than the present monstrosity, and in my opinion it is prettier as well as far more convenient. However, I should like to hear what they say about this second point. So far as my room at the House of Commons is concerned, there ought to be no question.

---

[1] Percy James Grigg, 1890–1964. Educated at Bournemouth School and St Johns College, Cambridge. Entered the Treasury, 1913. Served in the Royal Garrison Artillery, 1915–18. Principal Private Secretary to successive Chancellors of the Exchequer, 1921–30. Chairman, Board of Customs and Excise, 1930; Board of Inland Revenue, 1930–4. Knighted, 1932. Finance Member, Government of India, 1934–9. Elected to the Other Club, 1939. Permanent Under-Secretary of State for War, 1939–42. Secretary of State for War, 1942. Privy Councillor, 1942. National MP, East Cardiff, 1942–5. British Executive Director, International Bank for Reconstruction and Development, 1946–7. Subsequently a director of Imperial Tobacco, the Prudential Assurance Company and other companies. On 19 May 1930 Churchill wrote to Grigg: 'Your friendship is ever of great consequence to me, and my regard for you is deep. . . . I have the warmest feelings of admiration for your gifts and character.'

Winston S. Churchill to Lord Derby

(*Churchill papers: 18/1*)

23 December 1924
Private and Confidential

My dear Eddie,

Thank you so much for your letter and congratulations, which I greatly value.

I am very glad you approve of the way in which we have got round the food tax difficulty. It would indeed have been a pity to expose ourselves to all that cry with added complaints about a breach of faith for the sake of these petty taxes on tinned salmon etc. It gave me great pleasure to see the Cabinet move so sagaciously.

The question of safeguarding industries will also require much care. The Prime Minister stands very strictly to his pledge against using safeguarding provisions as a wedge to introduce a general tariff. Therefore the Bill must be very carefully drawn so as to prevent an ugly rush of claims. But on the other hand there is the risk that if it is so carefully drawn as all that, many will say it is a farce. However we have got round one great difficulty and I am very hopeful we shall surmount these others.

I am thinking a good deal about the Budget.

Thank you once again for writing.

With every good wish to you and yours,
Believe me,
Yours very sincerely
Winston S. Churchill

Winston S. Churchill to P. J. Grigg

(*Churchill papers: 18/3*)

23 December 1924

What has happened to my long minute about Pensions? One or two things were answered but I have not been told, for instance, of how it is proposed to deal with the Friendly Societies. What is happening to the Pensions Committee? When did it last meet? How many times have you attended on my behalf?

I should like to see Sir John Anderson and some of his principal colleagues myself and have a talk to them. I should be free to come to London on January 4th if that could be fitted in with other engagements.

Winston S. Churchill to L. S. Amery

(*Churchill papers: 18/2*)

23 December 1924
Private

My dear Leo,

I agree that you are bound to answer Bruce's[1] request about communicating with the other Dominions, and I think you are very wise in warning him of the chilly reception such a proposal would court. I understand the CID is to receive a statement on January 5 from Austen Chamberlain on the general aspect of our relations with Japan, and that thereafter there will be some discussion preliminary to the setting up of the CID sub-committee on the methods and tempo of the construction of Singapore. I think it would be premature in the interval for you to express official satisfaction either to Australia or New Zealand at the offers of contributions for Singapore they have so far made.

The Cabinet was very disappointed to find that this base, which is so vital an element in the ultimate security of Australasia, should apparently make so small an appeal to the imagination of these two Dominions, and that they seem quite content that practically the whole burden should be thrown on the Mother Country. Chamberlain in particular expressed a very strong view in this sense to me. Since my opinion has been invited, I can only say I hope very much you will defer such expression of approval until the CID or the Cabinet have been able to review the position.

All good wishes for Christmas,[2]

Yours very sincerely,
Winston S. Churchill

---

[1] Stanley Melbourne Bruce, 1883–1967. Born and educated in Melbourne, Australia. Called to the Bar (London), 1907. On active service with the Worcestershire Regiment, 1915 (severely wounded at Suvla Bay). Military Cross, 1915. Captain, Royal Fusiliers, France, 1916 (wounded). Prime Minister and Minister of External Affairs, Australia, 1923–9. Resident Minister in London, 1932–3; High Commissioner, 1933–45. Represented Australia at the Imperial Conferences of 1923, 1926 and 1937, and at the League of Nations Assembly, 1933–8. Created Viscount, 1947.

[2] Churchill spent Christmas 1924 at Chartwell. The visitors' book records an entirely family gathering. Those present were his brother Jack and sister-in-law Lady Gwendeline, with their three children, Peregrine, Johnnie and Clarissa; and Clementine Churchill's sister Nellie Romilly, with her husband Bertram and their children Giles and Esmond Romilly.

Clementine Churchill to Professor Lindemann
(*Cherwell papers*)

27 December 1924

Winston is immersed in thrilling new work with the Treasury officials, whom he says are a wonderful lot of men.

Winston S. Churchill to Sir Horace Hamilton
(*Treasury papers: T171/241*)

30 December 1924

THE McKENNA DUTIES

Without in the slightest degree committing myself to it in principle I should like to examine it in further detail. Can you analyse these duties for me. Take silk for instance. To what extent is it a raw material for protected industries? To what extent can it be described as a luxury? What is the import of raw, manufactured or artificial silk? Above all what is the production at home? Who are the classes and interests who would complain? Is this not a case in which it would be impracticable to impose a countervailing excise? If so, all the better.

In the absence of countervailing excise all these duties would have incidentally protective effects unless there was virtually no home production of a similar article. Such protective effects would be a serious defect in sound finance. On the other hand, with the present high rate of taxation every tax has its defects from that point of view. . . .

How much will be reaped by private interests at home compared with what is collected by the Exchequer? . . .

In short each of these suggested duties should be made the subject of a short story. Do not hesitate in confidence to avail yourself of the Board of Trade.

Winston S. Churchill to Brendan Bracken

(*Churchill papers: 1/172*)

28 December 1924

My dear Brendan,

I am telling Eddie to write to Lord D'Abernon[1] about you. Pagenstecker[2] was of course a world-famed German oculist, probably the greatest in his day. But I understood he was now very old indeed. I think it will be more helpful if you ask one of your doctors to write on half a sheet of note paper a brief account of your case. Eddie will then, with my authority, ask the Embassy in Berlin to advise who are the highest authorities available. I think you know D'Abernon personally, but if not, I will of course give you a letter of introduction to him. I am sure you should examine the bacteriological aspect very carefully before delivering yourself over to the surgeon. With your youth and vital force aided as it can now be, you ought to be able to throw off this poison yourself.

Winston S. Churchill: Cabinet memorandum[3]

(*Churchill papers: 22/22*)

30 December 1924   Treasury Chambers
Secret

EGYPT

I think it is precipitate to take the view that if Ziwar Pasha's Administration fails we must choose between the annexation and the evacuation of Egypt.[4] Our position in Egypt, except for the short period of the protectorate, has always rested on a fiction supported by force. We ruled for nearly forty

[1] Edgar Vincent, 1857–1941. Served in the Coldstream Guards, 1877–82. Financial Adviser to the Egyptian Government, 1883–9. Knighted, 1887 (at the age of thirty). Governor of the Imperial Ottoman Bank, 1889–97. Conservative MP, 1899–1906. Created Baron D'Abernon, 1914. Chairman, Central Control Board (Liquor Traffic), 1915–20. Mission to Poland, 1920. Ambassador to Berlin, 1920–6. Created Viscount, 1926. Chairman, Medical Research Council, 1929–33. In 1931 he published an account of the battle of Warsaw, *The Eighteenth Decisive Battle of the World.*

[2] Hermann Pagenstecker, 1844–1932. One of Germany's most distinguished eye surgeons: author of the definitive work on eye surgery, 1873–5. Professor of eye surgery at Wiesbaden from 1890. His brother Alexander (who died in 1879) and his son Hermann (who died in 1918) were both distinguished eye surgeons, with whom he was closely associated.

[3] Circulated to the Cabinet as Cabinet paper 555 of 1924.

[4] Ahmad Ziwar Pasha had become Prime Minister of Egypt on 24 November 1924 (in succession to Zaghlul Pasha). His administration lasted until 7 June 1926 (when Adli Yeghen Pasha became Prime Minister).

years on the theory that Egypt was 'a tributary province of the Turkish Empire in British military occupation'. I do not see why some similar formula should not be devised in the future. For instance, 'Egypt is an independent State acting in all matters of external and internal policy in accordance with British advice.' So far from agreeing that 'Cromerism' is impossible, I regard it as inevitable. We must not deem ourselves incapable of exercising a complete control over the whole administration of Egypt, while at the same time observing and respecting all the forms and procedure of a native Egyptian State.

In order to carry out such a policy successfully, we must have a persevering will of our own. The lamentable muddle into which Egypt has fallen of late years is due to the realisation by the Egyptian Nationalists that Great Britain for the time being no longer possesses such a will. It is sufficient to recite the acts of violence, of weakness and of vacillation which have marked our policy in Egypt since the Great War. We declared a protectorate over the country, and procured the assent of our Allies, including the United States, to this historic step. The ink of President Wilson's pen was hardly dry when we renounced our protectorate over Egypt and promised to set up an independent Egyptian Kingdom. We put Fuad Pasha[1] on the throne against the popular will, and guaranteed the crown, not only to himself, but to his son.[2] We had hardly made this solemn undertaking when we proceeded to throw Fuad and his dynasty to the mercies of an independent Egyptian National Government. Our nominee for one policy was left to face the swiftly approaching consequences of its reversal. We endeavoured to console him by making him a King. When this unfortunate puppet, whom we had hoisted into precarious eminence, was repeatedly assured that we were about to desert him, he naturally began to look about for a local foundation and to seek for friends among those forces hostile to British influence, to which Great Britain proposed to hand over the mastership of the country. When we saw him taking these reasonable precautions, we made naïve comments upon Oriental 'duplicity' and 'love of intrigue'. Duplicity is the natural resource

---

[1] Ahmed Fuad, 1869–1936. A great-grandson of Mehmed Ali. Studied at Geneva, and at the Military Academy of Turin. A Lieutenant in the Italian Army, 1889. Ottoman Military Attaché in Vienna, 1890–2. An advocate of scientific modernization for Egypt, he founded the Institute of Applied Hydrobiology and the Association of Feminist Industries. Khedive of Egypt, 1917; assumed the title of King, February 1922. Regarded by most Egyptian nationalists as a tool of Britain. Gradually increased his autocratic powers during the later 1920s.

[2] Farouk, 1920–65. Brought up by an English governess. Succeeded his father as King in 1936. Adopted the role of the 'pious king', visiting mosques and posing as the champion of the Muslim faith. Later he found himself in conflict with the Muslim authorities. Forced by the British to remove his pro-Axis advisers, 1942. Forced to abdicate in favour of his infant son, 1952. He died in Rome, at the age of 45.

of the weak when the strong fail in their duty. Intrigue may be the only resource when policy is non-existent. Thus we lost the King and such influence as he could command, and at the same time encouraged every hostile and subversive element in the country.

Our treatment of Zaghlul is a perfect cameo of 'how not to do it'. We first deport Zaghlul to Malta and make a martyr of him, while admitting the justice of the cause of Egyptian independence. We then allow him to return as a national hero and make a triumphal entry into Alexandria and Cairo. We then deport him again, this time to the Seychelles. We bring him back to Gibraltar, allow him to take the waters in Europe, and finally to return to Egypt a second time and make a second, and still more spectacular, triumphal entry. We knew all the time that Zaghlul was our bitter foe, and our treatment of him was certainly calculated to confirm him in this mood. By twice deporting him, we made him a martyr; by twice bringing him back, we made him a conqueror. If one had wished to prescribe a receipt for 'How to foment antagonism against oneself in an Oriental country,' one could not have set about it more skilfully or more successfully. Finally, we hand over the Government to Zaghlul the Conqueror, under an instrument which leaves every burning question between Britain and Egypt unsettled, and then we try to negotiate a treaty with him for our advantage in flat denial of his own cause. Here, again, everything worked out exactly as might have been expected. Consequences followed causes simply, swiftly and surely, until by an unbroken chain we reached the pistol volley which killed Sir Lee Stack on the 19th November.

Such is the situation to which the Foreign Secretary and His Majesty's present Government are the heirs. The strong, sober and successful action which has been taken since the murder of Sir Lee Stack has regained for us a fresh opportunity. We have now only to make up our minds what we mean to do, and then to carry out our purpose unswervingly for four or five years, to retrieve the disasters and blunders of the past. So far as policy is concerned, we really have very little choice. We cannot leave Egypt. We cannot allow any other European Power to set foot in Egypt. We cannot sit on the banks of the Suez Canal and allow Egypt to sink into anarchy, while forbidding all help and guidance from Europe or America. We have got to govern Egypt and to govern Egypt well. Finance, police, the army, railways, irrigation, education, sanitation—every one of these services must once again be made a credit to Great Britain. We have got to make the Egyptians feel that this is what we mean to do and that nothing will turn us from our resolve. We have got to use Egyptians as our instruments. We shall find plenty once our intentions are known. We may treat them with every form of ceremonial consideration. We may keep ourselves in the background as much as possible.

But if we are to succeed, no one in the Nile Valley must have the slightest doubt whose will is law throughout the land.

There is, however, one statement in the Foreign Office paper produced under Mr MacDonald's Administration which would seem to suggest that we are in a helpless position. We are told that 'a "down tools" movement in the public services and the railways and provincial services would leave the capital with its 600,000 inhabitants foodless in a few days and would force His Majesty's Government either to withdraw their troops from Cairo or take measures which would in fact amount to a reconquest of the country'. This is a matter on which the military authorities ought to have a word to say. It is, of course, quite easy to have food in Cairo sufficient for the British troops and European inhabitants for several weeks; and certainly it would be possible to bring more in up the Nile. If the Egyptians in the provinces chose to starve the 500,000 Egyptian inhabitants of the capital, they would be doing a very foolish thing. We should no doubt do our best to save these unfortunate people from the consequences of their countrymen's folly. But it would be their trouble, not ours. I have not the slightest doubt that the first pinch of scarcity would make all classes in Cairo co-operate actively in the pacification of the country and the restoration of the communications. The mere fact that it was known that the Europeans and the British troops had adequate food reserves would deter the Cairo agitators from any such scheme. We are surely not going to let ourselves be bounced out of Egypt by threats of this kind.

But there are certain perils which it would be well to avoid. We are at the present moment governing Egypt by arbitrary power. We are no doubt right to veil that power as much as possible. But it is no use trying to half-govern a country. We have pushed over the National Administration of Zaghlul. We have coerced the King into installing an Administration submissive to our wishes. The so-called Parliament which we laboriously brought into existence has been dissolved. It is hoped that the elections may be so worked as to produce a tame Parliament in its place. While our newly asserted will-power is producing these results—apparently quite easily—we cannot disclaim all responsibility for the internal good government of Egypt. We cannot acquiesce in, nay, encourage, the exodus of the British officials. We cannot contemplate with complacency the degeneration in every form of administrative life which is already swiftly overtaking the land we rescued from barbarism and shielded from invasion. Least of all can we meditate the withdrawal of our troops from Cairo in the despairing hope that the Egyptian Pashas and wealthy classes will be so terrified at the near approach of anarchy that they will beg us to remain. Someone must be responsible for the welfare of the State and people. We have got to shoulder the burden.

Why should we deem ourselves incapable of the toil? Why should we be found less capable of maintaining our interest in North Africa than France, or even than Italy? Are we really to be pushed out of Egypt as Spain is being ejected from Morocco? Surely now that we have stable conditions at home we ought to have the governing strength and ability to fulfil our mission in Egypt. Why is it that matters have so markedly improved in the last six weeks? No blood has been shed; not a shot has been fired; no state of siege even has yet been created. As long as we do not weaken or waver, the chances of a happy issue are good. I am firmly convinced that we have only to be resolved and persevering, we have only to point in one direction unchangingly over a definite period of years, to bring Egypt back to the path of progress and content.

WSC

Winston S. Churchill to Neville Chamberlain

(*Churchill papers: 18/2*)

30 December 1924   Treasury Chambers
Secret, Private & Personal

My dear Neville Chamberlain,

I promised when we had our talk to let you know about the end of February whether I thought it possible to make this year the reduction in direct taxation to which the insurance scheme would be the social and political counterpoise. Of course you know what the lot of the Chancellor of the Exchequer is at this time of year. The Estimates have still to be grappled with and it may be that the Naval demands, not particularly in 1925 but as certain to develop in succeeding years, will be such as to knock out all our plans. I am however hopeful after my talks with the Prime Minister and Austen that we may lower the temperature in regard to Japan sufficiently to bring Naval expense into reasonable relation with our other affairs. And on the whole I feel I ought to tell you at this stage that the chances are favourable to a diminution of direct taxation this year.

I think therefore that we ought to get our teeth into the insurance project. I do not think it is so formidable in detail as might be expected. Our reductions of debt by a £50 million sinking fund remorselessly applied, plus the economies of conversion if credit is maintained, plus the continuous diminution of the cost of war pensions afford a massive justification for laying the burden of the new insurance on future Parliaments and Ministries. Their load even with it, will be far lighter than ours.

I am wondering how you view the actual problem. Do you feel that we can trust ourselves to the figures of the Anderson Committee and to the Government Actuary? I have always been accustomed to rest myself on such foundations. But do you think any cross check is required?

Secondly, how would you deal with the existing working class insurance societies? How great is the scale of their work in the field of widowhood and Sixty-five old age? Not so very great, I think? Have you any data? If not, how shall we explore this essential feature? Health, I conceive, barged into them far more than widowhood and Sixty-five state insurance would do. Anyhow, we should have to know quite soon where we stand with them. I think myself they would not be injured by a State scheme which laid the foundations for widowhood and Sixty-five on a 10/- a week minimum basis. Any work they would do would be on top of this foundation—possibly even their work might be facilitated by the laying of the foundation, ie people in the higher ranks of labour who now think it hopeless to provide effectively against widowhood and Sixty-five might be stimulated by the 10/- compulsory national basis to take out voluntary policies to make the 10/- into 15/- or 20/- or more. Let us have a talk in the near future, and do tell me how you are viewing all this aspect.

Thirdly, what about the burden on employers and employed? So far as the employers are concerned, remember we shall be giving them simultaneous and substantial relief in the sphere of direct taxation. Snowden last year gave the employed classes a helping hand and I should certainly try to make him feel that he had a share in the architecture. But still 6d a week per man from both employers and employed is a pretty stiff poll tax, having regard to their existing obligations. This is the part of the scheme which pre-occupies me most. To what extent, for instance, would the Labour Party use the argument 'You are only making us live on our own tails'? On facts and figures we have a smashing reply. But we do not want to take all this trouble and incur all this expense and have the scheme ungratefully received. I do not think it would be. But it is a point to ponder over.

There are several Radicals who would be very good judges on a point like this—Masterman, Macnamara,[1] above all Ll G. How to elicit their true opinion without revealing our design? I thought even of employing Masterman to work up the social side of this for my own edification. I would like to have the Liberals with us in a thing like this. Ll G as the parent of insurance would, I am sure, be with us. Anyhow we do not want them all crabbing it

---

[1] Thomas James Macnamara, 1861–1931. A school teacher for sixteen years, and subsequently editor of the *Schoolmaster*, 1892–1907. President of the National Union of Teachers, 1896. Liberal MP, 1900–22 (National Liberal, 1922–4). Parliamentary Secretary, Local Government Board, 1907–8, and Admiralty, 1908–20. Minister of Labour, 1920–2.

and a little tact should avoid this. It is a fence to jump at a gallop. Once over with acclamation, and people start paying, everything will work out according to the actuaries, and the inestimable blessings which this measure may carry to the whole population will plead their own cause in every home.

Whoever we decide to consult, actuaries, politicians or experts (like Beveridge), we can always approach them on the basis that this is not for next year but for 1926 or even 1927. This would be quite straightforward because we have not ourselves settled the zero hour.

I should be grateful if you would weigh these matters and let me know when we meet how you feel about them. Personally, my instinct is all for it, and it is only experience and disillusionment that make me cautious.

With all good wishes for the New Year,

Believe me,
Yours vy sincerely
Winston S. Churchill

Winston S. Churchill to Austen Chamberlain

(*Churchill papers: 18/2*)

30 December 1924

WAR DEBTS AND THE UNITED STATES

The Lord Chancellor's[1] memorandum is very wise and I agree with nearly all of his marginal suggestions. I deprecate, however, the proposal to submit the question to 'a discussion by technically qualified representatives' of our two Governments. This is a point of policy rather than law and I greatly preferred the despatch as it originally stood in this respect. I do not think a discussion à quatre between, say, Leith Ross[2] and Niemeyer on our

[1] George Cave, 1856–1928. Conservative MP, 1906–18. Knighted, 1915. Solicitor-General, 1915–16. Home Secretary, 1916–19. Created Viscount, 1918. Lord Chancellor, 1922–4 and 1924–8. Chancellor of Oxford University, 1925–8. An Earldom was to have been conferred upon him in 1928, but he died before the patent was passed; his widow was accorded the title of Countess.

[2] Frederick William Leith-Ross, 1887–1968. Educated at Merchant Taylors' School and Balliol College, Oxford. Private Secretary to H. H. Asquith, 1911–13. British Representative on the Finance Board of the Reparations Commission, 1920–5. Deputy Controller of Finance, Treasury, 1925–32. Chief Economic Adviser to the Government, 1932–46. Knighted, 1933. Minister of the British War Debts Mission to Washington, 1933. Negotiated financial arrangements with Germany, October 1934, and with Italy, April 1935. Financial Mission to China, 1935–6. Chairman of the Economic Committee of the League of Nations, 1936 and 1937. Director-General, Ministry of Economic Warfare, 1939–42. Chairman, Inter-Allied Post-War Requirements Committee, 1941–3. Deputy Director-General of UNRRA, 1944–5. Governor of the National Bank of Egypt, 1946–51. Deputy Chairman, National Provincial Bank, 1951–66. In his memoirs, *Money Talks*, he wrote of Churchill: 'his vitality, his keen

side and Logan[1] and one of his subordinates on the other would carry matters forward towards a favourable solution at this stage. I should certainly prefer to go to Paris on the basis that we do not accept the American view either in law or in equity but are willing to arbitrate.

I do not contemplate a quarrel with the United States on this issue. I expect if we hold firm to receive some favourable definite proposition. Logan has made private approaches to me through a relative of mine who was a friend of his in Washington. He has also adopted a much more conciliatory tone in his conversations with Leith Ross. My information is that he is disquieted at having drawn his Government into a position of some embarrassment on ground which is at least questionable and uncertain. I think it very likely that if I can go into action on the basis of your despatch without the final amendment I shall have some proposal made to me which I can listen to without being committed and can promise to lay before the Cabinet. This would be carrying out your idea of Spenlow and Jorkins.[2]

Remember I have very little to play with. The Belgians and French for interested motives have admitted what they know to be a wrongful American claim. We are resisting it. On the other hand America threatens to press France about her debt. We shall also have to raise this uncomfortable point off the stage. At the same time both France and ourselves will have to squeeze the Belgians over their abuse of their 100 million priority on reparation. I cannot pretend to see how these difficult oppositions will relate to one another and I expect two or three days of disagreement before things begin to clear and we begin to see where the possibilities of agreement lie. Mean-

---

imagination and critical appreciation of any proposal put to him and his grasp of administration in the office, together with his generous temperament and genial expansiveness at Chartwell, won him the warm affection of all of us. I remember going into the Treasury board room with some urgent question and finding him dictating. He motioned me to a seat and when he had finished he said, with a schoolboyish grin, "I've been dictating an article for an American magazine. You don't know what a savour there is in dictating at a dollar a word." '

[1] James Addison Logan, 1879–1930. Born in Philadelphia. On active service with the Pennsylvania Volunteers in the Philippines during the Spanish–American War, 1898. Captain, US Army, 1901. Chief of the American Military Mission with the French Army, September 1914–June 1917. Colonel, 1917. Principal assistant to Herbert Hoover, European Relief Operations, 1918. American Representative, Supreme Economic Council, financial and communications sections, 1918–19. Adviser to the Russian Relief Section of the American Relief Administration, 1921–3. American unofficial delegate to the Reparations Commission, 1919–23; to the London Conference of Prime Ministers, 1924; to the Finance Ministers Conference, Paris, 1925.

[2] In *David Copperfield*, by Charles Dickens, Spenlow and Jorkins were a firm of solicitors to whom Copperfield was articled. Jorkins seldom appears in the narrative, but Spenlow frequently makes his supposed intractable character the ground for refusing any inconvenient request.

while we shall be in a very strong position, being quite independent and committed to no proposition which is not backed with massive arguments.

Winston S. Churchill to Sir Philip Cunliffe-Lister

(*Churchill papers: 18/2*)

30 December 1924

I have been ruminating a great deal over the Safeguarding of Industries Bill. With the assistance of the Customs I have prepared an alternative draft which I enclose. I like it better than the Board of Trade original but I do not like it very much. I feel that we run a considerable risk of Parliamentary embarrassment, and you particularly, as the Minister in charge, will have a very difficult task. The reason is that the policy of the Bill is a very small policy but the language very big. It is always difficult to know how much powder you should use to blow in the lock without bringing down the front of the building.

When you and the Prime Minister told me that you contemplated about half-a-dozen duties in the present Parliament I thought this was a very honest and reasonable fulfilment of our pledges. The problem is to put this moderate aim into the necessarily general language of a statute. The moment you try to put it into general language either you open the door to an ugly rush of interests, swiftly becoming vocal in every constituency, or we shall be accused of trying to make the Act a dead-letter, of teasing in the phrase and denying in the performance.

Then too in the House discord and division will immediately become apparent. On our own side the ardent tariff reformers will be greatly excited and feel it their duty to press for everything which widens the bounds. In this they will run up against free trade opinion, Lancashire and the Prime Minister's pledges about no general tariff. Meanwhile, the Opposition, Liberal and Labour, will of course attack all along the line.

Think it over very carefully I beg you, and do not get yourself drawn into a series of unfavourable debates through which we mean one thing and friends and foes alike mean another. One is frequently pushed into things in Parliament, and everybody says 'you must go on', but then if the Parliamentary situation turns out unfavourably to Party interests the blame is always thrown on the Minister directly involved. The only safety is to be downright and clear-cut, to have a defence effective in every direction, not to excite false hopes or arouse passions which cannot be allayed.

Forgive me with my very long experience writing in this way. Remember

I have lived in this controversy since 1903 and I think I know the country and its unhealthy spots as well as we know Lawrence Farm.[1] You told me how much rather you would be making Anglo-German Treaties and steel cartels than coming out into all this rigmarole which can neither sustain itself on the arguments for a scientific tariff nor on the arguments for free trade.

I know you will have been exercising your mind on all this and I thought I would like to let you know where my ideas have been leading me. I must however say at the outset that I have not made up my mind. I am only turning the matter over, and if I had the power—which I have not—to decide, I should not yet feel ripe for decision. For what it is worth, here is the argument:—

All safeguarding duties are to be general duties, ie they are to be exactly the same as McKenna Duties. If that be so, where is the justification for not imposing them through the Finance Bill with all the inquisitional procedure of the House of Commons in regard to new taxes. If there are only going to be, say, half-a-dozen duties, would not this procedure, cumbrous no doubt, be a simple and effective safeguard? I believe that the moment this principle was declared the Opposition would be ruptured. There would be sharp debates over the individual duties as each was proposed, but I think that if you and I work together we should be equal to that. No doubt keen tariff reformers would be disappointed, but then on the other hand they would soon find themselves called upon to support the Government upon particular propositions which would be very agreeable to them, instead of browsing about over the field of fiscal generalities.

But see what follows. If we use the procedure of the Finance Bill, or in case of urgency a separate Finance Bill, to carry any safeguarding duty or duties, what need is there for any special legislation? You, as President of the Board of Trade, can draw up your rules, form your Committee, hear complaints, weigh all the circumstances, advise the Cabinet, and the resulting action will issue directly in the form of a clause in the Finance Bill. You can lay your rules on the Table, or perhaps we could have an Order in Council (I have not examined this). But anyhow you would be master of the situation and we should have complete control at every stage over the whole affair. There would be no chance of the House being divided on vague general propositions. They would have to vote on some such proposition as 'ought we to

---

[1] From May to October 1916 Cunliffe-Lister had served on the western front as Brigade Intelligence Officer of the 124th Infantry Brigade (41st Division). From January to June 1916 Churchill had served as Commanding Officer of the 6th Royal Scots Fusiliers (9th Scottish Division), with his forward headquarters in the Belgian village of Ploegsteert. On 30 May 1916 the 41st Division had relieved the 9th Division in the Ploegsteert area. Lawrence farm was Churchill's advance headquarters, half-way between the village and the front line.

safeguard tyres, or lace'. We should have picked our grounds with the utmost discretion and come into action backed by heavy batteries.

Send me a line to let me know how this strikes you. I talked to Victor Cazalet a little in this sense and told him to tell you.

When do you return to London? We all assemble on the 5th, but I shall be up on Friday in case you want me.

Stanley Baldwin to Winston S. Churchill

(*Treasury papers: T171/247*)

30 December 1924

My dear Chancellor,

I have read your letter dated Friday with the keenest interest and pleasure. You are a Chancellor after my own heart!

You will observe the present tense. I have every hope that after accomplishing much I shall use the past when our term is completed.

Yours very sincerely,
Stanley Baldwin

Winston S. Churchill to A. C. Sheepshanks[1]

(*Churchill papers: 1/172*)

31 December 1924

Dear Mr Sheepshanks,

Many thanks for your long letter about Randolph which my wife and I have read with great interest.[2] I am very glad indeed that he has started well

---

[1] Arthur Charles Sheepshanks, 1884–1961. Educated at Eton and Trinity College, Cambridge. Assistant Master (Classics) at Eton, 1906–14. On active service in France, 1914–18 (despatches twice, wounded twice, DSO); Lieutenant-Colonel, 1917–18. Returned to Eton as Assistant Master (Classics), 1918–38. Housemaster, 1922–38. On 19 November 1924, after Sheepshanks had congratulated Churchill on entering the Government, Churchill replied: 'No one was more surprised than I.'

[2] In the course of his report on Randolph Churchill, Sheepshanks had written: 'There are mornings when he is clearly not in the mood for work, and on these occasions he is quite content to waste his time and do nothing. . . . I hope he will not relax his efforts at all. He is obviously possessed of a quick brain, and he must not be satisfied with anything but the best results. At present, he is rather inclined to go all out on anything he likes and not to bother much about things not so congenial. Also he must learn to adapt himself to all the different masters he is up to in School, and not to expect to find them all equally easy to get on with.'

at Eton. He has certainly come on a great deal as the result of his first term there. His manners are agreeable and he has become much more master of himself. At his age it is surely quite satisfactory that he should be in the Remove. I have talked to him about his French, which seems to be his least satisfactory field, and I hope he will show an improvement here next term. His Classical report is very good. That, I know, is the passport to scholastic success. His final place in the Form is also quite good. These little boys have to grow strong and compact and their will and purpose to develop. I think he has been very happy in his first half at Eton and that he is keen to resume his life there when the holidays are over.

We have been somewhat exercised in our minds about whether he should be a wet or dry bob. I should be so much obliged if you would give me your advice on the point. I do not think much of rowing as a pastime. If boys are not good at it they only loaf; if they are good they exhaust themselves and very likely strain their hearts. At the best it seems a monotonous form of recreation and one which leads to nothing in after life. I suppose that if a boy is a dry bob he nevertheless gets plenty of opportunities of swimming. Randolph is quite a good swimmer for his age, and I should like him to develop this.

With good wishes for the New Year
Believe me,
Yours sincerely
Winston S. Churchill

January 1925

Winston S. Churchill to Sir Otto Niemeyer

(Churchill papers: 18/12)

2 January 1925

Please see the 'Morning Post' of today.[1] I never intended that we should be bound to limit our demands by any settlement made between France and the United States. I rest myself on President Coolidge's[2] remarks that the less America takes from France the more that would leave for us. If France effects a settlement with the United States on easy terms, we shall at least claim *pari passu* payments. But that would not prevent us from effecting a settlement with France on stiffer terms if we are able to do so. The only limit I accept is that we will in any case not offer France worse terms than America exacts from us.

Winston S. Churchill to Sir Otto Niemeyer

(Churchill papers: 18/12)

2 January 1925

The United States has accumulated the greater part of the gold in the world and is suffering from a serious plethora. Are we sure that in trying to establish the gold standard we shall not be favouring American interests. Shall we not be making their hoard of gold more valuable than it is at present? Shall we not be relieving them from the consequences of their selfish and extortionate policy?

---

[1] The *Morning Post* of 2 January 1925 carried a report from the paper's Washington correspondent, who had learned of Britain's agreement to a United States plan to allow France a moratorium on her debt to the United States. Britain was given no such concession. The correspondent called Britain's action 'a generosity perhaps without parallel in history'.

[2] Calvin Coolidge, 1872–1933. A lawyer. Governor of Massachusetts, 1919 and 1920. Vice-President of the United States, 1920; President, 1923–9.

Is not this the sort of subject on which Mr Hawtrey[1] should be asked to draft a paper?

Winston S. Churchill to Sir George Barstow

(*Treasury papers: T172/1440*)

2 January 1925

SINGAPORE

I am quite sure that we ought to press for further investigation of the Defence Scheme, so as to be able to compare the respective merits of 15″ gun defence with aeroplane defence. Even if the latter were more costly it would at least be more mobile, therefore available for some other threatened point in an emergency.

Winston S. Churchill: departmental memorandum

(*Churchill papers: 18/12*)

3 January 1925

AIR ESTIMATES

(1) Over-estimating, resulting quite properly in under-spending, is an evil. That evil is not diminished by starting new works before their time. Once these works are started they develop automatically. I cannot consent to accelerate the Air Force expansion programme. No new works for which specific Parliamentary approval has not been obtained in 1924/25 can be started except as the result of the Estimates for the year 1925/6. I regret that I must adhere to this position. Upper Heyford, North Weald, Bicester and Sutton Farms are all proposals for which Estimates should be submitted in the normal course, and no money can be spent upon them before the expiration of the financial year 1924/5.

(2) If an abandoned aerodrome like Boscombe Down, which will certainly be needed in the course of the Air expansion programme, can be bought cheap, land and building, there is no objection to the bargain being made and paid for out of current under-spending. But this purchase does not commit us to beginning the development of the property except in accordance with the agreed temper of the expansion scheme.

---

[1] Ralph George Hawtrey, 1879–1975. Educated at Eton and Trinity College, Cambridge. Civil Servant, Admiralty, 1903–4; Treasury, 1904–45. Director of Financial Enquiries, Treasury, 1919–45. Knighted, 1956. Author and economist.

(3) The application of under-spending to the re-purchase of the site and building at Turnhouse for £45,000 is also approved. And there may be similar cases where a lump sum payment will put us in possession of war-time Air Force property. I should be ready to approve similar action in these cases. The question of the period within which these properties are to be worked up into going concerns can only be discussed in the Estimates of any given year.

Winston S. Churchill to Lord D'Abernon
(Churchill papers: 1/178)

4 January 1925

My dear Edgar,

A young friend of mine, Mr Bracken, is suffering from Sympathetic Ophthalmia [1] in a form which may conceivably produce grave consequence to his sight. He has been advised by some of the highest authorities here to have a serious operation. Before proceeding to take their advice he wishes to consult the best German authorities on his case. I have strongly recommended him to do this as, though the matter is urgent, a week or even month's delay could be accepted. I should be grateful to you if you would advise me as to who are the very best and latest authorities in Germany in this sphere and Mr Bracken will then come out and see them.

I am much concerned about this case. He is a very brilliant young Australian of quite exceptional powers, enterprise and vitality. He has recently founded 'English Life' which you may have seen, and at only 24 years is making himself with the greatest ease a considerable career. Now he is menaced by this very serious danger to his sight. Should he come out to Berlin I should be grateful if you would show him some kindness.

Yrs v sincerely
WSC

Winston S. Churchill: notes on the Paris Talks
(Churchill papers: 18/12)

4 January 1925

Somewhat exaggerated interest has been aroused over this Conference. The actual scope and official agenda are limited to the following questions:

[1] A condition of inflammation in one eye leading to the second eye; the second eye is then said to be the subject of 'sympathetic ophthalmia'. There is a danger in this situation of losing sight in both eyes. Sometimes the first eye is removed to preserve the sight of the second eye. When no eye is removed, the sight in both eyes may be impaired: as became the case with Bracken.

All these questions are extremely complicated but rather petty. The margins in dispute probably do not involve more than a couple of million one way or the other. I expect that we should secure about £10 millions in the first year and France about £24 millions.

There are a dozen ways of arriving at these results. The important thing is to find a simple and harmonious solution which will clear out of the way all the complicated special claims and leave the future to be regulated by percentage distributions of the total available sums received from Germany in any year.

I have a scheme fully prepared with several variants for simplifying the whole procedure and reducing the conflicting special claims of the different Allies for Armies of Occupation, Belgian Priority, Belgian Debt, Restitutions, etc to money values expressed in percentages of the available annuities. After two or three days haggling I shall hope to rally the Conference to some such treatment of the problem.

With regard to the American claim for a share in the Dawes annuities, I propose to adhere strictly to the position taken up in the last Foreign Office despatch, and I shall not depart from that position in any way without further instructions from the Cabinet. I shall endeavour, however, so to handle the matter as to avoid a painful or sharp dispute between the English-speaking representatives to the delectation of the European spectators. I think it highly probable from the information which has reached me that Mr Logan will in the course of the Conference make proposals for reducing the American claim to much more moderate limits; in which case I will transmit these proposals at once to the Cabinet, together with my recommendations upon them. If no proposals are made I shall rest on the despatch with its culminating offer of arbitration. Meanwhile the sharing up of the Dawes annuities according to the existing Spa percentages will go forward. Everything however leads me to believe that the Americans, and Mr Logan in particular, are extremely anxious for an amicable settlement off the stage. This, if it does not cost too much, is certainly in our interest to concede.

It will be necessary to point out quite clearly to M Clémentel that we will be bound to ask from France the same terms as America may concede to her. We preserve absolute independence in the matter, and the question of terms on which we settle with France will not be governed by decisions reached between France and the United States. I think, however, that this is an academic question as the Americans are scarcely likely to err on the side of over-generosity.

Cabinet minutes

(Cabinet papers: 23/49)

5 January 1925

THE CHANCELLOR OF THE EXCHEQUER said that the American reply to Mr Chamberlain's note of December 29th declined arbitration and repeated the previous arguments used . . . but indicated that the annual payments now asked for would not exceed by very much the annual payments to be made to the United States of America in respect of the cost of their Army of Occupation, though they would involve continuance of these payments for a greater number of years. He had reason to believe that the total amount involved to the Allies as a whole by accepting the American proposals would not be very large. . . .

The Press had rather exaggerated the scope and importance of the Conference, and since the amounts at stake were not very considerable, he proposed to take any opportunity that might offer in the opening meeting to indicate that the Conference was concerned rather with questions of detail.

THE CHANCELLOR OF THE EXCHEQUER made it clear to the Cabinet that he intended to hold the British Government free to make any arrangements with France independently in time or terms of America. . . .

He anticipated that the French finance Minister would raise the question with him. In that event he would impress on M Clémentel that we considered it the duty of France to pay her debt to us and expected her in the near future to make proposals for finding the debt and payment of interest. If she did not do so we should have to ask France officially to do so.

Winston S. Churchill: remarks at the Conference of Finance Ministers[1]

(Treasury papers: T188/6)

7 January 1925   Paris
3 pm

Monsieur the President and Gentlemen. The excellent and comprehensive speech which the President has made leaves very little to be said in response. The British Delegation associate themselves most cordially with the sentiments which he has expressed so happily and we are in full accord with the terms in which he has defined the tasks which lie before us.

[1] The Allied and Associated Powers representatives who were present were Clémentel (France), Churchill (Great Britain), Theunis (Belgium), Herrick (USA), Stefani (Italy) and Viscount Ishii (Japan).

I think at the outset however it is necessary for me to emphasise what Monsieur Clémentel has said about the limited and technical character of much of the work we have to do. The issues which are involved in the work of this Conference are no doubt extremely important, but they are not issues comparable to those which have been settled at many previous inter-Allied gatherings. They are not comparable, for instance, to those that were settled at Spa nor to those which have been so harmoniously adjusted by the Dawes Report and the recent Conference in London. The reason why there is so much interest aroused by our meeting is because the Dawes Report and the success of the London Conference have opened out a prospect of sure and reasonable advance towards a very much better state of things than has previously existed in Europe since the war. Hope flies on wings and international conferences plod afterwards along dusty roads, but still the conviction exists that progress is being made towards the reconstitution of the unity and prosperity of Europe, that the healing process is active and that problems are assuming increasingly simple form. That conviction is general and certainly nothing will be said or done here which will not tend to show that that conviction is well founded.

We have immediately to embark upon a series of complicated discussions. The subjects are varied in character and importance. The interests of the different Allied Powers are conflicting. Each of us naturally is bound to present his own country's case. But all of us will remember that we meet as friends and comrades and that our friendship and comradeship, continuing, and indissoluble, are of greater consequence than the exact achievement of our own particular point of view within the comparatively restricted limits within which our official work is confined.

Above and beyond the special claims of any power represented here stands the need for harmony in mood and for simplicity in method. We cannot leave the principles of the Dawes Report and decisions of the London Conference involved in a tangle of inconsistent interpretation and of ill-adjusted relationships and priorities. We must endeavour to reach a foundation which will enable the reparation and other payments made by Germany, in cash or in kind, under this head or that, to be distributed in future whatever their amount may be according to some simple plan based upon mathematical calculations and raising no issue which should require the summoning of conferences attended by the ministerial representatives of the various Powers. That is perhaps a modest aim. Let us achieve it. Let us clear up and wind up all these minor outstanding questions so that at any rate in our limited sphere the forward path is unobstructed.

In the background no doubt much larger issues still await decision and agreement. We will not complicate our immediate task with these. But we can so handle the business which is before us as to clear the field of minor obstructions and at the same time to create a spirit and an atmosphere which will bring the larger solutions nearer to the Allies, to all Europe and to the world.

Clementine Churchill to Winston S. Churchill

(*Churchill papers: 1/179*)

8 January 1925   2 Sussex Square

My Darling Winston,

The newspapers are full of you & Mr Sutcliffe![1]

Your departure from Victoria,[2] illustrated by snapshots of a débonnaire Pig, your arrival with lists of those who met you (amongst the names I notice that charming Mr Phipps[3] who dined with us in Loucheur's flat), your preliminary canters with Clémentel etc. Altogether you are the pet of the moment—I do not see how you *can* fulfill *all* the expectations that are entertained. I send you this amusing 'Poy'. . . ·

STANDING BY US.

WINSTON : "Excuse me, gentlemen, but a chap here has been run over, and I don't want to see him squashed."

[1] Herbert Sutcliffe, 1894–1978. The son of a cricketer, he played in Yorkshire's second eleven at the age of 16. On active service, 1915-18, first with the Sherwood Foresters, then with the Yorkshire Regiment, with whom he was commissioned. Chosen one of the five 'batsmen of the year', 1920. Between 1922 and 1936 he scored more than two thousand runs a year. In 1932 he set a record first-wicket partnership (with Holmes) of 555 runs.

[2] For the Paris Conference of Finance Ministers. Clementine Churchill added at the end of her letter: 'I do trust that everything is going well and that you will be able to make real headway.'

[3] Eric Clare Edmund Phipps, 1875–1945. Diplomat; Attaché in Paris, 1899; First Secretary in Petrograd, 1912; Counsellor of Embassy in Brussels, 1920–2; Minister in Paris, 1922–8. Knighted, 1927. Minister in Vienna, 1928–33. Privy Councillor, 1933. Ambassador in Berlin, 1933–7; Ambassador in Paris, 1937–9.

I am busy making lists of furniture to be moved from here to Downing Street.

Yesterday Moppett brought the children up & I took them to the big circus at Olympia. If you write address your letter to Chartwell as the PO forward anything directed here straight to Chartwell. Nothing addressed either to you or me ever reaches this house. I must say I'm sorry to leave it.[1]

I gave Venetia luncheon at Claridges on Tuesday—she starts on her travels tomorrow. She looked so white and shattered. If you have five minutes do write & thank her for that lovely jade & enamel box of Edwin's which she sent you with that charming letter. I remember always seeing it on his table. . . .

Winston S. Churchill to Clementine Churchill

(*Spencer-Churchill papers*)

10 January 1925   British Embassy
Evening   Paris

My darling Clemmie,

At last I have a quarter of an hour to myself! We have made vy good progress, & tonight after arduous wranglings on subjects as complicated as the rules of Mah Jongg when first you hear them, we have reached practically unanimous agreements on every important issue. Tomorrow and Monday the experts will draft in accordance with our agreements; on Tuesday we shall present our work to the plenary conference supported by all the six gt powers & on Wedy at noon (bar accidents) I start for home. (Where shall I spend the night?)

I have scarcely moved outside the Embassy except to the series of conferences & discussions & interviews wh have occupied the days. Even meal times have been devoted to meeting people of consequence. I had an interview with Herriot[2] in his sick room. Poor man—he seemed vy seedy & worn

---

[1] On 17 January 1925 Churchill completed the sale of 2 Sussex Square, for £10,750. Henceforth as Chancellor of the Exchequer he was to live at 11 Downing Street, while continuing to spend most of his weekends at Chartwell. Among his Chartwell visitors during 1925 were Lord Carson, Lord Balfour, Lord Birkenhead, Professor Lindemann, Sir Laming Worthington-Evans, the Duke of Westminster, Hilaire Belloc and Lord Linlithgow. P. J. Grigg, Sir Montagu Norman, Sir Otto Niemeyer and Walter Guinness were also among the guests. Also present, in August, were Ethel Barrymore and Nancy Mitford.

[2] Edouard Herriot, 1872–1957. Mayor of Lyon, 1905–40. Senator, 1912–19. Minister of Public Works, 1916–17. President of the Radical Party, 1919–40; of the Socialist-Radical Party, 1945–57. Deputy, 1919–40. Prime Minister, June 1924–April 1925 and July 1926. Held numerous Ministerial posts, 1926–36. President of the Chamber, 1936–40. Arrested by the Vichy Government, 1940. Interned near Berlin, 1944–5; liberated by Soviet troops. President of the National Assembly, 1947–54.

with worry & phlebites. We got on well. Tomorrow I am to see President Doumergue[1] in the morning; lunch with the Imbroglio[2]—watch the 'All Blacks' play France in the afternoon, & visit Clemenceau in the evening & dine with Loucheur. Last night & tonight big dinners at the Embassy. I have seen vy little of Peggy,[3] but she is most agreeable & amusing & you will be welcome here when you come over. She says even if she was not here they cd put you up. You need only fix the dates with her.

I have had tremendous battles with the Yanks, & have beaten them down inch by inch to a reasonable figure. In the end we were fighting over tripe like £100,000!

However there was never any ill will & I have now made quite a good arrangement with them wh will be announced on Tuesday with the rest. I think on the whole I have succeeded. Certainly I have had plenty of compliments. But that is not a vy trustworthy test.

I do not want to go to Wilton[4]—nor anywhere else but Chartwell. I expect to see a lot of progress on my return. The cottage, the book cases, the woodshed, the loggia: I shall be glad to prowl about them again. Give my fondest love to all the kittens. I hope they are good & well. And you my darling—Yr letter was a gt treat. I wish I cd have written earlier. But I know you will understand. With tender love & many kisses

Your ever devoted

W

[sketch of a pig]

PS. I will write to Venetia when I return.

---

[1] Gaston Doumergue, 1863–1937. Lawyer; magistrate in Indo-China, 1890–2, in Algeria, 1893. Minister of Colonies, 1902–5; of Commerce and Industry, 1906–8; of Public Instruction, 1908–10; of Foreign Affairs, 1913–14; of Colonies, 1914–17. President of the Senate, 1923–4. President of France, 1924–31; Prime Minister, February to November 1934.

[2] Marguerite Severine Philipinne, daughter of the 4th Duc Decazes and de Glücksbjerg. Known as 'Daisy'. In 1910 she married Prince Jean de Broglie (who died in 1918), hence her nickname 'the Imbroglio'. In 1919 she married the Hon Reginald Ailwyn Fellowes (who died in 1953, and whose mother was Lady Rosamond Spencer Churchill, 2nd daughter of the 7th Duke of Marlborough). In 1929 Daisy Fellowes published *Cats in the Isle of Man*. Her villa in the south of France was Les Zoraïdes; she also lived in Paris and Newbury.

[3] Lady Margaret Primrose, daughter of the 5th Earl of Rosebery. In 1899 she married (as his second wife) the Earl of Crewe.

[4] Near Salisbury, Wiltshire; the home of the Earl and Countess of Pembroke. Churchill often spent Whitsun at Wilton; indeed, Whitsuntide was known there as 'Winstontide'.

*Winston S. Churchill: note of a conversation with the President of the French
Republic*

(Churchill papers: 18/21) [1]

11 January 1925

The President of the Republic received me this morning. M Doumergue, after reminding me of the occasion during the war when we had previously met, proceeded to comment on the difficult questions which were occupying the Finance Ministers Conference.

I told him that in view of the progress made yesterday there was every probability of a complete agreement being reached, both among the European Allies and with the United States, in which case the proceedings at the Plenary Conference on Tuesday would afford a demonstration of unity among the Allied and Associated Powers such as had rarely been seen since the close of hostilities.

M Doumergue then led the conversation on to the importance of preserving the closest friendship and common action between England and France. The interests of the two countries did not clash at any important point, particularly in Asia, in which he apparently included North Africa. French and British interests were really one. Both were responsible for great Mahometan populations. Both were affected by the rapidly developing propaganda of Bolshevism among the coloured peoples. Each could render the other most important services. France could help in Asia with Turkey, and she thoroughly comprehended our vital interest in Egypt. The essential was a unity between our two countries which the Germans would realise was unbreakable.

I said that M Poincaré had done great harm to British sentiments towards France. We had not been in agreement with his policy. But, apart from that, many of his words and his manner towards our public men had chilled the sentiments of some of the warmest friends of France. Among these I included myself. His most unwise act was the reception he had accorded to the offer made by Mr Lloyd George at Cannes of a defensive pact. I had thought the reception of this proposal singularly ungracious. The opportunity had been thrown away, and it would not be easy to reconstitute so favourable a situation.

The President agreed with all this, but he said that M Poincaré's period of power had passed, and that he is not now a governing factor. He had a bad manner, but, as I would remember, before the war he had approved a policy based on the closest understanding with England. M Doumergue

---

[1] Churchill gave this note to Austen Chamberlain, who circulated it to the Cabinet on 5 February 1925.

then reverted to his theme of the vital importance of an accord between France and England which should convince Germany that she has no chance of splitting the Allies, and which would enable France to use her influence to assist England in Asia and North Africa.

I replied that the danger of German aggression in the west would not be so great were it not for the situation in the northern east. Germany would perhaps rest content with the arrangements of Versailles so far as her western frontiers were concerned. I was personally convinced that she would never acquiesce permanently in the condition of her eastern frontier. This then was the great cause of anxiety which brooded over Europe. The wars of Frederick the Great as well as those of Peter the Great had arisen from deep causes and ambitions which, so far from having passed away, were now associated with great historic memories.

M Doumergue said that the Russian policy was Imperialism under another form, and that, as in the days of Peter the Great, it would be over Asia that the Russian ambition would extend.

I replied that the wars which I had in mind were those which had led to Russian conquests towards the Baltic. Although many years might elapse before these dangers would raise their heads in a military form, one could not help feeling how deep and continuous was the shadow which lay over all the regions between Germany and Russia. England was not afraid of anything in the nature of a Russian descent on India; the incompetence, poverty and degradation of the Bolshevik régime would for many years strip that danger of reality. The attempts to poison the Asiatic and coloured populations which were being made were no doubt serious, and might at some point in the future lead to bloodshed. However, the improvement in technical apparatus had given great advantages to organised European forces, and I did not feel that the British position in Asia or Africa was subject to any grave danger at the present time, certainly not to any danger comparable to the awful risk we should run if a continuance of the age-long quarrel between France and Germany led, in some future generation, to our being involved in a renewal of the European war.

I said that of course I was only expressing a personal opinion, but one which I had expressed in public on many occasions, and which it was well known I had held for several years, namely, that one real security against a renewal of war would be a complete agreement between England, France and Germany. That alone would give the security which all were seeking, and that alone would enable the commerce of Europe to expand to such dimensions that the existing burden of debts and reparations would be supportable and not crushing.

M Doumergue hastened to reply that he did not put that prospect out of his thoughts, but that a close understanding between England and France was the indisputable preliminary. To which I replied, again speaking quite personally, that I had always felt that the best road from London to Berlin lay through Paris. This remark he appeared to appreciate, and he spoke frankly of the undoubted advantages which an agreement à *trois* would achieve. I said I thought that English people would feel that the risk attaching to a pact based on an effective arrangement with Germany was far less than a mere renewal of defensive relationship while the fundamental antagonism between France and Germany continued unappeased. I added that of course all these ideas were not merely personal but extremely speculative.

Winston S. Churchill: Cabinet memorandum

(*Churchill papers: 18/21*)

12 January 1925

More than once in our discussion M Clémentel has raised the question of the payment of the French debt to Great Britain. There is no doubt that this has become a very serious preoccupation in French Ministerial and financial circles and there is a sincere wish that the signature of France should not be exposed to reproach in this matter. M Clémentel asked whether His Majesty's Government still adhered to Lord Curzon's declaration upon the Balfour Note. This declaration contemplates at least an admixture of German Bonds in payment of French debt. To this enquiry and to all other references to the debt question, whether made by M Clémentel, M Herriot or M Loucheur (who is in close confabulation with Ministers) I have invariably answered in the following sense.

The Balfour declaration is a principle set up by Great Britain for her own guidance. It is not a bargain struck with France or any other Power in return for some consideration. At the same time it will remain for us a guide in dealing with any proposal we may receive.

As to the Curzon declaration, no statement has been made by the present Government on the point involved. The Cabinet have not considered the method by which an arrangement for the settlement of Anglo-French indebtedness should be reached. It is true that I have been instructed to make an inquiry as to French intentions. As M Clémentel has himself raised the question and informed me of the desire of France to make a proposal no such inquiry on my part has been necessary and the matter has been raised at the present time on the spontaneous initiative of the French. I have throughout declared myself without any instructions to discuss methods or terms. I have said that we should like to receive a proposal, even if it were unacceptable, that we would examine it with consideration and would possibly make a counter proposal. I have invited M Clémentel to put in writing for me the direct question about the validity in British eyes of the Curzon declaration. I am to see him this morning and receive this letter from him. I will then transmit it immediately to my colleagues.

M Loucheur, who came to see me yesterday evening after having been summoned by M Herriot to a Conference of Ministers and Ex-Ministers evidently intended to impart to me the kind of plan which the French had in mind and no doubt to sound me upon it. He said that in his opinion even if the Dawes reparation failed France would nevertheless do her best to pay something. If the Curzon declaration stood, the sort of proposal he would favour would be that France should cede to Britain a portion of the reparation percentages she was entitled to receive under the Dawes scheme. This portion she would guarantee herself. He said, for instance, France might take 48% instead of 52. To this démarche I made my stock reply that I would be glad to consider a scheme but that I had had no formal instructions as to terms or method.

Mr Leith Ross at my request had an interview with M Clémentel at which much the same ideas were advanced by the French Minister.

Speaking generally, I find the French Ministers and politicians depressed. Having seen them so often during the last ten years, often in tragic hours, I have never found them so tame and sad. For the moment there is no resentment towards us. All that has passed over to the United States. The wisdom and the justice of the Balfour Note enables me to stand here as a debt collector without odium. The Curzon declaration has now come to be regarded as an even more helpful and hopeful development. In my opinion this new attitude of France, amid all her difficulties, deserves recognition at the hands of His Majesty's Government.

The position of France ground between the upper and nether millstones of American avarice and German revenge affords full justification for her present sombre mood.

William Bridgeman to Winston S. Churchill
(*Churchill papers: 18/4*)

12 January 1925 Admiralty

My dear Chancellor,

Some time ago you said you wanted to send me some questions on certain naval matters on which you wanted information, and I said I should be very glad to provide you with what information we could give. I had been waiting in expectation of hearing from you, but I now find, somewhat to my surprise, that an official set of letters embodying these questions has been sent to the Secretary of the Admiralty. This seems to me rather an unusual proceeding, before we have even sent in our estimates to the Treasury. But I am quite willing to give you the information, as one Minister to another, for your guidance—I have, therefore, asked my advisers for the information in order that I may send it to you—and am glad to be able to forward it to you.

Yrs v sincerely
W. C. Bridgeman

Winston S. Churchill to Etienne Clémentel

(*Treasury papers: T188/7*)

13 January 1925   Paris

My dear M Clémentel,

During my visit here you have raised in an official and tentative form the question of the repayment of the French debt to Great Britain, and have expressed to me the desire of the French Government that this matter shall be the subject of future conversations. I have received these intimations with pleasure. His Majesty's Government had been inclined to expect the question to be raised, and it is certainly more appropriate that the initiative should have been spontaneously taken by France. I had not contemplated, during my visit here on this occasion, that any questions of method, terms, or conditions would present themselves, and therefore I have not so far obtained any instructions from the British Cabinet in this sphere. You have written me a letter asking that His Majesty's Government should define its position in regard to the Balfour note and the Curzon declaration of the 11th August, 1923. I have transmitted your letter to my colleagues, and I can assure you that as soon as I return to London we will take the whole matter into prompt and earnest consideration, and will endeavour to send you an answer which will place the French Government in a position to present us with definite proposals.

Meanwhile, I can only repeat that the Balfour note remains for us a dominating guide of principle set up freely by our own hands. We shall approach the discussion of the settlement of the French debt to Great Britain in the same spirit of loyal comradeship which led us safely through the agony and perils of the war, and will alone enable us to surmount the vexations and difficulties which remain after the military victory has been won.

> Believe me, &c
> Winston S. Churchill

Lord Beatty to his wife

(*Beatty papers*)

13 January 1925

Winston Churchill appears to have accomplished something by his trip to Paris and will return tomorrow flushed with victory. We have a very important meeting on Friday on Singapore and the Far East Policy, which I have no doubt will give him a full opportunity of letting himself go and it will be difficult to restrain him. He will, I know, be all for cutting everything down, which we shall have to resist.[1]

Cabinet minutes

(*Cabinet papers: 23/49*)

15 January 1925

The Cabinet expressed their high appreciation of the success of the Chancellor of the Exchequer's mission, which had resulted not only in clearing up very difficult and complicated financial questions but also in an improvement of the general political situation.[2]

Winston S. Churchill to William Bridgeman

(*Churchill papers: 18/4*)

15 January 1925   Treasury Chambers

My dear First Lord,

Many thanks for sending me the information for wh we asked.

I should have thought it hardly possible to have devised a more correct

---

[1] On 6 January 1925 Beatty had written to his wife: 'Yesterday I was vigorously engaged with Winston and I think on the whole got the better of him. I must say, although I had to say some pretty strong things, he never bears any malice and was good-humoured throughout the engagement.'

[2] During the Cabinet of 15 January 1925 Churchill told his Cabinet colleagues that: 'The outstanding feature was the anxiety of France as to her security, in view of the probable revival of Germany within the next five or ten years and the bad relations still existing between the two countries.'

& ceremonious form of interdepartmental communication than that wh we have followed: First, a private letter from me to you asking if we might apply for the information; secondly, your verbal assent; thirdly, official letters from the Treasury to the Admiralty such as the Treasury has an unquestioned right to send to any spending Department when it requires information, not about future Estimates but about the actual state of affairs. Such a right has never in my long experience been challenged, or reduced to the status of a favour. However, all is well that ends well.

WSC

Winston S. Churchill: Cabinet memorandum

(Churchill papers: 18/12)

15 January 1925

(1) I think the Secretary of State for War[1] might give the Cabinet some estimate of the financial profit likely to be reaped from the sales he has in mind in the next few years.

(2) I trust that there will be no sale even of old rifles. There is no greater security against vague and unmeasured dangers than a large store of rifles. At the time of the Agadir crisis it crossed my mind very strongly to urge Mr Haldane, then Secretary of State for War, to build up a reserve of at least one million rifles. It was not my business and I let the idea drop. But afterwards when the war came and we saw the terrible shifts to which we were reduced by want of rifles more than anything else, I repented bitterly of having let this idea slip.

Apparently nothing takes longer to make than a rifle: cannon, shells, aeroplanes, destroyers, submarines, monitors, quite large vessels can be made quicker than a supply of rifles. The most harassing problem of the early part of the war was the want of rifles. The possession of a large store of rifles in any country, especially after periods of prolonged peace, is an immense guarantee. It does not matter a bit whether the rifles are the modern kind or the oldest that will fire; the differences between one rifle and another are negligible when compared with the difference between the worst possible rifle and no rifle at all.

Taught by our bitter experiences I have always resolved to prevent any dispersion or destruction of old rifles that could possibly be made to fire. The French fought the Great War with a very old rifle. We more than any country depend on armies of expansion and improvisation in times of

[1] Sir Laming Worthington-Evans (see page 256, note 2).

trouble. We ought never to have less than 2 million rifles of all sorts and kinds in this country. I cannot believe there is any cheaper form of defence than keeping a store of rifles in a serviceable condition.

Winston S. Churchill to Sir George Barstow
(*Churchill papers: 18/12*)

15 January 1925

Have you looked through the Air Estimates in detail? Surely you ought to be able to formulate a score or a dozen criticisms of detail showing that they are asking for more than they need.

I do not wish to agree to this figure for the moment. What are the relations between the British and French Air Ministries? Are they working together in confidence and interchanging information, or are they looking at each other critically. I believe from my conversations in Paris that the French would be quite ready to discuss an Air Convention regulating British and French Air development. I am anxious that this should be explored in the future, and before assenting to the Estimates I propose to seek the agreement of the Air Ministry to the exploration of this possibility. Will you let me have some ideas for a letter on this point.

Lord George Hamilton to Winston S. Churchill
(*Churchill papers: 2/141*)

15 January 1925

My dear Winston,

As an old friend of your father's I must write to congratulate you upon the great success of your first big international adventure. I have always believed in your star, because you combine courage, industry and prescience.

Having achieved this great initial success, don't be in a hurry: rest on your oars and think well before you make another forward move.

You will excuse a typewritten letter; but most of my correspondents tell me that my writing is illegible, so I do not want to give you the task of deciphering it.

Don't trouble to answer this, as you must have heaps of similar letters.

Believe me,
Yours very truly,
George Hamilton

Eric Phipps to Winston S. Churchill

(*Churchill papers: 2/141*)

15 January 1925   British Embassy,
Personal   Paris

Dear Mr Churchill,

I send you the enclosed article by our friend Sauerwein,[1] which may interest you. It is certainly a relief to see such friendly words over the signature of one who has frequently in the past shown himself to be a most bitter enemy of ours.

I hear on all sides nothing but expressions of gratitude by the French for the consideration which you displayed towards them. I am personally delighted, for I have always urged that we must distinguish between the present very reasonable and friendly French Government and their noxious predecessors; otherwise 'ce serait à vous dégoûter de la vertu'.

Yours sincerely,
Eric Phipps[2]

Lord Grey of Fallodon to Winston S. Churchill

(*Churchill papers: 1/178*)

16 January 1925   Fallodon
                                                    Northumberland

My dear Winston,

The morning being a beautiful winter day I started off for a long walk & ate my lunch in a soft lair of winter grass under the lee of warm whins, which you Southerners call gorse; and lying there with a pipe I fell to meditating upon pleasant things; and amongst them on the success of the Paris Conference & upon your share in it.

It is a real pleasure to me, who has known the difficulties of such things,

[1] Jules August Sauerwein. French journalist; Foreign Editor of *Paris Soir*, 1933. A frequent correspondent of the *New York Times*, for which he worked for eight years. Author of *Que Va Faire l'Amérique* (1932) and *Les Événements de Septembre 1938* (1939). Commander of the Légion d'Honneur. The article referred to was published in *Le Matin* on 15 January 1925. 'If it were up to Churchill alone to decide,' wrote Sauerwein, 'I am certain that his reply would be generous and practical. I had the good fortune of speaking to him several times during his visit to Paris. This is a man of courage. He does not allow himself to be stopped by the arguments of demagogues. If the opposition tell him that he is giving up the English share of reparations in upholding the principles of the Balfour note, he replies that it is better to get rid of all cause of friction with France than to bind oneself to the illusory hopes of total repayment.'

[2] Churchill replied two days later: 'Thank you so much for sending me Sauerwein's article. It has been translated and published in the papers here. Certainly the very pleasant lunch you arranged bore rare and refreshing fruit.'

to read of so great a success; and when that is due to a man for whom one has feelings of personal friendship, it adds to the happiness of life. I gather from the Times that not only has the Conference been a success, but that your share in bringing that about has been great, & that the recognition of this is due to the spontaneous tribute of the foreigners with whom you have dealt. To uphold the interests of this country & at the same time to secure this recognition from the representatives of other countries is a rare achievement & a great public service. Such were my thoughts—as I should have liked to express them to you, if you had been lunching with me under the whin bushes. I send them by letter.

Yours ever
Edward Grey

Winston S. Churchill to Frederick Leith-Ross
(Leith-Ross: 'Money Talks')

16 January 1925

My dear Leith-Ross,

Your work at the Paris Conference was in every way admirable. Your knowledge, grasp and tact were equally distinguished. I was deeply impressed by the obvious ascendency of the British experts headed by yourself over their foreign colleagues.

You seemed to be accepted as trusted guides and exponents. Pray accept my congratulations and thanks.

Yours sincerely
Winston S. Churchill

Viscount Cecil of Chelwood to Winston S. Churchill
(Churchill papers: 18/8)

16 January 1925

My dear Winston,

May I make a suggestion very possibly superfluous—It is that you should issue a plain statement as to the results of the proceedings at Paris—perhaps as a White paper. The agreement itself is unintelligible except to highly skilled persons.

I am very anxious to talk with you about the Protocol. What I feel is this: European security is one whole & though you may be able to deal first with this or that particular case yet it must be done consistently with a general plan. That plan must include reduction of armaments. Otherwise no scheme for security will be effective. That again means a plan for piecemeal reduction is I fear impracticable. Finally, only a general plan will produce that general *détente* without which insecurity is certain to grow up again eg if you leave Poland in a condition of fear she will arm & that means sooner or later German armament. Partial alliances by themselves will only last as long as does the state of feeling which gave them birth. That may turn out also to be true of a General plan. If so, there is no hope. But the General plan has never been tried & it is worth a trial.

The great objection to a General plan is that it imposes such great obligations on its members that when the time comes they will not be discharged. That depends on what those obligations are. If the aim is to secure effective & immediate military action by everyone against our aggressor that probably is Utopian at least at present. But need one aim so high? The objects are (1) to have a framework into which special alliances can be fitted without risk of reviving grouping & balances of power &c which will not be open to the objections already alluded to & (2) to exert such pressure as is practicable against an aggressor. Suppose you had a general obligation to break off relations with the aggressor & no more, except a provision that each state would consider & consult with the others about what further could & should be done? Would something on those lines be too burdensome? I cannot think so. To that you might or might not add provisions to submit *all* quarrels to some form of arbitration, together with provisions as to demilitarised zones—which used to be a favourite device of Loucheur.[1] Then into that framework might be fitted such arrangements as you were speaking of in Cabinet yesterday.

'Curse the fellow' I hear you say 'why can't he leave me alone with all his chatter about disarmament & international Utopias?' The reason simply is that you are my only hope in the Cabinet. Austen seems to have become a mere phonograph of Crowe[2] & the PM for some reason resolutely refuses to apply his mind to these subjects. Of course many of our other colleagues

[1] And also one of Churchill's ideas, which he had perhaps derived from Loucheur (see pages 286–7).

[2] Eyre Alexander Barby Wichart Crowe, 1864–1925. Born in Leipzig; educated at Dusseldorf and Berlin (his mother was German, his father British). Entered Foreign Office as a Junior Clerk, 1906. Knighted, 1911. Assistant Under-Secretary of State, Foreign Office, 1912–19. Attacked by a section of the Press in 1915 for his German origins, his integrity was upheld publicly by Sir Edward Grey. One of the British plenipotentiaries at the Paris Peace Conference, 1919. Permanent Under-Secretary of State, Foreign Office, 1920–25.

are very able & admirable persons. But on questions of this kind the Ministers who really count apart from special cases must be the PM, the Foreign Minister & the Ch of Ex.

Yours ever
Cecil

Winston S. Churchill to William Bridgeman
(*Churchill papers: 18/10*)

19 January 1925   Treasury Chambers

My dear First Lord,

I am sorry there should have been some delay in answering your letter to Guinness, of January 6.

The policy of arming a certain number of merchant vessels for self-defensive purposes is one with which I fully agree. In fact I was responsible before the war for initiating this measure. I cannot, however, feel that there is the slightest urgency in completing the equipment of the hundred merchant ships at which the Board of Admiralty are aiming. I do not think either the Cabinet or the Committee of Imperial Defence have ever been consulted on the point of as many as a hundred vessels being so armed at any given date. The statement of the Foreign Secretary upon the improbability of any war with Japan for many years to come should make it possible to slow down the whole process of naval preparation. During the next fifteen years many ships now armed with 6-inch guns will necessarily be scrapped. It would in my opinion be a most prudent measure on the part of the Admiralty to preserve the guns, mountings and reserve ammunition of these vessels, and promote their armed merchant cruiser programme gradually by this means.

I cannot agree that any special provision, such as the ordering of new guns and mountings, is required. Moreover, I see no reason why you should not set aside a certain number of surplus serviceable 4·7-inch guns for the same purpose. Although these are not as good as 6-inch, they are of considerable value. The object of a self-defensive merchantman is not to fight a cruiser, or even a merchant cruiser; and she is quite incompetent to do this. Her role is solely to defend herself against a merchantman armed for commerce destruction. If you will examine the resources of the Japanese in 6-inch guns, you will, I am sure, see how very few they have to spare for this purpose. Therefore while I quite agree with you that 6-inch is the ideal, I should certainly not reject lower calibres of 4-inch and upwards. The Treasury will be quite ready to provide for the proper care and maintenance of such weapons as they become available through the scrapping of existing vessels.

Winston S. Churchill to Viscount Cecil of Chelwood

(*Churchill papers: 18/10*)

20 January 1925   Treasury Chambers

I think the Paris Conference has been so well accepted—possibly because it is unintelligible—that there is no immediate need for a White Paper. *Omne ignotum pro magnifico.* I dare say when Parliament meets there will be a debate which will give me an opportunity of explaining matters.

I will think carefully over all you write about the Protocol and disarmament. It seems to me all very unreal at the present time. Do you realise that the Navy Estimates are up more than ten millions, and that the new construction programme on which the Admiralty insist will raise them ten millions next year and five millions more on top of that, a total increase of twenty-five million pounds in three years, and an aggregate of over ninety millions in 1927–28 and following years? This is what I am trying to fight at the present time. The immediate question is not one of disarmament but of preventing Britain from leading the world in a vast expansion of naval armaments, accompanied to a lesser extent by a development of air power. From the moment these estimates are presented and the Admiralty designs disclosed to Parliament, we shall be irretrievably branded as a Jingo Armaments Administration. I do not envy you your task in preaching disarmament, to the French for instance, while we are in that plight. I do not propose to bring this grave matter before the Cabinet, if I can help it, before the beginning of February. I trust you will be home by then.

Winston S. Churchill to William Bridgeman

(*Churchill papers: 18/4*)

23 January 1925   Treasury Chambers

My dear First Lord,

I have carefully considered your letter of the 15 Jan in all its bearings; and also the very full information you have been so good as to give me on the Naval position generally during the last few weeks.

I find the situation created by the Admiralty requirements far too serious to be settled by departmental discussion between us. The requirements actual and prospective of which you have made me aware will absorb the whole available resources of the Exchequer not only this year but for two or three years to come. They preclude all possibility of relief to the taxpayer or of any schemes of social betterment. Thus these new Naval demands dominate the whole policy of the Government; and only the Cabinet can decide what they wish done.

Ever since the year 1908 I have followed with the best information the movement of Naval affairs and I am bound to say that I am convinced that the present policy and demand of the Admiralty are not warranted by any consideration of the safety of the country or of the adequate maintenance of our Naval power, and that they will be deeply injurious to the political foundations of the State.

In the circumstances I would suggest that you should follow the usual course of laying your proposals before the Cabinet. I will then put before them the other considerations which arise; and they must judge and settle what to do.

I cannot conclude without saying that I sympathise with your personal difficulties in having to bear the burden of this controversy at such short notice, and without having been able to shape the previous course of events; and let me also repeat my thanks for the courtesy and patience with which you have treated the Treasury. I am glad to feel that whatever consequences the decision of the Cabinet may entail nothing but the friendliest personal relations will subsist between us.

> Believe me,
> Yours very sincerely,
> Winston S. Churchill

Winston S. Churchill to Sir Otto Niemeyer and Sir George Barstow

(Churchill papers: 18/12)

23 January 1925

The Foreign Office policy is, I am afraid, to throw up the sponge in Egypt and to save the Soudan from the wreck at the expense of the British taxpayer. An alternative policy which I believe will impose itself upon us by the force of events is to control Egypt under such forms as may be necessary and while preserving order in the Soudan to prevent Egypt from interfering except nominally in the administration of that country. I do not agree with the policy of tearing the Soudan away from Egypt as a preliminary to letting Egypt sink into anarchy. Great as are the injuries which British and Egyptian interests have suffered through the policy with which the Foreign Office has been so largely associated in the last few years, I still hope and believe that the position may be retrieved.

Holding as I do that Egypt has a real interest in the Soudan and that a complete divorce between Egypt and the Soudan would be injurious and unjust, I see nothing obnoxious in accepting from Egypt the largest contribution she will make in aid of Soudan expenses. Write therefore to the Foreign Office pointing out that, in view of Sidki Pasha's[1] offers and wishes, there is no justification for throwing an increased charge upon the British taxpayer on account of Soudan. In our opinion the largest possible contribution should be obtained from Egypt, though the Foreign Office would no doubt stipulate against conditions which enabled an unfriendly Egyptian Government to hamper and obstruct Soudan administration.

With regard to the capital of £160,000 for the accommodation of British troops, that should clearly be paid out of Soudan revenues, which revenues will be fed to a large extent by an Egyptian contribution. I see no necessity in these circumstances for a loan. But if it is found that the Soudan cannot provide the necessary money at the moment, a temporary advance on loan might be made by the British Treasury. Our fundamental proposition must be that the Soudan should be self-supporting whether as regards black, Egyptian or white troops. Whatever it requires for its peace and order it must pay for. Only in the last resort can the Treasury be approached for assistance in the form of a grant-in-aid.

Thirdly, there is the £150,000 which we have had for forty years from the Egyptian Government on account of the British troops maintained in Egypt. Zaghlul's Government repudiated this as they repudiated the interest on a portion of the Egyptian debt. Our decision must be that we insist upon its payment, both for the instalment of last year and in future years. A further question has arisen owing to the increased cost of the garrison which it has been necessary to maintain in Egypt owing to the misconduct of the Egyptians. This in my judgment justifies a further claim upon the Egyptian Government. It ought to be made perfectly clear to them that disorder will be followed by an increase of the Army of Occupation and that the extra cost of maintaining this Army of Occupation as apart from its home charges will be one for which Egypt is responsible.

Pray unfold all these firm assertions in a draft letter for my consideration.

---

[1] Ismail Sidki Pasha, Egyptian Finance Minister, 1921–2; Minister of the Interior, 1924–5; Prime Minister, Minister of the Interior and Minister of Finance, 1930–3. Minister of Finance, 1937–8 and 1946. Prime Minister for the second time, February–December 1936.

Winston S. Churchill to Sir Warren Fisher

(*Churchill papers: 18/12*)

23 January 1925

You are mistaken in supposing that I have proposed any alteration in the system of registration. The directions which I have given relate solely to the method of preparing Minute papers and files. I attach to this Minute a docket and file in the form which long, and I think unequalled, experience of Public Offices has convinced me is the most convenient. Every feature of this was the result of long consideration, and it has been tested by much experience. I shall be delighted to explain to you personally its many advantages, not only to the Head of a Department but to those on whose advice he relies in administrative and executive matters. It will be sufficient for me here to point out the general principles.

(1) Minutes are intended to be brief steps towards decision, and not lengthy arguments. The latest Minute should in the form of the papers come uppermost to the eye, and the papers should reach whoever is the deciding authority in a form which enables that authority, if content, to dispose of them by placing an initial on the portion of the file which is presented to him. In many cases where the Head is fully acquainted with the course of the business it will not be even necessary to unfasten the tape binding the file.

(2) Memoranda of an informative and argumentative character, correspondence, drafts of letters, exhibits of all kinds should not interrupt the sequence of Minutes, but should be kept separate from the Minute sheets within the docket. A clear distinction is needed between the terseness and precision which are required in Minutes and the necessary more expansive forms of argument which are suitable to Memoranda. Whereas the Minutes read in chronological order from the first page to the latest Minute in the centre of the file, the exhibits, memoranda, documents, etc, begin at the last page and so bring the latest of their number, or possibly the draft letter which has to be sanctioned, immediately next the latest of the Minutes. Thus all action is apparent upon the upturned open face of the file.

The present method of presenting official papers at the Treasury is not convenient to the swift despatch of business. The papers are strung together with very little system; as often as not the latest is at the bottom of the file. The attempt to focus the decision is often entirely lacking. There is no distinction between Minutes leading up to decision and general disquisitions on complex matters. Enclosures are very often not attached by a fastener to the file, and consequently they drop out or lose their places. These strings of papers are simply thrust inside a thin paper docket which affords no strength to the file and is used by the Private Office for assisting the Minister in the day-to-day conduct of business. At the same time any Parliamentary Question, a creature of an hour, is given all to itself a brand new strong, effective docket. The great knowledge and ability which characterises all the memoranda I receive would be given a far more powerful and easy application if simple rules based on definite principles were introduced and scrupulously followed.

Winston S. Churchill to Sir Warren Fisher

(*Churchill papers: 18/12*)

23 January 1925

PRIME MINISTER'S PENSION

I am against the Prime Minister's pension. I think the position of Ministers is sufficiently safeguarded by the existing provision of Ministerial Pensions, and I much regret the prejudice which prevents these pensions from being resorted to by ex-Ministers who require them. I am sure this prejudice would be manifested in a lively form in regard to this proposal. The fact that the existing holder of the office proposes to exclude himself from all benefits would of course safeguard the personal aspect completely. I do not see, however, what from a public point of view is the distinction between the case of an ex-Prime Minister and the former occupant of some other great and prominent office. If public policy requires that persons who have held high positions under the State should thereafter lead lives of dignified affluence and should not engage in business or journalism, the argument would equally apply to others besides the holders of the Prime Minister's office. I do not believe, however, that any pension which a democratic Parliament would contemplate would be sufficient to induce men of eminence and ability to exclude themselves in these modern times from any legitimate forms of activity. The question of whether these forms of activity are dignified or not is one which can only be decided by the persons themselves. I should like therefore a note deprecating this proposal and showing the difficulties.

Winston S. Churchill to Sir Warren Fisher

(*Churchill papers: 18/12*)

23 January 1925

I am in favour in principle of raising the Ministries of Agriculture, Education, Labour and Scotland to the status of first class offices with salaries of

£5,000 a year. I would not, however, advise this change being proposed except on a basis that it did not apply during the existing Parliament. Any other course would certainly excite great prejudice and would embarrass us in effecting the needed reductions in pay and salaries throughout the Public Services.

I am not in favour of altering the salaries of the ceremonial quasi-sinecure offices, viz, the Lord President of the Council, the Lord Privy Seal and the Chancellor of the Duchy of Lancaster. None of these appointments can command the support of large national or public interests, such as champion the cause of the four Ministries above mentioned. Moreover their work is of a general and advisory character and does not correspond to the direct administrative duties and executive responsibility attached to the Departmental Ministers. I should not attempt to raise the Post Office whether in or out of the Cabinet. I do not concur in the principle that membership of the Cabinet should carry with it an equal salary. I am sure there would be an outcry if the three ceremonial offices mentioned were raised. The only conceivable exception to the above for which a strong case could be made is the Leadership of the House of Lords. I am sure, however, Lord Curzon would be exposed to much annoyance if such a question were pressed at the present time.

Winston S. Churchill to Stanley Baldwin
(Churchill papers: 18/4)

24 January 1925   Chartwell
Private

My dear PM,

I send you the earliest copy of a paper on the Navy Estimates which I shall have to circulate in a few days.

Perhaps you would like to have a talk with me early in the week. I should be grateful for any advice as to how to handle this extremely awkward business. I thought myself that after one or two Cabinets on the main issue, you would perhaps yourself mention certain figures for the next three years, and ask that plans should be made for working to them by a Cabinet Committee or by further discussions *on that basis* between the Admiralty and the Exchequer.

I would rather my paper were kept secret for the next few days.

Yours sincerely,
Winston S. Churchill

Lord Beatty to his wife

(Beatty papers)

26 January 1925

That extraordinary fellow Winston has gone mad. Economically mad, and no sacrifice is too great to achieve what, in his short-sightedness, is the panacea for all evils—to take one shilling off the income tax. Nobody outside a lunatic asylum expects a shilling off the income tax this budget. But he has made up his mind that it is the only thing he can do to justify his appointment as Chancellor of the Exchequer. The result will be a split in the Conservative Party and nothing else. As we, the Admiralty, are the principal Spending Department, he attacks us with virulence. . . .

Poor old Bridgeman, our First Lord, takes a very gloomy view and sees his job fading away from him. But I have heartened him up a lot, and I think he will stand firm. It's then a case of Winston coming off his perch, or a split in the Govt followed by the resignation of the Board of Admiralty. Every year it is the same struggle. We have won through up till now, but we are up against tougher stuff just now and it requires very careful watching.

William Bridgeman to Winston S. Churchill

(Churchill papers: 18/4)

26 January 1925   Admiralty

My dear Chancellor,

Many thanks for your letter of the 23rd inst. I am doing what you suggest and hope to put in a memorandum for the Cabinet in the next two days.

I greatly appreciate what you say as to the difficulty of my position, and fully realise that yours is not much easier—but I am sure the fact that our respective conceptions of our duty have brought us into strong departmental conflict will not impair the friendliest relations between us.

Yrs v sincerely

W. C. Bridgeman

Winston S. Churchill to L. S. Amery

(*Treasury papers: T171/241*)

27 January 1925   Treasury Chambers

My dear Leo,

The Treasury are looking into all the luxury articles you mentioned, by my directions. Much the best revenue getter is silk. I should not myself see much to object to in a tax of this kind, although unaccompanied by any countervailing excise. I am warned, however of the very grave and wide-spread unpopularity which would attach to it among the feminine section of the electorate.

William Bridgeman to Stanley Baldwin

(*Baldwin papers*)

28 January 1925   Admiralty

My dear Prime Minister,

As I am unable to come to any agreement with the Chancellor of the Exchequer over the Navy Estimates, I am sending a memorandum to the Cabinet today in support of our contentions—and he tells me he is preparing one from his point of view.

If the schedule of time prepared by the Whips is to be kept, it will be necessary to settle this matter by Wednesday next—I believe the approved practice, when differences of this kind occur is for the Prime Minister him-self to intervene—and I am very sorry to put you to this trouble—and at such short notice—I had been hoping to reach some agreement with the Chancellor and so avoid this procedure—and that has prevented my sending in my memorandum sooner.

There is one other question involved which is of great importance in itself—and that is the settlement of the Navy Officers' grievance as to Marriage Allowances which has been the subject of many questions in the House.

For two or three years the Admiralty have expressed their sympathy with the Naval Officers—and their belief in the substance of their grievance—and I have asked for a Cabinet Coordinating Cm to whom I can submit the figures which seem to prove the case for the Navy. It will create a very bitter feeling, I fear, if the matter is further postponed—and the settlement of it would do much to restore the popularity of the service & produce a better & more numerous list of candidates for Dartmouth. I enclose for your consideration a note from the First Sea Lord whom I have asked to let me know his opinion as to the urgency of the matter. It is stronger than even I had expected.

Yours ever
W. C. Bridgeman

Lord Beaverbrook to Sir Robert Borden[1]

(Beaverbrook papers)

28 January 1925

Things are very slack politically. Britain has at last attained Bonar Law's ideal of tranquillity—under Baldwin. So long as the Conservative Government do nothing they can go on for a very long time and could only be disturbed by those premonitions of coming fate which are contained in very adverse bye-elections.

Austen Chamberlain and Winston Churchill, who is very powerful, are already engaged in a kind of wrestle for the second place in the Cabinet. The immediate issue is one of foreign affairs, in which of course the Chancellor of the Exchequer is now deeply involved. The Protocol of the League of Nations being practically dead, Chamberlain favours an attempt to revive a 'Pact' guarantee for France and Belgium against any future aggression. Most of the Cabinet are likely to be opposed to this and I do not think the electorate would listen for a moment to any such suggestion. Churchill will head the anti-Pact forces.

Lord Birkenhead to Lord Reading

(Reading papers)

29 January 1925

Winston's position in the Government and Cabinet is very strong. He takes infinite trouble with the Prime Minister, who likes him and for whom he feels a very sincere gratitude.

---

[1] Robert Laird Borden, 1854–1937. Canadian Prime Minister, 1911–20. Knighted, 1914. First overseas Minister to receive summons to meeting of British Cabinet, 14 July 1915. Representative of Canada at Imperial War Cabinet, 1917–18. Chief Plenipotentiary Delegate of Canada at the Paris Peace Conference, 1919. Represented Canada on Council of League of Nations. Chairman of Sixth Committee of the League Assembly, 1930.

Winston S. Churchill: Cabinet memorandum[1]

(Churchill papers: 22/28)

29 January 1925   Treasury Chambers
Most Secret

NAVY ESTIMATES

The First Lord wishes to present Naval Estimates to Parliament for the year 1925–26 of £69,241,477 gross and £65,500,000 nett. This is described as an increase of £9,700,000 over the current financial year. As £580,000 of terminable Annuities fall in this year and are absorbed by fresh expenditure, it is really an increase of £10,280,000. This total comprises £1,323,000 for the Fleet Air Arm formerly borne on Air Force Votes without of course preventing a considerable increase on those Votes. Such an event will excite national and world-wide attention. It must necessarily become the outstanding feature of our policy, and it will be taken at home and abroad as indicating the spirit and policy of the new Government. It will play a prominent part in all the criticisms directed against us from every hostile quarter. It is therefore important that the Cabinet, before embarking upon such a policy of increased armament expenditure, should weigh the whole matter well.

The expansion for the year 1925–26 does not stand alone. It is part of a policy which, if adopted by the Cabinet, will irrevocably produce further great increases in succeeding years. For instance, the Admiralty ask on Vote A for an increase of 4,350 officers and men. This involves a continuing charge of £870,000 a year, of which only about half operates this year. The oil fuel and storage programme of £3,919,600 is estimated to rise steadily to £4,587,000 in 1928–29. The new construction programme of 5 cruisers, 8 submarines, 6 costly depôt, repair and victualling ships, and 11 minor vessels amounts to £21½ millions, less than 2 millions of which fall in the year 1925–26. Neither is it true that the increased expenditure for 1925–26 is caused by the working off of former new construction programmes. The increase under that head is stated by the First Lord to be no more than £550,000, and the total sum required for new construction in the proposed Estimates does not exceed £9½ millions. But this naval programme is only the forerunner of a succession of new construction programmes. The Admiralty have been good enough to furnish me with some information as to their plans for the next four years, from which it appears that expenditure on new construction in that period may be somewhat as follows:—

[1] Circulated to the Cabinet as Cabinet paper 39 of 1925.

					£ million
1925–26	...	...	...	...	9½
1926–27	...	...	...	...	18½
1927–28	...	...	...	...	22¾
1928–29	...	...	...	...	24½

This forecast shows that the cost of the new construction programmes will rise above the proposed figure for 1925–26 by approximately £9 millions additional in 1926–27, another £4 millions additional in 1927–28 and a further increase of £2 millions in 1928–29, a total super increase of £15 millions on new construction alone, fully operative in the fourth year. The First Lord has explained that in asking for no more addition to Vote A than 4,350 officers and men he is taking some risk. As larger and more complicated vessels are built, further considerable additions will of course be necessary year by year. There are also additions to be expected from the automatic increases in Navy Pay and marriage allowances; for the increase in non-effective Votes; from the gradual exhaustion of the reserves of wartime naval and victualling stores; and for the development of Singapore. Surveying the whole field with some experience of these matters, I cannot doubt that proceeding on the present lines the Naval estimates for 1926-27 will be about £12 millions above those of 1925–26 and those of 1927–28, perhaps £7 millions higher still. This would give us gross Naval Estimates in 1926–27 of £81½ millions, in 1927–28 of £88½ millions and in 1928–29 of over £90 millions.

If this policy of armament expansion and the reasoning on which it is based are adopted by the Cabinet, certain financial consequences must inevitably follow. First, there can be no possibility of any appreciable reduction in Direct Taxation, *not only this year but in the next three years.* Secondly, no effective funds can be available for social reform, housing, insurance, education and the like. I may reasonably expect a moderate expansion of the revenue through a better year coming into the average of the Income Tax returns; through increasingly severe collection; through the slow but steady growth of Death Duties; through the economies due to the reduction of the Debt charge by the operation of the Sinking Fund; and, so long as our credit is maintained, through certain economies of Conversion. But these sums will in the three years under review just about suffice to pay for the naval increases. To resort to borrowing in the shape of a Naval Loan would affect our credit and compromise the great operations of Conversion which will be upon us in 1928–29.

The Cabinet is therefore fortunate in finding the choice before it extremely simple. We can, if we choose, make this a Naval Parliament, the work and resources of which will have been wholly devoted to maintaining and developing our sea power, and which in consequence has had to demand the hardest sacrifices from the taxpayer, and to forgo all plans of social reform. On this basis I believe that we could meet the Admiralty requirements without any important increase in taxation. Is this, then, to be the decision to which we are to come?

Such a policy would of course concentrate upon us a most formidable agitation at home. The whole force of the Opposition Parties would be directed to denouncing the militarism of the Government, which it could truly be stated had closed the doors on social reform. But more dangerous than this will be the discontent of the direct taxpayer. Everyone will remember the outcry raised at the beginning of 1922 and its deeply injurious effects upon the Coalition Government. It will be unfortunate if in our efforts to sustain and develop the Navy we break up the present governing instrument and produce a political situation which restores a Socialist or Radical-Socialist Government to power; for then would come a wholesale and ruthless cutting down of the Navy, and all the money and efforts which to our own detriment we had devoted for three years would be undone in the fourth. This is an aspect of our Imperial safety which should perhaps be present to the minds of Admirals as well as of politicians.

The Foreign Secretary will no doubt judge the consequences which striking British Naval developments of this kind will have upon the external situation. Our League of Nations position will of course become ludicrous. It seems almost certain that the expansion of our Navy Estimates and the growth of our new construction will entail immediate rejoinders from Japan and still more from the United States. We might even find that building five more cruisers had merely called ten or twelve into existence against us, and so on.

It seems to be necessary to review our Naval position. The Admiralty consider that we are in great danger from Japan. The First Sea Lord has described the position as 'intolerable', and has expressed his relief that our present unclouded relations with that country accord us 'a breathing space' in which to prepare. I do not deny that the position of Japan in her own home waters and in the Northern Pacific is a very strong one, and I am still in favour of a gradual and discreet development of our fuel bases along the Eastern route, and in particular of Singapore. But I cannot regard the situation as urgent or critical. Certainly it is not sufficiently urgent or critical to call for action on our part so swift and far-reaching as largely to transform our naval organisation or to dislocate our whole finances. In the years preceding the Great War not only was the Japanese Fleet overwhelmingly superior to any force we could place on the China station, but the whole

British Fleet was riveted to the North Sea by the supreme German menace. In those days we scarcely dared to send our battle squadrons as far as the coast of Spain for their autumn cruise. Germany and Germany alone absorbed our thoughts; and nobody with whom I came in contact felt or showed the slightest anxiety about Japan. This danger has, in fact, become apparent only when greater dangers have passed away.

The present position is surely better in several aspects than it was in those days. The British Navy has no pre-occupations in home waters: the deadly peril to the Island is removed: the German Fleet is at the bottom of the sea. The great and powerful Navy of the United States, in appearance almost the equal of our own, has come into being and, though remote, is in fundamental antagonistic relation to that of Japan. The words which the Foreign Secretary and the Lord President have lately used to the Committee of Imperial Defence should also afford some reassurance:—

'*Mr Austen Chamberlain:* . . . I regard the prospect of war in the Far East as very remote. I cannot conceive of any circumstances in which, singlehanded, we are likely to go to war with Japan. I cannot conceive it possible that Japan, singlehanded, should seek a conflict with us. The only case in which I think Japan (which is an uneasy and rather restless Power, whose action is not always easy to predicate) might become dangerous is after a new regrouping of the European Powers. In other words, unless we see signs of a German-Russo-Japanese Alliance or agreement, I should not anticipate war between ourselves and Japan. I should regard the signs of such an agreement, such a new regrouping of the Powers as being a danger signal which would at once call our attention to the situation and would require that we should review it afresh. Of that regrouping there is no present sign. Germany is not yet in a position in which she can enter into engagements of that kind. There is no sign at present of an agreement between Russia and Japan, and I think it would be with difficulty that they would reconcile their interests for the purposes of such an agreement. Therefore, at the present time, I should regard the danger of war between ourselves and Japan as being as remote as the danger of war with any other Great Power. Japan has ambitions in China. I am quite certain that she is not seeking an occasion to make a war for the sake of China, and would be very reluctant to do so, but I cannot conceive at present of a development of Japanese policy in China which, if it were antagonistic to us or offensive to our sentiments, would not be even more offensive, or at least equally offensive, to America, and where we should not be acting with America instead of acting alone. As long as Japan is isolated, as she will be if she parts company with America and ourselves, it seems to me inconceivable that she should seek a quarrel or get into a position in which she cannot avoid a quarrel with America and ourselves. . . . I should strongly deprecate anything that can be read here or elsewhere as competitive building between ourselves and Japan in anticipation of a new struggle. If the danger of a struggle ever materialises, I think we shall have plenty of warning, and it would be a great mistake to disquiet the Japanese, to render them more nervous than they are. I think they would be rather frightened by any appearance of a hostile programme of naval shipbuilding, which they would interpret not as a measure of protection on our part, but as preparation for an aggressive attack upon them at some time. . . .'

'*Lord Curzon:* I do not think I have anything to add to the statement made by the Foreign Secretary, with which I cordially agree, except this, that all our evidence from Japan—and some of us have friends who write to us from there, apart from the official statements which we read—tends to show that, while Japan feels sore and sorry and rather sick at the loss of the British Alliance, she is anxious to replace it, as far as she possibly can, by intimate and cordial relations between ourselves, and therefore, quite apart from the remote risk of any such regrouping of the Powers as Mr Chamberlain has talked of, there is in Japan itself, the strongest pro-British sentiment at the present time, and it is scarcely possible, so far as I can judge, to conceive of any state of affairs in which the general trend of Japanese policy would for many years to come be anti-British. That is the only contribution, for what it is worth, I have to make to the discussion.'

Further reassurance is found by a comparison of British and Japanese Naval strengths. We have 18 Battleships against 6 Japanese and an equal number of Battle Cruisers (4) on each side. In addition, we are building the two strongest Battleship-Battle Cruisers in the world. We have, excluding 'Courageous' and 'Glorious', 57 Cruisers, British and Dominion, built and building against 24 Japanese; and 209 Flotilla Leaders and Destroyers against 118 Japanese. An analysis of the relative Cruiser strengths would emphasise these figures.

Although to our eyes the position of Japan (if she became aggressive) in the Far East may appear formidable, her own situation must cause her legitimate anxieties. She is webbed about on both sides of the world by the Naval apparatus of the two mighty English-speaking nations. She has agreed that our two Battle Fleets shall be to hers in the proportion of ten to three. She watches with anxious eyes the strong, though distant, development of American Naval Power in the Pacific and the remorseless advance of the renowned Navy of Britain towards her island home. Can we wonder that she builds light cruisers and is, in the Foreign Secretary's words, 'uneasy and restless'? What would our feelings be if we saw ourselves being laid hold of by a similar pair of tongs?

When we look across the Atlantic Ocean at the Navy of the United States, a different series of facts present themselves for consideration. Battleships, Battle Cruisers and Aircraft Carriers are regulated by the Washington Convention. There is absolutely no doubt that our Battle Fleet is the stronger, even on paper. The Americans have a certain superiority in Destroyers and Submarines, but in Cruisers they are astonishingly weak. The American Secretary to the Navy[1] has recently stated that the ratio of British to United States Cruisers is as 5 to 1. The United States have only nine modern Cruisers. Since our decision last year to lay down 5 10,000-ton cruisers, Congress has authorised the construction of 8 such vessels, which the United States Navy certainly requires. But the President has not yet taken the necessary steps to obtain the money. Whatever may happen about these 8 cruisers, a vigorous programme of Cruiser building on our part will lead either to our being confronted with the competition of a far superior wealth, to which we ourselves are forced to contribute, or, on the other hand, to our being led into another Naval Convention, in which we shall be compelled to settle on the basis of mere numerical equality and without regard for our special needs.

The Admiralty seems to be misconceiving the problem which is before them. That problem is to keep a Navy in being which over a long period of profound peace will, taken as a whole, not be inferior to the Navy either of the United States or of Japan. But this does not imply the immediate development of the means on the part of the British Navy to dominate either of these two Powers in their own quarter of the globe. In the case of the United States it must be recognised that no such attempt is being made by the Admiralty. In the case of Japan, however, a truly prodigious effort is absorbing the thoughts and exertions of the Admiralty staff. The Navy Estimates bear its imprint on almost every page. The construction of the naval base at Singapore, however desirable as a pillar in Imperial communications, has become a peg on which to hang the whole vast scheme of scientific naval control of Japan. Our Cruiser programme, with its formid-

[1] From March 1924 until March 1929 the United States Secretary of the Navy was Curtis D. Wilbur. On 20 January 1925, nine days before Churchill's memorandum was circulated to the Cabinet, the United States Senate had rejected a bellicose naval resolution, introduced by Senator McKellar of Tennessee, seeking to elevate the guns on thirteen United States battleships to correspond with the elevation of the guns on British battleships. The defeat of the McKellar Resolution was seen as proof of the determination of the United States not to go back on the provisions of the Washington Conference on naval disarmament.

able expense, is measured entirely against the Japanese. One hundred liners are to be equipped with 6-inch guns to act as auxiliary cruisers. The scale and rapidity with which the tremendous scheme of oil fuel installations is being pressed all along the Far Eastern route is a feature. So also are the developments which are taking place in the Naval ports along this route from Malta to Singapore. A costly development of Fleet auxiliaries, oilers, provision ships, Fleet repair ships, new depôt ships for destroyers, follows naturally from the same cause. It is proposed at the earliest possible moment to base a powerful submarine force at Hong Kong, and a Submarine Depôt Ship costing about £1,000,000 is included in the present programme for that express purpose. As soon as arrangements can be made a Battle Cruiser Squadron will be based upon Singapore. For this a new million pound Fleet Repair Ship is now required.

However desirable or well conceived in strategic theory these developments may be, I cannot feel that the existing international situation justifies either the rate or the scale on which they are now proceeding. If the cost of the policy becomes so great as to compromise the general action of the State and to expose us to other dangers of a very serious kind we should be bound to review it and control it.

Our naval situation to-day is in no way comparable in intensity or crisis to that which existed before the war. The only other two great naval Powers in the world are separated from us by oceans, and have no bases within thousands of miles of our home waters. They have no means of forcing a supreme naval battle upon us suddenly or within a short time. When we faced Germany across the narrow North Sea, we knew that we must always be ready to fight a decisive battle within a few days of the declaration of war, or perhaps simultaneously with the declaration of war. If, for instance, hostilities began on Monday, we could be threatened with invasion on Wednesday and have to engage the whole German Navy on Thursday or Friday. All our arrangements were aimed, to the best of our science and knowledge, at instant and continuous readiness for the supreme test. It was from such circumstances that the argument of 'the average versus the selected moment' was drawn. There is absolutely no resemblance between that tremendous situation and the secondary anxieties of the present time. Nothing could happen on the seas, however unpleasant, which could expose us to *mortal* danger in a short time, or oblige us to risk a decisive battle unless we were thoroughly ready.

Yet in spite of this, the whole of our naval organisation is being kept at a far higher pitch of preparedness and instant readiness than was deemed possible in 1914. Practically the whole Fleet, apart from destroyers and small craft, is maintained in full commission. The system of manning ships on the

Second Fleet scale, ie, 60 per cent full nucleus crews on board, and 40 per cent active service ratings requalifying in the schools ashore, has been entirely abandoned. Practically every ship not in dockyard hands refitting is kept permanently manned with its full complement of active service ratings. These complements have been largely increased *in the same ships* since 1914; for instance, the approved war complement of the *Iron Duke* in 1914 was 885, the approved peace complement is now 1,089, and the super-war complement (all of active service ratings to be provided without calling out reserves) is 1,212. Virtually the whole of the personnel are on a long-service basis of twelve years, with an option of continuing to twenty-one. We are therefore keeping our whole Fleet permanently manned during an indefinite period of peace with full complements of highly-trained long-service men. The reserve system, which every other military or naval organisation in the world has adopted to a greater or lesser extent, has practically ceased to play any effectual part in the British Navy. Only 15,000 Reservists are required for British warships on full mobilisation. Whereas the element of sudden, supreme, fatal danger has been entirely removed, our precautions against such danger have been carried, regardless of expense, to a far higher pitch of perfection. We are invited to live, perhaps for a quarter of a century of peace, with our pistol at full-cock and our finger on the trigger. I regard this not only as utterly unreasonable but as positively injurious to the main interests of the State.

The problem of keeping in being for an indefinite period a British Fleet not inferior, taken as a whole, to the next Naval Power—in other words, of maintaining a 'One-Power standard'—is in itself enough to absorb all the skill and science of the Admiralty and all the available resources of the taxpayer. I do not at all ignore the very serious difficulty which will in any case be upon us in future years of replacing a large proportion of the units of our Fleet as they become really worn out. This, in my judgment, is a call upon us far superior to the development of our naval position in the Pacific. If those claims compete within the limits of our available finance we may be forced to choose between them. In any case, if the task of gradual Fleet rebuilding is to be successfully accomplished without raising domestic and external complications, it can only be by rigorous thrift and great administrative contrivance on the part of the Admiralty. It is not necessary in the present state of the world that our Naval organisation should be complete and perfect in all respects, ready at a moment's notice to spring into full warlike action. During a long peace, such as follows in the wake of great wars, there must inevitably develop gaps in our structure of armaments. We have to select the essential elements of war power from amidst great quantities of ancillary and subsidiary improvements. These gaps can be gradually and unostentatiously filled up if deep international antagonisms, the invariable precursors of great wars, gradually become apparent in the world.

The task of maintaining the 'One Power Standard', even on a purely defensive and peace-time basis, will, in any case, having regard to all the burdens we have to bear, strain our resources to the utmost. It is a task which will much better be undertaken on a long rather than a short view. I should be quite willing, once the great questions of principle have been settled by the Cabinet, to consider with the Admiralty the increased financial provision which will inevitably be required, after every economy has been made, to rebuild that portion of the British Fleet likely to become finally unserviceable according to standards comparable to those of other Naval Powers in the next five years. There are great advantages in treating the subject in this way. Good reasons can be given to Parliament and the public for a sober and systematic policy of this kind. We should, of course, remain perfectly free ourselves to cope by new measures with unforeseeable tendencies. But the declaration of our intentions in normal circumstances over a lustrum would in itself exercise a steadying effect upon the programmes both of the United States and Japan. Japan particularly, if convinced that she is not being made the object of a scientific Naval approach, would probably rejoice in the relief from new construction thus afforded to her.

I do not feel justified in resting solely on criticism. Although conscious of the difficulties of making constructive proposals of economy, I would venture to propose to the Cabinet the following measures to arrest the expansion of Naval Expenditure before it is too late:—

(1) No new construction programme this year, except perhaps a few submarines: the whole Cruiser question to be examined meanwhile by a Sub-Committee of the Committee of Imperial Defence. [Saving (say) £1,800,000. Second year £8,000,000.]

(2) No addition to personnel. The 100,000 officers and men now borne on Vote A to be distributed by the Admiralty to the best advantage among the Fleets and Shore Establishments: the balance between home and foreign service to be reconsidered: a proportion of battleships and cruisers serving in home waters or the Mediterranean to be manned in peace with full nucleus crews on the pre-war Second Fleet Scale: the reserve system and the immediate reserve to be developed and utilised to a greater extent for mobilisation in time of war, a larger proportion of short-service men being engaged if necessary for this purpose: the schools to be closed on the outbreak of war, and their personnel made available for mobilisation, as in 1914. [Saving £427,000 in 1925–26, and £870,000 a year thereafter.]

(3) The expenditure on the Fleet Air Arm to be limited to £1,000,000 in 1925–26, the increase in Aircraft Carriers, in which we have an un-questioned lead, to be slowed down. [Saving £323,000.]

(4) The rate of the expansion of our oil-fuel installations to be spread over double the number of years, ie, the figure of 5 million tons to be reached only in 1933–34 instead of 1928–29; this to be effected in conjunction with economy in Fleet movement so as to reduce the prospective annual charges on Fuel and Fuel Reserve together by one-half. [Saving in 1925–26 £1,950,000. Second year £2,300,000.]

(5) The expenditure on Singapore to be spread over fifteen years instead of the present period.

(6) A reduction of at least £3 millions to be obtained from the Estimates of this year by internal economies, including the diminution in the number of depot ships, of new works, in the costs of shore establish-ments generally and for the invariable over-budgeting on approved services. [Saving £3,000,000.]

(7) The proposal of new marriage allowances to be negatived. [Saving £350,000.]

(8) The pay scales of the Navy to be revised for future entrants simul-taneously with the revision in the other services, and these results to be made effective from the year 1925–26 onwards.

These or alternative savings would still leave the Navy Estimates at £57,650,000 or nearly £2 millions above last year, despite the saving from the reduced terminable Annuities. No one can say this is not an ample supply.

I must, however, point out to the Cabinet that the serious character of this issue is not confined to the present year. It is far greater in the two years which follow. At the present moment a choice is open between alterna-tive policies, and future naval expenditure is still controllable. Once, how-ever, the programme of new construction now proposed by the Admiralty is sanctioned and begun and additions of officers and men to Vote A are approved, there can be no turning back. The Estimates for 1926–27 must certainly rise by at least 6, 7 or 8 millions above the increase now demanded. It will be impossible then, however great the outcry—unless we are prepared to leave ships unfinished on the stocks or buy out men newly engaged—to prevent Naval expenditure from becoming the main, and even the sole, feature of the policy of the Government. Whatever the decision, it should be taken with full realisation of the consequences.

                                                          WSC

Winston S. Churchill: Cabinet memorandum[1]

(Churchill papers: 22/29)

30 January 1925
Secret

INTER-ALLIED DEBTS

The only immediate question which the Cabinet have to settle is the answer we have promised to send in accordance with my letter of the 13th January to M Clémentel's letter of the 10th January. We do not therefore need at this stage to commit ourselves to any definite method for payment by the French of their debt, nor to decide upon terms or figures. Our task is simply to place the French Government in a position to propose a scheme for our consideration, and to indicate to them broadly the main principles by which we are guided and the scale and proportion we have in mind. When, and if, any proposals are made to us, we shall no doubt find them wholly inadequate; and it will be then, and not till then, that we shall have to formulate our counter-suggestions and that negotiations for a settlement will ensue. Let us not therefore complicate our immediate and comparatively easy task by discussions of the intricate and disputable issues which will be raised at a later stage, and which, even when decided, will themselves form only the basis of hard bargaining.

I have, however, for the purposes of our immediate answer to M Clémentel, been forced to arrive at some conclusions in my own mind of a general and provisional character, both as to method and amount. In particular it is necessary to have a clear idea of what is to happen in the event of a total failure of the Dawes annuities, and what is to happen after the possible cessation of those annuities in 1962. The full fruition of the Dawes scheme would probably enable us to secure from Europe a complete equivalent for our American payments. On the other hand, we must, as reasonable men, face the fact that a total failure of the Dawes plan would leave us with a heavy deficit. What, then, is the intermediate point in the yield of the Dawes annuities at which we should claim to be covered by France (and Italy) as against America? What is the minimum we should exact from France (and Italy) in the event of a total failure of all payments from Germany?

Opinions will differ on this. I find that whereas four years ago I was strongly opposed to waiving our claims against France and Italy (except as part of a general cancellation), I am now rather in opposition to those who from the other extreme wish to demand the fullest repayments from our Continental Allies. I have always thought that they, and France at any rate,

[1] Circulated to the Cabinet as Cabinet paper 46 of 1925.

can pay a substantial sum, and that they ought to pay a substantial sum. I have never thought they could pay the whole, or ought in any circumstances to be asked by us to pay the whole. I have therefore with some trepidation roughed out a purely tentative exposition of my own views as to how this problem should be handled and the sort of figures which we might reasonably try to obtain. I doubt whether we shall ever get so much. I do not doubt that we ought to try most resolutely to secure it.

The answer which the Cabinet should now approve for transmission to the French Government is not inconsistent with the method I have outlined; but it in no way commits us to that method. The statement that we should expect to be indemnified as against America, even if only half the Dawes reparations were received, goes considerably beyond the figures I have indicated in my table. This is no doubt only prudent at the outset of negotiations. On the other hand, we do not wish to send an answer which will chill and check any further proposal by France. We wish to encourage her to make a proposal, and so to take a step towards a practical result rather than to give satisfaction to our natural inclination to exact our strict legal or at least our full moral rights.[1]

WSC

Lord Beatty to his wife

(*Beatty papers*)

31 January 1925

I am very busy tackling the Chancellor of the Exchequer who has burst a bomb over us which he thinks will pulverise us, setting forth the extravagance of our claims. I am answering that tomorrow. In the meantime I've persuaded the First Lord to go and spend the weekend with the Prime Minister at Chequers and take him out for a long walk and talk sense to him. . . .

Winston and I are very good friends, and there is no malice or bad feeling attached to it.

[1] On 3 February 1925 L. S. Amery wrote in his diary: 'Cabinet Meeting on Allied Debts and adopted Winston's scheme with a modification suggested by myself' (*Amery papers*). For the final note as sent to Clémentel, see Churchill's Cabinet memorandum of 4 February 1925 (page 376).

February 1925

H. H. Asquith to Winston S. Churchill

(*Churchill papers: 1/178*)

1 February 1925

The Wharf,
Sutton Courtney

My dear Winston,

You wrote me a very kind letter which I greatly valued.[1] You have re-visited the scene in which, during many years of comradeship, we fought together side by side, just when I am quitting it for ever. I am sorry that I cannot look forward to seeing you again in your old place—even from the opposite side of the House. But I wish you with all my heart prosperity and long life.

I am most grateful for what you have written.

Yrs always
HHA

L. S. Amery: diary

(*Amery papers*)

2 February 1925

Winston and FE to dinner and a great evening's talk at the end of which FE went away protesting that he had not been allowed to get in more than ten percent of the talking. We discussed a great many topics, including naval expenditure, and my counter criticism that the only real way of meeting the burden was to increase production by protection and Imperial development.

[1] In February 1925 Asquith was created Earl of Oxford and Asquith. In June 1925 he was appointed a Knight of the Garter.

Sir George Barstow to Sir Warren Fisher

(*Baldwin papers*)

3 February 1925   Treasury

My dear Warren,

I hope very much that if you consult with Ministers on the subject of Navy Estimates you will drive home one point to which I attach great importance—the immense political value of an announcement that the Govt does not intend to initiate *any* new construction in the coming year. I am sure that as between even a low compromise figure of Cruisers say 2 or 1 even, and none, the advantage lies enormously in favour of *none*. It will, if the announcement is made in an effective way, be taken as a symbol of a really pacific attitude by Great Britain, and surely do a great deal to reassure a country like Japan, which is rendered anxious by the Singapore decision.

Is there really no higher policy that a state can pursue than to follow out obediently the staff calculations of its Naval advisers?

Even on a less idealist line of thought, I venture to think a policy of no new construction has immense tactical advantages at the present moment. Neither USA nor Japan has I believe laid down a single 10,000 ton Cruiser. President Coolidge has apparently resisted a raging propaganda in the USA to construct 8, and a British decision to build none would surely strengthen his hands. The Japanese Govt are I believe willing to enter into conference about naval construction and I cannot doubt would be willing to defer the cruisers which are nominally on their programme. At least, this method ought to be explored.

I believe our building resources are so much greater than theirs that if it came to a race we could always give them a start & pass them.

Finally, even on the Admiralty's own ground, I feel sure that the Cabinet ought to explore the cruiser policy of the Admiralty & satisfy itself that it is sound, before committing the country to vast expenditure. Matters of this importance ought not to be dealt with simply as a staff exercise, the answer to an Examination question:—'assuming a world war, what number of cruisers would be required to protect all trade routes of British seaborne commerce simultaneously?' Yet this is what is being done, without any collaboration by any department of Government with the Admiralty.

Yours ever

G. L. Barstow

Lord Beatty to his wife

(*Beatty papers*)

3 February 1925

Today I had a long and wearisome day going over all the old ground, finishing up with 2½ hours with Winston very amicable and friendly, but he says it is a very difficult position and it is not easy to bring our differences into line. Wires and letters pass in profusion, but I am bewildered by the change of plans and by the many proposals. . . .

I am so infernally harassed at present by the Government over Estimates and Singapore which they are now at the 11th hour jibbing at that I have no time to turn round. . . .

Winston S. Churchill to Lord Beatty

(*Churchill papers: 22/68*)

4 February 1925   Treasury Chambers
Private and Personal

I send these suggestions in the hope of our being able to come together with a view to finding some way out of the difficulty. It would be a great relief I am sure to you to know that you could count on a steady £60 millions in future years. It is far more than I realised would come on the Exchequer and it means more than £4 millions above this year in a period when everyone was looking for reductions. This is the absolute limit on which I could agree. It is the maximum limit compatible with the finance.

If we cannot agree we shall have to wrangle it out, and in that case these suggestions, and anything you may say to me about them, must be treated as entirely between ourselves.

Suggestions

(1) FLEET REBUILDING.

Taking the Admiralty graph and the figures in my memorandum as a basis and taking the present estimate of expenditure, viz £55,800,000, as a starting point, the burden of new building in the next four years would not be insupportable if it were halved. It would still be very heavy—an average of £6 millions up in the three years after 1925. If nothing else were added or taken away this would give Estimates of £62 millions. But if you could find another couple of millions from your own interior I would try to do the rest and make plans for Naval Estimates on the basis of a flat £60 millions for those three years. Once I know that these three years would not exceed that figure (barring utterly unforeseen developments abroad) any further economies you could make from your own interior within the £60 millions limit could in principle be used by you either to increase your new building or for any other approved services to which you attached special importance.

What sort of a programme of rebuilding could be made within these limits. Clearly it would either be your existing forecast with a blank year left between each annual programme, or a succession of half programmes, or any variant of these you may work out in the best interests of the Navy.

(2) ABOUT CRUISERS.

I recognise the importance of your being willing to go to Washington with a proposal to reduce cruisers to what I call the 7 inch size. This would immensely simplify the whole problem of cruiser rebuilding having regard to the extra number we must keep. If you could put off the next batch of cruisers till the Nelson and Rodney have been finished that would be one way of achieving the spreading out of the burden of new building. On the other hand, if you attach great importance to including some cruisers (if only as a bargaining counter with the United States and Japan) in the new Estimate, and we can agree on the general position, I will support you over this to the extent of three, it being understood, as you told me, that none are laid down on the 10,000 ton basis until we know for certain that we cannot get agreement on the 7,000 limit. (I think you could anyhow allow the United States a few 10,000 ton cruisers as she has none so far and is not a rival so far as cruisers are concerned.)

(3) HOW TO FIND THE MONEY?

Obviously the rate at which the oil fuel reserve is built up is the first hope. Taking the figures given by the Admiralty on the attached sheet (B) as a basis, I suggest that the limit should be a round million tons of oil each year. You could divide this between Fleet steaming and reserve, say, in the proportion of 7 to 3. But of course you could at your discretion take a little more for the Fleet in any year and build up the reserve a little slower. The tankage would of course have to be kept ahead of the reserves but by special efforts the margin should be reduced as much as possible. It would of course be understood that the CID would have to put on record a decision to accept a slower building up of reserves. This policy would give us £700,000 in 1925 and nearly £2 millions each year after that.

(4) WORKS.

There is not much to be done on the present year about works, but, having regard to the great stringency in the future, surely it would be wise not to start big new works. A little money has been spent both on the Malta storehouses and the Devonport basin entrance, but the sums are so small that nothing serious can have been done. If these and a few more not so big can stand over till the existing works programme is further worked off there would be substantial relief in the future from that cause.

(5) VOTE A.

Any increase in Vote A will be marked down against us as definite Naval expansion. Moreover, the expense once incurred is irrevocable. Surely by accepting some scheme of immediate reserve, by perhaps accepting lower quarter bills, by working a proportion of ships on full nucleus or reduced nucleus crews, by considering the schools available (in certain circumstances) for the war Fleet on mobilisation, and having regard to the possibility of getting a reduction in the size of cruisers in the future, it ought to be possible to keep to 100,000 without any appreciable loss of efficiency or any change in our naval strength apparent to foreign Powers or our own Dominions. If this could be managed by clever administration it would put me in a position to meet your strong wishes on the principle of a marriage allowance, subject to consideration in detail compared to the other Services, which I understand the First Lord is quite ready to agree to. The reduction in the pay of new entrants, which has been generally accepted but requires adjusting as between the Services, will tend to relieve future years, though of course very slowly on Navy Votes.

(6) With regard to the general cut I asked for on this year's Estimates, outside specific reductions there cannot be very great difficulty. The shadow cut of £2,250,000 made last year, apart from any reduction in services, could be repeated. But in addition it ought to be possible to find three-quarters of a million from the 'interior'. It is no good telling me the First Sea Lord cannot do this if he lets it be known that it is his wish. Even when First Lord, as you know, I often found this amount and larger amounts in a few mornings with a blue pencil.

(7) I will look into the question of the war airship you spoke to me about. But anyhow another quarter of a million could, I am sure, be got off the Fleet Air Arm.

(8) There are no serious differences between us about Singapore. At the

most I am pressing for it to be developed on a 15 year basis instead of 10 or 12, which is the present tempo. The figures in the early years are, as you so often said, not very heavy, and for the year immediately before us they are, thanks to Hong Kong, practically nil.

To sum up, you gain £580,000 extra from the end of the terminable annuities and lose, say, £1 million on account of the Fleet Air Arm—call it £400,000 down. It ought to be possible with a net increase of £3¼ millions to get through this year making the net Estimate just about £59 millions and the gross Estimate about £62¾ millions.

If we could agree generally and you wanted another half million to veer and haul upon I should have to find it, or perhaps you could take a bit more on the shadow cut.

Lord Beatty to his wife
(Beatty papers)

4 February 1925

I have to tackle Winston and had 2½ hours with him this evening. It takes a good deal out of me when dealing with a man of his calibre with a very quick brain. A false step, remark, or even gesture is immediately fastened upon, so I have to keep my wits about me. We of course arrived at nothing, but I think I impressed upon him the difficulties of the situation from the Admiralty point of view, and how it comes to the fact that the Government must either reaffirm their policy or alter it.

We are working up a case for the Prime Minister to adjudicate on the differences which exist between us at the Admiralty and the Air Ministry. It is a question of vital importance to us, and therefore we have to be very careful in the preparation of the arguments.

Winston S. Churchill: Cabinet memorandum
(Churchill papers: 22/29)

4 February 1925   Treasury Chambers
Secret

INTER-ALLIED DEBTS

I circulate to my colleagues a final draft of the note to M Clémentel. 'To improve is to change; to be perfect is to have changed often!'

Unless I receive further suggestions by to-morrow night (Thursday) the note will be despatched in this form.

WSC

His Majesty's Government adheres to the principle of the Balfour note. Much of the substance of this note was repeated in Lord Curzon's note of the 11th August, 1923, more particularly in paragraphs 2 and 8 to 11 of the enclosure. But paragraphs 6 and 7 of the enclosure, which refer to Mr Bonar Law's proposals of January 1923, are clearly no longer applicable to the existing facts of the situation. These paragraphs were written before the framing of the Dawes plan and on the assumptions that the total German liability would be fixed at a figure less than that adopted in the Dawes plan, particularly in the earlier years, and that bonds of the kind contemplated in Mr Bonar Law's plan, with the rights of redemption given in that plan, would be issued. These assumptions are not now tenable. It follows that Lord Curzon's statement cannot, therefore, in this respect serve as a basis for the policy of His Majesty's Government.

The principle of the Balfour note is that Great Britain should receive from Europe payments equivalent to those she is under obligation to make to the United States of America. His Majesty's Government cannot accept a position in which this principle could only be achieved upon the basis of the full normal yield of the Dawes annuities or by taking at their face value debts which cannot be at present treated as good assets.

His Majesty's Government have already consented not merely to reduce their claims against the Allies to an amount necessary to cover their own payments in respect of the British war debt to the United States Government, but actually to apply the whole of the United Kingdom share of German reparations to that purpose. This means that Great Britain not only takes to her own charge the whole of her own war damages, but also the £800,000,000 of foreign securities devoted to the general effort before the United States entered the war.

In the application of the Balfour note to the existing situation, His Majesty's Government, remembering that war debts between Allies have been incurred in a common cause, have been prepared to consider proposals under which the existing French debt to Great Britain would be reduced provided that the principle of a definite payment by France from her own national resources, fixed with due regard to her relative wealth and tax-paying capacity, is assured without reference to reparations.

In the view of His Majesty's Government, therefore, it might be found convenient that the French payments should be divided into—

(*a*) Fixed annual amounts to be paid by France irrespective of the actual receipts from the Dawes annuities in a particular year; and

(*b*) A further annual charge on the French share in the Dawes annuities.

It would, of course, be understood, *first* that all counter-claims by France against Great Britain would be superseded, and, *secondly*, that if and when the payments derived by Great Britain from European War Debts and Reparations were sufficient to provide for the full discharge of the British obligations towards the United States over the full period of such obligations, including the payments already made, any surplus would be used to diminish the burden resting upon Britain's Allies.

His Majesty's Government entertain the hope that if the French Government were prepared to make proposals for a settlement on the lines here suggested, a solution satisfactory to both countries might be reached.

Winston S. Churchill to William Bridgeman

(*Churchill papers: 18/4*)

5 February 1925

My dear First Lord,

I had another long talk yesterday with Beatty, for whom, as you know, I have not only admiration but warm personal regard. In these circumstances our conversation could not be unpleasant. It was however utterly unfruitful. The only suggestion which the First Sea Lord was able to make was that the Admiralty Estimates for this year should be reduced to £63,500,000 by a shadow cut of £2 millions; that we should treat the million and a quarter for the Air Arm as outside the discussion, reducing them to £62¼; and that by great efforts the Admiralty would try to get off by genuine economies another three quarters of a million, thus reducing their Estimate to £61½. You will see for yourself that a shadow cut is of no value to the Exchequer. It only implies that the Admiralty will not be able to spend all the money they wish on the services for which they will have obtained approval; and if, of course, at the end of the year the Admiralty can make better progress in spending than they now hope, the Treasury, having assented to the services, will be bound to approve the necessary Supplementary Estimates. Although therefore the shadow cut is of great value in preventing over-budgeting, it has nothing to do with the question of Naval expenditure. So far as 'not counting the Fleet Air Arm' is concerned, the proposal obviously adds nothing to the discussion because whether the Fleet Air Arm is counted or not, it has to be paid for. For the rest, all that is left is a positive economy of three-quarters of a million. This in no way bridges the gulf between our two Departments and affords no basis for an agreement.

When I looked to the future, none of my misgivings about the Estimate for 1926/27 was removed. The First Sea Lord considers that the increase of 4,350 men on Vote A will be unavoidable for this year. But he is willing to consider other methods of manning for the future to reduce further potential increases. But these would not apply to the present year. On new construction I got no definite offer of any kind, not even the acceptance of the principle that the programme shown on your graph should be spread over double the number of years beginning with the present year.

It is quite clear that the matter must go to the Cabinet. After all, it is their money, not mine, which has to be distributed. If they like to spend all the available funds in the next few years on Naval development, if they think that necessary to the safety of the country and in accordance with our deepest political and national interests, it is for them to say so. Hankey seems to think that Monday will be a good day for the Cabinet. I can be quite ready by then.

With many thanks for your courtesy in putting me in direct touch with your First Sea Lord,

Yours very sincerely,
Winston S. Churchill

Lord Beatty to his wife
(*Beatty papers*)

5 February 1925   Admiralty

I am having the devil's own time over Singapore. For $2\frac{1}{2}$ solid hours we argued and talked over a question which was settled, and has been again raised principally with the object of gaining time and indeed wasting time. It is simply monstrous. . . . I had to stop writing to you and go and see the PM about the Estimates, and so brought this home with me and am writing after dinner. Little Bridgeman is leaving all the conversations about the Estimates with me. I do not think Winston will go into the last ditch, and although we are a long way apart just at the present we shall come together and find agreement somehow.

Curzon told me he went to see you, but was unfortunate not finding you in. He has been very useful to me, and supported me nobly, principally because he dislikes Winston, so that he finds pleasure in our continued opposition.

Winston S. Churchill to Stanley Baldwin

(*Churchill papers: 18/8*)

5 February 1925   Treasury Chambers
Secret

My dear PM,

You will remember our talk with Austen abt intercepts. I pointed out that even if the FO wished to keep the intercept circulation entirely to themselves, the Ch of E ought at the very least to have the same knowledge of these vital telegrams as is necessarily possessed by the spending Depts, the Admy & the WO, with wh he is in continual official contact. I understood you to say that you wd specially consider this aspect.

Nothing has happened since then to lead me to suppose that you have given any directions on the subject. I still receive from time to time an intercept relating to some money question. But I remain entirely ignorant of the information possessed by the Admiralty and War Office. For instance, last week when I was discussing the great & vital question of the Navy Estimates with the Admiralty representatives they quoted to me freely & extensively the telegrams which have passed between the Japanese Embassy & Government. These telegrams, they said, showed the true intentions & feelings of Japan, particularly in regard to cruisers in the event of another Washington Conference: how they were willing to discuss the maximum size but certainly not to bind themselves about numbers etc.

I concealed my ignorance of these essential matters as well as I could; for I thought it hardly becoming that the Ch of the Exchequer should shew himself at such a disadvantage in secret information with the subordinate representatives of a spending Department. But the unfairness & impropriety of such a situation will, I am sure, appeal to you. How can I conduct the controversies on which the management of our finances depends unless at least I have the same knowledge of secret state affairs freely accessible to the officials of the Admiralty? The words 'monstrous' & 'intolerable' leap readily to my mind. I prefer to bury them in the cooler word 'absurd'.

I do trust however that you will at least procure me the telegrams which relate to the grave issues now under discussion with the Admiralty; & I hope that you will decide that the Ch of the Exchequer shall not be less well informed from this source (whatever is reserved to the Foreign Office) than are the spending Departments with which he has to deal.

Yours very sincerely
Winston S. Churchill

Winston S. Churchill to Stanley Baldwin

(*Churchill papers: 18/10*)

5 February 1925   Treasury Chambers
Private

My dear PM,

This is pretty tough reading[1] and I only suggest that you should skim through it at this stage. It will show you how the great Design is ripening. On this basis all the benefits we spoke of would be realised for additional contributions of no more from the employer than 2d for men and *nothing* for women; and in the case of workers of no more than 2d for men and 1d for women. The above rates of course only apply to trades within the ambit of Unemployment Insurance. Still that is the bulk. For Agriculture and the rest the rates will be a little stiffer—though much less than was originally thought.

The matter will however take much adjustment between the different funds, and possibly the final decisions will not be quite so favourable.

Still—my feeling is like yours—Is it not too good to be true.

Well this is after all the Government Actuary![2]

Let me have the paper back please.

Yours sincerely,
Winston S. Churchill

Winston S. Churchill to Austen Chamberlain

(*Churchill papers: 18/10*)

6 February 1925   Treasury Chambers

Since you took office you have resigned the Chairmanship of the Committee on the Currency and Bank of England Note Issues. That Committee has now reported. I enclose you a copy of its Report. As you had the opportunity of hearing all the evidence and were responsible for guiding the Committee through the major part of its deliberations, I should be greatly obliged if you would let me know whether, or to what extent, you agree with its Report. The matter is one of considerable urgency, and decision on

[1] A report by the Government Actuary, Sir Alfred Watson, on the details of the new insurance scheme, setting out the benefits and their cost.

[2] Alfred William Watson, 1870–1936. Actuary to several Provident Institutions. Chief Actuary to the National Health Insurance Joint Committee, 1912–19. Knighted, 1915. Government Actuary, 1917–36. President of the Institute of Actuaries, 1920–2. Member of the Royal Commissions on Decimal Coinage and National Health Insurance.

the question of the Gold Standard cannot long be delayed; and before I offer a definite recommendation to the Cabinet, I feel entitled to ask you for your advice. I am very sorry of course to throw any additional burden on you, for I well know how laborious the work of the Foreign Office is, especially in times like these.[1]

Committee of Imperial Defence: minutes

(Churchill papers: 22/31)

6 February 1925

ARTILLERY FOR INDIAN STATES

MR CHURCHILL said that although the Viceroy and the Secretary of State for India were really the responsible authorities with regard to this question his view had not been changed by anything that he had heard. He had always resisted the distribution of modern technical equipment to Indians. There was no outside danger to Indian States and he saw no reason why their armament should be improved. If 15-pr guns were issued to Indian States now there would shortly be a demand for more modern guns and also in time for aeroplanes and similar new types of modern equipment so that in course of time stronger forces would be built up in India which, instead of being valuable for purposes of Imperial defence might become an actual embarrassment to the Government in India.

He drew attention to the state of affairs during the Mutiny when small bodies of Englishmen, provided they were able to collect together in some moderately strong building, were able to hold their own unless artillery was brought against them. It was of great value in a large country like India for the scattered European population to be able to collect in previously arranged places of safety where they would be secure against attacks not supported by modern equipment. He strongly deprecated the issue of these guns to Indian States.[2]

[1] Austen Chamberlain gave his approval to the return to the Gold Standard two days later (see page 388).

[2] During this meeting of the Committee of Imperial Defence, Lord Birkenhead said there was no risk to the proposal 'provided the supply of ammunition was retained in the hands of the Government'. General Birdwood, Commander-in-Chief of the Army in India, told the meeting: 'these guns were obsolescent, were not quick-firers, and it should be noted that their ammunition was of such a nature that it did not keep well'. Amery supported the proposal, as it would help 'encourage the loyalty of the Indian Chiefs'. Curzon objected to the proposal. The Committee decided to supply the guns, but not artillery 'of the latest pattern'. The minutes noted that 'The Chancellor of the Exchequer wished his dissent from this recommendation to be recorded'.

Winston S. Churchill: Cabinet memorandum[1]

(*Churchill papers: 22/30*)

7 February 1925
Secret

NAVY ESTIMATES

1. The paper circulated by the First Lord to-day will put very plainly before the Cabinet the reality and gravity of the Naval position towards which we are moving. It should be observed first of all that no attempt is made by the Admiralty to dispute the broad truth of the forecast of Naval expenditure set out by me on page 2 of my CP 39 (25). In this I stated that proceeding on the present lines 'the Naval Estimates for 1926–27 would be about £12 millions above those of 1925–26 and those of 1927–28 perhaps £7 millions higher still. This would give us gross Naval Estimates in 1926–27 of £81½ millions, in 1927–28 of £88½ millions and in 1928–29 of over £90 millions.' It is, of course, impossible to forecast the future Naval expenditure of the United States or Japan; but the expenditure for next year of the United States is approximately £60 millions and that of Japan in the current year is about £20 millions. There can be no dispute that a naval policy on this scale will completely absorb our whole available surplus from existing taxation, will prevent any remissions of taxation, not only now, but in the next three years, and will exclude from our programme any appreciable measures of social reform. There can be no dispute that in these circumstances Naval development will become virtually the sole policy of the Government and that all our efforts will be required to vindicate it.

2. Such an immense sacrifice and exertion could be justified only upon the clearest evidence of mortal peril. Parliament and the country would consent to the policy only if convinced of the reality of the peril. They could only be convinced through the full exposure by the Prime Minister and the Foreign Secretary of the profound and incurable character of the antagonism subsisting between Great Britain and Japan and of the increasing menace of the Japanese preparations. Such evidence was adduced before the war, under the necessary reserves of public statement, in regard to Germany. If an equal conviction of mortal peril from Japan is established in the public mind, I am sure the sacrifices will be made, and of course the money must be found. But nothing short of this will suffice to defend Naval expenditure on the scale now demanded.

3. I wish to give a precise definition of the expression 'mortal peril', viz, *a physical assault so sudden and so violent as to deprive Great Britain finally of the power to convert to war purposes the latent energy of the Empire.* This was, in fact,

---

[1] Circulated to the Cabinet as Cabinet paper 71 of 1925.

the peril we faced from Germany before the war. Great as are the injuries which Japan, if she 'ran amok', could inflict upon our trade in the Northern Pacific, lamentable as would be the initial insults which she might offer to the British flag, I submit that it is beyond the power of Japan, in any period which we need now foresee, to take any action which would prevent the whole might of the British Empire being eventually brought to bear upon her. And I believe that this fact, if true, will exercise a dominating influence on the extremely sane and prudent counsels which we have learned over a long period of time to expect from the Japanese Government.

4. Against 'mortal perils' one must always be prepared, so far as national strength will go. We must, at all costs, be able to see our way, albeit through years of suffering, to a reasonable prospect of ultimate victory. But once the peril is not of a mortal character, the whole argument falls to a very important, but none the less secondary plane. We have to balance annoyance against expenditure, two or three years of vexation against many years of penury. And in casting such balances one is bound to consider not only the *degree*, but the *probability* of the danger. The First Lord in his Introductory Note seems to claim that the Admiralty must be the judge of the probabilities of war with Japan. I submit that in this sphere the Foreign Office have the prevailing voice. It is for them to judge whether deep and active antagonism exists between this country and Japan, or between any groups of Powers with which the fortunes of Great Britain or Japan are inextricably involved. Such antagonisms were plainly apparent between Great Britain and Germany and between the Triple Entente and the Triple Alliance for a long period before the war. If the Foreign Secretary considers that a conflict between Great Britain and Japan may well be inevitable, it is for him so to apprise the Cabinet; and it is for the Cabinet to prescribe to the Admiralty the responsibilities which are laid upon them in the circumstances. I demur to the claim of the Admiralty to judge the foreign situation.

5. I therefore submit to the Cabinet, first, that we are not in 'mortal peril' (as above defined) from Japan; secondly, that the statements of the Foreign Secretary to the Committee of Imperial Defence, supported by Lord Curzon, on the probability of a war with Japan ought to be taken as the ruling data on this subject; and, thirdly, that nothing less than clear proof of (a) 'mortal peril' or (b) the probability of war within a certain period will be sufficient to satisfy Parliament of the need to side-track all other aims of policy in favour of a vast naval expenditure.

6. Passing from these general observations, I address myself to certain points of detail arising from the Admiralty paper.

The tables on page 9 do not give a true picture of relative naval strengths, actual and potential. Take, for instance, *Cruisers*. It is true that Japan has laid down 18 cruisers since 1919. It is misleading to state that Great Britain has only increased her strength in the same period by laying down 5. We have, in fact, completed since the war 3 cruisers of 9,750 tons, these being incomparably the most powerful modern cruisers afloat in the world; we are completing another of 9,750 tons and two of 7,550 tons, and we are building 5 more of 10,000 tons. *These 11 British cruisers aggregate 104,100 tons; the 18 Japanese cruisers aggregate 102,230.* But the picture of relative naval strength cannot be understood if comparison is limited to the years since the war. During the war the Japanese arsenals were profitably occupied in making munitions for the Allies, and in the 5 years preceding 1919 Japan laid down only 2 cruisers. In the same period Great Britain laid down or completed no less than 32.[1] Therefore, taking a ten-year period, the total would become—

	Tons
Japan 20 cruisers, aggregating	109,230
Great Britain 43, aggregating	236,140

7. Again, consider the *Aircraft Carriers.* The Admiralty table on page 9 would seem to indicate that Japan possessed or was about to possess 3, the United States 2, while Great Britain was only converting 3. What are the facts? Great Britain at the present time has 4, the United States and Japan have each 1 small vessel. By the time that Japan and the United States have 3 each we shall have 6, with another completing. Very intricate arguments may be employed on either side upon the qualities of these various aircraft carriers, and the dates at which they will be commissioned for service. I will not complicate this paper with their discussion. I court an examination of the statement that our lead and superiority over either the United States or Japan in aircraft carriers and generally in naval aviation is not less marked than the figures here set out suggest.

8. I did not and do not contest the argument that further submarine construction is necessary. After all, a submarine is the only vessel in the Admiralty new construction programme (costing £21½ millions) which can strike a decisive blow at a capital unit. All the rest of that immense expense is devoted to ancillaries. None of it would count in that estimate of the strength of Navies on which the prestige and effectiveness of British diplomacy to a great extent depends through long years of peace.

9. The Admiralty paper on page 12 sets forth very truly the great shrinkage of our Fleet from the scale reached on the eve of the war with Germany. In 1914 we were able to maintain in the First and Second Fleets on the basis of full active service crews in war, 45 battleships, 7 battle cruisers and 60

[1] Churchill added a footnote at this point: 'Excluding the quasi-Battle-cruisers *Courageous, Furious* and *Glorious*, which are to be converted into aircraft carriers.'

cruisers; whereas now we are only maintaining 17 battleships, 3 battle cruisers, 32 cruisers and 10 flotilla leaders in the same status. Moreover, in 1914 we had 151,000 men in Vote A, as against 100,000 now. And finally, we had a new construction vote of £18½ millions, as against a new construction vote this year of less than £7 millions. In 1914 the enormous fleet and new construction were maintained at a cost of no more than £51½ millions nett; whereas the far smaller Fleets and Establishments of to-day cost in the present year nearly £56 millions. If we deduct from each of these totals the respective new construction votes, the comparable figures become £33 millions in 1914 and £49 millions in 1925. In other words, the general expense of naval administration has advanced so greatly that it costs in 1925 half as much again to maintain less than half the Fleets of 1914. Thus one might say that the cost of the Naval services in proportion to resultant war power has advanced more than three times beyond pre-war conditions. Of course, the cost of everything has gone up. The index figure ruling over the general field is 180 compared to 100 pre-war. But the index figure of Naval economy has deteriorated from 100 to something between 300 and 400. Making every allowance for the growth of non-effective votes, I am convinced that this altogether disproportionate increase in the cost of Naval power is largely due to the natural wish of the Admiralty to have everything superfine and perfect, to multiply every factor of safety at every stage, and to deny themselves nothing which they feel will improve the material and moral efficiency of the great instrument over which they preside.

10. The Admiralty are indisposed to reduce their demands for an addition of 4,350 men to Vote A. I am sure that there are at least half a dozen modes of manning the existing Fleet in peace or war on a basis of 100,000 officers and men. I have shown how the pre-war *war* complements of existing ships were greatly below their present *peace* complements, and still more below their approved super-war complements. A revision of the quarter bill of ships in commission, together with the same employment on mobilisation of the men of the Schools and shore establishments as was enforced in 1914, would enable our present Fleet to be maintained in a high standard of commission. But if this were not so, a small diminution of our cruisers on foreign service or of our ships maintained in full commission, and a transference of these vessels to something like the old Second Fleet scale, would provide the necessary saving in man power for peace purposes. The revival of the system of 'immediate reserves' for a portion of these ships might well be accepted on mobilisation in the strategic and political circumstances which prevail.

11. When we come to man power the Admiralty comparisons shift from Japan to the United States. They assert that the United States has 115,100

personnel,[1] and they are astonished at their moderation in asking for an increase of 4,350. But the United States terms of service are on a far lower scale than the British. Their men are enlisted for two, three, four or six years, with the option of re-engaging. Ours all serve for twelve years and a large proportion continue for twenty-one. There can be no comparison between complements containing a large proportion of men serving for only two, three and four years, with complements composed entirely of life-long professionals. We must further remember, when reviewing the personnel of the United States Navy for the purpose of a one-power standard, the enormous reserves of trained officers and men and the seafaring population which this island possesses. Finally, it is worth noting that in this year, when we are asked to increase our numbers by 4,350, the United States is proposing a reduction of 1,500.

---

12. I conclude by a general observation. I accept the *One-Power Standard*. I do not interpret that standard as meaning that we should maintain at least an equality in regard to the strongest points in both the American and Japanese navies. I do not interpret that standard in the sense that we should maintain a one-power standard against the United States and, in addition, be capable of levying war upon Japan in her own quarter of the globe. The one-power standard ought to be interpreted as the maintenance by us of a navy which will not, as a whole, be inferior or will not be regarded by foreign Powers or our Dominions as inferior to the navy of any other power, similarly considered as a whole.

Endless arguments can no doubt be raised on the different factors going to make up the naval strength of any country. Surely on the whole the truest measure ought to be the money provision. The pay of the personnel of the United States Navy is nearly double our own. By a frugal and searching employment of our naval funds we ought to be able to realise with the same sum of money a far higher development of war power than is possible in the United States. Japan, on the other hand, has very cheap labour and very cheap personnel; but the Japanese estimates are less than £20 millions in the present year and show a reduction to £18¼ millions for 1925–26. I cannot believe that on the basis of £57½ millions nett for 1925–26 and a rise to not more than £60 millions (including the Fleet Air Arm) in 1926–27 and succeeding years, it will not be possible for us to make adequate provision for Imperial Naval Defence. But to achieve these figures it is imperative (1) that there must be no serious commitments in new construction or new works which will be uncontrollable next year, (2) that there can be

---

[1] Churchill noted at this point: 'The US official figure seems to be 105,500.'

no addition to the numbers of men, and (3) that the accumulation of the Oil Fuel reserve must be spread over at least double the length of time now prescribed.

WSC

Austen Chamberlain to Winston S. Churchill

(*Treasury papers: T171/245*)

8 February 1925

I have read with profound interest and with complete agreement the report of the Currency Committee. They have exactly represented our views and our position up to the point in the summer when we decided to adjourn over the holidays without presenting a report in order that we might watch a little longer the development of events. Even then I had no doubt in my own mind of our power to restore and maintain the gold standard, but it seemed likely that there would be an early appreciation of the £ such as has taken place, and that it would be accompanied by at any rate some assimilation of price levels which would mitigate, if it did not altogether remove, the immediate difficulties of adjustment.

The subsequent course of events has fulfilled our expectations and in my opinion the committee are absolutely right in their recommendations. They are bound to take note of the possibilities and to make provision for them, but I feel sure that, if you make your announcement with *decisive confidence* on your part, the operation will now be found, all things considered, a very early omen and that to delay your decision much longer would be to expose you to a serious risk of a renewed fall in sterling. All the world is now expecting us to return to the gold standard and has become convinced that we can do it. If we do not do it we shall not stay where we were but inevitably start a *retrograde movement*.

Lord Rothermere to Winston S. Churchill

(*Churchill papers: 2/141*)

12 February 1925   South of France

My dear Winston,

I am here for a few days.

Be like an avenging angel. Spread terror and dismay in the ranks of the squandermaniacs.

Have you carefully considered that some of the sources of revenue are slowly but surely drying up? Are we not losing the heavy trades—iron & steel—shipbuilding—some forms of engineering with a big decline in coal exports? In my opinion in the year 1927—if not 1926—you will have to retrace any step you may take this year in tax reduction and not only reimpose the taxes you have reduced or taken off but impose further taxation.

It really looks every economic thing in England is going wrong. We are an old fashioned people whose leisurely methods are quite unsuited to the era of intensive competition which is now setting in.

We jibe at the Bricklayers Union. It takes three British bricklayers to do the work of one French bricklayer. But then it takes three British Ministers to do the work of one French Minister. When there is a change of Government in France eighteen new Ministers replace eighteen old Ministers. With us sixty Ministers replace the outgoing sixty Ministers. Yet France has a more centralised Government and her colonial foreign and defence problems are very much the same as ours.

Yours
Harold R.

Lord Beaverbrook to Lord Rothermere

(*Beaverbrook papers*)

12 February 1925

Winston came to dine with me the other night. He is a firm supporter of Baldwin and his debt settlement. He criticises [Lloyd] George very freely for the wicked Irish Treaty and declares that the Coalition Government ought to have continued to prosecute the war against Sinn Fein for another winter. I tried to shame him into acknowledgment of his leading part in making the Treaty. It is not easy to succeed.

I think he is over-hostile to Austen Chamberlain and sure to have a bust-up with that gentleman before long.

I hear that Lord Birkenhead proposes to give artillery to Bikaner[1] and to one or two other trusted Rajahs. Churchill is opposed very strongly and to the point of bad feeling between himself and Birkenhead.

[1] The Maharaja of Bikaner, 1880–1943. Succeeded as Maharaja at the age of seven; granted rank of Major in the British army, 1900; served in China, 1901; in charge of the Bikaner Camel Corps; knighted, 1901; represented India at the Imperial War Cabinet, 1917, and the Paris Peace Conference, 1919; led the Indian delegation to the League of Nations, 1930; first Chancellor of the Chamber of Princes, 1921–6; promoted General, 1927; Chancellor of Benares Hindu University, 1929–43; his Camel Corps was one of the famous martial sights of the sub-continent.

On the other hand, Chamberlain is supporting strongly the policy of Allenby in Egypt, which involves, I am told, another evacuation of Cairo. Birkenhead has supported Chamberlain and Baldwin has given his assent to the Foreign Office policy. Churchill, however, is bitterly opposed to it and gets much encouragement from the extreme group represented by those who support your North of Ireland policy for instance.

Lord Cecil of Chelwood to Winston S. Churchill

(*Churchill papers: 22/68*)

12 February 1925
Confidential

My dear Winston,

I am very sorry you thought I was jingo this morning, but it really is not so. I saw that the Cabinet was practically unanimously against Willy, and as he is a very old friend of mine I did not want to bear too hardly on him, since there was no danger of his views being adopted.[1]

As to the Washington Conference, my hesitation was due to this fact. It looks very much as if the League Conference on disarmament will be either discouraged or actually turned down by the Government. If at the same time they welcome a Conference at Washington I am afraid of the effect on League prestige. I quite realised after consideration that that is not sufficient reason for rejecting the possibility of a Washington Conference, but the event coming after several of the same tendency is unlucky. People are always saying to me that you must not put too much on the League until it has acquired reputation and position, and though I do not myself see any danger of the League undertaking too much, yet I recognise the force of the objec-

[1] At an earlier Cabinet on 11 February 1925 a majority of Ministers had agreed to Churchill's upper limit of £60 millions a year for all naval expenditure for several years. Baldwin sought to assuage Bridgeman's discontent by setting up a special Cabinet Committee under Lord Birkenhead to examine the whole question of future naval construction; but Bridgeman still insisted that no formal decision be reached until his naval advisers had been heard, and later that afternoon, having discussed the proposals with the Admiralty Board, he wrote to Baldwin threatening both his own and his Board's resignation unless a programme of four new cruisers to be laid down in 1925 were accepted without delay, 'subject to its modification later on'. Should the Board resign, Bridgeman added, 'I believe a very large proportion of our party will sympathise with their attitude'. But when the Cabinet reconvened on the morning of February 12 only Lord Cecil of Chelwood had supported Bridgeman's request, and Bridgeman had to agree, reluctantly, not to authorize any new construction 'at this stage', but to abide by the decisions of the proposed Cabinet Committee. He also agreed that the precise sum to be spent on the Navy in 1925–6 should be decided, not by the Cabinet, but by Baldwin, Churchill and himself (*Cabinet papers: 23/49*).

tion, for after all the League is out to do one of the biggest things that have ever been done in the history of the world. No one more than myself is conscious of the very many chances there are that the League might fail, and I am quite sure it cannot afford to give away the least point if it is to succeed. There are a good many of my colleagues who are intellectually favourable to the League but who are not prepared to take any really active or efficient steps in its support. That seems to me a very dangerous attitude of mind, and you must forgive me if I sometimes seem too anxious on the other side.

Yours ever,
Cecil

Winston S. Churchill to Lord Cecil of Chelwood: not sent
(*Churchill papers: 22/68*)

13 February 1925   Treasury Chambers

Many thanks for your letter. Others formed the same impression as I did as to the character of your advice, and I am very glad to know that we were mistaken.

The position is simple and serious. If the Navy Estimates go up by £6 or £7 millions this year and by another £8 or £9 millions next year (as is inevitable if certain decisions are taken), it will be idle for Great Britain to talk about Disarmament or a peaceful settlement of International disputes. We shall be leading the world in Naval expenditure and making active preparations to conduct a war against Japan in her own waters. This will reduce our position on the League of Nations to pure hypocrisy, and of course we shall be stigmatised by all the League of Nations people in this country as a Jingo Militarist Government. It is quite true that the overwhelming majority of the Cabinet take the Prime Minister's view against extraordinary Naval expenditure and are in favour of striking a note of peace and retrenchment at the outset of our career. But are they not right in this? Is it not a sure instinct which prompts them? Is it any kindness to a colleague to encourage him in an unwise direction, or ought kindness to come in in matters of such moment?

Again, is not your attitude about a Washington Conference rather like saying: 'If the League can't have their Disarmament Conference, no one else should have one'? When the issues at stake affect the whole outlook of the world, surely no feeling of *amour propre* as to the instruments employed for a good end ought to stand in the way of practical action. There is no comparison whatever between Naval armaments and Military. There are only three Naval Powers worth considering. America and Japan are building against each other; and we building against both. Every cruiser laid down by any one of the three starts the other two off; and this again re-acts on the original builder. A Conference between these Powers to reduce the size of vessels and to regulate and limit as far as possible the rate of Fleet replacements, is an obvious necessity. It is to the interest of all the three Naval Powers concerned to effect such an agreement which, while safeguarding their individual interests, reduces their common expenditure.

Things are entirely different with Armies, and all centre round the French anxieties about Germany. To insist on keeping Naval agreements waiting until Military agreements can be reached, to insist on preventing good partial agreements because one is in love with grand universal agreements, is surely no course to which you would lend your conscientious effort.

Forgive this lengthy letter but you know I weigh very carefully everything you write to me.

Winston S. Churchill to Austen Chamberlain

(*Austen Chamberlain papers*)

13 February 1925   Treasury Chambers
Private & Personal

My dear Austen,

I think the Soudan should pay back the £160,000 for Barracks when their finance allows. They will be quite rich some day, & able to meet their own loan charges. Subject to this, I accept your proposals, & am vy much obliged to you for having met the Treasury view to so great an extent. The simplest method of obtaining the money is to put £160,000 additional grant-in-aid in your Estimates (in the same way as the half million just voted).

I think it vy important not to encourage the War Office to come into the Soudan. None of these places—Nigeria (as you will remember)—Iraq & Palestine in more recent years—can stand the weight of the brass-hats. If they come to build these barracks, I am sure they will cost double what a local administration could build for. They are even now trying to get rid of Huddleston[1] in order to put a proper Major-General, with appropriate

---

[1] Hubert Jervoise Huddleston, 1880–1950. On active service in South Africa, 1899–1902, in the Sudan, 1910, and in the European War, 1914–18 (MC, DSO, CMG). Brigadier-General, 1918. General Officer Commanding Sudan, 1924–30. Major-General, 1933. Commanded Presidency District, Eastern Command, India, 1934–5; Baluchistan District, Western Command, 1935–8. Governor-General of the Sudan, 1940–7. Knighted, 1940.

retinue, into the billet. I should have thought that the cheapest way of keeping the Soudan was to let Trenchard run it as he does Iraq. It is astonishing that there is no flight of aeroplanes at Khartoum.

All these views are for your personal eye alone. An official letter will be written when your official letter arrives.

Yours very sincerely
Winston S. Churchill

Committee of Imperial Defence: minutes

(*Churchill papers: 22/31*)

13 February 1925

MR CHURCHILL: I seem to gather in the last few sentences exchanged across the table between the Foreign Secretary and the Chancellor of the Duchy they were both in agreement that we should send an answer and say we cannot accept the Protocol.[1]

LORD CECIL: In its present form.

MR CHURCHILL: I agree with that entirely.

LORD CURZON: That is the proposal of the Committee. It is contained in the latter part of their report.

MR CHURCHILL: I also agree with the Chancellor of the Duchy that the proposals of the Committee are not in themselves, a satisfactory basis for us to proceed upon. Great efforts have been made to find a solution by the Committee, but the solution is so moderate and so modest necessarily in the attempt to limit the liability of this country that it would never be taken by France as any substitute for strong national armaments. I feel we are really back where we were when this was first discussed here when the Government was formed and we looked at the original proposals of the Protocol.

We do not feel we should be justified in taking these great burdens upon the country in the absence of the United States. That is at the bottom of everybody's mind and at the back of the arguments of every department. Indefinite as are the liabilities, great as are the dangers, it might be worth

---

[1] A special Sub-Committee of the Committee of Imperial Defence, chaired by Sir Maurice Hankey, had examined the proposed League of Nations Protocol in detail in a twenty-eight-page report presented to the Committee of Imperial Defence on 23 January 1925 (CID paper 559-B). The Protocol, which had been under discussion for nearly a year, included among its proposals several items which this Sub-Committee, and subsequently the Cabinet, decided to reject 'entirely': compulsory arbitration, suspension of all defensive measures during proceedings for a peaceful settlement, and the maintenance 'in all circumstances' of the territorial integrity of all States (*Churchill papers: 22/31*).

while to run the risk if the whole fighting power of the United States were added to our own and all the friends we can get together in Europe. Without that we cannot come to any other conclusion really than the one everyone has come to now and which everyone had in their minds when the subject was first discussed. But when you come to the question of what answer you should send, how you can convey this conclusion to the outer world, you have the choice between sending a reasoned answer and sending a laconic answer.

We have all agreed we won't send an insincere answer, an answer putting the thing off for a few more months, making people think we have a wonderful scheme, when as a matter of fact we have all arrived at a different conclusion and a very negative conclusion. But as between a reasoned answer and a laconic answer I am strongly in favour of a reasoned answer.

LORD CURZON: At this stage?

MR CHURCHILL: At this stage, I am strongly in favour of a reasoned answer. First of all, because I think that a reasoned answer will tend to bring the United States public opinion more and more into line with our own. Lord Cecil does not agree, but I have an opposite opinion on that point, and I think that Lord Balfour's despatch, although I quite agree you might easily have to consider the answer to particular arguments, I think it is conceived from the point of view of gathering together a great volume of opinion not only throughout Great Britain and the United States, but throughout the British Empire. I believe if that despatch were read in Australia, in Canada, in New Zealand, as well as over wide areas of the United States, where after all Lord Balfour has shown himself an unequalled judge of American public opinion in the great matters he has handled over there,[1] I believe if this despatch were read—it may be altered—it would command a very great measure of comprehension and agreement. People would see our difficulties. They would see the justice of our case, and they would also see how vital it is for the United States to take a hand in this business, to come and shoulder their portion of the burden, if the world is to be saved from a renewal of these dangers. I am in favour of a reasoned despatch, not in these words, but on these lines.

Then I must say a word on the question to which the Foreign Secretary

[1] In April 1917, immediately following the entry of the United States into the war, Balfour had gone to Washington as head of a special diplomatic mission, in the course of which he revealed to Woodrow Wilson the existence of Britain's secret treaties with Russia and Italy— treaties which ran counter to the principle of nationality which was an integral part of 'Wilsonian' democracy. He also spoke before Congress, and played an important part in promoting the closest possible Anglo-American co-operation.

attached so much importance. Lord Cecil talks of the Protocol as being a sort of great foundation on which you can make your peace if it can be carried through, but he admitted you must have subsidiary agreements in order to procure disarmament. But it is the subsidiary agreements which are really the solid thing. They are really the solid thing, and I always argue you had far better approach the general conclusions you have in view, the grand conceptions, by taking practical steps along the line of getting first one and then another of these regional agreements, and then welding them together in the structure of a much greater agreement when the world is more reasonable and more peacefully disposed and more balanced than at the present time. I think that is the practical part, but I must admit that I feel it is a tremendous thing to ask the people of this country now, at this juncture, to bind themselves to go to war on the side of France without leaving to us a very full latitude of judging the circumstances and occasion of the quarrel. I have a little changed in my view.

MR AUSTEN CHAMBERLAIN: As far as I have contemplated an arrangement it would be one which would leave and must leave the British Government absolute judge of whether we should act or not, and the Belgian Ambassador[1] told me yesterday that is the character of the arrangement between France and Belgium to-day.

MR CHURCHILL: I do not wish to misrepresent that in any way, but I have a little changed in my view. I was three years ago firm in the wish that we should make good, as it were, the understanding to France on which she gave up her claim to the Rhine frontier, even in the default of the United States. I think that all the experiences we went through in the Poincaré epoch and a good deal we see in French policy at the present time makes one feel there is a tremendous risk in our being involved in that way in a policy which will simply keep alive this antagonism between Germany and France. France, with us, would feel strong enough to keep the antagonism alive, and after all, that is what is going to shatter the peace of the world. That is the danger. This war which has occurred between France and Germany several times has broken up the world. What guarantee have we got while things are going as they are that we shall not have another war. In fact, it seems as if we were moving towards it, although it may not be for twenty years, certainly not until Germany has been able to acquire some methods of waging war, chemically or otherwise. I do not think it is good enough at the present time for us to make a pact *à deux* with France. With all the disadvantages there are to the opposite course, I would be reluctant to see us do that now. On the

[1] Baron Moncheur, Belgian Ambassador to London from 1918 to 1928.

other hand, I think if you could get a real peace between France and Germany, it might be worth our while for that purpose and as part of that to run the great risks involved in signing a new instrument or making a new arrangement. I believe there is a large volume of opinion among thinking men in France which holds that France will be destroyed in another war unless she can make some sort of lasting arrangement of a friendly character with Germany. Of course, I see that cannot be done without a recasting of the arrangements of the Treaty of Versailles as far as the oriental frontiers of Germany are concerned. That again raises questions of the utmost difficulty and questions you could not solve in a few weeks or a few months. I am in favour of our not giving ourselves to France at this stage, but of our indicating that if as part of an arrangement between the three great nations we might well come in as a guarantor or as a partner. If you could, for instance, get France and Germany to make a real peace out of which Germany undoubtedly got not only the immediate evacuation of territories which are being held, but a substantial rectification of her Eastern frontiers, if you could get that, then I think the weight of England might well be thrown in to make that solid and enable it to be achieved. I do not think it is quite so absurd as it sounds. I had a talk to M Briand[1] when I was in Paris, and I found he had been for some time whole-heartedly in favour of that. At all events, it would avoid our being committed at this stage to an engagement which I am sure would cause enormous misgivings and anxiety throughout wide circles here. I say that, though in public I have defended the signing of a pact.

LORD BALFOUR: I understand in a certain sense the immediate question in front of us is between a brief answer and a reasoned answer. Can you avoid the sending of a reasoned answer whatever you do? In fact, will it not be much worse if you send it in the form of the report of a debate. I am not a member of the House of Commons now, but you cannot avoid a debate on the subject, and if you have a debate you must give your reasons.

MR AUSTEN CHAMBERLAIN: I think it is essential to have a reasoned answer, because otherwise there would be a debate on it and I should have to answer with infinitely less skill amidst all the difficulties of the House of Commons; I should state the reasons there infinitely worse than

[1] Aristide Briand, 1862–1932. French politician. Minister of Public Instruction and Worship, 1906–9. Prime Minister, 1909–10. Minister of Justice, 1912–13. Prime Minister, January–March 1913. Minister of Justice, 1914. Prime Minister, October 1915–March 1917. Prime Minister and Minister of Foreign Affairs, January 1921–January 1922. Minister of Foreign Affairs, April–July 1925. Prime Minister, November 1925–July 1926. Minister of Foreign Affairs, 1926–32. Awarded the Nobel Peace Prize for his part in the Locarno Agreements, 1926. Prime Minister for the sixth time, July–October 1929.

we shall state them in a form which has been passed by this Committee and the Cabinet.

MR AMERY: A reasoned despatch, giving reasons against signing, but not containing our future constructive policy?

MR AUSTEN CHAMBERLAIN: No.

MR AMERY: That was what I mean. We do not want to give our future policy.

LORD BALFOUR: I was only going to say I am afraid that the idea of tearing up the Treaty of Versailles and altering the frontiers of Poland and Czechoslovakia—I think we ought to put that on one side. I think it is hopeless.[1]

Winston S. Churchill to William Bridgeman

(*Churchill papers: 18/4*)

13 February 1925   Treasury Chambers

My dear First Lord,

This is only to remind you of my understanding of the way we finished up. We have agreed on the figure 60½, and you are going to make proposals for achieving this. It is agreed that there shall be an increase in Vote A, but much less than the 4,350. What exactly is the figure you now propose, you are going to let me know on Monday before we finally agree.

Ditto you will tell me about new works opening great commitments in future years.

Lastly the Marriage Allowance is to be co-ordinated with the other services as the result of an interdepartmental Committee of the Ministers concerned, which will in addition consider the pay of new entrants in all three services and bring the Departments into line.

Yours very sincerely,
Winston S. Churchill

[1] Following this meeting of the Committee of Imperial Defence, a letter was drafted in the Foreign Office to be sent from Austen Chamberlain to the League of Nations. The letter contained the sentence: '. . . if the danger should seriously threaten, they believe that the best way to meet it is not to stiffen the terms of the Covenant, but to provide special machinery for dealing with a special emergency. Examples of such machinery are already in existence. They consist essentially of defensive agreements, contracted under the aegis of the League, by States which conceive themselves, for whatever reason, to be in a position of peculiar peril'. Churchill redrafted this sentence to read: '. . . if the danger should seriously threaten, they believe that the best way to meet it is not to stiffen the terms of the Covenant, but to provide special machinery for dealing with a special danger, contracted under the aegis of the League, between States whose differences have in the past led to disastrous wars. Such machinery might comprise agreements for mutual defence and reassurance' (*Churchill papers: 22/31*).

William Bridgeman to Winston S. Churchill

(*Churchill papers: 18/4*)

13 February 1925   Admiralty

My dear Chancellor,

Your letter of today coincides with my understanding of what was settled this afternoon, subject to the following exception—viz that the question of the amount of Marriage Allowances is referred to a coordinating Committee presided over by an independent Cabinet Minister, and not to an inter-departmental Committee of Ministers. This was the arrangement to which I understood the PM to agree when I talked it over with him.

There is further proviso that if we exceed the £60,500,000 owing to greater progress on contract work, the Treasury undertake to make that good up to the £2,000,000 of the Shadow Cut by a Supplementary Estimate.

Yrs sincerely
W. C. Bridgeman

Winston S. Churchill to William Bridgeman

(*Churchill papers: 18/4*)

13 February 1925   Treasury Chambers

My dear First Lord,

I don't mind much about the form of the Committee on Marriage Allowances and I have no doubt we shall agree upon it. Of course it is understood that if the shadow-cut is not realised I must find the balance by Supplementary. On the other hand it is understood that the Admiralty made no undue effort to get rid of their money. I have no doubt Oswyn Murray and Barstow will know how to interpret this understanding.

You are going to let me see on Monday your revised plan of reaching £60½ millions and it is understood between us that our agreement is provisional until the figure of Vote A is settled.

Yours very sincerely,
Winston S. Churchill

William Bridgeman to Winston S. Churchill

(*Churchill papers: 18/4*)

14 February 1925   Admiralty
Private

My dear Chancellor,

Thanks for your second letter of yesterday.

I assure you we shall do everything we can to avoid having to draw upon the £2 million of the shadow cut: but the matter rests more with the contractors and their workmen than with us.

I am trying to make the reductions you ask for & to which we agreed, as far as possible in works which though not requiring very large expense this year do involve heavy future commitments.

You may rely upon my making every endeavour to use the time before us this year in investigating every possible means of economy and the staff here including the Parly Secretary[1] & Civil Lord[2] are genuinely anxious to avoid any extravagance.

I hope to let you have our proposals for meeting the reductions by Monday. We are going as far as we can to meet your wishes on Vote A—but the Sea Lords feel very strongly about it.

Yrs v sincerely
W. C. Bridgeman

Winston S. Churchill to William Bridgeman

(*Churchill papers: 18/4*)

16 February 1925   Treasury Chambers

My dear First Lord,

Many thanks for your letter and particularly for what you say about the way in which you and your Parliamentary colleagues will try to reduce unnecessary expenditure by a strict overhaul during the year. It is surely in

[1] J. C. C. Davidson, Parliamentary Secretary at the Admiralty from 1924 to 1927 (see page 235, note 1).

[2] James Richard Stanhope, 1880–1967. Educated at Eton and Magdalen College, Oxford. Grenadier Guards, 1901–8. Succeeded his father as 7th Earl Stanhope, 1905. Served with the Grenadier Guards in France, 1914–18 (despatches twice, Military Cross, 1916, DSO, 1917). Parliamentary Secretary, War Office, 1918–19. Civil Lord of Admiralty, 1924–9. Privy Councillor, 1929. Under-Secretary of State for War, 1931–4. Parliamentary Under-Secretary of State for Foreign Affairs, 1934–6. First Commissioner of Works, 1936–7. President of the Board of Education, 1937–8. First Lord of the Admiralty, 1938–9. Leader of the House of Lords, 1938–40. Lord President of the Council, 1939–40. His only brother, a Captain in the Grenadier Guards, was killed in action in France on 16 September 1916.

the interests of the Navy to concentrate on the rugged essentials of strength rather than upon a meticulous perfection or a standard of immediate readiness. A saving of 5 or 6 millions on existing charges would go very far towards meeting the problem of finding funds for new shipbuilding by the time Nelson and Rodney are completed without increase of total cost to the country.

Marriage Allowances. I should be ready to agree to a Committee of three of our colleagues not concerned in the fighting Departments to decide whether any and if so what augmentation is required to remove the alleged injustice to Naval Officers relatively to the other Services. I must make it clear that in assenting to this Committee the Treasury do not debar themselves from arguing the case before the Committee against an increase. I am however quite willing if you are, to accept the decision of the Committee provided that it is limited to 'levelling up' and does not involve new increases in the Army and Air. The Committee would also of course adjust the difference between the three fighting services and the Treasury about the pay and allowances of new entrants. Pray let me know that we are in agreement.

Yours very sincerely,
Winston S. Churchill

Winston S. Churchill: departmental memorandum[1]

(*Churchill papers: 18/12*)

16 February 1925

It was not the purpose of this taxation to ruin the producing power, but only to reclaim for the State a share in excess profits. It is contrary to public policy, and on the face of it absurd, that great Companies should go bankrupt because they cannot pay excess profits. Sir Richard Hopkins tells me that the Inland Revenue could not press these Companies for years, and would allow them an indefinite time to pull round. This practice of the Inland Revenue recognises the principle I have set out above. Why then does the difficulty arise in this case? It arises because the Companies wish to reconstruct. If they cannot reconstruct, they will go into liquidation; and they cannot reconstruct without affecting our claims. Then I am told that if they go into liquidation, we shall obtain £250,000 from the ruin. If, however, they reconstruct, our claim will be reduced in rank and value. If the

[1] Circulated to Sir Richard Hopkins (Chairman of the Board of Inland Revenue) and to Walter Guinness (Financial Secretary to the Treasury).

Companies prosper, it will be many years before we receive anything. If, as is thought at least likely, they fail, we shall get much less than we are getting now.

I cannot form any opinion on this difficult question without more knowledge.

(a) What will be the cost of the bankruptcy proceedings? How, for instance, do we get our £250,000? What process of sale or auction will be employed, and what real assets are available?

(b) What form would the new reconstruction take, and what are the chances of its revival?

(c) What amount of employment is involved in the alternative cases of (a) and (b)?

(d) Surely a wholesale liquidation of several Companies on a scale as big as this must affect the Income Tax to an appreciable extent. There must be a tremendous writing off among a number of people who, but for the crash, would have been substantial Income Tax payers.

(e) How great is the shock to the community in South Wales likely to be?

I should like to see Sir Richard Hopkins and the Financial Secretary at five today, and I should be glad if they could read this note before the meeting.

L. S. Amery: diary

(*Amery papers*)

17 February 1925

At the conference I was told Beatty completely talked round Winston and the figure agreed on was far better than the Admiralty hoped. So while the Press were giving headlines to Winston's victory over the Admiralty, the Sea Lords were quietly chortling over their successful defence.

Winston S. Churchill to Neville Chamberlain: unsent draft[1]

(*Churchill papers: 18/10*)

17 February 1925

My dear Minister of Health,

Your letter of the 9th February has caused me some concern.

The original proposal of the Anderson Committee was for a scheme of

---

[1] A note on the final typed draft of the letter states: 'withdrawn'. For the revised and shortened letter which Churchill sent Chamberlain three days later, see page 407.

'Sixty-five' and 'Widows and Orphans' Pensions at a contribution of a shilling (divided presumably between employers and workmen) for men; (I do not complicate the tale by discussing the consequential case of women), the whole cost of back payment being taken by the State, ie a new capital liability which cannot be less than £500,000,000.

This is a tremendous new financial burden for the Exchequer. It is expressed in the annual payments set out in the Table of the Committee's Report. These payments rise to £7 millions in 1930, £20 to £25 millions in 1940 and £25 to £35 millions in 1950. They do not include the cost of administering the scheme or the extra burden of Old Age Pensions involved in the disregard of the means limit in the case of all who have been pensioned under the scheme at the age of 65. These prodigious commitments will in my judgment strain to the full the future resources of the State. It is indeed a great vindication of our existing capitalist civilisation that we should be able to contemplate them.

Since this Report was first completed several mitigations have been suggested in the joint contribution of employer and employed. First of all it has been proposed that the contribution in respect of women, who are after all the main beneficiaries, should be increased and the contribution in respect of men reduced from 1/- to 10d. Next it is clear that Pensions at 65 will lighten or ought to lighten the burden in respect of people of the age of 65 upon the Health and Unemployment Insurance Funds. The relief to the new scheme from each of these sources is estimated at 1d—total 2d. Thus the total burden in respect of men can be reduced from the original shilling to 8d (or 9d in the case of the agricultural labourer). This will greatly alleviate the claims upon industry and the population. The State however neither asks nor receives any proportionate abatement of its new burden. That remains the same and towers up before the eyes of a future generation.

You point to the apparent differentiation against agriculture and you propose to meet this difficulty by an expedient. The Exchequer is to assume the burden of a penny a week for the whole of the men in insurance and a half-penny a week for the women, in exchange for a permanent reduction to the like extent in the State contribution to Unemployment Insurance. Such a plan would throw an extra burden of £600,000 a year on the taxpayer. It would prejudice the discussion now taking place between the Treasury and the Ministry of Labour to shift the contribution by the Exchequer to Unemployment Insurance from the present basis of the income of the Fund to the basis of the expenditure. Thirdly, it would destroy the logical basis of apportionment of expenditure recommended by the Anderson Committee for the new scheme. The broad principle that the workers and their employers should pay what the benefits are worth for young persons entering industry and that the State should take liability for all back payments is one of high consequence, easily understood by all.

I should be very sorry to mar the symmetry of our proposals in this respect. In any case every other method and device which ingenuity could suggest would have to be exhausted before we could adopt it.

If by the means which you suggest, or by some others which we may discover, the contribution for the new developments is reduced to 8d a week in respect of men, payable equally by employers and workmen, you now propose to make this great mitigation only the springboard of a far larger claim upon the Exchequer. For the sake of meeting the case of the agricultural labourer the contribution of employer and employed is to be reduced from 8d to 6d and in the apportionment of the 6d, 4d is to be left upon the employer and only 2d required of the worker. The remaining 2d is to be provided by the Exchequer.

Obviously the crux of the matter is whether 8d, equally divided between employer and worker, is too much for the weakest class of the insurable population, and whether, if so, the burden to the State must be raised over the whole area of the scheme, and this in order to give relief to the worker alone. As to the first of these points, we have on the one hand the Agricultural Wages Board fixing wages over nearly the whole of England and Wales at considerably higher figures than have recently obtained; on the other hand, we propose to offer benefits exceeding anything the agricultural workers can have contemplated. Eighteen shillings a week for a widow with two children, a pound a week for a man and his wife on their reaching the age of 65, represent in material comfort considerably more to the agricultural class than they do to the urban worker; and I should expect the agricultural labourer to be willing, as I am sure he will be able, under the new scales of wages, to pay his modest share (on the normal basis) of the cost of such a boon. Certainly we cannot for his sake open up the charge of 2d on the Exchequer over the whole Insurance field.

As regards the employers I think you will have great difficulty in securing their acquiescence on any other than a 'fifty fifty' basis, though, as I show below, you may have to ask for a little more in the case of the classes outside Unemployment Insurance. The risks to be covered by the new scheme do not, to say the least, demonstrably arise out of the insured persons occupations, and if a discrimination is to be made between the respective payments of the employers and the workers I should expect a claim to be advanced that the major part of the burden should fall upon the latter. We shall do well, in the circumstances, to secure that the workers shoulder no more than half the joint burden.

How little justification there is for giving all these Unemployment Insurance people an extra 2d at the expense of the State is shown by the fact that the present charges upon these are to be greatly reduced in the future. The present joint contribution for unemployment is 1/7 but when the debt of the Fund has been redeemed this joint contribution is to be reduced by Statute to 1/-. Your proposal would mean that in a comparatively short time 8 millions of men would be insured for all the benefits of the new scheme in addition to their present benefits, while they and their employers would be paying a penny a week less than they now pay. Even without the subsidy you ask me to provide, they will only be paying a penny more. I am sure that you will agree that this is not a case on which to base a demand for a new heavy contribution by the State.

It is clear that I cannot undertake the burden you ask me to shoulder. If a further reduction must be made and applied to agriculture as to other industries it must come from the reduction of the health insurance contribution by a further 1d a week.

On this I understand from your Memorandum that contemporaneously (or practically so) with the new plans of 'Sixty-five' and 'Widows and Orphans Insurance' it is proposed to start large schemes of improvement in the benefits under Health Insurance, advanced medical treatment, dentistry, and the like. Is this the time to put forward such plans? Our resources are limited. If it becomes a question of selecting between desirable objectives I am inclined to think that these improvements in medical treatment under Health Insurance, however good and desirable in themselves, will be quite lost sight of in the general movement of social life. I am sure they are not comparable as public objectives with the immense proposals comprised in 'Sixty-five' and 'Widows and Orphans'. I do not feel they ought to be allowed to stand in the way of the main scheme. Moreover surely it is bad policy to give everything away at once. Will you not want some new improvements to fill the window in later years.

I do not, however, think that such a further reduction in the contribution as would formally raise this question will be found necessary. I believe the boon to be offered is such a great one that there will be an overwhelming willingness upon the part of the nation to make the necessary sacrifices to secure it. I am convinced that a joint contribution of 8d a week from the classes in unemployment insurance and of 9d a week from other classes will not be deemed too heavy by those who are called upon to pay it; and I subjoin a statement showing how such a contribution could be divided in order that every employed man would pay 4d and every employed woman 2d.

This division also secures the 'fifty-fifty' principle as regards the whole of the population in the Unemployment Scheme; and as regards the others departs from it only to a small extent and that to secure two advantages—the larger one uniformity in the workers contribution over all industries, and the smaller one the avoidance of troublesome half-pence in the total of the workers contributions. I would ask you to give full consideration to this scheme of contributions. It appears to me to be the best that can be devised for the purpose in view. Its advantages are these

(i) It gives effect to the sound principle of apportionment as between the State and the other contributors proposed by the Anderson Committee.

(ii) It takes from Health and Unemployment Insurance contributions no more than is equivalent to the relief derived by these schemes from the stoppage of benefits at 65.

(iii) It places universally the same contribution on the workers in whatever industries they are employed.

(iv) It keeps a very reasonable relation between the respective contributions of the employers and the workers.

(v) It recognises the difference in the wage levels of men and women in the workers contributions, while as regards employers it goes as far as is possible in the direction of equality between the contributions levied for workers of either sex.

To sum up the situation, under your proposal the Exchequer is invited to contribute £5½ millions a year additional to the cost of the new Insurance schemes. This £5½ millions would begin next year. The Exchequer contribution would consequently be raised to £12½ millions in 1930, £25 to £30 millions in 1940, and £30 to £40 millions in 1950. The reason why I considered this great scheme practicable was because it did not throw too heavy a load upon the taxpayer in the early years; it gave time for the recovery of our trade after the war and for a diminution of debt and war pensions charges.

In the years with which we are immediately concerned the extra burden you suggest could not be assumed. I shall not be possessed of the funds to undertake it. Our plans for these years are cut to the finest point. If therefore this additional £5½ millions upon the Exchequer is indispensable to the scheme I do not think we can possibly face it. It entirely alters the standpoint from which I viewed the whole proposition. I should, however, deeply regret the failure, or even the postponement of the great development we have in view in this new scheme of social welfare and I sincerely hope that the proposals which I now put forward will commend themselves to you as providing the means by which it may be brought to fruition.

Yours sincerely,

Committee of Imperial Defence: minutes

(*Churchill papers: 22/31*)

19 February 1925

MR CHURCHILL: . . . I should like to say that, while I think I agree with him[1] in the end, I do believe that the time factor does not, at any rate from a layman's point of view—I have heard the Foreign Office view—the time factor does not press immediately. I think you may have France in a much better state of mind in the course of two or three years, and that an opportunity may occur, possibly not waiting so long as fifteen years, an opportunity may occur when you will get a better and more general solution. I do not wish to discuss this any further now because it is not before us to-day. I think we must go on to discuss it and have some opinion on the subject at a very early date, but my own feeling is that time may be on our side in the matter. I do not say an indefinite period of time, but certainly a longer period of time than apparently is envisaged at present.

MR AUSTEN CHAMBERLAIN: I want to make the point clear. I am vitally afraid that the whole situation would be poisoned and even ruined by the French remaining—

MR CHURCHILL: On the Rhine.

MR AUSTEN CHAMBERLAIN: In Cologne.

MR CHURCHILL: On the other hand, of course, you may be quite sure that, whether they remain in Cologne or not, whether their policy is the pacification of Germany or the irritation of Germany, nevertheless, French anxieties will be continuous and increasing, and that increasing French anxiety will make them all the more desirous of obtaining our assistance. We may be in a position at a later date to procure from the French concessions to Germany of a far more sweeping character than any they contemplate at the present time, which would be the foundation of a stable peace. We might be running a tremendous risk in attaching our signature to a pact of this kind. That is the only point. I admit the tremendous difficulty of it and I am very glad we are not going to discuss it to-day, although I think we ought to go boldly on and face it in the discussions which are to take place. I do not think we can leave it altogether.

LORD BIRKENHEAD: I hold entirely the same view.[2]

---

[1] The Foreign Secretary, Austen Chamberlain, who had spoken of the possibility of a Pact in which Britain would join France, Belgium and Germany in guaranteeing the Franco-German and Belgo-German frontiers.

[2] Following this meeting of the Committee of Imperial Defence, Churchill set out in detail his view of the future of the European balance of power (see his letter to Balfour of 22 February 1925, quoted on page 412, and his Cabinet memorandum of 24 February 1925, quoted on pages 413 to 417).

Winston S. Churchill to Neville Chamberlain
(*Churchill papers: 18/10*)

20 February 1925

My dear Minister of Health,

Your letter of the 9th February has received my careful consideration.

You point out that the Government Actuary advises that a contribution of 10d a week for a man and 5d a week for a woman is equivalent to and could, therefore, be substituted for the respective contributions of 1/- and 1d proposed by the Anderson Committee for pensions to widows and pensions to workers and their wives at the age of 65.

You draw attention to the fact, referred to also by the Anderson Committee, that in order to avoid overlap with the existing schemes of insurance health and unemployment, the benefits of these schemes would stop at the age of 65 on the adoption of the new proposals; and as regards Health insurance you state that this would enable a reduction of 1d a week to be made in the contribution for a man and ½d in the contribution for a woman, thus, in effect, bringing down the new contributions to 9d and 4½d. You then make two proposals. The first of these refers to Unemployment insurance. You suggest that instead of the contributions of either the worker or the employer being reduced by reason of the stoppage of benefits at 65, the State contribution to unemployment should be reduced by 1d a week for a man and ½d a week for a woman, the Exchequer assuming at the same time a liability to contribute the like amounts in aid of the weekly contributions for pensions, thus bringing the effective contribution under the new scheme down to 8d and 4d.

You put forward this proposal on the ground that to diminish the unemployment contribution of the worker or his employer would only relieve the classes that are in the unemployment scheme and consequently would not reduce the burden of contributions for the new benefits in the case of the agricultural industry. You are impressed by the difficulty of defending proposals which appear to place a greater charge in total on agriculture than is to be borne by other industries.

This line of criticism of our proposals would not, of course, be very logical. Agriculture is not bearing the burden of unemployment insurance and naturally, therefore, cannot share in any mitigation of that burden. But with you I realise the practical difficulty involved and have sympathetically considered your suggestion. My difficulties in the matter are two. In the first place, you suggest that I should be relieved of a charge in respect of some 11 million people who are insured against unemployment and accept a corresponding charge for 15 millions insured under the health scheme. This will cost the Exchequer £600,000 a year. Secondly, discussions are now taking place between the Treasury and the Ministry of Labour to shift the contribution by the Exchequer to unemployment insurance from the present basis of the income of the Fund to the basis of expenditure. I should be unwilling to do anything to prejudice this question, and while I do not think the grant of £600,000 a year need stand in the way, I must make my acceptance of your proposal conditional upon the working out of arrangements that on the new basis of State grant will secure to me the relief in respect of unemployment that you contemplate that I should have. Subject to the safeguarding of my position in this respect I concur in your proposal. At the same time I regret that we have to make a breach in the logical apportionment of the burden recommended by the Anderson Committee for the new scheme, under which the workers and their employers would have paid what the benefits are worth for young persons entering industry, and the liability of the State would have represented all back payments for the present insured population.

At this stage, therefore, we have a net additional contribution of 8d for a man and 4d for a woman divided equally, in each case, between employer and worker. You now raise the question as to whether this contribution is not too high and whether it should not be reduced to 6d (men) and 3d (women) by a reduction of the workers contribution to 2d (men) and 1d (women), the employers contribution remaining at 4d and 2d. You suggest that the reduction in the contributions of the workers should be made at the cost of the State, the Exchequer contributing the 2d and the 1d of which the workers are to be relieved. You base this proposal on the economic position of the agricultural worker, but as no discrimination can be made between one industry and another the effect of its adoption would be to reduce the workers contribution over the whole field of industry. Its effect as regards the Exchequer would be to add £5 millions a year to the charge from the beginning of the scheme and to bring up the State contribution in 1930 from £7½ millions to £12½ millions with a corresponding addition to the heavily rising charge on the State in subsequent years as set out in the estimates presented by the Anderson Committee. This is a grave proposal and I am not in a position to accept it. Our plans for the immediately coming years are cut to the finest point and the situation will not permit us to place such a burden on public funds. For the same reason I cannot agree to your modified proposal under which the contribution of the worker would be further reduced by 1d instead of 2d, at the cost of the Exchequer.

If the state of public finance allowed us to face the expedient you propose, the advisability of adopting it would still, I think, be very debatable. In the first place, I think that employers, who might as a class be willing to face a 'fifty fifty' division of the burden between themselves and their employees, would strongly oppose a plan under which their share of the charge was double that of the workers. Secondly, the proposal is based upon the assumption that the agricultural worker is unable to pay so heavy a contribution as 4d a week. On this we ought to have regard to the recent decisions of the Agricultural Wages Board under which the wages of the agricultural workers over nearly the whole of England and Wales have been substantially raised. We must also realise that the benefits we propose to offer are far in excess of anything that the agricultural worker can have contemplated; 18/- a week for a widow with two children or £1 a week for a man and his wife on their reaching the age of 65 represent in material comfort considerably more to the agricultural labourer than they do to the urban worker. With his improved wages I feel that he will be able to pay the 4d a week; with such a boon in prospect as the benefits represent he ought to be more than willing to do so. I am sure that we cannot in his economic conditions find a justification for reducing the contributions of 15 million workers at a further heavy cost to the taxpayer. I sincerely hope, therefore, that on consideration you will not think it necessary to press this second proposal.

Yours sincerely,
Winston S. Churchill

Winston S. Churchill to Stanley Baldwin
(*Churchill papers: 18/10*)

22 February 1925

My dear Prime Minister,

You have several times asked me my opinion about the Trade Union Political Levy, and I feel I have given you only uncertain, or even contradictory, replies. This is because the question is itself both uncertain and contradictory in character, and also because we were still in the period when weighing and balancing is not only possible but right. Now, however, we are at the point when decision is imperative, and I am glad to tell you that it finds me with an absolutely clear conviction.

If we recur to the main principles, we see that we have before us two worthy objects:—

First, to liberate working men from the unfair and humiliating position of being compelled under threat of ruin and starvation to subscribe to the propagation of political principles which they detest;

Secondly, not to hinder by want of funds the less wealthy classes in the nation from using to the full their Constitutional rights and so being continually assimilated into the British Parliamentary system.

Pages can be written in favour of these objects, and they are both of them right and true to the national interest. The difficulty of our problem resides in the fact that they seem to be opposed to each other. Can they be reconciled?

Surely they can be reconciled by a very simple course which proceeds at every step along the path of sound conviction. Let us pass the Bill to liberate workmen from the thraldom of the Levy, and let us at the same time reduce the cost of Parliamentary election to all classes and all Parties by substantial grants from the Exchequer. I would suggest that in supporting the Bill we announce that a sum of, say, £300 will be paid by the Exchequer to the expenses of any candidate who polls an adequate number of votes. If there were, say, fifteen hundred candidates, this would cost £450,000. The burden to the Exchequer could be accepted. Such a boon would take the edge off every *bona fide* candidature in the country. It would make men of all Parties more free from unwholesome excesses in Party discipline. It would pay the greater part of the expenses of many Labour candidatures. It would gratify every Member. It would free the charge that we are anxious to obstruct the entry of Labour men to Parliament from its sting. It would supply the new fact and makeweight which we must recognise is necessary to enable us to give effect to our convictions on the main issues. The Exchequer contribution can of course be considered both in respect to method and amount.

I believe that such a combined policy would gain overwhelming support in the House and would largely cut the ground from under the feet of the Socialists in the country. The policy would be one of 'fair play to the workman whatever his opinions, cheaper elections for all Parties, freedom of Members and candidates from undue reliance on Party funds'.

Such a policy must be contrasted with its alternative. When we last talked, I had not read the passage on page 7 of 'Looking Ahead' which Jackson showed me only on Thursday; nor did I know that you and your principal colleagues had all voted for such a Bill as this in the last Parliament. It seems to me in the light of these facts that it will be very difficult to find a successful Parliamentary argument for opposing the Bill. If there are any enemies lurking among our own supporters, or disappointed elements, it would be easy for them to accuse those who were in the last Parliament of not acting up to their convictions. Such information as I have been able to gather seems to show a very strong feeling in the rank and file of the Conservative Party. Surely we cannot be surprised at this, in view of the declaration in 'Looking Ahead'. Might it not be very harmful to the Government to disappoint the whole of this strong and natural feeling which has been encouraged by their leaders before the Election and is, moreover, logically and on its merits entirely sound?

If you thought well of this plan I would propose it when the matter comes before the Cabinet, and you could bring it safely into port. I think it might command practically the united support of Liberals, though this is the first time I have ever spoken of it. Perhaps you will let me know tomorrow morning what you think.

Winston S. Churchill to Sir Otto Niemeyer
(*Churchill papers: 18/12*)

22 February 1925
Private and Secret

RETURN TO THE GOLD STANDARD

The Treasury have never, it seems to me, faced the profound significance of what Mr Keynes[1] calls 'the paradox of unemployment amidst dearth'. The Governor[2] shows himself perfectly happy in the spectacle of Britain possessing the finest credit in the world simultaneously with a million and a quarter unemployed. Obviously if these million and a quarter were usefully and economically employed, they would produce at least £100 a year a head, instead of costing us at least £50 a year a head in doles. We should have at least £200 millions a year healthy net increase. These figures are of course purely illustrative. It is impossible not to regard such an object as at least equal, and probably superior, to the other valuable objectives you mention on your last page.

The community lacks goods, and a million and a quarter people lack work. It is certainly one of the highest functions of national finance and credit to bridge the gulf between the two. This is the only country in the world where this condition exists. The Treasury and Bank of England policy has been the only policy consistently pursued. It is a terrible responsibility for those who have shaped it, unless they can be sure that there is no con-

[1] John Maynard Keynes, 1883–1946. Educated at Eton and King's College, Cambridge. Economist. Editor of the *Economic Journal*, 1911–44. Served at the India Office, 1906–8; the Treasury, 1915–19. Principal Treasury Representative at the Paris Peace Conference, 1919. Created Baron, 1942. Leader of the British Delegation to Washington to negotiate the American Loan, 1945. Among his publications were *The Economic Consequences of the Peace* (1919) and *The Economic Consequences of Mr Churchill* (July 1925).

[2] Montagu Norman, Governor of the Bank of England (see page 302, note 2).

nection between the unique British phenomenon of chronic unemployment and the long, resolute consistency of a particular financial policy. I do not know whether France with her financial embarrassments can be said to be worse off than England with her unemployment. At any rate while that unemployment exists, no one is entitled to plume himself on the financial or credit policy which we have pursued.

It may be of course that you will argue that the unemployment would have been much greater but for the financial policy pursued; that there is no sufficient demand for commodities either internally or externally to require the services of this million and a quarter people; that there is nothing for them but to hang like a millstone round the neck of industry and on the public revenue until they become permanently demoralised. You may be right, but if so, it is one of the most sombre conclusions ever reached. On the other hand I do not pretend to see even 'through a glass darkly' how the financial and credit policy of the country could be handled so as to bridge the gap between a dearth of goods and a surplus of labour; and well I realise the danger of experiment to that end. The seas of history are full of famous wrecks. Still if I could see a way, I would far rather follow it than any other. I would rather see Finance less proud and Industry more content.

You and the Governor have managed this affair. Taken together I expect you know more about it than anyone else in the world. At any rate alone in the world you have had an opportunity over a definite period of years of seeing your policy carried out. That it is a great policy, greatly pursued, I have no doubt. But the fact that this island with its enormous extraneous resources is unable to maintain its population is surely a cause for the deepest heart-searching.

Forgive me adding to your labours by these Sunday morning reflections.[1]

Winston S. Churchill to Lord Balfour

(*Balfour papers*)

22 February 1925   11 Downing Street

My dear Arthur,

I set this down after our meeting on Thursday. It does not attempt to present an argument: it is merely thinking aloud. But I should so much like

---

[1] In his reply, Niemeyer urged that the alternative to the return to the Gold Standard was inflation; and that with increasing inflation the credit of the country would be destroyed, and money would 'cease to be acceptable as value'. As inflation grew, wage demands would increase, and there would be grave industrial unrest. 'I assume it to be admitted,' he wrote, 'that with Germany and Russia before us we do not think plenty can be found on this path' (*Churchill papers: 18/12*).

you to see it, if it would not give you too much trouble. I am sure France will come to us if we do not offer ourselves to her. Anyhow I agree with all you say about not concentrating our minds too much upon 'Armageddon No 2'. What is wanted is a better atmosphere, and that I believe is slowly coming.

Yours very sincerely,
Winston S.C.

Winston S. Churchill: Cabinet memorandum[1]

(Churchill papers: 22/31)

24 February 1925
Secret

FRENCH AND BELGIAN SECURITY

I agree with those who feel that we must first of all visualise decisively what we want. How to achieve it can then be considered in its turn. What do we want? We want to save ourselves from being involved in another Armageddon, victory in which would compass our ruin scarcely less surely than defeat. Nevertheless, if such a struggle comes shall we be safer fighting in it or standing out?

What is the cause which brings this dread possibility and choice before our minds? It is the quarrel between France and Germany. This antagonism, which has lasted through centuries, is unappeased. All the minor feuds of Europe group themselves around it. Everyone fears that it may lead to another World conflict. No one at any rate feels any assurance that it will not. We feel that we are deeply involved in this quarrel. Though we do not share its hatreds, though we cannot control its occasions, though all our interests and desires are to avoid it, we may irresistibly be drawn in. But this frightful possibility is happily some considerable way off. Germany is prostrate. In an age when lethal apparatus is almost everything she is disarmed. At the worst there is a breathing space, measured by decades. Our problem is how to use this breathing space to end the quarrel. That problem dominates all others.

Even if we saw clearly how to stop the quarrel we might not be able to

[1] On February 23 Churchill had sent a copy of this memorandum to Austen Chamberlain with the covering note: 'My dear Austen, I put down these rough notes on the tremendous problem of the Pact, & I thought you might care to see them before they assume their final form. They only represent "thinking aloud". I have sent a copy to AJB but otherwise no one else has seen them' *(Austen Chamberlain papers)*. The memorandum itself was subsequently circulated to the Cabinet as Cabinet paper 118 of 1925.

carry out our policy. We have, therefore, to seek not so much for the perfect way but for a practical way, the individual steps along which are unquestionably in our power. We have to seek a way which will not commit us beyond the limits of human foresight. It would be a great advantage if we could find a way which, even if it failed to stop the quarrel, did not necessarily commit us to a struggle in which we should almost certainly be defeated. No one will pretend that the affairs of nations can be conducted without many risks, or that any policy is free from uncertainty and danger. But certainly one would not be in a hurry in this rapidly changing world to bind one's self and to bind one's children to the obligation of fighting a disastrous war, the outbreak of which would occur through the working of forces outside our control.

Two plans have been suggested for stopping the new war between France and Germany. The first is a plan for elaborate paper declarations by an International Council at Geneva forbidding it to happen. Even this already ambitious hope is further weighted by a vast super-structure of general declarations to forbid all wars and settle all quarrels. The second plan is that England and France should join together to over-awe Germany, and that England should exact as a condition of her alliance with France that France should cease to harry and anger Germany. This is a much more practicable plan than the first. If union meant security in peace and victory in war the case would be complete. But if it seemed probable that England and France, in spite of standing together, would both be defeated by Germany on the mainland of Europe, it would not be much good. England, France and Russia were, indeed, an apparent counterpoise to the German power. England, France and the United States might also be a counterpoise. But England and France alone, with Belgium thrown in, is a combination which does not inspire much confidence so far as war on the Continent is concerned.

We have to contemplate a situation in which Germany will be rearmed either with existing military appliances or with new inventions. It is probable that such a process can only be accomplished gradually. Therefore one would expect that France would attack Germany at some moment before the process of rearming was complete. Do we wish to bind ourselves to march with her in such an attack; or are we to bind ourselves only to come to her aid when Germany thinks herself strong enough to attack when and if Germany is ripe and we are already too late? No doubt our pact would be phrased to involve us only in the case of deliberate aggression by Germany— a German invasion of French or Belgian soil. But this is the contingency least likely to occur. Far more probable is the steady revival of German military strength causing increasing terror in France, or alternatively

German agression against Poland which France would interpret as a compulsion to war. Therefore by making a pact we might range ourselves against Germany without over-aweing her, and yet when the struggle came, with all its inexorable consequences, we might not feel ourselves bound by treaty or sentiment to come in. In this case we should certainly encounter the hostility of whoever was the victor. On the other hand, if we held back from attacking Germany until Germany was really strong, we should condemn ourselves to participate in a disastrous enterprise. All these possibilities ought to be profoundly searched before we commit ourselves.

Have we any alternative? It is argued that we could never endure the possession of the Channel ports by a victorious Germany, ie, by the greatest European military Power. We dwelt, however, for centuries when these same Channel ports were in the possession of the greatest European military Power, and when that Power—France—was almost unceasingly hostile to us. It is said that the new weapons of war aggravate the danger. But that depends on who has the best and most powerful weapons. If, in addition to sea superiority we had air supremacy, we might maintain ourselves as we did in the days of Napoleon for indefinite periods, even when all the Channel ports and all the Low Countries were in the hands of a vast hostile military Power. It should never be admitted in this argument that England cannot, if the worst comes to the worst, stand alone. I decline to accept as an axiom that our fate is involved in that of France.

If therefore we have, as I believe, a choice, however grim, in the matter, ought we not to utilise that freedom to the full? Ought we not to use it in the way and at the time most calculated to achieve our primary object, viz, the prevention of the renewal of a Franco-German war? For the next ten or fifteen years France will be the strongest Power in Europe. She will be able to overrun Germany before we can bring any appreciable military forces to her aid. Shall we have more influence over her during this period if we are bound to her or if we are independent of her in a treaty sense? Would she be likely sensibly to mitigate her rigours towards Germany for the sake of any military aid she can expect from us during the period of her strength? Would she be justified in abandoning her strategic advantages on the Rhine for the sake of receiving a few British divisions in the first few months of a war? Should we not have just as great an influence, or perhaps an even greater influence, over her if we had still to be won, if she had still at every stage to convince us of her own rectitude and moderation and of the approach of growing danger?

It may be that as the German power revives and the French power sinks relatively, France will turn to Britain with an ever greater appeal. I cannot tell how soon this period will be reached; but that it has not yet been reached is certain. The contemptuous rejection by Poincaré and all the French forces he represents of our offer at Cannes convinces me that these are not days when France is willing to subordinate her own interests and ambitions to the cooler and more detached viewpoint of England.[1] She would like to have England bound to her by treaty and as a makeweight behind her, and no doubt would make certain concessions in her treatment of Germany to secure us. But she does not regard our aid as essential to her safety; she is counting far more on her own army, her black troops, her relations with Poland and, above all, on her strategic situation on the Rhine, than on the latent, tardy, if ultimately vast, forces which the British Empire could command.

I feel therefore that we have not got sufficient bargaining power and leverage at the present time to procure any decisive modification of French policy as the price of a British guarantee. At any rate it is by standing aloof and not by offering ourselves that we shall ascertain the degree of importance which France really attaches to our troth. Does anyone suppose that a British signature to a pact related only to the Western theatre would induce France to withdraw from the Rhine and evacuate Germany? Before she would do that she would require definite engagements in respect of numbers of troops and dates of arrival of a kind sufficient at least to compensate for the solid advantages she is asked to surrender. At the most she would consent to the evacuation of the first of the zones fixed by the treaty. The German grievance would continue unassuaged, and we should have squandered finally our bargaining power. We should have entered into dire obligations for the sake only of a partial and insufficient relief. For these reasons, among others, I cannot feel that this is a moment for a pact with France. I am sure we would do better, for the present at any rate, to keep ourselves free.

We must, however, have a policy which can be publicly expressed and explained to everyone. Might we not then hold the following language to France: 'We feel that your relations with Germany are at present too bitter for us to involve ourselves in the quarrel. Moreover, Germany is disarmed and you are strong. You are therefore not in any immediate danger. These are the years in which you have the opportunity of establishing much better

[1] At the Cannes Conference of January 1922 Britain was represented by Lloyd George, Lord Curzon, Sir Robert Horne, Sir Laming Worthington Evans and Churchill. At the Conference, Lloyd George and Briand (the French Prime Minister) had agreed to negotiate a Franco-British agreement in which Germany would be invited to join, and in which all the participants would undertake to refrain from aggression against their neighbours. But on being summoned back to Paris, while the Conference was still in session, Briand was forced to resign as a result of the combined pressure of both Poincaré (the President) and Barthou (the Foreign Secretary). On his return to Cannes, Briand turned to Barthou and asked: 'Can you tell me Monsieur Barthou, what is the equivalent of thirty pieces of silver at the current rate of exchange?'

relations with Germany, and so rendering a renewal of war less likely. We will do everything in our power to promote these improved relations. The better friends you are with Germany, the better friends we shall be with you. The more you can settle your quarrel with Germany, the more ready we shall be to associate ourselves with your fortunes in the event of all your efforts proving unavailing. If at any time you approach a real state of peace with Germany, we would be willing to come in in order to achieve, consolidate and render unbreakable that peace. We do not underrate the difficulties. We do not abandon our mistrust of Germany. You know well, as M Poincaré has reminded you, where some at least of our main interests lie. But it rests with you to accomplish the first part of the task; it rests with you to create that atmosphere in which Germany will have the least possible incentive to renew the war, and thereafter it may be our part to join with you in increasing the deterrents against her hostile action. We might well be partners in a genuine triple accord between England, France and Germany. Apart from such a triple accord, we cannot enter into specific obligations towards you. We can only watch the situation in the same spirit of hatred of aggression, of a respect for public law, which, together with our own national interests, led us to your side in 1914.'

I have only tried to set down thoughts, and not to find the diplomatic terms and forms in which the policy should be expressed. I believe that proceeding on these lines we should exert the maximum influence upon France, and that after a passing ebullition against us and Germany, and possibly a detachment from us for some years, she would come back in a far better mood. Meanwhile, we should not have cast away ineffectually what may be our one great lever to procure a general peace. I question, however, whether any alternative policy is really possible. I doubt whether in present circumstances the British people would be willing to accept definite obligations to France. Certainly to persuade them would require a great campaign of argument. The whole of this argument would dwell upon the possibility of what Lord Balfour calls 'Armageddon No 2'. Such an argument occupying the public mind would keep all thoughts on war and arouse great anxieties. It will delay the return to normal conditions. Very likely in the end we should not be able to carry an agreement. On all grounds, therefore, I rest upon the formula: 'When France has made a real peace with Germany, Britain will seal the bond with all her strength.'

WSC[1]

---

[1] When the Cabinet met on 4 March 1925 they agreed to tell Austen Chamberlain to make it clear to the French Government, as L. S. Amery noted in his diary, 'that there could be no question of an Anglo Franco Belgium Pact but that we favoured a joint pact with Germany, though as Winston insisted even this should involve no more than mutual consultation if one

Winston S. Churchill to Neville Chamberlain: not sent[1]

(Churchill papers: 18/8)

25 February 1925   Treasury Chambers

My dear Neville Chamberlain,

I read with great interest your Memorandum on the Weir houses. I feel very strongly that we must not let ourselves be crushed by the difficulties. We must conquer the difficulties. I am sure we can if we try. No great enterprise is free from risk. In this case not only is the prize well worth the risk, but the penalty for not succeeding is also a compulsive spur.

Let us recur to the primary facts.

(1) We need a million houses.
(2) We have got a million and a quarter unemployed.
(3) The Weir house can be built by mass production and unskilled labour.

Surely these three facts tower over all others. Compared to such facts, what are the hesitations and timidity of Local Authorities, the ignorance of the public on the subject, the interested hostility of the Building Trade Monopoly, the suggestions of favouritism of Weir, etc? If we march forward with a plan which mitigates at one stroke the Housing and the Employment shortage, I am sure we can smash the lot.

I agree entirely with your policy in taking the preliminary steps with caution. We must know that the Weir house is a sound house. I thought it very wise of you to arrange for a few hundred demonstration houses to be erected throughout the country. But I regard this as only the preliminary to the mass production of at least a quarter of a million Weir houses, the measures to render such production possible being undertaken in the next few months. When I remember the scale on which we were handling production at the Ministry of Munitions, I cannot feel that there is anything physically alarming in the programme. I doubt if the Trade will be able to place themselves in open opposition to a plan for building a quarter of a million houses to break the Housing monopoly and rescue the people from a cruel condition. A Government backed by the nation has overwhelming power. Of course you have to carry the Local Authorities with you; but not

---

party to the pact showed signs of breaking it. The definite adhesion of Curzon, Winston and FE to the anti-pactites of whom Hoare and I had so far been the protagonists has completely defeated the FO scheme (which captured Austen) for rushing the country (forgetting the Empire) with a definite commitment to defend France. . . .' (*Amery papers*).

[1] A note on this letter, signed by P. J. Grigg on 25 February 1925, states: 'Not sent—raised in Cabinet today.'

many of them in such circumstances would set themselves contumaciously against the State.

Could not the suggestion of 'favouring Weir houses' be overcome by creating a Public Trust for the direct construction of such houses, by which no profit is reaped on the capital employed? Three years have passed since Weir first discussed with me his plans for mass production of houses. At that time concrete was to be the medium, and steel is only an improvement upon that. I believe that Weir would be ready to contract himself out of all personal profit and give his extraordinary abilities to this cause for the honour alone. It would be quite easy to afford a similar opportunity to competing types, if they were equally sound and their advocates equally disinterested.

I must confess that I certainly have contemplated quite definitely the placing of a Government order for at least a quarter of a million emergency houses, and the whole life and strength of the Government being engaged behind the enterprise. I am ready at any time to discuss with you in detail the finance of such a scheme.

But we are not now concerned with any such gigantic plan. We are only at present experimenting on a tiny scale. You have taken £50,000 to procure the erection of a few hundred demonstration houses. Apparently we are not even to be allowed to do this without an immense series of manoeuvres and preliminaries. We are to set up a Court of Enquiry to interpret the Fair Wages clause, in the hopes that the progress of the Enquiry will arouse the interest of the public and convince them how very badly we are being treated by the obstructionists. The result of this Enquiry may apparently kill the steel houses altogether; or, secondly, it may hamper their construction sufficiently to make Weir abandon his plans. Even in the third alternative of our getting an entirely favourable verdict, very likely, we are told in your Memorandum, the Unions will not accept it—but then it is hoped we should have more public opinion with us than at present in fighting them. All this fight is not about the mass production of half a million or a quarter of a million houses; it is all about the demonstration for experimental purposes of a few hundreds. It is a depressing conclusion.

Why should we not adopt your No 3 alternative at once, so as to take at any rate the first preliminary step? No doubt all interested obstructionists will denounce our action. But the Government with its mighty power will defend its action; and as the Government has no motive at all except the national interest, it will rally both Press and public to its side. However that may be, the issue will come to a head in the House of Commons; and it is on this battle-ground that you would I am sure secure a decisive and resounding victory. Such a victory would give us the strength to move forward in a vastly greater sphere of effort.

March 1925

Winston S. Churchill to Lord Birkenhead

(*Churchill papers: 18/10*)

1 March 1925
Secret and Personal

My dear Fred,

I would suggest for tomorrow[1] that we do not want to get involved in immense discussions of strategy. We are called upon to make plans on a five years' basis. We want to know in the first instance what these plans involve in men, material and money. The Admiralty should be asked to supply these, showing sketch Estimates for the next five years. These Estimates necessarily cannot be exact. But if we know how many ships the Admiralty claim, how many men, how much oil, etc, we shall be in a position to judge the future demand on the State and the means of meeting it. No doubt Beatty will want to make a general statement, and no doubt it should be allowed to him; but I suggest that the questions which are interjected should as far as possible tend to bring out his actual requirements, rather than a general lecture on strategy.

Meanwhile I send you for your personal information a paper by Sir George Barstow, setting forth the Treasury view with which I am in general agreement. Will you kindly keep this paper entirely to yourself.[2]

---

[1] At the first meeting of the Naval Programme Committee. As Lord Birkenhead had been taken ill, Lord Salisbury (Lord Privy Seal) took the Chair at this first meeting. The others present were Churchill, Bridgeman, Edward Wood (Minister of Agriculture and Fisheries), Lord Peel (First Commissioner of Works), Lord Beatty and Captain Pound (Director of Plans, Admiralty).

[2] When the Naval Programme Committee of the Cabinet met on 2 March 1925 Churchill said, of the proposals for naval expansion put forward byWilliam Bridgeman: 'I am prepared to challenge this position which he has put forward in almost every particular, and I am prepared to show that these demands are unreasonable demands, and even if granted would not give us the security, which is sought for on the hypothesis which exists' (*Cabinet papers: 27/273*).

Winston S. Churchill to Sir Richard Hopkins

(Churchill papers: 18/2)

2 March 1925

Let me see the Royal Commission's Report. It is a new point to me that earned income probably rises with the cost of living and that unearned income is fixed. It does not alter my opinion, but it must be taken into account. The Royal Commission seem to have been rather against doing any more for the earned compared to the unearned.

I had not realised that the Super Tax had been raised after the war. What a cruel Budget that was of 1920, striking at the whole recuperative power of the country at the beginning of a great slump! I remember being staggered at the time.[1]

Winston S. Churchill: remarks to a Deputation[2]

(Treasury papers: T171/247)

4 March 1925

. . . The burdens which rest upon productive industry and upon the capital owning classes, the burdens which affect the enterprise and the thrift and saving power of the Nation are most formidable, and in regard to any extensions which we may contemplate during the present Parliament, we should have to consider very carefully what the re-action would be, and at the same time whether the actual financial position of the country justified reductions in that burden of taxation, which may conceivably make an extra load, if any, which had to be assumed by Industry, not only not more oncrous than the present, but less onerous than at present.

I am quite sure of this, that the first great aim should be to effect a reduction in the taxation of the country, and in regard to any further burdens which are laid upon Industry, it is to my mind essential that such a reduction should precede any imposition or should synchronise with the liability existing. What you say about the development of the psychological qualities

---

[1] In the 1920 Budget (introduced when Austen Chamberlain was Chancellor of the Exchequer), corporate income tax was raised from 40% to 60%; Super Tax payers earning over £2,500 had their scale of tax increased from 1 shilling to 1/6d, those earning over £10,400 from 3/6d to 4/6d, and for those earning over £32,500, from 4/6d to 6/-; duties on spirits were increased from 50/- to 72/6d a proof gallon; and Postage was increased from 1½d to 2d for domestic letters. But the 6d per gallon tax on motor spirit was abolished.

[2] A deputation from the National Conference of Employers' Organizations, led by Lord Weir.

of our race and how far they are being sapped by the social services to which you have referred, it may well be that people are becoming to a certain extent less self-reliant, and to a certain extent they expect to have things done for them, and to a certain extent in this country, unexampled in any other land, they expect benefits to be made available for them.

On the other hand, one must see the inevitability which characterised the legislation in the last 20 years. I do not think you could stand by and see disease proceeding utterly ungripped by the great machinery of Health Insurance. I do not think anybody could say that in the light of all they know—good and bad—of the things that have flowed from the decisions in 1909 and 1910 you would not develop this scheme of National Health Insurance, to which vastly the greater proportion is contributed by the working people. The same with unemployment insurance, you could not have got through these times without the existence of this scheme without putting a great burden on the industries which have suffered by the un-employment, but a great proportion has been contributed by the workers themselves; and it is surprising, if you cast your mind back to the position of this country 15 years ago, how this direct taxation of wages should have been so cheerfully accepted by the workers of the population; when we feel that they are not self-reliant because the burden has been taken from them, to a large extent, they are bearing their burdens themselves, and it must be remembered that there followed this enormous man-power when these individual savings are woven together in the form of national insurance.

Personally, I feel that that system of insurance, whatever may be the effects on the self-reliance of the individual, is going to be an absolutely inseparable element in our social life and eventually must have the effect of attaching the minds of the people, although their language and mood in many cases may not seem to indicate it—it must lead to the stability and order of the general structure. It is impossible to conceive that the very large numbers of people in this position who have earned by their own contributions—it is impossible to conceive that these people will not feel that their fortune is interwoven with the useful provisions which will enable them to be benefited by Old Age Pensions or Unemployment Insurance and that some of those qualities of self-reliance may be eliminated, yet at the same time you have a nation more nationalised and more firmly attached to orderly progression. That at any rate is an alternative view as far as Industry is concerned.

You have suffered most. 1/7d is the charge placed on industry as regards unemployment insurance, but it is known that that is to fall, we hope in a reasonable period, to 1/- when the debt which has been accumulated in unemployment has passed away and it has been reduced to a large extent as the diminution in unemployment proceeds, as it will proceed—it may be slowly, but still it is a steady progression—that relief will be non-existent, that relief will make a very considerable effect, especially if during the same period, when that relief has enured to the advantage of industry, it should be possible to make certain reductions, and it would give you a greater feeling of relief in the problems you have to face in the form of industrial production. I think it would be a great advantage to us if we could renew this discussion at some later period which is convenient to you and your colleagues. I know we should profit by it, and we should like to have time to go into details—I mean to discuss the matter of facts and figures.

Winston S. Churchill to Clementine Churchill[1]
(Spencer-Churchill papers)

8 March 1925

My darling,

We have just returned from the Zoo, where I took Diana and Sarah. The new aquarium is wonderful. Have you seen it? There are some new fish just arrived from Java, about three inches long and painted entirely with most brilliant yellow and white belts. No ordinary gold fish could look at them for shame.

The keepers made all the beasts do their tricks. The elephant took a bunch of keys as well as a lot of buns in his trunk and gave back the bunch of keys to the keeper every time without dropping the bun. We also saw in the insect house the scene of the great battle between the ants. The bridge is still there, and the whole colony was engaged in migrating—victors and vanquished—from one side of the river to the other. Every ant accustomed to work above ground carried one of the underground workers across the bridge in his mouth. Many other things, including the Mappin terraces, amused us very much.[2] We saw quantities of bears, two of them wrestling quite beautifully for a long time. I think the children enjoyed it very much.

Yesterday I paid my weekly visit to Chartwell. Wallace was away, his wife being ill. The second arch of the Palanquin is completed. I hope another fortnight will see this finished. Waterhouse has discovered a good

[1] Clementine Churchill was staying in the South of France at Consuelo Balsan's villa, Lou Seuil, at Eze.
[2] The Mappin Terraces, a four-tiered terrace, the funds for which had been given to the London Zoo by Mappin and Webb; these terraces were one of the Zoo's first major benefactions. On 2 July 1923 *The Times* reported: 'On each of the four hills of the Mappin Terraces at the Zoo a thriving herd has been established, showing that these artificial constructions are as satisfactory for animals as for visitors.'

yew tree in the garden, which he has planted at the head of the steps where you wished. They are working now on the bow window of the Palanquin. It is a serious undertaking. The cow is all right after her misadventure. We are lucky not to have lost her. She was two months before her time. I have managed to buy another little calf, Red Poll and high quality, only a week old for £5. It comes on Monday, and I am going to tell the cow it is her own. Perhaps she will believe it. If so, all the better for her. I brought back fourteen dozen eggs, and twenty dozen have been put in pickle. Great advance by the crocuses and snowdrops. All the other work is progressing, but very slowly, Alack! I am grappling with the dairy problem tomorrow, and I hope to be able to produce a reasonable scheme by the time you return. They have stripped off the inner lining of the peccant wing. I am going to see Tilden's man tomorrow about pressing forward. It will take us all our time to be ready by Easter.

Baldwin achieved a most remarkable success on Friday. He made about the only speech which could have restored the situation, and made it in exactly the right way.[1] I had no idea he could show such power. He has never done it before. The whole Conservative Party turned round and obeyed without one single mutineer. Poor Horne, willing to wound and yet afraid to strike, prudently sat mum. As Sieyès said of Napoleon when he and his fellow directors returned to Paris after the eighteenth Brumaire 'Nous avons un maitre.' I cease to be astonished at anything. However this is all to the good. A strong Conservative Party with an overwhelming majority and a moderate and even progressive leadership is a combination which has never been really tested before. It might well be the fulfilment of all that Dizzy and my father aimed at in their political work.

The revenue is coming in well; and if only I can win my battle with the Admiralty, I shall not be left penniless. In a fortnight they will be able to give me definite figures to work upon, instead of the vague forecasts which are all that are yet available.[2]

[1] During the debate on the Trade Unions Bill, a Private Member's bill which would have secured the right of union members to refuse to contribute to their union's political fund, Baldwin had moved that 'a measure of such far-reaching importance should not be introduced as a Private Member's Bill'. During his speech he made it clear that he thought the measure a just one, but he would not support it, because, as he declared: 'we are not going to push our political advantage home at a time like this. Suspicion which has prevented stability in Europe is the one poison that is preventing stability at home, and we offer the country to-day this: we, at any rate, are not going to fire the first shot. We stand for Peace.' Baldwin's motion passed, 325 to 153, and the bill was withdrawn. The debate took place on 6 March 1925.

[2] A second meeting of the Naval Programme Committee had been held on March 5 (see Main Volume V of this Biography, pages 102–3). Sir Roger Keyes stood in for the absent Lord Beatty. 'It is astonishing,' Churchill told the Committee, 'that the Japanese are able to preserve vessels which at 26 years of age are a source of anxiety to the Admiralty' (*Churchill papers: 22/65*).

Dinner with the Salisburys was very pleasant and the sort of one you would have liked to be at. Last night Philip[1] took me to see 'Old Lightnin'! What a good play, and what a life these Yankees lead! I have no doubt it is a very true picture.[2]

I have half done another article, and am now busy putting the library straight.

We are all anxious about poor George Curzon, who has haemorrhage of the bladder and is to have a somewhat serious operation tomorrow morning. I telephoned to enquire, and he sent his secretary round to give me rather a grave tale.

The work gets heavier every day. All this week I am to have a stream of deputations, and every morning my boxes are full of stiff papers about the Budget. I have decided not to try the third volume and to retire from the literary arena, at any rate for some time to come. I could not do justice to it and my other commitments. Moreover the taxes ate it nearly all.

Philip came here last night and fell into raptures over the Sargent[3] drawing. I was hard put to it to reconcile truth and politeness. I wanted to point out the awful concavity of my right cheek. However, one must not look a gift portrait in the mouth.

The children declared they were writing to you today, but they may be frauds. No—Sarah has just weighed in.

Tender love my darling one. I hope & pray you will have sunshine, peace & joy.

Your ever loving & devoted
W

[1] Sir Philip Sassoon (see page 53, note 1).

[2] The play *Lightnin'*, set in Nevada. According to the *Annual Register*, the success of the play 'owed probably more to the polished acting of Horace Hodges in a part exactly suited to his reticent style than anything it possessed in the way of atmosphere'.

[3] John Singer Sargent, 1856–1925. Son of a physician of Boston, USA. Born in Florence. Portrait painter: he gave his first exhibition in France, in 1879. Royal Academician, 1897. King George V declined to give him the Order of Merit on the grounds that he was an American. He lived in London at 31 Tite Street, Chelsea. He died on 15 April 1925.

Winston S. Churchill to Lord Birkenhead

(*Churchill papers: 18/10*)

8 March 1925
Secret

NAVAL COMMITTEE

My dear FE,

Everything really turns upon whether the Cabinet wish the Navy to be ready as soon as possible to put a superior battle fleet with all ancillaries in the Pacific in case of a war with Japan. If this is the policy, I do not think that the Admiralty requirements are excessive. If we are to beat Japan in her own home waters and ward off France while our Navy is at the other end of the world, and guard all the trade routes simultaneously through all the oceans and seas, even more, in my opinion will be needed. But this question of preparing to send the main Fleet into the Pacific as soon as possible in case of a war with Japan, has never been considered by any responsible authority outside the Admiralty.

I suggest that we should at our Committee decide to state a case for a ruling, in the first instance by the CID and subsequently for confirmation by the Cabinet, on this subject. No final decision can be taken by our Committee in the absence of such a ruling. Of course, however, it is possible to examine, as we are going to do, destroyers, submarines and ancillary vessels: oil, fuel storage and manning. So there would be no need for us to stop our work while the main issue of principle was being decided.

With regard to tomorrow's business, I think we might very likely cover both destroyers and submarines. It is for the Admiralty to explain what they want in these classes in the next few years. If they do this, I should be ready on Thursday to analyse their figures and make a counter proposal.

The PM jumped his big fence with a foot to spare. It was an amazing performance and constitutes a political event of first importance.

Yours always
W

Winston S. Churchill: Cabinet memorandum

(*Churchill papers: 22/67*)

10 March 1925
Confidential

I must ask my colleagues to persevere in their examination of the case of the six new British cruisers which, we are told, are already obsolete. Over

£10 million has been spent on these six ships, and three of them—*Effingham*, *Emerald* and *Enterprise*—are only at this moment on the point of completion. The arguments about the comparison between the 8-inch Japanese and the 7·5-inch British guns are fully explained in Appendix B of the Admiralty PD 02171, which has no doubt been read by my colleagues. In Table D, page 4, of this paper, a 'definite valuation of the offensive power' of the ships is set out. The Japanese 7,100-ton cruiser mounting 6-8-inch guns (*Furutaka* class) is given an offensive value of 600. The British 9,750-ton 7-7·5-inch gun (*Effingham* class) is given only an offensive value of 288 per ship. Thus it appears that the Japanese have been able to put more than double the offensive power into a 7,100-ton ship than the Admiralty has been able to put in a 9,750-ton ship. Full accounts are given in Appendix B aforesaid of the reasons why the 8-inch gun in its turret is 'crushingly' superior to the 7·5-inch gun behind its shield. But all these facts, if true, were surely apparent three years ago when the design and armament of the Japanese *Furutaka* class was known to the Admiralty. Why then did we proceed to spend over £2 million on the later *Effinghams*, which it was known would possess only half the 'offensive value' of a Japanese ship three-quarters of their size?

The *Emerald* and *Enterprise*, which are to be finished this year, are even more obsolete before they are born, according to the Admiralty argument. Their offensive value is estimated in Appendix B at only 168. Thus a British 7,500-ton ship compares with a Japanese 7,100-ton ship in offensive value only in the ratio of 168 to 600. It is a very serious matter that, year after year, money should have been poured out on these six vessels, when all the time the Admiralty knew how hopelessly inferior they were to even the smaller 8-inch gun cruisers which were being built by Japan.

These six British cruisers will cost, to keep in full commission, approximately £1,500,000 a year. Their total aggregate offensive value, according to the Admiralty figures, is 1,488, whereas the four smaller Japanese (*Furutakas*) have an offensive value of 2,400 and probably cost less than £200,000 a year to keep in commission. Such a story and such a result would produce a most unfavourable impression if it were realised by the public.

If the superiority of the 8-inch gun is as 'crushing' as set out in Appendix B, we must ask why the British vessels, the *Effingham* and the *Emerald*, were not armed with 8-inch guns during the process of construction. On the assumption that the Admiralty figures of the relative 'offensive values' are correct, the British ships should certainly be re-armed now. I am informed on high authority that the 7-7·5-inch guns of the *Effingham* could be replaced by 6-8-inch guns in turrets with the most modern mountings without an increase of weight sufficient to exceed the Washington 10,000-ton limit.

I am further informed that the two *Emeralds*, which are 7,500-ton ships of 33 knots, could also be rearmed with 4–8-inch guns in two turrets instead of their present 7–6-inch. I am assured that the rearming of these six vessels, particularly the 4 *Effinghams*, with 8-inch guns is perfectly practicable, and that the cost would not exceed £500,000 apiece. If these ships were in dockyard hands for eighteen months undergoing rearmament, there would be a gross saving of £400,000 on the cost of keeping each ship in commission. This saving aggregating £2,400,000 would almost pay for the rearmament. We should thus obtain six more 8-inch gun cruisers without any serious additional charge on Navy Votes. Whereas to build six new cruisers would cost us over £12 millions additional. The four rearmed *Effinghams* would carry 6 guns and the two rearmed *Emeralds* 4 guns compared to the *Furutaka* class 6 guns. The aggregate number of guns in the six British ships firing on the broadside compared to the four Japanese would be as 32 to 24. Their total offensive value would be 3,200 as against 2,400 Japanese. To this must be added the advantage of having 6 ships to 4.

It appears very necessary that this aspect should be the subject of detailed enquiry. I ask that it should be examined by the Committee. I propose to call high expert evidence. We cannot afford to have brand new British ships that cost over £10 millions written down as obsolete before they are commissioned because a rival has mounted a gun of a half-inch greater calibre, which we are assured is between $2\frac{1}{2}$ to 3 times as effective as our weapon.

WSC

Clementine Churchill to Winston S. Churchill

(*Churchill papers: 1/179*)

11 March 1925   Lou Sueil

My Darling,

I was delighted to get your letter.

No I have never seen the new Aquarium at the Zoo. It sounds lovely— How sweet of you to take the children there.

I had gathered from the papers that Mr Baldwin had achieved a personal triumph over the Levy Bill. I think he has a genuine feeling for the working people of the Country.

Now my lovely one—stand up to the Admiralty & don't be fascinated or flattered or cajoled by Beatty. I assure you the Country doesn't care two pins about him. This may be very unfair to our only War Hero, but it's a fact. Consuelo tells me that he lunched here a little time ago (when he came out to see Lady B[1] who is quite queer & mad) & that he said 'I'm on my way home to fight my big battle with Churchill'. Consuelo said 'Oh I expect Winston will win all right'—to which Beatty retorted 'I'm not so sure'—

Of course I think it would be not good to score a sensational Winstonian triumph over your former love, but do not get sentimental & too soft hearted. Beatty is a tight little screw & he will bargain with you & cheat you as tho he were selling you a dud horse which is I fear what the Navy is.

The Daily Mail is full of the Income Tax Deputation & I see Rothermere is off on another of his Near East scares or hares!

Thursday morning.

I was interrupted by having to go off to Monte Carlo to dine with a very rich fat lady who has a whole floor of the Hotel de Paris & entertains largely. Her name is Mrs Cameron & her Husband is Lord Inchcape's right hand man. He, Lord Inchcape is here & asked to be remembered to you.

What hard lives these old rich men do lead. Being ill (I suppose) he can't eat or drink & gambling bores him. I'm sure he does not read. He just goes for an hour's walk every day. I suppose the rest of the time he reflects upon his enormous business.

We are just off to Grasse to visit Louis Mallet[2] who has got a villa there.

Much love to you Darling
Clemmie

Winston S. Churchill to Clementine Churchill
(Spencer-Churchill papers)

12 March 1925

My darling,

All is well here. Your delightful letter arrived & gave me the greatest pleasure. What a delicate & jaunty pen you wield! Sweet pussy.

I am at work all day long now—8-8. Today & tomorrow I am leading the House of C in Baldwin's absence. He made a gt point of my doing so. I have not been formally in charge since 1910!

I lunched with Rothermere yesterday. He was most friendly—asked why Max was attacking me, said he was in no way under his influence, & would

[1] Ethel Newcomb Field, 1873–1932. Only daughter of the Chicago department store owner and millionaire, Marshall Field. She married Beatty (her second husband) in 1901.

[2] Louis du Pan Mallet, 1864–1936. Entered Foreign Office, 1888. Private Secretary to Sir Edward Grey, 1905-7. Under-Secretary of State for Foreign Affairs, 1907-13. Knighted, 1912. Ambassador at Constantinople, 1913-14. After his retirement from the Foreign Office in 1920, he lived at Mortefontaine, Peymeinade, near Grasse.

support my Budget whatever it was. If I took off taxes good—if not—then he wd applaud the courage of sound finance. He is vy angry with Baldwin on account of his contemptuous reference to the Press in the Albert Hall speech.[1] I duly reported all this to the PM who was surprised at having given offence. I am going to try and effect a reconciliation later on.

I have finished another article (7th) but I fear I shall not be able to do the 8th & last.

The work is almost continuous. I cannot get the little calf after all: but as I had not mentioned it to the cow, it does not matter.

Tender love my darling, I am glad you are in clover. Rest, recuperate & fatten.

Your ever devoted
W

Mary is vy well. She has just given me a beautiful kiss.

Sir Eyre Crowe to Austen Chamberlain

(*Austen Chamberlain papers*)

ANGLO-FRENCH RELATIONS

12 March 1925

. . . Later on in the afternoon I received a message from the Prime Minister at the House of Commons to the effect that he had decided to call together a number of his colleagues, not the whole Cabinet, in order to discuss the matter and to arrive at some decision, and he asked me to be present.

I went there at 5 o'clock and found assembled in the Prime Minister's room Mr Winston Churchill, Lord Birkenhead, Sir Samuel Hoare, Sir L. Worthington-Evans, Mr Amery, Mr Bridgeman, Lord Salisbury and Lord Cecil. I did not think it a very promising selection.

We sat till nearly 7, when, as I above explained, it was too late for me to write to you.

I cannot describe to you the deplorable impression made upon me by this discussion, nor the feeling, I may frankly say, of indignation in which I left it. I must give you, at the risk of being tedious, a short account of the sitting.

---

[1] Baldwin had spoken at a victory demonstration at the Albert Hall on 4 December 1924. During his speech he had given this advice to all the Conservative MPs: 'Don't ever lose touch with your constituency; don't ever mistake the voice of the clubman and the voice of the Pressman in London for the voice of the country.'

The Prime Minister opened by asking me to explain the situation as described in your letters. I began to do so, beginning with your last letter and pointing out that the immediate question raised, and on which you had expressed the desire for guidance from the Prime Minister and perhaps the Cabinet, was whether we should make the threat or intimation to Herriot concerning our possible withdrawal from the Rhine, to which I referred above. But, I said, whilst this was apparently the one immediate point, it was clear to me that the issue involved was a much wider and graver one, and I hoped the ministers would take the whole situation into consideration and review it once more.

Here I was interrupted, first by one minister, then another, and a debate was begun which lasted for about $1\frac{1}{2}$ hours, extending over every conceivable point, mostly entirely irrelevant,—in fact a discussion as vague and inconclusive and very much on the same lines as that I had listened to some weeks ago in the Defence Committee.

Mr Winston Churchill once more developed the theory on which he had then expatiated, the gist of it being that there was no reason why we should do anything at all; or why we should come to any arrangement with France, who could be left to stew in her own juice without its having any bad effect on anybody or anything; that there was no immediate hurry either to take action or to make any decision; all we had to do was to go our own way and in a few years time we should see France on her knees begging for assistance and allowing us to impose anything whatever on her. He could not see why such inaction on our part should lead to a quarrel with France. It was quite untrue that there was any danger of a breach with her; we should go on as before, France would ask for things, we should refuse them, and everyone would be perfectly happy.

Mr Amery, as usual, dilated on the impossibility of doing anything, because the Dominions would never agree to anything being done. All that was required was to avoid the danger of any talk of entanglements, and to restrict ourselves to developing moral atmospheres by pacific methods, to the exclusion of anything to do with war, or disarmaments, or force or violence. . . .

Lord Birkenhead took it up. He entirely agreed with both Mr Winston Churchill and Mr Amery in everything. He remained absolutely opposed to any pact of any kind whatever. Nor, he declared, had the Cabinet. . . .

It was quite clear to me that there was a determination on the part of these ministers to prevent the pursuit of any policy, and you will pardon me for saying quite frankly that the attitude of Mr Winston Churchill and Lord Birkenhead left me under the clear impression that their object was not the ostensible one of dealing with the problem on its merits, but that they had ulterior motives, which I could only believe to be to make your position impossible.

I began by repeating your warning concerning the serious situation with which we had to deal and by protesting very formally against the view taken of the situation either in France or Germany as being altogether opposed to the opinion and the considered judgment of the Foreign Office, which I believed was shared by the Secretary of State.

I desired to have it placed on record that a quarrel with France over this matter would, contrary to what Mr Winston Churchill believed, lead to a definite breach with France, with all the consequences on the general state of Europe to which I had before alluded.

Winston S. Churchill to Stanley Baldwin

(Churchill papers: 18/10)

13 March 1925

My dear Prime Minister,

I have now read the report of Sir Russell Scott's[1] Committee on the organisation of the Colonial Office. I am surprised that Amery should find the work so laborious. I personally found the Colonial Office very much quieter and easier, from the point of view of business, than almost any other Office I have held.

Coming from the War Office to the Colonial Office in the beginning of 1921, I was immediately struck by the great reduction in the daily burden. I was at once handed over Iraq and Palestine, then costing £40 millions a year and in a state of great confusion. At the beginning of the next year I had the whole business of setting up the Irish Free State and passing the necessary legislation placed in my hands.

Nevertheless I was not unduly burdened, and was able to devote a good deal of my time to Cabinet affairs, like the Committee on which we both sat on Navy, Army and Air Force Estimates. I find it very difficult therefore to believe that, now the Irish Free State has cut so much adrift and has so few questions of a routine character open with Great Britain, and now that the Middle East is reduced to an expenditure of £4 millions a year, there is

---

[1] Robert Russell Scott, 1877–1960. Entered the Admiralty as a Clerk, Class I, 1901; Private Secretary to the Civil Lord, 1904–7. Joint Secretary to the Royal Commission on Indian Public Services, 1912–15. Member of the Central Control Board (Liquor Traffic), 1915–16. Acting Assistant Secretary, Admiralty, 1917. Controller of Establishments, Treasury, 1921–32. Knighted, 1922. Permanent Under-Secretary of State at the Home Office, 1932–8.

any need or justification for the appointment of an additional Ministerial Under Secretary or of an additional Permanent Under Secretary. I am afraid therefore I must continue to be entirely unconvinced.

The matter has, however, been reduced to comparatively small dimensions. The appointment of a Deputy Permanent Secretary—I presume at £2,000 a year—would not raise any controversial issue. A change in the title of the Secretary of State is no doubt desirable and costs nothing. The question of an extra Minister is for you to decide. There are well known Parliamentary criticisms to be encountered when proposals to increase the number of Ministers are made. These criticisms will in this case be reinforced by what will be, I think, a widespread feeling that the Colonial Office is very lightly burdened with Parliamentary work, two or three debates usually sufficing for the whole session.

Still if you wish to make a new Ministerial appointment, it could, I think, be defended on a ground of the advantage of enabling one or other of the three Ministerial representatives of the Colonial Office to tour about the Empire and keep in personal touch with its various Governments.

If the matter is brought before the Cabinet and you have already made up your mind, I will support your decision. If on the other hand you wish for a free discussion, I should feel bound to argue in the general sense of this letter.[1]

Winston S. Churchill to Clementine Churchill

(Spencer-Churchill papers)

15 March 1925

My darling—

I enclose an account of some of my doings in a form wh saves me the effort of writing. I am tired & have rather a head at the end of a long week. I do hope you are having rest, peace & sunshine & that you will return really refreshed. I have polished off two more articles to help pay the Income Tax: & perhaps I may get another one out of myself this afternoon or tomorrow morning.[2]

[1] On 11 June 1925 L. S. Amery was appointed Secretary of State for Dominion Affairs, in addition to the post of Colonial Secretary which he already held. These two offices were separated in November 1931, when J. H. Thomas remained at the Dominions Office, and Sir Philip Cunliffe-Lister became Colonial Secretary.

[2] On 31 March 1925 Churchill completed an article, 'Consistency in Politics', which he sent to Curtis Brown in New York, where it was later published in *Cosmopolitan*. On 2 May 1925 the *Pictorial Magazine* published a further article by Churchill, 'The German Splendour', about his recollections of the German Army manoeuvres at Breslau which he had attended as the Kaiser's guest in 1906. Five further articles by Churchill, 'The Irish Treaty', 'The Battle

Mary is flourishing. She comes & sits with me in the mornings & is sometimes most gracious. Diana is just back from school & we are all planning to go to see Randolph this afternoon.

When do you think you will return my dear one. Do not abridge yr holiday if it is doing you good—But of course I feel far safer from worry and depression when you are with me & when I can confide in yr sweet soul. It has given me so much joy to see you becoming stronger & settling down in this new abode. Health & nerves are the first requisites of happiness. I *do* think you have made great progress since the year began, in spite of all the work & burdens I have put on you. The most precious thing I have in life is yr love for me. I reproach myself for many shortcomings. You are a rock & I depend on you & rest on you. Come back to me therefore as soon as you can.

Your ever loving & devoted
W

Winston S. Churchill to Clementine Churchill
(Spencer-Churchill papers)

15 March 1925

My darling,

The week has passed in a whirl of deputations, sometimes as many as four a day, and I have had to listen patiently to every kind of request for relief of taxation and to give answers which revealed nothing. I think, however, I have succeeded in making courtesy a substitute for more solid services.

We are still ignorant of what the revenue will be for this year or next. But in a week now trustworthy figures will be available, and from that moment I must lock every secret in my bosom until the 28th of April; and I weigh and balance all the possibilities of my plan.

The battle with the Admiralty continues ding dong in the Cabinet Committee. FE reveals continually his extraordinary mental powers. He sits like a stuck pig, hardly saying a word for hours, until I wondered whether he was really taking these to him unfamiliar topics in at all. But when the time came for him to draw up a series of questions to be remitted to the Committee of Imperial Defence, he showed a mastery and penetration of the difficulty of the argument, and a power of getting to the root of the matter, most profound and astonishing. For the rest, everything goes very quietly.

---

of Sidney Street', 'My Spy Story', 'Plugstreet', and 'In the Air', were published in *Cosmopolitan* during 1924: all seven articles were among those reprinted in *Thoughts and Adventures* (first published in November 1932).

I paid my weekly visit to Chartwell yesterday. The progress on the Palanquin is terribly slow. No doubt one ought to be there each day, and then I am sure it would get on. Wallace works very hard himself, but he does not seem to make the others do their part.

The frame of the bow window looking out over the valley is now in position, and I hope next week the walls will be complete. Some progress has also been made with the paving. Both the cottages are practically finished. There are some leaks in the roof of Best's cottage where the ivy has deranged the tiles, and this I am having put right. The nursery wing has been stripped of its inside lining and the wall everywhere exposed.

Tomorrow morning the waterproofing people begin their operations which consist in further spraying of the outside and in coating the whole of the inside with their special waterproof cement. They guarantee the result, and Wallace seems to have great confidence in them. They expect to finish their work this week, and Brown will then begin the re-papering. The thickening of the partition in the cock-loft is also to begin on Monday and will be completed in a week or ten days. The fitting up of the odd man's room in accordance with your orders is going forward. It seems to me a poor room to put two footmen in. Surely it would be better to put one in the spare room at the cottage when it is finished.

Waterhouse and his gardeners are busy stripping all the ivy off the grey wall and planting out the borders. I do trust they will be ready by the time you come back. A good deal of tidying up has been done, and I have got two extra men at work turfing the ugly bare parts of the dam.

I have been giving a great deal of thought to the dairy problem. If you have pasture, cows, a cottage, a cowman and a dairy maid, it seems inevitable to go one step further. I am quite sure the best thing will be to build a little dairy quite detached from any of the old buildings. Far the best place is where Topper's kennel now stands. A little oblong brick house with a nice tiled roof will cost about £50 and should be ready in five weeks. After the men have done the Palanquin, they would turn on this. I am sure this plan is much better than trying to adapt the laundry or wash-house or impinging upon your limited store-room accommodation in the kitchen wing. Nothing will be done until you return.

I could not get the little calf as I hoped. As I did not mention it to the cow, she was not disappointed. She is giving four quarts of milk a day, and this we are going to sell to the baker. If we get sixpence a quart, that will be fourteen shillings a week which is not to be sneezed at. I brought home sixteen dozen eggs last week and twelve dozen this, and thirty-one dozen are in pickle.

The five little pigs in the sty near the stables are to be sold to the butcher.

It is hoped they will make £30. The second old sow is on the verge of having another family. Their fertility is formidable. We shall have to get rid of all the little pigs as soon as they become marketable.

Such is my report.

Last night I dined with FE. He and Mr Solly Joel[1] having challenged Sir William Berry[2] and me to a contest of bridge—sixpenny points and £5 on the rubber—we met to play it off. You know I have not touched a bridge card for a year, and what a bad player I am. The other two were far better than my partner and myself. However, of course I held beautiful cards, played like a book, and won £25 on the rubber and came away with it.

Tonight I dine with Margaret Wodehouse[3] for Mah Jong. I have McKenna coming to dinner here on Tuesday, with Linky,[4] Keynes, Layton[5] and Niemeyer to argue about the gold standard, bank rate, etc. Jack and Goonie are coming to lunch today, and after that I am thinking of going down to Eton to see Randolph, taking Diana and Sarah with me.

I telegraphed you today to let me know when you are coming back. There is no reason why you should hurry back, if you are enjoying yourself

[1] Solomon Barnato Joel, diamond magnate. A nephew of the legendary Barney Barnato, pioneer of diamond mining in South Africa. Director of many mining companies, including de Beers Consolidated Mines. Director of (among others) the Standard Bank of South Africa, and of the City and South London Railway. He had houses in Mayfair, and at Newmarket. A Justice of the Peace. He died in 1931. His son Dudley Jack Barnato Joel was Conservative MP for Dudley from 1931 to 1941.

[2] William Ewer Berry, 1879–1954. Son of a Merthyr Tydfil Alderman. Founded the *Advertising World*, 1901. Editor-in-Chief of the *Sunday Times*, 1915–36. Created Baronet, 1921. Editor-in-Chief of the *Daily Telegraph* from 1928 until his death. Created Baron Camrose, 1929; Viscount, 1941. Chairman of the Financial Times Ltd and Chairman of the Associated Press. Principal Adviser to the Ministry of Information, 1939.

[3] Frances Margaret Montagu Irby, 1884–1950. Daughter of Colonel Leonard Irby, and great granddaughter of the 2nd Baron Boston. She married Lord Wodehouse (later 3rd Earl of Kimberley) as her third husband in 1922.

[4] Lord Hugh Richard Heathcote Gascoyne Cecil, 1869–1956. Known as 'Linky'. Fifth son of the 3rd Marquess of Salisbury. Educated at Eton and University College, Oxford. Conservative MP for Greenwich, 1895–1906; for Oxford University, 1910–37. Provost of Eton, 1936–44. Created Baron Quickswood, 1941. In 1908 he was the 'best man' at Churchill's wedding.

[5] Walter Thomas Layton, 1884–1966. Lecturer in economics, University College, London, 1909–12. Represented the Ministry of Munitions on the Milner Mission to Russia, 1917. Statistical Adviser, Ministry of Munitions, 1917–18. Unsuccessful Liberal candidate at the Elections of 1922 and 1923. Editor of *The Economist*, 1922–38. Knighted, 1930. Chairman, News Chronicle Ltd, 1930–50; Vice-Chairman, Daily News Ltd, 1930–63. Head of the Joint War Production Staff, 1942–3. Director, Reuters Ltd, 1945–53. Created Baron, 1947. Vice-President, Consultative Assembly of the Council of Europe, 1949–57. Deputy Leader of the Liberal Party in the House of Lords, 1952–5. Director, Tyne-Tees Television Ltd, 1958–61.

and it is doing you good. But let me know the date so that I can make my plans accordingly.

Your devoted

W

Winston S. Churchill to Sir George Barstow

(*Treasury papers: T172/1440*)

17 March 1925

After the figures were agreed at the CID, it was discovered that the Admiralty had added them up wrong and had omitted about £80,000. In response to repeated appeals, I agreed to waive further objection to this. . . .

Now after weeks of discussions have taken place, the Admiralty come forward and ask for £300,000 more. I propose to resist this and point out the consequences of Lord Curzon's speech in the Lords. Let me see it.[1]

P. J. Grigg: recollections

(*P. J. Grigg: 'Prejudice and Judgement'*)

17 March 1925

DINNER AT THE TREASURY

The Symposium lasted till midnight or after. I thought at the time that the ayes had it. Keynes's thesis, which was supported in every particular by McKenna, was that the discrepancy between American and British prices was not $2\frac{1}{2}$ per cent as the exchanges indicated, but 10 per cent. If we went back to gold at the old parity we should therefore have to deflate domestic prices by something of that order. This meant unemployment and downward adjustments of wages and prolonged strikes in some of the heavy industries, at the end of which it would be found that these industries had undergone a permanent contraction. It was much better, therefore, to try to keep domestic prices and nominal wage rates stable and allow the exchanges to fluctuate.

Bradbury made a great point of the fact that the Gold Standard was knave-proof. It could not be rigged for political or even more unworthy

---

[1] During a debate on 4 March 1925, Lord Curzon had called the Singapore base 'a necessary and indispensable link in the great chain of Imperial communications', and had warned that 'if there were a war in the Far East, and if you did not send your fleet to Singapore, the whole of your possessions would go, your trade routes would be destroyed, and your dominions exposed to attack'. This was Curzon's last speech in the House of Lords. He died on March 20.

reasons. It would prevent our living in a fool's paradise of false prosperity, and would ensure our keeping on a competitive basis in our export business, not by allowing what I believe the economists call the 'terms of trade' to go against us over the whole field, but by a reduction of costs in particular industries. In short, to anticipate a phrase which Winston afterwards used in answering a sneer about our having shackled ourselves to gold, we should be doing no more than shackling ourselves to reality.

To the suggestion that we should return to gold but at a lower parity, Bradbury's answer was that we were so near the old parity that it was silly to create a shock to confidence and to endanger our international reputation for so small and so ephemeral an easement.[1]

Neville Chamberlain to Winston S. Churchill

(*Treasury papers: T171/247*)

19 March 1925

My dear Chancellor,

I see that I never sent you a reply to your letter of the 20th February last, and perhaps this is really unnecessary now, seeing that we have come to a complete agreement as to the lines upon which we should proceed.

All the same, I think as I have to write to you, that I should like to correct the assumption in your letter that in my Memorandum I had definitely proposed to you the imposition upon the Exchequer of an additional charge of $5\frac{1}{2}$ millions a year in order to make up for the deficiency in the contributions of the insured workers necessitated by the inability of the agricultural labourer to meet the new burden. My view all along was that a true contributory scheme would involve full payment of the 4d by all insured men; but, in the absence of personal knowledge, I felt it was necessary to face the possibility that 4d might be more than the agricultural labourer could stand, and, in this case, it followed that one must consider what alternative there was to the abandonment of the scheme altogether.

I only want now to say that I was very much relieved to have a satisfactory

---

[1] The Governor of the Bank of England, Montagu Norman, was on holiday at the time of this dinner discussion. As soon as he returned to London, he set about obtaining both Churchill's and Baldwin's formal approval for an immediate return to the Gold Standard. Norman noted in his diary on March 19: 'Chancellor for lunch in Downing Street. Gold return to be announced April 6th–8th. Cushion to be meanwhile arranged by Bank. I warn him of 6% Bank rate next month.' And on March 20 Montagu Norman noted: 'Prime Minister, Chancellor, Austen Chamberlain, Bradbury, Niemeyer at 2.30. Free gold statement to be in Budget about April 28th.'

assurance about agriculture from the Minister[1] and other authorities, and that I feel well satisfied that we shall not impose upon the rural worker more than he can bear, or more than he will be willing to pay for the benefits received.

I now want to refer to the note which you passed to me in Cabinet yesterday. I always understood that you had in mind the introduction of a Bill on the day following your Budget speech, and my note to you was intended to show that this could not be done if secrecy was to be preserved up to the last moment. Your note, however, seems to point to a proposal which I had never thought of, namely, that I should explain the main provisions of a Bill to a House of Commons which would have no text before it. This seems to be a new kind of song without words, and I feel certain that it is quite impossible of achievement, even if it were desirable. We should have the whole opposition violently protesting, and our own people would be equally resentful. I cannot myself see what need there is for me to say anything until I bring in the Bill. I should have thought that a quarter of an hour from you on broad lines is all that you require; and if you have at any time thought that I should object to being silent during the Budget discussion, I beg you will put such an idea out of your mind.

I have to go to Edinburgh tonight, and shall not be back till Saturday, so that I shall not be able to attend the Cabinet. I think perhaps, however, it would be desirable that I should have some conversation with you on the subject, and I therefore will, if you like, come to your room on Monday afternoon.

Yours sincerely,
Neville Chamberlain

Winston S. Churchill to Neville Chamberlain

(*Churchill papers: 18/10*)

20 March 1925
Secret & Personal

My dear Neville Chamberlain,

I have been giving a good deal of thought to the later developments of the Anderson scheme, as explained to me by the Government Actuary. In my mind the scheme resolves itself into two parts, benefits (a) to the cove-

---

[1] From November 1924 to November 1925 the Minister of Agriculture was Edward Wood (see page 192, note 2).

nanted, and (b) to the uncovenanted. The covenanted are all plain sailing. They get what they pay for, and the Exchequer only intervenes for the purpose of enabling the scheme to start off immediately on equal terms for all contributors, whatever their age. It is true that a great gift is conferred by the State on contributors of advanced years, but that is inseparable from the initiation of any general contributory system.

When we come to the uncovenanted, quite a different series of circumstances exist. The uncovenanted have no claim, and whatever is done for them can only be done on grounds of public policy. It is clearly contrary to public policy to allow the present conditions to continue under which the dependent and often helpless children of a widow are deprived of the care and attention they ought to have because the mother is compelled to work long hours and laboriously to provide a bare maintenance for them. This then is the foundation on which our treatment of the uncovenanted should be built. I cannot, however, feel justified in following the uncovenanted widow further than her period of motherhood as defined by her having children dependent on her under a certain age. After the last child passes that age she is in no worse a position to gain her individual living than vast numbers of men, and there are no grounds of public policy for conferring upon her a special pension of 10/- a week towards which no contributions have been made on her behalf. In this particular I feel unable to accept the recommendation of the Anderson Committee.

It seems to me therefore that our scheme divides into (a) permanent pensions for all covenanted widows, and (b) temporary pensions for all uncovenanted widowed mothers. This is a good broad classification of principle, which can, I think, be defended against every assault.

What then should be the limiting age by which a dependent child should be defined? I understand that it has been proposed for your consideration that the uncovenanted benefit should be given to mothers with children under 11, and that the pension given in these circumstances should never be recalled, ie in the limiting case that a widow with one child and that child one day under 11 on January 1, 1926, should get 10/- a week for the rest of her life. In my view it would be better to raise the age of children for the purpose of the mother qualification of an uncovenanted widow and let her pension stop when the last child ceases to be dependent upon her. Dependence will be presumed where the child is under 16, unless the contrary appears. Thereafter the uncovenanted mother could resume her place in industry, and as a contributor would receive her pension at sixty-five.

The result of this change would be to bring in a very much larger number of widows now burdened with children (240,000 against 135,000) in the earlier years and at the same time clear the Fund more rapidly of the non-contributory cases. It would thus have the effect of adding to the charge in the earlier years and throwing less of an unjustifiable burden upon the Exchequer in later years. I am prepared to accept the earlier burden for the sake of the greater equity of the scheme and the larger number of immediate beneficiaries.

So far as the allowances to children are concerned, I think they should be continued to 14 in all cases, and thereafter to 16 if the child is still attending school. This would put a strong premium on better education and discourage early blind alley occupations. I do not think an allowance ought to be paid in respect of a child between 14 and 16 who is withdrawn from school and earning 7/- or 8/- a week running errands. This consideration should govern both covenanted and uncovenanted cases.

I understand that if all goes well it will be possible to bring this scheme into operation as regards widows from the beginning of January next, and as regards the 'Sixty-five's' from the following April 1. This will be quite agreeable to me.

Hitherto we have expressed the future costs of the scheme in two tables 'with lapse' and 'without lapse'. The true cost lies between these two extremes. It would be very confusing to argue the case on the basis of these alternative figures; in fact the financial position would become almost un-intelligible to anyone who did not give a special study to it. I have long felt we must have one set of figures. The Government Actuary therefore proposes to take certain arbitrary data giving the proportions, 'depending on age, etc' of those leaving employment who would become voluntary contributors. From these data he reaches a single column of figures about half way between the estimates on the two alternative bases. If this single line of figures is accepted for purposes of discussion, the necessary actuarial report for Parliament will show exactly how it was reached.

I append provisional estimates under these new conditions. A surplus to the Exchequer must arise in 1925–6, since no pensions to the 'Sixty-five's' will then be in course of payment: there will also be a small surplus in 1926–7. These surpluses I shall carry forward to diminish future contributions from the State.

With regard to your letter of the 19th I am in full agreement about procedure. I expect however that the Bill will be very far advanced if not ready at the date of the introduction of the Budget and that it could be introduced, if you wish, as soon as the Budget Resolutions have been passed. Assuming that we can agree on the general lines of this letter, it should be possible I understand to put a draft Bill before a small secret Cabinet Committee at the beginning of April. There is always a great safety in having two or three quite new minds applied to a business like this: the

kind of questions and difficulties they raise are often illuminating. Let us
have a talk on Monday: I shall be free after 5.30.

Yours very sincerely
Winston S. Churchill

Winston S. Churchill to Viscount French of Ypres
(French papers)

20 March 1925

My dear Friend,

This is only a line to tell you how much I rejoice at your wonderful
courage and strength and at the good reports the papers give of your
progress.

I have been thinking so much and often about you during this ordeal;
and I can never forget your kindness to me, and our comradeship and the
great matters in which we worked together.

If ever you feel inclined for a visit, command me.

With every good wish, Believe me,

Your faithful and devoted friend
Winston[1]

Sir Roger Keyes to Winston S. Churchill
(Churchill papers: 18/8)

21 March 1925   Admiralty

My dear Winston,

This is the book on the Far East which you promised to read. It was
written by a young Naval Officer[2] who has just spent 2½ years on the China
Station. I have marked passages which are of particular interest in connection with the steady and ruthless preparation for war on the part of Japan.[3]

---

[1] Viscount French of Ypres died on 22 May 1925.

[2] William Stephen Richard King-Hall, 1893–1966. Entered the Royal Navy, 1914. Served
with the Grand Fleet, 1914–17. Admiralty Naval Staff, 1919–20. China Squadron, 1921–3.
Intelligence Officer, Mediterranean Fleet (under Sir Roger Keyes), 1925–6; Atlantic Fleet,
1927–8. Founded the K. H. Newsletter Service, 1936. A writer and radio commentator on
current affairs. Independent MP for Ormskirk, 1939–44. Founded the Hansard Society for
Parliamentary Government, 1944. Knighted, 1954. Created Baron, 1966.

[3] The book was Western Civilization and the Far East, which had been published by Methuen
in October 1924. Stephen King-Hall had written four previous books under the pseudonym
'R. N. Etienne'. These were Verses From The Grand Fleet (1916), A Naval Lieutenant 1914–18
(1919), Strange Tales from the Fleet (1919) and The Diary of a U-Boat Commander (1920).

I was head of the Section of the Naval Intelligence Division which dealt with the Russo-Japanese war—I am a student of war, and I have access to all the information passed by the Foreign Office on the subject, and I think I am as well qualified to give an opinion on the possibility of a conflict in the Far East—*unless we insure against it*—as anyone in the Foreign Office.

Japan must know that she has nothing to fear from the United States or ourselves, if she is content to allow Europeans a fair field in the East. But, as surely as she turned China out of Korea, Russia out of Manchuria, Germany out of Tsingtau, she will turn Europeans out of China and, in time, Asia, unless we are sufficiently strong to make it not worth her while to attempt it.

I do see the other side very clearly, and I do realise that the country is in no mood to face the enormous expenditure which the provision of proper security will entail, but something must be done to check Japanese Naval Expansion or keep pace with it.

On pages 39 and 40 of the first volume of 'The World Crisis' you give a memorandum you wrote in 1909 on the German menace, and remarked—'this is, I think, the first sinister impression I was ever led to record'—it was prophetically true, but was only 2 years before Agadir and 6 before the Great War 1914.

I do hope you will bring home to the Government that there *is* a Japanese menace, for if this Government does not prepare to meet it or eliminate it, and is succeeded by a Labour Government the outlook is indeed black.

Yours ever,
Roger Keyes

Winston S. Churchill to Sir Roger Keyes

(*Keyes papers*)

22 March 1925   Treasury Chambers
Private

My dear Roger,

I am very grateful to you for sending me King Hall's book, and I will endeavour to read it as soon as possible.

Your letter distresses me because it shows how very differently we are viewing the position. I do not believe Japan has any idea of attacking the British Empire, or that there is any danger of her doing so for at least a generation to come. If, however, I am wrong and she did attack us 'out of the Blue', I do not think there would be any difficulty in defeating her. She would not, as was the case with Germany, have any chance of striking at the heart of the Empire and destroying its power to wage war. We should be put to great annoyance and expense, but in three or four years we could certainly sweep the Japanese from the seas and force them to make peace. The mere fact that in the opening years some of our Asiatic coaling stations or our Australasian colonies suffered annoyance, loss of trade, etc, would not make any difference to the final result. The fact that we were injured in the opening days of the war and that Japan was the aggressor, would certainly raise the issue of the Asiatic versus the European, and every country having interests in China—most especially the United States—would be thrown increasingly to our side. I am not therefore in the least afraid of a war with Japan if it should come; and it is because Japan knows perfectly well the risk she would run in attacking the British Empire, that I am convinced it will not come.

On the other hand the Admiralty policy of adding £25 or £30 millions to the Naval Estimates in the next few years in order to put a superior Fleet in the Pacific, will never be accepted by the country. I do not believe it will be accepted by the Government, or by the House of Commons. If it were, it would ruin the Government and lead to a Socialist House of Commons, returned for the express purpose of stopping such expenditure. This would mean that, even if you got your way now, your plans would be broken up before they had reached any effective fruition.

The great task before the Admiralty is to try to rebuild the Fleet in a sober and reasonable way, and without injuring the general interest to an excessive extent. To do this they must: (a) drop the idea of a war with Japan; (b) abandon the plan of putting a Fleet in the Pacific; (c) reduce the expense and maintenance of the Fleet by every possible means; (d) accept far more reasonable and moderate standards for replacement, and make every existing vessel last as long as possible. Even when all this has been done, there will still remain a serious extra charge to be borne by the Exchequer. I should be prepared to make an effort if the Admiralty on their side would try. I am very sorry to see that all they do is to exaggerate every danger, multiply every factor of safety, and put every one of their claims at the very highest.

Yours vy sincerely,
Winston S.C.

Winston S. Churchill to Clementine Churchill

(*Spencer-Churchill papers*)

22 March 1925

My dearest darling,

I have just got yr telegram.[1] I feel for you so much—& poor Nellie[2] too. Yr Mamma is a gt woman: & her life has been a noble life. When I think of all the courage & tenacity & self denial that she showed during the long hard years when she was fighting to bring up you & Nellie & Bill,[3] I feel what a true mother & grand woman she proved herself, & I am the more glad & proud to think her blood flows in the veins of our children.

My darling I grieve for you. An old & failing life going out on the tide, after the allotted span has been spent & after most joys have faded is not a case for human pity. It is only a part of the immense tragedy of our existence here below against wh both hope & faith have rebelled. It is only what we all expect & await—unless cut off untimely. But the loss of a mother severs a chord in the heart and makes life seem lonely & its duration fleeting. I know the sense of amputation from my own experience three years ago.[4] I deeply sorrow for yr pain. I greatly admired & liked yr mother. She was an ideal mother-in-law. Never shall I allow that relationship to be spoken of with mockery—for her sake. I am pleased to think that perhaps she wd also have given me a good character. At any rate I am sure our marriage & life together were one of the gt satisfactions of her life. My darling sweet I kiss you.

I have been working all day (Sunday) at pensions & am vy tired. Please telegraph me how events develop & whether there is anything that I can do.

Goodnight my dearest,

Your devoted husband

W

[1] Clementine Churchill had gone to Dieppe, where her mother, Lady Blanche Hozier, was dying. Lady Hozier died a week later, on 29 March 1925.

[2] Nellie Hozier, 1888–1957. Clementine Churchill's sister. While serving as a nurse in August 1914 she crossed over to Belgium, where she was captured by the Germans, but released almost immediately. In December 1915 she married Colonel Bertram Romilly. They had two children, Giles and Esmond (killed in Action in November 1941).

[3] William Ogilvy Hozier, 1888–1921. Clementine Churchill's brother. Entered the Navy, 1904. Lieutenant, 1909. Qualified as a German interpreter, 1910. Commanded the Destroyer *Thorn*, 1914–15, and the *Nubian*, 1915. First Lieutenant on board the cruiser *Edgar*, at the Dardanelles, 1915–16. Commanded the *Clematis*, 1916–18. Lieutenant-Commander, 1918.

[4] Churchill's mother had died on 29 June 1921, at the age of 67.

Winston S. Churchill: departmental note[1]

(*Churchill papers: 22/67*)

22 March 1925

The Singapore Sub Committee never considered the 1st April 1928 as a date of special significance. It was intended that the floating dock should be in position during 1928. The Cabinet have now asked the Naval Programme Committee whether a delay of three months in ordering the extra sections of the dock at the present time will in fact cause us to lose a year, as the Admiralty contend, ie whether a delay of three months now will prevent the dock from being in position at Singapore before 1929. This is the sole question before us.

The Admiralty paper states that 'owing to the south-west monsoon the sections cannot be towed across the Indian Ocean during the period May to September. Therefore the end of September 1927 is the first possible date in that year for the sections to leave Aden for Singapore.' On this basis the Admiralty expect to have all the sections across the Indian Ocean and available for assembling at Singapore by the end of January 1928, ie four months from the date of leaving Aden. If, however, this process is set back by three months, there will still be plenty of good weather. If, for instance, the dock sections left Aden at the end of December and took four months in transit, they would still reach Singapore by the end of April and the dock could be completed by August or September 1928. It is clear therefore on the Admiralty's time table that after making every conceivable allowance for delay and accidents they have three months in hand before the monsoon season of 1928 makes transportation across the Indian Ocean difficult.

Moreover, I do not myself see why it should take four months to transport these sections across the Indian Ocean; and I am sure that if the Admiralty wished to do so, they could quite easily shorten up this process by a month or six weeks. Even if we accept all their figures, it is clear that a three months' delay in authorising the construction of the dock sections would only produce a corresponding three months' delay in the construction of the dock in 1928, and would not push the completion over to the other side of the monsoon season in 1929.

The other parts of the Admiralty's time table similarly reveal very large margins. We are told that in order for the sections to leave Aden at the end of September 1927, they must leave England in the previous April, ie five months earlier. This seems an incredible length of time in which to move

[1] In a covering note to Sir George Barstow, Churchill wrote: 'Please look at the enclosed note which I have drafted on this Admiralty imposture. Please check my work, and let me have your corrections or confirmation before we go to the Committee tomorrow morning.'

these sections during the summer weather through the Mediterranean and the Red Sea. I have not the slightest doubt that two months could be economised on this portion of the journey if the Admiralty wished to do so.

Lastly, there is the question of the time taken for the construction of the sections from the date of ordering the material. For this two years are allowed by the Admiralty. I cannot believe that there would be the slightest difficulty in gaining three months on this, if it was desired to do so, without any appreciable addition to expenditure.

We have therefore at the present moment the following periods in hand:—

Saving in period of construction	3 months
Saving in passage from England to Aden	2 months
Saving by starting from Aden in December instead of September	3 months
Total saving	8 months

All we require for the purposes of our inquiry is three months. We must have it finished by June in order that Vote A may be debated in the House of Commons. On any showing we can afford to allow an inquiry to take place before authorising this new expenditure as an additional measure.

I suggest the following time table to the Admiralty:—

Decision to issue orders for the construction of the new sections, July 1, 1925.

Sections ready to leave England, April 1, 1927.

Sections arrive Aden, July 1, 1927.

Earliest date of leaving Aden, end of September, 1927.

Latest date of leaving Aden, if dock is to be in position in 1928, end of December, 1927.

Margin for contingencies, 6 months.

Add saving by more speedy passage of Indian Ocean, say $1\frac{1}{2}$ months, total margin even after allowing Cabinet Committee three months for decision of the question of principle, $7\frac{1}{2}$ months.

Winston S. Churchill: departmental note

(Churchill papers: 18/12)

24 March 1925

ROYAL MINT ISSUE OF SOVIET COINS[1]

Let me see the papers of the original decision to allow them to coin silver and copper. What are the designs of the coins and the translation of any inscriptions upon them? What is the amount of money and the profit involved in the silver and copper coinage? What is the profit involved in the proposed deal?

The policy of the late Government was to give the utmost countenance to the Soviets. That is certainly not the policy of the present Administration. It is at least paradoxical that the Royal Mint should be stamping coins with revolutionary emblems for the use of a Government pledged to the destruction of all Monarchies and the existing civilisation. Certainly it is a commercially minded incident.

Winston S. Churchill: remarks to a deputation[2]

(Treasury papers: T172/1452)

24 March 1925

TAX REMISSIONS

. . . as long as a working man is in good health and young, or in the prime of his life, and in employment at good wages, you need not really worry yourself about him, nor does he expect you to do so. He does not regard himself as an object of compassion: he regards himself as a healthy, strong, free citizen, and all is going well. It is when misfortune comes upon this

---

[1] In 1924 the Leningrad Mint approached the Royal Mint for help in supplying coins for Soviet Russia, designed to replace the paper money then in circulation. By the end of the year the Royal Mint had struck 40 million half-rouble pieces in fine silver. The Soviet Government provided the silver bullion for these coins; it was valued at £1,600,000. A further million copper five-copeck pieces were also struck in the Royal Mint. In its annual report for 1924 the Royal Mint pointed out that these coinages 'enabled the works to be continually engaged throughout the year'. In addition, as the Soviet lettering was new to the Mint, it 'afforded valuable experience for the Department'. Both coins showed the Arms of the Soviet Union on one side. On the reverse of the half-rouble was a smith at work forging metal. On the reverse of the five-copeck was an ornament composed of ears of barley.

[2] Requesting tax remissions. In his opening remarks, Churchill argued that tax remissions would be better spent 'for assisting some great scheme for dealing with the special cases of real hardship which are very numerous than as a general relief to the whole mass of the population'.

household, when prolonged unemployment, or old age, or sickness, or the death of the bread winner comes upon this household that you see how narrow was the margin on which he was apparently living so prosperously, and in a few months the result of the thrift of years may be swept away and the home broken up. . . .

I do not think myself that very bright years are in front of us. I do not think they are going to be any worse than what we have passed through. I think we are going to steadily get a little better each year. It will take very very careful national housekeeping. . . .

Winston S. Churchill to Clementine Churchill

(Spencer-Churchill papers)

25 March 1925

My darling,

The telephone talks are a comfort—in spite of the clippings & clickings & cuttings off.

I had rather hoped from what you said that if yr Mamma got through these two or three critical days, her lungs wd clear & she might recover. I am grieved that the doctor will not encourage this hope.

I marched in poor G. Curzon's cortege this morning.[1] The service was dull and dreary. He faced his end with fortitude & philosophy. I am vy sorry he is gone. I did not think the tributes were vy generous. I wd not have been grateful for such stuff. But he did not inspire affection, nor represent gt causes. Baba[2] looked a dream in crape. Much the best memorial.

I must take you to see Hamlet. Diana DC[3] took me. It is vy impressive. Barrymore[4] is an agreeable fellow—vy polished & worldly wise. I think he makes a fine interpretation of the part. LG has returned—walked out to Westminster—I had a pleasant talk with him. He is going to the Canaries for a cruise. He said he ought not to come to the House—but it was like not

---

[1] Lord Curzon had died on 20 March 1925.

[2] Grace Elvina Hinds, daughter of J. Monroe Hinds, of Alabama, USA, United States Minister to Brazil, and widow of Alfred Duggan of Buenos Aires. She married Curzon in 1917, and was created GBE in 1922. She died in 1958.

[3] Lady Diana Olivia Winifred Maud Manners, 1892–   . Daughter of the 8th Duke of Rutland. In 1919 she married Alfred Duff Cooper (later Viscount Norwich). After her husband's death in 1954 she was known as Lady Diana Cooper.

[4] John Barrymore, 1882–1942. Actor. First appeared on the stage in Chicago, 1903. He produced and played Hamlet at the Haymarket, London, in 1925. Subsequently he appeared in many films and radio programmes in the United States.

being able to keep away from the 'pub'. He made a speech on foreign affairs full of truth & knowledge—but lacking any clear purpose.[1] Austen did the heavy father in rebuke: & Baldwin professed to be much scandalized. It is now a convention that Foreign affairs are only to be treated in unctuous platitudes wh bear no relation to what is really going on. This is called 'Open diplomacy'.

Really the offer about the house wh I enclosed is exhilarating. I expect I cd get 80 guineas a week for 17 weeks—nearly £1,400. But where shd we go?

It is like offering a snail a fine rent for his shell. He wd like to take it: but what the hell is he to do without the shell?

Think it over—we cd go to Dinard or some beautiful place for the childrens' holiday & have Chartwell for nothing for the whole year.

On the whole I am for living there ourselves.

Tender love my sweet
Yr ever devoted
W

PS. See Goonie's letter enclosed. Will you telegraph to her. My dearest—I just add this line to say how I am thinking of yr dear mamma & of all her goodness & rare qualities. I always felt what a gt lady she was, how endowed with dignity, how dowered with amiability. She knew I had a deep regard for her.

---

[1] Speaking in the debate on the Geneva Protocol on 24 March 1925, Lloyd George had said, of the European situation: 'With regard to the questions between France and Germany, I am very hopeful that there will be no conflict. The French peasant has had enough of war. His losses have been so colossal that he will not go to war for the Saar, or the bridgeheads of the Rhine, or Reparations, and there I am hopeful, although not altogether confident. That is not the case with regard to the East. The Eastern frontiers are throbbing with trouble from the Bosphorus to the Baltic. Every European frontier is marked in red, but the frontiers of Central and Eastern Europe are a deeper red than any. There is none of these borderlines that has not been fought over for centuries. There is not a tract of territory in regard to which any country cannot claim precedents for saying that it belonged to them at one time, and there have been conquests and reconquests.'

Winston S. Churchill: note[1]

(*Churchill papers: 22/68*)

31 March 1925   Treasury Chambers

SINGAPORE

The Admiralty should, so soon as the floating dock is in position, make arrangements to base a squadron of battle-cruisers, or a fast division of battle-ships, or if possible both, upon Singapore during the period of strained relations, or as soon as may be after War has begun. This force shd be provided with a due proportion of the latest light Cruisers, with two flotillas of the newest destroyers, and not less than 20 of the best submarines.

The role of this force would be defensive, and it shd not be drawn into battle with superior Japanese forces unless or until these have been reduced by submarines, by mines, by aeroplane action or by the batteries of Singapore. It is believed that such a force wd prove an effectual deterrent against a Japanese attack upon Singapore, having regard to its distance (2,300 miles) from any Japanese base. In no case however shd we attempt offensive operations in Japanese home waters, nor risk capital ships in aid of the defence of Hong Kong. All the rest of our naval forces shd be utilized to secure the trade-routes through the Indian Ocean, round the Cape of Good Hope, and so far as may be necessary in the Atlantic.

Simultaneously with the declaration of war, a preconceived programme of new construction shd be begun according to a plan kept constantly up to date. The object of this programme shd be the continued reinforcement of the fleet at Singapore, and secondly the preparation of a floating base capable of sustaining a superior battle fleet with all ancillary vessels in Japanese waters.

Such base must comprise floating docks, repair-ships, store ships, victual-ling ships, armament ships, guardship monitors, depot-ships both for sub-marines and destroyers, together with an ample fleet of tankers, the whole capable of being moved forward from point to point by selected anchorages with the movement of the battle fleet. The time-table of this scheme of construction shd be compressed into a maximum of two years from the outbreak of the war.

In the event, which is not admitted as a reasonably probable contingency, of Singapore falling before the forces based on it are capable of delivering

---

[1] In sending this note to Sir Maurice Hankey, Edward Marsh wrote: 'This is for your eye alone. Winston has just jotted down what he thinks the Admiralty ought to reply to Question (4) in the proposed terms of reference to the CID arising out of the Naval Programme Committee—without of course wishing to hold them down to particular figures and details. He wd like to know what you think of it.'

decisive battle, our covering forces hitherto based on Singapore should, unless a favourable opportunity has been offered to them, withdraw without being drawn into decisive action at an inferiority to Colombo, to Bombay, or to Aden & the Red Sea, beginning their advance from this point as soon as the Floating Base for the whole fleet has been completed.

April 1925

Winston S. Churchill to William Bridgeman

(*Churchill papers: 22/68*)

1 April 1925

My dear First Lord,

Sir Philip Watts[1] has sent me his correspondence with Lord Chelmsford, of which there is no doubt a copy in the Admiralty, on the subject of fitting bulges to the five 'Queen Elizabeths'.

It is evident that very great expense will be involved in this questionable policy. Not only is the expense incurred upon the ships it is proposed to alter, but the whole question of dock accommodation is affected thereby. Particularly is this the case at Singapore. I understand that without these bulges these five ships could all use the existing commercial dock in Keppel Harbour as well as the floating dock which is to be installed. If the decision of the Committee of Imperial Defence should be against sending the main Battlefleet to Singapore for a decisive battle in the Pacific, at any rate for a considerable number of years, it would be all the more important that any capital ships stationed at Singapore should possess superior speed to the Japanese Battlefleet. The loss of speed by fitting the bulges appears therefore to be a serious disadvantage. It seems a pity to cripple this fast division of capital ships, the arguments for which were held to be so powerful at the time when great sacrifices were made for their creation.

I propose to bring this matter before Lord Birkenhead's Committee and also to raise it in the Committee of Imperial Defence. Before doing so I should be very much obliged to you if you would let me know what steps have already been taken to fit the bulges to these ships, what expense is involved and how this expense is distributed over the various years and what

---

[1] Philip Watts, 1846–1926. Naval architect. Served in the Construction Department of the Admiralty, 1870–85. Director of the War Shipbuilding Department of Armstrong, Whitworth, 1885–1901. Chairman of the Federation of Shipbuilders. Director of Naval Construction, Admiralty, 1901–12. Knighted, 1905. Adviser on Naval Construction to the Board of Admiralty, 1912–22. Fellow of the Royal Society.

consequential expenditure is entailed through widening docks at Devonport, Singapore or elsewhere.

Yours very sincerely,
Winston S. Churchill

Cornelia, Lady Wimborne to Winston S. Churchill
(*Churchill papers: 2/141*)

3 April 1925

Dearest Winston,

I have not written to you to congratulate you before, partly because I find it very difficult to know what to say. My feelings are as you may imagine mixed, but I do rejoice in whatever gives you pleasure and prosperity and although it is difficult to be logical in life, I wish you personally all success & would not like you to think I was wanting in love & affection for you for I am very fond of you & your life revives all the memories of the dearest of brothers.

Don't trouble to write as you must have more than enough on your shoulders. I am also not unmindful of your good offices in the past for Ivor. Life rushes on. To me at least it seems nothing but memories.

Yr affectionate
Aunt C.

Winston S. Churchill to Neville Chamberlain
(*Churchill papers: 18/10*)

3 April 1925   Treasury Chambers

My dear Neville Chamberlain,

I have been thinking continually over our conversation of Monday. I feel increasingly convinced that the uncovenanted man of 65 ought to pay something before receiving a free gift from the State. The man of 65 has paid nothing, has been promised nothing, is expecting nothing; and he is suddenly to be presented with £25 a year, as well as having his wife provided for in the event of his death. I do not believe he would regard it as a hardship to be made to contribute for two or three years before receiving his pension at 65. He would have to pay £1 a year for three years in order to receive £25 a year for two years, from 68 to 70. He would thus get back £50 for £3, and his would be the least favoured case.

The whole principle of contribution is valuable: it avoids pauperisation and the stigma of doles; it will promote each man's self-respect and make him value his pension the more when he gets it. I have therefore asked the Actuary to work out an alternative scheme requiring: (a) one year, (b) two years and (c) three years of contributions before the pre-seventy pension comes into operation.

You will see from the enclosed note that there is a very large saving in the earlier years after the necessary adjustments have been made in respect of the increased charges for Health and Unemployment Insurance Funds. This saving I should utilise in the following manner. I should equalise the Government contributions over the whole of the first ten-year period, thus showing that this Parliament is not simply trying to be generous at the expense of the next. You will see that on the three years basis I could do this by ten instalments of £4,300,000, and on a two years basis by similar payments of £5,200,000.

The former of these two would be convenient to my finance. The Treasury like the method of presentation on grounds of financial decorum. It avoids the puzzle of the small early surpluses under our present scheme. There is of course also a clear saving to the taxpayer in the next ten years of £20 millions. Politically I do not feel that there is any disadvantage. On the contrary there may be a gain of having two joy days instead of one, and the second of them falling not very far off a General Election. Everyone will have his sixty-five pension by then. The widows will be provided for from the very outset, and I shall be able to sweep away all the anomalies of the existing seventy Old Age Pension system and clean that branch up entirely.

I propose therefore to circulate this alternative, together with the other papers. I send you this line to advise you of it beforehand. It is only for discussion, as I am still balancing it.

Winston S. Churchill to Etienne Clémentel

(*Churchill papers: 18/10*)

6 April 1925   Treasury Chambers

My dear Monsieur Clémentel,

It is not my duty to express opinions upon the politics of any other country but my own; but I am sure you will allow me to say on personal grounds how much I regret your departure from the Ministry of Finance.[1] The

---

[1] On 3 April 1925 Clémentel had been succeeded as Minister of Finance by Anatole de Monzie. Two weeks later, de Monzie was succeeded by Joseph Caillaux. During Churchill's five years as Chancellor of the Exchequer, he had twelve opposite numbers in France (and six in Germany).

pleasant relations which we had established were a real advantage in the discussions of the various difficult questions which are open between Great Britain and France; and I shall always preserve most agreeable memories of our long discussions, and of the great consideration with which you always treated me.

Permit me to assure you of my highest respect and regard, and believe me,

Dear Monsieur Clémentel,
Yours very sincerely,
Winston S. Churchill

Sir Arthur Steel-Maitland to Winston S. Churchill

(*Churchill papers: 18/19*)

6 April 1925   Ministry of Labour

Dear Churchill,

I have been seedy all day and fear I shall be unable to come at 6.30. The two main points which strike me are:—

(1) Unless it disturbs the balance of your Budget proposals too much, I would sooner see the Bill brought in *next* year than this. Apart from any other reasons, benefits are soon forgotten and the nearer this is to the next Election the better.

(2) If it were still possible to make this a children's bill—not a widow's bill— there are great reasons for doing so.

    (a) Public sentiment is for it because of the *children* emphatically, rather than the women

    (b) You avoid the anomaly of a pre-contributory widow of 60 with no pension and a contributory widow of 40 with pension. The anomaly is a passing one but one on which we will give way sometime, I am sure

    (c) A woman of 40 with a pension of 10/- is either a subsidized wage earner which is bad or discouraged from earning which is worse

    (d) What about children orphaned of *both* father & mother? They should get more than the present children's rate.

Yours sincerely
Arthur Steel-Maitland

Winston S. Churchill to Sir Arthur Steel-Maitland

(*Churchill papers: 18/10*)

6 April 1925   Treasury Chambers

My dear Steel-Maitland,

I am very sorry to hear you are not well. In reply to your points: (1) It would fatally derange the balance of the Budget, and I should have to recast every plan if Insurance were postponed.

(2) We are committed to pensions for *Widows*; that is the whole character of the pledges which have been given.

(a) Surely also it would be invidious to leave the Mother with the care of the children without any provision of her own, and solely dependent upon what she could make out of their keep.

(b) There are anomalies in the inauguration of every new plan; but it is surely an important distinction that the covenanted widow will have paid for her benefits through her husband, and the uncovenanted will not.

(c) A covenanted widow is only very partially 'subsidized'.

(d) The Bill provides 7/6 for the eldest orphan and 6/- each for the rest of the family.

Yours very sincerely,
Winston S. Churchill

*Winston S. Churchill to Sir Otto Niemeyer, Sir George Barstow
and Sir Warren Fisher*

(*Churchill papers: 18/12*)

8 April 1925

I am a little out of sympathy with your general view of this question. The importance of a good telephone system to the trade of the country is surely enormous. I should have thought that it was far more important than 1d postage. It is shocking that we should be so low down in the scale.

Next, the telephone service has at last begun to make a slight profit. Does this profit include the usual percentage of interest on capital or not? If so the new capital expenditure is directly remunerative as well as indirectly reproductive. I would rather curtail some of the other loans under the Trade Facilities than check the natural expansion of the telephone system in response to growing public demand.

Thirdly, I do not see how the difference between borrowing £12½ millions or borrowing £10 millions can surely affect our conversion prospects. You point out that the Post Office exaggerate the effects of the difference between our offer and their demand but we for argumentative purposes seem likely to fall into the same habit.

Broadly speaking, I should think that this was thoroughly good expenditure and that it would be very reactionary to check the normal expansion of a scientific system of communication in a crowded island like this. Our only chance is to have a first class outfit and apparatus.

Stanley Baldwin to King George V

(*Baldwin papers*)

8 April 1925   House of Commons

The Prime Minister with his humble duty to Your Majesty.

Mr Churchill was yesterday given an opportunity of showing his paces in a debate which formed a sort of parliamentary canter in the difficult art of exposition. No Minister can be faced with a more difficult task than to expound with clearness and simplicity a financial subject which bristles with so many technicalities and economic difficulties that he may only have an imperfect understanding of them himself. The subject which Mr Churchill had to tackle yesterday was a Resolution giving effect to an agreement recently arrived at with the German Government by which the operation of the Reparations Recovery Act was to be suspended and a new and more practical scheme for the collection of German reparations substituted for it. . . .

Even the Treasury would have found it difficult to present a Minister with a more complicated and technical subject, but Mr Churchill steered a wonderful course through all the shoals and reefs which might have beset him, and gave an illustration of the most lucid exposition which won for him the respectful admiration of the House and must hearten Mr Churchill for the more serious ordeal which awaits him.[1]

Widows' Pensions Committee: minutes

(*Cabinet papers: 27/276*)

9 April 1925

It had been agreed to lift payments a penny at each three succeeding decades up to 1956 and then stop. This arrangement would avoid charge

---

[1] The forthcoming Budget, Churchill's first.

of breach of faith against the State. The Government Actuary suggested stopping at two decades, as new entrants at 1956 would be paying the whole cost of non-contributory pensions.

The Chancellor of the Exchequer thought, on the other hand, that this was a salutory arrangement, a good example of Conservative Social Reform, and that the Government should openly avow it. It should be pointed out that the State was bearing the cost of the transition from non contributory to contributory pensions.

Frederick Guest to Winston S. Churchill

(*Churchill papers: 2/141*)

12 April 1925

Dear Winnie,

Best of luck on Thursday & remember that you will have a very friendly house to speak to.

It is *almost* the biggest day that we have been looking forward to for, now, nearly a generation. There can only be *one* bigger.

Yrs
Freddie

Winston S. Churchill to P. J. Grigg

(*Churchill papers: 18/12*)

16 April 1925

1. The 'Daily Express' has again today a lot of alarmist stuff about Japan. Some time ago I asked you to ask the Foreign Office if they would telegraph to the Ambassador[1] for a full and precise account of the present condition of Japanese ship-building and programmes. Surely this is an enquiry they can put quite easily. The Ambassador must know the position. You had better go and see Eyre Crowe yourself, so that he can ask the Foreign Secretary. If there is any difficulty about it, I will ask the Foreign Secretary myself.

[1] Charles Norton Edgecumbe Eliot, 1862–1931. Boden Sanskrit scholar, Oxford, 1883; Syriac Prize, 1884. Entered the diplomatic service, 1886. Consul-General, Zanzibar, 1900–4. Resigned from the diplomatic service, 1904. Member of the Royal Commission on Electoral Systems, 1909. Knighted, 1910. Principal of the University of Hong Kong, 1912. British High Commissioner in Siberia, 1918–19. Privy Councillor, 1919. Ambassador to Japan, 1919–26. Among his publications were a *Finnish Grammar* (1908) and *Hinduism and Buddhism* (1921).

2. For the Cabinet on Wednesday I shall want to have printed (probably at Hopkins's private press) twenty copies of the three columns of figures: New Pensions Scheme, Old Age Pensions, and War Pensions, with the totals. I will distribute these myself to the Cabinet at the right moment. Nothing else is needed for this Cabinet.

3. For Monday's Cabinet I shall have to have my scales ready on each point. Here again I will give them out in the room and recall them as soon as they have been read.

4. How is Barstow getting on with his analysis of the Japanese Estimates? We really must have the most careful search made in these Estimates for the total amount available for new construction. This can be reached by the exhaustive process of deducting pay of men, oil, maintenance, etc. How are we to get information as to the cost of building warships in Japan? Probably some of the British shipbuilders could give you accurate information. I believe that a great many things required for building warships in Japan have to be purchased from outside. For instance, Lord Weir told me that they were ordering their pumps from him. How about armour? Where do they get that from, and where do they make their engines? Anything they have to buy outside the country must cost them a great deal now that the yen is so depreciated.

While I am busy at the Budget, Barstow should make a minute study of this. Do not hesitate to spend money in engaging extra staff or prosecuting enquiries.

WSC

Winston S. Churchill to Neville Chamberlain

16 April 1925
Secret

My dear Neville Chamberlain,

At our last meeting you said that you wished to postpone the removal of Old Age Pensioners' disabilities until July 1, 1926. This is a relief to me from a financial point of view. But I think there should be very good reasons to explain why this step, which we are admitting to be one of justice, should not take place for nearly fifteen months, during which time so many of these old men and women will die. I wish you would let me know what are the reasons. Will there be a great deal of work in tracing these men and women and in investigating their conditions, ages, etc? If so, no doubt we could make out a perfectly good case.

Forgive me for troubling you in your holidays, but this point has recurred to my mind several times.

Yours very sincerely,
Winston S. Churchill

Winston S. Churchill to Stanley Baldwin

(*Churchill papers: 18/8*)

17 April 1925

My dear Prime Minister,

Everything is moving 'according to plan'; and all will be in readiness by zero hour. You asked me to give you a note about the origin of the Insurance Scheme.

You yourself set up the Anderson Committee in the summer of 1922, as you felt that this was an indispensable line of advance in social reform for the Conservative Party. Not to introduce a contributory scheme means, and can only mean, that either it will be introduced by some other Government or that a non-contributory scheme with all its measureless injury to our finances will some day be carried. After more than a year's study, the Anderson Committee produced a series of reports. These reports laid bare the whole of the information available upon the subject.

The Government Actuary was a member of the Committee, and he more than anyone else is master of every detail and of the whole problem. He has behind him, as you know, a whole staff of actuaries (more than twenty in number), and his Department possesses the only authoritative statistics available in the field of State Insurance.

When you went out of office, the Conservative Shadow Cabinet, equally keen on solving the Pensions problem, set up a Committee of ex-Ministers who formulated a scheme which they submitted to an outside actuary.[1] On our assumption of office in November last the results of this unofficial Committee were pooled with those of the official Committee, and thoroughly examined. Of course no outside actuary could have at his disposal the same amount of material as the Government Actuary. But all his work and material were fully considered by the Anderson Committee who decided that there was nothing in it which required them to modify their own scheme.

Within a fortnight of Neville and me taking up our duties, we both addressed you upon this question. We obtained from you the strongest possible encouragement to proceed. We have worked together in complete

[1] Duncan Fraser (see page 263, note 1).

harmony ever since, keeping you informed at every stage of the development of our plans. These plans, though built upon the information of the Anderson Committee, are different in many respects. They are far less costly to the State, and they only involve contributions of fourpence in the first ten years instead of sixpence as contemplated by the Anderson Committee. Everything has been done through the medium and with the machinery of the Government Actuary, who takes full responsibility for all the statistical data on which we are working. In February it became necessary for Neville and me to consult the Minister of Agriculture and the Minister of Labour,[1] and we obtained their general concurrence from the special points of view they represented.

A month ago matters had so far ripened that we asked you to appoint a secret Cabinet Committee consisting of the four Ministers already privy, Lord Salisbury and Sir Laming Worthington Evans. This Committee held three prolonged meetings, and a general agreement was reached not only in principle but on detail. The Insurance Scheme is complete in every respect. The Bill has been prepared by the Ministry of Health, and will, I understand, be circulated to Ministers on Saturday night together with an explanatory memorandum. The report by the Government Actuary will be circulated on the following Saturday night. The Insurance Scheme forms an integral and inseparable part of the Budget, as it is the counterpoise in social legislation which balances the remissions of direct taxation which I propose to submit to the Cabinet on Monday April 27th.

The Cabinet should perhaps be asked on Wednesday to give a general and provisional consent to the Scheme in principle, reserving if they will a final judgment till they have read the Actuary's Report which will be circulated on the night of the 25th, and till they have heard the full Budget statement on Monday the 27th.

I hope you will open on Wednesday with a statement which will include something of this kind. I would then suggest that Neville should be asked by you to explain the scope of the Bill, the benefits, the time table, etc. I will then explain the big finance. It will take me a quarter of an hour. I cannot conceive that proceeding on these lines we shall not get a thoroughly good response from our colleagues. It would of course be disastrous if hesitation and division arose now that we are so very near to the battlefield.

I have also carried out all the negotiations with the Federal Reserve Bank and Messrs Morgan on the lines which you and Austen approved at our conference. . . .[2]

---

[1] Edward Wood and Sir Arthur Steel-Maitland.
[2] For the restoration of the Gold Standard.

Winston S. Churchill to King George V

(*Churchill papers: 18/7*)

23 April 1925

The Chancellor of the Exchequer with his humble duty to Your Majesty.

From the first weeks of taking office Mr Churchill has laboured in the closest accord with the Prime Minister upon the preparation of a Budget aimed at achieving the following two main objectives. First, security for the wage earning population and their dependants against exceptional misfortune; and secondly, encouragement to the enterprise of the nation by the remission of taxes upon income. Mr Churchill is now in a position to make appreciable advances in both these directions.

The finance of 1924 realised a surplus of £3,659,000, and Mr Snowden has been pluming himself on his accurate budgetting. The details, however, show that he was, to say the least, fortunate, as the dying Excess Profits Duty and Corporation Profits Tax fell short of the Budget figure by £9·2 millions and the situation was only retrieved by the remarkable expansion of the Income Tax, Super-tax and Death Duties, which yielded no less than £16 millions above Mr Snowden's estimate.

For the finance of 1925 Mr Churchill has not thought fit to take a sanguine view. He has not counted on any sudden expansion of trade. On the other hand he feels sure that there will be a steady if gradual improvement. 1924 was better than 1923 and 1925 should maintain this slow but satisfactory progression. In particular, a bad year drops out of the three years' average of Income Tax. And in all the circumstances Mr Churchill has felt able on a conservative basis to budget for a total revenue from existing taxes of £826 millions.

Against this he has to find nearly £799½ millions of expenditure. This includes an additional £5 millions for the raising of the new Sinking Fund to £50 millions a year. Deducting the expenditure from the estimated revenue the prospective surplus for 1925 becomes £26,600,000. This is a good deal more than even the best informed people have been able to forecast and it again affords an impressive demonstration of the immense financial power of Great Britain.

Good as this surplus is, it is not enough for the objects which Mr Churchill has already mentioned to Your Majesty. He therefore proposes to fortify the revenue in the following way. First of all, the scale of Estate Duty will be increased. Small estates under £12,500 will not be affected, nor will estates over £1 million have to pay more than their present extremely onerous duty. It is upon the medium estates that the increase will fall. It is a moderate increase, not exceeding at the highest point six per cent. The yield of this increased tax will be £4·5 millions in the first year and £10 millions in a full year.

Mr Churchill next turns to a series of taxes upon articles of luxury the consumption of which is optional, so no one need pay the taxes unless they like. In the forefront of these stands the new duty on Silk, natural, artificial, raw, manufactured, etc. For a generation the Treasury have been examining the possibilities of a duty on Silk, and it is due to the ingenuity of the Customs authorities that Mr Churchill is in possession of what is believed to be a really satisfactory solution. The revenue will gain practically the whole of the tax which will be borne by the consumer. A countervailing duty will be imposed on artificial silk manufactured in Great Britain. On the whole, however, the Silk trade are compensated by a slightly protective adjustment of the rates between foreign and home-made silk goods. The yield of this duty will be £4 millions in 1925 and £7 millions in a full year.

A small duty on Hops has also been included as the control which has preserved the Hop industry for the last five years expires in August.

Lastly, Mr Churchill proposes to reimpose the McKenna Duties. Mr Churchill cannot afford the loss of revenue involved in the destruction of these duties. He requires every penny he can scrape together. The yield of the Hop Duty and the McKenna Duties together will be in the first year £1,730,000 and in a full year £3,050,000.

This completes the new taxes. They yield in the aggregate £10,230,000 in the first year, and, what is of even greater importance, over £20 millions in a full year. The prospective surplus for 1925 is by these measures increased to £36,830,000, with a further £10 millions of new revenue for 1926.

Thus armed it is possible to approach the first of the two main objectives already mentioned, namely, security for the wage-earners through instituting a compulsory contributory system of widows' pensions and of pensions at 65. Mr Churchill will not burden Your Majesty with more than the barest outlines of this enormous and far-reaching scheme of social betterment. The area of the population affected will be that covered by the present Health Insurance, namely, 15 million insured persons representing with their dependants 30 million souls.

From January 1st, 1926, an extra 4d a week will be paid by all insured males and 4d a week by their employers, women being at half rates in both cases. On this basis the scheme would be nearly self-supporting if everybody had begun to subscribe at 16 years of age. But no one has subscribed and if we were to wait until the fund were strong enough in itself to pay out the benefits few of this generation would see the slightest return for their money.

Here is where the capitalist State with its sure credit and carefully guarded finance is able to come to the rescue. The Exchequer makes a contribution sufficient to take off the back payments and enable the whole scheme to start at once. The cost to the Exchequer will not be heavy during the first ten years. Mr Churchill proposes to defray it by ten approximately equal payments of £5½ millions a year. At the tenth year the cost of the scheme to the State will have risen to £15 millions, and in 1956 it is no less than £24 millions. Mr Churchill has however felt justified in incurring this heavy new liability because the War Pensions are being paid regularly out of the taxes each year and are of course steadily dwindling away.

Mr Churchill thinks the tables which he encloses will be of great interest to Your Majesty.

The most serious feature is of course the quite unexpected swelling of the non-contributory Old Age Pensions, which nearly doubles in thirty years from now. In spite of this however, the decline in the War Pensions practically equates the increased cost of the Old Age Pensions and the new Pensions Scheme. Moreover, as it is provided that the contributions for the new Scheme are to rise by 1d from both employer and employed at every tenth year until a total of 7d for both parties is reached, the contributor of 16 who begins in 1956 to subscribe will with the aid of his employer be paying not only for all the benefits under the new Scheme but in addition will be paying for his own share of the existing non-contributory Old Age Pensions scheme. The whole sphere of national Insurance will thus be dominated eventually by sound social and financial principles.

Your Majesty will naturally enquire what are the benefits. They are indeed remarkable: 10/- a week for life will be paid to every widow of an insured person who dies after 1st January 1926, together with 5/- for the first child and 3/- for other children until they reach the age of 14. Existing widows who are also mothers with children under 14, although their husbands will have paid no contributions will nevertheless receive the same benefits as long as they have children dependent on them under 14. Orphans of insured parents will receive 7/6 for the eldest and 6/- for other members of the family. Pensions of 10/- a week will be given to insured men and their wives, and insured women, who reach the age of 65. These pensions will merge in the Old Age Pensions at 70. All the restrictions of means disqualification, etc, which have been so much grumbled at will disappear so far as insured persons are concerned and this advantage will also be extended from July 1st, 1926, to all persons over 70 within the insurable class.

Many years ago immediately after the introduction in 1906 of the original scheme of non-contributory Old Age Pensions, when Mr Churchill was President of the Board of Trade, he was struck by the immense opportunities which the State gift of pensions at 70 offered for a contributory Insurance Scheme for pensions at 65. By providing for people after 70 the State virtually took off all the bad risks, and the actuarial possibilities of a scheme providing for the earlier period became extraordinary. It is strange that this should so long have been neglected. A treasure almost measureless could be made available for the people by contributions which at any rate in the earlier years are comparatively very small.

The Government Actuary has provided Mr Churchill with a few illustrations: under a scheme of collective insurance an employed man of 20 will obtain for 4d a week benefits for himself and his family which are actuarially worth 1/0½d; the same benefits would be worth for a man of 30 1/8½d, for the man of 40 2/8½d, for the man of 50 4/11d, and for the man of 60 16/6d a week. They will all equally get this for 4d a week. Women who will actually receive the major part of the benefits will under the collective scheme pay half the contribution of a man.

A supreme example is the case, common enough, of an insured man who dies at 35 and leaves a widow with three children under 5 years of age. The benefits which this widow and her children will receive allowing for her pension stopping if she remarries are worth in capital value £600, ie the maximum sum for which the Workmen's Compensation Act provides in the case of a man killed in an industrial accident. Such are the miracles of nation wide insurance.

The effect of such a scheme must be to give millions of people a stake in the country which they will have created largely by their own contributory efforts. The position of every wage-earner's wife will be definitely improved; she will know that if her husband dies she will not be left penniless but that she and her children will be provided for to a very large extent. On the other hand, everyone will realise that violent disorder, confusion, revolutionary disturbance, repudiation of liabilities, injury to public credit, confiscatory finance, etc, will endanger the insurance arrangements from which the vast majority expect to derive benefits. This must increase the sense of responsibility among all voters. Whether the scheme will be immediately popular is a secondary question. The important fact is that it will anchor the mass of the nation to an ordered system of society and to continuity in national life.

Mr Churchill has regarded the foregoing scheme as a necessary counterpoise to the remissions of direct taxation which he proposes simultaneously to make and as the means of striking the balance fairly between class and class. He proposes first of all to reduce the Super-tax by an amount equal to the increase in the Estate Duty, namely, £10 millions in a full year. There is no doubt that the Super-tax is very burdensome and hampers initiative and enterprise throughout the country. There is a great difference between the position of the highly paid brain worker who has nothing behind him but his earnings and the man with equal income derived from investments. This difference, already recognised by the Estate Duty, will be further mitigated by the new proposals. The reductions in the Super-tax correspond as nearly as possible with the increase in the Estate Duty. The scale of Super-tax reductions halves the existing rates up to £3,000 a year and thereafter diminishes in advantage until it reaches the region of incomes denoting a capital where no increase of Estate Duty has been imposed. The cost of the Super-tax remissions will be £6,700,000, and £10 millions in the full year.

A principle somewhat similar will be applied by Mr Churchill to the Income Taxpayers by a further relief to earned as against investment incomes, mainly in the lower ranges. The relief here will also be very substantial. A married man with no children with an income all earned of £300 a year will have his tax reduced by the equivalent of from 4/6d to 2/6d; a man with an income from £500 to £750 will get his tax reduced by the equivalent of an 8d reduction; a man with £1,000 will be relieved by the equivalent of nearly 7d; a married man with three children under 16 with an income from £500 to £750 a year all earned will get a relief of about 1/- in the £. Your Majesty will realise what a very large class of deserving people who have to maintain a certain status of living, who are sometimes called 'the black coated working men', will be relieved in this way. The cost of this remission will be £3 millions in the first year and £7½ millions in the full year.

Finally there is the question of the standard rate of Income Tax. The growth in the yield of Income Tax increases the cost of a remission on the standard rate. To take 6d off the Income Tax will cost in 1925 no less than £24 millions, and £32 millions in a full year. Mr Churchill however finds it possible to do this in addition to the other remissions he has described.

Increased Imperial Preference will be granted on existing duties, particularly Sugar and Tobacco, involving a cost to the revenue of £1,470,000 in 1925 and £1,720,000 in a full year. This is in fulfilment of the Government policy towards the Dominions and India.

The effect of these remissions of taxation and the Imperial Preference after allowing for the increased taxation leaves the estimate of revenue for 1925 at £801,060,000. Deducting from this an estimated expenditure of £799,400,000 Mr Churchill has in hand for contingencies a prospective surplus of £1,660,000.

Finally it has been decided to revert to the gold standard as from April 28. All arrangements have been made during the last few months by the Treasury for this purpose. 166 million dollars have been accumulated to pay not only the June but the December instalments of the American Debt. £153 millions of gold are being concentrated in the hands of the Bank of England. Lastly, credits of 300 million dollars have been arranged by the Chancellor of the Exchequer and the Governor of the Bank of England with the Federal Reserve Bank and through Messrs Morgan in the United States. It is not expected that these will have to be used as we are quite strong enough ourselves to resume the gold standard. But these reserve credits are intended as a warning to speculators of the impregnable character of the British exchange, and are a measure of additional precaution.

Germany and the United States are already on the gold standard. It is believed that Holland will move to a gold basis in conformity with Great Britain. As far as the British Empire is concerned, the step will be taken unitedly. Canada is already on the gold standard, South Africa, Australia and New Zealand only await the British signal. The importance of a uniform standard of value to which all transactions can be referred throughout the British Empire and through a very large part of the world cannot be over-estimated. It benefits all countries, but it benefits no country more than our crowded island with its vast world trade and finance by which it lives.

The Chancellor of the Exchequer regrets to have trespassed so long upon Your Majesty's time but he felt that a full account of these considerable public matters would be desired by Your Majesty when out of the Kingdom,[1] and with his humble duty has the honour to remain Your Majesty's devoted servant

Winston S. Churchill

Winston S. Churchill to P. J. Grigg

(*Churchill papers: 18/12*)

23 April 1925

I see that the 'Daily Mail' and the 'Daily Telegraph' have got hold of the contributory Insurance policy within a few hours of its being disclosed to the Cabinet. This makes me chary of circulating the gold papers on Saturday night as Cabinet circulation involves at least 100 persons being informed. I propose therefore to make no circulation but to explain by word of mouth to the Cabinet on Monday.

---

[1] Following a bronchial attack in February, King George V had been ordered by his doctors to seek the sun. Despite what his biographer Harold Nicolson described as the King's 'repugnance to foreign travel', he had, reluctantly, agreed to his doctor's advice, and on March 19 had joined the Royal Yacht *Victoria and Albert* at Genoa for a cruise off Sicily. He returned to London on April 25.

Winston S. Churchill to Stanley Baldwin

(*Churchill papers: 18/7*)

24 April 1925

My dear Prime Minister,

There are two small points on which I ask your agreement.

I shall be pointing out that I have counted in my estimates on no increase for reparations and no payments of Inter-Allied debts. If these come, they will be in the nature of a windfall. I wish to add:

'Neither am I counting on any receipts from Ireland in the current year in fulfilment of Article 5 of the Treaty. But I by no means abandon that serious claim. The honour of both islands is engaged in the strict and punctual fulfilment of the Treaty as a whole.'

Besides the obvious wish to safeguard our rights in this matter I have always had in mind the possibility that if the Irish Free State should treat us unreasonably over Article 11 (the Boundary), we should keep as a guard the power to press them severely over Article 5. I think such a possibility being disclosed at this stage might be found of great value to us as a Party should, which I cannot believe, a wrong-headed decision emerge from the Boundary Commission.

Secondly, I want to use words on economy to the following effect:

'I have further obtained the assent of the Prime Minister to the setting up of a Standing Committee of the Cabinet not for the purpose of dealing with new expenditure but before which blocks of old and recurring expenditure may be overhauled irrespective of the annual scrutiny of the Estimates by the Treasury. In my opinion we ought to aim at a further net reduction of Supply expenditure of at least £10 millions a year.'

Perhaps you will let me know on Monday whether you approve of my holding this language and whether these points should be mentioned to the Cabinet.

Yours vy sincerely
Winston S. Churchill

Lord Stamfordham[1] to Winston S. Churchill

(*Churchill papers: 18/7*)

25 April 1925   Buckingham Palace
Private

My dear Churchill,

The King desires me to thank you very much for the full and very clear
explanation of the leading features of your Budget which you have so kindly
sent for His Majesty's information. The King has read it with deep interest
and, I may add, much approval, and congratulates you upon the results of
your anxious labours of the past 5 months.

Yours very sincerely,
Stamfordham

J. E. B. Seely to Winston S. Churchill

(*Churchill papers: 2/141*)

27 April 1925   Isle of Wight

My dear Winston,

One line to wish you all possible success tomorrow in the House of
Commons—indeed I am certain that success is assured.

But it is such a splendidly romantic episode that you should complete
what your Father was robbed of doing that a word of good wishes from your
oldest friend may be permitted.

I am going up to London this evening to Brooks's Club. If you are free
on Wednesday come and be rejoiced at lunch at the Carlton and bring
Eddie Marsh too—ask him to send me a line or telephone message to
Brooks's.

Again every good wish.

Yours ever
Jack

---

[1] Arthur John Bigge, 1849–1931. Entered Army, 1869. Entered the Royal Household,
1880. Private Secretary to Queen Victoria, 1895–1901; to George V, 1910–31. Created
Baron Stamfordham, 1911. His only son was killed in action on 15 May 1915.

Charles Trevelyan[1] *to Winston S. Churchill*

(*Churchill papers: 2/141*)

28 April 1925   House of Commons

Congratulations on a fine performance, greater even than 1887 might have been.

Charles Trevelyan

Lord Mildmay[2] *to Winston S. Churchill*

(*Churchill papers: 2/141*)

28 April 1925

My dear Winston,

I have heard 40 Budget statements exactly: & I have never heard one that so kept my unflagging interest all through. It is almost impertinent in me to tell you how admirable it was in manner & delivery, as well, of course, as in construction. You so deftly anticipated & countered all prospective criticism—& then, above all, the whole scheme was statesmanlike as well as attractive.

I was sitting very near your wife & children, and it made one happy to see *their* happiness in your success.

I expect that you will have a great press tomorrow!

Please don't acknowledge this.

Yrs Ever
Frank Mildmay

[1] Charles Philips Trevelyan, 1870–1958. Educated at Harrow and Trinity College, Cambridge. Liberal MP, 1899–1918. Charity Commissioner, 1906–8. Parliamentary Secretary, Board of Education, 1908–14. President of the Board of Education, 1924 and 1929–31. Succeeded his father as 3rd Baronet, 1928. His father Sir George Otto Trevelyan (who died in 1928 at the age of 90) had been a friend of Lord Randolph, and Chief Secretary for Scotland in 1886, the year before Lord Randolph's budget-less five months at the Exchequer.

[2] Francis Bingham Mildmay, 1861–1947. Educated at Eton and Trinity College, Cambridge. Unionist MP for Totnes, 1885–1922. On active service in South Africa, 1899–1901, and in Europe, 1914–19 (despatches four times). A Director of the Great Western Railway Company, 1914–45. Privy Councillor, 1916. Created Baron, 1922. President of the National Unionist Association, 1922–3. Lord Lieutenant of Devon, 1928–36.

Colonel Jackson to Winston S. Churchill
(*Churchill papers: 2/141*)

28 April 1925

My dear Winston,

Please let me offer Heartiest Congratulations. Quite splendid—I knew it would be.

Yours ever
F. Stanley Jackson

Montagu Norman to Winston S. Churchill
(*Churchill papers: 2/141*)

28 April 1925

Dear Mr Chancellor,

As I was not able to see you this evening, I would like, without delay, to thank you for the clear & helpful gold statement & to take off my hat to the Budget Statement.

I think you must in turn, have nettled & tickled all parties! Pray count on me to try to do my little bit.

I am, with regards
Yours sincerely,
M. Norman

Stanley Baldwin to King George V
(*Baldwin papers*)

28 April 1925   House of Commons

The general impression was that Mr Churchill rose magnificently to the occasion. His speech was not only a great feat of endurance, lasting as it did for two hours and forty minutes, but was a first-rate example of Mr Churchill's characteristic style. At one moment he would be expounding quietly and lucidly facts and figures relating to the financial position during the past and current years. At another moment, inspired and animated by the old political controversies on the subject of tariff reform, he indulged in witty levity and humour which comes as a refreshing relief in the dry atmosphere of a Budget speech. At another moment, when announcing the introduction of a scheme for widows and mothers pensions, he soared into emotional flights of rhetoric in which he has few equals; and throughout the speech he showed that he is not only possessed of consummate ability as a parliamentarian, but also all the versatility of an actor.

In the case of such a masterly performance criticism would seem to be superfluous and almost unfair, but, if a critic wished to assail any weak points in the speech, it might perhaps be said that the speech would have been even more effective if Mr Churchill had been able to limit its length, and that he devoted either too much or too little time to the propounding of the new pensions scheme. It might perhaps be suggested that the prosaic nature of the Budget does not present a suitable background for some of the rhetorical flights which Mr Churchill undertook. It is doubtful whether these dramatic declarations, impressive as they were from the purely oratorical point of view, were such as to carry conviction in the minds of the Opposition Members who tend to be more impressed with quiet sincerity than impassioned declamation.

It might also be argued that Mr Churchill endeavoured to go into too great detail in regard to the pensions scheme. His task was extremely difficult. The scheme is one which bristles with technicalities and complications, and in order to present it clearly in all its details it would have been necessary to devote far more time than Mr Churchill had available in the course of a Budget speech. Another course open to him would have been to have confined himself to a brief statement on the most general lines, setting out only the broad principles of the scheme and leaving a more elaborate exposition to the Minister of Health who will have to undertake the introduction of the Bill. As it was Mr Churchill took a path midway between these two courses, and the details which he endeavoured to give the House in order to make the whole position clear were inevitably hardly sufficient to serve their purpose. This was the only period during his speech when he failed to grip the complete attention of the House.

These criticisms, however, are of small account if the speech be looked at as a whole. In its arrangement, in its marshalling of facts and arguments, in the picturesque, dramatic and humorous presentation, it was one of the most striking Budget speeches of recent years.

It would be premature at this stage to forecast the reception which his Budget proposals will meet with both in the country and in the House of Commons, but it was recognised on all sides that Mr Churchill had framed a comprehensive scheme, bold in its character and conception, which would establish his reputation as Chancellor of the Exchequer.

Lucy, Countess of St. Aldwyn[1] to Winston S. Churchill

(*Churchill papers: 2/141*)

29 April 1925

Dear Mr Churchill,

May I venture—as a very old friend—to send you my warmest congratulations on your success of yesterday. I wish I could have heard your speech having heard so many Budget speeches in old days.

If there is any ground for Mr Snowden's wonder 'whether the spirits of former occupants of the treasury bench still hover round the scene of their earthly conflicts', the spirits of your father & of my husband must surely have rejoiced last night.

Yrs very sincerely,
Lucy St. Aldwyn

Lord Wimborne to Winston S. Churchill

(*Churchill papers: 2/141*)

29 April 1925

Dear Winston,

Just a line to offer you my congratulations on the very distinguished success which your budget has gained you.

Reading this morning's papers has been a source of immense pleasure to me: (I do not refer to Income or Supertax reductions)—but to the satisfaction on personal family grounds which this last achievement of yours has accorded me.

I heard your speech described as Gladstonian and I suppose no higher praise could be found for a budget statement: may it lead on to all the greater things that I am sure the future holds for you.

Yr affectionate Cousin
Ivor

[1] Lady Lucy Catherine Fortescue, 1851–1940. Daughter of the 3rd Earl Fortescue. In 1874 she married Michael Edward Hicks-Beach, 1st Earl St Aldwyn, Chancellor of the Exchequer, 1885–6, and in 1895–1902, and a close friend of Churchill's father. St Aldwyn died on 30 April 1916, seven days after his only son, Viscount Quenington, Conservative MP for Tewkesbury, had been killed in action in Egypt. One of Lady St Aldwyn's brothers, the Hon Lionel Fortescue, had been killed in action in South Africa in 1900, and one of her nephews, Grenville Fortescue, had been killed in action on the western front in 1915.

Lord Beaverbrook to Sir Robert Borden

(*Beaverbrook papers*)

29 April 1925

Churchill now lives next door to Baldwin and sees him more frequently than any other members of the Cabinet—and, in my belief, influences him more. It would not be too much to say that Churchill keeps him straight. For he has the capacity for doing this for others, though he cannot do it for himself, and is sure to fly off at some wild tangent before long.

Lord Reading to Winston S. Churchill

(*Churchill papers: 2/141*)

30 April 1925

My dear Winston,

My warmest congratulations on your speech & its reception. It was good to see you yesterday & I rejoice in the great success of an old friend & colleague—may good fortune attend you!

Yours always
Sincerely
Rufus

May 1925

Neville Chamberlain: diary

(*Neville Chamberlain papers*)

1 May 1925

Winston's exposition of the Budget was a masterly performance, and though my office and some of my colleagues are indignant at his taking to himself the credit for a scheme which belongs to the Ministry of Health, I did not myself think that I had any reason to complain of what he said. In a sense it *is* his scheme. We were pledged to something of the kind, but I don't think we should have done it this year if he had not made it part of his Budget scheme, and in my opinion he does deserve special personal credit for his initiative and drive.

Stanley Baldwin to King George V

(*Baldwin papers*)

1 May 1925   House of Commons

The Prime Minister with his humble duty to Your Majesty.

The end of the first stage of the Budget debates was marred by a most deplorable scene. Mr Churchill had risen to reply to his critics. It was obvious from the opening of his speech that he was in good fighting fettle, but there did not seem to be any intention on his part to be unfair or unduly provocative. He had spent a few minutes in twitting Mr Ramsay MacDonald for his attitude in regard to the pensions scheme. Mr MacDonald when in Office had contributed nothing to the subject but now that another Government had introduced a scheme Mr MacDonald, while not prepared to accept the unpopularity of opposing it, took the line that he would give the authors of the scheme an opportunity of testifying to their sincerity by asking them at every stage of the Bill to perform what are known to be impossibilities, namely to put the whole cost to the Exchequer and to raise the benefits to an impracticable level.

This was a perfectly fair criticism of Mr Ramsay MacDonald's attitude towards the Government proposals.

Mr Churchill had then proceeded to make some general observations in regard to the unemployment situation, and had stated that it was a very strange thing that the rate of unemployment should be increasing when exports were showing an increase. Despite this increase the rate of unemployment continued to keep very curiously high and was growing. It was in the interests of trades unionists as well as the employers in industries to make sure that there was not growing up a certain habit of learning how to qualify for the unemployment insurance.

There can be no doubt whatsoever that the suggestions which Mr Churchill made, and this observation in particular, were not intended by him to be in any way offensive, but the hypersensitiveness of some of the Labour extremists produced an unwarranted display of resentment which found expression in a noisy demand for the withdrawal of Mr Churchill's statement. They resented in particular Mr Churchill's suggestion that some of the unemployment was due to malingering, partly because it came from Mr Churchill, and partly because they must have been only too conscious that the suggestion had some foundation in fact.

It was, however, unfortunate that Mr Churchill, faced with such a situation, notwithstanding the fact that he was innocent of any guilty intention, did not adopt a more conciliatory attitude. It is true that at this moment and during the scenes which followed, he retained complete control of his temper, but his attitude of bold defiance undoubtedly helped to stimulate the anger of his opponents. He rose to his feet and exclaimed 'are we really not to have free speech in this House. I do not intend to withdraw my statement for one moment. On the contrary we intend to probe it.' Shortly afterward he made the observation that he really was not aware that this was such a sore subject, and asked if the representatives of the Labour Party were really incapable of listening to a debating retort.

In ordinary circumstances no exception could possibly have been taken to such statements or to Mr Churchill's attitude, but considerations of parliamentary expedience ought to have led him, when dealing with such sensitive and troublesome mentalities, perhaps even to go out of his way in the direction of conciliation. As it was his bold and defiant attitude added fuel to the flames with the result that the extremists on the opposite side by their noisy clamour refused to allow him to continue his speech.

After some ten minutes tumult Mr Churchill obtained a brief hearing in order to announce that he was perfectly prepared not to conclude his speech and to arrange for an immediate division. He then attempted to move the

Closure, but the Chairman withheld his assent. Mr Saklatvala[1] then appeared as a deus ex machina to quell the tumult. Undue credit should not be given to him for this performance, seeing that it was only his intervention in the debate which served to empty the House, and gave Members some twenty minutes in which to cool the heat of their anger. His unconscious mediation served the purpose and, immediately he concluded, the Prime Minister moved the Closure, and the outstanding Budget Resolution was agreed to.

Regarding the incident as a whole, it would be impossible not to sympathise with Mr Churchill who was not responsible for the original outbreak, but from the point of view of the future Budget debates it is unfortunate that such an atmosphere should have been created in the very initial stages.

George Cornwallis-West[2] to Winston S. Churchill

(*Churchill papers: 2/141*)

2 May 1925

My dear Winston,

You have probably received thousands of congratulatory letters upon your Budget 'Tour de Force' in the H of C last Tues. But none can be more sincere than this, & I know you will not think it impertinent of me to write it.

I do congratulate most heartily. Your speech was a masterpiece of lucidity. I only wish your Mother had been alive to have heard you.

Yrs ever

G. Cornwallis-West

[1] Shapurji Saklatvala, 1874–1936. A Parsi, born in Bombay. Joined his family firm of Tata and Sons, and helped to establish the Tata Iron and Steel Works in India. Came to England, 1905. Active in the Independent Labour Party from 1910. Communist MP for North Battersea, 1922–3 and 1924–9. Imprisoned for two months in 1926, after being charged with a breach of the peace during a May Day speech, and after refusing to find sureties for good behaviour.

[2] George Frederick Myddelton Cornwallis-West, 1874–1951. Lieutenant, Scots Guards, 1895–1900. Married Lady Randolph Churchill, 1900; the marriage was dissolved, 1913. Married the actress Mrs Patrick Campbell, April 1914. Lieutenant-Colonel, commanding a battalion of the Royal Naval Division at Antwerp, October 1914. Married Georgette, widow of Adolph Hirsch, 1940.

Stanley Baldwin to King George V

(Baldwin papers)

5 May 1925 House of Commons

SECOND READING OF THE GOLD STANDARD BILL

The Prime Minister with his humble duty to Your Majesty.

Members who took part in the debate yesterday on the Second Reading of the Gold Standard Bill seemed to be suffering from an extreme form of inferiority complex, but, considering the technical nature of the subject under discussion, their professions of humility were neither unreasonable nor unjustified. There can be few, if any, Members who have sufficient confidence in their knowledge and understanding of political economy not to show traces of diffidence when faced with such an abstruse and thorny problem as the restoration of the gold standard. . . .

It remained for Mr Churchill to contribute the best speech of the Sitting. He probably approached the subject with a sense of deep humility, but the eloquence which he brought to bear and the effectiveness of his arguments might have created the impression that he had a complete mastery of the technicalities of the subject. He was not content with walking on a tight-rope: he seemed to revel in the dangers of dancing on it.

He opened his speech by pulverising the arguments advanced by Mr Snowden. No step of such a character had ever been taken by any Government which had been more characterised by design, forethought, and careful and laborious preparation. Even Mr Keynes the most formidable brilliant opponent of the gold standard had openly expressed the view that, if this country must return to the gold standard, the Treasury were endeavouring to do so on the most prudent and far sighted lines open to them. The fact was that Mr Snowden wished to have the best of both worlds, and his attitude was based on considerations of Party manoeuvres and exigencies.

The Chancellor then proceeded to justify his action by advancing three arguments of a general and non-technical character. There was the economic reason that this crowded island, unable to be self-supporting, must at all costs keep in close touch with world wide economic reality: there was the social reason that this country, depending as it did upon overseas for food and raw material, must work to obtain stability of prices which could only come through the restoration of a common value in international trans-actions: there was the imperial reason that when the dominions had decided to return to the gold standard this country must not be left in the back-ground. It had been suggested that the gold standard would shackle this country to the United States. His answer was that it would shackle us to reality, which was the only basis that offered any permanent security for our affairs.

Sir Alfred Mond, appearing in his customary role as the foe of all economic theorists, endeavoured to shatter the effect of Mr Churchill's brilliant speech by woeful prognostications in regard to the effect of his action on the industries of the country, but the opposition to the Bill was not sufficiently serious to enable him to make much headway as was shown by the fact that the Bill was allowed to receive its Second Reading without a division after a debate of unexpected brevity.

Stanley Baldwin to King George V

(Baldwin papers)

6 May 1925   House of Commons

. . . There was a good deal of sympathy shown with the plea made by Lord Hugh Cecil for gold coinage instead of paper currency, and this question, coming as it does within more every day experience, might have led more speakers to rediscover their eloquence had not Mr Churchill emphasised the uselessness of pursuing such a discussion. He urged the impracticability of diminishing at the present time our national wealth and credit by the unwarrantable expense of going back to the gold coinage. Indeed this could hardly be looked for during the lifetime of the present House of Commons, and we have far to travel on the road of retrenchment before such a course can come within the scope of practical politics.

Stanley Baldwin to King George V

(Baldwin papers)

8 May 1925   House of Commons

The Opposition may possibly have complaints to make in regard to the proposals contained in the Budget, but there is no one who ought not to be grateful to Mr Churchill for the liveliness and humour which he imparts to the debates. The dryness and solidity which usually attaches to debates on financial subjects is immediately swept away by his ardent enthusiasm and his powerful rhetoric.

His defence of the McKenna Duties yesterday was ingenious, subtle, and amusing, and was characterised by a hearty and vigorous pugnacity which aroused the enthusiasm of all his supporters. He opened his speech by developing the argument that the reintroduction of the McKenna Duties should not be in any way confused with the wider question of Free Trade versus Protection. The duties had originally been introduced by a confirmed Free Trader, and he based his position on the declaration made by Mr McKenna when the duties were originally imposed. As for the pledges made by the Prime Minister since the Election, they were never intended to limit in any way the full freedom of the Chancellor of the Exchequer to propose in any year duties which had for their bona fide object the service of the revenue of the country.

Then, acting on the theory that attack is the best method of defence, Mr Churchill delighted the House with the most humorous raillery at the expense of his opponents. When the duties were introduced they were supported by Sir John Simon otherwise almost impeccable, this being the only stain upon his orthodox escutcheon. The Government could also call to their aid the attitude of Sir Alfred Mond. He, however, had a variegated record in this matter. Originally he opposed the duties, but, when he came into Office, he developed into one of their strongest supporters. While leading the House to believe that it was rather against his will, but that he acquiesced for the sake of larger things, he bowed the knee in the Temple of Rimmon—he in fact led the chants, and when it came to the safeguarding of Industries Act he very nearly conducted the service. The Chancellor pertinently added that he would be quite ready to contrast his record in this respect with that of Sir Alfred Mond.

Mr Snowden was his next victim. He had deplored the raising of this issue. Mr Churchill retorted by asserting that the real villain of the piece was Mr Snowden himself, who had used the abolition of the McKenna Duties last year as a Party manoeuvre, and as an act of strategy to obtain Liberal support in order to divide Liberals from Conservatives, so that he and his Party might more effectively destroy them at leisure.

He concluded by producing some interesting and useful statistics which showed that the abolition of the duties had led to a large increase in the foreign importation of finished articles and a noticeable decline in the importation of parts, showing that the work of assembling the parts in this country had been diminished with consequent loss of employment.

Mr Snowden feels strongly on the subject of the McKenna Duties and has always expressed himself with proportionate candour and vigour, but Mr Churchill's speech seems to have goaded him into unaccustomed fury. At one moment during the speech it almost looked as though Mr Snowden, remembering the action taken last week by his own Party in silencing Mr Churchill, was intent on stirring the Conservative Party to such wrath that they would adopt similar tactics against himself. At one moment he declared that Mr Churchill was incapable of appreciating honest political motives.

The remark produced angry and noisy resentment, but fortunately the Conservatives possess greater self restraint than some of their opponents, and Mr Snowden was allowed to proceed after a brief interruption. His vigorous denunciation of the Chancellor and his present protectionist leanings could not, however, affect the inevitable result which was a majority of 161 in favour of the duties.

After this animated interlude the debate relapsed once more into lethargic realities.

Winston S. Churchill: notes dictated for his wife's use

(Churchill papers: 18/2)

undated

You must look at the policy of the Budget and the Widows Pensions as a whole and not simply pick out what you like and criticise what you do not. All stand together as part of a definite scheme for financial and social reform. This scheme, vast as it is, is only a portion of the full design of the new Government. They have plenty of time and can unfold their policy step by step.

You must not be misled too much by the attitude of some of the popular newspapers. The headlines of these papers and the extracts from the debates given prominence by them do not represent the opinion of Parliament or the feeling of the country but only what the proprietors of these great newspapers decide shall be the lines for the time being. For instance, the 'Daily Mail' this morning is headed: 'Revolt against the Pensions Bill', 'Government Alarm', 'Sir Robert Horne's Warning', etc; and then in a little note is added: 'the muster of Conservatives to vote for the Pensions Bill was the largest seen this Session and no Conservative voted against the measure'.[1]

This country is governed and is going to be governed for the next four years at least by the Cabinet resting on Parliament and the Members of Parliament in touch with their constituencies all over the country.

On the Budget some people condemn the Silk Tax, but they were quite glad to take the money which the Silk Tax produced in the shape of a

[1] On 20 May 1925, the following headlines appeared in the *Daily Mail*:

> PENSIONS BILL REVOLT
> SIR R. HORNE ON ITS DISASTROUS EFFECTS
> DON'T BREAK OUR HEARTS
> SIR ALFRED MOND'S WARNING
> GOVERNMENT ALARM

reduction of the Income Tax on earned incomes for the smaller class of Income Taxpayers. You cannot make a remission of taxation of this kind without finding the money from some other quarter.

On the whole the Budget took off over £30 millions of taxation and at the same time maintained our national credit.

On the Pensions Scheme with the exception of the Socialists the whole of the rest of the House of Commons had voted for it. The Socialists were very sore and their position was extremely weak on the subject. They had promised Widows Pensions, etc, but when they were in office they never made the slightest step to try to procure them. If it had not been for the Committee set up by Mr Baldwin in the last Conservative administration no progress would have been made at all in studying the problem. The Labour Party in their manifesto stated that they had a complete, detailed scheme of Pensions for Widows and Orphans ready and would have introduced it this year. All they had was the Report of the Committee set up by Mr Baldwin. This Report was for a contributory Scheme of Old Age Pensions which the Socialists now pretended they would have nothing to do with.

Mr Wheatley[1] denounced the Pensions Bill as fiendish and heartless, but when he was Minister of Health and responsible for the Pensions Scheme which his Party had promised he took so little interest in the subject that according to his own statement he never even knew or took the slightest trouble to enquire whether the 'detailed Scheme' which the Labour Party promised in their Election Manifesto was contributory or non-contributory. He simply took no interest in the matter at all while he had the chance and the place of power and then when other men came forward and tried to carry the reform he denounced their efforts in unmeasured terms. But the electors would judge whether such words as 'fiendish' and 'heartless' could be justly applied to a Government earnestly and faithfully and punctually redeeming its promises and working hard at a great and beneficent reform, or whether they were not more appropriate to a Socialist Minister who showed himself in office utterly indifferent to a promise of his Party or to the sufferings of the widows and orphans and, although he was the Minister specially in charge never even took the trouble to make an enquiry on their behalf.

At any rate the Electors would be able to judge. No doubt Parliament would most carefully discuss both the Budget and the Pensions Bill and any improvements that suggested themselves after full discussion could be incorporated. But they might be sure that in the main both the Budget and the Pensions Bill will be carried into law before the House of Commons separates.

[1] John Wheatley, see page 162, note 2.

That will mean that an important measure of relief will be given to the Income Taxpayers of the country; that from the 4th January 250,000 widows and 350,000 children will be receiving the new pensions allowance; and that from the same date 6 million wives will know that if their husbands die they have this security behind them and will not be left penniless and friendless in a hard world. On the 1st July next all the disabilities of the Old Age Pensioners which the Socialists promised to remove but only tinkered with, including the means test and inquisitorial examination, will be swept away, and by the 6th January 1928 pensions at 65 will be universal through-out the whole area covered by the Health Insurance; that is to say, 15 million insured persons, representing over 30 million of British people.

I am very glad that in this great scheme of Pensions, whatever differences there may be about method, the Liberal Party, led by Mr Lloyd George the pioneer of the Insurance policy, has voted with the Government. That is another proof that in the main lines of his policy Mr Baldwin was pursuing a national rather than a Party policy. The Government would continue to do this and would welcome sincere help from any quarter. But if help was not forthcoming but only opposition, then the Government would be strong enough with its great majority to go forth alone with sincere hearts and strong hands.

Stanley Baldwin to King George V

(Baldwin papers)

12 May 1925   House of Commons

. . . Before the debate itself opened, Captain Wedgwood Benn endeavoured to embarrass the Chancellor by indulging in skirmishing tactics. He tried to suspend the debate by raising the question whether it was proper, according to the forms of the House, for the Chancellor of the Exchequer to move a resolution imposing a tax on an article which was not clearly defined in the resolution. He had apparently been informed by experts in the trade that artificial silk had no precise meaning at all.

In support of his argument he suddenly produced, to the great amusement of the House, an assorted collection of brightly-coloured articles and challenged the Chancellor of the Exchequer to differentiate the silk articles from those made of artificial silk. This argument did not prove very effective as the Chancellor of the Exchequer immediately opened a Despatch-box and produced an even better assortment, consisting of handkerchiefs, ladies' stockings and other samples of wonderful hue. During the conversation which followed, Mr Austin Hopkinson came to the rescue of the Chancellor by asserting that it was perfectly well-known, both in the trade and outside it, what constituted silk within the meaning of the resolution, whether natural or artificial. It was a fibre produced by the extension of a viscous substance through minute orifices in such a way as to make filaments of a homogeneous nature.

This lucid definition might perhaps have failed to prove conclusive, but the dispute was settled by the intervention of the Speaker, who came down definitely on the side of the Chancellor that the definition would be more properly contained in the Finance Bill than in the resolution. . . .

Mr Churchill then turned his attention to Mr Runciman and disposed of his argument that artificial silk was not a luxury by the most effective use of a quotation from Mr Courtauld[1] himself which had appeared in a supplement of the Manchester Guardian shortly before the introduction of the Budget. In any event, silk and artificial silk must be treated on the same basis. Waving his collection of samples, he challenged Mr Ramsay MacDonald to succeed in differentiating where a jury of ladies had already failed and emphatically declared that, if artificial silk were to be excluded from the scheme, the whole tax would inevitably have to be dropped. During the remainder of his speech he devoted himself mainly to arguments of a more technical character to show that the tax had been devised in such a way as to impose no handicap on the home producer as compared with the foreign competitor and to hold the balance evenly between natural and artificial production.

The general impression conveyed by Mr Churchill's defence was so satisfactory that, when Mr Snowden rose to reply, the majority of Members trooped off to the Dining Rooms. He had very little instructive criticism to offer and amply justified Mr Churchill's prophesy by indulging in a Jeremiad in regard to the damaging effect which these taxes would exercise on an expanding industry.

[1] Samuel Courtauld, 1876–1947. Chairman of Courtaulds Limited, 1921–46. A Trustee of the Tate Gallery from 1927 and of the National Gallery from 1931.

Sir Douglas Hogg to Winston S. Churchill

(*Churchill papers: 1/178*)

13 May 1925

Dear Chancellor,

Thank you for writing. Your knowledge of my wife[1] goes back further even than my own. She often spoke to me of you, & she was glad when the old association was renewed two years ago. No man ever had a wife who was so completely a comrade & partner: she shared every interest in my life; her pleasure made success pleasant & her companionship lightened trouble. She would like to know that you had written. My wife liked & admired your wife so much, & we thought sometimes that your partnership was something like our own. I cant say any more.

Yours sincerely,
Douglas McGarel Hogg

Winston S. Churchill: remarks to a deputation

(*Treasury papers: T172/1517*)

14 May 1925

SILK DUTY

You do not imagine I am putting this tax on for fun, out of mischief? . . .

I am putting it on because I have to try and find money in order to give remissions of taxation in other directions which I consider press more severely upon the population and upon the business of the country than this would. . . .

I regard all taxation with distaste, but having to balance the whole of it I have not the slightest doubt which is the least harmful to the country and which would be the greatest measure of relief. . . .

I have to produce a balanced Budget. It gives me the greatest pain to interfere with your affairs.

You see silk is the only commodity I could call a luxury commodity which would produce sufficient revenue.

---

[1] Elizabeth Brown, daughter of Judge James Trimble Brown of Nashville, Tennessee, USA. In 1897 she married Archibald John Marjoribanks (whose brother was married to Churchill's aunt, Lady Fanny Spencer-Churchill). He died three years after their marriage, and in 1905 she married Sir Douglas Hogg (later Viscount Hailsham). She died on 10 May 1925: their son Quintin Hogg, after a long political career, was appointed Lord Chancellor in 1970.

Lord Birkenhead to Winston S. Churchill

(*Churchill papers: 2/141*)

18 May 1925
Secret

My dear Winston,

I have often for many years given many hours of my time to your private affairs. Busy as you are, you must give a little to mine now. I gave up £30,000 a year when I became LC. I gave up my claim to the woolsack to make things easier for the PM. I can earn without the slightest prejudice to my ministerial work £10,000 a year by writing. I agree to your formula but unless this thing is decided that way, I want you quite clearly to understand that when I have been a year at the IO & Indian things are straighter I shall resign & become merely a judge & an author. I have responsibilities to my family which I have too long neglected.[1]

Yours as ever
F

Stanley Baldwin to King George V

(*Baldwin papers*)

26 May 1925   House of Commons

The Prime Minister with his humble duty to Your Majesty.

There is an old maxim 'Money is like muck, not good except it be spread.' To judge from yesterday's debate on the Second Reading of the Finance Bill there would seem to be general agreement amongst all Parties that taxation has the same attributes, but there would seem to be differences of opinion in regard to the method of its distribution. Perhaps yesterday's debate showed that those differences are not in reality as substantial as the glamour of rhetoric would make them appear to be. From the point of view of parliamentary criticism the debate was a disappointment, but from the point of view of the Government it was thoroughly satisfactory. Speakers on the Opposition side made a very poor case against the Budget proposals, and their speeches were for the most part flimsy and unconvincing. Mr Churchill can therefore feel proportionately gratified.

---

[1] Lord Birkenhead remained Secretary of State for India until October 1928, when he resigned in order to earn money by writing. He had already published *Law, Life and Letters* in 1927. In 1929 he published his collected speeches, and in 1930 *The World in 2030*. Published posthumously were *Turning Points in History* and *Last Essays* (both in 1930) and *Fifty Famous Fights in Fact and Fiction* (in 1932).

Mr Churchill, who rose shortly before dinner, was in his very best form. It was essentially a debating speech, but it was full of cleverness and ingenuity, and was delivered with all the picturesqueness of expression, rhetoric power, and vigour of gesture which form part of Mr Churchill's inimitable style. If anything he was more forceful than usual, and both the Liberals and the Opposition came in for some vigorous punishment.

In routing his opponents he was eminently successful. He produced a formidable array of ingenious facts and subtle statistics with which he successfully showed that Mr Snowden's Party cry had absolutely no foundation in fact. His rout of Mr Lloyd George was equally effective, and was really achieved in a single sentence. He opened his attack on the Liberal amendment by challenging Mr Lloyd George to say whether he had taken any part in drafting that amendment, whether he had approved of it, or whether he had even read it. Mr Lloyd George's spontaneous action in endeavouring to obtain a copy of the Order Paper from the friends around him, and the look of guilt on his face were quite sufficient to convince the House that Mr Churchill had made a very accurate guess.

Winston S. Churchill to Stanley Baldwin

(*Baldwin papers*)

29 May 1925   Treasury Chambers
Personal and Private

My dear Prime Minister,

Although I agree absolutely with the decision of the Cabinet Committee and of the Cabinet in turning down Marriage Allowances for the Navy on the merits, I do not feel quite easy about the political situation created thereby. Bridgeman insisted upon taking £350,000 provisionally in the Estimates, and although he used language which showed that the whole matter was under consideration, nevertheless this money has actually been voted for this purpose by the House of Commons. I expect that all over the Navy the married officers have taken it as settled and have been counting on getting at any rate something. If they are completely disappointed, we shall certainly be asked: 'Why did you excite false hopes; why couldn't you wait till your enquiries were complete and you had made up your minds, instead of playing with these poor fellows?' We have not got a satisfactory answer to such a question, in view of the precipitate action which the Admiralty took.

It is impossible for me as Chancellor to raise such a point, because it would destroy my power of insisting on other economies; and those members of the Cabinet who have taken such a firm stand against unwarranted demands would be much offended if the Minister, who of all others ought to insist, appeared to throw them over. All the same, I feel this matter will require to be handled by you in the direction of a compromise. It will not be easy, because the Air and the Army will both be angry if the Navy get anything more without their getting something too. Still I think you might put it to Bridgeman that you would back him up for, say, £100,000 (instead of £350,000), provided he made adjustments in the pay and (or) collected something from the untaxed liquor consumed on board HM ships, and from these various sources constructed a certain reduced scheme of Marriage Allowances. We were on thoroughly good ground about the ex-ranker officers. But owing to the course adopted by the Admiralty, I cannot feel our hands are quite free in this Naval business.

Perhaps having regard to the by-elections[1] and the Unemployed demonstration on the 21st,[2] it would be better to leave till the end of June our new departure in Unemployment Insurance in the vague and general language which I used in the House of Commons. I must admit I am in two minds about it; and of course if Steel-Maitland feels very strongly that the announcement ought to be delayed for a few weeks, that ought to weigh in the decision.

Yours vy sincerely,
Winston S. Churchill

[1] By-elections were held at Ayr Burghs on June 12 (held by the Conservatives); at Eastbourne on June 17 (held by the Conservatives); at Oldham on June 2 (held by the Liberals, with no Conservative standing); and at the Forest of Dean on July 14 (held by Labour).

[2] The Trade Union Congress had declared Sunday, 22 June 1925, 'Unemployed Sunday', and a manifesto had been circulated calling for the support of the demonstration, and stating that during the previous four years the workers had suffered 'unparallelled unemployment, widespread short time, and drastic reductions in wages'. The London meeting was held in Trafalgar Square. *The Times* called it 'the largest gathering of its kind seen there in recent years'. Among the speakers was the Labour MP Clement Attlee, who called upon the Government to establish a National Employment and Development Board to 'develop the National resources for the common good', and to reopen trade with the Soviet Union.

June 1925

Lord Beaverbrook to Sir Robert Borden

(*Beaverbrook papers*)

10 June 1925

Baldwin goes on the placid tenor of his way—following Winston Churchill's advice. In this way he is not ill-advised, for Churchill is a good judge in every matter which does not concern himself. There, his judgment is hopeless, and he is sure to come to a big crash in time. He really had a lucky escape over his Budget which might easily have ruined him. As it is, he is riding out that tempest more or less successfully. But he is born to trouble for like Jehovah in the hymn—'He plants his footsteps on the deep and rides upon the storm.'

Winston S. Churchill to Stanley Baldwin

(*Churchill papers: 18/11*)

12 June 1925

My dear Prime Minister,

Before we make up our minds whether or not to grant an Enquiry under the Safeguarding of Industries procedure into the claims of the Steel trade for protection, it is necessary for the Cabinet to see exactly where we are going and where the Enquiry may lead us. Hitherto the SG procedure has only touched articles of small consequence to the general trade of the country, and those have been of a finished or luxury class. Steel, however, is one of the fundamental basic raw materials of national industry. It affects in one way or another all the greatest trades in the country: shipbuilding, factory and house building, railways and tramways, bridges, engineering of all kinds and every form of machinery. Most of those trades are themselves hard pressed by foreign competition, and all of them are increasingly making use of cheap foreign steel. If British steel is to be protected, it will be impossible to resist a demand for a corresponding measure of protection against foreign competition to all the users of steel. This again will only lead to further consequential developments. All the trades dependent upon machinery for agricultural implements or for large Works of construction, etc, will also claim, with reason, that they are prejudiced by an increase in their costs of production and that they are entitled to a measure of protection for their own special benefit. We may thus rouse complaints both of Agriculture and Textiles. In other words, the whole field of British industry would be involved in a protective duty on Steel. I do not attempt to argue the merits of the policy here; I am only drawing attention to its vast scope.

It is said that all these aspects will be examined by the proposed Committee of Enquiry. All the interests who conceive themselves prejudicially affected will have access under our scheme and will be able to argue their case. It is expected that the adverse effects on other industries would be so great that the claims of the Steel trade, however good in themselves, would have to be overridden. But from the moment that an Enquiry under the SG procedure about Steel has been started, the whole controversy of Free Trade as against Protection will, for good or for ill, have been raised in the most direct and serious form.

A decision to protect Steel cannot possibly be taken apart from the question of a general tariff on foreign imports. Nothing could be more unscientific or indeed manifestly absurd and unjust than to assist one particular basic industry and to give it protection, while leaving those dependent upon it unsheltered. Everyone—Protectionists and Free Traders alike—would see this. Thus from the moment the Enquiry is announced this great disruptive fiscal issue will become the dominant feature of British politics. I am sure you do not want this.

We are told that in all probability the Enquiry would lead to a denial of the Steel trade claims on grounds of the adverse effects on other industries. But if the Enquiry yields a negative result, what good is that to the Steel trade whose lamentable condition is after all the great problem? There will only have been a long tariff wrangle with the usual rise of temperature inseparable from the main fiscal controversy, and then at the end the Steel trade will be left with nothing.

If on the other hand the Committee have advised us that the Steel trade should be protected—and protected irrespective of the consequences to other industries—that will create a political situation of the gravest and most critical kind. I can understand a general tariff on all foreign imports, scientifically graded, being carried through a Parliament which had received a mandate for that purpose. I cannot conceive an isolated duty on Steel being carried through in the teeth of the opposition of all the users of Steel and of Free Trade opinion generally. I am sure it would be riddled in detail and that those responsible for it would have to face all the arguments of Free Traders without being able to use their counter-arguments which sustain the case for a general tariff. I ought not at this very early stage to leave you in any doubt of the serious view which I personally should take of such a proposal.

I am sure that if this situation were reached and it was decided to go forward with a protective tariff on Steel, the whole Protectionist opinion of the country would be irresistibly drawn into widening the issue and dealing with the problem in a logical and scientific manner through the agency of a general tariff. From a Protectionist point of view this is unquestionably right, and from any point of view far more reasonable. But we are inhibited from adopting this course in the present Parliament by your own and other most explicit pledges. Therefore the Cabinet would be confronted at this point either with a demand to pass an isolated Steel duty through the House or of making a fresh appeal to the country.

Surely this is not a conclusion towards which you wish to move. The vital interests of the British Empire and of the stability of this country, alike require a steady period of settled government, which alone can give time for the recovery from our exhaustion. To plunge into violent fiscal controversy, leading certainly in a short time to another General Election, would be little less than a crime against the central foundation of the State.

I am sure you will be in full agreement with this. But if so, we ought not lightly to enter upon paths or lend ourselves to currents which will inevitably conduct to such an ill-starred conclusion.

To sum up, either the claims of the Steel trade will be turned down by the Committee, in which case their difficulties will be left quite unremedied; or on the other hand, we should be involved in another political crisis. Therefore either way, nothing but misfortune can attend the decision to set up the Enquiry. Happily we are under no obligation to grant this Enquiry. Clause 4, Section I, of the White Paper gives full powers to the Board of Trade to refuse the application:

'The Board of Trade will, in their discretion reserve the right to refuse an enquiry, irrespective of other conditions obtaining in the industry, if they are of opinion that the industry is not carried on in this country with reasonable efficiency and economy, or *that the imposition of a duty on goods of the class or description in question would exert a seriously adverse effect on employment in any other industry using goods of that class or description in production.*'

In these circumstances the Cabinet should themselves make up their minds whether the Enquiry under the SG procedure should be granted or not, and should not agree to it unless they see their way to carry the matter to its full conclusion.

The problem of the Steel trade, which within certain minimum limits is a key industry vital to our war-making power if we are attacked, rightly deserves profound and immediate study. Such study should be given by a procedure entirely different and totally divorced from the political aspects of the SG policy. A Royal Commission on the State of the Steel trade and its relation to national defence would not in my opinion raise the fiscal issues inseparable from the SG procedure. It would be placed in a special category. It may well be that wide recommendations would result—concentration on the latest plants, a cartel, within limits State Assistance—in which reasonable Free Traders as well as Protectionists would join. And whatever the recommendations, the Government would remain completely free to adopt or reject them in whole or in part, on grounds not of economics but of high State policy.

Winston S. Churchill to Sir Alfred Watson
and Sir George Barstow

(*Churchill papers: 18/12*)

19 June 1925

The disciplinary and social effects of the provisions of this Bill are of such importance to the State, and so conducive to sound national economy, that they justify an exertion by the Exchequer. We must not accept the calculations of the Ministry of Labour without careful scrutiny.

Two important factors are at work in aggravating Unemployment. The first is that people occasionally and temporarily employed have learned to take advantage of the benefit in a way never practised in earlier years. The astringent clauses of the Bill will produce a salutary effect, which I think the Ministry of Labour are naturally prone to underrate. I should not be surprised if the effects of the various restrictions were to influence the whole tone of the Unemployment administration, and if the consequent reduction in numbers far exceeded the 80,000 now estimated.

The second factor is the crisis in the Coal Trade. This is now acute, and must settle itself in a few months either by a new agreement on a more highly competitive basis or by a strike. Probably by the autumn the Coal Mines will be working on a new basis. It would be very illogical to mix up the 120,000 coal miners now on the Fund with the ordinary seasonal unemployment. I think it is fair to assume that employment in the Coal Trade will be normal by the time the new obligations in respect of Unemployment Insurance fall upon the Exchequer.

From these two causes I look for a reduction of at least 200,000 in the general figures by January. I want to know how the Ministry of Labour have calculated the coal factor in Unemployment.

I do not feel that a reduction of twopence employer and a penny workman would justify the expectations we have roused. I therefore wish plans to be made for financing a scheme on its present basis. If the gloomy estimates of the Ministry of Labour are made good, then we must make use of our borrowing powers under the Act. Or, alternatively, a scheme may be devised for respreading the payments in regard to the new pension scheme so as to enable us to make a larger contribution to Unemployment during the years when this scheme showed surpluses. In the event of Unemployment remaining chronic on its present high figure, the whole question of Unemployed benefits will have to be reconsidered. Possibly the benefits will have to be reduced throughout the whole area, from 18/- to 15/-. I do not consider that the Cabinet view about not using the borrowing powers need be taken as final. I think I could have guided them to a different decision, had it been necessary.

On this basis please make me the best alternative proposals you can for discussion tomorrow at 12.30.

WSC

Winston S. Churchill to Stanley Baldwin

(*Baldwin papers*)

19 June 1925   Chartwell Manor
Personal and Private

My dear Prime Minister,

I have been all day clearing away jungle, and at the same time clearing my thoughts. In my sphere now there are three large questions ripening for decision.

First of all the Unemployment Bill. Owing to the bad returns of the last two weeks, the Ministry of Labour now estimate for an average thirteen hundred thousand in the next twelve months, instead of eleven eighty which was the basis of all our calculations. This would mean that I should have to find not £4 millions, but nearly double, in order to make the reduction in the contributions of employers and workers. I could not afford this unless I made use of the statutory borrowing powers during this exceptional period of Unemployment and let the Debt increase each year by the difference between my £4 millions and the annual Unemployment demand. Alternatively, I might somewhat vary the finance of the New Pensions scheme: pay less to the New Pensions in the first three years when there are actual surpluses in the new Fund, and more for Unemployment.

One way or another I consider we are bound to go ahead with the scheme, and I do not think it would be handling the matter effectively to reduce only by twopence employer and a penny workman, instead of threepence and twopence as we now intend. I am going into the basis of the Ministry of Labour's estimates tomorrow with the Government Actuary and others. I do not think they make sufficient allowance for the special conditions which have led to the increase in Unemployment among miners, or to the possibility of its clearing off before January when our payment begins. I think the disciplinary and social values of the new restrictions are so great that the expense will be fully justified. I think, however, we shall have to have another meeting of our small Unemployment Committee on the new finance and on the new Ministry of Labour's estimates on Unemployment.

The second question is the Navy. I am sure they are going to make a great push to have four or five cruisers laid down this year. This means £4 or £5 millions addition on the Estimates next year, to say nothing of the cost of small craft. I am convinced that this is not justified by any real danger, and that it will be criticised not merely by our opponents but by many friends, and some who should be our political friends but are our active foes. My proposal would be not to have any cruisers this year. This would make a great impression and tend more than anything else to slow down naval competition. We would, however, declare a replacement programme of about three cruisers a year, together with a quota of destroyers and submarines beginning next year. Even this will bring the Naval Estimates up to £63 or £64 millions after every Admiralty economy has been made.

The Air Force also think they are going up a million or two. All this issue must be fought out, first on FE's Committee and then at the Cabinet in the first ten days of July at the latest.

Thirdly there is Steel. The more I think about it, the more sure I am that a protective duty on Steel, in isolation from everything else, would be indefensible from a Protectionist point of view. It would be the signal for the reopening of the old controversy in its sharpest form. It would be unworkable apart from a general tariff, and the general tariff is impossible without the General Election. Our Safeguarding policy is far too restricted to carry the weight of a fundamental issue of this kind. The moment such an Enquiry is started, everyone will be set by the ears. And if in the end the Enquiry turns the application down, Steel will be none the better for all the agitation. A Royal Commission, on the other hand, to report on the extent and importance of the depression in the Steel Trade, on the remedies that are possible, and on the minimum facilities that must be preserved in this country in the interest of national defence, would not raise the fiscal issue in an acute form and would give us far more chance of reaching a practicable solution.

I am sure you will be pondering over this. A forest fire is so easily started in this dry weather.

Yours vy sincerely
Winston S. Churchill

PS. The quotations from Mond about steel during the SG Bill debates, all related to SG proposals wh were concerned with discriminating duties agst particular countries, & it cd not be fairly argued that they applied to the present proposed general protection duty.

Winston S. Churchill: Cabinet memorandum[1]

(*Churchill papers: 22/38*)

20 June 1925   Treasury Chambers
Secret

EXPORT OF ARMS TO SOVIET RUSSIA

COMPENSATION FOR THE WITHDRAWAL AND NON-RENEWAL OF LICENCES

The Cabinet will recall that, following their decision of the 5th January to maintain their refusal to license the export of arms to Russia and to withdraw or to decline to renew, where they had lapsed, licences previously granted, applications were received from the firms concerned for compensation for losses suffered by them as a consequence of this decision. Upon this being reported to the Cabinet on the 21st January, I, with the President of the Board of Trade, undertook, at the invitation of our colleagues, 'to consider favourably the grant of compensation up to reasonable amounts to *bonâ fide* applicants who were able to substantiate their claims'.

The firms concerned are two only, viz, the Birmingham Small Arms Company and Messrs Vickers, Limited, and the amounts in question are as follows:—

	Value.
BIRMINGHAM SMALL ARMS COMPANY	£
200 Lewis Guns and spare parts, Russian 7·62 mm calibre	19,992
270 sets of Lewis Gun parts, English ·303-inch calibre ...	16,605
3 Thompson Automatic Rifles, Russian calibre ...	463
	37,060

[1] Circulated to the Cabinet as Cabinet paper 300 of 1925.

VICKERS, LIMITED

    136 sets of spare parts, 7·62 mm Russian calibre Vickers
        Hand-service Machine Guns   9,100

The total amount involved, assuming that none of the material can be disposed of elsewhere, is thus £46,160.

Neither the Admiralty nor the War Office nor the Air Ministry, all of whom have been consulted, are able to make use of any of the above material; and I have accordingly given very careful consideration to the question of compensation.

No funds are available for the purpose, and it is clear therefore that any proposal of the kind would need a special Vote of Parliament by means of a Supplementary Estimate. There can be no doubt that such a Vote would be very difficult to justify and would be most unpopular in the House of Commons, where it would certainly be argued against the proposal—

1. That the firms were engaged in what was admittedly a risky business in supplying arms to Soviet Russia under terminable licences, and that having accepted the risk they should be prepared to face the results.
2. That for the sake of the large profits involved firms are always prepared to spend large sums of money in connection with contracts of this kind, and that a loss such as this is one of the risks incidental to the business of armament supply to foreign States.
3. That they might be able to dispose of their munitions elsewhere.

Finally, it seems to me that, in admitting the claim of an individual or firm to be compensated for failure to carry out a contract owing to the intervention of the Government on grounds of national interest, we should be creating a most dangerous precedent for the future and one that in its implications might have the most serious consequences upon the liberty of action of the Executive Government.

I have therefore come to the conclusion that these claims should be refused, and I invite my colleagues to concur in this view.

WSC

Lord Rothermere to Lord Beaverbrook

(*Beaverbrook papers*)

22 June 1925   South of France

I feel Winston has treated me with great incivility. To me more than any one else he owes his return to the political arena. Yet he brings in a budget taxing artificial silk without consulting me who outside the actual manufacturer knows more about this trade than possibly anyone living. When he took me down to his home at Westerham, he must have had this design in his mind and when I gave him a half promise to back his budget candour required him to get my views about such a tax. I should have pointed out the absurdity of the proposed impost and put him right, so his is the loss not mine.

Our feeble politicians are past praying for.

Yours

Harold

Regarding Winston I remember he came to me and asked whether I thought Trenchard would make a good Inspector General of the Air Force. I said Yes. Next week he made Trenchard Chief of the Air Staff. This was uncandid.

The result of this appointment is that for the money spent, we have the worst Air Force in the World. Our machines are bad so we are hopelessly outdistanced in world flights and I am told the number of young officers killed in training is more than all the other air forces together.

C. P. Scott[1] *to Winston S. Churchill*

(*Churchill papers: 2/142*)

22 June 1925   The Guardian Office, Manchester

My dear Churchill,

I am grieved about that paragraph.[2] It is of course of a kind that should never have appeared.

As I wired you this afternoon we shall publish a correction tomorrow and expression of regret.[3]

Yours sincerely

C. P. Scott

[1] Charles Prestwich Scott, 1846–1932. Editor of the *Manchester Guardian*, 1872–1929. Liberal MP, 1895–1906. A friend of Lloyd George, who often sought his advice.

[2] On 20 June 1925 the 'London Correspondent' of the *Manchester Guardian*, in an article entitled 'Statesman in the Smoking Room', had written of Churchill's 'persistent efforts' in the smoking room to 'acquire and extend his personal popularity among members of all ranks, even the most obscure of back benchers on the Government side of the House'. The article stated that even during 'the continuous work of the Committee stage of the Finance Bill, Mr Churchill has found time to appear each day in the smoking room'. The correspondent added: 'Though there are few Government or Liberal members whom the Chancellor has not found an opportunity of engaging in conversation, there are probably not more than half a dozen who have exchanged even a word with the Prime Minister.'

[3] On 23 June 1925 the *Manchester Guardian* published the following paragraph, headed 'Statesman in the Smoking Room': 'In a paragraph of our London Correspondence under this heading there were some observations relating to Mr Churchill which we are assured are entirely without foundation. We much regret the error.'

Stanley Baldwin to King George V

(*Baldwin papers*)

26 June 1925   House of Commons

The Finance Bill was finally laid to rest yesterday amid the blare of oratory and the clash of opinions. . . . .

As was to be expected Mr Churchill maintained the high standard which had been set in the course of the debate. In the course of his speech he collected together in summarised form all the main arguments which had been levelled against the various proposals contained in the Finance Bill, and successively repeated in abbreviated and potted terms the justification of his policy. In many respects it was a speech which was calculated to make a greater appeal to his readers outside the House than to the actual listeners, and, from this point of view, it ought to have a great influence. For the most part there was an absence of the usual fireworks, although, on one occasion during the speech, the vigour of his gestures caused him to hit the Financial Secretary[1] in the face—an incident which caused considerable amusement and enabled him to pay a most graceful and well deserved compliment to the victim of his exuberation. Looking at it as a whole his speech was a fitting termination to crown the brilliance which Mr Churchill has shown in piloting the Finance Bill through the House.

Clementine Churchill to Professor Lindemann

(*Cherwell papers*)

28 June 1925   11 Downing Street

My dear 'Prof',

As I write I picture that lucky little Randolph buzzing off with you to the Eclipse.

It is good of you to take him.

Now when will you come to Chartwell in August?

Could you by any chance come to us for a week or ten days on Friday August the 12th. I have picked out this period as Winston & the children are being rather frivolous & are visiting & yachting at various times, but between the 12th & 19th the whole family will be assembled under the home roof. They all want to be there when you come if possible.

[1] From November 1924 to November 1925 Walter Guinness was the Financial Secretary to the Treasury. He was succeeded in November 1925 by Ronald McNeill, who was himself succeeded in November 1927 by Arthur Samuel.

Winston S. Churchill to Sir Horace Hamilton

(*Treasury papers: T172/1474*)

29 June 1925

Now that the Budget is through the House of Commons, I must send you my most sincere and heart-felt thanks for the help you gave me. I cannot express too strongly my sense of the ability and resource which you have shown, or your power of continuous hard work in exacting circumstances, and I think myself most fortunate to have had such a Lieutenant.

C. P. Scott: diary

(*Scott papers*)

30 June 1925

Brendan Bracken, manager of Eyre and Spottiswoode's, whom I did not know, had asked me to dinner to meet Churchill (who he said wanted to see me and would come any [time] that I liked) so I offered the day before the other. I thought we should have been almost alone, but there were a dozen other people. . . .

Sat next Churchill who talked incessantly. He professed himself entirely at home in the Tory party. In foreign policy it was now a peace party. In home politics he differed from it only on Protection. Its errors on that subject were only small and for his own part he always frankly admitted them. They would not go much further. . . . Insufficient attention had been paid to his insurance scheme. It was a very big thing and meant great alleviation to the risks and hardships of the working class. It would no doubt have received more notice if brought in as a separate measure, but he was obliged to include it in his Budget because of the costs it involved to the Exchequer. . . .

The Polish ambassador,[1] whose English was imperfect and talked with Churchill and me partly in French, was very friendly in spite of the sins of the Manchester Guardian and pressed me to come to see him when next I was in London.

Churchill, who was as rhetorical as ever in his anti-Bolshevism, argued strongly that Poland should by all means cultivate the friendship of Germany.

---

[1] Konstanty Skirmunt, 1866–1951. Born in Russian Poland; studied law at the University of St Petersburg. A member of the Russian Council of State, 1909–17; of the Polish National Committee, 1918–19; of the Polish Delegation to the Paris Peace Conference, 1919. Minister of Foreign Affairs, Warsaw, 1921–2. Ambassador to London, 1922–34. Polish representative to the League of Nations, 1934–9.

Else, if Germany were driven back on Russian support, Poland in the end would be crushed between them. But the ambassador was not inclined to take so long a view and could only reiterate that Poland was quite ready to be friends with Germany provided only that she was asked to give nothing up.

July 1925

Thomas Jones: diary

(*Jones papers*)

1 July 1925

LORD HALDANE: Had I seen Winston's speech last Saturday to the girls at a school in Essex? Even Winston was convinced though he was Chancellor of the Exchequer, that there must be no stinting of funds for education. I told this to the Duchess of Atholl last night at dinner and she was going to circulate Winston's speech to the Chiefs of the Board of Education.

Sir Horace Hamilton to Winston S. Churchill

(*Treasury papers: T172/1474*)

3 July 1925

In sending you the enclosed Minute thanking you for your message to the Department, I should like to say how greatly I appreciate your very kind letter to myself. . . .

This is by far the most noteworthy budget that we have had since the war. I share your view that future Chancellors will think many times before taking off the silk duties. An entirely novel scheme of this kind may well require amendments in future Finance Bills but modifications will I venture to think, take the form of perfecting the scheme rather than of reducing it.

Lord Beatty to his wife

(*Beatty papers*)

4 July 1925

I am glad you are reading Winston's book,[1] which is very well written, but I do not think you are fair to him when you abuse him because he

---

[1] *The World Crisis 1915*, which had been published in October 1923 (see pages 65–6).

appointed Jellicoe to be C-in-C. Everybody thought in those days that Jellicoe was the best admiral we had. He certainly was the cleverest, and because he failed on one particular occasion, which would have proved the greatness or otherwise of the man, I do not think can be put down to Winston. He has been a very good friend to me and has backed me many times under circumstances of great difficulty.

Lord Beatty to his wife

(*Beatty papers*)

7 July 1925

We have reached an *impasse* with the Government on the cruiser question, and I do not see the way out. We have made our proposals as being the very lowest we can agree to, and they won't have them, with the result that somebody has got to give way completely and Willie Bridgeman is as firm as a rock. Therefore the whole of the Admiralty is with him *en bloc* and I suppose we shall have to go. There can be no other way out.

Winston S. Churchill to Austen Chamberlain

(*Churchill papers: 18/11*)

7 July 1925

My dear Austen,

I have read with much interest the note by Mr Lampson[1] of the points which the French Ambassador[2] proposes to raise with you this afternoon: and I understand that you would like to know my views as to your reply.

As regards the French debt to the United States, we must take strong exception to the suggestion made by the Ambassador that the British and American debts 'do not rest on an identic basis'. We could not regard this statement as having any foundation in fact and it would moreover seem to

[1] Miles Wedderburn Lampson, 1880–1964. Entered Foreign Office, 1903. 2nd Secretary, Tokyo, 1908–10. High Commissioner in Siberia, 1920. Foreign Office, 1924–6. Minister to China, 1926–33. Knighted, 1927. High Commissioner for Egypt and the Sudan, 1934–6; Ambassador in Cairo, 1936–46. Created Baron Killearn, 1943. Special Commissioner, South-East Asia, 1946–8.

[2] Aimé Joseph de Fleuriau, 1870–1938. Entered the French Diplomatic Service, 1895. Counsellor of Embassy, London, 1913–20, and close friend of Paul Cambon, the Ambassador. Minister to Peking, 1921–4. Ambassador to London, 1924–33.

be inconsistent with the assurance that in its negotiations with America 'the French Government will carefully abstain from any settlement such as would place the United States of America in a position of advantage over His Majesty's Government'. I should be glad if you would take note of this assurance with satisfaction, and inform the Ambassador that we were somewhat surprised that no such assurance was given in the official reply which he sent, in the name of the French Government, on the 2nd instant.

While we would be glad to see the French get good terms from the United States of America, I do not understand how it is supposed that we can intervene with this object.

As regards the French debt to this country, the position is less satisfactory. It is true that M de Fleuriau placed some representatives of the French Treasury in touch with the British Treasury last March and that some conversations took place. But their conversations related chiefly to the interpretation of my correspondence with M Clémentel: no *official* proposal of any kind was put forward and the *personal* suggestions made by the French officials could not be regarded as a serious basis of negotiation. I do not think that we can accept the statement that the Ambassador 'had tried, and failed, to come to a direct settlement with His Majesty's Government'. The French representatives were informed of the lines on which their proposals should have been framed under the Clémentel note and we had hoped that they would have been sent back ere this with a more satisfactory offer.

As regards the best method of continuing the discussions with this country, what we want is an *official* proposal by the French Government, (a) of *substantial* payments on account of their debt, independent of reparation receipts (which should begin immediately though the scale of payments might be graduated for a few years before reaching the normal figure), together with (b) a further payment which may be contingent on the yield of the Dawes Annuities. Perhaps the best course would be for the French Government to put forward in writing the proposals which they can make. This would give a definite basis for conversation—which has so far been lacking from their side. Such a communication could be regarded as informal, if they so desired, but it ought to come from the French Government and be reasonably precise. So far the French Government have made no real suggestion at all.

I enclose herewith an official letter which we were addressing to you in regard to M de Fleuriau's note of the 2nd instant, which supplements what I write now.

I shd be glad to explain this position to de Fleuriau at any time,

Yours sincerely,
Winston S. Churchill

Notes of a conversation between Winston S. Churchill and the French Ambassador

(*Treasury papers: T188/7*)

9 July 1925

The French Ambassador called at the Treasury on the 9th July and was received by the Chancellor of the Exchequer.

The Chancellor began by referring to the British note of the 26th June, and he emphasised that we could not tolerate the French Government giving better treatment to the United States debt than they gave to our debt. If such a situation arose, we should have to cancel the Balfour offer and to insist on exacting from France the full measure of the obligations which we held.

The French Ambassador was very upset at this declaration. He protested, however, that the French Government had never any intention of pursuing such a policy. He asked what had led the British Government to raise the point.

The Chancellor referred to the attempt which M Poincaré had made to differentiate between the two debts, and stated frankly that reports had reached him to the effect that this point of view was still held in France. (M de Fleuriau had himself spoken of the two debts as not being 'on an identic basis' in his conversation with Mr Lampson on the 7th instant, but the Chancellor did not mention this.)

The Chancellor finally stated that, if His Majesty's Government were to come to an arrangement with France about her debt, they would have to stipulate in some form or other that, in the event of any better terms being accorded to the United States by France, we should be entitled to revise the arrangement made with us so as to secure the same terms as those accorded to the United States.

The Chancellor repeated this statement, at M de Fleuriau's request, in order that there might be no mistake about it. He also pointed out to the French Ambassador that such a stipulation might in fact materially strengthen the hands of the French Government in their negotiations with the United States.

The French Ambassador urged that the settlement between the two countries could not be on precisely the same lines. For example, he understood that the British Government was willing to accept a proportion of their payments in the form of a share in the Dawes annuities which the United States declined to accept.

The Chancellor replied that we must have equality in substance, not necessarily in form. We could not assent to any arrangement under which similar payments were made to the United States and to Great Britain, but those offered to the United States were to be payments by France, whereas those offered to Great Britain were to be contingent on German payments. If the security were different, the payments must differ in proportion to the value of the security, so that there should be a real equality between the two settlements. While laying down this general principle, the Chancellor did not commit himself to any rigid system.

The French Ambassador mentioned that the arrangement contemplated with the United States would include a long moratorium. The Chancellor did not reply to this, but obviously if we accept in part settlement of the French debt a share in the German payments, no moratorium would apply.

The French Ambassador said he might ask for a memorandum of the Chancellor's declarations and he hoped that it might be put in such a form as to be helpful to the French Government in its negotiations with the United States. He also asked what form of delegation His Majesty's Government would prefer to receive, and when it should come, with a view to the further discussion of the question. He thought it might be preferable to await the result of the negotiations in the United States of America.

The Chancellor dissented from the suggestion that the negotiations with Great Britain should be deferred until after a settlement had been reached with the United States, and he stated that he thought the French delegation should come to London at least as soon as, if not before, one was sent to the United States. As regards the form of the delegation, this seemed to be primarily a question for the French Government, but he thought the best course was for M Caillaux[1] to come here as soon as his duties in France allowed him the opportunity. Obviously, any settlement of the debt involved heavy political responsibilities. Any Ministers who sign such an agreement would be attacked on both sides of the Channel as having sacrificed the interests of their countries. It was essential, therefore, that Ministers should confer together with a view to arriving at a fair deal.

It was agreed that the conversation should be regarded as private unless the French Ambassador asked for a memorandum.

[1] Joseph Caillaux, 1862–1944. Born in Le Mans. A Socialist-Radical Deputy from 1898. Minister of Finance, 1899–1902, 1906–9, 1911 and 1913–14. Prime Minister, 1911–12. Arrested for treason on Clemenceau's orders, 1918; sentenced to 3 years in prison and 10 years deprivation of political rights. Amnestied, 1924. Senator, 1925. Minister of Finance, April–October 1925, June–July 1926 and June 1935. In June 1937 he played a major part in the Senate in bringing about the fall of Blum's Government. Chairman for the Commission for Finances, 1937–40.

Winston S. Churchill: note of a conversation with the French Ambassador

(*Treasury papers: T188/7*)

17 July 1925[1]

M de Fleuriau came again to see me on the 17th on the subject of inter-Allied debts. He asked me how I reconciled the position of the Balfour note and other British declarations with the statement that we must receive payments from France *pari passu* and proportionately with any she made to the United States and with my further statement that in no circumstances would we acquiesce in France settling with America on better terms than with us. I replied that at the time of the Balfour note and of all subsequent declarations we had never conceived it possible that anything so unfair as that France should give more favourable terms to the United States than to us could be contemplated, and that we should resist such a proceeding in the strongest manner, to the extent of withdrawing completely from any voluntary declarations which we had made out of consideration and magnanimity. Such a situation, if it arose, would overrule the Balfour declaration. He then said that their difficulty with America was that she would probably refuse to take any proportion of French payments in German reparation, whereas we had again and again indicated our readiness to do so. I said that we did not stipulate for exact similarity in form between the settlements, but only that, judged as a whole, they must be equal in value. The form might be varied to suit the views of the two creditor countries, but if we took an inferior security for a proportion of our payments that would have to be taken into consideration in the rest of the terms. M de Fleuriau did not effectively challenge this position.

I then asked him whether it was the interest of France to come to a settlement with America earlier than with Great Britain; surely her interest would be to come to terms with us and then tell the United States that they could not give her any better terms in substance (apart from form) than those they had made with us, and that we had stipulated if they did that our position should be improved up to the American level. Seeing that M de Fleuriau evidently felt the truth of this, I suggested to him that the best course was to send a debt funding commission to the United States to negotiate and then at the same time let M Caillaux come over here and discuss the problem with me. If we reached an agreement here, that could be used as a means of limiting American demands on France. We had shown ourselves far more ready to consider European difficulties than the United States, and they would be well advised to carry the matter as far forward as possible with us before becoming too deeply committed in the American

[1] Churchill prepared this account for the Cabinet on 21 July 1925.

negotiations. Whereas if they made terms with America, who would certainly be most severe, those more severe terms would govern any settlement subsequently to be effected with us.

M de Fleuriau expressed himself as in cordial agreement with this. I had offered at our previous interview to give him an *aide-mémoire* if he so desired. He now said that M Briand thought it better that nothing should be set in writing at this stage, and that both our conversations should be treated as personal and private.

WSC

L. S. Amery: diary

(*Amery papers*)

17 July 1925

Cabinet on the report of the Navy Committee. This report, with FE in the chair to back up Winston almost inevitably took the little Navy point of view. . . .

The Cabinet supported Winston's view that it [two-thirds of the programme agreed in 1923] should be postponed a year. Willie led off stating his case very well and was followed by Winston who was also effective and made a great appeal to the weaker elements in the Cabinet generally.

Winston S. Churchill to Austen Chamberlain

(*Austen Chamberlain papers*)

17 July 1925

My dear Austen,

Vy many thanks for yr invaluable help this afternoon in keeping the door from being closed. I tried my best too, but I have now come to the end of my resources. I still hope that the compromise will be accepted.

Yours ever,

W

Winston S. Churchill to William Bridgeman

(*Churchill papers: 22/69*)

17 July 1925

My dear First Lord,

The Prime Minister authorises me to send you the enclosed draft statement which it is suggested might be used in the House by you to make plain your position and that of the naval Lords, I should be very much obliged if you would send it tonight to Beatty. I promised to furnish him with it.

Yours very sincerely,
Winston S. Churchill

Draft statement for William Bridgeman

(*Churchill papers: 22/69*)

17 July 1925

I ought not to lead the House to suppose that this solution is (wholly) satisfactory to the Board of Admiralty. The Board would have preferred that the process of replacing obsolescent cruisers should have been undertaken on a larger scale both this year and next. They have advised the construction of four cruisers this year and three next year. HMG after a full review of the international situation and with due consideration of the present financial position assume the responsibility for the modifications upon which they have decided. The Board of Admiralty have accepted these modifications subject only to this clear statement of their view.

Winston S. Churchill to William Bridgeman

(*Churchill papers: 22/69*)

18 July 1925

My dear First Lord,

The Prime Minister wishes me to add to my letter to you of last night that of course the formula about responsibility that we have suggested to you would have to be approved by the Cabinet before it could be finally offered. At present it is only tentative and subject to Cabinet approval. The Prime Minister thinks, and I agree with him, that the Cabinet would readily approve it, if it were acceptable to the Admiralty. But it might be thought wanting in respect to the Cabinet if we presumed to make it formally without their prior sanction.

William Bridgeman to Stanley Baldwin

(*Churchill papers: 22/69*)

18 July 1925

My dear Prime Minister,

I have laid the letter and draft statement which you directed the Chancellor of the Exchequer to send me before the Sea Lords. They feel that the only course that they can take at the moment is to enter an emphatic protest against any further delay in the reduced programme which they have agreed to under pressure as the minimum immediate addition to our naval strength that will fulfil the responsibility laid upon them of safeguarding our territories and sea communications.

W. C. Bridgeman

Austen Chamberlain to Winston S. Churchill

(*Churchill papers: 22/69*)

18 July 1925   Foreign Office
Private & Personal

My dear Winston,

I thought your tone & temper on our Friday conference admirable.[1]

I can & do feel sympathy with both sides, & I want a compromise & tried to put the case for compromise in a way that might appeal to Beatty.

You led straight up to the same goal.

As I said in Cabinet, the Chancellor often has to play a very lonely hand, & I felt so much the lack of support by my immediate predecessor[2] when I was last Chancellor in 1920 that I have tried throughout to help you where I could.

Yours ever
Austen

PS. I believe it is the first time that you & I have signed 'yours ever' to each other. It is a solemn form of signature, but after so many years of friendship I follow your example with confidence.

[1] At the end of a three-day conference, summoned by Baldwin to bring the Naval Estimates dispute to an end, Churchill had put forward a compromise suggestion that the Admiralty should build its first four new cruisers over two years instead of one. But neither Bridgeman nor Beatty had been willing to agree to this.

[2] Andrew Bonar Law (who was Chancellor of the Exchequer from December 1916 to January 1919).

Winston S. Churchill to Austen Chamberlain

(Austen Chamberlain papers)

20 July 1925   Treasury Chambers
Private

My dear Austen,

I am very grateful to you for yr most kind & welcome letter. Yr influence & help at Friday's conference wd have achieved its purpose, if we were not in presence of unreasoning obstinacy.

Believe me
Yours ever
W

Winston S. Churchill: Cabinet memorandum[1]

(Churchill papers: 22/41)

20 July 1925
Secret

NAVY ESTIMATES

New Construction Programme

It will be well to set out clearly the final issues on which the decision on Naval policy turns. I accept the figures of expenditure set forth on page 5 of the Committee's Report, plus the existing maintenance expenditure of the Navy, as the maximum contribution to which the Exchequer can be committed in present circumstances.

—	1925–26	1926–27	1927–28	1928–29	1929–30
	£	£	£	£	£
Old Programme	7,647,877	6,953,950	2,197,634	68,055	Nil
New Programme	Nil	1,280,950	6,626,850	11,558,736	12,949,431
Total	7,647,877	8,234,900	8,824,484	11,626,791	12,949,431

If to these are added the present cost of maintenance at approximately

[1] Circulated to the Cabinet as Cabinet paper 360 of 1925.

£53 millions plus the shadow cut of £2 millions, it would give net Naval Estimates for the period under review of—

1925–26	1926–27	1927–28	1928–29	1929–30
£ 62,647,877	£ 63,234,900	£ 63,824,484	£ 66,626,791	£ 67,949,431

or making allowance for the shadow cut carried forward from year to year—

1925–26	1926–27	1927–28	1928–29	1929–30
£ 60½	£ 61,234,900	£ 61,824,484	£ 64,626,791	£ 65,949,431

This I regard as the utmost limit of finance which we can contemplate unless some great adverse change takes place in the world situation.

On Friday, at the desire of the Prime Minister, I proposed to the First Lord that he should begin two cruisers (and the four China gunboats—a very small matter) this year and thus spread the programme of four proposed for next year over two years instead of having a blank year, always provided that no increase of expenditure above the Committee's total was incurred in either year. The increased cost of beginning these two cruisers this year instead of next year (plus China gunboats) would be approximately £600,000 more this year and about £1,200,000 next year. There would be a corresponding relief in later years. The Treasury are of opinion that the £600,000 required for this year could be found without taking anything more than a token Supplementary Vote. The Treasury estimate that in spite of the shadow cut of £2,000,000 it is safe to allow for a further under-spending of at least £300,000. The present Vote contains £350,000 for marriage allowances which two Cabinet Committees and the Cabinet have rejected. The number of men coming on to charge during the year, namely, 103,025, would offer, the Treasury suggest, a reduction of £50,000 to £75,000 on the original estimate.

A very moderate slowing down in the rate of building up the reserve of oil would provide a substantial increased margin. Similar calculations have been made for next year. It is, of course, evident that if the vessels are laid down earlier the money will have to be found from one source or another, and that there can be no question of delaying construction once put in hand.

That there is great room for interior economies may be inferred from the following calculation: In 1914, on the eve of the German war, our total estimates were £51½ millions net. These Estimates included £18½ millions of new construction, leaving £33 millions for maintenance. Our present Estimates of £62½ millions (including £2 millions 'shadow' cut) contain only £7½ millions of new construction and provide for costs of maintenance £55 millions. To make an exact comparison between the 1914 figure of £33 millions and the present figure of £55 millions it is necessary first of all to strike out the non-effective votes on both sides. These were in 1914 £3 millions and in 1925 £8 millions. The increase in cost of the maintenance of the Navy is therefore measured by the difference between £30 millions and £47 millions. On the other hand, the purchasing power of the sovereign has diminished in the proportion of 175 to 100. If the £30 millions of 1914 are increased by 75 per cent to allow for this we obtain a figure of £52½ millions, which compares with £47 millions of today; in other words, there has been a reduction of 10½ per cent only upon the maintenance charges of 1914. But for the equivalent £52½ millions of 1914 after all allowances have been made the Admiralty maintained 45 battleships, 7 battle cruisers and 60 cruisers manned with full active reserve ratings, as against only 17 battleships, 3 battle cruisers and 42 cruisers and flotilla leaders in the same state as the present time. It is difficult to compare these Fleets exactly, but it is certainly true that the present Fleet is less than half what was maintained in 1914. In 1914 also 151,000 men were borne on Vote A, as against 100,000 now. It will be seen, after making every allowance for the decline in purchasing power, ie, the increase in the cost of everything, the interior economy of Naval administration, judged by results in war power, has deteriorated by something between one-third and one-half. Even a 10 per cent further economy in maintenance expenditure would save over £5 millions.

If the Admiralty were able to effect economies, it would be possible for them, with Cabinet approval, in any year or over a series of years to accelerate new construction. They could do this in two ways: either by laying down their ships at an earlier period in the year than is now allowed for, or, secondly, by constructing their cruisers, as is quite practicable, in thirty months instead of thirty-six. One of the advantages of proceeding on a programme agreed over a series of years is that designs, contracts, and, even within certain limits, the accumulation of materials can be proceeded with in advance. By each of these two methods 6 months at least can be saved, thus together making up the period of 12 months, and fully overtaking, if indeed it be thought necessary, the period of delay of 1 year involved in the Committee's recommendations.

The Cabinet in endorsing the Committee's report have therefore placed it in the power of the Admiralty to give full and exact expression to the

programme of requirements as set out by the First Sea Lord. It is not a
question of whether the view of the Board of Admiralty on the scale of new
construction and the dates at which it should be completed is to be modified,
it is only a question of whether the Admiralty attach sufficient importance
to an earlier execution of their own programme to make the moderate
sacrifices of reducing some of the excessive costs of their interior administration. It is obvious that they have a great latitude in this sphere.

                                                                    WSC

Winston S. Churchill to Lord Birkenhead

(Churchill papers: 22/69)

22 July 1925   Treasury Chambers
Private but official!

My dear Fred,
    You will remember that the question of the Oil Fuel Reserves was specific-
ally referred to yr Ctee, but that we came to no decision upon it, & in the
clash of conclusion it played no part. On the other hand all the members of
the Ctee, headed by Salisbury, had I think formed the strong opinion that
the rate of accumulation of these reserves cd be greatly diminished in future
years, having regard to our large existing stock. The Admy on the other
hand claim that they are governed by the existing decision of the CID. I
suggest that you shd write officially to the PM stating the position, & recommending that the subject shd be referred to an early meeting of the CID,
having regard to the recent decision of that body upon the probability of
war etc.

                                                              Yours ever
                                                                    W

William Bridgeman to Stanley Baldwin

(Churchill papers: 22/69)

22 July 1925   Admiralty

My dear Prime Minister,
    The Board met at 4 pm today, and I put before them the proposals con-
tained in the Cabinet decision of this morning.
    I told them that I could not refuse to accede to your appeal, and that I
should agree with my colleagues in the Cabinet in their decision.
    They accepted my view—and only asked that I should forward to you a

memorandum from them pointing out the very inferior position we should be placed in by the postponement of the submarine and destroyer programme.

Of the four alternatives suggested by you we were unanimously of the opinion that the second should be adopted.
ie

2 Cruisers to be laid down					Oct 1925
2	,,	,, ,,	,,	,,	Feb 1926
2	,,	,, ,,	,,	,,	Oct 1926
1	,,	,, ,,	,,	,,	Feb 1927

With many thanks
Yours very sincerely,
W. C. Bridgeman

The Sea Lords' memorandum on the submarine position will follow.

Winston S. Churchill to Stanley Baldwin

(*Churchill papers: 22/69*)

24 July 1925

My dear Prime Minister,
    Don't read this until you come back in the train tomorrow. I shall have to press for a settlement of the figures in strict accordance with the Cabinet decision, and this is what I am sure you would wish. I am sending a copy to the First Lord; and perhaps you will be able to adjust any differences between us without a Cabinet. The difficulty is Time.

Yours very sincerely,
Winston S. Churchill

Winston S. Churchill to William Bridgeman

(*Churchill papers: 22/69*)

24 July 1925

My dear First Lord,
    I enclose a copy of a memorandum which I am sending to the Prime Minister tonight. I shall be available tomorrow morning if you want to see

me, but I am afraid you will be too deeply involved in the Coal-strike.[1] On the other hand we must have a decision on Monday at the latest.

Yours sincerely,
Winston S. Churchill

Winston S. Churchill: memorandum

(*Churchill papers: 22/69*)

24 July 1925

The estimates of expenditure on new construction supplied by the Admiralty require several important amendments to bring them within the scope of the Cabinet decision (appended).

(1) The cost of the Old programme as given in Lord Beatty's estimates on page 3 of the Committee's Report which were the basis of all discussions has been increased as follows:

	1925–26	*1926–27*	*1927–28*	*1928–29*
Estimates now presented:	7,647,877	7,020,090	2,974,296	102,100
Lord Beatty's Estimates:	7,647,877	6,953,950	2,197,634	68,055
Increase		+66,140	+776,662	+34,045

The Admiralty explain that the gunmountings for the 5 Kents ordered last year will probably cost £1,075,000 more than they had previously estimated. This was apparently discovered before Lord Beatty's estimate of the 1st July was given to the Committee; for the increased cost was added to the new cruisers, but no mention of the effect upon the old programme was made to the Committee or to the Treasury. The Treasury consider that if this increased expenditure cannot be avoided an equivalent sum should be retrenched in each year by other economies or postponements. The principal effect is in 1927–28.

(2) The Admiralty figures include the laying down of 9 destroyers in the

---

[1] For more than a month Churchill himself had been active in trying to avert the threatened Coal Strike. But at a meeting with the Coal Owners on June 14 he had failed to persuade them to accept voluntarily an extra hour of work in the mines, together with the same wage as for the shorter, seven-hour day, and with an upward revision of wages to reach the national minimum in those districts where wages had already fallen. On the following day, June 15, the Government had informed the House of Commons that it had therefore decided to introduce a Bill legalizing the eight-hour working day. The Eight Hours Bill received the Royal Assent on July 8. The owners, however, still refused to put forward new wage scales for the longer day, and on July 10 the miners' leader, A. J. Cook, announced defiantly: 'Not a penny off the pay, not a second on the day.'

financial year 1926–27 whereas the figures on page 5 of the Committee's Report show clearly that this construction was not to begin until 1927–28. . . .

The Cabinet decision was 'that, with the exception of the 4 China Gun-boats and the 3 Dock Sections, the rest of the Admiralty programme shall begin next year and not this year, and shall thereafter be in accordance with the recommendations of the Committee Report (CP–342 (25)) on page 5'. That the Cabinet decision was so read and accepted by the Admiralty is evident from the letter of the First Lord to the Prime Minister of 22nd July, in which it is stated that the Board of Admiralty while accepting the Cabinet decision, 'asked that I should forward to you a memorandum from them pointing out the very inferior position we should be placed in by the postponement of the submarine *and destroyer* programme'. The statement made by the Prime Minister in the House which was intended to summarise the decision of the Cabinet upon the new programme used the following words:—

'We have also decided that an annual construction of nine destroyers and six submarines, together with certain ancillary vessels, will be required, beginning in the financial year 1926/7, and likewise continuing during the normal life of the present Parliament.'

To be strictly accurate this statement should have read '*the submarines and certain ancillary vessels* beginning in the financial year 1926–27, and *the destroyers in 1928–29*, and likewise continuing during the normal life of the present Parliament'. I must take responsibility for any lack of precision. The draft of the statement was shown to the Admiralty for checking in the ordinary way and in conjunction with their preparation of the figures. They made certain minor corrections in the text, but did not think it necessary to point out that it might be read as giving them 9 more destroyers in the period than they had accepted under the Cabinet decision. They merely increased their figures accordingly as follows:–

1926/27	525,515
1927/28	1,756,100
1928/29	912,240
1929/30	21,600

The statement was therefore made by the Prime Minister as inadvertently drafted. It is to be noted that in all other respects so far as the minor pro-gramme is concerned the Admiralty estimates follow the Cabinet decision on page 5, the ante-dating of the 9 destroyers being a solitary exception.

It is clear that the figures must be revised in conformity with the decision as made by the Cabinet and as accepted by the Board of Admiralty.

(3) Lord Beatty's figures on p. 3 of the Report contain the following charges for the three dock sections:—

1925/26	90,000
1926/27	210,000
1927/28	100,000
total	310,000

The figures now included in the new estimates are as follows:—

1925/26	30,000
1926/27	400,000
1927/28	150,000
1928/29	95,000
total	675,000

Increase 365,000

The original estimate for the floating dock and for its despatch to Singapore were the subject of prolonged examination by the Committee of Imperial Defence and precise statements were made to Parliament by the late Lord Curzon. These estimates have already been once increased without Parliament being informed and are now to be the subject of a further heavy addition. No communication has been made by the Admiralty to the Treasury other than a remark thrown across the table by the First Lord in the course of recent discussions. It may be that there are very good reasons for making the change but the usual departmental discussions on new expenditure need not be anticipated. For the purposes of the White Paper we are confined by the Cabinet decision to the figures included on pages 2 and 3 of the Birkenhead Committee's report. Any further increases upon these owing to unavoidable or unforeseeable events must be the subject of ordinary departmental discussion.

(4) It will be seen from the Cabinet decision (Section (a)) that the 'actual dates of laying down the 7 cruisers of the first two years' were accepted in principle by the Cabinet 'subject to discussion between the Chancellor of the Exchequer and the First Lord'. The Board of Admiralty expressed a desire for the Prime Minister's second alternative, viz:—

2 plus 2 for 1925/26 and for the sub-alternative 2 plus 1 for 1926/27. I prefer the sub-alternative '1 plus 2' as it saves about £300,000 in the difficult year 1926/27. The form of the Prime Minister's statement 'an annual construction of 3 cruisers thereafter' leaves this point open.

Lord Rothermere to Winston S. Churchill

(*Churchill papers: 2/142*)

25 July 1925

My dear Winston,

You are taking life far too seriously.

We are having the most brilliant summer on record and instead of enjoying this—the Gods greatest gift—you are fretting and fuming in Downing St.[1]

I have not ceased to entertain a great regard for you but please do not be perturbed because I like to indulge a vagrant fancy, so far very occasionally, to take a hand in politics.

I don't imagine my amateur antics interest anyone except a small circle of wrong headed people who think that without searching economy in national and local finance Britain is doomed, for has not the Prime Minister with all his sagacity, authority and prestige told his countrymen not to take any notice of what Pressmen say (Albert Hall Victory Demonstration).

I have not altered my belief that the present administration will come to grief early or late in 1927 and for one who is taking life so hardly as you are this prospect I am sure must be a most welcome one.

We shall meet again.

Yours always sincerely
Harold Rothermere

Regarding provisions for Industrial widows with dependent children about which I expressed a measure of approval never did I for one moment think you would place further burdens on industry to provide the cost when within a stones throw of your office there are Ministers and Ministries among whom economies of many tens of millions of pounds per annum can be affected.

Winston S. Churchill to Stanley Baldwin

(*Baldwin papers*)

27 July 1925   House of Commons

Prime Minister,

It has been proved to the satisfaction of two Cabinet Committees that Naval Officers are *better* paid without Marriage Allowance than Army & Air

---

[1] In fact, Churchill was taking a short holiday, at Wilton House, near Salisbury, the home of the Earl and Countess of Pembroke, from July 25 to July 27. Among the other guests were Muriel Beckett, Edward Wood, Victor Cazalet and the Countess of Dalkieth, later Duchess of Buccleuch. Churchill was again at Wilton two years later, between June 4 and June 7, when the other guests included Oliver Lyttelton (later Viscount Chandos).

Force Officers with their Marriage Allowance. At this time when we are reducing the pay of the Services for future entrants, when every class is being urged to make sacrifices (including miners), when the cost of living has undergone reductions far greater than the $5\frac{1}{2}\%$ cut since the pay rates were fixed, and when the need of retrenchment & reduction is admitted on all hands, there is no justification for spending this very large annual sum. The Cabinet reached a definite decision against it and I think they have a right to be consulted before that decision is departed from. I doubt very much whether the Cabinet will be found to have changed its mind.

In these circumstances the First Lord ought to inform Parliament of the findings of the Gilmour Committee and state that the original proposals which were made under all reserves are now withdrawn. In view of the expectations which have been aroused the Cabinet might consent to, say, £100,000 a year being used to increase the allowances of Officers over a certain age & under a certain rank who marry with the approval of the Admiralty while their emoluments are below a certain minimum.

An undertaking from the Ministers representing the other Services not to press consequential claims would be indispensable.

WSC

Cabinet minutes

(*Cabinet papers: 23/50*)

29 July 1925

CHURCHILL'S REPORT ON THE NEGOTIATIONS WITH FRANCE

Without going into details, we had tried to make the Ambassador understand that while the British Government had no objection to the United States of America giving the French Government better terms than they had given to us, we could not agree that France should give more favourable terms for the repayment of her debt to America than to ourselves; further, that if the British Government reached agreement with France before an agreement was reached between France and America, we should have to insist on a clause entitling us to reopen the question if better terms of payment were accorded to the United States.

The result of the conversations with the French was that the French Government had now made a proposal which, though not satisfactory, was at any rate serious. They assumed that we were paying £3,500,000 a year to the United States of America, and that, on the basis that the Dawes payment would realise 75 per cent of their face value, we should receive £15,000,000 from Germany. That would leave 20,000,000 to be recovered from other sources. The French government were prepared to assume responsibility for half of this £20,000,000. They proposed to pay £4,000,000 in cash, and a percent out of the 52 per cent of the total Dawes payment to which they were entitled: that is to say, about £6,000,000 on the assumption that the realised value of the Dawes payments was 75 per cent of their face value, making a total of about £525,000,000 in gold which had been deposited in this country during the war and had been despatched to America for payments there, and to the return of which France was entitled only after the whole of her debt to this country had been paid. Insomuch as this amount stood in the credit of the Bank of France as an asset, they wished the British Government to pay them a sum of about £275,000 annually until 1984 under this head.

These proposals, though not unsatisfactory, were a great advance on anything that had been deemed possible three years ago. If we refused them, the French would be entitled to ask us what we proposed.

The Chancellor of the Exchequer then proposed to the Cabinet that the French Government should be asked to pay a sum of £10,000,000 during the period of our payments to the United States of America, of which £10,000 would be from the resources of France's share in the Dawes payment.

ON 28 JULY 1925 Baldwin had appointed Churchill to be Chairman of a special Cabinet Committee[1] to investigate one possibility of a long-term solution, the state control of all mining royalties. This would cost the Government some £100 million. In its report two days later, Churchill's Committee recommended a scheme 'of gradual acquisition of mineral royalties for the State by purchase'. The Committee also suggested that Baldwin should appoint 'an expert Committee' which would 'consider and advise whatever any or what steps can be taken to bring about an improvement in the organisation, development and management of the mining industry'.

The mine owners maintained their intention to cut wages, and during July 30 the Trade Union General Council issued

[1] The other members of the Mining Royalties Committee were Lord Birkenhead, Sir Laming Worthington-Evans, Sir Philip Cunliffe-Lister, Edward Wood, Sir Douglas Hogg and George Lane-Fox (Secretary for Mines).

instructions for a nation-wide embargo on the movement of coal. In retaliation, the owners prepared to issue dismissal notices. That afternoon Churchill spent three-quarters of an hour with Baldwin discussing his Cabinet Committee's recommendations, and working out details of the proposed Government subsidy. Thomas Jones, who saw Baldwin immediately afterwards, noted in his diary that the idea was for the subsidy to be spread over nine months 'and to be used to fill such gap as would remain between the terms offered by the owners and the terms which the men were willing to accept'. Baldwin also accepted Churchill's proposal for a Royal Commission, to examine the complete reorganization of the mining industry.

In Cabinet that evening, Baldwin proposed a subsidy, estimated at £10 million, and covering the next nine months. Several Ministers were opposed to such action on the part of a Conservative Government, but Churchill strongly supported Baldwin, and the subsidy was accepted.

Walter Citrine: [1] *recollections*

('*Men and Work*')

31 July 1925   Ministry of Labour

At 3.50 pm, when Herbert[2] was right in the middle of one of his stories, the door opened and the Prime Minister walked in, accompanied by Winston Churchill and Lane-Fox[3] and one or two departmental officials.

[1] Walter McLennan Citrine, 1887–   . Secretary of the Electrical Trades Union, 1914–20; Assistant General Secretary, 1920–3. Assistant Secretary, Trade Union Congress, 1924–5; General Secretary, 1926–46. Director of the *Daily Herald*, 1929–46. Knighted, 1935. Visited Russia, 1936 and 1938. Privy Councillor, 1940. Member of the National Production Advisory Council, 1942–6 and 1949–57. Created Baron, 1946. Member of the National Coal Board, 1946–7. Chairman of the Central Electricity Authority, 1947–57.

[2] Herbert Smith, 1876–1938. Born in a Lancashire workhouse, the posthumous son of a miner killed in a pit accident. Began work in the mines at the age of ten; Vice-President of the Yorkshire Miners' Association, 1904; President, 1906–38. Frequently led rescue parties down the mines after pit accidents. President of the National Association, 1922–9.

[3] George Richard Lane-Fox, 1870–1940. Educated at Eton and New College, Oxford. Barrister, 1896. Conservative MP for Barkston Ash (Yorkshire), 1906–31. Served in the Great War, 1914–17 (wounded). Secretary for Mines, October 1922–January 1924 and November 1924–January 1928. Member of the Indian Statutory Commission, 1928–9. Chairman, Pig Products Commission, 1932; Fat Stock Reorganization Commission, 1933. Created Baron Bingley, 1933. President of the National Union of Conservative and Unionist Associations, 1937. In 1903 he married Mary Wood, 2nd daughter of the 2nd Viscount Halifax and sister of Edward Wood (later Viceroy of India and Foreign Secretary).

The Prime Minister looked tired and worn. He had been up practically all the previous night, trying to make a settlement. He told us that the Government had arranged with the mine-owners that notices should be suspended for a fortnight and that the Government would give financial assistance to the industry until May 1st, 1926. A few questions were asked, after which Baldwin hurried away, as he had to speak in the House of Commons on the situation. We then had our own separate meeting and the miners heartily thanked us for what we had done. . . .[1]

It was arranged that we should send out immediately a telegram to all the transport unions, telling them that the dispute was settled and that their members should remain at work. We were not sure of the exact terms of the settlement, because there was no signed document concluding the negotiations which in my opinion, and that of several of my colleagues, was a little curious. I wrote out a telegram and at one part I said, 'Notices are suspended for a fortnight in order to allow the Government and the owners to discuss the matter in detail.'

Winston Churchill just came out of the room where the Ministers had been and I handed him the telegram, saying, 'Is this all right?' He did not express any surprise, although I don't know whether he remembered seeing me in the conference room.

He replied, 'Yes, that is splendid; that just hits it off.'

'I want to send it out to our people,' I explained.

Just as I said this Arthur Cook[2] came up and remarked, 'Well, sir, I am glad we have settled it.'

'Yes,' replied Churchill, 'it is a good job it is over, but you have done it over my blood-stained corpse. I have got to find the money for it now.'

Then Evan Williams,[3] the chairman of the Mining Association, came up. He was a different style of individual from what I expected. I had imagined him to be keen, young, and alert-looking. Instead, he was well past middle

[1] The Coal subsidy, which Churchill defended in the House of Commons on August 7.

[2] Arthur James Cook, 1885–1931. After elementary school, he worked underground as a miner for 21 years. Won a scholarship to the Central Labour College, 1911. Miners' Agent, Rhondda district; imprisoned 1918 and 1921 for taking part in strikes and lock-outs. Member of the Executive of the Miners' Federation of Great Britain, 1918–31; subsequently General Secretary. Member of the General Council of the TUC. Member of the Executive of the Labour Party. Member of the Government Mines Welfare Committee and Advisory Board, 1929–31. A member of the 1917 and Trade Union Clubs.

[3] Evan Williams, 1871–1959. Educated at Clare College, Cambridge. Coal owner. Chairman of the Monmouth and South Wales Coalowners' Association, 1913. President of the Mining Association of Great Britain, 1919–44. President of the National Board for the Coal Mining Industry, 1921–5. President of the National Confederation of Employers' Organizations, 1925–6. Chairman of the Joint Standing Consultative Committee for the Coal Mining Industry, 1926–44. Chairman of the Central Council under the Coal Mines Act, 1930–8. Created Baronet, 1935.

age and not very neatly dressed or smart-looking. He said to Cook: 'Look here, Mr Cook, now you should help us. You ought to tell some of these sheltered trades that they have got to make some sacrifice.' I could see Williams's game straight away, so I interjected, 'It is my business, Mr Williams, to look after both the sheltered and unsheltered trades, so it is no use your asking for sacrifices there.' He looked at me for a second or so and didn't continue the conversation.

Churchill did not seem at all affected by the negotiations. He was fresh-faced and very much like the cartoons in the newspapers. He was smoking a long cigar all the time. I noticed that when he was in the room with Baldwin, during the negotiations, he put his tall silk hat on the table in front of him, with his gloves and walking stick alongside it. Possibly some of these actions were characteristics of his journalist days.

Purcell[1] told me that Churchill was a decent chap to speak to. Churchill had told Purcell that some of his friends should be in gaol, but they didn't matter.

---

[1] Albert Arthur Purcell, 1872–1935. Secretary of the Manchester and Salford Trades Council. Labour MP for Coventry, 1923–4; for the Forest of Dean, 1925–9. President of the International Federation of Trade Unions, 1924–7.

August 1925

Stanley Baldwin to King George V

(Baldwin papers)

6 August 1925

Mr Keynes believed that manipulated currency was the best shock absorber for the fluctuations of world trade. In the most amusing and enlivening manner, Mr Churchill likened this process to the manipulation of weights and measures by grocers and drapers in order to make both ends meet, but surely the Labour Party did not want secret juggling and manipulation of this kind which was entirely contrary to the sound and rugged principles which had built up British financial policy. It was far more in accord with British traditions to face the true facts and from the industrial and economic point of view it was far more advantageous to aim at fixity and stability.

To judge from the applause which greeted Mr Churchill when he resumed his seat the speech did much to raise the spirits of the Government supporters which are at a somewhat low level pending to-day's debate on the coal dispute.

Stanley Baldwin to King George V

(Baldwin papers)

7 August 1925

Mr Clynes wound up the debate on behalf of the Opposition with a speech which was rather more spirited than usual. He condemned the Prime Minister for issuing a warning based on a supposition that the recent crisis had had relation to factors other than the simple problem of wages, and, while welcoming the settlement, taunted the Government for its cowardice in surrendering to fear.

Mr Churchill who wound up for the Government was again in brilliant form. While extremely eloquent he avoided any incautious or contentious remarks which might have caused ill-feeling in the ranks of the Opposition; on the contrary he won their support and sympathy by warmly repudiating the suggestion that any challenge had come from the mining community as a whole. His sympathetic references to the distress in the mining field and his emphatic insistence on the point that they were justly concerned with wage problems and not with political considerations was warmly applauded by the Labour Party. In another phase of his speech he gave an illustration of his powers of wit and humour when he vividly portrayed the criticisms to which the Government would have been subjected in the popular press if they had taken the only other course open to them. In his general presentation of the arguments in favour of the Government's policy he was masterful, cogent and convincing, and his speech did much to remove for good and all any languishing feeling of disquiet in the ranks of his own supporters.[1]

The debate concluded with a few courageous and helpful words from Mr J. H. Thomas who declared that the attitude of the railwaymen in no way constituted a challenge to authority but was actuated solely by a feeling that the miners were not obtaining justice. . . .

Winston S. Churchill to Sir Warren Fisher
(Churchill papers: 18/12)

10 August 1925

Now that we are so seriously involved in Coal finance, I think we ought to establish (without any addition to the staff) a small section of the Treasury to deal with the finance of the subvention,[2] so as to secure the very greatest economy and keep it within the smallest limits. It is also important we should understand the whole of the way this Coal finance works. Will you make me proposals to this end?

WSC

[1] Speaking on 6 August 1925, during the debate on the temporary subvention of the coal-mining industry, Churchill said, of the attitude of the miners: 'I do not believe that an attitude of challenge is the mood of the great mass of the mining population. The mass of the mineworking community are in no mood for a challenge. They are passing through a period of great depression. They see themselves confronted with extinction, in many parts of the country, of their means of livelihood. They are passing through a time, not of arrogant challenge; they do not know which way to turn, or how to deal with the problem of their industry. While many workers in sheltered trades have vastly improved their wages, miners have seen their superior position largely disappear since the War. Their wages have risen less compared with pre-War standards than many less arduous and far less dangerous occupations.'

[2] The Coal Subsidy.

Winston S. Churchill to Sir Warren Fisher

(*Churchill papers: 1/178*)

10 August 1925

My dear Fisher,

I went to see Masterton-Smith a little while ago, and I find it very difficult to believe that with proper treatment he could not be rescued from his present terrible sufferings. I found myself in close personal relation with him for more than an hour. Although from time to time his appalling melancholia overwhelmed him and quite mad lapses occurred, yet the main structure of his mind and memory seemed to me quite unimpaired.

I wonder very much whether he is getting the proper treatment. I think it would drive most of us into melancholia if we were simply shut up with nothing to do but brood, and no attempt made to build up the counter-interests of the mind. I should like the specialist who examined him to come and have another talk with you and me, and see if a more scientific and modern treatment cannot be devised. I am sure his friends would be able to subscribe the comparatively small sums which might perhaps be needed. I would certainly do my utmost, and I know every Chief under whom he has served would assist. I think that what is wanted is almost daily instruction from some specialist skilled in mind troubles, coupled, if thought well, with visits from some of those with whom he worked and who could revive his interest in that official work which was so great a part of his life.

I shall be in London all Thursday.

Winston S. Churchill to Lord Wodehouse

(*Churchill papers: 1/178*)

10 August 1925

I have finally decided to give up Polo, and I wonder whether you could find me a purchaser for 'Bay Rum' and 'Ostrich' in the next two months. If not, I will keep them till the spring. But I should prefer to get rid of them at once. They are really fine ponies to play, the best I have ever ridden in my life. They are not quite up to the speed standard of the best match, but even with my weight on their backs they are most excellent and serviceable playing ponies and are a pleasure and comfort to ride. I should be so much obliged if you could settle this for me.

Will you let me know what you think I ought to pay Balding for having mounted me I think nine times, two chukkers a time. In addition to this there would be the expense of sending that unplayable grey pony from Rugby to London and back.

I hope you are enjoying yourself at Deauville.

Sir Philip Cunliffe-Lister to Winston S. Churchill

(*Churchill papers: 2/142*)

14 August 1925

My dear Winston,

I have spent a good many days trying to see things, as you would have me see them. I just can't.

If I were to concur, I should do so without conviction & indeed with the conviction that I was doing the wrong thing. The line of least resistance is to do what you suggest. I cant convince myself that it is right; & I cant give good service, if I honestly feel that I ought not to be doing the job at all.[1]

The transfer of mines to another Minister, is really the same in effect though less practically convenient than transferring me to another office. I am afraid that is a camouflage I cant accept. I agreed to it with a good deal of hesitation, when a short period of reformation might have brought a settlement. Now as events have turned out, coal has become a dominant issue over the next 9 months. Either I am in a position to take charge of the policy, as my office demands, or I ought to be replaced.

I believe you wd feel & do the same in my place.

Yours ever
P. Cunliffe-Lister

Winston S. Churchill to Stanley Baldwin

(*Baldwin papers*)

14 August 1925   Treasury Chambers

My dear Prime Minister,

I do not feel this morning that Hilton Young will be big enough if Samuel[2] fails. But I hope and believe the latter will accept. I should think he

[1] As President of the Board of Trade, Cunliffe-Lister was in overall charge of the Mines Department. He was also married to a mine-owner.
[2] Herbert Louis Samuel, 1870–1963. Educated at University College School and Balliol College, Oxford. Liberal MP, 1902–18; 1929–35. Chancellor of the Duchy of Lancaster,

would be sure to accept.[1] All the rest of the tableau seems quite good: if not impressive, workmanlike and sound. I think it would be better to know who the Chairman is before approaching the others. I am sure I shall be able to set the Commission up all right in your absence. As soon as I know about Samuel, I will come up to London and see all the members myself, communicating with you if any difficulty arises.

About Philip. I hope he may be persuaded to remain. If it made things easier, I could perfectly well take charge of the Mines Department pro tem and any Coal business that arose; and this could be stated publicly. Now that we are paying the subsidy, I shall in any case have to give a good deal of time to Coal. If you think this is a solution, do not hesitate to adopt it. I am not overburdened at present.

I think you are quite right to try to get off on Sunday. You will be lucky if you can take a month. I presume you will take a cipher and a secretary with you, so that communications will be easy and secret.

Yours vy sincerely,
Winston S. Churchill

Sir Philip Cunliffe-Lister to Winston S. Churchill
(*Churchill papers: 2/142*)

17 August 1925   Swinton Park, Yorkshire

My dear Winston,

I have promised the PM to postpone a final decision till he returns from Aix.

If I honestly feel I can, I will stay; & I will try to see my way through, as my colleagues wish. I do appreciate enormously the wish of you all to keep me as a colleague. If it were the case of a contract or a control, or any issue that can be decided once & for all, I shd feel so differently. But this wretched coal business has become a dominating factor in politics. It & its effects will spread everywhere in the next year. That is what makes the choice so hard; & I am so afraid that you will wish one thing now & the others six months hence.

Yours ever
PCL

1909–10. Postmaster-General, 1910–14. President of the Local Government Board, 1914–15. Home Secretary, 1916. Chairman of the Select Committee on National Expenditure, 1917–18. Knighted, 1920. High Commissioner for Palestine, 1920–5. Chairman of the Royal Commission on the Coal Industry, 1925–6. Home Secretary, 1931–2. Leader of the Parliamentary Liberal Party, 1931–5. Created Viscount, 1937.

[1] The Chairmanship of the Royal Commission on the Coal Industry. Both Hilton Young and Samuel were, at that time, Liberals (Hilton Young joined the Conservative Party in 1926).

Winston S. Churchill to Sir Philip Cunliffe-Lister

(*Churchill papers: 2/142*)

Private   Treasury
18 August 1925

My dear Philip,

The Prime Minister told me that he had arranged to allow the question of your resignation to stand over till he returned from abroad. In these circumstances the responsibility is clearly on your shoulders for the time being.

Candidly I do not understand your view or agree with it: and I shall strongly urge the PM that if ultimately he is forced to bow to your wishes he will make it plain the HMG do not consider that they are well or wisely founded. Otherwise you wd be pronouncing a sentence of exclusion from public life upon men like Londonderry whom we all hope to see with us in the future.

My steady opinion is that so long as you are not personally in charge of the negotiations with a great industry in wh you have a legitimate interest & so long as that interest is known & declared, there is no reason whatever why you shd not take part in Cabinet decisions affecting it, still less in all other manifold business of Government. I write this on public grounds alone.

I do hope that cool reflection will lead you to allow yr judgment & sense of delicacy to fall along the broad lines of public precedent & policy; & that you will not take exceptional views wh wd interfere with your career & deprive us all of a valued colleague & friend.

Yours always, very sincerely,
Winston S. Churchill

Stanley Baldwin to Winston S. Churchill

(*Churchill papers: 18/9*)

21 August 1925   Aix les Bains[1]

My dear Winston,

The infant Samuel duly arrived as the clock was striking six on Monday evening.

Cool, competent and precise as when he was first lent to this temporary

[1] Where Baldwin regularly took his summer holiday. The letter itself was written on 10 Downing Street notepaper.

world by an inscrutable providence, it was the work of a moment for him to grasp our problem in all its manifold implications.

But he would have none of it and for 'worthy reasons', if I may borrow a happy phrase of the Marquess Curzon which he employed in accounting for Sir Laming's adherence to the coalition at the Carlton Club and subsequent acceptance of a modest office. Suddenly conscious of a parananasia (if I remember that boss word correctly) he substituted 'proper' for 'worthy'. Whether he realised the admirable choice of the first epithet, I shall never know!

To resume. He (the original subject) had been counting the hours until his release from office,[1] hoping to get to work on a monumental volume he wished to write. He had retired into Tirol and had actually started on it. He had already taken his passage to India where he had arranged to study divers aspects of his subject for several months etc etc. Very strong private reasons with which I sympathise. Would we do our utmost to find a substitute? Until we could assure him we had done so, he couldn't look at it. Hence the fevered telegrams which passed and now all is well.

I think he is quite the best man we could have. The brief talk we had convinced me.

Now all he wants to know is—when will he be needed in London? I have told him that you will communicate with him and if you are able to give him a date, that will ease his mind.

Aix is very full: so are most of the people here. The hotel buses discharge 'em at the baths and they look, many of them, as if you stuck a fork in them, a rich gravy would burst forth.

But the beauty of the country is unchanged and unchangeable, and there is enough to make everybody happy. For those who would go from the trough to the straw and back again, well, there never were troughs so filled or so often and never straw softer or cleaner.

Yours very sincerely
Stanley Baldwin

Winston S. Churchill: departmental minute
(Churchill papers: 18/12)

25 August 1925

It is clear to me that the Customs are allowing themselves to be led into positions where the whole administration of the Silk Tax will be exposed to

[1] As British High Commissioner in Palestine, a post he held from 1920 to 1925.

ridicule. After the brilliant work done by the Board in devising this tax and in assisting its passage through Parliament, it is lamentable that short-sighted and trifling administrative conduct should discredit the broad and solid results.

I am determined to bring this state of things to an end, even though I strain to the utmost my legal powers. More than a fortnight has passed since in successive Minutes I asked for proposals to eliminate altogether from the area of the Tax any commodity in which the silk contained was less than 1%. This alone will save the administration of the Tax from the ludicrous task of writing essays on the taxability of Golliwogs' eyelashes, etc.

The proposals for which I have called must now be submitted, at latest during the present week. No consultation with the Silk Trade or Chambers of Commerce must delay their completion. I do not admit the right of these bodies to interfere with the reasonable administration of an Act of Parliament.

Victor Cazalet: diary

(*Robert Rhodes James: ' Victor Cazalet, A Portrait'*)

26 August 1925

I had a long talk with Winston. No one has such charm when he cares to exert it. We talked of the Coalition Government. He defended their Indian policy, and their conduct in Ireland, where the military gave way, *not* the politicians. The latter promised the former anything they wanted. But if you are up against cold-blooded deeds and horrors committed by people whom it is impossible either to catch or punish, you can only reply by similar methods, and the British public will not tolerate indiscriminate reprisals.

Frederick Guest to Winston S. Churchill

(*Churchill papers: 18/9*)

27 August 1925

Dear Winston,

I think you had done very well with Caillaux—I had a talk with Blum[1]

---

[1] Ralph D. Blumenfeld, 1864–1948. Born in the United States. Entered journalism as a reporter on the *Chicago Herald*, 1884. London Correspondent of the *New York Herald*, 1887–93. News Editor of the *Daily Mail*, 1900–2. Editor of the *Daily Express*, 1902–32. Founder of the Anti-Socialist Union. Author of several volumes of memoirs, including *All in a Lifetime* (1931). Chairman of the *Daily Express* from 1933 until his death.

today who told me that he strongly disapproved of Max's persecution[1] & watered it down whenever he could—or whenever he was left in charge. He doubted the French ability to pay. He felt sure the Yanks would demand stiffish terms. . . . .

Neville Chamberlain to Stanley Baldwin

(*Baldwin papers*)

30 August 1925   Perthshire

Looking back over our final session I think our Chancellor has done very well, all the better because he hasn't been what he was expected to be. He hasn't dominated the Cabinet, though undoubtedly he has influenced it; he hasn't tied us up to pedantic Free Trade, though he is a bit sticky about safeguarding of Industries. He hasn't intrigued for the Leadership, but he has been a tower of debating strength in the House of Commons. And taking him all round I dont think there can be any dispute but that he has been a source of increased influence & prestige to the government as a whole.

I have often thought about the incidents with which I was concerned in the formation of the Cabinet. Of course when I saw you I did not know who was in the next room and it was only some considerable time afterwards that I came to the conclusions which have satisfied themselves in my mind. Perhaps some day you will tell me whether they are right. If they are, I should feel some satisfaction in having reached them and having penetrated into the workings of your mind. And in my view the judgement and the motives thus revealed are such as no man need hesitate to acknowledge for they were all thoroughly sound.

It seems then to me that once having decided to bring Winston into the Cabinet, you had been driven to the conclusion that the position in which he could be of most use (& do least harm) was at the Treasury. There however you found yourself in the difficulty that I had been Chancellor already and that it would be said that I had been slighted if I were passed over. On the whole you felt bound to offer it to me and *you* made up your mind that I should probably take it. But you thought there was a chance I might refuse it for the Ministry of Health and you said to yourself that if I did take that line & so allowed you with a clear conscience to put Winston at the Treasury

[1] A leading article in the *Daily Express* on 26 August 1925, headlined 'The Tangle of War Debts', had declared: 'There can be no justification for reducing our demand below the sum of twenty millions per annum.' On August 27 the settlement of twelve and a half millions per annum was announced. A *Daily Express* editorial concluded: 'We could almost wish that Mr Churchill were head of the French Treasury and M Caillaux the guardian of our own financial affairs. M Caillaux would assuredly have done a better day's business for Great Britain.'

you would then have both Ministers in the ideal positions. Accordingly you were proportionately delighted when I did take the line and I remember you sounded me as to W's being Chancellor and I said that the idea rather appeals to me and that I didn't think it would cause more 'row' in our party than the fact of taking him in at all.

Well, whether you had thought things out in this sort of way beforehand or not, there is no doubt that you made us both happy, and I for one have never for a moment regretted the decision I made then or envied Winston his pre-eminence. What a brilliant creature he is! But there is somehow a great gulf fixed between him and me which I don't think I shall ever cross. I like him. I like his humour and his vitality. I like his courage. I like the way he took that to me very unexpected line over the coal crisis in Cabinet. But not for all the joys of Paradise would I be a member of his staff! Mercurial! a much abused word, but it is the literal description of his temperament.

Sir Harry Goschen to Winston S. Churchill

(*Treasury papers: T172/1504*)

31 August 1925

. . . A line to congratulate you on the result of your negotiations for the settlement of the French debt—of course the usual abuse is forthcoming from the same quarters as before, but it seems to me a very sensible business arrangement.

It is the very kind of arrangement that we in the city often, unfortunately, have to make to ascertain how much our debtor can pay. Well, we will accept that, provided you don't give anyone else better terms.

In any case it was the best you could get.

Esmond Harmsworth to Winston S. Churchill

(*Churchill papers: 18/9*)

31 August 1925

Dear Churchill,

My father has asked me to write and say how sorry he is that an article appeared in last Monday's Daily Mail (written by Lovat Fraser[1]) which

---

[1] Lovat Fraser, 1871–1926. Editor, *Times of India*, 1902–6. On his return to London in 1907 he joined the Editorial Staff of *The Times*, remaining with the paper until 1922. Chief Literary Adviser, *Sunday Pictorial* and *Daily Mirror*, 1922–6.

was very antagonistic to yourself. Had he known that it was to appear he would have forbidden its publication. It is especially regrettable in view of the fact that it coincided with the visit of the French Finance Minister.[1]

Hoping that you are keeping well under the cares of office.

Yours sincerely
Esmond Harmsworth

[1] Lovat Fraser's article had appeared in the *Daily Mail* of 24 August 1925, claiming that 'the most conspicuous failure of the Parliamentary session which has now been adjourned is the failure of Mr Winston Churchill. He had the greatest chance of restoring himself in popular estimation ever given a statesman with a record full of blemishes, and he has thrown it away.' Lovat Fraser had criticized Churchill's Contributory Pensions Bill, and the rate of taxation in the new budget.

September 1925

Winston S. Churchill to Austen Chamberlain

(*Austen Chamberlain papers*)

1 September 1925
Private

My dear Austen,

I never had the slightest doubt of what the reception of the Anglo-French debt arrangement would be in the United States. Although sunk in selfishness in the present period, the American people have an extremely uncomfortable conscience, and when this conscience is being stirred, as it is now, they are naturally very resentful. I think you will find everything will calm down in a short time, and I am pretty sure that the secondary reaction will not be unfavourable. There is a very sensible article in the 'Baltimore Sun', a copy of which appears in the 'Manchester Guardian' of August 29, which I enclose. I will, however, watch the situation attentively and will try my hand at a communiqué if I think the situation requires it.

Do you think I shall collaborate easily with Wellesley?[1]

Good luck to you at Geneva.

Yours vy sincerely
Winston S. Churchill

PS. It is all calming down. I will see if I can say something usefully when I speak on the 16th to the Midland Conservative Club![2]

[1] Victor Alexander Augustus Henry Wellesley, 1876–1954. A godson of Queen Victoria; Page of Honour to the Queen, 1887–92. Educated in Germany. Entered Foreign Office, 1899; Superintendent, Treaty Department, 1913–16; Controller of Commercial and Consular Affairs, 1916–19; Counsellor in charge of the Far Eastern Department, 1920–4; Deputy Under-Secretary of State, 1925–36. Knighted, 1926. A painter of landscapes and portraits, his pictures were frequently exhibited in the Royal Academy. He published his memoirs and reflections, *Diplomacy in Fetters*, in 1944.

[2] On 16 September 1925, during a speech to the Midland Conservative Club on the general aims of Conservative policy, Churchill said, of the question of France's debt to the United States: 'I was asked, during the summer, by prominent American official personages whether we should complain if the United States decided to grant more favourable terms to France than had been arranged with Britain. I invariably replied, with the assent of His Majesty's

Austen Chamberlain to Winston S. Churchill

(*Austen Chamberlain papers*)

2 September 1925
Confidential

British Delegation
Geneva

My dear Chancellor,

I am asking Wellesley to send you a copy of a letter received by him from Phipps dated the 30th August and a memorandum by Wigram[1] of information given to him by Poliakoff[2] on the 31st. I am rather uneasy as to what Caillaux has reported to his colleagues lest he is encouraging them to hope for a solution which the Cabinet definitely rejected. You will remember how strongly our colleagues opposed the suggestion that French payments should be dependent on the amount of the receipts from the Dawes annuities, except in the form of making a part of the payment to us in Dawes points. If Caillaux has told the French Cabinet that we were ready to accept payment entirely dependent upon Dawes, we may easily find ourselves face to face with an impassable obstacle whenever the conversations are renewed.

I see from Phipps' letter that you have had some correspondence with Caillaux. I should be grateful if you would keep me informed of anything that it would be useful for me to know while I am here. I do not, of course, propose to start a discussion of the debts with Briand, or with Loucheur who is also here, but either of them may say something to me, and I should like to be sure that I am on firm ground in any reply that I may make. I had thought that it might help if I found an opportunity to say something to the effect that the Cabinet had been rather shocked by our proposal, and

---

Government, that a creditor has the right to discriminate between debtors, but that debtors have not the right, in our view, to discriminate between creditors.' Later in his speech, Churchill added: 'These great affairs between nations have to be judged with a historic sense, and with due respect for the majesty of vast, organized communities of men and women. To-day, the French Minister, who in a resolute spirit is facing the problems of French finance, starts upon his mission to the United States. I am sure I can say, on behalf of this country, that we wish him well, and that we hope a good arrangement will be arrived at in accordance with the declared policy of the United States, and also in harmony with the general interests of the whole world, in which the United States, its fortunes and its policy, have become a dominant, and indeed, in some respects, a dominating influence.'

[1] Ralph Follett Wigram, 1890–1936. Educated at Eton and University College, Oxford. Temporary Secretary, British Embassy, Washington, 1916–19. 3rd Secretary, Foreign Office, 1919; 2nd Secretary, 1920. 1st Secretary, British Embassy, Paris, 1924–33. CMG, 1933. A Counsellor in the Foreign Office, 1934, and head of the Central Department (1934–36). In 1925 he married Ava, daughter of J. E. C. Bodley (she married again, in 1941, John Anderson, 1st Viscount Waverley).

[2] A French journalist, famous for his scoops.

that we had had a great deal of difficulty in getting them to go as far as they did.

I could, of course, add that there was one point upon which they were rigid, and that was that a substantial part of the French payment must depend upon French credit alone. If you think it would be useful for me to say anything of this kind I can, no doubt, easily create the opportunity. On the other hand, as I have said, I need say nothing (if you prefer that course) unless they speak to me; but in any case I should be glad to have your views, and to know whether anything of consequence has passed since I last saw you.

Yours sincerely
Austen Chamberlain

Austen Chamberlain to Winston S. Churchill

(*Austen Chamberlain papers*)

4 September 1925   British Delegation
Private and Personal   Geneva

My dear Winston,

Many thanks for your letter of the 1st. Like you I expected an explosion, but at the moment when I first wrote to you it looked to me as if it were taking dangerous proportions, and I did not like to leave England without just bringing the matter to your attention. I am confident that if you have need of him you will find Wellesley very helpful—a man of sound judgment, long experience and perfect loyalty.

Since writing to you from this place, I have seen Niemeyer who tells me that up to his departure you had sent no letter to Caillaux, and that Berthelot[1] must have referred to the half-sheet of paper containing the Cabinet decision which you gave to him in London.

I was lunching yesterday with Briand and Loucheur, and the latter made some enquiry about the impression we had formed of Caillaux in London. I said that he had impressed us as an able man and with a real desire to do business, that you yourself had met him generously and were a good man to do business with, but that you and I had had considerable difficulty in

---

[1] Philippe Berthelot, 1866–1934. Entered the French Foreign Ministry, 1904; Assistant Director, Political and Commercial Department, 1913. Served as a Liaison Officer between the Allied Staffs, 1914–18. Head of the Political Department, Foreign Ministry, 1919–20; Secretary-General, 1920–1. Resigned after being accused of using his influence to help the Industrial Bank of China, of which his brother was a Director. Re-appointed Secretary-General of the Foreign Ministry, 1925; subsequently he accompanied Briand to Locarno, and conducted the French negotiations for the recognition of Soviet Russia.

getting the Cabinet to swallow our proposals. They said that they fully understood that that had been so, and Briand added something to the effect that the Cabinet had not consented to accept a limitation to such amounts as France might receive from Germany.

I only shook my head and made a face to indicate that that was an impossible proposition, and the conversation passed to other subjects. We are not likely to renew it, but if there should be any developments I hope you will let me know.

Amery made an admirable statement to the Council yesterday, and has I think been equally good to-day, but this morning I was not present to hear him.

Yours sincerely,
Austen Chamberlain

PS. This letter got lost among other papers. I have since had your telegram and have dwelt a little more insistently on the extreme length to which we had gone in making concessions.

AC 8.9.25

Winston S. Churchill to Austen Chamberlain

(Austen Chamberlain papers)

7 September 1925

My dear Austen,

I received on Saturday a letter from Caillaux, of which I enclose a copy. Oddly enough, it was neither dated nor signed, but that, I am sure, is merely a clerical oversight. I think the letter is very satisfactory so far as it goes. I have no doubt that Caillaux will not wish to go further in the matter with us until he has gone through his American ordeal. This is to our advantage because the subsidiary points on which he has yet to settle with me are all points on which the Americans will be extremely stiff; in fact, I do not think the event could flow out more conveniently.

Mr Strong[1] of the Federal Reserve Bank came to see me here on Saturday, and we had a long and very pleasant talk. He thinks we have acted very wisely in making a moderate settlement with France and he will use all his influence in America to procure a similarly reasonable solution.

I have been rather concerned at the way in which the Iraq mandate policy has been received here. There is no doubt that people are much alarmed. The Press is very hostile, not only our habitual critics but our

[1] Benjamin Strong, 1872–1928. Entered banking as a clerk; subsequently Secretary of the Atlantic Trust Corporation, and President of the Bankers Trust Corporation. Governor of the Federal Reserve Bank, New York, from 1914 until his death.

friends. I am sure that we should not be supported by the nation in any military exertions to defend Mosul, and I am personally altogether opposed to risking a single British unit in defence of Mesopotamia; it is an independent state and ought to fight its own battles. The furthest we can go in my opinion is benevolent bottle-holding; it would be madness to get entangled there. I am sure you will have been watching all this in your mind.

Everything otherwise seems very quiet here and the Coal Commission names have been extremely well received.

Yours vy sincerely,
Winston S. Churchill

Winston S. Churchill to Stanley Baldwin[1]

(Churchill papers: 18/11)

7 September 1925   Chartwell Manor

My dear Prime Minister,

The Coal Commission names have been extremely well received in all sections of the Press, and I am sure they could not have been better. I think even that Kenneth Lee[2] is an improvement on Alan Anderson,[3] as with Lawrence[4] we had already one banker.[5]

---

[1] Baldwin was still at Aix-les-Bains.

[2] Kenneth Lee, 1879–1967. A Manchester cotton manufacturer. Member of the Advisory Committee to the Department of Overseas Trade, 1918–25. Chairman of the British Cotton Industry Research Association, 1920–9. Chairman of the Inter-Departmental Committee on Patents, 1921. Member of the Royal Commission on the Coal Industry, 1925, and of the Home Office Committee on the Factory Inspectorate, 1929. Member of the Fuel Research Board, 1931–5; and of the Royal Commission on the Manufacture of and Trade in Private Arms, 1935–6. Knighted, 1934. Director-General of the Ministry of Information, 1939–45. Created Baronet, 1941.

[3] Alan Garrett Anderson, 1877–1952. A marine engineer. Knighted, 1917. President of the United Kingdom Chamber of Shipping, 1924–5. President of the Association of Chambers of Commerce, 1933–4. Conservative MP for the City of London, 1935–40. A Director of the Suez Canal Company.

[4] Herbert Alexander Lawrence, 1861–1943. 4th son of the 1st Baron Lawrence. Entered the Army, 1882. Served as an Intelligence Officer at the War Office and in South Africa, 1897–1902. Retired from the Army, 1903, and entered the City. A Member of the Committee of the Ottoman Bank, 1906, and a Director of the Midland Railway, 1913. Rejoined the Army, 1914. Major-General, 1915, on active service at Gallipoli, in command of the 127th (Manchester) Brigade. In the summer of 1916 he commanded the troops that drove the Turks from Sinai. Commanded the 66th Division at Passchendaele, 1917. Knighted, 1917. Chief of Staff, GHQ, France, January–November 1918. Lieutenant-General, 1918. General, 1919. Chairman of Vickers, 1926. Chairman and Managing Director of Glyn Mills & Co, merchant bankers, 1934–43. Both his sons were killed in action, one in May 1915, the other in September 1916.

[5] The other member of the Coal Commission was Sir William Beveridge. The expert assessors were William Brace (Chief Labour Adviser, Mines Department), Dr W. Gibson

I have been rather worried about the Iraq mandate and the Turkish menace there. Like you, I agreed at the Cabinet to Amery's 25 years proposal, but I understood that such a proposal involved no new commitments or responsibilities, either military or financial. It would be fatal to us to get drawn into a war with Turkey on the Upper Tigris about Mosul or Mesopotamia; I do not think we should get any support at all in any part of the country. I have been rather wondering whether we were not a little precipitate in accepting the 25 years proposal. It was, you remember, a very long Cabinet at the end of the Session, when we were all dominated by the Coal crisis, and when at least a dozen considerable topics had to be dealt with.

I hope on your return you will see that the whole position is reviewed. I am sure we should never get the support necessary to afford any effective military aid to Iraq: the furthest we could go would be benevolent bottle-holding; and that, as I understand it, is all we are committed to. I was, as you know, prepared to run great risks in 1922 to prevent the Turks relighting the flames of war in Europe, but I certainly would not jeopardise the great domestic interests which the Government have to guard for the sake of Mesopotamia.

FE has been spending the week-end with me. I do not know whether you saw some disagreeable comments in the 'Morning Post' upon an article which has appeared over his name.[1] He wished me to tell you that this series was all arranged for before he took office and the articles were written before your statement on the subject was made in the House. However, as the people who purchased the articles published them in a form quite different from what the original contract contemplated, FE, under threat of legal proceedings compelled them to cancel the whole of the rest of the series. So there will be no difficulty on that account.

(former Assistant to the Director of the Geological Survey) and Dr C. H. H. Lander (Director of Fuel Research, Department of Scientific and Industrial Research). The Commission's Secretary was C. S. Hurst (Assistant Under-Secretary, Mines Department). On September 1 *The Times* had reported that the Government was finding it difficult to select suitable members for the Commission. The names were announced to the Press on September 4.

[1] On 7 September 1925 the *Morning Post* had quoted extensively from the *Saturday Review*'s comments on Lord Birkenhead's association with 'the literature of puffery'. The *Review* article had appeared on September 5, and was headlined 'Chance It, Smith!' It had complained of an article Lord Birkenhead had written in the *Mayfair Cartoon* endorsing a firm of electrical condenser manufacturers. The *Review* had concluded: 'If Lord Birkenhead, whose earnings were at one time very large, finds it impossible to gratify his tastes on his present income, the remedy is for him to seek out a career in which ampler rewards await his great abilities. There is nothing discreditable to him in the fact, if it be a fact, that he is not Spartan in his tastes. But he must not combine office with the kind of journalism to which he has descended.'

The days have slipped away very quickly here. I have passed them almost entirely in the open air, making a dam, which largely extends my lake and finally, I hope, removes it from the category of ponds. I trust you have had good weather and are restored and refreshed by the break of routine. I am still intending, though somewhat doubtfully, to go to Florence for a fortnight on the 17th, but I shall be here when you return and will come up to London to meet you.

Sir Edward Grigg to Winston S. Churchill
(Churchill papers: 18/9)

17 September 1925   off Port Said[1]

My dear Winston,

I meant to write to you before leaving England about our conversation regarding *The Times* and Geoffrey Dawson's attitude to you. Better now than never, as I am sure he bears you no ill will.

I had a long talk to him on the subject—particularly on the leader of July 22nd, to which you took exception.[2] He pointed out—I think, fairly— that the offending passage towards the end of that leader dealt only with the use which anti-Baldwinites made of your name. It was in no way intended to suggest any doubt as to your own loyalty to the PM. To confirm this, he quoted his second leader of July 30th. He has since sent me copies of both these leaders which I enclose. I consider certainly that if there was any danger of the first leader being misread to your prejudice (and I agree that there was) the second makes full amends to you.[3]

I hope Irak is not going to take away money badly needed for the develop-

---

[1] Sir Edward Grigg was on his way to Kenya, to take up his post as Governor and Commander-in-Chief, and High Commissioner for Transport, Kenya Colony. He returned to England in 1931.

[2] On 22 July 1925 *The Times*, under the heading 'A Critical Cabinet', wrote of dissension inside the Cabinet over naval expenditure, and of a 'campaign of rumour' which it claimed 'coincides also with a fitful and calculated projection across the screen of the figure of the Chancellor of the Exchequer as the heir apparent'. The article continued: 'Mr Churchill of all men has most reason at this moment to avoid the charge that he has been the protagonist, however unwilling, in breaking the front of a party which is still traditionally suspicious of him.'

[3] In a leading article on 30 July 1925, *The Times* wrote, of the previous day's debate in the House of Commons: 'If, however, neither Mr MacDonald nor Mr Lloyd George was able to contribute anything constructive to the discussion, they served the purpose of providing Mr Churchill with the opportunity of delivering an extraordinary, loyal, eloquent, and convincing vindication of the Government policy.'

ment of the rest of the tropical Empire—productive expenditure, if any expenditure ever was. Being out of politics, I look at the Mosul business with an impartial eye, and as politics it looks very bad business to me. If the country would not stand up to the Chanak crisis in 1922, it does not seem likely to stand up to a much more remote challenge in Mosul in 1925, when we are feeling the pinch far more than in 1922. I am thinking, I admit, mainly of our 10 million East African loan. We shall need that money very badly.

I don't suppose you will get much chance of leave during my time in Kenya, but come and pay us a visit if you can. You know the country, and a second survey after many years ought to be very interesting to you.

My best regards to your lady.

Yours ever,
Scribe

Winston S. Churchill: departmental note
(Churchill papers: 18/12)

19 September 1925   Chartwell Manor
Most Secret

This is an important telegram and should be considered by the Department.

I am increasingly impressed with the difficulty of carrying out any economy which causes real hardship to large numbers of people at home while we are spending £4 millions a year on these sulky and greedy Arabs. I do not see what the retention of Basra has to do with the Persian Oil supplies which come from Mohammerah, and I cannot think there is much danger of the Turks establishing a naval base in the Persian Gulf which would be any menace to our naval communications with the Awaz oilfields. A decision by the League of Nations to give us the Zab frontier might therefore be a welcome release from obligations which it is very difficult to reconcile with the main interests of the Government. Pray consider this.

Let me see the telegram when I come up on Tuesday with any comments which Sir G. Barstow may make on it and on this minute.

Let me have a map showing the frontier ready on Tuesday.

Winston S. Churchill: notes for a Cabinet meeting[1]

(*Churchill papers: 22/27*)

19 September 1925

Original intention of Treaty was that we should be under no obligation defend soil Iraq. Text of Treaty. Text of Military Agreement. My clear declarations that reduced Garrison was not capable defending Iraq. I contend we have no *legal* obligation at moment towards Iraq. Have we any moral obligation? No. All give and no take. Sovereign independent State. Animated deep hostility to foreigners. Euphrates tribes liable rise against us at any moment, even while we are defending their frontier. No strategic value—a source of weakness. No profit or advantage to Britain. Pure quixotic philanthropy. What we have spent already. Expense increasing. Air Force £2 millions. Vitiates economy. If brought home, will be in reduction of cost of carrying out our expansion programme. Estimates this year up. We have given Iraq advantages denied to every one of our own Crown Colonies. Fancy if we had spent Iraq money in developing railways in Africa! More than discharged any moral obligation. Therefore my view not bound Iraq either legally, morally or by common interests.

However, well known that if in spring Turkey attacks Iraq, we shall have to go to war with Turkey. League of Nations will do nothing but pass Resolutions. We shall be drawn into most expensive and unsatisfactory operations in Iraq, and probably be compelled to attack Turkey in Europe to get some sort of solution. This will be putting immense strain upon Government and arming Socialist Party with great advantages. Although if Turkey attacks us and affronts British flag, we shall have to fight, the anger against Ministers who have created the situation where this contingency became inevitable will be deep and just. However, that is present position, and apparently it is bound to continue until 1928. At any moment up to then the Turks may cross, or the Bolsheviks may push them to cross, the frontier and invade Iraq. All our finances would be thrown into confu-

---

[1] On 7 August 1925 a special League of Nations Commission had issued a report which, while accepting the Turkish Government's claim that the Mosul region of Iraq was, in fact, 'an integral part of Turkey', proposed, nevertheless, to keep the region inside Iraq, on condition that Britain, the Mandatory of Iraq, extended her Mandate for a further twenty-five years. On 3 September 1925 the Colonial Secretary, L. S. Amery, on behalf of Britain, agreed publicly to continue the Iraq Mandate 'for as long as necessary' in order to keep the Mosul region inside Iraq. On 15 September 1925 the British delegation at the League of Nations, in Geneva, accused the Turks of forcibly removing the Christian population from the northernmost section of the disputed area. This accusation was upheld by an independent enquiry, under the Estonian General Laidoner, who reported that the Turks had been responsible for mass deportations, violence and even massacre in the area.

sion, and the whole political fortunes of the Government compromised. We may at any time—most inconvenient time—be involved in thoroughly disastrous quarrel; and I admit that if it arises, we shall have to fight.

The Colonial Secretary[1] laboured to prove that we are trapped. Although those who drafted the Treaty did all they could to avoid any suggestion that we should have to fight for Iraq, he now has woven a skilful web of argument and pledge, moral deductions from these pledges, indirect obligations, etc, the effect of which is that we must admit that until 1928 we must continue to live in this horrible position of wasting our money on these ungrateful Arabs, and of having the Turk continually pointing a loaded pistol at us with a shaky finger and a hair trigger. Well, if that be true, we have got to put up with it until 1928, to hope with the Foreign Secretary that the Turk will not attack us and will only bluff, and threaten, and worry and blackmail us. But in 1928 the hour of liberation comes.

Even the policy which I declared to Parliament was based upon our being free from any obligation to defend Iraq, and upon our getting into a position where we could in a few years wind up our commitments, terminate our expenditure and reduce our connection with the country to one only of friendship and commerce. But the present Prime Minister and Mr Bonar Law before him went much further and indicated most precisely 1928 as a definite date. It is to this that everyone has been looking forward.

As to what should happen after that date, I can see no objection to our extending friendly offices to them, to our lending them British officers and officials in the same way as we have sent military missions to Greece and the Argentine, and acquiring exceptional influence in consequence. But what is absolutely vital is that after 1928, not only shall the expense to which we are now put come to an end—except perhaps some very small sum—but that it should be made absolutely plain that we are in no way involved in the defence of Iraq as we are now. To do this is not in any way to vary the decision of the Cabinet last summer. That decision was only given on a most clear understanding that we were not to be involved in any responsibility to defend Iraq or to spend money upon Iraq. At this point there is a quibble about words.

The Colonial Secretary's view is that at the present moment we are bound to fight to the last man to defend Iraq, and therefore he will be quite content if we do not take any further responsibility than that for the next twenty-five years. But I am quite certain that Parliament will not allow him to continue that situation beyond 1928. It is of the utmost importance to make it perfectly clear that after 1928 we shall take no more responsibility for the defence of Iraq and make no more exertions for Iraq than any other

[1] L. S. Amery.

member of the League of Nations. Why should we be so squeamish about seeing Mosul invaded by the Turks? We sat still with folded hands and saw the vast horrors that have taken place in Asia Minor where millions of Christians lost their lives, although we had been very responsible in inducing the Greek Armies to go into Asia Minor.

I think we should give full notice that after 1928 our responsibilities towards Iraq will be no greater than those of any other member of the League of Nations. More than that, we must reduce our expenditure on Iraq every year, and work up steadily to the position of being quit of the country on that date, apart, that is to say, from any influence that our previous work and commercial connections may give us in it.

Winston S. Churchill to Sir Arthur Steel-Maitland

(Churchill papers: 18/11)

19 September 1925

I hear we are to meet on Tuesday afternoon with Gilmour about steel houses, etc, and I would like an opportunity of discussing with you the following proposition, which I express in the shortest possible terms as you will readily appreciate its implication.

The existing Unemployment Insurance Act lapses during 1926 and a new Bill has to be produced. Far better than tampering with the rate of benefit, eg reducing it from 18/- to 15/-, would be the bold stroke of abolishing absolutely uncovenanted benefit. It is profoundly injurious to the State that this system should continue; it is demoralising to the whole working class population, not only those who receive it, but also those who feel they have it behind them.

As the original author of the Unemployment Insurance Act I have some qualification to speak on this subject. Covenanted Unemployment Insurance is a wholesome earned right for which a man or woman has paid with State encouragement adequate contributions; but uncovenanted benefit is nothing more or less than charitable relief; and charitable relief should never be enjoyed as a legal right.

Do not imagine that I am only seeking to save the Exchequer. The cost to the Exchequer is a very small part of the evil. I should be ready to place at your disposal a contribution almost equal to the present charges provided it were administered throughout under discretionary power instead of being taken for granted. You could make grants to Local Committees or to newly constituted ad hoc bodies, which would deal with all genuine cases of distress at least as fully as they are dealt with now. But each case should be judged on its merits, and this cultivation of a class of dole qualifiers in water-tight compartments at the tail of every industry ought to be brought to an end by any Government that dares to do its duty.

My proposal would be threefold.

(1) Denounce the principle of uncovenanted benefit.

(2) Provide from the Insurance Fund in part and from the Exchequer adequate funds to relieve *bona fide* and inevitable distress (perhaps by grants to Necessitous Areas, or Poor Law Authorities, or by any other machinery).

(3) Decree that no person under, say, 25 shall receive such relief without doing a full days work, which of course the State would have to organise and pay for.

Proceeding on the present lines we are rotting the youth of the country and rupturing the mainspring of its energies. No country in the world has ever attempted such a policy of keeping this waiting list of unemployed in strict trade union compartments at the root of every separate industry. I do beg you to consider this and talk to me about it when we meet.

Winston S. Churchill to Sir Samuel Hoare

(*Churchill papers: 18/11*)

20 September 1925
Personal

I proposed to the Prime Minister that the Economy Committee of the Cabinet should begin its work about the middle of October. I shall have a series of main proposals to put before it, one of which will certainly be a reconsideration of the rate at which the execution of the Air programme should be effected. It would probably be convenient to bring this forward at a very early stage, certainly before the end of October. This will not of course prejudice subsequent Cabinet consideration if there are still out-standing differences. In the meanwhile the Treasury do not feel able to agree to being committed to the construction of the additional aerodromes of which you write. It is surely only reasonable that the review of policy should precede these further commitments as only a few weeks' delay will be involved.

I should be perfectly content to accept the principle of block figures for the Air Ministry for the next three years, subject to ordinary criticism of administrative expense; but I expect we should have different ideas about the figures. What sort of figures have you in your mind? The pressure upon me to effect economies is enormous. The House of Commons, the Press and the business world are all up in arms against our increasing expenditure. The Air Force is now costing under all heads, Air, Military, Naval and Iraq expenditure £25 millions. Both the Army and the Navy never cease to declare that at least £5 millions a year is lost through a separate Air Ministry, and they point to the obvious and hideous duplication and triplication of so many services. Worthy, who is very good at figures and a most friendly and unaggressive colleague, told me that he was sure £3 or £4 millions could be saved if the transport and other services of the Army were made available for the Air, and if the military wing was placed under the War Office. The Admiralty say the same thing only in much more violent language. There is no doubt an interest and an appetite on the part of both these older Services for which allowance must be made. The fact however remains that both Navy and Army could so easily provide the after permanent career of the airman when he has ceased to fly, while you have to try to provide for it by far greater rewards and multiplication of senior non-flying posts.

Up to the present the Treasury view has been favourable to the maintenance of a separate Air Force, but you would be surprised to hear all the quarters in which misgivings are felt upon the subject. My own view is strictly in favour of a separate Air Force on the merits, subject only to the query, 'can we afford it'. All expenditure is now coming into criticism, and I am sure you will have a very heavy concentration upon you unless you walk warily and reduce your demands upon the Exchequer to a minimum. As you know I am animated by the most friendly feeling to you and to Trenchard, and am most earnestly desirous of maintaining that close co-operation of which you speak.

Winston S. Churchill to Stanley Baldwin
(*Churchill papers: 18/11*)

20 September 1925

My dear Prime Minister,

I do not suppose many of our colleagues will be continuously in London until the middle of October. As I told you, I propose to be back by October 10th. I hope you will find it possible to convene the Cabinet Committee on Economy shortly after October 15th. I shall have prepared a series of proposals all involving policy to lay before them. I give you a very brief outline of them for your *personal* consideration beforehand.

A. A 5% reduction on the salaries and pay of all Government and Municipal employees from the highest to the humblest. There is at least £8 millions in this, and of course if Ministers penalise themselves their moral position would be strong for dealing with others. There is no doubt that such a step would receive great support in the Press, in the business world and generally outside official circles. Against it are two very grave arguments.

(1) The possibility of offending the armed forces and the police in the advent of what may be a considerable social and industrial tussle. The hostility of all these official classes is capable of course of a definite voting expression.

(2) The difficulty of imposing such a cut on so many persons with modest or small remuneration in order to save £8 millions when we are spending, eg £4 millions a year on the greedy and ungrateful Arabs in Iraq. Others would adduce Singapore, cruisers, coal subsidy, the dole, etc.

B. A system of reducing the number, or at any rate countervailing the increase in the official employees of the Government by instituting an establishment say 25% lower than the present establishment and working down to that over a long period of years as vacancies occur. This would involve the principle of 'acting rank' in certain higher appointments on the lower scale of salary, etc, which is quite well understood. Fisher will deploy you very serious arguments against either of these two changes, and no doubt they would be steadfastly opposed by the whole of the Civil Service. The question before you to decide is, how far are you prepared to go, and what efforts are you prepared to make, counting the cost well beforehand.

C. The Navy is being overhauled by Lord Colwyn's Committee.[1] They have begun to make considerable economies on their own account. Some of these economies might well have been selected from the point of view of exciting the greatest possible irritation. With one gesture Scotland is offended at Rosyth, and with another Wales at Pembroke, for a saving which is very small. Whereas the large reductions which are possible on the Admiralty staff and generally on the staff maintained throughout the Fleet; on the building up of the oil fuel reserve; on the numbers on Vote A, which should certainly not be allowed to exceed 100,000; and on the number of cruisers and battleships kept in commission, have not yet made their appearance. Still I think it is better to await the Colwyn Committee Report before attempting any investigation of naval expenditure. I must however again point out the difficulty of shutting up establishments like Pembroke and Rosyth, and perhaps Sheerness or even Chatham when the total savings from all these sources, with all the suffering they entail, are far less than the

[1] A Committee set up in April 1925, under the Chairmanship of Lord Colwyn, to make recommendations on defence spending.

£4 millions a year spent on Iraq, etc. The uncomfortable conviction is dawning upon me that one unthrifty item of expenditure entails not only its own loss but 'dulls the edge of husbandry' simultaneously in every direction.

D. Sam Hoare is pressing for early review of the Air Force expansion scheme. He is aware of the pressures which are mounting against the separate Air Force, and he does not at all deny the consequential reaction of the pact with France and increased friendly relations. My view is that the Air should not have more next year than they have had this year, and that they should be made to delay their expansion scheme accordingly. Alternatively we might fix the figures for two years at the present level and let Trenchard and Co do their best within those limits.

E. I think Worthy should be prepared to get at least £2 millions off the Army Estimates. He has already, I know, in a praise-worthy spirit effected certain savings (eg the costly costing system). But I suspect that these savings are mostly with an eye to compensating improvements in other directions, whereas a net reduction is essential. In my view, resulting from more than 20 years of study of Army politics and finance, the completion of the reduction of the historic pre-war cavalry regiments to one squadron each and the grouping of such squadrons into complete regiments of three offers a substantial saving and is absolutely justified by the modern developments of war and of new arms of the Service, tanks, gas, tractors, signals, etc, to say nothing of aviation.

F. I should hope that the Cabinet Committee, after some discussion among themselves, would assign to each of the other Departments a certain proportion of reduction. In most cases it cannot be a very large reduction. I will submit a draft scheme on which the Committee can work when they assemble. When this draft as amended has been approved I suggest that each Departmental Minister should be asked to furnish them with proposals for effecting the assigned economies, and that they should show what disadvantages to the Public Service would necessarily be entailed therefrom. This would enable the Committee about a month later to make definite recommendations to the Cabinet.

G. My thought comes back again and again to this. There must be reduction in expenditure on Iraq in any case; but if the League of Nations gives us any excuse for escaping from the mandate and laying it at their feet, we ought to embrace the opportunity. No one knows better than I do all the arguments on the other side. But having regard to the vital consequences of the political success of the constitutional cause which is in our charge, we must be ready to subordinate even very important minor considerations to the main end. We do not seem to have a single friend on the subject of

Mesopotamia. I could unearth letters I wrote in the later Coalition days to Lloyd George on this subject. There is no doubt it is a grievous handicap for any Government to sustain.

Lastly, there is the question of the uncovenanted dole. I enclose you a copy of a private letter I have written to Steel-Maitland on this subject. You will see that I am thinking less about saving the exchequer than about saving the moral fibre of our working classes.

Summing up the whole of these main headings on which I must ask for decisions from the Cabinet Committee or the Cabinet, the one simple question emerges, which I know you will not shrink from facing squarely: do we, or do we not mean to make a strong and resolute effort to cut down expenditure. If we do, it will be easier and safer to cut it down in all sorts of directions at once. There will be vehement resistance and much unpopularity, but there will also be tremendous support and a real easement of our finance at the end. Have we the manhood and command to plunge into the fierce battle against the current, or is it only open to us to drift with the stream? You must know what you feel about this. The big policy applied all round might be carried through to triumph, but a little pinching here and there with a few Pembrokes and Rosyths thrown in will perish miserably under the combined reprobation of the angered vested interests and the disappointed economy enthusiasts.

Yours vy sincerely,
Winston S. Churchill

October 1925

Winston S. Churchill to Sir Edward Grigg

(Churchill papers: 18/9)

1 October 1925   Florence

My dear Scribe,

Many thanks for your letter. I read both the articles at the time, and I certainly think the first constituted a most unwarrantable reflection. I am much obliged to you all the same for the trouble which you took to send them.

I agree with what you say about Mosul, but I don't think there is any likelihood of our being drawn into war or increased expenditure in that quarter.

The question of the development of the loan in East Africa will be considered on its merits; and, as you know, the project has many supporters. I repeatedly asked the Colonial Office for a well considered plan of Railway development. It is no use spending money except in relation to some carefully laid plan which affords a reasonable prospect of at any rate a partial return. Some of our friends seem to think that so long as orders are placed for railway material in England, and railways are built anywhere in East Africa, there is a nett gain. We have, however, only a limited supply of credit to distribute between many claimants. Still I think your business ranks very high in the minds of most of the Cabinet.

All good wishes to you in taking up your important duties. I was so sorry to read of the *contretemps* which delayed your departure.[1]

---

[1] The delay in Grigg's departure had been caused by the illness of his seventeen-month-old son, John Grigg (later a political journalist of distinction, and biographer of Lloyd George. On succeeding to his father's barony in 1955, John Grigg did *not* apply for a Writ of Summons to the House of Lords, and eight years later was among the very first Peers to disclaim his title, under the new legislation).

Winston S. Churchill to P. J. Grigg
(*Churchill papers: 18/9*)

2 October 1925   Florence

My dear Grigg,

I see reports in the papers that I am to meet Caillaux on my way through Paris on the 9th. I am inclined to think this would not be prudent procedure. The Italian papers say today that only a *modus vivendi* has been reached in America, and that Caillaux is returning without a settlement. I think we ought to review very carefully the whole position disclosed by the American negotiations so far as we know them, and that the Cabinet should be consulted before we proceed to address the French formally on the subject. In the meanwhile a private conversation would be embarrassing. Perhaps you will read this to the Prime Minister; and unless he disagrees, I shall travel straight through, reaching England on Friday evening. I shall motor straight from Folkestone to Chartwell.

I am delighted about the Bank Rate and that our twin spoil-sports have not been able to prevent this easement. I should be very glad if you could come to Chartwell on Saturday night for the week-end. You could then bring me up to date, and we could rehearse the Steel cross-examination. Would Niemeyer like to come too? I shall be quite alone, as my wife is remaining in Italy. Wire me.

Yours sincerely,
Winston S. Churchill

Lord Trenchard to Winston S. Churchill
(*Churchill papers: 18/9*)

10 October 1925   Air Ministry

My dear Mr Churchill,

You wrote a letter to Sir Samuel Hoare dated the 20th, which you said he might show to me. I am writing this letter personally to you, because I am really seriously worried and alarmed.

You know when you got me back to run the Air Force how very diffident I was—how I was doubtful as to whether I could do the job successfully— how I thought it would be too great a task for me—and how I was dubious of getting enough support to enable me to carry it through. And no one remembers better than I do your wonderful kindness and assistance, your constant assurance that I should carry it through and make a success of it.

And now, I ask you to look at the Service that has been formed and is growing up. Have you any idea of the spirit which obtains in the Air Force?

Wherever you go, whether it is in a punch-and-judy show or in grand opera, in the highest circles or the lowest, you will hear the opinion that the Air Force do better than anyone else. Take the Tattoo; take Olympia; take the Hendon Display; take flying generally; take what all foreign powers say of us; take the wonderful improvement there has been regarding accidents; the improvement in the upkeep of machines; the spirit animating the whole Service; take Iraq and the saving of millions; and will you say that, because a few people with a little knowledge like Worthington-Evans state to you that they can save 4 or 5 millions by taking over the air and running it differently, you think we may have made a mistake? We have already saved you 15 millions a year in one place alone—Iraq.

I can quite easily state and substantiate that there is not 3 or 4 millions to save in what they propose, and that not a penny piece would be saved in doing away with what you call 'the hideous duplication and triplication of many services'. The Mond Committee explored this very thoroughly, and reported, to put it baldly, that there was nothing in it. How is Worthington-Evans going to make the Army Transport and other services available for the Air? We work in with the Army and Navy already as far as is possible. As you know we have no transport depots, supply depots and the like but rely on the other Services. Neither Worthington-Evans nor anyone else could make the Army transport deal with the local work of our scattered units all over the country, and mostly a long way from Army stations. The same applies to the other services. The three Medical Services for instance work closely together and pool hospital accommodation, and splitting up the Air Service would not save a penny in this direction.

Then look at the other side of the picture. As a separate Service we can and do have common training arrangements for all purposes. You know as well as I do that the Army and Navy, should they take over, would never do this, and that training machinery, a very costly item, would be duplicated to a large extent. They could not even train their Cadets to fly at Woolwich, Sandhurst or Dartmouth. If the Army and Navy had each their own Air Service I am certain that no saving would result. It would, on the other hand, increase expenditure by 6 or 7 millions in order to produce the same efficiency. And I would ask you if I have ever been far wrong in my calculations of expenditure.

I feel that you do not really mean that you are exercised that we are making appointments for higher officers, when you remember the Short Service System which was like the judgement of Solomon in cutting the baby in two—this system whereby we got rid of having to find a career for a large number of officers, did away with having a large number of officers on half-pay, dispensed with having unnecessary senior appointments, and got a Reserve of young officers. You know that the only true way of economy in the defensive services of this country is not to do away with the Army or the Navy, but the substitution of Air in part of their duties and responsibilities, and you know this can never come about, (you have seen it yourself), without a separate Air Service.

The Navy and Army will, of course, say they are just as ready to substitute as we are, but they will never do it. Did the Army favour substitution in Iraq when it came to a concrete case? Are the Admiralty ready to substitute at Singapore? They will both give lip service to substitution, but in fact they will only add. Where does the economy come in?

I realise that the economical question is undoubtedly the outstanding question of the day and I feel sure you will believe me when I say that I personally, and all here, are perfectly convinced that economy is the most important thing at the present time and, as an ordinary tax-payer, I agree that we should try to reduce the cost of the Services. I hope that you will agree, at any rate, that I have tried to play the game over this, and, as far as I am concerned I should be perfectly prepared, as you know, to be very reasonable in any suggestions to reduce cost. As you know economy never comes in the first year of making the arrangements.

I have written all this to you and you may say I had no right to do so but as you said in your note to my Secretary of State 'You may show this to HT' and having worked under you I have presumed on this thing for once. I do not want the Air Ministry to get into the odour that the Admiralty got into over the Cruiser programme, and I want to show you that as far as the permanent servants of the Air are concerned you will not find them in any way not out to assist you in your tremendous task.

May I give you lunch at Brooks's Club on any day you like? I know you are busy, but I would so much like to talk to you personally.

Yours very sincerely,
Trenchard

Winston S. Churchill to Lord Trenchard
(Churchill papers: 18/9)

11 October 1925
Private

My dear Trenchard,

Of course always write to me on anything.

I have not at all altered my views as to the desirability of a separate Air Force so far as efficiency and leadership in the air are concerned. The expense is another matter, and I am not convinced that large savings would not result from the less satisfactory solution of division. Everything now turns on finance, and I am sure that if the Air Force is going to continue to swell our expenditure upon armaments from year to year it will draw upon itself a volume of criticism which will bring the question of division into the forefront of defence problems.

The Navy reproach me bitterly for only criticising and attacking their expenditure while the Air Force they say is favoured and the Army let alone. You have only to read the papers to see how cruel is the pressure to which I am subjected. We are at present heading straight for large increases in expenditure next year with consequent reimposition of taxation. I am sure the Cabinet will recoil from this prospect when they are confronted with it and that desperate efforts will be made to cut down. I do trust that you will be able to help the Treasury in their task. You have many friends there who have confidence in your own frugality of administration and see the usefulness of your intervention against the extravagances both of the Navy and of the Army. I am sure that the present relations with France not only justify but demand a complete reconsideration of the rate of the expansion scheme, and I should be bound to resist by every means in my power any attempt to carry the total of Air Votes in the coming year beyond the figure under all heads for this.

Certainly let us lunch together. But since I am installed at Downing Street, let me be the host. Wednesday, 1.30? Let me know.

Yours v sincerely,
Winston S. Churchill

L. S. Amery: diary

(*Amery papers*)

12 October 1925

Attended the Civil Research Committee and spent one hour listening to Winston cross-examining the Iron industry representatives and trying to trip them up. At the end I got in one minute of questions, which I think undid his efforts.

L. S. Amery: diary

(*Amery papers*)

13 October 1925

Agricultural Policy Committee where we spent an hour while Winston criticised Edward's[1] proposals for small holdings and occupying ownership. I fear Winston is a pure Cobdenite in his outlook and his long dissertations make it very difficult to get ahead with the business.

Cabinet Standing Committee on Expenditure:[2] *minutes*

(*Cabinet papers: 27/303*)

14 October 1925

CHURCHILL: It seemed probable that the budget estimates of the current financial year would in the main be realised. . . .

Because of the coal subsidy the deficit for the current year might therefore amount to between £12,000,000 and £15,000,000 which would have to be met by temporary borrowing. This state of affairs made it all the more essential that every step should be taken to endeavour to reduce, so far as possible, the amount of the 1925–26 deficit and provide for a balanced budget on sound financial lines for 1926–27.[3]

Winston S. Churchill to Neville Chamberlain

(*Churchill papers: 18/11*)

15 October 1925
Private

My dear Neville,
    The review of our financial position which I gave yesterday to the Cabinet Economy Committee[4] was sufficiently gloomy to convince them that the

---

[1] Edward Wood, Minister of Agriculture.
[2] Consisting of Baldwin (in the Chair), Churchill, Lord Salisbury (Lord Privy Seal), Joynson-Hicks (Home Secretary) and Lord Birkenhead (Secretary of State for India).
[3] In his detailed survey to the Committee, Churchill advocated cuts of £10 million in the fighting services, but he opposed a reduction of 5 per cent in the pay of all civil servants, on the grounds that: 'Not merely had pledges been given which would have to be overridden, but it would be a serious thing to give members of the Services and the Police cause for discontent at a time of industrial crisis' (*Cabinet papers: 27/303*). Churchill also opposed reductions in the grants for elementary education, in the war pensions pledge, and in the Northern Ireland unemployment grant. For his proposals on the National Health Insurance Scheme, see Churchill's letter to Neville Chamberlain of 15 October 1925.
[4] Otherwise known as the Standing Committee on Expenditure.

most strenuous efforts have to be made if we are to avoid additional taxation next year. Among the various proposals which I laid before them were two relating to the National Health Insurance Scheme, which I know you have been thinking over; and the Committee asked me to explore them further in consultation with you. These are:

(1) that the State grant to the Scheme, of two-ninths of the expenditure, should be limited to the initial benefits of the Act and the cost of administration thereof, and should not extend to the additional benefits which are being declared by many Societies from time to time after valuation (saving £2,000,000);

(2) that the whole cost of central, as well as of local, administration should, as in the case of Unemployment Insurance, be borne on the Insurance Fund subject of course to the usual State grant (saving £800,000).

The prosperity of the Health Insurance Scheme contrasts favourably with the general position. While the Cabinet Committee is now forced to contemplate drastic reductions in services hitherto regarded as essential, involving sacrifices in every department of the State, the Health Insurance Scheme continues to yield vast surpluses of almost embarrassing magnitude. The Exchequer does not claim these surpluses; but I feel most strongly they should not operate to *increase* the financial difficulties of the State.

Further, the cost of central administration was accepted as a State charge when the scheme was in its infancy and the national finances were flourishing. Now the scheme is prosperous, while we are in difficulties. No small part of these difficulties can be attributed to the cost of launching another great scheme of social reform: Widows' and Old Age Pensions. We have planned for that scheme to be self-supporting in time, but at present, having regard to the consequential relief given by the Exchequer to the Unemployment Insurance Fund, it is costing us altogether nearly £10 millions a year. If we now seek some relief from our liabilities to the Health Insurance Scheme and in doing so take a step towards making that scheme also self-supporting, we can hardly be regarded either as unreasonable or inconsistent.

These are my suggestions for doing this; but if you think it would be preferable to proceed by the simpler way of altering the 2/9ths proportion for our grant to 1/9th, I should of course welcome the greater saving, for we need all that we can get. There are serious political difficulties to be faced in every direction, and I know of no proposal of similar financial significance which would involve so little real hardship.

There is no analogy between the Health Insurance Scheme and that of Unemployment Insurance. If the health of this country were as bad as its industrial position and if approved societies were labouring under the heavy charges of serious epidemics, I should not be making these suggestions. But largely owing to the lavish expenditure of the Government and municipalities in recent decades in tackling the root causes of disease: ignorance, bad sanitation and housing, no segregation of cases of infectious disease, etc, the national health was never better and the case for reducing our assistance to the scheme presents itself with exceptional force.

Yours vy sincerely,
Winston S. Churchill

House of Lords Reform Committee: [1] *minutes*
(*Churchill papers: 22/58*)

16 October 1925
11 am

Lord Chancellor's Room
House of Lords

THE CHANCELLOR OF THE EXCHEQUER emphasized the advantages of the Referendum as compared with a General Election. The Labour Party favoured frequent General Elections, a policy highly detrimental to the interests of the public. No one could impugn the democratic character of the referendum which had been found to work well in countries which had adopted it. He suggested that the Committee's recommendation to the Cabinet should be to the effect that in the event of a satisfactory constitution for the House of Lords being devised, the question of differences between the two Houses could best be solved by recourse to referendum. He also suggested that the legislation creating the referendum system should make provision for its detailed machinery.

THE SECRETARY OF STATE FOR INDIA was doubtful as to the desirability of introducing so novel an expedient as the referendum into the constitution. The public were tenacious of methods in which they had been bred and the referendum might well prove a two-edged weapon. It was, moreover, wholly alien to English habit and conception, but in view of the general feeling of the Committee, he did not wish to insist on his objection.

---

[1] Those present were Lord Cave (the Lord Chancellor, and Chairman of the Committee), Lord Salisbury (Lord Privy Seal), Lord Peel (First Commissioner of Works), Lord Birkenhead (Secretary of State for India), Lord Cecil of Chelwood (Chancellor of the Duchy of Lancaster), Joynson-Hicks (Home Secretary) and Churchill.

Winston S. Churchill to Lord Beaverbrook

(*Beaverbrook papers*)

19 October 1925   Treasury Chambers

My dear Max,

I am very much obliged to you for sending me through Freddie[1] the passages in your Book which relate to me. You will not expect me to agree with all of them, but I have no complaint to make about any. I do not think you are accurate in saying that I proposed a consultation with you before the Budget. It was on the morrow of that event. Otherwise, I have no comments.

You once told me that you had written some account of our talk together with FE at the Admiralty the night Germany declared war upon Russia, and I was a little alarmed at the description you gave of my attitude. I gather that you are not dealing with this episode in the present volume, but if you should do so perhaps you would let me see the reference.

My view was that if war was inevitable this was by far the most favourable opportunity and the only one that would bring France, Russia and ourselves together. But I should not like that put in a way that would suggest I wished for war and was glad when the decisive steps were taken. I was only glad that they were taken in circumstances so favourable. A very little alteration of the emphasis would make my true position clear. I gather however you are holding the earlier volume of your Memoirs in suspense.[2]

Yours vy sincerely,
Winston S. Churchill

Lord Beaverbrook to Winston S. Churchill

(*Churchill papers: 2/142*)

22 October 1925

My dear Winston,

Very many thanks for your letter. I am very glad that you do not object to the publication of the narrative as a whole, while differing from it on various points.

[1] Frederick Guest, to whom Beaverbrook had written, on 15 October 1925: 'Would you mind reading the passages in my MS relating to Winston? If you think there is anything which should be referred to him, I hope you will do me the kindness of acting as intermediary. In fact, on reflection, I have no hesitation in saying that I would be very grateful if you would take the whole text to Winston, and let him have an opportunity of reading it' (*Churchill papers: 2/142*).

[2] Beaverbrook's first volume, *Politicians and the War 1914–1916*, was published in two parts, in 1928 and 1932. His second volume, *Men and Power 1917–18*, was not published until 1956, and its successor, *The Decline and Fall of Lloyd George*, until 1963. His proposed volume on the Bonar Law and Baldwin premierships was never completed.

Referring to the suggested talk that never took place—whether before or after the Budget; I will recall what happened to your memory, because I think you are wrong on this point. On the Friday morning you rang me up from your country house, Chartwell, and asked me to go out and lunch with you; but I said I could not go. I had heard at that time of your conversations with (1) Rothermere in March (2) McKenna and the other Bankers about Gold for Notes, etc.

The day after the Budget you rang me up from the Treasury and we had a talk. I feel sure you are confusing the two conversations. Anyhow it does not matter very much—provided I am right—for my narrative is quite innocuous.

As to my diary narrative of events leading up to the War and continued through the war period—the publication of which is postponed more or less indefinitely—I will show it you some day. For you take a dominating part in the drama. I have not been keen to produce it for you, because it is full of extremely valuable first hand material and evidence in the form of letters. And no man who writes books on the history of the period, as you do, can help using—quite unconsciously—any information which has come before him. His intellect in fact would revolt against giving an incomplete picture when he could make a complete one, & I want to be first in the field.

I have a large collection of private letters from public men in this diary— given me by Lloyd George and several others. And Bonar Law also let me consult his letter files at the time. Of course he subsequently willed his papers to me.

But what I think the most interesting documents of this period are, I regret to say, not in my possession. They are a series of letters of Asquith written from the Cabinet room from May of 1914 up to early in 1915.[1] I have been allowed to use the material. But that is not the same thing.

Turning to the particular point you raise about the midnight sitting at Admiralty House, I can assure you that there is nothing in it which you need mind in the very least. No doubt I give 'another version of the same'— as we say in the Presbyterian Psalm Book.

As a matter of fact in the same section of the story, I give a description of your attitude towards the War which is similar with that contained in your letter.

Yours sincerely,
Max

---

[1] Letters from Asquith to Venetia Stanley. Extracts from eighty of these letters are quoted in Main Volume III of this biography.

Winston S. Churchill to Lord Beaverbrook

(Beaverbrook papers)

25 October 1925   Treasury Chambers

My dear Max,

I am quite sure that you are wrong about my proposing a conversation on the Friday before the Budget. I knew that you were an implacable opponent of the Gold Standard, and besides I did not wish to discuss my plans beforehand with anyone. After the Budget had been launched and appeared to be a great success, I should have liked very much to have had a friendly argument with you about it. But this project, through no fault of mine, got no further than our talk on the telephone. Your passage seems to suggest that I was anxious to convert you beforehand. This is really not so. I knew it was hopeless. You can, I am sure, quite easily adjust the passage without interrupting the sequence of your narrative.

I do not know when I shall be able to publish my third volume. A great deal was done before I took office; and of course as soon as I am turned out, I shall finish it off. It covers the period 1916 to the end of the war, and afterwards so far as the Russian, Greek and Turkish business is concerned. I expect, therefore, I shall be running over a good deal of your ground, and naturally I ought not to see your own secret materials beforehand. As you say, I could not help being influenced by them.[1] But I shall certainly look forward to reading your work when it appears. All I would ask is that, if you quote me in any private conversation, you will let me check the words quoted. I have always done this for other people, and I have found they made no requests which detracted from the story.

I am glad you think that trade is on the turn upwards. I agree with you, and will do my best to help.

Yours vy sincerely
Winston S. Churchill

[1] Churchill published *The World Crisis 1916–1918* in two parts, in March 1927; *The World Cisis: The Aftermath* in March 1929; and *The World Crisis: The Eastern Front* in November 1931.

Winston S. Churchill to Sir Francis Lloyd

(*Churchill papers: 2/142*)

27 October 1925

My dear General,

Thank you so much for your letter. I am very glad to rejoin the Carlton, and tho' I don't use any club much I hope I may see you there from time to time.[1]

Yours ever,
WSC

W. A. S. Hewins: [2] *diary*

('*The Apologia of an Imperialist*')

28 October 1925

INTERVIEW WITH BALDWIN

He agreed about the urgency of the iron and steel position. He said the Cabinet Committee had not yet come to a decision. Winston Churchill took the view that the extension of safeguarding duties to that industry was a violation of his (the PM's) pledge, not I gathered in principle, but because it would involve so many duties and would affect so many other trades that it would be a practical violation of the pledge not to introduce what Winston understands by a 'general' tariff.

The PM said that was not his view: he held that he could safeguard any industry which made out its case.

[1] Churchill had resigned from the Carlton Club in April 1905, after he had crossed the floor of the House of Commons from the Conservative to the Liberal benches. On learning of his re-election he had also written to Lord Younger, on October 25: 'I am very much obliged for the trouble you have taken. I think I shall have to get you to come personally and lead me in on the first occasion that I recross those once well-known portals.'

[2] William Albert Samuel Hewins, 1865–1931. Director of the London School of Economics, 1895–1903. Advocate of Imperial Preference, he was Secretary of the Tariff Commission, 1903–17, and Chairman, 1920–2. Conservative MP for Hereford, 1912–18. Under-Secretary of State for the Colonies, 1917–19. Unsuccessful Parliamentary candidate, 1922, 1923 and 1924. Author of several books on Empire, trade and tariffs. Adviser on political matters to Cardinal Bourne, Cardinal Archbishop of Westminster.

Winston S. Churchill to Lord Balfour

(*Balfour papers*)

30 October 1925   Treasury
Personal & Secret

My dear Arthur,

I send you herewith a paper on Steel wh I have prepared with the aid of the Customs. It would be disastrous if this controversy, dividing friends and uniting foes, were set alight again. Quite a number of our Colleagues take this view, & so do Jackson & Linlithgow.[1] I expect the issue of whether an enquiry shall be allowed will have to be settled by the Cabinet in the next three weeks. I suppose you will be South by then.

I am sending you on the Report of the Civil Research Sub Committee on the Loan Embargo. You will remember that this Ctee was set up in view of Amery's demand that the Embargo shd be removed, & the Treasury resistance. As we are ready now to meet these wishes, & as the pressure of the City is growing extremely strong, the Prime Minister has agreed to my making the announcement early next week. I hope you will not mind action being taken before we have been able to discuss the matter formally. I am sure the Cabinet will be delighted to know that this step can now be taken. It will be a double event if we can at once remove the Embargo and hold a Bank Rate of 4%. I cannot guarantee it; but I am not without hopes.

                                                    Yours ever
                                                    Winston S.C.

Lord Beaverbrook to Winston S. Churchill

(*Churchill papers: 2/142*)

30 October 1925

My dear Winston,

Many thanks for your letter. I have made enquiries and am quite satisfied that we did have a telephone conversation on the Friday from Chartwell. The effect of the conversation was that you asked me down, and that I

---

[1] Lord Alexander John Hope, Earl of Hopetoun, 1887–1952. Educated at Eton. Succeeded his father as 2nd Marquess of Linlithgow, 1908. On active service, 1914–18 (despatches). Commanded the Border Armoured Car Company, 1920–6. Civil Lord of Admiralty, 1922–4. Deputy Chairman of the Conservative Party Organization, 1924–6. Chairman, Royal Commission on Indian Agriculture, 1926–8. Chairman, Joint Select Committee on Indian Constitutional Reform, 1933–4. Chairman, Medical Research Council, 1934–6. Privy Councillor, 1935. Viceroy of India, 1936–43. Knight of the Garter, 1943.

regretted I could not go. But of course it would not be justifiable to draw from this fact the public inference that you wished to tell me about the Budget. It would be natural for you to think me too impenitent an opponent of the return to the Gold Standard, to make any overtures to me to support the Budget; just as it was natural in me to think that you still hoped to convert me.

I have therefore redrafted the passages concerned in this sense, and I send back the new draft.

I am sorry to trouble you—but it is important to me that the passages in my book referring to you should not be regarded in the nature of revelations or indiscretions. I cannot tolerate that sort of thing.

Yours sincerely,
Max

Winston S. Churchill to Joseph Caillaux

(*Churchill papers: 18/11*)

30 October 1925   Treasury Chambers
Personal and Private

My dear Monsieur Caillaux,

I have from time to time the melancholy duty of writing valedictory letters to French Ministers of Finance when the political kaleidoscope revolves.[1] But it is in no formal sense that I express to you my regret on personal grounds that our agreeable conversations on disagreeable subjects have been so prematurely interrupted. It was a pleasure to me to make your acquaintance, and I preserve a vivid impression of your courtesy and charm.

Ministers change, but difficulties remain, and grimly demand solution without respect to persons. It is quite impossible for anyone to understand the politics of another country; and very difficult even to understand one's own. But I hope that when you next come to England you will let me know; and whether I am at Downing Street or in a humbler abode, I should like to gather a small, select and cheerful company to welcome a statesman who faces facts and foes.

Yours very sincerely,
Winston S. Churchill

[1] On 29 October 1925 Caillaux had been succeeded as Minister of Finance by Paul Painlevé. A month later, on November 28, Painlevé was succeeded by Louis Loucheur; and two weeks later Loucheur was succeeded by Paul Doumer.

November 1925

Winston S. Churchill to Stanley Baldwin

(*Baldwin papers*)

1 November 1925   Chartwell Manor
Private

My dear PM,

I saw Austen this morning & found him not only agreeable to, but attracted by the Ronald McNeill[1] plan. He said that RM had no sphere at the FO: & wd be vy disappointed if left there; & that he thought RM wd welcome the promotion modest tho it be. I do not of course know for certain how RM wd view it; but I have no doubt that it wd be the best arrangement from my own and the Treasury standpoint. It wd give me much more help than any of the other alternatives. Since you were kind enough to consult me, I am able to give a perfectly clear answer.

It is a year almost to a day since you asked me to work with you. We know each other better than we did then, & I have been very happy under yr leadership. I am sure that you have a winning hand to play if only you have the firmness & patience to play it regularly through. Gradually but surely the nation will revive its strength, & be conscious of an increased well being. Time will vindicate all the principal action we have taken, whether it be yr forbearing attitude to Labour provocations, or the Widows Pensions, or the Gold Standard. The Rothermere–Beaverbrook attack will be repulsed, not by speeches, not by disdain; but by events. What about that Roman Fabius Maximus Cunctator—was there not some famous quotation

---

[1] Ronald John McNeill, 1861–1936. Educated at Harrow and Christ Church, Oxford. Editor of the *St James's Gazette*, 1900–4. Assistant Editor, *Encyclopaedia Britannica*, 1906–11. Unsuccessful Conservative candidate, 1906, 1907 and 1910 (twice). Conservative MP for the St Augustine Division of Kent, 1911–18; for Canterbury, 1918–27. A leading 'die-hard' and opponent of Home Rule for Ireland: in 1912 he threw a book at Churchill's head during a Parliamentary debate. Parliamentary Under-Secretary of State for Foreign Affairs, 1922–4 and 1924–5. Financial Secretary to the Treasury, 1925–7. Created Baron Cushendun, 1927. Chancellor of the Duchy of Lancaster, 1927–9. Acting Secretary of State for Foreign Affairs, August–December 1928. Chief British Representative to the League of Nations.

about him?[1] Did he not give his country a chance to pull round & realise its mighty strength & let the deep long forces work for him—instead of being lured into desperate & premature struggles?

As long as we stick to the platform of the General Election all will be well & we shall wear down all our foes, & what is more important do our duty in securing the country its promised breathing space. But if Amery—who publicly repudiated yr declarations of fiscal policy before the election—is allowed to rush the Conservative party on to the slippery slope of Protection, then friends will be divided & enemies united & all the vultures will gather for the prey.

A general Tariff wd encounter no more reproaches of departure from pledges, & a less effectual resistance, than an isolated general protective duty on Steel. One is a policy—the other a meaningless & unrelated episode, the result not of scientific thought on Trade conditions, but only of drifting from one half measure & compromise to another.

I expect that if these Steel men knew that the tariff was off for this Parliament, and if you let me get into direct touch with them, we cd find a way of helping them to regional concentrations on the most profitable plants.

At any rate I wd gladly try.

Yours vy sincerely
Winston S. Churchill

Winston S. Churchill to Lord Beaverbrook

(*Beaverbrook papers*)

2 November 1925   Treasury Chambers
Private and Personal

My dear Max,

You are entirely in error in supposing that I told Rothermere any secrets connected with the Budget. When I saw him (I think early in March), he made a point of not asking for any information, but merely said good-humouredly that he would give me a helping hand with my first Budget. So far as the Gold Standard was concerned, it was of course necessary both for me and the Governor of the Bank to consult with a certain number of financial authorities beforehand. Still I think that the announcement to be made in the Budget was very well kept.

---

[1] The three best-known quotations of Fabius Maximus are: 'A wise and good man can suffer no disgrace', 'He will have true glory who despises glory' and 'To avoid all mistakes in the conduct of great enterprises is beyond man's powers'.

I do not remember asking you to Chartwell before the Budget, but I have no record. FE was with me at the time, and it would have been quite natural that we should have wished you to join us. But any such message—of which I have no recollection—would have been purely personal and devoid of political intention.

While I do not complain of the general tone of the extracts from your new book which you have been good enough to send me, you will, I am sure, realise that my own account of these matters would in many cases be different. What particularly stands in my memory is the last time we dined together at the Vineyard—I think at the end of February. Here indeed we had a long talk; and you advised me most strongly against adopting the Gold Standard, on which point you used many, if not most, of the arguments which have since been employed by its opponents. I reflected a great deal on what you said, but in the end the counter-arguments prevailed.

You also then advised me to tell Rothermere and Burnham,[1] and presumably yourself, the outline of the Budget some time before it was announced to Parliament. You said—and I do not doubt it—that strict secrecy would have been preserved and that a friendly reception would in all probability have been assured. You told me that Bonar had disclosed Baldwin's Budget to you and Rothermere, and that you had backed it up and secured it a favourable reception, with much else of an intimate and private character.

I weighed carefully all you said, but I could not feel that my position was in any way the same as Bonar Law's. He was Prime Minister and Party Leader, and therefore free to use his judgment in the communication of secrets as he thought best for the interests of the Government and the country. An ordinary Chancellor of the Exchequer has no such latitude and would be bound to obtain the assent of the Prime Minister before adopting any such course. You and Bonar lived not only on friendly, but fraternal, terms; and you were devoted to his political interests, which in turn were identical with those of the Government. Very different indeed was, and is, your attitude towards the Chief it is my duty to serve.

I therefore made up my mind definitely not to impart my plans to anyone outside the indispensable official circle. I had hoped that such a decision, which indeed was no more than my obvious duty, would not have prevented the pleasant social relations we have enjoyed with some lapses for a number

[1] Harry Lawson Webster Levy Lawson, 1862–1933. Educated at Eton and Balliol College, Oxford. Conservative MP, 1885–1906 and 1910–16. Mayor of Stepney, 1907–9. President of the Institute of Journalists, 1910. Succeeded his father (the principal proprietor of the *Daily Telegraph*) as 2nd Baron Burnham, 1916. President of the Empire Press Union, 1916–28. Created Viscount, May 1919. President of the International Labour Conference, Geneva, 1921–2 and 1926; of the Press Experts Conference, 1927 and 1929; and of the Public Health Congress, 1924 and 1927.

of years; and it is not my fault that these did not continue. It is perhaps better, however, as Joe Chamberlain used to hold, to suspend personal relations during a period of sharp political controversy.

Neither is it in my view a true description of our relations to imply, as some of your passages seem to do, that I was your friend only when my political fortunes were not prosperous. On the contrary, after the 1923 Election and the Freddie Guest incident, I broke off all relations with you for many months, and they were only renewed through the offices of common friends after you were kind enough to come and call on me.

But seriously and amicably, are you not making a mistake in writing about these personal affairs in public? So long as your narrative confines itself to public points of difference, you have a perfectly watertight explanation of the line you have adopted. The moment you suggest that you thought you were going to be told the secrets of the Budget, you suggest proceedings the public would regard with violent disapproval and make statements which I should certainly have to declare unfounded. Very little alteration is needed to make your narrative conform to the line I recommend, and the last sentence of your letter shows that this is also most strongly your own wish. In this way public differences can be fought out and private friendship left to right itself again when times are better.

Yours sincerely
Winston S. Churchill

Lord Beaverbrook to Winston S. Churchill

(*Churchill papers: 2/142*)

3 November 1925

My dear Winston,

I have received your letter and I accept, of course, your statement as to the nature of your interview with Rothermere. I will at once strike out all reference to this whatsoever.

As to the telephone conversation from Chartwell prior to the Budget, you say you have no record about it and do not remember; whereas I remember very well and have a record. But, of course, as you say, Birkenhead was with you at the time and it was quite natural to ask me down simply for a friendly visit. This view is embodied in the new text.

Forgive me if, in reply to your letter, I re-raise some of the points of friendly controversy you mention yourself:

In the first place, I cannot remember the exact details of our happy reconciliation in 1923. I thought it arose out of your kindness to me, but quite possibly it was the other way about. But you are quite wrong in thinking that the moral of my story in this connection is that you only came to me when your political prospects were not flourishing. What I say is something quite different—that I like you best under the least fortunate political circumstances.

To continue our very agreeable argument, I do not think you will find anything in the text of the book in the way of 'revelations' or discussions of 'private affairs'. That is far from being my intention.

All references to conversations about public affairs have been submitted, as in your own case, to the people concerned and they have all said, as you did, that they do not object to publication while reserving their right to put their own construction on conversations or events. Nobody, except yourself, has suggested any alteration whatsoever.

I rather gather that you consider this question of private conversations about public affairs important—and I quite agree. Certainly our best talks have been concerned with politics. And here I have noticed what is to me one of the most interesting aspects of your character—that on one occasion you will be absolutely frank and unreserved—and that on another you can display the most astonishing self-restraint. I confess I like the alternating moods, which do not always coincide with your periods of opposition—as when you told me before your last Budget that you were considering a reduction in the supertax. You showed the other quality on the night of the day that you became Chancellor—an evening I will not attempt to record.

The next important point you raise seems to involve the whole question as to under what circumstance, if at all, the secrets of the Budget ought to be disclosed outside the strict official circle—this in connection with the story I told you about the Baldwin Budget of 1923.

The conversation you mention arose in relation to how you could best get newspaper support. As an instance I gave you an account of the preliminaries to that Budget. At that time a strong effort was being made by the dissident Conservatives—with whom you were working—to discredit Baldwin's Budget in advance by getting hold of the popular press and inducing it to attack on the fateful day. Nor was the Government over-strong. Under these circumstances Bonar Law, Baldwin, J. C. C. Davidson and McKenna, myself and Rothermere all worked together to fight off this attack. I will send you a full, written account of all this someday. And if your suggestion is that Bonar Law did anything wrong, I must dispute it.

My object in telling you was, as you say, to suggest that you should see Rothermere and Burnham, tell them your plans and secure, if you could, their support. I particularly did not mean you to tell me because I was irrevocably opposed to you on the Gold Standard—whereas there was no reason to suppose that either Rothermere or Burnham would be hostile on this account.

Of course, I thought you would tell me what was in the Budget if I asked you. But I particularly did not want to know, because it would have been awkward for me to have this knowledge when I knew I had to oppose you. And that is why I would not come to Chartwell—being afraid, as it turns out quite wrongly, that you meant to tell me.

Now this question of 'telling' seems to be the crux of your whole letter. For you suggest towards the end exactly what your private secretaries are always saying in public—namely that I have opposed you because you would not tell me what was in your Budget. As long as other people say this I do not mind. But if you advance it yourself as a real reason for my opposition to the Budget, I should have to defend myself against the charge. I think it quite possible that I have misread your letter on this point and that you do not mean what I seem to read into this passage.

I am sorry to write you such a long letter. I assure you I have no desire to dispute any conversations.

In fact the original purpose in writing you was to avoid anything in the nature of controversy. I unfortunately quarrelled with Freddie Guest because I thought he made a threat in a letter he wrote me. He tells me now there was no such intention. How easy it is to be misunderstood in the written word or on the telephone. Nearly all my trials in personal relationships begin with misunderstanding on the telephone.

Yours sincerely,
Max

Ronald McNeill to Winston S. Churchill

(*Churchill papers 2/142*)

3 November 1925

My dear Churchill,

Although I still feel the gravest misgiving as to my unfitness for the duties of Financial Secretary to the Treasury, and while my own preference is for the Under Secretaryship at the Foreign Office rather than any other place outside the Cabinet, I yet have come to the decision that it would be very ungrateful both to you & the Prime Minister to persist in declining an important post which you have offered me in such very complimentary terms. I have therefore written to the PM accepting the office.

I will do my best to help you. There is one thing at any rate I can promise.
I have never served under, or with, any man without serving him loyally; &
I can promise you loyalty if nothing else.

Yours sincerely,
Ronald McNeill

House of Lords Reform Committee: minutes

(*Churchill papers: 22/58*)

4 November 1925
Secret

THE CHANCELLOR OF THE EXCHEQUER warned the Committee
of the danger of amending the Parliament Act in this particular respect.[1] A
Labour Government with an independent majority in the House of Commons could attain their ends by administrative action and would be encouraged to so do by the existence of statutory provisions fettering their
liberty of action. Substantial amendment of the Act would unite the parties
of the Left on the pretext that the House of Lords were endeavouring to
exercise rights over Money Bills.

The Government should endeavour to enlist in support of their proposals
those great masses of public opinion which desired some constitutional check
against revolutionary measures. It should, he thought, suffice if an indication
were given to the Appointed Authority that the decisions of the Speaker
were not to be regarded as precedents.

THE CHANCELLOR OF THE EXCHEQUER said that on the assump-
tion that the ultimate solution of differences between the two Houses would
be left to the machinery of a Referendum and *not* to that of a Joint Session
he was in favour of the principle of indirect election rather than that of
nomination, which had no tradition or authority behind it. The electors
might be members of the House of Commons grouped in panels who would
choose say 400 members of the Second Chamber from a panel of 1,200
candidates all of whom would have to possess certain qualifications.

[1] By amending the definition of Money Bills, as proposed to the Committee by Lord
Salisbury.

Winston S. Churchill to Lord Beaverbrook
(*Beaverbrook papers*)

6 November 1925   Treasury Chambers
Private

My dear Max,

Many thanks for what you say about the alterations you are going to make in your new text.

If you will re-read my last letter, you will see that I do not attempt to judge Bonar's action. On the contrary my argument was directed to showing that a Prime Minister has a latitude which a subordinate does not possess. You are wrong in supposing that I was working 'to discredit Baldwin's Budget in advance', etc. I did not return from abroad till late in April, and I never heard of any such plan on the part of my political friends.

I have never authorised or encouraged anyone to state that your attacks on me are due to my having declined to disclose to you the Budget secrets. You yourself gave great publicity to this suggestion three or four months ago in the 'Sunday Express', but it is not one for which I accept any responsibility or which was in any way suggested by my letter.

On the contrary the whole of our relations during the present year have been those of the Wolf and the Lamb. The Wolf has made repeated and extremely spiteful attacks upon the Lamb, and has avowedly compassed his destruction. The Lamb, on the other hand, conscious not only of his innocence but of the strength of the fold, and sustained by the sympathy of the Shepherd and the other Sheep, has preserved a moody silence not, however, unaccompanied by some complacency.

Yours sincerely,
Winston S. Churchill

Joseph Caillaux to Winston S. Churchill
(*Churchill papers: 2/142*) [1]

7 November 1925
Personal

Do you know, my dear Mr Churchill, it could be difficult to write a more delicate & charming letter than the one you have sent me? It touched me greatly—it even rather moved me.

Well well! the job of a Finance Minister is complicated in all countries &

[1] Caillaux's original letter was in French: this is the translation done for Churchill by Edward Marsh.

at all times. It is infinitely difficult for a man who takes upon himself to tell the truth, the whole truth, to any nation which has for a long time been diligently culled with illusions. It is human nature to dislike the wretch who dispels the delightful mirages, and speaks roughly to the dupes; & sometimes they make haste to show him the door.

But pshaw! Talleyrand said that 'in politics one only dies to rise again'. Haven't we both experienced the truth of this maxim?

My fifth sojourn—this time a very short one—at the Finance Ministry will at best have given me the chance of paying a most agreeable visit to London, altho' as you observe the subject of discussion was disagreeable. But you showed me such courtesy throughout—you received me with so much grace, & had such a happy touch in vivifying & brightening our conversations, that they left me with the impression that we were in complete agreement.

You give me the most kindly invitation to come & see you when next I am in London. I certainly will. I could not deny myself the pleasure of tasting the charm of further intercourse with a man of your culture & high quality. But I must make one condition: that you for your part will knock at my door when you come to Paris. Is what has come round to me true—that you have been on the banks of the Seine several times in the last few months? If so it would be very wrong of you not to have made a sign to your then colleague. He wd punish you for it (if he didn't know the burden which rests on yr shoulders) by insisting on your coming at once to shoot the partridge with him in this Sarthe country where he has taken refuge, & which autumn is embroidering with such pretty colours. In any case, please keep in mind the definite invitation which he hereby sends you for next summer—and above all, please believe that it gave me a very lively pleasure to make the acquaintance of a statesman like yourself, for whom I feel no less admiration than profound sympathy.

Yours in all friendship
J. Caillaux

Winston S. Churchill to Sir Warren Fisher, Sir Otto Niemeyer and Sir Richard Hopkins

(*Churchill papers: 18/13*)

7 November 1925
Most Secret

I wish the Treasury to hold in mind the importance of vindicating the figures presented in the Budget. A surplus of between £1 and £2 millions, apart from the Coal Subsidy, would achieve this. The Coal Subsidy, which will, I fear, not be less than £17 millions, minus the budgetted surplus, should constitute the deficit. No pressure of collection should be resorted to beyond what is necessary to realise this result. As much collection power as possible must be saved for 1926. The fact that there is a slight increase in special receipts should make it possible to keep our collection power reserve largely intact. I am determined not to impose new taxation for revenue purposes next year, and every effort must be made to reduce expenditure. If, however, we should succeed in balancing the Budget without the imposition of new taxation, though using to the full our collection power, I should then feel free to study special taxes on luxuries, with a view to making remission from existing taxation.

In order that you may all see what is in my mind, I put this on record at this early period; and if there are any arguments against my course, I shall be glad if you will take an opportunity of seeing me together on the subject, so as to arrive at action in every direction in harmony with a complete understanding.

Winston S. Churchill to Sir Aylmer Hunter-Weston[1]

(Churchill papers: 18/11)

10 November 1925
Private

My dear General,

No one can possibly defend a system which would allow expenditure upon luxury roads to proceed out of all relation to national wealth or to other considerations of public policy. The Government will have to balance one class of expenditure against another, and it is their duty to try to make proposals to Parliament which comprehend the whole interest of the State.

I do not know what decision will be reached about the Road Fund. My own view is that some increased relief is needed for rural roads, but that the development of the main roads is proceeding at the present time as fast as the community can afford. Would you, for instance, propose to build joy

[1] Aylmer Hunter-Weston, 1864–1940. Entered Royal Engineers, 1884. Served on Kitchener's staff in the Sudan, 1898. Chief Staff Officer to Sir John French's Cavalry Division in South Africa, 1900. Brigadier-General commanding 11th Infantry Brigade, August 1914; promoted Major-General for distinguished service in the field. Commanded the 29th Division at the landing on Cape Helles, April 1915; promoted Lieutenant-General for the successful landing. Commanded the VIIIth Corps at the Dardanelles and in France, 1915–18. Knighted, 1915. Conservative MP for Ayrshire, 1916–35. Known as 'Hunter-Bunter'.

roads to Brighton or Ascot at a time when you could not afford to build cruisers? Would you prefer to see the strength of the Army further reduced, or on the other hand do you favour a reimposition of the direct or indirect taxation recently remitted? It is no use adopting an intransigent attitude on one point, unless you are prepared with alternative suggestions on others. The just sense of proportion which arises from a study of war will, I am sure, convince you on reflection that a decision to vote against the Finance Bill of the Government—the most serious form of opposition which one of its supporters can take—ought not to be taken upon any single point but only upon a general review of the whole financial situation and the measures proposed by the Government for meeting it.

House of Lords Reform Committee: minutes
(Churchill papers: 22/58)

11 November 1925
Secret

THE CHANCELLOR OF THE EXCHEQUER said that he did not differ very substantially from the Lord Chancellor's proposals but he was convinced that it would be found necessary to have a panel of notables from out of which the members of the reformed House of Lords would be selected. Normally the panel might consist of about 1,200 persons and should include the whole of the hereditary peerage, all members of the Privy Council, all persons who had filled certain important public or municipal officers, Chairman of the County Councils, Lord Mayors, Chairmen of Royal Commissions, Members of the House of Commons of 12 years standing and persons nominated to the panel by the Crown on the advice of the Joint Committee on Financial Bills. The Committee might indeed have power to extend the 1,200 members of the panel to 1,500 if occasion so required.

From this panel the Members of the House of Commons grouped in the areas specified in the Bryce Report[1] sitting in separate Committees would choose the Members of the Second Chamber who would sit for 12 years, one-third of them retiring at each dissolution of Parliament or every 4 years.

[1] In 1918 Lord Bryce, the Liberal statesman and former Ambassador to Washington, had been appointed chairman of a joint conference, selected from members of the two Houses of Parliament, to report on the reform of the House of Lords. Owing to the wide differences of opinion in the conference, the report took the unusual form of a letter from the chairman to the Prime Minister, Lloyd George, putting forward a somewhat complicated plan for constituting a second chamber of some 330 members by indirect election or nomination, and indicating the arguments for and against the more controversial parts of the plan.

Hereditary peers on the panel but not elected to the reformed House of Lords would be entitled to sit and speak but not to vote in that Chamber. In addition to the elected peers of Parliament, the Princes of the Blood, Spiritual Peers and Law Lords would for all purposes be members of the Assembly.

The advantage of a scheme on these lines was that it would provide an Assembly based on and moving with the national will, different in character from the House of Commons but fully capable of properly using the Referendum. The scheme requires no new machinery, retains the form and much of the substance of the existing House of Lords, and at the same time gives a chance of that constitutional equality which the Parties of the Left demanded.

THE CHANCELLOR OF THE EXCHEQUER did not believe that election by Local Authorities would give either a strong or a representative basis for the Second Chamber. The Labour Party could never secure effective representation by this means. Moreover to give the Local Authorities this power must inevitably affect the whole character of Local Government. Either elections to the County Councils will be conducted on political lines or the House of Lords will be based on an electoral choice having no relation to the questions on which they will be called upon to deliberate.

Winston S. Churchill: Cabinet memorandum

(Churchill papers: 22/60)

17 November 1925
Confidential

HOUSE OF LORDS REFORM

1. To deal successfully with large controversies it is important to understand the reasoning and feelings of opponents. In the pre-war dispute between two historic Parties, who did not disagree about fundamentals, the grievance of the Liberals against the House of Lords might be summed up in the words 'Constitutional inequality'. Their objection was not so much to a brake to put on the wheel, but that this brake was in the hands of one particular Party and was applied only in accordance with one view of the national interests. Thus the Education Bill of 1902 and the Licensing Bill of 1904 were passed without demur by the House of Lords, although these measures were certainly not before the country in 1900, and pledges had been given that the mandate of a war Election would not be used for ordinary

Party purposes: whereas as soon as the Liberals were returned with an enormous majority, their similar measures, although they had formed part of the controversies on which the nation had pronounced, were immediately mutilated or destroyed.

This, it was argued, divided the State into two sets of citizens each numbering many millions, one of which possessed superior and the other inferior rights under the Constitution; and this was denounced as invidious, contrary to the spirit of the Constitution, and dangerous to good government. In practice it appeared that the House of Lords' brake was turned on and turned off, not as a result of deliberations in the Chamber, but in accordance with decisions taken by the leaders of the Conservative Party, who naturally thought the success of their Party was identical with the national welfare.

Nothing could prevent this controversy from going forward to some sort of solution. It afforded at once an irritant and a unifying bond to all the so-called Progressive forces in the country. Liberal Governments had the solid advantages of official power without losing much of the popularity inherent in opposition. They were in a position to say: 'This law is good and we have passed it; that law is evil, but the House of Lords will not let us sweep it away.' In my opinion the action of the House of Lords and the antagonism to it in the country were the main cause of the continued Liberal ascendancy in the years before the war, in spite of the preponderating Conservative instincts of the English people. The operation of the Parliament Act would for the first time have stripped the Liberals of their grievance and, with their grievance, of their advantage. It was on the threshold of this phase in our Constitutional history that we were all plunged into the Great War.

2. The situation which we now survey is vastly changed. One of the historic Parties has been destroyed as a potential governing instrument. The caprice of the electoral laws has reduced the representation of this Party out of all proportion to its popular strength. All the forces of the Left previously contained within the Liberal fold have rejected the traditional guidance and formed a new, immense and rapidly growing Party composed of millions of our own fellow-countrymen, who nevertheless espouse and proclaim doctrines fundamentally subversive, not only of the State and of the Empire, but of economic civilisation.

3. Meanwhile changes scarcely less far-reaching have occurred in the Conservative Party. The franchise has been extended and is now nearly universal. The final step will not be long delayed.[1] All the old questions which formed the basis of pre-war Party warfare have been settled in one way or another by the joint action of Conservatives and Liberals. The Conservative

[1] Under the 1928 Equal Franchise Act, the voting age of women was lowered from 30 (as established by the 1918 Representation of the People Act) to 21.

Party has adapted itself to this new basis with remarkable success, and no one who knows the present House of Commons can doubt that the Conservative Members reflect the intensely democratic character of the modern franchise. On the other hand the extension of the franchise has greatly strengthened the forces of the Left at the expense of those of the Centre. In the nick of time the presiding genius of the British Empire removed the hostile Irish element from Westminster.[1]

4. But though the whole face of politics has been completely transformed, the Constitutional questions connected with the Reform of the House of Lords will, I believe, raise an issue which, though differently circumstanced, will not be wholly dissimilar to the pre-war issue. The mass of Liberals will make common cause with the Socialists in resisting what they will call an attempt 'to load the dice' against what, even in the favourable circumstances of the last Election, constituted the larger part of the electorate. The cry for 'equal rights under the Constitution for all His Majesty's subjects' will make a formidable appeal to those forces of logic and justice inherent in the human heart, for the satisfaction of which so many wasteful conflicts have been waged.

Because I regard effectual resistance to Socialism—revolutionary or evolutionary—as a prime duty for those who wish to preserve the greatness of Britain, because I am ready to take all measures which circumstances may require to avert the establishment of a Socialist tyranny, I feel profoundly the need not only for prudence in the degree of action, but for continued contact with Constitutional equality. We are confronted with the steady increase of forces which will deprive us, not only of national greatness and prosperity, but of individual freedom. We shall be safe only as long as we march along the high road of fair play to all parties.

5. So long as the changes proposed to be made in the powers of the House of Lords are not important and do not challenge the main structure of the Parliament Act, viz, the right of the House of Commons to legislate freely within the lifetime of a single Parliament, no serious question is raised about the composition of the House of Lords. But the moment it is proposed to arm the House of Lords with a power so far reaching as the Referendum (a measure which, if other conditions are satisfactory, I am prepared to support), the composition of the House of Lords becomes the main issue in a great controversy.

There are millions of people outside the Conservative Party who wish to be protected against sudden, violent, irreparable changes in the structure of

---

[1] Within a month of the British General Election of December 1918, the Sinn Fein MPs, 76 in all, refused to take their seats in the Westminster Parliament, and sat, instead, in an assembly of their own in Dublin.

the State and of society, who would not be prepared to entrust this protection to the leaders at any given period of the Conservative Party. If these great powers are assumed by the Chamber of review, that Chamber must be placed upon a national and not upon a Party basis, and must be so clothed with representative authority and animated by the public will as to be above sectional partisanship. For otherwise it will be said:

'No sooner have you extended the franchise than you seek to take away with one hand what you have given with the other. While everyone is urging the Socialist masses to proceed by the Constitutional path rather than by direct action, and while these masses are themselves being continually assimilated by our wonderful Parliamentary system, you are introducing a Constitutional change the object of which is to prevent the Labour Party from ever having an equal opportunity of governing the country. A Labour Government might have every one of its important measures sent to a direct vote of the people, while the Conservative Government could pass legislation abolishing all the privileges of Trade Unions, or introducing conscription, or limiting the franchise, with the certainty that it would pass immediately into law.'

Such a controversy would be deeply injurious in the long run to Conservative interests. On the other hand we must have some provision in the Constitution which will prevent the violent and revolutionary overturn by legislative action of the whole basis of society, and obviate the danger of a resort to force such as has occurred in various European countries.

6. These general observations are an indispensable preliminary to the consideration of the composition of the House of Lords as a Second Chamber capable of wielding the power of Referendum.

An authoritative Second Chamber can of course be erected on the basis of direct election. This character would not be lost if the franchise were different; if, for instance, it represented the views of all classes and parties of electors over a certain age, say thirty or thirty-five. It would then have an authority not indeed co-equal with the House of Commons, but a different measure of the same kind of authority. Again, a system of election based on grouped Constituencies or on proportional representation, apart from or combined with any alteration in the age for the franchise, would not be open to any objection on the score of class or party inequality.

But coming from theoretical principle to practical considerations, a system of direct election would certainly not meet the highest requirements of good government. Many of the elements on which the dignity or wisdom of a Second Chamber depends would never face the whirlpool of popular election. The idea of a Chamber of Elder Statesmen, in itself inherently sound, just and logical, would never play its part under such a system. The Second

Chamber would be very like the First. The exigencies of electioneers would rule it in as great a degree. The State and Empire would not gain the invaluable influence of age, experience and pre-eminence in the varied walks of life. Nor would it possess that detached view, or that superiority to passing moods and vulgar errors inseparable from a great senate. We shall not find the solution of our problems in any system of direct election.

7. The next question is the choice between nomination and indirect election. It is difficult to believe that a nominated Chamber could ever have the authority necessary to wield so powerful an instrument as the Referendum, or indeed the immense existing powers of the Parliament Act. The present House of Lords, in spite of every anomaly and defect, stands as an august institution of the Realm, second only to the Monarchy itself. But once a chasm has been cut between past and present and it is sought to create a new Assembly with novel powers and new relationships, mere nomination would be found a trumpery foundation. The nominated 'Senators', or whatever they were called, would owe their position solely to the favour of a Party leader. The hereditary sanction would be entirely lacking. The Monarchy would be deprived of the patriarchate without having in its place a body which rested either upon ancient or modern sanctions.

8. If we are to leave the venerable, if somewhat crumbled, rock on which the House of Lords now stands, there is no safe foothold until we come to an elected Chamber.

We have discussed various modes of indirect election, of which the two most practicable seem at present to be election by the County Councils or County Boroughs, or election, as proposed in the Bryce Report, by the House of Commons. It is hard to believe that election by the County Councils or Boroughs, or by groups of them, would afford either a strong or a representative basis for the Second Chamber. How could it produce a body which in any period we can now foresee would afford effective representation to the Labour Party? The County Councils are overwhelmingly Conservative. In the County Boroughs Liberals and Conservatives are increasingly combining against Labour; and this process will certainly continue. A Second Chamber elected by the County Councils would be denounced as unrepresentative of the national wish and as an appanage of the Conservative Party. Such a plan would encounter the hostility of all outside the regular Conservative ranks.

9. I imagine that serious objections would also be taken to making local authorities the instrument by which one branch of the legislature is produced. It would be said that this distorted their purpose and could not fail to transform their character and the character of their elections. The whole procedure of electing Peers by County Councils or grouped County Councils

will be found fraught with many difficulties in practical working. The spectacle of members of the House of Lords competing against each other all over the country for the good graces of County and Borough Councils seems very odd. A much more powerful and dignified basis is needed. If grouped County and Borough Councils are used, some difficulties disappear. But then, on the other hand, a number of other difficulties connected with the convening of these hitherto unassociated bodies would immediately arise.

Finally, what is the escape from the following dilemma? Either the County Councils will be elected for national purposes, in which case the whole character of local government is transformed; or the new House of Lords will sit as a consequence of an electoral choice which has no relation to the matters upon which they are to deliberate. How could a body elected on such an irrelevant basis wield a moral authority comparable with that which antiquity and custom give to the present Assembly?

10. These rejections lead to the proposal that the House of Commons should be used for the purpose of choosing the members of the House of Lords. This idea, after all, has the advantage of being familiar to the public through the Recommendations of the Bryce Committee. It therefore has behind it a certain sanction of moderate non-Party, and liberal public opinion. If the House of Lords wishes to base itself in some way or other upon the national will in political matters, how in existing circumstances, apart from direct election, can it achieve this result otherwise than through the House of Commons? It is admitted on all hands that the new House of Lords could not select itself out of its own body in a satisfactory manner. It is also agreed that direct election is unsuitable. What else remains? Contact must either be retained with long tradition or established with the modern electorate. Why should it be thought derogatory to the House of Lords to be chosen by the representatives of twenty million electors?

The House of Commons in this respect would be doing the House of Lords the service, which only they can do, of putting them in contact with the authority of the electorate. Still less can I understand the argument that such a principle is derogatory when it is put forward by those who favour the Peerage of Britain dancing attendance upon the present various local bodies. Moreover, the machinery in the case of election by the House of Commons would be swift, simple and convenient. The choosing body would not only wield and confer the authority of the whole electorate, but also it would be well informed. Men's reputations and services are fairly well known at Westminster. If the system were once accepted, each of the organised parties would be anxious to have the most effective and respectable representation possible; and there can be no doubt that the whole influence of the leaders of each Party and their powerful organisations would be used to secure creditable lists. Thus the quality of the Second Chamber would be effectually sustained.

11. But if the choosing body is to have an unlimited choice, how can we ensure any long-lasting representation of the present Peerage? Apart from influence exerted by the organization of the Conservative Party, there would be no force tending to the selection of Peers. The older Peers and the great mass who do not take much interest in politics would soon drift out of the public view. The Peerage, shorn of all connection with legislative function, would sink, as in France, to a mere titled class divorced from all connection with Government. In fact any system of election which does not in the first instance operate upon the hereditary Peerage spells nothing less than the obliteration of that order as a political reality. Such reasoning leads to the conclusion that the choice of the House of Commons (or other choosing body) must be limited, and must operate mainly within the limits of the existing Peerage.

However, the existing Peerage is overwhelmingly Conservative, and a choice so limited would give no opportunity to the Liberal or the Labour Party to find suitable representatives for their opinions. Moreover, some worthy people do not care about titles, and the multiplication of hereditary Peerages to suit the changing requirements of political parties would be absurd. Therefore, if the hereditary peerage is to serve as the body upon which the selection is to be exercised, it must first of all be allied with other elements of distinction fairly representative of the nation as a whole. It is this process of reasoning which leads to what is called 'The Panel'. The House of Lords has in fact to be reformed by being made much larger and far more representative of the whole country, and from this House so reformed there should be chosen a smaller working body associated with the movements of the electorate to transact public business.

Having now traced the successive steps by which my own thought has moved on this question, I propose for discussion the following plan.

12. The House of Lords to consist of 315 members to be chosen from a panel of 1,200. The panel to consist of all the hereditary Peerage and of all the Privy Council present and future, and, in addition, of persons who have filled certain important Public or Municipal offices (such as Chairman of a County Council, Lord Mayor, Lord Provost, Chairman of a Royal Commission, &c), or who have sat twelve years in the House of Commons; and lastly, of persons nominated to the panel by the Crown on the advice of the Joint Committee of Privileges (proposed to be set up to decide what are money bills), which Committee shall be charged expressly with the duty of making sure that the panel contains the names of at least sufficient persons of all political opinions to enable any Party to select its quota therefrom. This

Committee would have power to exceed the number of 1,200 to the extent of 300, should such expansion be necessary to carry out the aforesaid object.

As soon as possible after a General Election the Members of the House of Commons for the fifteen areas specified in the Bryce Report, sitting in separate Committees, should each choose [by proportional representation] in the first instance twenty-one members of the Second Chamber, and thereafter seven, from those persons whose names are on the Peerage panel.

Those persons so elected shall become Peers of Parliament for twelve years, subject to the following condition:—One-third, selected by ballot, shall retire at each dissolution of Parliament [or every four years, whichever period is the shorter].

No person (Peer or Commoner) shall be placed on the panel against his wish, and any person not chosen from the panel to serve in any Parliament may retire from the panel, and after retiring shall be eligible to vote or sit in the House of Commons.

Any hereditary Peer who allows his name to remain upon the panel, but is not elected a 'Peer of Parliament', may, notwithstanding all the foregoing, sit and speak, but not vote, in all the proceedings of the House of Lords.

In addition to the 315 elected Peers of Parliament, the Princes of the Blood and the Bishops (possibly reduced in number) and the Law Lords shall be for all purposes members of the Assembly.

13. It is submitted that a scheme on the above lines or some variant of it meets a great many of the conflicting desiderata:—

First, it provides an Assembly which rests on and moves, albeit slowly, with the national will; and which, in times of political stress with frequent General Elections, would increasingly adapt itself to the settled purposes of the electorate.

Secondly, it provides an Assembly of notables different in character from the House of Commons, fully capable of wielding the responsible power of arresting legislation subject to the right of the Government to demand a Referendum.

Thirdly, it sets up no expensive, novel or inconvenient machinery, and no new ceremonial and hardly any new nomenclature.

Fourthly, it secures the effective representation in the House of Lords, if they so desire it, of all the vital elements in the present Assembly.

Fifthly, while securing contact with the whole electorate, it exposes no one to the strain and burden of electioneering.

Sixthly, it makes the smallest possible change in appearances.

Seventhly, it enables all the hereditary Peers, and particularly the younger Peers, to take their part in the debates of the Assembly as they do now, and thus affords them a platform from which the younger men can make themselves known.

Eighthly, it is fair to all Parties in accordance with their numerical House of Commons strength, as evidenced in successive elections.

*   *   *   *   *

14. Even the above scheme contains the defect of undue influence by the party machines, and with the best will in the world to solve the problem, everyone who tries must feel the obstinacy of the objections to every plan.

This leads me to wonder whether it may not be easier to deal with the subject if the sphere of action were greatly enlarged and if other institutions besides the House of Lords were brought into the discussion. I therefore take as a fresh starting point the Lord Chancellor's amplification of the Brycc Committee's proposal for sixteen electoral colleges to be composed of the local Peers and Members of Parliament with representatives of the County Council, &c. If it were necessary to create larger units of local government for the purpose of selecting a Second Chamber, would it not be worth while to keep them in being for other purposes as well?

The need for larger units of local government is deep and obvious. The two most active commercial nations, before the War, Germany and the United States, conducted their affairs by means of scores of powerful local governments woven together in a federal system, and in the United States at any rate these local units are the foundation of the Senate. The attempt to transact all affairs small and great at Westminster is attended by grave inconveniences, nor can a Parliament charged with such a multiplicity of business really fulfil the functions of an Imperial or even of a national assembly. Every thinking man must be struck with the extreme shallowness of the rivulets by which Parliament is fed with personalities. The overwhelming power of party machinery is at once a proof of the weakness of our political life and the only means by which such weakness can be shielded. Quite apart from any question of the House of Lords there has long been a need for the erection of far larger, more powerful and more strongly characteristic local bodies than any we have yet devised, except in London or in Northern Ireland.

15. Suppose we had sixteen units on the same scale as the London County Council, whether they were called Provincial Councils or Local Parliaments, representing all the well marked historical and geographical areas of Great Britain, should we not vary, enrich and strengthen our public life in a remarkable degree? Would a career not be offered of far greater interest and importance to persons of wide local influence? Would not the Imperial Government find itself recruited and invigorated by a continuous flow of

men who had attained eminence in national counsels not merely by House of Commons sword-play or successful electioneering, aided by Party machinery, but also by records of administrative achievement, by years of service and of proved capacity in powerful local bodies? We have not seen, since the days of Mr Joseph Chamberlain, a man attain the first rank in politics by municipal service and move like him quite easily and naturally from the head of a great municipal body to a situation in the Cabinet.[1] I have for twenty years wished to see Great Britain equipped with modern bodies of great local authority. I believe such a system might be attended by a diminution in the multiplicity of elections and by much simplification over the whole field of local government.

16. By another road we are led simultaneously to the same conclusion. The time has come when it is urgent to re-cast the relation of Imperial and local finance, both revenue and expenditure. The present system of percentage grants, where the central government provides the greater part and the local bodies spend all the money, is condemned as being wasteful in the last degree. The spending by one authority of funds provided by another is bound to be subversive of thrifty housekeeping.

The Minister of Health is moving with a very great body of argument towards the establishment of a 'block grant' system which cannot, however, be achieved until 1928 or 1929. The question arises, ought we not to go further? Ought we not to lay our foundations deeper and broader and raise up a far more spacious structure of local government? Ought we not to build up these larger local bodies and confer upon them responsibilities and powers much beyond those which are devolved at present? Ought we not to assign them, together with the discharge of these responsibilities, a share in revenues they do not now possess, but which revenues rise or fall with the general prosperity of the nation? Would not the Imperial Exchequer be relieved of ill-adjusted burdens at the same time as the Imperial Parliament was relieved of ill-assorted and disproportionate functions? Is not this a path along which great and memorable reform might well be achieved by a Conservative Administration? Is there not a storey missing in the fabric of our national life? Could not the top-heavy character of the present structure be remedied and the whole edifice vastly strengthened if the missing storey were properly built in? Would this reform not afford a sphere in which the Peers through their local influence might acquire new and full authority in the Provinces as a compensation for a partial diminution of old rights at the centre?

17. Lastly, might not a policy on these lines, occupying the mind of the

[1] Joseph Chamberlain had been elected Mayor of Birmingham in 1873, 1874 and 1875. In 1880 he joined Gladstone's second administration as President of the Board of Trade.

present Parliament, afford an opportunity of presenting the reform of the House of Lords, not as an isolated episode in our constitutional history, designed to be a check on the results of popular election and democratic franchise, but as an integral part in a broad and salutary reconstruction of our constitutional machinery, affecting beneficially both Houses of Parliament and every aspect of our public life? In so wide a treatment of the problem the old controversies about Lords and Commons would fall into their proper place and cease to exercise the same dominance upon our view; and at the same time might we not bring into closer harmony ancient forms and modern realities? Might not the evolution be at once conservative (with a small c) and democratic, and leave our country far better fitted to surmount the ever-growing complexities and stresses of scientific civilisation?

18. Into such a policy the question of the Reform of the House of Lords would fall as follows:—

The local Parliaments, like the States of the American Union, would choose the Second Chamber. The Panel from which they should choose would be their own members *plus* the hereditary peerage. In practice of course those Peers who concerned themselves with local affairs, sat in the local Parliaments, and carried great weight in their counties and districts, as well as those who played an active part in the national politics, would have a great and desirable advantage over those who rested in retirement; but the connection between the Hereditary Peerage and legislative function would be preserved, and new roads of useful service opened in which men might prove their capacity. The constituencies of the Peers would be the local Parliaments, of which they might or might not be members, as they desired. A man could be a member simultaneously of either House of Parliament and of the local Parliament. Thus over the whole area—House of Lords, House of Commons and local Parliaments—there would be, within prescribed limits, a free movement, and no one who felt ability to enter the public service would be deprived of a real and useful field.

19. The Second Chamber resulting from such a process would be competent in every respect to exercise the power of referring all changes which it deemed to be profound to the vote of the whole people. While preserving a conservative (with a small c) character, while being wholly different from the House of Commons, differently composed, with elections differently timed, it would, nevertheless, reflect another facet of the national will and afford a guarantee to the whole nation against violent change either in the direction of Communist Revolution or Fascist reaction.

Far reaching as these projects may seem, I do not believe that in achievement they would require more than the two or three years at our disposal.

WSC

Winston S. Churchill to Stanley Baldwin

(Baldwin papers)

17 November 1925   Treasury Chambers

My dear Prime Minister,

Referring to our conversation last night about business, I feel that you will be on very strong ground in refusing to give any time for debates on general topics except in cases where it can be shown that it will be unfair to the House to make them wait until the Debate on the Address in February. The Debate on the Address has always been intended to be the vehicle for all these kinds of challenges to questions of policy; and in an autumn session it is, in my judgment, contrary to the spirit of Parliamentary procedure to anticipate the impending debates in the Address to the Crown at the beginning of a new session. A case like the Administration of Justice controversy arising suddenly and urgently fully justifies a special debate. So also do Locarno and Rosyth and Pembroke. The Coal Subsidy must have one, on account of the finance. But Mosul, Unemployment in general, Debt Settlements and National Expenditure ought all to wait their turn in the Debate on the Address, and cannot be prejudiced by so doing.

Yours vy sincerely,
Winston S. Churchill

Lord Beaverbrook to Winston S. Churchill

(Churchill papers: 2/142)

17 November 1925

My dear Winston,

Many thanks for your letter. I will tell you my exact attitude—though I expect you will think that I deceive myself.

I have no personal ill-feeling against Baldwin whatsoever. I have never felt the slightest rancour. I simply think of him in exactly the same terms that you and I did (this is not a debating score) in 1923. You take a 1925 view of him, whereas I remain fixed in my 1923 and 1924 opinion. It is quite possible or probable that you are right and I am wrong; but my judgment then had, and my judgment now has, nothing to do with personal feelings. It is based on a cold analysis of public qualities.

As to my opposition to you, you know very well that it is not a personal matter at all. I felt very strongly about the return to the Gold Standard and fought you for that reason.

Now that controversy is for good or ill definitely settled, for there can be no going back. The damage is done or the good accomplished, according to our separate viewpoints. Putting that issue aside, my political attitude to your next measures depend on what I think about them. They depend on the future policy of the Government. I have simply been fighting for the things I believe in. My fundamental beliefs are well known and I shall not put them in this letter.

Believe me, I would far rather be in harmony with than opposed to a Conservative executive. But if I am expected to conform blindly to anything that executive may choose to do, however wrong I may think it, I would rather go back to my own little village in Canada—where there is good fishing.[1]

I admired your bit of imagery about the shepherd, his sheep and the wolf. Do not believe too much in some of the sheep that are in the pasture with you. The wolf does not bite—just howls.

The Baldwin Budget was published on the 17th April 1923—the campaign was carried on for many days. You dined at the Embassy Club on the 19th.

Anyhow I think our correspondence has cleared up the points mentioned in the book.

Do not bother to answer this letter.

Yours sincerely,
Max

Cabinet Standing Committee on Expenditure: minutes

(*Churchill papers: 22/50*)

18 November 1925
Secret

THE GRANT FOR MARKETING EMPIRE FOOD PRODUCTS IN BRITAIN

THE CHANCELLOR OF THE EXCHEQUER stated that while there was no question of any departure in principle from the pledges which had been given, there should also be no question of squandering money merely for the purpose of satisfying the letter of the pledges. He suggested that the Government should decide that money would be provided next year only to the extent for which reasonable and acceptable schemes can be produced,

---

[1] Beaverbrook had been born in the parish of Maple, Ontario. Before his first birthday, his parents moved to Newcastle, New Brunswick, a township with 1,500 inhabitants, on the Miramichi river.

that the provision made in 1926/27 should be limited to £500,000 and that if the experiment was found satisfactory the full provision should be made in 1927/28. After emphasizing the serious set back to trade revival of any increase in taxation and pointing out various directions in which he had met the wishes of the Secretary of State for the Dominions[1] in financial matters, he made a special appeal for the acceptance of his proposals in regard to this particular item of expenditure.

THE CHANCELLOR OF THE EXCHEQUER stated categorically that no question could arise as to any provision being made for the service in the present financial year, nor would he in any circumstances agree to the proposal that unexpended balances of the grant should be carried forward from year to year. He would not accept any scheme for spending money unless it was one which reasonable business men would enthusiastically support.

UNEMPLOYMENT INSURANCE

THE CHANCELLOR OF THE EXCHEQUER stated that the decision to be taken on the Ministry of Labour Provisional Estimates was of decisive importance. There was no question here of diminishing the benefits of an existing social service. What was proposed was an alteration of the basis of calculating the Exchequer contribution. The Treasury would assume full responsibility for the consequences of their proposals. The Ministry's Estimates were based on an estimated average live register for the financial year 1926/27 of 1,250,000; on this basis the estimated Exchequer contribution for that year was £17,265,000, representing an average payment of 12/8¼d per person per week in respect of 1,250,000 unemployed.

The actual number of unemployed on 2nd November 1925 was 1,207,700. After pointing out that the unemployment curves for 1922, 1923 and 1924 were very similar and that special factors such as the coal situation accounted for the abnormality of 1925, the Chancellor of the Exchequer advised the Committee to disregard the 1925 curve and base the 1926 unemployment estimate on deductions to be drawn from the uniform tendencies of the preceding years. The Committee would observe from the Table at the head of page 4 of Part II of NE 12, that the average live registers of the years 1922/23, 1923/24 and 1924/25 were 87% of the November figures for 1921, 1922 and 1923 respectively. If this average decline of 13% was applied to

[1] L. S. Amery (who was also Secretary of State for the Colonies).

the November 1925 figure (1,207,700) an estimated average figure of 1,050,000 would result for 1926/27.

There was no reason to suppose that trade generally would be worse next year than in 1925, on the contrary, with the exception of the heavy trades there was a general steady improvement; the Revenue figures were being well maintained; the Exchange conditions were more favourable and Germany's competitive capacity was receding. Good harvests throughout the world were another encouraging feature of the outlook.

Of course the situation would be entirely altered if a great labour crisis developed next Spring. This might indeed involve an increase of direct taxation and a return to War budgeting. The best chance of averting a crisis next Spring would be a trade revival and nothing would chill such a revival so much as the fear of a reimposition of taxation.

Provided the Unemployment estimate was taken at 1,050,000 and not 1,250,000, a saving in the Exchequer contribution of £5¼ millions could, in his opinion, be obtained in 1926/27 and yet leave a substantial balance on the year. Even if the number of unemployed in 1926/27 exceeded the Treasury estimate by 100,000 the deficit on the Fund for the year would be relatively small.

The justification for his proposals were the serious financial situation; the reduction in unemployment and the Coal Subsidy. A great coal strike in August last would have added enormously to the liabilities of the Fund. If it should be decided to estimate for 1,050,000 unemployed as proposed, legislation will be necessary and the necessary clauses could be incorporated in the contemplated Economy Provisions Bill.

Winston S. Churchill: departmental minute

(*Churchill papers: 22/55*)

19 November 1925

I think we should oppose this altogether.[1] It is of course impossible to decide finally until we know the Boundary Commission's award. We ought not to encourage people to migrate. If there are some who think they are in danger of their lives, they ought not to be treated any better than the Loyalists in Southern Ireland generally. Please marshal a case. There can be no question of this matter being considered by a Sub-Committee of the

---

[1] A proposal by Sir William Joynson-Hicks, the Home Secretary, to pay compensation 'to persons transferred from Northern Ireland under the Boundary award'.

Irish Committee of the Cabinet. It must be considered by the Treasury, and decided upon by the whole Cabinet.

Let me have a table showing the finance of Ulster towards the United Kingdom since the passing of the 1920 Act, showing: (a) the contribution agreed for each year and its revisions, (b) the counter-payments, and (c) the resulting balance; together with forecasts for the next two years. This table should include the latest economies in the cost of the public buildings.

WSC

Winston S. Churchill: note

(*Churchill papers: 22/55*)

19 November 1925

The proposal of the Home Secretary that 'compensation' should be paid out of British funds to persons who may suffer 'direct financial loss' as the result of a transfer of territory under the award of the Boundary Commission is likely to have far-reaching consequences. The grant of compensation for the results of a change in the form of government within His Majesty's Dominions seems to be a novel thing and it will be difficult to maintain the view that persons who were adversely affected by the establishment of the Irish Free State have no similar claim to consideration.

It is surely a paradox to assert that persons in Northern Ireland will 'find themselves transferred without warning to the Free State', whereas residents in the 26 Counties have known for years that their political future was in jeopardy. On the contrary any persons likely to be affected by the Boundary award have now had four years' warning of the possibility, while residents in the 26 counties had only a few months' notice of the likelihood of so fundamental a change as the establishment of the Free State. All that the latter had previously any reason to expect was the grant to Ireland of some form of limited Home Rule, and the Government of Ireland Act, which was in fact the law up to the signing of the Treaty, reserved to Imperial control, either permanently or for varying periods, such important matters as the main forms of taxation, the judiciary, the police and Land legislation.

The Home Secretary refers, by way of example, to landowners who will get less favourable terms under the Free State Land Act of 1923 than under the recent Northern Ireland Land Act. It is necessary to remember that the Southern Irish landlords claim a grant of at least £5 millions from the British Exchequer as compensation for the difference between Free State terms and Convention terms which they contend the Government of 1920 promised to carry into effect before the Treaty. Their claim is powerfully supported in the House of Lords, and Lord Oranmore and Browne[1] has a motion on the paper on the subject.

Many ex-Royal Irish Constables and others were compelled to leave Southern Ireland in 1922 and thereby sustained financial losses, including in a number of cases property or businesses for which they have received little or no compensation. It will be difficult to convince such sufferers that their claims are weaker than those of Northern Irish Special Constables. The Government have still to await the report of the recently established Committee on the Southern Loyalists who claim additional compensation from the British Exchequer for actual destruction of their property since the Truce.

It can hardly be doubted that the admission of any right to compensation for consequences of Boundary changes would greatly strengthen the foregoing claims. Moreover any precise definitions of the expression 'direct financial loss' (to which the Home Secretary appears to attach a wide meaning), or of the persons who should be regarded as entitled to compensation would be extremely difficult.

The Irish Grants Committee was set up to give ex-gratia assistance to refugees who had been forced to fly from Ireland for safety and who were in genuine distress. It has never been empowered to award compensation to such persons for their losses and it is suggested that its procedure affords no precedent for the present proposal.

Cabinet Committee on Civil Research: minutes

(Churchill papers: 22/46)

19 November 1925
Secret

POSITION OF THE IRON AND STEEL INDUSTRY

MR CHURCHILL agreed that it was not possible then to discuss either the political aspect of the question or the conditions created by the Government pledges in regard to this matter. He welcomed, however, the statement of the President of the Board of Trade[2] that the White Paper setting out the

---

[1] Geoffrey Henry Browne Browne, 1861–1927. Succeeded his father as 3rd Baron Oranmore and Browne (Ireland), 1900. A Member of the Irish Convention, 1917–18. Elected a Senator for Southern Ireland, 1921. Privy Councillor, Ireland, 1921. A Representative Peer for Ireland. Created Baron Mereworth (United Kingdom), 1926. Owner of some 8,000 acres: he lived at 21 Portland Place, London; Mereworth Castle, Kent; and Castle MacGarrett, County Mayo.

[2] Sir Philip Cunliffe-Lister.

procedure to be followed in the Safeguarding of Industries Act gave the Government full power, even if a *primâ facie* case had been established, to refuse to grant an enquiry on the ground of the probable repercussions on other industries of a Safeguarding duty. He had firmly relied on this provision when the terms of the White Paper were under consideration. The express object of that provision had, in his view, been to enable the Government to avoid being forced to give lop-sided Protection or, by being led into a large number of consequential duties, to break their pledges on the question of Free Trade. He believed that it was open to the Government to refuse the Steel Industry's application for a Safeguarding enquiry on the ground of repercussion, and in his opinion this was the course which ought to be adopted.

Many of the witnesses who had appeared before the Committee were deeply and legitimately interested in the manufacture of steel, and there was no doubt that they would obtain great and immediate advantages from a duty. The Committee had also considered evidence from the Re-Rollers, from the shipowners (but not from the shipbuilders, so far as the tariff aspect of the problem was concerned) and from the engineering industry. He felt sure, however, that if there was a public discussion there would be a great marshalling of the interests affected who would demand compensation or corresponding Protection. The experience of the Silk Duty had convinced him that Protection to the last iota would be demanded by interests affected if it were once decided to protect raw steel. This would raise an economic controversy of the first consequence.

The cyclical periods of depression through which the steel industry had successfully emerged in the past was striking. As far back as 1884 Lord Randolph Churchill had proclaimed the immediate ruin of the steel trade, and the same arguments had been put forward in the great controversy in 1903. As regards the present depression, he believed that, if more prudent councils had prevailed in the years 1919 and 1920, when large profits had been made, many of the present difficulties would have been avoided. Many of the chief steel companies had, however, made immense distributions of profits in the form of bonus shares. Clearly, if these profits had been carried to reserve, these firms would have been in a better position than they are to-day to meet world competition.

A paper recently circulated to the Committee (CR (H) 43) showed that Professor Bone, FRS,[1] held the view that it was probable that the world

[1] William Arthur Bone, 1871–1938. Lecturer in Chemistry, Owens College, Manchester, 1898–1905. Professor of Applied Chemistry, Leeds University, 1905–12. Chief Professor, and Head of the Department of Chemical Technology, Imperial College, London, 1912–36. Chairman of the British Association Committee on Fuel Economy, 1915–22. Consultant to the Government Fuel Research Board, 1917–18. Medallist of the Royal Society of Arts for his work on brown coals and lignites, 1922. Fellow of the Royal Society.

appetite for steel would increase within a comparatively short period, and some statisticians even held that this country might in time be faced with a labour famine. For these reasons he did not accept the view that without assistance by the Government the British steel industry would pass away. He was not convinced that any defence interests were involved to the extent of making Government action essential. The proper way to assist the industry was to lead them along the path of further concentration. This would involve amalgamation, either general or by regions, the setting up of an effective selling organisation, and the distribution of orders among the most profitable works. The Government should, he considered, refuse to grant a Safeguarding enquiry, but at the same time indicate their willingness to help the industry, perhaps through the Trade Facilities procedure, towards securing further amalgamation. It was obvious that until the question of Safeguarding was definitely settled, the industry would take no steps towards that end.

He wished to record his opinion that it was impossible to grant a Safeguarding enquiry owing to its indirect reactions on other industries, but that, as regards amalgamation, if the trade desired to pursue this question further, they should be assured by the Government of immediate and sympathetic consideration.

When the Safeguarding question had been disposed of, he would be glad to confer with the President of the Board of Trade and the Secretary of State for War[1] with a view to preparing a scheme or schemes of amalgamation to increase the efficiency of the trade, and thereby help them to emerge from their present difficulties, which were largely the aftermath of the War. If after their application were refused the industry were to sulk and refuse to consider the question of further concentration, the Government could only await the working of economic forces, but, even in that event, he believed that the steel industry would survive.

Cabinet Committee: minutes

(*Cabinet papers: 27/294*)

20 November 1925

AIR FORCE EXPENDITURE

MR AUSTEN CHAMBERLAIN saw no reason why the programme of expansion should not be spread over a number of years. All expansion might be held up for one year and then it could be seen how other Powers responded

---

[1] Sir Laming Worthington-Evans.

to this gesture. It might be possible to suggest a holiday in aerial armament like that proposed in the past by Mr Winston Churchill for Naval armaments.[1]

MR WINSTON CHURCHILL thought that that policy would not be applicable in this case. A sudden stop would entail organisations being broken down, and designing staffs disbanded which might have a far-reaching effect on the powers of future expansion. He drew attention to the violent alterations in policy to which the Air Service had been subjected in the past. With all his responsibilities towards the Treasury he did not wish to see violent swings in policy again. Drastic cuts were often succeeded by feverish increases which resulted in vastly enhanced expenditure. He thought the object should be to aim at an effective equality with France, and for this reason he was in favour of extending the period of the expansion. This, he was sure, was the cheapest method in the end. The present programme was due to be completed in 1931; in view of all the considerations he suggested that the period might be extended to 1940. If the Committee decided on 1940 he was confident that the Air Ministry could effect very considerable economies. Any such recommendation would not preclude a clause being inserted whereby the situation could be reviewed yearly. In his view we should never be safe or independent if we did not have a high class Air Force.

SIR SAMUEL HOARE thought that an extension of the period to 1940 would introduce much of the waste which the policy of shutting down completely involved. Buildings would be left derelict and the training of the personnel would have to be arrested. Moreover, was it possible for us to remain in so vulnerable a position for so long a time?

MR AUSTEN CHAMBERLAIN said that he did not contemplate a complete closing down such as had followed from the application of the Geddes recommendations[2] but rather that we should go on with work already in operation and should not embark on any new construction. . . .

MR WINSTON CHURCHILL stated that the Committee might decide, after hearing the views of the Foreign Secretary, that on purely international

---

[1] In April 1912, on the eve of the new German Navy Law, Churchill had proposed to the German Kaiser a 'naval holiday', whereby both Britain and Germany would agree not to embark on any new naval construction for an agreed period. The Kaiser replied that such an arrangement could only be made between allies.

[2] The rigorous expenditure cut-back recommendations of the Geddes Committee (Chaired by Sir Eric Geddes in 1921–2), and known as the 'Geddes Axe'. On 2 August 1921 the then Secretary of State for Education, H. A. L. Fisher, had written in his diary: 'PM proposes a business committee under E. Geddes to recommend economies. I oppose; so does Churchill very vehemently. Baldwin also. However the thing is carried' (*Fisher papers*). The Prime Minister at that time was Lloyd George. The Committee reported on 22 February 1922 (Command Paper 1589 of 1922).

grounds there was no reason why 1940 should not be substituted for 1931 as the date of completion of the expansion of the Air Forces but that the actual extension in time depended upon the economies which could thereby be made effective.

SIR HUGH TRENCHARD thought that so long a delay would result in a certain amount of waste. It would probably mean that at least two aerodromes and new buildings costing roughly £130,000 to £200,000 each would lie empty and derelict and one other would be only partially utilised.

SIR SAMUEL HOARE hoped that the Committee would not decide on an extension beyond the year 1935; he thought it was extending the period rather too far and there was a risk if progress was too slow of a newspaper panic being created.

Winston S. Churchill to Alfred Hurst[1] *and Donald Fergusson*[2]

(*Treasury papers: T171/250*)

22 November 1925

ROAD FUND

1. We must really go into the question of pledges. Let me have them looked up. There can be no question of the power of Parliament to sweep away the whole system of taxation and reimpose entirely new taxation, and to assign out of the yields of new taxation any sums it may choose for the upkeep of roads through any authorities, central or local.

Who ever said that the motorists were to contribute nothing for all time to the general Revenue of the country, or that, however great their luxury and wealth or the inroad they make on the convenience of pedestrians, they were to be exempt for all time through their character of motorists from the smallest contribution to our Revenue? Entertainments may be taxed; public houses may be taxed; race horses may be taxed; the possession of armorial bearings and men servants may be taxed—and the yield devoted to the

[1] Alfred William Hurst, 1884–1975. Educated at Emmanuel College, Cambridge. Entered the Treasury, 1907 (first place in the Civil Service examination); Assistant Secretary, 1921–7; CB, 1926; Principal Assistant Secretary, 1928–9; knighted, 1929; Under-Secretary, 1932. Under-Secretary for Mines, 1940–2, in charge of reconstruction. Member of the Secretariat, War Cabinet, 1942–4.

[2] John Donald Balfour Fergusson, 1891–1963. Educated at Berkhamsted School and Magdalen College, Oxford. On active service, 1914–18. Entered Treasury, 1919; Private Secretary to successive Chancellors of the Exchequer, 1920–38. Permanent Secretary, Ministry of Agriculture and Fisheries, 1936–45; Ministry of Fuel and Power, 1945–52. Knighted, 1937. One of his three sons was killed on active service in the Second World War.

general Revenue. But motorists are to be privileged for all time to have the whole yield of the tax on motors devoted to roads.

Obviously this is all nonsense. Who ever said that, whatever the yield of these taxes and whatever the poverty of the country, we were to build roads, and nothing but roads, from this yield? We might have to cripple our trade by increased taxation of income. We might have to mutilate our Education for the sake of economy. We might even be unable to pay for the upkeep of our Fleet. But never mind, whatever happens, the whole yield of the taxes on motors must be spent on roads! We might, for instance, be compelled to spend £50 millions a year on roads and be unable to find more than £20 millions a year for Education. Such contentions are absurd and constitute at once an outrage upon the sovereignty of Parliament and upon common-sense.

What were the pledges made by Mr Lloyd George when he originally introduced the tax, and what was the yield estimated to be? Were not these pledges broken in the war and all work on the roads stopped? If so, this constitutes a precedent to reinforce the obvious.

2. Another line of enquiry arises from the fatuous intervention of the Unemployment Committee in the general policy of road construction. Is it not a fact that no form of Public Work is less productive of employment for the workless than the Roads? All that happens is that large sums of money, which might otherwise relieve the general taxpayer and are therefore in every sense 'taken from him', which he would otherwise have used to give remunerative employment in every trade of the country, are devoted to keeping a comparatively small corps of road-making specialists at full, and even over, time employment.

3. We make these great roads. Everyone would like to see them made, if money was no object. But after they are made the local authorities have to keep them up, have to keep them tarred. They are not concrete as in America, but tarred with a composition the main constituents of which involves an oversea purchase from the United States prejudicially affecting our exchange.

Local authorities are encouraged to make roads above the needs of the district, in order to earn higher grants from the Road Board. Thus road expenditure and central expenditure are deliberately fomented together. In many cases local authorities undertake to make a road which is not required, which is a luxury road, the up-keep of which will afterwards form a serious charge against them, in order to get the superior grant payable from head-quarters. Are there not instances of scandalous waste, ie where it has been agreed to tar a road simply in order to get the higher grant?

You will develop all this argument, I am sure, as well as the case for the local authorities having a greater discretionary power.

Winston S. Churchill: remarks to a deputation of motorists' representatives

(Treasury papers: T161/250)

23 November 1925

ROAD FUND

Let me say clearly I have an expensive motor car and use it a great deal and I have nothing personal in my argument. . . .

I can assure you I will not be intimidated by any amount of worked up agitation or resolutions. . . . We cannot go on having super first class roads if as a result we are forced to have inferior education, or an insufficient Fleet, or could not make adequate provision for public health, or were compelled to dump some tax upon the business people of this country which would hamper the chance of a trade revival.

You mean Parliament would hesitate to tax beer, spirits, sugar, tea or anything affecting the comfort of the people, or put the income tax or super tax on if they came in contact with this particular class who have the great good fortune to rush about the Country, if they have to get permission of that class before doing anything?

Of course we have to tax all sorts of people who are not at all satisfied by it. . . .

Personally I am very glad that you have come to see me, but I rather resent the attitude of some of the newspapers which seems to proceed from an idea that you have only got to intimidate Ministers or the Government, and they will not do such a thing. . . .

I can assure you I will not be intimidated by any amount of worked up agitation or resolutions.

I think it would be a great mistake for the motoring interests to put themselves outside the ebb and flow of national fortunes.[1]

---

[1] Churchill told a further Motorists' deputation on 27 January 1926: 'If anything could reduce a politician to a proper state of submissiveness and trepidation it would be such an accumulation of representative forces as those which are gathered round this table, forces which can, from every quarter of the country, from every constituency and through every possible channel, bring their views into prominence and can influence political and parliamentary opinion. Therefore, I assure you that if I am not able in every respect to see eye to eye with all those that have spoken, it is only because other pressures, other arguments, other forces, which I cannot help feeling, lead me to take a somewhat—I will not say wider but—more general view of our problem' (*Treasury papers: T171/250*).

December 1925

Winston S. Churchill to Sir Warren Fisher

(Churchill papers: 18/13)

1 December 1925

I am obliged to you for your Minute which does not in any essential indicate a course different from that which I proposed, or throw a new light upon the problem.

It may be that among the alternatives we discussed last year was a Budget containing no remission of taxation; but this was by no means the only alternative examined in the early and very few conversations we had.

I gathered that from some points of view you thought a remission of taxation causing financial stringency later would be beneficial to the cause of economy, and put us in a strong position as against the Spending Departments who would be confronted with the certainty that taxation would have to be re-imposed unless their estimates were reduced.

One remark of yours, made on the occasion when the Budget was presented to the Cabinet Committee, rests particularly in my mind. You told me that you had 'seen the making of a great many Budgets and you never remembered one where people had not predicted all sorts of evil consequences for the second year, but that if the Budget for the first year fairly balanced, the second year nearly always worked out all right' or words to that effect.

However you need not be apprehensive that I shall seek to share my responsibilities with you or put any burden upon you which it would not be your duty to assume.

During the year I have been at the Treasury I have received scarcely any assistance from you in the very difficult task I have been endeavouring to discharge. I only recall three Minutes which dealt with Treasury business. The first a rather facetious rejection by you of some suggestion on the improving and regularizing of the form of office papers in accordance with the practice of other Departments; the second a Minute proposing to spend a considerable sum of money on the purchase in this overburdened year of recreation grounds for Civil Servants; the third showing the impossibility of any reduction in the emoluments or numbers of the Civil Service.

Sometimes as much as three months have passed without my even seeing you or receiving any official paper from you, and on any of the occasions when we have met, it has only been because I have directly summoned you.

I am well aware that you do not regard yourself in any way responsible for assisting the Chancellor of the Exchequer and that you reserve your functions entirely for the First Lord of the Treasury. You have been careful to impress this upon me and I have not challenged your interpretation of your duties. I must say however that it is an interpretation very different from that which after nearly twenty years experience in Ministerial Office I had supposed was the practice, and I cannot conceive that any of your distinguished predecessors have not been accustomed to give more constant and effective assistance to the Chancellor of the day, whether in regard to the controlling of expenditure or the framing of finance.[1] Such knowledge as I possessed led me to suppose that the Secretary to the Treasury was the right-hand man and fellow-worker of the Chancellor of the Exchequer and the leading official figure in the whole business of the Treasury.

I do not record this for the purpose of framing any complaint, because I have been most ably and loyally assisted by the very accomplished heads of the five great branches of the Treasury, for whose selection you are I believe entitled to much credit. I record these facts only because I do not think that a Minute such as you have addressed to me is couched in a tone which should be used by an official, aloof from the labour and anxiety of financial business, to the Minister who, whatever his shortcomings, has actually to conduct it. Had you chosen, and I should have welcomed it, to throw yourself wholeheartedly into the stress and strain of our work, you would not have found me at all averse to remonstrances or implied censure; but in the circumstances which actually exist, I do not consider that such fitful interventions on your part rest upon a sufficiently solid foundation of aid and guidance.

Addressing myself to the substance of your remarks, it is of course obvious that if we had not taken off 26 million of taxation this year, we should, apart from the Coal Subsidy, have had a surplus of about that amount. It would, in my opinion, have been unjustifiable to propose to take this large sum of money from the pockets of the hard-pressed tax-payer, if it was not actually needed for the approved service of the year. It was hoped that by making an early remission of taxation, some stimulus would be contributed to trade

---

[1] Sir Warren Fisher's predecessors as Permanent Secretary to the Treasury between 1903 and 1919 were Sir George Murray (1903–11), Sir Robert Chalmers (1911–13), and, as Joint Permanent Secretaries, Sir Thomas Heath (1913–19) and Sir John Bradbury (1913–19). Sir Warren Fisher remained head of the Treasury for twenty years (as well as head of the Civil Service), and was succeeded, in 1939, by Sir Horace Wilson.

revival and nothing that has happened since has led me to doubt the soundness of that view.

So far as the year 1926–27 is concerned, you speak of a deficit of 39 millions
being 'in sight'; but you know perfectly well, or you should know, that this
figure is reached only by estimating revenue at its minimum and expenditure
at the maximum unpruned demands of all Departments. An increase of 29
millions in the expenditure, assumes for instance a failure by the Admiralty
to keep their undertaking not to increase their total for this year in consequence of the cruiser programme £M 3¾. It assumes an increase for the Air
Force of £M 3. It assumes that the Ministry of Health will not reduce their
estimates by £M 2¼ which they have already agreed to do, that Agriculture
and Education will not each carry out the already agreed reductions, which
together aggregate £M 1½.

From these sources alone there is 'in sight' a reduction of £M 10¾ and
there are several important blocks of expenditure still to be examined.

On the revenue side also your assumptions are decidedly and legitimately
(having regard to the season of the year) conservative.

I am glad to learn from your Minute that you are in favour of the proposed
treatment of the Road Fund, which if handled in the way proposed by Sir
George Barstow, will very nearly efface altogether the deficit which is 'in
sight'.

In these circumstances, although our task is full of difficulty and much
very hard fighting and personal effort lies before me, there is certainly no
ground whatever for the suggestion which inspires your Minute, that some
grave miscalculation has been made which would entitle a person in your
position to exclaim 'I told you so'.

When you say that the Americans think that we are 'down and out', I
am bound to suggest to you that in this case they must be extremely ill-
informed of our affairs and that it is possible that the erroneous impression
you say they have formed, is largely due to the weak and unhelpful pessimism
in which it is fashionable at the present time to indulge.

There remains the question of the Coal Subsidy and its possible repercussion on the finance of next year. I have always regarded this as entirely outside the Budget calculations and forecasts on which I have been working.
Either the continuation of such a Subsidy or the disaster of a prolonged
general strike would of course require a complete review of our financial
measures. The decisions in this sphere lie either in the province of the
Cabinet or in events which are outside our control. Every step that we have
taken so far has received the over-whelming approval of Parliament and I
should see no difficulty in obtaining the assent of the Cabinet and Parliament
to the consequential reactions of any future decision that they may take.

In all the circumstances I see no reason to alter the indications of general Treasury policy which I gave to the responsible officials in my Minute of the 7th inst and which out of courtesy I also marked to you. That policy comprises the execution of all measures necessary to sustain the surplus of £1,100,000 available, apart from the Coal Subsidy, at the completion of the Budget Debate, but not to exceed it and to allow the Coal Subsidy accruing in this year to be met by temporary borrowing, as explained by me in the House of Commons; secondly—a continuance of the strenuous effort we are making to enforce a general reduction in the first estimates presented by the Departments, and thirdly, not to hesitate to re-impose such portion of the income tax as may be necessary (though I do not expect it) to balance the finance of next year, and lastly only to impose any novel form of taxation (many of which must be studied) for the purpose not of balancing the new Budget but of giving alternative relief to the tax-payer. With this policy I gather you are in general agreement.

Irish Boundary Commission:[1] *notes of a Conference*

(*Churchill papers: 22/56*)

1 December 1925   Treasury Board Room
12 noon
Secret

MR CHURCHILL suggested that it would be convenient if at this stage he were to state the views of the British Government in regard to Article 5. The British Government had throughout strictly adhered to the Treaty and when eighteen months ago great difficulties had arisen they had, none the less, carried legislation appointing the Boundary Commission over the head of Ulster's objections. The British Parliament had thus rigidly carried out the conditions of Article 12. There then followed the protracted labours of the Commission and the position now was that Free State Ministers were disappointed at what they understood to be that Commission's finding. He was bound to say that having now seen the map prepared by the Commission (which he had not seen when he had last seen Mr Cosgrave) he could truly say that the result of the Commission's labours was very much what he had

---

[1] The British members of the Irish Boundary Commission were Churchill (in the Chair), Lord Salisbury (Lord Privy Seal), Lord Birkenhead (Secretary of State for India), Sir John Anderson (Permanent Under-Secretary of State, Home Office), G. G. Whiskard (Assistant Secretary, Dominions Office) and P. J. Grigg (Treasury). The Irish Free State members were William Cosgrave (President of the Executive Council), Kevin O'Higgins (Vice-President) and J. O'Byrne (Attorney-General).

expected and meant when he signed the Treaty. The British Government felt that they had done everything to carry out the letter of the Treaty, and as regards the spirit of it their conscience was quite clear. They had from the beginning stated that they anticipated a finding of this character.

As regards Article 5 the Treaty was perfectly clear, when Article 12 had been disposed of, it followed under the Treaty that discussion on Article 5 should begin. It was impossible to forecast the result of the arbitration under that Article, though each side naturally had confidence in its case. The view of the British Treasury, after a full examination, was that an arbitrator might reasonably be expected to award Great Britain the sum of $155\frac{3}{4}$ million and if that sum were paid over a period of 60 years it would mean an annual annuity of £$8\frac{1}{4}$ millions at 5%. If, however, following the analogy of recent International agreements the rate of interest were reduced to $3\frac{1}{2}$%, the annuity for the same period would be $6\frac{1}{4}$ millions.

It would be a very serious step for a British Government to renounce on behalf of the British taxpayer so substantial a claim, especially at a time like the present when economy in every field of national expenditure was being rigidly carried out.

Retrenchments were being pressed in education, health, services, unemployment allowances and the armed forces of the Crown. Such economies naturally created dissatisfaction and all those affected would certainly attack the Government if the latter were to forego what they regarded as important claims of the British Government under this Article. There was not only this to be considered but there were also possible reactions to be borne in mind on the Northern Irish contribution. There was very little doubt that the waiving of Article 5 would strengthen the movement in Ulster to reduce or abolish the Northern Irish contribution.

There were also reactions in the other Dominions to be feared. Large repayments were now being made, for example by Australia, of money borrowed during the war for war purposes. Finally, there was the position of the loyalists in Southern Ireland who were very discontented at their position. They would certainly object to any waiving of British rights while the damages they had sustained had, in their view, only been met to an inconsiderable extent.

The British Government had considered this question on Monday afternoon and they took a grave and adverse view of the consequences of waiving Article 5. The British Ministers at the present meeting were not authorised to do more than open discussion and to exchange views. It would be their duty to report their discussion to the Cabinet. It was important in considering the financial position of Great Britain to remember not only the internal debt, the service of which more than covered the yield of income tax and super-tax, but also the unexampled payments amounting to £34 million per annum which were being made to the United States. The interest charged by the United States would in 1933 be increased by $\frac{1}{2}$ with a consequent annual increase of £4,400,000, in the annuities to be paid.

With this prospect in view it was essential that all the resources at the disposal of the British Government should be husbanded. There would, he believed, be an explosion of public opinion if the British Government were to abandon Article 5 although they had carried out to the letter the terms of Article 12.

MR COSGRAVE reminded the Conference that the Treaty had been signed for two purposes. In the first place it was to make peace between the South of Ireland and Great Britain and in the second place to secure peace in Ireland itself. Article 12 and the proposed Award under it gave no satisfaction either in Northern Ireland or in the Free State. He had gathered that Sir James Craig was prepared to allow Article 12 to drop. The trouble had been of twelve or fourteen years standing and had been the cause of much bitterness. Peace over the whole of Ireland as the result of agreement between Northern Ireland and the Free State was, he believed, possible. Such peace would be of importance to the British Government also.

As regards the sum of £150 (odd) million, this was based upon a total figure of £7,840 million for national debt, but of this £2,000 million were due from the Dominions and foreign countries. On this account the figure of £150 (odd) million should be at once reduced to £120 million. Assuming, however, for a moment that the arbitrator decided that an annuity of £6 millions was due by the Free State how could they possibly pay such a sum? They had not succeeded in existing circumstances in balancing their budget and they would not be able even to maintain services at the figure estimated in this year's Budget.

Irish Boundary Commission: notes of a Conference

(*Churchill papers: 22/56*)

1 December 1925   Treasury Board Room
4 pm
Secret

MR CHURCHILL thought that it was desirable to consider the question not only strictly from the financial point of view. It might be possible in that regard for the British Government to go some distance, but not as far as the Free State desired. Sir James Craig for his part might also be able to do something, but not as much as the Free State wished. A combination of the two lines of solution, namely, amelioration of the lot of the Catholics in Northern Ireland, and easement of Free State finance in relation to Article 5, might be to the interest of the Free State. He was anxious to know what ideas Free State ministers held as to the lines that assistance could take. The Prime Minister had agreed that he should discuss the question further with Sir James Craig, and for his part, he thought that this course might be more fruitful than direct negotiations between Northern Ireland and Free State Ministers.

As regards proportional representation, there were many obvious objections, and it might well be that other more satisfactory means could be devised for protecting the Catholic minority in the North, eg (though he had no authority to make such a suggestion) an arrangement might be made whereby additional members were nominated to the Northern Parliament to secure better representations of the minority.

MR CHURCHILL pointed to the tremendous payments that this country was called upon to make to America. These payments would increase in 1933. If, however, the attitude of the United States were to become less rigid, the atmosphere would be easier for this country, and it would thus place us in a position to deal more generously.

In reply to a question by LORD BIRKENHEAD, MR COSGRAVE said that if he were to accept a moratorium on the lines proposed, his action would be riddled with criticisms. He would much prefer to secure improved conditions for the Roman Catholics in Northern Ireland, but failing this he looked for more than a moratorium of the provisions of Article 5.

MR O'HIGGINS[1] said that in order to ride the political storm, it was essential to have regard to the feeling of the electorate in the 26 counties. The Government could only survive if one or other of the two conditions to which he had referred were secured, either the improvement of the position of the Northern Catholics, or the elimination of Article 5. He believed that the Government could maintain their position if they were to stand on the territorial *status quo*, were to secure the release of the prisoners to which Sir James Craig had agreed, and if Article 5 were to disappear.

---

[1] Kevin Christopher O'Higgins, 1862–1927. MP (Sinn Fein) for Queen's County, 1918– 22. Minister for Home Affairs, Irish Free State, 1922–3; Vice-President and Minister of Justice from 1923 until his death.

Irish Boundary Commission: notes of a Conference

(*Churchill papers: 22/56*)

1 December 1925   Treasury Board Room
6.15 pm
Secret

MR CHURCHILL said that in his view the proposal for the joint meeting of the two Irish Executives was a matter of enormous importance. The Executive Officers of both parts of Ireland had a vital interest in achieving success. This proposal was, however, only a fraction of the task with which the British and Irish Governments were faced to-day.

MR COSGRAVE enquired what business could be transacted by a joint meeting of the two Irish Cabinets. He foresaw great difficulties if it were to act by (say) a majority vote.

MR CHURCHILL agreed that to achieve success mutual agreement was essential. He was anxious to know whether Sir James Craig's suggestion would be valued in the Free State.

MR COSGRAVE thought that joint meetings would in themselves be excellent, but if they were brought forward at this stage as a contribution to the present discussions they would certainly be regarded as a piece of eye-wash. . . .

MR COSGRAVE thought that it would be a mistake to define a proposal to this end in the form of a definite agreement. It would be better to allow it to be the natural outcome of a growing improvement of mutual understanding.

MR CHURCHILL said that for his part he was most anxious to see joint action by the two Irish executives. The practical question was, however, to meet the immediate emergency. He suggested that the Free State Government might make it stand on the following points. (i) Article 12 had been abrogated. (ii) As regards Article 5, a Moratorium had been agreed to for x years. (iii) A responsible liaison Officer had been appointed by the Catholics in Northern Ireland to represent them and to defend their interests. (iv) Agreement had been reached for periodical joint consultation between the two Irish Governments.

Such a scheme in his view was a general proposition that was worthy of consideration. All were agreed that unity in Ireland was the goal to be aimed at and that the results of partition were bad. A definite declaration on the part of the Irish Governments that they would meet in joint Council from time to time might do good to the cause of unity.

SIR JAMES CRAIG feared that such a proposal might in the present circumstances be a source of embarrassment to Mr Cosgrave. . . .

MR CHURCHILL suggested that the questions at issue should be further considered to-morrow when he hoped it would be possible to reach a definite agreement. He accordingly suggested that the present meeting should be resumed at 12 noon. He would himself see Sir James Craig at 11 am.

The Conference then adjourned.

Cabinet Committee on the Irish Negotiations:[1] *minutes*

(Churchill papers: 22/55)

2 December 1925   Treasury Board Room
11 am
Secret

MR CHURCHILL informed the Committee that he had seen Sir James Craig after his interview the previous evening with the Free State Ministers. It appeared that Sir James had tried to act in the role of mediator between the Irish Free State and the British Treasury and had accordingly suggested that the British Government should waive the advantages contained in Article 5 of the Treaty. He had naturally asked whether in return, Sir James Craig was prepared to grant proportional representation in Northern Ireland in order to meet the wishes of the Free State.

MR WHISKARD[2] said that he had seen Sir James Craig late the previous evening and had found him a strong advocate of the Free State cause. He had argued that the Irish Free State was a poverty stricken country which could not possibly pay more than a sum of £400,000 a year for a few years.

THE CHANCELLOR OF THE EXCHEQUER thought that in the next meeting with Irish Ministers it would be desirable to take a fairly stiff stand in regard to Article 5.

LORD BIRKENHEAD agreed with that provided his colleagues were satisfied that there was a reasonable possibility of obtaining money from the Free State: he personally had been much impressed by the picture of poverty in Southern Ireland that had been drawn up by Mr Cosgrave on

---

[1] Those present were Churchill (in the Chair), Lord Salisbury, Sir John Anderson, Lord Birkenhead, G. G. Whiskard, P. J. Grigg, G. C. Upcott (Deputy Controller of Establishments, Treasury) and F. W. Leith Ross (Deputy Controller of Finance, Treasury). The Secretaries were Thomas Jones and A. F. Hemming.

[2] Geoffrey Granville Whiskard, 1886–1957. Entered the Home Office, 1911. Assistant Secretary, Dublin Castle, 1920–2; Colonial Office, 1922–5; Dominions Office, 1925–9. Vice-Chairman, Overseas Settlement Committee, 1929–30. Assistant Under-Secretary of State, Dominions Office, 1930–5. Knighted, 1933. United Kingdom High Commissioner in the Commonwealth of Australia, 1936–41. Permanent Secretary, Ministry of Works and Building, 1941–3; Ministry of Town and Country Planning, 1943–6.

the previous day. If that was a true representation of the case, he would be opposed to any attempt to exact stringent conditions.

THE CHANCELLOR OF THE EXCHEQUER pointed out that Southern Ireland formerly yielded a substantial revenue. It was true that since the Treaty it had fallen, but it might reasonably be expected to recover. He suggested that the Free State might be asked to pay, say, £1,000,000 a year for 20 years, if at the same time they were given a moratorium by which the actual commencement of payment would be postponed. A settlement even on these lines would of course produce a sum much lower than our legitimate claims.

Irish Boundary Commission: notes of a Conference

(Churchill papers: 22/56)

2 December 1925   Treasury Board Room
12.15 pm
Secret

MR CHURCHILL thought that the question could most conveniently be dealt with in two stages. In the first place, it was necessary to determine the amount due, and in the second place, the capacity of the debtor to pay. He cited the example of the Italian debt to the United States. In that case there was no dispute whatever in regard to the actual sum due. The question at issue, however, was how much they were able to pay to the United States.

MR COSGRAVE suggested that while Article 5 might not admit an arbitrator to have regard to such considerations, the fact that Ireland was a poor country must necessarily result in weight being given to arguments of this kind.

MR CHURCHILL pointed out that no state in Europe was at the present time paying less than 10% of its Budget in the service of public debt. If those conditions obtained in Ireland, the Irish Free State would be paying £2·6 millions a year for debt charges out of a total revenue of £26 millions.

LORD BIRKENHEAD enquired whether the Free State Ministers had considered the question of spreading the payment of the debt over a long period.

MR COSGRAVE said that this point had been considered by his colleagues and himself.

MR CHURCHILL assured the Free State Ministers that they would not find any difficulties raised on that aspect of the question. He again cited the example of the Italian debt where payment was to be spread over an immense period of years. He reminded the Conference that the British Government were paying nearly 50% of their Budget in the service of debt.

MR COSGRAVE drew a distinction between payment of foreign debt and the payment of interest on sinking fund in respect of internal debt.

MR CHURCHILL agreed that this was so, but pointed out the onerous character of the British debt payments to the United States.

MR COSGRAVE referred to the payments amounting to £3¼ millions per annum being paid by the Free State mainly to persons not living in that country in respect of land purchase. No other example could be cited of a country paying such large sums for its land.

MR CHURCHILL suggested that the question of capacity to pay did not arise until after the actual amount of debt due had been agreed. In the present instance there could be no question of coercion, but the Free State could not fail to be sensible of the advantages to their credit that would follow a debt settlement. It was considerations of this kind that had led France and Italy to change their ideas and to cause them within the last year to attempt to settle their foreign debts.

The British and Free State Governments were not in the same position as, say, Italy and the United States, because they had already agreed to the terms embodied in Article 5 of the Treaty. The British Government could not compel the Free State to carry out that Agreement, but there was the self compulsion of their own feelings. The British Government in dealing with debt questions were always ready to take a much lower figure than their paper claim. The British settlement of the American debt whereby the whole amount was to be repaid stood alone in such transactions.

The British Government were anxious for a statesmanlike settlement of the present difficulties. Irish interests were dear to them, but if there was to be an agreement, it must take the form of a real and not a derisory settlement. If Free State Ministers felt in a position to make any suggestion, he would at once consult his colleagues in the Cabinet.

LORD BIRKENHEAD said that ever since the Treaty, he had watched anxiously the fortunes of the Irish Free State, and he entreated the Free State Ministers to put forward for discussion a figure of a character that the British Government would have some chance of successfully defending. It would not be necessary to put forward at the present time a binding figure, but merely a figure as a basis of discussion. He suggested that Irish Ministers might care to consider this question among themselves.

MR CHURCHILL said that the British Government were in a position to offer a moratorium to the Free State, but if this was of no use to them, there remained the alternative of a definite figure on which to reach a settlement. If Free State Ministers would put forward such a figure, he and his colleagues would at once consider it and then set to work in regard to devising a method of payment.

The debt settlement terms exacted from Great Britain by the United States were severe, and there was no need to take that transaction as a model. If a figure could be fixed as the total amount of the debt, he did not anticipate any difficulty in regard to the period of payment.

Irish Boundary Commission: notes of a Conference[1]

(Churchill papers: 22/56)

2 December 1925   Treasury Board Room
Secret

At 3.30 pm when the meeting was about to begin, Mr Cosgrave stated that he saw no basis for a proposal from his side. Neither he nor Mr O'Higgins were expert financiers. He was satisfied that Sir James Craig would not meet them with adequate concessions. He then indicated that he desired a private conversation with the Chancellor of the Exchequer. They adjourned to the room of the Financial Secretary to the Treasury and returned about 3.50 pm.

On their return, the Chancellor of the Exchequer said that two alternative proposals had been suggested by Mr Cosgrave:

(a) The debt of the Free State should be fixed at £6 millions, the payment spread over an agreed period, or

(b) Article 5 should be waived and the Free State should repay the British Government moneys paid for compensation since 1921 plus 10 per cent on the awards made by the Courts under the Damage to Property Act 1923.

LORD SALISBURY, who had to leave at this point for the House of Lords, said that as then advised he was unable to accept either of these proposals.

THE CHANCELLOR OF THE EXCHEQUER emphasised that outside these payments there were others which would not be affected and he referred specifically to the importance of reaching agreement on the payment of income tax deducted by the Free State from the Land Purchase Annuities.

[1] Only three Ministers from each side were present at this afternoon meeting: Churchill, Salisbury and Birkenhead for Great Britain; Cosgrave, O'Higgins and O'Byrne for the Irish Free State.

THE CHANCELLOR OF THE EXCHEQUER undertook to place the Free State proposals before the Cabinet at a special meeting which had been summoned for six o'clock that evening.

After the Free State representatives had withdrawn, LORD BIRKEN-HEAD called attention to the unfortunate economic situation of the Free State and to the undesirability of fixing payments which they could not possibly hope to discharge.

Irish Boundary Commission: notes of a Conference[1]

(Jones papers)

2 December 1925   Treasury Board Room
7.45 pm
Secret

THE CHANCELLOR OF THE EXCHEQUER stated that he had explained to the Cabinet the alternative proposals made earlier that day by the Free State representatives. The Cabinet had carefully considered them and had accepted them in principle. They had done so in order to give one more manifestation of their desire to make the Treaty policy a permanent success. There were certain outstanding matters apart from Article 5 which it was desirable should be settled now once for all. He suggested that the Free State Minister of Finance[2] and his advisers should be summoned to London at the earliest moment. The Cabinet preferred the alternative proposal which was based on compensation. It would be necessary to define it in more detail than had been possible that day and to agree a method of payment.

He wished to repeat the expression of his satisfaction in making this announcement of the Cabinet's agreement to the representatives of the Free State and to have been authorised to make it in the most friendly and generous temper.

MR COSGRAVE agreed that his Finance Minister should be summoned immediately and that among the outstanding matters to be fixed up should be the Income Tax deductions on Land Purchase Annuity payments.

MR COSGRAVE (continuing) said that he most gladly welcomed the action of the British Cabinet. It would go far to cement the friendship of

---

[1] Those present at this evening meeting were Churchill, Sir John Anderson and P. J. Grigg for Great Britain; Cosgrave, O'Higgins and O'Byrne for the Irish Free State.

[2] In December 1925 the Finance Minister of the Irish Free State was Earnán de Blaghd (Ernest Blythe).

the two peoples. He appreciated fully the great care the question had received at the hands of His Majesty's Government and from the Chancellor personally. He knew something of the financial troubles which weighed upon him. His own Irish burdens were colossal. The arrangement now proposed showed a spirit of neighbourly comradeship which had never before been revealed. The active cooperation of Sir James Craig in promoting this spirit was also most welcome.

THE CHANCELLOR OF THE EXCHEQUER said that he understood the two alternative proposals were to be regarded as roughly equivalent in respect of the payment to be made. The details could be arranged on the next day. It would be a triple arrangement involving the acceptance of the present boundary, the waiving of Article 5, and the recognition that the burden of compensation would be assumed by the Free State.

MR O'HIGGINS said that the Cabinet had chosen the form of payment which would be the better, politically, for the Executive Council. It would enable them to say that they were prepared to shoulder their own burdens arising out of the disturbances in Ireland.

THE CHANCELLOR OF THE EXCHEQUER said that he had informed the Cabinet of Sir James Craig's concurrence in the proposed arrangement so far as Northern Ireland was concerned.

MR O'HIGGINS promised that what seven men could do to clothe the agreement with the spirit of friendship should be done, and they would also use what influence they possessed to induce the Nationalist members in Ulster to take their place in the Northern Parliament.

After MR COSGRAVE had again expressed his gratitude for the generosity of the terms proposed and his recognition of the courage and resource of the Chancellor, the conference adjourned until 10.30 am on Thursday, December 3rd.

Thomas Jones: diary

(*Jones papers*)

2 December 1925

Discussions throughout the day on Article 5; Craig and Birkenhead very helpful to the Free State, Salisbury also willing to grant concessions but on less generous terms, Churchill presiding and tilting the balance towards the Irishmen with much skill.

Churchill put the proposals through the Cabinet in principle. Churchill advised the Cabinet that a settlement was a paramount interest.

Irish Boundary Commission : notes of a Conference

(*Churchill papers: 22/56*)

3 December 1925   Treasury Board Room
10.45 am
Secret

THE CHANCELLOR OF THE EXCHEQUER raised the question of the Prime Minister seeing the members of the Boundary Commission with a view to asking them to suppress or postpone the issue of their Report and Award. He proposed that in the first instance the Prime Minister should see the Commission and that later, if agreeable to the Commission, the three Prime Ministers should meet the Commission and make a formal application to them to suppress the Award. It could be published later as a matter of historical interest.

Some discussion took place as to the time when legislation should be introduced in the British and Free State Parliaments to give effect to the Agreement. MR COSGRAVE's view that there should be no avoidable delay and that action should be taken if possible in the course of next week was generally shared by those present.

Thomas Jones : diary

(*Jones papers*)

3 December 1925

Churchill at 11.25 saw Craig at the Treasury Board Room and formally told him of the agreement reached last night. 'You have done the right thing in a big way' observed Craig.

Irish Boundary Commission: notes of a Conference

(*Churchill papers: 22/56*)

3 December 1925   Prime Minister's Room
7.50 pm   House of Commons
Secret

THE PRIME MINISTER read to the Conference the Agreement as finally approved at the Conference held at 6.40 pm that evening (CA/H/48—9th Minutes) at the Treasury.

MR CHURCHILL read the following supplementary financial agreement that had been initialled at that meeting by Mr Cosgrave and himself.

For the purpose of giving effect to Article 3 of the Agreement between the Governments concerned dated the third day of December 1925, it is hereby agreed that payment shall be made by the Irish Free State Government to the British Government of (a) a sum of £150,000 on the 1st January, 1926, and (b) an annuity of £250,000 for 60 years, of which the first payment shall be made on the 1st April, 1926, and subsequent payments on the 1st April in each succeeding year.

MR CHURCHILL further announced that an agreement had at the same meeting been initialled by Sir James Craig, Mr Cosgrave and the Secretary of State for the Dominions providing that the cases of prisoners convicted in Northern Ireland in respect of offences during the period of disturbance should be reviewed by the British Government whose decision in each case should be accepted by the Government of Northern Ireland.

The Agreement between the British Government, the Government of the Irish Free State and the Government of Northern Ireland was then signed in triplicate. . . .[1]

Irish Boundary Commission: notes of a Conference[2]

(*Churchill papers: 22/56*)

3 December 1925   Prime Minister's Room
5.15 pm   House of Commons
Secret

MR CHURCHILL said that he had been mixed up with Irish negotiations since 1910. It was this very question of Tyrone and Fermanagh which had throughout been found most insoluble. Even when we were on the verge of Civil War and confronted with a situation which had no parallel for generations, the Buckingham Palace Conference broke down. Then came the Great War in the course of which Empires disappeared, and after the War a controversy about these same parishes emerged again and nothing would induce the two Governments to agree.

The Bill of 1920 was nearly wrecked on this issue and it had so nearly wrecked the settlement reached in the Treaty that the question was left

[1] The British Government signatories were Baldwin, Churchill, Joynson-Hicks, Lord Birkenhead and L. S. Amery.

[2] Four Ministers were present at this final Conference of the Irish negotiations: Baldwin, Churchill, Cosgrave and Craig. Also present was Justice Feetham (the Chairman of the Irish Boundary Commission) and J. R. Fisher (a Member of the Irish Boundary Commission).

uncleared, one side understanding one thing and the other side another. It was inherent in the circumstances of the case and inevitable that it should be left in a certain vagueness. Then came the labours of the Boundary Commission, and now suddenly the two Parties have settled the matter out of Court.

The issue is finished, and so is the work of the Commission. The work of the Commission had led to this settlement. Neither he nor the Prime Minister had met Mr Justice Feetham[1] before that day. The only question that could possibly be in the minds of right thinking people was the peace of Ireland. It was a great sacrifice that this admirable report should not be published.

Over the whole area of the Empire it will be felt that something has happened which has brought peace, and it will be recognised that these secret labours of the Commission have profoundly helped that peace. The withholding of publication was therefore a sacrifice that in the circumstances the Commissioners might properly make. Not the slightest slur on their integrity would rest on them.

THE PRIME MINISTER said he was satisfied that a solution would never have been reached without the Commission.

MR CHURCHILL, continuing, said he would beg the Commission to leave their reputation in the hands of the three Governments. Let them make their report to the British Government and leave it to their discretion. As an historical document it might some day appear. At present it was absolutely in the public interest to merge it in the happier prospect, although it had been the vehicle and agency by which the miracle of peace had come about.

L. S. Amery: diary

(*Amery papers*)

4 December 1925

When Winston had settled the terms I went up with him, Craig and Cosgrave in a taxi from H of C to Treasury. As we got out Craig and Cosgrave both rushed forward to pay the fare. I pulled Winston back, and told

---

[1] Richard Feetham, 1874–1965. Born in Wales. Educated at Marlborough and New College, Oxford. Called to the Bar, Inner Temple, 1899. Town Clerk, Johannesburg, 1902–5. Member of the Transvaal Legislative Council, 1907–10. Member of the South African Parliament, 1915–23. Lieutenant, 1st Battalion Cape Corps, 1916–19. Judge of the South African Supreme Court, Transvaal Provincial Division, 1923–30. Chairman of the Irish Boundary Commission, 1924–5. CMG, 1924. Chairman of the Local Government Commission, Kenya Colony, 1926. Adviser to the Shanghai Municipal Council, 1930–1. Vice-Chancellor, University of Witwatersrand, Johannesburg, 1938–48; Chancellor, 1949–61.

him not to interfere with the first occasion in history in which the two factions in Ireland had ever joined to pay for England.

When the draft agreement was finally corrected and retyped we took it down to Stanley's room at H of C, and there all those who had been concerned in the negotiations assembled to sign.

The Irish had got to catch the 8.45 from Euston, but Winston and I gave them dinner. They ate the first course or two, and we drank to each others' healths before they and I left, myself to address a meeting in Mile End, where I told them, and incidentally the Press, the news of the new Irish Locarno. The whole business has been an immense relief to me.

Winston really did all the work of negotiating the deal, which was as well, as I should have been out of place as a representative of the British side, and equally so, when the Irish were present, as their champion. But I think I can credit myself with having during the year done much to create the atmosphere without which the settlement would never have been possible. As to the ultimate end no one can say. But if the Free State settlement is to succeed at all, or succeed for a generation, this new agreement has given it its chance.

Winston S. Churchill to James Hawkey

(*Hawkey papers*)

10 December 1925 Treasury Chambers

My dear Hawkey,

I wish I could be with you at the meeting tomorrow. I hear on all hands of the splendid work which the Junior Imperial and Constitutional League is doing, in proving to the young blood of the country that there can be progress without revolution, & that the energy, the courage, & the high ideals of youth can find full scope in the service of the party which seeks to maintain all that is good in our great national tradition.

Yours very sincerely
Winston S. Churchill

Winston S. Churchill to Randolph Churchill

(*Churchill papers: 1/178*)

11 December 1925

My dearest Randolph,

I have read the paper and your answers to it. I do not think you have done badly but it would have been very easy to do better.

Take for instance the question about 'Why Rome won?' What you say is all right so far as it goes, but surely you ought to have mentioned sea power. Quite one of the most astonishing things in history is the way in which Rome, a nation of soldiers and agriculture, beat the Carthaginians on sea in the first Punic war, and thereafter had the command of the sea. Without this Rome and her Legionaries might indeed have defended themselves in Italy, but they never could have conquered Carthage, still less the world.

Lastly you might have added a word on the moral power of Rome. Both rivals were cruel, but Rome gave the impression of a stronger sense of Justice, of law, of keeping faith; and notice how she punishes four years afterwards the mutinous legions which seized Reggio. If the Latin cities had all turned against Rome as an oppressor, nothing could have saved her. Carthage could not even keep faith with her own mercenaries. See the terrible war, the African war, after the first Punic war came to an end. (The 'Inexpiable War') a frightful war. Can anyone doubt that it was better for the world that Rome should win? It was not only a victory of natural and national forces against mercenary forces, but a victory of a higher, though still primitive form of civilization.

I wonder you did not trouble to answer the question about whether Hannibal was over-cautious after Cannae. This is a most interesting topic, and I should like to see what you would have put down about it.

You are quite good at taking a decision as to what your opinion is on these different points, but I am sure to win a prize like this it is necessary to be fuller in your answers.

Take the question 'Who was the best Roman General?' This is your best answer, and clearly the Examiner thought so too. A little more about Fabius and Scipio was necessary to do yourself justice. Although Fabius was quite right in delaying when he did, he was quite wrong at the end, and he tried all he could to prevent Scipio going to Africa, prophesied ruin, and hampered him in every way. When Scipio got there he had an almost immediate success; still there is no doubt you were right in assigning the greater part to Fabius.

When will it be known what is to be the subject for next year? You ought certainly to go in for it next time, and if we can get the books early we can read it up together.

Winston S. Churchill to Louis Loucheur

(*Loucheur papers*)

18 December 1925
Private & Personal

My dear Loucheur,

I am most grieved on every personal ground to read the news of your resignation from the office which you had undertaken amid such difficulties & with so much courage.[1] I had looked forward to collaborating with you in the settlement of the Anglo-French Debt question; & our friendship, extending over so many years & born amid war-time scenes, wd I am sure have rendered the discussion even of such a disagreeable topic easy & fruitful.

Political life is full of ups & downs on both sides of the Channel. I have had my share; & as you know I have never accepted a hostile decision without carrying matters forward into another battlefield. This is only what will be expected of you by all who know you, & especially by yr friends, among whom permit me with kind regards to subscribe myself.

Yours vy sincerely
Winston S. Churchill

Winston S. Churchill to Stanley Baldwin

(*Baldwin papers*)

20 December 1925   Treasury Chambers
Private

My dear Prime Minister,

Percy's[2] letter to you and me admits that he has 'gravely miscalculated', and that the Local Authorities have with his acquiescence committed us to expenditure for which there has been neither Treasury nor Cabinet authority and which is directly contrary to our policy at the present time. Moreover,

---

[1] Loucheur had resigned as French Finance Minister after only seventeen days in Office. He was succeeded by Paul Doumer.

[2] Lord Eustace Sutherland Campbell Percy, 1887–1958. 7th son of the 7th Duke of Northumberland. Entered the Diplomatic Service, 1909; served in the Foreign Office, 1914–19. Conservative MP for Hastings, 1921–37. Parliamentary Secretary, Board of Education, 1923; Ministry of Health, 1923–4. President of the Board of Education, 1924–9. Minister without Portfolio, 1935–6. Created Baron Percy of Newcastle, 1953. His brother-in-law, Lieutenant-Colonel A. E. Maxwell, was killed in action at Antwerp, 8 October 1914.

he evidently contemplates 'launching an Educational Programme involving substantial extra expenditure before the next General Election and the advantage of a block grant based upon a programme of expansion for the years 1927–30'. Such a policy is incompatible with relief of taxation in the closing years of the Parliament.

A Conservative Education policy, instead of allowing the automatic growth of expenditure on primary education, ought surely to concentrate any additional aid from the Exchequer upon developing the higher forms and the cleverest pupils, etc.

On all these grounds I feel bound to resist the present Education proposals and estimates. I hope especially that you will not press me to accept a Cabinet decision on them, as Percy suggests, before Christmas. A decision by the Cabinet on Tuesday to present these largely increased Education estimates might well lead to a general drawing back by other Departments from economies to which they have already agreed. Neville, for instance, would be quite entitled to point out that his condition about sacrifices all round had been voided.

Percy's haste in plunging out with his Circular in advance of the reductions on other Departments has certainly not conduced to economy. What is needed now is not haste but patient investigation and steady pressure. Such investigation can be undertaken during January by a Committee, and then the Cabinet will be able to decide its policy at the beginning of February with a definite report to guide them.

One alternative would be to refer the Education estimates to the Colwyn Committee (who have now practically finished with the fighting Departments). There is much to be said for this. The Committee bring a great deal of cool influence to bear, not only on the Ministers affected, but on the Departmental officials behind them, and can make a more thorough examination. Another plan would be to pick three Ministers from the Economy Committee to make us a special report at the end of January. Either method would be salutary. Perhaps the former would be the more convenient.

I suggest that we discuss this question at the outset of the Economy Committee at five o'clock tomorrow afternoon, take the Health Insurance question at five thirty and turn back to Education at six fifteen or thereabouts, the Education and Health Ministers being invited at six fifteen and five thirty respectively. I will arrange this programme early tomorrow morning, subject to your confirmation later in the day.

I am sure you know that I would not be hard on a young Minister who had got into financial difficulties with his estimates. But the decision *now* to grant largely increased estimates to Education might be fatal to all our economy schemes at present steadily moving forward to success. Every Department will say 'Those who resist, escape.'

Send for me when you have read this, if you require me. I shall be in the Treasury.

Yours vy sincerely,
Winston S. Churchill

Winston S. Churchill: suggested answer to a Parliamentary Question

(*Churchill papers: 18/13*)

20 December 1925

My Rt Hon Friend, the Chancellor of the Exchequer, informs me that he is correctly reported in making the following statement at Battersea on the 11th instant:

'Behind Socialism stands Communism; behind Communism stands Moscow, that dark, sinister, evil power which has made its appearance in the world. This band of Cosmopolitan conspirators are aiming constantly to overthrow all civilised countries and reduce every nation to the level of misery in which they have plunged the great people of Russia. They strike everywhere, by every method, through every channel which is open to them. But there is no country at which they strike so much as at this island of ours.'

No facts known to the Government are at variance with the general truth of this statement. It is the avowed policy of the Russian Soviet Government to bring about a world revolution, and to interfere in the affairs of other countries in a manner unprecedented by any friendly foreign State. In spite of this, however, in an endeavour to foster trade between Great Britain and Russia and as a *modus vivendi*, we have resumed and are maintaining diplomatic relations with the Soviet Government. Such a relationship in the existing circumstances has never prevented, and must not prevent, the country being kept fully informed of the actual situation.[1]

[1] At Question Time in the House of Commons on 21 December 1925, a Labour MP, R. A. Taylor, asked the Prime Minister 'whether his attention had been drawn to the references, made by the Chancellor of the Exchequer at Battersea, on 11 December, to the heads of a friendly foreign State, and whether the opinions expressed by the Chancellor represent the considered views of the Cabinet?' Baldwin replied: 'The answer to the first part of the question is in the affirmative. His Majesty's Government endorse the principle involved in the Chancellor of the Exchequer's statement, having regard to the well-known activities of the Third International, but it is our hope that the Soviet Government will eventually dissociate itself from that body, and thus render possible a continuous improvement in the relations between the two countries.'

Winston S. Churchill to Sir Otto Niemeyer and Sir Horace Hamilton

(Churchill papers: 18/13)

20 December 1925

The question of a betting tax must now be grappled with in earnest, and we must examine it thoroughly so as to ascertain whether it is practicable or not. Let me see the report of the Parliamentary Committee, together with any ideas you have or scheme the Treasury has proposed for dealing with it. I am to receive a deputation from a number of Peers on the subject shortly. Lord D'Abernon, whom I saw yesterday, was very interesting on the question. He pointed out the right way and the wrong way of dealing with luxury expenditure. The wrong way: legal Prohibition with wholesale disregard of the law, many abuses and much fraud by the law-breaking public, no revenue to the State. The right way: high taxation, abolition of abuses, and large revenue to the State.

We have followed the right way in regard to liquor and the wrong way with regard to betting. We have greatly diminished drunkenness by taxation, raised an enormous revenue, and made the law rigidly respected. This is exactly opposite to what the United States do, where the law is everywhere broken and the bootleggers get the revenue of the State. He argued we ought to apply the same principle to betting as we do to drink, ie recognise the evil and reduce it by taxation.

Lord D'Abernon did not say all this, but his observations led me on to this line of thought.

So far as the betting shop is concerned, it would be essential to prohibit any notice, placard, list of betting odds, or other street sign which would flaunt itself before the passer-by. A registered bookmaker would be entitled to transact business behind a plain house front and in a building used for no other purpose.

How do these schemes fit in with the totalisator, and how would the State secure a share in the totalisator?

Do not suppose that I have in the slightest degree made up my mind on this proposal, about which I entertain the gravest doubts. I am only examining the subject.

J. L. Garvin to Winston S. Churchill

(Churchill papers: 2/147

24 December 1925

My dear Winston,

Here enclosed is the *Encyclopaedia Britannica* article, and anything you think advisable, as doing more justice to your own point of view 1912–1914—and also to Fisher's different point of view—shall be inserted by my direction as an editorial footnote—unless you care personally to initial. I want you to come out right in this standard record of 1910–1925.[1]

Only the tersest additions needed.

How great a pleasure it was to see you both again the other day. You know well that although we don't pretend to see eye to eye on every little thing, I am much more humanly attached to you than to any other statesmen; and this is to wish you and your wife & your children & everybody you care for the best Christmas & New Year that can be.

Ever yours
J. L. Garvin

Commander Arthur Marsden[2] to Winston S. Churchill

(Churchill papers: 2/142)

26 December 1925

Dear Mr Churchill,

I write, rather belatedly I fear, to thank you very much for your kindness in coming down to speak at N. Battersea the other day.

I can't help feeling that the undercurrent of Communism & 'Red-Flagism' that is so prevalent there, is largely due to the fact that Conservatism as the Imperial Spirit has never been properly expounded to the Electorate who

---

[1] In the thirteenth edition of the *Encyclopaedia Britannica* the Dardanelles section of the Churchill entry read: 'Mr Churchill presently found himself the leader of a minority and opposition school of war strategy of which the Antwerp expedition and the Dardanelles enterprise were the main products. In both cases the strategical conception was not only sound but brilliant, but the forces against their success were too strong, and Churchill's own impatience contributed to their failure.' The thirteenth edition did not include the sentence in the 12th (1922) edition which read: 'Mr Churchill had shown enormous vigour, industry, imagination and patriotism; but insufficient judgement and discretion.'

[2] Arthur Marsden, 1883–1960. Entered the Royal Navy, 1898. Royal Humane Society Silver Medal for saving life at sea, 1910. Commanded HMS *Ardent* at the Battle of Jutland. Commander, retired, 1920. Unsuccessful Conservative Candidate at North Battersea, 1929. Conservative MP for North Battersea, 1931–5; for Chertsey, 1937–50. Served in the Royal Navy, 1939–45; Captain, 1939.

only read their own papers & have had little opportunity of hearing real British & straightforward constructive addresses, such as yours & others on Dec 11th last. I do feel very confident that when the chance occurs Communism will be renounced by the majority of the voters.[1]

Again thanking you.

I am yours truly
A. Marsden

Winston S. Churchill to Sir Warren Fisher, Sir Otto Niemeyer
and Sir George Barstow

(*Churchill papers: 18/25*)

26 December 1925

We have now made sufficient progress with the estimates for 1926–7 to enable us to make a preliminary survey of the expenditure of 1927–8. To this end Sir George Barstow and Mr Hurst should assume as a basis the achievement of a 40 million reduction, as set out in Mr Hurst's latest summary; and should then proceed to trace the consequences of these reductions on the estimates for 1927–8.

If the basis for the Navy is taken as 58 with a shadow cut of 2 for 1926–7, it would be fair to add any increase on the agreed expenditure on new construction in 1927–8 in excess of the amount included in 1926–7. With the Army at 41 this New Year we cannot look for any further reduction next. I expect half a million more will be required for the Air Force. Anyhow adopt this basis for the Fighting Services.

We ought to get a certain reduction in Education from the estimates we shall have to find this year, of say, $41\frac{1}{2}$—perhaps another 500,000 might be achieved. Is there not some relief to be expected owing to some arrangement about the Pension scale?

We cannot expect any further relief on Unemployment Insurance before further improvement will inure to the benefit of the Employers' Penny. Health will not get any better. Old Age Pensions should be susceptible of some reduction in view of the cut the Actuary has been willing to make this year. At any rate make me a sketch on these lines for 1927–8.

---

[1] In the 1929 General Election the Communist MP for North Battersea, Shapurji Saklatvala, was pushed into third place by the Labour candidate, with Marsden in second place. Marsden was elected in 1931, but defeated again in 1935.

January 1926

Winston S. Churchill to Sir Roger Keyes

(*Keyes papers*)

5 January 1926
Personal & Secret

My dear Roger,

I expect you will have been thinking a lot about some of those places we used to take an interest in a few years ago. In fact I said to Beatty at the CID that I was quite sure that in certain circumstances you might be enjoying yourself very much.[1]

I hate Irak. I have done everything I could from the Cairo Conference onwards to reduce our commitments and expense. I wish we had never gone there, and I hope we shall in a few years get into the position of an entirely detached bottle-holder. But England cannot bend to lawless and violent aggression. If it should come (perhaps in the spring) and we should be the object of an unprovoked attack, you may be pretty sure we shall defend ourselves—and I trust with vigour.

I presume that you have got all your plans worked out, not only for going through, but for making yourself both comfortable and objectionable when you get there; and that you have also been thinking over the second move. We must assume that the League of Nations will be actively with us, in which case Constanza would be available for victualling and training a Flotilla or Squadron in the Black Sea.

In my view we should, if the Air cannot stop them, let them overrun Mosul, and hold on to the far more valuable gages in Europe until they come to their senses. It might be a good thing for you to have an impressive and comprehensive Report drawn up on all the possibilities, showing what you

[1] With the continuing Turkish threat to the province of Mosul, in Iraq, the British Government was in a position, as Mandatory for Iraq, of possibly having to challenge Turkey militarily. It was thus on Sir Roger Keyes, as Commander-in-Chief Mediterranean, that would fall the responsibility of any naval action in the Aegean, Dardanelles or Black Sea. In 1915 Keyes had been Chief of Staff of the Eastern Mediterranean Squadron at the Dardanelles, and had been an advocate of a more vigorous attacking policy than that actually pursued by the Commanding Admiral.

think feasible. We could then ask for such a paper to be laid before us on the CID. Personally I do not believe that anything will happen, and I hope that we shall come to some amicable arrangement with the Turks. But it is always well to have everything thought out beforehand, and to have a document which at a critical moment can be laid before those who have to decide.

All the above is of course absolutely personal and unofficial. Do not mention the fact that I have written to you.

The Admiralty seem to be trying to make economies; and I hope we shall get through this coming year without a serious clash.

Please commend me to your wife and give her, and accept for yourself, my very warmest good wishes for the New Year.

Your sincere friend,
Winston S. Churchill

Winston S. Churchill to Sir George Barstow
(*Churchill papers: 18/30*)

6 January 1926

Please see the passage marked in red. I am not prepared to agree to any expenditure on Airships beyond what is necessary to complete the two experimental airships which are now far advanced. Let me know actually what the position is. I do not want to abrogate my right to criticise all this waste of money.

Winston S. Churchill to Sir Richard Hopkins
(*Churchill papers: 18/30*)

7 January 1926

Ask your Committee of five to turn over in their minds the following extremely revolutionary scheme, with a view to throwing light upon the discussion from every conceivable angle.

The first principle is the separation of earned from investment income. They are treated as entirely different sources of revenue, with their own rates, scales and methods of collection. Upon the whole, the emphasis of favour will be shown to the earned; and the emphasis of burden to the investment. This is in accordance with our general policy in the lower scales of taxation. The new rates would of course be fixed in each case so as to secure at least the existing revenue to the Exchequer. Dismiss from your mind at this stage the complications at the year of change. Contrast simply the new system with the existing system.

We leave for the present earned income in all its forms, and direct attention solely to investment income now deducted at the source. This constitutes approximately 75% of the whole yield of the Income Tax, and an even larger proportion of the Super-tax. It is proposed to levy a combined impost of Income and Super-tax upon the whole of this investment income as it arises.

A National Register of taxpayers deriving investment income will be formed. When a Company pays a dividend, the dividend warrant will first be sent to Somerset House, the rate of deduction will be ascertained, the amount will be deducted, and the sum thus reduced will be entered in the Register and paid into the taxpayer's bank or, if desired, to him direct.

For example:—a taxpayer receives dividend warrants at irregular intervals throughout the year. His first dividend is £500. There is deducted by the Treasury from his dividend warrant, before it reaches him, the tax appropriate to an income of £500, and no more for the whole year, say, £15. In June he receives a £1,000 dividend. His income for the *current year* has therefore amounted to £1,500. On £1,500 investment income the appropriate tax is, say, £150, in respect of which he has already paid £15.

There is therefore deducted £135 from his £1,000 dividend. In September he receives a dividend of £4,000, making his total income for the year £5,500. The appropriate charge upon an income of this amount in any year is, say, £1,600, of which he has already paid £150. Therefore there falls to be deducted from this dividend £1,540. He gets no more dividends till January, when he receives £500, making his total investment income for the year £6,000, on which the tax charged is, say, £1,800. Of this he has already paid £1,600. £200 is therefore deducted from this dividend. A total is thus obtained by the Exchequer from a £6,000 a year investment income of, say, £1,800.

Omitting for the moment the complications connected with the unearned profits of Real Estate, we now turn to earned income. This will be collected in the current year at the rate appropriate to the income of the previous year on the income. It is common ground between us that this is practical.

Under this dual system the taxpayer could be made to benefit the most who derived his whole income from earnings, and the taxpayer would suffer the most who derived his whole income from investments. In so far as earned and investment income were mixed, no matter in what degree, the effectual rate would emerge from the deductions made from both forms of income.

Of course the rates in regard to both earned and investment incomes would be adjusted so as to produce at least the existing and estimated yield of the taxes. The ratio of the earned and investment income scales would require most careful study and no doubt many feasible variations upon it exist.

ADVANTAGE

(1) A clear distinction is drawn between earned and investment income.

(2) The rates on either source can be varied without further complications to produce the revenue required by the State.

(3) All investment income is taxed at the source both for Income Tax and for Super-Tax on the basis of the current year.

(4) All evasion is rendered impossible, for the dividend does not reach the taxpayer until after the deduction has been made.

(5) The distinction between Income Tax and Super-tax is swept away.

(6) No assessment of any kind would be necessary, except for earned income; and the assessment of earned income would not react upon the rates appropriate to investment income, this point having already been settled by the interplay of the scales already fixed.

(7) Apart from the question of a National Register in respect of taxpayers, which will be examined later, an immense simplification of the whole system of Income Tax and Super-tax collection should be achieved.

(8) All questions of rebates and reclaims would automatically disappear as far as investment income was concerned, because on the earliest dividend warrants being paid the exemptions appropriate to the individual would operate.

(9) The taxpayers would pay their investment Income and Super-tax instantaneously as received. No arrears could accumulate, and the Revenue would sustain no loss through subsequently impoverished taxpayers.

The whole of the above plan turns on whether it is feasible to deduct at the source at other than the standard rate, and to deduct at rates appropriate to each individual, ie to keep an individual account in the Register. This might well imply the complete centralisation of the machinery of compiling the Register. Do not complicate the argument by the political difficulties attaching to any abrogation of the existing powers of Local Commissioners of Income Tax. Could such a Register be compiled? Could it be kept up to date? Is it practicable? On this it is to be observed that dividend warrants are a perfectly definite and already taxed article. Everyone knows where they are, when they are paid, and whom they reach. In practice they are now almost invariably dealt with through the Banks. It would be easy to make this compulsory. Even now dividend warrants passing from hand to hand in accordance with the dates when shares were sold cum-dividend are traced, sometimes through seven and eight different holders.

The great bulk of the machinery is therefore in existence. The Companies now declare their dividends, the Banks now receive their payments, the Exchequer now deducts its tax at source. The only new feature would be that each new dividend warrant would first of all have to be sent to Somerset House (or some other suitable building) where the Revenue officer would look up the owner's name in the National Register (or Card Index), ascertain the rate at which the tax should be deducted, issue a new warrant for the reduced sum and send it either to the owner or to his Bank, as desired by him.

All this process would be governed by perfectly simple tables and by equally simple facts fixing the position of each taxpayer. We have to imagine an organisation like that of a Bank, though existing for one purpose alone and therefore much less complicated, but containing many more clients. A great simplification could of course be obtained by confining the Register to persons possessing an investment income in the previous year of over £1,000. This would reduce the numbers to probably one hundred and fifty thousand. How many clients do the 'Big Five' Banks serve together?

WSC

Winston S. Churchill to J. B. Atkins[1]

(*Churchill papers: 1/188*)

7 January 1926   Chartwell Manor[2]

My dear Atkins,
    It was not until after the Deputation on the Betting Tax had left my room and I saw your name on the list, that I realised who the tall, clean-shaven,

---

[1] John Black Atkins, 1871–1954. Journalist. Special Correspondent of the *Manchester Guardian* in the Graeco-Turkish war, 1897; in the Spanish–American war, 1898; and in South Africa, 1899–1900. London editor of the *Manchester Guardian*, 1901–5. Assistant Editor of the *Spectator*, 1907–26. Editor of *A Monthly Bulletin*, which he founded for the improvement of public houses, 1931–48, and a vigorous advocate of poetry and play readings in public houses.
[2] During 1926 Churchill's overnight guests at Chartwell included Professor Lindemann (January 4–11, February 13–19, March 27–29, August 20–30 and September 20), Sir Philip Cunliffe-Lister (February 6–8), Sir Samuel Hoare (February 13–19), E. L. Spears (July 10), Bernard Baruch (August 8) and Lord Birkenhead (August 20–22). The guests over Christmas and the New Year were Jack, Gwendeline and Clarissa Churchill, Diana Mitford, Professor Lindemann and his brother, and Nellie, Giles and Esmond Romilly. Edward Marsh stayed overnight on December 28, and Lord Riddell on December 31.

I think I may still say 'young' man was whose face had seemed familiar to me. We had not met for so many years, and I had been meaning to write to congratulate you on having succeeded to the Editorship of 'The Spectator'. Suddenly you appeared in the flesh in my room at the Treasury, and I did not greet you as I wished to do.

I never forget our experiences in South Africa, nor your extremely sympathetic and appreciative references to my character and conduct when you supposed I had been killed in the Armoured Train affair. Do come and see me some time after Parliament resumes and I am again in London.[1]

Cabinet Luxury Tax Committee: minutes

(Cabinet papers: 27/300)

13 January 1926

STREET BETTING

CHURCHILL: The present conditions were disgraceful, but he believed that the Labour party, the Trade Unions and the Non-Conformist churches would come out against a general Betting Tax in great preponderance. It might be argued against this view that it was not right that there should be one law for the rich and another for the poor. . . .

The real difficulty was that street Betting Houses might become a real evil if they tended to become local casinoes. His suggestion was, therefore, that street betting should be left alone. If at a later stage, after a tax had been imposed, a demand grew up for equality of treatment for the rich and the poor, this aspect might be further considered.

He regarded his proposed tax as an anti-betting measure and an attempt to discourage expenditure on what was a luxury and an extravagance. The moral force of public opinion could not be maintained against a tax of this kind.

Winston S. Churchill to Sir Richard Hopkins and Sir Horace Hamilton

(Churchill papers: 18/38)

12 January 1926

The Cabinet Committee must be satisfied that I am not criticising other Departments and cutting down their staff, without having done everything in my power to arrest the continued expansion at the Treasury.

---

[1] J. B. Atkins replied on 9 January 1926: 'Those days when we pitched our tent together in the Railway Triangle at Estcourt and, in particular perhaps, the dinner party in our tent at which you persuaded Long not to withdraw the guns, are as vivid to me as ever.'

At the root of the whole of this matter lies the only possible remedy in a revolutionary alteration of the methods of Income Tax law and collection. I am entirely unconvinced by the report of the Royal Commission on this subject. Under the present system we are rapidly developing a tremendous class of persons whose livelihood consists in showing the public how to avoid unnecessary taxation, and of course a counter-development on the part of the Revenue officers to meet these activities. The system of allowances, rebates, the various methods of assessment, the immense labour attaching to recoveries of excess tax—all aggravate and complicate themselves from year to year.

The fact that nearly £7 millions is spent on the collection of Inland Revenue is staggering. I yield to none in admiration for the efficiency, loyalty and courtesy of the staff. But the system is an impossible one, and I am determined to search continually during the present year for the means of effecting fundamental simplification.

It had occurred to me that as the Collectors of Income Tax must know the most about the subject, a standing offer of a hundred pounds, or some greater sum, might be made annually for the best series of proposals for effecting simplification and economy in the law. Perhaps you will let me have your views on this.

L. S. Amery: diary

(*Amery papers*)

19 January 1926

In the afternoon I attended a meeting of the Standing Committee on Expenditure and agreed with Winston as to the very considerable number of economies on Middle East and Colonial votes.

Winston S. Churchill: departmental note

(*Churchill papers: 18/30*)

19 January 1926

POST OFFICE ESTIMATES

(1) Is it not possible to introduce a system of deferred telegrams, so as to maintain a more even flow over the wires during the twenty-four hours? If so, the deferred telegram might be charged at existing rates and the urgent

telegram, obtaining priority, might pay an extra sixpence. We would not of course speak of deferred telegrams. There would simply be 'Telegrams' and 'Priority Telegrams', just as we speak of eggs and new laid eggs. Perhaps Mr Hurst will find out what the Post Office have to say to this before the meeting.

(2) I should like to know what has been done about substituting less skilled labour now that the machinery for sending telegrams by typewriter has been developed.

(3) Let me have a short note of the proposals which Sir George Barstow considers can be made about broadcasting.

(4) I do not think it wise to tamper with deliveries.

Winston S. Churchill to Sir George Barstow
(*Churchill papers: 18/30*)

20 January 1926

All that you have written only confirms me in the view that there should be a single allocating authority in regard to research. It would take into consideration all that you have written, and would know where to draw the line between an experimental aeroplane and an experimental submarine, which are really large works of construction, and the more theoretical forms of experimental research. I see no objection to the gas and flying experimental establishments being included in the scope of the proposal. I am quite sure that a block vote of £3 millions to cover all forms of research, to be apportioned under the direction of Lord Balfour's Department, would be in every way a useful measure.

Pray now endeavour to support my view on this subject, and let us talk it over when I return.

Winston S. Churchill to Sir Arthur Steel-Maitland: not sent
(*Churchill papers: 18/30*)

23 January 1926

I ought to have mentioned to you last night two others ways in which a reversal of the decision to reduce the Exchequer contribution to approximately 12 million would frustrate the work of the Cabinet Committee on Economy. Neville Chamberlain has only agreed to make his reduction in Health on the understanding of similar efforts being made by other Departments. If Unemployment Insurance were taken out of the Economy Bill there really would be nothing left in it worth speaking of except the Health Insurance reduction, and I am quite sure that the Minister of Health would not consent to go forward in isolation. Therefore it seems to me the Bill which has been already announced would be virtually destroyed, only details of a few hundred thousand pounds remaining.

The second point would not be less disturbing. In all our efforts to curb expenditure we have only just succeeded in stemming the upward tide. Still we have done so, and the estimates of this year, in spite of new decisions of policy taken last year (Widows' Pensions, Cruisers, Beet Sugar, etc) will in fact, as at present arranged, show no advance on 1925/6. The whole cry about increasing expenditure will be silenced. But if your view of the contribution to be made to the Insurance Fund by the Treasury this year were to prevail all the efforts of the Cabinet Committee to prevent an increase in expenditure would have failed.

I am having all the different variances of the past figures worked out this morning eg the average fall from the January peak figure in the last four years, three complete years prior to the last year, in the two least favourable of the three years prior to last year. All these are being worked out, with or without Coal, I have not the slightest doubt that they will all sustain the cost for a live register for 1,050,000, and that any estimate in excess of this would be unwarrantable.

When the Cabinet Committee discussed this matter on Tuesday I was asked what new facts led the Ministry of Labour to wish to recede from its previous provisional view. I could only instance the higher 'individual cost' which you claim to have worked out. On every other ground the prospect is surely better now than it was in November. I have no doubt that the President of the Board of Trade would record a responsible opinion to this effect.

I do hope you will try to help the interests of the Government, not the Chancellor of the Exchequer, by taking a general view.

Winston S. Churchill to Sir Robert Horne
(*Churchill papers: 18/29*)

26 January 1926

My dear Horne,

I had been meaning to write to you on purpose to thank you for your most excellent statement of our rubber case. I have heard from every quarter what good it did in the United States. The enclosed letter, which has just reached me, is only one additional evidence of this fact.

I am very grateful to you for your friendly note. You will, I am sure, enjoy the Nile. I have followed the whole course of the Nile from its source to the sea, with the exception of the Dongola Loop and the last few miles of the Delta. It is more like a god than a river. I suppose you will see the great dam. It would interest me so much. The accumulation of water has always fascinated me, and this is the most tremendous work of its kind ever executed. Do try to form a definite opinion about the cotton prospects there.

How long will you be away? The first phase of Parliament will be interesting. The Economy Bill will contain several unpopular provisions, with one of which at any rate I know you will most cordially agree. I must get this through before the Budget, as one depends on the other. If by any chance you are back by the 13th of February, do come and stay with me for that week-end. I have Walter Guinness and Sam Hoare. We shall be a bachelor party. Still I suppose you can put up with that.

With every good wish for a pleasant journey and a speedy return, believe me

Cabinet Luxury Tax Committee: minutes

(Cabinet papers: 27/300)

27 January 1926

CHURCHILL: If the rate were reduced to $2\frac{1}{2}\%$ it would not be worth the trouble involved, but the duty had great attractions at 5% if it yielded so huge a sum as £6,000,000 a year. There was, he believed, a substantial fund of new money that the public was always ready to devote to this form of self-indulgence. The size of the sums involved were shewn by the fact that the bookmakers' profits amounted to £1,500,000 a year. . . . There could be no doubt that those who bet regularly could not fail to lose in the long run.

Winston S. Churchill to Sir Alfred Mond

(Melchett papers)

29 January 1926   Treasury Chambers
Private

My dear Mond,

I have been thinking a great deal about the step wh you have decided to take, & it is my deliberate opinion that no other course was honourably open to you.[1] It is perfectly certain that LG will move steadily to the left, & that those who wish to offer effectual resistance to Socialism must join or co-operate with the Conservative Party. That Party now stands upon a broad democratic basis. It is the largest party in the country, & the only one strong enough to make head against the new destructive doctrines. Moreover, both the Government & its supporters in the House of Commons are animated by an extremely tolerant & progressive spirit, & sincerely desire to improve the conditions of the working masses. I am sure they will give a cordial welcome to yr parliamentary gifts & wide experience, & that you will find yrself, as I have done, in genuine sympathy with them in our fight against what LG used to call 'the common foe'.

Yours very sincerely,
Winston S. Churchill

Winston S. Churchill to Sir Austen Chamberlain[2]

(Churchill papers: 18/29)

29 January 1926

The estimates of every Department of the Government have as you know been the subject this year of a prolonged scrutiny and in nearly every case reductions have been effected in expenditure. Even the India Office which has always occupied a quasi independent position is inclined to meet me to the extent of a reduction of £35,000 a year upon the staff expenses.

I know how greatly the business of the Foreign Office has increased owing to the immersion of this country in European policies which resulted from the war. But you have been Chancellor of the Exchequer for so long that I am sure you will not take it amiss if I ask you to give your personal attention to the cost of the Foreign Office in order to effect such savings as are possible. I am sure our joint experience, which covers practically the last thirty years of official life, shows that a request by the Head of a Department for a certain degree of retrenchment in the office is nearly always attended by the dis-covery and lopping off of some superfluous item, and unless such a process is from time to time applied, there is nothing to check the steady growth of the Bureaucracy. It is for these reasons that I ask the Foreign Office not to exclude itself from the sacrifices and efforts at economy which all other Departments are making.

[1] Sir Alfred Mond was about to leave the Liberal Party and to join the Conservatives.
[2] Austen Chamberlain had become a Knight of the Garter on 1 December 1925.

I have not specified any particular item because I have felt that the most fruitful prospects lay in a personal direction given by you; [but if you were to invite detailed suggestions I would of course readily supply them.]¹

P. J. Grigg to Winston S. Churchill

(*Treasury papers: T172/1505*)

30 January 1926

I am anxious that you shd not get into the position of having it said by Briand that while you are treating Italy with great generosity you are chivvying France at a time when they are in great distress. Is it quite certain that a little forbearance now will not make it easier to preserve the $12\frac{1}{2}\%$ basis?²

---

¹ Churchill deleted the words in square brackets in the final version of this letter, as sent on 2 February 1926 (*Austen Chamberlain papers*).

² Churchill minuted on Grigg's suggestion: 'My instinct is the other way. But I have weighed yr point carefully.'

February 1926

Winston S. Churchill to Paul Doumer[1]

(*Churchill papers: 18/29*)

1 February 1926

Dear Monsieur Doumer,

In your letter of the 5th January you expressed the hope that you would be able in about a fortnight to fix a date for your projected visit to London for the purpose of reaching a final and definite settlement of the French debt. I realise of course that the financial measures which you have been so arduously championing have made but slow progress in the French Chamber and I cannot but feel the greatest sympathy for you in your work. Nevertheless events move forward and I feel bound to point out the very great embarrassment that will be caused by any further postponement of the debt funding.

I explained to Monsieur Caillaux that we regard it as essential that our respective Governments should conclude a definite settlement which will include provision for a first payment within the current financial year, ending 31st March next. The arrangements agreed between the French and British Governments as the result of Monsieur Caillaux's visit were based on this understanding. I hope therefore that the situation in France now enables you to fix a definite date for the renewal of conversations early in February. It will make, I fear, a disagreeable impression on Parliament if contemporaneously with the settlement of the Italian debt, I have to admit that the final steps to complete the settlement with France are not yet concluded, or at least on the way to a definite conclusion.

---

[1] Paul Doumer, 1857–1932. Son of a railway foreman. Professor of Mathematics, 1879. In the first year of his professorship he took up journalism, and founded the *Tribune de l'Aisne*, a radical newspaper. Entered politics in 1888. Minister of Finance, 1895. In 1896 he guided the first French income tax through the Chamber of Deputies, but the Senate refused to pass it. Governor-General of Indo-China, 1897–1902. President of the Chamber of Deputies, 1905. Member of the Senate, 1912–25. Minister of Finance, 16 December 1925 to 9 March 1926. President of the Senate, 1927; of the French Republic, 1931. He was assassinated by a man calling himself a 'Russian Fascist' on 7 May 1932. Doumer had lost four sons in the Great War.

Six months have passed since the negotiations originally started. Nearly five months have passed since a definite agreement was publicly declared upon the actual figure of the Annuities. All the time the French Treasury Bills that we hold are being automatically renewed and interest is being added to capital at the rate of over thirty millions a year. This will all have to be taken into account in the final adjustments that have to be made of the settlement with Monsieur Caillaux.

I am sure you will understand that I am bound by my duty to make this serious communication, which I do, as I trust you will believe, in no want of good-will either to yourself or to France.

L. S. Amery: diary

(*Amery papers*)

1 February 1926

PM's dinner. I sat between Winston and Willie.[1] Winston very cheery and much interested in discussing climbing and the psychology of climbing. . . . Fear in his view is quite definitely grey in colour.

Winston S. Churchill to Lord Beaverbrook

(*Beaverbrook papers*)

1 February 1926   Treasury Chambers

My dear Max,

I have a tiny party—men only—at Chartwell on Feb 13 for the week end. Fred[2] is coming, Sam Hoare & other friends. If you are free I shd so much like you to come.

I expect Fred & you cd arrange some golf or tennis.

Yours vy sincerely
Winston S.C.

[1] William Bridgeman, First Lord of the Admiralty.
[2] Lord Birkenhead, Secretary of State for India.

Sir Austen Chamberlain to Winston S. Churchill

(*Austen Chamberlain papers*)

2 February 1926

My dear Winston,

Quite apart from my recognition of the need for the strictest economy in every Department of the Government Service an appeal from you in such terms as you use in your letter makes me most anxious to meet your wishes if it be in any way possible. Indeed I think my views are already known to the Department and that they have realised that these are days in which we must all go on the shortest commons compatible with the efficient discharge of our work. You, I know, will realise how much depends on that efficiency. The more we cut our army and navy the greater is the responsibility placed on our diplomacy, and my own experience teaches me, and I think must show to others, how very greatly the success of diplomacy depends upon personal influence exercised not only by the Secretary of State himself and his responsible officials in London but by the Ambassadors and Ministers and members of their staffs. Much of the most valuable information that I get comes in letters which recount conversations held when some foreign Minister receives hospitality from a member of the Embassy staff or offers that hospitality in return. Their salaries must be commensurate to these obligations and we get a real return for the money which we pay to make them possible.

Again, at more than one place we are represented by a Minister only where one or more foreign Powers are represented by Ambassadors. I am constantly being pressed to raise the status of this or that Legation. Only yesterday I had before me a very strong representation from the Commercial Community in the Argentine and it is not unlikely that the Prince of Wales will press the same proposal on me.[1]

I am resisting all these demands and am fortified in doing so by financial exigencies. You will see, therefore, that we are not unmindful of the need for economy and I think that you will find that your Treasury advisers recognise that we are not extravagant or wasteful. I do not know whether when writing you were aware of the careful scrutiny which our whole establishment has undergone at the hands of some of your Treasury officials, in consultation with Tyrrell and the Chief Clerk.[2] If, after enquiring about

[1] The British Legation in the Argentine was raised to the status of an Embassy on 7 July 1927, when Sir Malcolm Robertson (the British Minister to the Argentine since 1925) presented his credentials as Britain's first Ambassador.

[2] Charles Hubert Montgomery, 1876–1942. Entered the Foreign Office, 1900. Précis-writer to Sir Edward Grey, 1907 and 1908–10. Assistant Private Secretary to the Prime

this, you still think that more ought to be done I am ready to join with you in establishing a further enquiry. I am satisfied that there is no large item at the present moment on which I could easily place my finger and direct a saving; if savings are to be made, they could only be effected in detail and it would be very difficult, if not impossible, to find the time required for that kind of detailed survey.

If, therefore, you think further enquiry necessary I would propose, that you should nominate the Financial Secretary and Scott,[1] or whoever would be the proper Treasury Officer, that I on my side should nominate Locker-Lampson and the Chief Clerk of the Foreign Office and that together they should again subject our votes to an exhaustive examination.

I would instruct my representatives that it is my desire that the strictest economy should be exercised and that if anything can be saved without the sacrifice of efficiency this saving should be effected.[2]

Yours sincerely,
Austen Chamberlain

Winston S. Churchill to Clementine Churchill[3]
(*Spencer-Churchill papers*)

4 February 1926   11 Downing Street

My darling,

Nearly a week has flashed away with functions, a wrangle with Ulster, Betting tax report, Chartwell problems etc. I have just given Craig & his Ministers dinner here & made peace again with them on the vy unusual basis of *my* getting a little bone out of the dog's mouth: & now I am off to Chartwell for a Friday's digging. . . .

The session opened like a doped lamb. A feeble bleat about the Italians, but no challenge in debate. A much milder Socialist amendt & a half empty

---

Minister (Campbell-Bannerman), 1908. Marshal of the Ceremonies, 1913. Chief Clerk and Assistant Secretary, Foreign Office, 1919; Assistant Under-Secretary of State, 1922; Deputy Under-Secretary of State, 1930. Knighted, 1927. Minister at the Hague, 1933–8.

[1] Sir Robert Scott, Controller of Establishments at the Treasury (see page 432, note 1).

[2] Churchill replied on 8 February 1927: 'I greatly appreciate the sympathetic spirit in which you write and you correctly interpret the view held in this Department of the Foreign Office. I think that your idea of a committee has much to commend it, because we could then say that every branch of the Service, abroad no less than at home, has been included in our review. I have asked McNeill and Scott to serve on the Committee, as you suggest' (*Austen Chamberlain papers*).

[3] Clementine Churchill was in the South of France, staying with Consuelo Balsan at Eze.

H of C. LG dined with me *à deux* on the first night. I found him rather bothered, & quite astonishingly empty of knowledge & ideas, but vy genial and plucky. It surprised me to see how far adrift he was from the actual detailed prospect of Government business. It was vy nice to see him again.

My big plans are steadily falling into their combination; & I now see my way through.

Last night I dined at Grillions—after 4 yrs—& found myself opposite the Archb of Canterbury.[1] We had a delightful talk—the first I have ever had with him—78! & he plays squash racquets often.

My little party arrives Saturday.

AJB alas is still in his sick room—but we are six. FE too is laid up perhaps for 3 weeks with colic wh has affected kidney & bladder. Margaret[2] says there is no danger—but gt pain. The Cabinet is vy attenuated.

I do not attempt Chartwell shop—but things are working out fairly well & I shall have a good account to give when you return.

My beloved I do hope you are enjoying yrself—free from care—& lapt in sunshine & luxury. Give my love to Consuelo & tell her how I wish I was with you all—reviving in Riviera brightness, with just an occasional flutter at trente et quarante, in the evenings or even the afternoon as soon as they open.

I will write you more on Sunday & report about Sarah & Maria.

Good night my sweet Clemmie
Ever in the thoughts of yr devoted
W

Winston S. Churchill to William Bridgeman
(*Churchill papers: 18/29*)

5 February 1926
Private

My dear First Lord,

I certainly do not anticipate any serious differences with you in settling the Navy estimates this year. You will, I am sure, remember that at the present moment the Cabinet Committee on Economy have asked the Admiralty to realise the figure of £57,500,000; and it is surely only my duty

---

[1] Randall Thomas Davidson, 1848–1930. Dean of Windsor and Domestic Chaplain to Queen Victoria, 1883–91. Bishop of Rochester, 1891–5. Bishop of Winchester, 1895–1903. Archbishop of Canterbury, 1903–28. Created Baron, 1928.

[2] Margaret Eleanor Furneaux, 1878–1968. Daughter of the classical scholar Henry Furneaux. In 1901 she married F. E. Smith (later 1st Earl of Birkenhead).

to act in accordance with what the Prime Minister and the Committee have asked for. But you are so near achieving that figure that I am sure in the end we shall be in agreement.

On the Oil Fuel Reserve, we might have a talk before the CID to see exactly how far we are apart.

On the Fleet Air Arm the Air Ministry made a very elaborate case to me, and I am surprised you have not been informed of it. Their case, as explained to me, was not at all dependent on any retardation of the air-carrier programme, but only on actual dates at which the vessels would in fact be finished. The possibility of further saving in the dockyards came to me from your own lips. I am sorry that you do not think they will materialise this year.

With regard to Vote A, I recognise that you have tried very hard to economise men; and although I do not myself agree that further reduction is not possible, I will content myself this year at any rate with merely leaving my opinion on record.

I am much obliged to you for meeting my views about our talk on Votes 9 and 10.

Thanking you once more for all the efforts you have made to assist the Government in its financial difficulties, and with a lively sense of still a few remaining favours to come, believe me

Yours very sincerely,

Winston S. Churchill to Clementine Churchill
(*Spencer-Churchill papers*)

5 February 1926   Chartwell Manor

I came down here last night, Thursday, Baldwin having agreed to let me pair for the Division on the Socialist amendment today. A certain amount of progress has been made, in spite of much rain. Nearly all the holes are dug for the apple trees, and about twenty more are planted. I ordered from Bunyard one hundred; and in consideration of our taking this number, he let us have them at five shillings apiece, instead of seven shillings which is the ordinary price. They have all arrived and will be, I hope, all planted before you return. A few extra ones might, I thought, go in between those you have now planted and my new little lake. They will be quite inoffensive there.

My work on the dam is practically finished, and only a little turfing remains to do. Today we were hampered by rain, but we did a certain amount of tidying up and path making. The cutting on the far side of the lake has been put right, and there is now a smooth grass slope running into the water which looks as if it had been there for a thousand years.

Wallace has sent in his new plan for the kitchen wing ground floor. It would be rather difficult to send it out to you by post, and you will be home so soon that I am keeping it for your return.

Leaning has furnished his report on the house, and Tilden sent down a firm of surveyors of his own who inspected the foundations.

All agreed that there is no danger but that the foundations were not laid in accordance with the best principles. I had an interview between Leaning and Mr Osborne of Nicholl, Manisty; and all matters are being pressed forward on the lines of my letter to Leaning which you liked.

Your stone wall is finished. It cost about £3 and looks very handsome. I am laying one line of paving stones at the foot of the garden steps in front of the garden house door at about the same cost.

The Bachelor's Party arrive tomorrow, minus, alas, AJB. As he was not coming, I did not ask Lindemann, and now find Mary extremely disappointed at the non-arrival of the 'Fesser'.

I have had a good deal of work this week, as I am driving forward at least ten large questions, and many smaller ones all inter-related and centering on the Budget. So far I am getting my own way in nearly everything. But it is a most laborious business, so many stages having to be gone through, so many people having to be consulted, and so much detail having to be mastered or explored in one way or another.

I had an awful tussle with Craig and Co about their Unemployment Insurance. I had promised them £650,000 for this year, and they sent in a bill for £1,300,000 owing to the fact that their estimates on which our previous agreement was based were all wrong. They stood on the agreement, and I stood on the £650,000. We had some very troublesome interviews, but in the end they behaved extremely well and accepted my point of view with good grace. Indeed I think they were quite chivalrous, because they had a sort of case against me on the letter though not in the spirit of our relations.

I got them all four to dine at Downing Street last night before coming down here. They are nearly all teetotallers and non-smokers. I suppose this is what makes them such stern politicians!

I am seeing a great deal of my colleagues now through the week-end parties, and also at lunch and dinner in Downing Street. It is really very necessary, when one has so much controversial business about money matters with them, to take the edge off things by a little friendly post-prandial talk across a dining room table.

I asked LG why he was so down on Mond and had never reproached me in any way. He said that he read Mond for the first time in the newspapers, and what particularly annoyed him was that Mond attributed his quitting the Party to LG's land reform scheme which is quite untrue, and then went on to express his great gratitude to Mr Asquith who had never thought him worthy of any office, while he, LG, had in the face of great prejudice appointed and promoted him on every occasion. He is tragically isolated in the present House, with hardly a friend and still fewer supporters. Moreover, tied up as he is in this wretched bundle of squabbling Liberal factions, he never gets the chance to speak with the clear bold counsel of a great Statesman thinking only of the merits of the question and his country's good. He has all the disadvantages of Party politics, without a Party to back him up. If he let his so-called followers drop with a flop and spoke to the House as a whole, he would at a stroke, in my opinion, regain a great measure of his vanished prestige. Max (I have not seen him again) says the difficulty is the Party fund. He does not want to give up the Fund; and if you have a Fund, you must have a Party to justify it. Such is the mill-stone to which he has tied himself.

Winston S. Churchill to Philip Snowden
(*Churchill papers: 18/29*)

6 February 1926

My dear Snowden,

It would give me so much pleasure if you could come and dine with me at 11, Downing Street on Thursday next, at 8.15. I am asking Haldane, Grigg and perhaps another of your Treasury friends. My wife is abroad, and we should be only men. Do not bother to dress, as we shall probably have to go back and vote after dinner.

Perhaps you will telephone an answer to the Treasury.

Clementine Churchill to Winston S. Churchill
(*Churchill papers: 1/179*)

7 February 1926   Eze

My Darling,

It is Sunday & ten o'clock in the morning & I picture you & your guests sitting (I hope) in the sun having a delicious breakfast & interesting conversation. I fear AJB is not with you as I saw he was ill. I am afraid this will have been a disappointment.

To-day is brilliant—How you would love it. You would be out now painting in the shimmering air.

Your picture of Eze has been hung in a place of honour. It is the only work of art in a little guest house they have built on a point overlooking the sea.

I am feeling so well & fresh. We are out all day—Golf in the morning, tennis in the afternoon. I return home on the 16th reaching London on the 17th. . . .

All the Riviera habitués come & go in this hospitable house—Consuelo's excellent Austrian woman cook who had been with her 17 years died the other day—But they have now got a superlative chef. How you would enjoy the delicious yet simple food. I wish I could provide for you at home like this. Chickens after your own heart, roasted a golden brown with plump melting white bosoms—Every time I eat one which is once or twice a day I think of you! I think of you at other times too, but the 'Ching of a Wicken' conjures you up in a life-like manner.

I am rather intrigued by this International Conference on the hours of work? Is it a good thing? Of course if English people *won't* work hard, perhaps it's a good thing to try & prevent Foreigners from doing so—but I should think there would be a good deal of black-legging—I think one ought to form a Black Leg's Trade Union. I give you the idea as I am not standing for Parliament.

Aurevoir—your loving
Clemmie

How Tory I am getting. It's all this luxury sapping my moral fibre!

Winston S. Churchill: Cabinet memorandum[1]
(Churchill papers: 22/87)

8 February 1926   Treasury Chambers
Secret

UNEMPLOYMENT INSURANCE (NORTHERN IRELAND) AGREEMENT

I have arrived at a provisional arrangement in this matter with Sir James Craig and his colleagues which I have undertaken to put forward for the approval of the Cabinet. I am still personally in favour of the amalgamation of the Unemployment Funds of Great Britain and Northern Ireland and

[1] Circulated to the Cabinet as Cabinet paper 47 of 1926.

such an arrangement would also be acceptable to Northern Ireland Ministers as it would of course transfer the whole of the excess deficiency of their Fund to the amalgamated Fund. But on the assumption that the Cabinet remain unwilling to adopt this solution Sir James Craig offers to postpone the initial date of the agreement made last August from 1st April last to 1st October, the excess debt incurred by the Northern Ireland Fund during the intervening six months being added to the amount to be placed to the Suspense Account, and the interest charges thereon being brought into account in future years. The effect of this postponement will be to reduce the estimated contribution to be made by the Exchequer this year to approximately the figure of £650,000 which I had originally contemplated.

As regards future years Sir James Craig is unwilling to agree to the insertion in the Agreement of an over-riding maximum for the contribution as I had desired, but he undertakes to give me for publication a letter agreeing that, if in any year the contribution exceeds £1,000,000, the Imperial Government shall be free, without breach of agreement, to reopen the question on its merits. He also agrees to observe strictly the regulations adopted by the Ministry of Labour in this country and he invites the fullest possible inspection by their representatives of the Northern Ireland administration. (See correspondence annexed.)

In these circumstances I ask the Cabinet to approve the Agreement as now embodied in the Schedule to the Draft Bill attached.

WSC

Winston S. Churchill to Clementine Churchill

(*Spencer-Churchill papers*)

8 February 1926

My Beloved,

I am in yr burry & the party has arrived. The House is vy warm & comfortable & everything seems to work smoothly & easily.

Yr letter reached me yesterday. I have never climbed up to the golf links, but I have heard tell of the view. Yr account is enticing, but for my part the attractions of the Casino seem more compelling.

At work all day in the garden: fruit trees being planted every quarter of an hour, & pattern progressing swiftly. The rain held off.

Poor Fred is vy seedy—'Coli' a bug has quitted his colon (where it ought to live) & entered his kidney where it has caused inflammation of the bladder, but Margaret says not dangerous.

Mary is vy gracious to me & spends $\frac{1}{2}$ an hour each morning in my bed while I breakfast. Some of her comments are made in the tone & style of a woman of thirty. She is a sweet.

Give cordial messages to Consuelo & others from me. I wish I were with you. Don't play singles, & avoid any form of worry.

Tell Jacques[1] I am reading *his* copy of 'Les Rois Arcugles'. The opening is thrilling.

Tender love my darling one—

I enclose (with some trepidation) a rather substantial Memo on various affairs.

Miss Fisher is going to stay, after having a rest cure on medical certification!

Yours ever,
W

Winston S. Churchill to Lord Derby

(*Treasury papers: T171/250*)

8 February 1926

My dear Eddie,

Many thanks for your letter.[2] I certainly did not intend, that there shd be no limitation on the amount spent constructing these gt new race-tracks. I believe there is a great deal of waste in this sphere of the Road Board's activities, & also that the general financial position of the Country requires economy and 'value for money' here as everywhere else. The assurance wh I gave the Dept was therefore limited to upkeep, or as I clumsily put it 'upkeep and maintenance'. It is indeed from keeping a tight hand on the expenditure that I hope to obtain some of the money to supply the funds with wh the Local Authorities are primarily concerned. Neither do I intend myself to go entirely empty away. We have of course a large programme of commitments (Mersey Tunnel etc) wh of course we shall carry out. But

[1] Colonel Jacques Balsan, Consuelo Vanderbilt's second husband, whom she married in 1921, the year after her marriage to the 9th Duke of Marlborough had been dissolved. A balloonist and aviator, in 1899 he had flown a balloon from France to Prussia, and in 1909 had received his aeroplane pilot's licence. On active service as a pilot in Morocco (1913–14; Captain, Legion d'Honneur), and in the first world war. He died in 1956.

[2] On 6 February 1926 Lord Derby had written to Churchill to say that after the previous Motorists' deputation to Churchill at the Treasury, the deputation had come away 'understanding that what you had proposed to us was this, that the Road Board should receive for all purposes—construction, maintenance and repair—not only the same sum that they had received this last year, but an increase'.

the days when Sir Hy Maybury[1] can go careering abt the country in a desperate effort to get rid of as many millions as possible before the close of each financial year ought to what is called 'cease & determine'.

The schemes on wh we are working are both novel & far-reaching, & will I believe be approved by the Cabinet & pressed forward with our united strength. I shd be delighted to tell you about them if you wd come and see me. Meanwhile I hope you will not commit yrself prematurely against what may be a vy important & hopeful development of policy.

I think you might at any rate say that the Govt have a right to state their case as a whole, & that you wd certainly not lend yrself to prevent or prejudice the deliberate constitutional explanation of their policy at the present time.

If you can lunch with Robert Donald,[2] why can you not lunch with me? What abt Thursday, 1.30 at 11 Downing St. You will be glad to know I have come to a satisfactory arrangement with Worthy on the Army Estimates about wh you were anxious.

Yours ever
W

Winston S. Churchill to Sir Arthur Steel-Maitland

(*Churchill papers: 18/29*)

9 February 1926
Private

My dear Steel-Maitland,

I am very much obliged to you for having effected the additional £117,000 savings on some portions of your Votes. Not only the Chancellor of the Exchequer but the Government is greatly indebted to you for the manner in which you have considered the general interest.

I do not think the Unemployment Insurance position, as disclosed by your later view, is really serious. Of course by screwing up the individual

---

[1] Henry Percy Maybury, 1864–1943. A Civil Engineer. On active service in France and Flanders, 1914–18. Brigadier-General, 1918. Knighted, 1919. Director-General of Roads, Ministry of Transport, 1919–28. President of the Institute of Transport, 1921–2. Chairman, London and Home Counties Traffic Advisory Committee, 1924–33. Consulting Engineer and Adviser on Road and Traffic questions, Ministry of Transport, 1928–32. President of the Institution of Civil Engineers, 1933–4.

[2] Robert Donald, 1861–1933. Editor, *Daily Chronicle*, 1902–18. Chairman, Empire Press Union, 1915–26. A Director, Department of Information, 1917. A strong advocate of dropping leaflets over enemy territory. Knighted, 1924. A friend of the first Labour Prime Minister, Ramsay MacDonald, for whom he undertook publicity work.

cost as well as the total Live Register, it is easy to show a Fund running £5 or £6 millions into debt during the year. Even if this were the case, I could certainly defend such a policy at the present juncture, because of the great contributions the Exchequer has made to help the Miners through their crisis this winter. This, you will find, is an argument which will carry conviction to all fair-minded men, and I propose to rely upon it in regard to both the diminutions of Unemployment and Health Insurance contributions. But quite apart from this, the whole object of the £30 millions borrowing power of the Unemployment Insurance Fund is to allow for the exceptional stresses of periods like this; and surely a deficiency of £5 millions in a year to a Fund with statutory borrowing powers up to £30 millions, and an income of about £50 millions, is a perfectly reasonable proposal. You must not be more of a financial purist than the Treasury, and I am of course prepared to take the fullest responsibility as Chancellor of the Exchequer for the financial aspect. Thus even if we assumed your 14/- individual cost and your 1,200,000 Live Register, there would be no reason to depart from the basis we had previously reached.

The Treasury do, however, most strenuously protest against the estimates you put forward as needlessly pessimistic. You will recollect that in November last we gave figures to the Economy Committee based on the course of employment in previous years, on which we arrived at an estimate for the live register for 1926 of 1,050,000. Applying the same line of argument to your latest figure of 1,175,000, our case is greatly strengthened as you will see from the attached statement. The current financial year has been wholly exceptional for various reasons, but the average of the two less favourable of the three previous financial years yields a figure under 1,050,000. This line of argument proceeds on the assumption that our prospects of trade improvement in 1926 are as good as and no better than they were in 1923 and 1924. Personally I think that we have every ground for looking for a more favourable result. I myself believe that 1,000,000 would be a perfectly safe and prudent estimate for the live register of 1926.

This is, of course, on the assumption that there is no Coal Strike. If there is a Coal Strike all calculations would be vitiated. We are bound to make our estimates on the basis of industrial peace and not of industrial war.

This, again, is only sensible and prudent. Our contention, therefore, is that 1,050,000 is a sound conservative estimate of the live register for 1926. So far as the individual cost is concerned, we are not in a position to challenge your estimate of 14/- for the year, but we note that the figure is subject to wide variation and also that it is by no means to be taken for granted that it will rise as unemployment falls further. Indeed, a contrary movement appears to have occurred in the early part of last year. If we adopt the basis of 1,050,000 as the live register, the average weekly cost will apparently need to be 13/9, to balance the account. Alternatively, 14/- would balance on the basis of a live register of 1,030,000. I think that we should be justified in accepting either basis.

By framing the estimates on this basis there will be no need to budget for an increased deficiency in the fund and none of the questions mentioned in the first part of my letter will arise.

Should the events of the year be more unfavourable to the fund than the Treasury estimate, the resulting increase in this debt would not be serious or out of proportion to the strength of the fund or the strain which it ought to bear in these difficult years. But we do not believe that, apart from a great struggle, there is any danger of this. I hope, therefore, that you will be able to agree with me on these points and to make no alteration in the provisional basis we have reached in the Economy Committee.

I should be very glad to confer with you and your experts some time this week. Tomorrow evening would suit me very well. If we are still in disagreement I suggest we put our points to the Prime Minister and accept his decision; but I hope that will not be necessary.

Lord Beaverbrook to William Mackenzie King[1]

(Beaverbrook papers)

9 February 1926

Churchill, whom I saw the other night, gave me the impression that he was in favour of renewing the Coal Subsidy when it expires at the end of April. And Churchill practically is the Government. He has got a complete strangle-hold on the younger reactionary Tories, who used to move Baldwin about as they liked, and now keeps the Prime Minister in a padded room of his own. The latter even goes into Churchill's bedroom (for WC is a late riser) on the mornings he is leaving for the country, to get the last word.

This is really a wonderful performance on Churchill's part, for so recently as 1923, when Baldwin formed his first administration he would not hear of Churchill's inclusion in any capacity. He told people that Churchill would

---

[1] William Lyon Mackenzie King, 1874–1950. Born in Ontario, Canada. Fellow in Political Science, Harvard University, 1897–1900. Editor of the *Labour Gazette*, Canada, 1900–8. Liberal MP in the Canadian Parliament, 1908–49. Leader of the Liberal Party of Canada, 1919. Leader of the Opposition, 1919–21. Prime Minister of Canada, 1921–6, 1926–30 and 1935–48. Secretary of State for External Affairs, 1935–46. Order of Merit, 1947.

do far less harm outside than inside, and that he feared his support more than his opposition.

I am going to stay with Churchill next weekend. I do this because I like him so much, though I am sure the proceedings will partake of the nature of a wrangle.

Winston S. Churchill to Lord Balfour

(*Balfour papers*)

9 February 1926   Treasury Chambers

My dear Arthur,

It was a gt disappointment to me that you cd not come, & still more do I grieve for the cause. You really must give me another chance later on. I have so many things to tell you wh wd interest you.

In the main everything is going well. We have agreed on the enclosed report wh will now go to the Cabinet. The figures at the end are all you need look at. They show that the deficit of 40 millions has now been stemmed; & it now rests with me to find the means of gaining a surplus & of making an attractive plan. I am pretty sure I shall succeed. However for the time being we must all wear serious faces.

Do let us meet so soon as you return to town.

Yours ever
W

Winston S. Churchill to Clementine Churchill

(*Spencer-Churchill papers*)

10 February 1926

My darling,

Yr letter about the succulent chickens has just arrived. Time slips so quickly away that I expect this will be about my last letter to reach you before you quit yr Capuan perch. I am gradually getting my public affairs into order. You shd read the vy amusing account in todays DT of Eddy Derby's meeting about the Road Fund. He was brought to curse but instead he blessed—like Balaam—or was it the Ass? It was vy friendly of him.

FE is definitely better this morning, & I hope to be allowed to see him this afternoon. He has had a vy bad time, & will *still* be ten days in *bed*. The K gave me a most lurid account of his dining on the Royal Yacht last autumn at Cowes. But this is better repeated than written.

The orchard is being planted at (I hope) almost 35 trees a day, & ought to be all finished when you return. The Laming–Tilden–Brown–Waterex–Nicoll Manisty affair is being slowly pressed forward.

Knight F. & Rutley ask whether we will let Chartwell for May June July—They say they have a likely tenant. I have said this will suit us—if the rent was adequate. Even at 40 gs a week it wd be £500: a substantial contribution to the kitchen wing—or at least to pay bills.

My dearest one it will be nice to have you back here. Yr room is vy desolate & empty. My indigestion is yielding to a new medicine by Gorman: but I have a tummy ache. I hope there is no real cause for my chronic troubles.

Your devoted
W

Winston S. Churchill to Randolph S. Churchill

(*Randolph Churchill papers*)

10 February 1926   Treasury Chambers

I am so glad to hear from you and that you like the amenities of an Upper boy's life. Your mother returns on the 18th so there will be plenty of time to arrange for a Chartwell weekend at your long leave. You will find we have made a good deal of progress. The orchard will be planted and the drains in good order. But one thing leads to another and 'le mieux est l'ennemie du bien'.

Have you read 'The Long Roll' 'Cease Firing',[1] and 'Dracula' by Bram Stoker?[2] They interested me very much when I read them. There is a very

---

[1] *Long Roll* (published in July 1911) and *Cease Firing* (published in November 1912) were both written by Mary Johnston, an American novelist born in Virginia, many of whose novels were set in the pre-Civil War period. Her two most popular novels were *To Have and To Hold* (1900) and *Audrey* (1902). She died in 1936, at the age of 66.

[2] Abraham (Bram) Stoker. A Dubliner; civil servant at Dublin Castle and Inspector of Petty Sessions in Ireland, 1877–8. Art and dramatic critic of several newspapers. Joined Henry Irving at the Lyceum Theatre, 1878. Novelist: he published *Dracula* in 1897. He died in 1912.

good book of a different character called 'The Caravaners' by the author of Elizabeth and her German garden[1] which perhaps might amuse you. Let me know.

The Budget will probably be introduced about the middle of April.

With best love,
Your loving father,
Winston S. Churchill

Winston S. Churchill to Sir Henry Cautley[2]

(*Treasury papers: T171/250*)

10 February 1926

My dear Cautley,

I must claim on behalf of His Majesty's Government and on my own account as Chancellor of the Exchequer the ordinary constitutional freedom in framing the Budget proposals for submission to Parliament in due course. I am sure that the House of Commons would never approve of attempts to fetter the ordinary freedom and responsibility of Ministers in such a case. Therefore I am not able to make partial disclosures or give limited assurances beyond those which I have already given publicly. I can however repeat them.

I do not contemplate any proposals which will reduce the grants now made to local authorities for the maintenance of roads. On the contrary these grants, particularly those to rural authorities, ought in my view to be increased: and the fund from which they are supplied ought not to be a fixed fund but one which will grow with 'wear and tear'.

These statements by no means cover the whole field, but they are all that I can make at present. They are, I hope, sufficient to enable your Committee to give a reasonable measure of confidence to the Government in the preparation of their plans.

Yours very sincerely,
Winston S. Churchill

[1] Elizabeth Mary Russell. Married, first, Count Arnim, who died in 1910, and, second, the 2nd Earl Russell, brother of Bertrand Russell. Her publications include *Elizabeth and her German Garden* (1898), *The Solitary Summer* (1899), *The Princess Priscilla's Fortnight* (1906), *In the Mountains* (1920), *Love* (1925) and *All the Dogs of my Life* (1936). She died in 1941 aged 75.

[2] Henry Strother Cautley, 1863–1946. Called to the Bar, 1886. Unsuccessful Conservative candidate, 1892 and 1895. Conservative MP for East Leeds, 1900–6; for East Grinstead, 1910–36. Recorder of Sunderland, 1918–35. King's Council, 1919. Created Baronet, 1924; Baron, 1936.

Winston S. Churchill to Sir Austen Chamberlain

(*Churchill papers: 18/29*)

10 February 1926

You will no doubt remember the contribution of £150,000 a year paid by Egypt to the War Office since 1907 and discontinued under Zagloul Pasha. Worthington Evans tells me that he can reach the figure prescribed by the Colwyn Committee for Army Estimates for 1926/27 subject to certain assumptions, one of which is that he is given credit for this payment. It seems clear that if we now let this payment go by default we shall never succeed in obtaining it from Egypt.

I am aware, and the Financial Secretary from his Foreign Office experience has been able to explain very fully, how great are the difficulties which would beset even a friendly Egyptian Government in making such a payment; and I conclude that the Foreign Office would be unwilling to press them. But I would appeal to you to do your utmost to secure for the British taxpayer this slight relief. It is a trifling sum compared with the cost of the forces we maintain in Egypt and with the profit derived by Egypt from our occupation even in the narrowest sense of the word profit.

I am informed by the War Office that they have a further financial point outstanding with Egypt, in which the sum at stake is £240,000. There seems a possibility that it may be acceded to by Egypt, or failing that, that they might agree to an arbitration. All I have to ask you on this point is that should the point itself not be conceded, you would use your influence to support the War Office in their claim for an arbitration. A copy of a War Office memorandum is enclosed.

Winston S. Churchill to Sir Horace Hamilton

(*Churchill papers: 18/30*)

12 February 1926

1. For next week the important work must be to deal with the Motor Taxation and its substitutes. I can give an hour and a half on Tuesday, Wednesday and Thursday afternoons. A full Committee should be convened for Tuesday afternoon so that we may discuss the Spirit proposal. On this, as I know you wish, I could compensate small users of illuminants. But how am I to deal with the stationary or farm engine? I thought I might take all the horse power of such engines and divide it into the gallons of petrol estimated to be consumed thereby, and then make a payment equal to the

quotient per horse power to every stationary engine that claims it and proves it was in bona fide use. The owner of said engine would pay, or part pay, his fuel tax out of this.

Have you any better idea? Something will certainly have to be done.

2. Consider for the Luxury Cars the following—a 5% per annum ad valorem on so much of the purchase price of any car that exceeds £1,000 (£800?); the value to be written down each year by 5%. This gets over all difficulties for the sale of second-hand cars, etc.

3. What are your ideas about taxing the heavy lorries, particularly steam driven who will not pay the Petrol tax, and also ought anything extra to be put on non-indiarubber tyred vehicles? Clearly weight and road smashing must be the governing factors.

4. I want to survey quite minutely the intervening scale of skeleton licence duties on motor cars. Let me see a table showing exactly how they are taxed now. It is important to bear in mind that some foreign cars happen to be penalised by the present scale. We do not want to confer any benefit on them if we can help it.

5. Finally, consider very carefully how much weight we should put on the petrol leg and how much on the licence leg.

Will you be ready to talk to me about these points on Tuesday.

WSC

Sir Samuel Hoare to Lord Beaverbrook

(*Beaverbrook papers*)

15 February 1926
Private and Personal

It might amuse you to hear about our Sunday. The party was Walter, Hugh Cecil, Phillip Sassoon and Lindemann. I had never seen Winston before in the role of landed proprietor. Most of Sunday morning we inspected the property, and the engineering works upon which he is engaged. These engineering works consist of making a series of ponds in a valley, and Winston appeared to be a great deal more interested in them than in anything else in the world.

The House struck me as being very comfortable, but rather gaunt to look at from the outside. It certainly has a pleasant situation and Winston seems blissfully happy over it all. He scarcely stopped talking the whole time, though occasionally Hugh Cecil talked at the same time.

He is convinced that he is to be the prophet to lead us into the Promised

Land in which there will be no income tax and everyone will live happily ever afterwards. The trouble is that he has got so many schemes tumbling over each other in his mind, that I am beginning to wonder whether he will be able to pull any one of them out of the heap.

I was very much impressed by Lindemann. He is one of the few scientists I have ever met, who is articulate and intelligible to other people. He evidently has a good deal of influence with Winston in putting ideas into his head.

Winston S. Churchill to Sir Horace Hamilton
(Churchill papers: 18/30)

16 February 1926

Several weeks ago I sent you a message through Mr Grigg about Sir William Wiseman's[1] suggestion to me that American Films could be much more effectively taxed if the tax was in proportion to the amount of money spent on the preparation of the film instead of on the length of the roll, etc.

I have not heard anything from you on this point.

On Sunday in the 'News of the World' was a leading article suggesting that 25 millions a year is taken out of this country by American Film Producers and advocating some form of tax reclaiming a portion of this profit. It would naturally give great pleasure in this country if any revenue could be derived from the profits of American Film Producers and I should like to hear from you soon on both these matters.

Winston S. Churchill: departmental memorandum
(Churchill papers: 18/30)

18 February 1926

The working of the Coal Subsidy and the grossly defective estimates and forecasts made by the Ministry of Mines, together with the fact that their reasoning and argument is found to have been entirely illusory, and that the course taken by the Subsidy has not been governed in the slightest by any

---

[1] William George Eden Wiseman, 1885–1962. Educated at Winchester and Jesus College, Cambridge. Succeeded his father as 10th Baronet, 1893. Member of the Purchasing Commission of the Ministry of Munitions in the United States, 1915–17, during which time he had conducted British Intelligence activities in the United States. Lieutenant-Colonel, Military Intelligence, 1917. Chief Adviser on American Affairs to the British Delegation in Paris, 1918–19. A member of the banking firm of Kuhn, Loeb and Company, New York.

of the considerations they originally propounded, is extremely unsatisfactory. The whole matter must now be examined by the Economy Committee in order that we may see what has taken place and what I have to meet.

We are now over 2½ millions on the wrong side on this coal estimate compared to the Black Budget. Let a paper be prepared showing how the estimates of the Ministry of Mines have been successively falsified, and let me see it in draft.

Winston S. Churchill to Major George Tryon[1]

(Churchill papers: 18/20)

20 February 1926

A year ago a most careful forecast was made by the Government Actuary of the future annual expense of War Pensions. This forecast served as one of the bases of our calculation in the Widows' Pension and Contributory Old Age Pension schemes. The figures were published to Parliament in the Report of the Government Actuary. I now learn that although such a short time has intervened, the Treasury, as the result of their communications with the Ministry of Pensions, has come to the conclusion that the rate of expenditure upon pensions is such that an increase of from two to three millions a year upon the forecast of the Government Actuary must be expected. This is a most serious matter as it upsets the whole of our calculation. Moreover, when the new increased figures become known they will be contrasted with the Actuary's forecast and the discrepancy will tend to throw doubt upon the whole of the calculations upon wh we acted.

Your Department was, I understand, fully cognizant of the estimates formed by the Actuary as these estimates were based on data which they had furnished him. Obviously something has happened since this time last year which has led to this very heavy increase in expense. The question is what has happened? What new fact is present that was not known a year ago? Observe, it is not a mere fluctuation between one year and another such as might arise from the falling in of an extra pay day, but a steady substantial lag in the whole downward scale. You will I am sure agree that

---

[1] George Clement Tryon, 1871–1940. A nephew of the 1st Earl of Ancaster. Educated at Eton and Sandhurst. Entered the Grenadier Guards, 1890. On active service in South Africa, 1899–1900. Conservative MP for Brighton, 1910–40. Under-Secretary of State for Air, 1919. Parliamentary Secretary, Ministry of Pensions, 1920–2. Privy Councillor, 1922. Minister of Pensions, 1922–4, 1924–9 and 1931–5. Postmaster-General, 1935–40. Chancellor of the Duchy of Lancaster, 1940. First Commissioner of Works, 1940. Created Baron, 1940. Parliamentary Secretary, Ministry of Pensions, 1940.

this grave discrepancy requires immediate attention and the fullest possible explanation. I am, therefore, drawing the attention of the Cabinet Committee on Economy to the new situation in the hopes that they may authorise such administration measures, if taken in good time, as will be necessary to bring expense into reasonable relation with the Actuary's estimates.

I quite realise the difficulty you have in maintaining a tight hand over pension expenditure and that it is a thankless and painful task, nevertheless so serious a deterioration in the pensions forecast is a most disconcerting event and the finances of the country cannot afford such unexpected losses.

You objected to my applying the word 'lax' to the Pensions administration. I certainly did not intend to use it in the sense of 'careless' or 'slovenly'. I know how unjust that would be. I used it in the sense of 'less stringent' or 'more generous'. I can quite understand the temptations to this and that it would be prompted by the very highest motives. In the absence, however, of any new decision of policy I cannot see what other explanation is possible. I shall be very glad if you can help me.

It is not a pleasant thing to call in question the Departmental affairs of a colleague and friend. But neither is it a pleasant thing to see the public burden increased by two or three millions a year; and I am sure you will see that I should be failing in my duty if I did not draw attention immediately to this danger.

Winston S. Churchill to Sir George Barstow

(*Churchill papers: 18/30*)

23 February 1926

I am much disconcerted by this increase of burdens and I think it reflects upon the preparation of these estimates that within a few months such large discrepancies should be revealed. I am struck, however, with your general approval of the Ministry of Pensions administration; nevertheless I think it would be a good thing to apply some pressure as no doubt the tendency to expansion is very great. Will you see how my letter could be modified to meet your views?

Winston S. Churchill to Sir Otto Niemeyer

(*Churchill papers: 18/30*)

23 February 1926

The way in which we should like this movement to develop would be that all the Continental nations should lower their tariffs and make a Zollverein to which England would be a party and would share the benefits under the most favoured nation clause while remaining Free Trade and in contact with all the world.

We cannot wall ourselves in but we have no objection to others reducing their walls inter se.

Winston S. Churchill to Sir Leslie Wilson

(Churchill papers: 2/147)

24 February 1926

Looking through a box of old letters to-day I came across your very kind letter to me of the 19th April, 1924, and let me tell you how very sorry I am that this letter should have gone so long unanswered. It sometimes happens that a letter which one puts away because one attaches particular importance to it slips out of the regular routine of correspondence.

Many things have happened since you wrote to me which no one could at that time have foreseen, and certainly the Westminster election was, as you rightly divined, an episode of great importance in my political fortunes.

As you know I felt very much indeed the circumstances attending the break up of the Coalition, and scarcely less the melancholy election of 1923. It seemed almost impossible after that that things should go as I had for the last ten years wished them to go. But out of extraordinary reverses and chaotic plunging the Convervative party has once again obtained—I hope for a long period—a dominant responsibility in the State.

Although I was vexed at the course you took in 1922, I have never forgotten my friendship for your gallant brother,[1] and I shall always be proud of having placed you at the head of a battalion of the Naval Division where you too rendered devoted service to the country,[2] and with every good wish,

Believe me,

[1] Ernest Orme Wilson, 1879–97. He was killed in action on the north-west frontier of India, a year after leaving St Paul's School: at St Paul's he was commemorated in a stained glass window that was destroyed in the Blitz. Churchill, who fought in the same action, had written to his own mother, Lady Randolph Churchill (on 5 September 1897): 'I have faith in my star—that is that I am intended to do something in the world. If I am mistaken—what does it matter? My life has been a pleasant one and though I should regret to leave it—it would be a regret that perhaps I should never know'.

[2] In December 1914 Leslie Wilson, then a Lieutenant-Colonel, had been given command of the Hawke Battalion of the Royal Naval Division, and in June 1915 he had commanded the Battalion on the Gallipoli Peninsula, being himself invalided in August 1915, and later receiving the CMG for his services at Gallipoli. In June 1916 he took command of the Battalion on the western front (as part of the 188th Brigade), taking his men into action on the Ancre on 12 June 1916, when he was wounded.

Winston S. Churchill to Major George Tryon

(*Churchill papers: 18/29*)

25 February 1926

Since speaking to you the other night, I have gone more fully into the forecasts prepared by your Department and the Government Actuary respectively as to the future course of pensions expenditure, and while the difference between them is very disconcerting to a Chancellor of the Exchequer, I do not feel that the basis on which the Actuary's figures have been prepared gives me sound ground for criticism.

The position would appear to be, first, that he proceeded on data which have since proved to be partly incorrect, and, secondly, that he appears to have received an erroneous impression as to the possibility of undoing the effects of the Roberts[1] regime. I recognise only too well that some of those effects cannot be otherwise than enduring in character and that as regards those which are within your power to remove, the task is one of extraordinary delicacy and difficulty which can only be carried through with great circumspection.

As regards your estimates for next year, I have come to the conclusion that my first suggestion to fix the total at £63·1 millions went too far, and after looking into the details it is proposed to reduce them only to £63·5 millions. I trust you will make a strong effort to conform to this figure. It is true that, compared with the revised estimate of the current year, this total shows a reduction of £4 millions, but if allowance is made for pay day irregularities and arrears of payment overseas, I understand that the difference is only about £2·7 millions, and in all probability this figure will be reduced still further by savings on the current year's estimate.

The reduction between 1923–4 and 1924–5 was almost as great as this (about £2·6 millions excluding pay day adjustments etc), and on this occasion you have two important factors in your favour; the operation of the seven years' time limit, and the declining effects of your predecessor's term of office. I do not think therefore that this will set you too difficult a task, and it may be that you will be able to improve the total.

In concluding let me congratulate you on your able and spirited defence

---

[1] Frederick Owen Roberts, 1876–1941. Educated at a National School. Member of the Northampton Town Council. Labour MP for West Bromwich, 1918–31 and 1935–41. Member of the Executive Council of the Printing Trades Federation. Minister of Pensions with first Labour Government, January to November 1924, and in the second Labour Government, June 1929 to September 1931. Privy Councillor, 1924. Member of the Labour Party National Executive (Chairman, 1926–7).

on Tuesday night of the vital positions in the pensions system. It was high time that the methods of the British Legion should be exposed and no one could have done it better or more courageously.[1]

Stanley Baldwin to King George V

(*Baldwin papers*)

23 February 1926   House of Commons

That the House of Commons should be able to spend many hours discussing Irish affairs in an atmosphere of calm and moderation is a pleasant contrast compared with former times. The debate yesterday enabling the Imperial Exchequer to make grants to Ulster during the next few years in order to cover the deficit in their Unemployment Insurance Fund showed the extent to which former passions and prejudices have been allayed. It was illustrated in the character of Mr Churchill's opening statement. He spoke with the confidence of a man who knows that he is armed with a very strong case, and, although his friendly feeling towards Ulster was reflected in his speech, he relied rather on the clear and unadorned presentation of substantial arguments than on the rhetorical gifts which he has at his command.

His presentation of the case was logical, restrained and almost prosaic. The controversial note was studiously avoided, and there was only one occasion during his speech when he came into active conflict with the Opposition. This incident arose out of an interruption made by one of the Labour Members. Mr Batey[2] by way of interruption asked Mr Churchill why the money should be given to Ireland. Mr Churchill pertinently retorted that Mr Batey wished to give money to Russia. This retort, which was entirely justifiable from a debating point of view, caused unwarranted

---

[1] The British Legion had presented the Government with a petition, supported by 800,000 signatures, criticizing the Government's administration of war pensions. Major Tryon, the Minister of Pensions, speaking on a motion for an enquiry on war pensions on 23 February 1926, replied that 800,000 was a small number compared with the 10 million ex-servicemen and their wives now in the country. He went on to charge the British Legion with attempting to conceal the true opinions of ex-servicemen, declaring: 'While attempts are made by various organizations to create similar opinions all over the country, I find that there are committees all over the country that prefer to think for themselves.'

[2] Joseph Batey, 1867–1949. Son of a coal miner. Educated at a Colliery School. Began work in a coal mine on the day after his 12th birthday, 1879. Miners' Secretary, St Hilda Colliery, South Shields, 1896. Member of the Durham Miners' Executive Committee, 1901–15. President of the South Shields Co-operative Society, 1906. Miners' Agent, Durham, 1915. Member of the Executive Committee of the Miners' Federation of Great Britain, 1919–22. Labour MP for the Spennymoor Division of Durham, 1922–42.

disturbance in the minds of the Labour Party, and there were indignant demands that Mr Churchill should withdraw the statement.

There is no Party so fond of interruption as the Labour Party or so susceptible when a retort is turned against them. Moreover the subject of Russia is not unnaturally a particularly sore point. Mr Churchill, faced with this clamour, stood his ground firmly, and quite properly declared that, if it was not the fact that Mr Batey wished to give money to Russia, he would withdraw his statement.

March 1926

Stanley Baldwin to Winston S. Churchill

(*Churchill papers: 18/27*)

5 March 1926

My dear Winston,

I have had close on an hour with Anderson fighting your battle for the £50,000, and I can't get it for you. It is a difficult task when you have thoroughly scraped the ham and have lifted £100,000 off it, to set me to scrape a rind of fat from the naked bone!

I have been into figures very carefully and have gone thoroughly into the whole question.

I hope you won't worry over these frills for you have done mighty well and have accomplished more than you dreamed of when you started.

Yours ever
SB

Winston S. Churchill to Sir Horace Hamilton and Alfred Hurst

(*Churchill papers: 18/30*)

7 March 1926
Absolutely secret

We must have some more figures about Fuel imports and consumption of all kinds. Some officer must be separately charged with the task of collecting these statistics and presenting them in the most instructive and convenient form. He should at the same time indicate the gaps in our knowledge where no precise figures exist.

Particularly I want to know how tea and lamp oil bulk in the cottage budget. All these facts must be readily available; but if necessary, discreet new enquiries may be made. We must have a complete explanation of the figures. Propose me a plan for achieving this.

Winston S. Churchill to Sir Horace Hamilton

(*Churchill papers: 18/30*)

7 March 1926
Absolutely secret

Let me have your views, after consultation with the Ministry of Transport, on the possibility of increasing the Licence duty on motor drivers so as to yield an appreciable revenue. The present duty of five shillings a year is surely farcical.[1]

Winston S. Churchill to Sir Horace Hamilton

(*Treasury papers: T171/251*)

7 March 1926
Absolutely secret

(1) Do not mix up arguments about the desirability of a tax on Motor Spirit with the difficulties of evolving a practical scheme. You should assume at the present stage that the arguments in favour of the Fuel duty are overwhelming, and that your task is limited to producing three or four alternative methods of collecting the duty.

(2) I therefore put aside what you write about: (a) the Licence duties not having warped engine design; (b) about the duty as proposed not being large enough to bridge the gap between the scientific and commercial liquifaction of coal; and (c) about the uncertain yield of a new duty while in the year of change. I have never relied upon '(a)' as an important argument. '(b)' has always been stated by me as merely narrowing the gap. As for '(c)', I intend to take ample precautions that the error, if any, shall not leave the Revenue stranded.

(3) I proclaim to you that a Motor Spirit tax, if it can be devised in a practical shape, is from every point of view desirable and in harmony with the largest and longest conceptions of the national interest. This covers the financial, political, economic and scientific aspects equally. I expect the Customs to produce various alternatives for surmounting the difficulties— great though they be. To every one of these alternatives there will no doubt be attached serious objections. These objections will have to be balanced

---

[1] No increase was made in motor licence duties in the 1926 Budget. But taxation of vehicles above two tons was increased, to yield an expected £2,345,000 in the first full year. At the same time, Churchill took £7 million from the Road Fund for general Exchequer purposes.

at a subsequent stage against the value of the prize to be won. They must not be allowed to weaken the resolve to solve the problem.

(4) Mr Ricardo's[1] opinion that there is no danger of lamp oil being used extensively as motor spirit is an important favourable fact. We must not accept the melancholy conclusion that it is impossible to frame a definition which excludes lamp oil while including white spirit and petrol. A group of chemists of the highest authority must be concentrated upon this task and paid whatever fees are necessary. Even supposing that an absolutely perfect solution has not been reached before the Budget, we should not be precluded from going forward. The erection of cracking plants, the large scale manufacture of white spirit, etc, will require time to develop. And by the time the leak has become formidable, the plug will be ready for it. I will not accept defeat in this field or see the whole policy wrecked on such small issues as a definition of 'uniformity or approximate uniformity'. After all, you have only got to arrive at a definition that is reasonably watertight for one year. The definition can easily be amended or extended in the light of actual experience and for the practices of evasion that develop. Consider the leakage that is taking place at this moment in the field of direct taxation.

(5) I do not consider that the Treaty argument is serious. There is only one cracking establishment in this country at present. What is its total capacity? Surely it is infinitesimal. How long would it take to produce others on a scale capable of affecting the problem? Is it likely that such production would be undertaken in the face of a clear intimation that they would be smitten by taxation either through the Customs duty or in some other way as soon as they developed? Are we really going to be stopped in our advance by one single cracking plant?

(6) The achievement of a Motor Spirit duty would be well worth an additional £200,000 a year in collection and the extra staff involved. But I must not be taken as admitting that this would be necessary.

(7) I am quite ready to abandon the Detector. You proposed it to me, and I reasoned on that basis. But it is obviously running a great risk to hang the whole scheme of taxation on a single peg which may at any moment break.

(8) I hope the Customs will not make too heavy weather over the rebates to stationary, marine engines and the like. How many claimants do you estimate would be involved? I do not believe there would be eighty thousand,

[1] Harry Ralph Ricardo, 1885–1974. A consulting engineer. Concerned with locomotives, steam plant and Diesel engines, 1906–15. Consulting Engineer, Mechanical Warfare Department, Ministry of Munitions (designing petrol engines for tanks), 1916–17. Consulting Engineer to the Air Ministry (on aero engines), 1918. Member of the Motor Spirit Specification Committee of the Board of Customs and Excise, 1926 and 1927–8. Fellow of the Royal Society, 1929. President of the Institution of Mechanical Engineers, 1944–5. Knighted, 1948.

nor that it would be necessary to have more than ten categories of use. A single sheet of a Blue Book should suffice to set forth the maximum allowances for rebates claimable for *bona fide* use. These maxima would be fixed on the stingy side in most cases. Within the limits of the maxima we should not trouble ourselves what use was made of the fuel, ie if a man may claim in consequence of possessing a stationary engine or of manufacturing paint, we should not fret ourselves if he occasionally used a can of such rebated fuel for his motor car. I cannot believe there would be any difficulty about this, once lamp oil is excluded. Someone must explain to me verbally the process set forth in your Appendix to your Second Report on the question of Rebates. Perhaps you could do this yourself in half an hour at 7.30 on Monday.

(9) We must concentrate our efforts on the exclusion of lamp oil from the scope of the duty. Why should you not obtain information from the Oil Companies? Why should the Government Chemist[1] not continue his search? Why stop at eighteen samples? Let him be reinforced by other chemists and test many more samples. I am prepared to face the prospect of having it known that we are strenuously endeavouring to find a basis for a Motor Spirit duty.

(10) Tuesday and Wednesday I am busy in the House. But I am keeping Thursday afternoon, and if necessary will clear the whole of Thursday, for this subject. I wish to see Mr Ricardo at 11 on Thursday. Meanwhile you should get into touch with Lord Weir and show him this Minute, and I will see him thereafter on Thursday before the meeting of those concerned, in the afternoon at, say, 4.30.

(11) So convinced am I of the necessity of advancing in this direction that, if everything else fails, I am prepared to re-open the whole question of taxing all fuel oils entering this country. In that case I may have to think of other forms of compensation, apart from this tax, to the other class of non Motor Spirit users incidentally affected by the enlarged scope. Do not, however, trouble yourself with these forms of compensation at this stage.

---

[1] Robert Robertson, 1869–1949. Educated at St Andrew's University. Chemist in charge of laboratory and sections of manufacture, Royal Gunpowder Factory, Waltham Abbey. Director of Explosives Research, Royal Arsenal, Woolwich. Knighted, 1918. Government Chemist, 1921–36. Treasurer of the Royal Institution, 1929–46. Director of the Armaments Research Department, Woolwich, 1939–46. Davy Medal, Royal Society, 1944.

Winston S. Churchill to Sir Richard Hopkins

(*Churchill papers: 18/30*)

7 March 1926
Absolutely secret

(1) Have I in my possession your scheme for spending, say, £8 or £10 millions in giving relief to the reserves of Companies together with the objections thereto? If not, let me have it.

(2) Pray examine the following:

The spending of a sum not exceeding £12 millions on giving Income Tax relief to employers of labour by, for instance: (a) allowing, say, 1/10th of the Wages Bill for all employees (other than domestic servants) to be deducted from Income Tax; or (b) a *per capita* reduction of, say, £10 a year to be deducted from assessable income; or (c) a much smaller *per capita* sum actually to be deducted from the ascertained tax.

Let me have your views on this line of thought. I can see the obvious objection that it would not help those who were making no income. The object would be to lighten the burden on those whose businesses involve the possession of large rateable properties and the employment of large numbers of employees. There is no doubt that this class are at a great disadvantage compared to the *rentier* merchant or financier.

Winston S. Churchill to Walter Guinness

(*Churchill papers: 1/188*)

8 March 1926

My dear Walter,

It is most awfully kind of you to have installed the artificial sunlight in Downing Street. I have had two doses, and already I feel decidedly more energetic. The man who came to explain it said five minutes each for the obverse and reverse of the medal (total: 10) for the first day, and then go up by a minute every other day. But I thought you were doing much longer spells than this, and I began myself with half an hour on the first day. However, no evil results to the cuticle have yet manifested themselves.

Once more very many thanks.

Yours very sincerely,
Winston S. Churchill

Winston S. Churchill to Raoul Peret[1]

(*Churchill papers: 18/29*)

12 March 1926

My dear Monsieur Peret,

May I be permitted to offer you my best wishes for your success in the thankless and difficult task which you have assumed?

You will, I presume, be conversant with the correspondence which has taken place between me and your predecessors in regard to the settlement of the French Debt to this country, beginning with the Agreement of Principle arrived at with Monsieur Caillaux last August. I had hoped that before now it would have been possible for our two Governments to have completed a definite settlement of this question, which is causing much misgiving in this country. As I said in writing to Monsieur Doumer last December, a settlement of this Debt is as much in the interest of France as of this country, as the funding of the War Debts is obviously essential to any programme of Budget equilibrium and stabilisation.

Since the negotiations began last autumn over £15 millions of interest has accrued: and though I have endeavoured to restrain Parliamentary expression of opinion here it is becoming impossible to allow the matter to drift further. I sincerely hope, therefore, that you will be able to arrange to come over to London at an early date and resume conversations with a view to completing the Agreement.

Yours very faithfully,
Winston S. Churchill

Winston S. Churchill to Neville Chamberlain

(*Churchill papers: 18/29*)

15 March 1926   Treasury Chambers

Now that the debate is not to be finished till Wednesday after dinner I expect you will feel inclined to keep yourself free on the general aspects (apart from Health Insurance) until we see how the attack develops. The dawn of the second day of battle often reveals the true situation. It seems to me however that one of the most vicious forms of attack which will be employed will be the following:—

'You have deliberately driven 100,000 men from the Unemployment Insurance Fund to out-door relief, and it is only because you have thrown

[1] Raoul Peret. French Minister of Finance, March–June 1926. Minister of Justice, March–November 1930.

this extra burden on the Local Authorities that you are able to cut down the State contribution to the Unemployment Insurance Fund. You are therefore saving only at the expense of the rates.'

The Ministry of Labour have a considered argument dealing with, or at any rate minimising, this point. Hurst of the Treasury is asking them to put it in shape for you tomorrow.

I am so glad you are going to wind up the Second Reading.

Winston S. Churchill: Cabinet memorandum[1]

(*Churchill papers: 22/90*)

17 March 1926   Treasury Chambers
Secret
To Be Kept Under Lock and Key

EMPIRE MARKETING GRANT

Mr Bruce's telegram of the 6th March is surely couched in a tone unusual in communications between the Governments of the British Empire. It is difficult to believe that this telegram really represents the views of the Australian people or even the true feelings of Mr Bruce himself. It seems to me very probable that he has been urged, perhaps by representatives on the Imperial Economic Committee, to back them up in their effort to obtain as much money as possible from the Imperial Exchequer; and that the impulse behind this telegram has not originated in Australia. However it may be, the document is certainly one which, if it ever became public, would be derogatory to the dignity of the Australian Commonwealth. It is to be hoped therefore that the strictest secrecy will be preserved in regard to it.

It is necessary to re-examine for a moment the contention of breach of faith and failure to keep 'obligations' towards Australia which Mr Bruce advances. The Imperial Economic Conference of 1923 made certain declarations about extended preferences. These declarations were not the result of a bilateral bargain in return for which we received certain measured advantages. They were simply a spontaneous announcement by the Imperial Government of the policy it intended to pursue. This policy has been carried out except in a few minor particulars, the inclusion of which would have created disproportionate political difficulty here and compromised far graver interests at a critical period. Tinned salmon and the crayfish group,

[1] Circulated to the Cabinet as Cabinet paper 115 of 1926.

apples, tinned fruit and honey were all adjudged to be articles of food, and in consequence it was impossible to put new taxes on these commodities for the purpose of giving preference to the Dominions. But tinned salmon (and the crayfish group) comes mainly from Canada and in particular from British Columbia. It does not affect Australia in the slightest degree. Apples also to a large extent come from Canada. Tinned fruit affects South Africa and Canada as well as Australia, and honey is so small as to be negligible.

Therefore, if we are to make Shylock calculations, Mr Bruce is only a loser to the extent of a portion of the preference on apples and on tinned fruits. Although these together constitute more than two-thirds of the total of the omitted food duties, the Australian share of them constitutes less than one-third. As against this, owing to the Snowden reduction of the sugar duty in 1924 (and so large and so early a reduction was certainly not foreseen in 1923), the effective rate of preference upon sugar has been raised from one-sixth to over one-third, and this confers a benefit upon Australian sugar, the money value of which is substantially greater than the Australian share of the proposed preferences on apples and tinned fruit. There are, moreover, the additional expenditure upon the Wembley Exhibition amounting to over £1,100,000 and, from a general Imperial point of view, the new preferences created by the present Government on Silk, on the various articles comprised within the Safeguarding of Industries procedure and— though this was mentioned at the Conference—the important Merchandise Marks Bill together with the restored preferences on the McKenna group.

If we are to be forced by Mr Bruce to make these meticulous calculations of profit and loss in order to vindicate our good faith, if that is to be the kind of groove into which Imperial discussions are to be directed, then it is perhaps reasonable for us to remember that it can be demonstrated arithmetically that Australia is at the present moment in a better position in consequence of the policy of His Majesty's Government than she could reasonably have expected at the time of the Imperial Conference of 1923. So much for the charge of breach of faith.

The Cabinet have, after profound reflection, arrived at certain definite decisions upon the Empire Marketing Grant, and it is scarcely consonant with our own self-respect that we should allow such an aspersion to be cast upon our good faith without pointing out in the mildest and meekest manner possible what are the true facts of the case. It is rendering but poor service to the cause of Empire consolidation for the British Government to remain silent and abashed in the face of this unmerited girding.

Mr Bruce speaks of the preferences which Australia has given to Great Britain as being worth £8 millions a year. The main step which Australia has taken since the 1923 Conference has been to increase substantially many of her protective duties against British goods. Although the preference in our favour against foreign goods has been somewhat improved, this feature of the latest Australia tariff is entirely subordinate to the main object of domestic protection. The President of the Board of Trade has told us that the advantages of this Act to British trade are at the best negative.

It is a striking comment upon Mr Bruce's claims that, in spite of the fact that we are continually lending very large sums to Australia which presumably go out in the shape of exports and the interest of which comes back in imports of Australian produce, British exports to Australia have remained stagnant in the last three years whereas imports from Australia have increased by 50 per cent in the same period.

But the main object of this paper is not to dwell on the comparatively restricted and even petty scope of the existing preference duties on either side. The original policy of Mr Chamberlain in 1903 was to give preferences to the Dominions on bread, meat and dairy produce and also presumably on certain raw materials like wool through the imposition of a new series of taxes on these articles of basic consumption and manufacture. Since circumstances make it impossible for that policy to be adopted in any future we can reasonably foresee, ought we not to seek for some new means of carrying forward the further development of Imperial consolidation?

From this point of view, the telegram which Mr Bruce has sent about improved and accelerated shipping services between Great Britain and Australia is worthy of the most careful examination. Here we are dealing not with the often questionable and still more often inappreciable results to be achieved by haggling over the restricted preferences which are now alone possible, but with the achievement by the Empire of a new cohesion arising from a natural advantage.

The reduction of the distance from Australia to London by a week or ten days if it were commercially and technically possible would be an event of practical and historic moment far exceeding any results which can ever be obtained by the present limited system of preferences. If such an acceleration of sea transport were combined with efficient air services from Bombay, still higher possibilities are opened to passenger traffic. It is indeed a melancholy fact that in 25 years practically no curtailment of the length of the voyages to and fro has been achieved, and that Australia still remains as deeply plunged in the abyss of ocean as at the end of the last century.

I do not attempt to express an opinion about the business aspects of Mr Bruce's proposal or its effects upon existing vested shipping interests, but upon the principle there can surely be no doubt of the magnitude of the policy revealed. The remoteness of Australia and New Zealand is the greatest impediment to closer union. It may be in our power to reduce by more than a quarter that wasteful gulf. A subsidy for such a line of steamers as Mr Bruce suggests would be only in a very minor degree a subsidy to shipping.

If the scheme is practicable it would help every industry concerned in Anglo-Australian trade. It would facilitate the outward movement of our population and mitigate the sense of distance. It would make the whole Empire more compact and coherent and render possible far more intimate and constant intermingling of their leading citizens. It would cause no opposition in Great Britain which could not easily be overcome and certainly no division which would place any appreciable mass of the wage-earning population in antagonism to the idea of closer Imperial unity. Is it not the time to open this new door to Imperial consolidation?

WSC

Winston S. Churchill to Stanley Baldwin

(*Churchill papers: 18/30*)

19 March 1926

1. In connection with this and future Budgets it is necessary from several points of view to grapple with the question of combined Defence Services. When an able, distinguished young soldier MP like General Davidson[1] states in Parliament that he will vote against the Estimates of the Fighting Services next year if they aggregate the present total, that is surely an indication of the point to which instructed Conservative opinion has advanced.

Having myself an unequalled experience of all three Fighting Departments,[2] I am quite sure that without any weakening of our standards of security a substantial saving could be achieved through effectual combination. I would guarantee myself that £10 millions could be saved by this means, not only without reduction in true defensive power but with a positive

---

[1] John Humphrey Davidson, 1876–1954. Educated at Harrow and Sandhurst. On active service in South Africa, 1899–1902. Instructor, Staff College, 1911–14. General Staff, BEF, 1914; subsequently, under Sir Douglas Haig, Director of Military Operations in France. Major-General, 1918. Conservative MP for Fareham, 1918–31. Knighted, 1919. A Director of the national Bank of Egypt, 1925–49. A Director of Vickers Ltd, 1935–49. In 1953 he published *Haig: Master of the Field*.

[2] Churchill had been First Lord of the Admiralty from 1911 to 1915, and Secretary of State for War and Air from 1919 to 1921.

enhancement. I know how strong your own views are upon the need of a higher concentration of effort in the Fighting Forces.

The declaration which you recently made to the House and the approaching debate which you have encouraged on the question of a 'Ministry of Defence' are indispensable steps on the road on which we ought to march. What is the next practical step?

2. Combination, co-operation, union between persons, forces or departments are best achieved not by paper constitutions but by common efforts to meet common difficulties. The particularism which now dominates and distorts the organisation of the three Services will only be melted in a common purpose if all three are forced to face together a simultaneous and common pressure.

I suggest therefore that the figure of £110 millions should be fixed by you, with Cabinet endorsement, as the maximum of the Estimates of 1927/28, and that the three Departments should be requested to set to work almost immediately to prepare a plan achieving this result for submission to the Cabinet not later than October next. It would of course be open to them to set forth together with the plan reasons against it, and therefore no difference of a crucial character could arise at the present stage.

This suggestion follows generally the most important recommendation of the Colwyn Committee, and it would seem proper that while the figure aimed at should be kept secret, the fact that such a joint study of the problem has been set on foot should be disclosed either in the debate on the 'Ministry of Defence' or in the Budget statement.

3. It would be necessary in the first place to constitute the organism. There already exists the Committee of the three Chiefs of the Staff which was constituted after the war. But the weakness of this body arises from the fact that, although they consider strategic and tactical problems from a general standpoint, each Chief of the Staff regards himself as responsible only for his own particular service and as the champion of its interests, and feels not only no impulse but rather a positive inhibition to meddle in the technical business of the others. We have in fact the meeting of three tribal chiefs, all working for the common victory, but allowing no inroad upon the vested interests of their tribe. In place of this we ought to have three war-experts all equally responsible for the whole problem and for the outlay of the limited resources available to the best possible advantage.

It seems to me therefore that additional Patents should be made out in a most formal manner for each of these officers vesting this extended responsibility in them jointly and severally. They should *each* also be equipped with a small staff group of officers of middle rank drawn from the three Services, and should have the fullest access to all inter-departmental information. I believe that the assignment of such responsibility to these three Chiefs would unquestionably be followed by their adoption of the new mental attitude.

4. Side by side with the Committee of Chiefs of the Staff should be the Committee of the three Ministerial heads, whose conception of their duties on this Committee should follow similar lines to those prescribed for the Chiefs of the Staff. The two bodies would meet either separately or jointly entirely as they might consider convenient. The senior Privy Councillor or the senior officer would preside over each of the Committees and the senior Privy Councillor over joint meetings. This is the new step that should be taken at the present time.

5. One of the earliest tasks of the joint Defence Committee, Ministers and experts together, would be to call into being a joint staff training organisation to create near the summit a band of officers of general attainments and habits of thought and also to create a staff college or system of study for officers of middle rank to secure a more deeply laid foundation in the future. All this is the essential preliminary of a joint general staff.

There is nothing startling or untried in this conception. Infantry, artillery and cavalry officers, proud of their own arms and with the stamp of these arms imprinted on them by their earlier training, nevertheless are considered equally qualified to direct armies composed of all three arms and many others. The joint study and in time of peace joint direction of strategic and tactical preparation is only the extension of this principle and its application upon a higher plane that is required to secure an enormous advance in the organisation of Imperial Defence.

6. I would not at this stage bring any outsider into the business. Let them fight their own battles within the new organism. But this organism itself must of course be brought into harmonious relation with the Committee of Imperial Defence, with the Cabinet and with the head of the Government. The existing machinery is well adapted for this purpose. The Committee of Imperial Defence is merely the organism now described with the addition of Ministers like the Foreign Secretary and the Chancellor of the Exchequer whose departmental view is indispensable to the final solution. The relations between the Committee of Imperial Defence and the Cabinet are well understood and fully safeguard the supreme authority of the Cabinet with the Prime Minister at its head. There would be no rupture of continuity or startling departure in our procedure. We should merely be advancing one more stage in a steady and inevitable evolution.

Clementine Churchill to Winston S. Churchill

(*Spencer-Churchill papers*)

20 March 1926   British Embassy
                                                        Rome

My Darling,

Since we arrived on Wednesday evening we have been living in such a turmoil of excitement over Ancient Mediaeval & Modern Rome that this is the first moment that I have had to myself. . . .

To begin with Modern Rome; I have seen Mussolini—He came very privately to tea with Sybil[1] the day after we arrived—He is most impressive —quite simple & *natural*, very dignified, has a charming smile & the most beautiful golden brown piercing eyes which you see but can't look at—When he came in everyone (women too) got up as if he were a King—You couldn't help doing it. It seemed the natural thing to do—He fills you with a sort of pleasurable awe—

You feel at once you would like to do something for him or at least quickly carry out his wishes.

He loves music & plays the violin himself. Sybil had arranged a lovely little concert for him—I had a few minutes talk with him—He sent you friendly messages & said he would like to meet you. I am sure he is a very great person—I do hope nothing happens to him.[2] He looked pale & thin but not I thought ill—It is certain that he inspires fanatical devotion in his followers—He is speaking next week to 50,000 people in the open air—It will be the 5th anniversary of 'Fascismo'.

Goonie & I are going to hear him. We shan't understand a word, but it will be interesting all the same—He seems to like the Grahams very much.

Last night we dined with the Volpis.[3] Very pleasant. Tomorrow they are taking us to Tivoli to see Hadrian's Villa. News trickles thro' to me slowly

---

[1] Lady Sybil Brodrick, daughter of the 1st Earl of Midleton. She married Sir Ronald Graham in 1912, and died in 1934. Her husband was Ambassador to Italy from 1921 to 1933.

[2] For Clementine Churchill's later view of Mussolini, see her letter to her husband of 28 September 1927, quoted on page 1058 of this volume.

[3] Giuseppe Volpi, Conte di Misurata, 1877–1941. Born in Venice. Financier and industrialist. Founded the Società Adriatica di Elettricità, 1905, which established control of the electric energy grid of fifteen Italian provinces. Took part in the Italo-Turkish peace negotiations, 1912. Governor of Tripolitania (Libya), 1921–5. Senator, 1922. Minister of Finance, July 1925–July 1928. Podestà of Venice. President of the Fascist Chamber of Manufacturers; dismissed from this post by Mussolini in 1943. Fled to Switzerland. Returned to Italy, and was arrested by the German occupation authorities; escaped to Switzerland, 1944. Returned to Italy after the war; was tried for 'carrying on fascist activities', and acquitted.

owing to my not being able to read the Italian newspapers. Mussolini said he had heard a rumour that *you* were going to the Foreign Office! Tender Love. Kiss the Kittens for me

Clemmie

Winston S. Churchill to Clementine Churchill

(*Spencer-Churchill papers*)

20 March 1926

My darling Clemmie,

. . . I have had a vy laborious but quite successful week:[1] & am now at Chartwell with Jack. Nellie came down to lunch & to see her offspring, with whose condition she appeared content. She is off to Egypt next week, as Bertram[2] has been clamouring for her. I tried to induce her to stay the night, but she had other plans.

All is well here. Mary breakfasted & Sarah dined with me. Diana talked quite intelligently about politics & seemed to have a lot of information derived from the newspapers. They are all vy sweet & it is a joy to have them down here. They love every minute of it. I don't know wh I love most. But Diana is going to be a gt feature in our lives in the next few years. Nature is mysteriously arming her for the ancient conflict. She has a wonderful charm & grace, wh grows now perceptibly from month to month.

I have heard nothing of Randolph since you saw him. I am inquiring today & will give you news in my next letter.

---

[1] On 10 March 1926 the Royal Commission headed by Sir Herbert Samuel had published its Report, in which the Owners were told to institute long-term reforms in working conditions, and the Miners were told that there should be an end to the Government subsidy. This, the Owners hastened to point out, would lead to an immediate reduction of Miners' wages. On March 17 Churchill had been appointed a member of a special Cabinet Committee, headed by Baldwin, to discuss the Samuel Report. The other members were Sir Laming Worthington-Evans, Lord Birkenhead, William Bridgeman, Sir Philip Cunliffe-Lister, Sir Arthur Steel-Maitland and Colonel Lane-Fox. On March 19 the Committee agreed to accept the Samuel Report, and urged 'the co-operation of all parties'. But at subsequent meetings between the Miners, the Owners and the Government, it was clear that a serious crisis could not be avoided. Churchill took no part in these later discussions, which were conducted principally by Baldwin himself, Lord Birkenhead and Sir Horace Wilson.

[2] Bertram Henry Samuel Romilly, 1878–1940. 2nd Lieutenant, Scots Guards, 1898. On active service in South Africa, 1900–2 (DSO). Attached to the Egyptian Camel Corps, 1903. On active service 1914–17; Lieutenant-Colonel, 1915. Military Governor of the Galilee, 1919–20. Chief Instructor, Cairo Military School, Egyptian Army, 1925–8. He had married Clementine Churchill's sister, Nellie Hozier, in 1915: they had two sons, Giles and Esmond. Colonel Romilly died four days before Churchill became Prime Minister.

It is frigid here, with icy blasts & snow & hail hurled in the North wind & occasional gleams of Arctic sunshine. I worked at the cement stones all day & have finished all in the water gardens. The effect is quite good. In a vy little while you will not be able to tell them from stone. Moss, lichen, weather stains will all vary their tones. I shall have this garden completely finished by yr return. All yr own work is going forward in the week.

Poor Austen has returned—the Manchester Guardian unkindly suggesting that this time he shd receive the Thistle! And on Wednesday we are all to go to the Guildhall to see him made a free man. As a matter of fact both the Locarno triumph & the Geneva disaster are impostures. Things have improved a gt deal & he has done a lot to help. But when praise & rewards are excessive at one moment, the reaction has a certain justice in it. Anyhow it is rather ridiculous.

I don't like FEs looks at all. He is listless & his eye dull. He does not seem to have rallied from his illness. We must make him go away for a six week voyage.

Lord Riddell is motoring over to lunch. The revenue continues to fulfil all expectations & a little more. It will be a little better than what I said at Belfast.[1] The Italians paid their 2 m to the minute. I sent round to inquire, & there it was!

I got yr telegram with gt delight on Friday. I am sure you will have a lovely time. I shd so like to be with you. Both politics & painting are specially exciting in Rome. I expect they are making a lot of the Cat.[2] But not more than she deserves when she is good. Give my love to Goonie. And darling one think now and again of your loving devoted

W

[1] During a speech to the Belfast Chamber of Commerce on 2 March 1926, Churchill had applauded the Conservative's total reduction in taxation of £202½ millions since 1922. 'In fact,' he continued, 'the question that people have been asking during the last few months is whether I did not go too far last year and show my characteristic rashness and impulsiveness in taking sixpence more off the income tax. So high an authority as the Federation of British Industries, for instance, estimated a week or so ago that there would be a deficit in this year's budget of 44 millions. I have not been dismayed by these predictions. When I spoke to the Leeds Chamber of Commerce in January, I expressed my conviction that the Budget calculations and forecasts would be found to be correct. Now we are getting very close to the end of the year; in fact we have only four more weeks to run, and I repeat again the belief I expressed at Leeds that, apart from coal—a matter which could not be foreseen a year ago—the forecast of income and expenditure on which the budget was based will be found to be extremely accurate. I budgeted for a surplus of one million and this I expect to be realized.'

[2] On March 25 Clementine Churchill wrote to her husband: 'I have just received a beautiful signed photograph from Mussolini! "A la Signora Winston Churchill Devotamente B. Mussolini Roma 25 Marzo 1926" is inscribed on it. All the Embassy ladies are dying of jealousy!'

Winston S. Churchill to Sir Horace Hamilton, Sir George Barstow and
Alfred Hurst

(*Treasury papers: T171/251*)

27 March 1926
Secret

(1) Tuesday afternoon we must deal with the Petrol. I will keep the whole afternoon for this alone. I wish to see: first, the Government Chemist, Mr Tizard,[1] Mr Ricardo and Mr Dunstan,[2] at four o'clock, at the Treasury, in the presence of yourself, Colonel Moore-Brabazon[3] and his permanent secretary[4] if he wishes to come. Thereafter, at half past five, after the chemists have gone, we will take the necessary decision for submission to Cabinet.

(2) The specification report clearly affords ground for the skeleton duty— I presume at twopence. If this is decided on, I agree with the Ministry of Transport's view that no changes of any kind should be made in the Licence scale this year. It would be necessary, however, to unfold the whole scheme sufficiently fully to show Parliament and the country the policy on which we have embarked. Let me see the finance of this limited scheme, and how the new skeleton duty works in with the current Licences.

I must tell you, however, that I should regard the adoption of the skeleton duty as a misfortune and a confession of weakness, and that my inclination is to go forward with the whole programme. If we impose a two-penny duty

---

[1] Henry Thomas Tizard, 1885–1959. Educated at Westminster School, Magdalen College, Oxford, and Imperial College. Lecturer in Natural Science, Oxford, 1911–21. Royal Garrison Artillery, 1914; Royal Flying Corps, 1915–18. Lieutenant-Colonel, and Assistant Controller of Experiments and Research, RAF, 1918–19. Permanent Secretary, Department of Scientific and Industrial Research, 1927–9. Rector of Imperial College, 1929–42. Chairman, Aeronautical Research Committee, 1933–43. Knighted, 1937. Member of Council, Ministry of Aircraft Production, 1941–3. President of Magdalen College, Oxford, 1942–6. Chairman, Advisory Council on Scientific Policy and Defence Research Policy, 1946–52.

[2] Albert Ernest Dunstan, 1878–1964. Doctor of Science, London, 1910. Chief Chemist of the Anglo-Iranian Oil Company. Examiner in Petroleum Technology at the Universities of Oxford London, Birmingham and Sheffield. President of the British Association of Chemists. Chairman of the Committee on Petroleum Products. Director, National Oil Refineries, Ltd. Cantor Lecturer on Petroleum, 1928. Jubilee Memorial Lecturer, Society of the Chemical Industry, 1932.

[3] John Theodore Cuthbert Moore-Brabazon, 1884–1964. Educated at Harrow and Trinity College, Cambridge. Pioneer motorist and aviator; holder of pilot's Certificate No 1. Won the *Daily Mail* £1,000 for flying a circular mile, 1909. Lieutenant-Colonel in charge of the Royal Flying Corps Photographic Section, 1914–18 (Military Cross, despatches thrice). Conservative MP for Chatham, 1918–29; for Wallasey, 1931–42. Chairman, Air Mails Committee, 1923. Parliamentary Secretary, Ministry of Transport, 1924–7. Elected to the Other Club, 1936. Minister of Transport, 1940–1. Minister of Aircraft Production, 1941–2. Created Baron, 1942. He published *The Brabazon Story* in 1956.

[4] John Reeve Brooke, 1880–1937. Secretary, Ministry of Transport, 1923–7. Secretary, Central Electricity Board, 1927–9. Knighted, 1928. An Electricity Commissioner, 1929–37.

now, the Oil Companies will almost certainly increase the impending advance in price and our skeleton duty will be saddled with all the unpopularity. An agitation against dear petrol will be set on foot, and much of the support now forthcoming for a Petrol tax may be dissipated before the time comes to put the whole tax into operation. All the while we shall have been unable to give any relief on Licences. Nor will the Exchequer get the revenues it expected: (a) from a well managed overlap as between the full Petrol and Licence duties; and (b) from the taxation of luxury vehicles. The heavies will remain threatened but untaxed, and we shall have a whole year in which to face their growing opposition. I strongly incline to the belief that it will be wiser, and in the end safer, to take the plunge. The systematic and general treatment of a great question often go through where tentative tinkering and tampering fall short. I do not wish to press you beyond your better judgment; but if you say that you believe the proposal is practicable, as far as human foresight can go, I will take the responsibility of coming into action with it.

Let me have the finance of the full scheme, and its effects upon the present year also, set out.

WSC

Winston S. Churchill to Stanley Baldwin

(*Baldwin papers*)

28 March 1926
Secret & Personal

Treasury Chambers

My dear Prime Minister,

Percy[1] has written to you that he is already discussing in a preliminary way with the Local Authorities the best method of substituting block grants for expenditure grants, and he says that these discussions are reaching a point where he may have to 'formulate tentative proposals as to the *method*' without, however, 'committing himself as to the *amount* of grant'.

The Treasury are very much alarmed about this. The substitution of a general system of block grants, not based on expenditure, for the present percentage grants is a great scheme of policy and, if achieved in the present Parliament, would be a memorable event. You know yourself how immensely important it is to the Exchequer, and indeed to true economy, in the spending of these large sums.

Every step in this field should be taken with foresight and design. Above all, contact should be preserved with Neville Chamberlain, who is deeply

[1] Lord Eustace Percy, President of the Board of Education (see page 619, note 2).

interested in the problem and whose general method of approach commends itself much more to the Treasury than Percy's.

I dread to see Percy plunge out precipitately into this field. The experience of Circular 1371, which he was so eager to launch, is fresh in my mind. It would be a disaster, alike to finance and administration, if the whole policy of block grants were compromised by partial, precipitate and inexperienced handling.

I do not believe that the Board of Education wish to economise. I think they are determined—as Percy has repeatedly avowed—to commit us to very much larger expenditure and to a new extensive programme before the Parliament is over. I shall ask, therefore, when the matter is raised, that there should be set up an Inter-departmental Committee of experts representing the different Departments, to devise for eventual submission to the Cabinet a comprehensive scheme and time-table for effecting the change from percentage to block grants; and that, pending the report of this Committee, no individual Minister or Department shall commit us either to method or amount. As nothing can be achieved until 1928, it cannot be urged that the few weeks required for this examination cannot be spared.

I shall be ready Thursday morning, if you like, to outline the Budget proposals, with approximate figures, to you, Neville and Austen, and to bring the Budget before the Cabinet at our first meeting after Easter. I am asking Hankey to obtain your approval to putting down the Betting Tax for Wednesday next, and I am asking that no reference to it by name be made on the Agenda. A decision on the principle is now necessary for me.

The figures are not turning out as well as I had hoped. Customs and Excise will not even hold their own; and the profits for Income Tax are substantially less than we had hoped. Having regard to the continued falling away of moribund taxes and special receipts, I cannot see any appreciable expansion in the Revenue for the next few years. Unless further economies can be effected, the outlook for the taxpayer is cheerless.

Yours vy sincerely,
Winston S. Churchill

E. L. Spears to Winston S. Churchill

(*Treasury papers: T172/1505*)

28 March 1926

I saw Loucheur before leaving Paris yesterday, and he asked me to tell you that he had that morning on behalf of the Groups of the Left come to an understanding with the Finance Minister and that although the taxes proposed by the Minister would not be passed, substitute ones acceptable to him would receive the assent of the Chamber. All this to take place next week. He considers that except for quite unforeseen emergencies the Government is therefore safe and that Monsieur Peret would be free to come to England fairly soon to discuss the settlement of the debt.

It is however evidently the opinion of Loucheur that Caillaux's offer was too optimistic and that France is incapable of making immediate heavy cash payments. Loucheur says there is going to be a balanced budget and wished me to explain to you that he had got over all his own difficulties and was now firmly in the saddle again and working in the closest touch with his successor.

Winston S. Churchill to Sir Warren Fisher and Sir Russell Scott

(*Churchill papers: 18/30*)

28 March 1926
Secret

With regard to the case of the Treasury clerk, Counter, who has confessed to systematically selling Government secrets to the newspapers, the Cabinet decided to leave to me the decision of whether and how any official announcement should be made to the Service, the general opinion being clearly in favour of such an announcement. In view of the circumstances under which this man's guilt was detected and the restrictions upon our freedom of action arising therefrom, it would be necessary for the announcement to be worded very carefully and moderately. Indeed it may not be possible to make any announcement at all. There is always to be borne in mind the questions that will be asked once publicity is given: Why did you not prosecute the criminal? Why did you not prosecute the tempter? etc. On the other hand it seems most desirable that the warning arising from this discovery should be circulated. Pray let me have your draft announcement, together with your views on the desirability of making one.

Considerable hilarity was expressed at the Cabinet, reflecting what I gather is the mood among those who have been informed in the other Departments, that the delinquent should have been discovered in the Treasury serving under the eye of the head of the Civil Service and in the Department which sits in judgment over all the others. The Attorney-General stated that the guilty clerk was described as 'a searcher' and that his duties were to wander from room to room in the Treasury looking for papers which had been lost by high officials. It was stated that in no other Department was such an official needed, and that they did not exist. How many 'searchers' are there in the Treasury? What are the reasons which have made their inclusion in the staff necessary? Is it true that there are none in other Departments?

With regard to papers getting lost or mislaid in the Treasury. More than a year ago I drew Sir Warren Fisher's attention to the extremely informal manner in which the official files of the Treasury are handled. I only received a somewhat flippant reply. Having served for nearly twenty years in many Public Departments, I am of opinion that the lack of system in docketing and minuting in the Treasury is unique. Questions are raised and minuted on any odd piece of paper and have no regular routine of dockets and Minute sheets. The introduction of such a routine would, I believe, quickly repay the initial trouble. It is a curious thing that Memoranda and Minutes which are more informative and more able than any I have seen in any Department, should be circulated in such a happy-go-lucky fashion. Let me see my previous Minute on this subject, together with the Departmental answers which were received.

The attention of Mr Meiklejohn[1] should be drawn to the statements which Counter makes that the greater part of the confidential documents which he betrayed were found in Mr Meiklejohn's room; and he should be invited to make an explanation of this fact.

The use of locked boxes for the conveyance of secret papers is indispensable. Moreover, these boxes should all have snap locks. In addition, every officer into whose hands confidential papers come should have in his room a full-sized box with a snap lock. This is the only protection against forgetting to lock a box. It is an absolutely effective protection, as the box is bound to be open unless it is locked, and cannot remain at once closed and unlocked. Pray make me proposals without delay for giving effect to this order.

---

[1] Roderick Sinclair Meiklejohn, 1876–1962. Educated at St Paul's School and Hertford College, Oxford. Entered the War Office, 1899. Transferred to the Treasury, 1902. Private Secretary to H. H. Asquith, first as Chancellor of the Exchequer and then as Prime Minister, 1905–11. Deputy Controller of Supply Services, Treasury, 1922–7. First Civil Service Commissioner, 1928–39. Knighted, 1931.

Winston S. Churchill to Sir Horace Hamilton

(*Churchill papers: 18/30*)

26 March 1926

ENTERTAINMENTS TAX

As you know, I think the London theatres, the home of the Drama in this country, are roughly treated by this tax, and still more so by the invidious Snowden remissions to the cheap and trashy Cinema entertainments, etc. It is, however, impossible to deal with this at the present time; and indeed our general policy of increasing optional as against compulsory taxation runs contrary to any reduction.

Winston S. Churchill to L. S. Amery

(*Churchill papers: 18/27*)

31 March 1926
Personal and Private

My dear Leo,

I learn from the Inland Revenue that the outlook for 1926–7 is less expansive than we had hoped, and the low price prevailing for Rubber is a factor of serious concern for me. I am greatly disturbed to hear rumours that you contemplate opening the restriction scheme beyond 100%. It would surely be taking a very grave responsibility to inflict this loss on Britain in the hopes of conciliating the extortionate Americans. May I have your assurance that no further relaxation will be allowed by you without the Cabinet being consulted in good time beforehand? The Prime Minister told me when last I mentioned this to him two months ago that the working of the Rubber Restriction Scheme must be a matter of Cabinet policy. I have had a talk with Stevenson, but this letter is entirely due to my own anxiety.

Yours very sincerely,
Winston S. Churchill

April 1926

Winston S. Churchill to Raoul Peret

(*Treasury papers: T172/1505*)

1 April 1926

I hope that the passage of the Budget through the Chamber will enable you to come over here on or about the 7 April when I shall be at your disposal. . . .

I am to open my Budget on the 26 April and the uncertainty about the Anglo-French debt settlement makes it difficult for me to know what to say or do. After the Budget is opened I shall be gripped by the House of Commons, and therefore the end of the month would be almost impossible for me.

Winston S. Churchill to Professor Lindemann

(*Cherwell papers*)

4 April 1926

I was so much interested in your book that I have consumed a morning which ought to have been devoted to the Budget in dictating this note while the impression was still fresh in my mind. I would be so much obliged to you if you would correct it for me, and I shall then have a true general view in my mind.

There are a great many points which I want to ask you about, and I look forward very much to our next meeting. I will only mention one now. Have the relations between music and mathematics been examined in the same way as those between mathematics and physics? Is there any sort of correspondence? If so, there will be a correspondence between music and physics other than mere sound-waves. Might there not be a notation which would cover not merely sound-waves but harmonies and discords, rhythms and cadences; and might not this notation be found in the absolute?

With all good wishes
Winston S. Churchill

Winston S. Churchill to P. J. Grigg

(*Grigg papers*)

11 April 1926   Chartwell Manor
Secret

My dear Grigg,

I send you herewith the outline of what I wish to say on the Budget. Do not show it entire to anyone but Niemeyer. You may show particular passages to those whom they concern. I have sent Hurst a copy of the Road Fund 'piece'.

Niemeyer should be asked to supply something about the working of the Gold Standard. 'At any rate our prosperity, such as it is, stands on an absolutely sound foundation. Having deliberately thrown ourselves out of a top story window, we have at least the assurance that we can start fair again from the pavement.' Niemeyer's observations should play around this theme. Two or three sentences about national thrift, and four or five about debt repayments, floating debt, etc.

Hopkins should be asked for a short draft, not exceeding three or, at the outside, four of these pages on his Income Tax manoeuvres, leading up to the basis of the preceding year.

Hamilton should see what I thought of saying about Petrol, about the dodging of the Bowles Act, and about Amery's consolation prize.

Barstow should say what is to be said on economy, and brace himself for further struggles in the coming year.

You may tell Niemeyer (but no one else) that I am inclined to think £17 millions is too large a surplus in view of the greedy appetites of the Coal Trade. I think, if nothing goes wrong with the French debt, I will be content with £14 millions, leaving £3 millions for the Miners and £1 million for myself. This would enable me to give back £2 millions to Hopkins and £1 million to Hamilton.

I shall return Tuesday. I am quite ready for a fight this time with the Coal Miners. I feel quite differently about it to what I did last August. All my inclinations also are to fight for the full Petrol duties.

Winston S. Churchill to Sir Richard Hopkins and Sir Otto Niemeyer

(*Churchill papers: 18/30*)

15 April 1926

These figures in their adjusted form are deeply interesting. They illustrate very clearly the commonly accepted view, ie that the distributive trades and, above all, finance and insurance have greatly improved their position, while the basic industries have fallen back or only just held their own. Where there has been an improvement in manufacture, it is in all the miscellaneous manufactures rather than in the great trades which employ large masses of labour.

The contrast between the fortunes of the mining and metal industries on the one hand and finance and insurance on the other is most glaring. It would furnish powerful support for the argument of those who contend that the policy of the Treasury and the Bank of England has consistently, during and after the war period, favoured finance at the expense of production.

I do not understand the relations of the wholesale price test to that of the cost of living index. Is there no single test combining the two? Do not, however, trouble to prepare further figures.

There is no objection to the Colwyn Committee seeing them, but they should be regarded as confidential for the present.

Winston S. Churchill to Sir George Barstow
(*Churchill papers: 18/30*)

22 April 1926

The point should be put to the Ministry of Transport. Generally speaking, I propose to organise a far more strict system of Treasury control for the expenditure on the Roads. There can be no question of allowing the present waste to continue. Lord Salisbury was speaking with indignation in the Cabinet the other day of cases which had come to his notice. When every other part of the National Service is the subject of increasing retrenchment, it is impossible to throw the money about as they do.

Pray make me proposals including, if necessary, the engagement of a special staff for bringing a most searching scrutiny and supervision to bear upon the expenditure of the Road Board.

Stanley Baldwin to King George V
(*Baldwin papers*)

23 April 1926   House of Commons

Among the prominent soloists on the Opposition side were Sir John Simon and Mr J. H. Thomas who repeated the familiar accusations. But there was nothing in the debate really to thrill the House until Mr Churchill rose in order to deliver the final defence.[1]

Mr Churchill was in his happiest mood and imparted that happiness to the House in full measure. Obviously revelling in his task, he delivered a joyous and slashing attack on his opponents. The debates, he said, had revealed the hopeless insincerity of the Liberal and Socialist platitudinous pleas for economy. As a matter of fact the Socialists did not wish for economy —their policy had always been in favour of prodigality of expenditure.

Mr Churchill then set the House rocking with laughter with an analysis of the epithets which had been used by Opposition speakers during previous debates. The words robbery or robbed had been used 67 times, confiscation 10, plunder 10, steal 3—it had been used once more since by Mr Thomas but that addition had arrived after the list was closed—theft 2, filch 1, grab 1, cheat 1, breach of faith 19 and so on.

He himself had also received the following compliments: the villain of the piece, robber, marauder, cat-burglar and artful dodger. As, however, the Labour Party had for some years saluted him with the expression murderer, the title robber seemed to him to be a form of promotion.

Having set the House in a thoroughly good and exhilarated humour by this extremely amusing analysis Mr Churchill, taking full advantage of the atmosphere which he had thus created, delivered a first rate fighting speech in justification of the Government's policy, and, having dealt devastatingly with the vagueness and flimsiness of the Opposition's arguments, wound up on a note of defiance by declaring that the Government would be judged not by the violence of their opponents' language but by the consequences of their own actions.

If the Bill produced all the evil consequences which the Opposition had foreshadowed and resulted in a great contraction of the social services of the country, then some of the wild language used might find some excuse in the public mind. If, however, as would assuredly happen, a greater sum was spent on social services and a more efficient public and social life was developed, then all this violent language would recoil upon the heads of those who had used it.

It was a crushing rejoinder delivered in Mr Churchill's best manner, with all the rhetorical power and devices which make him one of the most formidable debaters in the House of Commons.

On a division being taken, the Economy Bill was consigned to its resting place by a majority of 388 to 138 votes.

All of which is submitted by Your Majesty's humble, obedient Servant,

[1] This being the third and final reading of the Economy Bill.

Stanley Baldwin to King George V

(*Baldwin papers*)

27 April 1926   House of Commons[1]

The Prime Minister with his humble duty to Your Majesty.

Mr Churchill had every reason to be pleased with the setting provided for the introduction of his second Budget. Every portion of the House was filled to its utmost capacity. There was a large array of peers present; the Strangers' Galleries were full to overflowing; and there has seldom been seen a larger array of Members in the Galleries running along the side of the House.

The general atmosphere was exceptionally good-tempered and good-humoured, and, as usually happens on such occasions, Members allowed political prejudice to give place to sympathy for the individual who is faced with an extremely difficult task.

Mr Churchill's speech was universally thought to be entirely worthy of the setting. It possessed the two cardinal virtues which make for success on such occasions—clearness and brevity. A modern House of Commons expects a businesslike statement, and does not appreciate, upon the opening of a Budget statement, superfluous flights of imagination or prolixity of language. Mr Churchill in his presentation of the balance sheet was concise and practical which showed that he has a better understanding of the damned dots than his father before him. In his presentation of new proposals and marshalling of argument he was equally concise and to the point.

The feature of the speech, however, which redounds greatly to his credit was the very happy way in which from time to time he succeeded in introducing light touches of wit with a view to enlivening a dry and material subject. In this he was undoubtedly assisted by the prevailing good-humour of Members on all sides who were quick to seize upon any points which were in any way calculated to provoke amusement.

Some of Mr Churchill's witticisms were the products of thought and preparation, and were included in his notes, but his nimbleness of mind was shown on many occasions by the spontaneous introduction of some happy epithet or phrase tending to brighten what must be a dull theme. One of his happiest phrases came towards the end of the speech when, having referred

---

[1] Churchill introduced his second Budget in the House of Commons on 26 April 1926. His most controversial measure was a betting tax, amounting to 5 per cent on all bets. Income Tax remained unchanged. 'The economic picture,' he said, 'is not black—it is not grey; it is piebald, and on the whole the dark patches are less prominent this year than last.' He urged thrift and economy, and warned that if there were a coal strike, he would have to ask the House of Commons for additional powers to levy new taxes, both direct and indirect, on a substantial scale.

to certain windfalls which had fallen into his lap, he added that these windfalls had been produced not only by the wind but by a certain judicious shaking of the trees.[1]

Sir Samuel Hoare to Lord Irwin

(*Irwin papers*)

29 April 1926

The Budget has been completely overshadowed by the coal business. Perhaps it is not a bad thing, as whilst it is a very ingenious affair, it is not the kind of Budget to excite much enthusiasm. Winston's speech was subdued, but on the whole successful. Indeed, he has been speaking very well in the House, particularly on the Second and Third Readings of the Economy Bill, where he had very difficult country to defend. I do not think he will have much trouble with the Budget in the House, and I believe that it is getting into peoples' heads that unless you scrap things that really matter, it is almost impossible to get expenditure below about £800 millions.

Winston S. Churchill to Sir Warren Fisher

(*Churchill papers: 18/30*)

30 April 1926

Your minute of the 27th April does not give me the information for which I asked. . . . I asked you specifically to define the functions of the Permanent Secretary in relation to the Chancellor of the Exchequer. You do not refer to this in any way. You tell me that 'the functions of the Official Secretary of the Board include responsibility for the organisation of the Treasury, for the general supervision and co-ordination of the work of the Treasury as a whole, and for advising the Board'.

Responsibility to whom? The Treasury Board never meets to transact business and is for this purpose only a fiction. If therefore your answer is

[1] During the Budget debate both Snowden and Lloyd George praised the 'rhetorical quality' of Churchill's speech, Snowden saying: 'The right hon Gentleman deserves—and this is no formal matter, as I believe I am expressing the wish of every member of the Committee—our warmest congratulations upon the rhetorical success of his speech, and the clearness with which he has put very complicated matters of detail before us.' Criticism of the Budget centred on the new taxes—principally the motor tax and the betting duty—and upon the rise in expenditure. Snowden claimed that Churchill had raised the level of expenditure by £30,000,000 in 18 months time, but only after 'raiding the sick, the disabled, and the unemployed'.

that you are responsible to the Board for matters connected with the interior organisation of the Treasury, that answer is tantamount to saying you are responsible to no one. This would clearly be unconstitutional, and you would not be covered by Ministerial responsibility.

On the other hand, your answer may be that you are responsible to the Prime Minister, and indeed we all are in our respective spheres. I certainly did not suppose that the Prime Minister would wish to exercise executive responsibility over the domestic routine and control of the Treasury. I imagined, as I stated in my last minute, that this was in practice invariably exercised by the Chancellor of the Exchequer. On consulting the Prime Minister I found that this was also his view. It therefore seems to me that while you are in practice responsible to the Prime Minister for advising him in general matters affecting the Civil Service and for such other matters as he may entrust to you, you are so far as the administration of the Treasury is concerned responsible to me.

I am of course always ready to see you, and I am sorry we have met so rarely during the 18 months I have been at the Treasury. But I think it would be more useful if you replied in writing to these perfectly plain questions. It may be that your answer will be such as to make it unnecessary for me to take the action which in other circumstances I should contemplate, namely, of obtaining a Treasury Minute defining our relationship precisely.

As an instance of the practical difficulty which has brought this matter to my notice I may mention the issue by you on March 23rd of a minute to the Department in connection with the recent leakage of information on which you had not previously consulted me. As this was a matter quite outside routine, and as I had in fact been instructed by the Cabinet to consider what action should be taken upon it, it is clear that on the assumption that you are responsible to me for the interior control of the Treasury, I should have been consulted.

I should myself have expressed the minute somewhat differently. But the point in question is that you issued this minute without consulting the Prime Minister or the Chancellor of the Exchequer, or, I need scarcely say, the Treasury Board. In other words you exercised some independent authority which you conceive to be resident in your office. This is obviously unconstitutional.

May 1926

L. S. Amery: diary

(Amery papers)

2 May 1926

... at 9.30 we assembled in Winston's room and passed the evening as best we could until about 11. Then Stanley came in very tired and threw himself into an armchair leaving it to FE to read out as far as they had got with the discussions. ...

While we were discussing the news arrived that the Daily Mail had been suppressed altogether by the printers because they did not like its leading article. We had already had information that in the Sunday Express and other papers articles had been considerably censored or dropped out. This turned the scale.[1]

---

[1] In a note written ten days later, J. C. C. Davidson recorded that, at the meetings on 2 May 1926, 'Churchill, Neville Chamberlain, Balfour, Bridgeman and Hogg successively made it clear that it must be the result of the General Strike instructions that had already been dispatched, and the Cabinet came to the conclusion that they could no longer negotiate under the threat of a General Strike, particularly now that this had resulted in an action to silence the press. The negotiations were promptly suspended and the Government demanded the repudiation of the actions that had taken place and an immediate and unconditional withdrawal of the instructions for a General Strike.' Davidson added: 'It is a point worth making that there was no dissension on this point. It has often been written that the extremists forced Baldwin's hand, but nothing could be further from the truth' (Davidson papers).

Winston S. Churchill: notes for a meeting with Newspaper Proprietors[1]

(*Churchill papers: 22/142*)

3 May 1926

The Government has decided upon the immediate issue of a daily bulletin as suggested by the Newspaper Proprietors' Association.[2] The matter is of the utmost urgency as the first issue should be made tomorrow morning. The following questions should be considered:—

(1) The name. ?'The London Gazette.'

(2) The printing offices which should be used should be selected.

(3) The editorial and journalistic staff.

(4) The arrangements for procuring the necessary volunteers.

(5) The status of the paper in relation to the Government. The Government will take full responsibility and use its powers of requisition as may be thought advisable.

(6) The channel of communication between the Government and the editorial staff will be the Parliamentary Secretary to the Admiralty[3] working under direct instructions from the Cabinet.

(7) The question of distribution.

(8) What use can be made of the broadcasting arrangements? Is it possible to have several local editions of the London Gazette published in parts of the country where a large portion of the newspaper trade unions will continue?

(9) What is to be the price? Experience shows that what is not paid for is not valued. Suggested price 1d, the receipts to go in aid of the expenses of production. The Government assume the whole responsibility for the balance expense. Side by side with the copies sold there will of course be a large free distribution to all authorities throughout the country. The Air Ministry will no doubt co-operate in deliveries.

[1] As soon as the Government had broken off negotiations with the TUC there was no further chance of averting a general strike, and on Monday, May 3, the Government finalized its preparations. Executive authority for all measures in confronting the strikers was given to the Home Secretary, Sir William Joynson-Hicks, who prepared to send troops to wherever they were needed to protect vehicles carrying food and fuel. All strike-breaking plans were discussed by a special Cabinet Committee, the Supply and Transport Committee, presided over by Joynson-Hicks. During the morning of May 3, this Committee decided that as the strike was likely to affect all newspapers, the leading newspaper editors should be asked to co-operate in the publication of a single emergency news-sheet, and that Sir Samuel Hoare, L. S. Amery and J. C. C. Davidson should arrange for its distribution by road and air. At the Committee's request, Churchill prepared a ten-point programme on the nature of the proposed news-sheet.

[2] The Government's decision was made in anticipation of the General Strike, which was to begin at one minute before midnight on 3 May 1926. It was expected that once the Strike began, no newspapers whatsoever would be published.

[3] J. C. C. Davidson.

(10) The editorial staff would of course not be confined to the official communications but make the publication as interesting as possible with the object of encouraging and helping the action of all loyal men.

The Government is considering the issue of regulations forbidding any newspaper to appear during the crisis without a licence. Licences will however be granted to all well-disposed newspapers, which should do their best to appear, however abridged.

All papers should be urged to do their best to produce even the smallest sheet either singly or in groups.

WSC

Notes of a meeting held at the Treasury

(Churchill papers: 22/142)

3 May 1926   Chancellor of the Exchequer's Room

THE CHANCELLOR OF THE EXCHEQUER opened the Meeting by thanking the Members of the Newspaper Proprietors' Association and the Newspaper Society for having come at so short notice. He then proceeded to read the note which had been prepared with regard to the issue of a daily bulletin. He explained that the matter was extremely urgent and that while details would be left to them to arrange with Mr Davidson there were certain important questions of principle which he wished to discuss with them. Having read the note, he explained that these were merely rough ideas which had been put together in order to show the various aspects of the problem, that they were not then meeting to take any definite decisions but only to put forward suggestions which might form the basis of prompt decisions.

LORD BURNHAM replied by referring to the resolutions which the Newspaper Proprietors' Association had passed at their Meeting yesterday, a copy of which had been forwarded to the Prime Minister. They were glad to observe that the Government had been largely guided by them in the scheme which they had in view. He pointed out that in the last resolution they had offered to confer with the Government in regard to the carrying out of the second resolution. He said that he understood that the Government wished to refer these matters to the newspapers for consideration among themselves. He explained that there would be a meeting at 3 o'clock that day of the Newspaper Proprietors' Association. He did not of course know what was being done by the Newspaper Society. He went on to say 'I am sure we shall be prepared to implement this assurance and to let you know later, on the points you put up, how we think we can give you the best assistance.

'In regard to the question of distribution, although of course there are men who are expert in that branch of the newspaper trade, it would also be a case for the big wholesale agents to help you—W. H. Smith and H. Marshall being the principle ones. But I have no doubt you are in communication with them. I do not know whether there is any idea of commandeering the vans and cars which we all have in varying extent for this service. Perhaps that is a point about which you would like to hear from us later. I do not think you will expect us to suggest anything in regard to this at the moment.

'The best means of carrying out your proposal would be either by an advisory committee or by obtaining the services of good journalists to help, but that is a question which can be discussed by ourselves or with the particular newspaper.'

MR CHURCHILL: There is not the slightest objection to an advisory committee, but the essential thing is that we should produce a really powerful readable broadsheet not merely to contain news but in order to relieve the minds of the people. Something must be done to prevent alarming news from being spread about and there is no reason why it should not be done as well as possible. I do not contemplate violent partisanship, but fair, strong encouragement to the great mass of loyal people.

LORD BURNHAM: . . . As far as our newspapers are concerned, the position is very difficult. We decided to carry out very much what you suggest in your notes this afternoon and to recommend all newspaper printers to publish as long as they can. We are ready to give such assistance as is in our power—that is as far as the London committee is concerned—but I do not think we can do very much.

MR CHURCHILL: I am told a number of Provincial papers will come out.

LORD RIDDELL: How do you propose to provide labour?

MR CHURCHILL: Volunteers.

LORD RIDDELL: But I mean the printing itself.

LORD BURNHAM pointed out that notices from all the trade unions would be in this afternoon.

The Secretary of the NEWSPAPER SOCIETY said that most of the trade unions are instructing their members to finish their jobs tonight.

THE CHANCELLOR enquired whether an edition would be brought out tomorrow.

LORD BURNHAM said that they would but that they did not know whether trains starting before 12 o'clock would continue after that time.

The Secretary of the NEWSPAPER SOCIETY said that those trains starting before midnight would complete their journey before 6 o'clock but that it was not clear what would happen to trains starting after 6 o'clock, and that many important papers go on them.

MR CHURCHILL: I certainly contemplated that this advisory committee would decide on the selection of the highly competent editorial staff, and that this staff would have a free hand to run the paper according to their own idea.

LORD RIDDELL: But how are you going to print the paper?

MR CHURCHILL: I contemplate getting volunteers and also contemplate making use of the Government printing arrangements.

MR DAVIDSON: I do not think we could spare the Government printers.

MR CHURCHILL: Anyhow when the premises are taken back after all this is over if amateurs have been using the machines and damage is done I will be responsible.

LORD BURNHAM: There is no difficulty about the journalistic side.

MR DAVIDSON enquired whether it would be possible to arrange for over-seers to be available.

LORD BURNHAM said that this was quite impossible, that these men were wholly trade union, and that as far as London was concerned it was im-possible to provide mechanical skill.

It was suggested that the only way to provide such labour would be by the use of non-union labour belonging to houses in the country.

MR CHURCHILL: How many men do you want?

MR DAVIDSON: Would it not be better to take staff bodily from non-union houses and deposit them in the building and produce a small paper?

LORD BURNHAM: I think it would be better to ask what staff would be required for the production of an eight page paper.

SIR A. CAIRD:[1] I should think that would require 200 men. The difficulty is in getting them to work the press. It is highly complicated and very difficult to handle. There would be great difficulty in getting volunteers and they would most likely damage the press. It is the question of volun-teers that is really the crux of the whole thing. We have been going into that matter in my house, we have been discussing whether the 'Evening News' is to be stopped. I understand the 'Evening Standard' is also dis-cussing the question with its men. We are asking our men when the

[1] Andrew Caird, 1870–1956. Educated at Montrose Academy and Dundee University College. Administrator, New York Headquarters, British (Northcliffe) War Mission to the United States, 1917–18. Knighted, 1918. Managing Director of the *Daily Mail*, 1922–6. Chairman and Managing Director of the *Calcutta Statesman*, 1927–8. Unsuccessful Conservative candidate for St Ives, 1928 and 1929.

'Evening News' has stopped if there are any who are willing to volunteer to carry on the 'Evening News' tonight and we shall get some indication of the spirit of the men.

We ought to try to bring out a four page standard size paper. But the question of getting men to man the press is extraordinarily difficult. If there is a non-union office in the country the thing to do is to lift the whole crew and bring them to London. There is a great difficulty with regard to good men, all of them who would be loyal do not dare to for fear of not being allowed to work once the trouble is over.

MR CHURCHILL: Tell me where the difficulty is.

SIR A. CAIRD: There is no difficulty with regard to the editorial, the compositors or the stereotypers. There is no real difficulty about distribution. Packers, distributors, compositors and stereotypers are all right. The great difficulty is in turning the press.

MR CHURCHILL: Is that so difficult? Is it quite impossible to teach a highly educated person with a good teacher?

SIR A. CAIRD: It is impossible if they have never worked on a machine before.

MR CHURCHILL: Are there not at the university people who know how to print?

Someone said that this was not so.

MR DAVIDSON: If you are printing a comparatively small four sheet paper would it be the most efficient to use the biggest machine?

LORD RIDDELL: It is much easier to get men to work machines of that sort. Rotary machines are complicated. There are few men in the country able to work them. But if it is your intention only to bring out a small sheet a number of non union houses could turn out a flat sheet.

MR CODLING:[1] It is quite unnecessary to run these big machines on this small job.

MR CHURCHILL made some suggestion about aiming at a million to begin with.

SIR A. CAIRD: I think that idea is the best one, that we turn it into a two page sheet.

LORD RIDDELL: The same size as the 'Evening Standard'?

SIR A. CAIRD: Find out the best size. 'The Evening Standard' would do quite well.

MR CHURCHILL: Only two pages?

---

[1] William Richard Codling, 1879–1947. Educated at Enfield Grammar School and King's College, London. Entered the Stationery Office, 1898; Superintendent of Publications, 1916–17; Deputy Controller, 1917–19; Controller, 1919–42. Knighted, 1935. Member of the Statute Law Committee of the United Kingdom and Northern Ireland.

SIR A. CAIRD: You could get all you want on that. You could send moulds and proofs of it all over the country. Every newspaper that could print could adopt these two pages.

LORD RIDDELL: One rotary press will turn out an enormous number of copies. Directly you begin to add copies difficulties increase. If you only want to bring out four pages—

MR CHURCHILL: What is the size of the print you mean?

LORD RIDDELL indicated the size.

MR CHURCHILL: We can begin on that. Now as to time. If you are certain that you can give some sort of paper tomorrow and not after we must assume that Wednesday is the day on which there will be nothing.

LORD RIDDELL: To what extent does this print consist of comments? A great many different points of view are represented here, and I am not expressing any opinion, but you quite understand it will be necessary for us to understand what sort of comment is going into the paper. Is it to be solely of news and speeches, proclamations, or is it to have something in the nature of a leading article, and what is to be the policy of that article?

MR CHURCHILL: Obviously mainly of news, speeches, etc, also recruiting going on, anything occurring in the country, organisations. But it should have a leading article, not violently partisan, but agreeable to the great majority of the people of our side. Constitutional, the hope for peace, Parliament maintain authority in the country, injury to trade and reputation of the country.

LORD BURNHAM: Is this to be a Government publication for which the Government are responsible, or is it suggested that these two associations should assume responsibility?

MR CHURCHILL: How would you like it? We are ready to take any action.

LORD BURNHAM: I am only expressing individual opinion, but it must be a Government publication. It would not be fair to make us particularly responsible. The Government ought to take the responsibility.

MR CHURCHILL: I contemplate the whole of the responsibility to any stage you wish to enable people to work together. It would not be sectional in any way.

LORD RIDDELL: We suggested the best way of keeping the public informed is by means of daily bulletins. Is it not for the Government to carry this out?

MR CHURCHILL: You do what you like.

LORD BURNHAM: There is no doubt I think we could take immediate action. No doubt about our being able to take action.

MR HARMSWORTH: There are two ways out of the difficulty. We are perfectly willing to go to any expense on our own and any trouble to produce with non-Union labour if necessary provided the Government will give us protection. If that is not done the Government must take entire responsibility for the publication of all newspapers.

MR CHURCHILL: If you were successful you would produce reduced editions of the 'Daily Mail'?

MR HARMSWORTH: Yes.

LORD RIDDELL: If the leading article were from the Government point of view it would be difficult for our paper to be directly associated with such a publication for fear that the persons associated with it might be involved in its views. The question of individual assistance is another matter. We had better talk this over this afternoon.

SIR A. CAIRD: It must be a Government publication and you must confine it to news. If you call upon a London paper to write an article—

LORD BURNHAM: When we come to practical consideration, surely speeches by Ministers would be much better than a leading article. You can get all you want in another way.

LORD RIDDELL: You could get it printed a great deal easier if you can find news. They (the printers) would regard for example, speeches by the Prime Minister as news.

MR CHURCHILL: The thing that matters is to get it started—to get something out on Wednesday morning.

LORD RIDDELL: Instruct Mr Codling to arrange for printing which he is quite able to do. He knows the capacity of the general printing offices and where to lay his hands on various presses.

MR CODLING: I do not know where the provincial presses are.

LORD RIDDELL: I am talking about the general printing trade.

LORD BURNHAM: No office could be aggrieved if it were commandeered. That would be a general printing office.

MR CHURCHILL: We want you to help us. We are prepared to take full responsibility for the character of the newspaper and for the costs and for all defence measures. As for the exact form and as to the character of the article and so forth, we are ready to take your guide after you have considered it among yourselves. Give us a plan of action, what you want, where we are to put our hands on paper.

LORD RIDDELL: The matter is quite simple. Mr Codling is greatly experienced in getting large things done under emergency, how to get the sheet printed and how to buy paper. When you have made those arrangements the production of matter to put in it is a matter of arrangement.

MR CHURCHILL: Can you do that? And that would not prevent independent arrangements?

LORD RIDDELL: That is another matter. As far as printing is concerned Mr Codling can find out where that is to be done. No elaborate staff would be wanted for news.

LORD BURNHAM: You could get paper at once.

MR CODLING: The paper in existence is not suitable for the machines in the office. Your paper would not take my rotaries.

MR CHURCHILL: It is no good doing it unless you start on a million.

MR DAVIDSON: It is for us to take full responsibility for all things including requisitioning of premises. We want you to help the Government by producing the paper. We take full responsibility for it and for distributing it. We want you to think out a scheme and to decide what Government help is necessary. We want the newspaper to be produced, edited and distributed as far as possible, with all the help we can give, by the people who are accustomed to do it. If we print the thing we probably will not know all the ramifications. Without your help it is impossible. We want a common newspaper to keep alive the idea that a newspaper exists.

MR CHURCHILL: Can you not get 200 men? With all the wealth of the country this should be possible.

LORD RIDDELL: There is no difficulty in getting the paper printed if you go about it in the right way. Mr Codling can easily get it done. Distribution is not a very difficult matter. I have no doubt you would be able to get the paper printed. But there is the practical question of management. I do not know that we are the best people under the circumstances to do this. The ordinary means of printing and distribution are taken away from us. Therefore it is really a question for practical printers like Mr Codling.

MR CODLING: I have got all the miscellaneous other printing of the Government, and I do not want this.

MR HARMSWORTH: We are going to print as much as possible. If you will provide the protection and if you will get the men something will be produced.

MR CHURCHILL: I cannot get the men. But I am prepared if you put forward a scheme for getting men, to finance it.

LORD BURNHAM: I understand that Sir Charles Hyde's[1] (the Birmingham Post) is a non-union house, and they have a big plant. We have been listening to London almost exclusively.

The President of the NEWSPAPER SOCIETY here indicated that Sir Charles

---

[1] Charles Hyde, 1876–1942. Proprietor of the *Birmingham Post*. Created Baronet, 1922. Chairman, Birmingham Pensions Hospitals and Queen's Hospital, Birmingham. Warden of the Guild of Undergraduates, Birmingham University, 1923–5. High Sheriff of Warwickshire, 1933–4.

Hyde was not a member of his Society and that he did not know what he was a member of.

PRESIDENT OF NEWSPAPER SOCIETY: I think there are enough machine men to supply the country if they are wired for.

MR DAVIDSON: I raised that point some time ago.

MR CHURCHILL: Would you work at the London Gazette?

SIR A. CAIRD: That I cannot say.

MR HARMSWORTH: We could certainly work at the London Gazette, but if there is an appeal for newspapers to produce what they can naturally they will do so.

MR CHURCHILL: Where is your meeting?

LORD BURNHAM: At 3 o'clock at Bouverie Street.

MR CHURCHILL: Would it not be more convenient to meet here?

LORD BURNHAM: I think it would be better at Bouverie Street.

MR CHURCHILL: Will you ask for a small committee?

LORD BURNHAM: I think that would be better. Meanwhile cannot you put yourselves into communication at once with Sir Charles Hyde at Birmingham. . . .

LORD RIDDELL: Do you promise protection for newspapers willing to produce on their own account?

MR CHURCHILL: Certainly. An enquiry was made as to whether the Government would promise any number of men that if they took the risk and worked they would be looked after afterwards. Some men would work if assured of that.

MR CHURCHILL: I am perfectly prepared but I must have your proposal made to me in writing. We want 200 men to work. I am prepared to guarantee these 200 men to an extent which we can discuss, but which would certainly be ample.

LORD BURNHAM: I would again suggest the importance of getting into touch with these big non-union men in Birmingham and Edinburgh.

MR CHURCHILL then handed round copies of the note which he had read out and asked the meeting to discuss it and let him have something in writing.

MR DAVIDSON raised the question of the title which had been suggested of the 'London Gazette' and pointed out that the present 'London Gazette' would have to go on.

THE CHANCELLOR said that the proposed paper could be called the 'London Gazette Extraordinary'.

Stanley Baldwin to King George V

(*Baldwin papers*)

4 May 1926   House of Commons

Mr Churchill followed with a speech in which his natural exuberance was noticeably tempered by self imposed restraint and a tremendous sense of responsibility. He re-stated the Government's position clearly, directly and precisely with little attempt to conceal the ugly facts of the situation. He declared that the trade union leaders had as their object the indefinite continuance of the Government subsidy and emphatically repudiated any possibility of such a step.[1]

In his denunciation of the general strike and his firm declaration that this was a threat to which no Government could yield, he combined dignity, gravity and courage. He made it clear that in no circumstances would the Government hesitate in facing the challenge unflinchingly and resolutely to the end, but he combined this firm declaration with the more peaceful announcement that the door was still open to negotiation provided that the Trades Union Congress cancelled the notices which they had issued as a necessary preliminary step.

Mr Thomas at once seized upon this statement in order to ascertain whether the Government in such circumstances would arrange for the lock-out notices to be withdrawn in order to permit of further negotiations.

Mr Churchill replied that the threat must first be removed and that the withdrawal of the lock-out notices would be a matter for subsequent negotiation.

---

[1] In his speech, Churchill had pointed out that while the miners' strike was a legitimate one, 'that is an entirely different thing from the concerted, deliberate organised menace of a General Strike in order to compel Parliament to do something which otherwise it would not do'. If fought out to a conclusion the conflict between the strikers and the Government could only end 'in the overthrow of Parliamentary Government or in its decisive victory'. There was no middle course open. 'The Government may be bundled out of the way,' he said, 'but the other forces, enemies to the Parliamentary constitutional system of this country, forces which deserve and require the consistent control of democrats in every land, would emerge and carry on the struggle in infinitely more disastrous and tragical forms than with which we are now threatened.' During his speech Churchill sought to maintain a balance between firmness and compromise, telling the House of Common: 'We are seeking peace, we are defending ourselves, we are bound to defend ourselves from the terrible menace which is levied upon us from tomorrow morning, but we are still perfectly unchanged in our attitude as it was last week. The door is always open. . . . There is no question of there being a gulf across which no negotiator can pass—certainly not . . . it is our duty to parley.'

Thomas Jones: diary

(*Jones papers*)

4 May 1926   10 Downing Street

The PM said he felt Ramsay was feeling the position acutely. None of the leaders were strong enough to turn and tell their followers the truth. 'We shall have to find some way,' the PM went on, 'to deal with all this Trade Union business, and revise its powers and machinery so far as the Government is concerned in the light of this tremendous centralising of their powers. We must get some way by which the voice of the rank and file can be made effective.'

At this point Winston came in and announced that he had commandeered the offices and machinery of the 'Morning Post' with a view to bringing out some sort of Government news sheet. I asked both what was to be my line in any private conversations to-day with any of the Labour folk. Winston said 'There are two disputes on: there is the General Strike which is a challenge to the Government and with which we cannot compromise. Strike Notices must be withdrawn unconditionally. There is also a trade dispute in the coal industry: on that we are prepared to take the utmost pains to reach a settlement in the most conciliatory spirit.'

Sir Samuel Hoare: diary

(*Templewood papers*)

4 May 1926.

Visit to Max.[1] Winston there. Blood and Iron. [Winston in his element].[2] Drive round papers with him after midnight. My idea of 'British' in title.[3]

---

[1] At the offices of the *Daily Express* in Fleet Street.

[2] This sentence appears to have been added later by Sir Samuel Hoare to his diary entry. Of the Cabinet meeting on the eve of the General Strike, Hoare wrote in his diary notes: 'There were no divisions among Ministers and it is incorrect to say that a Churchill–Birkenhead section were determined upon a fight to the finish.'

[3] The title finally chosen was *British Gazette*. The first copies were on sale on the morning of May 5. Copies were flown to the North by special volunteer pilots. Of this first number, a total of 230,000 copies were printed, distributed and sold.

Frederick Guest to Winston S. Churchill

(*Churchill papers: 22/141*)

5 May 1926   Civil Servants' Hospitality Office

Dear Winston,

I gather from reliable sources that the tone of the Broadcast service is 'defeatist'—

Today it opened:

'Cross channel service cut off'

It gave the impression that we were cut off from Europe. It turned out to be the Irish Channel!!

Then—

British Gazette 2 sheets

Times limited sheet

British Worker News *8 sheets*

Several other papers got out editions to which no reference was made, Express, Telegraph etc. I don't know who runs the Broadcast but some other Govt news ought to be set up by an expert journalist & psychologist—

This is illustration enough for your quick mind.

At present I have 50 beds & no takers, (only 14 to be exact).

Winston S. Churchill: draft article for the 'British Gazette'

(*Churchill papers: 22/142*)

5 May 1926

A few words are needed to explain the appearance of the 'British Gazette'.

There are at present two quite different disputes which are holding up the country. The first is the stoppage in the Coal Industry. This is a Trade dispute which could be settled in the ordinary way. The Government have already paid a subsidy of £23 millions to give time for this industry to put its affairs on a sound basis. They cannot, however, continue paying out between £2 and £3 millions a month of the taxpayers' money to the employers and workers in one particular trade. Moreover, exporting Coal at a loss to our rivals only increases their unfair competition with British manufactures. Lastly, if we go on subsidising our export Coal, Germany and other rivals will have to do the same. Thus every nation will be impoverishing itself in uneconomic competition. The Coal Industry must therefore come on to an economic basis.

The Coal Commission has shown how this can be done. The Government have accepted their proposals and will carry out the Recommendations affecting the State, even where this particular Government does not agree with them. But the Owners and the Miners must do their part as well. The Owners have agreed to nearly everything recommended by the Commission; and it is certain that the small part to which they have not yet agreed would never be allowed to be the sole block to the scientific re-organisation of the Coal Industry. The Miners' Leaders have not, however, made the slightest real advance towards an acceptance of those recommendations in the Report which do not call for any sacrifice from them.

In spite of the nine months breathing space which has been obtained, or the £23 millions of public money which has been spent, or the fact that even with the subsidy there have never been less than a hundred thousand miners unemployed in the coal fields, the Leaders remain in exactly the same position as they were in last July. This may be natural, and one cannot help sympathising with the Miners themselves in their difficulty. But it is no use making these difficulties worse by prolonging the subsidy or trying to carry on the Coal Trade month after month at a heavy loss. All three parties— Government, Owners and Miners—ought to accept unreservedly the whole of the Recommendations of the Coal Commission. And if they do, and when they do, the Government, apart from doing its share, will not refuse a helping hand. So much for the Trade dispute which has caused the stoppage of the Coal Industry.

On the top of this has now come a second dispute. The Trade Union Leaders, having failed to induce the Miners to make any concessions, have felt bound nevertheless to support them. They have therefore declared a General Strike and called out millions of men in carefully selected vital trades throughout the country. This has for the time being paralysed the whole business of the nation, and prevented this crowded island from earning its daily bread by manufacture and commerce.

If the General Strike is prolonged for many weeks, the prosperity of Great Britain will be ruined for probably as many years. Our foreign rivals will eagerly supplant us in overseas markets. Unemployment, which had just dipped below the million, will rise again at an unprecedented rate. Unemployment Insurance and all the working class funds will be exhausted; and hard times, such as were not known even during the worst of the war, will descend for a long period on the whole community.

The Trade Union Leaders believe that this threat will compel the Government to grant an indefinite prolongation of the subsidy to the Coal Trade at the expense of the general taxpayer. This has been shown to be a foolish and useless policy, no better than drinking salt water to relieve thirst. No one has pointed this out more strongly than the wiser and more responsible Labour leaders [like Mr Ramsay MacDonald and Mr J. H. Thomas].[1] If Parliament were to allow its considered judgment to be overborne under the cruel assault of a General Strike, the economic disaster would only be a part of a much greater disaster. It would be definitely established that the weapon of a General Strike which the Trade Union Leaders at present wield is irresistible. These men, although it is certainly not the object of the great majority of them, would in fact become the masters of the whole country, and the power of government would have passed from Parliament into their hands. This would involve the virtual supersession of Paraliament and of the representative institutions which we have established in our island after three hundred years of struggle, which we have preserved almost alone among the nations of Europe, and which are the foundation of our democratic freedom. Instead of the representatives of the nation duly elected on a franchise almost universal, our rights and destinies would be in the hands of a body of men who, however well meaning most of them may be, represent only a section of the public and have derived no authority from the people comparable to that of the House of Commons.

We must never forget, even in the heat and height of this struggle, that we are all fellow citizens. But the democratic State cannot possibly submit to sectional dictation. It is bound to defend and assert, no matter at what cost, the National and Constitutional authority. While, therefore, there is plenty of room for negotiation and a spirit of compromise about the Coal Trade, there can be absolutely none about a General Strike. That is not a dispute between employers and workmen. It is a conflict between the Trade Union Leaders and Parliament. And that conflict must only end, and can only end, in the decisive and unmistakable victory of Parliament. This victory His Majesty's Government is definitely resolved to secure.

Ample force to preserve the laws and the life of the nation is at the disposal of the State. But force is not the instrument on which a British Government should rely. We rely on reason, on public opinion and on the will of the people. In this crisis the organisers of the General Strike have made it their first care to paralyse public opinion by breaking down and muzzling the newspapers on which the whole people have been accustomed to rely for information about what is going on at home and abroad. Nearly all the newspapers have been silenced by violent concerted action. And this great nation, on the whole the strongest community which civilisation can show, is for the moment reduced in this respect to the level of African natives dependent only on the rumours which are carried from place to place.

[1] Before printing this article in the *British Gazette*, Churchill deleted the words in square brackets.

In a few days, if this were allowed to continue, rumours would poison the air, raise panics and disorders, inflame fears and passions together, and carry us all to depths which no sane man of any Party or class would care even to contemplate. The Government have therefore decided not only to use Broadcasting for spreading information, but to bring out a paper of their own on a sufficient scale to carry full and timely news throughout all parts of the country.

The 'British Gazette' is run without profit on the authority and, if necessary, at the expense of the Government. It begins necessarily on a small scale, and its first issue cannot exceed 700,000 copies. It is proposed, however, to use the unlimited resources of the State, with the assistance of all loyal persons, to raise the circulation day after day until it provides sure and sufficient means of information and a guide for action for all British citizens.

Winston S. Churchill: draft article for the 'British Gazette'

(*Churchill papers: 22/142*)

5 May 1926

Everyone must realise that, so far as the General Strike is concerned, there can be no question of compromise of any kind. Either the country will break the General Strike, or the General Strike will break the country. Not only is the prosperity of the country gravely injured; not only is immense and increasing loss and suffering inflicted upon the whole mass of the people; but the foundations of the lawful Constitution of Great Britain are assailed. His Majesty's Government will not flinch from the issue, and will use all the resources at their disposal and whatever measures may be necessary to secure in a decisive manner the authority of Parliamentary government.

The Prime Minister's message to 'The British Gazette' expresses a decision from which there can be no withdrawal.[1] All loyal citizens, without respect to Party or class, should forthwith range themselves behind His Majesty's Government and Parliament in the task of defeating in an exemplary fashion the deliberate and organised assault upon the rights and freedom of the

---

[1] The second and third issues of the *British Gazette* on May 5 and May 6 contained the following message from Baldwin: 'Constitutional Government is being attacked. Let all good citizens whose livelihood and labour have thus been put in peril bear with fortitude and patience the hardships with which they have been so suddenly confronted. Stand behind the Government, who are doing their part, confident that you will co-operate in the measures they have undertaken to preserve the liberties and privileges of the people of these islands. The laws of England are the people's birthright. The laws are in your keeping. You have made Parliament their guardian. The General Strike is a challenge to Parliament and is the road to anarchy and ruin.'

nation. The stronger the rally of loyal and faithful men to the cause of Parliamentary government, the sooner will the victory be achieved and the shorter the period of waste and suffering.

No doubt it is true that the majority of the Trades Union leaders did not intend, when they launched the General Strike, to raise the Constitutional issue. They drifted weakly forward under the pressure of more extreme men. Perhaps they thought that the Government would collapse and Parliament bow down before the threat of so much injury to the commonwealth. But whatever they may have wished or thought, a national issue has been raised of supreme magnitude.

Moreover, the responsibility of these Trades Union leaders is grievous. It is also a personal responsibility. They made no attempt to consult by ballot those whom they claim to represent. They broke in many directions contracts and engagements to which their good name was pledged; and they yielded themselves to a course of action reckless, violent and, but for the strength and good sense of the British nation, immeasurable in its possibilities. It would be the manly course on their part, and one which they have a perfect right to take, to reconsider their action now that they can see into what deep and deepening waters it is daily carrying them. It is not yet too late.

But whatever they may do, the authority of Parliamentary government over any sectional combination must be vindicated. Every man and every woman must consider where duty lies and, where duties seem to conflict, where the greater duty lies. The first of all duties, a duty greater than all others put together, is owed to the nation as a whole and to that system of democratic and representative Parliamentary government which has for so many generations been the mainstay of British progress and of British freedom.

Winston S. Churchill to Professor Lindemann: telegram

(*Treasury papers: T172/1558*)

5 May 1926

Your volunteers should report to Locker-Lampson's office St Stephen's House where full arrangements are made to put them up. Whole fourteen should report at Treasury Whitehall this evening. If you care to come can put you up at Downing Street.

Sir Philip Sassoon[1] to Sir Samuel Hoare

(*Templewood papers*)

6 May 1926   Cambridge

The publication of the Government newspaper is the finest thing that cd have happened & has impressed & heartened people all over the country enormously.[2]

J. C. C. Davidson to Stanley Baldwin

(*Baldwin papers*)

6 May 1926
Secret and Personal

The failure to some extent in the details of distribution of the British Gazette has been due entirely to the fact that the Chancellor occupied the attention of practically the whole of the staff who normally would have been thinking out the details. Of course he was anxious, but it was unfortunate that he tried so persistently to force a scratch staff beyond its capacity. So long as he does not come to the Morning Post Offices to-night the staff will be able to do what it is there to do, viz organize the printing, the production and distribution of the Gazette. I must depend on you, and the staff are relying on me, to find some means of preventing his coming. By all means let him put what pressure he can personally upon Sir Malcolm Fraser,[3] who is in general control, and the Stationery Office, by interview or letter, but the technical staff should be left to do their job. He rattled them very badly last night. He thinks he is Napoleon, but curiously enough the men who have

---

[1] Sassoon had been appointed one of the Government's special Regional Commissioners for the duration of the General Strike.

[2] Three days later Sassoon wrote to Hoare: 'our organisation for distributing the Gazette is working perfectly & we can do with as many more copies as you can spare for us. I am getting it down as far as possible into the villages & all those who received this morning's leaflet are putting it up in their windows' (*Templewood papers*).

[3] John Malcolm Fraser, 1878–1949. Journalist. Adviser on Press matters to the Conservative Party, 1910. Lieutenant, Royal Navy Air Service, 1915; Captain, 1918. Deputy-Director of Airship Production at the Admiralty, 1918–19 (when over a hundred airships were completed). Reorganized the Literature Department of the Conservative Party Headquarters, 1919. Knighted, 1919. Principal Agent of the Conservative Party, 1920–3; Vice-Chairman, 1937–8. Appointed by the Government to produce the *British Gazette* during the General Strike of May 1926. At different times, editor of the *Evening Standard*, the *St James Gazette*, the *Daily Express* (Day Editor) and the *Birmingham Gazette* (Editor-in-Chief).

been printing all their life in the various processes happen to know more about their job than he does. May I suggest that you should enlist the services of Jix in urging that it is not safe for him to come.[1]

Lord Wodehouse to Winston S. Churchill
(Churchill papers: 22/141)

7 May 1926   Treasury Chambers

I took down copies of the British Gazette to Woodford this morning, and they were distributed in the Constituency. I visited Volunteer Service Committees in Woodford & Wanstead with Hawkey, also Ilford, Walthamstow & Leytonstone which are in the area Hawkey controls.

These centres are all working well though a shortage of meat and flour is anticipated owing to refusal to allow delivery by TUC.

Arrangements have been made for regular supply of British Gazette & distribution in the Constituency from tomorrow morning.

Everyone very pleased that you are dealing with the Strike. They all have the greatest confidence in you.

Hawkey's report is attached.

Winston S. Churchill to Sir Laming Worthington-Evans
(Churchill papers: 22/141)

7 May 1926   Treasury Chambers

I am seriously concerned at several important things. I am sure you have not got enough force, and this may entail the use of lethal force unnecessarily. The Home Office are far behind in Special Constables. We ought to have at least 300,000 trustworthy men under our hands during the next week. You and they will incur an enormous responsibility unless you are able to devise effectual schemes for increasing the forces at your disposal. If in the meanwhile any wide-spread disorder occurs which hampers the movement of essential foodstuffs and the situation threatens to go out of control, there is only one course open to you—you must embody the Territorial Army.

[1] On 14 June 1926 J. C. C. Davidson wrote to Lord Irwin (the Viceroy of India): 'Winston is really a most remarkable creature. His energy was boundless and he ran entirely on his own lines. Whether it was right or wrong he desired to produce a newspaper rather than a news sheet. He, in fact conceived that the *British Gazette* should be a better newspaper than any of the great journals whose operations had been temporarily suspended' (*India Office papers*).

Do not, I beg you, speaking with the knowledge of so many years of military affairs, be misled by silly War Office objections against this necessary measure. The Territorial Army will recover after the conflict is over, but even if it suffers for some years it will not have suffered in vain. Such an embodiment will immediately give you the necessary mass of men to afford the wide-spread protection which is essential, and will enable you to keep the regular units concentrated. It is far better to take too many precautions than too few. I am not suggesting that this measure need be decided upon for the next two or three days, but only begging you to prepare your mind for it.

You should look at the last supplementary bulletin, which shows that all our vaunted railway services do not exceed one-twentieth of the normal.

Winston S. Churchill: draft article for the 'British Gazette'

(*Churchill papers: 22/142*)

7 May 1926

No one must underrate the prodigious task which is before us. The trade and business of the country will soon come to a standstill. But merely to carry on the supply of food and milk and power and to maintain the necessary communications of 45 millions of people when those who should do this task have deserted their posts is of immense difficulty. It is being successfully solved at the present time. But these services on which the life—not the prosperity but the life—of millions of the nation depend can only be carried on if there is unfailing and active support of the authorities by the large majority of citizens. The success which has hitherto attended the maintenance of vital services must not lead people into imagining that very grave dangers do not threaten the State and the whole community, or that any relaxation of effort or weakness of purpose is possible. Above all, there must be no over-confidence.

There can be no question of impartiality between the public and the strikers, or between the Government and the trade unions. The Government and Parliament represent the whole nation, the trade unions less than one-tenth of it. The Government is constitutionally established; the trade unions are wielding an illegitimate power.

The Government is toiling to feed the people; the trade unions are toiling to starve them. The Government is trying to preserve the health and life of the public; the trade unions are recklessly and wantonly endangering both in order to usurp power. The picketing which is taking place all over the country is deliberately intended to prevent the necessary movement of food and fuel. The plan of the general strike is progressively to stop all forms of livelihood and employment and to throw enormous masses of the people into the streets and strikes or on to the dole as unemployed.

Should the efforts of the Government and its volunteers to preserve the vital services in any large area of the country be frustrated, a great and terrible disaster will occur and the lives of very large numbers of people will be in jeopardy. If the organism of Government in any large area were to be successfully broken down by the trade unions, immense suffering and help-less confusion in that area would follow. To restore such a situation would entail the use of armed force. If this is to be avoided public opinion must range itself without hesitation and vehemently upon the side of established authority.

It is possible for the Government to protect vehicles, power, food stores and other essentials. Only a strong and active public opinion can give pro-tection to loyal workers and their families in their homes, and only a strong tide of public resentment against the evil-doers can recall the mass of strikers to their duty and hold in awe the malignant elements which are now so active.

It would be altogether wrong for an official newspaper like this to lull the public into a false security, or lead them to suppose that their homes and daily bread can be preserved apart from a strong and resolute attitude on their part. A terrible responsibility rests upon any man who associates him-self with the organised attempt now going on to ruin and subvert the State. Every man and woman can do something to convince the strikers of the error and peril of their actions. It is far better that this should be accom-plished by waves of public opinion than by other measures.

Thomas Jones: diary

(*Jones papers*)

7 May 1926

I then hurried to see Winston and had one of the fiercest and hottest inter-views in my life. I put to him the policy I put to the PM a few minutes earlier, but before I had got any distance with it and when he saw what was coming, he overwhelmed me with a cataract of boiling eloquence, impossible to reproduce. 'We were at war. Matters had changed from Sunday morning. We were a long way from our position then. We must go through with it. You must have the nerve.' I shouted back 'I have plenty of moral nerve, but we want something besides nerve.' He retorted, 'You have a terrible responsibility in advising a man so sympathetic like the Prime Minister.' I tried to say that I stood absolutely firm on the constitutional issues, but that we at the centre failed to realise the importance of making the Government's position absolutely plain to every man and woman in the country.

The PM should make a statement in the House which would be something the moderates could take hold of, and even if it failed to divide Eccleston Square it would divide the Trade Unionists. 'Pugh[1] and Thomas and Poulton[2] are as loyal as you are to the State.' This infuriated him, and he broke out into a fresh tempest in the corridor, and I felt tossed about like a small boat in an angry sea. 'Well, I have done my duty by you' was my parting shot as he left well after 11 am to go down to the Cabinet.

I followed, walking down with P. J. Grigg, who told me that last night Winston had dictated a wild article about embodying the Territorial troops, etc, etc, but Grigg had succeeded in persuading Winston 'to sleep over it' before sending it to the Press.

Sir Thomas Inskip[3] to Lord Irwin

(*Irwin papers*)

9 May 1926

Winston is enjoying himself in editing the *British Gazette*. His Budget of 820 millions no longer interests him very much. I don't say he is wrong in his instinct for the dominant issue of the moment, but he is entertaining in his absorption in 'publicity'.

[1] Arthur Pugh, 1870–1955. Educated at elementary school. Lost both his parents in infancy. Apprenticed to a farmer and butcher at the age of 13. Took up the trade of a steel smelter in Wales, 1894. Assistant Secretary, British Steel Smelters' Association, 1906. General Secretary of the Iron and Steel Trades Federation, 1917–36. Knighted, 1935. Chairman of the General Congress of the Trade Union Congress, 1925.

[2] Edward Lawrence Poulton, 1865–1937. Joined the National Union of Boot and Shoe Operatives, in Northampton, 1887. Mayor of Northampton, 1906. General Secretary to the National Union of Boot and Shoe Operatives, 1908–31. OBE, 1917. British Workers Delegate on the Governing Body of the International Labour Office, Geneva, 1921–31. Vice President of Trade Union Congress.

[3] Thomas Walker Hobart Inskip, 1876–1947. Educated at Clifton and King's College, Cambridge. Barrister, 1899. Served in the Naval Intelligence Division, Admiralty, 1915–18. Conservative MP for Central Bristol, 1918–29, and for Fareham, 1931–9. Knighted, 1922. Solicitor-General, October 1922–January 1924, November 1924–March 1928 and September 1931–January 1932. Attorney-General, 1928–9 and 1932–6. Minister for the Co-ordination of Defence, 1936–9. Secretary of State for Dominion Affairs, January–September 1939 and May–October 1940. Lord Chancellor, September 1939–May 1940. Created Viscount Caldecote, 1939. Lord Chief Justice, 1940–6.

Thomas Jones: diary

(*Jones papers*)

9 May 1926

I ran into Winston who asked me if I had seen the letter which Steel-Maitland had given Samuel. It was very hard and had been drafted by FE with the concurrence of the PM. Winston implied that it was almost too stiff and final. But probably this was just to appease me. Winston was certain that three or four days of firm handling would bring the TUC to its senses.

The Private Secretaries at No 10 are all trying to get Winston to be put in charge of Transport. Gwynne of the 'Morning Post' has sent several messages begging that Winston should be kept away from that office where the 'British Gazette' is being printed. He butts in at the busiest hours and insists on changing commas and full stops until the staff is furious.

Went to lunch with P. J. Grigg (Winston's private secretary) entirely out of sympathy with his chief's wild ways. . . .

I hear the Trade Union Bill will appear on Tuesday. Grigg thinks it is less bad now than we believed it would be. It is a declaratory Bill. Winston is trying to see Sir John Simon to-night, to secure his support for it.

I have been trying during the day to get the PM's statement printed as a small bulletin to be posted up in the East End and the poorer districts throughout the country. The 'British Gazette' is a paper for suburbia not for the working man.

Sir Malcolm Fraser to Winston S. Churchill

(*Churchill papers: 2/143*)

9 May 1926   The British Gazette

My dear Chancellor,

This is to remind you of our conversation this evening.

You were going to be kind enough to instruct your Secretary to send for Lord Burnham, Mr Cadbury,[1] Major Astor and those of the Newspaper Proprietors who are not assisting us at the present moment. Also Sir William Berry, whose 'Financial Times' is our size & who can spare men from their Clements Printing Works.

Sir Andrew Caird has, I understand, explained to you how much the 'Daily Mail' resent depleting their resources in giving us the very excellent

[1] Edward Cadbury, 1873–1948. Educated at Quaker schools. Director of the British Cocoa and Chocolate Co Ltd. A Life Governor of Birmingham University. Owner, *Daily News*.

aid which they have already done, and that they feel they are placing themselves at a disadvantage in producing their paper at the earliest possible moment unless other Newspaper Owners do the same thing.

I am afraid, unless other Newspaper Owners are included to assist, the 'Daily Mail' will withdraw some of the important Key men whom they have been good enough to lend.

Yours sincerely,
Malcolm Fraser

Winston S. Churchill: telegram[1]

(*Churchill papers: 2/143*)

9 May 1926

Earnestly request you give any assistance in your power to the Government newspaper to work the new office and double circulation. Churchill.

J. E. B. Seely to Winston S. Churchill

(*Treasury papers: T172/1558*)

9 May 1926   Hampshire

My dear Winston,

The Chairman designate of the National War Savings Committee must report to his chief, if only to say that he is 'otherwise engaged'.

This you knew before, but I know you will be glad to hear that in this county there has been complete order, no single conflict with the police, no single case of the stopping of any vehicle or individual on the King's highway, since the strike began. I have had the police reports daily from every City and Borough as well as from the whole county, and have been from end to end of it more than once, and it is good to be able to say that complete order prevails.

Southampton is a great port, Portsmouth has $\frac{1}{4}$ of a million inhabitants, Eastleigh is a big railway centre—all trams are running, all omnibuses, all traffic except the railways, without let or hindrance. . . .

---

[1] This telegram was sent to Major Astor, Viscount Burnham, Lord Beaverbrook, Sir William Berry and Edward Cadbury.

Thomas Jones: diary

(*Jones papers*)

10 May 1926

About 10.45 I saw the PM at No 10, and walked up and down with him on the Terrace. I entreated him to pause before rushing the new Trade Union legislation through Parliament. When I pressed him to define the exact scope of the Bill he was not at all clear. He thought it made a sympathetic strike illegal, and a General Strike illegal, but later I was told that it made a sympathetic strike illegal only when it assumed the aspect of a General Strike. I told him that in my belief Eccleston Square was already beaten, and knew it was beaten, that it had taken some time to get the country to appreciate what the General Strike was, but this new Bill would come as a thunder-clap on the country which was utterly unprepared for it, and would greatly confuse its mind. It would be held to be an attack on Trade Unions, and would profoundly change the quite peaceful temper of the men now on strike. Could he not give two or three more days before introducing it?

The only remark that the PM made was that Winston had seen Simon who endorsed the Bill with the exception of two or three words. In the middle of this conversation Winston joined us and Bobby Monsell, and we paraded up and down while I pleaded with fierce energy for delay. Winston said hardly a word, except to defend the 'British Gazette' which I had attacked, but went off to the Treasury, cursed me to his Private Secretary, but sat down and wrote a note to the PM admitting that it might be wise to consider further timetable and procedure, adding that light sometimes came in a Cabinet, and also comfort when taking an important decision. The PM then decided to call a Cabinet this afternoon. . . .

Niemeyer told me that the Chancellor had been trying to press the Governor of the Bank of England to arrest the Unions' funds even before the passing of the Bill, and that the Governor had refused.

John Reith:[1] *recollections*

(*Lord Reith: 'Into The Wind'*)

10 May 1926

Lord Grey of Fallodon was to speak on Monday night, May 10, and a message came asking if someone would collect him from Churchill's house, 11

[1] J. C. W. Reith, 1889–1971. Managing Director, BBC, 1923–7; Director-General, 1927–38. Knighted, 1927. Minister of Information, 1939–40; of Transport, 1940. Created Baron, 1940.

Downing Street. I went myself. A few days earlier Churchill had sent me a personal message; he wanted the noises of the production of the *British Gazette* to be broadcast that night; but the noises were not broadcast.[1]

Now, hearing that someone had come for Lord Grey, Churchill came out and invited me to join them for coffee. In due course he enquired if I were connected with the BBC. Yes. In what capacity? Managing director. He swung round in his chair: '*Are you Mr Reith?*' Perhaps I had not come up, or rather down, to what he had been expecting.[2] He said he was greatly interested to meet me; had been trying to do so all week. I replied that I had been on the job every day and most of every night, and would have been very glad to meet him.

As an instance of his indignation he cited an item in the news the day before about Lord Knutsford[3] having arranged with a TUC official to have power maintained at the London Hospital. From this a general argument developed, Mrs Churchill supporting him, Lord Grey supporting me. He was polite to me; I wished we had had a proper set-to at the beginning of the strike. He came to the car with us; said he was very glad to have met me; he had heard I had been badly wounded in the war—'In the head, wasn't it?' I said yes, but that my present attitude was not traceable thereto.

Another embarrassment next day. Ramsay MacDonald telephoned to ask if he might broadcast; he knew I was not entirely a free agent, but might he send along a draft? This he did with a friendly note offering to make any alterations. I asked Davidson to show it to the Prime Minister and to say I strongly recommended letting it go out. Davidson told me it certainly could not go; it would set Churchill off again.

Winston S. Churchill to Stanley Baldwin: draft letter

(*Cherwell papers*)

11 May 1926

Dear PM,

The point to which I wish to draw your mind is that there must be a clear interval between the calling off of the General Strike and the resumption of

[1] On 14 June 1926 J. C. C. Davidson wrote to Lord Irwin: 'the Prime Minister played a very skilful game in postponing a decision by the Cabinet, on the question repeatedly raised by Winston and FE of taking over the BBC and running it as a governmental propaganda agency. Winston was very strong in his insistence that the Government ought to assume complete possession. I was equally strong and Jix shared my view that it would be fatal to do so' (*Irwin papers*).

[2] John Reith was over 6 feet 6 inches tall.

[3] Sydney Holland, 1855–1931. 2nd Viscount Knutsford, 1914. Director of the Underground Electric Railways Company. Chairman of the London Hospital.

the coal negotiations. The first tonight--the second to-morrow. But nothing simultaneous and concurrent. That will I am sure be fatal.

No question of subsidy even for a fortnight can be mixed with the withdrawal of the General Strike. To-night surrender. Tomorrow magnanimity. On the interval between these two depends the whole result of this deep national conflict.

Stanley Baldwin to King George V

(*Baldwin papers*)

11 May 1926   House of Commons

The Prime Minister with his humble duty to Your Majesty.

Criticism of the 'British Gazette' may perhaps act as a beneficial check on the exuberant editorial enthusiasm of Mr Churchill, who is finding that an editor's task is almost as much open to criticism as that of Chancellor of the Exchequer, but it does not redound to the credit of Mr Lloyd George that he should indulge in petty attacks of this character.

At Question time Mr Churchill had been heckled in regard to the policy followed by those responsible for the production of this newspaper. It was alleged that it was not sufficiently impartial, that it omitted statements made by responsible men which might possibly be considered detrimental to the Government, and in this connection particular reference was made by Mr Lloyd George to the omission of the declaration made by the Archbishop of Canterbury on Friday in regard to the attitude of the Churches. The omission of this declaration was probably a mistake of policy and Mr Churchill had to draw fully on his inherent ingenuity in order to justify his action. One of his lines of defence was that he had also omitted the very firm and helpful declaration made by Cardinal Bourne[1] on Sunday.

Subsequently in the debate on the Home Office Vote Mr Lloyd George returned to the charge and strongly criticised the omission of the Archbishop's appeal. Mr Churchill in his defence laid emphasis on the stupendous nature of the task which had been achieved by those responsible for the production of the newspaper. In the face of exceptional difficulties they had brought the circulation already to a figure exceeding one million copies, and the circulation was being increased daily. The staff was working under the severest pressure imaginable, and, in circumstances like the present, it was impossible to avoid the omission of news even of an important character.

[1] Francis Bourne, 1861-1931. Born in London. Educated in Paris and at the University of Louvain. Ordained Priest, 1884; Domestic Prelate to Pope Leo XIII, 1895. Bishop of Southwark, 1897-1903. Archbishop of Westminster from 1903 until his death. Cardinal, 1911.

After indicating that it might be possible to include in a later issue the declarations made both by the Archbishop and by Cardinal Bourne, Mr Churchill rightly voiced the feeling of the Conservative Party when he expressed a hope that Mr Lloyd George would make some contribution to meeting the present difficulties other than selecting small points which he could criticise. Mr Lloyd George has thoroughly earned this rebuke, and his attitude during this crisis has lowered his stock in the House of Commons very considerably.

Winston S. Churchill to Lord Beaverbrook

(Beaverbrook papers)

11 May 1926   Treasury Chambers

My dear Max,

We are trying to solve the news-print difficulty as quickly as possible. The rapidly increasing circulation of 'The British Gazette' will make the paper shortage very acute. We are expecting to publish over three millions tonight, and we shall probably have to requisition every scrap of news-print which is available and suitable. I hope, however, that by the middle of next week our supplies will be coming forward well, and I hope it may be possible to help both you and Rothermere to start then. I hope you will not attempt to do so beforehand, as it would then be necessary for me to release all the key-men that Rothermere's people have contributed and this would gravely cripple the Government organ during the days when its influence may be indispensable to the successful termination of the crisis.

In accordance with your wishes, I have of course made no mention of this to Caird or Esmond Harmsworth. I think, however, you ought to enable me to discuss the position with them, so that a joint plan can be made for next week.

I have in confidence told Sir Malcolm Fraser of the position and of your wish, and have asked him to facilitate your resumption on or after Wednesday, the 19th, if the news-print situation can possibly be adjusted. We are also training understudies for all the key-men sent us by 'The Daily Mail', as well as for the three splendid fellows you so kindly lent us at the beginning. It would be convenient if you would have any business matters dealt with between your staff and Sir Malcolm Fraser; but I shall of course be delighted to talk these matters over with you privately at any time.

Yours very sincerely,
Winston S. Churchill

Cabinet minutes

(Cabinet papers: 23/52)

11 May 1926

THE CHANCELLOR OF THE EXCHEQUER expressed his desire to bring the Gazette to an end as soon as the daily newspapers were in a position to resume normal publication but he insisted that this resumption must be carried out on terms fair to all and that those papers which had given help to the Government in the crisis should not suffer prejudice because of their patriotism. . . .

He had promised the 'Daily Mail' that if they lent their staff for the production of the 'British Gazette', he would see that their rivals did not get started ahead of them . . . he might, pending a decision by the Cabinet, have to use his discretionary powers to secure fair play in accordance with his promise.

General appreciation was expressed of the success achieved by the Chancellor of the Exchequer.

L. S. Amery: diary[1]

(Amery papers)

11 May 1926

This let loose Winston in a magnificent tirade on the wonders achieved, the selfishness of the Times in wishing to increase its circulation at expense of others during the crisis, the impossibility of letting go at the moment without unfairness to one or other newspaper and ended with his determination to suppress the Daily Express, if, as they intended, they started an evening paper in the next few days. Against his vigour and enthusiasm nobody except Eustace Percy had the courage to say anything and most of those who for days had been going round and complaining rather left me alone when I belled the cat.

---

[1] Amery had proposed, in the Cabinet of May 11, an early return to 'normal newspaper publication' (*Amery papers*).

Winston S. Churchill to Lord Beaverbrook

(*Beaverbrook papers*)

12 May 1926   Treasury Chambers
Private & Confidential

My dear Max,

Many thanks for your letter of last night.[1] I have also received a letter from Andrew Caird telling me that you have informed him that you intend to start printing the 'Daily Express' at the 'Evening Standard' offices at any time after the 48 hours agreed upon between you has expired.

As I told you, I am doing everything in my power to facilitate your resumption and that of the 'Daily Mail', if you both wish to do so, as from Wednesday the 19th. By that time the supplies of paper will be more abundant and the understudies will be sufficiently trained to release most at any rate of the key men you and the 'Daily Mail' so kindly lent us. An earlier start on your part would completely cripple the 'British Gazette' at the moment when it may be of the greatest consequence in the country and before the independent press could have grown strong enough to discharge adequately the task of public guidance and information throughout the country.

If you start before Wednesday I must immediately release all the 'Daily Mail' staff who are with us, and this would practically bring the 'British Gazette' to an end. I hope therefore, and I earnestly request in the public interest, that you will defer your intentions until Wednesday the 19th. I am of course referring to large scale production and not to the various small sheets which you have in the face of so many difficulties been producing by one expedient and another.

If I could be assured that both you and the 'Daily Mail' could start up next Wednesday at, say, half a million each produced in London, I should be quite ready to face a curtailment of the 'British Gazette' of at least an equal amount. The withdrawal of your key men and those of the 'Daily Mail' at the present time would practically bring us to a standstill.

It is possible however that none of these situations may arise. There are persistent rumours that a crisis has been reached on the TUC. Within 48 hours we shall know a great deal more than we know now. Therefore I beg

---

[1] In his letter of 11 May 1926, Beaverbrook had pointed out the extent of the help he had given to the *British Gazette*. 'We have made immense sacrifices at this end,' he wrote, 'and personally guaranteed the employees of this office who took on the task of producing the *British Gazette*, at a time when no other London newspaper, except the *Morning Post* was giving material assistance.' Nevertheless, Beaverbrook added, he would be willing to hand over his final two hundred tons of paper 'if it is absolutely necessary for the Government'.

of you to defer, as you have so consistently done hitherto, to my wish in the public interest, and take no fresh departure at any rate until we have had some further conversation.

Yours vy sincerely
Winston S. Churchill

Walter Citrine: recollections

('*Men and Work*')

12 May 1926   10 Downing Street

THE GENERAL STRIKE CALLED OFF

While we were talking, Churchill, Baldwin, and Steel Maitland were pacing rapidly up and down the garden, talking animatedly. There was no sign of jubilation amongst them, and Pugh muttered to me: 'I saw Churchill a few minutes ago, and he said, "Thank God it is over, Mr Pugh." '

Thomas Jones: diary

(*Jones papers*)

13 May 1926

1.45 lunch with Geoffrey Dawson at the Travellers' Club.

He had heard some wild rumour that the Cabinet were divided in two on the Samuel proposals, and that a critical situation was developing. I told him that this was the first news I had of it. He was very sarcastic about the penny *Morning Post* which appears to-morrow, and about Winston's military organisation of the *British Gazette*.

Geoffrey Dawson said that Winston had posted up in the Printing Office a list of the General Staff of the paper, with Winston as Commander-in-Chief, etc, etc. He described a meeting of newspaper owners held at the Treasury yesterday which was harangued by Winston. He wanted the views of his audience on how long the *British Gazette* ought to be continued. *The Times* had sent Pybus[1] to represent it. He is a little terrier and not afraid to

---

[1] John Pybus, 1880–1935. An electrical engineer: Managing Director of the English Electrical Company and a director of several Ordnance and Cement works. Unsuccessful Liberal candidate in the 1923 and 1924 elections. In August and September 1923 he contributed to *The Times* a remarkable series of articles on Trade Union policy, urging a scheme of 'payment by results'. Liberal MP, 1929–35. Minister of Transport in the National Government, 1931–3, when he piloted the London Passenger Transport Bill through the House of Commons. Knighted, 1934. A director of *The Times* Publishing Company.

bite, and very different from the docile and obliging Lord Burnham. The *British Gazette* was sentenced to immediate death. In today's issue, No 8 and the last, its story is told in epic style.[1]

Winston S. Churchill to Sir Austen Chamberlain

(*Austen Chamberlain papers*)

14 May 1926
Private

My dear Austen,

Despite long official experience, I was not only surprised but startled at the character of the proposal which was explained to me yesterday for bribing the Turks to let us alone in Iraq. I see no objection to the independent Iraq Government making a concession out of their oil royalties to their powerful neighbour. In order to facilitate this I was willing to waive certain rather shadowy British claims on Iraq revenues. It is a matter of indifference whether Iraq makes a payment to Turkey in the shape of a share in oil royalties or commutes that payment to a capital sum. But that is quite a different thing from the suggestion that the British Treasury should promise to pay £500,000 to the Turks in order to induce them to keep the treaties that they have already signed or to sign another.

This is nothing less than 'Danegelt', and nothing could to my mind be more fatal than for Great Britain to embark on such a policy with a faithless and rapacious Government like that which now rules Turkey. I should be very much surprised if the Cabinet would assent to it, and the publication of such an arrangement would certainly smirch the reputation of the Government for firmness where the national interest is concerned.

Moreover I do not believe it is necessary to the preservation of peace. As far as I can judge, the reasons which have actuated the Turks in suddenly becoming so conciliatory towards us are obvious. It is not Lindsay's[2] skill, but Mussolini's menaces that have produced the change.

Turkey has now definitely to consider as a main and growing preoccupation a potential attack on Adalia or Smyrna, or both, by the Italians, probably supported by a Greek movement against Thrace. This may not materialise,

---

[1] The final *British Gazette* article contained the Churchillian sentence: 'It becomes a memory; but it remains a monument.'

[2] Ronald Charles Lindsay, 1877–1945. 5th son of the 26th Earl of Crawford. Entered Diplomatic Service, 1898. Knighted, 1925. Ambassador to Turkey, 1925–6; Berlin, 1926–8. Permanent Under-Secretary of State at the Foreign Office, 1928–30. Ambassador in Washington, 1930–9.

at any rate for a long time. But Turkey will be bound to subordinate all Iraq ambitions to being ready to meet an actual invasion. This turn of events is very favourable to us, and has completely altered the situation as we saw it last autumn.

It is necessary also to consider the eventual destination of this £500,000 Great Britain is to pay. Lindsay's Angora despatch shows the financial straits to which this xenophobe Turkish Government, which humiliated us so much at Lausanne, has now been reduced. They need the money, either to pay their officials or to organise their forces against our friends the Italians. In these circumstances not only do I believe it to be a great mistake to give them money through British funds but I consider the blackmailing of Iraq should also be reviewed.

Finally, what is the lasting value of an engagement signed with this crumbling and treacherous Turkish Government? If they were free from the Italian anxiety they could at any time increase their forces on the Iraq border and by raids and menaces force us to heavy further expense. Once we have started on the principle of bribing them off, they or their successors will know very well where to turn when they are short of money.

It is clear to me that such issues cannot possibly be settled apart from the Cabinet. They are issues on which the Treasury officials have no instructions from me and which go far beyond the sphere in which they have expert competence.

Believe me,
Yours very sincerely,
Winston S. Churchill

Stanley Baldwin to King George V

(*Baldwin papers*)

19 May 1926   House of Commons

The Prime Minister with his humble duty to Your Majesty.

The proceedings yesterday opened with another lively interchange of question and answer between the Chancellor of the Exchequer and his critics on the subject of the 'British Gazette'.

The Chancellor, who was in a very witty mood, emerged from the engagement with flying colours. His most important announcement was to the effect that the net loss on the 'British Gazette' was approximately estimated at £10,000. He amused the House by adding that if the general strike had lasted for another three days there was every reason to expect an actual profit. It was no doubt better, however, that the strike should have ended when it did.

Winston S. Churchill to Sir Austen Chamberlain

(Austen Chamberlain papers)

21 May 1926

My dear Austen,

You are always so good in consulting the Cabinet on Foreign Office questions that I cannot help feeling vy much surprised that the decision about Zagloul shd not have been submitted for Cabinet discussion. Lloyd's telegram shows that he had weighed & balanced the pros & cons with full knowledge & great care, & to overrule the considered judgment of the 'man on the spot' on a question of first-rate importance was a step on wh I shd certainly have thought the Cabinet had a right to be consulted.[1]

I write this without in any way undervaluing the strength of the arguments wh have influenced you. But I remember the disasters wh have followed from Milner's[2] neglect to consult the Cabinet in 1920, & the vy unfair treatment wh we then received. In the present case I fear that you will be purchasing a short spell of correctitude at the expense of a shock and set-back to our own position in Egypt, leading to a violent crisis in the near future. However this may be, I am sure you wd have been right to gather yr colleagues behind you on a difference with the High Commissioner & at a crucial point in policy. Will it be possible for us to discuss the matter before the event actually takes place?

Yours vy sincerely
Winston S. Churchill

[1] The result of the Egyptian elections, the first to be held there by direct voting under universal male suffrage, had been announced on May 14. The Government members had won only 14 seats, the smaller opposition groups 36 seats and the Zaghloulist opposition *164* seats. Zaghloul himself announced his intention to become Prime Minister, but following the intervention of the High Commissioner (Lord Lloyd), Zaghloul was persuaded to renounce office, and to nominate Adly Pasha in his place. The Cabinet eventually upheld Lloyd's decision, which Churchill strongly endorsed.

[2] Alfred Milner, 1854–1925. Under-Secretary for Finance, Egypt, 1889–92. Chairman of the Board of Inland Revenue, 1892–5. Knighted, 1895. High Commissioner for South Africa, 1897–1905. Created Baron, 1901. Created Viscount, 1902. Member of the War Cabinet, December 1916–18. Secretary of State for War, 1918–19; for the Colonies, 1919–21.

Sir Austen Chamberlain to Winston S. Churchill

(*Churchill papers: 22/84*)

21 May 1926

My dear Winston,

Most certainly I intend to consult the Cabinet before giving a final decision about Zagloul. I have not any telegram here as I write, but it does I think contain words indicating this intention. If not, they were certainly in an earlier telegram.

My message about which you write was intended to elicit a further expression of his views & an answer to my questions so that the Cabinet might be in the best position to decide a very grave & difficult problem.

Yrs sincerely
Austen Chamberlain

PS. I have in any case made the point of Cabinet consultation clear in another telegram approved tonight in answer to Lloyd's 221, which is satisfactory as indicating about the best that we can expect.

Sir Philip Cunliffe-Lister and Winston S. Churchill: joint note for the Cabinet

(*Churchill papers: 22/113*)

21 May 1926
Secret

THE COAL NEGOTIATIONS

Following upon the proposal made by the Chancellor yesterday, it would seem that the modification set out hereafter ought to be considered.

(1) The minimum percentage rate and the subsistence wage should be fixed at a figure below which on social grounds miners ought not to work.

(2) The Commission reported that any reduction in wages should be offset by a reduction in owners' profits, ie there should be a sacrifice by both parties.

If a minimum rate is fixed, say at 20%, and the owners are allowed to retain their present proportion of surplus proceeds, the sacrifice is not mutual. It is therefore suggested that the minimum rate and the subsistence wage should be fixed at whatever is considered to be a fair figure for a minimum wage. But above this figure, until the men are receiving the same wages which they would have received under the 1924 Agreement, a larger percentage of surplus proceeds should go in wages and a smaller proportion in owners' profits.

This would work out somewhat as follows:

(1) An eight-hour day.
(2) A minimum percentage rate of 20% above standard base rates, and a subsistence wage of, say, eight shillings per day.
(3) Until wages are paid at the 1924 Agreement rates, ie $32\frac{1}{2}$% minimum rate and the subsistence wages ruling under that Agreement in each district, surplus proceeds would be divided in the proportion of 8% or 10% to owners and 90% or 92% to men.
(4) When in any district wages have reached the minimum level of the 1924 Agreement, surplus proceeds to be divided between wages and profits in the recognised proportions of 87 to 13.

Can this general basis be examined by the Ministry of Mines so as to show, broadly speaking, what proportion of mines would be forced out of production through its enforcement by legislation? Are there also any objections to be urged against it on its merits; and if so, what modifications in figures would be suggested?

PC-L
WSC

Winston S. Churchill to Sir Douglas Hogg
(Churchill papers: 2/147)

26 May 1926   Chartwell Manor
Private

My dear Hogg,

I wish you would look at the enclosed article.[1] I do not attach any importance to the title, or to the travesty of facts, which the article contains. But there is one very serious statement which I have underlined in red. It is wholly untrue and unfounded. As you will know, my arguments in Cabinet

[1] On 22 May 1926 the *New Statesman*, under the heading 'Should we hang Mr Churchill or not?', set out a detailed account of the alleged activities of the 'war party' in the Cabinet on the night of May 2. According to the paper, Churchill had led this group in the threat of immediate resignation if negotiations with the TUC were continued, and had been throughout that critical day 'in favour of war at all costs'. The newspaper continued: 'Mr Churchill was the villain of the piece. He is reported to have remarked that he thought "a little blood-letting" would be all to the good. Whether he actually used this phrase or not there is no doubt about his tireless efforts to seize the providential opportunity for a fight.'

were all directed to keeping the Military out of the business, and to using, even at great expense, very large numbers of citizens unarmed. I am sure I have never used any language not entirely consistent with this. The charge appears to be a gross libel upon a Minister in the execution of his duty, and I certainly do not feel inclined to allow such a lie to pass into the general currency of Labour incriminations.

I should be very glad to know what you think about it, and whether you think it is a case on which a criminal information could be founded. They would, I should expect, collapse at once, make a full apology in Court, and pay £1,000 to some charity.

I hope you are enjoying this delicious weather.

Yours vy sincerely,
Winston S. Churchill

Sir Douglas Hogg to Winston Churchill
(*Churchill papers: 2/147*)

28 May 1926

My dear Chancellor,

I have received your letter and enclosure of the 26th. On a first perusal I think the passage you have underlined is defamatory and could be made the subject of a criminal prosecution for libel. But I am not so sure of the wisdom of instituting such a prosecution.

Personally I am inclined to reserve the machinery of a criminal prosecution for very extreme and grave cases; and whilst I can well understand, and indeed share, your indignation at a most unjustifiable attack I am doubtful whether it merits being elevated to a 'cause célèbre'.

In such a prosecution cross-examination would be admissible to discuss in detail the Cabinet discussion upon the Trade Union document (falsely described in the article as an agreed formula). You will remember that there was some diversity of opinion about this document and about the negotiations which led up to it, and except in cases of absolute necessity I should be reluctant to have all that thrashed out in Court.

I am writing to the Director of Public Prosecutions to ask him to see me on Monday so that I may obtain his view, and perhaps you would have a talk to me next week before reaching a final decision.

If you saw fit to consult either FE or the Lord Chancellor their experience and judgment might also be useful.[1]

---

[1] Churchill decided not to take action against the *New Statesman*.

June 1926

Legislation Committee of the Cabinet: minutes

(Cabinet papers: 27/326)

3 June 1926

THE CHANCELLOR OF THE EXCHEQUER hoped that the contemplated legislation would be confined to declaring general strikes to be illegal, and to secure that no strike should take place unless a majority of those affected was in favour of it. . . .

He hoped, however, that the Bill would not attempt to deal with matters such as peaceful picketing or the repeal of any part of the Trade Disputes Act 1906.[1] He doubted whether any ballot conducted otherwise than on the lines of a Parliamentary Ballot would be satisfactory.

Winston S. Churchill to Stanley Baldwin

(Churchill papers: 18/29)

9 June 1926   Treasury Chambers
Private

My dear PM,

I am very glad to hear you are better. In case I do not see you to-night I write you this.

The coal stoppage is now beginning to cut deep into our prosperity & finance. I do not feel convinced that the right course is being taken to give it the best chance of being ended.

More than 3 weeks have passed since our talk on the eve of the holidays without any progress except by the slow process of attrition. I believe that

---

[1] The Trade Disputes Act of 1906, one of the first pieces of Liberal legislation to be passed through the House of Commons after Churchill had become a member of the Liberal Government. The Act made Trade Unions, but not individual members of Unions, secure against legal liability. The Act had been fiercely attacked in the House of Lords, where the Conservative Leader, Lord Lansdowne, was systematically opposing the Government's social reform measures.

if we had legislated on June 1 to the effect that any mine that can pay the existing rate (or some lesser quite defensible rate) may work 8 hours during (say) a 3-years period of reorganization—we should now be nearer to a break away in the coalfields & to a series of district settlements. But if I am wrong how could we be worse off than we are? We are relying solely upon economic pressure administered regardless of cost. That remains after all the final process. We ought to avoid it & save the country & the mines from it, if it be in human power.

I wish therefore now to bring this issue before the Coal Cte[1] in the first instance & thereafter before the Cabinet—if you will permit me to do so.

Hopkinson[2] & the owners make out that your subsidy reference has hardened the miners. Whether this has any foundation or not—& no doubt it is exaggerated—it makes it all the more desirable to formulate a Government policy. How are you going to bring the men—not their leaders—up against the definite issue of 8 hours, except by legislation? Is it not much easier for them to accept it from Parlt than for their leaders to agree voluntarily to repudiate a cherished slogan.

The Ministers of Mines & Labour are content to wait on from day to day & week to week in the hopes of the miners resistance collapsing. But I am bound to point out to you the *terrible* cost to the nation of these time units wh are being so lavishly & passively paid out. The Trade future is being compromised for a whole year in advance. As to Finance, conceive the effects upon an Income tax no longer based on the 3 years average.

I feel strongly on this matter & against a policy of continuous waiting from day to day. Even if in a fortnight there is a settlement, I shall still believe that guidance by the Govt & H of C wd have produced it earlier. But if it lasts still longer, as well it may, then a grave injury will be done to us all. Even if Government legislation were rejected by both sides, nothing wd happen worse than that.

Anyhow I shall be grateful if you will give facilities for the issue being brought to Cabinet decision.

Yours vy sincerely,
Winston S. Churchill

[1] The official title of this Committee was: Committee on the Report of the Royal Commission on the Coal Industry. Known as the Coal Committee, its chairman was Stanley Baldwin, and its members Churchill, Birkenhead (Secretary of State for India), Cunliffe-Lister (President of the Board of Trade), Worthington-Evans (Secretary of State for War), Bridgeman (First Lord of the Admiralty), Steel-Maitland (Minister of Labour) and Lane-Fox (Parliamentary Secretary, Mines Department).

[2] Austen Hopkinson, Conservative MP for Mossley, and a coal owner. Speaking in the House of Commons on 1 June 1926, he had called the subsidy 'a bar to the prosperity of the coal mining industry of this country'.

Cabinet Coal Committee: minutes

(*Churchill papers: 22/116*)

14 June 1926   Prime Minister's Room
Secret   House of Commons

THE CHANCELLOR OF THE EXCHEQUER gave an account of a conference which he and other Ministers had just had with representatives of the Mining Association. The meeting, which had been held at the House of Commons, had lasted for nearly two hours. The owners had been told that the Government might find themselves driven to legislate over the heads of both parties to the dispute, that the miners would not be very willing to lose on both hours and wages, and that some advance on the position hitherto taken up by the owners was most desirable and urgent in view of the debate which was to take place on the following day.

The conference had been adjourned to enable the mine-owners to consider, in consultation with the Secretary for Mines and Mr Gowers,[1] what offer they could make which would serve as a counterpoise to the suspension of the Seven Hours Act, and the terms in which the offer could best be expressed.

MR GOWERS read a draft of the statement to which the owners were prepared to agree, and certain verbal amendments were suggested for further discussion with the owners.

THE MINISTER OF LABOUR stated that in his view it would not be possible at present to obtain any better offer from the owners.

THE SECRETARY FOR MINES pointed out that it was implicit in the offer that there would be no Government subsidy.

THE CHANCELLOR OF THE EXCHEQUER agreed and said that it would be preferable to use the money which had been promised to help to provide steel houses in mining areas, and for training schemes and other forms of assistance for displaced miners.

THE MINISTER OF LABOUR urged that care should be taken to hold out no prospect of financial assistance to pits at work. The money originally intended 'to ease the hump' would not now be required for that purpose and could be better used to help miners thrown out of work.

---

[1] Ernest Arthur Gowers, 1880–1966. Educated at Rugby and Clare College, Cambridge. Entered the Inland Revenue, 1903; transferred to the India Office, 1904. Principal Private Secretary to Lloyd George (at the Exchequer), 1911–12. Chief Inspector, National Health Insurance Commission, 1912–17. Secretary, Civil Service Arbitration Board, 1917–19. Director of Production, Coal Mines Department, 1919–20. Permanent Under-Secretary for Mines, 1920–7. Knighted, 1926. Chairman, Board of Inland Revenue, 1927–30. Chairman, Coal Mines Reorganization Commission, 1930–5; the Coal Commission, 1938–46. Chairman of the Royal Commission on Capital Punishment, 1949–53. Author of *Plain Words* (1948).

THE PRIME MINISTER said it would be necessary to undertake in the Debate to proceed with the Government proposals for reorganisation on the lines already submitted to the owners and miners, and to say that Bills would be immediately introduced dealing with working facilities, amalgamations, recruitment, and the setting up of a National Wages Board.

The Committee were reminded that neither owners nor miners desired to have a National Wages Board on the railway model, but it was generally agreed that the Government should adhere to its announcement on the subject and that if it should be found that when legislation is introduced there is strong opposition from both sides, the matter could be further considered.

THE SECRETARY OF STATE FOR WAR suggested that the Prime Minister in announcing the Government's policy should lay stress on the distinction between a minimum wage and actual earnings, and to the profit-sharing character of the present wage agreement.

THE CHANCELLOR OF THE EXCHEQUER thought the Prime Minister should call attention to the economic loss involved in the continuance of the struggle and to the vast displacement of labour in certain areas which would admittedly follow if the policy of the miners' leaders were adopted.

George Lambton[1] to Winston S. Churchill

(*Churchill papers: 18/27*)

15 June 1926

My dear Winston,

I am disgusted with the attitude of the Sporting Life re: Betting Tax; in wh it wrote, 'that you are doing your best to endanger the industry of racing'.

I must tell you that the Sporting Life is a paper of no account, and is looked on with contempt by all racing people.

I have written a short letter to the Editor for Publication, but from what I know of him, it will not be published.

Yours,
George Lambton

[1] George Lambton, 1860–1945. 5th son of the 2nd Earl of Durham. Lieutenant, Derbyshire Militia, 1880. A racing enthusiast, he lived at Newmarket, and published, in 1924, his memoirs, *Men and Horses I Have Known*.

Winston S. Churchill to George Lambton

(*Churchill papers: 18/27*)

16 June 1926

So many thanks for your letter.

I do not mind in the least the newspaper criticism. It is impossible to deal with any question of taxation without causing dissatisfaction. One has to do the best one can. You may be quite sure that no newspaper criticism would prevent my doing my very best in the general interest.

Sir Samuel Hoare to Lord Irwin

(*Irwin papers*)

18 June 1926

. . . I have not had a very easy time in sticking to my airship programme in face of the demands for reduction of expenditure. Moreover, Winston, on the totally irrelevant evidence of the war, is still dead against airships and loses no chance of a dig at the programme. The more, therefore, that you help me with your support, even though for the time being it is little more than moral, the stronger will be my position. . . .

Since then we have had a set battle over Russia. Winston and FE have been violently urging the breaking off of relations. . . . I am sure myself that from both points of view, the immediate effect upon the miners and the more distant effect upon trade and Europe generally, it would be a great mistake to make a dramatic act that whilst it will please the Die-hards for a few months, will leave every kind of difficulty behind it. This was the view taken by every member of the House of Commons in the Cabinet except Winston and Co, and although Stanley will have some difficulty with the Die-hards, I believe it is the view generally held in the country.

Legislation Committee of the Cabinet: minutes

(*Cabinet papers: 27/326*)

22 June 1926

THE CHANCELLOR OF THE EXCHEQUER said that in effect Lord Weir, after drawing attention to the almost desperate condition of industry, had rejected the various remedies which had been suggested and apparently was prepared to rely on the acceptance by the working man of the advice and guidance of politicians.

It was disappointing to hear that in the view of Lord Weir and Dr Andrew Duncan[1] the result of the institution of the secret ballot would be an increase in the number of strikes. He, personally, was not prepared to accept this view.

He was convinced that the majority of working men would adopt a sound and sensible attitude and that a secret ballot would be a most effective method of restricting the influence of the young and extremist members of the union.

Winston S. Churchill to Stanley Baldwin

(*Churchill papers: 18/29*)

26 June 1926   Treasury Chambers

My dear Prime Minister,

I am very sorry to trespass on your week end but I am seriously concerned about the delay in the Mineowners' posting the new wage scales on an eight hours basis at the pits. It was a fortnight last Thursday since we took the decision to introduce the Bill and they for their part assured us of the wage scales they would offer. We were told they were meeting on the Saturday and that early in the next week the notices would be issued. Since then nothing has appeared. The miners have been left with nothing but the proposed increase of hours, and your general statement of the wage position. We were I thought counting on definite wage offers in each district, and in more than half of a satisfactory character to bring about district cleavages. But this process has so far been wholly inoperative, and meanwhile losses and misery are rolling up thicker and thicker.

Some misunderstanding was we are told caused by the postponement of the Bill. But this could have been prevented by a direct assurance of the resolve of the Government to the mineowners. It would not have taken the Minister of Labour ten minutes to explain the reasons of the postponement. The Cabinet last Wednesday did not quite understand why this was not done, and I personally am completely at a loss.

[1] Andrew Rae Duncan, 1884–1952. Coal Controller, 1919–20. Chairman of the Advisory Committee of the Mines Department, 1920–9. Vice-President, Shipbuilding Employers' Federation, 1920–7. Knighted, 1921. Chairman of the Central Electricity Board, 1927–35. A Director of the Bank of England, 1929–40. Chairman of the Executive Committee of the British Iron and Steel Federations, 1935–40 and 1945–52. MP for the City of London, 1940–50. President of the Board of Trade, 1940 and 1941. Minister of Supply, 1940–1 and 1942–5. A Director of Imperial Chemical Industries, and of the Dunlop Rubber Company. One of his two sons was killed in action in the Second World War.

Last night Bridgeman told me that he had heard that Steel-Maitland had raised with the mineowners some point about eight hours and the Washington Convention: and that in consequence they did not intend to post the new wage scales till after the *third* reading of the Bill. The First Lord expressed anxiety at this; so does Lane-Fox, and so has Gowers privately to P. J. Grigg.

It seems to me that very good reasons not known to me would be required to justify this long and hideously costly delay. If of course you have plans and are in negotiations with which I am not acquainted there is no doubt a perfectly satisfactory explanation; and my misgivings are groundless. But if it is just drift on the part of the Ministry of Labour, then I feel they are taking a good deal of responsibility.

Nothing would be easier for me than to leave these events to take their course, and confine my gaze to the depleted Exchequer, and it is only my earnest desire for the success of your Government which induces me to write this letter.

Yours sincerely,
Winston S. Churchill

PS. Would it not be well to have a Coal Cabinet Committee meeting on Monday morning?

Winston S. Churchill to Lord Salisbury
(*Salisbury papers*)

29 June 1926

My dear Salisbury,

I enclose a copy of my reply to Amery about the proposal to make a grant of £20,000 to relieve the distress among unemployed ex-Service men in the Irish Free State. Prima facie I felt a great deal of sympathy with this suggestion, but on considering it carefully I have come to the conclusion that we could do no real good by making such a grant. It could only be a gesture and one which would be fraught with many difficulties and dangers. The Free State Government's new road scheme ought to relieve the position materially. Meanwhile in this country unemployment and distress grow worse each week.

Yours vy sincerely,
Winston S. Churchill

July 1926

Stanley Baldwin to King George V

(Baldwin papers)

3 July 1926

The House always crowds in to hear Mr Churchill, who, quite apart from the entertainment which any 'bonny fechter' affords, is always worth hearing as an orator after the old school and of the grand manner. His performance on this occasion was admirable, and although in his exposition he emphasised the facts of the situation—a proceeding which is always repugnant to the feelings of the Opposition—yet his consideration for those feelings and his good humour gave them no opportunity to denounce him as 'provocative'. He observed that, however mild a use might be made of the powers given by these emergency regulations, no responsible person could say that in a stoppage like this they were not necessary or that their necessity did not increase as the continuance of the dispute aggravated conditions in the country.

It was easy to criticise the handling of a big dispute. At any stage some other decision might have been taken, and since the dispute continued irresponsible critics could always say that the decision taken was the wrong one. If the Government are firm, they say, 'How stubborn!': if they are conciliatory, 'How weak!': if they act, 'How precipitate!': if they wait, 'How dilatory!'.

Mr Churchill proceeded to review the course which the coal dispute had taken from its earliest beginnings, exposing as he went along how vain was the criticism that, at the time of the General Strike, the Government had broken off negotiations when 'everything was nearly settled', seeing that in fact eight weeks afterwards we found ourselves as far away as ever from a settlement. . . .

How could it be reasonably maintained that the Eight Hours Bill was provocative? The Report implies a reduction in wages: all the Eight Hours Bill does is to make it possible to express the necessary reduction in wages, if desired and where desired, in terms of longer hours.

Winston S. Churchill to Lord Beaverbrook

(*Beaverbrook papers*)

5 July 1926   Treasury Chambers
Private

My dear Max,

I am much concerned about the matter, wh I had imagined was satisfactorily settled.[1] I have not in the least receded from my undertaking to do
all in my power; & I am continuing & shall continue my efforts.

I may have more to tell you shortly.

Yours ever
W

Winston S. Churchill to Stanley Baldwin

(*Baldwin papers*)

5 July 1926   Treasury Chambers
Private

My dear Prime Minister,

I am vy much distressed & embarrassed by the omission from the Honours
List of my recommendations of the humble printers etc who faced such fierce
pressures at the time of the starting of the British Gazette. The moment was
vy critical & I committed myself no doubt beyond my authority but in the
stress of the emergency both to Beaverbrook & to his three men who were
the key men that their action would be rewarded. Accordingly I spoke most
seriously of this matter to Fisher, & left it to him to present the list to you with
the definite understanding that if there was any difficulty, I was to be informed by him beforehand so that I could myself explain to you how the case
stood & appeal to you not to repudiate the expectations I had created. I
naturally assumed, since I heard no word, that all wd be well. I never even
searched the Honours List. I was sure that before my recommendations were
rejected, I should at least have the opportunity in a personal matter of this
kind of laying my case before you. No communication of any kind reached
me. Fisher now (this morning) shows me the draft of a letter wh you approved
to the Home Secretary & other ministers declining to accept any representations arising out of the general strike. Had this reached me, I shd have

---

[1] Churchill's promise, made during the printing of the *British Gazette*, that the senior *Daily
Express* technicians who worked on the emergency paper would receive some recognition in
the next Honours List.

come to you at once with the confidence that you wd not have turned a deaf ear to a colleague thus situated through exceeding his authority in an emergency by right action taken in the public interest. At any rate you wd have heard what I had to say, & I cd have conscientiously told those concerned that I had striven my utmost & had been unsuccessful.

While of course in these questions the decision rests absolutely with the Prime Minister, & while no other authority can commit him, it is I am sure in accordance with long usage that some opportunity of discussion shd be accorded to a Minister if he desires it on special grounds.

I understand that the letters of wh I was to have had one have now been found unopened in yr office. I do hope still that you will not take a final decision without hearing what I have to say.

Yours vy sincerely,
Winston S. Churchill

Winston S. Churchill: departmental minute

(*Churchill papers: 18/30*)

6 July 1926

The question is not of the readiness of the Ministry of Transport to adjust the main block of their finances in accordance with Cabinet decision, nor of their kindness in meeting the needs of the Treasury, but whether public money is being wasted or spent without proper scrutiny and criticism upon road services.

I am quite clear that there is a great deal of waste throughout the proceedings of the Ministry of Transport, and the enormous sums with which they are provided ought to be the subject of a most strict control. Some time ago I gave directions on other papers, which I have not by me now but which Mr Grigg will perhaps be able to find, for the institution of a definite group of officials in the Treasury for the purpose of subjecting these estimates to a detailed and continuous control.

I have no intention whatever of approving the estimates without being guided by the results of an examination of this kind. If the control is strict enough, it is probable that £2 or £3 millions could be saved in the year, all of which would go to strengthen the reserves available for the future. I have assented to nothing so far, except the gross figure up to which the Ministry of Transport is entitled to spend provided that they show good cause and get the utmost value for their money. I am therefore unable to accept the advice of these papers.

Winston S. Churchill: departmental memorandum

(*Churchill papers: 18/30*)

8 July 1926

No part of the Parliamentary Session is consumed to less advantage than the long time spent on the Spring Supplementary Estimates. This year no fewer than ten days were required to dispose of them. The discussions are, or ought to be, strictly confined to limited points. They conduce neither to the control of expenditure nor to the ventilation of grievance, but merely afford pegs for aimless discussion of a petty character.

The attempts we are making to reach a higher and closer standard of budgeting necessarily involve that there will be fewer surrenders of money by Departments at the end of the year, and more small Supplementaries. If this is so, we must expect each year a very large block of Supplementaries not aggregating any formidable sum. To devote ten days of Parliamentary time to discussing a block of expenditure which in the aggregate this year did not exceed £4 millions was surely a very unthrifty use of the limited time available for financial control by Parliament. It was in fact one-fifth of the number of Parliamentary days available for finance in all its forms, and was devoted to a frittering discussion covering only one two-hundredth part of the expenditure.

I am sure it would be possible to explain this matter to the House in a manner that would gain their general support, more especially if the ground were prepared beforehand for discussion say by Mr Runciman and Mr Snowden. My suggestion would be that the Supply Rule should be remodelled to cover Supplementary Estimates, not more than five nor less than three days being devoted to these, and the Opposition given the choice of specifying the subjects and arranging the time, after which the Supplementaries would be closured just in the same way as the main supply.

The Summer Supplementaries have not caused any serious difficulty or delay, and it is not certain that they require to be brought into the ambit of a revised Supply Rule. The saving of time on the Supplementaries should make it possible for the discussion of the report of the Estimates Committee on the block of estimates of the current year which has yet to be examined, as well as, if desired, for a day on the estimates of the three Fighting Services combined.[1]

---

[1] On 12 July 1926 Churchill circulated this departmental memorandum to the Cabinet, as part of Cabinet paper 267 of 1926 (*Churchill papers: 22/97*).

Stanley Baldwin to King George V

(*Baldwin papers*)

8 July 1926

. . . Mr Churchill made the most dazzling and brilliant use of his opportunity. In the earlier part of his speech there was a slight scene because some Members of the Opposition, notably Mr Lansbury,[1] stigmatised one of his statements as to the publication of the 'Daily Herald' during the General Strike as a lie.

There was slight uproar for two or three minutes, but when calm had been restored Mr Churchill seized the occasion to administer a sharp and well deserved rebuke to the Labour Party for their general attitude in recent debates. He pointed out that it was a matter of absolute indifference to him whether he was allowed to state his case to the House or not. If it were thought better to pass the remaining seventeen minutes of the debate in howling rather than in arguing, he was perfectly prepared to facilitate the general wish. But if the House was to be allowed a debate, it must also be allowed liberty of debate. It was impossible to conduct parliamentary discussion if the Labour Party continually shouted down and interrupted because Conservative Members made use of expressions which annoyed them.

Why, he asked, should the Labour Party be so mealy-mouthed about parliamentary debates? Why should revolutionary and advanced politicians be afraid of hard words? . . .

He had been accused of not producing an entirely impartial paper. But, said Mr Churchill, 'I decline utterly to be impartial as between the fire brigade and the fire'. He was not prepared to fill the paper with a lot of defeatist trash. When organising a newspaper it was necessary to make up one's mind first of all whether it was desirable to fortify the faithful or to convert the heathen.

But the climax to it all came in the last sentence of Mr Churchill's speech when he turned his attention to the revolutionary threats uttered by Mr Purcell. Speaking in the most dramatic tones in which defiance and solemnity were mingled and shaking his finger in a threatening manner at the Members of the Opposition, Mr Churchill, in a House that was tense with anticipation, delivered this solemn pronouncement. 'One last word. The Honourable Member for the Forest of Dean has indicated that a time may come when

[1] George Lansbury, 1859–1940. Left school at the age of 14. Was employed unloading coal trucks for the Great Eastern Railway. First attempted to enter Parliament, 1895. Labour MP for Bow and Bromley, 1910–12. Resigned to fight the seat as a supporter of women's suffrage. Not re-elected until 1922. Mayor of Poplar, 1919–20 and 1936–7. Editor of the *Daily Herald*, 1919–25. First Commissioner of Works in the second Labour Government, 1929–31. Leader of the Labour Party, 1931–5.

another trial of strength will occur and when something like this will be tried again upon the country or the community. I have no wish to make threats or to use language which would disturb the House and cause bad blood. But this I must say; make your minds perfectly clear that if ever you let loose upon us again a general strike, we will loose upon you—another "British Gazette".'

The anti-climax was perfect. The shouts of angry defiance which were waiting on the lips of the Labour Party gave way to an outburst of un-restrained laughter in which the House was convulsed. Mr Churchill's whole attitude had led the Labour Party to believe that they might expect one of his fulminatory and warlike declarations with reference to tanks, machine-guns and all the armed forces of the State, and the complete bathos contained in his final words was a consummate jest which no one appreciated more than the victims at whose expense it was effected. It was a happy ending to a good humoured debate which was only marred in its earlier stages by the offensiveness of Mr Mardy Jones.[1]

Lord Beaverbrook to Sir Robert Borden

(*Beaverbrook papers*)

12 July 1926

Birkenhead tells me that he is about to publish a book on President Wilson. It should add a new terror to death. Winston Churchill also has a book nearly ready for publication. He is terrified lest Birkenhead should get out first, and so compel the Cabinet to introduce an embargo on Ministers publishing books while in office. Birkenhead tells me that Churchill has given him the most earnest and sincere advice not to publish his President Wilson book.

[1] On July 7 Thomas Isaac Mardy Jones, Labour MP for Pontypridd, stated in the House of Commons that the President of the Board of Trade, Sir Philip Cunliffe-Lister, 'is directly interested in the coal industry in this country'. Later he offered to withdraw the remark if it was incorrect, but he added: 'I understood that the President of the Board of Trade is married to a lady who is the chief owner of one of the largest mines.' A few moments later he declared: 'It has been a most unhappy choice, from the point of view of public opinion, that the Government should have selected the President of the Board of Trade to insult the miners of Britain by asking for this Vote here to-day. Why did not the Government put up the Secretary for Mines? I suppose because he is a royalty owner himself. Why did they not put up the Parliamentary Secretary to the Board of Trade? He is only a shipowner.'

Winston S. Churchill to Sir Richard Hopkins

(*Churchill papers: 1/191*)

20 July 1926   Treasury Chambers

My dear Hopkins,

At the time when I took office as Chancellor of the Exchequer, under-standing that by the very fact of holding such an office I was precluded from continuing in any way my previous profession as a journalist & author, I took immediate steps to wind my profession up. I ceased all journalistic work, & although I had entered into contracts to publish two books both of wh were nearly completed, I cancelled the contracts, foregoing both serial rights & royalties. I also assigned to other people copyrights from which a few royalties were still due to come in in respect of earlier publications.

Just recently I have found that I was to some extent under a misapprehension, & that the embargo does not of necessity extend to the publication of a book, ie to authorship as opposed to current journalism.

In these circumstances I am now proposing to complete the two books wh I had in preparation, & to publish one in the spring and the other either in the autumn or in the following year. I have no other work of authorship (or journalism) in view, except that possibly I may give permission for republication of some old articles (the copyright in wh I had treated as worthless), & receive some honorarium therefore.

I assume that if I take this course I shall be liable to be charged to Income Tax on my receipts as casual profits under Case I, or alternatively as a new business under Case IV, of Schedule D & that my past liability will not be altered; but I shd be vy glad if you wd let me know authoritatively what my position is under the law & the existing practice.[1]

Stanley Baldwin to King George V

(*Baldwin papers*)

20 July 1926   House of Commons

He (Mr Snowden) wound up by chastising the Chancellor for his alleged weakness in negotiating with foreign Ministers of Finance which resulted in

---

[1] *The World Crisis 1916–1918*, in two parts, was published on 3 March 1927. A total of 12,894 were sold by the end of 1927. Churchill received an advance of £2,000, as against a royalty of 14 shillings per copy. He thus earned more than £9,000 from his book alone in the tax year 1927–8. On July 30 Hopkins replied that Churchill's past liability 'would not be altered by the circumstances now contemplated', which could indeed be dealt with under Case IV of Schedule D.

his obtaining for this country worse conditions than those secured by his more astute rivals the Americans.

Mr Churchill in his defence was in a quiet, logical and reasoning frame of mind. He contended that the correspondence with Monsieur Caillaux did not in any way vitiate the Agreement, but merely opened the door for reconsideration without in any way committing the Government of this country to any definite policy. Without that correspondence no settlement could have been arrived at and the need for stability in European affairs was such that a settlement was the paramount consideration.

Dealing with the subject of the Anglo-American debt, Mr Churchill seized the opportunity to refute a statement which had recently been made by Mr Mellon,[1] the Secretary to the United States Treasury, to the effect that some of the British war borrowings from the United States had been used for purely commercial and selfish interests. As regards the general question, he provoked Mr Lloyd George's hostility by declaring that no one had had a better chance of settling the debt on the principle of equality of sacrifice, not only in regard to money, but also in regard to blood than Mr Lloyd George. That opportunity had, however, gone by and it was futile at this stage to indulge in idle recrimination in regard to the past.

Winston S. Churchill to Lord Balfour

(*Balfour papers*)

26 July 1926   10 Downing Street

I was so pleased to read yr vy gt compliment of my work at the Exchequer wh you paid in yr speech in the H of L.[2]

It was like being 'mentioned in despatches'.

WSC

[1] Andrew William Mellon, 1855–1937. Industrialist and financier. Born in Pittsburgh, Pennsylvania. Owner of T. Mellon and Sons, bankers, 1882. Co-founder of Alcoa Corporation, 1882, and of Gulf Oil and Union Steel, 1891. Secretary of the United States Treasury, 1921–32, under three Presidents, Harding, Coolidge and Hoover. United States Ambassador to Britain, February 1932–January 1933. Founder of the National Gallery of Art, Washington, 1935, and of the Mellon Institute of Industrial Research.

[2] On 26 July 1926, during a debate on the Finance Bill in the House of Lords, Lord Balfour remarked that: 'so far as my judgement goes, at a very difficult period, under conditions of unusual difficulty, our finances have been directed by the Chancellor of the Exchequer with singular courage, great caution, great invention and, as I think, great success'.

August 1926

George Lane-Fox to Lord Irwin

(Irwin papers)

9 August 1926

The PM had been getting rather weary lately, and as the coal trouble continues without our being able to settle it, I am afraid it weighs on him considerably.

Neville Chamberlain: diary

(Neville Chamberlain papers)

10 August 1926

SB has suffered most from the strike . . . he too is worn out, and has no spirit left, but he remains the one with the greatest influence in the country.

Winston has decidedly improved his position and is very popular, I believe, with our side, as he is really with the whole House for the wonderful entertainment he gives them.

Winston S. Churchill to Robert Boothby[1]

(Boothby papers)

10 August 1926   Chartwell Manor

My dear Boothby,

How very kind of you to send me the article which you wrote to the Spectator about my book.[2] I have read it with the greatest pleasure, all the

---

[1] Robert John Graham Boothby, 1900– . Educated at Eton and Magdalen College, Oxford. Conservative MP for East Aberdeenshire, 1924–58. Parliamentary Private Secretary to the Chancellor of the Exchequer (Churchill), 1926–9. Elected to the Other Club, 1928. Parliamentary Secretary, Ministry of Food, 1940–1. A British Delegate to the Consultative Assembly, Council of Europe, 1949–57. Knighted, 1953. Created Baron, 1958. President of the Anglo-Israel Association. Rector of St Andrews University, 1958–61. Chairman, Royal Philharmonic Orchestra, 1961–3. Published *The New Economy* (1943), *I Fight to Live* (1947) and *My Yesterday, Your Tomorrow* (1962).

[2] On 10 November 1923 a letter from Robert Boothby had been published in *The Spectator* defending the second volume of Churchill's *The World Crisis* against a hostile review by

more because it was written before we were friends—before we even knew each other—& when you might, as so many other people have done, have formed unfavourable views of my character & performance.

You must not mind my chaff about the Bolsheviks. It has a serious underside however. I do not want to see you get mixed up with these snakes or their servitors in this country just for the sake of herrings, & so prejudice what I daresay will be a prosperous political career.

With good wishes,
Yours sincerely,
Winston S. Churchill

Neville Chamberlain to Lord Irwin

(*Irwin papers*)

15 August 1926

THE CABINET FILM

. . . at a sort of preparatory blare of trumpets, the words 'Winston' appeared on the screen and immediately the letters of which it was composed all separated themselves and, moving about by some jugglery which enchanted me, although I could not understand, finally settled themselves into a caricature of our Chancellor with the well-known beetling brows and bald head.

This was funny without being vulgar and while we were still in a good humour the door flew open and in burst Winston himself (all in the film you understand). By Jove! how things hum in that office. The table groaned under mountains of books, secretaries rushed in and out. Ronnie McNeill sat him down in an attitude of respectful attention and then, lighting a cigar of Brobdingnagian proportions, Winston grimaced, stormed, graticulated (??!!), and orated until the film man got paralysed or his film burst. . . .

Winston constantly improves his position in the House and in the Party. His speeches are extraordinarily brilliant and men flock in to hear him as they would to a first class entertainment at the theatre. The best show in London, they say, and there is the weak point. So far as I can judge they

---

General Sir Frederick Maurice which the magazine had published the previous week. Maurice had ended his review: 'This second volume leaves us thanking God that he ceased to have anything to do with the conduct of the war before he had brought us to perdition.' Defending Churchill and the Dardanelles, Boothby wrote: 'Undaunted, he fought on—a lone hand—attacked by all, while he saw the prize, of which he alone perhaps realized the full value, slip from his grasp through no fault of his own.'

think of it as a show and they are not prepared at present to trust his character and still less his judgment.

Personally, I can't help liking and admiring him more, the more I see of him, but it is always accompanied by a diminution of my intellectual respect for him. I have noticed that in all disputes of a departmental character that I had with him he has had to give way because his case was not really well founded.

George Lane-Fox to Lord Irwin

(*Irwin papers*)

18 August 1926

Winston seems to me to be playing the game very well, he is an affectionate creature at heart, and I really think he has a deep affection for SB. I think he feels he owes unexpectedly high office to him, and the possible conspiracy that you and I once dreaded, when Winston and FE might rally the Diehards and break up the Cabinet, seems to me to be more unlikely now, partly because FE is still bibulous and I think Winston would not feel him to be a very reliable ally, but mainly I believe because of Winston's own personal feelings for SB.

Thomas Jones: diary

(*Jones papers*)

25 August 1926

At 5.30 pm the Chancellor spoke to me on the phone from Chartwell, and asked me to come down and spend the night there. He would send a car to Oxted to meet a train due just before 8.0 pm: dinner would be at 8.30 pm. Besides the Churchill family, I found at Chartwell two cousins, the Misses White, old Paulinas, and Lindemann, Professor of Experimental Philosophy at Oxford, who had been Director of the RAF Laboratory at Farnborough.

Winston plunged into the coal business at once, and I tried in vain to postpone the subject until after dinner when I could have talked in private with my host, but he is the most unsubtle and expansive person. He talked with the greatest freedom and frankness before Lindemann and the rest, making several little speeches in the course of dinner, one especially in defence of a change of opinion which Mrs Churchill alleged against him. The two elder children were with us, Diana about 17, and Randolph about 15.

Nothing could be more charming than Winston's handling of the children throughout my short visit. Lindemann, I quickly discovered, regarded all miners, if not all the working classes, as a species of sub-humans. This drove me to the Extreme Left with Winston at the Right Centre. The ladies left at about 10 pm and we carried on till past midnight, Randolph being allowed to stay to the end as a special privilege, and his father frequently deferring to him for his opinion on some phase or other of the coal crisis: the boy was extremely intelligent, and obviously under the influence of the Prof (as he was called).

Winston is dictating Volume III of the World Crisis, and has been working out comparative figures of British and German casualties with the help of Lindemann and the small boy. I made him talk about the book, and he gave us a brilliant summary of it, especially of the 'beautiful preparations' which we were making in 1918 for bombing German aerodromes far behind the German front. Every sentence of the book is dictated, so his secretary told me. At one stage he digressed into an account of the two occasions on which he had stayed with Joseph Chamberlain; he was gathering material for the Life of his father. Chamberlain he described as a man of most domineering temper and narrow vision, who saw with great clearness along the line of that vision. He had destroyed the Liberal Party by his Protectionist frenzy, to which Gladstone's failure to take Chamberlain into his confidence had contributed.

Shortly after midnight, on my way to my room, my host showed me his bedroom and work-room where I saw the famous bust of Napoleon on his writing-table.[1] My room had been occupied by Henry VIII when he used to pay court to Ann Boleyn at Hever, a few miles away. Winston's modern house incorporates what was left of the old Manor of Chartwell. It was built by Philip Tilden who built Churt for Lloyd George, and did a lot at Lympne for Philip Sassoon. Tilden forgot to put a scullery at Churt: what he forgot at Chartwell I did not discover because he was a subject to be avoided. I think he does fine design and leaves all the roofs leaking, and ends up by presenting a bill to his client two or three times the original estimate; that much I gathered from Mrs Churchill.

I was out and about before 9.0 am, and found the Chancellor attired in dungarees and high Wellington boots superintending the building of a dam by a dozen navvies. This is the third lake, and the children are wondering what their father will do next year, as there is room for no more lakes.

As I was going away, he told me 'I am very glad you expounded the democratic faith last night, as the small boy does not often hear it, and it will be

[1] A small white china bust of Napoleon, which had been a gift to Churchill from Lord Northcliffe. For the incident in 1916 which led Churchill briefly to return it, see Companion Volume III of this biography, pages 1512–13 and 1516–17.

very good for him.' I agreed, and said that in view of what was likely to happen in the next twenty years it was desirable he should not be unduly Lindemannised. The father agreed and said he was eager that the boy should get a scientific outlook.

Sir Philip Cunliffe-Lister to Winston S. Churchill

(*Churchill papers: 22/112*)

25 August 1926
Personal

My dear Winston,

I hope very much that you will speak in the debate on Monday. If the Prime Minister is not back[1] you will presumably be leading the House, but in any case I think a speech from you will be very useful. It will help greatly in getting men back to work if a first-class speech is made and fully reported, which shows the futility of the men waiting for Cook to produce a settlement from some undisclosed quarter, and which gives assurance in firm but unprovocative terms that ample protection will be forthcoming everywhere. You are also the right person to dispose again and finally of any question of a subsidy, and you are the right person to answer Lloyd George. I thought the lines of your last speech excellent.

I presume the course of the debate will be that we shall give formal notice to consider the regulations to-morrow, and that the debate on the adjournment will then begin. You would, I suppose, speak at about half past six or seven and so be sure not only of a full report but of considered leading articles in the papers.

I saw Lane-Fox yesterday and he too is very keen that you should speak.

Yrs ever
P. Cunliffe-Lister

[1] From Aix-les-Bains, to which the Cabinet had persuaded Baldwin to go (see George Lane-Fox's letter of 1 September 1926 to Lord Irwin, quoted on page 761 of this volume).

Cabinet Coal Committee: minutes[1]

(*Churchill papers: 22/116*)

26 August 1926   10 Downing Street

1. THE COMMITTEE took note of the following telegram which had just been received from the Secretary of State for India:—[2]

'Regret was away and message not received in time. Cook's most recent speech repeats so-called slogan and suggests that he is merely making an impudent tactical attempt to save his face. I think he should be sharply reminded that his own perverse obstinacy has greatly altered the position to the prejudice of the miners so that the terms obtainable in May are no longer open. He might also usefully be reminded of his insulting references to the Prime Minister. I think a representative of the Home Office should be present and the question of protection treated as one of urgent importance.'

2. SIR ERNEST GOWERS, at the request of the Chairman, gave his views of the position now reached. Mr Cook had held out before the Miners the prospect of fresh negotiations in order to prevent their returning to work. He had probably in mind nothing more than the conversations with Lord Wimborne. The coalowners refused to confer with Lord Wimborne; the miners having failed to establish contact with the owners had sought a meeting with the Government. In this way the appearance of negotiations would be kept up until the meeting of Parliament on Monday. He understood that Mr Cook would endeavour to prolong the mystery by objecting to any press report being given out of the conference with Ministers.

THE CHANCELLOR OF THE EXCHEQUER said that it was important to avoid any misconception arising as to the character of the conference, and the Government must reserve the right to publish a clear statement of the position.

THE MINISTER OF LABOUR said it was important to elicit whether any fresh proposals were forthcoming from the miners' leaders and to make plain to them that the Government could not entertain a further subsidy or a rigid seven hours or a postponement pending reorganisation, or a national agreement with no prior district discussions.

---

[1] Those present were Churchill (in the chair), Sir Arthur Steel-Maitland (Minister of Labour) and George Lane-Fox (Parliamentary Secretary, Mines Department). Also present were Sir Ernest Gowers (Permanent Under-Secretary, Mines Department), A. L. Dixon (Home Office) and J. D. B. Fergusson (Treasury). The Secretary to the Committee was Thomas Jones. Two days earlier Sir William Joynson-Hicks had written to Baldwin: 'I am quite happy that SM & Winston should deal with coal, & I will deal with Cook & his merry men' (*Baldwin papers*).

[2] Lord Birkenhead.

THE SECRETARY FOR MINES thought district arrangements must play an important part in any settlement reached.

THE CHANCELLOR OF THE EXCHEQUER said he had no wish to see the Government assist in breaking up the Miners' Federation. The sound position for the Government was to refuse further financial help. Other aspects of the dispute were on a different plane. If the Miners' leaders attached great importance to a national agreement it was not the business of the Government to oppose, provided there was the necessary elasticity for dealing with exceptional districts. If the men continue unreasonable and break up in the field, there would be district settlements but they were not likely to be permanent.

MR DIXON[1] reported on behalf of the Home Secretary that, apart from sporadic outbreaks trouble had been confined to the Nottinghamshire and Derby district where the miners' leaders had conducted an intensive campaign. The police had been reinforced on Monday and Tuesday and were now believed to be in ample strength in both counties. None had been sent from London. There had been a change in the attitude of pickets. Up to midday reports showed that Derby was quiet and an increase of men employed was reported.

Winston S. Churchill: remarks during a meeting of Ministers and the Miners' Federation[2]

(Churchill papers: 22/100)

26 August 1926   10 Downing Street
5 pm

MR CHURCHILL: I think I had better at the very outset clear out of the field any proposition which we should not be in any circumstances likely to entertain because the question of giving any financial help to the industry has long passed out of the sphere of practical politics. We gave twenty three millions, when I last saw Mr Cook. I told him that, we gave

[1] Arthur Lewis Dixon, 1881–1969. Educated Kingswood School, Bath, and Sidney Sussex College, Cambridge. Entered the Home Office, 1903; Private Secretary to the Parliamentary Under-Secretary of State, 1908; to the Permanent Under-Secretary, 1910. Assistant Secretary, 1919–33. Assistant Under-Secretary of State, 1933–42. Knighted, 1941. Principal Assistant Under-Secretary of State, 1942–6.

[2] The following were present at this meeting: for the Government, Churchill, Sir Arthur Steel-Maitland (Minister of Labour), Colonel George Lane-Fox (Secretary for Mines), Sir Ernest Gowers (Permanent Under-Secretary, Mines Department) and Thomas Jones (Deputy Secretary, Cabinet). For the Miners' Federation: Herbert Smith (President), Thomas Richards, W. P. Richardson and A. J. Cook (Secretary).

23 millions to secure nine months in which to try and come to some sort of settlement of this position. It was a very questionable thing for the Government to do to use the taxpayers' money in that way and we had the greatest difficulty in justifying it. That was the end, absolutely the end. There was of course the three millions which I reserved in the budget of this year because if we could have avoided this struggle it might have been thrown in to make a taper to ease matters off or assist in the removal of miners from pits that might be closed. There was the three millions but as there has been all this long stoppage and such tremendous expenses thrown upon us that was entirely withdrawn, but we have said that what is left out of that after the various expenses we are now being put to have been defrayed it will be available for aiding the movement of miners from any pits which may be closed, and we have actually earmarked £250,000 for the development of Scientific research, the attempt to develop liquid fuel from coal and other projects with which you are very well acquainted. But of course we have bought a good deal of foreign coal and if the stoppage comes to an end, whenever it does come to an end, we are bound to be left with a certain amount of this on our hands and as coal will certainly fall in price we shall have a loss on that. Therefore I cannot say it will be three millions. It may be half but whatever is left will be available to carry out the recommendations of the Royal Commission that the Government should assist the removal of miners from pits no longer in working order, no longer able to pay the rate of wages that is decided upon, and that is the end. Nothing in the nature of a subsidy however small, however temporary and nothing in the nature of a loan by the Government, which is after all exactly the same as a subsidy, would be possible to us now. It is not our money: we are answerable to the taxpayers of the country as a whole, and there are 750,000 men out of work who would now be working apart from miners but for this prolonged stoppage. There is an immense amount of suffering throughout the country in many districts particularly in the working class districts in the big basic industries. The revenue is affected, everything is affected. We made an effort last year to avoid these evils, but now these evils have happened. We could not possibly consider anything in the nature of financial help.

MR CHURCHILL: I think we would all agree with you in thinking that it would be very much better for you to terminate this matter if possible, if you find you can terminate it by a general act of your own volition, than that it should simply go forward indefinitely until finally the force of circumstances and events prevail and there is no sort of agreement to which you are parties, but what I want to ask you, if you will allow me to do so, is how will your position in the matter be benefited supposing we go on for another six weeks or two months. We have learned a good deal since this began. If you had asked me when the coal stoppage began what I thought the loss to the country would be after the twelfth week I should have given you figures ten times as high as those I now know to be the case. As a matter of fact the country has shown a most extraordinary power of carrying on except in the great basic trades in which so many of your own people and your own friends and people who have suffered a great deal to help you, are engaged. Generally speaking the country as a whole, the exports for July, for instance, were better than a year ago making allowance for the fact that no coal was exported and making allowance for prices. Unemployment is better—of course the harvest has something to do with that—but the minister of Labour has reported a diminution—between six and seven hundred thousand men were unemployed during the general strike—but since the general strike, we are 50,000 better than we were then. People are buying coal. We are not called upon to buy coal to any extent now. It is coming in freely, nearly one million tons a week. It could easily be increased, no doubt, if the cold weather came. On the other hand, there is a certain output here and outcrop workings are being used, and there is no doubt whatever that we are in a position where we have no difficulty in carrying on the life of the country, a large proportion of the trade of the country and all the vital services. As to its prosperity, I agree there is suffering every day, but as far as carrying on the thing for another six weeks or two months is concerned there is not the slightest compulsion or pressure on the Government such as we should have imagined would have been operating on us when we looked at it sixteen weeks ago. That is a very remarkable new fact, a very extraordinary fact and what I want you to consider is this—how will you be better, supposing we come and meet again when the Prime Minister is back, how will it be better for your people than it is today and for your organisation? As far as we are concerned you may be sure we shall give no money. On that we are absolutely clear, but you need not think we wish to humiliate you or the miners. As a Government we have no such idea or feeling in our mind at all, nothing of the sort. There is nothing we should rejoice in more than that you should make a good working arrangement in the industry. We should rejoice in that. Whether there should be national or district settlements is not for us to decide—I cannot see why the two cannot be reconciled; but that is for you. All I would say is that we do not see how you benefit your position by a further postponement of the settlement.

MR RICHARDS:[1] I regret very much that speech which I interpret as say-

[1] Thomas Richards, 1859–1931. Born in Ebbw Vale. Left elementary school at the age of ten to work in the mines. In 1884, while still working at the coal face, he formed the Ebbw

ing to us this, you cannot hurt us, carry on. That is the sum and substance of that speech. Now I wanted you to regard us in the capacity today, as we expected to find you, desirous of trying to find a way out of this great difficulty.

MR CHURCHILL: We are.

SIR A. STEEL-MAITLAND: I think everyone is anxious to find a way out of the difficulty. It is only that the subsidy is left out of the question.

MR CHURCHILL: Mr Richards, I must not mislead you into supposing that because we say we can give no financial assistance, our good offices are not available. They would be available freely to enable the country yourselves, ourselves, and all of us to get out of this very lamentable state of affairs. But it is no use good offices being available unless you know what they are to work upon, and I am bound to say when I heard you were coming to see us today I hoped you would put before us certain quite new and definite suggestions which we could consider and if we thought there was any real practicable chance of a solution being reached by them then as we have said over and over again, the Prime Minister and everybody, our good offices would be available in whatever way they would be most useful. Therefore if I turn down anything in the nature of a subsidy it does not at all mean that we would not use our good offices provided that there was some chance of their coming to some useful result. That is where it is really up to you, if I may say so at this moment. Have you anything in your minds that alters the present situation, anything that can be put forward? If so, do so now. But let me say that it has been agreed that what has been said shall be recorded. We can agree among ourselves that if there is any special thing you wish to say you wish to be excluded from the report, it can be excluded. We would trust you in the matter, but I think it better that the whole transcript should be made. We feel it is up to you to tell us what is in your minds and what is the practical contribution you make to stop the present deadlock. Our contribution has been made, 23 millions.

Vale Miners' Association. Miners' Agent, Ebbw Vale District, 1888–1901. General Secretary of the South Wales Miners' Federation from 1898 until his death. Labour MP for West Monmouth and Ebbw Vale, 1904–20; resigned to devote his services to the Miners' Federation, of which he became Vice-President (President, 1930–1). Privy Councillor, 1918. Member of the TUC General Council, 1925–31, and of the National Executive of the Labour Party. On 9 November 1931 *The Times* wrote: 'Moderate, cautious, and conciliatory in his counsel to the miners on all occasions, and often dissenting profoundly from the policy they were bent on pursuing, he held their loyalty and confidence by the courage and firmness he displayed when the battle was joined. Beneath his mild and deprecating demeanour there were surprising reserves of strength and determination. He could not be browbeaten. He met intimidation with outspokenness and candour.'

MR RICHARDS: We say you threw the 23 millions away. That is our interpretation of that. If closely examined it can be pretty strongly verified. It did not help the industry one bit.

MR CHURCHILL: It gave nine months.

MR RICHARDS: Nine months' work of course.

MR CHURCHILL: It gave nine months in which to think things over.

MR COOK: . . . We all make mistakes in propaganda speeches. I am as guilty as anybody else. Everybody puts their own point of view, but it is not the whole truth. Isn't there some way of calling the two sides together with a view to discussing a national agreement to see what we can arrive at? We can then see if there is any accommodation for disagreements instead of starting by saying hard and fast, we cannot do this and we cannot do that. It should not be taken as a sign of weakness that people want to negotiate a settlement.

MR CHURCHILL: Certainly not.

MR COOK: Because we have got to agree some time. Either we have got to have an agreement that is going to be signed by both sides, or an agreement that is going to be imposed, and you know enough of the world and of men to know that an imposed agreement would be kept as long as it could be imposed and constant agitation would be going on to remove it. It means no kind of developed stability in an industry that, for development, needs some continuity.

MR RICHARDS: . . . I have understood that the big thing the Government were sticking against is that if 'we do find money there will be no hope of a settlement'. I think there is some hope of a settlement, and we think it is not unreasonable to ask that the money which is being used for fighting should be used for establishing peace.

MR CHURCHILL: We are not finding money for fighting in this. The employers and you are fighting each other, and we find that owing to the fight going on between you the country is in such a situation that we have to spend money to ensure that the people get their food and that businesses are carried on as far as possible. We are bound to do our best to carry that on. That is quite a different thing to paying a special subsidy to a particular industry, because then all the other industries would have claims too, and there are industries other than coal that would jump at a subsidy at the present time.

MR COOK: And what about the hours?

MR CHURCHILL: As far as the Eight Hours Bill was concerned, we have said again and again that the miners ought to have a choice in certain districts between an extra hour or half hour or a very low rate of wages. They ought to have the choice, and the law said they should not have the choice, and we took steps to remove that restriction. When you say that obsolete mines should be shut down, I agree. But we have first to see how many are to be shut down at once. Are they to be shut down before there are others to take the miners, and so on? We have been told—and the Commission made a careful report on the subject—that on the basis of a uniform 7 hours and the rate of wages which the men got, as many as over a third of the pits would be shut down either permanently or for a very long time. That is a frightful thing to contemplate. You gentlemen have to manage your affairs, and I know how difficult they are. Apart from everything else, I sympathise with you in your task; But it seems to me we were not going beyond where it was right for a Government to go to say at any rate if it is a question of whole districts being blotted out with all the local industries dependent upon them—all blotted out, or some increase in the working day as a temporary measure in a particular industry, that is a matter that may fairly be put to you for consideration at the present time. That is our position. I know you do not agree with it, as you have taken up this other line, but it comes to this. Supposing we were to go to the owners tonight and say 'You come and meet the miners at a three-cornered conference and see if we can hammer out a settlement,' they would say at once 'Is there anything new; we have explored all this for months, but there is nothing new.' I wondered if there was something new on the tip of your tongues except this old demand for a subsidy. We cannot do this now; we have been put to all this suffering and struggling, and we have tried very hard—the Minister of Labour and the Prime Minister—and everyone knows it would be a great feather in the cap of the Government if the matter could have been settled and avoided and so on, but nothing new has come forward. I certainly did hope—I did not expect it, but I did hope—that perhaps to-day you or perhaps Mr Smith or Mr Richards would have said straight out across this table 'This thing has got to be stopped; we know we have to give something here and there, and this is what we can do if we can get a settlement.' If that was a real advance, then our good offices would be used to explore and further the matter with the utmost desire that good might result, but we have heard nothing new this evening; the only thing we have heard is a request for financial assistance.

MR COOK: Upon what terms; what do you mean by something new? Shall we get down to brass tacks?

MR CHURCHILL: Have you anything to suggest to us: would you like to consult with one another in another room? Have you anything to suggest which in your opinion as practical men is likely to alter the situation?

MR RICHARDS: The suppositions have been that with reorganisation and with better selling arrangements and with some amalgamations and other things this industry could be put on a very much better basis than it was when we stopped work, and you ask us what we specially put to you? We have to emphasise this. We have been asked to make the whole of the sacrifice from our wages until those things are put right, and that very fact removes the pressure from employers, and they will go on in their old slipshod fashion as they have gone since I have known it. I have been actively engaged in South Wales for 40 years, and for the whole of that time the best coal in the world has been recklessly drawn and sent away at nothing like its commercial value.

MR CHURCHILL: You mean the transferred coal?

MR RICHARDS: No, between 50 and 60 million tons a year produced and nobody making anything out of it, only the Managing Directors and their friends and agents and their ships and railways and other industries they are interested in. Remove this pressure from them by lowering wages, and there will be no reorganisation done to put the industry into a better position. . . .

MR CHURCHILL: Let me say once again what I said at the outset, that if you have some proposals to make to us in any way you like to make them, confidentially, openly or verbally—if you have any proposals to put to us which will constitute a new situation, we shall see that those proposals are transmitted to the other side, and naturally we shall do our best to take advantage of anything in those proposals that show that the two sides were coming together on the issues at stake. Do not let me lead you into the misconception that I do not realise how greatly the country is suffering by what is going on. You are suffering, the country is suffering, everybody is suffering, but there is no doubt of the country's capacity to continue. That is all I wish to say to indicate the difference between being and well-being.

MR COOK: What do you mean by new proposals—some proposal for a lower national minimum for instance than what existed?

MR CHURCHILL: We thought really that these proposals ought to come from you. We can easily suggest what is the best solution for both sides, but we have not the power of enforcing it, and it is really for you to say what you think. We have made many proposals in the past. The Prime Minister wrote a letter making suggestions, but it is really for you to do that now. And let me say that the door is open if you have proposals to make at any time, but after all, we are looking at realities. They may seem rather dour. We are looking at the realities of the case; you have to face the hard facts of the case, and you know the facts as well as we do. You know what matters and what does not matter, and if at any time you feel able to make a proposal which alters the position in a manner which is substantial naturally, if we are satisfied that it is something that leads to a hope of bringing the two sides nearer to an agreement, we should exert ourselves at once, but we cannot give you or the other side in the matter assurances. We have to try and carry on as well as we can during your quarrel.

MR RICHARDS: Supposing we are prepared to give some proposals, are you then prepared not to rule out among these proposals the question of some financial assistance?

MR CHURCHILL: No, we cannot give financial assistance, I mean Government financial assistance. If the industry arranged a loan in its own way, that does not affect the Government, but there can be no loan from the Government, nor a subsidy.

MR RICHARDS: So your lifeboat is not going to be launched?

MR CHURCHILL: My lifeboat has already sunk.

MR RICHARDS: You wasted a lot of money on the lifeboat last year, and we claim that every man is entitled to a decent living wage.

MR CHURCHILL: I do not really quite understand why you don't consider that the Bill—I am now only on the point of re-organisation—I do not understand why you consider the Act of Parliament we have passed is not in any way a means of carrying forward the re-organisation. Let me point out so far as I may—I am prepared to be contradicted, I am only aware of one important point on which it departs from the recommendations of the Royal Commission and that is the point about mining royalties. Now I can quite see it would help the miners if the royalties were bought by the State and the whole of the proceeds given the miners. That is not the proposal of the Royal Commission. The proposal of the Royal Commission is that a fair market value should be paid for these royalties and that I as Chancellor of the Exchequer on behalf of the State should receive what the royalty owners receive now having given them public money instead. I have had it worked out. I believe it could be done so that in the first few years there would be no great loss to the State. On the other hand it would be very inconvenient to borrow the necessary money at the present time. From a financial point of view it may not make a great difference to the State. It makes no difference to you and the only thing is the psychological effect. Why the miners should feel it would be better psychologically because a hundred millions in hard cash is handed over to the royalty owners I cannot understand. I should not feel psychologically improved in my mood.

Our sincere and honest belief is that our Act, apart from the question of mining royalties which would not be any financial service to the miners at the present time, does fully meet the proposals of the Commission and we are determined to put them into operation with the utmost vigour in our power. That is on this particular point of re-organisation.

MR RICHARDS: Of course the royalties would have paid off the loan would they not?

MR COOK: It is a lot more than psychological, the reduction that is being asked of the lower paid men who are the first to be sacrificed all the time. One does not want to make propaganda; we want a settlement.

MR CHURCHILL: Let me finish by saying there is no reason why our discussion this afternoon should be the last word at all. If at any time you feel you need the help of the Government of the country you are entitled to come, but so far nothing has appeared which in any way arms us with the means to advance matters towards a settlement. The only request that has been made, the only request—and it has now been made by all four of you gentlemen—has been for a renewal of financial assistance and we have definitely stated that after all that has happened—after the financial assistance we have given, after the great loss we have suffered—we are not prepared to ask Parliament to do that. But on other matters if you wish to come to see us or to see the Minister of Labour it is our duty to see you and you know perfectly well how we should rejoice if a settlement could be reached. We would rather have a settlement reached by an agreement to which both parties put their names than by the struggle being fought out to the bitter end.

MR COOK: That is better for everybody.

MR CHURCHILL: It is better for everybody, but we have made our financial contribution and we cannot make any further one. So far as re-organisation is concerned you are powerfully represented in Parliament, and if you can show us we are falling short in vigour in putting that Act into operation you can bring it to our attention in the proper place, but certainly our intention is to put it into operation at full speed. Any settlement you can make with the owners will be better than what is going on now from our point of view, but we see no reason why district settlements and a national settlement should not be combined in the same way as you have a schedule to an Act of Parliament.

MR HERBERT SMITH: The difficulty is this: your saying you will help puts me in mind of a man in the river drowning and a man on the bank saying if you come in to the side and drag yourself out I will wipe your feet. We are not going to settle on any terms. I am going to fight a bit yet. I am nearly 65 and there is a bit of fight in the old dog still. We have said all that the Report has asked us to say, examine it, take it from front to back and take its results and I say when we come to the sixth point we are prepared to deal with the sixth point but we are not prepared to say at once we will give a reduction of wages to help the employers.

MR CHURCHILL: We will provide you with a copy of the transcript. I must tell you I propose on behalf of the Government to publish a statement saying in short what we consider has occurred here, but if we can agree upon the statement that would be more satisfactory, but something has got to be done. I want to talk quite frankly. We do not believe there is any advantage gained by an air of mystery hanging over the whole scene and people thinking a lot is going on and we are negotiating. We think it should be known that there is an advance to a solution or that there is no advance.

MR COOK: My point is this, in order that nobody shall say *this* has been said and *that* has been said I would rather the whole report was published.

MR CHURCHILL: I have not a word to say against that.

MR COOK: So much gets manufactured. The imagination of some pressmen is wonderful.

MR CHURCHILL: Shall we agree on a statement or if not, shall we decide on what statement we are going to make? We will send you a copy. If there is anything you object to in it you can check it. Perhaps you would have a meeting with Mr Jones.

As the report is going to be published it is not of very great consequence but I think it is important that it should be made clear there is no change in the situation so far as we are concerned because the only thing we have been asked specifically upon we are not able to do.

MR COOK: But let us not start at the opening now on a stunt which may be propagated by the press of different colours before the full report is published. It does give the idea we have come simply on that.

MR CHURCHILL: I think we should agree on some neutral words and then publish the report. The alternative is for you to give your version, for you to say we met the Government, we were very disgusted with their attitude, but if we can agree on something neutral I think it would be better. Anyhow we do not want to do anything to damage the prospect of our meeting again.

MR COOK: That is my idea.

MR CHURCHILL: It is agreed the report, while giving the truth, should not be coloured in either way and Mr Cook and Mr Jones will just rough up something and if they wish to consult the others they will do so, but if they are both agreed on the matter the statement can be published.

SIR A. STEEL-MAITLAND: It is impossible for a dozen people to discuss it.

MR CHURCHILL: We will give you a copy of the proceedings. You can look through them and if you are misreported in any way you can correct it. We will make a perfectly fair, honourable and readable report of what has taken place.

(The proceedings then terminated.)

Thomas Jones to Stanley Baldwin

(*Jones papers*)

26 August 1926

The meeting lasted about an hour and a half. Herbert Smith was uncompromising throughout and reiterated the old demands. All four pressed the Chancellor hard over and over again for temporary financial assistance. The Chancellor firmly resisted further help either by way of subsidy, loan, or guarantee. He made quite plain that the Government would gladly help to resume negotiations with the Owners if proposals from the men were such as to create a really new situation. No such proposals emerged but it was evident that Cook especially was anxious to get out some such proposals; but Herbert Smith had his foot on Cook's neck. . . .

Most of the running for our side was done of course by the Chancellor, and most admirably done as I think you will agree when you see the shorthand note. The Minister of Labour with his greater knowledge of detail was also first-rate, I thought, and there is nothing to regret in the conduct of to-day's meeting by our side.

Winston S. Churchill to John Reith: telegram

(*Churchill papers: 2/147*)

28 August 1926

I have received a request from Mr Havelock Wilson[1] to ask you to let him intervene tonight in the entertainment programme for ten minutes with an appeal for industrial peace. You are no doubt aware of the fact. In the absence of the Prime Minister I trust you will be able to make an exception in this case provided of course that the controversial tone is not adopted.

[1] Joseph Havelock Wilson, 1859–1929. A seaman: subsequently President of the National Seamen's Union. A Liberal MP from 1892–1900, 1906–10 and 1918–22. Secretary of the Merchant Seaman's League. In 1925 he published his memoirs, *My Stormy Voyages Through Life*.

Thomas Jones: diary

(*Jones papers*)

30 August 1926

The Cabinet Coal Committee met at 12.0 to-day. In addition to the Chancellor (in the Chair) we had Steel-Maitland, Lane-Fox, Sir Laming, Jix, Cunliffe-Lister, Horace Wilson,[1] and Gowers. . . .

The Home Secretary had no news of an exciting kind from the Midlands, beyond the fact that nearly 3,000 additional men had gone to work. Had he remained in the North he would have shot 200 birds or brace (I am not sure which) on somebody's moors. Lane-Fox then pulled out of his pocket a letter from Evan Williams to which the Committee did not take at all kindly.

Every Minister present, with the doubtful exception of the Secretary for Mines, was quite firm on one point: that if by any chance the miners leaders' tabled to the Government proposals which showed a substantial return to sanity, the Government would be bound to transmit these proposals to the Mining Association, and to warn the Association that if they refused to deal nationally with such proposals, they could not count on the Government supporting them in such a course. Several very confidential letters from owners were read to the Committee—one important one by Cunliffe-Lister—which showed a considerable minority of owners in the districts to be in favour of a $7\frac{1}{2}$ hours day and of a national agreement with local variations. . . .

The Chancellor wanted throughout the discussion to make plain to the owners that the Government could not endorse the attitude of Evan Williams in his letter, and was keen to tell Evan Williams at once that if the owners were unreasonable the Government would not shrink from modifying the Eight Hours Act in the direction suggested by Cunliffe-Lister, viz, inserting district boards with an independent Chairman, and a national minimum. Ultimately it was agreed to telegraph to Evan Williams at Frinton bidding him to come up to meet the Committee this evening, but I have just heard (5 pm) that the meeting will not take place until tomorrow afternoon.

The discussion was thoroughly amicable throughout.

[1] Horace John Wilson, 1882–1972. Entered the Civil Service, 1900; Permanent Secretary, Ministry of Labour, 1921–30. Knighted, 1924. Chief Industrial Adviser to the Government, 1930–9. Seconded to the Treasury for special service with Stanley Baldwin, 1935–7, and with Neville Chamberlain, 1937–40 (when he had a room at 10 Downing Street). Permanent Secretary of the Treasury and Head of the Civil Service, 1939–42.

September 1926

George Lane-Fox to Lord Irwin

(Irwin papers)

1 September 1926

We persuaded the PM to go abroad, and His Majesty was induced to waive his objection. I am sure that was wise. He would have done no good by staying here, and nothing has occurred since he went away that has made any of us regret his going. Winston is here in charge and has certainly done extremely well, tactful and conciliatory, and with a keen flair for public opinion which has prevented him making the kind of 'thinking aloud' lapses, that SB is rather given to. In fact my fear is that many people may begin to compare the rather woolly and hesitating line of SB who never really seems to know where he is going, with the really clever and definite line which Winston has seemed to follow. Of course he will probably go off in to some wild error before long, but I can only tell you how things seems to me to stand now.

Winston took charge rather against the wish of Steel Maitland, but encouraged by me, as I thought a change of bowling might be effective. And he definitely put the miners in the wrong by begging them to make some suggestions of their own, and pointing out that all they had said was to ask for a renewal of subsidy. They went away, conferred with their Executive, and with the Labour Party, but could agree on nothing, though Ramsay was dying to get something out of them which he could use in the debate of yesterday. . . .

If Winston works up to a settlement of the coal trouble, I wonder how it may affect SB's position. But I think Winston is very loyal and will give SB a proper chance and not take advantage of being in charge just when the settlement is bound to come along.

Sir William Joynson-Hicks to King George V

(*Baldwin papers*)

1 September 1926

Mr Churchill's reply could hardly have been excelled.[1] It is almost sufficient to say that he has seldom appeared to better advantage in the House.
There were no polemics; there were no statements or arguments which
could reasonably provoke resentment or interruption—although on a few
occasions individual back-benchers on the opposite side made futile attempts
to lower the standard of the debate, which met with a well deserved and
dignified rebuke from Mr Churchill. Instead Mr Churchill reviewed the
whole problem in the most calm, unprovocative and dispassionate manner
that was possible, regarding it mainly from the point of view as to what
steps on the part of the Government were practicable in order to bring about
an improvement in the situation.

The main purpose of his speech was to make it clear that the Government
could not profitably intervene until there was some semblance of an offer
made by one side or the other which would provide definite and tangible
evidence that the parties interested were disposed to face the facts of the
situation and to negotiate on a businesslike footing. He hoped that the conference of the miners' delegates on Thursday might be productive of some
result. In any event the Government would continue to watch the situation
in the hope that some development might arise which would enable them to
take useful and profitable action. It was a speech of conciliation, reasonableness and good-will which undoubtedly made a considerable impression on
Members of the Labour Party.

Mr Smillie,[2] who followed, dealt mainly with the sentimental aspects of
the problem, but concluded by expressing a hope that the Chancellor of the

---

[1] Speaking in the House of Commons on August 31, Churchill had declared: 'The object
is to secure the greatest amount of employment and the largest sum of money paid in wages
throughout the coal industry under decent conditions, with the prospect of amelioration.
That is the object. . . . We want the greatest good for the greatest number. I had hoped that
the conference which the miners' leaders sought with the Government last week would lead
to some offer which would create a new situation, and there was one moment when I thought
I saw it on the tip of their tongue: but nothing actually emerged.' A few moments later he
said: 'One set of criticism is that the Prime Minister is always anxious to be very tender-
hearted and make peaceful settlements, and that I am the marplot who frequently comes
forward and intervenes to obstruct.' Churchill went on: 'It may be our fault if we failed, or
our misfortune from the obduracy of the situation. Nothing that you can do by an Act of
Parliament could compel miners to work or would compel owners to keep their pits open.
You may lead the horses to the water, but you cannot make them drink.'

[2] Robert Smillie, 1857–1940. President of the Scottish Miners' Federation, 1894–1918 and
1921–40. President of the Miners' Federation of Great Britain, 1912–21. Labour MP for
Morpeth, 1923–9.

Exchequer would follow up some of the hints which he had dropped in the course of his speech.

Thus the debate came to an end. It showed the House of Commons at its best. The poison and rancour which have characterised previous debates on this subject and have tended to embitter the controversy were almost entirely absent, and so great was the improvement in the atmosphere that it must be regarded as a hopeful sign and an indication of the growth of a spirit which may shortly bring to an end what Mr Churchill described as the most melancholy and ignominious breakdown of British common-sense ever exhibited.

Thomas Jones to Stanley Baldwin

(*Baldwin papers*)

1 September 1926   Offices of the Cabinet

Prime Minister,

The newspapers may have reached you before this does as owing to a meeting last night I missed the bag.

Yesterday's Debate at the House was undoubtedly one of the best we have had during the dispute. 'Ramsay', despite some raucous criticism at the outset, dropped to pianissimo before the close. LG was in his most seductive mood, and the Chancellor made a brilliant speech, dignified, conciliatory and fair. It made an immediate impression, and I believe has set several people at work trying once more to persuade the miners to table some sensible proposals. The Government has a very good Press to-day.[1]

At 5 pm last night the Chancellor and his colleagues met Evan Williams and half a dozen coal owners. The Chancellor outlined the main points of the speech he had made in the House and told the owners quite plainly that if hours and wages could be surmounted the Government would not allow a squabble over national agreements to block a settlement. The owners did

---

[1] Another account of the Debate was sent on 2 September 1926 by Baldwin's Private Secretary, Sir Patrick Gower, to J. C. C. Davidson, who was with Baldwin at Aix-les-Bains. Gower wrote: 'Ramsay started off badly with some cheap criticisms of the usual kind in regard to the Government, but the bulk of his speech, while not teeming with constructive suggestions, showed moderation and sincerity which has been lacking in most of his contributions on the subject of the coal strike. The general impression in regard to Steel-Maitland's speech was that it was deplorable, as it was much too provocative in tone and language. Ll G was at his mildest and best, and Winston achieved remarkable success. His speech seems to have convinced even the critics of the Government and, what is more, the most sanctimonious liberal critics, that the Government cannot profitably intervene at this stage and that it is really up to the miners' leaders to put forward some proposals however tentative in character before any advance can be made. . . .' (*Davidson papers*).

not like this and repeated that in their view we were within sight of the end, and that other districts would quickly follow Notts and Derby. This morning I belive Ramsay has been in touch with the miners whose Delegate Conference meets to-morrow (Thursday).

At 3 pm this afternoon Ramsay phoned asking if he could see the Chancellor, and there was some attempt to arrange a private dinner in Town. Ultimately Fergusson fixed up a car to take Ramsay down to Chartwell where the Chancellor is, and Lane-Fox and Gowers are going down by train. Horace Wilson is at Swanage, and Steel-Maitland was playing golf with Jix, so I could not get in touch with them, and in any case they had not been invited to Chartwell, and my task was much simplified by their absence!

Ramsay, I imagine, will try to extract from the Chancellor how far the Government want the men to go in order to secure the resumption of negotiations. I heard this afternoon through an intermediary that Cook was willing to swallow the eight points on the attached slip, but I have not had confirmation of this. I have sent a copy of this down to the Chancellor, as I am nervous of his too readily giving points away to JRM.

Winston S. Churchill to Stanley Baldwin: telegram

(*Churchill papers: 22/112*)

1 September 1926

Things are moving a little favourably but nothing definite yet. Am keeping close touch with George and Arthur.[1] Shall know by Saturday and will wire you again. General position quite satisfactory.

Winston

Memorandum of Conversations at Chartwell[2]

(*Baldwin papers*)

1 September 1926
Secret

Mr MacDonald explained that the object of his visit was to see if he could develop the situation along the lines of the invitation in Mr Churchill's

---

[1] George Lane-Fox (Secretary for Mines) and Sir Arthur Steel-Maitland (Minister of Labour).

[2] Those present were Ramsay Macdonald, Churchill, Sir Arthur Steel-Maitland (Minister of Labour), George Lane-Fox (Secretary for Mines) and Sir Ernest Gowers (Permanent Under-Secretary, Mines Department).

speech in the House of Commons—'If the miners have any real proposals, let me say to them "Come on, and make them in any form you like, through any channel you like. We are ready to share in the risk of seeing that those proposals get a fair chance." ' He did not come as the authorised agent of the miners. No-one knew and no-one would know that he had come. But he had been with the miners that day and was confident that he had much influence with them, especially with Mr Herbert Smith. If, however, he was to undertake the task of trying to persuade the Delegate Conference to make 'real proposals', he thought that it was only right that he should have some private assurance as to what the Government would regard as proposals of such a nature as to require them to fulfil their promise to call a conference. Would some general undertaking to discuss wages and hours be sufficient? He did not suggest that proposals that ruled out any discussion of hours could be expected to be treated as 'real proposals'. As to district variations he saw no difficulty. He would not disclose the fact that he had the authority of the Government for saying that the formula agreed upon would be acceptable, but would consider himself at liberty to say that he had good reason to believe that that was so.

Mr Churchill said that this was a request which it was quite impossible for the Government to refuse; indeed they welcomed it. But it must be understood that all the Government could commit themselves to if the formula was accepted by the men was to invite the owners and men to a tripartite conference. It was quite likely that the owners, in view of the present attitude, might refuse to come, or, if they did come, might take a line that would make progress impossible. If they put themselves in the wrong in this way, the Government would make no secret of their opinion that they were in the wrong, but the powers of actual coercion that the Government possessed were very limited.

Mr MacDonald said that he quite understood that all the Government were committing themselves to was an invitation to a conference, and was quite content with that.

After discussion the following words were agreed:

'We are prepared to negotiate on wages and hours to meet the immediate needs of the industry. We stand for a national settlement, in accordance with the established custom of the Federation, but we recognise the need for district variations.'

Thomas Jones to Stanley Baldwin

(*Baldwin papers*)

2 September 1926   Offices of the Cabinet
5 pm

Prime Minister,

I send you a Note which Gowers has made of the conversation which took place at Chartwell last night. You will be glad to notice that Steel-Maitland was present. The Chancellor had the good sense, a little late in the day, to telephone to Cadogan Square asking S-M to join the party at dinner. The formula, I think you will agree, is perfectly safe.

The Miners had their first meeting this morning, and adjourned until 4.30 this afternoon. I learn from Tom Richards that he is so far satisfied with the way things have gone, and he is still hoping to have plenary powers, perhaps tomorrow morning. Meanwhile great pressure is being put privately on Herbert Smith to be reasonable. At 4.0 pm this afternoon JRM sent a message to the Chancellor to the effect that preliminaries had gone well but 'there are still many obstacles to be surmounted'.

Thomas Jones to J. C. C. Davidson

(*Davidson papers*)

2 September 1926   Offices of the Cabinet

The Miners' Executive met this morning and adjourned until 4.30. So far so good. If the delegates give the executive plenary powers, negotiations with owners via the Government will start at once and will be pushed forward by the Chancellor of the Exchequer with the utmost vigour. The question which is exercising me is, at what point should the PM be called back? I don't want to curtail his holiday by an hour; on the other hand I should naturally like him to be here if we are really going to settle.

The Chancellor of the Exchequer is doing excellently. You will see from the note that he kept well within the bounds in his talk with JRM, and of course nothing must be done to prejudice peace. The Chancellor should share in any kudos to be got out of a settlement. On the other hand I don't like to contemplate a settlement sealed and signed in the PM's absence, for personal and Party reasons obvious to you.

You must on no account read this as a summons to the PM to return. The time for that has not yet come anyway, and if the Conference refuses plenary powers, negotiations will be delayed. Even if they give the powers the negotiations may be prolonged owing to the attitude of the Owners. But I want the foregoing to be in your mind, should I think it necessary in the next day or two to send you or the Chief a telegram. I will sign it 'Microbe'.

Winston S. Churchill to Stanley Baldwin: telegram
(*Churchill papers: 22/112*)

2 September 1926
9.20 pm

We have offered miners to press owners to negotiate in three-cornered conference with Government providing miners assent to our formula involving adjustment of wages and hours to meet immediate economic needs. MacDonald who is helping told me good progress today and probable desire consult me tomorrow. Owners' opposition to national negotiations will be serious and if miners really make honest offer a clash will occur with them. I shall probably have more definite information for you to-morrow or Saturday. Meanwhile everything is well in hand.

Winston

Sir Maurice Hankey to Thomas Jones
(*Jones papers*)

3 September 1926

Many thanks for your ample and really hopeful news. As regards the PM, I am sure your rightful course is to keep the PM very fully informed by letter and when necessary by telegram, and to get Downing Street to let it be known through the usual channels that the PM is in close touch. You might get Winston to let you put his name to some telegrams. Then leave it to the PM to decide. After all, the main object is to get a settlement. The true statesmanship is to get the PM to use his best agent in the matter.

Of course I see the danger of Winston's 'reaping the harvest'. But the PM will get more kudos by effecting a settlement through Winston than by 'swapping horses while crossing the stream'. From the point of view of the Government, and even of the head of the Government, the settlement is the thing. The PM is a big man in this sort of matter, and I really think he is the proper judge of when he should come—unless you see a moment coming when his presence is really essential, which might well happen.

Stanley Baldwin to Winston S. Churchill: telegram

(*Baldwin papers*)

3 September 1926   Aix-les-Bains
Cyphered and sent 2.25 pm
Received 5 pm

Assume your conference has object of bringing parties together and not making government a partner. If district settlements wages and hours can be included in national agreement well and good. You on spot can alone judge when to jump in but be careful of Ramsay. Awaiting further news.

Winston S. Churchill to Stanley Baldwin: telegram

(*Baldwin papers*)

3 September 1926
received 11 pm

We have offered Miners to press owners to negotiate in three cornered Conference with Government provided that Miners assent to our formula involving adjustment of wages and hours to meet immediate Economic Needs.

Ramsay MacDonald who is helping, tells me good progress today and probably desires to consult me tomorrow. Owners opposition to National Negotiations will be serious & if Miners really make an honest offer a clash will occur with them.

I shall have more definite information for you tomorrow or Saturday. Meanwhile everything is well in hand. Winston

Thomas Jones: diary

(*Baldwin papers*)

3 September 1926

3.0   At 3.0 pm Mr Churchill saw Mr Ramsay MacDonald alone in Sir Abe Bailey's house, 38 Bryanston Square. They discussed the sort of formula which the Miners might use in writing to the Government. The formula assumed various shapes, an early one being:

A. 'We are prepared to meet to discuss a national agreement having regard to the present necessities of the industry in relation to wages and the future prospect of reorganisation.'

3.15 At about 3.15 pm as the news agencies kept phoning about a meeting which they alleged the Miners had arranged for 4.0 pm with the Government, I spoke to Mr Cook who denied having told the Press anything about such meeting. Mr Cook then said he would very much like a private talk with me this evening. He was desperately afraid that the chance which the Miners now had might be ruined at the very first meeting unless the ground were prepared properly. He was having a terrific fight, etc etc. I agreed to meet him at Geoffrey Fry's[1] house, and later altered it to Baillie Hamilton's[2] flat.

Mr Churchill pressed for a more specific reference to 'hours and wages'
4.15 and returned to the Treasury at 4.15 to consult his colleagues (Sir Arthur Steel-Maitland, Colonel Lane-Fox and Sir Ernest Gowers) on the following:

> B. 'We are prepared to meet to discuss a national agreement on the issues of the dispute having regard to the present necessities of the industry.'

5.15 This was amended to read:

> C. 'We are prepared to enter into negotiations for a new national agreement with a view to an immediate reduction in labour costs to meet the present necessities of the industry. We recognise the need for district variations.'

All who were present at this Treasury Conference were agreed that this formula must be understood to mean negotiations on hours and wages.

It was felt desirable[3] that the Chancellor should now meet the four Miners' officials with or without Mr MacDonald, in a purely informal way on neutral ground in order to be sure there was no misunderstanding as to the meaning of the formula. I spoke to Mr Cook and Mr Fergusson spoke to Mr MacDonald, suggesting a meeting at Bryanston Square with or without Mr MacDonald, whichever was preferred. After consultation at Russell Square, a message came that Mr MacDonald

---

[1] Geoffrey Storrs Fry, 1888–1960. Educated at Harrow and King's College, Cambridge. Called to the Bar, 1913. Served in the Home Office, 1915–17, and at the Treasury, 1917–19. Private Secretary to Bonar Law, 1919–21, 1922–3, and to Baldwin, 1923–39. Created Baronet, 1929.

[2] Charles William Baillie-Hamilton, 1900–39. Brother of the 12th Earl of Haddington. Educated at Eton and Balliol College, Oxford. Private Secretary to Stanley Baldwin 1924–9. Conservative MP for Bath, 1929–31. His father, Brigadier-General Lord Binning, had died in 1917 while on active service with the Royal Horse Guards.

[3] By Thomas Jones himself.

would bring the four Miners' officials at once to Bryanston Square.

6.15 They were met there by Mr Churchill and me at 6.15 pm. No notes were taken.

Mr Churchill explained that the meeting was in no sense official, but solely intended to assist in bringing the parties into official relations again. No one would be bound by what was said. Mr Churchill then produced Formula C above. Exception was at once taken by Mr Smith to the open reference to district variations. Mr Richards said the point was implied in a reduction in labour costs. Mr Churchill laid great stress on it being clearly understood that the phrase about labour costs involved negotiations on hours and wages, and this was fully accepted. Mr Smith indicated that in his view the line of advance would be found along a low national minimum.

Mr Churchill and I withdrew to an adjoining room. Presently Mr MacDonald joined us and suggested the omission of 'immediate' as being redundant. Mr Churchill agreed to omit 'immediate' before reduction and to substitute it for 'present' later in the sentence. We rejoined the officials and finally agreed the formula as follows:

D. 'We are prepared to enter into negotiations for a new national agreement with a view to a reduction in labour costs to meet the immediate necessities of the industry.'

Mr Cook undertook to let us have at Downing Street within an hour a letter emobodying it. Mr Churchill said he would then send it to the owners and to the Press. He would invite the owners to a joint conference but expected that Mr Williams would reply that the Mining Association had no power to negotiate nationally.

Mr Churchill and I returned to the Treasury and reported what had taken place to Sir Arthur Steel-Maitland, Colonel Lane-Fox, and Sir Ernest Gowers. Some regret was expressed at the transference of the word 'immediate' in the formula. Gowers was instructed to write to the owners and Mr Churchill said he would issue a communiqué to the Press stating that in the Government's opinion the letter from the Miners afforded a basis for asking owners to resume negotiations.

Between 7 and 8 o'clock the following letter was received from Mr Cook:

Dear Sir,

I beg to inform you that the Executive Committee and the Special Delegate Conference of the Miners' Federation, having again carefully considered the present deadlock in the mining dispute, have resolved to ask you to convene and attend a Conference of the Mining Association and the Federation. We are prepared to enter into negotiations for a new national agreement with a view to a reduction in labour costs to meet the immediate necessities of the industry.

Yours faithfully,
A. J. Cook.[1]

8.15   At 8.15 Mr Churchill, Sir Arthur Steel-Maitland, Colonel Lane-Fox, Fergusson and I dined at the Savoy Grill. Gowers had in the meantime seen Evan Williams who was quite firm in refusing to enter into a joint conference. It was then agreed that on receipt of his refusal the owners should be asked to meet the Cabinet Coal Committee on Monday, September 6th at 3 pm.

9.45   The Chancellor had two hours conversation with Mr Evan Williams at the Treasury.

Winston S. Churchill to Stanley Baldwin: telegram[2]
(Churchill papers: 22/112)

3 September 1926
11.15 pm
No Distribution

Miners having received full power by vote of Federation have sent us the following letter saying:—

'The Executive Committee and the Special Delegate Conference of the Miners' Federation, having again carefully considered the present deadlock in the mining dispute, have resolved to ask you to convene and attend a Conference of the Mining Association and the Federation. We are prepared to enter into negotiations for a new national agreement with a view to a reduction in labour costs to meet the immediate necessities of the industry.'

It was clearly understood at informal meeting I had with them and MacDonald that the phrase 'reduction in labour costs' meant hours as well as wages. On this Coal Committee decided that sufficient ground existed for government to request owners to resume negotiation. We all felt that any

---

[1] The original of this letter, written on the notepaper of the Miners' Federation of Great Britain, is in the Churchill papers (*Churchill papers: 22/113*). It is signed by Cook in his capacity as Secretary to the Miners' Federation.

[2] This telegram was received by Baldwin at Aix-les-Bains at 10.30 am on 4 September 1926 (*Baldwin papers*).

conference to be useful must be three-cornered with the government presiding. Next step will be refusal of coal owners to negotiate nationally and we shall argue they are already committed by the assurance they gave before you introduced the eight hours. I expect we shall meet them Monday. Public opinion seems unanimous in approving and even demanding government intervention and its pressure upon coal owners will be very strong. I do not think stoppage will collapse by itself. 2,000 or 3,000 men a day are going back in Midlands but quarrel might easily slough along for many weeks. Earnest efforts on our part even with risk of failure are imperative.

Thomas Jones to Sir Maurice Hankey

(Jones papers)

4 September 1926

I send you a chronicle of yesterday's events and also a most secret note which has reached me this morning, showing the direction in which the Miners are prepared to move if properly coaxed along.

I am going now to Chartwell for the week-end and have arranged for Sir David Llewellyn[1] to dine there tomorrow night. Gowers will be there also. I spoke to the Chancellor yesterday quite frankly about the PM's return and he was most correct and loyal in every way. The PM is being kept fully informed and I shall not suggest his returning until we have made some progress for the negotiations. We shall meet the owners alone on Monday at 3 o'clock.

Thomas Jones to Sir David Llewellyn

(Jones papers)

4 September 1926

... The Chancellor feels very strongly that it will neither be right nor possible for the owners to refuse to negotiate nationally and I have told him that you take the same view. I believe the men are in a mood now to go a long way to meet your district requirements and if this can be secured, why not have a peace with some elements of permanence in it.

[1] David Richard Llewellyn, 1874–1940. Educated at University College, Cardiff. Deputy Chairman of Amalgamated Anthracite Collieries. A Justice of the Peace for Glamorgan, 1920. Created Baronet, 1922.

Sir Patrick Gower to J. C. C. Davidson

(*Davidson papers*)

4 September 1926

. . . Knowing Winston as you do you may entertain fears lest he should use every endeavour in the Prime Minister's absence to effect a settlement of the dispute in order that all the kudos should fall into his lap. You need not, however, worry on this score. Winston has shown a most loyal and sporting attitude and has on many occasions in private conversation expressed a very sincere anxiety lest his activities while the Prime Minister is away should lead people to give him undue credit for anything which he may be able to do. What is more, he has on many occasions expressed his determination to call the Prime Minister home as soon as the necessity arises. It is only fair to Winston to mention this, because otherwise there might be misunderstandings as to his attitude.

In the meantime, I rather gather that Steel-Maitland is a bit disgruntled because he feels that his nose is put out of joint by Winston's predominance in the negotiations. I do not put it higher than that, but the position was not improved by the fact that Steel-Maitland made a very poor speech on Tuesday while Winston excelled himself. One cannot help feeling sorry for Steel-Maitland, because he has borne much of the burden during the past few months. But on the other hand, he seems to be more nervy than usual and hardly in a fit state to take charge of the negotiations. In some ways it is almost a pity that his doctor does not advise him to take a few weeks' holiday. The poor devil has certainly deserved one, and is I think unquestionably in need of one.

Stanley Baldwin to Winston S. Churchill

(*Churchill papers: 22/112*)

5 September 1926   Aix-les-Bains

My dear Winston,

I am grateful for your telegrams which, with sundry précis I have received, keep me posted as well as is possible at this distance.

Your speech in the House I thought admirable, and I think that you have probably followed the only course available and followed it with skill and success. But it is just at the moment that one seems in a fair way to pass through a difficult channel that one has to look out for sunken rocks. I wish it had been possible to see a separate Notts agreement drawn up before we came in, but I dare say it was really impossible to wait. I am a great believer in paying out rope to the last, but I recognise, as I said in my telegram, that only the man on the spot can judge when the moment is come to jerk it in.

No doubt the immediate apprehension of a break in the Federation caused the swing round of the vote. Now where I am anxious is just here at the point where the tripartite Conference begins. My desire, and I think the desire of all of us, is to wean the Coal Industry from the Government, and that any agreement must be between owners and men. The men will be eager to have the Government a party to any agreement, because: (A) if anything goes wrong, they can curse 'em; and (B) so long as Government can be indicated as a partner, so long is there a peg for nationalization and all that the dreams of the wild men stand for. If any declaration of Government policy is involved, eg help for displaced men, it should be a separate undertaking.

And unless we are clear that a settlement contains—as far as human foresight can tell—no seeds of future trouble in it, it is far better not to pursue it: for any momentary kudos will be soon lost, and failure in twelve months time would fall on us like a load of bricks within a measurable distance of the general election.

I am sure these points are as clear to your mind as they are to mine; but being 800 miles away and ignorant of the shifting of the sands which are very quick just now, I cannot refrain from writing. I intend in any case to be in London on the 15th inst which will have given me three clear weeks and a day, and if I can adhere to that date, I shall of course be very happy. But I need not say I am ready to return any day that I am really wanted.

It is a great relief to me to feel what a strong Committee I have left in charge to handle this most difficult situation.

Yours ever,
Stanley Baldwin

Stanley Baldwin to Thomas Jones: telegram[1]

(Jones papers)

5 September 1926   Aix-les-Bains

Are we right to assume that Government intend only to bring parties together if possible and that actual negotiations on terms of settlement will be between miners and owners alone under independent chairman if desirable?

[1] This telegram was sent to Jones at Chartwell.

Winston S. Churchill to Stanley Baldwin: telegram

(*Churchill papers: 22/112*)

5 September 1926
8 pm

Your telegram to Mr Tom Jones who is with me. I am trying to procure a three cornered conference with representatives of both parties and ministers. Miners have directly asked me to undertake this task. It will certainly be several days before opposition of owners is overcome and perhaps this may never be overcome. Should we however get the three cornered conference first series of important questions to be decided will not be details of wages and hours but procedure to be followed in the negotiations in order to secure earliest possible resumption. It is at this stage that the help of the government is indispensable. Once agreement has been reached on the broad principles of procedure it would certainly be convenient to substitute one or more independent chairmen for the negotiating body or bodies. I certainly do not contemplate myself sitting to fix hours or wage conditions but only to settle the order and method of dealing with these points and the relation of national to district agreements. Of course one cannot see very far into the way things may develop and there are so many obstacles that they may not develop at all.

It is very important I should know that you approve this procedure. Without active Government help involving serious risk and labour no progress will be made.

Thomas Jones to Stanley Baldwin: telegram

(*Churchill papers: 22/112*)

5 September 1926
8 pm

Gowers and I agree that procedure indicated by Chancellor of Exchequer is right in present circumstances. Politically impossible to act otherwise now. Londonderry and Llewellyn here to-day.

Thomas Jones to a friend
(*Jones papers*)

5 September 1926 Chartwell

. . . Remained yesterday at office until 4.0 when Gowers of the Mines Dept picked me up in his car and brought me down here by 5.15 in time for tea. Mrs C in Scotland, Randolph in Yorkshire, other children here and schoolfriend of Diana's. Winston 'humming' with coal all the time—discussing it from every conceivable angle.

Lord Londonderry arrived for dinner and is still here. It was 12.45 am when our host showed us to our rooms. I found a bat flying about the room and got it out through the door, not through the window. Then I slaughtered three mosquitos and fell asleep until 7.0 when I was awakened by rather noisy servants. Slept again until tea arrived at 8.30.

Breakfast 9.30. Heavy mist early over the valley. It has lifted a bit but the day is dull and grey. At the moment Winston is walking in the grounds with 'Charlie' Londonderry and owing to the echo his voice can be heard a quarter of a mile away. They have been friends since L was a boy at Eton and Winston at Harrow.

W is a most brilliant and incessant talker—his sentences full of colour and alliteration and frequent military metaphor. He is always deploying guns or barrages on the owners or the men. He gave us last night a wonderful description of his visit to East Africa when Under-Secretary for the Colonies— the train passing through endless zoological gardens with rhinos and crocodiles, twenty sorts of antelopes, lions which never brushed their teeth or cleaned their claws so that it was desirable to avoid them. Lakes as big as Scotland, the Mountains of the Moon—why go shooting grouse on Yorkshire moors when you can go pig-sticking in Kenya? He stuck a pig, chasing him on horseback; the spear broke in two, it was Winston's last, and he had to shoot with a revolver, etc, etc, etc.[1]

Lots of political talk of course. Man has two lobes to his brain but only thinks with one and the other looks after his stomach. Great thing is to think with both sides—complementary. Rarely find men who can be defiant in defeat and magnanimous in victory. From this on to comparisons of Botha[2]

[1] Following his visit to East Africa in 1908, Churchill had published an account of his experiences in the *Strand* magazine. This account, somewhat expanded, was then issued in book form, entitled *My African Journey*, published in London by Hodder and Stoughton in December 1908, and in New York by Doubleday, Doran in April 1909. A cheap paperback edition, published in March 1919, sold 20,000 copies.

[2] Louis Botha, 1862–1919. Born in Natal. Commander-in-Chief of the Boer Forces, 1900–2. Visited England, 1902, 1907 and 1909. Prime Minister of the Transvaal, 1907–10. Commanded the South African Forces in South-West Africa, 1914–15, receiving the surrender of the German army. A General in the British Army, and a British Privy Counsellor. Prime Minister of South Africa, 1910–19.

and Smuts,[1] Herbert Smith and Cook, Arthur Griffith[2] and Collins. So I mischievously said: 'LG and Bonar.' 'Pooh! Bonar was just a Glasgow man of business—no statesman—a parliamentarian, yes.' He called me the 'thyroid gland of the Cabinet, supplying the organism with secretions not otherwise provided by the Central Office or party machinery'. Said it may be necessary for me to 'nip over to Aix to see the PM' if we come up against a crisis with owners.

This morning I drew him on to talk of Foch[3] and Haig and Pétain[4] and the great battles of the war. He knows all the places and dates and details and pictures it all most vividly to his listeners. Told us how the French only got news of the terrific attack of the Germans on Chemin des Dames the day before it was to take place, through 2 German prisoners—how the Allied line was weak and tired and there was no way or time to bring reinforcements, and the French were swept back for miles over the Aisne. But I must not attempt to retell this. I think Vol III will be exciting. He showed me the 'lay-out' of it and said he found it himself exciting to write. He has lots of black boxes filled with papers here all catalogued by secretaries.

He was very amusing about the building of the house. Said another time

[1] Jan Christian Smuts, 1870–1950. Born in Cape Colony. General, commanding Boer Commando Forces, Cape Colony, 1901. Colonial Secretary, Transvaal, 1907. Minister of Defence, Union of South Africa, 1910–20. Second-in-Command of the South African forces that defeated the Germans in South-West Africa, July 1915. Honorary Lieutenant-General commanding the imperial forces in East Africa, 1916–17. South African Representative at the Imperial War Cabinet, 1917 and 1918. Prime Minister of South Africa, 1919–24. Minister of Justice, 1933–9. Prime Minister, 1939–48.

[2] Arthur Griffith, 1872–1922. Born in Dublin. Worked as a miner on the Rand (South Africa) in the 1890s. Returned to Dublin, where he published a study of the Hungarian national movement. Editor of the *United Irishman*, 1899–1906; of *Sinn Fein*, 1906–14; of *Nationality*, 1915–22. Imprisoned in Wandsworth, 1916. President of the Sinn Fein Party, 1917. Elected to Parliament as a Sinn Fein candidate, 1918. Imprisoned at Gloucester, 1918. Acting President of the Dail, 1919. Imprisoned at Mountjoy, 1920–1. President of the Dail, 1922.

[3] Ferdinand Foch, 1851–1929. Lieutenant, French Army, 1873. Professor, Ecole Superieure de Guerre, 1894–1900; General Commanding the Ecole, 1907–11. Commanded the XXth Corps, based on Nancy, 1913–14. Commanded the 9th Army, at the battle of the Marne, September 1914. Deputy to the Commander-in-Chief, during the 'race to the sea', October 1914. Honorary knighthood, 1914. Commanded the Group of Armies of the North, 1915–16. Deprived of his command after the battle of the Somme. Recalled, as Generalissimo of the Allied Forces, France, April–November 1918. Marshal of France, August 1918. Appointed British Field-Marshal, 1919. His only son was killed in action on 22 August 1914.

[4] Henri Philippe Benoni Omer Joseph Pétain, 1856–1951. Commanded an Infantry Regiment, August 1914; an Army Corps, October 1914; the 2nd Army, June 1915. In charge at the siege of Verdun, 1916. Chief of the General Staff, April 1917. Commander-in-Chief, May 1917–November 1918. Vice-President of the Supreme War Council, 1920–30. War Minister, 1934. Ambassador in Madrid, 1939–40. Prime Minister, 16 June 1940; he negotiated the armistice with Germany, 22 June 1940. Chief of State, 1940–4. Condemned to death after the liberation of France, 14 August 1945; the sentence was commuted to life imprisonment.

he'd have nothing to do with drawings. He'd spend £100 on having an exact model made, and having agreed it he would never go near the house during its building. Every time he had done so it had cost him £100. His wife suffered from 'arboricidal mania'. They removed the vegetable garden to make a tennis court, and then moved the garden again.

Lord Londonderry to Winston S. Churchill

(*Churchill papers: 22/112*)

6 September 1926

My dear Winston,

It was a real pleasure to stay at Chartwell and I was delighted at the opportunity. I was charmed with your house and surroundings.

I do hope your meeting today has not been altogether unsatisfactory. I expect that Evan Williams will have gone away saying he wants to meet his larger committee of District representatives. This is all he can do. Cook and Smith can do what they want in the name of the Federation when it suits them but Williams cannot do this by the character and constitution of the Mining Association. So far he has refused to meet the Federation on national lines as he is bound to oppose a National agreement, but I am hopeful that you will have been able to overcome his quite legitimate attitude by interposing your support for District variations within the ambit of a National agreement.

I attended our meeting to-day and with difficulty I was able to carry the meeting with me on these lines. I accepted the Federation as a body which in some form was bound to be in existence, and we agreed that our district arrangement should be subject to the acceptance or rejection of the Federation, but not if we could help it to variation by the Federation. That means that wages, hours and conditions of working should be district arrangements, and that other matters should be for the Federation to discuss and arrange with the Association. I think this is really embodied in William's letter to Lane-Fox of the 29th. I had our recognition of the Federation on these lines telephoned up to Guthrie,[1] our district representative, in the hope of

---

[1] Reginald Guthrie. Born in 1855. Educated at Newcastle upon Tyne Grammar School. Secretary of the Northumberland and Durham Coal Owners Association, 1888. Associate Member of the Institute of Mining Engineers. Member of the Central Committee of the Mining Association of Great Britain, 1925, and the National Board for the Coal Industry, 1925. District Representative of the Durham Coal Owners Association. He retired in 1939.

it reaching him before 3 pm and Gainford[1] will put our attitude at the meeting to-morrow.

I fancy that we are more tractable than other districts and if that is so Williams will be in a difficult position. We all have our different points of view. You approach it as a Minister, a statesman and as one who naturally wants a settlement for every reason. I approach it as one who is in politics, has a certain experience of conferences and administration etc etc, and also as an owner. Cook and Smith want nationalisation and to save their faces; the owners want to get back to work and make money but are obsessed with the idea that they cannot make money on National lines. They trace all the trouble to the growth of the National idea and the case is a very strong one indeed. The railway arrangement is a failure because the porter at a wayside station gets the same wage as the porter at a big and profitable station. To illustrate what I mean further, when I pressed my friends as to how far they would go on National lines, the answer was, they could accept a National agreement which allowed for the working at a profit of the poorest district.

I do feel however that if you will consider the owners point of view as sympathetically as you consider the point of view of Cook and Smith—not more and not less—and bring your great powers of exposition of the pros and the cons, the merits and the demerits, I feel you can manage it. The great point for district settlements which is being lost sight of is that a trivial local dispute would not have the effect of holding the country up to ransom which is what Cook and Smith want, by the power of the Federation, to be able to do.

My idea is that if the Federation (Cook and Smith) were judiciously handled that Cook and Smith will be only too glad to climb out on the bare recognition of the Miners' Federation, but if you give them the smallest inkling that your mind is moving from the equilibrium away from the owners side of the table even by a hair's breadth then they will fight like tigers for the National agreement and nothing but the National Agreement. If I were in their place I should probably do the same.[2]

[1] Joseph Albert Pease, 1860–1943. Liberal MP, 1892–1917. Chancellor of the Duchy of Lancaster, 1910–11. President of the Board of Education, 1911–15. Postmaster-General, 1916. Created Baron Gainford, 1917. Chairman of the British Broadcasting Company, 1922–6. President of the Federation of British Industries, 1927–8. Deputy Chairman, Durham Coal Owners' Association. Chairman of Durham Coke Owners, and of several Colliery companies.

[2] A leading article in the *Morning Post* of 6 September 1926 attacked Cook's statement that: 'We are prepared to enter into negotiations for a new national agreement with a view to a reduction in labour costs to meet the immediate necessities of the industry.' The paper thought this a device to get national work stoppages, and called Cook a 'disciple of Lenin'. Nor did the paper approve of Churchill's statement in the House of Commons on August 31 that 'a national settlement is still possible', believing it had indirectly prompted Cook's statement.

Please forgive the length of this letter and its somewhat disjointed composition, but I have not a typist with me and I have dictated letters for so long now that I am helpless with a pen.

Yours

L

Cabinet Coal Committee: minutes[1]

(*Churchill papers: 22/117*)

6 September 1926   10 Downing Street
2.45 pm

THE CHANCELLOR OF THE EXCHEQUER gave the Committee a summary of the private and informal conversations which had taken place on Friday last (3rd September) with Mr Ramsay MacDonald and the four chief officials of the Miners' Federation. At these conversations the formula agreed with Mr Churchill was clearly understood to embrace negotiations on hours, wages and reorganisation. No relevant issue was barred from the discussions at the conference with the owners which the Government were asked to convene.

THE CHANCELLOR OF THE EXCHEQUER stated that he had also seen Mr Evan Williams privately on Friday September 3rd and had urged him in his reply to the Government's invitation to a joint conference to avoid closing the door upon further meetings with the Government.

A general discussion followed as to the course to be adopted in the meeting about to take place with representatives of the Mining Association.

THE CHANCELLOR OF THE EXCHEQUER said he proposed to press the owners to seek release from the embargo on national negotiations and obtain authority from their constituent bodies to meet in joint conference.

THE MINISTER OF LABOUR stated that according to information which had reached him the owners would not give way.

THE FIRST LORD said in that event the Chairman, without in any way threatening the owners, should indicate that the Government could not leave the matter to rest there and would have to consider the position very seriously.

THE SECRETARY OF STATE FOR WAR mentioned the possibility of proceeding by means of an Industrial Court Enquiry.

THE CHANCELLOR OF THE EXCHEQUER outlined the course

[1] Those present were Churchill, Sir Arthur Steel-Maitland (Minister of Labour), William Bridgeman (First Lord of the Admiralty), Sir Laming Worthington-Evans (Secretary of State for War) and Sir Philip Cunliffe-Lister (President of the Board of Trade).

which the negotiations might take in the event of the parties agreeing to come together. The Miners' leaders had themselves suggested that the Agenda should be drawn up by the Government. The Government should keep hold of procedure and endeavour to obtain agreement on general principles for the guidance of the local organisations. District agreements, embracing hours and wages, on which miners should return to work, would have to be made. They should be provisional in character and be later brought up for review and co-ordination by a national body. This task would involve much detail and would be better handled by an independent chairman than by the Government.

THE PRESIDENT OF THE BOARD OF TRADE suggested courses open to the Government in the event of the owners refusing to negotiate nationally.

The consideration of these suggestions was postponed pending the result of the conference with the owners.

Stenographic Notes of a Meeting between Cabinet Ministers and the Mining Association[1]

(Churchill papers: 22/101)

6 September 1926   10 Downing Street
3.15 pm

MR CHURCHILL: I cannot say that we were surprised to receive the answer which you sent to our letter proposing the three-cornered conference, because we had before us your statement at the meeting ten days ago with the men and also the letter that you have been good enough to write us telling us what your view is and the great importance you attach to it. But if the Government were not surprised by the answer they are deeply concerned at it and we have various considerations which we should like to put before you. The consideration which takes priority over everything else and which if established I am sure would weigh the most heavily in your mind is the question of the general understanding on this point, the basis of understanding, which has subsisted between His Majesty's Government and the Mining Association during this long-drawn and protracted dispute.

[1] The Cabinet Ministers present were Churchill, Worthington-Evans, Bridgeman, Steel-Maitland and Lane-Fox. The civil servants present were Sir Horace Wilson, Sir Ernest Gowers, C. S. Hurst and Thomas Jones. The Mining Association was represented by twelve members, headed by its Chairman, Evan Williams, and its Vice-Chairman, Sir Adam Nimmo.

MR EVAN WILLIAMS: Did you say Miners or Mineowners?

MR CHURCHILL: The Mining Association.

Now there are two quite distinct points which are habitually confused. The first is this. Assuming that there will continue to be, as there has been since 1921, a National Agreement dealing with certain aspects of the wage question and District Agreements dealing with others, what subjects are to be dealt with in each? In particular, is the minimum percentage to continue to find a place in the National Agreement, as the men claim, or is it to be transferred to the District Agreements, as the owners claim? That is what I may call one question. That is the first question. The second question is this. Is there to be any National Agreement at all or is the industry in future to be regulated purely by District Agreements without any National Wage Negotiating bodies? That is the second, the alternative, question. Now up to the meeting between yourselves and the men on the 19th August the issue was No 1, the issue was the first of those questions. On the 19th August, owing to your declaration, the issue became No 2; it became the second of those questions. That is the point with which we are concerned at the present moment and that is the only point with which we are concerned at the present moment and it is very important that that point should not be obscured by being mixed up with the first and more complicated point. Let me state what, in my judgment, is the issue across the table at the moment. It is, is there to be any National Agreement at all, or is the industry in future to be regulated purely by District Agreements without any National Wage negotiating body? Now that is the only point to which I want to ask you to address yourselves this afternoon. As to details it is perfectly clear that there must be District Agreements. It is perfectly clear that this matter can never be settled in all its details of wages and hours by a conference in London; it has got to be settled in the districts, but the extent to which the District Agreements are related to a National structure, the extent to which national machinery on both sides is to be preserved, that is the issue before us at the present time. Now I should like, if you will allow me, to make some quotations from your declarations in the past, Mr Williams. When this question first arose you argued before the Royal Commission that any form of National Agreement was wrong and that the industry ought to revert to the pre-war system of regulation by District Agreements. Well, the Royal Commission did not accept that view. I am not one of those who consider that the Royal Commission Report is a sort of bible, from which everything that is quoted is necessarily absolutely authoritative, because I think that would be putting its credentials too high, but still it is the fact that you argued in that sense and the Royal Commission said on page 236 'We consider it essential that there should be, as there always have been hitherto, considerable variations in the rates of wages in the several districts, but we are strongly of the opinion that National Wage Agreements should continue.' Now in the face of this declaration the Mining Association withdrew from the position which they had taken up in giving evidence before the Commission and at your meeting with the men on the 31st March, you will permit me to quote your words, you said:—

'I say quite frankly that we are making a sacrifice of our conviction, which is not a thing to boast about or to take any credit for, from that point of view. But we are not going to stand on the ground which we have taken up in the past in regard to this matter, and we are prepared, in order that we may get on with the real problem that faces us, to sit down with you and to carry on negotiations on a national basis, upon general principles, and upon such things as are of general application to the industry, and to enter into a national agreement with you on the same lines.'

Later on in the same meeting you said, Mr Evan Williams:—

'If we had any desire or intention at all either to break up, or even to weaken the influence of the Miners' Federation, we should not have been doing what we have done today—sitting down with you to consider this question nationally and telling you what you probably did not expect to hear, that, notwithstanding what we said to the Commission, we are prepared to negotiate a national agreement with you between the Miners' Federation and the Mining Association.'

On the 13th April you met again and reaffirmed your position in the following words:—

'We have said that we are prepared to discuss and arrange with you a National Agreement. We are prepared to do that, and to determine the principles upon which the ascertainments of wages should be made in the different districts, and that all that is necessary to enable those ascertainments to be made should be determined on a national basis as between you and us on lines similar to those which have been in operation in the past, with the one qualification which we have put to you and which is I think you must agree, inevitable, that a national minimum is no longer possible.'

That would probably mean 'a national uniform minimum is no longer possible'. Finally on the 22nd April, the last meeting that took place before the Stoppage you went so far as to put before the men the draft of a National Agreement and in handing this draft to Mr Herbert Smith you said:—

'Mr Smith and gentlemen, as we indicated to you at our last meeting, that we were prepared to discuss with you the terms of a national agreement, we proceeded at the earliest opportunity to get into shape proposals in a definite form, insofar as its main lines are concerned, at any rate, for the agreement which, in our view, should be made as between the Miners' Federation and the Mining Association. We had this submitted in draft to our districts last week, and yesterday we were in a position to send to you, in a form approved by the districts, the proposals which we make in regard to it. I do not know whether the better procedure would not be to go through the agreement in detail and to discuss its clauses as we proceed, so that we may have your views upon them and so that you may have our explanations insofar as they are necessary.'

Up to the date, therefore, when the General Strike and the National Coal Stoppage begin, it is perfectly clear, and I am sure it will not be disputed between us, that the owners' position was that, although they disliked the idea of a National Agreement, they were prepared to enter into one. It is now necessary to turn to the proceedings which took place after the stoppage had begun. You had an interview with the Prime Minister and other Ministers on the 14th May at which you pressed strongly for the introduction of an Eight Hours Bill. You have told the Miners, when you met them on the last occasion—and I do not complain about it at all—that you strongly advocated this and used every argument you commanded to impress upon the Government the importance to the industry of imparting to it that elasticity which a lengthening of hours in certain circumstances could alone give and the Prime Minister and his colleagues were impressed with the arguments which were put forward and also as a result of their own enquiries and the advice which they received from their highly skilled technical experts. At this meeting on the 14th May when the Eight Hours Bill was under discussion you gave no indication to us of any change in your attitude as defined in the quotations I have read out. On the contrary you said 'As to the basis of negotiations we are quite prepared to meet the Miners' Federation at any time on a perfectly open situation.' That is a very good phrase 'a perfectly open situation'. It is what I have in my mind and what I am asking you to do today. The next thing that happened was the issue two or three days later of the Government proposals for a settlement. Comprised in these proposals was the suggestion that a National Board should 'frame a National Wage and Hours Agreement'. To this your Association sent in a long elaborate and argumentative written reply; but it contained no specific comment or demurrer on this point. Then we come to the 21st May and you defined the position, in an interview with the Minister of Labour, in the following words:—

'I want to make this quite clear. It may not be very palatable, but I think it only right that I should tell you exactly how we feel in this matter. The Mining Association, as such, as you know, has no powers to deal with wages questions except at the direct request of the District Associations, and all that it is necessary for the districts to do, or even one district to do to prevent any negotiations being carried on centrally is to say that they withdraw their authority to the Mining Association to deal with the matter for them. We hold the same view as we have always done, that as long as there is a national body on the owners' side and a national body on the men's side dealing with questions of wages, so long will it be difficult to keep wage questions in the industry out of the political arena, and the greatest safeguard that could be brought about for peace in the industry and for a real settlement of the whole of these questions is to get away from national settlements altogether and leave each District to deal with the question for itself. It may be that there is a line which may have to be taken in this matter. I am not suggesting in any way that that is the position that we want to take up at the present moment, but rather than have any question of having terms imposed upon us from outside. . . .'

Evidently you were subjected to some argumentative pressure from the Government at that moment—

'I feel perfectly certain that that is the line of action which the District Associations would take in regard to this matter.'

Now that I think was intended and was interpreted as a warning, perhaps even more than a warning, a veiled threat, that if the Government interfered too much with the freedom of negotiations between the parties, the Mining Association would have to depart from their attitude towards National negotiations and insist on district negotiations only, but it is also a clear proof that at that date, May 21st, they were still willing to negotiate nationally and implied an assurance that in the absence of such interference by the Government such as they deprecated that would continue to be their attitude. Now that was the position when the Eight Hours Bill was introduced and, as you know, it was a very serious thing for His Majesty's Government to introduce a measure facilitating the lengthening of the hours of labour in coalmines. It undoubtedly is a step which is greatly resented by large masses of the industrial population, a step which was bound to be represented as part of a regular scheme and policy of lengthening hours. We arrived at the conclusion that it was necessary and right after careful consideration, but many of us, most of us I think I may say were very much inclined to insert in the Bill a series of conditions under which the facility of working the extra hour could be permitted and we had a discussion with you, which was animated, on that point. You strongly argued against the insertion of any limiting condition and we considered the matter among ourselves and came to the conclusion that if you were willing to give us certain assurances in general terms we would waive the question of inserting those conditions. Then the Prime Minister made a statement, in introducing the Eight Hours Bill, which is reported in Hansard, stating that there would be offers on a district basis which would amount to all that the industry could possibly pay at that time and which would be very much better offers than would be possible on the seven hours basis, and so forth, but the statement ended with the following sentence 'In any case under the proposals already made by the owners they could not in any district fall below the 1921 minimum which the owners point out, having regard to the change in the cost of living, would now give a real wage thirty per cent higher than at the time when it was agreed to, five years ago, and would meet the miners' desire for a national settlement.' Now we shall not get into any dispute about personal good faith, or anything like that,—put that entirely outside the discussion,—but we did understand that you had agreed to those words beforehand. In any case there can be no question that after those words were published we received no protest of any kind from you. Many of your most prominent Members were in the House when the Prime Minister used those words and those words were never the subject of any sort of adverse comment, from you. The matter was dealt with entirely as a reproduction, as you might say, of a passage which had been submitted to you. Now take the whole of this chain of quotations and facts—I am not making the slightest reproach against you—You will see, if you put yourselves in our position, that we, as Ministers of the Crown, were justified in our belief that at the time we introduced the Mines Eight Hours Bill there was no question of departing from the negotiation of a National Agreement. Now let me say this. We were quite in favour of district agreements. We are still, if they can be arrived at, and we were very glad that you were going to negotiate in the districts, if you could arrive at agreements in that way, but we never contemplated for one moment that opening the district settlements door meant shutting the door to a National settlement. We wished both doors to be open and for settlements to advance through whichever one could most expeditiously be approached.

I must, on behalf of His Majesty's Government, record the fact that it was our perfectly clear impression that both these doors were open and that peace could be reached through either of them. I am quite sure of this, that if we had known that following the passage of the Eight Hours Bill into law a new obstacle to a settlement, a new complication, would arise through the closing of one of those doors to peace we never should have passed the Bill or proceeded with it. Therefore if you take up the attitude that you have now no more power to negotiate and that there can be no national negotiations of any kind, if you take up that *non possumus* attitude, while I am not for a moment making a charge of breach of faith I do think you will see that we shall have been placed in a position which is, from our point of view at any rate, extremely unfortunate and even, as it might be thought unfair—and that, I know, will weigh with you perhaps more than any other argument that I am going to use.

Now let me just touch on a point which requires a little blunt speaking.

The most important and specific of these quotations which I have read from your speeches, were before the Stoppage began, and of course it stands to reason that in the hope of averting a great misfortune like that everything is offered, even things that one does not think desirable are offered, if they can possibly be the means of staving off the catastrophe. But when for eighteen weeks the country has been thrown into its present condition and when you gentlemen, as I know well, have been suffering in a very formidable manner losses perhaps of £600,000 or even £700,000 a week, in keeping the pits from falling to pieces and being flooded, when peace has not been secured, I am quite prepared to say that a new situation arises. If two States are negotiating and then they go to war, it is idle to suppose that negotiations can be taken up after a prolonged campaign at the point at which they left off. That is perfectly clear, but the issue today is whether there shall be national negotiations or not—the issue, whether the national negotiation door shall be closed or open. That issue, does not depend on your relations with the men, with those I do not wish to deal at this moment at all. I wish to establish, by reasonable argument, that there is a relationship between yourselves and the Government, that it is on the point of your relations with the Government, that I earnestly ask you to consider very carefully what your attitude should be in regard to our formal, deliberate request that you should come with us and meet the men in an open, unprejudiced discussion.

Now I have to say a word about the men. Naturally I am not here to speak for them or to give any guarantee on their behalf. I do not know how far they are prepared to go; that we can only ascertain when we come to closer quarters, but His Majesty's Government required, after the many futile negotiations which have been attempted, some evidence which was satisfactory to us that the Miners Federation had made a definite change of spirit and that they were earnestly desirous of making a peaceful and lasting settlement. Now I am not going to give a guarantee, I am in no position to do so, but honestly I believe there has been a change of heart and that there is a wish, an earnest wish, for peace, and that there is a willingness to discuss on the merits, with a sincere desire to secure the greatest benefits for all concerned, every aspect of this question. Now in the letter which they have written to us there occurs this expression, 'a reduction in labour costs'. That expression has evidently been very carefully chosen because it is what, to use a homely term, I might call a 'portmanteau' expression, it covers everything, it is chosen because it covers everything. It covers wages, it covers hours, it covers reorganisation, and it was chosen deliberately.

That, I think, indicates a very distinct alteration in the position that was disclosed even at your last meeting with the men, and on that it seems to me that we are bound—and I trust that you will also feel a similar obligation—to come to closer quarters with the matter, to hear what is said under the most favourable circumstances, under an impartial Chairmanship, on both sides, and to see what practical steps can be taken to terminate this stoppage.

Naturally, I have not gone so far in this matter with my colleagues without having considered the second steps which at the proper time the Government will be prepared to suggest; but this would only complicate the issue now. You should not suppose however that we are pushing forward in this matter without having seen some distance ahead along the various alternative courses which may be forced upon us or which may be open to us.

To sum up, I ask you to address yourselves to the perfectly simple question, is there to be any national agreement at all, or is the industry in future to be regulated purely by district agreement without any national wage negotiating body. Secondly, will you meet us with the men, being properly authorised and retaining your perfect freedom to refuse any unreasonable proposition or to break off the negotiations if it is found there is no change of heart, and no desire to reach a settlement.

Will you meet us with the men and let us see what are the practical steps, by national discussion and by district discussion—for both will unquestionably be necessary, to bring this trouble to an end; and on behalf of His Majesty's Government, with whom you have been so long in close and amicable discussion and negotiation, who are after all the trustees of the public as a whole, on their behalf I most earnestly venture to express the hope that you will defer to our wishes.

MR EVAN WILLIAMS: You have a considerable advantage over me in this discussion this afternoon in that you knew, having prepared it, what you were going to say, and I have to reply only after hearing what you have said.

MR CHURCHILL: Would you like to withdraw for a few minutes?

MR EVAN WILLIAMS: I do not think there is any necessity.

I agree with you that there is only one issue that is open for discussion between us this afternoon, and that is as to whether or not the Mining Association is prepared to enter into negotiations with the Miners Federation to set up a national agreement. To put this in its true aspect it is this, as to whether the coalowners of the country are prepared to authorise the Mining Association to enter into negotiations with the miners, with the Government standing by and taking part in the discussions, not that the question would assume any different phase at all whether the Government does or does not come in in this particular matter. I think I must, even at the cost of repeating what has been said many times before, say what the position of the Mining Association is in regard to questions of this kind and what its position is as between itself and the coalowners who, after all, compose it through their District Associations in general. The Mining Association has been in existence for a large number of years, since 1854. It was set up to deal with questions of legislation, of questions affecting the owners of the collieries throughout the country which did not affect their relations between themselves and the men they employed. Up to 1919 there was no definite constitution that would be a constitution for the Mining Association. In 1919 a new constitution was established of which I believe the Mines Department generally have knowledge, and in that agreement it is specifically laid down that the Mining Association shall not have any power or authority to deal with wages questions affecting any district except at the direct request of that particular district. That clearly debarred the Mining Association from dealing with wages questions at all except by the direct request and unanimous consent of every District Association of the country forming it. When the war came and the mines were taken under control, questions arose affecting all sorts of things concerning the collieries, and it was necessary, as the industry was treated as a whole under the control of the Government, that there should be some body with which the Government could be in touch and make such arrangements as were called for for the regulation of the multitude of matters which required consideration and decisions, among them questions of wages. The Mining Association, being in existence for other purposes, was the only body available at the time, and without any questions at all in the emergency which existed the District Associations agreed at once that it should deal with any questions as between it and the Government relating to the industry; the industry had been treated as a whole by the Government and there was no choice for the coalowners except to fall in with the position which had been created and agree to all questions that were put to it as affecting the industry being put through the only body which was in existence. It was after the war that the new constitution was arranged, but the mines were still under control, and it was definitely the view to put an end to all national agreements of this kind at the earliest possible moment and with one voice the coalowners of the country insisted upon having such a clause as I have mentioned inserted in this constitution. Obviously, during the time the industry was under control it could not get away from dealing with matters on a national basis, and when we came to 1921 there were so many questions involving so much difficulty that had to be dealt with that it was obviously impracticable at that moment to resolve the problem of the coal industry into its component parts district by district, and the coalowners agreed that for the time being it was inevitable that they should continue to be dealt with on a national basis, to some extent to have general principles laid down and have a National Board set up to deal with the many questions which cropped up on de-control and on the formulation of a new basis for the regulation of wages in the industry. The basis was new to every district in the country. As a matter of fact, I think it was necessary perhaps at that time to have an over-riding National Board which was to deal with questions which arose under and out of the new method of dealing with the industry. It is no secret that at the backs of their minds the coalowners felt that as soon as this new method, this new scheme, of regulating wages had been formally established there would no longer be any necessity in the industry for a national supervision of any kind at all, and there has been no disguise right through of their desire at the earliest possible moment to get away from national agreements and back to those district agreements which prior to the war had been the regular method of dealing with wages in the industry and which had brought about prosperity in the industry to both the owners and the men. It was the miners who put an end to the 1921 agreement at a time when there was a Labour Government in power, and a crisis was brought about through the national determination of the whole of the wage arrangements in the country at the same time by the Miners Federation in the early months of 1924. At that time, the feeling in the districts against a continuance of the national agreement was exceedingly strong, and it was only the very extreme pressure which was put upon the coalowners of the country through the Mining Association that led to the mineowners, to avoid a crisis similar to that which we have gone through and are going through, to accept the position and make a new national agreement with the miners and to continue for a period, which was limited to twelve months, this arrangement of dealing with questions through a National Board in so far as they concerned general treatment and through the districts themselves as to the details of the actual arrangements to be made. It was with the greatest difficulty, as I said, that the coalowners were got to see that at that time force of circumstances was so great, that the risk of the country of being held up in this way was so great, at a time when we were emerging from a period of temporary and quite accidental disturbance, that, as I say, we entered into an agreement the terms of which we distinctly stated at that time were in our opinion certain to prove disastrous to the industry and which, as a matter of fact, bore out everything and even more of those things that we prophesied for it when the agreement was made. The experience we had of national agreements up to that time, during the course of that year, produced such unanimity of feeling among coalowners that they must, in the interests of peace and prosperity in the industry, revert to their old methods of settling their affairs district by district between those people who knew completely what they were dealing with and through people who had to carry out such agreements as they were dealing with, that they determined that no further national agreements would be entered into on their behalf by any body for them, and, as I have said, the view that was put to the Royal Commission on this particular point was on the lines that I have just indicated. The Commission did not accept the view that we put forward, and I submit that it was not altogether on the merits of the question that they came to this conclusion but, being human, they could not be blind to the position that would arise with the Miners' Federation if they accepted the owners' view on a point to which the Miners' Federation very naturally attached so very much importance.

Then we come to the point at which the Government and the owners and the men had to consider the Report of the Commission. We were faced with a position, at the end of April, when all arrangements between the Government and the industry came to an end. There had been no national agreement in existence between the owners and the men from the 31st July 1925 up to that time. We were in the position of having no national agreement with the men, we were faced with a crisis in the industry, the Government felt the seriousness of it quite as much as we did, and in order to avert the disaster which has happened the Government decided to accept a good many things which they themselves said were objectionable to their principles, and the owners as well said that the lead the Government had given could not but be followed by them in the hope and the very sincere desire of trying to avert what has happened. I do not think we should be, I will not say 'taunted', because we did not do it in that form, that it should be held up as an argument against us at the present moment that we swallowed a good many things which were very distasteful to us in the hope that we might thereby avert this general stoppage of work in this industry and also the general strike which was clearly threatened at the time we were discussing this question, and that with a feeling that we could not very well stand up before the country and say that though a national agreement may prevent this terrible thing happening we are not going to have a national agreement which followed our predictions, we agreed to continue with the Miners Federation some form—I am wrong when I say 'we should continue', that we should re-establish some form of national agreement to regulate certain general questions in the industry in future. It has got to be borne in mind that we have been pressed, not only by the Miners Federation but by the Government through the Mines Department to enter into a national agreement covering the period during which the subsidy was to be paid, but we stead-fastly and absolutely refused to do anything of the kind. In order, as I have said, to try to avert this calamity we agreed to offer a national agreement the terms of which were simply refused by the Miners Federation. Under pressure from the Government we went further and said that for an eight hour day, a universal uniform eight hour day, we would be prepared to insert in that agreement a uniform national minimum, and I think it is only right that I should quote what the Prime Minister himself said to us at that time, on the 30th April, when we announced our decision, which had been brought about with very great difficulty, with very great mis-givings and reluctance amongst the coalowners. On the eve of the 1st May, the Prime Minister said in this room:—

'First of all, Mr Evan Williams, I do want to thank you for the trouble you have given to this. I do recognise that you have made an enormous effort, and I think that a good many members of your Association have come a long way, and I do want to say that I think you have done a great deal to help things. That, I think, is only fair to you, and it is the truth.'

It is a recognition on the part of the Prime Minister at that time of the difficulties which we had had to face and of the efforts which we had made to overcome those difficulties so that nothing we could do on our part at that time could be said to have stood in the way of averting the general strike which followed upon the stoppage of work in the industry. And right through from that, right on I think, we have met the Government fairly and reasonably in everything that has been asked of us, up to the time when the Eight Hours Bill was introduced in the House of Commons. I do want to make this perfectly clear, that even on the 30th April, when a National Agreement, or a national minimum was offered, it was conditional upon a uniform eight-hour day throughout the whole of the industry.

MR CHURCHILL: You mean not that a National Agreement was conditional upon a uniform eight-hour day throughout the industry, but the 1921 minimum percentage?

MR EVAN WILLIAMS: Specifically that, but coupled with it—you see we had told the Prime Minister quite definitely and I may say the Prime Minister did not demur, that there was no possibility of re-establishing the industry on sound economic lines except by an eight-hour day. I do not think there was any question at all about it.

MR CHURCHILL: We certainly thought, we still think that the principle of some extension of hours is a necessary feature of any settlement which will meet the present condition. We have not the slightest reason to depart from our conviction that that is the right and proper thing to do, but we certainly assumed that you were not going to close the door to national negotiations—that would have made no difference.

MR EVAN WILLIAMS: I am perfectly certain of this, that neither the Government, nor the majority in the House of Commons who passed this, would have made it law if they were not convinced it was absolutely necessary.

MR CHURCHILL: Do you mean to say that if the House of Commons had been informed that when this had been introduced the owners were going back on the whole of their position on national negotiations—

MR EVAN WILLIAMS: I have not come to that yet. There were meetings, the verbatim notes of some of which you have quoted, which took place right up to the 14th May, up to the point at which the Government made definite proposals to both sides, proposals which were rejected by both sides. The Government definitely declared at that time, on the 21st May, that it was free from all the offers which it had made and had a perfectly free hand and was not committed to anything. The Government did make that announcement to the Miners' Federation. We had marched step by step with the Government up to that point. I think we had done, up to that point, everything that the Government had pressed us to do. I do not think there can be any question about that and when the Government, which had taken a very active part in the discussions which had taken place and in such negotiations as had taken place up to that time, declared themselves free from all their offers and no longer bound in any way by any of the proposals which had been made by them, they cannot expect that the same freedom was not accorded to the other two parties at the same time.

MR CHURCHILL: No, I make no reproach about that; it is the relationship between the Mining Association and His Majesty's Government, on which I rest because, as I say, if you were going to make so great a departure and change from the basis on which matters had been proceeding, we ought to have been told specifically that you were going to do so, in the clearest possible way, before we met your strong wish that you had publicly expressed that we should pass the Eight Hours Bill. You should have said—'clearly understand that when you have passed that Bill, we are going to shut the door on the idea of a National settlement'.

MR EVAN WILLIAMS: You have rather anticipated the point I want to deal with. That is on the 21st May. There was an interval during which nothing took place, no negotiations between the Government and the Mining Association, until we come to some time towards the end of June when, as the result of representations and arguments which we put forward, the Government began to consider seriously the question of an eight-hour day. We entered then upon a new phase and I defy anybody to say that during those new negotiations, from the end of June and right on until July, until the Eight Hours Bill became law, there was any suggestion from the Government that this was conditional upon a National Agreement, or any suggestion at all that there should be anything but separate district offers made by the Coalowners' Associations throughout the districts, determined on an eight-hour basis.

MR CHURCHILL: I cannot possibly accept that. The assumption on which we proceeded was that district negotiations would be undertaken but that, of course, there was no narrowing of the possibilities of peace and, if there had been, the initiative in announcing them should have come from you, because you were changing the basis on which we were acting and therefore you should have informed us that you were changing that basis. We assumed the basis remained the same unless we were informed of a change.

MR EVAN WILLIAMS: We were starting upon an entirely new basis, a basis which gave freedom to the districts to make new offers in an entirely new condition of things. In our reply to you on the 14th May we said that we indicated the action we were prepared to take with a view to giving effect as far as possible to the objects aimed at in the Royal Commission's recommendations if a settlement could thereby be reached without a stoppage of work. (That was on the 14th May.) These negotiations broke down. Then there was a period during which nothing took place between us until we began to talk about eight hours. I do not know what may have been at the backs of the minds of the Government. If they had that condition at the back of their minds they never mentioned it to us. We had no indication of any kind at all that the introduction of an Eight Hours Bill in the House of Commons was to be conditional upon a National settlement. They urged us very strongly and one of the meetings to which you referred at which some feeling was developed was on the very point that we had not put forward these separate district offers on the eight-hour basis by the time we were going to.

MR CHURCHILL: It was on the point of delay in putting forward the proposals.

MR EVAN WILLIAMS: On the point of the delay in putting forward those offers, the offers on the eight-hour basis, and we told you quite clearly they had to be considered by each district separately. Each district had to make up its mind what was the very best it could offer on the eight-hour basis, without any reference at all to any other district. That was the whole basis upon which these discussions between us took place, that offers on the eight-hour basis were put forward absolutely independently by districts without any suggestion of any kind that there was an overriding or collateral National settlement.

MR CHURCHILL: But you see, Mr Williams, where two parties are in relation, whoever makes the change in the general basis must declare it and at the moment when the Government were taking action, on its merits I admit, but action for which you had most strongly pressed, in passing this Bill, if at that moment you were all the time contemplating making a change in the basis you should immediately have said—we are going to depart from our principle and all previous declarations are null and we shall not entertain national negotiations. You should not have let a thing like that pass silently.

MR EVAN WILLIAMS: It did not pass by any means silently. The District Associations, each one of them, made proposals. That was made known to the Government. We kept the Government aware of every step we took.

MR CHURCHILL: Perfectly true.

MR EVAN WILLIAMS: And the only thing that was contemplated between the two sides at that time was that there should be definite offers made, district by district, settled by each district without reference to any national body or any other body.

SIR A. STEEL-MAITLAND: May I interrupt for one moment. I would like to say a word about this. The fact that the districts were making their offers and having their negotiations, from our point of view was not incompatible with the National Agreement. I think there must be some misunderstanding, but I will deal with that afterwards.

MR EVAN WILLIAMS: There was no suggestion of any sort or kind; there was no mention of a National Agreement.

MR CHURCHILL: It is mentioned in the very words the Prime Minister used in his speech.

MR EVAN WILLIAMS: It did not occur to me when I read those words that there was any very serious collision of opinion. The only construction to be put upon the Prime Minister's words is—'now you have obtained in these district offers, minima each one of which is not less than twenty per cent, conditional upon its district circumstances being adjusted. Having obtained that twenty per cent minimum in each of the individual districts, your aspiration for a national settlement is fully met without there being a national agreement. The substance is there without the form.' That is the only construction which I think we may put upon the Prime Minister's words. It has met the desire of the miners for a national settlement and if the desire of the miners for a national settlement has been met in that way, what further question is there of a national agreement? There is no further question and there never was during the whole of that time, no suggestion from you that there should be an Eight Hours Bill conditional upon a national agreement. There was no talk of a national settlement. The whole discussion took place upon the basis of there being separate district offers made by the District Associations on certain lines and when those were made, national agreements were not necessary. These offers were made, you know perfectly well, with the direct object and hope that in each district separately there would be a return to work. I think it was perfectly clearly indicated to you as far as the Midland counties were concerned, where there was no reduction of wages, where there was in some cases even a higher minimum offer than the twenty per cent, that in those districts there would be, first of all, a return to work and the return would spread piecemeal throughout the country. It was clearly understood between us that there was no question of a general resumption of work simultaneously, that it would be district by district.

MR CHURCHILL: That is perfectly true, by way of district settlement.

MR EVAN WILLIAMS: If that is so, how can you say you understand that the question of a national settlement was still open? If these districts made offers and these offers were accepted, one by one, then a national agreement goes overboard altogether. That was the only interpretation that could be put upon the whole of these negotiations.

MR CHURCHILL: Not at all. There were two doors and we were perfectly ready to reach a settlement through the district door if there was no possibility of reaching a settlement through the national door, but no-one ever intended or contemplated that the national door would be closed and that the district door should fail to open.

MR EVAN WILLIAMS: I say quite definitely that in our opinion the national door had been closed and the only door that was open at that time was the district door and it was to open those district doors that we were urged and we agreed to make those district offers, one by one. We were urged to make these offers as high as possible, differing district by district, in order to get the resumption of work in detail throughout the country. How can you reconcile that with a statement that at that time you were still expecting a national settlement? It is contrary to the facts, I say definitely it is contrary to the whole of the facts.

The important question is, however, not as to whether an understanding existed or did not exist between the Government and the employers. The real question is what is the position of the Mining Association, and what are the merits of a national settlement.

MR CHURCHILL: I submitted it to you as an argument to show that in the opinion of His Majesty's Government a national settlement was not barred though district settlements were being attempted, and that was our honest impression, and you singularly failed to undeceive us at the moment we introduced the Eight Hours Bill, I do not put the point at more than that, but I take the chain of statements which you made and say it was a natural and reasonable assumption for us to make that while we knew you were going ahead to make district settlements yet at the same time no door to peace was closed, and if he had known that the introduction of the Eight Hours Bill would synchronise with a decision on your part the moment you got it to close the national door, never should we have allowed ourselves to be placed in that position. It was due to us that you should tell us you were going to make that change at that moment.

MR EVAN WILLIAMS: I say definitely there was no suggestion of a national settlement; everything pointed to the contrary. We were urged to make offers district by district; the only common element in those district offers were the Eight Hours and the 20% minimum, and they did not synchronise with the passing of the Bill. It was all preliminary to the passing of the Bill. I should have said there was no minimum less than 20%; the 20% was a minimum of the district minima. There could not have been a national settlement in the minds of either you or ourselves at a time when we were being urged if possible to give a higher minimum than 20% in those districts which could put it forward, and in order to bring about the very thing which a national settlement could not have brought about, that is to say, a break away piecemeal district by district.

A general resumption of work simultaneously throughout the country was impossible and the only way to settle this strike was to do it in detail and get it settled district by district and in that way once there had been a considerable number of districts with a resumption of work on a tolerably large scale the remainder of the district would very soon follow. From that time forward there has been no suggestion by the Government to us, and certainly no word from us to the Government, in the contrary direction.

MR CHURCHILL: Pardon me, we never knew you had taken this step until you met the men on the 19th August, and then you wrote a letter to the Minister of Mines shortly after the interview we had with the miners the week before last. Immediately then we drew your attention to it.

MR EVAN WILLIAMS: I say there was no necessity for any intimation in a formal way. The whole of the discussions—and I repeat this again—prior to the introduction of the Eight Hours Bill had been on a district basis, with which a national agreement was incompatible. Then nothing more transpired until we got a request from the men to meet them. I say the Government were aware, before that meeting was held, that we were going to say definitely to the men that no national settlement was possible, no national discussions could take place, and after the meeting was held on the 19th August a whole week elapsed with no suggestion from the Government in any shape or form.

It was only when I read the verbatim notes of your interview with the Miners Federation on the 26th that I felt that the position which the owners had taken up, of which the Government were fully aware and were an assenting party to, was being changed, that I wrote the letter to Col Lane Fox. I say quite emphatically that so far from there being a change of front at the end of last month, the 19th August, between us and the Government or between us and the men, everything that was said at that time was consistent with the whole of the transactions between the Government and the mineowners right back to the two or three weeks preceding the passing of the Eight Hours Bill.

Coming now to the actual situation the position is, as has been distinctly stated to you, the Mining Association has no authority to enter into any negotiations with the Miners Federation, and that position arises out of the constitution of the Mining Association, under which it is only by direct requests from each and every one of the districts that the Mining Association could be endowed with any power or authority to make this agreement. I ought to say that there are districts in the country which have withdrawn from the Mining Association, and the Mining Association does not represent in any shape or form the whole of the country at the present time, and I may say that it is the fact that the Mining Association entered into such a disastrous agreement with the Miners Federation in June 1924 that has caused these districts to give up their membership of the Association. So strong is the feeling on the merits of the position in these districts that I say definitely that it is not possible for those districts to so change their minds, no matter what may be the position, as to give the Association power and authority to meet the Miners Federation and discuss matters, and a meeting held between the Mining Association and the Miners Federation in those circumstances would not be honest because all they could say to them if they met them would be, 'We are very sorry, our position is exactly the same as it was when we met you last on August 19th, and we cannot enter into any negotiations.' I do want to make this perfectly clear, that there is no desire on the part of the Mining Association, or on the part of the coalowners of the country, to break up the Miners Federation. Nothing is further from our thoughts. It existed before the war. The Mining Association had dealings with it before the war on many occasion. In 1911 we sat for weeks considering the details of the Mines Acts which were then brought forward. We have never refused, and we shall not refuse, to meet them upon any general questions affecting the safety, health or welfare of the miners or of those engaged in the mines. We are prepared to meet them upon any question of general importance of that kind, but the question of the wages arrangements, the terms and conditions of employment of the worker with his own colliery company is a matter which cannot be dealt with except in the districts by those who know the conditions in the districts, and by those who are to carry out the arrangements when they are made.

As I said, it was with the greatest reluctance that we had at any time entered upon national agreements and national negotiations. It is the experience which we in the country have had of those agreements that has strengthened us so much in the view that we put forward, that we say quite definitely and emphatically that the Mining Association will not enter into negotiations with the Miners Federation on this point. What has been the position? There has never been peace in this industry since we had national agreements, since the industry has been dealt with on a national basis. If you look up the Ministry of Labour figures you will find that in the 22 years prior to the war, the only ones for which the Ministry of Labour have particulars, there was an average loss of time in the industry through disputes, of 5·30 days per person per annum. In the years during which there have been national arrangements there have been losses per man per annum, including this year up to the end of August, of 23·36 days per annum, and if you exclude this year, the whole of 1926, there have been losses of over 12 days per man per annum through disputes which shows clearly what a change there has been in the number of days lost in that way. We have been faced with crisis after crisis whenever an agreement has come to an end. In 1924 we were faced with a crisis through a national settlement, and it was only averted by the owners giving way to the representatives of the Labour Government of that day. In 1925 there was another crisis and that was only settled by the Government giving way to the threats of the miners. In 1926 a similar position was brought about which was not averted because neither the Government nor the owners gave way. As certain as there is a national agreement which brings all the districts of the country under one arrangement, so certain will there be crises of that character, and looking not only at the interests of the coalowners themselves but the industry as a whole and the country as a whole—only we feel that we should be acting most detrimentally to the community as a whole if we again entered into an arrangement which inevitably makes every industrial question in the mining industry a political issue. The very things that are happening this week end and to-day are in themselves proofs of the undesirable character of national agreements. If it had not been for the question of national agreements, does anyone suppose there would have been a stoppage in Cannock Chase, Notts, Derby and Leicester, where the men were not asked to accept any reduction of wages at all? The effect of a national agreement has been to bring about a stoppage even where there is no dispute as regards wages between the owners and the men. I say it is a political issue pure and simple, and the moment you have set up a national agreement with a National Board you bring every question that is relevant to that Board forward as a political issue, with debates in the House of Commons, and you get the Government involved and you put the industry as a whole on a different plane from every other industry, and such accusations as have been made that there are troubles in the coal industry and that they are more numerous and more bitter than in any other industry of the country are due solely and entirely to the fact that they are dealt with on a national basis and not on a district basis. It gives the opportunity to direct national strikes not against the industry or the owners, but against the whole community, and I should have thought the experience we have had since April of this year ought to be enough to convince the Government and the whole country that the sooner it gets away from these national arrangements in this or any other industry the better for the country. It may be thought that by entering into discussions with the Miners Federation in some way we should solve this problem. We hold the contrary view absolutely. There are districts where the owners' offer has been accepted without reference in any way at all to national agreements. That movement is spreading rapidly. Even to-day, which is a Monday and not the kind of day on which large resumption of works generally take place, there are in those three districts of Notts and Derby, Warwick and Cannock Chase, over 2,750 more men at work than on Friday.

MR CHURCHILL: Perfectly clearly, the discussions that we have been having have not deterred men from returning because the largest returns have been since the peace discussions have been reopened.

MR EVAN WILLIAMS: No. The rate of increase was itself progressive up to Friday. To-day it has dropped.

MR CHURCHILL: I thought a moment ago you were rather heartened by what had taken place.

MR EVAN WILLIAMS: No, I was going to say that in spite of this there have been resumptions of work on an increased scale, and while resumptions may continue to increase in those districts where it has started, it is quite certain they will not begin in those districts which would have had resumptions on a considerable scale by this time. I say that even if the refusal of the Mining Association were to prolong the strike—which I think is not going to be the case—it is in the interests of the country in the long run that it should get away from these national arrangements which have held the country to ransom over and over again, and will continue to do so so long as they exist. You have said of the miners that there is evidence of a change of heart. That was on Friday, as the result of a meeting which they held probably on Thursday. But on Saturday there is an article by Mr Cook in 'The Miner', in leaded type:—

'Neither I nor my colleagues will sign any agreement for longer hours. On that question or on the question of a national settlement there can be no compromise.'

I say solemnly with conviction that I regard this move on the part of the Miners Federation not as a movement in the direction of peace in the industry, but as a deliberate attempt to create difficulty between the Coalowners and the Prime Minister.

MR EVAN WILLIAMS: I want to make it perfectly clear to you that our objection, the objection of the coalowners throughout the country, is not one of form, it is one of substance. The Minister of Labour has spoken of a lasting peace. That is what we want, a lasting peace, and it is because we are convinced that we cannot get a lasting peace that we are so determined. After all, you cannot ignore experience. The man who will not pay attention to history in dealing with the present situation is not doing himself justice, and it is the experience we have had of the cramping effect of a national agreement upon district arrangements, of the inevitable effect of dealing with the question as a whole which makes it become a political question and not an industrial question, that causes us to feel so strongly upon this matter. The problem is a district problem, it is a very big problem in many districts, a problem that some districts would have the very greatest difficulty in settling for themselves without any interference at all or any restrictions imposed upon them from any central authority, and to suggest that a district problem which varies so much from district to district can be helped in the very least by negotiations of a national character, in which district considerations cannot be taken into consideration in any shape or form.—

SIR LAMING WORTHINGTON-EVANS: The cardinal principle is laid down.

MR EVAN WILLIAMS: The principles are already embodied in all the district offers. Can anybody suggest any advantage to the industry or to the country from the superposition, as you put it, of a national agreement upon a series of district agreements which have already been made.

MR BRIDGEMAN: What I said was 'ratification'.

MR EVAN WILLIAMS: How long is it going to take? I have not heard anybody who has been able to point out a single element of national advantage, of national benefit, I mean from the point of view of the community as a whole, in having national settlements.

MR CHURCHILL: Surely it would be an advantage if by national negotiations at the present time we ended this terrible dispute and got the men back to work and the industries of the country going. Surely that is our object? What we are here for is to find a way of ending the dispute.

MR EVAN WILLIAMS: It is because we feel so confident that anything in the nature of national negotiations, quite apart from merits or demerits, is going to prolong the strike that we are reinforced in our opinion that it would be a national disaster. It is in the interests of the country as a whole that we feel so strongly in this matter.

MR BRIDGEMAN: Supposing you got district settlements made which were perfectly satisfactory to all of you, to you and to the men, discussed in the districts, they must contain some elements that are common all round. What would you or they lose, or what would anybody lose, by collecting those district arrangements together and saying, 'These are made according to what each district can do, and we as a whole ratify them with all their variations.'

MR EVAN WILLIAMS: What does anybody gain?

MR BRIDGEMAN: Peace, probably.

MR EVAN WILLIAMS: No. You will have had peace with the district agreements. What are you going to gain?

MR BRIDGEMAN: You ratify peace.

MR CHURCHILL: You may not succeed in making district agreements apart from a national understanding. In June you were confident that district agreements would be made on an eight hour basis, but nothing has occurred, and as long as there is this veto on a national agreement the struggle may go on for weeks.

MR EVAN WILLIAMS: I do not want to make any further reference to the Bishops. The jocular remark which I made the other day has been misinterpreted, though it was received with laughter at the time, but I say quite definitely we cannot lay the blame for any of the delay that has taken place on the coalowners; a great deal of blame can be laid on people outside, and I feel quite sure the industry—and other industries who support us to the hilt on this point, the big industries of the country—are perfectly confident that the only lasting solution of this difficulty, and the quickest solution after all, is by dealing with the matter in the districts where the problems are known and where they have to be faced; whatever might be done in the way of a national preliminary or subsequent national agreement these problems have got to be faced, and the districts feel that they are not going to be hampered by national agreements which may have been entered into before they make these agreements, and they are not going to subject agreements which they may have made locally, and which are satisfactory to both sides, to the veto or even to the registration of any other body.

MR CHURCHILL: Mr Williams, I must most earnestly beg you not at this meeting to use language which will preclude you from seeking from your constituent bodies the necessary authority to enable you to meet with us and the Miners Federation.

If you were to take that step you would be taking an immense responsibility upon yourselves. I think that the impression undoubtedly will be that, you feel yourselves in a position to close a door which, in the opinion of His Majesty's Government, may be found—may, I only say 'may'—may be found to give the means of reaching a peace—that, to my mind, would be a grave position, and I implore you not to take that step. I have gone back upon the past, not at all for the purpose of recrimination, but I have discussed the attitude which your Association have had towards a national agreement from the beginning because I wanted to convey to you the impression which that series of events has produced upon His Majesty's Government.

If you will study what I have ventured to say when it appears in the transcript, you will see that it casts a very significant light upon the position of His Majesty's Government. We were not aware that doors would be closed and would remain closed even if the other side showed a disposition to knock at them or to enter in them. We were not aware that at this stage, after the country has suffered for so many weeks, the dispute would be prolonged, in the opinion of a great many people, through the closing of these doors, or any door national or district. After all, if it is your view that district settlements are much better than national settlements and that district settlements would remove the necessity for national settlements, surely it is at least your duty to appear in the presence of the other party and to argue your case.

But to take the course of saying, 'We are out of action altogether for the purposes of national negotiations as an Association, and the matter no longer rests with us in any way,' is to take a most serious attitude. After all, the question of a national agreement is an industrial issue in the dispute as much as wages and hours, and if the Government thought fit to set up an Industrial Court you would have to attend as a national body before that Court or else see your case go by default. The matter is really not one when a body, which for a whole year has been before the public as the united spokesman of one side in the industry, should suddenly say 'We have dissolved ourselves, our powers have gone, there is nothing but the void to talk to now.'

An attitude of that kind is bound to array against you a mass of public opinion in the country.

So far as the Government is concerned, after what has passed and what has been said, and after the long recital of our honest understanding of the general position, it is quite clear that if we receive, as I earnestly hope we shall not receive—certainly not to-day—but after you have consulted your constituents, if we receive in the course of the next day or two—I agree with you that matters must be pressed forward—a definite refusal to do business on any terms, or even to discuss whether business should be done,—if we did receive that it is perfectly clear that we could not leave matters where they are. We have come into the open definitely in the last few days and have accepted a new situation and the force and power of His Majesty's Government are engaged behind that position, and it is essential that that should be realised because we have great responsibility in this matter, we have legislated in this matter and legislated, as you have pointed out, in accordance with your advice and wishes, and therefore our responsibility is a very grave one.

If a final decision on your part never to negotiate again with anybody on a national basis, never even to enter into a discussion with anyone on a national basis, was going to be the last word in the matter, if that should unhappily be your position—and I most devoutly and earnestly hope it will not be your decision—if it should be then it seems to me quite clear that we shall have to move forward upon our own course of action in your absence. But I would earnestly hope that you would seek from your constituents authority to enter into discussion in order that the position may be explored. It is not being explored in the districts today. Rightly or wrongly, however it may be, the Miners Federation have been able to impose a veto except in the Midland area upon any effectual resumption and upon the making of district agreements. For you to take up at this time an unalterable attitude would be a very serious disaster. So may I take it in conclusion that while you adhere very strongly to the views which you have expressed, nevertheless you will seek from your constituents their opinion. You say the stoppage has continued because of the various peace movements. Otherwise the men would have come in. I do not believe that for a moment, but whether that be true or false, in this country unquestionably a prolonged dispute of this kind, causing all the suffering and the distress which it does, will be attended by repeated efforts for peace and that is a fact you must take into consideration. Now I do ask you to convene your constituents and to recover the power which you had. Use it as you think fit and only if you see there is an improved situation. If there is not an improved situation we shall not be in any attitude of antagonism to you. It is becase we believe that there is a change and because we hope that it may be developed into the means of peace and into removing the deadlock and into releasing the possibility of district settlements from the effective veto under which they now lie that we have taken this step.

MR EVAN WILLIAMS: I am sorry that in your concluding remarks you referred to the point which we discussed at such great length to begin with and that you again suggested we are seeking to take advantage, after it took place, of the fact that the Eight Hours Act is now on the Statute Book. I do most emphatically deny that that is the position in any shape or form. Our position has been perfectly clear and I maintain there was a complete understanding between us and the Government and that the passing of the Eight Hours Act did not constitute a bargain of any sort between us and the Government. Unless the House of Commons thought it was a right thing to release the industry from the Seven Hours Act, it would not have done so. It was because it was the right thing to do. It was not contingent upon anything the owners did or were prepared to do.

While the whole of the question in the districts is an industrial one, the moment it is made national then it becomes political. We are firmly convinced that to start national negotiations, which we know cannot possibly come to any conclusion, would delay for an appreciable period settling down in the districts to considering their own problems and solving them. We are convinced that that would be the worst step we could possibly take at the present time. That is one of our reasons. The other main reason is that on its merits, in the interests of the country as a whole, you should put an end to the means of bringing about these national crises. Through this question of a National Agreement, districts in which the owners have never given notice to the men were called out by the Miners Federation, a thing which could never happen except on a national basis.

MR BRIDGEMAN: Nobody has suggested that you should begin with a National Agreement before you have the district settlements.

MR EVAN WILLIAMS: You have asked us to seek powers from our constituents, if I may so use the word. We cannot seek powers to do what we feel is wrong. We have a meeting in the ordinary way tomorrow of our Central Committee. We will certainly put the whole of the facts before them and we shall take their opinion.

MR CHURCHILL: I hope you will put before them the earnest considered request of the Government that they should empower you to come and meet the Miners Federation with a view to discussing what are the most expeditious means of ending the present deadlock. That is all I am asking at the moment. The Miners will say—make a National Agreement. It will be open to you to say—no, we think district agreements will be better, but at any rate come to the point where that issue can be raised.

SIR L. WORTHINGTON-EVANS: And to discuss what they mean by National Agreement. Let us see what the real difference is.

MR EVAN WILLIAMS: You know perfectly well the stand the Miners Federation has taken, there must be the national settlement and simultaneous resumption of work. That is the position they take up.

If, as is practically certain when we discuss this matter tomorrow,—our Central Committee which consists of members of every district, and will have before them the whole of this discussion which is going to be made public, are still of the same view, it will be dishonest on our part to enter into a semblance of discussion with the Miners Federation; we should have to tell them definitely that it is the view of our District Associations that they will not permit the Mining Association to enter into national discussion, or national negotiations at all. You realise what the position is? A national settlement is impossible unless every district in the country comes into it. National negotiations by the Mining Association are impossible except with the consent of every district in the Association. If one large district, for instance Yorkshire, were to say—no, we are unalterably opposed to it, we will not authorise you to deal with this question nationally on our behalf, then the Mining Association could not deal with it.

MR CHURCHILL: It is no use carrying the matter any further at the moment. The only thing to do is to wait until tomorrow when you will let us know what your final position is. I cannot add anything to what I have said.

Thomas Jones to Stanley Baldwin

(*Baldwin papers*)

6 September 1926   Offices of the Cabinet
6.30 pm
Secret

Prime Minister,
    The meeting of the Cabinet Coal Committee with the Mining Association lasted from 3.15 pm until 6.0 pm this afternoon. For the Government there were present the Chancellor (in the Chair), Sir Laming Worthington-Evans, Bridgeman, Steel-Maitland, Lane-Fox, Horace Wilson and Gowers. These Ministers, plus Cunliffe-Lister had met half an hour earlier and discussed the general position. The Chancellor confined himself to enforcing an appeal to the owners to come into negotiations with the men. In doing this he reviewed the history of the relations which have existed between the Mining Association and the Government immediately before and since the stoppage. This led to an acute, and at times rather acrimonious, debate between Winston and Evan Williams as to the attitude of the Government and the owners to a national agreement at the time of the passing of the Eight Hours' Bill. Winston urged that we assumed that two doors, District and National, to a settlement were open, and that we had specific assurance in writing which you quoted in the House on the introduction of the Bill. This led to some cross-swearing as to what had taken place in St Stephen's Club, etc, which I hope it will be possible to keep out of the Press. Winston urged that the owners had raised no protest to the words used by you. EW maintained that they were capable of the interpretation that there were to be no further national negotiations. EW also urged that at a luncheon with Lane-Fox and Steel-Maitland on the day before the final meeting (August 19th) with the miners, it was assumed that no further national negotiations would take place. This was denied by the two Ministers. Then there was a reference to a private conversation between you and Evan Williams where there was a similar assumption. It was agreed that there should be no reference to this in the Notes. Presently we got away from all this to the main point, and Evan

Williams repeated in the most emphatic language that the owners would *not* resume national discussions. Winston then made a final and eloquent appeal and at the close EW said he would put the matter before his Central Committee which meets in London to-morrow morning, but such indications as he gave left it open to no doubt that the reply would be in the negative.

The Coal Committee will meet to-morrow afternoon at 5.0 pm to consider the position which will then have been reached.

I think it not unlikely that the Cabinet Committee will then send for the four Miners' officials and see how far they are really prepared to go in the matter of district agreements, and how far it will be possible for the Government to undertake on their part to give a national character to such district agreements. Cunliffe-Lister and Gowers are thinking out various ways by which effect can be given to this. If we should reach a decision to bring any sort of legal compulsion on the owners it will of course be necessary for you to return. Someone suggested to-day that it might be worth while having a meeting of all the owners in London at which you could make a personal appeal. But we shall first see how public opinion moves. . . .[1]

Winston S. Churchill to Stanley Baldwin

(*Churchill papers: 22/112*)

6 September 1926

My dear PM,

I am glad you are sending me a full expression of your views.

We were met to-day, as TJ will tell you, with a complete refusal from the owners to enter into any sort of negotiation on a national basis. There is a slight chance this may be modified tomorrow, as they have promised to discuss the whole affair with their members. Still we must count on a final refusal. What to do? I should propose in that event going to the miners and sounding them without committing the Government to action on the following proposition:—If you will order your men to begin district negotiations and to resume work as and when these negotiations are complete we will amend the Eight Hours Act so as to deny its indulgence to any pit which does not conform to certain conditions. These conditions are being carefully studied by Gowers. They cannot be very drastic or else the Eight Hours Act

---

[1] In a leading article of 5 September 1926, the *Sunday Times* had praised the Miners' Delegate Conference for their decision to give their executive committee plenary powers to negotiate a settlement. Former recalcitrance in the Union, the paper believed, had come from the 'extreme Socialists', and not from the 'vast majority of the men'. On the same page, an article by 'Scrutator' applauded Churchill's speech of 31 August 1926 as one of the causes of the miner's decision.

would remain a dead letter, but they may be sufficient to keep alive the principle of a national structure within which district settlements are comprised. If the miners refuse, then we shall have shown a perfect readiness to implement our undertaking to the very best of our ability and power, and that will be the end of this peace effort. No one will be able to say that we have not tried or that we have not played fair with the men. We shall not be worse off than we are now, which is pretty bad. If on the other hand the miners play up, then I shall have to ask you to come home and convene a Cabinet at which action must be decided. This contingency will certainly not arise during the present week. As far as I can make out we have overwhelming public support for the line we are taking, and I think we shall retain that support so long as we act in a straightforward and resolute spirit.

I do hope you are having a good rest, which is more than I am getting, and with all good wishes,

Sir Arthur Steel-Maitland to J. C. C. Davidson
(*Davidson papers*)

6 September 1926

. . . Winston is a great study. His speech was awfully good. He swung with a will from a negative attitude at our meeting with the miners to the Government anxious for a chance to intervene. I can hear him in imagination rehearsing his speech and finding how telling it would be. And it was—awfully good. The trouble is that:

1. He has really put us in rather a false position. The miners should have come to us saying, 'peccavemus. But will you get a national settlement.' And we say 'We will try.' But Winston started out by letting us be put by the miners into an anti-owner position. Also it is no good bullying the miners, until at any rate they have failed to be reasonable when appealed to.

2. He altered the formula he agreed on. He did this when talking to MacDonald and the miners. It may do no harm, but it opens a serious loophole. He's jolly difficult when he's in a napoleonesque attitude, dictating instructions in military metaphors, and the spotlight full on him. He threw himself all over JRM, who is an untrustworthy beggar. But with these vagaries, he generally, after a lot of talking to, swings round to safety all right. . . .

As I read through this it looks as if I was crabbing Winston. I don't mean to, as I set myself to work with him though he is a bit trying, similarly let the PM see anything you think wd interest him though I don't want to bother him.

Patrick Duff[1] to J. C. C. Davidson

(Davidson papers)

7 September 1926

. . . I am sending you the notes of yesterday's meeting with the owners. This agreed report was issued to the press, but it is so long that you will probably not have seen any full report. It was not a satisfactory meeting. Winston, considering the very disingenuous and provocative attitude of the owners, was comparatively restrained, although he always puts his points aggressively and every now and then jumped on Evan Williams. The latter at one point stated that he had had an interview with the Prime Minister at which he had made it quite clear that the owners were no longer prepared to consider any form of national agreement, and that the Prime Minister made no demur to this. He said also that Steel-Maitland and Lane-Fox had been definitely so informed as well, but in reply to this George Fox only 'indicated dissent' and Steel-Maitland denied it in an unconvincing and rambling statement. All this part was, by agreement, omitted from the notes.

To sum up my earlier remarks, I don't think Winston's activities are at present beyond what the circumstances of the situation call for, or are actuated by any desire for self-advertisement.

Cabinet Coal Committee: minutes

(Churchill papers: 22/117)

7 September 1926   10 Downing Street
5 pm

. . . A general discussion took place on the course to be followed in the next few days pending the decision of the Mining Association on Monday next, 13th September.

THE CHANCELLOR OF THE EXCHEQUER stated that in his view the Government should avoid being drawn into the discussion of details of hours and wages but should seek a three cornered conference in order to

---

[1] Charles Patrick Duff, 1889–1972. Educated at Blundell's School and Balliol College, Oxford. Entered Board of Trade, 1912. On active service, Gallipoli, France and Mesopotamia, 1914–18 (wounded, despatches twice). Private Secretary to successive Presidents of the Board of Trade, 1919–23; to successive Prime Ministers (Baldwin, MacDonald, Baldwin, MacDonald), 1923–33. Knighted, 1932. Secretary, Ministry of Works and Public Buildings, 1933–41. Deputy High Commissioner, Canada, 1941–4; High Commissioner, New Zealand, 1945–9. A Church Commissioner for England, 1949–54.

establish certain broad general principles and the steps to be taken to enable district settlements to proceed and be brought back to London for co-ordination. Two or three resolutions might be agreed for the regulation of district discussions, and an effort made to get the men back to work on a provisional basis, leaving the work of co-ordination to be done later by the national body. This co-ordinating body should be presided over by an independent chairman.

It was important, MR CHURCHILL continued, that the owners should be given a lead and he would like a letter sent to the Mining Association suitable for publication. This letter should indicate the character of the preliminary tripartite conference.

THE FIRST LORD, while not sanguine of a favourable response from the mineowners, agreed that a statement ought to be issued by the Government before Monday explaining the purpose and scope of the preliminary conference.

THE MINISTER OF LABOUR thought it might be worth while seeing the Miners' Leaders again with a view to making quite certain what their attitude was on hours and wages and district agreements. It was premature to introduce the subject of arbitration.

THE CHANCELLOR OF THE EXCHEQUER stated that in the event of the Owners persisting in their refusal it would be necessary to summon the Cabinet and to ask the Prime Minister to return to London. If legislation were determined upon Parliament would have to be assembled. He agreed that the Miners' Leaders ought to be seen privately and informally and he had taken steps to that end.

THE FIRST LORD thought that there should be no pressure nor threat of legislation at this stage especially as the Prime Minister was away. The best line to take with the Miners was to tell them that the possibility of an early and good settlement would depend on how far they armed the Government with satisfactory terms.

THE SECRETARY OF STATE FOR WAR asked how general, how limited and how preliminary was it intended the joint conference should be. Could the scope of the conference be more precisely defined?

SIR ERNEST GOWERS read a memorandum dealing with the procedure suggested by the Ministry of Mines in the event of a three cornered conference being found possible. (This will be circulated later, after revision).

At this point the Chancellor, the President of the Board of Trade and Sir Ernest Gowers withdrew to draft a letter to Mr Evan Williams and during their absence the First Lord read to the Committee a letter dated 5th September, which the Prime Minister had sent to the Chancellor of the Exchequer.

MR CHURCHILL read to the Committee the draft of a letter to Mr Evan Williams.

The Committee agreed—

(a) To authorise the Chancellor of the Exchequer, the Minister of Labour, the Secretary for Mines, and Mr T. Jones to see the Miners' Leaders that evening.

(b) That the Miners' Leaders should be told that a letter was about to be sent to Mr Evan Williams but that it had been decided to discuss its terms with them in advance, so as to make it as little objectionable to them as was compatible with its purpose of moderating the opposition of the Owners to a joint conference.

(c) Subject to any amendments arising under (b) the Chancellor of the Exchequer was authorised to send the letter to Mr Evan Williams and to the Press.

Winston S. Churchill to Evan Williams

(Churchill papers: 22/113)

7 September 1926

Dear Mr Evan Williams,

I have to thank you on behalf of His Majesty's Government for having deferred to our earnestly expressed wish that the Mining Association should consult its constituents upon the question of resuming national negotiations for a settlement of the coal dispute. I take this opportunity of explaining the kind of three party conference that the Government have in view and the scope of its work. It is obviously quite impossible for any conference sitting in London to settle the wages, hours and conditions in the various coal-mining districts throughout the country. All we could hope to do in the first instance would be to lay down certain broad principles and to recommend the practical steps necessary to secure an early and universal resumption of work. With this guidance the task of making district agreements could be undertaken with the assent of both parties under favourable conditions and without any further delay. We cannot afford any further delay or long ceremonial procedure. At least 1,700,000 families affected by the dispute are looking for the opportunity of regaining their weekly wages. Our procedure must be planned to bring this about as quickly as possible on fair and sound terms.

These district settlements would form a basis on which work would be immediately resumed. In so far as they dealt with matters which by custom are settled nationally they would require to be referred to the central body for confirmation or where necessary for reference back to the district. There should eventually be no practical difficulty or objection of principle to framing a national agreement governing many, if not all, of the points that have hitherto been dealt with in that way.

After prolonged thought His Majesty's Government believe that this is about the best and shortest path that can be found to reach the vital object in view, namely a businesslike and honourable settlement for a good long time.

Winston S. Churchill to Stanley Baldwin: not sent[1]

(*Churchill papers: 22/112*)

7 September 1926   Treasury Chambers

My dear Prime Minister,

I got your letter last night, and I do not think there is any difference in our views. I do not think we shall get the tripartite Conference, on account of the Owners' obstinate refusal. Should we do so, however, all that would be settled there in the first instance would be certain general preliminaries and principles in order to start the district settlements. Then when the district settlements had been made, they would be referred to the national body for ratification or modification. At this stage the Government would be out of the business and their place taken by an outside Chairman.

On the other hand the final refusal of the Owners will, as I wrote you last night, make it necessary to sound the men. They will perhaps be ready to go a good deal further now that the Government are for the moment ranged adversely to the Owners. We have only one card to play, ie to attach conditions to the 8-hours Act, and through these conditions to secure something of the structure of a national settlement. It would only be worth while doing this if the men would agree to order the beginning of district negotiations. If they will not do so, I should feel that we had done all in our power, and the dispute will just drag on. With the approach of winter the demand for coal and the difficulties of buying it across the Atlantic will both greatly increase. It will be most important to us that the country should feel we have done everything in human power, and that even if we have failed, it has not been through neglect or weakness. If, however, the men will definitely order the opening of district negotiations and the resumption of work thereupon, I think we ought to be ready to legislate immediately by an amendment of the 8-hours Act.

[1] Instead of sending this letter, Churchill sent Baldwin a telegram at 8 pm.

I see no need for you to come home before the 15th, because I believe that both parties will continue unreasonable. It will only be if the men are ready to take steps which will effectively and immediately produce a resumption of work through district settlements, both on wages and hours, that the important decision about legislation will have to be taken.

Worthy, Bridgeman and Cunliffe-Lister all turned up yesterday, and there was general agreement on the course to be taken. The Press, with the exception of 'The Sunday Times' and 'The Morning Post' (Northumberland[1]), is unanimous and strong in support of our line. The big country papers, like 'The Yorkshire Post' and 'The Birmingham Daily Post', are particularly favourable. The anxiety throughout the country is acute.

Believe me

Thomas Jones to Stanley Baldwin

(*Baldwin papers*)

7 September 1926   Offices of the Cabinet
7.30 pm

The Chancellor has just dictated in my hearing a telegram to you summarising the arrangements reached at the Coal Committee this afternoon. The four Miners are down at the TUC at Bournemouth. Smith, Richardson[2] and Cook are due to arrive at 9.0 pm to-night, and Richards is due at 11.0 pm. We are to meet at 9.30 pm at Bryanston Square, and on this occasion the Chancellor will have with him the Minister of Labour and Lane-Fox, plus TJ. I enclose a copy of the draft letter to Evan Williams which will be put before the miners.

[1] Lord Alan Ian Percy, 1880–1930. Captain, Grenadier Guards, on active service in South Africa, 1901–2. Employed with the Egyptian army, 1907–10. Earl Percy, 1909. On active service in France, 1914–16. Succeeded his father as 8th Duke of Northumberland, 1918. An owner of substantial coalfields, he became Chairman of the Board of Directors of the *Morning Post* in 1926. When he died, *The Times* obituary (of 25 August 1930) described him as 'a strong Tory, militant and uncompromising . . . an ardent patriot, a keen party man, a patron of art and education, and a ready champion of that order of industry and society of which it was his lot to be so typical a representative'. His eldest son, who succeeded him as 9th Duke, was killed in action at Tournai on 21 May 1940.

[2] William Pallister Richardson, 1873–1930. Educated at elementary school. Lost his father in a pit accident in March 1885. Began work in the pits himself in August 1885, at the age of twelve. Worked underground until 1915. Member of the Durham Mining Federation Board, 1912; Miners' Agent, Durham, 1915. Treasurer of the Miners' Federation, 1921–30. An active member of the Independent Labour Party, and a noted advocate of the minimum wage. His brother, T. Richardson, was Labour MP for Whitehaven, 1910–18.

It is clearly the Government's duty to exploit the next few days to the utmost and put all the pressure possible on the miners to help us to make it easier for the owners to come into a joint conference. The Press, so far as I have seen it to-day, including the Birmingham and Yorkshire papers, are supporting the Government, but they will be more definite to-morrow, as we were only able to send out the verbatim report very late last night.

Winston S. Churchill to Stanley Baldwin: telegram

(*Churchill papers: 22/112*)

7 September 1926
8 pm

Owners while maintaining their attitude of opposition have decided in deference to our wishes to consult their constituents. This puts off result till Monday 13th. I am content with this and fairly confident that they will act rightly. In the interval both to help owners to wisdom and put pressure on miners we are writing Evan Williams explaining our general idea of three-cornered conference, namely not try settle in London wages, hours, etc, but lay down a few broad principles and practical steps to early resumption work as a guide for district negotiations, results of which will be thereafter referred to central body as explained in my telegram of Sunday 5th. Am seeing four miners tonight to apprise them of intended letter and endeavour secure least possible outcry. Letter may be repudiated by them but if so responsibility for breakdown theirs. Risk must be accepted. Our position with men today should be strong and we must profit by it. These developments fully approved by all colleagues make it certain that you need not return before 15th and then only if question of coercing employers arises.

William Bridgeman to Stanley Baldwin

(*Baldwin papers*)

7 September 1926

I only wish I could be as sanguine as Winston that the Mineowners would avoid any further folly—they never miss a chance of putting themselves in the wrong with the public.

George Lane-Fox to Winston S. Churchill

(*Churchill papers: 22/113*)

8 September 1925   Mines Department

. . . I had luncheon with Evan Williams today—he told me that there was no chance whatever of the local coal-miners reversing the owner's decision as to national negotiations—and that the main reason for their referring this question to the local association was to show to the Govt & the Country how overwhelming was the support for that decision.

I told him he was laying up a great store of trouble for coalowners—& that we were already starting to draft bills to coerce them—this is true as I had this morning told our Mr Hurst[1] to get busy with it—But I am prepared to lay 5 to 1 on a refusal next Thursday.

Meanwhile I hope we shall not get the mens' tails up too much—Last night's interview has left me a little troubled—& will have restored their spirits considerably. I think we put rather too much into the national negotiations. They will be much easier to deal with if they remain what they in fact are, a hopelessly defeated body.

Yours ever,
G. R. Lane-Fox

Thomas Jones to William Bridgeman

(*Jones papers*)

8 September 1926

The meeting began at 10 pm, with Smith, Richardson, and Cook present for the men, the Chancellor, Steel-Maitland, and Lane-Fox for the Government. The Chancellor tabled the draft letter right away, and for 3½ hours it was discussed from every conceivable angle with occasional adjournments for private consultation. The miners were naturally very critical of the frequent emphasis on district agreements in the document, and it was to meet them that we inserted the 'national' paragraph.

The Chancellor, as you would expect, was more emphatic than his two colleagues about making the national agreement real and not a mere camouflage, but he carried them with him completely in the draft which was

---

[1] Christopher Salkeld Hurst, 1886–1963. Educated at Uppingham and Exeter College, Oxford. Public Trustee Office, 1910; Ministry of Munitions, 1915; Ministry of Labour, 1919; Coal Control Department, 1919; Mines Department, 1925. Secretary to the Royal Commission on the Coal Industry, 1925. Principal Assistant Secretary, Mines Department, 1930–8. Secretary and Controller, Coal Commission, 1938–47.

finally tabled. The miners were not asked of course to accept the letter in any sense. The letter was from the Government to the owners. But they did say that the publication of the letter would not be allowed to prevent their attending a joint conference.

At 1.40 am the Chancellor motored Smith and Cook to their hotel whilst Steel-Maitland took Richardson to his—all in a friendly mood.

This morning Gowers and I saw the Chancellor at Chartwell, and he agreed to re-arrange the order of some of the sentences, but its substance was not changed from where we left it last night. It was sent to Mr Evan Williams and to the Press at about 5.0 pm.

I am keeping the PM fully informed.

Clementine Churchill to Winston S. Churchill

(Churchill papers: 1/179)

8 September 1926
Grantully Castle[1]
Aberfeldy
Perthshire

My Darling,

I read carefully the official account of your interview with the Officers of the Mining Association. I suppose they want District Settlements so as to break up the solidarity of the Federation? I suppose it would be more difficult to call another strike with District Settlements. It is most depressing reading as it reveals such cold anger. However the papers seem hopeful & I see Ramsay is optimstic.

Nothing happening here—Scotland is in the occupation of the Americans until all the grouse are shot. These little birds have been causing great anxiety. They so dislike being shot by parvenu foreigners that they are practising Birth Control among themselves, & their population is diminished by half since the war. However they have been told by the impoverished Scotch Landowners that such conduct is reprehensible & the patriotic little creatures are considering their future policy. A universal 'Ca Canny' policy is favoured as against the present strike which operates only in certain districts!

Your loving
Clemmie

---

[1] The home of the Scrymsoure–Steuart–Fothringham family; from 1919 to 1936 the castle was rented by Lord Beatty.

Thomas Jones to Stanley Baldwin

(*Baldwin papers*)

8 September 1926   Offices of the Cabinet
10 am

The 'conversation' with the Miners' Leaders (Smith, Cook and Richardson) began at 10 and ended at 1.40 am. The Coal Committee Draft letter to Evan Williams was put before them at once by the Chancellor of the Exchequer and it emerged out of the 3½ hours discussion in the form marked No 2. We did not ask that they should agree the terms of No 2. We tried to make it as helpful to them as possible while keeping in view the owners' difficulties. They did agree that this letter would not be allowed to prevent their coming to a joint conference. AS-M and Lane-Fox present and fully co-operating throughout. I have now to see Gowers and HJW so that they may pass it 'technically' and then it will be given to EW and the Press. Miners' Executive will meet on Monday, on the same day as Mining Association. Your letter to Chancellor of Exchequer was read to the Coal Committee yesterday.

Sir Arthur Steel-Maitland to Stanley Baldwin

(*Baldwin papers*)

8 September 1926   Ministry of Labour
Private

My dear Prime Minister,
    . . . The stage is set for a conference on Tuesday. It is not at all clear that the owners will attend. But if they do, I am pretty certain that this first meeting will break down. If it doesn't break, no harm is done by your coming the next day. If it does, it had far better do so without your being present, both for your own sake and because you will be greater use too.
    Winston is far too optimistic. He thinks that because the owners have referred the matter to districts that they will of course come round, and will in any case attend on Monday. It is not so. They will only attend if Weir persuades EW that it is better so. They are not only really keen on the principle but very sore and angry. And again the miners have stiffened. They were pretty down & out a week ago but have perked their tails up since then.
    I think that ultimately we shall probably get an agreement. But the men will have to come more under the harrow first and we shall have an awkward time with the owners. On balance I think they are mistaken in disliking *my* national agreement in my form. But it ought to be decided on sheer industrial grounds.

Thomas Jones to Stanley Baldwin

(*Baldwin papers*)

8 September 1926   Offices of the Cabinet
3 pm

Gowers and I motored down to Chartwell at mid-day, and have just returned with No 3 draft. The letter has now been sent in this form to Evan Williams, and I am about to take a copy personally to Herbert Smith. The Chancellor is more optimistic than the Mines Department, and thinks it is 6 to 4 (as he put it) that the Owners will cave in.

The Chancellor was turning over in his mind at luncheon the desirability of your sending a brief message for publication in which you would say that in view of the prolonged stoppage, suffering & loss you hoped no door which might lead to a peaceful outcome of the strife would be closed. He may write or telegraph to you about this.

Sir Arthur Steel-Maitland to J. C. C. Davidson

(*Davidson papers*)

8 September 1926

. . . One reason for my not writing was that I didn't want to criticize Winston or let the PM think we were at loggerheads. The PM knows WC and with his position as PM can control him. But he is difficult to 'hand or to bind' otherwise. He will let himself be talked round, by officials or by a personal friend, if there is time enough for the process. But his impulsiveness and combativeness are an awful danger in negotiations. He has been more than a little trying as you wd find if you could get Wilson or Gowers or Lane-Fox to talk. But that was part of the day's work to be put up with. And I think, between us all, we have prevented most harm being done.

One trouble is that we jumped in too soon. . . . The miners were nearly down and out & ready to agree to anything.

A few days more and perhaps the Notts and Derby agreement would have clinched it. As it was Winston jumped in too readily and it was impossible to stop. With his impulsiveness he was all over the miners. Cook is able to quote him as ready, with them, to make peace and of course the miners have in turn stiffened a lot. On the other hand, the interview with the owners was lamentable. The strong hand may need to be shown, but not in a way that put all their backs up. If they were in a weak position (as during the passing of the Eight Hours Act) it wd be different. But they are not, and coercive measures by the Govt are not *at all* easy and they probably know it. . . .

What has also put their backs up is that they think WC is actuated by political and not industrial reasons and of course it is true. He thinks out industrial policy in terms of making a political speech. . . .

I have had to write quickly, and I may have over-emphasized Winston's failings in the present difficulties. I have got along with him all right, and have been determined to do so, though he doesn't like independent advice from another Cabinet Minister when there isn't time to do so very slowly and we aren't old colleagues. He is a most brilliant fellow, but his gifts aren't those of judgement, nor of appreciating industry, nor of a negotiator. Only don't let yourself or the PM get troubled. We have worked along all right. We have got some troubles ahead and as Gower said to me today 'The Party will be glad when the PM is back.' But it is worth everything to have him fit and sound and himself again. . . . He won't come back to a triumphant smooth path to peace. But he won't come back to a horrid time as before. The difficulties can quite well be overcome with just prudence & patience and as I said to Worthy, 'If the PM tells the coal owners what he thinks as a businessman himself, and what is their duty as citizens, he can do more with them than all of us rolled together,' and Worthy heartily agreed. . . .

Clementine Churchill to Winston S. Churchill

(*Churchill papers: 1/179*)

9 September 1926   Grantully Castle

My Darling,

. . . I fear you are having a very anxious & difficult time.

The Coal position is hard & cruel. It seems as though it could not be settled with good will & compromise, but only on a strict economic basis.

I return on the afternoon of next Monday so do not alter your Sunday plans! . . .

If you are in London Monday afternoon perhaps we could go down together in the little car.

Your loving
Clemmie

Thomas Jones to Stanley Baldwin

(*Baldwin papers*)

10 September 1926   Offices of the Cabinet

. . . The essence of the position with which you will be confronted on your return will be something like this:—

(a) The Chancellor made a speech renewing the offer of Government help if the miners would make a substantial advance. You could not have done less and you have approved the speech in your letter to the Chancellor. I believe the broad lines of this speech had been agreed the night before with several ministers who were available including Cunliffe-Lister and Sir L. Worthington-Evans. I am not certain about the presence of Lane-Fox and Sir S. Hoare—I think they were there. Gowers and I agreed then, and still think, that politically the speech was right.

(b) Immediately after the speech the Chancellor and his colleagues met the owners and the Chancellor went over the same ground with them and there was no questioning of the policy by ministers.

(c) On the next day came a request for an interview with the Chancellor from Ramsay Macdonald during which a 'formula' was discussed. This was revised and accepted on the clear understanding that 'reduction of labour costs' meant negotiations on hours and wages and district variations.

(d) At the next meeting with the owners the Government's request for a joint conference was reiterated with Worthington-Evans, Bridgeman, Steel-Maitland and Lane-Fox present and participating. All ministers pressed for a joint conference and though all ministers were not unanimous as to the scope of the conference, all assumed that at some stage there must be a national agreement.

(e) The Coal Committee decided that a letter should be sent to Evan Williams with the object of moderating the opposition of the owners and of forcing the hands of the miners. This letter was agreed to by the Chancellor of the Exchequer, the Minister of Labour, and the Secretary for Mines. It defined the relation of national and district negotiations and explicitly mentioned hours and wages. The public rightly guessed that the letter had been submitted in advance to the Miners' Leaders and marked a further stage.

(f) Gowers, who saw Evan Williams for two hours yesterday, is satisfied that the owners will not budge on Monday next, and all the Press says the same thing. The Press is less enthusiastic in its support of the Chancellor than it was. My own view is that this is due in large measure to the hostility which the personality of the Chancellor excites. He has hinted at what the Government will do to the owners if they prove obdurate. The newspapers ask: Is it conceivable that a Conservative Government will coerce the owners, however foolish, and the assumption is, No.

(g) But has the Chancellor in fact a plan? What compulsion can the Government put on the owners, assuming the Cabinet agrees to go ahead? There's the rub. The Mines Department is engaged upon this problem but has reached no satisfactory solution. You cannot directly impose a national agreement but indirectly you can do something. You could say that no district shall work eight hours which is not prepared to go to arbitration on hours and wages in those cases where no agreement is reached. But this would be just as distasteful to the men as to the owners. Another method would be this: if the owners refuse a joint conference, then turn to the men and endeavour to persuade them to play up. Let them instruct the districts to make provisional agreements on some general principles agreed to centrally. Let the Government undertake to give some national character to such agreements by scheduling them to the Eight Hours Act and by confining the advantages of that Act to those areas approved by the Board of Trade.

(h) You will not like travelling into this region, but the Government cannot recede now without throwing over the Chancellor and his approving colleagues. The Government's way of escape will probably come through the failure of the miners to exploit the situation in their own interest, as has so often happened. It is unlikely that they will arm the Government with terms good enough to enable the Government to go ahead in spite of the owners. They will haggle and boggle and once more defeat your efforts to give them a square deal.

(i) If, as I gather, you leave Aix on Tuesday evening and arrive here on Wednesday afternoon, then I think there should be a Cabinet on Thursday morning. That would give you time for personal conversations beforehand with ministers. One purpose I have had in mind in recounting the above is to bring out the fact that though the language of the Chancellor has been more vigorous than some of his colleagues would use, the course he has followed has had their approval and cannot now be disowned.

Winston S. Churchill to Lord Stamfordham

(*Churchill papers: 18/29*)

10 September 1926   Treasury Chambers

My dear Stamfordham,

It was extremely kind of the King to release me from my duty at Balmoral on account of the political situation here and the absence of the Prime

Minister. I should so much have liked to have come from the 13th to the 17th. However, as you will see from the newspapers, the Prime Minister does not return till the 15th, and the 16th and 17th will be very important days for the Cabinet. I fear therefore that it will be impossible for me to leave the neighbourhood of London.

The coal dispute is a cause of real anxiety. The miners have hitherto had the power to veto district settlements, and the owners are very likely determined to veto a national settlement. Meanwhile the injury to the wealth of the country is progressing. The Governor of the Bank was speaking to me last night in terms of grave concern. Although we are carrying on far better than I should have expected or hoped, the weekly loss is frightful—1,700,000 families earning nothing, and industry after industry closing down or running at a loss on costly and nasty foreign coal. Even if the deadlock were broken now, the effects will manifest themselves on our trade during the whole of next year. People are living from hand to mouth, and all the future exploitations on which the steady flow of our business depend are crippled or prevented. This will have serious reactions upon the exchange position. It is sad to see industrial England tearing itself to pieces while the rest of the country is only just about able to keep its head above water.

I presume the King realises that the difficulties of bringing in foreign coal by sea will greatly increase in the winter season, and at the same time the national requirements will enormously increase. I do not see any sign so far of the miners giving in. Less than 50,000 working miners, out of nearly a million, have returned; and with the modern methods of local relief there is no decisive pressure upon them to return. The situation therefore causes me the very greatest anxiety. I was never in the least frightened of the General Strike, and felt sure that, if taken by the throat, it would be speedily broken. But a Coal Strike, prolonged as this has been, is like a ship sinking slowly in a calm sea.

Clementine Churchill to Winston S. Churchill

(Churchill papers: 1/179)

10 September 1926   Grantully Castle

My Darling,

I am anxiously awaiting further news after your telegram saying that Owners' action involves 'serious collision, with political reaction next week'.

The last public news is your letter to Mr Evan Williams explaining how a National & District Settlement can be combined. Has he refused to meet.

The papers say that the answer from the Districts cannot arrive till next week so I wonder what has meanwhile happened. I gather that the Districts are expected to agree with the Mining Association.

There is a nice tennis court & when there is no shooting we disport ourselves there. I have also taken to golf! . . .

I am looking forward so much to seeing you again my Darling. You are having an anxious but a thrilling & engrossing time with power & scope which is what the Pig likes—I suppose Steel-Maitland & Lane-Fox are not often allowed near the trough? I hope you let them have a tit-bit now & again. If the Cat were Minister of Labour or Mines she would not give up her place there without a few 'miaows'. She would scratch the pig's topsy & run between his legs & get her little paws in the said trough.

I hope your 'lamp-post' Party on Sunday will be pleasant. Please do not allow any very low conversation before the children! I don't necessarily mean 'improper' but Lord B[1] does manage to defile any subject he touches & I hope the relationship between him & Mrs Norton[2] will not be apparent to Randolph & Diana's inquisitive marmoset-like eyes & ears.

Consuelo is much relieved to hear that Mrs Norton is not travelling abroad with her little Ivor!, who refused to come here & took himself off to France in his car!

Tender love from
Clemmie

Lord Londonderry to Winston S. Churchill

(*Churchill papers: 22/112*)

11 September 1926

My dear Winston,

You know how much we agree on so many points that I have a difficulty in persuading myself that I do not agree with you now: and I feel very sorry about it.

I regret these verbatim reports; I think they are a great mistake: a communiqué is infinitely better.

I know you want to be impartial but you really have come down on the side of Cook and Smith; not on the side of the men nor on the side of the owners.

It is only Cook and Smith to save their faces, who were clinging to the

---

[1] Lord Beaverbrook.   [2] Jean Norton (see page 60, note 2).

shadow of a National Agreement, now of course their stock has advanced by 100%.

I have urged the Durham Association to stand by the resolution we agreed to last Monday, and to accept your invitation to the Conference. Public opinion as you know is uninstructed and is swayed hither and thither—and of course the Government siding with Cook and Smith is a tremendous factor. You speak of a change of heart: there is no change of heart, and the change of voice was solely due to one district being determined to make their own arrangements.

The subsidy was wrong and the 8 hours Bill was wrong. You will retort that the owners asked for the 8 hours Bill; so they did but it was very unwise and if you probed deep into their minds you would probably find that their idea was that 8 hours in the end would mean district agreements. The Government goes with them on the 8 hours, but you have not helped towards district agreements, which for future peace are essential. However important a settlement on any terms is, the rescue of Cook and Smith is fraught with fresh disaster.

I hope I am entirely wrong. I shall be the first to say so if I am; you may be sure of that. I don't ask you to do anything for the owners; what I do really ask is, that if you believe in district settlements, and believe as I do that a National settlement is only a device to keep the Federation (the executive of which is our worst political enemy) alive, you will let Cook and Smith fail: and notwithstanding the wonderful spirit shewn by the miners in the war, and the clap-trap talked on platforms about their marvellous loyalty, you will find they will leave Cook and Smith like rats leave a sinking ship. These Conferences are mainly tactics, and so far Cook and Smith have gained on the tactics; when it comes to strategy which the Government has to consider and we the lieutenants in the counties have also to consider, we shall be up against the full force of the victorious Federation.

You are an optimist and you say that everything produces a vaccine, a reaction, an antidote or whatever you like to call it. I sincerely hope you are right: but I beg of you not to buttress Cook and Smith because you are impatient with the owners. The owners are absolutely right in theory, as a Capitalist State sees the question, but they are bad tacticians. Evan Williams made an excellent statement the other day and without knowing exactly what you were going to say. He showed very clearly how the Association had been forced to take up a position vis à vis the Federation to oblige the Government; and everything they have done, every concession has been used as a jumping off ground by the Federation, for demanding more.

You know quite well that I have often been impatient with the Association and that is why I do not take a more prominent part but I am certain as time goes on you will find that the Association attitude on this occasion has been a correct one, and that they can only very reluctantly attend a joint conference, on the reference laid down by you in agreement with Cook and Smith because it is they who to save their skins and not only their faces are pressing for a National Agreement.

Tom Jones is dead against the owners point of view because he is not of your or my political belief; and the Ministry of Mines like many ministries and many people follows the line of what seems to be the least resistance, vide that pitiable bill the re-organization Bill which I had to go into the Government Lobby and support because I am so anxious to support you in public that I accept all you do. You may compel the owners to do what you want and what Cook and Smith want them to do; the Government have invariably gained their point with the owners but invariably attach all the blame to the owners when anything goes wrong.

I am sorry to write in a somewhat bitter spirit but when the trouble begins again in a year, all this will be forgotten and the owners will be held up as stubborn and unyielding when for the last 10 years they have done everything to fall in with policies of successive Governments.

I am, yours,
Londonderry

Lord Birkenhead to Winston S. Churchill: telegram
(*Churchill papers: 18/28*)

12 September 1926   Biarritz

I am not happy about your attitude. Why should we impose upon owners national settlement if they are strong enough to obtain district settlements. Why should we enable men's leaders who have done their best to ruin England to escape without the brand of failure. Be careful of TJ whom I like but whose advice may easily be unsound.

Fred

Winston S. Churchill to Lord Birkenhead: telegram
(*Churchill papers: 18/28*)

13 September 1926

Very sorry you were not with us to advise. All others agreed with steps taken. Your telegram begs question whether owners strong enough win on all points. Consequences stoppage worse each week. Cabinet Thursday. Are you coming? Wire.

W

Evan Williams to Winston S. Churchill

(*Churchill papers: 22/113*)

13 September 1926
By Hand

Dear Chancellor of the Exchequer,

I am now in a position to reply to your letter of the 8th instant, the receipt of which I formally acknowledged on the same day.

Copies of your letter were at once circulated to the district associations so that they might have it before them when they gave consideration to the question which we both agreed at the meeting on the 6th instant was the only one at issue at the moment, and which you expressed in the following words:—

'Is there to be any national agreement at all, or is the industry in future to be regulated purely by district agreements without any national wage negotiating body.'

With the exception of one small inland district the twenty-four district associations have replied clearly and emphatically declining to give the Mining Association power or authority to enter into agreements on their behalf in regard to terms of employment of the workmen in their respective districts.

You will accordingly see that the meeting which you propose in your letter could serve no useful purpose. There is no person who would be entitled to speak or to listen on behalf of the coalowners, and I am sure you will agree that no good, but harm, would result from a meeting held under conditions which would expose the parties to a charge of insincerity.

The district coalowners' associations have been and are willing and anxious to meet the miners' associations in their districts at any time without ceremony or any preliminary procedure whatsoever. There is no valid obstacle to this. There is no question of principle that need delay them. None of the district associations raises any objection to the principle of wage regulation by reference to ascertained results, the principle of a minimum percentage below which wages cannot fall, or the principle of subsistence wages. The quantitative determinations on these and all other points can only be made in the light of the circumstances of the districts by those who know them and have to face the results.

A realisation of these facts is imperative, and it is failure to recognise them that stands in the way of these negotiations being entered into at once and is alone responsible for the prolongation of the stoppage.

I desire to add that the decisions of the districts, which re-affirm the declarations made to you last Monday, arise from a deep and earnest conviction that settlements on a national basis, by linking the industry with politics, inevitably take the consideration of purely industrial questions out of their proper economic sphere, have been destructive of peace and prosperity to those engaged in the industry, and, as experience of the immediate past has shewn, are a menace to the community as a whole.

Yours sincerely,
Evan Williams

Cabinet Coal Committee: minutes

(Churchill papers: 22/117)

14 September 1926   10 Downing Street
4.15 pm

The CHANCELLOR OF THE EXCHEQUER gave an account of the recent private conversations with the miners' leaders which had preceded the publication of the letter from the Government to Mr Evan Williams.

The Chancellor in the course of his statement laid stress on the growing gravity of the country's position owing to the continuance of the stoppage and referred to the anxiety which had been expressed by the Governor of the Bank as to the outlook for next spring. Primary processes usually put in hand now and maturing next spring were arrested and the results would be severely felt in February and March. It was therefore of the utmost importance in the interests of the country's finances to secure a resumption of work in the collieries at the earliest possible moment. It was vital that the situation should be quickly cleared up.

A discussion followed on the course which the Government should take in view of the owners' refusal to meet in a tripartite conference. It was suggested, on the one hand, that a letter should be addressed at once to the Miners' Federation the object of which should be to discover what coercive action the miners desired the Government to take and how far the miners, in return, would be prepared to go in the way of a satisfactory offer on hours, wages and district settlements. It was urged, on the other hand, by the majority of ministers present, to be preferable to postpone further action until the meeting of the Cabinet on Thursday next.

COERCION OF OWNERS

The Committee considered at length various suggestions for bringing pressure to bear on the mineowners, and had before them some draft clauses prepared by the Mines Department.

SIR ERNEST GOWERS stated that in the opinion of the Mines Department there were very great if not insuperable difficulties to proceeding by imposing a National Agreement either before or after district settlements. The purpose of a National Agreement was to secure for the miners the fairest wages the coal industry could economically pay. If there had to be legislation the best form it could take would be to use the machinery of the Coal Mines (Minimum Wage) Act 1921 and apply it to district percentages. This he had attempted to do in the draft clauses which he had circulated.

To this proposal it was objected that it would offer no inducement to the miners.

After other proposals had been examined the discussion was adjourned.

Winston S. Churchill to Lord Londonderry

(*Churchill papers: 22/112*)

14 September 1926

My dear Charlie,

If the owners had deferred to the Government wish to attend a Conference, it could have been held last Wednesday; and by Thursday last either the men would have shown they were ready to face the economic facts and we should be approaching an end to this disastrous period, or the Conference would have been broken off and a perfectly clear cut situation been established. As it is, there must be a continued uncertainty till the Prime Minister returns, till the Cabinet assembles and action is decided upon. This is certainly detrimental, but I personally accept no responsibility for it. The injury of the stoppage to the nation deepens progressively week by week, and there is no longer any question of a swift recovery.

Winston S. Churchill to Sir Roger Keyes

(*Keyes papers*)

16 September 1926
Private

My dear Roger,

I feel very remiss about not having answered your former charming letter nor the fascinating invitation which it contained. Pray forgive me.

I have not been neglectful about the Income Tax point, but I am sorry to say my alguazils[1] report in the following sour terms and I cannot but administer the law as they interpret it. . . .[2]

With regard to Beatty, I thought at the time of the Estimates fight and when he appeared to be banking so heavily on a war with Japan, which I believe to be nonsense in itself and also very bad policy on our part, that a change ought to take place. But now that Singapore is so satisfactorily settled for several years to come and the new programme has been agreed upon, the position is entirely changed. On every personal ground I have always wished Beatty to remain and now I am glad to say public as well as private considerations flow together. I am sorry that Haig has not been kept at the head of the British Army in the same way, for I am sure it is right after a war that the successful Commanders should leave a definite stamp upon the Services of which they were the heads in the struggle.

So far from not having found time to get on with the book, it is now nearly finished and will come out in the Spring. I send you herewith the two chapters which deal with Jutland. Beatty put Commander Kenneth Dewar[3] at my disposal, and I have been having some lively arguments with him. The two chapters are not yet in their final form and I shall particularly welcome any corrections, improvements or criticisms you may care to make upon them. I shall probably have a page or two of general conclusions at the end of the second chapter in order to focus the moral.

---

[1] Alguazil: the Spanish form of the Arabic word *al-vazir*, or vizier, meaning a minister, or officer: thus, an official who carries out orders. In a speech at Blackpool on 24 January 1884, Churchill's father, Lord Randolph Churchill, commenting on a Press report that Gladstone was 'guarded as usual' when he went to Church, had gone on to declare: 'Surely the art of government must have sunk to a very low ebb when the first servant of the Crown has to be watched night and day by alguazils armed to the teeth.'

[2] The Treasury reported that whereas Sir Roger Keyes was accepted as a non-resident for tax-purposes, Lady Keyes had been refused any tax repayment for the period June to October 1925 'on the ground that she had not ceased to be resident here until the later date'.

[3] Kenneth Gilbert Balmain Dewar, 1879–1964. Entered HMS *Britannia*, 1893. Commander, 1911. Assistant Director, Plans Division, Admiralty Naval Staff, 1917. Deputy Director, Naval Intelligence Division, 1925–7. Commanded HMS *Royal Oak* and *Tiger*, 1924–9. Rear-Admiral, retired, 1929; Vice-Admiral, 1934.

Your sacred book is strictly under lock and key, and I hope to send it back to you before the end of the year.

It is a great pleasure to me to hear from you and to learn how much you are enjoying your great Command. If at any time I should find myself in Rome, which is not an impossibility next month, I may telegraph to you on the chance of proposing a flying visit. I suppose you could pick me up somewhere in your despatch vessel. I should like very much to see the Fleet. It is more than eleven years since I stood on the deck of the unfinished 'Queen Elizabeth', and I have never been on board a battleship since.

with all good wishes
from
your sincere friend,
Winston S. Churchill

Cabinet Coal Committee: minutes

(Churchill papers: 2/117)

16 September 1926   10 Downing Street
11.30 am

THE CHANCELLOR OF THE EXCHEQUER explained the scope and purpose of the Draft Clauses, prepared by the Mines Department, for a Bill to bring pressure to bear on the owners. The intention was to deny the benefit of the Eight Hours Act to owners unless wages etc in their mines were determined in accordance with the Agreement of 1924, as amended by the new Bill. Any divergence from the Agreement thus amended would be reviewed after an interval of six months by a National Board and its decision would be deemed to be the decision of the District Board. The National Board would have the task of judging in relation to other districts whether a particular variation was justified. Unless owners conformed to the decision of the National Board they should not be allowed to work their mines for more than seven hours a day.

THE PRESIDENT OF THE BOARD OF TRADE said that a cardinal aim should be to get the men back to work at the earliest moment and the Draft Clauses did not appear to limit the right of appeal to men who were at work. Both sides had been unreasonable in the dispute and the Government should put forward what they regarded as a fair settlement. There should be district negotiations based on general principles nationally agreed. If the men were dissatisfied with local terms, provided they went back to work, they should be given the right to go to an arbitral court. The Government should legislate to provide that if the Court awarded terms better than those of the owners, the owners should not be allowed the advantage of the Eight Hours Act, unless they accepted the Court's award.

THE CHANCELLOR OF THE EXCHEQUER reminded the Committee that the Government's letter to Mr Evan Williams had envisaged three stages:

(a) The outline of broad general principles of a national settlement.
(b) District agreements concluded with a view to the immediate resumption of work.
(c) Review of district agreements in order to see how they diverged from national principles, and where necessary reference back to districts.

Beyond that there might be arbitration.

THE CHANCELLOR OF THE EXCHEQUER said the position at the moment was that the Government had been rebuffed by the owners. The men would repeat that they were prepared to go into open conference with no issue barred and would press to know what the Government proposed to do in the matter of a national agreement. The Government could not simply go to the men and ask them to make further disclosures of their position and be silent on its own attitude to the owners.

Montagu Norman to Winston S. Churchill

(Churchill papers: 22/113)

16 September 1926   Bank of England

Dear Mr Chancellor,

When I was speaking to you last week the particular point that I had in mind was more or less as follows:—Owing to the Coal Strike we have slowed down our manufactures and exports have therefore suffered. This seems not only obvious but likely to continue at least until the production of coal is again normal. Meanwhile it must affect our exchange position.

But, over and above this, I wonder whether the adverse effect upon our exchange position is not going to continue for many months after the Coal Strike comes to an end, not because of the time taken to secure the full resumption of normal coal production but because manufacture is, in many cases, a process of months. If in the early stages this process is checked, the completion of the manufactured article will be delayed, exports will continue to suffer and the adverse effect upon our exchange position be prolonged.

Hence, I have fears for the exchanges during and beyond the continuance of the Coal Strike. But I write as a financial onlooker and not as an industrial expert.

Believe me to be,
Dear Mr Chancellor,
Yours most faithfully,
M. Norman

Lord Londonderry to Winston S. Churchill

(*Churchill papers: 22/112*)

17 September 1926
Private

My dear Winston,

Many thanks for your letter. I feel very sorry that the negotiations broke down because I would have been so delighted for you to have succeeded and settled the strike.

I wish all the districts had taken the line of Durham and urged their representatives to meet at all events.

The real thing is that every concession made by the owners has been used as a jumping off ground for something else and they all know it. Conciliation and acceptance of the new ideas of the Federation developing solely as a political body and *nothing else,* has compelled them to feel that nothing could be worse so perhaps firmness may be better.

My men at one pit are making overtures to go back on our terms; but the management are fearful of the new sinkings being wrecked by the Bolshevist element. I have wired for a full report, because unless there is a good number of brave men, it is no good doing anything: and as I have to work that pit at a loss anyhow, I am not so anxious to start it again.

I repeat that I wish the verbatim reports were not published. There may be some good reason for them, but I am sure without verbatim reports you could have prevailed on Evan Williams to approach the Districts in a totally different way. I have a great difficulty with Evan Williams and his colleagues. They are very jealous of me and they are terrified of my getting any credit. When I wrote to him in London, I received no answer. I am fearful of becoming prejudiced against him on petty grounds, but I fear I have no opinion of him at all. The post I think is an impossible one. It should really be an office and nothing more and the districts should run their own shows. Evan Williams did show very well what is quite true but what everybody forgets that the Government forced this position on the Association and to oblige they shouldered the burden.

I did hope that you were going to bring this off and I wish I could have helped you, but it would have been wrong of me to drive a wedge into the Association and it would have only heartened Cook. I would have got great credit from the public but it would have been wrong. However don't let us lose heart.

Yours affectionately,
Charley

Winston S. Churchill to H. A. Gwynne

(*Churchill papers: 2/147*)

20 September 1926
Private and Confidential

My dear Mr Gwynne,

I am shocked to find your letter of the 6th September has, in the tangle of the coal negotiations, been mislaid until now. It would have been a pleasure to me to come to your Luncheon and to say a few words to your miner emigrants, if I could have found the time. Unhappily the date is passed. I hope your not receiving any answer from me was not a cause of inconvenience. Pray accept my excuses.[1]

I saw you were worried about the line that I took in the coal business, though I noted with appreciation that you did not allow yourself your old vigour of criticism. I am sure the Owners made a great mistake in not coming to a joint conference. The men are undoubtedly prepared to go a considerable distance. I do not think they are prepared to go the necessary distance, but this could only have been ascertained at such a conference as we had in view. It would have emerged in the first day or two and I should have confronted the men with the economic issues in the most unmistakable manner. Thus all would have been over in a few days and the situation would again have been quite clear cut on a fighting basis, unless, that is to say, there had been real progress to a settlement. Now the situation has been clarified again to a very considerable extent and I am very grateful to the Cabinet and the Prime Minister for endorsing the course which, in the circumstances of the

---

[1] The scheme supported and sponsored by Gwynne and the *Morning Post* was aimed at settling two hundred British miners in Australia. The first group of forty miners left England on September 18: Gwynne had invited Churchill to speak at their farewell luncheon on the previous day.

Owners' refusal, I felt bound to recommend. But it is always a mistake for people to refuse to come to a conference, especially people in the responsible position of coal owners. It is the duty of all classes to give reasonable aid to the lawfully constituted authorities in the discharge of their responsibilities to the nation as a whole. This does not of course mean that anybody is under any obligation to agree to arrangements which they think prejudicial.

It will not be very pleasant if this thing goes on another six weeks or two months, and I feel no assurance that it will not. I have never been frightened of a General Strike or a Railway Strike, or any strike that leads to action and collision; but a Coal Strike is like going down in a calm sea. Very deep injury is being wrought in the economic structure of the country.

Lord Beaverbrook to Lord Derby

(*Beaverbrook papers*)

20 September 1926

I have been with Winston a lot lately. I met him the night of the meeting with the coal-owners. We dined at the Savoy Grill. He explained his plans. I pointed out to him the Conservative objections. He became eloquent and of course would not tolerate any opposition. However, he did promise me that he would not use any threats. Then he showed me what he had already said that afternoon—full of threats, of course. Yet he was perfectly unaware that he had said anything extreme. Since then we have met again and again. He is, of course, now in full flight, and only wants his retreat covered— which the Cabinet is doing.

I must say that I am not quite sure he is right from the point of view of his own interest, in climbing down. (I did not dare tell him this for fear of damaging national interests). But I believe that if he had gone the full length of resignation and suffered shame in this cause, he might have got a rally of moderate opinion round him and emerged at the end with a political halo and a stronger general position. . . .

It is curious to reflect that Baldwin, who is undoubtedly a man of peace at heart—if only he had a nature sufficiently violent to impose his will to peace on others—worked in with Birkenhead over the General Strike, and with Winston over this business, and made them accessories to a policy of moderation. Each time the move went wrong. And since Baldwin, as the titular leader of the Conservative Party, cannot—and rightly so—do wrong, FE and Winston in succession have had to take the blame and suffer the rebuff, while Baldwin gets scot-free.

I do not suggest that they have been put in the forefront of the battle like Uriah. For our modern Joab, while he retires from before the wall all right, at least carries his wounded Hittites off the field with him.

Thomas Jones: diary

(*Jones papers*)

21 September 1926

6.50 pm. Baldwin, Winston, Gowers, Grigg discuss Winston's draft letter. I tell PM that Gowers and Grigg are against it going. . . .

8.55 pm. Back at No 10. Miners in Treasury Board Room.

9.00 pm. Baldwin, Winston, Steel-Maitland, Lane-Fox, Horace Wilson, Gowers. Amend Winston's letter and retype.

9.30 pm. I see Herbert Smith and Cook and arrange for four only of them to come to Cabinet Room. Provide cigars, the four come in. PM reads the letter to them. Winston justifies his course of action.

10.40 pm. Four miners' representatives withdraw to Duff's room. Horace Wilson and I see the Four on the question of a national façade. Winston to threaten 'Proposals—or in ten minutes PM's letter goes to the Press.'

Sir Horace Wilson and C. S. Hurst: draft proposals

(*Churchill papers: 22/113*)

21 September 1926
11 pm

1. The Miners Federation offer the following as a basis of settlement and immediate resumption of work:—

(a) There shall be a national minimum of X per cent upon standard, of general application;

(b) The principle of joint ascertainment and the principle of division of proceeds in ratio of Y to wages and Z to profits shall apply to all districts;

(c) The principle of subsistence allowances shall apply generally, with district decision as in the past;

(d) Temporary variations from the general national conditions settled under (a) and (b), may be agreed by local discussion, subject to appeal to and review by the Tribunal established by (2) below.

2. The Government to set up immediately a National Tribunal (as in existing scheme).

Thomas Jones: diary

(*Jones papers*)

21 September 1926

11.10 pm. Miners given five more minutes.

11.35 pm. Miners back. Temperature rapidly rising. Winston: You have not come into the open with anything.

11.50 pm. Herbert Smith begins to approach proposals with much preliminary preparation of the ground.

HS: If we make suggestions it bain't an auctioneering process. News gets out on placards.

Winston: We'll keep them absolutely secret and tell you what we can or cannot do.

11.55 pm. Proposals. Immediate resumption on 1921 minimum and Samuel Report. Arbitration by agreed tribunal. Anything due to the men to be recoverable.

12.10 am. Men withdraw. Should we adjourn at once or cross-examine with leading questions?

12.20 am. Men return for cross-examination on meaning of Proposals. I get copies made and return original.

12.55 am. Press Notice.

Thomas Jones: diary

(*Jones papers*)

22 September 1926

A few minutes after 8.0 am I telegraphed and later telephoned to Birkenhead and Worthington-Evans, summoning them to a meeting of the Coal Committee at 11 am. I found Birkenhead was in town, and the clerk spoke to the butler who said his lordship was in the house, and would be told about the meeting. This was between 9.0 and 10.0. Between 10 and 11 Duff was told that Birkenhead had started for Southampton at 9.0 am.

When I told Churchill this he was very angry and mentioned it to the PM. Churchill was genuinely anxious to get Birkenhead's counsel, and as cross-examiner with the miners he would have been much more helpful than any other Minister on the Committee. At 10.20 I asked the PM if I should summon the four miners, and have them available in an adjoining room for a rapid consultation, but he was against doing this.

At 11.0 am the Committee met. Horace Wilson and Gowers gave their views on the proposals tabled at midnight by Herbert Smith. One course would be to elucidate the meaning of these proposals with greater precision than was possible in the late hours last night, and then the Government, taking no responsibility for them, could act as mediators and convey them to the owners. The owners would be certain to turn them down. Alternatively the Government could take last night's proposals and endeavour to fit them in to its own scheme of coercing the owners.

A most rambling discussion followed for an hour and a half, the PM doing nothing whatever to guide its course, and contributing nothing more than a weary ejaculation to the effect that we seemed deeper in the soup than ever, and that if we coerced the owners they could also refuse to open their pits, and the result would be dear coal.

The Chancellor, as always, was eager to continue negotiating and to put the best face possible on the midnight proposals. He was quite prepared to go to great lengths in the way of legislation on hours, wages, and conditions—which terrified his colleagues. Steel-Maitland was sceptical of the men's intentions, and wanted to confront them plainly with the question, would they discuss the variation of the minimum in the districts? Lane-Fox as usual said hardly anything and Sir Laming on the whole backed Churchill.

By the end of the meeting Churchill was back to his earlier position of giving the men a national façade, ie a body of principles which should guide the district negotiations and these to be given the form and force of law.

About 11.20 all officials were asked to withdraw at the prompting of the Chancellor, and about 10 minutes later the bell went and we went back into the Cabinet Room to find Winston and Worthy vanished. The PM told Horace Wilson and Gowers that they were to get in touch with the four miners' officials at once, cross-examine them closely on the midnight proposals and report later to a meeting of the Ministers at 3.15.

It was plain that things were not moving easily, and a few minutes afterwards the Chancellor asked me into his room where he had already begun to dictate his views. He turned the typist out, and then told me the situation was becoming impossible for him and that he would not come to the 3.15 meeting. It was hopeless exploring one device after another in the confused fashion of the meeting we had just attended with the Prime Minister thoroughly sound at heart and in intention, doing nothing to pilot the discussion, and with Steel-Maitland and Lane-Fox quite futile. 'It is quite easy to understand why the stoppage has lasted all these months. They are now sending Wilson and Gowers, to see the miners: they have not the prestige even if they had the knowledge, and they cannot adjust themselves to the course of the talk with the miners, and perhaps get into a new and better position; they will simply come back and report all the difficulties.

I wanted the PM to let Worthy and me see them, but that was turned down, so I will clear out of it. I will put down my views in writing. I can do a job of work if it is given to me to do, and I can work with a colleague putting it through, but I can't go meandering all over the place and arrive nowhere in the way we are now doing.'

I said that I thought the bottom fact which paralysed the discussions was that Steel-Maitland, Lane-Fox, and Gowers did not believe settlement with the men possible, that there was no settlement which the men would accept which the owners would look at. I then said that if he carried out his threat of not going to the 3.15 meeting it would get about at once, fill the papers, and its importance would be vastly exaggerated; that infinite patience was required at a time like this, especially as the PM himself was suffering from sciatica and obviously did not know which way to turn in the midst of his conflicting advisers.

I gradually calmed him down, and before I came away he had promised to turn up this afternoon.

Winston S. Churchill: discussion with Herbert Smith and A. J. Cook

(Jones papers)

22 September 1926
12.30 pm

C of Ex. The National Tribunal would be set up by law and its findings would have to be enforced by law?

HS. We are not necessarily seeking compulsory arbitration. We suggest both parties should agree on a Tribunal. If we fail to agree we would have to come back to Government. Government would have the final word.

C of Ex. Supposing the owners refuse, all we can do is to pass a law. What about the terms of reference to the Tribunal? The Samuel Report? Do you mean the application of the Samuel Report to owners and miners on hours, wages and conditions, or do you mean reorganisation, royalties, municipal selling? Parliament is not likely to submit itself to a Tribunal.

HS. We rather thought of the things in the way of immediate dispute—stopping this industry getting to work.

C of Ex. This is an awkward question now. You take the 1926 Report for purposes of settlement by the Tribunal. Is all arbitration on hours barred?

HS. If you take Commission Report on hours, they put in proviso. We will resist as far as we can all extension of hours.

C of Ex. While you would resist it would not be outside the scope of the Tribunal.

Cook. It is in the Report.

Winston S. Churchill: Cabinet memorandum

(*Churchill papers: 22/113*)

22 September 1926
3.15 pm

1. A practical method of ending the stoppage was outlined in our letter to Evan Williams of September 8, namely,

(1) the laying down nationally of certain broad principles;
(2) district negotiations in the light of (1);
(3) subsequent review by an impartial Tribunal.

The owners refusal to attend the conference (for the purposes of (1)) has led the Government to proceed merely on the basis of (2) and (3). This we have done in the Prime Minister's letter of September 17.

2. The miners now make counter-proposals which differ widely from, but are not unrelated to, the proposals of the Prime Minister's letter. They ask for a National Tribunal at once to adjudicate on the application of the Samuel Commission Report to wages and conditions. They propose in the meanwhile a resumption on the temporary basis of the 1921 minimum.

3. Sir Ernest Gowers has drafted a paper translating the miners' proposals into a precise and reasonable form. We have also before us the unofficial sketch of the kind of principles that should govern national agreements drawn up by Mr Jones and Sir Horace Wilson and shown to the miners informally last night. Finally we have the draft Bill prepared by the Ministry of Mines and subsequently discarded by the Cabinet in favour of Cunliffe-Lister's plan.

4. If it is desired to advance towards a settlement I believe that the most hopeful course lies in a combination of elements taken from the three aforesaid documents. I would therefore propose that we should say to the miners:

'You wish for a national settlement as the preliminary to district negotiations, but the owners will not make one with you. In these circumstances we will make one with you, provided we can agree upon its principles and also upon all the other steps which must be taken. Our idea of the national principles is as follows: [Here we get to Mr Jones' paper]. Are you prepared to fill in the blanks, or what alterations do you suggest? Clearly understand that if we reach an agreement on this, it means that if all other matters are satisfactorily settled you will have to order district negotiations to begin.'

5. Assuming the above surmounted, the next question is, how should these agreed national principles be promulgated or enforced? Here we should offer to set up the Tribunal by law at once and to direct it after an interval to review district settlements in accordance with the declared national prin-

ciples. This is no more than the plan of the discarded Bill, to which may be added the suggestion that the 'national principles' need not be in the text but can be an instruction to the Tribunal imparted through the Mines Department.

6. Once we have decided to act in this way if need be, and subject to all other conditions being satisfactory, we should tell the owners that we are now going to settle national principles with the men, and if they do not choose to take part in the discussions we shall proceed without them and carry them into law over their heads. As there is very little real difference about these national principles no very serious consequences can arise.

7. On the above basis, each of the foregoing steps having been taken, the miners would order their men to begin district negotiations, or failing district negotiations to offer to resume work on the basis of the 1921 minimum and the $7\frac{1}{2}$ hours day. It would have to be made clear that in the temporary period following immediate resumption there would be at least three different bases on which resumption would take place:—

(a) district agreements duly concluded;

(b) return to work without agreements on the rough and ready $7\frac{1}{2}$ hours and 1921 minimum; and

(c) whatever has been arranged locally in the pits and districts which have re-opened and which must continue. But this is only a feature of an interim period.

8. Finally the Tribunal which will have been set up will be charged, after an interval of, say, six months, with the duty of reviewing the district settlements of all kinds and of bringing them into accord with the national principles previously proclaimed.

9. If everything else were satisfactorily settled and an immediate resumption were certain, I should be prepared to follow the Lord Chancellor in making the 'sanctions' extend not merely to the difference between 7 and 8 hours but to the whole industry.

10. All the above to be presented as the reluctant alternative to a national settlement between the parties, and of course every part of the process and agreement to be dependent on every other part.

Lord Birkenhead to Stanley Baldwin

(*Baldwin papers*)

23 September 1926

I must make my apologies for not having attended the two Meetings of the Coal Committee. But I deliberately abstained from doing so because I have a great personal contempt both for Cook and Smith, and was apprehensive that intervening in the discussions at rather a late stage owing to my absence abroad, I might be a source of disharmony rather than of harmony.

Thomas Jones: diary

(*Jones papers*)

24 September 1926

CABINET COAL COMMITTEE

PM met his colleagues this afternoon to talk Coal once more. [He said] Difficulties between owners and miners unbridgeable. Nothing on earth will bring them together. Miners are beaten and rattled. Cook badly rattled. They don't know what to do. House meets on Monday. They have their eye on that. They produced proposals with air of great secrecy, but two things are hopeless: men are to go back at once on 1921 minimum and the old seven hours. They begged the whole question of the Act and fact that owners would not have opened the pits, not for cussedness but because they wanted to know terms on which they were opening them. They went as far as the Samuel Report. The more we examined their offer the less hope we saw of a basis of settlement. Evan Williams says: Leave us alone and we'll get settlements, if there is no interference we'll get them quickly, some will be longer than others. The men know they are beaten. They'll come in soon in some districts but not in South Wales, Northumberland, or Herbert Smith's district. The issue is simple: either leave things alone or do something. Good deal to be said for both. If you leave things alone you don't know how long pits will remain idle. Days are getting shorter. Cold coming. Public not pinched yet. If we take action we can't see any action other than compulsory arbitration: a very strong measure. If no action, many will feel that the Government has left a mass of miners to be beaten to their knees by the owners. That bad for us as we still have to deal with Trade Unions. If you lay down terms on which men are to go back you keep men waiting while award is being made. The Coal Committee have come very slowly to the conclusion that there are less disadvantages from action than inaction.

Winston stressed the remarkable advance of the men's proposals. They would have ended the strike in May and the men would now have had millions in their pockets. But they have not faced the full economic position required, they have taken a strong political position with public opinion. At the moment the owners have taken a wholly wrong and unreasonable position, and refused to come to a three-cornered conference, an attitude without precedent in recent times. The Whips had been at some of the Ministers urging them to do nothing. Owners were satisfied that the Government were the stumbling block. Suppose Tribunal formulated wages rates and owners refused to open pits, the result would be a demand for nationalisation. And it would give men right to demand unemployment benefit. Is every industrial dispute to come to the PM and to lead ultimately to arbitration? Better for Government to disinterest itself and refuse to see Evan Williams or Cook again.

These and many more difficulties emerged in the course of the discussion and the opposition to positive action grew as the obstacles to making the Bill work were envisaged. Birkenhead felt it was the most difficult decision since the evacuation of the Dardanelles.[1]

Winston S. Churchill: draft Heads of an Agreement between His Majesty's Government and the Miners' Federation

(*Churchill papers: 22/113*)

24 September 1926

(1) The Miners' Federation to do all in their power to promote district settlements and immediate resumption of work thereupon.

(2) District settlements to be final, if they conform to the following principles: viz

(a) The 20% minimum percentage for a $7\frac{1}{2}$-hour day; $33\frac{1}{3}$% minimum for a 8-hour day; and 15% for a $7\frac{3}{4}$-hour day.
(b) Ratio 87:13.
(c) Subsistence wages as at April 30, 1926.
(d) Approved prices for transferred coal, etc.
(e) Agreed methods of ascertainment.

[1] Birkenhead (as F. E. Smith) had entered Asquith's Cabinet on 3 November 1915. Churchill (then Chancellor of the Duchy of Lancaster) had left the Cabinet on 12 November 1915. The decision to evacuate the Dardanelles was taken, after much discussion, on 7 December 1915, and the evacuation itself was completed by 9 January 1916.

(3) If the district settlement does not conform to any of the above principles, it may nevertheless operate pro tem subject to an appeal by either party to the National Tribunal.

Winston S. Churchill: draft statement

(Churchill papers: 22/113)

24 September 1926

The Miners are in our sincere belief prepared to negotiate with the Government for an immediate ending of the dispute by district settlements provided that satisfactory conditions can be arranged with the Government for the subsequent review and co-ordination of such district settlements in accordance with certain agreed national principles. Failing agreement with the Government all offers are withdrawn.

L. S. Amery: diary

(Amery papers)

24 September 1926

Winston unfolded the scheme[1] at considerable length but it soon became obvious nobody liked it very much. I championed the extreme opposite view that we ought not only not to take up the scheme but announce definitely that we did not mean to intervene in the matter again believing that the more definite our announcement the quicker the men will come in.

Winston S. Churchill to Neville Chamberlain

(Churchill papers: 18/29)

27 September 1926

My dear Neville,

Holidays and Coal have made me remiss in replying to your letter of July 30th. I sympathise with your wish and would gladly meet it if the serious objections of the Treasury could be overcome.

We feel that there is grave risk to the Exchequer in opening a new door

[1] For an immediate Parliamentary Bill to bring about compulsory arbitration on district settlements.

of principle in Grants to local authorities. From grants for the after-care of tuberculous patients to grants for home assistance of the tuberculous who have not been in sanatoria is only a step, and thence to grants for assistance to other diseased and disabled persons only another step. We do not feel the rationing device you have suggested by way of safeguard would long be effectual. 'Virement' is a useful process to meet an unforeseen and exceptional discrepancy, but to found a system on a 'virement' would inevitably lead to the acceptance of a principle. Pending a general grant for all local services of national importance it is surely important to maintain a clear distinction between health expenditure and public assistance.

Assistance in institutions is free from some of the objections which attach to assistance in the home. It is at any rate clearly confined within definite limits. I should be quite ready to provide the sum of money for which you ask in aid of the establishment of two or three experimental workshops and possibly a new village centre on the lines of Papworth. It is not the sum of money which is in question, nor the cause itself, but the entry by the State upon another of these slippery slopes of expenditure down which we are always sliding without any recorded instance of recovery.

Thomas Jones: diary

(*Jones papers*)

27 September 1926

11.30 went to the Treasury and read through the Chancellor's draft of the speech he was to deliver this evening in the House. He prepares most carefully, well in advance, and circulates drafts for criticism. Hurst, of the Mines Department, was to read this draft also. My chief criticism was that the Chancellor did not face up to what is sure to be the chief line of attack, namely, the omission of the national façade in the Government's offer to the men. It would be much better to anticipate LG, who is sure to make capital out of this backing out of the Government's offer in their letter to Evan Williams.

I then went to No 10 where I found the PM working at his speech. He will open the debate. I had sent him to Chequers on Saturday a chronological history of the dispute from June 1925, and his speech will just be a narrative of the main events with some comment. He had written hardly anything but proceeded to walk up and down rehearsing what he proposed to say—all very colourless and piano, and all harping on his favourite maxims about the impotence of the Government. He will leave the tale of recent negotiations to Winston, but will indicate that the Government is pretty well at the end of its tether.

I put to him the same point as I had criticised in Winston's draft, but he did not take it up. At this point Winston himself came in, and he told the PM that he proposed to use a portion of a letter which he had sent to the PM at Aix which would prove that quite early in September Winston had a clear-cut policy, and had not since seriously departed from it.

Soon after 3.0 I went down to the House and heard SB, Ramsay, LG, and Winston. The PM was hissed as he got up by the Labour Benches, and there were cries of 'What about the square deal!' The speech was a dull historical record but unprovocative. Ramsay followed and was studiously polite to Winston, and very careful to give nothing away of our private conversations. He did at one point talk of a breach of faith, but Winston quickly brushed that aside.

LG followed, plausible, conciliatory, carrying Labour with him and bringing clearly into the foreground the fact that we were asking the men to begin district negotiations without giving them any declaration of national principles in advance. One striking difference between him and Ramsay is the way in which he compels you to feel that he is speaking with his whole heart and mind with deep conviction, whereas about the Labour Leader there is always a certain hollow theatricality.

I whispered to Grigg, the Chancellor's Secretary, that Winston ought to rise at once and reply to LG but Grigg remarked 'Winston can't do that, hates doing it, he likes an interval to gather his material,' so the PM and Winston got up and went together to the Chancellor's room.

It was now about 6 pm. The Whips found it difficult to carry on the debate, and in a quarter of an hour or so Winston was back in the House, and on his feet invigorated, I surmise, by a pint of champagne. He was in splendid form, and though he had his manuscript on the table, he moved quite freely, dealing wittily with interruptions, and by imperceptible stages heightening the Government's policy in favour of the Miners, appealing to them not to turn down the offer of arbitration now made to them. In their heart of hearts the Cabinet hate this offer, and are dreadfully afraid it may be accepted. During this brilliant performance, the PM's face was turned towards the Official Gallery, and covered with one of his hands. He looked utterly wretched, much as Ramsay does when LG is on his legs.

I went to the Strangers' Room, and dined with David Davies.[1] Cook was

[1] David Davies, 1880–1944. Landed proprietor. Liberal MP for Montgomeryshire, 1906–29. Commanded the 14th Battalion, Royal Welsh Fusiliers, in France, 1915–16. Parliamentary Private Secretary to Lloyd George, 1916–22. Created Baron, 1932. Director of several colliery and railway companies. Founder and Chairman of the New Commonwealth Society.

at a neighbouring table drinking a cocktail with George Barker.[1] He came across presently, excited and expansive, shook hands with David Davies, told him that wages had been forced up in the past too rapidly in S Wales, told him that the men were quite prepared to do a deal on hours, but he hoped the Government would meet them on the point of a national agreement.

While we were talking, Winston came up, and hauled me away to his table. Cook followed, and threw his arm round Winston's neck in a most embarrassing fashion, as the dining room was full. Winston bade me get busy tomorrow with the Miners' Leaders with a view to securing their acceptance of the Government's offer. I could go some distance to meet them on the façade and on extending the scope of arbitration to include those districts working seven hours.

Winston S. Churchill to the Portuguese Ambassador[2]

(*Churchill papers: 18/29*)

27 September 1926

My dear Ambassador,

I have to thank you for your very frank and cordial letter of the 13th instant in which you have been good enough to explain your difficulties in regard to the settlement of the Portuguese war debts.

If I, on my side, cannot accept your point of view, believe me, it is not from any lack of sympathy with the Portuguese Government or from any desire to belittle their contribution to the Allied cause. We must each of us necessarily look on these questions from the different standpoints of our respective nations. I have already explained the general position which must be maintained, and it would seem that the next step is for you to formulate your revised proposals and discuss them with Sir Otto Niemeyer. It will then be possible to see better the extent of the difference which remains to be bridged: and I should be prepared to consider, with an open mind, whether any accommodation can then be found.

It is indispensable that your revised proposals should represent a substantial advance on either of the proposals you put forward last month, and that they should be formulated on the credit of Portugal and not made dependent on the Dawes Annuities. This latter condition is not one, as I had intended

---

[1] George Barker, 1858–1936. On active service for seven years, including the Zulu War of 1879 (medal and clasp). Labour MP for Abertillery, 1920–9.

[2] From 1925 to 1928 the Portuguese Ambassador in London was José Mendes Ribeiro Norton de Mattos, GCMG.

to indicate, that His Majesty's Government can accept. I trust that you will be able to fall in with this suggestion, and that some further progress will be made towards the settlement which we both desire.

Thomas Jones: diary

(*Jones papers*)

28 September 1926

I went and saw Tawney[1] at Mecklenburgh Square. I showed him the draft of the National principles. He thought they would be acceptable and that it would materially help the miners to swallow the Government's offer. We then got on the phone with Cook and made an appointment for 1.15.

I took a taxi to No 10. The Coal Committee was just ending, so I put before the Ministers present (SB, Worthy, C-L, S-M, L-F) the draft and asked for definite confirmation of Winston's instructions. With the exception of Worthy they were all alarmed. 'It was going beyond the views of Friday's Cabinet; it would suggest to the miners that the Government were most anxious to get the Tribunal accepted,' etc.

I went to the phone and cancelled my appointment with Tawney and Cook. At this moment Winston came through on the private wire from Chartwell. I told him what had taken place. He boiled up at once, called Steel-Maitland a bloody fool, said they were all afraid of the owners, that he had taken up a public position which he must maintain—he demanded another meeting of the Coal Committee to be called for 6.0 pm. This presently I fixed up with the PM and went off to lunch. . . .

4.30. Tea with Sir David Llewellyn. I put to him the same ideas of reorganising his relations with the miners of the Cambrian Companies as I had put to David Davies for the Ocean Company. But DRL thinks the suspicion and hatred are such that permanent good relations with the men are impossible. He rather counts on a very prosperous spell during which a lot of money can be made, then a moderate spell, then bad times. He regards this as an inevitable sequence in the coal trade. . . .

A few minutes before 6.0 pm I saw the Chancellor who was much quieter than on the telephone at lunch time, and it was possible to reason with him.

---

[1] Richard Henry Tawney, 1880–1962. Educated at Rugby and Balliol College, Oxford. Lecturer, author and economic historian. Member of the Executive of the Workers' Educational Association, 1905–47 (President, 1928–44). Member of the Board of Education Consultative Committee, 1912–31. Member of the Coal Industry Commission, 1919. Member of the Cotton Trade Conciliation Commission, 1936–9. Professor of Economic History at the University of London, 1931–49.

The meeting began at 6.0 pm in the PM's room. Bridgeman was there and Birkenhead, who under private pressure from Winston had been brought back from some Club in Kingston; during most of the meeting he was fast asleep.

Winston put his point: he wanted the men to be helped and guided privately; 'I don't like leaving this flapping in the wind; if we are to have legislation there must be a swift surrender and resumption of work. Force the pace, but don't force it unfairly; tell the leaders to-night that the Government's offer is our last friendly gesture, and won't be open beyond this week. Let Wilson or Jones or Gowers tell them they can have the national principles (ratio, subsistence, and minimum) put, not on the face of the Bill, but in a schedule as a guide to the Tribunal.' He produced a letter sent him on the previous day by Steel-Maitland approving of this procedure, and the Minister of Labour, who was so emphatic in his opposition this morning, was now silent, and left Bridgeman, Lane-Fox, and the others to oppose the Chancellor.

Winston insisted that he was suggesting nothing which had not been publicly offered, but he was gradually worn down in the course of over an hour's discussion, especially when it became clear that the declaration of national principles, to which his colleagues were now willing to assent, were so platitudinous as to be futile. He himself would have put a specific figure for the national minimum in the Bill, while allowing variations in exceptional districts, but this frightened the others.

The PM by way of compromise suggested that none of us Civil Servants should seek out the miners' leaders, but if they came to us we should be free to give them information. Towards the end, Birkenhead woke up and as the discussion was still very much at the point where he had left it when he fell asleep, he had only to listen for a minute, and then join in. 'Cook and Smith,' he said, 'have treated us very badly. We ought not to go further than we have gone. Don't let us go to them, let them come to us,' and that was the finding of the Committee.

George Lane-Fox to Lord Irwin

(*Irwin papers*)

29 September 1926

Most of our party dislike Government interference and believe that Winston had started a new and unnecessary stage of interference, and were not at all cordial to him. . . .

Then Winston, who had been doing his best to persuade us of the Coal Committee just before to do a bit more negotiations, wound up the debate in a most unexpected speech, hitting Macdonald and LG hard, urging the house to get down to realities and reminding them that the offer which the Government have made that if the men will go back to work in provisional district agreement, they shall be allowed an appeal to an arbitration tribunal, was not open for more than two or three days, and that they must decide on that at once or expect nothing more.

It has been very necessary to bring the dispute really to a point and this has done it. Our people were very restless.

Winston S. Churchill to Clementine Churchill
(*Spencer-Churchill papers*)

30 September 1926   Chartwell Manor

Beloved,

I telegraphed to poor Ettie & got the enclosed from Willie.[1] What a tragic fate pursues these people—so equipped for a pleasant life! Poor Ivo— his head was not his strongest point.

Mary & Sarah are both well & send you their love.

I have had rather a crisis with the dam & vy strong measures have had to be taken to correct percolation. These are now succeeding. We must start yr garden on yr return. When will that be? I do hope you will be home for Sunday—I am not asking anyone in the hopes you will be here. The weather today has been divine. It has been a lovely autumn, I do not remember such another.

How I have enjoyed my weeks here. But for Coal I shd have had unbroken holiday. Never move from home. Much love to Diana.

                                    Always yr loving & devoted husband
                                                        Winston
                    [Drawing of a pig]

PS. The car will meet you at Dover.

---

[1] News of the motor accident to Ivo Grenfell. William Henry Grenfell (later 1st Baron Desborough) had married Ethel Anne Priscilla Fane (known as 'Ettie'). Of their three sons and two daughters, their son Julian was killed in action at Ypres in May 1915; their son Gerald was killed in action in Flanders in July 1915; and their third son, Ivo, died on 8 October 1926, as a result of this motor accident, a month after his 28th birthday.

October 1926

Cabinet Coal Committee: minutes

(Churchill papers: 22/117)

5 October 1926   10 Downing Street
6 pm

THE CHANCELLOR OF THE EXCHEQUER urged that, in view of recent developments, the Miners' Federation should be informed forthwith that, in the absence of acceptance within, say, 48 hours, of the Government's offer of the 17th September, the offer would be withdrawn. He would enter into no discussions of detail unless the Federation were prepared to accept the offer in principle and without qualification.

Robert Boothby to Winston S. Churchill

(Churchill papers: 18/28)

9 October 1926   Carlton Club
Private

Dear Mr Churchill,

I must apologise for writing to you. But I am so troubled about the present trend of affairs that I would beg you to consider one or two aspects of the situation as they have struck me of late in Scotland. We are losing ground at a rate that is alarming, and the reason is not far to seek.

It is the impression, growing every day, that the Government has now divested itself of all responsibility for the conduct of our national industries in the interests of the country as a whole; that it has capitulated to the demands of one of the parties engaged in industry, and is now preparing legislative action at their behest, in order to compass the destruction of the other. In short that, despite the promise of the first months, it has become what the people of Scotland have never tolerated, and will never tolerate— a Government of reaction.

You know far better than I do, the mind of the average Scottish elector when it is not confused by side issues. It is imbued with the spirit of true Liberalism. At the last election thousands of life-long members of the Liberal Party voted for us for the first time. There are also those 'wise men who gaze without self-deception at the failings and follies of both parties; of brave and earnest men who find in neither faction fair scope for the effort that is in them; of 'poor men' who increasingly doubt the sincerity of party philanthropy'.[1] They, too, voted for us.

It would be difficult to exaggerate the effect of your vigorous intervention in the mining dispute last month upon the average moderate-minded person in Scotland; or the disappointment which attended the failure of your efforts. There are many who consider (I can really answer for this) that at the time you wrote to the Prime Minister the letter which you quoted in the House of Commons, you were resolved to go forward and to compel the owners (not necessarily the Mining Association) to meet the executive of the Federation, using, if necessary, the threat of suspension of the Eight Hours Act; but that you subsequently succumbed to pressure from many quarters.

Moreover the miners leaders assert in speech after speech that you gave them positive assurances that if they made such an offer as their last one 'the whole force and authority of His Majesty's Government' would be brought into action in their support. This has never been publicly contradicted.

To put it quite frankly, there is a widespread feeling even amongst those who most strongly disapprove of the policy and performances of the Miners Federation, that you made a great attempt to obtain a fair and reasonable peace in the interests of the nation; that the miners went a long way to meet you; but that the owners, supported by a section of the Conservative Party, contemptuously declined even to negotiate, and that you did not feel yourself strong enough to hold on the right course. Great hope has been replaced by great disillusionment.

Imagine the effect, in such a situation of Hopkinson's article in the 'English Review'. He points out that the owners have been following, from the start, a clearly defined policy designed not merely from the point of view of the interests of the industry, but 'after careful consideration of the national interests involved'. He accuses the Conservative Party of being prepared to 'tear the Constitution to shreds in order to induce a few more voters to support its candidates' and refers to the 'folly and ambition of all politicians'.

---

[1] A quotation from the conclusion of Churchill's own book, *Lord Randolph Churchill*, first published in 1906. Churchill's final sentence had continued: 'It was to that England that Lord Randolph Churchill appealed; it was that England he so nearly won; it is by that England he will be justly judged.'

He accuses you personally of hatching 'plots' and of deliberate falsehood. Finally, at the conclusion of an article which, for callous cynicism and open defiance not only of the Government but of democracy itself, exceeds anything that Cook has ever imagined, he states that the present policy of the owners, for which he is largely responsible, is 'to make the position of interfering politicians so unpleasant that they will for the future think twice before they meddle with the basic industries of the country'. The calm cheek of it. Who are the owners that they should decide what is in the national interests, in opposition to the Government and the elected representatives of the people?

Hopkinson does not believe in democracy. But the Scottish people do. And they are not prepared to allow themselves to be insulted, and their prosperity wrecked, by a few fanatics, whether they be owners or miners.

The effect of this article has been disastrous. It proves, once and for all, that the owners have throughout treated the Government with a contempt which has at no time been accorded to it by the Federation.

Meanwhile, the miners in the exporting districts are observed doggedly awaiting their fate. Obstinate, stubborn, and stupid. Misled by their leaders, abandoned by the Government. But loyal according to their lights, peaceable, and, despite increasing hunger, resisting (in Scotland almost to a man) what is to them the temptation to return to work. Is it to be wondered at that, with the cold weather now rapidly approaching such a spectacle has excited widespread sympathy?

It is generally recognised that there are certain abuses in connexion with the Trades Unions which it is the duty of the Government to remedy, but the Scarborough conference had given rise to an uneasy feeling that a massed attack on Trade Unionism is now contemplated.

There are many good Conservatives in Scotland who do not forget the speech of Mr Whitelaw,[1] the Chairman of the LNER at the Scottish Unionist conference in Edinburgh last year, condemning any attempt at a general repeal of the Trades Disputes Act as utter folly. His warning against meddling with the political funds of the Unions was as trenchant as it was impressive, and as a result of his speech Macquisten's motion on the subject of Trades Unions was rejected by the conference.

Surely the Government will not allow itself to be stampeded by a few English Tory agents gathered together at Scarborough for the purpose of passing some idiotic resolutions about drink in clubs and corporal punishment? The vast mass of those who support the Government do not go to

---

[1] William Whitelaw, 1868–1946. Conservative MP for Perth City, 1892–5. A Director of the Forth Bridge Railway Company, and of the Bank of Scotland. Chairman of the London and North Eastern Railway Company.

conferences. Nor are their opinions to be discovered in the leading articles of the Rothermere press. But if they are inarticulate, they decide elections.

I apologise for writing at such length. My only excuse is my anxiety, and please do not think that I want a written reply.

A Scottish owner observed to me the other day 'The sooner you bloody politicians realize that there is only one tougher set of men in the country than the Miners' Federation, and that's the owners, the better.'

How, in the face of that sort of thing, and Hopkinson's article, can the Government, having placed the weapon in the hands of the owners, stand by and allow the miners to be bludgeoned and battered back, district by district?

Bludgeoned and battered they will be, in parts of Scotland at any rate. And the instruments? Longer legal hours, cold, and starvation. No. As Lord Hermiston[1] once observed 'There is a kind of decency to be obsairvit.'

If this is to be followed by legislative action calculated to convey the impression that the Conservative Party has utilised the power given to it by the electors to plunder the funds of the principal opposition party, and smash the Trade Unions, then, in Scotland at least, a terrible retribution awaits it at the polls. I cannot help concluding with a quotation which will be familiar to you.

'Labour in this modern movement has against it the prejudices of property, the resources of capital, and all the numerous forces—social, professional, and journalist—which those prejudices and resources can influence. It is our business, as Tory politicians, to uphold the Constitution. If under the Constitution as it now exists, and as we wish to see it preserved, the Labour interest finds that it can obtain its objects and secure its own advantage, then that interest will be reconciled to the Constitution, will find faith in it, and will maintain it. But if it should unfortunately occur that the Constitutional Party, to which you and I belong, are deaf to hear and slow to meet the demands of Labour, are stubborn in opposition to those demands, and are persistent in ranging themselves in unreasoning and short-sighted support of all the present rights of property and capital, the result may be that the Labour interest may identify what it will take to be defects in the Constitutional Party with the Constitution itself, and in a moment of indiscriminate impulse may use its power to sweep both away.'

---

[1] Lord Hermiston was the central figure in Robert Louis Stevenson's last, and unfinished, novel *Weir of Hermiston*. He was Lord Justice Clerk, the equivalent in Scotland of the Lord Chief Justice in England. The portrait of Lord Hermiston is widely believed to have been drawn from Lord Braxfield, who was in fact a Lord Justice Clerk, and who was known in Scotland as 'the Hanging Judge'. Robert Louis Stevenson was often seen gazing at the painting of Lord Braxfield in the Advocates Library in Edinburgh.

Written by one, who in the year 1892, regarded the Miner's Eight Hours Bill as of greater importance than 'the Monarchy, the Church, the House of Lords, or the Union'.[1]

Yours very sincerely,
Robert Boothby

Cabinet Coal Committee: minutes

(Churchill papers: 22/117)

12 October 1926   10 Downing Street
6.15 pm

THE CHANCELLOR OF THE EXCHEQUER drew attention to the serious effect on the Revenue of the continuance of the strike. Receipts from Excise and Income Tax were substantially below the budget estimates; there had also been heavy realisation of War Savings Certificates. He hoped that the coal reserve would be utilized when it was safe to do so and that representations would be made to the South Yorkshire owners to expedite their offer.

Winston S. Churchill to Robert Boothby

(Churchill papers: 18/29)

16 October 1926
Private

My dear Boothby,

Thank you so much for your letter and I am sorry not to have answered it before. The Miners get $10\frac{1}{2}$d out of every shilling of profits calculated on an agreed basis. If this is not good enough for them, they ought to find something else to do. There are twelve hundred thousand living on the same coal-output which sustained a million twenty years ago. There are too many miners. In trying to divide work they have divided wages. The Eight Hours will I hope enable them gradually to reduce numbers and share the wages in a smaller circle. Such a general comb-out is much less harsh than the blotting out of whole districts on the Cook-Smith plan. Anyhow the rest of the country is not going to pay a shilling to keep the miners on an artificial level. So much for the economics.

I never promised anybody to procure a joint conference or agreement. Such a promise would be inherently impossible and absurd. I always con-

[1] The 'familiar' quotation was from a letter written by Churchill's father, Lord Randolph Churchill, to the Liberal-Unionist candidate for Tyneside, Arnold White.

templated meeting an Owners' refusal by a conditional amendment of the new Eight Hours Act. The Cabinet supported me in this. 'Twas all I got, 'twas all I asked. I told MacDonald and the Miners at the outset that that was the limit of any coercion we could put on the Owners, and that we would only do that to settle the business promptly. Subsequently the men's leaders went back on lengthening hours, and made other proposals which though a great advance did not bridge the gap.

Now I am afraid it must be fought out. These people think themselves stronger than the State. But that is a mistake. There is a similar attitude among the Owners, as to which I share your feelings; but after all the $10\frac{1}{2}$d in the shilling is a pretty considerable fact.

As to Trade Union Law, I do not feel that concessions—contrary to good principles but made out of compassion to working men in days when Trade Unions were purely industrial bodies—apply to a gigantic political development which as we saw in the General Strike tends to challenge the constitutional foundations.

The issue is not one between Government and Opposition, but what are good laws for the community. Intimidatory picketing, privileged immunity, political levies under pain of boycott, are not—once the issue is raised—compatible with any form of good government. The General Strike constituted a direct challenge, and is a milestone in British politics.

I shall certainly not let Hopkinson's extravagances cloud the mirrors of thought. He is sour to himself for the sour purpose of being sourer to others—a melancholy regime!

I quite understand your pangs and anxieties. But don't let them draw you from a coherent view. Let me know when you are in London and we can have a talk.

Yours sincerely,
Winston S. Churchill

Winston S. Churchill to Sir Otto Niemeyer

(*Churchill papers: 18/30*)

25 October 1926

Sir O. Niemeyer to see. An early discussion of the Colwyn Cte.

FROM 'THE YOUNG DUKE' BY DISRAELI

'I look upon Pitt as the first man that ever lived,' said the third.

'What!' said the first. 'The man who worked up the National Debt to nearly eight hundred millions!'

'What of that?' said the third. 'I look upon the National Debt as the source of all our prosperity.'

'The source of all our taxes, you mean.'

'What is the harm of taxes?'

'The harm is, that you will soon have no trade; and when you have no trade, you will have no duties; and when you have no duties, you will have no dividends; and when you have no dividends, you will have no law; and then, where is your source of prosperity?' said the first.

Winston S. Churchill: Cabinet memorandum[1]

(Churchill papers: 22/103)

27 October 1926   Treasury Chambers
Most Secret
To be kept under Lock and Key

TRADE UNION LEGISLATION

I venture to submit to my colleagues the conclusions which I have gradually reached upon the necessary Trade Union legislation.

I assume that there will be general agreement with the proposals of the Lord Chancellor's Committee about (1) strikes against the community or the State; (2) 'peaceful picketing'; and (3) 'the tortious act'. I am strongly in favour of (4) compulsory ballot before a privileged strike, but I recognise the divisions of opinion on this point. But if (1), (2) and (3) are satisfactorily dealt with, the ballot question sinks into unimportance. I am, however, attracted by a suggestion which was made in the Lord Chancellor's Committee that we should set up the State machinery for Trade Union ballots and leave it open to any Trade Union to use it at a very moderate cost per member if and when they choose. Later on, when passions have cooled, it is possible they will find it of great convenience. At any rate, it is an innocent method of not entirely ignoring a subject upon which so many people are aroused.

It would be a great pity to deal by legislation with the above four questions without at the same time dealing with the political levy. This is a real and dangerous abuse, and, as we shall in any case encounter the violent hostility of the Labour Socialist Party, it is surely worth while to do our work thoroughly in the general interest. I therefore renew the suggestion which I made in February of last year of combining the reform of the political levy

[1] Circulated to the Cabinet as Cabinet paper 365 of 1926.

with a reduction at the cost of the Exchequer in Election expenses. I venture to repeat what I then wrote:—

'If we recur to the main principles, we see that we have before us two worthy objects:—

First, to liberate working men from the unfair and humiliating position of being compelled under threat of ruin and starvation to subscribe to the propagation of political principles which they detest.

Secondly, not to hinder by want of funds the less wealthy classes in the nation from using to the full their Constitutional rights and so being continually assimilated into the British Parliamentary system.

Pages can be written in favour of these objects, and they are both of them right and true to the national interest. The difficulty of our problem resides in the fact that they seem to be opposed to each other. Can they be reconciled?

Surely they can be reconciled by a very simple course which proceeds at every step along the path of sound conviction. Let us pass the Bill to liberate workmen from the thraldom of the Levy, and let us at the same time reduce the cost of Parliamentary election to all classes and all Parties by substantial grants from the Exchequer. I would suggest that in supporting the Bill we announce that a sum of, say, £300 will be paid by the Exchequer to the expenses of any candidate who polls an adequate number of votes. If there were, say, fifteen hundred candidates, this would cost £450,000. The burden to the Exchequer could be accepted. Such a boon would take the edge off every *bonâ fide* candidature in the country. It would make men of all Parties more free from unwholesome excesses in Party discipline. It would pay the greater part of the expenses of many Labour candidatures. It would gratify every Member. It would free the charge that we are anxious to obstruct the entry of Labour men to Parliament from its sting. It would supply the new fact and makeweight which we must recognise is necessary to enable us to give effect to our convictions on the main issues. The Exchequer contribution can of course be considered both in respect to method and amount.

I believe that such a combined policy would gain overwhelming support in the House and would largely cut the ground from under the feet of the Socialists in the country. The policy would be one of "fair play to the workman whatever his opinions, cheaper elections for all Parties, freedom of Members and candidates from undue reliance on Party funds".'

The Cabinet Committee which examined the question in February 1925 did not think such a proposal suitable to a Bill dealing only with the political levy, nor did they feel it would have met the House of Commons' situation.

But in a general Bill the position is surely different. The diminution in the cost of elections would be a part of a general policy and would redeem that policy from an accusation of being aimed at working class institutions. I am very anxious indeed that we should safeguard ourselves against any charge of hampering working class representation in Parliament, which is the alternative we offer to all forms of Direct Action. I beg that the matter may be reconsidered anew as a part of our general policy.

WSC

Winston S. Churchill to Sir Otto Niemeyer

(*Churchill papers: 18/30*)

28 October 1926

Your spirited note extols the salutary and even life-giving qualities of taxation in every form.[1] This is no doubt a characteristic and appropriate Treasury view; but it does not touch the points on which I wanted enlightenment, ie the effect of a reduction or increase of Income Tax upon the price of gilt edged Government stocks, with consequent reactions upon conversion possibilities. For instance, the following train of ideas has occurred to me. When the Income Tax was 6/-, the rate of interest for Government stocks was 6%. Now that we have reduced the Income Tax to 4/-, we are able to borrow at $4\frac{1}{2}$%. The Income Tax is deducted at the source from the coupons paid on the Government securities. At 4/- in the pound this is equivalent to 1% in the rate of interest. Thus at the present time the Government pays only about $3\frac{1}{2}$% for its money. As the tax is reduced the yield of the Government stocks to their owners improves, and the value of the stock rises. In fact you will see that the rise of the stock has, broadly speaking, corresponded to the reduction in the tax. It is not suggested that the relations of cause and effect are complete, but the coincidence is indisputable.[2] From this point of view it might be argued that the lowering of Income Tax by increasing the value of Government stocks (as of all other stocks) made the process of debt redemption more costly to the Government in the case of stocks which have not already reached par; and conversely that an increase in the Income Tax, depressing the prices of stocks, will at once give the Government more money to purchase its paper with and enable it to obtain that paper at a reduced value. However, there is no question of our being able to redeem by taxation

[1] P. J. Grigg wrote in the margin at this point: 'It doesn't. It says that if you have money available it is better from the point of view of conversion to use it to redeem debt than to reducing tax.'

[2] P. J. Grigg wrote in the margin at this point: 'I believe it is only a coincidence.'

to any appreciable extent.[1] We have to convert by new borrowing; and from this point of view the high price of existing Government securities and consequent low rate of interest constitutes a direct aid to conversion. Perhaps you will expatiate on these various propositions.

Your theory that taxation is no burden overlooks the argument that a very large proportion of all taxation is ultimately passed on to the mass of consumers.[2] I certainly believe that a high rate of Income Tax means that a high rate of profit is demanded by the Income Tax payers, and is in a great many instances obtained by them. Are not all money increases traceable with the burden of taxation? The charge for all services is raised to meet the extra cost of taxation by all classes of workers who have the power to pass the burden on—and they are numerous. Doctors' fees, lawyers' fees, Civil Servants' salaries and a thousand other factors—all move in a mysterious harmony with the rate of taxation.[3] In direct taxation we know that the trade always succeeds not only in passing on the tax, but in making larger profits on the basis of high taxation than on low taxation. Beer, spirits and tobacco are noteworthy instances. High taxation, whether direct or indirect, is the shelter of the middleman. The whole weight of the taxation falls with force upon the mass of the consumers. Hence the talk we hear about the 'increased cost of living' and the 'arrest or stagnation of the consuming power'.

The expression 'perishables' is misleading. Everything that is produced is consumed, and the vast proportion that is produced is consumed within the year. An active state of consumption means prosperity. The act of consumption is the realisation of prosperity. There is no prosperity in hoarding. There may be prudence, but prudence is not prosperity. National saving is the gathering of economic power by self-denial.[4] In this world of shock and change it must always be a strong feature in State policy. In an ideal State production and consumption on ever increasing scales would obviate the necessity for hoarding.[5] The consumption[6] of perishables is not injurious but beneficial. Even economically it is a proof of increasing economic productive

[1] P. J. Grigg wrote in the margin at this point: 'I think there is a point to be examined here but you have compressed so much that it is not clearly brought out & anyhow it is of a much smaller magnitude than the conversion problem.'

[2] P. J. Grigg wrote in the margin at this point: 'This isn't his theory. Everybody knows that all taxation is a burden—on somebody or something.'

[3] P. J. Grigg wrote in the margin at this point: 'I believe this is only a secondary influence. Changes in money values are much more important. (Of course indirect tax^n enters to some extent into cost of living)'.

[4] P. J. Grigg wrote in the margin at this point: 'But there is the cause of true prosperity. And anyhow saving involves spending by somebody else.'

[5] P. J. Grigg wrote in the margin at this point: 'Where does Capital come from?'

[6] P. J. Grigg wrote in the margin at this point: 'Isn't it a question of the kind of consumption?'

power, and at the same time a stimulus to future production. The Socialist error does not consist in taking the consuming power as the standard by which prosperity can be measured. In this the economist is quite right, and the Socialists for once have followed a good doctrine. Their error consists in assuming that if the consuming power is stimulated artificially by un-economic wages, the favourable reactions will follow. However, they only follow when the process grows naturally and not when it is faked.

I am startled by all this folly you have been shoving in Colwyn's mouth. It may be all right to teach Socialists to pay off the National Debt. So far as I am concerned I think a £50 million sinking fund is already excessive, and that the removal of artificial checks upon the consuming power which result from over taxation[1] will add to our economic strength more rapidly than the comparatively small increases which are recommended in the speed of amortisation.

To sum up, a reduction of taxation is the greatest economic service which a State can render to the population and the surest means of creating prosperity.[2]

---

[1] P. J. Grigg wrote in the margin at this point: 'If taxation means compulsory saving it may mean cheaper capital, increased prodⁿ & therefore increased consuming power.'

[2] On 28 October 1926 P. J. Grigg noted on Churchill's letter to Niemeyer: 'It seems to me that a whole book will be required to examine adequately the issues you have raised. There are so many q'ns of balancing the future against the present and so many secondary reactions which complicate the primary effects. I have never had time or brain enough to think through these things.'

November 1926

Winston S. Churchill: Cabinet memorandum[1]

(*Churchill papers: 22/103*)

2 November 1926
Secret
To Be Kept Under Lock and Key

THE COAL SITUATION

1. Mr Neville Chamberlain's paper (CP 362/26) shows that since the 1st May Boards of Guardians in England and Wales have borrowed, in addition to any money raised by increase of rates, over £7 millions sterling, of which £5½ millions have been supplied by the banks and £2 millions by the Exchequer—the latter only doubtfully recoverable. The advances from the Exchequer are now nearly £250,000 a week. No doubt the bulk of this money has gone to the mining districts and this is the explanation of the protraction of the dispute with consequently increasing injuries to the nation. These reliefs, turned to the best advantage by communal kitchens, enable the married miner to live upon the food of his family. No wonder the struggle continues! It is difficult to see why it should not continue indefinitely, the miners adhering to their principles while subsisting on the outdoor relief of their families and becoming gradually habituated to an indigent idleness.

2. The owners also are seeking to demonstrate 'a principle' which was not asserted when the dispute first began, viz, that there should be no national negotiations or settlement. They have even unwarrantably refused the invitation of the Government to come to a joint conference. They have invariably been wrong in their predictions about the return of the miners. A very large number of owners are heavily in debt to the banks, and now feel that the banks must carry them to the end. Therefore the incentives to settlement are on both sides simultaneously weakened.

3. Sooner or later the Government will have to face the question 'Is this the end of the story? Is there nothing for it but to go on like this week after week and month after month, keeping the process alive on the one hand

[1] Circulated to the Cabinet as Cabinet paper 368 of 1926.

and reckoning up the monthly impoverishment of the nation on the other? Is that to be the last word which the Government can speak? Or if not, for how much longer must it continue to be our position?'

4. Is it not clear that a certain point will be reached when the Government ought to say 'This thing has got to stop, and we are going to stop it immediately.' I am not for the moment examining whether that point has yet been reached. But on the assumption that the moment had come when we decided to act in that spirit, how should we act? I propose for discussion the following outline.

5.—(a) Override the owners by passing the Compulsory Arbitration Bill already submitted to the Cabinet covering all agreements in the coalfields, and set up the Arbitration Tribunal.

(b) In the meanwhile, until the arbitrations are concluded, prescribe by law the interim conditions of immediate resumption of work, to wit, not more than $7\frac{1}{2}$ hours except where men are already at work on an 8 hours basis and the wages of last April.

(c) No employer shall be allowed to open his pit in the interim period except on these conditions; nor after the arbitration except in accordance with the award. In any case where the men are willing to return on these conditions and the conditions are refused by the owners, the men to be considered as unemployed and eligible for full scale benefit. Where the employers open the pits on the prescribed terms and the men or any men refuse to return, all relief to their families to cease within one week of the passage of the Bill.

The Cabinet must balance the exertions and dangers of such a policy against the really frightful injuries to national wealth and character inherent in indefinite prolongation of the stoppage over very large portions of the coalfields.

WSC

Cabinet Standing Committee on Expenditure: minutes

(Cabinet papers: 23/53)

3 November 1926

THE CHANCELLOR OF THE EXCHEQUER, while recognising the great economies already effected within the last few years in the Service Estimates, appealed to his colleagues, in view of the very serious financial outlook, which he explained to the Cabinet, to do their utmost towards realisation of the maximum figure of £110,000,000 suggested in Cabinet 48/(26) conclusion 16. [The Chancellor of the Exchequer] asked that the

Service Departments should carry out their programmes with all convenience and speed, without at present making adjustments between this year and next, leaving to the Treasury such minor adjustments as it might be found convenient to make at the last moment.

Lord Londonderry to Winston S. Churchill

(*Churchill papers: 18/28*)

2 November 1926

My dear Winston,

I am reading your speeches with many regrets and they make it very difficult for me in my humble capacity of trying to take a part in the nation's affairs. However crudely and however stupidly, as you and the PM put it, the Owners may put their case, they are fighting Socialism and every time you attack them, you are helping Cook. Neither you nor the PM specify why they are stupid. Owners are bound to be unpopular because everybody really resents paying for anything and that really is the main reason, and has nothing to do with the present situation.

Do you suggest that Owners should offer terms which would mean running certain pits at a loss? I did this mainly for philanthropy before the strike but I do not propose to do it again and short of that, I do not know what the Owners can do.

I am afraid your prejudice was strengthened by the refusal of the Owners to join your conference. I think on the merits, they were perfectly right, but I should have done it quite differently tho' far less honestly. I should have got all the kudos of joining the conference and done nothing when I got there. That is the Lloyd-Georgian form of conference for which we are all paying heavily now.

I feel sure you know the distinction between the Association and the Federation. The association is the mouthpiece of the Districts and nothing more; it has no power of any sort and is not intended to have power because we all believe in the policy of Districts. The Federation is nothing but a Communist Central Office, with plenipotentiary powers, because they have got the best grip on their so-called followers, the grip of being able to get their money, and make them forfeit it at will. It is a very cleverly composed organisation, and a very small minority, if well organised, can wield immense power.

With the greatest respect and deference you seem to me, reading your speeches as one of the public, to forget all this and to look on the Association and the Federation as two organisations formed for the same purpose on their respective sides, with the same powers and with the same outlook on general things. This is wholly wide of the mark and still with respect, and I say it with diffidence I can assure you, you are making a great mistake if you want to come in at all, in prejudicing the public against the Owners.

You will have to fight Socialism in the very near future and the Federation is one of the powerful army corps in the field against us, controlled as an army should be, whilst we have to hope that a disorganised force which does not know how to intimidate, will stand up against the forces of Socialism. The attitude of the Labour leaders is very interesting. They see the value of the Federation and that is why they are toeing the line, as far as they possibly can no matter what they tell us in private. Russia is a standing example of what a very small minority can do, and we shall have the same struggle and no doubt we shall win, but we shall be a sorry spectacle after our victory.

We are still a Capitalist country and if we believe in it, we had best fight for our convictions, but this decrying of one set of champions of Capitalism, however unattractive the word may be, is suicidal. I write in all earnestness because I know we are dealing with vital issues, in which this controversy is only a symptom and nothing more.

The coal issue matters very little to me personally; if I was out of it to-morrow, I should have few regrets, but I know we are in a real crisis and the way to meet this crisis is by following our convictions and not subsidizing the forces of Socialism and Communism by dividing our own Army. The Coal Owners are one class of the captains of industry, and while you may not desire a victory for the owners over the men, which really is not the issue at all, we want a victory over the strongest Communistic force in the country.

You yourself have said the Coal Industry is the real essence of co-partnership and profit sharing so I ask again, what more can the Owners do?

Yours ever,
Charlie

Winston S. Churchill to Lord Londonderry
(*Churchill papers: 18/28*)

3 November 1926
Private and Personal

My dear Charlie,

You ask me what the Owners ought to have done. They ought to have obeyed the summons of His Majesty's Government to a tripartite conference. By not doing so they have done harm to their own position and still greater harm to the country. Secondly, they ought not to have aggravated the dispute by introducing, after obtaining the Mines (Eight Hours) Act, a new cause of difference in the shape of a refusal to negotiate a national agreement.

A national agreement or provision for the review and co-ordination of district settlements is indispensable and ultimately inevitable. Nothing that the Owners can do will destroy a National Federation among the Miners. All other great trades are organised nationally, and there is no body of workers more accustomed to take their guidance from a national body than the Miners. All this embarrassment and needless friction is therefore being caused for an object which will not in the end be permanently achieved.

In speaking of the Owners I am speaking of course of the Owners' representatives. Both sides are represented by their worst and most unreasonable elements and by people selected for their obstinacy and combative qualities. In my opinion they both share the discredit of leading their industry and the country into their present lamentable position.

With those parts of your letter which deal with the necessity for combatting Bolshevism I am in entire accord. But there could be no worse way of combating Bolshevism than to identify the Conservative Party and His Majesty's Government with the employers, and particularly with a body of employers like those headed by Mr Evan Williams and Sir Adam Nimmo.[1] The duty of the Government is to occupy an impartial position in the interests of the State and of the whole community. The unfortunate results of the Municipal Elections should show you the folly of trying to fight on a purely class issue.[2]

You say that the Owners are fighting Socialism. It is not the business of Coal Owners as Coal Owners to fight Socialism. If they declare it their duty, how can they blame the Miners' Federation for pursuing political ends? The business of the Coal Owners is to manage their industry successfully, to insist upon sound economic conditions as regards hours and wages, and to fight Socialism as citizens and not as owners of a particular class of property.

---

[1] Adam Nimmo, 1867–1939. Coal owner. Chairman of the Fife Coal Co Ltd. President of the Mining Association of Great Britain. Chairman of the Board of Trade Committee on the Coal Trade After the War, and a member of the Coal and Coke Supplies Committee, 1915–18. Knighted, 1918.

[2] Elections for councillors in over 300 counties and municipal boroughs of England and Wales had taken place on 1 November 1926. The Conservatives gained 18 seats, while losing 86; the Liberals gained 7, while losing 55; Labour gained 145, while losing only 8. On November 2 *The Times* called the election 'a sweeping Socialist success', attributing it to the disruptions in the coal industry and to the Labour Party's intensive campaigning. On 13 November 1926 Baldwin declared in a written message to a Conservative meeting in Scotland: 'The results of the recent municipal elections have shown that in many cases the Socialists have gained ground merely through the failure of men and women of moderate views to record their votes. The times are too serious for such a lack of civic duty to pass unnoticed.'

I may add that by far the greater part of every speech I have made in my constituency on the Coal dispute has been devoted to showing the unreasonable character of the Miners' claims and the wrongfulness of their leaders' conduct. But no one with the slightest spark of impartiality could avoid reference to the faults and errors of the other party to the dispute.

Many thanks for your letter, and I am sure you will not mind my replying to it with equal frankness and sincerity.

Yours affectionately,
W

Stenographic Notes of a Meeting between Cabinet Ministers and the Miners'
Federation[1]

(*Churchill papers: 22/125*)

5 November 1926   10 Downing Street
1.15 pm
Most Secret

MR BALDWIN: I think you know the origin of this meeting. I do not think it is a meeting which need take long, it is an awkward time of day for it, but we thought it best to suit your convenience in the matter. We have been told by the Trades Union Council this morning that you are prepared to order immediate district negotiations, subject to certain principles being satisfactory, and what I wanted to ask you was to tell us quite clearly, if you will, what those principles are so that we may consider them and see whether they can be made the basis for agreement.

MR HERBERT SMITH: We were rather waiting to hear certain principles which you were going to ask us to consider.

MR WINSTON CHURCHILL: It was not a question of who would put the suggestions forward first, it is a matter of what is at the back of your minds, so that we can consider them and see how far the Prime Minister can endorse them. If you put forward a proposal or suggestion, you must remember that after all it is your business and not ours. You surely must know what you have in your minds. It may be that what you have in your minds may not be worth going further with; on the other hand it may be worth going further with.

[1] The Ministers present were Baldwin, Churchill, Worthington-Evans, Birkenhead, Bridgeman, Steel-Maitland and Lane-Fox. The civil servants present were Sir Ernest Gowers and C. S. Hurst. The Executive Committee of the Miners' Federation was headed by Herbert Smith (the President), Tom Richards (Vice-President), W. P. Richardson (Treasurer) and A. J. Cook (Secretary). The same people were present at the second meeting, held at 4.15 pm (see pages 870–1).

MR COOK: The Chancellor of the Exchequer will remember that he put forward certain proposals when we were talking about national principles and he will remember that he put down certain national principles which in fact you knew so clearly that you embodied them in a letter to Mr Evan Williams, and therefore I gather that when you do meet our colleagues you have expressed willingness to go on with them.

MR BALDWIN: I remember those principles—the minimum and district wages.

MR RICHARDS: There is the National Board.

MR COOK: It is the letter of the 8th September.

MR CHURCHILL reads portions of this letter.

MR BALDWIN: What other point arises except those specified in the letter. You used the phrase 'safeguards', Mr Smith. What safeguards do you suggest would be satisfactory to you, because you must remember that every offer we have made up to now has been turned down, and I want to know where your mind is at the present moment in regard to that. That is a very important thing, something we can get or something we can come to some agreement upon.

MR SMITH: We do not agree that every proposal you have made has been turned down. If you people would tell us in language what your position is, as to the minimum and as regards hours, if you people could put that in black and white we should know what your proposal is.

MR CHURCHILL: I cannot understand how there can be any doubt about the option as to hours. Take district settlements if you began to negotiate on district settlements. The owners are anxious to get the men back to work and the men are anxious also to go back to work. In one particular district the men may have a distinct objection to working 8 hours but no objection to working $7\frac{1}{2}$ hours. That is a matter which the district negotiations will thrash out. The option would be exercised by the district negotiations. When you say district negotiations it does not at all mean that the employers simply say 'Here are our terms; take them or leave them'; it is intended to be a close, intimate, sustained attempt by the two parties in a district to come to an agreement, and one of the factors would be the question of hours. Some districts would take one view and other districts another. In various districts arrangements have been arrived at to work $7\frac{1}{2}$ hours or 8 hours, so it is perfectly clear there is the option.

MR SMITH: Let us get back. That is not the way to approach the thing. First there has been no agreement entered into where men have gone back to work. That is the first thing you had better disabuse your mind of. You said when the Government passed this Act, it passed it as an optional measure. It seems that your option is this, as between $7\frac{1}{2}$ hours or 8 hours, so it is going to be that they will work some extra time.

MR CHURCHILL: Not at all.

MR SMITH: Just listen to me. Your statement implies that there has got to be some extension of hours. Now, I want you to say what you mean by optional. Does it mean between 7 hours and 8 hours, or that they work 7 hours, or work $7\frac{1}{4}$ hours, or $7\frac{1}{2}$ hours, or 8 hours, because once I sign the contract there is the winding time when I go down, and winding time when I come out. It is not a factory; I cannot labour when I want.

MR CHURCHILL: The negotiations which would take place in a district would obviously fix the hours and the Miners' Representatives would be a party to that agreement as well as the Owners, and would present the best arguments they could in the district negotiations. That is what we mean by option in hours. It might be that a district negotiation would not come to an agreement at first, but later on they might agree to work 7 or 8 hours, or whatever it might be. That would be a matter to be thrashed out in the district settlement.

MR SMITH: It only goes to prove what Mr Winston Churchill was saying. He leads off that there have been various agreements made with districts. There has been none, and it is known as wrong. I want to put it that it is wrong, as I know it is wrong. That is why I say that the next thing we want to find is what you mean by the word option. That is what we want to find, what you mean by the word option.

MR CHURCHILL: It would be open to the miners in a district to bargain with the employers as to what hours they should work, not exceeding 8.

MR SMITH: Or more than 7.

MR CHURCHILL: In my opinion it is perfectly optional to say that the Miners shall not work more than 7.

MR SMITH: It is now, we are doing it now as we are out. We want a solution which will set the machinery going.

MR CHURCHILL: Have you got in mind the letter of 17th September?

MR SMITH: I have not. I have come here with an open mind, but what I have been told is that I would listen to proposals which would safeguard ——.[1] I have come. I am taking full responsibility and have come into this room now to discuss national principles with the object of district settlements with national safeguards. I cannot get away from that. I have already received national agreements if I get satisfactory safeguards. What are the satisfactory safeguards? When I know this, I can see whether we can accept or not.

[1] Left blank in the original stenographic account.

MR BALDWIN: You cannot tell us what you consider would be a satisfactory safeguard yourself.

MR SMITH: We could tell you a lot. The most important thing to do is to find what is your opinion on district settlements in your safeguards and what is your opinion on hours in your safeguards. Is it going to be a mutual agreement between us or is it to be a forced agreement between us, because if so, I want to make it quite clear that it has to be mutuality. We are on a long way if we get mutuality, if the districts can choose which they like. Now, what is clear to me is hours, I will tell you the honest truth. There need not be any question of fear on either side, because if we cannot get to an agreement neither side will be committed. If we do not settle, I have the right to ——[1] or be shot at.

MR WINSTON CHURCHILL: I do not think there is any very great importance between whether we suggest some sort of draft to begin talking about or whether you should, but we thought we would take yours as you would naturally know the importance you attach to different points. If you feel that is open to very grave difficulty, we might talk among ourselves and offer you something that makes a basis for us to begin to bite at, something that is very general, and then we can go on.

MR BALDWIN: You might come back at 3 o'clock.

MR SMITH: We are at your service at any time.

*Stenographic Notes of a Meeting between Cabinet Ministers and the Miners'
Federation*

(*Churchill papers: 22/125*)

5 November 1926   10 Downing Street
4.15 pm
Most Secret

MR COOK: There is one other point. I have not heard you say a word about any co-ordinating machinery. I understood you had been consulting with your colleagues as regards co-ordination. You said something about subsequent co-ordination after agreements had been arrived at.

MR CHURCHILL: The idea was that if there had been a tribunal, supposing the Government were willing to renew their offer of a tribunal, the tribunal, when it considered an appeal from any district against a district settlement saying 'We are being treated unfairly, they have put these hours on us and wages are only so and so,' and asking 'Is that

---

[1] Left blank in the original stenographic account.

fair?' the tribunal would consider whether that was fair, and they would answer that question not only in relation to that district but they would see what the other districts round about the country were doing, and so they would be co-ordinating one with the other. That is how it is meant to work.

MR SMITH: Is that the only co-ordination you meant then? Did it not go further than that?

MR CHURCHILL: In what way do you think it went further?

MR SMITH: I should have thought you were going to co-ordinate the method of working, that is, under groups, etc.

MR CHURCHILL: That is another side of the question altogether, that is a scientific reorganisation of the industry.

MR COOK: You would not object to our raising the point about capital expenditure—anything that is a question of removing suspicion that they are putting costs down as capital expenditure?

MR CHURCHILL: I think that is a thoroughly bad point to raise. I have made some enquiries and I am told there is not very much in it. If the two parties are working on a basis that the profits are to be divided according to a certain arrangement and ascertainment, and one of the parties thinks the facts are not being clearly stated in a certain number of cases, on the face of it there is ground for examination of that, but you will remember that when it has been mentioned between us across the table I have always reminded you of the very strong body of miners Members of Parliament, and that if ever there was a question to which I am certain the House of Commons would give the closest attention it would be a well stated case claiming that the facts required the light turned on to them by some means or another so that they could be elucidated.

George Lane-Fox to Lord Irwin

(*Irwin papers*)

9 November 1926

Winston has been a great trouble all through these coal discussions. Just as his enthusiasm has let him down at the Treasury, through his determination to make figures mean what he wants them to mean, rather than what they do mean, so he deliberately ignores real difficulties and tried to find short cuts to settlement, through impossible country. He ignores that tiresome fact that the pit belongs to the owner, and says this miserable man must conform to the will of Parliament, &c, &c.

The Prime Minister sits dumb and bored while Winston makes flowery speeches to the miners, who wait until the inevitable mistake occurs and then pin him to it.

Cabinet Coal Committee: [1] *minutes*

(*Churchill papers: 22/117*)

10 November 1926   Prime Minister's Room
7 pm   House of Commons
Secret

THE CHANCELLOR OF THE EXCHEQUER observed that on the next occasion when the Committee met the Executive of the Miners' Federation the latter might say that they were not at liberty to discuss the question of hours. In this event they must be told that negotiations were at an end. If, however, as seemed probable, the Miners' Executive definitely undertook that nothing should be ruled out from the discussions, and that they had full power to negotiate on all outstanding issues including the question of hours, then the Committee should be ready to submit written proposals to the Miners' Executive and give them time to consider those proposals. There was no doubt that the proposals of the 17th September were open to serious disadvantages. For example, the tendency under those proposals would be for the owners to offer less than they were really prepared to give, so that in effect a subsequent application to the Tribunal would only result in the men obtaining what the owners would have given in the first instance had there been no appeal to the Tribunal. The 17th September plan would also have resulted in considerable uncertainty and confusion.

He therefore now proposed an arrangement which would not be open to these objections. He suggested that certain broad conditions should be laid down and that in districts where these conditions were accepted settlements based upon them should be final, and should be outside the jurisdiction of the national Tribunal. The conditions would be such as would enable from one half to three quarters of the coal industry to contract itself out of the jurisdiction of the Tribunal. In the case, however, of the export districts and of certain other districts which could not conform to the standard

[1] The Coal Committee members present were Baldwin (in the Chair), Churchill, Birkenhead, Cunliffe-Lister, Worthington-Evans, Bridgeman, Steel-Maitland and Lane-Fox. Also present were Sir Ernest Gowers, C. S. Hurst and P. J. Grigg.

conditions an appeal to the Tribunal would be given. The new proposals represented substantial concessions to the owners as compared with the 17th September proposals, gave the owners every inducement to offer good terms and did not involve the setting out of minimum conditions in the terms of settlement. Under the new proposals the industry would be freed from uncertainty, and the arrangements would be so stabilised as to secure that it could be carried on for a substantial period on sound and economic lines.

THE CHANCELLOR OF THE EXCHEQUER read to the Committee the draft memorandum of settlement; a copy of this memorandum, incorporating certain drafting alterations made by the Committee, is appended to these Minutes.

THE SECRETARY OF STATE FOR WAR informed the Committee that he had just heard that the Delegate Conference was prepared to give the Miners' Executive full powers to negotiate if the Executive desired such powers. At the moment it was doubtful whether the Executive would accept unfettered liberty of action. If it did so it would press most strongly for a national Tribunal and for the submission to that Tribunal of all questions at issue.

THE FIRST LORD OF THE ADMIRALTY was doubtful whether a national Tribunal would be likely to give the men better terms than they could obtain by appeal to the district Tribunals.

THE CHANCELLOR OF THE EXCHEQUER pointed out that in the districts the men had largely lost their power to negotiate effectively.

Winston S. Churchill: Draft Memorandum of Settlement

(Churchill papers: 22/117)

10 November 1926

(1) The Miners' Federation undertake to do all in their power to promote an immediate resumption of work by means of district settlements: no subject at present in dispute between the parties being excluded from the district negotiations.

(2) As regards the provisions of such settlements for the wages on which work is to be immediately resumed, the Owners have informed the Government that, subject to agreement on other matters, they are willing to start work for not less than the April percentages in all districts except in Northumberland, Durham and North Wales and the April subsistence wages in all districts.

(3) As regards the provisions of such settlements, for the permanent terms

of employment, any district agreement that embodies certain general principles shall be regarded as a 'standard' agreement, that is to say any agreement that contains provision for all the following matters:—

(a) A Conciliation Board with an Independent Chairman.

(b) Periodical determination of the trading results of the industry, ascertained jointly by accountants appointed by each side, with provision for test audits and the reference of any question arising therefrom to the Independent Chairman.

(c) Periodical regulation of the district percentage in accordance with the results of (b), the ratio of division of 'net proceeds' (as defined in the 1924 agreement) being not less favourable to the owners than 87:13 and not less favourable to the miners than 85:15.

(d) A minimum percentage below which the district percentage shall not fall, being fixed at or above the following figures:

(15% on standard where 7 hours are worked)
20% „   „ $7\frac{1}{2}$ „ „   „
25% „   „ 8 „ „   „

(e) Subsistence wages payable to low-paid daywagemen, to be determined in default of agreement by the Independent Chairman.

(f) A duration of at least four years, without prejudice to any agreed provision for the alteration of any of its terms within that period by District Arbitration.

(4) The Government, as soon as they are satisfied that paragraph (1) has been complied with, undertake to introduce legislation by which any district agreement, other than a 'standard' agreement may be made the subject of appeal by either side to a national arbitral authority in respect of any of the matters set out in paragraph (3). No appeal will lie as respects any 'standard' district agreement.

(5) The national arbitral authority will consist of such members of the Industrial Court (not having any connexion with the coal-mining industry) as the Minister of Labour may direct.

(6) When an agreement is made the subject of appeal to the Industrial Court, the Court may make such modifications as they think fit in it in respect of all or any of the matters set out in paragraph (3) in respect of which it does not conform to a 'standard' agreement, or may, if they think fit, confirm it.

(7) The Act giving these powers to the Industrial Court will have effect for six months only.

Winston S. Churchill: notes on the Coal Situation

(*Churchill papers: 22/113*)

11 November 1926

1. Originally to avoid the stoppage we offered, and so did the owners, to accept the Report and to take all the necessary steps to carry it out. But this offer was rejected and the stoppage began. On this all parties regained their liberty and all offers were withdrawn. A settlement on the basis of the Report is no longer possible.

2. After the stoppage had gone on for nearly four months negotiations were re-opened. The Government endeavoured to procure a three-party conference, understanding that the men were prepared to deal with hours as well as with wages. The owners however refused to consider a national settlement and to attend such a conference. The Government holding that the owners were wrong, made their offer contained in the Prime Minister's letter of September 17th to set up an arbitration Tribunal. This was the only substitute which it was in the power of the Government to offer in the absence of a willingness on the part of the owners to make a national agreement. It was an important and substantial offer but it was incontinently turned down, not on detail but in principle, and the negotiations came to an end. The men then made an offer of their own which it was quite clear would not lead to an agreement. The Government made it clear that they would not attempt to legislate unless it was certain that the dispute would be brought to an end as a result.

3. The present position. Since then there have been no negotiations or fresh proposals of any kind. No negotiations are now going on or are pending. The Government has not at present any proposals for ending the matter nationally. We have made our proposals. They have been rejected and they are now withdrawn. It is very wrong to mock people with false hopes and suggestions that negotiations are in progress or likely to be begun. There are none.

4. The Government's proposals having been rejected by the men and the men's counter proposals having been rejected by the owners as offering no means of settlement, it is still open to the men to make any new proposal that they choose, and any proposal they make will of course be examined with a sincere desire to reach an agreement. But the Government have themselves no further proposals to make. The door is always open, but our contribution is already made and we have nothing further to suggest.

5. Meanwhile the country is suffering very severely, bleeding internally. Impoverishment of the Trades Union world proceeds apace and great

injuries are done to the structure of our trade and finance. No one under-rates these.

6. On the other hand the power of the country to maintain not merely its prosperity but its life and a considerable proportion of its trade in the face of this stoppage far exceeds anything that could have been believed. The unemployment is only a quarter of a million more after six months' stoppage of a fundamental industry than it was this time last year. The exports, if you deduct coal and make allowance for the fall in prices, are very little below what they were in the corresponding months last year. Since we last met, over 100,000 miners have resumed work. The country and the Government have found no difficulty in importing, no doubt at heavy expense, nearly 1 million tons a week, and another million tons is being produced by the quarter of a million miners who are at work. From this it is clear that the power of the community to endure the great mis-fortunes which are inflicted upon it is indefinite.

7. A great many people seem to think that they would like to have both sides compelled to resume work. Let us see what that means. We have no intention of taking over the mines or becoming responsible for them in any circumstances. We are entirely opposed to allowing an act of nationalisation to be forced upon us by this method. It is not in our power to compel owners to work their pits at a loss, nor to compel miners to hew coal against their will. What then is the extreme limit to which in the last resort the Govern-ment might well be compelled to go? We could pass an Act of universal arbitration on all the conditions other than wages in the coal trade, and when the arbitration was completed we could forbid any owner to work his pit otherwise than in accordance with the awards. But that would carry with it an obligation on the part of the men to accept these awards, otherwise it is a purely one-sided process. That would mean that the continuance of any agitation or attempt to prevent men from going to work, even by peaceful picketing or persuasion of any kind, would be wrong. It would also mean that the families of men who did not go to work in accordance with the arbitration could not receive help out of any fund. That is a perfectly even-handed proposal for putting compulsion on both sides, and as both sides have been most unreasonable there are many people who would like to see that, or something like it, done. But it is obvious that this is going to lengths much greater than have ever been done before in regard to the compulsion by the State upon owners and workers and we are reluctant to do this if it can be avoided. First of all it means a further immense delay in reaching a conclusion; and in the second place it is by no means clear that such a process would be supported by the mass of labour opinion. In view of the fact that men have returned in the month and that there are many indications

that this number will steadily increase we do not feel that the facts warrant our coming forth with so drastic a policy, and it is perhaps better for the country to pay a still heavier price in its general trade and prosperity than for us to be committed to such very large inroads upon the liberty of individuals that would be involved by such a process. Obviously if it went on for ever we should have to do it. If we were satisfied that the thing were going on indefinitely, that is to say for another year, it is obvious that the Government would be forced to act. But we would not in any circumstances nationalise the mines. Something like the above would be the only way in which we could proceed. But we do not see that the situation is so desperate, and it is probably better for the general well-being of the country that the freedom on both sides should not be over-ridden.

The only source of their income is that they live on the relief given to their women and children.

Both parties have exhausted every credit resource at their disposal. A very large proportion of the mines are mortgaged to the Banks and really do not belong to their owners. Every form of trade union thrift has been disorganised.

Frederick Guest to Winston S. Churchill

(*Churchill papers: 2/147*)

11 November 1926
Private and Confidential

Dear Winston,

I must send you a piece of news that has come to me through my Agent in Bristol. He attended an open-air Socialist Meeting where the coal question was being discussed and the speaker, by no means an irresponsible person, having twice been a Labour Parliamentary candidate, told his audience that if only the matter had been left in your hands some weeks ago it would have been settled and the men would have had a square deal.

I think this is good hearing from such a source and is likely to be an indication of a much wider and similar feeling in the country.

Yrs
Freddie

Winston S. Churchill to Sir Roger Keyes

(*Churchill papers: 1/188*)

15 November 1926

My dear Roger,

If it would be in every way convenient I will start from here on January 4th which ought to bring me to Messina some time on the 6th, where perhaps you could pick me up. (Please not that despatch vessel of yours. I have had a terrible account from Beatty of her rolling capacities which seem to break all records short of actually turning turtle.) This would give me the 7th, 8th and 9th at Malta, and I could start with you on your cruise on the 10th and push off on the 11th or 12th to some Italian port. If this causes the slightest difficulty you have only to let me know. I could come two days earlier if it would be better for me not to start on your Athens voyage.

Now I have another favour to ask you which you need not have the slightest scruple in refusing if it does not fit. On leaving you I am going to stay in Rome for a few days to see Mussolini (while he lasts), and I am taking with me my brother Jack, whom you know, and my boy Randolph. Could you manage to receive us all three with one servant? If we went to sea I daresay Randolph could be accommodated in the gunroom. He is 15 and your Middies are very little older. I should very much like him to see the Fleet as early impressions are so important. Do not, however, hesitate, I beseech you, to say quite frankly if this would be a bore. I shall quite understand and will come in any case myself.

One other point. Congreve[1] and his lady are old friends of mine. Perhaps you could explain to him that I am coming out only to see you and the Fleet and in a purely private capacity, and that I hope he will let me come and dine with him one night. I shall write to him myself when everything is settled but perhaps you will prepare the way and see that there is no offence given.

As to Polo, of course I should love to have a game. It is awfully kind of you to offer to mount me. It would have to be a mild one as I have not played all this season. However I will arrange to have a gallop or two beforehand so as to 'calibrate' my tailor muscles. Anyhow I will bring a couple of sticks and do my best. If I expire on the ground it will at any rate be a worthy end!

---

[1] Walter Norris Congreve, 1862–1927. 2nd Lieutenant, Rifle Brigade, 1885. Married, 1890, Celia, daughter of Captain C. B. La Touche. Major, 1901. Served in South Africa, 1899–1902, when he won the Victoria Cross. Major-General, 1915. Knighted, 1917; Lieutenant-General, 1918. General Officer Commanding the Troops in Egypt and Palestine, 1921–3. C-in-C, Southern Command, 1923–4. Governor and C-in-C, Malta, 1924–7. His son won the Victoria Cross on the Somme in 1916.

Cabinet Committee: minutes

(Cabinet papers: 27/326)

15 November 1926

REPEAL OF TRADE DISPUTES ACT

CHURCHILL: He was in favour of the Lord Chancellor's proposals as he was convinced that the Government were bound to deal with a privilege which the Trade Unions had grossly abused, and which had been shown to be contrary to the public interest.[1]

PICKETING

CHURCHILL: Considered that a picket should be allowed the same liberty of persuasion as was open to a political canvasser.

Winston S. Churchill to Sir James Hawkey

(Churchill papers: 2/147)

16 November 1926

The year that is passing away has been harassing to the Government and deeply injurious to the nation. We have been confronted with the most destructive industrial disturbances which this country has experienced for generations. The fact that the Trade Unions have become the tool of the Socialist Party has brought politics into industry in a manner hitherto unknown in any country. Although many of the older Trade Union leaders are men of goodwill and patriotism, and although the majority of Trade Unionists wish to be good citizens of the country and Empire, the spirit of faction for political and Party ends pervades and dominates the Trade Union world. The extremists are able on nearly every occasion to force the majority into violent courses, to repulse all efforts at compromise and conciliation, and to levy the class war inside the industries in order to procure by an increase of misery the triumph of Socialist or Communist doctrines.

We have seen these extremists sway the miners' Councils to the general misfortune at every critical moment in the ruinous dispute now probably ending. But for that the miners could have obtained seven months ago, and without suffering to themselves or the mass of their fellow-countrymen, terms incomparably better than those which they will now have to accept.

[1] The Cabinet decided not to repeal the Trade Disputes Act, only Churchill and Lord Cave dissenting.

Even three months ago they could have had from the Government terms greatly superior to those of which their leaders have now advised acceptance. But the Moscow influence and the Moscow money have been powerful enough to drown the voice of reason and good feeling.[1]

The struggle has been fought to the bitter end. All classes have suffered much; no class has suffered more than the members of the great Trade Unions, and among them the greatest sufferers have been the miners themselves. Their credit is exhausted; their funds, like those of all the other Unions, have been dissipated; they and their homes have lost at least £100 millions of wages which they could have earned; and in the result they have gained nothing—indeed have lost much which they could easily have secured—[and there remains to them only the evil consolation of gloating on][2] and in addition there is all the harm which has been done to others. The miners ought not to have allowed themselves to be led by the nose in this shocking manner. Anyone can see the reasons for the policy of the Russian Bolsheviks. They argue that the more miserable and impoverished the working classes of Britain become, the better is the chance of a bloody revolution and general collapse which would reduce this country to the social and economical level of the Russian Republic. Besides this they saw the chance of grabbing British markets for their own coal exports. A lot of sensible British working men ought not to let themselves be used as pawns in these deep foreign intrigues.

There is the greatest difference between an industrial dispute, however lamentable, and a general strike. An industrial dispute about wages, hours, conditions, etc, in a particular industry ought to be settled in a spirit of compromise, with give and take on both sides. As you know, I have always tried to bring about a friendly settlement in industrial disputes. But a general strike is a challenge to the State, to the Constitution and to the [majesty of][3]

---

[1] Churchill wrote with authority, as he had received from January to November 1926 a series of secret reports from Special Branch, New Scotland Yard, titled 'Report on Revolutionary Organisations in the United Kingdom'. One of these reports (No. 329, dated 21 January 1926) stated that the British Communist Party had received only £1,000 during 1925 from domestic subscriptions, but that it had received £16,000 from the Moscow-based Communist International (*Churchill papers: 22/147*). Report No. 354, dated 9 September 1926, stated: 'Communist propaganda against any compromise in the mining dispute continues in the coalfields and in the Party Press' (*Churchill papers: 22/149*). Report No. 362 of 4 November 1926 stated that on October 28 A. J. Cook had telegraphed to the President of the Central Council of Trade Unions in Moscow, Dogadov, that the mining situation was 'very desperate' and asking for further financial help. On November 3 Cook had telegraphed to the Communist leader Tomsky, in Moscow: 'Last instalment one million roubles just received: note next installment to be remitted next week-end': making a total of £250,000, and bringing the total Soviet aid since the coal strike began to £1,100,000 (*Churchill papers: 22/150*).

[2] Churchill deleted this phrase in the final draft of his letter.

[3] Words deleted in the final draft.

the nation. Here there is no room for compromise. Any section of citizens, however powerful or well organised, who set themselves against the common-wealth must be made to surrender unconditionally. The loyal active response of the strongest forces in all classes of our island life, and the good arrange-ments made by the Government, enabled the first general strike in Britain to be smashed so decisively that it will not be repeated soon; and if ever it is repeated, we know now that it can certainly be smashed. There is no humiliation in a citizen who has been misled into a wrong position having to submit unconditionally to the will of the people and the law of the land. On the contrary he honours himself by submitting and by owning himself in the wrong.

I am well aware that a large number of the Trade Union leaders only acquiesced in the General Strike in order to prevent violent men taking their places and pushing things to extremes. Therefore I do not pass harsh judgment upon them. Their difficulties were enormous. But after all there has to be somewhere in every community stern and superior resisting power against an unlawful challenge to the State. After our experiences of May we know that this will not be found wanting in our country. I offer you my congratulations and thanks for the exemplary manner in which all your local services were organised in that crisis, and law and order strictly main-tained.

The power and fame of Britain and her Empire have been built up by hundreds of years of faithful and valiant efforts. We must never let them be squandered, whatever may have to be done, while life and strength remain.

The events of this year, the malicious spirit at work in the industries by which we live, the subversive doctrines of the Socialist Party, the obvious foreign influences, the recklessness and folly, the impoverishment of all which has resulted, have forced us to reconsider the privileged position of Trade Unions under the law. As long as Trade Unions confine themselves to looking after the interests of their members and of the industries out of which those members earn their wages, the issue is merely one of Labour versus Capital. But when the privileges of Trade Unions are used, not for any industrial purpose but for unconstitutional political action and to starve the public into submission, then the issue is between the citizens and the State.

It is our duty therefore to make sure that the laws of Britain are such as to do justice between all classes. Privileges are sometimes allowed to slumber and survive as long as they do not work serious public injury. When they are abused, it becomes necessary to recur to first principles and regulate matters accordingly. I can assure you that this question is now under a searching review by His Majesty's Government and that at the proper time we shall make our proposals to Parliament about them.

The British Empire, for some time to come at any rate, is not likely to be wrecked by any warlike assault from outside; it will certainly not be weakened by any Constitutional issue between the Dominions and the Mother Country or between the Dominions and each other. It is here at the heart of the Empire that the present danger threatens. The attempt to establish in this island a Socialist State in sympathy and alliance with Moscow will be resisted by whatever Constitutional means and measures may be found necessary. I am sure in such an issue we may rely with invincible confidence on the electors of West Essex.

Winston S. Churchill to Stanley Baldwin

(Baldwin papers)

16 November 1926   Treasury Chambers
Private

My dear Prime Minister,

It is my duty to write to you about Oliver Locker-Lampson. Last time when Austen spoke to you on this subject, you indicated that there was a serious allegation about the use of some funds entrusted to him for political purposes, & that this allegation was a bar to his having an appointment. But all this was entirely disproved in the conversations wh followed, & he was known to have acted with complete personal integrity.

Of course his loyalty to Austen conflicted in those days with his loyalty to you as Party Leader. But he was by no means alone in this, & you have shown a wise & generous superiority to such considerations, & have formed a Government without reference to past differences. Oliver L-L seems now to be the one exception to the act of Indemnity. This naturally distresses his friends who are now linked to you by ties wh strengthen every year. Hence these lines.

On merits his Parlt record experience & standing are thoroughly adequate. He has made several most successful H of C interventions. He has as I can testify good administrative abilities; & wd I am sure do credit to an official position.

I know this suggestion will not be particularly of relevance to you, & that many objections will be made. Nevertheless I feel bound to write to you on the subject, knowing that you will consider the matter in all its bearings.[1]

Yours vy sincerely,
Winston S. Churchill

---

[1] Although Locker-Lampson remained a Member of Parliament until 1945, he held no Government office under Baldwin, Chamberlain or Churchill. In his *Who's Who* entry he gave one of his recreations as 'refusing honours'.

Randolph Churchill to Winston S. Churchill

(*Churchill papers: 1/188*)

17 November 1926   Eton College

My dear Papa,

. . . I am so very sorry that I have been doing so badly and have disappointed you so much. But it has been very difficult to apply myself to Greek, since I know that after the end of this half I will never do anymore, and that the whole of the last two years' work has been wasted.

It is true that all four masters were displeased with me, but two of them teach me Greek, and the other two were not really annoyed with me.

But next half I shall be specialising in History and will stop learning Greek. It is true that I shall be at a slight disadvantage with the other boys in Latin, as I have done none for the last year, but I shall be able to make up on the History.

I succeeded in getting my 'white ticket' signed by all the masters, and since then I have been doing considerably better.

Have you yet read 'Some Experiences of an Irish RM'?[1] If you have, do you think you could send me some hints on it, as the paper is in about a fortnight.

Your very loving son
Randolph

George Lane-Fox to Lord Irwin

(*Irwin papers*)

18 November 1926

The miners agreed to accept a very much modified form of arbitration tribunal, not affecting any districts except those which under very exceptional circumstances had to offer less than 'standard terms'. This was what we got Winston's unfortunate efforts reduced to.

---

[1] *Some Experiences of an Irish RM*, by Edith Somerville and Martin Ross, first published in 1899. The novel gave a humorous account of Irish country life, as seen through the eyes of an Irish 'Resident Magistrate'. In 1908 Somerville and Ross published a sequel, *Further Experiences of an Irish RM*.

Winston S. Churchill to Lord Haig

(*Haig papers*)

20 November 1926   Treasury Chambers
Private

My dear Field-Marshal,

The Third Volume of my book on the war which is coming out early next
year contains two or three references to some conversations we had during
1918, and reproduces a telegram you were good enough to send me. These
references are both innocent and unessential. I however have always held
to the rule—all the more important in these days—of never printing anything
said in conversation without the permission of the speaker. I therefore send
you these passages marked in their context, and I need scarcely say that if
you have the slightest objection they will be deleted. The four chapters in
which they occur may perhaps interest you, and I dare say you will not be
discontented with them. They endeavour with other chapters to give almost
for the first time an account of the achievements of our army in 1918.
Even knowing what I did about the facts I have been astonished by my
studies.

On the other hand, as you may perhaps remember, I was a convinced
and outspoken opponent to our offensive policy at Loos, on the Somme and
at Passchendaele, and the argument of the book turns strongly against it.
Therefore, in considering whether you care to allow these personal quotations
to appear in the latter part you ought to bear in mind the criticisms of the
earlier years which are also included in the work. I need scarcely say that
these criticisms are expressed in terms appropriate to the pleasant personal
relations which have for so many years and in such varied circumstances
existed between us.

I have marked the passages in red, the publication of which your permission
is necessary.

Yours very sincerely
Winston S. Churchill

Winston S. Churchill to Lord Beaverbrook

(*Beaverbrook papers*)

23 November 1926   11 Downing Street

My dear Max,

It is very good of you to have written me such an extremely well considered criticism. Of course there are great difficulties in writing this kind

of contemporary history when one has friendly relations with the actors, and still more when one is a Minister. There is no doubt that both Jellicoe and Haig were absolutely at the top of their professions from every point of view; and apart from the erroneous doctrines which led one to fight as little, and the other as much, as possible, they played worthy parts and rendered great services and bore a noteworthy share in the eventual success. Therefore it would not be just, apart from other considerations, to frame a hard partisan indictment and omit all recognition of the other side.

I do not seek to condemn individuals, but to establish certain impersonal views upon the war by sea and land. If I can do this satisfactorily while avoiding recriminations, I am quite content. As a matter of fact my subsequent study of the war has led me to think a good deal better of Haig than I did at the time. It is absolutely certain there was no one who could have taken his place.

I did not mean the Julian Grenfell[1] quotation to be ironical. Perhaps, however, it would do better at the end of the chapter than at the beginning.

With regard to the German General Staff and the British, there was a great difference. Haig ran the war mainly with his Army Commanders. Byng, Horne, Plumer, and Rawlinson were a pretty good lot,[2] and their staff officers would never have presumed to ignore them as did the German staff officers who ran Hindenburg, the Crown Prince, Rupprecht, etc.

I quite agree about Kitchener's power and had already reduced it before I got your letter. I was rather thinking of the number of men whose fortunes he dominated than of the quality of his power over them.

After all George did give me office within a few weeks of the debate. I am sure it will always be of lasting pleasure to you to remember how much Colonel Churchill enjoyed using your car, and how freely you placed it at his disposal at a time when it was certainly his most important possession.

Yours ever
W

PS. The second instalment has just arrived.

---

[1] Julian Henry Francis Grenfell, 1888–1915. Eldest son of the 1st Baron Desborough. Lieutenant, 1st Royal Dragoons, 1910. On active service, 1914–15 (Despatches, DSO). His poem *Into Battle* was one of the first famous poems of the Great War. He was killed in action on the western front on 26 May 1915.

[2] General Sir Julian Byng commanded the 3rd Army, 1917–18; General Sir Henry Horne commanded the 1st Army, 1917–18; General Sir Herbert Plumer commanded the 2nd Army, 1915–17 and March–November 1918; and General Sir Henry Rawlinson commanded the 4th Army, 1916–18.

Sir Roger Keyes to Winston S. Churchill

(*Churchill papers: 1/188*)

23 November 1926   Admiralty House, Malta

My dear Winston,

Of course we will be delighted to see you all 3 and your man on 7th January and I will send you to an Italian Port from the lee of some Greek Island if you don't want to go as far as Athens—tho' could run you over from there through the Corinth Canal to Brindisi.

The Congreves and I have often talked over this visit of yours and they'll come here and we'll go there. Randolph can of course go and play about with the midshipmen—we've got a very good lot—but of course he will live with us—tho' he will probably have to swing in a cot on the ½ deck! Both this house and the Palace are very short of bed rooms—I can certainly put up you, Randolph and your man—but we may have to send your brother to the Palace tho' I doubt their having a room just then. Anyhow I can get one in the hotel or in one of the Staff's houses near by.

Don't bother to bring polo sticks: you will find all kinds and lengths here. What is your Hurlingham handicap?—We'll get up a four chucker match for one day after you've had a bit of practice. I expect 4 would be about enough if you haven't been playing—also where do you like playing?

About your XII chapter. I became Director of Plans on 28th Sept 1917— and my C of C head of the Planning Section of Operation Division in June 1917—then he became my Assistant. Prior to that nothing was really worked out by a proper qualified staff—Bayly's,[1] Aston's[2] Borkum plan simply wasn't *War* under modern conditions.

It is difficult to find time here at the moment to go into things very deeply but with the assistance of my COS[3] I am producing an Appreciation of your

---

[1] Lewis Bayly, 1857–1938. Entered Navy, 1870. Vice-Admiral commanding the 3rd Battle Squadron, 1913–14. Knighted, 1914. Commanded the 1st Battle Squadron, 1914–15. Commander-in-Chief of the Western Approaches, 1915–19. Admiral, 1917.

[2] George Grey Aston, 1861–1938. Entered Royal Marine Artillery, 1879. Brigadier-General, General Staff, South Africa, 1908–12. Knighted, 1913. Admiralty War Staff, 1913–14. Commanded the Marine expeditions to Ostend and Dunkirk, 1914. War Cabinet Secretariat, 1918–19. Military historian and biographer.

[3] Alfred Dudley Pickman Rogers Pound, 1877–1943. Entered Navy, 1891. Torpedo Lieutenant, 1902. Captain, 1914. Second Naval Assistant to Lord Fisher, December 1914– May 1915. Flag Captain, HMS *Colossus*, 1915–17. Took part in the Battle of Jutland. Served on the Admiralty Staff, 1917–19. Director of Plans Division, Admiralty, 1922. Chief of Staff to Sir Roger Keyes, Commander-in-Chief Mediterranean, on board HMS *Warspite*, 1925–9. Commanded the Battle Cruiser Squadron, 1929–32. Knighted, 1933. Second Sea Lord, 1932–5. Commander-in-Chief, Mediterranean, 1936–9. Admiral of the Fleet, 1939. First Sea Lord and Chief of the Naval Staff, 1939–43. He declined a peerage in 1943, on account of his lack of means. On the day before he died, Churchill personally handed him the insignia of the Order of Merit.

Chapter XII which I hope will induce you to eliminate it! I can't think who were the younger Staff Officers at the Admiralty who were working at exactly the same objectives, unless they were the young bloods we collected in 1917. We worked at every conceivable scheme and considered them in the light of Gallipoli and Western Front experience. However the letter to you on the subject is practically finished—and this is just to tell you how welcome you will be. We can fight over Chapter XII here or onboard after you have had time to study my answer.[1]

I think the quickest thing for you to do is come right through to Syracuse in the train de luxe—ferry from Messina—A destroyer can run you over in 4 or 5 hours—unless it is set free—then the much maligned Despatch vessel would bring you more comfortably.

Yours v sincerely
Roger Keyes

Winston S. Churchill to Geoffrey Dawson

('*The Times*' archive)

25 November 1926

My dear Dawson,

I had a talk with Mr Lloyd,[2] and have now been through all the extracts which he has made. Further consideration made me realise the difficulties of his task and how judicious and skilful his selections have been. I have, however, a few comments to make.

(1) I am sure that 'The Blood Test' is worth two articles and that the argument cannot possibly be done justice to within the limits of one. I have cut out the extracts which I think are necessary to sustain the interest of this important topic. I have prefixed to the first article the opening page of the book, which makes a good *lever de rideau*. You realise no doubt that this subject will be extremely controversial. The figures will be somewhat modified in their final form, but the alterations will not in the slightest degree affect the argument or the conclusion. . . .

(6) The later selections seem to make up very good articles, though here

---

[1] Churchill decided to delete altogether his proposed chapter on naval warfare after the battle of Jutland. The principal document, which he had intended to publish almost in full, was his memorandum of 7 July 1917 on Naval War Policy. This memorandum is published in full in an earlier volume of this biography, Companion Volume IV, pages 77–99.

[2] Thomas John Lloyd, 1873–1949. Assistant Editor and Dramatic Critic of the *Birmingham Gazette*; later Assistant (and acting) Editor of the *Evening Standard*. Joined the staff of *The Times*, 1918: served as a 'special writer' from 1918 to 1944. Collator of Lord Esher's memoirs.

and there the argument or narrative requires a little more amplifying. But do you not think it would be better to break the military matter by one article at least on the political or general aspects? The two chapters, 'The Intervention of the United States' and 'A Political Interlude', seem to me to be above the average interest; and I expect some of your readers would rather like a change from battle diet. Will you look through these from this point of view?

(7) Could I have a revised proof of the articles I am now sending you, on the lines I indicate? It would be easy then to adjust them to the length you find necessary.

(8) Will you also let me have back my own clean proofs which I am now sending you, on which I have marked in double red lines the additions suggested? This will enable me to mark off the passages you have selected upon the final proof which should be ready in a fortnight. Thus there will be no difficulty in your setting up from the final version, and we shall not have to make all the numerous corrections individually by reference to the latest text.

(9) I am expecting your selection from the final chapters.

Yours vy sincerely,
Winston S. Churchill

Winston S. Churchill to Lord Beaverbrook

(*Beaverbrook papers*)

27 November 1926   11 Downing Street
Private

My dear Max,

I have now had time to think over your second letter about Volume III. I am very grateful to you for the attention you have given it. Nothing can obscure the fact that I was a much less important person in this period than in the former ones. The point of view is subordinate and the amount of first-hand narrative less. This explains the effect you notice. I am glad, however, you think the style has not become slovenly.

(2) *LG.* I have added a short passage of appreciation at the end of 'A Political Interlude' which I trust will repair the deficiency you notice. I will see if I can soften the reference to him you criticise about praising Foch at the expense of the British. It is quite true and was bitterly resented by GHQ at the time.

(3) *Robertson's resignation.* I only learned the details of this from his recent

book, and was not aware that Derby had resigned. Being in France during this disturbance I only received subsequent accounts from various actors who all seemed panting from their exertions and scornful of Derby's conduct. Can you give me a short dictated note about the political aspect, so that I can amplify the paragraph accordingly and do justice to LG's determined stand?

I agree that Haig's resignation would not have overturned the Government at this moment.

(4) *The Maurice Debate.* This seems to have made no impression upon me. I may have been in Paris. All I recollect is being horrified to hear Bonar offer Asquith a judicial enquiry. I was with him on the bench and implored that this offer should be withdrawn. I think I was the one who convinced both him and LG that same afternoon. It would have been a frightful trap, and no Government ought to put up a set of judges to say whether they are liars or not. Asquith saved the situation by boggling about the enquiry, most foolishly from his point of view; and the Government were able to withdraw their offer in good style.

Certainly I must refer to the Maurice Debate.[1] Again could you give me a short note of your recollections, out of which with the published materials I can make a paragraph or two?

(5) I have from the beginning had great misgivings about the stodgy mass of 'past official documents' which figure from Chapter XII to XVI. Of course they were written with my heart's blood and explain my ideas about the war better than anything else. Your view, however, decides me. Three-quarters will go into the Appendix or be ousted altogether. Of the four chapters the 'Naval Offensive' one vanishes to the Appendix, two are compressed into one, and the fourth is shortened to half. I am indebted to you for giving me the impulse to overcome my affection for these documents. It is like tearing a bit of skin off one's thumb. Never mind, it is done. Perhaps you would glance at these chapters in their abridged form in a week or two?

Many thanks for a delightful dinner and film the other night. I am so sorry you cannot come to my birthday party.

Yours vy sincerely
Winston S.C.

---

[1] On 9 May 1918 the House of Commons had debated a public letter written by the outgoing Director of Military Operations, Major-General Sir Frederick Maurice, in which Maurice accused Lloyd George of deceiving the House about the strength of the British Army on the western front. As a result of his speech in the debate, Lloyd George was left in undisputed control of the war-making machine, while the position of the Asquith Liberals, who had attempted to gain advantage from Maurice's letter, was much weakened. Maurice himself was at once retired from the Army, and was refused both the court martial and the enquiry which he demanded.

Winston S. Churchill to Lord Beaverbrook

(*Beaverbrook papers*)

30 November 1926   11 Downing Street
Private

My dear Max,

Many thanks for your two notes. It is good of you to take so much trouble. I return you the 'Evening Standard' review written by an eminent journalist. It is very shrewd and penetrating.

I am grieved that the story should produce the impression on your mind of hostility to LG. I think now, as I said then, that he was utterly wrong about Nivelle,[1] about not stopping Passchendaele and about not reinforcing the army in the winter of 1918. He would have had far more authority over GHQ if he had not chopped and changed so much about offensives in the west. Every three or four months he was in a new mood. They at any rate were consistent in always wanting to attack. I was consistent in always trying to stop them. LG figures on both sides of the account with a contradiction which history is bound to note, because all the documents exist. In the upshot he was always wrong. He encouraged the Nivelle offensive which ended in disaster. He discouraged the final advance in 1918 which ended in success. He gave way about the prolongation of Passchendaele against a true conviction. Still there is no doubt he was much better as No 1 than anybody else. The same may be said of Haig. The truth is that Armageddon was quite beyond the compass of anybody, even including you and me.

You had better look at the passages you question in the book in its final form, as it alters a great deal under successive revisions.

I am so glad you are coming tonight.

Yours ever
W

I have made a few marks on the copy.

[1] In May 1916 General Nivelle had replaced General Pétain in command of the French troops at Verdun, and had halted the German forces within six weeks. A year later, in April 1917, with Lloyd George's strong support, Nivelle was given command of the first major offensive of 1917 on the western front: it was this 'Nivelle offensive' that left the French army terribly weakened, and on the verge of mutiny.

Thomas Jones: diary

(*Jones papers*)

30 November 1926

Winston has circulated a memorandum on Trade Union legislation. He wants to set up State machinery for Trade Union ballots and leave it open to any Trade Union to use it at a moderate cost whenever they choose.

He wants also to tackle the political levy, which is now a dangerous abuse. He would pass a Bill which would liberate workmen from the thraldom of the levy and at the same time reduce the cost of Parliamentary election to all classes and Parties by a Treasury grant of, say, £300 towards the expenses of every candidate who polls an adequate number of votes.

This is really a revival of a proposal he put forward in February 1925 and is meant to be fitted into the proposals of the Cave Committee on strikes, picketing, etc.

December 1926

Winston S. Churchill: private note passed to a colleague[1] in Cabinet
(*Churchill papers: 18/28*)

[1] December 1926

I do not think that it wd be right or wise to shelve legislation on

    a. General strike
    b. picketing
and c. political levy

because of whines from the Labour leaders or suggestions that they will all again be united by this sort of thing. I hope this procedure does not portend such a decision. To simplify the bill may be quite good policy. But I certainly think the essentials ought to be insisted on and fought for whatever may be said by Labour leaders. I did not express my view publicly just now because I did not wish to seem to criticise yr proposal. But I feel I ought not to fail to put it on record.

WSC

Winston S. Churchill to Sir Roger Keyes
(*Churchill papers: 1/188*)

5 December 1926

So many thanks for your letter. I will start on the 3rd and come straight through to Syracuse, as you suggest. It is a delightful prospect, and I greatly look forward to such a complete change from my grind here, and still more to fighting old battles over again in your company. I am planning to be in Rome by the 15th at latest. Much though I should like to go to Athens, I think I am better out of the Greek arena at the present time. Could you give me some outline of your cruise, so that I can drop off at a convenient moment when, it is to be hoped, the sea will be fairly flat.

[1] Possibly L. S. Amery, who wrote against (*a*) and (*b*): 'quite agree', and against (*c*): 'have not yet made up my mind'.

Stanley Baldwin to King George V

(*Baldwin papers*)

9 December 1926 House of Commons[1]

The coup de grace was delivered by Mr Churchill, who, in a winding up speech lasting forty five minutes, excelled himself. It was a debating speech, but a debating speech of such skill and power that it probably could not have been delivered by any other Member in the House. In its orderly array of arguments presented with all Mr Churchill's pugnacity and force, in its well arranged sequence of thought, and, above all, in its parliamentary strategy, it was a masterpiece of its kind.

Nothing perhaps was cleverer than the tactics adopted by Mr Churchill in order to secure a fair hearing for some of the very acid comments which he directed against his political opponents. On many occasions he created considerable amusement by prefacing such comments with a somewhat flippant warning to Members of the Opposition as to what they were to expect. It was the warning of a dentist who is about to inflict pain on his patient, and it had the effect either of putting Opposition Members into such a good frame of mind that they did not wish to interrupt, or of putting them on their metal to the extent of convincing them that interruption would be derogatory to their dignity and prestige.

Above all Mr Churchill was at times delightful in his humour, especially in his sarcasm at the expense of Mr Cook. On one occasion he referred to a statement which had been made by Mr Ramsay MacDonald to the effect that Mr Cook was incompetent. 'Whether "incompetence",' he went on to say 'is an exhaustive description of Mr Cook's attributes I will not presume to say, but I notice that the Right Honourable Gentleman let him get as far as Moscow before he uttered that word. Perhaps, if Mr Cook should, unhappily, continue his journey to Siberia, we shall have the rest of the epithet.' On another occasion he brought the House down by stating that Mr Cook had gone to Moscow, he presumed, to report progress and ask leave to strike again. These comments were, however, merely bright and flippant adornments which served to embellish a speech, which, in its destructive criticism and in the constructive ideas in regard to industrial peace, was super-excellent.

The division resulted in the very satisfactory majority of 339 to 131—figures which were greeted with loud ministerial laughter, and sent Members of the Conservative Party home with feelings of gratification not unmingled with amusement over the parliamentary tactics of the discordant Party.

[1] During a Labour motion of censure on the Government's conduct of the Coal negotiations.

Winston S. Churchill to Randolph S. Churchill

(*Randolph Churchill papers*)

13 December 1926   House of Commons

I send you herewith £2 to wind up the term, but please keep account of the money you have to give in tips and explain it to me later.

We are spending Christmas at Chartwell and I am going to take you to Malta on Jan 4. It was very disappointing to me while arranging this very interesting expedition for you to learn how little you are using your abilities and opportunities at Eton.

You will certainly not go to Oxford unless you show some aptitude and love for learning.

Many thanks for your letter on my birthday and for the cigarettes. It would give me much more pleasure to hear something creditable about you from your masters.

Your loving father,
Winston S. Churchill

Winston S. Churchill to Lord Beaverbrook

(*Beaverbrook papers*)

13 December 1926   House of Commons

My dear Max,

The Frigidaire laid beautiful ice eggs all yesterday. But even more important it reduces soda water & champagne to exactly the right level, & no dilution by ice of the latter is required. Thank you once more for installing it. It is a most welcome gift.

You will be glad to know that young Boothby whom you praised the other day is coming to me as parlty private secretary.

Looking forward to the community singing.

Yours ever
W

Sir Philip Sassoon to Winston S. Churchill
(*Churchill papers: 1/188*)

13 December 1926

My dear Winston,

You have often admired the picture by John Lewis Brown[1] of the two horsemen that hung at Trent, so I am sending it to you with my *best* wishes in the hope that you may find a corner for it at Chartwell. I am also sending the little Sargent picture wh you asked for. He painted it when he was 18!

Yrs affectionately
Philip

Lord Beaverbrook to Winston S. Churchill
(*Churchill papers: 1/188*)

17 December 1926

My dear Winston,

On Monday night I propose to look at a film at 23 St Bride Street. The name of it is 'Tell That to the Marines'. I believe it is a thrilling drama produced under the auspices of the American Government for the purpose of aiding their naval recruiting schemes. I am told it is a really great picture.

Will you and your wife come and dine and see it afterwards?[2]

Everything is all set for the Community Singing on Saturday night. I am glad to hear that Randolph is coming. I hope you will reach the Box by 8 o'clock. We dine afterwards.

Yours ever,
Max

Winston S. Churchill to Sir Roger Keyes
(*Churchill papers: 1/188*)

18 December 1926

My dear Roger,

All our plans are now made. It happens there is a magnificent Italian steamer the 'Hesperia', leaving Genoa on the afternoon of the 6th which reaches Syracuse at 7 am on the 8th. This is far more convenient for us than

---

[1] John Lewis Brown, 1829–90. A painter and engraver, he lived for most of his life in Paris. He was best known for his military and sporting scenes.
[2] P. J. Grigg noted on this letter: 'Answered Yes for C of E. No for Mrs Ch.'

the train journey. It avoids a delay of 24 hours in Rome and is, therefore, actually quicker as well as more comfortable, and gives us five hours in Naples during the best of the 7th. If you can pick us up in Syracuse Harbour on the morning of the 8th we could arrive in Malta by lunch.

If you want me to play a game of Polo that afternoon, I shall be quite ready to do so without a preliminary 'knock up'. I thought it might be inconvenient playing on Monday as you state the Fleet would probably be sailing that day. You must realise I am very bad at Polo. I think my latest handicap was 2.

I telegraphed to you to-day to let you know the exact date and hour of arrival.

So many thanks for your searching criticism of my Borkum plan. It has proved fatal to the enclosing of the chapter in any form, which is probably a good thing. I am bringing your paper out and will try to argue the matter with you. I agree that the 'slipping round the edges' point is very hard for me to meet.

Looking forward very much to seeing you both,

I am,

Winston S. Churchill to Lord Haig

(*Haig papers*)

18 December 1926   Treasury Chambers
Private

My dear Field-Marshal,

Many thanks for all the notes that you have sent me. I am in many cases altering the text to bring it into accordance with the facts you adduce. I am very glad you are agreeable to the publication in fac-simile of your celebrated Order. I will certainly have 100, or as many more as you like, pulled off for you. I think you will find they will be greatly sought after among the ex-service men. It will be quite easy to make more if necessary later on. The expense is inappreciable.

Philip[1] told me you wished for some information about the application of Death Duties. I am looking into this and will let you know.

With all good wishes for Christmas and the New Year. Believe me,

Yours sincerely,
Winston S. Churchill

[1] Sir Philip Sassoon, who had been Private Secretary to Sir Douglas Haig from 1914 to 1918.

A. C. Sheepshanks to Winston S. Churchill

(*Churchill papers: 1/88*)

[19] December 1926   Eton College

Dear Mr Churchill,

I enclose Randolph's reports and trials marks.

The reports are of the usual type, too little concentration, and too much chatter. I am not going to repeat what I have already said and written on these two faults—I am glad to read Whitfield's[1] remarks about the History—This augurs well for next Half.

I have been trying to persuade him not to be so obstinate, and to make him realise that it is essential sometimes to believe that the other person is right although he holds an opinion diametrically opposed to his own. He will never persuade himself that he is wrong, and this becomes quite intolerable for everyone.

He has done creditably in Trials and obviously worked well at the revision.

I hope for good results next Half.

Yrs sincerely
A. C. Sheepshanks

I am glad he has been elected to the Debate.

William Bridgeman to Winston S. Churchill

(*Churchill papers: 18/32*)

19 December 1926
Private

My dear Winston,

In sending you my best wishes for Christmas, I hope my card may remind you of some happy days in your old haunt—the Board Room.

I do hope your throat is getting all right and that your sea trip will complete the cure. After seeing you on Friday evening I got a formal letter from the PM informing me of the conclusions of the Estimates Committee—and asking me to produce estimates cut down by 3% from last year. But

[1] Brian Whitfield, 1897–1969. A schoolmaster at St Lawrence's, Ramsgate, before the First World War. On active service, 1914–18, when he was badly gassed. Caius College, Cambridge, 1920–3 (1st Class Classical Tripos and Captain of the University Hockey Team). Taught Classics at Eton, 1923–59. According to his obituary in the Eton College Chronicle: 'he was wise and kind and a shrewd wielder of the carrot and the goad in due proportion'.

there was a saving clause which pointed out that the case of the Admiralty differed from the others in some respects.

I must say I do not think the plan of setting up an Estimates Committee which does not even hear the case of the department which is under criticism, and then pronounces an ex cathedra judgement that all that is necessary is to take up your pen & sit down quickly and write 97 per cent, is a very good one.

Some of those who sat there with you know nothing whatever about the Navy and its requirements—and the man in the street could have pronounced the same conclusion as that which these able colleagues of ours have reached —I don't suppose that any of them except you are aware that the Admiralty are faced—before beginning any cuts—with an increase of over £2 millions from retardation and automatic additions for which they are in no way responsible. This sum is more than the whole estimates of either the Pres of the B of T or B of Agr and I cannot believe they were aware of it.

I much prefer the old plan of letting the Department make its own estimates subject to the strictest injunctions for economy from the PM and then discuss them with the Chancellor of the Exchequer with a view to reducing them to the lowest possible figure—as you know & have often acknowledged I have worked like a black to cut out every superfluity, and on the other hand I know that you, while striving hard to do your duty as Chancellor, understood the Admiralty's difficulties, and approach them with sympathy.

I am writing to the PM to say it is absolutely impossible to reduce to the figure of £56,350,000 which he names without putting the Navy in the position of being unable to fulfil the obligations which have been imposed upon it quite properly by the Government—and that I should much prefer to continue negotiations with you—

I am working away with Murray and the Board to make reductions on the figures I first gave you, which will bring our figures (after taking a £2 millions shadow cut) down below £59 millions—and if you allow for retardation which I put at £1,400,000, for the extra week's pay £374,000, for the money taken from me & given to the United States £200,000, and for the increase in the non-effective vote for pension £240,000, that brings me nearly to his figure—But even if you allowed half of this amount it would in fact though not on paper bring me below last year's estimate which I consider a great feat.

It seems to me very hard that after we have more than fulfilled our undertaking to balance the cost of the new constructions by economies & got well below the figures which you told the Birkenhead Ctee were the most you could afford, we should only be rewarded by being asked for further reductions by people who if they have made any reductions at all have done nothing comparable with what the Admiralty have done when faced with the expenses of new constructions.

I am off home tomorrow, and wish I could go & enjoy a holiday with the knowledge that other people understood our case as well as you do.

All good wishes
Yours vy sincerely,
W. C. Bridgeman

PS. It must also be remembered that the field over which reductions are possible at all is not £50,000,000 but less than half of that—and therefore I am asked to reduce by over 6% on those votes which are capable of reduction.

Winston S. Churchill to William Bridgeman
(Churchill papers: 18/32)

22 December 1926
Private

You must make allowances for the difficulties of the Estimates Committee. The Cabinet asked the three Services to consider jointly their estimates with a view to effecting a reduction of £6 millions on last year's figure. As a result the said three Services proposed estimates showing an increase of £2 millions on last year's figure. These estimates only reached the Treasury, admittedly in a provisional form, during the second week in December. It was necessary for the Committee before dispersing for Christmas to make it quite clear that in their view we ought not to contemplate any increase in the total Service estimates over last year, and to ask the three Departments to make proposals rendering possible a 3% cut.

I think the Departments ought to make the best possible proposals for effecting this, while at the same time preserving their full right of arguing against these proposals in so far as they go beyond what is in their view advisable. The Committee of course have no power over any Department: nothing can abrogate the right of the Minister to appeal to the full Cabinet. But if we had not asked for this reduction, the whole matter would have stood over as far as the Committee was concerned till the end of January. Worthy was quite agreeable to such a request being made, and said it would help him with his Council. Sam Hoare's position is known to you. I say all this on behalf of the Committee, for whose actions I have of course a very great deal of responsibility.

But nothing in this letter need prevent or supersede discussions between you and me. The Admiralty have so often wallopped and humiliated the Treasury that the poor devil naturally attempts to get what strength and countenance it can. Nevertheless I do not think you will find me using false arguments. For instance if, owing to the Strike, you cannot spend what it was your duty to spend this year, you should obviously be credited next year with whatever monies are surrendered before the 31st of March. This will not enter into any argument between us. Whatever is surrendered will be deducted from your total of next year and treated as a simple re-issue by the Treasury. I wrote you a note that it might be £800,000. It may well be a million. For this reason I myself suggested this saving clause in the letter which the Prime Minister wrote on behalf of the Committee.

To make out a case for your being credited with the £200,000 you say we have taken from you to give to America, you ought to show: first, that it was one of the ordinary kind of windfalls which figure as appropriation-in-aid; and secondly, that you would have got it in the financial year 1927–28 but for our deal with the Yankees. The incidence of a Leap Year pay day is a good argument for the House of Commons. But in administration it ought, I think, to be balanced as far as possible by spreading, ie delaying, purchases of stores. Still it is evident that out of these factors a certain amount of elbow room can be made.

Now for a few positive suggestions. It would be of very great advantage if you found it possible to postpone the rest of your programme from October to February. I would not ask you to push any part of it out of the year, but only to begin it as late as possible in the year. This ought to give you considerable relief. I expect your Intelligence Department could give you very strong military justification, if you asked them to compare the dates apprehended for the completion of the corresponding batch of Japanese cruisers as they were reported two years ago, and their present estimated dates.

Here I am drawing a bow at a venture; but I am sure they are late and lagging. It has never been our policy to build against foreign programmes, but only against vessels which are actually under construction. If you would look up the figures you gave the Birkenhead Committee of the dates when the Japanese batch would finish construction, I am pretty sure you would find that justification now exists for taking another four or five months before beginning our corresponding quota.

> 'Build late, build fast,
> Each year better than the last.'

There is a great deal in old Fisher's wisdom. Always begin at the last possible moment. Always carry the construction out at the highest economical speed.

I was very glad to see that you were proposing a diminution of Vote A by 400. It would seem that a five or six months' retardation of the new programme for economy and the retardation of the current programme through the Strike would justify another 500 or 600 off this Vote. Personally I would stick to 100,000 which was the figure which Baldwin and I fixed five years ago and with which Beatty was then quite content. Things have not got worse in those five years. They have got better. A reduction of 1,000 in Vote A and the retardation of the whole programme for one cause or another by five or six months will, I am sure, have a beneficial effect in chilling off Japanese, and still more American, competition. It is a profound interest of Britain to keep the naval temperature low. The damnable thing is that they all want to have navies now, instead of leaving it to us who managed so well and behaved so well for a hundred years of supremacy. The smallest turn on the side of diminution and retardation will, I am sure, bring about favourable reactions.

However, as you know, I am not prepared to accept dictation from the United States; and if they attempt to bully us by threatening a large programme, I shall hope to be able to range myself with you and Beatty as to the manner in which such a threat should be dealt with. They have such a rotten cruiser outfit at the present time, compared to Japan, that they have a considerable case on merits. What I should resent is any attempt to force our hand by such a threat. Obviously the President does not want to build but only to bluff and bluster.

I was also very glad to hear you suggest skipping the 100,000 tons addition to the oil fuel reserve this year. You might very well set that against the Leap Year pay day. But cannot something be done to reduce the enormous current expenditure of oil fuel? If only 100,000 tons could be scraped off this, it would be a substantial help. And would the Fleet be any weaker or less efficient at the end of the year?

[Here let me say that you are entitled to present a quite separate account for the *extra* expense of sending vessels to China. That is *quasi* war expenditure and can quite properly be mentioned as an exceptional factor.][1]

I am sure a further overhaul of stores and retardation of the deliveries of later ammunition outfits will provide you with further relief. A retardation is an economy, for the same year never recurs and everything rolls forward. I presume you have gone all through the depot ships and shore establishments, in which such a tremendous amount of money is eaten up? There is nothing like a depot ship for eating money and men. Even the smallest tender devours men, each man costing up to £200 a year.

Dockyard economies:—Something will have to be done in view of the very searching report of that Committee.

[1] At P. J. Grigg's suggestion, Churchill deleted the sentence in square brackets.

Lastly, there are Works. I was always able to get something off them. It is always possible to make a certain number of things do for another year, and so save the capital outlay and subsequent interest on that outlay involved in their immediate replacement. The philosophy of the 'second best' must play its part in everything that is not vital. Everyone puts up with a lot in his own housekeeping, and so must great Departments. I must say the much abused Air put up with a devil of a lot, if you look at the dwellings they live in and compare them with the fine permanent barracks of the Navy and Army, particularly the Navy.

These, I think, are all the suggestions that I can make to you at this stage. I should like to have the full details of Votes 9 and 10 at your convenience during January. At present I have no means of judging detail.

Of course it is a very trying business to reduce estimates in face of the automatic non-effective increases, etc. But the resulting process of compression is really not unhealthy: and unless it took place every year, you would find a very ridiculous and dangerous situation developing, everyone making two fountain pens flow where one flew before.

From your own point of view I would certainly recommend cutting £20,000 or £30,000 a year off the Admiralty office vote. I cannot believe the present figure is justified. You always retort about the Treasury, and I wish I knew the way to deal with its continuous increase. They always reduce me to submission by threatening a falling off in the revenue and by offering definite increases in the yield of direct taxation in return for additional staff. Certainly we are collecting a much larger and a much more complicated revenue than formerly, while you are providing a much smaller, though a more scientific, Fleet.

This brings me to the end of a letter which ill requites your Christmas card and kindly wishes. Let me reciprocate them most heartily from my wife and myself, and may the country have a chance to get upon her feet next year.

Believe me

Winston S. Churchill to Lady Leslie[1]
(Shane Leslie papers)

23 December 1926   Blenheim

Dear Aunt Leonie,

Just a line to wish you a 'Merry Christmas'. I was so sorry not to come to Ireland as I was looking forward to it so much. Perhaps you are astonished

---

[1] Leonie Blanche Jerome, 1859–1943. Sister of Lady Randolph Churchill. She married Colonel John Leslie in 1884. Their younger son Norman was killed in action on 18 October 1914.

at the paper. Sunny very kindly asked me down here for the Christmas week. He is such an interesting companion and anything but the idiot I was taught to believe him to be. I went out hunting today for the first time and succeeded in getting the brush. Nothing but personal news must bore you— so, thanking you for being so kind to me while I was at Sandhurst and wishing you everything amiable.

I remain yr affectionate nephew
Winston S. Churchill

Winston S. Churchill to Sir Roger Keyes
(*Churchill papers: 1/188*)

24 December 1926

My dear Roger,

I am grieved to think I may have deranged your plans by arriving the morning of the 8th instead of the afternoon of the 6th; but the chance of a passage in the *Esperia* and of seeing Naples on the way makes the journey so much less tedious. I shall be with you (DV) in plenty of time to play on Saturday afternoon. I do not think one day's practice would do me much good; in fact it would only make one stiff. I hope to do a little hacking in the next few days, if the snow which now overlays us should permit.

The Foreign Office do not see any objection to my visiting Athens. I do not wish, however, to take part in any of your festivities there, as I should only be in the way and the Greeks would no doubt try to nobble me about their debt on which we are pressing them rather hard. I dare say you could arrange to send us on shore quietly, so that we could look at the Acropolis during the day.

About returning to Brindisi in a destroyer. (1) Are there very heavy dues to be paid going through the Corinth Canal? (2) Would the expense in oil be very serious? I have to look at these things very carefully. If the destroyer had any other mission to perform which took her over the same route, that of course would be very satisfactory. We can discuss this when we meet. After all an Admiral Commander-in-Chief has a reasonable discretion in regard to the movement of small craft.

Everything that I do will probably be the subject of a question. But a good answer could always be made, and after all I suppose it is a good thing that the Chancellor of the Exchequer should from time to time see the Fleet.

Fancy it will be more than twelve years since I have set foot on a British battleship; and I used to know them as well as I know my back garden. Actually I designed or paid for in my time all the capital ships, except the

Hood, now in commission. But this should not encourage you to ask for any new ones! They are so good, they will certainly last a great deal longer.

Alas, the twelve years have made such a gap that I cannot pick from your list with any certainty. I remember Meade[1] and Pound, and I think Franklin;[2] and surely I know Hodges.[3] But the young ones were all babies in those far off pre-war days.

Randolph is thrilled at the idea of going. We are bringing a large supply of Mothersills, so that we shall not flinch even from the Wry Neck, or is it Wyburn?

With all good wishes to your wife.

Lord Beaverbrook to Winston S. Churchill

(*Churchill papers: 1/188*)

27 December 1926

My dear Winston,

Here is a box of cigars—Good—but not the best in the world. Just the right brand for a sea journey. The cigars are better than most speeches you hear in the H of C particularly from the Front Bench.

The Community singing at Fulham Football Field today was a remarkable performance. Thirty thousand people—I should think—sang Land of Hope & Glory & God save the King with a display of patriotism which made my heart glad.

The most successful song was the old nursery rhyme 'Who killed Cock Robin'.

[1] Herbert Meade, 1875–1964 (assumed the additional name Fetherstonhaugh, 1931). Heir presumptive to the 6th Earl of Clanwilliam. Mobilization Division, Admiralty War Staff, 1912–14. On active service in the Royal Navy, 1914–18 (battle of the Heligoland Bight, 1914; Dogger Bank, 1915; Jutland, 1916). Naval Assistant to the Second Sea Lord, 1918–19. Commanded HMS *Renown*, 1921–3. Commanded the Royal Naval College, Dartmouth, 1923–5. Rear-Admiral Commanding the Destroyer Flotillas of the Mediterranean Fleet, 1926–8. Knighted, 1929. Commanded the Royal Yacht, 1931–4. Commodore of Convoys, Royal Naval Reserve, 1939–45, and Sergeant-at-Arms, House of Lords, 1939–46.

[2] Charles S. P. Franklin. Lieutenant, 1899. Naval Instructor, HMS *Cornwall* (a training cruiser for naval cadets), 1912. Instructor Captain, HMS *Warspite*, 1925–35. Retired from the Royal Navy, 1935.

[3] Michael Henry Hodges, 1874–1951. Entered the Royal Navy in 1887; on active service at the defence of Ladysmith, 1899–1900 (despatches). Naval Attaché, Paris, 1914. Principal Naval Transport Officer, Salonica, 1915–16. Commanded HMS *Indomitable*, and HMS *Renown*, Grand Fleet, 1916–18. Naval Secretary to the First Lord, 1923–5. Vice-Admiral, 1925. Knighted, 1925. Second-in-Command, Mediterranean Fleet, 1925–7. Second Sea Lord, 1927–30. Admiral, 1929. Commander-in-Chief, Atlantic Fleet, 1930–1. Retired, 1932. Flag Officer in Charge, Trinidad, 1941–2.

I am off in the morning & staying at the Carlton Hotel Cannes. I have plenty of room & if your plans are unformed I will be glad to have you & Mrs Churchill there for a few days.

With sincere & affectionate wishes for your New Year,

I am, Yours ever

Max

Winston S. Churchill to Lord Beaverbrook

(*Beaverbrook papers*)

28 December 1926   Chartwell Manor

My dear Max,

Many thanks for yr letter & the cigars to wh I will do full justice.

I am sincerely glad that the year wh is passing has been one of such pleasant relations between us. I have a vy deep regard for you and feel the full attraction of yr vivid, genial, loyal & dominating personality. I always enjoy myself in yr company & look forward to all our meetings.

The difficulty of my being in the centre of a govt to wh you have every right to be opposed, has I rejoice to think ceased to be any obstacle to our personal intimacy. Whatever differences we may have on public matters—& look at the differences I had with Fred for years—we ought to keep our friendship clear & intact.

As life flows on one does not make many new friends, or meet many people from whose society real pleasure is to be gained. It is vital to preserve & cherish those associations wh are mellowed by time & by common experiences & adventures. Some day the wheel may turn—it surely will—& political action may superimpose itself on bright companionship. In the main & on the greatest issues I expect we shd be together.

You have had wonderful success in yr eventful life while still quite young, & everything you have touched has prospered. All yr direct & finite ambitions have been attained. What lies before you now, properly understood holds I believe greater possibilities & deeper satisfactions than any you have known—even in the fierce battle-days of youth.

The best part of life lies before you: & the hardest & fiercest work. Splendid opportunities will reward the earlier risks & toils. Personally I have so far enjoyed life more every year. But I do not think that wd continue if I felt that the future was closed or cabined. I do not feel that it is—either in my own case or in yours.

There are vy great things to be done by those who reach a certain scale of comprehension & of power in their early prime. As long as health & life are ours, we must try to do them,—not to be content except with the best & truest solutions—But I am writing a tract & not the New Years' Greeting I set out to pen.

With all good wishes then for that New Year & may we get things going a little better in it.

Believe me
Your sincere friend
Winston S.C.

I am fixed up as follows: Jan 4, start. Jan 8, Malta. Jan 13, Athens. Jan 15, Rome. Jan 20, Madame Balsan. Jan 28, England, Home, & deficit. If you are still on the Riviera during the 4th week of Jan—we will foregather. If not—we will have a dinner as soon as I get back. I have got some views about Community singing. It is a vy big thing.

January 1927

Victor Cazalet: diary
(*Robert Rhodes James: 'Victor Cazalet, A Portrait'*)

2 January 1927

AT CHARTWELL

I never knew Winston in better form. He's magnificent, full of fun and talk, charming, affectionate and vivacious. We talked of the Budget, and the deficit: there will, I think be no extra taxation this year. Spender-Clay[1] was there and Professor Lindemann. I love all the children, and my god-daughter Mary is growing apace in looks and intelligence.

Winston was very much against my becoming Political Correspondent of the *Evening Standard*. He explained how life in The House would be impossible on those lines. No one would tell me anything. I saw his point and wrote off accordingly. I stayed till nearly midnight as Winston simply would not let me go.

Winston S. Churchill to Clementine Churchill
(*Spencer-Churchill papers*)

6 January 1927   Esperia

My darling one,

We are just off & I send you this line by the Fasciste. They have been saluting in their impressive manner all over the place, & the Esperia staff gave us a most cordial welcome.

I worked till 2.30 this morning & again from 8 till now at the proofs. They have all been left with the Hotel to post tomorrow (Everything is shut

---

[1] Herbert Henry Spender-Clay, 1875–1937. Educated at Eton and Sandhurst. Joined the 2nd Life Guards, 1896. On active service in South Africa, 1899–1900, and on the Western Front, 1914–18 (Military Cross, despatches three times). Lieutenant-Colonel, 1910. Conservative MP for Tonbridge from 1910 until his death. Charity Commissioner, 1923–4 and 1924–9. Privy Councillor, 1929.

today): under threats of vengeance from Mussolini if anything goes wrong. Thank God the book is finished. It is now off my mind for good or ill for ever. It will I hope secure us an easy two years without having to derange our Chartwell plans: & by that time I will think of something else.[1]

Randolph is vy well behaved, & I am looking after his health carefully. We have lovely cabins—no extra charge—the best in the ship—& the sea is as flat as a pancake. Tomorrow Naples. I wish you were here. You can always join me at Rome if you arrange with Sybil Graham.

This country gives the impression of discipline, order, good will, smiling faces. A happy strict school—or no talking among the pupils. Great changes have taken place since you & I disembarked from this ship nearly 6 years ago.[2]

I sent the nasty letter to the unsettled Bel aigles with some compunction.[3] I think you shd go to Paris two or three days before you leave for Consuelo's and find a place for Diana for *4* months.

I will write again from Naples.

Your ever devoted
W

Winston S. Churchill to Clementine Churchill
(*Spencer-Churchill papers*)

7 January 1927   Esperia
                                                 Off Naples

My darling,

I had literally to work till the last minute yesterday in order to get the proofs off before the ship sailed. But it is all done now, & I trust I shall not see its face again. So I write a few more lines to you to complete my last letter.

Butterworth told me that the Lawrence books were worth today more than £100. So will you have a leather case or box made with a lock in wh

---

[1] Volume 3 of *The World Crisis*, published on 3 March 1927, as *The World Crisis 1916–18*. Among the first printed copies which Churchill sent out was one to General Smuts, on 21 February 1927 (see page 953). Volume 4, entitled *The World Crisis: The Aftermath*, was published on 7 March 1929.

[2] On 31 March 1921 Churchill (then Secretary of State for the Colonies) and his wife had embarked on the *Esperia* at Alexandria, and sailed to Genoa. Churchill had taken the first boat possible from Egypt, hoping to reach London before a successor had been found to Austen Chamberlain, who had ceased to be Chancellor of the Exchequer. But he arrived back only after Sir Robert Horne had been chosen as Chamberlain's successor.

[3] Withdrawing his daughter Diana from an educational establishment in Paris with which she was going to stay in order to learn French.

this book can live safely without getting damaged. Also I do not think we need lend it to too many people. It is a literary curio of the first rank.[1]

The voyage has been quite smooth & we are now approaching Naples.

The Rabbit is a vy good travelling companion. He curls up in the cabin most silently & tidily. We have played a great deal of chess in wh I give him either a Queen, or two castles, or even castle, bishop & knight—& still wallop him. I am shocked to see him wear nothing under his little linen shirts, & go about without a coat on every occasion. He is *hardy*, but surely a vest is a necessity to white people. I am going to buy him some.

There is no news at all—except that Sir A. Mond's brother[2] is on board & I am bound to have a good long talk with him some time or other.

You shd ask Miss Fisher to get you a copy of my amended letter to the Bel aigles. It certainly carries the war into their camp with a vengeance. I do not expect you will have any difficulty in finding another home for Diana. I expect there is much more solid educational value in establishments with not quite such high pretensions to culture etc.

It is an immense relief to have ended my task. I am not going to think any more about it—or the mioulings that will attend its publication.

As soon as yr garden is done two of the extra men shd be got rid of, (Townshend & the tall man) & the others can stay till I come back.

Tender love my darling pussy cat

from yr ever devoted

W

Jack is clamouring for me to come and look at Vesuvius. It is erupting mildly.

---

[1] T. E. Lawrence's book *Seven Pillars of Wisdom*, published in London in 1926. Fifty years later, this book was valued at £1,900 (*Current Book Prices*, 1977 edition).

[2] Robert Ludwig Mond, 1867–1938. An industrial chemist; President of the French Society of the Chemical Industry. A Director of the South Staffordshire Mond Gas Company, the Mond Staffordshire Refining Company and the International Nickel Company of Canada. Knighted, 1932. Fellow of the Royal Society, 1938. A patron of music, the arts, and archaeology; President of the Egypt Exploration Society, Treasurer of the Palestine Exploration Fund, Honorary Treasurer of the British School of Archaeology at Jerusalem and Vice-President of the Archaeological Institute. Founder of the Infant's Hospital, Westminster (in memory of his first wife, who died in 1905, seven years after their marriage). The historian W. J. Reader wrote (*Imperial Chemical Industries, A History*, 1970) that Robert Mond was 'possessed of an easy charm which Alfred could never attain'.

Winston S. Churchill to Clementine Churchill

(*Spencer-Churchill papers*)

10 January 1927   Admiralty House
                                                              Malta

My darling,

We had a calm voyage here & all was pleasant.

The Professor who presides over the excavations of Pompei showed & explained us everything. We saw the actual earth being removed from these long buried walls. He translated all the inscriptions painted on the houses. An election for the Aedileship was in progress when the volcano intervened. The candidates' appeals remained uncancelled & unanswered for two thousand years!

It is a new pleasure to me to show the world to Randolph. He is vy well, vy good mannered & seems to take things in. It is or ought to be a wonderful experience for him. Every day something entirely novel & of fascinating interest.

We dined last night with the Congreves' and they lit up that splendid palace & armoury. The night before the Keyes's gave a dance to the fleet & garrison. Bright uniforms & quite a lot of pretty women. I met a Mrs Hastings—wife of the captain[1] of the notorious despatch vessel Bryony. She was a Miss Hozier & her mother is a niece of yr Aunt Mary! They are an extremely agreeable couple. He runs the polo for the Admiralty as well as his yacht.

Many inquiries are made after you & requests that we shd return next year together. This afternoon we go afloat in the Warspite. It is blowing half a gale, but they say the great ships do not move unpleasantly.

I got through the polo without shame or distinction & enjoyed it so much.

I have telegraphed to Sheepshanks *requesting* leave for R to return by the 22nd. Jack evidently did not want to go home before the 20th & his holidays are few & far between. Eton does not resume its regular studies till the 21st & the big boys only return on that day. I don't think any harm will be done if Sheepshanks agrees. I am sure R is getting as useful education here as there.

The house is full of the Keyes children[2] & midshipmen & all yesterday

[1] Edward G. G. Hastings, Lieutenant Royal Navy, 1909. Commander, 1925. Commanding Officer from May 1925 to October 1927 of HMS *Bryony*, a sloop of 1,290 tons in the Mediterranean Fleet. He subsequently served in the Naval Intelligence Division of the Admiralty.

[2] Geoffrey Keyes (born, 1917; killed in action in Libya, 1941; posthumous VC); Roger Keyes (born, 1919; served in the Royal Navy, 1939–45; succeeded his father as 2nd Baron in 1945); Diana (born, 1910; married, 1936, Colonel J. R. Johnson, DSO, MC); Katherine (born, 1911; married 1935, Major Peter William-Powlett, MC); and Elizabeth (born, 1915; served in the second world war with the VAD).

they played 'Bear' in wh pursuit R was an active figure. I have seen more of him in these few days than all the rest of the holidays. Evidently he is a gt success with the others.

I am planning to join Bendor at Dieppe on the 26th for a couple of days after the pig before the Cabinets begin. I have written to Baldwin hoping this will not be before Wed Feb 2. But I may have to be back on the 26 in London, if he decides otherwise.

Anyway we shall meet 21st at Eze.

We reach Allesso on the morning of the 13th & *luckily* as it happens so conveniently there is a destroyer wh has to go to Gibraltar from Athens, & this destroyer will drop us at Brindisi in time to catch the night train to Rome on the 14th. So there will be no cost to the public!

I am reading such an amusing book about George Washington wh Seymour Leslie[1] sent me. It is a real contribution to literature, if not to history. What a tough raw boned Colonial he was! The book is candid beyond audacity. I will lend it to you at Lou Seuil.

Tender love my darling & I am wondering vy much whether it will be Purrr! or only Wow! However it may be I long to see you again & kiss your dear face my sweet pussy cat.

Your devoted
W

Winston S. Churchill to Stanley Baldwin

(*Baldwin papers*)

10 January 1927

Admiralty House
Malta

My dear PM,

I have been hoping that you will not require to have a cabinet—unless for some emergency—before Wednesday Feb 2: & I am planning to return on Jan 31. If you must have it a week earlier, will you tell yr people to have me wired to on receipt of this as all my plans must be recast. I must be there when the final decision is taken about the Poor Law & the Trade Union Bills. On the whole I am in favour of going forward with the Poor Law + Block Grants, wh will be a vy big thing indeed & a landmark in Conservative social legislation. Even tho it means 7 or 8 millions a year more for whoever is at the Treasury in 1930, it is worth it from several points of view. But if you do this, then I think the Factory Bill shd be dropped for this year.

[1] Seymour William Leslie, 1889–   . Churchill's cousin. Son of Sir John and Leonie Leslie. Secretary, Queen Charlotte's Maternity Hospital. In 1964 he published *The Jerome Connection*.

Our Factory laws are the most advanced & far the most strictly enforced in Europe; & our manufacturers are certainly not the most prosperous employers in Europe. Therefore I wd advise making the Poor Law the only large constructive measure of the Session.

You will perhaps remember we had a talk about the Home Affairs Cte; & you seemed to like my suggestion that it shd be presided over in the future by a member of the House of Commons like Jack Gilmour; & also reconstituted of really trustworthy butchers. I think this is vy important. All those little Bills cost money & lose votes.

About the TU's:—My view is that we are bound to have a Bill, that we *ought* to have a Bill, even the most perfunctory will excite united Labour Opposition; that therefore we shd have a real Bill which rallies our own forces for the fight & wh when passed will have cut into the vitals of our enemies, & given them something to cry out for.

To be precise I hold most strongly that the political levy shd be included; & that to leave it out will be to discourage supporters without mitigating the anger of foes.

I do not think that arguments about—not uniting the moderates & the extremist, not blighting the alleged impending lion-lying-down-with-the-lamb performance—ought to influence action. Immense injury has been done this year to the whole country, & a deliberate assault made upon its institutions by the forces resting upon the political activity of the TUs. These activities have been unhealthily developed by privilege legislation. And the privilege in its harmful aspects shd now be removed. I am sure this is an issue wh we ought to face sternly; & that once it is dealt with the path will be clear for soothing processes. I am rather afraid this may not make you relish particularly my eagerness to be present when the issues are decided!

I agree with you vy much that the Bill shd be simple & not loaded up with nagging little points interfering with ordinary TU life. Two or three broad real applications of principle—in wh battle can be joined. I do not believe it will be a vy severe battle. These nettles are best grasped firmly.

I am having a vy interesting trip & it is a new pleasure to me to show the world to Randolph. We sail after lunch for three days exercises with the whole Fleet—sixty ships—& arrive at Athens 13th,[1] whence I go to Rome

---

[1] On January 31 Randolph Churchill wrote to Professor Lindemann: 'We reached Athens on the 13th in the morning and drove straight to the Acropolis where Papa painted. Uncle Jack and I went to inspect the Parthenon' (*Cherwell papers*). Noting Churchill's arrival in Athens, *The Times* of January 15 had reported his talks with Andreas Michalakopoulos, the Greek Foreign Minister, to whom he 'expressed his pleasure at the restoration of Parliamentary Government in Greece'. During his visit Churchill also discussed Greece's war debts to Britain.

15th (British Embassy). Roger Keyes is in gt form out here. A splendid figure & looks a boy. After 12 years it interests me greatly to revive all three topics in wh I used to dwell—& see the ships we planned in the far-off thrilling pre-war days.

They had a dance here on Sat night & I met yr daughter[1] who was looking extremely well & dancing energetically. She made many enquiries about you. To these I made suitable & satisfactory replies.

The Malta Chronicle wh is my only source of information looks vy disagreeable in its Chinese news.[2] As you know I do not set up as authority on this question, & I am glad it does not fall to me to propose a policy. We shall soon have no more cheeks to turn. I see my cock Chang Tso-Lin[3] is not yet out of the pit.

With all good wishes for the New Year.

Believe me, your sincere friend,
Winston S. Churchill

PS. Have me word sent to the Br Emb Rome about yr Cabinet plans.

Winston S. Churchill to Sir Roger Keyes

(*Keyes papers*)

16 January 1927   British Embassy
                                                   Rome

My dear Roger,

It was a vy gt pleasure to me to visit you in yr splendid command & to have such long good talks about the past & the future. I do not know when

[1] Pamela Margaret Baldwin. Born in 1897, she married in 1919 Commander Herbert Maurice Huntington-Whiteley, Royal Navy. One of their three sons, Herbert, a Captain, Royal Marines, was killed in action in France in September 1944.

[2] On 4 January 1927, a Chinese mob had stormed the British and other Foreign Concessions in Hankow. At the same time, the Royal Marines guarding the Concession area were warned that if any shots were fired at the Chinese, every foreigner in the city would be killed. Two days later, on January 6, the Royal Marines transferred control of the British Concession area to the Nationalist Chinese forces. The Nationalists, however, proved incapable of controlling the mobs, who remained on the rampage, forcing all banks and businesses to close down. Two weeks later, on January 21, the Cabinet authorized the despatch of an additional Marine battalion from Portsmouth to protect British lives and property in Hankow.

[3] Chang Tso-Lin. Born in Manchuria in about 1875. Leader of armed bands harrassing the flanks of the Russian Army during the Russo-Japanese War, 1904–5. Governor of Fengtien and Manchuria, 1914. Leader of the Manchurian rebellion against the Peking Government, 1922. Seized Peking, 1926, and assumed the title 'Generalissimo of China'. A strong opponent of Bolshevism during his rule of Peking, 1926–8. Mortally wounded by an explosion on board his train, he relinquished control of Peking on 4 June 1928, and died seventeen days later.

I have enjoyed any expedition more, & Jack & Randolph were absolutely delighted with their experiences. Nothing cd exceed yr kindness to us nor yr princely hospitality. We are also vy grateful to yr wife for her warm welcome ashore. Altogether it has been a most happy & bright page in the book of recollection. I liked also vy much to see again the ships & men, I was once proudly associated with, & to feel that they are in sure, strong & experienced hands, under leadership worthy of the finest traditions of the Fleet.

Once more thanking you, believe me,

Your sincere friend,
Winston S. Churchill

Stanley Baldwin to Winston S. Churchill
(*Churchill papers: 22/151*)

18 January 1927   10 Downing Street

My dear Winston,

In full agreement with the Malta Chronicle that the Chinese situation is very disagreeable. Fired by your statement that we ought to have a policy and recognising that we shall soon have no more cheeks to turn, and taking their courage in both hands after your refusal to set up as an authority on these matters (what a preamble!), the Cabinet therefore decided yesterday afternoon on the course of action laid down in the minutes herein enclosed. I am arranging for a special messenger to take this on at once as I find the bag for Rome does not normally leave till next Monday.

I think if you are back on the 31st that will give us time enough to discuss the sessional business. I have had a long talk with Grigg on block grants and I am clear that if the Poor Law Bill is to be our principal measure you will never have time to do that together with a long Budget. I think you should consider the possibility of postponing intricate and novel propositions until 1928 when they may be useful as material for the General Election.

We shall be bound to tackle Unemployment Relief which will need a certain amount of time and I see no prospect of avoiding a substantial amount of work in the autumn. And of course, not to take Poor Law means putting it off till the next Parliament. Ponder these things in your heart. I am looking forward keenly to hearing your account of your talk with Mussolini, tempered only with a natural regret that I shall never hear his impressions. The picture will be vivid but incomplete.

You must be having a glorious time and I rejoice to think of you flinging a loose leg around the Mediterranean littoral. I have heard indirectly that your talks at Athens have given great pleasure in the FO.

Well, I won't bore you any more. You will find a welcome awaiting you on your return.

Yours ever,
Stanley Baldwin

Winston S. Churchill to Sir Horace Hamilton

(*Churchill papers: 18/50*)

19 January 1927

I see no objection, in principle or in practice, to our eventually collecting the extra $\frac{1}{2}$% for the Jockey Club and utilising the money for the encouragement of horse breeding and the improvement of sport. But while I think this will be the final result, I entirely agree with you that we should proceed by stages and gradually, and that it is now too early for us to tamper with the tax. It is of course open to the Jockey Club to try to collect the $\frac{1}{2}$% themselves, and this is what I should in principle recommend them to do. At the same time I should advise their waiting at least one year, so that the full effects of the tax may be seen when it is in actual operation. I should be quite ready to receive a deputation on this subject in connection with the Budget deputations, and in my reply I should not go further than the sentence which immediately precedes this one.

The figures of the blood stock sales are most satisfactory and encouraging. Pray let me have some other figures showing how much revenue has been collected this year and what you now estimate the total yield this year will be; secondly how many bookmakers have registered, etc; and thirdly, any information on the general working of the tax.

There will certainly be a demand to pay the tax on winnings instead of on turnover. As this only makes a difference of about 3%, it is obvious that we could concede the point provided that the concession were attended by an improvement of sentiment. I should like to have figures worked out on this basis for my consideration, together with a statement of any difficulties that would arise in the change.

My strong inclination at present is to do absolutely nothing during the whole of the year 1927, but simply to let the tax work itself into the life of the community. Later on I should, as you know, like to legalise cash betting by correspondence and suppress with extreme rigour the street betting which exists today.

Sir Ronald Graham[1] to Austen Chamberlain

(*Austen Chamberlain papers*)

21 January 1927   British Embassy
Private & Personal   Rome

My dear Sir Austen,

Churchill's visit has been a great success, at any rate from the Italian point of view. I took him to see Mussolini and left him alone there once the ball was well going. They had another good talk at the Embassy the next night. There was much mutual appreciation. The press were a perfect nuisance and simply besieged the Embassy, while photographers dogged Churchill's every step.

In order to get rid of them Churchill said he would see them collectively on his last morning and he did so. He thought it best not to answer questions but to write out a sort of statement of the answers he would have given if questioned and to hand it to them. We translated it into Italian.

From fifty to sixty Italian, British and foreign journalists came to the Embassy and received copies. It has been reproduced textually in the Italian press but in case this has not been done in the British press I enclose a copy. Churchill dictated it, and it seemed to me extremely good as well as striking an original note. Mussolini was perfectly delighted with it,[2] but I cannot say the same as regards the Russian press representative!

---

[1] Ronald William Graham, 1870–1949. Educated at Eton. Entered the Diplomatic Service, 1892. Adviser to the Ministry of the Interior, Government of Egypt, 1910–16. Knighted, 1915. Assistant Under-Secretary, Foreign Office, 1916–19. Minister to Holland, 1919–21. Ambassador to Italy, 1921–33. Privy Councillor, 1921. British Government Director, Suez Canal Co, 1939–45.

[2] In his Press statement Churchill stressed the traditional friendship of Britain and Italy. Commenting on the personal impression which Mussolini had made on him, Churchill said: 'I could not help being charmed, like so many other people have been, by his gentle and simple bearing and by his calm, detached poise in spite of so many burdens and dangers. Secondly, anyone could see that he thought of nothing but the lasting good, as he understood it, of the Italian people, and that no lesser interest was of the slightest consequence to him.' It was, Churchill continued, 'quite absurd to suggest that the Italian Government does not stand upon a popular basis or that it is not upheld by the active and practical assent of the great masses'. No political issue could be judged 'apart from its atmosphere and environment'. As for Fascism, he continued: 'If I had been an Italian, I am sure I should have been wholeheartedly with you from the start to finish in your triumphant struggle against the bestial appetites and passions of Leninism. But in England we have not yet had to face this danger in the same deadly form. We have our own way of doing things. But that we shall succeed in grappling with Communism and choking the life out of it—of that I am absolutely sure.'

I am doing my best to rope the Italians in to our Chinese policy, but they are a little sticky over it. Although they cannot do much in the business their whole-hearted support would have a moral value, and I hope to obtain it.

Yrs v sincerely,
R. Graham

Winston S. Churchill to Stanley Baldwin

(*Churchill papers: 22/151*)

22 January 1927

Lou Sueil,
Eze

My dear PM,

It was a relief to get the Cabinet Minutes and to learn that a deplorable series of telegrams had come to an end. Short of being actually conquered, there is no evil worse than submitting to wrong and violence for fear of war. Once you take the position of not being able in any circumstances to defend your rights against the agression of some particular set of people, there is no end to the demands that will be made or to the humiliations that must be accepted.

But now that the Cabinet have as you say taken their courage in both hands, I hope that the very great but almost invariable mistake will not be made of using inadequate forces and of running risks by halves. Nothing is more likely to force the Japanese to send plenty of troops than the knowledge that England will otherwise have the largest numbers in a theatre so vital to Japan. A little manoeuvring to avoid if possible our incurring the onus of being the first to disembark troops is wise, but secondary. The important thing is to put at least *two* divisions under orders for the East, to take up the transport and go steadily ahead with the preparations; and to announce this intention to the Japanese. They will immediately respond. They cannot possibly cede the *military* preponderance in the Far East to G Britain. And after all it may not be necessary to send the later Brigades. It is so easy to stop troops and so lengthy to get them started. There is nothing so costly as inadequate forces. Must we always have to learn that lesson fresh every time?

I do not believe the Canton Army will be found very formidable. Systematic bombing of their bivouacs would probably reduce their numbers considerably. And I trust there will be no false logic and false sentiment and false humanity against using Gas.

I write this because I am so very anxious you should not get involved in *unsuccessful* military operations. These are the ones that cost the money—and the votes. There is never any harm in having more force than you need. And there will be no more political opposition to *two* Divisions than to one being sent.

On the other hand I hope the question of using Singapore as a strategic base for troops will not be decided till I come back. It has nothing to do with the present issue, and is just dragged in by Beatty. I should have thought there could hardly be a worse, more expensive, unhealthy place to keep a large garrison than Singapore. There are no barracks etc—whereas in India there is everything on a permanent footing; and what are a few more days on a voyage once transports have been fitted and troops are embarked.

I will not write now about the Block Grant and Poor Law question, because we shall meet so soon. But I hope I shall not be asked to provide several millions for a scheme which has no lasting financial advantages, and will in other ways be very unpopular. It will be better to leave it till the next Parliament.

Many thanks for your very kind remarks and wishes. You will see I had to give an interview in Rome to the journalists, but I daresay it will be found helpful. I stay here till 25th and then to Dieppe where Westminster has organised a pack of hounds to chase the wild boars of a very large forest near by—none of which I thought existed in these parts.

With every good wish,
Believe me,
Yours very sincerely,
Winston S.C.

P. J. Grigg to Winston S. Churchill

(*Churchill papers: 18/41*)

22 January 1927   Treasury Chambers

My dear Chancellor,

The pouch only arrived this morning and so there isn't much time to fulfil all your behests in time for a messenger who is to reach Eze not later than the day after tomorrow. However I will do the best I can.

The Prime Minister sent you a personal letter to Rome containing the Cabinet Minutes setting out the main decisions on China. I enclose CP's and telegrams subsequent to this and also the conclusions of a Cabinet meeting held yesterday.

You will see that we have now definitely embarked on sending very considerable Naval and Military reinforcements to China. It is quite clear that these forces will involve millions of extra money on the Fighting Services Votes, most of which will fall on next year. Is it not then rather futile to continue your discussion with Bridgeman on an entirely unreal basis? Would it not be better to wait until you return and have had time to take stock of a new situation? My own belief is that this will finally make the budgetary position unadjustable next year, and that the issue will be presented to you in the crudest possible form, viz:—substantial additions to taxation or suspension in part even of the current Baldwin sinking fund. Of course there never was such cruel luck as yours—first the coal subsidy, then the 7 months' coal strike, and now 'heavily-armed neutrality' in China.

There is nothing else to tell you except that Hurst seems to take rather a cheerful view of the progress which is being made on the Block Grants Committee. I have just received your request to hold up the Percy letter. I am glad of this because Percy is beginning to realise the attractions of the Block Grant scheme and it would be a pity to trail your coat before you have got him through that wood, and anyhow I am inclined to think that you will find his letter to you already out-of-date.

By the way, I sent to you at Eze (under cover to Madame Balsan) a letter from Niemeyer about the Conversion and also a note on your idea of reducing the nominal total (NB not the cost) of the debt by extinguishing $2\frac{1}{2}\%$ Consols.

You ought to read every word of Salisbury's report on his visit to Australia. It is magnificent! I don't think I told you (but perhaps the PM did) that I was sent for to tell the PM all about Block Grants. He seemed inclined to go on with it but was rather leaning to curtailing the legislative programme as much as possible in other directions in order to find Parliamentary time for the big reform.

This is all rather scrappy & flatulent but I am feeling rather depressed & influenza-ish.

Yours
P. J. Grigg

Winston S. Churchill to P. J. Grigg

(*Churchill papers: 18/43*)

25 January 1927   Eze

My dear Grigg,

I return on Sunday by the boat from Dieppe which reaches Newhaven at 4.40 pm. Will you order my car from Chartwell to meet me there? Aley can bring an official box with him. If you are doing nothing, it will be nice if you will come down to Chartwell on Sunday afternoon and dine and sleep, and we can talk over things and come up Monday for lunch.[1] If this suits you, please inform Chartwell.

I do not take the financial complications arising out of China very seriously. There are many ways of dealing with war expenditure. I attach great importance, however, to a special account of war expenditure being kept by the three fighting Ministries. Will you give directions about this? It must not be brought into the ordinary estimates in any way. The transport of troops, the extra cost of maintaining them abroad, the charges for the Indian Brigade, the ship movements—all must be kept entirely separate. I shall then endeavour to procure economies on some other branches of these fighting Services to ease the extra charge of war on a small scale. I think the Admiralty should give up their 100,000 tons of oil, the Army their new artillery plans, etc. Similarly we must make demands on other Departments for cuts in aid of Chinese education. Now do get busy and let me have every penny of Chinese expenditure accounted for.

I am sure the way to force the hand of the Japanese is to send plenty of British troops. The real wish of Japan is to see all British, American and European influence eliminated in the yellow world, and all their actions and advice to us will be in accord with that main end. On the other hand they will not be able to stand by idly and see England taking the lead.

You should see a copy of the letter I am sending to Worthy.

Yours vy sincerely,
Winston S. Churchill

[1] P. J. Grigg did go to Chartwell at the end of January, and again in both August and October. Among Churchill's other guests during 1927 were Professor Lindemann (April 19–23, August 12–16, October 5 and December 30–January 3), Robert Boothby (February 18–19), Venetia Montagu (March 12–13 and September 16–19), Edward Marsh (July 29–August 2 and August 26–29), the painter Neville Lewis (painting Mary Churchill's portrait, July 29–August 2 and August 5–9), Richard Sickert (August 29 and September 24–25) and Maurice Baring (September 16–19). The Christmas and New Year guests were Nellie, Giles and Esmond Romilly. Edward Marsh and Professor Lindemann both stayed over the New Year.

Winston S. Churchill to Sir Laming Worthington-Evans

(*Churchill papers: 18/43*)

25 January 1927 Eze’

My dear Worthy,

I hope the Chinese developments will in no way lead you to relax your efforts to effect a reduction in the *normal* Army estimates. I am asking that all the special Chinese expenditure shall be kept in a separate account, and you will have no difficulty in obtaining Treasury sanction for all you need. On the other hand, for that very reason and my difficulties being so great, I am sure I can count upon you to do your utmost to ease the burden in other directions.

This, however, is by the way, for my motive in writing is to urge you to send out plenty of Tanks to Shanghai. A dozen of those fast tanks we saw at Aldershot would do more to keep order in a great Chinese city than 20,000 infantry soldiers. Moreover, how are Chinese troops going to resist an attack by tanks? Unless they have really good artillerists—like the German officer who shot six tanks in succession single-handed before being killed[1]—they will be quite helpless against these vehicles.

I was very glad to see that you had carried your point about Gas. ‘Gas for Asia’ may be a phrase of great significance. But I believe you will find Tanks even more effective, both for street fighting and operations in open country. The worst thing in the world is trying to fight Chinese by mere numbers of infantrymen. Give them a dose of what you gave the Colonial Premiers and you will find there will be very little blood shed, for the great bulk will run away. I hope that firm action and *adequate forces* will lead to a peaceful solution. But if not, I beseech you at the outset of what may well be great responsibilities to use the right tackle.

I venture to make one more point. The Military are accustomed to think in Divisions. They were the bricks out of which the Western Front was built. A General of a certain rank commands a Division; it takes a certain length on the road in line of march; etc. But it does not follow at all that a Division as constituted for the Western Front is the proper unit for the defence of our interests in China. What you want is to make up a ‘Force’ for China, fitted as accurately as possible to the work you think it may have to do.

---

[1] The officer was Lieutenant Müller of the 108th Regiment. The incident took place on 20 November 1917, during the Battle of Cambrai. According to Sir Douglas Haig’s despatch of 20 February 1918: ‘Many of the hits on our tanks at Flesquières were obtained by a German artillery officer who, remaining alone at his battery, served a field gun single-handed until killed at his gun. The great bravery of this officer aroused the admiration of all ranks.’ Lieutenant Müller was the only individual German officer ever to be mentioned in British despatches.

Such a 'Force' should, I think, be stronger than an ordinary Division unit
in tanks and armoured cars and in gas units and machine gunners. Anyhow
it should not be a conventional formation. And above all, choose a good
General, for all our fortunes depend on that.

I shall be in London on Monday next.

With good wishes, believe me
Yours vy sincerely,
Winston S. Churchill

PS. I hope the right decisions have not been taken *Too Late!*[1]

Winston S. Churchill to Clementine Churchill

(*Spencer-Churchill papers*)

25 January 1927   In the train

My darling Clemmie,

Only a line to tell you how sad I feel at leaving you & how lonely: & to
send you back a kiss of deep & true love. It was sweet to hear you say I was
'the ami of yr life'. Well I know how unworthy I am to play that part &
how many are my shortcomings. You must make many allowances my
darling & above all do not lose heart over trifles. At the present moment
our affairs are by no means in an unsatisfactory state. Indeed I am hoping
that with care & prudence we may have a couple of peaceful years, &
consolidate our Chartwell position. Try to rest & recuperate at Lou Seuil &
come back reinvigorated.

I will send you a full report of the progress of yr garden & of other
Chartwell projects; & will also tell you about the hunting at Eu.

With tender love yr ever devoted
W

[1] A reference to a speech by Lloyd George during the First World War, when he told the
House of Commons on 20 December 1915, at the time of the Gallipoli evacuations: 'I wonder
whether it will be Too Late! Ah, fatal words of this war! Too Late in moving here! Too Late
in arriving there! Too Late in coming to this decision! Too Late in starting with that enterprise! Too Late in preparing! In this war the footsteps of the Allied forces have been dogged
by the mocking spectre of "Too Late" and unless we quicken our movements, damnation will
fall on the sacred cause for which so much gallant blood has flowed!'

Lord Crewe to Sir Austen Chamberlain

(*Austen Chamberlain papers*)

26 January 1927   British Embassy
Private & Personal   Paris

My dear Austen,

Winston came to see me this morning on his hasty journey through Paris. He was going to lunch with Loucheur, who had asked some politicians of different Parties to meet him.

As he will no doubt tell you when you see him, he is not a little exercised at the reply which Poincaré gave yesterday at the meeting of the Finance Committee of the Chamber, when asked by M Margaine[1] if the inter-allied debts would soon be the subject of a vote in Parliament. Poincaré replied 'Qu'il n'était pas pressé', saying that the Government would not ask for an immediate examination of the inter-allied agreements, all the more as Parliamentary business in the United States will be suspended for a time, during the replacement of part of the Senate.

Winston feels that he may be placed in a difficult position in the House of Commons if he is cross-questioned, as he very likely may be, about the English share of the Debt. And he asked me, therefore, if I saw Poincaré to point this out to him, there being no ostensible reason for not funding the Debt on the agreed terms. I promised to do this whenever I met Poincaré, or, if I do not get a chance of this soon, to drop a word in the same sense to Briand.

Winston was anxious not to make a personal complaint, and he agreed that I could not well ask for an interview simply to make it on his behalf. The fact of a parliamentary difficulty being created makes it easy enough to say a word about it. You get, of course, the full report of Poincaré's statement by despatch today.

Yours sincerely
Crewe

[1] Alfred Margaine, 1870–1942. Entered the National Assembly as a Radical Socialist in 1910. Under-Secretary of State for War for three days in June 1914. Active in the 1920s in seeking closer French relations with the Danube states, and with the Soviet Union. Under-Secretary of State for Public Works, June–December 1932. In 1940 he was one of the eighty Deputies who refused to vote Marshal Pétain plenipotentiary powers.

Winston S. Churchill to Sir Otto Niemeyer

(*Churchill papers: 18/40*)

26 January 1927   Paris

While agreeing with your arguments against a gradual purchase of 2½% Consols, I cannot feel convinced that you are right in speaking of an addition of £37 millions to the total deadweight debt as 'an imaginary evil'. After all £37 millions will have to be paid by our children and raised by taxation from them. Moreover, the dead hand of the debt will continue to rest for a longer period and with greater weight upon the productive energies of the country. It might be argued that a large reduction in the annual interest was a full compensation; but the interest has only been reduced, I gather, by about £150,000 a year.

Greatly as I admire the skill and knowledge of market conditions which has characterised this last Conversion and welcome our success in meeting the maturities, I cannot feel that we have done anything but mark time and hold our own, and that for this we have laid a heavy fresh burden upon posterity.

I do not see how we can afford to regard the steady growth of the deadweight debt as an insignificant factor. The Colwyn Committee certainly take the opposite view. I shall certainly have to meet the criticism that the policy of the Treasury and the Bank favours the Capitalists' interests and in particular the *rentier* class to such an extent that the nation will never be free from the debt in any period which can be foreseen. Even in a hundred years it will go on increasing, in spite of enormous annual sacrifices to pay it off.

I am of course well aware that within certain limits time and money are interchangeable terms. But surely a Conversion like this raises fundamental issues in an extremely controversial form. Compare for instance the Germans and French who are either wholly or to a large extent already free from their debts. In Germany particularly credit has greatly recovered and large sums of newly created capital are available for the support of industry. Great industrial activity prevails, in spite of all the terrible experiences they have gone through and the horrible financial expedients they have perpetrated.

Britain, on the other hand, after paying off by direct taxation £500 or £600 millions of debt, actually owes more than she did at the beginning. All she has done is to obtain a certain reduction in interest at the cost of throwing a far heavier burden on posterity. I cannot believe that this is a position that will be generally accepted by the public and by Parliament.

In a few years time you will see on the one hand Germany free from debt with a strong credit, a most active industry and low taxation, and Britain with gigantic taxation and an enormous *rentier* class growing with the growth of the debt the taxpayer is forever being spurred on to reduce but only succeeds in postponing and increasing.

The fact that such a policy obtains keen approval among the banking classes and in the City of London is no answer. Indeed it might be considered quite natural that they should welcome a policy which undoubtedly tends to foster to its highest point the interests of creditors and inert citizens of all kinds at the expense of all those forces which by fresh efforts are perennially replacing what is consumed. Everything in fact under this system is consumed and replaced except the debt which towers up higher and higher.

Your argument has hitherto been that it is to the saving in annual interest rather than to the deadweight total that we should look. But the very small saving effected by our latest Conversion really deprives me of this argument. All I can say is that it is right to count upon greatly improved conditions in the future which will carry in their train a reduced rent of money. Shall we not be forced to meet the great impending maturities by similar devices which will throw very much increased burdens forward and produce only a minor saving for this generation? If this is so, shall we not be told that the Treasury is exalting the interests of the 'Money Trust' above all other interests in the State: social, moral or manufacturing? After all there is more in the life of a nation than the development of an immense *rentier* class quartered in perpetuity upon the struggling producer of new wealth.

I think I should either be furnished with very massive, easily understood arguments in a contrary sense or with suggestions for some timely modification of our policy, at least so as not to raise these issues in their most acute and glaring form.

This brings me to what I have repeatedly asked you to discuss, though without any result so far, ie the question of a forced loan at a low rate of interest as a part of our system of taxation. Why for instance should not the taxpayers whose incomes have over a period of say five years averaged more than a certain amount, say £3,000 a year, be required to take up a certain graduated proportion of $2\frac{1}{2}\%$ or 3% Government bonds? I am well aware that this would be a new direct tax measured by the difference between the market and the par value of these bonds. On the other hand wealthy people have a power to wait for values to improve far greater than the smaller taxpayer. They could put these bonds away and wait for their steady recovery before the period of maturity arrives.

Do not try to pull my argument to pieces with superior knowledge of these technical matters. But try on the other hand to present the most reasonable variants and solutions while reserving, if you will, your own opinion as to their soundness. I have no doubt you can put what I want to put in a far better form than any of which I am capable. Endeavour therefore to work out something like this:

A graduated scale of obligations to take up $2\frac{1}{2}$% Government bonds in accordance with five years average income, such bonds to be either redeemable at say fifty years, or (and) acceptable at par value in payment of death duties after they have been held for so many years. There might even be a sliding scale of the values at which they should be accepted in payment of death duties.

These reflections are also forced on me by the report which I have been reading of the Income Tax Simplification proposals. Have you read this report? If not, please do so and consider whether the occasion of a change over to the current year and a consequent deferment of taxation might not be accompanied by a considerable loan tax of this kind.

I am quite sure that a really well argued political campaign to get clear of a process by which the total of the debt is continually increasing would be irresistible if it were launched with sufficient knowledge and skill. And I do not want to see such a development against us.

Winston S. Churchill to Sir Richard Hopkins

(*Treasury papers: T171/255*)

26 January 1927   Paris

I have now read and re-read the whole of these Income Tax Simplification papers. Let me first of all thank you and the Committee for the great care and thought they have given to this subject and congratulate them upon the result, albeit modest, which they have achieved. I should like to see the Committee and yourself as soon as Parliament meets and I have got through the political speeches I have to make at the end of next week. Perhaps Grigg will arrange a night when you and they will come and dine with me at Downing St. In the meanwhile there are a few points which occur to me.

(1) For the expression 'wealthy taxpayer' the expression 'larger taxpayer' should invariably be adopted.

(2) For the expression 'untaxed income' I should prefer the phrase 'undeductable income'. 'Untaxed income' connotes at least ambiguously the idea of tax free income, whereas it is only tax deferred income.

(3) When you speak of a change to the current year being attended by a 'deferment' of £175 millions in one year and £64 millions in the next, what do you mean? Deferment till when? Is it, for instance, deferment to the end of time, a sort of pushing on that is never caught up until death or

cessation of business; or is the amount recovered in the following year, and should the deferment be added to the total figures in your tables, eg should £251 millions for year 10 be increased by £175 millions deferment from year 9, etc? I am afraid this is not the case, but the context does not explain it to me. If it were the case, it seems to me that a variety of operations might be possible to meet the contingency.

(4) Please see a copy of the paper I have sent to Niemeyer on this subject. The last suggestion, although rejected for achieving the basis of the current year by means of a Government bond, appears to me deserving of further examination by you and Niemeyer jointly. I will not repeat here what I have written to him, but pray give it your best consideration. I do not want to give up the current year basis without a further struggle, and without having exhausted every possible variant including those outside the scope of the Inland Revenue.

I do not see myself why the larger, and still more the largest, taxpayers should not make a special contribution to debt extinction; and I believe they would prefer to do this through the obligatory taking up of Government stock at a low rate of interest rather than by an addition to direct taxation. Are there no means of forestalling the revenue of future years for the purpose of the earlier cancellation of debt?

I know the difficulty of trying to lift oneself by one's boot tabs and how many illusions are founded on that process. Nevertheless I am sure the state of affairs described in my Minute to Niemeyer will not be allowed to continue indefinitely in a country based on adult suffrage.

Winston S. Churchill to Clementine Churchill

(Spencer-Churchill papers)

28 January 1927   Grand Hotel
                                                      Dieppe

My darling—

Benny came with me this afternoon when I laid two wreaths on yr Mama's grave, & Bill's. Both were well kept—tho of course at this black season the plants do not grow—& the old woman at the lodge led us to them immediately. The military graves close by are now all finished, with their orderly lines of tombstones & the high cross of sacrifice. We wandered among them reading the inscriptions wh recall the history we know so well.

Loucheur's luncheon in Paris was a considerable affair. Briand, Peret,

Vincent Auriol,[1] about 15 MPs representing leading elements in all parties— & vy advanced politicians. I conducted a general conversation in my best French, & defended Debt demands & Mussolini interviews with some spirit. All vy friendly.

I saw Crewe beforehand & did some business with him. He begged that you wd propose yrself to the Embassy when you passed through Paris. It wd be silly not to do this, if you have any occasion to break yr journey. You have only to write.

Yesterday we hunted the penwiper.[2] A dramatic moment occurred when he appeared from a lake where he had refreshed himself & galloped into our midst. The wire netting round a covert prevented his escape. He turned to bay. Colonel Hunter[3] fired repeatedly & missed. Benny advanced pistol in hand—but luckily on horseback—to fire the final shot. The pistol in bad order wd not cock. The penwiper charged—grazed the horse, scatters the company & eventually made good his retreat & escape into the depths of the forest. Tomorrow we hunt again. There are plenty of pigs & the country people of all classes are enchanted at the hunt & follow it on foot in motors or on any kind of quadruped. They are as eager to kill them as if they were Germans. It is all quite novel to them so far.

The famous Coco[4] turned up & I took a gt fancy to her—A most capable

---

[1] Vincent Auriol, 1884–1966. The son of a village baker, he founded a local newspaper, *Le Midi Socialiste*, at the age of 21. Elected to the Chamber of Deputies in 1914. General Secretary of the socialist group in the Chamber, 1919–36, and principal financial expert of the Socialist Party. Minister of Finance in Léon Blum's Popular Front Government, 1936. Minister of Justice, 1937. Co-ordinator of the Prime Minister's Department, 1938. One of the few Socialist Deputies to vote against Marshal Pétain, 1940. Imprisoned by the Vichy regime, but escaped. Worked with the Resistance; then joined de Gaulle in London. Vice-Premier in de Gaulle's Provisional Government, 1945. First President of the Fourth Republic, 1947–54. Active in persuading the Socialists to work with de Gaulle in 1958, and a member of de Gaulle's Constitutional Council, 1958–9.

[2] Churchill's nickname for the wild boar.

[3] Charles Finlayson Hunter, born 1880. On active service, 1914–18; DSO, 1916; Lieutenant-Colonel, 1917. Assistant Quarter-Master General, British Mission to French Army Headquarters, 1917–19. Commanded the 4th Dragoon Guards, 1919–23.

[4] Gabrielle Jeanne Chanel, 1883–1971. Known as 'Coco'. She opened her first shop, for hats, in Paris in 1910, and soon became known also for her sportswear, and simple jersey dresses and suits. In 1920 *The Times* reported that she had been left £40,000 in the will of her lover, Captain Arthur 'Boy' Capel, a British Liaison Officer at the Paris Peace Conference (he left a further £40,000 to a second mistress, an Italian Countess whose husband had been killed at Verdun). A dress designer, famed for simple, comfortable clothes, in muted colours, she designed theatrical costumes in Paris from 1922; introduced 'English Hour' fashions to France in 1927; and prepared costumes for the film *Tonight or Never* in 1931. A friend of Picasso, Diaghilev and Stravinsky, from 1925 to 1930 she lived with the 2nd Duke of Westminster. Her villa in the South of France was La Pausa (which she sold in 1953 to Emery Reeves, Churchill's Literary Agent). In 1943, while living in German-occupied France, she suggested to the Germans that she act as a go-between with Churchill

& agreeable woman—much the strongest personality Benny has yet been up against. She hunted vigorously all day, motored to Paris after dinner, & is today engaged in passing & improving dresses on endless streams of mannequins. Altogether 200 models have to be settled in almost 3 weeks. Some have to be altered ten times. She does it with her own fingers, pinning, cutting, looping etc. With her—Vera Bate[1] née Arkwright 'Yr Chief of Staff?' Non—'One of yr lieutenants?' Non 'Elle est là. Voilà tout.' However the said Vera, whom we used to know, has been there 7 years & has a vy presentable husband an American on the Reparations Cte. All hunted.

Last night arrived Neville Lytton[2] with his flute & his new wife—Both charming. Very consoling to him after the towering severities of his former spouse. She is French, but looks Italian—as Benny told her—exactly suited to organs, canary birds, etc. They are vy happy & Bohemian. She says 'Married 3 years, but friends for 10: & each day "Plus qu'hier, moins que demain".' A high standard wh we must endeavour to emulate.

I am going back by the night boat tomorrow night, so as to have all Sunday at Chartwell. The speeches are 'peser'ing on me. Why do I ever agree to make any! I shall bring Diana down to Chartwell to keep me company & will send her early to school Monday.

The Sherwoods have lost over £1,000 since we parted, so do not fret over my peccadilos at the Casino.

Tender love my sweet Clemmie. Think kindly of yr ever loving & devoted

W

Write London.

---

for a negotiated peace (and was actually allowed to travel to Lisbon for this purpose). Having closed her fashion house in 1939, she reopened it in 1954, when she relaunched a vogue for easy-fitting suits.

[1] Sarah Gertrude Arkwright, 1885–1947. Known as 'Vera'. Born in London. Her birth certificate stated that her father was a stonemason; but she believed herself (and was by many believed to be) the illegitimate daughter of a descendent of the Duke of Cambridge. Served as a nurse in France during the first world war, and also with Clementine Churchill, in London, providing canteen facilities for women munition workers. She married her American husband in 1919; they were divorced in 1927. She remarried, in 1929, Alberto Lombardi, an Italian officer and one of the finest horsemen of his day. During the second world war she lived in the South of France, and encouraged Chanel's unsuccessful attempt to act as a 'go-between' between the Germans and the British; arrested by the Gestapo, and imprisoned in Rome, November 1943. Accompanied Chanel to Madrid, on a German safe-conduct, 1944, and then refused to return to German-occupied France.

[2] Neville Stephen Lytton, 1879–1951. Fourth son of the 1st Earl of Lytton. Painter. Amateur Tennis Champion, 1911 and 1913. On active service, 1914–18 (wounded). In 1924 he married, as his second wife, Alexandra Fortel, of St Rambert-en-Bugey, Ain, France. In 1947 he succeeded his elder brother as 3rd Earl of Lytton.

Winston S. Churchill to Clementine Churchill
(Spencer-Churchill papers)

30 January 1927   Chartwell

My darling,

A vy rough night passage: but thanks to Mothersill, I did not succumb, & am now returned to England, Home & Downpour. We killed our pig yesterday in the open fields, & I began to lose my heart to Mrs Neville Lytton. But my purpose in writing to you is not to impart news but to discuss business.

I am sure the best thing wd be for you to stop in Paris with the Crewe's for two or three days & fix Diana up with some new family, & let her come over immediately afterwards. I dont think this school will do her any good and it interrupts her French. I shd try to get her back to Paris as soon as possible. This is what she wd like, & is really best for her. Write me yr views. There must be scores of suitable families.

The new passage is splendid, but the hammering in putting down the carpet caused another heavy fall of plaster in the Drawing Room. I am seeing about it. It is vy vexing. A lot of wood has been cut, but otherwise progress has been lamentably slow. I am so sleepy that I am going to doze off now & then work at a speech & then up to London with Diana to dine (me) at Philip Sassoon's. A vy hard bunk & violent motion robbed me of my minimum sleep ration.

Tender love,
Yr devoted
W

All is well with the kittens.

February 1927

Lord Birkenhead to Winston S. Churchill
(*Churchill papers: 1/194*)

1 February 1927

My dear Winston,

I absolutely grovel for having forgotten your lunch. My head is like a sieve; I foolishly did not put it down and it simply went out of my head until 7.30 tonight.

Do believe me that I am both contrite & ashamed. You cannot add to my self reproach.

The only thing I can do is to support you right or wrong tomorrow.

Yours
F

Clementine Churchill to Winston S. Churchill
(*Spencer-Churchill papers*)

2 February 1927

Lou Sueil
Eze

My Darling,

I *loved* getting a letter from you so quickly.

It was sweet of you to write. I expect you are arriving at Dieppe about now.

When I left you at the station I was about to telegraph to Eddie about a wreath for your Aunt Cornelia when I saw by the 'Times' which Serjeant Thompson had just bought me that she was being buried today & that the train for people attending the funeral (& for flowers) left Waterloo at 9.30 this morning.

The girl at the Post Office said a telegram would not be delivered till this morning so it was Alas! too late. But we could send a wreath a little later, which will be really just as nice as by then all the other flowers will be faded—I expect you are writing to Ivor.

There was rather a nice memoir of her in the 'Times' I thought. . . .[1]

I shall love to hear your news—Give Bennie my love. I do hope you get a pen-wiper. But do not let him gore you.

Your loving
Clemmie

Winston S. Churchill to Stanley Baldwin

(*Churchill papers: 22/151*)

2 February 1927

My dear Prime Minister,

As I gather that it is unlikely that a serious decision will be required on China at Friday's Cabinet I propose to carry out my public engagements.[2] But in case the main issue should arise I should be very much obliged if you would read these few notes of mine to the Cabinet.

We ought not to make any alteration in the movement of our troops to Shanghai in order to reach an agreement with Chen[3] about Hankow or

---

[1] Lady Wimborne had died on 22 January 1927. An obituary notice, published in *The Times* two days later, mentioned her reputation for 'politico-social' gatherings, which 'were of much service to the Liberal Party, which was by no means so well provided as its rival with hostesses of rank, wealth, and social gifts'. The obituary also quoted from the late Lord Wimborne's will, who left 'to my darling wife, everything of which I die possessed for her own use and benefit absolutely, and I thank God He has given me a wife so sweet, so loving, and so capable'.

[2] On Thursday, 3 February 1927, Churchill was to speak in Oldham, and on the following day in Manchester. He carried out both engagements, speaking in Oldham at the annual dinner of the Oldham Chamber of Commerce. 'The simple blunt truths of finance,' he said, 'apply equally to the economy of the humblest cottage, the most wealthy corporation, and the most powerful state. Balance your budget. Pay your way. Pay your debts. Make your expenditure less than your income. Let your word be your bond. Save. Buy war certificates (laughter). Do a fair day's work for the money you earn, and make sure you are paid in an honest and stable currency.' And he added: 'I will give you an infallible test by which you can tell whether any financial measure is sound or unsound: If it is sound, is it disagreeable.' On Friday, 4 February 1927, Churchill made two speeches in Manchester, one to a luncheon meeting of the Constitutional Club, and the other to an evening meeting in the Free Trade Hall. In both speeches he spoke of the continuing ill effects of the disruptions in the coal industry during 1926.

[3] Eugene Chen, 1878–1944. Born in the British West Indies, of Chinese parents. Educated at St Mary's College, Trinidad. While practising as a Barrister in London in 1912, he met Sun Yat-sen, whose protégé he became, and whom he accompanied to China. Editor of the *Peking Gazette*, 1913–17. Imprisoned in 1917 for opposing Japanese influence in China. Foreign adviser to Sun Yat-sen when the latter gained control of Canton in 1923. Member of the Central Executive of Kuomintang, 1926. Nationalist Minister for Foreign Affairs (at Canton), 1926. Ruler of Hankow, 1926. After being forced to resign all posts, in April 1927, he fled to the Soviet Union, and then to Western Europe, where he lived from 1928 to 1931. In Hong Kong, 1931. Foreign Minister to Chiang Kai-Shek, 1931. Forced to flee again when convicted of rebellion, 1934. He went briefly to Paris, and then returned to Shanghai, where he lived until his death.

Kiukiang. We have little to gain in signing the proposed agreement with Chen. It may be the best we can seek in the unhappy circumstances, but in fact it constitutes an almost complete surrender of our special position in China.

We have been expelled by mob violence from our treaty rights at Hankow and Kiukiang and we have now offered to make an agreement condoning this great wrong and accepting for ever the brutal usurpation of which we have been the victim. If in these circumstances Chen refuses to sign, we need not be disappointed. As the American papers say, we have gone to the full limit and this will effectually prevent other Powers from under-cutting us. Therefore if Chen refuses to sign, or exacts fresh conditions, or tries to dictate to us about the movements of our troops to parts of China far beyond his control, I think that we should let the negotiations languish, saying 'We have done our best to meet you, and this is all that has come of it.'

Chen seems to me to be a figure very much like Kerensky,[1] half kicking against the extremists, always dominated by them, and in the result offering no basis for straight-forward dealing. Moreover, as the telegrams show, he or those behind him are trying to take a hand in British Party politics, playing off our Labour Party against us and endeavouring to humiliate HMG to their advantage. Even leaving Moscow out of it altogether, this is an extremely disagreeable feature, and one which would aggravate our British public feeling.

Moreover there is no immediate hurry. By all means let the earliest units disembark at Hong-Kong if there is no immediate danger at Shanghai. But do that without saying a word in public and simply as a part of the ordinary programme of War Office movements. This will give us at least a fortnight during which we can survey the situation and Chen can be kept guessing. During that fortnight we shall have taken no steps of an aggressive character and have closed no door on future action.

Meanwhile it seems to me that the movement of our troops steadily continuing across the ocean might well be used as a lever for further parleys with Japan and the United States. If Japan is really anxious that we should not disembark a substantial force at Shanghai she might be willing, if it were put in the right way, to make us a proposal or to accept a proposal from us that if we did not land further troops at Shanghai she would guarantee to send equal forces with us at three or four days notice should

---

[1] Alexander Feodorovich Kerensky, 1881–1970. A Labour member of the Russian Duma, 1912. Minister of Justice in the Provisional Government, February 1917; Minister of War and the Navy, May 1917. Urged the continuing prosecution of the war, and sought to raise army morale, May–July 1917. Prime Minister, July–October 1917, and Supreme Commander-in-Chief, September–October 1917. Fled from Petrograd, October 1917. In exile in France, 1918–40, and then in the United States.

the situation at any moment become critical. The same is true in a lesser degree of the United States. This seems to be a prudent and hopeful course, and it, or something like it, has been suggested to me by a conversation which I had with Lord Balfour. Above all, do not let us make a bargain with Chen about the troops for Shanghai.

Yours vy sincerely,
WSC

Clementine Churchill to Winston S. Churchill

(*Spencer-Churchill papers*)

6 February 1927 Lou Sueil
Eze

My Darling,

I hope that after your labours in the Midlands you had a pleasant & restful weekend at Chartwell.

I see the reports (not very full) of your two Manchester speeches in the 'Times'.

Your comparison of Mr Cook & Mr Chen amused me![1] The Oxfords have been here since last Thursday. The old boy is most friendly but getting very very old.[2] His surly, disagreeable manner to you at our dinner party *must* be purely his bad manners as he has spoken of you most affectionately & admiringly. He told me that his contribution (during the General Strike) to the British Gazette was prompted solely, by his 'penchant' for you![3]

---

[1] Speaking to the Manchester Constitutional Club on 4 February 1927, Churchill said, as reported in *The Times* on the following day: 'It seems that this year our trade, gravely prejudiced by the prolonged coal stoppage last year, would be affected, to some extent at any rate, by the disturbances which had broken out in China. Last year we had Mr Cook. This year we have Mr Chen. The one arose amid the musky coal pits of Britain; the other was nurtured in the balmy air of far Cathay. When I say balmy air of far Cathy I am not sure that the balmy element may not have found its representation in both cases. Both gentlemen seem to have been studying at the same school. Both seem to draw their inspirations from the same fount. They preach the same doctrine, they use the same language, and they seem to be pursuing the same objects.'

[2] Asquith died a year later, on 15 February 1928, aged 75.

[3] The front page of the fourth issue of the *British Gazette*, of Saturday, 8 May 1926, contained a message from Asquith, in the course of which he declared: 'We should have lost all sense of self-respect if we were to allow any section of the community at its own will, and for whatever motives, to bring to a standstill the industrial and social life of the whole nation. It would be to acquiesce in the substitution for Free Government of a Dictatorship. This the British people will never do. We desire at the earliest moment the resumption of negotiations to bring peace and reconstruction to our coalfields. But the anti-social weapon, which has been so unadvisedly drawn, must first be sheathed.'

He is of course rather sad about Wedgwood Benn's defection.[1] It seems unreasonable to be driven into the Labour Party by Lloyd George, when Lloyd George will so very soon join him there! Margot is as sprightly as a grasshopper, very amusing but most fatiguing.

I have enjoyed my holiday but I now long for England—Home and—Winston—

Your most loving
Clemmie

Winston S. Churchill to William Bridgeman

(*Churchill papers: 18/32*)

7 February 1927

My dear First Lord,

Very many thanks for your long letter. It reached me just as I was leaving the 'Warspite' after a three days' deeply interesting but somewhat stormy cruise and manoeuvres.

I have now had time to consider it here with the figures of our previous discussions before me. Let me say without delay that I recognise fully the efforts you and your Naval colleagues are making to meet the public difficulty at the present time, and I particularly appreciate their decision to postpone till February 1 the new construction programme of 1927. I am sure that if this is effectively stated, it will tend to encourage a Naval *détente.*

I am sorry your Board do not like the idea of dropping the 100,000 tons of Oil Reserve, though I quite understand their desire to keep the principle of building up the Reserve alive. In view of the alternative reduction in reserves which you propose, I shall not press you further on this item during the discussion of the 1927 estimates, although our contention could quite legitimately be that both were practicable.

'My withers are quite unwrung' (whatever that far fetched expression means) by all you say about my inconsistency in regard to Vote A. The programme of new construction we were then discussing was a very different one from that upon which we finally agreed. It was natural for me to argue that a demand for new ships on such a scale would be accompanied by a

---

[1] Having been a Liberal MP since January 1906, and having served in Asquith's Government as a Junior Lord of the Treasury between 1910 and 1915, Wedgwood Benn resigned his seat in February 1927 in order to join the Labour Party. He was elected as Labour MP for North Aberdeen in August 1928.

demand for a larger personnel; and it was my duty to resist both. But there would have been no inconsistency, even had the new programme been agreed to in its original form, in my arguing that its burden should be reduced by economies in personnel in other branches of the Navy. Now that the construction programmes are settled, I attach more importance to Vote A than to anything else.

I am in favour of an active new construction within the limits agreed. But the very fact that a Navy has a better and more modern plant should enable reductions in the lower grades of personnel to be effected. The inconsistency lies with anyone who says: Because we have better and more powerful weapons, we must have more men. Machine power within certain limits should be a substitute for man power, and we should enable this to be effected by the continued laying up of obsolete types and by the development of reserve systems.

Although the saving in the first year must be comparatively small, I must most earnestly press you to consider once again the possibility of making a further reduction in Vote A of say 250 men. I am sure that such a figure can easily be reduced from the shore establishments, or from the very liberal allowance made by the Admiralty for men in transit on relief.

There remains only the question of the shadow cut. For the last three years the Treasury have always argued that the Admiralty were, no doubt from the highest motives, over-budgeting, and each year there has been an interdepartmental dispute about the amount. Every year, however, for one reason or another our view has been vindicated in the result, and considerable surrenders have been made in spite of the shadow cut.

No doubt exceptional circumstances have been at work this year, but I feel sure your surrender will be (apart from China special expenditure) nearer a million than half a million, in spite of a shadow cut of 2 millions. There is of course no question of diminishing any of the approved Admiralty services. The obligation of the Treasury to finance these remains unaltered. But at this particular juncture it is specially desirable to avoid asking for more money from the taxpayer than will actually be spent in the course of the year. Moreover, (pace all your arguments) bringing the actual published figure of the naval estimates below the comparable figure of last year makes everything easier and smoother.

I should propose therefore to make a shadow cut of £2,500,000; for which, if need be, you will be entitled to a supplementary estimate. We could then agree to estimates of approximately £58 millions without further correspondence or discussion.

Let me however conclude as I began by expressing my very cordial thanks to you and your Board for the perseverance and ingenuity with which you have laboured to assist the Government in the difficult circumstances of the present time. It is certainly under the impression that the two outstanding points I have mentioned will be discussed by me.

Yours vy sincerely,
Winston S. Churchill

Winston S. Churchill: draft Cabinet declaration

(Churchill papers: 22/151)

8 February 1927   10 Downing Street

Our troops were sent to the Far East to safeguard British life in China & particularly at Shanghai. That was & is the only policy of HMG. The question of the time at which & the manner & numbers in which the troops shd be landed at Shanghai must obviously depend upon the local situation & the advice we receive from our representatives on the spot. If they consider that the emergency requires immediate disembarkation at Shanghai we shall act accordingly. If not, the leading Brigade will be held in readiness at Hong Kong, while the rest of the force is approaching. There can of course be no question of entering into any arrangement with Mr Chen or anyone else in connexion with the movement of troops despatched to protect British life & property.

Winston S. Churchill: draft Cabinet telegram to General Duncan[1]

(Churchill papers: 22/151)

8 February 1927

You are authorized to draw on the troops arriving & approaching if & as you think necessary for the defence of British life at Shanghai. We cannot judge the local situation from here. If however there is no immediate danger locally then it would be convenient from the international point of view to disembark the leading brigade at Hong Kong. But in no case must such

---

[1] John Duncan, 1872–1948. Entered the Army, 1891. On active service on the North-West Frontier of India, 1897–8; in South Africa, 1899–1901; at Gallipoli, 1915, and on the western front, 1916–17. Commanded the 22nd Division in Macedonia, 1917–19. Major-General, General Staff, Army of the Black Sea, April–December, 1919. Major-General Commanding the Shanghai Military Force, 1927–8. Knighted, 1928. General Officer Commanding, First Division, Aldershot, 1928. Retired from the Army, 1928. Chief Commissioner, St John's Ambulance Brigade, 1931–43.

considerations stand against the safeguarding of British life and property for which you are responsible. Ask therefore what you require for the arm purpose.

Winston S. Churchill to Clementine Churchill
(Spencer-Churchill papers)

9 February 1927

My darling,

You will see by the papers how hunted I have been. But it all went off well. The meetings were a gt success, & the crowds & interest all that they **S** shd be. I returned to find the Cabinet divided into 2 equal halves on **e** whether the troops shd go on to Shanghai or stop at Hong Kong: & I **c** am glad to say I provided a formula—wh B read out in Parl on wh all **r** **e** agreed, & wh has been approved alike by the Manchester Guardian & **t** the Morning Post.

No ruffle of discontent has yet manifested itself about the Times articles. They seem to take it for granted.[1]

I hope by yr letters you will come straight on to Chartwell arriving some-time Friday. I shall be there with Diana & the Prof. Wire when you want the car at Dover.

I am doubtful about Diana's Italian aspirations. It is so much better to learn *one* foreign language thoroughly than to fritter away time & money on smatterings. The object of learning a language is to get a key to a new library—with all its boundless possibilities of culture & pleasure. I told her I will gladly facilitate her going to Italy (wh she had in her eye) when she cd talk French easily, write it correctly, & read it with pleasure.

She is getting vy pretty, & I have been taking her about everywhere— We go to plays every night! She is vy swcct.

I won't burden myself to write all about Chartwell. It is as usual a picture of shade as well as light. You will see it all when you come. Mary blossoming.

I send you a note from Eddie to show you an invitation wh I have accepted for us both.

---

[1] On 7 February 1927 *The Times* had begun its serialization of Volume III of Churchill's *World Crisis*, extracts from which appeared daily until March 1. On February 15 Arthur Conan Doyle wrote to *The Times*: 'One could not read the last paragraph of Mr Winston Churchill's accounts of the Somme Battles, as given in your issue of February 12, without rejoicing that Kitchener's Army has at last received a worthy panegyric. Personally, I have long recognized that Winston Churchill had the finest prose style of any contemporary, and it is indeed a splendid thing that he should use it to do that which seemed impossible— namely to give an adequate appreciation of that glorious Army of patriotic volunteers who gave themselves so ungrudgingly to their country's service.'

I have been busy with my Will & have some new arrangements to discuss with you, wh I hope you will think right. We *must* be careful. I am addressing this caution to myself primarily. There is just enough—but it does not bear trenching on any more.

Tender love my dearest
Your ever devoted
W

PS. I have to wind up the debate this evening.[1]

Winston S. Churchill to Sir Laming Worthington-Evans

(*Churchill papers: 18/34*)[2]

9 February 1927   Treasury Chambers
Most Secret

My dear Secretary of State for War,

I have now been able to study your paper NE 45. I realise all that you say of the reductions which have been made in Army expenditure in recent years, and that the margins on which you are working are not wide. I appreciate the efforts which you have made to achieve the figure for next year of £41,900,000 (apart of course from special China expense). I hope, however, you will not mind my making you a few suggestions.

The Army List shows that, apart from three Cavalry Regiments in Egypt and the Soudan (? Palestine), you have two Guard and twelve Line Cavalry Regiments at home. You are incurring, rightly, a heavy expenditure in the development of tanks and mechanisation. In these circumstances I am sure you would be justified in amalgamating without delay eight more Line Cavalry Regiments. You mention the 10th and 11th Hussars and the 7th and 8th Hussars as the first on the roster for amalgamation. Perhaps you would let me know what you put as the next four. The effect of amalgamation on the 1922 principle on these Regiments is well described on page 31

---

[1] The Debate on the King's Address. Churchill rose at seven in the evening, and spoke for half an hour. Much of his speech was devoted to the Trades Union Bill, and the Government's policy towards the Chinese Civil War. He concluded with a defence of the Government's statements against Soviet Russia, declaring that: 'We believe ourselves to be the object of insidious hostile propaganda in every part of the world, and we are determined that, if this is to continue or at any time come to a head, it shall be encountered by a British public opinion in which the constitutional and patriotic elements are fully apprised of what is taking place; are vigilant, warned, ready for action, and ready to meet danger when it comes.'

[2] On 9 February 1927 Churchill circulated this letter to the Cabinet Committee on Expenditure. It was discussed at the Committee's meeting on February 10.

of 'Army Estimates 1926'. 'The identity of the original Regiments was preserved by maintaining within each unit two squadrons of the original Regiment and one squadron of the junior, and by giving to the new Regiment a title combining the designation of the two Regiments from which it was formed.'

The War Office inform me that the annual cost of a Cavalry Regiment is about £130,000 a year, of which £22,000 is for non-effective charges. Amalgamating eight Regiments into four would therefore effect an ultimate and permanent economy of £520,000, if action were immediate and recruiting for the Cavalry restricted accordingly. This in my opinion is only a fair counterpoise to the development of fast tanks, armoured cars and mechanisation. You have frequently told me that you contemplate action in this direction. I am bound to urge that it should not be delayed and that we should not be forced to face a lengthy over-lapping of the new and the old Arms.

I do not think that a desire to keep one complete cavalry division at home for a year or two more ought to obstruct this natural and inevitable transition. The composition of a cavalry division is purely arbitrary. No principle of war which has the slightest application to modern conditions requires either that a brigade should contain four regiments or that a division should contain three brigades. Where, might I ask, is it likely or indeed conceivable that one complete British cavalry division would be required to act as a unit? We can I am sure exclude for the next two or three years our one cavalry division operating upon the Rhine!

I cannot imagine any circumstances which would make it necessary, or possible, to employ such a large specialised unit in Egypt or Palestine. But, if so, there are already three regiments in this theatre which would be available, to say nothing of the two Guards Cavalry regiments at home. The only theatre where a mounted war on a great scale and the use of the largest cavalry formations is within the bounds—I will not say of reason, but of fond imagination—is in India. But here there is no lack of cavalry. On the contrary not only are there I believe five British cavalry regiments in garrison but very large numbers of efficient Indian cavalry units, both regular and irregular. If it became necessary to send all our available cavalry forces to India they would surely be far better used in forming several mixed divisions with Indian regiments than concentrated as a purely British force.

I do not think, in view of the need of developing mechanical arms, that the sentimental desire to preserve the conventional organisation of an old style cavalry division ought to stand in the way of the immediate amalgamation I propose. I know well that the social influences which may be marshalled in favour of the independent existence of famous cavalry regiments are very strong; but I cannot see why what has been enforced upon the 17th and 21st Lancers should not equally be made applicable to the 10th and 11th Hussars, &c. In the pass we are come to about money, and in the rapidly changing character of military science, we cannot afford to allow such considerations to weigh against realities.

Is it not in every way preferable to reduce the number of regular cavalry units, as suggested, rather than to reduce the number of troops, as you propose, in the existing units? I have always been brought up to believe that a weak unit, under strength and with few horses or effective sabres or lances is from every point of view undesirable. All the overhead charges, regimental headquarters, &c, remain constant, while the practical fighting strength and the facilities of training are seriously and uneconomically impaired. I should have thought that a further step in amalgamation was a salutary measure in harmony with the movement of military science and producing a substantial economy and was in every way to be preferred to clipping the already attenuated peace-time fighting strength of existing units.

I see that you propose to disband two well-known Scottish scout yeomanry regiments and two English yeomanry regiments for the purpose of saving the exiguous sum of £27,000. To do this in preference to the amalgamation of regular cavalry regiments is surely to raise the issue of the value of regular *versus* territorial units in the most questionable form.

As one regular cavalry regiment costs £130,000 a year and reducing four yeomanry regiments together saves only £27,000 in the first year and £40,000 thereafter, we reach the conclusion that the War Office regard one regular cavalry regiment, measured in terms of money, as worth approximately eight or ten times a regiment like Lovat's Scouts. This is a standard of values which I am confident could never face the light of day. Unless I am wrongly informed, most of the remaining yeomanry regiments have accepted the obligation for foreign service in an emergency. They would therefore be embodied at the outset of a war. Their efficiency must therefore be measured not by peace-time standards but as it would be (say) after four months' continuous training.

Surely any scheme which you have as yet prepared for the despatch of an expeditionary force, including an entire cavalry division, would allow at least this period before the transport for the later units would be available. Not only on military grounds but on those of domestic stability I am entirely opposed on merits to the disbandment of these four yeomanry regiments in order to save so small a sum as £27,000 this year; and whatever may be decided by the Cabinet about the estimates, I should strongly oppose such a step. It is the very acme of improvidence.

Similarly I could not support the abolition of the Grant to Cadet units to save £15,000, and I really cannot understand how you could give disbandment of the Irish and Welsh Guards at the saving of £70,000 priority over the amalgamation of the 10th and 11th Hussars at a saving of £130,000.

A reduction of 30 men on the establishment of Line Battalions at home is a feasible measure and produces a substantial saving of £126,000. The amalgamation of the two London Territorial Divisions at a saving of £114,000 yields also appreciable results. But I should be very reluctant to press you on either of these points at the present time, and certainly it would be absurd to consider such melancholy steps in priority to the amalgamation of even only four Regular Cavalry Regiments, which yields a slightly greater saving, viz, £260,000 a year against £240,000.

To sum up, the suggestion I venture to make to you with absolute conviction of its wisdom and timeliness, is the amalgamation of the eight Cavalry Regiments yielding an ultimate saving of £520,000; the maintenance of every Regular Cavalry Regiment at its present strength, increasing your proposed Estimates for 1927 about £35,500, and the preservation of the four Scout and Yeomanry Regiments, reducing your saving by a further £27,000. Total net saving £458,000.

I recognise of course that this could not all become immediately effective. I do not suggest the 'axing' of men and officers below the rank of Captain. You have only to restrict the recruitments for the Cavalry and the entrance of officers from Sandhurst, &c, to effect the amalgamations in a comparatively painless manner.

I earnestly hope you will give unprejudiced consideration to these suggestions.

There are some points of detail on which I must comment. You say, page 6, section (d), paragraph 1, that you have saved £885,000 on the Regular Army by postponement of 'various very desirable "new services"'. But surely this includes £302,000 for Aden, transferred to the Middle East Vote, £130,000 for sea transport yet to be adjudicated on by Lord Cave, and £92,500 contribution towards Singapore from the Federated Malay States, total £524,000, which can hardly accurately be described as 'postponement of various very desirable new services mainly in connection with buildings and armaments'.

I should be obliged if you would let me have the full details of the Works Vote. I understand that it includes a figure of £100,000 for Imber. I must press that this should not be incurred in the present year of exceptional strain.

These suggestions would not, it is true, reach the figure of £41,250,000 which the Prime Minister mentioned to you in his letter on behalf of the

Estimates Committee. They would however appreciably diminish the gap and still further help future years. A shadow cut of £200,000 was, as you mention (paragraph 5), agreed to between us last year and whatever the explanation will be shown to be fully justified by the events. I do not yet know the total amount of the Surrender which in spite of this shadow cut the War Office will make at the end of the year. It will however, apart from China, certainly be substantial. In these circumstances a further allowance for under-spending could certainly be made next year without of course involving you in any further reduction of services. I would far rather face a supplementary estimate within moderate limits than over-budget at the present time.

The financial situation discloses not only a heavy deficit this year, but a large prospective deficit involving serious new taxation. It is the more essential that Parliament should have real and unmistakable economies presented to them in all departments.

Yours very sincerely,
Winston S. Churchill

William Bridgeman to Winston S. Churchill

(*Churchill papers: 18/32*)

9 February 1927 Admiralty

My dear Chancellor,

Many thanks for your letter of the 7th inst. I am very glad to think we are practically agreed on my Estimates—and it is gratifying to receive your assurance that you recognise the greatness of the effort we have made to assist you in this time of stringency.

As regards the two points you mention, I am sorry I do not agree with you. When the larger ships take the place of the old ones, there must be an increase in vote A and a reduction of 250 now, while not saving more than perhaps £10,000 this year will make a further increase look bigger—But we are all the time doing our best to keep Vote A as low as is compatible with requirements.

As for the Shadow Cut, it is really more your affair than mine. I am convinced that 2½ millions is too large for this year. Last year 2 millions would have been too large, but for the coal stoppage, and this year the probability of retardation is not great. Indeed there seems to me a possibility of catching up some arrears. If you make it as high as 2½, I should have to say in introducing the Estimates that we had put it very high & that a supplementary estimate was not improbable—otherwise we should be accused of bad calculation. I think that everyone is expecting some increase in Navy Estimates, and that they will be pleased to find it under half a million— and I should much prefer that to the risk, amounting almost to a certainty in my opinion, of a supplementary estimate in the Spring.

Cabinet Standing Committee on Expenditure: minutes[1]

(*Churchill papers: 22/168*)

10 February 1927   Prime Minister's Room
6.30 pm   House of Commons
Most Secret

THE CHANCELLOR OF THE EXCHEQUER stated that, in view of the very serious financial position, it was imperative that the Government should be able to show that they had done everything possible to reduce expenditure, particularly on armaments.

He hoped to be able to arrange with the Admiralty for Naval Estimates for 1927–28 on the basis of a figure of £58 millions. While this figure was in excess of the figure (£56,350,000) which he had hoped to attain, it was materially lower than the provisional Estimate originally submitted by the Admiralty (£61,420,000). The reduction had been possible because the Admiralty had voluntarily agreed to postpone their new building programme for seven months. No new ships would be laid down until February 1928; this decision when known would certainly have favourable reactions on other foreign naval programmes. The Admiralty were also proposing to reduce the number of men in Vote A.

Although the Air Ministry were working on a programme of expansion, nevertheless it was hoped that the Air Estimates for 1927–28 would show a reduction of £500,000 on the Estimates for 1926–27.

With regard to the Army Estimates the Committee would remember that the Prime Minister had suggested a figure of £41,250,000. In NE 45 the Secretary of State for War made suggestions involving an estimate of £41,900,000. The difference between the two figures was not an important one, but he would ask the Committee to give careful consideration to the proposals.

[1] The Standing Committee members, all of whom were present, were Baldwin (in the Chair), Lord Salisbury (Lord Privy Seal), Sir Philip Cunliffe-Lister (President of the Board of Trade), Churchill, Walter Guinness (Minister of Agriculture and Fisheries) and Lord Peel (First Commissioner of Works). Also present at this particular meeting were Sir Laming Worthington-Evans (Secretary of State for War), Ronald McNeill (Financial Secretary to the Treasury), Sir George Barstow (Controller of Supply Services, Treasury) and P. J. Grigg.

The Committee would observe that among other suggestions the Secretary of State for War was prepared to disband two Scottish yeomanry and two English yeomanry regiments for a saving of £27,000. For the reasons set out in his letter of the 7th February Mr Churchill stated that he was unable to accept this suggestion and indeed would strenuously oppose the disbandment of these yeomanry units.

His, Mr Churchill's, alternative suggestion was the amalgamation of eight line cavalry regiments into four regiments. This would give a saving in the first year of about £100,000, and an ultimate saving of £520,000 per annum. In so important a matter social and sentimental considerations must be disregarded. The War Office was committed rightly to the policy of the substitution of tanks and other mechanical inventions for cavalry.

In his opinion the Army would be greatly strengthened by reducing the cavalry and increasing our resources in the matter of mechanical apparatus. The country could not afford the expenditure incidental to an overlapping of the two systems. Assuming that in any event cavalry reorganisation would be effected in two years' time, it was grossly extravagant to train recruits for the cavalry. Personally he would like to see his proposal with regard to the cavalry given priority to the other proposals of the Secretary of State for War. If Sir Laming was prepared to meet him in the matter of cavalry he would give favourable consideration to the proposal that £100,000 should be provided for Imber.

THE SECRETARY OF STATE FOR WAR observed that between the Chancellor of the Exchequer's suggestion and his own the difference in the saving in respect of 1927/28 was small. If the cavalry regiments to be amalgamated were all stationed at home, the saving in the first year would be £84,000, but following precedent it would be the junior regiments which would have to be amalgamated, and as four of these were abroad, transport charges would absorb the whole saving so that there would be no economy in the first year. . . .

THE CHANCELLOR OF THE EXCHEQUER repeated his objections for the disbandment of the yeomanry regiments and questioned the desirability of the abolition of the Territorial army bounty. He also viewed with reluctance the proposal for reducing the establishments of infantry battalions at home, for abolishing the grant to cadet units and for telescoping two London divisions of the Territorial Army. The proposal to reduce the establishment of Privates in Territorial units would mean that in the north of England where the battalions were at full strength men would actually have to be discharged. This, in his opinion, would be most regrettable.

THE SECRETARY OF STATE FOR WAR said that the proposal of

the Chancellor of the Exchequer would in effect mean a reduction of about 2,000 men in the cavalry. He was quite prepared to see how far such a reduction could be obtained by the cessation of recruiting.[1]

Winston S. Churchill to William Bridgeman
(*Churchill papers: 18/32*)

11 February 1927

My dear First Lord,

My advisers are definitely of opinion that we should be justified in taking the risk of a 2½ million shadow-cut. No doubt the day will come when the Treasury view of such things will be falsified, but it has not been falsified yet.

I hope you will therefore proceed to prepare Estimates in the neighbourhood of 58 millions.

Yours very sincerely,
Winston S. Churchill

Winston S. Churchill to Sir Laming Worthington-Evans
(*Churchill papers: 18/34*)

11 February 1927
Private and Personal

My dear Worthy,

I beg you to consider the very serious disadvantage at which you put yourself, and indeed the Government, by the proposals and relative valuations of your paper. The abolition of the four Yeomanry Regiments, at a saving of only £27,000 rising to £40,000; and the reduction of 35,000 men in the well-recruited units of the TF at a saving of only £140,000 this year and £73,000 pa subsequently, seem to me to be as improvident as they will be unpopular. The contrast between this and keeping 14 Cavalry Regiments at home at a cost of nearly two millions, at a time when it is admitted that the whole Cavalry position must be reviewed, is glaring. I am quite sure I

[1] That same day, at a meeting of the Cabinet Revision Committee (on tax evasion), with Churchill in the Chair, Churchill argued in favour of distinguishing between 'the one man company established legitimately by a land owner to protect his estate, and the one man company created by the financier, the sole purpose of which was to avoid taxation'. A few moments later he went on to observe 'that it would be very much better for the present Government to deal with the more glaring cases of avoidance than to allow the abuse to grow into a public scandal to be dealt with on very drastic lines, possibly by some future Socialist Government' (*Cabinet papers: 27/338*).

could convince the Cabinet that the necessary savings could far better be made in the latter sphere.

You must remember there are a great many members of the Cabinet who have a great deal more experience of modern fighting than many of your professional advisers;[1] and there is so much knowledge of military matters in the country nowadays that mere assertions by the Army Council that eg 2,000 Cavalry men are worth more than 35,000 Territorials plus 2,000 Lovat Scouts etc, will not carry conviction. Everyone knows the professional bias. Moreover the social influence of the Cavalry, the education of Prince Henry,[2] etc will not appeal to the modern public either in Parliament or out of doors.

It amazes me that the War Office should take up such a position after all the lessons of the War. The argument against training several thousand Cavalrymen during the next few years at great expense for work which they will never do was considered overwhelming by all our colleagues yesterday, and I think you yourself felt its force. I beg you to consider the following practical readjustments:—

(1) Abolish the bounty, which yields £64,000 rising to £322,000, if you are sure that it will not stop recruiting.

(2) See what happens about this before you reduce the establishment of the TF by 35,000, ie, get all the recruits you can without the bounty inducement (up to present limits), losing a saving of £140,000 this year and £73,000 thereafter.

(3) Retain the four Yeomanry Regts, if necessary strengthening their cadres somewhat from the Regulars.

(4) Check recruiting for the Cavalry, so as to save 1,500 men; make what adjustments of a transitional character are best calculated to effect this with the minimum injury to your Cavalry force. I do not believe that you will find any better way than the amalgamation of eight Regiments. I cannot feel the 'juniority' argument can really stand against heavy expense.

(5) Examine further the proposals to amalgamate the two London Territorial Divisions at a saving of £114,000 this year and possibly more in future

[1] Churchill himself had been on active service in India (1897), the Sudan (1898), South Africa (1900) and the western front (1916). Of his Cabinet colleagues, Walter Guinness (Minister of Agriculture and Fisheries) had been on active service in South Africa, where he was wounded, and on the western front, where he had been mentioned in despatches three times; Sir Douglas Hogg (the Attorney-General) had been on active service in South Africa; L. S. Amery (Secretary of State for the Colonies and the Dominions) had been an intelligence officer in the Balkans and Eastern Mediterranean, 1915–16; John Gilmour (Secretary of State for Scotland) had been on active service in South Africa, where he was twice mentioned in despatches, and on the western front, where he won the DSO; and Sir Philip Cunliffe-Lister (President of the Board of Trade) had served on the western front, winning the MC.

[2] Third son of King George V. Created Duke of Gloucester, 1928.

years. These Divisions are, I believe, under strength, and after the withdrawal of the bounty may be still more so.

(6) Postpone Imber until the future of the Cavalry unit has been adjusted to provide the greater part of its future expense.

I was concerned to see that your TF plans have already become public property.[1]

Will you kindly send me over the full details of the Works Vote No 10, and also of Votes 8, 9, 11, and 12. I should be glad if these could reach me some time today, as I wish to study them during the week-end.

Yours very sincerely,
Winston S. Churchill

Winston S. Churchill to Sir Laming Worthington-Evans

(*Churchill papers: 18/34*)

13 February 1927

My dear Secretary of State for War,

I have been looking through Votes 7 to 11, and offer you the following general suggestions for savings.

Vote 7. Ask for proposals to save £10,000.

Vote 8. Ask for proposals to save £30,000.

Vote 9. It seems an extraordinary thing that when the manufacture and purchase of Warlike Stores does not exceed £1,733,000, no less than £1,050,000 should be annually expended on research and inspection. The disproportion is so striking that with every sympathy for research I would ask you to call for proposals effecting a reduction on Sub-head A of £30,000 and on Sub-head B of £30,000.

Vote 10. This vote shows a nominal decrease of £545,000; but as a matter of fact, after making allowances for the cessation of the Military Works annuity, there is an increase of nearly £300,000. I am bound to resist an increase on this vote. Upwards of £3 millions a year, year after year, in time of peace ought certainly to provide the necessary works for the Army; and new projects ought to be met out of savings on the old. You cannot count as savings the final completion by the taxpayer of long annuities for previous military work. I suggest to you a reduction of Sub-head A by £30,000; of

---

[1] Press predictions about the Territorial Army changes continued: on February 14 *The Times* predicted cuts from 636 to 500 per battalion, a cutback in the number of horses and the elimination of bounties for recruits. The War Office formally announced the ending of the bounties on 1 March 1927.

Sub-head C by £170,000; and I am of course opposing the purchases of land at Imber and Bordon of £100,000 on Sub-head E. Total £300,000. I should be much obliged if you would ask for proposals showing what would be involved in carrying out a reduction in the least injurious manner of £170,000 on Sub-head C. I note an item of £80,000 for land at Singapore. I understood that most of the land had been given by the Malay States or by Singapore itself. Could you explain the position?

Vote 11. An increase of nearly £20,000 in the cost of field training in a year when we are exposed to the special expense of the Chinese Expedition ought surely to be met by savings on other heads of this vote. I therefore suggest a reduction of £20,000.

Vote 12. From every quarter I have heard criticisms of the cost of the War Office compared to pre war. Could you let me have figures showing the proportion of this vote: (a) to the total Army expenditure; (b) to Vote A; and (c) to the strength of the Expeditionary Force in your proposed estimates and in 1914? I think you will find that with a smaller Army, a much smaller Expeditionary Force, and after being relieved of the Air administration the War Office cost has increased far beyond the decline in the purchasing power of money. You are wisely making a *pro forma* reduction of £10,000 in the estimates for 1927. I suggest to you that a further reduction of £20,000 on this vote, a sum almost equal to what would preserve the four Yeomanry regiments this year, is perfectly practicable.

The total of these reductions comes to £450,000. I have not the slightest doubt they can all be made without affecting the strength or efficiency of the Army and without unfitting it to meet any emergency likely to present itself in the next twelve months. I should be prepared, if need be, to suggest for your consideration the details of the various reductions. But this would involve some delay in the estimates, and I always found it myself preferable to ask the Departmental officers responsible for the various votes or sub-heads to show how the economies could be effected themselves. Perhaps you will talk to me about this when you come at twelve tomorrow.

L. S. Amery: diary

(*Amery papers*)

16 February 1927

CABINET

Winston just before we separated produced the suggestion that we should launch a document of protest threatening to turn them [the Russians] out if any bloodshed occurred in China as a result of their mischief making.

Winston S. Churchill: Cabinet memorandum[1]

(Churchill papers: 2/155)

16 February 1927
Confidential

RELATIONS WITH THE SOVIET GOVERNMENT

As suggested at the Cabinet, I have drafted the following alternative concluding paragraph to the draft note to the Soviet Government prepared by the Foreign Office. The actual wording is, of course, merely suggestive.

In my view if serious loss of British life occurred in China, by which I mean, a number of soldiers, traders or missionaries killed or massacred, feeling in this country and in Parliament would attribute such a result in no small measure to the machinations of the Soviets and would not tolerate the continuance of relations with them. It would be impossible for English families to receive the news of the killing of their sons and brothers by mobs or armed forces spurred on and instructed by Russian Bolshevists and yet acquiesce in the authors of these wrongs being accorded not merely the means to continue their propaganda in our midst but even the ceremonial usages of the Court and of the Foreign Office. The shedding of blood and the loss of life would be a signal which none could ignore.

If this be true, ought we not to say so in advance? Do we not thereby give to our people in China the best chance of escaping without maltreatment? Do we not give to the Soviets the best chance of proving a desire for better relations? Do we not propound a policy which the country and Parliament will understand and would regard at once as practical and prudent? Do we not gain the maximum security against a future evil, postpone for the time being an admittedly extremely difficult decision, and at the same time prepare a foundation upon which—should the worst come to the worst—action would be clear and simple?

If no catastrophe occurs, our hands are free, nay indeed Russian relations may enter upon a better phase. If on the other hand there is serious bloodshed, we are threatening nothing that we shall not be irresistibly forced to do, and we are only threatening it in time to give the best chance of averting the evil.

WSC

[1] Circulated to the Cabinet as Cabinet paper 61 of 1927.

Winston S. Churchill: draft paragraph to note to the Soviet Government

(Churchill papers: 2/155)

16 February 1927

It is the hope and firm belief of His Majesty's Government that a peaceful and bloodless settlement of the present difficulties will be achieved, though possibly not until after a lengthy and difficult period has been traversed. In the meantime they feel it their duty to make it clear to the Union of Socialist Soviet Republics that should the hopes of a peaceful and favourable outcome in China be frustrated and should in fact any serious collision or loss of life to British subjects or British soldiers occur, they will hold themselves the sole judges of the responsibility of the Soviet Government in the matter, and unless they are satisfied that the Union of Socialist Soviet Republics have done everything in their power from this time forward to avert lamentable incidents will feel themselves unable to continue any longer the efforts they have made and are making to maintain the machinery of diplomatic and commercial relations between the two Governments. His Majesty's Government utter this warning while there is time for the Soviet Government, if they attach any value to their relations with Great Britain, to prove by practical steps and their consequences that they desire their continuance.

Winston S. Churchill to Lord Birkenhead

(Treasury papers: T172/1569)

18 February 1927

I hope you will not resist my suggestion for an examination of the issues arising out of the possible Russian threat to Afghanistan and India. I did not contemplate at all a detailed discussion in the full committee, but only that a sub-committee of four or five ministers should be set up to study the matter and to set it definitely in the same position as was occupied before the war by the German menace to France.

To show you how necessary this is, I could not for instance make up my mind whether we ought to assist Afghanistan to defend her northern territories without knowing what military consequences and commitments were involved. This knowledge can only be obtained by secret and thorough study with maps and experts. The principal ministers in my opinion ought to know as much now about the conditions of such a conflict as they did about a German invasion of Belgium. Otherwise a sudden emergency will produce pure babel. I think you would be unwise with your responsibilities not to see that at least a portion of your colleagues have the means of informing themselves on matters of such gravity.

There is of course no hurry, and there would be quite time enough when Jacob[1] returns about the middle of March.

Winston S. Churchill to Stanley Baldwin
(Churchill papers: 18/43)

18 February 1927

My dear Prime Minister,

I am much obliged to you for meeting my wish to be chairman of the Cabinet Committee on Block Grants as recorded in the Cabinet Minute of Wednesday. Nevertheless it is well to put on record the reasons which justified such a course.

Originally the Minister of Health proposed a Poor Law scheme which involved a fresh charge upon the Treasury of £1½ millions. From a purely departmental standpoint it would have been my duty to criticise this increase in relation to our general financial position in the same way as other departmental expenditure is canvassed. The Treasury however put forward a larger scheme by which a far better financial arrangement would be made of a permanent character although at a higher cost. This cost may ultimately amount to £7 or £8 millions a year which the Treasury do not reject in view of the lasting reform in the relations between national and local finance which would follow. Obviously however the offer which we have made must be conditional upon the securing of satisfactory terms.

The Treasury proposal is made in no narrow departmental interest but solely for the general good. If, as the result of our further enquiries, it should be found that the agreement of the other Departments cannot be obtained, the Treasury are of course free to withdraw their offer. The Block Grants policy would fall to the ground and we should revert to the original proposals of the Minister of Health and to the need of examining them from the financial standpoint. The worst therefore that the Committee can do to the other Departments represented upon it is to leave them in the same position as they are now and that they would have been in if no Treasury proposal

---

[1] Claud William Jacob, 1863–1948. Entered the Army, 1882. Major, Indian Army, 1901. Brigade-Commander, Dehra Dun Brigade BEF, 1914–15. Divisional Commander, Meerut Division, 1915; 21st Division, 1915–16. Commanded the II Army Corps, 1916–19. Lieutenant-General, 1917. Knighted, 1917. General, 1920. Chief of the General Staff, India, 1920–4. Commander-in-Chief, India, 1925. Field-Marshal, 1926. Secretary of the Military Department, India Office, 1926–30.

had been made. On the other hand the report of such a Committee advocating a £7 or £8 millions charge upon the Exchequer for what we should regard as an unsatisfactory scheme would leave the Treasury in a far worse position than it is at the present time. There is therefore no parity as far as this question is concerned between the position of, say, the Home Office or the Board of Education on the one hand and that of the Chancellor of the Exchequer upon the other.

Moreover the question of the future treatment of rates and taxes must be a vital feature in the Treasury policy of the next few years. It lies in the very centre of our affairs and is an essential and integral part of Budget proposals. It would be entirely contrary to custom for the initiative in such matters to be undertaken by any other Minister than the Chancellor of the Exchequer. It seems therefore that if the Treasury were to be included in the Committee, it could only be by presiding over it.

Alternatively, a Committee could be formed without Treasury representation to study this or any other question involving expenditure. As long as the Treasury were not represented I should remain perfectly free to criticise the resultant recommendations in the Cabinet uncompromised by association with any preceding Committee report.

I am sending a copy of this to the Minister of Health, and I am sure you and he will believe that no personal consideration has entered into my views.

Winston S. Churchill to General Smuts
(Churchill papers: 1/194)

21 February 1927

My dear Smuts,

Some months ago you sent me a deeply interesting book on Philosophy, into which I have peered with awe. I now venture to retaliate by sending you a couple of volumes in which I am sure you will find yourself much more at home.[1]

I follow always the course of your affairs with that enduring sympathy which springs from wartime comradeship. I hope it will not be long before you pay us a visit. You will find a very warm welcome awaiting you from your many friends, and from none more than those who with you have faced the battle and the breeze of the 20th century of the Christian era.

[1] *The World Crisis 1916–18*, published on March 3 in two parts. 7,523 sets were printed, but the demand was such that on February 28, three days before publication, a further 2,600 were ordered by the publisher. By April 28 the total number of sets printed was 13,963. On March 5 J. M. Keynes praised Churchill in *The Nation* because he 'pursues no vendettas, discloses no malice', and Keynes went on to describe the book as 'a tractate against war—more effective than the work of a pacifist could be'.

Winston S. Churchill to Professor Lindemann
(*Churchill papers: 18/43*)

22 February 1927

My dear Prof,

I send you some comments on your formula and memo which have reached me from the Inland Revenue. You are no doubt used to the asperities of scientific discussion. I have found the mathematical argument thrilling.

Standing Committee on Expenditure: minutes
(*Cabinet papers: 27/339*)

23 February 1927

BLOCK GRANTS

CHURCHILL: The Treasury favoured the change from the percentage to a Block Grant system, mainly as an escape from the present unsatisfactory position under which year after year the Exchequer was forced to find large sums of money in respect of the activities of Local Authorities the policy of which could not be effectively controlled by the Government. The Government got no credit for their large grants. The pound for pound principle was a great incentive to expenditure, and easily lent itself to expenditure and waste. For these, among other reasons the Exchequer was prepared to find the large sum of £8,400,000, representing the total cost of the scheme, but the money would only be found as part of a comprehensive scheme of reform and reorganisation of the relations between the local and Central Governments.[1]

Committee of Imperial Defence: minutes
(*Churchill papers: 2/155*)

25 February 1927
Secret

IRAQ

MR CHURCHILL said that the maintenance of internal order in Iraq depended fundamentally on the squadrons of aircraft, whether seven, ten or

---

[1] Neville Chamberlain told the Standing Committee on Expenditure that he liked Churchill's scheme as 'it relieves the Local Authority from that minute scrutiny of its expenditure by the Central Government which was an inevitable feature of the Percentage Grant System'.

twelve, located in the main Air Force station at Hinaidi. As long as this entrenched camp for aircraft was kept secure, air power could operate all over the country; although he did not suggest that this air power would be sufficient to prevent invasion, it would act as a deterrent, and in any case enable the local Government to maintain internal order. The maintenance of British aircraft in Iraq also enabled any part of the Middle East to be reinforced without trouble or expense, and without any ostentatious movement of force. This aspect was, he suggested, the centre and foundation of the whole question under consideration.

Mr Churchill stated he accepted the idea that the Middle East, ie, Egypt, the Sudan, Aden and Iraq, should be considered as one military sphere for aircraft in Imperial defence. He looked on the Air Force in Iraq as an integral part of the air power of Great Britain, and for this reason he did not consider that the local Government should be asked to pay more than the difference in cost between maintaining air units at home and abroad. Future capital expenditure, he suggested, should be made the subject of a legitimate claim on the local revenues, or a loan charge to be recovered in due course.

On the other hand, the year 1928 was looked forward to as the time when Iraq would bear the whole cost of her administration, paying for all levies and forces used in that country, except the air force, for reasons already given. An exception to this principle might be necessary if an Imperial battalion had to be retained in Iraq for the security of the Hinaidi aerodrome.

Apart from this, Mr Churchill said that in his opinion it would be wrong to continue giving financial assistance to Iraq for defence purposes after 1928. It seemed to him that a new treaty allowing for the presence of British air forces in Iraq on the lines he had indicated should be made. We could inform Iraq that the British air forces would normally be there, and that they could make arrangements for local defence on that assumption. Such an arrangement would provide, firstly, for the maintenance of internal order in Iraq based on our air power, and, secondly, the necessary facilities for a British air scheme in the Middle East. It would not, however, afford any guarantee for defence against serious invasion by Turkey, and, in his opinion, air, supplemented by native troops, could not be expected to deal alone with such an eventuality. The external defence of Iraq must be undertaken by the League of Nations, who might bring pressure to bear on Turkey elsewhere, either at Constantinople by arrangement with Greece or Bulgaria, or by other means.

Finally, Mr Churchill suggested that the proposed scheme should now be worked out, and that negotiations with Iraq should be entered on during the coming year.

Winston S. Churchill to Edward Carson
(*Carson papers*)

28 February 1927   Treasury Chambers

My dear Carson,

I hope you will accept from me a copy of my new book about the War. We lived through a good deal of it together & hoped the same, suffered the same & did not always think differently. You will find a few words, very inadequate, of reference to your work at the Admiralty where you actually had to live through the worst period during which the great remedial decisions were taken. It is strange how kind Ulster men have been to me. I think they have treated me better than I have been treated by anybody else in public life—& I might almost say better than they have treated anyone else who is not one of themselves, & I was indeed at one time very much the contrary. You in particular have always been a good friend to me, both in the War & afterwards, as much as you possibly could & I take this opportunity which affords itself to authors, of making a very small acknowledgement.

Believe me
Yrs very sincerely
Winston S. Churchill

Winston S. Churchill to Earl Haig
(*Haig papers*)

28 February 1927   Treasury Chambers

My dear Field Marshal,

Although I cannot expect that you will share the opinions which this book contains, I believe you will regard them as the result of reflection devoid of ill-will. I therefore venture to send you a copy, with many thanks for your kind & broad-minded assistance.

I also send you 100 facsimiles of yr 'Back to the Wall' letter, wh I am sure will be much treasured by the ex-servicemen to whom they are given.[1]

Believe me
Yours vy sincerely
Winston S. Churchill

[1] On 11 April 1918, three weeks after the German breakthrough on the western front, Haig had issued an order to 'all ranks' of the British forces in France, in which he declared: 'with our backs to the wall, and believing in the justice of our cause each one of us must fight to the end. The safety of our Homes and the Freedom of mankind alike depend upon the conduct of each of us at this critical moment.' Churchill reproduced a facsimile of the whole message, as drafted by Haig himself, as a special insert between pages 434 and 435 of *The World Crisis 1916–1918*.

March 1927

Winston S. Churchill to J. C. C. Davidson[1]

(Churchill papers: 18/51)

2 March 1927

BETTING TAX

Dear Davidson,

Many thanks for your letter.

I do not think it is likely that the tax will be altered until at any rate it has run through one whole flat racing season. All Governments have to put up with a certain amount of underground attacks by vested interests, which manifest themselves at bye-elections.[2] It is not possible to alter legislation because a handful of people move out from place to place with money and motor cars. Everything goes to show that the tax will produce a substantial revenue without doing the slightest harm to sport.

Winston S. Churchill to Robert Boothby

(Boothby papers)

7 March 1927

My dear Boothby,

I should not let Snowden's remarks ruffle or influence you in the slightest degree.[3] It was unchivalrous and unworthy in a politician of his standing to

---

[1] Davidson, who had served as Parliamentary Secretary at the Admiralty from 1924 to 1926, had become Chairman of the Conservative Party in November 1926. He held this post until May 1930, when he was succeeded by Neville Chamberlain.

[2] On 23 February 1927 the Conservatives had lost Stourbridge to Labour, the Conservative majority of 1,910 having been transformed into a Labour majority of 3,099.

[3] During a debate on Anglo-Russian relations on 3 March 1927, Snowden accused Boothby of inconsistency in his attitude towards Russia. Boothby had visited Russia during the previous year, and had written an optimistic report on prospects of Anglo-Russian friendship. But on 3 March 1927, speaking just before Snowden, Boothby had condemned the Soviet Union for agitation in China, and for influencing the TUC during the General Strike. Snowden replied: 'The honourable Member's complete change of attitude in regard to Russia may

make an attack of that character upon a young Member who had not assailed him in any way. It was very unlike Snowden, and I expect he regrets it already. I should certainly not advise any explanations. If one is conscious of having acted in accordance with his convictions, one can always afford to disdain taunts until at least a thoroughly convenient opportunity comes for repaying. I thought you spoke very well, and was most pleased to be able to hear you. I read with suitable emotion your very kind and very excellent review.

Winston S. Churchill: Cabinet memorandum

(Churchill papers: 22/155)

8 March 1927
Secret

THE QUESTION OF EXTENDING FEMALE SUFFRAGE

1. It has been said that every extension of the franchise has benefited the Conservative Party, and it is certainly true that the latest election on the widest franchise has produced the largest homogeneous Conservative majority. There is, however, a danger that such generalisations do not take sufficient account of times and circumstances. The gradual extension of the franchise over a century has been steadily accompanied by a general improvement in prosperity and by the rallying of new classes to Constitutional government, to the defence of property and to the maintenance of the Empire. The consequences of the gigantic extension of the franchise in 1918 have been masked by two very important facts; first of all the withdrawal of 80 adverse Irish votes, and secondly, the splitting for the time being into two unequal but substantial parts of the pre-war anti-Conservative British vote. But for these two facts, ie, if parties had continued on pre-war lines, Conservatism would probably be still in a minority. Even under the super-favourable circumstances of the last election, a majority of 600,000 votes was cast against us. If the adverse vote[1] had its proper numerical representation, we should even now be in a minority in the House of

---

be regarded as a result of the mesmeric influence of association with the Chancellor of the Exchequer. I would suggest to the honourable Member that he should continue that association and if he continues to crawl along the hedge-bottoms he will be an Under-Secretary before very long.'

[1] At the General Election in October 1924, 5,489,077 voters had cast their votes for the Labour Party and 2,929,747 for the Liberal Party: a total 'adverse vote' of 8,418,824, as against 8,039,598 votes cast for the Conservative Party.

Commons of about 20; and if to this had been added the 80 adverse Irish, of 100. It would therefore seem that the 1918 extension would not necessarily in itself have been favourable to Conservatism.

2. The Irish exclusion is no doubt permanent; but it would be very rash to assume that the adverse vote against us in 1924 will indefinitely fail to secure adequate representation in Parliament. Even on the existing basis any mistake on our part which created a '*Bloc des Gauches*' would by that very fact alone place us in a minority. In any case we must expect a continuous approximation of the adverse voting strength towards its arithmetical representation in Parliament. Some sort of arrangement between Liberals and Labour against vote splitting will almost certainly play a part in the next election. Is this the moment for us to increase the electorate by approximately 25 per cent? A mathematical survey is hardly encouraging! If in an electorate of 21 millions we are in a minority of 600,000, we should in an electorate of 26 millions be in a minority over 750,000 votes. Elections are decided by the margins and a 25 per cent larger adverse margin would be thrown against us *even if the new electorate was no less favourable to us than the old*.

3. The quite decided reports received from the Chairman of the Party as to the complexion of the extended electorate will no doubt have been read by the Cabinet. They seem to have taken a good many members of the Cabinet Committee by surprise. In so far as they are well-founded they reinforce the purely mathematical tendencies mentioned above. It was moreover pointed out to us that any extension of the franchise on a large scale would create such extraordinary discrepancies between the size of constituencies—ranging perhaps from 100,000 to 35,000—that a Redistribution Bill, with all its disturbance and unpopularity and with all its undermining effects upon the personal relation of individual Members to their constituencies, would be inevitable in the present Parliament. Since the greatest numbers of the new voters would be found in the industrial areas, such a measure must undoubtedly give a large number of additional safe seats to the Socialists at the expense of existing country constituencies. Along this path we may easily march to a decisive and long-lasting defeat.

4. Such considerations cannot be brushed aside as immaterial or unworthy by those who are responsible for the guidance of the one great organised Party capable at the present time of affording a solid and integral basis for British Government. There is no country so devoid of any form of constitutional safeguards as ours, nor is there any in which the influence of a passing mood upon the electorate is so direct and decisive. Neither is there any community of equal magnitude whose economic life is so artificial and complex or whose affairs are so vast, delicate and varied. Moreover, the facts of the particular period through which we are passing—the aftermath

of the war, the general strike and the subversive movement in the industrial population, the enthronement of a revolutionary faction in Moscow devoted to the cause of world revolution, the disorganised condition and flimsy structure of the ever-growing Labour Party at home—all enjoin prudence and impose responsibility upon us in an unusual degree. In a few years the assimilative power of British institutions, the healing process of peace, the revival of world prosperity, may ease the whole position. Above all, the Labour party, amalgamating with Liberal elements, may well be steadily developing into a trustworthy though unpalatable alternative administrative instrument. Its programme will become more solidly defined. A Socialist majority at the next election might claim a mandate for anything between a sort of milk-and-water sentimentalism and a general overturn. As time passes the extreme elements will be driven out of the Labour party and a 'Bloc des Gauches' formed which will not be very different in character and intention from the Radical majority of 1906. But that position will not be reached by the next election. The good of the nation as a whole requires a step by step advance and forbids a violent alteration in the existing wide political basis. Certainly before any such plunge is taken there ought to be a reasonable certainty that the vast new electorate of 1918 has been digested and properly incorporated in the various Party organisations. Above all, no such adventure should be decided upon without long, earnest study and discussion by the responsible Government.

5. I cannot feel that there is any deep or forceful popular movement in favour of a further immediate extension of the franchise. Nearly a quarter of the present electorate do not even trouble to use their votes. The decision to enfranchise 5 or 6 million additional electors, and finally to transfer the control of our affairs to a majority of women,[1] is surely one of the greatest events of our history. I have never heard it discussed except casually in any council of which I have been a member. The House of Commons has only chattered about it in the irresponsible atmosphere of a private Member's Friday. It was in no sense an issue at the last election. I do not believe it counted in the slightest degree in the decision which men and women all over the country then took. When I fought the Westminster election in the spring of 1924, I declared flatly against any further extension for at least ten years without being conscious of any appreciable loss of support. In the General Election so little was the matter in the public mind that I do not remember having referred to the declaration of the Leader of the Conservative Party and I certainly continued to answer the routine questions of the women's societies by general statements to the effect that 'while the principle

---

[1] In the General Election of 1929 there were 15,193,000 registered women voters, and 13,665,000 registered men voters.

of an equal franchise for both sexes was indisputable it was too soon to make a new large expansion of the electorate'. No one seemed the least upset at this.

6. The Prime Minister's declaration was as follows:—

'The Unionist Party are in favour of equal political rights for men and women, and desire that the question of the extension of the franchise should, if possible, be settled by agreement. With this in view they would, if returned to power, propose that the matter be referred to a conference of all political parties on the lines of the Ullswater Committee.'[1]

Here we have a statement of the general intentions and outlook of the Conservative Party the essential point of which is not disputed to-day by any important section of public opinion, namely, the principle of equal rights for men and women. No one disputes that this is bound to come, but as to when the goal is to be reached we are, according to the Prime Minister's statement, entirely free. There are many planks in Party platforms which, owing to changing circumstances, very often and very happily are rendered entirely obsolete. The greatest and most vital of our pledges at the last Election was to give steady and stable Government and to combat the Socialist movement. Although, therefore, we were bound in principle, we were perfectly free so far as Election pledges are concerned as to time, degree and method.

7. On the 18th February, 1925, the Cabinet Minutes record that we considered the Prime Minister's pledge in relation to a Private Member's Bill to be introduced on Friday, the 20th February.[2] The Minute concludes as follows:—

'Summarising the discussion, the Home Secretary proposed, in opposing the Second Reading, to refer to the Prime Minister's pledge as quoted above, and to state that the Government intended to give effect to it later in the life of the present Parliament by proposing a Conference of all political parties.'

[1] The Ullswater Committee was a Speaker's Conference, made up of Members of Parliament and Peers, which met in 1916 and 1917 to discuss electoral reforms. Among its recommendations were Women's Suffrage. Viscount Ullswater (1885–1949), a Conservative MP, was at that time also Speaker of the House of Commons. In 1929 he became Chairman of the Lords and Commons Committee on Electoral Reform.

[2] The private member's Bill was introduced by William Whiteley, Labour MP for the Blaydon Division of Durham. Among those who had supported the Bill were five leading Labour MPs, Arthur Henderson, Ellen Wilkinson, F. W. Pethick-Lawrence, George Lansbury and Philip Snowden. The Bill did not proceed to a Division.

Such were the views and intentions of the Cabinet. But, speaking in the House, the Home Secretary used the following language:—

'We do mean to carry out that pledge. We do mean to give equal political rights to men and women, but we desire to do it by agreement. . . . The Prime Minister adheres to his statement. It will be carried out. (Hon Members: "When?") It will be carried out by this Parliament.

Viscountess Astor:[1] . . . does the Right Hon Gentleman mean equal votes at 21?

Sir W. Joynson-Hicks: It means exactly what it says. (Hon Members: "Answer!") No, it would be wrong of me to pre-judge the views which hon Members opposite might put before the conference. It means that a conference will be held—that is my proposal—at which all parties will be asked to be present, and they will then be asked to consider how the Prime Minister's pledge can best be carried out.'

So far so good; but observe what followed:—

'*The Prime Minister's pledge is for equal rights and at the next election. I will say quite definitely that means that no difference will take place in the ages at which men and women will go to the poll at the next election.*'

The italics are mine.

The House thereafter on a Government amendment resolved as follows:—

'That this House declines in the early stages of a new Parliament to accord a Second Reading to a Franchise Bill, involving as it would a General Election with the consequent interruption of important legislative and administrative work, and records its opinion that a considered scheme of franchise reform should be brought before this House at a suitable opportunity within the lifetime of the present Parliament.'

8. It is clear from the Home Secretary's speech that the 'considered scheme of franchise reform' was not to be brought before the House except as the result of a Speaker's Conference, and there is a strong implication in the words 'we desire to do it by agreement' that a general agreement between parties was a condition. Mr Ramsay MacDonald, speaking after the Home Secretary, showed how he interpreted the position—'Next year

---

[1] Nancy Witcher Langhorne, 1879–1964. Born in Virginia. Married first, in 1897, Robert Gould Shaw (divorced, 1903); second, in 1906, the 2nd Viscount Astor. Conservative MP for Plymouth Sutton, 1919–45 (the first woman to take her seat in the Westminster Parliament). Companion of Honour, 1937.

we are promised not a bill, not a principle, not a declaration of policy, but simply an enquiry, upon what we do not know. . . .' And further on 'It would be a waste of time and a farce for two or three people to go into consultation with a principle like this left open in this way.' It would therefore seem that the Leader of the Opposition did not take a serious view of the language used by the Home Secretary. Captain Wedgwood Benn spoke for the Liberal party on this point in the same sense. There was evidently a good deal of confusion as between the pledge of the Prime Minister for a conference or enquiry, the language of the Home Secretary and the Government amendment about legislation in the present Parliament, and also about the ages of 21 and 25. In the upshot the Leader of the Opposition rejected the Government declaration.

9. However, the conclusion which emerges from reading the whole Debate is undoubtedly—

First, that the Home Secretary, in the passage underlined, put an interpretation on the Prime Minister's pre-election declaration which went far beyond what the party was committed to or the Cabinet had sanctioned, and also beyond anything which had ever been discussed in a grave or practical manner by any body of responsible Ministers. Secondly, that this declaration was over-laid by and mixed up with a number of emphatic but vague statements about a Speaker's Conference and the need of a 'general agreement' and 'a considered bill . . . carried unanimously'. Thirdly, that none of these declarations, authorised or unauthorised, considered or impromptu, was accepted by the spokesmen of either the Labour or Liberal parties. They remain on record to be judged on their merits as party and Government commitments: but they were no part of a 'Parliamentary bargain' or of any compact entered into with any section of the Opposition. Nevertheless one cannot doubt that the position has been greatly changed by the Home Secretary's words, and it may well happen that the whole course of history will have been deflected by the chance utterances in the pressure of debate of a single Minister speaking beyond Cabinet authority during a Friday afternoon on a Private Member's Bill.

10. Let me say that by acquiescing in the Home Secretary's statement we have clearly made our moral position towards the House of Commons the same as his, and that he is in no way isolated in responsibility. Moreover, the Prime Minister himself, speaking at the end of the Debate, while avoiding the precise and peccant statement of our colleague, did not restrict or modify it in any way.

11. What then are the courses open to us? I feel that while the Prime Minister's declaration must and can be made good, we must hold ourselves free at this moment to take an independent decision upon the expansions

given to it. The Home Secretary's statements were made to the House of Commons and the same House of Commons can, if it pleases, relieve us from them. The Parliament has still nearly three years to run, and in consequence it cannot be said that it is too late for us to seek any relief we may require. I hold therefore that unless we are convinced on the merits that absolutely equal rights for both sexes *at the next election* would be in the main interest of the British nation and Empire we ought, without losing time, to restate our position to Parliament. Such a course, though fraught with some unpleasantness, is far less questionable than to drive the country against our convictions into a decision which may not be for its good and may even prove disastrous to its peace and power. Once we have decided where out duty lies we ought not to be turned from it by the derision and reproaches in which it is the natural function of our opponents to indulge.

12. The Prime Minister's promise was to set up a conference of all Parties on the Ullswater model.

Lord Ullswater gave the following account of his conference in 1917:—

'I accepted an invitation from the Prime Minister to convene a conference of Members of both Houses of Parliament and to preside over it. The Members of Parliament and Peers whom I selected appeared to me to be eminently representative of the various shades of political opinion in Parliament and in the country upon the special topics connected with electoral reform. Their numbers were as nearly as possible proportionate to the strength of pre-war Parties in the House of Commons.'

The Conference, by its terms of reference, was asked to examine '*and if possible submit agreed resolutions* on' the various questions submitted to it. Most of its resolutions appear as unanimous but in some cases, eg, Women's Suffrage, the resolutions are stated to be the decision of the majority only.

13. The Prime Minister's promise to set up such a conference did not commit us in any way to accept its conclusions nor to accept them at any particular time, certainly not in the lifetime of the present Parliament. Nor did it commit us to any particular method nor to action of any kind in the event of disagreement. We could therefore set up such a conference without in any way prejudging our action, if we thought its advice was bad for the country. There are serious dangers in this conference: it will change the question for the first time from an academic to a practical issue and greatly increase such agitation as exists in favour of a wide departure. If it is to be set up it would be imperative that we should first of all—

(a) restate our position to the House of Commons so far as may be necessary in respect of the Home Secretary's *obiter dicta*;

(b) make it perfectly clear that we shall be bound by no decisions of the conference which are not decisions agreed upon between all three Parties; and

(c) that failing such agreement we hold ourselves free to take no action in the present Parliament.

14. I am sure that the Cabinet Committee will not be able to make any further progress on this question. It would seem that the Cabinet ought in the near future to come to a very difficult and grave decision. Much as I apprehend the dangers of this conference, I think on the whole, after much hesitation, it may prove to be the inevitable step. The promise of a conference was precise and practical, and the mere disinclination of any particular Speaker to undertake to preside over it would not be held a sufficient bar.

15. I summarise the alternatives which, in my opinion, are still open to us:—

(A) To set up a Conference like the Ullswater Conference, as promised by the Prime Minister, and as promised by the Home Secretary *in the session of* 1926, after having regained the necessary liberty of action by a Resolution in the House of Commons; and thereafter upon this Conference so far as it is open to us through representatives of our views, to refuse to agree—

(a) to anything beyond the sex equalisation of the franchise of persons over 30;

or   (b) to anything beyond 25 for both sexes;

(c) to anything beyond the compromise proposal of an equal residential qualification at 25 and an equal occupational qualification at 21 for both sexes.

(Of these subsidiary alternatives I prefer the last. I beg that it may be most earnestly examined, and that the objections to it may be weighed against the objections to other courses and not taken as decisive in themselves.)

Failing agreement to hold ourselves free to refuse to legislate in the present Parliament, or alternatively to legislate on our own solution, either (a), (b) or (c),

or (B) To throw ourselves boldly and with as much confidence as we can muster, into universal suffrage with the consequent inseparable

Redistribution Bill, both to be made effective before the General Election.

In this case a Conference would be unnecessary. All would have been conceded, and the greater includes the less.

WSC

Winston S. Churchill to P. J. Grigg

(*Churchill papers: 18/40*)

14 March 1927

I observe with pleasure a statement in today's 'Evening Standard' that we ate 50% more meat during this, the Strike year. Pray have this verified. And also what has been the consumption of bread? We certainly know how to do ourselves well.

Winston S. Churchill: remarks to a deputation

(*Churchill papers: 18/55*)

15 March 1927

DEPUTATION FROM HORSE BREEDING SOCIETIES[1]

MR CHURCHILL: My Lord D'Abernon, I am very much obliged to you for coming to see me today and for bringing so influential a deputation and also for having arranged with the other important interests who are concerned in this matter to come with you in a joint deputation. I need scarcely say at the outset that His Majesty's Government recognises the importance to this island and to its repute of the very remarkable prestige which it has so long enjoyed in consequence of its breed of blood and stock horses. It is an industry and an art and a possession linked for long generations with the evolution of English national life and character and has brought us fame all over the world.

I am sure you would be the last to accuse us of having, by the recent legislation imposing a tax on betting, injured that industry. In fact many

[1] The following Societies were represented on this delegation: the Hunters' Improvement Society, the Thoroughbred Breeders' Association (led by Lord D'Abernon), the Hackney Horse Society, the National Horse Association of Great Britain, the National Pony Society, the Shire Horse Society, the Clydesdale Horse Society and the Percheron Horse Society. In all, there were fifteen members of the delegation.

things are disputed about the betting tax and there is much controversy about it—not ended yet, indeed likely to be renewed very shortly—but the one thing which cannot be disputed is that it has not injured in any way horse breeding in this country. I notice that the Newmarket sales last December of blood stock, after the duty had commenced, when the bookmakers were in full swing in their campaign against the duty, recorded the highest results ever known, the yield being 449,000 guineas as against 380,000 guineas, the highest figure in any preceding year and 353,000 guineas in 1925. Further the number of lots sold rose from 761 in the previous year to 827, a figure only once exceeded in recent years.

The average was the best on record and it cannot therefore be said that the mere advent of the betting tax has in any way affected this most important industry. I see the average price in 1926 for the Doncaster sales of yearlings was 1,055 guineas, which is also the largest average price ever paid, and the number sold was 327 or only two less than the previous best. . . .

I make these points not in the least to diminish the force of the argument you have brought forward today, but only in order that we may make it perfectly clear that the Government do not admit and I do not admit that the tax that has been imposed has adversely affected the horse breeding industry in this country, either in thoroughbreds or in hunters. When you come to the question of whether the State should, directly or indirectly, offer some assistance to horse breeders in consequence of the tax being put upon betting that raises a number of very much more difficult questions.

The newspapers are full of reports and rumours of how the betting tax imposed last year is going to be modified in the forthcoming Budget. How they know these things I cannot tell because I certainly do not know myself. I have promised to receive a deputation from those representing various Betting Associations and I have also arranged to meet the Stewards of the Jockey Club. I have promised to receive them and to hear anything that may be said and any suggestions that may be made for improving the working of the tax, but I am not aware at present of any suggestion which has been made or which is likely to be made which is going to secure to the State anything like the revenue which we are certain to gain from the tax on its present basis, and that being so, I maintain an attitude of reserve singularly in contrast with the very confident statements which you see on every side about the proposed changes.

But I am bound to say there is one modification which it seems to me requires careful study and attention from those who are interested in the turf and those who are interested in the breeding of horses: those who occasionally indulge in betting and those who are concerned with the maintenance of the revenue, that is the totalisator. I do not know whether you have formed definite views upon that, but you have certainly quoted to me examples of the use of the pari-mutuel in France and in New Zealand; I think in India also, and in many parts of the world which seem to show that that system has been tried and developed in such a way as to give every encouragement to sport and a real support to it, at the same time yielding a substantial revenue to the State.

However, I am not committing myself in any way on that matter, but it certainly appears to me that if at any time the totalisator were legalised and became an important feature in racing in this country, that would be the moment for those who are interested in the breeding of blood stock horses and others, to press their claims equally with those of the race course proprietors for a share in whatever was left over after the Government had taken what, no doubt, would be recognised as its prior due. But I should like to point out that even in the absence of such a development which certainly may be brought much nearer by the somewhat unreasonable attitude of some of those who are concerned in working the tax, in the absence of such a development I should like to point out that we last year made a very marked distinction between the rate of tax on betting on the race course and the rate of tax on office betting. It is the difference between two per cent and three and a half per cent that was done with the direct intention of making it easier for sport to live and to put a premium on those who can go to the race course and actually see the horses run and enjoy the sport which has played so large a part in our national life. . . .

The betting tax is admittedly a fiscal experiment of an entirely novel kind, and many wise and prudent people counselled me strongly against it, but the opposition to it was practically nil either from the saints or the sinners and the revenue, even in this experimental period, although not what we hoped, is at any rate substantial and I am strongly of the opinion that this tax should be allowed a fair trial during the flat racing season with reasonable weather and unhampered by the evil effects of the strike period from which we have just emerged.

I may say that be the fortune for the future good or ill you may count upon my looking upon the interests you represent with a most sympathetic eye, and although it may not be possible for me in any direct way to assist them I should be very glad to see developments taking place which would be to their advantage and certainly, I can assure you, if I cannot give you any direct help you need not at any stage fear my obstructing any development which is favourable to the interests you represent.

Winston S. Churchill to Robert Somervell[1]

(Churchill papers: 1/194)

19 March 1927

My dear Mr Somervell,

Many thanks for your letter and what you say about my new book. I find that we subscribe to the Edenbridge Cottage Hospital, and I therefore cannot give an annual subscription to the one whose interests you watch. I send, however, a cheque for two guineas and wish it could be more.

I wonder if among your papers you have got one showing the method you used to employ in teaching the lowest boys at Harrow to analyse English sentences with the different coloured inks and so on? If you have, I should very much like to see it. I have always thought that the instruction you gave in English analysis was of great advantage to me and enabled me to learn to write passable English in spite of my aversion to the classics. I hold most strongly that boys should be taught English first of all, and that the clever ones or those who like it should afterwards as a privilege be allowed to learn Latin and Greek, but certainly not compelled.

With all good wishes, believe me

Winston S. Churchill to Cortlandt MacMahon[2]

(Churchill papers: 1/194)

21 March 1927

Dear Mr Cortlandt MacMahon,

Considering how enormously I have benefited by your treatment—to the extent almost of a perfect cure—it is only my duty to spread the good tidings to others who may be similarly helped. I am hoping that my friend, Sir

[1] Robert Somervell, 1851–1933. English and History master at Harrow from 1887 to 1911. He was Churchill's first form-master. On 12 July 1888 the assistant master at Harrow had written to Lady Randolph Churchill: 'I do not think, nor does Mr Somervell, that he is in any way *wilfully* troublesome; but his forgetfulness, carelessness, unpunctuality, and irregularity in every way, have really been so serious, that I write to ask you, when he is at home to speak very gravely to him on the subject.'

[2] Cortlandt MacMahon, 1875–1954. Instructor for Speech Defects and Breathing Exercises at St Bartholomew's Hospital, 1911–39. Treated many cases of gunshot wounds in the chest, and cases of speech damage due to the war, on behalf of the Ministry of Pensions, 1918–26. Author of several papers on stammering, published in medical journals.

Archibald Sinclair, will shortly come to you. He has a stammer which hampers him in public speaking and also suffers occasionally, though not chronically, from indigestion. I am so glad about Mrs Dudley Ward.[1]

Winston S. Churchill to Sir Archibald Sinclair

(*Churchill papers: 1/194*)

21 March 1927

My dear Archie,

I send you these papers which Cortlandt MacMahon sent me. I believe you might find him a help in more ways than one, and anyhow there would be very little expense and no risk. It stands to reason, when one thinks of it, that the internal muscles of the stomach ought to be as fit as the external, and only exercise can develop them. He has been wonderfully successful in curing stammer; and though yours is so slight as not to be a barrier to successful speaking, it is an impediment. Anyhow he has done me so much good that I am anxious to spread the good tidings to my friends.

Winston S. Churchill to Lord Beaverbrook

(*Beaverbrook papers*)

23 March 1927   Treasury Chambers
Private

My dear Max,

I have looked through the proofs you sent me. I have not had time to read them as a whole, as I should like to do, but I am very busy and feel you wish to have them back.

I have checked the various references to myself. There is only one alteration of any significance—it is on page 5. I have suggested an amendment, or alternately the two paragraphs at 'X' might be omitted altogether. They would only be used to suggest that I wanted the war.

With regard to my telegram from Antwerp. I do not know how it came into your possession. I possess no copy of it myself. I have no personal objection to it being published. It was a sporting offer, and I was very lucky

---

[1] Winifred (Freda) Birkin, daughter of Colonel Charles Birkin. In 1913 she married the Rt Hon William Dudley Ward (from whom she obtained a divorce in 1931). She subsequently married the Marquis de Casa Maury.

not to be taken at my word! The responsibility of the publication must be yours.[1]

I gather you are going to send me some more proofs and that your letter covers not only this batch but a further instalment. I shall look forward to reading them with great interest.

Would you care to give me lunch on Tuesday or Wednesday next, the 29th or 30th? I try to be away in the country as much as possible at the present moment.

Yours ever
W

L. S. Amery: diary

(*Amery papers*)

28 March 1927

Winston in very good form and rather amusing on the subject of Austen's triumphs which have mainly been forced upon him as against the policy of a purely defensive treaty with France, and Shanghai when FE and I had to fight for our lives to prevent the FO stopping the troops at Hong Kong.

Winston S. Churchill: remarks to a deputation

(*Churchill papers: 18/56*)

29 March 1927

THE BETTING TAX

Gentlemen, let me first of all thank you for the brevity with which you have stated your points of view, and also for having consented to come in one deputation instead of making it necessary for me to traverse the whole ground three times over with separate bodies.[2] I quite appreciate that each

---

[1] The telegram was one sent by Churchill to Asquith from the siege of Antwerp. Dated 5 October 1914, it stated: 'I am willing to resign my office and undertake command of relieving and defensive forces assigned to Antwerp in conjunction with Belgian Army, provided that I am given necessary military rank and authority, and full powers of a commander of a detached force in the field,' and suggesting Walter Runciman as his successor as First Lord of the Admiralty. The telegram was given by Asquith to Venetia Stanley, who later sold it to Lord Beaverbrook. It is published in full in volume III of this biography, pages 111–12.

[2] The Deputation was made up of representatives for the Turf Guardian Society, the Betting Duty Reform Association, and the Northern Bookmakers and Backers Protection Association.

speaker has spoken only for those whom he represents, and that all your points of view are not in full accord, but I have no doubt that you are all in accord in thinking that the tax at any rate is pressing heavily upon you at the present time.

That leads me to ask first of all whether a really wise policy has been adopted by the Bookmakers generally and the Turf Commission Agents in regard to the betting tax? Of course every time that in your agitation you dwell upon the crushing effect of the tax, how it will ruin sport, how it will prevent betting altogether, and so on, you tend to alarm the betting public and discourage your clientele. I do not in the least complain of criticism or agitation as long as it is fair, but I think you must yourselves consider the depressing effect which some of the incidents and propaganda of this autumn must have had upon the betting public. I do not say that is the sole cause, but it is a cause that has played its part. There is always a certain amount of friction and disturbance in bringing new taxes into operation, and I do not think you have helped yourselves to face the initial difficulties in the best possible way.

But now let us see what has been the effect. Of course opinions differ about this, and I cannot expect that you will agree with the view which I take on the evidence supplied to me, but I will tell you what it is. First of all it is clear to us that the tax has not seriously injured racing. I am informed that at the sales in the autumn bloodstock realised the highest records that have ever been known. I have seen it said that that was only because of the foreign buyers over here, but that is not true; the purely British money paid exceeded all previous records; and in addition it is not true to say that the best horses were bought for foreign countries. Far and away the largest number of the highest priced horses were bought by English owners for the British Turf.

Then we come to the question of the attendances at the different meetings. The Jockey Club have prepared most careful statistics comparing this year with the year before, and the period after the tax was imposed with the period before it was imposed. There is no doubt that these statistics show a considerable decline in attendances, but there are several causes which have led to that. No doubt the betting tax is one of them. But in our opinion it appears from an examination of these figures that the industrial depression caused by the aftermath of the recent coal dispute has had a far more serious effect than the imposition of the tax.

The weather is evidently a more important factor than either, as between one race meeting and another. For instance, in November after the tax was imposed, there was a serious falling off in attendances as compared with the previous year, but then it appears that the weather in November, 1926, was twice as bad as in the previous year. On the other hand when we get to December, there has been an actual increase in the attendances this last year as compared with the attendance at all the comparable meetings the year before. But then again the weather this last December was three times as good as in the preceding December. . . .

It is far from the intention of the Government to do a permanent injury to sport—we have every desire to avoid that—and from that point of view our interests are not at all opposed to yours. What I strongly urge and strongly advise is to give the Tax a fair trial over the Flat Racing season, or a large part of it. If then it is seen that no harm is being done, or very little harm is being done, because nobody can pretend a tax can do any good— I have not pretended this tax would do anybody any good—but if the harm is not serious and the tax is working well, we shall not be so much in disagreement as we are at the present time. If, on the other hand, it is found that there is an injury to racing as measured by the attendances at race meetings then I shall be willing to reconsider both the method and the weight of the tax in the light of the experience which will have been obtained.

Finally, I must say that there are some forms of subterranean agitation which, though legitimate in a free country, nevertheless are apt to harden opinion and rouse a combative spirit on both sides and I should strongly advise you and urge you to let us have a fair trial in a good atmosphere of the Tax during the summer of the Flat Racing season and, for my part, I promise a review of the whole position in the light of the data which then will have been obtained.

Winston S. Churchill to Sir Archibald Salvidge

(Churchill papers: 2/151)

31 March 1927   Treasury Chambers
Personal and secret

My dear Salvidge,

I have just had a vy satisfactory talk with the PM. He said he knew what was going on in Liverpool but did not wish himself or the Central Office to be involved in any way. He spoke vy appreciatively of all you had done for L'pool & the Party, & he went out of his way to say that he wd not think of allowing any personal feeling to influence his judgement. He thought that in the interests not so much of the present as of the future you wd probably be well-advised to broaden and strengthen the basis of L'pool politics, attract & enlist the younger lot, etc. But he hopes all this wd be settled with yr guidance & without dragging him in.

I said I knew you were not in the least inclined to adopt a stone-wall attitude, & that if the thing had been properly put to you, & by the proper procedures, you wd have handled it like the wise tactician yr life's work proved you to be. But it had not been presented properly. Leslie Scott[1] had seen him (the PM) & had used his name, & conveyed an impression that the Central Office was also favourable to the Scott movement.[2] The PM replied 'How cd he help seeing Scott, who was an MP, an ex-Minister, & cd come up to him in the H of C at any time. He wd have been equally ready to see you if you had asked him'. I said 'Well, after all, you were a PC.' He said 'Yes indeed, & he wd gladly see you if you wished it. You had only to ask.'

Now this is what I want you to do. The next Election will be one of deep import to the Country & the Empire, & my only wish is: 'we must be all together'. Baldwin has treated me well, & we have got on better & better every day. I want you to feel in the same way abt him as I do, & I am sure that personal contact is what is needed, & all that is needed. What I hope you will do is, to ask to see him, quoting me if you like as having suggested it, & have a full & friendly talk as soon as possible. Now do do this, & let me know when you are coming up to London so that we can meet.

Yours vy sincerely
Winston S. Churchill

[1] Leslie Frederic Scott, 1869–1950. Conservative MP for Liverpool Exchange, 1910–29. President of the Central Association for Mental Welfare, 1914–47. Chairman of the Agricultural Organization Society, 1917–22, and of the Acquisition of Land Committee, 1917–19. Solicitor-General, 1922. Knighted, 1922. Privy Councillor, 1927. Chairman of the Committee on Ministers' Powers, 1931–2, and of the Land Utilization in Rural Areas Committee, 1941–2.

[2] The Scott movement was an attempt, led by Sir Leslie Scott, to break Salvidge's dominance of Liverpool politics. One of its manifestations was a demand for full-time constituency agents in each of the seven Liverpool seats, to undermine the authority of the central agent. The movement was welcomed by the Liverpool Chamber of Commerce, and by the local trade associations, and in May Salvidge conceded the point about separate agents. Salvidge died in September 1928. Scott himself was an advocate of women's suffrage, proportional representation, and a land transfer system that would be simple enough and cheap enough to enable more of the working class to become property owners. He was also a believer in what he called 'the complete bona fides' of the Labour Party, so much so that the Labour Party seriously considered proposing him for Speaker of the House of Commons in 1928.

April 1927

Winston S. Churchill: Cabinet note[1]

(Churchill papers: 22/169)

2 April 1927   Treasury Chambers
Secret

REDUCTION OF EXPENDITURE IN 1928

We have to make up our minds on the question:—'Are we going to give up the fight for economy or are we going to make a new effort?' It seems to me that to announce that nothing more can be done, that the automatic growth of expenditure is irresistible, that the expense will steadily increase and that as far as we are concerned the taxes will never be lower would be to create quite a bad impression among people who do not know the difficulties. Moreover I do not believe such an attitude is justified: I am sure that the Cabinet could if it chose cut down the Estimates by 20 millions in the course of the present year and by so doing set an example to the Local Authorities which example, properly inculcated, would result in proportionate savings to the Ratepayers. Are we going to try or not? If not, it is no use my holding out vague hopes of future reductions; there will only be future increases. It would be better to explain that we have done our best and can do no more.

I am sure that Parliament and the country will require a further resolute effort on our part and I ask my colleagues to authorise me to speak in this sense on the Budget.

In order to show the kind of possibilities of retrenchment that are open I have caused the attached paper to be prepared in the Treasury as a basis for discussion. These proposals represent the best suggestions which the Treasury can make. Every one will have to be fought over, but personally I believe that even larger cuts would be possible provided we made up our minds to act while there is still time for the wounds to heal before the end of the Parliament.

WSC

[1] Churchill circulated this note to the Cabinet's Standing Committee on Expenditure, for consideration at its forthcoming meeting on 5 April 1927 (see page 977).

Winston S. Churchill to Sir Warren Fisher, Sir Otto Niemeyer and
Sir Richard Hopkins

(*Churchill papers: 18/40*)

3 April 1927
Most Secret

After prolonged weighing, I have decided that an increase of the Income Tax this year cannot be justified. The yield of the new Indirect Taxes is sufficient to balance the Budget of 1928 on a £50 millions Sinking Fund. If another £10 millions are needed, the right course is to find them by economy, on which we must concentrate our efforts, and some of which may be made to play a part in reducing the Estimates of this year. The character of the Indirect Taxation leaves a very fair balance between wage earning and other classes, and in addition B and A weight the scale heavily in favour of the non-wage earning classes.

The falling off in the Income Tax in 1925 coincident upon the measures taken to restore the Gold Standard shows how hard the traders and manufacturers are being ridden at the present time. To add an additional burden when the tax is already failing will be very undesirable. Moreover, we should not long have the benefit of the extra 2d. It would have to be the first item to disappear, probably next year, certainly the year after. We could not keep it on simply to keep the Sinking Fund above 50, and it is not necessary for any other purposes in our prospective finance.

This decision involves the Sinking Fund being fixed at 60 or 65. I would accept 60, but 65 would be preferable. It will, however, be necessary to show a final prospective surplus of at least £5 millions in view of China and the speculative character of the Betting Tax estimate. On the previous basis of 2d and £70 millions Sinking Fund the prospective final surplus was only £3½ millions. If only £5 millions is taken from the Sinking Fund and £7·1 millions sacrificed in Income Tax, the prospective surplus would be reduced to £1½ millions on a Sinking Fund of 65.

If a final revision of the forecast of revenue or Consolidated Fund Expenditure can be made to show an extra £4 millions for the final surplus, I am prepared to fix the Sinking Fund at 65. If no advance can be made on forecast, it will have to be 60, which will leave us with £6½ millions in hand. I think we might count on £3 or £4 millions saving *this year* to balance China, as the results of the new economy campaign. Please try therefore to adjust the figures accordingly. If nothing can be done we must be content with £60 millions, which I am sure will be regarded as an astonishingly satisfactory result in all the circumstances. I am recasting my speech on this basis.

I have also decided definitely not to deal with the Estate Duty evasion provisions this year or with the Amenity Value concession or with 'letting out the small fry'. All this stands over for next year. But the intention to deal with the Estate Duties and to remove unspecified unfairness in the basis of these Duties on Agricultural Properties will be definitely announced for simultaneous action with the other evasion provisions next year. Action accordingly.

I should be glad to see you all on Monday evening at 6.

Standing Committee on Expenditure: minutes

(*Churchill papers: 18/40*)

5 April 1927   Prime Minister's Room,
5 pm   House of Commons

THE CHANCELLOR OF THE EXCHEQUER drew attention to the very strong and widespread feeling that further efforts should be made to reduce expenditure during 1927/28. After the war, expenditure had fallen steadily for five years to the £790,000,000 of 1924, since then there had been a rise to the £818,000,000 of 1927/28, an increase of £28,000,000. As the period of automatic increases had come to an end the Exchequer should reap the full benefit of any reductions that could be made in future.

Since the Government took office they had had to face £40,000,000 of increased expenditure for which previous Governments were alone responsible. Automatic reductions of expenditure brought this figure down to £28,000,000 to which must be added the increased expenditure of £17,000,000 (mainly Widows' Pensions and the Sugar Beet subsidy) for which the Government were responsible. This £17,000,000 had been provided as to £13,000,000 by economies and as to £4,000,000 by the Road Fund. The Government could therefore justly claim that they had more than held their own.

Of the £28,000,000 of increased expenditure, £15,000,000 was attributable to the Post Office and the Road Fund both revenue producers, £8,000,000 was due to automatic increases in Old Age and other Pension services and £5,000,000 to the increased Sinking Fund. These figures were a good answer to the critics. Unfortunately the Revenue was not expanding, the forthcoming Budget would represent the limits of what could be done by way of taxation without checking a trade revival and endangering further conversion operations. Immediate economies must be realised if further taxation was to be avoided next year. It had not been practicable to repeat in 1926 the economy campaign of 1925, but the time was now ripe for a resumption of that campaign.

THE CHANCELLOR OF THE EXCHEQUER read to the Committee the draft of a statement which he suggested might be incorporated in the Budget Speech relative to the question of the abolition of the Post War Departments which was recently revived by the Earl of Oxford and Asquith in the House of Lords on 22nd March 1927. While proposing to retain the Ministries of Labour and Pensions, the statement contemplates the termination as separate Departments of the Ministry of Transport, the Mines Department and the Department of Overseas Trade.

THE PRIME MINISTER thought that the remaining proposals would give rise to no difficulty but that objection might be again raised to the abolition of the Overseas Trade Department, and in this connection he reminded the Committee that in 1922 the then Government had been forced to withdraw similar proposals based on the recommendations of the Geddes Committee. The question of which Departments should take over responsibility for the various functions of the abolished Departments would require careful consideration before any definite announcement was made. . . .

THE CHANCELLOR OF THE EXCHEQUER read to the Committee a statement (Appendix II) which he suggested should be incorporated in his Budget Speech relative to a reduction of recruitment for the Civil Service by 50% during the remaining years of the present Parliament.

THE SECRETARY TO THE TREASURY[1] warned the Committee that the proposed percentage reduction had no scientific basis and could only be a figure to be aimed at, but one which could not in fact be achieved. The Ministry of Health and the Revenue Departments for instance (including the Post Office where the big numbers were to be found) could not possibly suppress vacancies without grave prejudice to the work entrusted to them and indeed would require additional staff. He hoped that any statement would be so worded as not to commit the Government definitely to a reduction of intake of 50% because he was satisfied that such an undertaking could not be implemented.

THE CHANCELLOR OF THE EXCHEQUER thought that the position was sufficiently safeguarded by the qualifications contained in the proposed statement; the country would be reassured by a proposal of this kind. He hoped that it would be possible in the near future to hold a conference of Local Authority representatives to consider ways and means of inculcating economy in details of local administration.

[1] Ronald McNeill (see page 566, note 1).

THE MINISTER OF HEALTH[1] thought it would be very unwise for the Government to enter into a commitment unless they were sure it could be carried out.

Winston S. Churchill to King George V

(Churchill papers: 18/40)

8 April 1927

The Chancellor of the Exchequer, with his humble duty to Your Majesty, has the honour to unfold the main scheme of the Budget for 1927.

The finance of 1925 has been deranged by the Coal Subsidy and that of 1926 by the Coal Stoppage. No less than £19 millions additional expenditure was incurred on this account in 1925, and £32 millions in 1926. Apart from this the estimates of revenue and expenditure for both these years would have shown, upon a £50 millions Sinking Fund, a surplus of £5 millions in each year.

In the result the Chancellor of the Exchequer has to meet a situation of some difficulty in the present year. The change of the Income Tax from the three years' basis to that of the preceding year concentrates the losses of the strike year upon the revenue of 1927. On the other hand, the same change will concentrate the improvement of 1927 upon the finance of 1928. The worst part of our difficulty is therefore temporary, and by 1929 the revenue will fully have recovered its normal strength.

The expenditure of 1927 is estimated at £818 millions. This is £19 millions above the expenditure, namely, £799 millions, in the year of the Labour Government. But this increase is easily explained. It is common ground between all Parties, as Your Majesty will have noticed from the speeches of Lord Oxford and Mr Snowden, that the healthy growth of the Road Fund and Post Office expenditure and revenue ought not to be included in the ordinary expense of the year. This is accountable for £10 millions of the increase, while the increased Sinking Fund has added another £5 millions, leaving only £4 millions to be explained. The growth of pre-War Old Age Pensions and ordinary Service Pensions far more than cover this. All this talk about wild increases of expenditure is therefore grotesquely exaggerated. Nevertheless, resolute efforts must be made to effect further economies, and it is to be noted that the automatic growth of expenditure consequent on the pledges and promises of the three General Elections and upon the bright ideas of three successive Administrations newly arriving in

[1] Neville Chamberlain.

power is now passing away. In 1928 the automatic decreases will balance, and more than balance, the automatic increases. There are therefore good hopes that further economies will emerge as definite reductions of the total bill.

Though the Chancellor of the Exchequer estimates the revenue for 1927 at 796½ millions, subtracting this from an expenditure of £818 millions, there remains a deficit of £21½ millions. This is on the assumption that the Sinking Fund is maintained at £50 millions. Mr Churchill has never even dreamed of reducing the Sinking Fund below the statutory £50 millions. He is resolved to maintain it at that figure. But neither can he leave behind him the deficit of £36½ millions of last year, which measures the short-fall in our efforts to maintain a £50 millions Sinking Fund during the present Parliament. He feels it necessary to make an effort to pay off at least a substantial proportion, something like half, of the arrears. It is therefore not with a sum of £22½ millions, but with a deficit of between £35 and £40 millions, that he conceives himself to be confronted.

How to find the money? The Chancellor of the Exchequer will first propose a Safeguarding Duty on Translucent and Vitrified Table Ware Pottery, yielding £150,000 in the first and £200,000 in a full year.

He will propose a Duty of 33⅓% on imported Motor Car Tyres. A Duty on Tyres formed part of the original conception of the so-called McKenna Duties, which were introduced in 1917 under the aegis of Lord Oxford himself. It was omitted only in consequence of a war-time arrangement with American manufacturers, whereby we obtained the power of diverting all American Tyres passing to Europe from enemy countries. Mr Churchill now proposes to rectify this omission, with the result that the revenue will gain £700,000 in 1927 and £750,000 thereafter.

Mr Churchill will also propose a slight addition to the tax on Matches, which is favoured by the Match-making Trade, will not weigh seriously upon the consumer, and brings to the revenue £600,000 in the first, and £700,000 in a full year.

The denunciation of the Anglo-Spanish Commercial Treaty some months ago offered the opportunity of re-grading the Wine Duties by lowering the dividing line between light and heavy Wines from 30° to 25°. Full and carefully conceived preferences are given to the Dominions, with the result that Australian Wines will receive a notable advantage. An overhead increase of 6d a gallon on light Wines and 2/- a gallon on heavy Wines will also be proposed. The Wine Trade have throughout been carefully consulted. The results to the Exchequer of this treatment of the Wine Duties yield £1,330,000 in the first, and £1,500,000 in a full year. These figures include a small Duty on so-called British wines, manufactured here by the ingenious process of importing Grape Juice, which, though they have hitherto borne no tax addition have nevertheless in some cases an intoxicating value measured as high as 28° or even 29°.

Finally, in the sphere of Customs and Excise, Mr Churchill is forced to deal with Tobacco. He proposes to raise the rate of tax upon Tobacco by 8d a lb. The yield of this Duty will be £3,100,000 in the first, and £3,400,000 in a full year. It is believed that at least half of it will be found from the extraordinary profits of the Imperial Tobacco Company, and that only a portion of the tax will fall upon the consumer. Mr Churchill has reason to express very solid doubts that the price of cigarettes, the main bulk of the consumption, will be raised in consequence of the extra tax.

The total increase of the revenue through these new indirect taxes will amount to £5,880,000 in 1927 and £6¾ millions thereafter.

In the sphere of direct taxation Mr Churchill proposes to rectify a small anomaly of a highly technical character in respect of Estate Duty, which will yield £300,000 this year, and £800,000 for many years to come.

The above comprise all the permanent additions to taxation which the Chancellor of the Exchequer now desires to impose. There remains the task of finding about £30 millions of revenue. Mr Churchill proposes in the first instance to transfer the reserve of the Road Fund, which amounts to £12 millions, to the National Debt Commissioners. The revenue from the Road Fund is increasing by leaps and bounds, and there is ample money to defray all the undertakings entered into. The reserve is used as the working capital of the Road Fund to finance its commitments throughout the financial year. This is necessary as the bulk of the receipts from licences is collected in the last quarter of the year. Mr Churchill proposes that the Exchequer shall become the banker of the Road Fund and that it shall finance them in the same way as it finances all other public departments, and consequently that their local reserve shall be pooled with the general financial resources of the State.

Your Majesty will remember how the withdrawal last year of one month of the extended credit allowed to Brewers was gracefully accepted by the Trade and yielded no less than £5 millions to the revenue. This year Mr Churchill proposes to take one month more, yielding a like sum in 1927. He has reason to believe that this also will be borne by the Trade without any serious complaint and without any diminution of the gravity of Beer.

Finally, the attention of the Chancellor of the Exchequer has been drawn to Schedule A, 'the Landlord and Property' section of the Income Tax. Before the War this tax was paid in one instalment on the 1st January, the tenant paying the tax out of the first quarter's rent and remitting the balance to the landlord. However, when the tax rose in 1918 to 5/- and upwards, such a procedure was no longer possible for the amount of the tax exceeded the amount of the quarter's rent. A concession, unnoticed in those days of immense figures, was made to the Schedule A taxpayers, and they were allowed to pay their tax in two instalments, one on the 1st January and the other on the 1st July. Now that the standard rate of Income Tax has fallen to 4/- the reasons for this concession have disappeared, and Mr Churchill proposes that in future the Income Tax on Schedule A shall be payable on or after the 1st January in any year. This change will impose upon the class of taxpayers affected only a moderate burden. They will in effect lose the interest on half the tax for 6 months. In the case of a man with £10,000 a year from rents, this will amount to £25.

There remains, of course, the inconvenience to the individual of finding a larger sum of money at an earlier period. Mr Churchill does not under-rate this. Nevertheless, he has no doubt that, as compared with a heavy addition to the standard rate of the Income Tax, the new burden will be thankfully accepted, especially by those who do not have to share it. The total additional burden upon the Schedule A tax-payers will be the equiva-lent of an amount of £500,000 a year. But the results to the revenue are far more important. No injury is done to the revenue of future years; the whole series of payments are pulled forward in a manner very similar to what has been done about the Brewers' Credit; all that will happen is that when the world comes to an end, if that date should fall between December and July in any financial year, the Chancellor of the Exchequer of the day, whoever he may be, will be found in possession of one additional instalment of Schedule A. That instalment is worth to the revenue no less than £14,800,000 in the current year.

Thus Mr Churchill proposes to raise by permanent taxes approximately £6 millions a year (£7½ millions in a full year) and by these windfalls, or once-for-all acquisitions, no less than £32 millions—a total addition to the revenue of 1927–28 of £38 millions.

This is much the best way of bridging the awkward gap caused in the revenue returns by the aftermath of the follies and disasters of last year. It converts a prospective deficit of £21½ millions into a prospective surplus of £16½ millions. It enables the Chancellor of the Exchequer so far from raiding the statutory £50 millions Sinking Fund, as many shrewd judges have believed inevitable and have even counselled, to raise it to the un-precedented level of £65 millions, and to provide in addition a small balance of £1½ millions as a final prospective surplus.

The increase of the Sinking Fund to £65 millions is especially important to the financial prestige of the country at a time when enormous conversion possibilities are converging upon us year after year. It is about the only feature of a Budget which makes its impression on foreign countries, and it is well worth while making exertions to present to the world the spectacle of Great Britain emerging from all her troubles with her financial flag still flying, still discharging all her obligations in an unexampled manner and maintaining those signs of evident strength which are indispensable to our increasingly threatened sovereignty in international finance.

Your Majesty's Servants at the Cabinet Meeting this morning showed themselves extremely relieved, and even gratified, at this unexpected escape from the ugly alternatives which otherwise alone remained of either raiding the Sinking Fund or putting 6d on the Income Tax.

All of which is submitted to Your Majesty with the Chancellor of the Exchequer's most humble duty by Your Majesty's faithful and devoted servant and subject.

Lord Stamfordham to Winston S. Churchill

(*Churchill papers: 18/40*)

8 April 1927   Windsor Castle

My dear Churchill,

The King is most grateful for your interesting letter of today, explaining the general scheme of your Budget for this year. Although, as you will appreciate, His Majesty finds it difficult, without further study, to grasp completely some of the more technical points, he congratulates you upon the ingenious manner in which you have met so formidable an undertaking in dealing with a situation seriously aggravated by the complications in the coal industry in 1925 and 26: and the King feels that the public will share his relief that you will have accomplished your task without either raiding the Sinking Fund or putting an additional 6d on the income tax.

Yours very sincerely
Stamfordham

L. S. Amery to Stanley Baldwin

(*Baldwin papers*)

9 April 1927

My dear Stanley,

I don't know what the House and the country are going to say to Winston's Budget tomorrow. All I can say is that his exposition to us on Thursday left me profoundly disquieted both on economic and political grounds, and compels me to write to you very frankly about the whole situation as I see it ahead of us.

We are confronted by a problem of appalling difficulty, which calls for an immense effort at the reconstruction of the whole base of our industrial and financial system. It is the solving of that problem which alone can save this country and the Empire. It is by our contribution to its solution that we as a Party are going to be judged when we next go to the country. The effort to find it is the supreme task before us as a Government, and falls in a peculiar sense upon one of its members, the Chancellor, who does not even realize that the problem exists.

A few hand to mouth dodges for picking up odd windfalls, a hope that better trade and a few millions saved by cheese-paring here and there may tide matters over next year: that is the beginning and end of it. Not the glimmering of an idea how the paralysing burden of our present direct taxation is to be progressively reduced, not a suggestion for helping the productive industries from which the revenue after all is derived, still less any inkling of the difficulties threatened by our growing adverse trade balance and by the repercussion of this on our power of investment overseas, on our bank rate at home, or of the effect of a high bank rate on the recovery of industry and on the possibility of debt conversion. . . .

The more I see of Winston, the more I like and enjoy him, and the higher I rate his military instinct. But I do care about policy, and would much sooner go out and preach what I believe in at the street corners than acquiesce in the drift to disaster for the sake of staying in office.

Stanley Baldwin to King George V

(*Baldwin papers*)

12 April 1927   House of Commons

During the early part of Question Time, long before the Chancellor's statement was due to begin, Members of Parliament were flocking into the side galleries upstairs in order to make sure of an advantageous position. The Strangers' galleries were packed at a very early stage of the proceedings, while the large assembly of Peers showed that they were taking an unwonted interest in the proceedings of the House of Commons. The only vacant place seemed to be the seat above the clock, but that did not remain empty long as His Royal Highness the Prince of Wales was seen to take his seat just before the Chancellor began his speech. The scene was quite sufficient to show that Mr Churchill as a star turn has a power of attraction which nobody in the House of Commons can excel.

In the meantime, Members on the Floor of the House had been in a boisterous and cheerful mood, a sure indication of great events to come. The Socialists in particular seemed to be overcome with gaiety and hilarity. Hence the boisterous reception which they accorded to Mr Snowden as he advanced slowly to his seat, which was presently countered by the enthusiastic welcome given to the Chancellor of the Exchequer when he came into the House beaming with smiles, having apparently filled the role of a Pied Piper of Hamlin from Downing Street to the House of Commons.

The Budget speech was in every respect a complete justification of the audience which the Chancellor's personality had collected. It was a masterpiece of cleverness and ingenuity which was only matched by the subtlety and ingenuity of the framework of his Budget proposals. Seldom has a Chancellor been faced with a more difficult or unenviable task. The picture which he had to present was of the gloomiest possible description. Thanks to the coal stoppage there was a decrease of revenue in 1926 amounting to £17,500,000, and an increase of expenditure of about £14,500,000. In consequence there was a deficit on the year of over £36,000,000; but that was not the whole story. During the current year, on the existing basis of taxation, the Chancellor found himself left with a prospective deficit of £21,500,000, quite apart from the obligation which he imposed upon himself to make some provision for the deficit of 1926. In short, the task which he set before himself was to find £36,000,000 of new revenue during the current year. Over and above all this the profits of trade during 1926 were no less than £150,000,000 below the original expectation, and the results of the coal stoppage would be felt not only during the current year but also to a smaller extent in future years.

Such was the formidable task with which Mr Churchill was faced. Nevertheless, this gloomy background only served to enhance his buoyant optimism, just as the severity of his subject served to intensify the flashes of irrepressible gaiety and humour which, at oft-recurring intervals, brought a touch of life and humanity into his soulless theme.

There is in Mr Churchill an undercurrent of buoyant mischievousness which frequently makes its appearance on the surface in some picturesque phrase or playful sally at the expense of his opponents. Thus, when describing the lamentable effects of the coal stoppage, he represents himself not as an impartial judge but only the public executioner whose task it is to apportion the burden but not the blame. . . .

If there is one criticism that might be levelled against the speech, which was otherwise perfect, it is that some of Mr Churchill's observations on the subject of national economy and retrenchment were characterised by a slight appearance of flippancy which might have been better dispensed with, having regard to the strong feelings of Members on this subject.

Mr Churchill's speech also served to illustrate his cheerful and buoyant optimism. Notwithstanding the lamentable results of last year's events, Mr Churchill cheered himself with the thought that the sufferings arising from the shocking breakdown in our civilisation were not as intense as they might have been. . . .

Then again there was Mr Churchill's wonderful sense of the dramatic touch. In order to maintain interest, all Chancellors have to arrange their speeches so as to keep their most important secrets up their sleeves to the last moment; but nobody could have practised the art of tantalisation better than did Mr Churchill. Having set before the House the nature of the task with which they were confronted, he showed the most deft manipulation in the order and arrangement of his proposals, so as to keep Members keyed up to the highest pitch.

These qualities, however, were merely the ornaments and embellishments which helped to place the speech in the very front rank. The framework of the speech which constituted the background exhibited all the practised skill of the perfect craftsman which is the product of intensive training and hereditary ability.

It was not until the speech was concluded that Members were able fully to realise the marvellous ingenuity of the Budget. The trepidation of the Conservatives rapidly turned into intense rejoicing and intense admiration for the cleverness exhibited by Mr Churchill.

His enemies will say that this year's Budget is a mischievous piece of manipulation and juggling with the country's finances, but his friends will say that it is a masterpiece of ingenuity. The only criticism which may be heard from his own supporters is whether it might not have been more politic to reserve such a popular Budget for next year when political considerations will make such popularity a matter of considerable expediency. The hidden reserves have now been exhausted and if any unfortunate events during the current year should lead to increased expenditure, the Chancellor of the Exchequer cannot have recourse to such methods again. That, however, is a political consideration which does not minimise the extent of Mr Churchill's triumph.

All of which is submitted by Your Majesty's humble, obedient Servant,

Hazel Lavery[1] to Winston S. Churchill

(*Churchill papers: 2/151*)

12 April 1927

My dear Winston,

This is just a word of impulsive admiration and affection. Your speech was so brilliant, so courageous and fine. I hope you won't mind my applauding it and sending you my very constant friendship—and love to you and Clemmie always,

from John and Hazel Lavery

Thomas Jones: diary

(*Jones papers*)

12 April 1927

Papers full of Winston's Budget speech. *The Times* calls it ingenious, but most of the other papers speak of trickery. Everyone is surprised at the absence of fresh direct taxation. The Imperial Tobacco Company advertise that the price of their products will not be raised.

I crossed to No 10 at 10.15, and met the Governor of the Bank looking thoroughly ill and disconsolate. I suggested that the Chancellor had bemused the public with a false sense of security. The Governor recalled Blondin[2] and tried to recall the name of a famous juggler.

In a few minutes Winston joined us, all smiles and buoyancy. 'It was as good a get-out as we could get' was his salutation to the Governor, who made no reply. Winston moved in to see the PM for a few minutes and when he came out he and the Governor went out together, and I went into the Cabinet room with J. C. C. Davidson.

I had not seen the PM for some days and he was horribly tired and once again twitching restlessly. As a work of art he thought Winston's speech as good as it could possibly be. There was a general sense of bewilderment at the end of it.

---

[1] Hazel Martyn, 1887–1935. Second wife of the painter Sir John Lavery, whom she married in 1910. Active in seeking to reconcile Sinn Fein with the British, 1920–2. In recognition of the part she had played in the Irish settlement, the Free State Government put her likeness on their banknotes.

[2] Jean François Gravelet, 1824–97. Known as 'Charles Blondin'. A French rope-dancer, in 1859 he crossed Niagara Falls on a tightrope. Later he repeated this feat blindfold, then with a wheelbarrow, then with a man on his back, and finally on stilts.

Lord George Hamilton to Winston S. Churchill

(*Churchill papers: 2/151*)

13 April 1927

My dear Churchill,

I must heartily congratulate you upon the excellent Budget you have drawn up out of very unpromising data. I always predicted for you a prosperous business career, because you combine industry, ability & courage, & with those three qualities in combination almost any difficulty can be surmounted.

Don't trouble to answer this.

Wishing you all success in your subsequent undertakings.

Believe me,
Yours very truly,
George Hamilton

Ronald McNeill to Winston S. Churchill

(*Churchill papers: 2/151*)

14 April 1927

My dear Winston,

Now that we have a break I really must congratulate you on your two really brilliant speeches this week on the Budget. I think you must have been going in for Cone's system, for you seem to me every day to get better & better. You seem to me to have very decidedly increased in brilliancy since you returned from riotous living with the Liberal harlots to your own Spiritual Home. If you don't leave too much to my ineffectual blundering, the Budget ought to go through with ease & credit. . . .[1]

I hope you'll have a good rest.

I'm going tonight to Ireland till Tuesday.

Yours ever,
Ronald McNeill

[1] On April 14 George Lane-Fox wrote to Lord Irwin about Churchill's budget: 'the city had reacted favourably to it, and the Opposition are obviously disappointed at the plausible way in which Winston extricated himself from his difficulties. . . . It has certainly revived the flagging spirits of the Conservative Party' (*Irwin papers*). On May 19 during the second reading of the Finance Bill, David Grenfell, the Labour MP for the Gower Division of Glamorganshire, wrote in the *Daily Chronicle*: 'A smiling Chancellor of the Exchequer is a public danger. He should keep a straight and hard face, suppress human kindness and deal stiffly with his colleagues. This is an impossible counsel for Winston. His own laugh and the gusto with which he provokes laughter in others are among his chief assets. He encourages the Labour backbenchers to laugh with him rather than howl at him.'

Winston S. Churchill to Sir George Barstow and Alfred Hurst

(Churchill papers: 18/45)

15 April 1927

Let me have a report showing exactly how all pensions, other than war pensions, are paid. Has each Department of State got a Pension Branch of its own, ie War Office, Admiralty, etc? If so, let me have the staff of each of these departments, together with the amount of money they distribute and the number of pensioners they serve. Compare the over-head charges in each case with those of the Ministry of Pensions.

The idea I propose to test exhaustively is whether a saving would not be achieved by pooling the whole of the pensions of all the departments in one office, viz the Ministry of Pensions.

Winston S. Churchill to Sir Otto Niemeyer

(Churchill papers: 18/45)

16 April 1927
Most Secret

I am deeply concerned at the Debt position. You will have noticed that practically every responsible Conservative speaker on the Budget protested against the Sinking Fund of over 50 millions, and you may take it as absolutely certain that it will not be possible in the present Government to impose permanent taxation for that purpose. You may take it therefore that 50 millions is the maximum of future Sinking Funds, as far as I am concerned. On the other hand the danger of leaving debt redemption in its present unsatisfactory condition, and to give a Socialist Government the opportunity of meeting a public need obvious to all by some unsound expedient like a forced loan or a capital levy, veiled in the form of a surtax, is grave.

In my opinion the Socialists ought to, and easily may, concentrate upon the admitted failure of the Capitalist system and our present policy to deal adequately with the debt and to liberate the country from its thralls. It is only their lack of ability which prevents them from doing this.

On the other hand, in these circumstances it seems unwise to let the opportunity afforded this year by the 65 millions Sinking Fund slip away. I wish therefore to begin immediately all preparations for a Conversion operation on the largest possible scale. It is not necessary now either to decide whether this is practicable or not, or to fix the date. I wish you to prepare—in the first instance for my eye alone—the best method.

I suggest for your consideration as a starting point the conversion of 2,000 millions of the 5% Loan into a 4% stock, to be redeemable at par in 25 or 30 years. The stock would be immune from all future income tax taxation as the threatened Socialist sur-tax. It would therefore be peculiarly a stock on which Banks, Insurance Companies and Trustees could rely. Other stock beside the 5% War Loan could be accepted under suitable conditions.

In order to set the board for such an operation all necessary measures must be taken to reduce borrowing by the Post Office, etc, and to warn Australians off the market for five or six months. Every effort should be made to secure a period of cheap money. You should advise me on what method would be possible and would be justifiable in such circumstances.

The loan would be called the Liberation Loan. I should propose to engineer an immense campaign, and to enlist all the forces of the Press, London and Provincial. I have reason to believe that ardent co-operation could be expected. I have already received assurances to this effect from the proprietors of the popular newspapers. It is hoped that the Banks, etc would, in a suitable atmosphere, be willing to exchange the old security for the new, at par; and that very large numbers of private individuals would do their bit if a sufficient movement is set on foot. Every agency would be employed for two or three months.

The matter is extremely urgent. Once you have given me the outline of the plan we can together address the Governor. I am to dine with the Bankers on May 11, and this might well be a good moment to fire the first shot.

Winston S. Churchill to Lord George Hamilton

(*Churchill papers: 2/151*)

23 April 1927

My dear George Hamilton,

How very kind of you to write to me about the Budget. It gives me great pleasure to receive a letter of approval from one of my father's contemporaries. The immediate results of the Budget have fully sustained its favourable reception, and as you will see, there has been no loss of confidence or check to the business revival such as it is.

With my best wishes, believe me
Winston S. Churchill[1]

[1] Lord George Hamilton died on 22 September 1927, at the age of 73.

Winston S. Churchill to Lord Beatty

(*Shane Leslie papers*)

24 April 1927   Windsor Castle
Personal, Private and Secret

My dear Beatty,

I have been reading the latest reports of your Committee on China and Austen Chamberlain's note upon them. I agree with your views about not frittering away forces or getting involved in unnecessary commitments. Nevertheless I am sure Chamberlain is right in thinking Hankow the place above all others at which to strike.

The situation is changing so quickly that all our judgements have to be modified, certainly at least from week to week. But on political grounds I have no doubt what our immediate objective should be. It was at Hankow that we received an affront and injury far greater than the disorders of Nanking. Owing to our weakness we were thrown out of our Concession and forced to sign a most unworthy agreement with Chen—since proved to be quite valueless for our protection, but still remaining as a most dangerous model affecting all other British and foreign Concessions.

It is this injury I wish to repair rather than what happened at Nanking. It could only be repaired by our denouncing the violated Hankow Agreement and by our re-taking and holding our Concession. That is an event which would tell its own tale throughout China, and would in addition afford us a solid and lasting satisfaction, quite different from that obtainable by firing off cannons at abandoned, obsolete and inefficient Chinese forts.

Moreover, the Japanese have made a most determined stand at Hankow, and in spite of being booted out of their Concession as we were out of ours, they fired with rifles and machine guns upon the mob and held their own without serious loss of life either to themselves or the Chinese. They have only a few men there, and their ships. But they do not seem anxious about their position, knowing the Chinese better than we do. They seem resolute to maintain themselves at this point, and I should like to see us take our stand at their side.

The questions are: What force should we require, and how long could we stay? I should have thought, judging by the Japanese proceedings, that a brigade and some batteries with the strong Naval concentration already effected would have been amply sufficient as long as the river is high. I presume the river does not fall until the late autumn. We should therefore have about six months in which to survey the scene. And if, when the river began to fall, we found no improvement and thought it too dangerous to leave our troops there, we could depart in good time, 'saving our face' to use a Chinese expression, if we pleased, by blowing up the Hankow Arsenal or taking other retaliatory measures elsewhere.

It does not seem to me that 'six hundred miles up the river' is so serious as fifty miles inland, as long as the river is navigable. It sounds very formidable, but so long as there is open navigation for armed ships, the distance does not really count as much as it seems.

The final reason for acting against Hankow is that we do not at this critical moment drive Chiang[1] off his anti-Bolshevik line. I think myself his split with the Reds is real. At any rate it is real enough for him to have shed a great deal of red blood. If he should demand the expulsion of the Bolshevist Russians, clearly there would be an enormous advantage gained. In an arrangement between Chiang Kai-Shek and Chang Tso-lin on an anti-Bolshevik basis lies far and away the best hope of our making good and honourable new treaties with the Chinese. What happened at Nanking is quite unimportant compared to such hopes.

By acting at Hankow we leave Chiang alone and concentrate only upon his new foes. We obtain a fruitful sanction instead of barren sanctions, and get out of the bad position into which our weakness at the outset compelled us to fall. There is always also the possibility—though I am not counting on this—of Chang Tso-lin's troops coming down from Honan and reaching Hankow themselves, in which case if we had already regained possession of our Settlement, we should probably make a far better treaty about Hankow with him than if our agreement with Chen still ruled.

I have ventured to put all these points before you as I see them, because although they are political issues rather than military, it is nevertheless essential that we should each in our sphere act with comprehension of the other's point of view. I am going to propose to the Cabinet that both Tyrwhitt on the spot and your Committee here should be asked simultaneously a question on the following lines:

Assuming that HMG consider the re-occupation of the Hankow concession and its retention during the high water indispensable, what are the minimum forces which would be required? I hope you will be able to give us a helpful answer to such a question.

[1] Chiang Kai-Shek, 1887–1975. Joined Sun Yat-sen's revolutionary party in 1907. A member of the revolutionary army, Shanghai, on the outbreak of the Chinese revolution, 1911. Served at Chinese General Headquarters, 1918–20. Visited the Soviet Union to study its military and social systems, 1923. Founder and Principal, Whanpoa Military Academy, Canton, 1924. Member of the Central Executive Committee of the Kuomintang, 1926. Commander-in-Chief, Northern Expeditionary Forces, 1926–8. Chairman of State, and Generalissimo of all fighting services, 1928–31. Resigned, 1931. Director-General of the Kuomintang Party, 1938. Chairman of the Supreme National Defence Council, 1939–47. President of the Republic of China, 1948. Retired, 1948. Formed a Government on behalf of the Chinese Nationalists in Formosa (Taiwan), 1949.

Turning to another topic, I am glad to hear from Dewar that the Admiralty would not be indisposed to publishing the Harper Report[1] if a question was asked upon it in the House of Commons. I think it very unfair to you that it should be so repeatedly suggested in the Press, and apparently by Harper[2] himself, that this Report is held up because you fear the publication of its contents; when all the time there is absolutely nothing in the Report (according to Dewar for I have not seen it) which in the slightest degree reflects upon your tactics or is in any way sensational.

I shall be in London tomorrow, in case you would like to discuss the China situation.

Yours very sincerely,
Winston S. Churchill

Winston S. Churchill to Lord Beaverbrook

(Beaverbrook papers)

27 April 1927   Treasury Chambers

My dear Max,

I telephoned last night to you to let you know that, contrary to my expectations, the Budget grips me on the bench all Thursday as well as Tuesday & Wednesday. Therefore I cannot dine with you as I had hoped. I am quite free on Friday, in case you have no plans.

Yours ever
W

[1] *The Record of the Battle of Jutland*, by Vice-Admiral J. E. T. Harper, was published later in 1927. Beatty, who feared that the Report would censure him for not having closed to a more decisive range, had persuaded Harper to make certain small alterations in the report to his advantage.

[2] John Ernest Troyte Harper, 1874–1945. Entered the Royal Navy, 1888. On active service in South Africa, 1899–1900; in the Ogaden, 1900–1. Commander of the Royal Yacht *Victoria and Albert*, 1911–14. Captain, 1913. Master-of-the-Fleet for Naval Review, 20 July 1914. On active service at sea, 1914–18. Compiler of the official record of the Battle of Jutland. Director of Navigation, Admiralty, 1919–21. Member of the Anglo-American Arbitration Board, 1921–2. Rear-Admiral, 1924; Vice-Admiral, retired, 1929. Nautical Assessor to the House of Lords, 1934–46. Author of two books on Jutland (published in 1927 and 1935).

Sir Hugh Trenchard to Winston S. Churchill
(Churchill papers: 2/151)

27 April 1927   Air Ministry

My dear Mr Churchill,

With reference to your remarks to me about the inaccuracy of our bomb-dropping, and also your suggestions with regard to a bomb-sight, anything that can make bomb-dropping simpler or more accurate is of value to us in the Air Service.

I have been wondering therefore if there was anybody who had an idea for a bomb-sight such as you explained to me (or whether it was only yourself), whom you could ask to come round and talk to me on the subject, so that we could try to see if something new could be developed in this direction. I am always doing my best to encourage people to give us ideas of this kind.

I feel that one of our greatest troubles is that we have never been able to practise sufficiently owing to the absence of bomb-ranges. However, I am all for trying out improved bomb-sights. If therefore there is anybody whom you could get to come and talk to me on this important subject, I would be grateful. You know me well enough to know that I like outside suggestions.

Yours v sincerely,
H. Trenchard

Winston S. Churchill to Sir Hugh Trenchard
(Churchill papers: 2/151)

28 April 1927
Private   11 Downing Street

My dear Trenchard,

The process was explained to me by my friend, Professor Lindemann, who spoke with some anxiety about the slow development of accurate bomb-dropping. He is, as you know, Professor of Physics at Oxford, and in addition is a high practical authority on bombing from the air. I am sending your letter to him, and perhaps you will communicate with him yourself. He is very often in London, and I dare say I could arrange for him to come and meet you here at lunch one day.

Winston S. Churchill to Sir Laming Worthington-Evans

(*Churchill papers: 18/41*)

29 April 1927

My dear Secretary of State for War,

More than three months have now passed since you informed the Economy Committee of your intention to effect far-reaching changes in the character of the Cavalry Arm, on which nearly £2 millions a year is now being spent. I am not prepared in any circumstances to agree to the building of a new Cavalry barracks at British expense in Cairo and to the construction of Horse Lines of a permanent character, until the decisions have been taken at the War Office affecting the general character and composition of Cavalry units.

It would be unpardonable to waste the large sum of money involved in constructing Cavalry Lines when probably half a dozen Whippet Tanks or an armoured car detachment would give far greater security to public order in Cairo than a mass of Horse soldiers. The extent of the delay involved in the construction of permanent quarters for whatever form of unit is necessary rests therefore with the War Office, and it is their duty to face the general question as speedily as possible instead of allowing money to flow out month after month for the unreformed Cavalry units while policy remains undecided.

If you wish to discuss the matter before the Economy Committee, I shall be quite prepared to do so; and perhaps in that case you will notify the Prime Minister of your wish for a meeting.

Winston S. Churchill to L. S. Amery

(*Churchill papers: 18/41*)

30 April 1927

My dear Leo,

There is no excuse whatever for Palestine being a burden on the Exchequer of this country. It is quite as capable of paying its own way in every respect as most of the Crown Colonies. I cannot understand why the idea of keeping Palestine in a dole-fed condition at the expense of our taxpayers attracts you. I should have strained every nerve to secure solvency and independence at the earliest possible moment. There is no credit, whatever, in making one country swim at the expense of another. The credit is to make it self-supporting. At the present moment the policies of which you are the special advocate are costing us considerably more than 2d on the Income Tax and I hope the return is adequate and will be judged adequate in retrospect.

May 1927

Winston S. Churchill to Sir Austen Chamberlain

(*Austen Chamberlain papers*)

16 May 1927

My dear Austen,

I fear that it will not be possible to make any concession in regard to tyres in transit or ordered before the Budget Statement. I am not surprised to learn that the American interests have been hit as I heard just before the Budget that enormous consignments of American tyres were on the way to this country in the hope of escaping a possible duty. The Ambassador's[1] complaints would appear merely to emphasise the rightness of the decision to make the duty immediately operative. Otherwise we might very well have had a repetition of what happened in 1925.

Yours vy sincerely
Winston S. Churchill

Winston S. Churchill to Sir Otto Niemeyer

(*Churchill papers: 18/71*)

20 May 1927

I have never suggested or imagined that Germany was 'financially and industrially in a better position than this country' at the present time, and I agree with all you have written on this point. Nevertheless the relative prospects of the two countries in the next fifteen or twenty years cannot be

[1] Alanson Bigelow Houghton, 1863–1941. Educated at Harvard. A glass manufacturer from 1889; President of the Corning Glass Works, 1910–18. Director of the Metropolitan Life Insurance Co, of the Carnegie Endowment for International Peace, of the Brookings Institution (Washington) and the Institute for Advanced Studies (Princeton). United States Ambassador to Germany, 1922–5; to Britain, 1925–9.

viewed with complacency by us. We have assumed since the war, largely under the guidance of the Bank of England, a policy of deflation, debt repayment, high taxation, large sinking funds and Gold Standard. This has raised our credit, restored our exchange and lowered the cost of living. On the other hand it has produced bad trade, hard times, an immense increase in unemployment involving costly and unwise remedial measures, attempts to reduce wages in conformity with the cost of living and so increase the competitive power, fierce labour disputes arising therefrom, with expense to the State and community measured by hundreds of millions.

Our debt policy has now reached a complete *impasse*. So far as the present Government is concerned there is no question of a higher sinking fund than £50 millions. The industrial disturbances have delayed the fall in the rent of money, and consequently no fruitful conversion possibilities are open. The £600 or £700 millions we have provided from the taxes or from the sales of war stores for the amortisation of the debt have been largely countervailed by increases in its nominal deadweight value which, however explicable, are baffling to public opinion and disappointing. The increase in the nominal deadweight cost of the debt is sustained by an increase in its real value and actual weight due to the fall of prices and the consequent augmentation of the bondholders' claim. I have seen it stated that the increase on this head in real value is over £1,000 millions since the war.

These tendencies will operate increasingly in the future. The nominal total of the debt will grow year by year in spite of the heavy sacrifices of the taxpayer, and the property of the bondholders will increase in value with every lowering in the cost of living and, where long term loans are concerned, with every fall in the rent of money. We have to look forward, as a definite part of the Bank of England policy, to an indefinite period of high taxation, of immense repayments and of no progress towards liberation either nominal or real, only a continued enhancement of the bondholders' claim.

This debt and taxation lie like a vast wet blanket across the whole process of creating new wealth by new enterprise. Moreover, however desirable from many points of view a gradual steady decline in the cost of living may be, it must be recognised that such a process means continuous bad trade. An era like the early years of the century in which the South African gold discoveries moved prices slightly upwards year after year, was accompanied by very good trade and employment and general contentment.

The course on which we are now steering offers on the other hand contentment only to the national bondholders. This will certainly produce political reactions in the next ten years which may well undo what good has been achieved by the rigid policy of the Bank of England. It must be admitted that in one respect the period of high taxation and slowly falling prices, with bad trade and great unemployment, into which we conceive it our duty to move may be of assistance to debt conversion, for when trade is bad there is plenty of money for Government stocks. On the other hand a trade revival would bring the forces creating new wealth into serious competition with the interests of the old wealth as represented by the bondholders.

To sum up, the financial policy of Great Britain since the war has been directed by the Governor of the Bank of England and distinguished Treasury permanent officials who, amid the repeated changes of Government and of Chancellors, have pursued inflexibly a strict, rigid, highly particularist line of action, entirely satisfactory when judged from within the sphere in which they move and for which they are responsible, and almost entirely unsatisfactory in its reactions upon the wider social, industrial and political spheres. It must, however, be admitted that any policy, even the most rigid and narrow, consistently pursued is less disastrous than successive alterations and reversals.

Germany represents the exact opposite to the above picture. The headlong torrent of events and the compulsion of defeat led to a financial collapse without parallel in history. The flight of the Mark effected a vast act of national repudiation extinguishing the *rentier* class, devouring the savings of every class except the speculative, and ultimately obliterating all internal debt and debenture charges.

It is unnecessary to dwell upon the evil and injustice of such a process. Nevertheless it is already apparent that the consequences, apart from the injustice and the suffering to individuals, are incomparably less disastrous than had been expected. German credit has not been ruined. Her power to borrow abroad has, as you point out, been abundantly proved. Her trade is extremely active. The competitive power of her industries, freed from deadweight charges, is already intense and only just beginning to come into play on the post-war world. The willingness to save and invest has not been destroyed in the German people by their previous act of repudiation. The rates at which they can borrow both at home and abroad are steadily improving. Their science and their industry are certain in a very few years to recuperate their wealth. The Reparations burden remains the only heavy bar. Even though relieved from Naval, Military and Colonial expenditure, the German people must be terribly obstructed by this, and it is by no means certain that, however great their internal wealth, it is possible for them to pass all the actual payments across the frontier.

It may well be that in the next ten years—perhaps much sooner—some very substantial mitigation of German Reparations will be forced upon the Allies, largely through the agency of the United States whose interest in her commercial loans to Germany is continually increasing.[1] In ten years' time therefore if the policy which the Treasury and the Bank have with such remarkable ability and skill pursued be carried to its logical conclusion, we may well see Great Britain with a debt still heavier—nominally and in reality—with crushing taxation, bad trade, high unemployment and great discontent; and on the other hand Germany with no internal debt, with reduced Reparations, with far lighter taxation, ever expanding trade and the contentment which comes from a sense of returning prosperity. That will be a strange contrast to be produced by military victory and financial orthodoxy on the one hand, and by decisive defeat and dishonourable repudiation on the other. It is a contrast from which most misleading deductions might easily be drawn by a democratic electorate.

WSC

Winston S. Churchill to E. L. Spears

(*Churchill papers: 2/152*)

27 May 1927   Treasury Chambers

My dear Spears,

You are wise to place boldly before the electors of the Bosworth Division[2] the twin questions of the day: Ought Trade Unions to mix themselves up so much with Party politics? and, Ought Russian Bolsheviks to meddle with British affairs?

Electors in every walk of life should ask themselves whether this mixing up of things that ought to be kept separate has not already done us all a great deal of harm. Minding one's own business is an extremely useful rule. The business of Trade Unions is to look after the interests of their members irrespective of Party, to exercise the power of collective bargaining in trade matters, to protect individual workmen from being unjustly treated, to give

---

[1] Five years later, in June 1932, sixteen countries, including Germany, met at Lausanne to discuss bringing reparations effectively to an end. Ramsay MacDonald was the senior British negotiator, von Papen represented Germany and Herriot represented France. While the Conference was sitting, the Nazi Party increased its vote from 37 per cent to 44 per cent in the provincial election in Hesse, and at the General Election held three weeks after the Conference had successfully ended reparations, the Nazis won 13½ million votes, becoming the largest single Party in Germany (the Social Democrats winning nearly 8 million, and the Communists just over 5 million votes).

[2] Spears was standing as a Conservative candidate at the Bosworth by-election. In 1922 he had been elected (with Churchill's encouragement) as a National Liberal, for Loughborough, but had been defeated by the Conservative candidate in 1924 (and had come bottom of the poll).

them additional benefits in sickness and unemployment, and to understand and watch over the life of the industries by which their members get their daily bread. It is surely not their business to go plunging into furious political battles to decide whether Conservatives, Liberals or Socialists should get into office; or to waste the time of Lodge meetings arguing, as Mr Spencer,[1] a Miners' leader, has well put it, whether Mussolini should come to England, or whether British troops should be sent to protect our people in Shanghai, or what our relations with Russia should be.

All these matters are the proper concern of working men and women as citizens and as electors, but not as Trade Unionists. For industrial matters there are the Trade Unions; for politics there are elections, Parliament, Party clubs and Organisations of all kinds. It is very important to the good government of our country and to working class prosperity to keep these things separate and to use the right tools for each task.

Still less ought Trade Unions to band themselves together to use the industrial weapon of strikes in order to coerce lawfully elected Governments, or decide great questions of national or international politics, or bring about the Socialist millennium, *et cetera*. A Parliament freely chosen on a democratic franchise is the only authority under the British Constitution for settling political issues. To bring ordinary Party politics into the factories is to do great injury to our industries already hard pressed in the competition of the modern world. To use the industrial weapon against the Constitution is either to injure the Constitution or, which is much more probable, to blunt or break the industrial weapon. It is against the interests of the country, and still more is it against the interests of Trade Unionists.

If you want to see how true this is, you have only to compare the feeling that was aroused against the Taff Vale judgment in 1904, 1905 and 1906 with the very strong support which the Government is receiving now all over the country for its Trade Disputes Bill. In those earlier years Trade Unions, having pursued a responsible non-Party line, had wide support outside their own ranks and in every class and Party; and a Bill giving them quite exceptional privileges was passed through Parliament without even a division on its third reading. But now that the extremists in the Trade Union Movement have daubed it all over with red paint and exploited it for their own political careers and advancing their own pet fads and theories and have tried to set it up as a rival to the free Parliamentary Constitution of Britain, they do not find anything like the same support in the general

---

[1] George Alfred Spencer, 1872–1957. A coal miner; President of the Nottinghamshire Miners' Association. President of the National Federation of Industrial Unions. Member of the North Midland Regional Coal Board, and the National Coal Board. Labour MP for the Broxtowe Division of Nottinghamshire, 1918–29.

mass of the nation. All this comes of mixing up things that ought to be kept separate and using the wrong tool for a job.

But the harm which has been done to our industries, and consequently through them to the prosperity of the wage earners and their wives and families, is even more apparent. Mr Lloyd George pointed out in the House of Commons with what terrible rapidity the number of days' wages lost through strikes was increasing in this country. I have had the figures calculated. They are as follows:—In the seven years ending in 1906 20 million days' wages were lost through strikes; in the seven years ending in 1913 this was more than quadrupled, 87 million days' wages being lost; and after the war in the seven years ending in 1926, no fewer than 322 million days' wages have been lost through trade disputes. In fact the number of days' wages lost has quadrupled twice over or multiplied sixteen fold.

This is the bitter fruit which has been brought to the wage earners by the extremists increasingly getting hold of the old Trade Union Movement and using it for class warfare and political ambitions. No wonder the general public throughout the whole country is deeply anxious and you hear thoughtful people everywhere saying, 'We are sick and tired of all these strikes which eat up the wages and savings of countless homes, which squander the funds of Trade Unions, including their benefit funds, and which are breaking down the industries without which this overcrowded island could not buy from abroad what it needs to keep it alive.' It is only another proof that the Red Flag Socialists ought to keep their hot heads and hot air for the Party platform and for Parliament, and for God's sake give the industries of the country a chance to recover and give ordinary working people a chance to build up a little prosperity in their homes and better themselves.

The fact that we are falling behind other countries in recovering from the war is due more than anything else to the misuse of the great Trade Union Movement by the Socialists. Unless they are checked, they will ruin the country. In fact some of them want to ruin the country, because they hope to clamber on top of the wreckage. Anyone who has heard them talk knows that this is true.

Just as the Trade Unionists have let themselves be led by the nose by the Socialist extremists, so the Socialist extremists have fallen increasingly under the influence of Moscow. Many of them are fascinated by the spectacle of a gang of conspirators having succeeded in toppling over the Russian Empire and now ruling it with a rod of iron. They think they might with a little luck do the same sort of thing here and get the country into their grip by violence, and hold it down afterwards by terror. The Russian Bolsheviks are always urging them to try. They send them money, they help them to organise, they teach them how to poison people's minds, and how to spread the propaganda of Revolution.[1]

They will not succeed! That will not be for want of trying. It will be because the British nation is on its guard. But what impudence it is that they should try!

The British people which has spread the ideas of self-government, of personal liberty and of Parliamentary institutions throughout the world has nothing to learn from these Asiatic minds, except what to avoid. Nevertheless they have done us great harm; they have embittered every British controversy, whether social, political or industrial; they have hampered progress, delayed reform and diminished prosperity. Their malignant plottings have been repeatedly exposed.

We have shown patience beyond that of Job. Perhaps contempt has led us to show more patience than was wise. But at last, after every warning had been disregarded and their bad faith was shown to be bottomless, the House of Commons by an overwhelming majority has resolved to utter the short, simple but useful word—'Go!' [I am only sorry that we cannot pack off with them their tail of spoon-fed intriguers, parasites, dupes and decoys. These however can be dealt with in their turn, according to the laws of the land they have spurned.][2]

It is lamentable that the Liberal Party has no guidance to give the British people on such a clear-cut issue. They are so busy finding fault both with Conservatives and Labour men, and also with each other, that they cannot act unitedly or with decision on any of the big practical questions of the day. Their many able leaders are at variance and speak with different voices on even the plainest matters. Mr Lloyd George who used to be so sure of himself and gave us such able leadership in bye-gone years cannot even make up his mind which Lobby to vote in. On the blunt question—Should the Russians go or stay? he could vote neither 'Aye' nor 'No'. [He could only walk out.][3] Tugged at by opposing sections of his followers, he could

---

[1] On 21 April 1927 Churchill had received Special Branch Report No 384, 'Report on Revolutionary Organisations in the United Kingdom', which referred to 'a frenzy of indignation' roused in the Communist Party by the proposed Trade Union Bill. The Report quoted a Communist Party circular of April 14, which declared: 'The aim of our party must therefore be to mobilise the workers in order to force the leaders to fight in every sphere of activity, and to use every weapon up to and including a real general strike of all workers to secure the withdrawal of the bill. Nothing less than a real general strike will be sufficient to force this government to withdraw the bill, and all the measures of agitation and propaganda of the party must be conceived with this end in view.' Similar exhortations were quoted in the Special Branch Reports No 385 of April 28, No 386 of May 5 and No 387 of May 12, all of which Churchill had studied (*Churchill papers: 22/187*).

[2] The two sentences in square brackets were deleted by Churchill in the letter as finally sent.

[3] Churchill deleted this sentence in the letter as sent, and added the sentence that follows.

only walk out of the House of Commons and take refuge at Margate; and if Sir William Edge[1] had been at his side he would have had to walk out too and sit on the beach with him.

The problems with which the British people are now confronted will not be solved by 'walkers out'. The causes which are at stake require resolute men and Parties who know their minds. You with your four wounds have proved your resolution in the field of war, and your abilities and experience would—as the Prime Minister has assured you—be welcome to the one strong, united Party upon which the stability, the freedom, and the progress of Great Britain and her Empire now mainly depend.[2]

[1] William Edge, 1880–1948. Liberal MP, 1916–23 and 1927–31. National Liberal MP, 1931–45. A Junior Lord of the Treasury, August 1919–February 1920. A National Liberal Whip, 1922–3. Knighted, 1922. A Charity Commissioner, 1932–5. Created Baronet, 1937.

[2] The by-election at Bosworth was held on 31 May 1927. Spears (Conservative) came bottom of the poll with 7,685 votes. Sir William Edge (Liberal) was elected, with 11,981 votes, and held the seat until 1945. The Labour candidate, J. Minto, came second, with 11,710 votes. Spears himself was re-elected to Parliament for Carlisle in 1931, as a Conservative.

June 1927

Sir Samuel Hoare to Winston S. Churchill
(Churchill papers: 2/152)

3 June 1927
Private & Personal

Dear Winston,

Now that the GBE is actually announced I must add this line of thanks to what I have already told you by word of mouth.[1] I am most genuinely grateful to you for what you have done.

It was the act of a very kind friend, and I shall always remember it with gratitude.

Yours ever,
Samuel Hoare

H. A. Gwynne to Winston S. Churchill
(Churchill papers: 2/152)

3 June 1927   The Morning Post

My dear Chancellor,

I must take this opportunity of thanking you on behalf of those who worked for the BRITISH GAZETTE, for your kindness in remembering them in the Honours List.[2]

Truly it may be said of you that your word is as good as a bond.

Yours very sincerely,
H. A. Gwynne

---

[1] Sir Samuel Hoare was made GBE (Grand Cross of the Order of the British Empire) on 3 June 1927. In January 1934 he was made GCSI (Grand Cross of the Star of India).

[2] Among those who had worked on the *British Gazette*, and who received the OBE in the June 1927 honours list, were Alfred Hawkins, the Chief Stereotyper of the *Daily Mail*, and Sydney Long, Night Production Superintendent of the *Daily Express*. Both honours were stated to be 'for public services', no specific mention being made of the *British Gazette*.

Winston S. Churchill to Alfred Hurst

(*Churchill papers: 18/64*)

4 June 1927
Secret

I have been wondering whether it will not be possible, and indeed necessary, to effect a great reduction in Rates next year, coupled with far-reaching reforms. I wish you to block in the picture for me. For this purpose you should assume that the changes would be on so large a scale as to dwarf the existing controversies about Block Grants, etc. The main object in view is to help productive industry and agriculture by an immense reduction in the burden of Local Rates. There are many ways of dealing with this, ie alterations in the basis of assessment. But all resolve themselves into a question of money.

You may assume in outlining the plan that I have formed a mass of manoeuvre of £30 millions a year: say, £16 millions by economies, £12 millions from a tax on petrol, and £3 millions from other sources; total £30 millions. How is this to be applied: (a) so as to give the greatest relief to production; (b) so as to achieve the greatest measure of reform in the rating system, the sweeping away of all petty obstructions and outworn relics and the establishment of absolutely modern symmetrical machinery; and (c) the enforcement of a far higher economy.

Assume therefore that you possess this tremendous leverage of £30 millions a year. Show how it could be used to the greatest advantage. You need not make detailed calculations. At this stage I only want a picture and a desideratum. We have nothing to put before the country next year; and the way is therefore clear for a vast campaign against the Rates with forces large enough to overbear the obstruction fatal to smaller measures. Also suggest me some literature upon the subject.

Lord Winterton[1] to Lord Irwin

(*Irwin papers*)

6 June 1927

... The great Parliamentary event was Winston's Budget speech, I thought it a masterpiece, and about the best I have ever heard.

---

[1] Edward Turnour, 1883–1962. Educated at Eton and New College, Oxford. Conservative MP, 1904–18, 1918–40 and 1940–51. Succeeded his father as 6th Earl Winterton, 1907. As an Irish peer, he continued to sit in the House of Commons. An original member of the Other Club, 1911. Served at Gallipoli, in Palestine and in Arabia, 1915–18. Under-Secretary of State for India, 1922–4 and 1924–9. Chancellor of the Duchy of Lancaster, 1937–9. Paymaster-General, 1939. Chairman, Inter-Governmental Committee for Refugees, 1938–45.

Winston is a wonderful fellow, I consider that he is head and shoulders above anyone else in the House (not excluding Lloyd George) in Parliamentary position, and both orational and debating skill, at the present moment. The remarkable thing about him is the way in which he has suddenly acquired, quite late in his Parliamentary life, an immense kind of tact, patience, good humour and banter on almost all occasions; no one used to 'suffer fools ungladly' more fully than Winston, now he is friendly and accessible to everyone, both in the House, and in the lobbies, with the result that he has become what he never was before the war, very popular in the House generally—a great accretion to his already formidable parliamentary powers.

Winston S. Churchill to Stanley Baldwin

(*Churchill papers: 18/64*)

6 June 1927
Secret and Personal

My dear Prime Minister,

I have been pondering on our position and prospects, and in particular on the great need we have to dominate events lest we be submerged by them. Each year it is necessary for a modern British Government to place some large issue or measure before the country, or to be engaged in some struggle which holds the public mind. In our first year we had the Widows' Pensions and Locarno; in our second we gained our victory over the General Strike; this year we have the Trade Unions Bill, Shanghai and the Russian expulsion.[1]

All these three have appealed very strongly to our own people, but gain us no support beyond the Party limits. They have enabled us to retain the initiative and keep our forces in good heart. But what are the prospects for next year?

It seems to me that in their present showing they are very bleak. We shall

---

[1] On 12 May 1927 a large number of plain-clothes policemen had raided the London premises of Arcos, the Russian State trading agency, had seized a large quantity of documents and had continued to search the building for four days, looking for a document alleged to have been stolen from the War Office. On May 24 Baldwin told the House of Commons that although no stolen War Office document had been discovered, a 'photostat' room had been found in the building, and in it a man 'known to be a secret service agent of the Soviet Government'. Both the trading agency and the Russian Delegation, housed in the same building, had carried out, according to Baldwin, military espionage and subversive activities throughout the British Empire and the Americas. Baldwin had gone on to announce that, as a result, the Anglo-Soviet Agreement would be ended, that both the Trade Delegation and the Soviet Mission must withdraw from London and that the British Mission would be recalled from Moscow.

be in our fourth Session; and the Opposition forces will have every inducement to such common action as is possible to them. On the other hand what have we to offer to our supporters or to the wider public with whom the decision rests?

We cannot pretend to have been successful in our treatment of labour. All your efforts have not secured 'peace in our time'. The state of the coal fields is certainly nothing for us to be proud of. We have not succeeded in economising and reducing expenditure. All my efforts, such as they have been, have failed and were, I think, bound to fail. We have no Agricultural policy, and the grumbling of the farmers will certainly continue and grow. What then is to be our new legislation?

We are to have a Factory Bill made up of a host of minor improvements, but with no great feature or principle on which opinion can be rallied. It will not be popular with the employers or with the Party, and the Labour and Liberal Parties will of course look at it only to crab. We are to have a Poor Law Bill which will equally fall between two stools, disturbing many things and settling few. Lastly, there is the Franchise. You know my views about that, I fear, only too well. Whatever its merits, it will arouse only dislike and discouragement in the Conservative Party. Nobody wants it, and many fear it. Forgive me for marshalling the disagreeable facts as I see them. I do so only to see how they can be overcome.

Not the least difficulty about the Franchise, and to a lesser extent the Factory Bill, is that they arm your very doubtful friends of the popular Press with just the sort of weapon they have been looking for. I am pretty sure they intend to work these grievances for all they are worth month after month, and to try to create an atmosphere of despondency and unrest among our supporters in the great group of trustworthy Constituencies—chiefly around London—where their influence is so strong. If we have only such unappetising fare to set before the public, if we have the inevitable swing of the pendulum to sustain, if it seems that our message is exhausted, we may easily find the Session of 1928 unpleasant to ourselves and injurious to the national interests we guard.

It is for these reasons that I have been casting about for some large new constructive measure which, by its importance and scope, by its antagonisms as well as by its appeal, will lift us above the ruck of current affairs. I see the plan at present only in the barest outline. To complete it and to achieve it involves an enormous amount of effort; and I inflict this tiresome letter upon you because, unless it commends itself to your judgment, it would be no use wasting time and strength upon it. The plan constitutes the main conception of the Budget of next year, and indeed of the remaining finance of this Parliament. Here it is.

£15 millions at least must be saved from expenditure, ie the Estimates of 1928 must, apart from the extra Sinking Fund, be £15 millions less than 1927. I am sure this is practicable, if we try. The bulk of it must come off the Fighting Services, principally the Navy. I believe they could yield together £10 millions without endangering our security, and I shall be prepared at the proper time to make detailed proposals to effect this. I should propose to raise another £15 millions by a tax upon petrol—not as a substitute for the Motor Licence Duties, but as an additional burden upon the motoring public. I feel this is just. The motorists are on the whole the most fortunate representatives of every class from the motor bicycle to the Rolls Royce car. They are making an immense demand upon the roads, upon the Police, upon traffic arrangements in London, upon the railways, upon the rural rates, and upon the goodwill of pedestrians. We cannot be overrun with motorists or forced into an expenditure upon roads and bridges, both upon the rates and the taxes, disproportionate to the growth of the national wealth and in striking contrast to the adversity of our basic industries. In spite of this heavy addition to their burdens, motor traffic will still steadily increase. It is so buoyant that in my opinion it will easily support and bear upwards this new charge.

I have some other resources of taxation, including possibly treating the other Schedules of Income Tax as we treated Schedule A. But these I shall probably need to balance the ordinary expense. In the upshot therefore I should seek to accumulate what in war-time parlance would be called a 'mass of manoeuvre' of £30 millions a year.

Now here is a lever, if we can obtain it, big enough to shift things with. It would be a tremendous instrument in our hands. Where shall we use it? It is no use using it to reduce the Income Tax. That is really not justified in the present state of the debt. Moreover, it would be regarded at the present time by the non-Income Taxpaying masses as class favouritism. Your plans about the women, if carried through, relegate cheaper beer to the limbo of discarded ambitions. Pensions and doles of all kinds have had their day. But there is one field which of all the others calls for action on the greatest scale. I mean the Rates.

A substantial reduction in the Rates would help every class. But it would help above all the producing class, be they manufacturers or agriculturists; and no one would it help more than those very basic industries that employ the greatest mass of labour and have to use the largest quantities of real property. It would also relieve every household, and would, I presume, directly influence the cost of living of the masses.

£30 millions applied to the Rates would enable us to make Neville Chamberlain's Bill the greatest measure of the Parliament. It would be a steam roller flattening out all the petty interests which have obstructed Block Grants and rating reform. With the power to pay such a price we should not need to be content with anything less than the very best arrangements which can be devised. The relief which the manufacturers would gain would brush away their minor grievances about the Factory Bill. Industry would be stimulated, Agriculture placated, and the immense mass of the ratepayers would be astonished and gratified. Every town and every part of the country, as well as every class, would share the boon. It might even be possible, without starving local services, to shift the basis of assessment from property to profits; and if this could be done, the relief would come with increasing effect to the depressed and struggling industries and factories, with reactions upon our competitive power and upon employment of the utmost benefit.

Of course you will see that, whereas the economies and a part at least of the Petrol Tax will bear fruit in the financial year 1928, the expense of the rating reliefs would not come upon me until 1929. Consequently I should have in 1928 the means of keeping up a good Sinking Fund to cover any conversion operations which may be opened. Moreover, I shall be better off in 1929 than in 1928, so that if £5 millions less was secured by economy, or alternatively £5 millions more was required to make the rating plan effective, I could probably manage all the same.

I have searched the field up hill and down dale, and can see nothing else comparable in advantage to the country or to the repute of your Administration. Pray let me know how you feel about it. It is really not worth while being content with half measures, or indeed with anything less than the best solutions. If we start at all, let us make a workmanlike job of it and one that will be long remembered.

There is one other point which I venture again to press upon you. You have carefully left the door open for a free vote as between 25 and 21. I attach an importance to this which I really cannot measure. It would relieve you of pressures which ought not to be personal. It relieves me of a vote which I should have more difficulty over and dislike more than anything that has ever happened in my public life. As you know, my hope is that the Lords will reject the Bill. If they did, certainly no one who voted for the Parliament Act could reproach them for using their great and newly acquired power in a case for which they seem expressly designed. But what is the advantage of keeping the question of an open vote in suspense and making a mystery about it? Why is it necessary to wait for pressure in order to take this very simple course? At the present time no one knows what to say: and we are simply waiting to be hustled, and courting it.

If, on the other hand, attention is relaxed by the promise of an open vote on this particular issue of the Franchise, and at the same time we recover command of the public mind by a great relieving operation upon the Rates, I do not see why we should not wind up the Parliament in good style.

I hope you are getting a good rest. I was delighted to see how quickly you recovered your vigour by a little care.

Believe me
Yours very sincerely,
Winston S. Churchill

Winston S. Churchill to Neville Chamberlain

(*Churchill papers: 18/43*)

7 June 1927
Personal and Secret

My dear Neville,

I have been worrying about next year which will be critical for our fortunes. The Franchise Bill will be thoroughly unpopular with the Conservative Party. It will discourage many of our workers, and be a very dangerous weapon in the unfriendly hands of the masters of the popular Press. The Factory Bill will irritate the employers, and is all made up of minor improvements without any large principle. Your Poor Law Bill, however desirable and necessary, will disturb lots of people and yet not effect any decisive reform. A fourth Session with only such unappetising fare to set before the public, with probably an adverse trend of bye-elections and a feeling that our mission has run threadbare, seems to me to be full of menace.

I have therefore been casting about for some large act of policy which will dominate the political field and enable us to retain the initiative and command indispensable to the successful conduct of affairs. I have written at length to the Prime Minister on the ideas which have occurred to me. At present they are both vague and tentative. Nevertheless as they would affect your plans in a most decided manner, I venture to open them to you in the strictest secrecy at this very early stage.

If I can get the necessary support from the Prime Minister and our colleagues, I should hope to save £15 millions in 1928 upon the expenditure of this year. I could get another £15 millions by an additional tax on petrol, which I believe the buoyant motoring public could easily bear. I have a few other ideas of taxation which will be needed to ensure the ordinary balance of the Budget on a £60 million Sinking Fund. In the upshot I should aim at securing a 'mass of manoeuvre' of £30 millions, the greater part of which would be available in 1928, and all of which would be realised in 1929.

It would not be justifiable in the present condition of the debt to use such a surplus revenue to reduce the Income Tax. The non-Income Taxpaying masses would only regard that as class favouritism. If all these millions of women get the vote—which God forfend—a reduction in the Beer duty ceases to be attractive as a political measure. Pensions of all kinds have run their course. Housing is provided for. There remains only one sphere in which action on the largest scale is open.

£30 millions is a lever strong enough to shift things. Properly used, it should enable us to find superior solutions of any group of problems which we attack. There is, as no one knows better than you, one immense sphere gaping open before us. I am inclined to think that we should use these £30 millions for a great operation in relief of Rates. With forces like that at our disposal we ought to be able to put the rating system on to a thoroughly sound and workmanlike basis and to bring it into true relation to modern conditions.

Whether it would be possible to shift the basis of rating from property to profits or not, I am not yet sufficiently informed. But of course a substantial reduction in the Rates, however achieved, would help every class, all parts of the country, every town, every Constituency. It would help in an appreciable manner every class of producer in agriculture or manufacturing alike. Mines, railways, shipyards—all the great basic industries—the very ones now most heavily burdened and hardest pressed, would gain the greatest relief. The competitive power of our industries would be stimulated, and employment should be improved. It would in fact be a Trade and an Agricultural policy. The relief given to the manufacturers would cover the vexations of the Factory Bill. The money power we should be using would enable you to make your Rating Bill thoroughly satisfactory from every point of view. We should override the petty opposition and establish a sound relation between national and local finance, with proper incentive to economy and real responsibility for the local bodies. In fact it seems to me that Rates are the key which will unlock our difficulties.

Of course you will realise what a struggle it will be to gather the £30 millions of revenue. Nevertheless I am sure it can be done, if we have enough resolution. Will you therefore but without holding me committed— turn the whole matter over in your mind and let me know how such a policy appeals to you. I do not propose at this stage to open it to anyone except yourself and the Prime Minister, and possibly later Walter Guinness; and of course unless there is very earnest support, it would not be worth while embarking on the enterprise.

Believe me
Yours very sincerely,
Winston S. Churchill

Winston S. Churchill to E. L. Spears

(*Churchill papers: 2/152*

8 June 1927

My dear Louis,

Many thanks for your letter.[1] I am very sorry you did not succeed; but I am sure it was no fault of yours and that in all the circumstances no other Conservative candidate could have sustained the onslaught. I warned you beforehand to make it perfectly clear to the Central Office that it was no favour to you, but only an arduous duty which fell to your lot. I hope you did so, because human nature is prone to many weaknesses, among which criticising an unsuccessful candidate often emerges.

Come and see me after the holidays are over, and let me know your further plans.

Winston S. Churchill to Sir Philip Sassoon

(*Churchill papers: 1/194*)

9 June 1927

My dear Philip,

The black swans arrived safely, and I conducted them to their pool. The next day they were driven off by the irate Jupiter. But a wire fence has now been constructed which will protect them from his aggression until the novelty of their presence has worn off. They look lovely, and their beaks have got much redder since they arrived. They sing to one another beautifully, and dance minuets with their necks. I am so glad to have them, and it was charming of you to send them to me. Could you let me know whether they have been mated before, or whether their journey in the crate was their first introduction to one another? Secondly, is there any chance of their breeding

---

[1] On June 2 Spears had written to Churchill: 'We have been beaten, but considering the facts the local people think it was a good effort. There was no sign of an organisation when we came down, and the fact that the Member was absent was being rubbed in by Socialists and Liberals alike. Edge has been spending at least £10,000 of Lloyd George's money in the division, and thirty paid organisers have been at work on his behalf for many months. We gave them such a run for their money that Edge and his organisers were persuaded that they were beaten.' Spears ended his letter: 'I cannot tell you how much I appreciated your letter to me. I am sure it did a great deal of good. It struck the right note and heartened the Conservatives. The Arcos raid certainly did help us, but the attitude of the Liberals in the House had not had time to sink in to the mentality of these very slow people.'

this year? Thirdly, could your bird man at Trent say what steps ought to be taken to look after them in the winter?[1] Ought they to have a house to live in, and how do you teach them to go into the house?

Once more with thanks.

Yours ever,

Winston S. Churchill to Lord Beaverbrook

(*Beaverbrook papers*)

9 June 1927   Chartwell Manor

My dear Max,

Your letter lay here for days, but I have now had time to meditate upon its extremely attractive proposition. I am afraid I cannot get away at all in June or July. Every week-end is fixed one way or another. There are large patches of Finance Bill, & my movements are pegged by Cabinets, public dinners, Unionist demonstrations etc. August then it must be, or never. How would Thursday Aug 18th suit you? I cd come then for a few days if that wd be convenient to you, & shd greatly look forward to doing so.

You ask me to suggest a cruise—North, East or South. What is the matter with Holland? The Dutch are a respectable people. I have never seen them in their homes amid their dykes & dams. Their coastline appears to be furnished with harbours affording secure & handy refuges from the turbulence of the sea. Moreover, they can be got at in a single night of open sea from Harwich. Altogether, since you ask me, I pronounce for Holland. Ja! ja! as Motley[2] said in his admirable history of these Batavians.

Yours ever,

W

---

[1] Sir Philip Sassoon's sister, The Dowager Countess of Cholmondeley, writes: 'The "bird man" was called Osborne and looked after the golf course as well as the birds. He has been dead a long time. At that time my brother had a wonderful collection of rare birds in a small lake including *tree* ducks which he said had a high note like Tetrazzini! It was always the custom of guests to feed these birds and see what new additions had been made. I should think he had 40 different species of ducks and geese.' (*Letter to the author, 14 July 1978.*)

[2] John Lothrop Motley, 1814–77. Born in Massachusetts. Educated at Harvard, Göttingen and Berlin. A friend of Bismarck. American Minister in Vienna, 1861–7, and in London, 1869–70. He published *The Rise of the Dutch Republic* in 1856 and the *History of the United Netherlands* in 1860–7.

T. E. Lawrence to Edward Marsh

(*Lawrence papers*)

10 June 1927

Winston wrote me a gorgeous letter. Called his Crisis a pot-boiler! Some pot! and probably some boil, too. I suppose he recalls that he's the only high person, since Thucydides & Clarendon, who has put his generation, imaginatively in his debt. Incidentally neither T or C was impartial! That doesn't matter, as long as you write better than anybody of your rivals.

He alarms me a little bit, for I feel that he wants to go for Russia, and the ex-bear hasn't yet come into the open. It's hard to attack, for its neighbours, except Germany, aren't very good allies for us. We can only get at her, here, through Turkey, or Persia, or Afghanistan, or China, and I fancy the Red Army is probably good enough to turn any one of those into a bit of herself, as the Germans did Rumania.

Winston S. Churchill to H. A. Gwynne

(*Churchill papers: 2/152*)

10 June 1927

My dear Gwynne,

I am very glad you are satisfied with the Honours Gazette. I wish it had been possible to recognise the services of many others, although I know that you yourself had declined to be considered. It took me a good deal of time and trouble to secure an exception being made in the case of the printers and others in their class who really bore the brunt in the crisis. I hear they are quite pleased at the recognition which has at last been accorded to them. Personally I feel deeply indebted to the Prime Minister for having departed from his general decision in order that I might not fail in the promise which I made to some of them.

I was sorry not to see you at the British Gazette luncheon this year, and I shall always look back to that extraordinary ten days. They form one of the most vivid experiences of my somewhat variegated life, and were utterly different from every other episode. I am glad to think they have left behind them a better understanding between us.

Come and see me some time and let us have a talk. I am much in the House of Commons in the afternoons, and nearly always free.

Winston S. Churchill to Sir Richard Hopkins and Alfred Hurst
(Churchill papers: 18/64)

10 June 1927

I am deeply interested in Mr Hurst's admirable note which forms a very good starting point for our scheme. I gather from it that the producing classes to be relieved would obtain an easement to the extent of half their rates under the plan proposed. I should like the Inland Revenue to select a certain number of sample firms, in order that I may see exactly how they would be affected. Would the relief be really substantial? Would it in some cases make the difference between carrying on their business and shutting down? Take also some farmers and agricultural proprietors, and let us see how they would be affected—small as well as big.

I should like Mr Hurst to apply his critical faculty to the existing rating system. His remark about the location of factories not being decided on economic merits but because of the local incidence of rates, is most valuable. I should like him to write a few pages showing the blemishes of the existing system. The principles underlying his paper seem to me incontestable.

WSC

Neville Chamberlain to Winston S. Churchill
(Churchill papers: 18/64)

10 June 1927   Birmingham
Personal

My dear Winston,

Your interesting letter of the 7th was sent on & reached me here yesterday.

I will certainly turn over what you have written, but I think it will be necessary to have a talk before I can express any opinion on your ideas.

At present for instance I don't see why you want as much as thirty millions for your purpose and I am disposed to think at first sight that the disposal of so large a sum would provoke quite as much criticism as approval.

Possibly I may have some suggestions of my own to make when I know a little more precisely what you have in mind.

I return to town on Monday.

Yours sincerely,
N. Chamberlain

Winston S. Churchill to Neville Chamberlain
(*Churchill papers: 18/64*)

11 June 1927

My dear Neville,

Many thanks for your acknowledgment of my letter. As I wrote you, my ideas are not fixed on any aspect of method or detail but only in the two fundamental points of

(a) the direction of the effort, and
(b) its large scale.

I should take no interest in a petty handling of this subject which would only bring us back into the shallows of the Block Grants Committee. Thirty millions is, after all, only one-fifth of the total amount of the rates and I cannot believe that any figure less than that would effect a first-class reform of the existing system.

I am anxious to examine the subject at closer quarters with a view to formulating a plan for discussion between us. I shall be much obliged if you will allow my advisers to have access on the most helpful terms to your experts in Rating. I should welcome a talk and of course without your constructive collaboration I should not attempt the toils which are involved in the financing of any large scheme.[1]

Yours vy sincerely,
Winston S. Churchill

Winston S. Churchill to Frederick Leith-Ross
(*Churchill papers: 18/45*)

11 June 1927

Your very interesting paper on recent French transactions leads me to ask you to consider the following point. The French apparently had and have a strangle-hold upon us enabling them to demand payment of £20 millions of gold to our great inconvenience. This strangle-hold resulted not from any genuine increase in French financial strength but was solely due to the esteem in which a world speculation held the franc. It is also true that this esteem related not to the intrinsic value of the franc but merely to what was

[1] On 15 July 1927 Neville Chamberlain wrote to Churchill from the Ministry of Health: '. . . it seems to me that a scheme which would offer a definite reduction of rates, especially in those industrial areas where the rate burden falls with crushing weight on the very shoulders least able to bear it would appeal very strongly to our supporters in the country and even to many who do not share our political views' (*Churchill papers: 18/63*).

expected to be its speculative future. As a consequence France has become possessed, as you rightly say, of large temporary resources withdrawable at call by world speculators.

Obviously therefore the foundation of the strangle-hold is extremely precarious as shock to French credit like, for instance, advent of a Socialist Government to power in France, break-up of the National Ministry, cessation or diminution of German reparations, outbreak of war between Russia and Poland, would instantly lead to an equally rapid and equally uncontrollable withdrawal of this speculative support from the franc. How then is it possible for Monsieur Poincaré to consider paying 400 million dollars to the United States when the only dollars he has to pay are these same speculative and temporary assets which may be taken from him next week? Testing the position by the only sound measures of real merits and economic values, it appears that the French strangle-hold is really not so formidable as it is assumed to be even in your excellent paper.

It seems to me that had the French persisted in their demand for the 20 millions of gold we should have sent it to them and should at the same time have replaced it by a gold credit obtained at the necessary cost in the United States. The Governor told me there would have been no difficulty in this, though I suppose it might cost say 21 millions, or a loss of a million at the outside. Pray follow up the re-actions which such a step would have had upon the French, American and European position.

With regard to the loss we should make on purchasing the gold on credit in the United States, it must be borne in mind that we are sustaining at the present time the heavy direct loss of borrowing on Treasury Bills at the rate of £4. 7. 6d, and in addition we have the set-back to trade by totally artificial and uneconomic means through the tightening of our money markets. There is even the prospect that the Bank Rate may have to be advanced. The losses would far exceed the cost of purchasing the gold. Prima facie it would seem to me that the obvious corrective on the gold basis for action such as the Bank of France would take would be a re-shufflement of gold reserves between the other important banks, subject to the necessary discount being paid.

Winston S. Churchill to Sir Richard Hopkins and Sir Horace Hamilton
(Churchill papers: 18/45)

13 June 1927
Secret and Personal

We must look ahead without delay into all possible sources of fresh taxation for next year.

We may count, I think, on about one million from some safeguarding duties.

I must bring a million from a hotel luxury tax case once again into the area of discussion.

What about powders and perfumes so increasingly enjoyed by the future electorate?

The United Kingdom Alliance suggestion about the Brewers' allowance for wastage being curtailed is well worth probing. I would be ready to gild this pill by making that small concession on the licence duty for the benefit of the public that the Brewers so high-mindedly asked for this year. This tariff should be worked for consideration on the basis of yielding $1\frac{1}{2}$ millions net to me.

The Customs should also examine all the possibilities of a tax on imported liquid fuel (not merely petrol). Show me as soon as convenient, but without consulting outsiders, how 10, 15 or 20 millions respectively could be raised on this, and especially what rates of tax would be necessary to produce the various totals.

In the sphere of the Inland Revenue we must consider very earnestly applying the Schedule A performance to the other Schedules, yielding a windfall of, say, 5 millions. I cannot exclude a slight stiffening of the Super tax scale on the higher ranges, yielding, say, 3 millions. Lastly at present there is a plan for charging interest on arrears while refusing it when we are ourselves guilty. From this 2 millions at least should be obtainable.

Here are some 8 millions odd of annual revenue and 5 millions windfall, apart from 10, 15 or 20 millions from liquid fuel, all good and worthy to be examined. But further I need not say that I welcome all suggestions which the inexhaustible ingenuity of both departments can produce. I must aim at a disposable surplus on a 50 million sinking fund of 40 or 50 millions to enable us to wind up the Parliament satisfactorily in the Spring of 1929 and with a view to the great operation upon the Rates with which you should both be acquainted.

I have marked this to the Heads of the Departments and it should not go beyond them as a connected scheme. They should simply follow out these ideas and find any new ones without involving me. Of course Sir Ernest Gowers and Sir Francis Floud[1] should be made acquainted with *everything*.

---

[1] Francis Lewis Castle Floud, 1875–1965. Educated at Cranleigh School and King's College, London. Entered the Board of Agriculture, 1894; Head of the Land Branch, 1907–14; Assistant Secretary, 1914–19. Permanent Secretary, Ministry of Agriculture and Fisheries, 1920–7. Knighted, 1921. Chairman of the Board of Customs and Excise, 1927–30. Permanent Secretary, Ministry of Labour, 1930–4. United Kingdom High Commissioner in Canada, 1934–8. Chairman, Bengal Land Revenue Commission, 1938–40. Chairman, Appeal Tribunal for Conscientious Objectors, 1940–6.

Cabinet minutes

(*Cabinet papers: 23/55*)

15 June 1927

THE CHANCELLOR OF THE EXCHEQUER made a statement to the Cabinet with regard to certain funds held in London banks to the credit of the late Imperial and Provisional Government, now amounting to upwards of £5,000,000 on which, under Article 10 of the Russian Trade Agreement the Soviet Government had undertaken to make no claims. Mr Churchill pointed out that, now that the Russian Trade Agreement had been terminated, the Soviet Government are no longer debarred from claiming this money and that, as they have been recognised by His Majesty's Government as the *de jure* Government of Russia, such a claim would very likely succeed in the British Courts. The whole of these funds had been supplied by British Tax-payers for the purpose of enabling the Imperial Russian Government to carry on the war. They formed part of the assets of the former Russian Government, and it was essential that they should not be allowed to fall into Soviet hands.[1]

Winston S. Churchill to Sir Otto Niemeyer and Frederick Leith-Ross

(*Churchill papers: 18/45*)

19 June 1927

I regard the general development of Poincaré's French policy about ratification as extremely unsatisfactory. In order to obtain a settlement we made immense concessions upon the debt, concessions which many may think in the light of current events exceeded what was right. I was authorised by M Poincaré to assure the House of Commons last year that speedy ratification would be proposed. Now apparently ratification is to be postponed and probably discarded.

I consider that we should send a formal note without delay to the French Government, expressing our concern at the statements which have been made, drawing attention to the pledge which was given, rehearsing the repeated concessions we have made, and asking for a speedy completion of the arrangement. Let me see a communication of this kind in draft. It should not be too long, very suave but at the same time very grim.

If we are not careful we shall find ourselves cheated out of everything. The question of publication will only arise in the event of an unfavourable answer.

[1] Churchill's proposal was accepted.

Edward Marsh to the Commissioner of Police
(*Churchill papers: 1/194*)

21 June 1927

Dear Sir,

I am desired by Mr Churchill to draw your attention to the danger to pedestrians crossing the Brompton Road outside No 38, the London Joint City and Midland Bank, from motor vehicles coming eastwards. As you are no doubt aware, the road widens just beyond this point, and consequently the vehicles draw in here very close to the curb. This is especially noticeable in the case of motor buses, as they have a stopping place a few yards farther on. Mr Churchill wonders whether a stone pillar could not be erected here in order to prevent accidents similar to that which happened to Mrs Churchill last week, when she was knocked down by a bus just as she was about to cross the street. Mr Churchill understands that other accidents have occurred at this point recently, and therefore feels you will agree with him that something should be done to keep the traffic from passing too close to the curb here.

Yours truly,
Private Secretary

Winston S. Churchill to Sir Richard Hopkins
(*Churchill papers: 18/45*)

22 June 1927

I was astonished to read in the papers of Sunday and Monday about the treatment meted out by the Revenue authorities to the fat Jazz Band conductor, Teddy Brown.[1] It seems to me extremely harsh to arrest a man on a Saturday afternoon, to refuse to accept a cheque or to allow any delay in which he could obtain the money, and then to fling him into prison for the week-end although there were people ready with the money to pay the whole debt. I wish a full report upon the circumstances. Considering that nearly £20 millions of Income Tax and Super-tax is owed, I cannot understand why such extreme rigour was used in the case of this unfortunate comedian.

[1] On 21 June 1927 *The Times* had reported: 'Payment to the Deputy-Sheriff of the necessary sum in cash yesterday secured the release of Mr "Teddy" Brown, an American orchestra director, who was taken to Brixton Prison on Saturday for non-payment of income tax, a tender by cheque of the sum claimed not being accepted.' Born in New York City, Teddy Brown had acted in Variety since the age of nine, and had been a member of the New York Philharmonic Symphony Orchestra for four years. He was also a noted xylophonist, and, while resident in London, had played before the Royal Family.

It is quite right to collect the taxes from such people with the utmost vigilance. Nevertheless I do not think that arrest without the option of payment and confinement over the week-end should be resorted to unless the man is expected to leave the country. I think that we should communicate with the Sheriff's officer and find out why this rough method was employed.

Winston S. Churchill: remarks to a deputation

(Churchill papers: 18/52)

27 June 1927
3 pm

BETTING DUTY

THE CHANCELLOR OF THE EXCHEQUER replied that their arguments weighed with him very much. He quite recognised that the bookmakers were in a position to foment agitation amongst what might be called the public house crowd of poor Tories. The Labour party, in putting down their clause to abolish the duty, were out to catch votes and expected that their action in so doing would have a great effect. This was, of course, a menace which could not be overlooked.

But what was the position? The duty was certainly vindicating itself by producing a substantial revenue. It is true that the estimate of £6 millions would not be reached, but it might yield something between £3 million and £4 million. This was between half and two-thirds of the tea duty and more than the duty on cheques about which so much had been heard lately.

As to the complaint that the estimate was wrong, the figure of £6 million was originally based upon a proposed duty of 5%. But when the bookmakers appealed last year for a reduced duty, they gave increased figures of turnover and in consequence when the proposed rate of 5% was reduced to $3\frac{1}{2}$% (office) and 2% (course) the estimate was allowed to stand. That was the history of the speculative estimate. The figures of yield for the month of June would be of importance.

The deputation would realise that criticisms were made whatever a Chancellor did in matters of finance. So far as expenditure went, cutting down on the Navy and Education Votes caused disturbance, and if he were to put another 6d in the £ on income tax there would be a great row. The fact was that he could not afford to dispense with £3 million or £4 million of revenue.

He mentioned that the duty had had none of the disastrous effects that were prophesied for it. The prices of bloodstock since the tax were the highest ever recorded. So far as attendances at race meetings were concerned, he had compared 1927 with 1925 attendances and had found that though there had been a certain falling off in attendances at north country meetings where the effects of the strike were much felt, he was not satisfied that in general the betting duty had caused any slackening of attendances. He quoted the figures for the Epsom meeting which showed a large increase in 1927 as compared with 1925.

On the point of the falling off in betting he quoted recent advertisements of Mr John to the effect that he had had the biggest turnover on the Derby for 37 years and Mr Douglas Stuart to the effect that he had cheerfully paid out £100,000 on winnings.[1] This did not show that bookmakers were losing business.

He must have the results of a complete year's operation of the duty before any adequate survey of the position could be made. It was important to placate voters and to do what was possible to allay irritation, but too much weight could be given to public house propaganda. He would close no door to possible changes but he must have a year's results before deciding upon any change.

He reminded the deputation that deliberately he had not touched the betting laws—indeed it was not possible to do so in a Finance Bill. But if public opinion was such that it gave opening for the introduction of a Bill amending the betting laws, his own opinion was that such a Bill might authorise the setting up of the Totalisator, the legalisation of cash betting by post and possibly some reservation of the right to refuse licences in certain cases.

---

[1] J. John Ltd, and Douglas Stuart Ltd, were both credit office bookmakers, not represented on the racecourse. Douglas Stuart Ltd had been formed in October 1926, with offices at 162 Shaftesbury Avenue, London, and did much of its business by advertising in 'quality' periodicals such as *The Illustrated London News*, with its slogan of 'no limit'. The firm's directors were Martin Benson and Sidney Freeman. Between 1930 and 1936 Benson and Freeman, as members of a syndicate comprising several other bookmakers, made a great deal of money from buying shares in Irish Hospitals Sweepstake tickets drawn for horses running in the English Grand National. In 1938 Benson bought for £60,000 the stallion, Nearco. Unbeaten winner of fourteen races, Nearco was twice champion sire in England and had immense influence on bloodstock breeding both in England and America.

Winston S. Churchill: Cabinet note during a discussion on House of Lords reform

(*Churchill papers: 22/151*)

29 June 1927 10 Downing Street

a wave of negativism.
People don't want anything done in
any direction.
'fed-uppism'.

Winston S. Churchill to John Baker[1]

(*Churchill papers: 2/152*)

30 June 1927

Dear Mr Baker,

It has come to my knowledge, since our 'breeze' in the House about the Civil Service Clause in the Trade Union Bill, that you have reason to be pre-occupied about your health. I hope you will allow me to express my very great regret on personal grounds at this, and to say that had I been aware of your trouble I should never have allowed myself to be provoked into sharp controversy.[2]

Believe me
Yours very truly,

[1] Walter John Baker, 1876–1930. Assistant General Secretary, Union of Post Office Workers. Unsuccessful Labour candidate, 1918 and 1922. Labour MP for East Bristol from 1923 until his death.

[2] On 22 June 1927 Baker had attacked Churchill's position on a clause of the Trade Disputes Bill. The Bill limited the right of civil servants to engage in certain types of political activity. Baker had himself been a civil servant, and during his speech attributed his own election to Parliament to 'the contributions of his colleagues in a similarly lowly status in life'. A few moments later, Churchill called Baker's speech a 'rasping speech, a speech which certainly showed how very far as a political representative of the Civil Service his flagrant partisanship allowed him to go'.

July 1927

Winston S. Churchill to Sir George Barstow and Sir Richard Hopkins
(Churchill papers: 18/46)

1 July 1927

CAVALRY REDUCTIONS

I am anxious you should understand the manner in which I approach this subject. The War Office have agreed pending further developments of mechanisation to make further large reductions in the strength of individual Cavalry Units. I assented to this in order less to gain an economy than to further the important transition from the horse to the machine which I consider essential. But the fact that each unit is now so reduced constitutes a still stronger case for further amalgamations.

If you will recall the arguments which had vogue in the days of Sir Arthur Haliburton[1] you will see that it was then the pride of the War Office to show the increasing cheapness of each bayonet or sabre as compared with non-combatant staffs. Applying these tests to the present depleted Cavalry Units will show how inexcusably extravagant is the present practice and how irresistible is the case for amalgamation. We have a large number of Cavalry Units each of which has its Colonel, its second in Command, its regimental staff, its band, its signallers, its medical arrangements, its barracks accommodation and all the usual overhead charges but none of which is able to produce any substantial output of immediate fighting men. It would probably be possible to give the War Office the same number of fighting sabres that they have at the present time and yet effect very substantial

[1] Arthur Laurence Haliburton, 1832–1907. Born and educated in Nova Scotia. Barrister, Nova Scotia, 1855. Served on the Commissariat Staff of the Army in the Crimea, 1855. Assistant Director, Supplies and Transport, War Office, 1870; Director, 1878. Knighted, 1885. Assistant Under-Secretary of State for War, 1888–95; Permanent Under-Secretary, 1895–7. Created Baron, 1898. After his retirement, he emerged as a strong critic of the War Office reforms of 1903 (which had been effected partly from Churchill's own criticisms of military extravagance), maintaining that any inefficiency had been the result, not of flaws in the system itself, but of political interference. He was also known for his advocacy of the maxim: 'Measure for measure it is more important to maintain the strength of the Regular Army in the field than to provide for an army of expansion.'

economy through the merging of Units. It would be very difficult for them to resist an attack on these lines, although of course in certain contingencies it is important to have a great number of cadres, some on a skeleton basis in order to permit of rapid expansion.

This argument does not apply to the present conditions; first the Cavalry is admittedly an arm in a state of impending transition and great expansive power is not required; second, the 'no great European War for ten years' rule is still in force and is being renewed; third, the remaining Yeomanry Regiments, ten of which cost only as much as one regular Cavalry Regiment, provide in the background an adequate element of potential expansion.

I therefore propose to ask the War Office during August to agree to the amalgamation of all the remaining Cavalry Regiments on the basis of three being screwed into one, or alternatively as a compromise of two into one. I should like this to be worked out on the basis that the sabre power remains undiminished. We should then have a smaller number of regiments but each regiment would be an effective military unit and the general upshot would be an equal immediate fighting power. For this purpose I must first of all have the present approved ration strength for a Cavalry Regiment during the year *after* the reductions of strength agreed to in January have been effected. The return must show in exact detail the functions of every officer and man and the number of horses. The latter of course reveals the limits of the sabre strength, which is probably actually 15% below the horse strength.

Next I should like to see the ration strength of a Cavalry Regiment before the Great War and also its pre-war approved war strength, again in full detail. This will enable us to ascertain how many sabres can conveniently and indisputably be carried upon a single regimental organisation. Although I have not checked any of the figures my present impression is that the Cavalry Regiments as reduced can mount with difficulty 200 sabres whereas the barrack accommodation and all the overhead plant of the unit could quite easily carry 400 sabres.

You will see the bearing of this argument upon the Helmieh barrack accommodation question. There are three Cavalry Regiments in Egypt, one at Helmieh and two at Abbassia. The reductions approved this year cut, as General Strickland[1] shows, 11 officers and 265 men from these three regiments. In fact almost one regiment is suppressed in fighting strength. You should obtain privately from the War Office the full limit of accommodation at

[1] Edward Peter Strickland, 1869–1951. 2nd Lieutenant, 1888; on active service in Upper Burma (1887–9), Dongola (1896), the Sudan (1897), Omdurman (1898), Northern Nigeria (1906) and on the western front (1914–18). Major-General, 1916. Commanded the 6th Division, Ireland, 1919–22. Knighted, 1919. Lieutenant-General, 1926. General Officer Commanding the British Troops in Egypt, 1927–31. General, 1931.

Abbassia barracks for horses and men, especially horses. It will then be found, I suspect from my recollections of the size of Abbassia, that the same sabre strength now borne by three Cavalry Units could be accommodated in the Abbassia barracks and borne on two Cavalry Units. Thus there will be no need to construct new barracks at Helmieh for Cavalry or armoured cars or anything else and the skeleton cadres of that Regiment could come home and be merged in some other unamalgamated Cavalry Unit here.

Please let these figures be procured as quickly as possible. I imagine they must all be in print in the old returns, which of course show with minute exactness the disposition of every single man. It will then be possible to show the cost per sabre in peace time under present conditions and how perfectly wasteful and indefensible it is. We are at great expense keeping a large number of trees which only grow a few oranges, whereas by better arrangement the same number of oranges can be grown from half the number of trees and the rest of the ground used for other purposes.

It is important that the War Office should not gather from any enquiries you may make the kind of argument to which they will shortly be exposed.

Stanley Baldwin to King George V
(*Baldwin papers*)

5 July 1927   House of Commons

On the resumption of the Committee stage of the Finance Bill yesterday the Chancellor of the Exchequer encountered one of the stiffest fences on the course. He was faced with the revolt of a large section of his own followers and in consequence he was placed in the embarrassing position of fighting in alliance with Socialists and Liberals against some very stubborn and antagonistic Conservatives.

The clauses under discussion contained new provisions for the prevention of super-tax evasion by means of Limited Companies. Provisions with this object were first introduced in 1922, but subsequent experience had shown that the net which had then been set was not sufficiently large and that evasion continued to be practised in different forms.

It was in order to meet this increasing danger to the revenue that the Chancellor had introduced new proposals bringing within their scope a much greater number of Companies than had been included in the scheme of 1922. Partly owing to misconception, partly owing to a distrust of bureaucratic devices, a large section of Conservatives representing industrial interests and headed by Sir Henry Buckingham[1] had worked up a strong agitation against this portion of the Budget. In their view the proposals would hamper legitimate business, would discourage the legitimate allocation of profits to reserve funds, and would give to Civil Servants who knew little of business the power to dictate to Companies the proper distribution of profits.

Their fears were undoubtedly genuine, and with a view to allaying their anxiety the Chancellor of the Exchequer had been in negotiation with them prior to the debate, and had promised certain amendments by way of providing additional safeguards. He was only partially successful in his object, as was illustrated by yesterday's debate. . . .

If oratorical ability and the power of speech were omnipotent Mr Churchill need have had little to fear. His defence of the Clause was masterly and courageous. It is safe to say that nobody in the House could have stated the case more lucidly, more forcibly, or more convincingly. Nevertheless the energy and forcefulness of his speech may in the long run have been a weakness. If he had been more meek and more conciliatory, perhaps the Opposition might have shown signs of being pacified, and it is possible that the courageous defiance with which he declared that he had given away the maximum in the way of concessions and that he could not recede from the policy which he had laid down aroused rather than mollified the temper of the Opposition.

Perhaps the rebellious element was further encouraged by the strong support which the Chancellor received from Mr William Graham,[2] who has always taken a firm line on this subject of evasion, and he not only welcomed the Chancellor's action but actually urged the adoption of more drastic methods.

---

[1] Henry Cecil Buckingham, 1867–1931. Educated at Harrow. Chairman, Commissioners of Taxes, Holborn. Sheriff of London, 1910–11. Knighted, 1911. Member of the City of London Advisory Committee, 1916; of the Military Service Committee of the Ministry of Munitions, 1917–19. Adviser on Press Recruiting, 1918. Member of the Committee to Enquire into the Methods of the Ministry of Munitions, 1920. Conservative MP for Guildford from 1922 until his death.

[2] William Graham, 1887–1932. Junior Clerk, War Office, 1903. Entered Edinburgh University, 1911; Economist and statistician. Labour MP for Edinburgh Central, 1918–31. Member of the Royal Commission on Income Tax, 1919. Member of the Medical Research Council, 1920–8. Financial Secretary to the Treasury in the First Labour Government, 1924. Privy Councillor, 1924. Adviser on economic and statistical questions to Schwab and Snelling, Stockbrokers, from 1931 until his death.

Colonel Spender Clay to Winston S. Churchill

(*Churchill papers: 18/42*)

7 July 1927

My dear Winston,

Please allow an old friend to congratulate you on the result of a singularly hard political week. I know what a strain the supertax clauses of the finance Bill must have entailed & after two days of battle over them you had to face a situation last night which was fraught with dangerous possibilities from which you emerged so triumphantly.[1]

All good luck to you.

Yours ever
Spender Clay

Winston S. Churchill to Stanley Baldwin and Austen Chamberlain

(*Churchill papers: 22/182*)

11 July 1927

I should be greatly obliged if the following telegram, or something like it, could go to the First Lord.

'The Chancellor of the Exchequer shares your view that a possible solution may be found in agreement of three Powers to specific programmes by numbers and quality of cruisers for three or four years to come. He thinks this should certainly be explored. He presumes, however, that we shall not be committed to any increase in numbers and quality beyond the programmes settled between you and him in 1925, without Treasury and Cabinet being first consulted and having a perfectly free decision in the matter uncompromised by anything said at Geneva. His own personal view is that it would be better for all parties to remain free for the next few years—at any rate in the smaller types—rather than to have to concede both increased British naval estimates and American parity as the price of an agreement.'

---

[1] On 6 July 1927 the House of Commons debated a motion brought by Ramsay MacDonald which called the Conservative Government's House of Lords Bill an 'outrage upon the constitution'. In winding up the debate for the Government, Churchill declared: 'if these proposals had been received in a sincere desire to examine this problem and carry it forward, and if we had been reproached with any fault in the manner or method in which we brought them before the public, we should have been wounded by the censure; but when we see there is nothing in this except hungry partisanship, and that it expresses itself in the gross, harsh and insulting language of censure, we shall show ourselves able to repel it'. The question was then put; 167 votes being in favour of MacDonald's motion, and 362 against.

Winston S. Churchill to Lord Beaverbrook

(*Beaverbrook papers*)

12 July 1927   Chartwell Manor

My dear Max,

My wife says she wd like vy much to come on the cruise. I have been so hunted lately with the Budget etc, that I fear I have kept you waiting for a reply to yr delightful invitation a long time.[1] Nor have I been able to see yr German war film. I have just been studying my card, and find that Monday 25 is my first free evening. What about that?

I am distressed about poor K. O'Higgins.[2] 'It is better to be a poor fisher, than to meddle with the Government of men.'

Yours vy sincerely
Winston S.C.

[1] On 10 July 1927 the *Weekly Despatch* reported: 'The Chancellor of the Exchequer must have filled more pages in Hansard this week than any other six members put together. . . . More and more the task of defending Government and getting them out of their difficulties is put upon the shoulders of the Chancellor. . . . He also has a way of dealing with the Socialists which, while it never lacks anything in force or directness, yet appeals to their sense of fair play and good humour. "Winston is up!" empties the smoking room quicker than any other announcement.' The article ended: 'Yet with all his talents and his force of character, the main body of Conservatives would never follow him as Prime Minister.'

[2] Kevin O'Higgins was shot dead by gunmen while on his way to mass in Dublin on 10 July 1927. He was attacked while walking down the street by five men and shot several times. The IRA later denied responsibility, but the Government held them responsible, introducing a Public Safety Act in the Dail giving them drastic powers to detain suspected IRA members. Speaking at the Mansion House on the evening of July 12, Churchill said of O'Higgins: 'History will relate with pride how in that perilous time the Irish people found the men whose courage, whose will power, whose stern and sober moderation, whose sagacity, and whose iron determination enabled the Irish people to assume with dignity the rights of self-government which they so passionately claimed, and to keep in the strictest faith the Treaty obligations to which the honour of Ireland was pledged. Among these men scarcely one played a greater part than the late Vice-President, who has fallen, like a grander figure in the United States, at the hand of the vile assassin, and at the moment when he piloted the people he loved so well through the worst perils of their voyage.'

L. S. Amery: diary

(*Amery papers*)

20 July 1927

W is convinced that this Empire tour[1] can be made a big thing and I think rather envies me the opportunity. He also talked a bit about Geneva on which he is all out for defying the Yanks and saying that we will not allow anyone to build up a parity with us. . . . He thinks that if we tell the Yanks sharply to mind their own business and not to presume to compete with us at sea they will take it lying down and we can then afford not to build more than a minimum ourselves.

Winston S. Churchill: Cabinet memorandum

(*Churchill papers: 22/182*)

20 July 1927
Secret

CRUISERS AND PARITY

1. I have never accepted the 70 cruiser programme or the reasoning on which it stood, and Cabinet assent in 1925 was given only to an instalment of that programme up to 1929, large reductions being made by the Admiralty through an arbitrary extension of the life of cruisers. Seventy cruisers is not, as is stated, an absolute requirement. If, for instance, no other Navy existed it would be excessive, or, alternatively, if the Japanese or Americans had 100 or even 70 it would not be sufficient. Our special cruiser requirements can only be measured in relation to other Powers. I question whether 70 cruisers would be sufficient even if the Americans had only 47. I doubt whether the solution of our food supply in time of war can even be achieved in terms of cruisers or by multiplying cruisers. The advantages of a raider preying on commerce against a number of defending ships are enormous, and the seas are so large that the stronger defenders cannot make sure of hunting down

---

[1] Amery left Britain on 22 July 1927, accompanied by his wife, by two civil servants, Geoffrey Whiskard and William Brass, and by Gervas Huxley, of the Empire Marketing Foundation. On August 8 they reached South Africa, in September they were in Swaziland, in October in Australia, in November in New Zealand, on December 23 in Fiji and on December 30 in Hawaii. On 5 January 1928 they reached Victoria, Canada. Travelling through Vancouver, Edmonton, Calgary, Winnipeg, Toronto and Ottawa, they arrived in Quebec on January 24, leaving Canada for Britain on February 1. In the Canadian Rockies a 10,940-feet peak was named 'Mount Amery' in his honour: he was himself an avid mountaineer.

the raiders. There is no parity whatever in the tasks of defending trade and attacking trade. Less than 10 German cruisers, loose in the great waters, were not destroyed till after several months of serious depredations by more than 100 British and Allied vessels. I believe, therefore, that the safeguard of our food supply will be found not in multiplying cruisers beyond a certain point, but in instituting convoys. The kind of vessels used for convoy guard might be quite different from the costly unarmoured cruiser type now in vogue. They might well be tougher ships of much slower speed, but with more powerful guns than the hostile cruisers. It is possible that eventually our special dangers might be recognised by our being allowed to build a class of vessel of limited speed for the purpose of convoy guards over and above the ordinary cruiser forces of Britain and the United States. At any rate, this is the line which in the future should be explored and certainly not closed. It affords a means by which our special needs might be met without at the same time securing to us what other Powers would regard as Naval supremacy in aggressive weapons.

2. The undue stereotyping of Naval architecture arising from these various Naval agreements excludes all those novel developments of Naval design which mitigate and obscure the sharpness of numerical comparisons of strength. I cannot believe on general grounds that stereotyping makes either for domestic economy or international goodwill. I believe that freedom used in moderation will be more beneficial to all Naval Powers, but especially to us, and to the peace of the world. We are also by our great lead in cruisers at the present time in a position to set a good example for a year or two while America indulges in a sensational cruiser programme. At the end of such a slack period we should have not only public justification for a renewed effort, but also could build a much better type of cruiser or other class of vessel, tending to render obsolete the lavish conventional constructions of other Powers. Moreover, it has always been found that other nations follow the British lead in the design of warships, and thus our superior Naval science confers upon us a considerable advantage.

3. Altogether, on every ground, national and international, moral, military and financial, I dislike rigid meticulous bindings-down in Naval architecture. The type of 10,000-ton 8-inch cruiser is fixed as a maximum. The remedy for a hostile 10,000-ton 8-inch cruiser fleet is not more of the same kind, but probably a smaller number of a larger kind, &c. We are, in fact, gravely endangering the foundations of British sea power and our security by entering into entangling engagements. Moreover, the Americans and their press will mar the workings of any such agreement by continued friction, together with reproaches, that we are not acting fairly, that we are 'stealing a march', 'pulling the wool over their eyes', &c—all of which, translated into endless

technical complications, enables a fine case to be made out for local consumption.

4. For all these reasons I fear very much the attempt to extend the principles of the Washington Agreement beyond the battleship class. These comparatively few monsters alone lend themselves to accurate definition and limitation. If, however, it were decided to extend a treaty to cruisers over, say, 7,500 tons, we should have to accept, but even this is contrary to a long view of our interests.

I am sure that it is against our interest to enter into any agreement restricting our full freedom of minor construction in numbers or type.

5. These general observations explain the basis on which we should approach the present Conference.

Up till Geneva the Admiralty view has always been that we could not agree to parity with the United States in cruisers. Their memorandum of the 14th April (No 808–B) showed that they thought we ought to have 70 cruisers if the United States only had 47. It was clearly understood that American building beyond 47 would react upon our total of 70. Such was the position, apart from other factors, on which our representatives went to Geneva. As soon as this position was revealed to the American delegates they set on foot a press campaign in the United States, declaring that we denied them parity. Nobody in England paid the slightest attention. But the Cabinet, becoming alarmed about Anglo-American relations, sent on June 29 the following telegram to our delegates at Geneva:—

> 'For diplomatic reasons we think it most desirable to say publicly and at once what we believe to be the line on which you are working, namely, that while we mean to build cruisers up to our needs, we lay down no conditions limiting America's cruisers to a smaller number.
> Do you see any objection?'

This telegram did not sufficiently explain our point of view. We never meant to say that the United States are justified in building up to parity with us in cruisers or that we would sign a treaty authorising them to do so. All we meant was that if they choose to build up to our level we should not make it a ground of quarrel, ie, as long as we remained free their naval programme would not upset our relations with them.

6. All this was very bad ground. Our delegates at Geneva[1] treated the telegram above quoted as a final decision to submit to absolute parity by treaty with the United States. Some of the blame for this misunderstanding rests with us. Nevertheless, it is difficult to understand why in the light of the past

[1] The British delegates to the Three Power Naval Conference at Geneva were William Bridgeman and Lord Cecil of Chelwood.

history of the question our delegates did not react against the interpretation they put upon our message. It has been, as I have shown, the fundamental basis of the Admiralty position all these years that we could not consent to parity with the United States in the minor construction. How much we could do in any single year to resist must depend on our moral power and our finance. But obviously, since numerical parity means British inferiority and potential British subjugation, we cannot consent to it. Anxious to put our whole mind before our delegates, we sent eight days later (the 7th July) the considered message for publication drafted by Lord Balfour. It is impossible to reconcile their interpretation of the telegram of the 29th June with the acquiescence by the delegation in our publishing the Balfour message. The full Balfour message explains quite clearly the imperfections of the original telegram. It is entirely inconsistent with the idea of our consenting by treaty to general Naval parity with the United States. In the upshot we are deeply committed to the principle of absolute parity by treaty, although such a principle is fatal to British Naval security.

7. No doubt it is quite right in the interests of peace to go on talking about war with the United States being 'unthinkable'. Everyone knows that this is not true. However foolish and disastrous such a war would be, it is in fact, the only basis upon which the Naval discussions at Geneva are proceeding. We do not wish to put ourselves in the power of the United States. We cannot tell what they might do if at some future date they were in a position to give us orders about our policy, say, in India, or Egypt, or Canada, or on any other great matter behind which their electioneering forces were marshalled. Moreover, tonnage parity means that Britain can be starved into obedience to any American decree. I would neither trust America to command, nor England to submit. Evidently on the basis of American Naval superiority speciously disguised as parity immense dangers overhang the future of the world.

8. What to do? I know there will be some who argue we have gone so far, we must not go back: we have said this, or implied that, we must make it good: our consistency is at stake: we may be subject to reproach: America will be angry with us, etc, etc. But all these considerations sink into insignificance compared to the foundations of British security and independence. For these touch the foundations of the peace of the world.

9. Mercifully there is still time to break away from the net which is closing on us. We have no right to sacrifice the vital interests of the country to any misunderstandings among ourselves or to any failure on our part at a given moment to express our position clearly. Let us now, with the added knowledge that these discussions have given, draw up our own charter of the freedom of the seas. Let us select as if we had a clean sheet the points essential to

our 'right to live'. Never mind whether these points, if just and necessary in themselves, should make agreement at Geneva impossible. Let us hold on to them at all costs. After all, who called the Conference? Who called it for political motives? Who is most interested in producing something that can be hawked about the American platforms in 1928 as an English submission to American parity, ie, supremacy? That is surely not our affair. Let us stick to the truth and to our needs. It may well be that the American Government in their anxiety for some sort of an agreement will gradually conform to our view. We have certainly not lost anything by not immediately casting our-selves at their feet. The stout resistance made by the First Lord and his col-leagues so far from infuriating the United States press has led them to lower their note day by day. But anyhow we cannot consent to be ruled by the United States press. The only chance of a good Naval Agreement is that the United States shall accept our considered and sober view. If they want an agreement, let them pay the price for it in fair accommodation. They risk nothing, we risk everything. They are trying to buy the sovereignty of the seas by mere money power, and this has never been done in the history of the world. They do not even expect to have to cash the cheque.

10. The American newspapers tell us, and this mood is reflected in their delegation at Geneva, that we shall have to submit to *force majeure*. We have to pay more than half the cost of their Navy as a war indemnity in addition to the upkeep of our own. They are the world's steelmaster. Therefore it is argued we had better give in now and come along quietly. But this takes altogether too narrow a view of the resources of the British Empire and of the sacrifices which an island people is prepared to make for vital objects. A poor man may pay for dear life what a rich man will not pay for mere prestige. They do not know much about shipbuilding. They do not know much about the sea. They do not like it. Naval competition would be a great evil, but it does not at all follow that over a long period of years we should emerge from it with inferior means of self-defence.

11. I do not believe myself that this would be the result. I believe they would blow off steam in a few programmes of aggressive cruisers, and that if we lay quiet and calm and studied scientific improvements we should find in a few years a strong reaction in the United States against unnecessary expenditure and a strong revival of Anglo-Japanese association. Anyhow, it is a very long business. Supreme Navies cannot be made with a stroke of a wand or the signing of a cheque. All sorts of intermediate processes come into operation, and at every stage there is room for negotiation and goodwill. I can imagine no more disagreeable proposition for the Government of the United States than that they should have to embark upon a ten or fifteen-year pro-gramme of building a supreme fleet from the 50 millions a year war indem-

nity which they are extracting through various channels from the German people. But why should we save them from this ugly, salutory corrective? Why should we sacrifice our title-deeds to save them the embarrassments which properly attend a wrongful national assertion? Let us not depart from what we regard as our minimum. Let us not part with the essentials of our security to enable them to gratify their prestige, or to protect them from the consequences of a wrong and imprudent policy.

WSC

Winston S. Churchill: Cabinet memorandum

(*Churchill papers: 22/182*)

25 July 1927

In the year 1924/5 the Labour Government began 5 10,000 ton 8-8″ gun cruisers. In our first year 1925/6 we began 4 of these cruisers. In the same year the Dominions began 2. In the year 1926/7 we began 2 10,000 ton 8-8″ gun cruisers and 1 7,500 ton 8-8″ gun cruiser. In the current year we are committed to 1 10,000 ton 8-8″ gun cruiser and 2 7,500 ton 8-8″ gun cruisers. Total new British 8-8″ gun cruisers since 1924 17 incl 14 10,000 ton 8-8″ gun cruisers + 3 7,500 ton 8-8″ gun cruisers.

In the same period Japan began 4 Nachi class 10,000 ton 8-8″ gun cruisers and sanctioned in December 1926 4 more similar ships for completion about 1931. If nothing more is built or scrapped on either side the two Powers will have in 1931 of 10,000 ton 8-8″ gun cruisers—British Empire 14 and Japan 8. All these cruisers are the best that can be built.

In addition Japan has the 4 Furutakas 7,100 ton 6-8″ gun cruisers and Great Britain has and will have the following: 4 'Hawkins' class 10,000 ton 7·5″ ships and 3 latest 7,500 ton 8-8″ gun cruisers. If no new cruisers of any kind are begun either by Britain or Japan till after the programme of 1931 the above figures define the relative strengths of the modern cruisers possessed by the two Powers until the year 1934 or 1935.

This assumes 3 years for building a cruiser, but we can if need be build one in a little more than 2½ years. There are of course besides these new cruisers 20 older Japanese cruisers and 46 older and much more powerful British cruisers at the present time all under 16 years of age. Of these an arbitrary 16 years rule would reduce the British by 16 and the Japanese by 3 by 1931. For the purposes of the Birkenhead Report the Admiralty were willing to increase the life of cruisers to 20 years. On this basis none would drop out on either side.

Surveying the cruiser fleets in their entirety it is submitted that, as compared with Japan, if nothing new is built, we have an adequate superiority until the year 1934 or 1935.

There never has been any question of cruiser competition with the United States. They are hopelessly behind, having only of cruisers under 16 years old the 10 'Omaha's' with 6″ guns and 2 10,000 ton 8-8″ gun cruisers begun in 1926. In addition they have 22 pre-war cruisers from 19 to 34 years old ranging from 15 to 23 knots speed. It is evident therefore that both Great Britain and Japan could afford to allow the United States to build if she wished up to the 12–12–8 ratio in 10,000 ton 8″ gun cruisers which ratio we already exceed, provided they both marked time themselves. It may well be that the United States will also wish to build a few smaller cruisers to match the Japanese 'Furutaka's' and the British 'Hawkins' and new B-class 8″ vessels. It is for them to state their wishes and for Britain and Japan to see what reaction if any this would produce in their construction of similar vessels.

WSC

Winston S. Churchill to John Gretton[1]

(Churchill papers: 18/46)

26 July 1927

My dear Gretton,

The Prime Minister asked me to undertake the duty of replying to your last letter.

We have given the most careful consideration to your proposal that there should be a new Committee of Enquiry into the expenditure of the country. We do not feel able to recede from the position taken up by the Prime Minister in his previous letter. The enquiry would not we believe yield fruitful results and might well impede the efforts which the Government is itself making to effect every possible economy, not only upon the next year's estimates but upon those already voted for the current year.

You will remember that in the Budget Speech I indicated that the cost of the Shanghai Defence Forces would have to be met to a large extent by savings on the approved expenditure if a deficit was to be avoided. Substantial progress has already been made towards this object, and savings

---

[1] John Gretton, 1867–1947. Educated at Harrow. Conservative MP, 1895–1906 and 1907–43. Chairman of Bass, Ratcliffe and Gretton Ltd, brewers. Colonel, Territorial Army, 1912. Privy Councillor, 1926. Created Baron, 1944. One of his two brothers, a Captain in the Bedfordshire Regiment, was killed in action at Ypres on 18 December 1915.

greater than those which would have resulted from all the suggestions of your original letter are already in sight.

With regard to next year, a comprehensive scheme for effecting a reduction in the expenditure has been prepared and has been approved in principle by the Economy Committee of the Cabinet. All the departments concerned have been addressed personally by the Prime Minister and requested to effect the reductions proposed or to suggest alternatives equally fruitful. The influence exerted by a strong Parliamentary opinion in favour of economy, such as exercised by your Committee, strengthens the hands of the Treasury and is useful to the State. It is through no lack of appreciation of your work that His Majesty's Government find themselves unable at this moment to accept your advice about the appointing of a new Committee of Enquiry.

I note that you say in your last letter that 'there will be profound disappointment if a Budget next year is presented which proposes taxation much in excess of 800 millions'. You will I am sure remember that if the Sinking Fund were reduced by 20 millions to the figure of 45 millions at which it stood under the late Government, and if the beneficial increase of the Road Fund and Post Office expenditure of 11 millions which has taken place since we took office, is also allowed for, 31 out of the 40 millions of increase of expenditure are already accounted for.

It would of course be quite easy by reducing the Sinking Fund and by separating the beneficial expenditure from the ordinary accounts, as many high authorities think should be done, to achieve a paper result considerably below the figure that you mention. Such a presentation would however be of no advantage unless accompanied by a substantial curtailment of actual expense, and it is upon this aspect that our efforts are at the present time mainly directed.[1]

J. C. C. Davidson to Stanley Baldwin[2]

(*Baldwin papers*)

27 July 1927

I was very frightened on Monday the 25th, because Austen apparently allowed Winston to reopen the whole question of the cruiser programme. Willie was not only very worried but exceedingly angry, and at one time

[1] Churchill noted on the draft of this letter, for his advisers: 'Check, verify etc.'
[2] Baldwin had left England for his annual holiday at Aix-les-Bains, and for an official visit to Canada and the United States.

was in a minority of one. I gather that they pressed him again to go back to Geneva admitting that he had exceeded his instructions with regard to parity, to which he replied bluntly that he would do no such thing, but that he was quite prepared to announce that the British Government had changed its mind. All these things however, apparently passed off, and now he is going back to Geneva to stand firm on the six inch gun in the defensive cruiser.

I have tried to find out what happened at the Cabinet last night but apart from that fact and the fact that Jix and Winston have got their way, which means I imagine reversing the decision of the Cabinet last Friday over which you presided, I failed to get any details. No doubt, however, you have a full account from Hankey of everything that passed.

There are a certain number of cross currents and I feel very much as though we were sitting on the edge of a volcano, while Winston, FE, and Austen are in control. Austen had no business to give in to Winston yesterday.[1]

Winston S. Churchill to Sir Austen Chamberlain

(*Austen Chamberlain papers*)

28 July 1928
Confidential

My dear Austen,

You will remember that last March I wrote to you suggesting that pressure should be put on the Egyptians to terminate their default over the 1855 Loan. In your reply of the 11th April you indicated that the best course might be 'to induce the Egyptian Government to resume payment as part of a bargain covering other issues, for example, in return for some concession in respect of the Capitulations'.

Having regard to this, I hope that you agree with what I said in Cabinet this morning viz: that we must take the opportunity afforded by the discussion of a Treaty of Alliance to secure definite satisfaction on this question. The precise form is immaterial ie whether it is embodied in the Treaty itself

---

[1] As a result of the Cabinet decision of 26 July 1927, the final British compromise proposal was for a total cruiser and destroyer force of 590,000 tons each for Britain and the United States, and 385,000 tons for Japan; with a maximum size of 6-inch for all new secondary cruiser guns. After the senior United States delegate, Hugh Gibson, had rejected this proposal, and the negotiations had broken down, Bridgeman wrote to King George V: 'It became evident that no agreement which did not humiliate the British Empire, was likely to find acceptance with Gibson and his colleagues and there was no course open but to wind it up in as dignified a way as we could' (*Baldwin papers*).

or in a separate instrument signed at the same time. But it is essential, when we are prepared to offer the Egyptians very important concessions on other points, to end the present impasse and ensure the resumption by Egypt of the service of the debt.

I understand that Sarwat Pasha[1] threw out the suggestion that the question might be referred to a Debts Commission. While I would not object to the reference to a Commission of such subsidiary points as eg the creation of a Sinking Fund for the extinction of this debt, I submit that the principle of the payment by Egypt of her share in the service of the Loan cannot be left open to discussion and that the acceptance of this principle should be made a definite stipulation in any new arrangement for regulating our future relations with Egypt.

[1] Abd al-Khalek Sarwat Pasha, 1873–1928. Educated at Cairo Law School. Governor of Assiut Province, 1908. First entered the Egyptian Cabinet as Minister of Justice, 1915. Minister of the Interior, 1921. Egyptian Foreign Minister from March to November 1922, and from June 1926 to April 1927; Prime Minister from March to November 1922, and from April 1927 to March 1928. He died in September 1928. *The Times* noted in his obituary: 'When the history of post-war Egypt comes to be written, two names will stand out, those of Zaghlul Pasha and Sarwat Pasha. And Sarwat's, without doubt, will be accorded the higher place.'

August 1927

Winston S. Churchill to Commander Kenworthy[1]

(Churchill papers: 18/44)

3 August 1927

My dear Commander Kenworthy,

As I thought you would be wishing to have your proofs back as soon as possible, I have already looked them through. I need scarcely say that I find them most interesting and even startling.[2] In fact they seem to me to bristle with grave statements upon the most dangerous and explosive topics. I should think myself it was no service to peace to dwell morbidly upon the nightmares of future wars or to expatiate upon all the disagreeable things great nations might do to one another if they should happen to go mad again. I therefore hope that you will re-read these interesting proofs with an intention at any rate of pruning out admissions which would tell against British interests. Would it not be well for instance to show them to Ramsay MacDonald?

[1] Joseph Montague Kenworthy, 1886–1953. Entered Royal Navy, 1902. Commanded HMS *Bullfinch*, 1914; HMS *Commonwealth*, 1916. Lieutenant-Commander, 1916. Admiralty War Staff, 1917. Assistant Chief of Staff, Gibraltar, 1918. Retired from the Navy, 1920. Liberal MP, 1919–26. Labour MP, 1926–31. Succeeded his father as 10th Baron Strabolgi, 1934. Opposition Chief Whip, House of Lords, 1938–42. President of the United Kingdom Pilots' Association, 1922–5. Chairman of the Advisory Committee on Sea Fisheries, 1926–32.

[2] Commander Kenworthy's book *Will Civilization Crash?* was published in London by Ernest Benn in October 1927, with an introduction by H. G. Wells. In his book, Kenworthy argued that: 'If this present world state of affairs continues, another great war is inevitable.' Of Churchill, Kenworthy wrote: 'Winston Churchill is one of our ablest Parliamentarians, and a very brilliant man. A former big Navy advocate, he is now the watchdog of the Treasury.' In Asia, Kenworthy believed, war was made more likely by the consolidation of the Chinese into one people, speaking a single language. 'The ex-Kaiser's nightmare of the Yellow Peril is likely to come true, after all.' Later he wrote: 'The more ignorant and primitive the mob, the greater the danger. And China, with her great city populations is fertile ground for the unscrupulous demagogue.' Writing on 'Why an Anglo-American War Is Possible', he cited American anger at European unrest, and English anger at America's debt policy as possible causes of conflict. A nation, Kenworthy wrote, 'is an organized mob. If suitable appeals are made to tune the mind of a mob for war, and if the right slogans, catchwords, and war cries are uttered at the appropriate moment, the mob will desire to fight.'

I need scarcely say after this jobation[1] that I could not possibly in an official position seem to approve or associate myself with the stirring up of these very dangerous matters. I hope we shall by good sense and good will get along from day to day and from year to year until the nightmares have faded in the distance.

> I return you your proofs,
> With many thanks,
> Believe me.

Winston S. Churchill to Lord Beaverbrook

(*Beaverbrook papers*)

7 August 1927   Treasury Chambers

My dear Max,

I am grieved to learn of the death of yr mother[2] & offer you my deep sympathy. It must have been a gt pleasure in yr life to have had her to watch yr successes & to be able by yr own exertions to make the path of life smooth for her. Eighty-four is a venerable age & no one wd wish to live forever. Nevertheless as I know well the death of one's mother breaks links with the past that can never be revived & without wh the world is different. I thought you wd not mind my writing these few lines; for I know you will be in the shadows.

Do not I beg you hesitate to put us off for the 18th, if you wd rather be alone. In fact I shall assume that you will do so.

> With deep sympathy,
> Believe me,
> Yours ever,
> W

---

[1] Jobation (pronounced *jaw*-bation): a rebuke or a reproof, especially one of a long or tedious nature; a 'talking to'. Its origin is the lengthy reproofs addressed to Job by his friends.

[2] Jane Noble, daughter of a Canadian storekeeper and farmer, who had married William Aitken, a Church of Scotland Minister, in 1867. Beaverbrook's wife Gladys died soon afterwards, on 1 December 1927.

Lord Beaverbrook to Winston S. Churchill

(Churchill papers: 1/194)

10 August 1927

My dear Winston,

It was like you to take the trouble to write me such a long, sympathetic and above all understanding letter in my bereavement. As a matter of fact you put the case for consolation almost exactly as I have put it to myself.

Once the first shock & wrench is over I do feel that I have been fortunate in keeping my mother so long, for 84 is a great age.

She died in full possession of her faculties & especially of her sense of humour which she applied to every object in her ken—& in particular to me.

Yours ever
Max

Victor Cazalet: diary

(Robert Rhodes James: 'Victor Cazalet, A Portrait')

10 August 1927

With Winston—a wonderful day. Peter and I were alone with him after dinner till midnight. He was in a marvellous mood, and just would not let us go. I played the piano and we talked on cricket, on music and politics. I told him of my row with Birkenhead. He says I ought to have replied, 'Go to blazes, you're trying to insult me.' One should never be non-plussed, or allow oneself to be sworn at without replying. He told us he had a great respect for Christian Science. He admires the book *Mother India* and would have no mercy with the Hindus who marry little girls aged ten.[1] But his conversation is unrepeatable because of its brilliance—its metaphors, its quotations, its gorgeous language, and its political interest. He had two talks

[1] Katherine Mayo, an American writer, had visited India in the autumn of 1925, to observe the practice of the Indian masses in matters affecting public health. She published her findings in May 1927, under the title *Mother India*, in which she was particularly critical of the custom of child-marriage among Hindus, and stressed its crueller physical aspects. The book went through forty printings in three and a half years. In 1931 she published a further book, *Volume Two*, based on the report of an unofficial committee of Indians, known as the Age of Consent Committee, which, in an enquiry in 1928, upheld her findings. She also published a picture book, highly critical of Hinduism and the caste-system, entitled *The Face of Mother India*. On 16 August 1927 the Viceroy of India, Lord Irwin, had written to Neville Chamberlain of *Mother India*: 'I think the general effect may be useful if it gives a shock re the unsatisfactory conditions of Hindu thought on many of these subjects' *(Irwin papers)*.

with the great Lord Salisbury.[1] Salisbury said to him—'For the last fifty years we have been living through a period of unbelievable expansion, but anyone who thinks it can continue will be left high and dry.'

Winston S. Churchill to Lord Londonderry

(Churchill papers: 18/44)

14 August 1927   Treasury Chambers

It is not true to say that taxation is more onerous and exacting than ever before. Both the Income Tax and the Super Tax have in fact been substantially reduced since the present Government came into office.

The provisions of the Finance Act against evasion will not affect any private company carrying on a bona fide business in an honest manner, as they are no different in principle from those under which more than half the private companies have been working since Horne's Budget of 1922. In fact they will tend to preserve to private companies the great privileges which they at present enjoy over private firms and individuals by freeing that privilege from the dangerous infection of an ever-growing abuse.

With regard to your remarks about 'immediate and drastic economy' and for 'a policy of retrenchment conceived not in a spirit of fear of the self styled Labour Party', and your desire that the situation should be 'tackled fairly and in the right way', I should be very much obliged if you will inform me what practical suggestions you have in mind behind this general exhortation. It does not add to my enlightenment merely to receive vague requests to 'act fairly and in the right way, and not in a spirit of fear of the self styled Labour Party'. I try my best and am not supposed to be particularly 'under the fear of the self styled Labour Party', and I always hope that my friends when they write to me on public business will have some definite and reasonable suggestions to make.

Yours ever,

---

[1] Lord Salisbury (the 3rd Marquess of Salisbury) had been Prime Minister from 1897 to 1902. Churchill was a lifelong friend of three of his sons, the 4th Marquess, Viscount Cecil of Chelwood and Lord Hugh Cecil, and his father had been a good friend of Salisbury. On 16 March 1886 Salisbury had written to Lord Randolph Churchill (after the 11-year-old Winston had nearly died of fever): 'I am very sorry indeed to have just heard that you have had anxiety about one of your sons.' In 1900, Churchill had dedicated his book *The River War* to Lord Salisbury, 'under whose direction the Conservative Party have long enjoyed power and the Nation prosperity. During whose administrations the reorganisation of Egypt has been mainly accomplished and upon whose advice Her Majesty determined to order the reconquest of the Soudan.'

Winston S. Churchill to Stanley Baldwin

(*Baldwin papers*)

18 August 1927   Treasury Chambers
Private

My dear Prime Minister,

Welcome home! I trust that you will have benefited by the change—though not I fear by the rest—of your Canadian excursion. It all seems to have gone off very well, judging by the reports which have reached this country.[1]

I am just off for a week's cruise with Max, and am dreading considerably the rough weather which is our fate at this and other times of the year. We are going to visit Amsterdam and perhaps go through the Kiel Canal. I shall, however, in any case be back in time for the Cabinet on the 25th.

I enclose you a copy of a letter I have written to Bridgeman, which explains itself. I shall be much obliged if you will allow the question of a renewed enquiry into the cruiser position to take its place on the agenda for the 25th. I have ventured to mention the matter to the Cabinet Office, so that I expect it will already be included.

With all good wishes, believe me
Yours vy sincerely
Winston S. Churchill

Winston S. Churchill to William Bridgeman

(*Baldwin papers*)

18 August 1927
Private

My dear Willie,

I hear that you have written to Austen proposing to begin the DORSET-SHIRE but to reduce her from 10,000 to 8,000 tons. At the last Cabinet,

---

[1] Baldwin's biographers, Keith Middlemas and John Barnes, have written (*Baldwin*, 1969): 'The tour of Canada, on which Baldwin had staked a great deal of hope, was diminished by this coldness with the United States. The visits to New York and Washington, which he had proposed to Houghton, the American ambassador in London, had to be precipitately abandoned because the public and press in the United States blamed Britain as unanimously as the British press and public blamed them. The collapse of the Conference boosted the "Big Navy" League and the American cruiser-building programme, it disillusioned Kellogg, the Secretary of State, with European politics, and it deprived the President of his diplomatic triumph. At the opening of the Peace Bridge above Niagara, which Baldwin attended, Vice-President Dawes openly blamed the lack of diplomatic preparation for the failure of the Conference, to the consternation of the State Department and the embarrassment of the Canadians.'

while you were away at Geneva, it was decided that there should be a fresh enquiry into our cruiser position, and the Admiralty and the Treasury were directed to prepare material so that this could begin in the Autumn.

Since the last enquiry several important things have happened. First and foremost, the Japanese have stopped building and do not propose to add appreciably to what they have now planned for the next eight or nine years. Secondly, we have expressed our willingness to allow the United States to build to parity with us in 10,000-ton cruisers. Thirdly, the Admiralty were willing, for the sake of an agreement, to postpone the whole of this year's programme.

These three facts seem to deal with the only three possible reasons for cruiser building this year, ie (1) danger from Japan; (2) danger from the United States; and (3) the rate at which the Fleet is wearing out. I am bound therefore to press that there should be a halt in our cruiser construction. This would bring a very substantial relief to our finance next year, and some relief this year. On even larger grounds it seems, however, most desirable—and I know this is Austen's view—that we should give every opportunity for the Navy party in the United States to cool down; and if for a couple of programmes they build, say, six cruisers a year while we stand still, we shall perhaps have taken the most practical step to prevent a naval race developing. They will have put themselves in the worst position and us in a fairly good one.

You will understand of course that I am not asking for an immediate decision on this issue. I only ask that the question should be re-examined by the strongest possible Committee of our colleagues in the light of all that has taken place.

In these circumstances I am asking the Prime Minister that the subject should be on the agenda for the Cabinet on the 25th, and meanwhile I am sure you will consent not to take any irrevocable step about beginning the reduced DORSETSHIRE.

Yours very sincerely,
Winston S. Churchill

Neville Chamberlain to Lord Irwin

(*Irwin papers*)

25 August 1927

Winston remains the figure most interesting to the general public. I think he has materially improved his position in the party, and it is admitted on all sides that he has no equal in the House of Commons. His manner with the opposition is so good-humoured that although they often interrupt him, they look forward to his speeches as the finest entertainment the House can offer.

I watched an excitable creature called Salter[1] recently while Winston was on his feet. His features were distorted by the convulsions of his mirth; at intervals he relieved the overwhelming pressure by a series of resounding slaps on his own thigh. At other times I have seen this man totally unable to control his temper shouting out 'Liar, coward, murderer', and any other similar abuse that entered his mind. I think it was on the third reading of the TU Bill that Winston was much interrupted by an excited opposition in a full house as he neared the end of his peroration. 'Of course it is perfectly possible,' he said, 'for Hon'ble members to prevent my speaking, and indeed I do not want to cast my pearls before . . .'—he paused and then concluded 'those who do not want them,' in a roar of delight that lasted several minutes.

Winston S. Churchill to William Bridgeman
(Churchill papers: 22/175)

26 August 1927

I hold the view that with our slender resources we must spend every penny in the best possible way, so as to produce the highest war power. If therefore your Naval advisers consider that the war qualities of Class A are substantially in advance of Class B and well worth the extra money from a Naval point of view, I shall not press you on grounds of expense.

Neville Chamberlain to Lord Irwin
(Irwin papers)

27 August 1927

ON CHURCHILL'S 'SUCCESSES' IN THE HOUSE OF COMMONS

They are tremendous and yet they don't escape criticism. You remember the old children's game when you pretend to be very angry with the young rascals. You throw them across your knee and spank them fiercely. But you insert your own left hand between the instrument of punishment and the

---

[1] Alfred Salter, 1873–1945. A doctor of medicine; Resident Obstetric Physician, Guy's Hospital, 1896. Bacteriologist, British Institute of Preventative Medicine, 1897–1900. Labour MP for West Bermondsey, 1922–3 and 1924–45.

place of application with the result that the noise is multiplied, but the child feels none of the inconveniences generally attaching to the process. It is an amazing game, the child enjoys it thoroughly, so do you and most of the on-lookers. Only the maiden aunt who thinks the child is really in need of a corrective disapproves and says sonorously that this is only encouraging it to be naughty again. For the child, read the Labour Party—for the maiden aunt, read the stricter sects of the Conservative party, and you see the point of the criticism. And Winston's greatest admirers still distrust his judgement.

September 1927

Winston S. Churchill to Richard Sickert [1]

(Churchill papers: 1/194)

8 September 1927

My dear Mr Sickert,

I have been assiduously practising your system. I have executed the preliminary stage of the photograph of St Paul's Cathedral which you sent me, and I have also made another quite successful representation of a Daily Mail photograph.

The Professor insisted on presenting me with a beautiful camera, and I have already taken several photographs which have been developed and enlarged, and which, together with the other sketches, will form the basis of future efforts. I am really enormously obliged to you for your kindness and interest; and when I return to London you must let me have another long consultation with you. When it comes to doing the face on a photograph, or any intricate piece of work, it is quite possible to sub-divide the square or to put criss-cross lines; while the ordinary parts of the picture can be done on the large square.

Winston S. Churchill to Lord Cecil of Chelwood

(Cecil of Chelwood papers)

14 September 1927

My dear Bob,

I was grieved to get yr valedictory note, & am vy sorry indeed that you have left the Government. [2] Your withdrawal is a gt loss to us & in several

---

[1] Walter Richard Sickert, 1860–1942. A friend of Clementine Churchill's mother, Lady Blanche Hozier. Painter. Royal Academy, 1934 (resigned, 1935). He taught Churchill the 'Panafieu technique', of painting in oils on top of a black and white photograph whose image was projected on to a canvas screen. Many of the photographs on which Churchill and Sickert worked were taken by Professor Lindemann.

[2] On August 28 Lord Cecil (the Chancellor of the Duchy of Lancaster) had resigned in protest at the failure to reach an agreement on disarmament at the Three Power Naval Con-

special ways to me. Moreover I do not believe that the League of Nations cause will be the gainer by yr laying aside the Britannic ensign—even tho it will be carried forward by Lord Onslow.[1] I know how sincere is yr devotion to the League, & how little any thought of yrself or yr own interests ever affects yr action. Such a resignation as yrs helps to dignify public life & to strengthen the position & repute of politicians generally. But nevertheless the balance of loss is to my mind heavy, & once again let me repeat my deep regret.

It is not I think true that a concession on the 8″ gun wd have turned the scale at Geneva. The basis of agreement never existed.

I have just returned from Holker[2] where yr recent visit had given so much pleasure. I do hope that official severance will not prevent our seeing each other and talking things over; & you know I am sure that I never allowed even fierce & hurtful political opposition to affect valued personal friendships.

With evy good wish,
Believe me,
Yours always,
Winston S.C.

ference at Geneva. He was the only British Cabinet Minister in more than seventy-five years to have resigned from the Cabinet *twice*, having already done so, over Welsh Disestablishment, in November 1918. He never held Cabinet Office again.

[1] Richard William Alan Onslow, 1876–1945. Served abroad in the Diplomatic Service, 1901–9; Commercial Secretary, Berlin, 1908. Assistant Private Secretary to Sir Edward Grey, 1909. Succeeded his father as 5th Earl of Onslow, 1911. Assistant Clerk, Foreign Office, 1913–14. On active service, 1914–18; Major, 1918. Director of Staff Duties, BEF, France, 1918. Civil Lord of the Admiralty, 1920–1. Parliamentary Secretary, Ministry of Health, 1921–3; Board of Education, 1923–4. Under-Secretary for War, 1924–8. Civil Commissioner, South Wales, General Strike of 1926. Paymaster-General, 1928–9. Deputy Speaker, House of Lords, 1931–4. Chairman of the Burnham Committee on Teachers' Salaries, 1934–43.

[2] Holker Hall, Cark-in-Cartmel, Lancashire: the home of the Rt Hon Lord Richard Cavendish, brother of the 9th Duke of Devonshire, and a former Liberal Unionist MP. His brother, Lord John Spencer Cavendish, was killed in action on 20 October 1914. His daughter Elizabeth married, in 1915, the 5th Marquess of Salisbury (Lord Cecil of Chelwood's brother). His daughter Diana married, in 1935, Robert Boothby. In his memoirs *Twenty-One Years*, Raldolph Churchill recalled: 'One summer, when I was about fourteen, my father and mother took all us children up to Holker, to spend ten days with Lord Richard and Lady Moyra Cavendish. My father spent most of the time damming streams. Holker, which is on the west coast of Lancashire, is a most attractive residence.'

Stanley Baldwin to Lord Irwin

(*Irwin papers*)

15 September 1927

Winston's position is curious. Our people like him. They love listening to him in the House, look on him as a star turn and settle down in the stalls with anticipatory grins. But for the leadership, they would turn him down every time. If anything happened to me, the best men are Neville and Hogg, and I think on the whole the second would be chosen.[1]

Winston S. Churchill to Sir Warren Fisher

(*Churchill papers: 18/71*)

17 September 1927

Please let me have a list showing the gains and losses on the half year. There are certainly a great many gains achieved or in prospect, eg sale of the British Celanese; Lady Houston's death duties;[2] savings on the reduced steel house; savings through no cruisers this year, which should be assumed; savings through the reduction of the Civil Service bonus; windfalls through the settlement with Canada and the East African loan arrangements; savings on the British Empire Marketing Board £500,000; savings through Departmental economies already agreed to £2 millions; savings from the £3,500,000 estimate through the reduction in the Shanghai forces.

Altogether I have made out a very respectable list. What is there on the other side? I have not agreed to much, I think. There is the supplementary for the London University and some small charges about Cyprus. Anyhow let me have a detailed list of all the possibles and probables—good or bad—the test being that they were not included in the Budget estimates.

---

[1] But Baldwin himself insured that Sir Douglas Hogg would not succeed to the Leadership of the Conservative Party (and hence to the Premiership) when he was created Baron Hailsham on 5 April 1928, on his becoming Lord Chancellor (see page 1239).

[2] Sir Robert Houston, the shipowner, had died on 14 April 1926. As he had taken domicile in Jersey, there were legal complications as to the liability for estate tax. *The Times* reported lengthy, 'secret' meetings between Churchill and Lady Houston at the Treasury on 31 October 1927 and on November 11. On November 16 Churchill told the House of Commons: 'Lady Houston has paid to the Exchequer the sum of £1,600,000 as an act of grace, and without admitting legal liability. I have accepted this sum, which in its amount is unprecedented, which was offered spontaneously and from a public spirited desire to help the finances of the country in a munificent way.'

Lord Beaverbrook to Winston S. Churchill

(Churchill papers: 1/194)

20 September 1927

My dear Winston,

The American Telephone and Telegraph Co, which is the biggest corporation in the world, has perfected a process of talking pictures which is beyond description.

I have seen a picture of President Coolidge which beats anything in my experience.

The first exhibition of these talking pictures is to take place in London on October 11 at the New Gallery Cinema, under the auspices of my friend Mr Evans.

He asked me today to indicate the name of a prominent person in England who might be pictured and added to the President Coolidge-Mussolini-Poincaré trio. Only one Englishman is to appear.

I asked Mr Evans to allow me to make the offer to you and I strongly urge you to accept.

You can see the Coolidge picture at any time at a private view at the New Gallery, except when the theatre is open.

If you approve, the picture of you will have to be taken by Thursday or Friday of this week so that it can be sent to America on Saturday for development.

Again I emphasise that this is the greatest advance in cinematography that has taken place since its invention. Further, it must not be confused with previous talking pictures, for the American Telephone and Telegraph method is something quite different and so perfect in its synchronisation and in its rendering of the human voice that it is a startling and astonishing manifestation.

Please reply by telegraph, as if the arrangements are not convenient to you I propose to telegraph to our old friend Lloyd George.

Yours ever,
Max

Winston S. Churchill to Lord Beaverbrook

(Beaverbrook papers)

20 September 1927   Chartwell Manor

My dear Max,

It is very kind of you to give me an opportunity of figuring in such distinguished company, and I have most carefully considered your proposition.

On the whole, however, I think I would rather not. I am in a far humbler class than the individuals you mention, and have no right to such prominence. Lloyd George, as a war figure and as a world statesman, would be far more appropriate. Moreover, I am not sure I could do it very well, and perhaps the exhibition would make me as many enemies as friends. Finally, here I am and here I stay as long as I possibly can. So for all these reasons—which I admit are somewhat disconnected—pray excuse me from your flattering offer.

I shall be here alone all next week. Clemmie has to go to Venice for a rest and change. Why do you not come down and spend a night, see my works of construction and discuss the situation at home and abroad over a sound bottle of 1906?

Thank you so much also for the book, but much more if you will come. *Do*

Yours vy sincerely
Winston S.C.

PS. I ought to have added that I have decided to eschew Ambition & Advertisement for the future.

Winston S. Churchill to Lord Stamfordham

(*Churchill papers: 1/194*)

20 September 1927

My dear Stamfordham,

I was much amused by the cutting which the King sent me. If I could be sure of equally skilful auctioneering, I really might endeavour to reduce our national liabilities by turning out a few pictures. I am so glad that a substantial contribution to the Fund was realised.[1]

I enjoyed myself very much at Balmoral. It is not often that the paths of duty and enjoyment fall so naturally together. I had a particularly pleasant

[1] At the beginning of September, a Churchill painting had been auctioned at Balmoral. The 'auctioneer' was Sir Frederick Ponsonby, who had written to Churchill on 10 September 1927: 'In a raucous voice I explained what I was doing. I said that although there were innumerable instances of the King of Scotland giving commissions to famous artists, I defied anyone to find an instance in history of the Sovereign of this Country asking a Chancellor of the Exchequer to paint a picture to be sold for charitable purposes. . . . I ended by saying that in order that there should be no jealousy amongst the artists of Scotland I would suggest the President of the Scottish Academy being asked to join the Treasury in order that he might help you to think out some way of reducing taxation' (*Churchill papers: 1/194*). The painting, which sold for 115 guineas, was presented to the buyer by Queen Mary.

luncheon with the King when we went out deer driving, and a very good talk about all sorts of things. I am very glad he did not disapprove of my using the Ministerial room as a studio, and I took particular care to leave no spots on the Victorian tartans.

With all good wishes, believe me

Winston S. Churchill to Richard Sickert

(*Churchill papers: 1/194*)

20 September 1927

My dear Mr Sickert,

I have to acknowledge another most interesting letter from you, and also a telegram which reached Balmoral after I had left and which apparently caused much perplexity to those who forwarded it. The picture was of course your beau-ideal of a landscape which I turned into a camaïeu[1] according to your command, and subsequently coloured as well as I could from imagination.

I am deeply interested in all you have shown me, and am most anxious to have a further conclave. Clemmie has been ordered abroad for a rest, and leaves for Venice on Friday. I wonder whether there would be any chance of your coming for the week-end? I would have several camaïeus in various stages of preparation for your inspection, and you could then show me how the colouring stage proceeds. This, you will remember, was only very lightly touched on in our discussion.

The studio will be in working order, and strong, permanent easels and immovable tables will be available instead of the gimcrack structure on which you found me working.

Once more thanking you for so many kindnesses,

believe me

PS. I need scarcely say that it will give me very great pleasure if Mrs Sickert[2] will come with you.

---

[1] Camaïeu (also spelt camayeu), a method of painting in only a single colour.

[2] Therese Lessore, died 1945. A landscape, portrait and figure painter. In May 1914, when she was married to Bernard Adeney, Sickert wrote of her: 'Her pictures are seemingly not painted from models pretending to do things. By some strange alchemy of genius, the essentials of their being and movement are torn from them, and presented in ordered and rhythmical arrangement of the highest technical brevity and beauty.' She married Sickert, as his third wife, in June 1926.

Sir George Lloyd to Lord Irwin

(*Irwin papers*)

25 September 1927

I was staying a weekend recently with Winston who was immensely struck with Mother India—Miss Mayo's book. It is all true.

Winston S. Churchill to Clementine Churchill

(*Spencer-Churchill papers*)

26 September 1927
'Chartwell Bulletin'
Published weekly—or bi-weekly.

I was delighted to get your telegram and to hear that you have lovely weather at Venice. Here we have had a fair proportion of sunshine and storm.

Sickert arrived on Friday night and we worked very hard at various paintings and had many discussions. I am really thrilled by the field he is opening to me. I see my way to paint far better pictures than I ever thought possible before. He is really giving me a new lease of life as a painter.

Jack proposed himself for the week-end, Abe came to lunch on the Sunday.[1] So I had plenty of company. Jack brought with him his portable wireless and we had a wonderful concert each night. I had no idea that they could produce such results; no blare, no clack, just quiet, fine music. We turned out the lights and listened by the hour together. These sets cost £30, but there are better ones and by fixing even this one to an aerial you get an enormous increase of choice.

I am asking Harrods tentatively whether they will take back the electric piano, and on what terms. I am quite sure we should get far more value out of a good wireless instrument like Jack's, also it would be much cheaper. There is still another instalment of £13.9.0. to pay on the piano. There would be no difficulty about Sarah as our Downing Street piano could come down. Let me know what you think of this idea.

Hill has three extra men, including the two old fellows, who have all accepted at 35/-d a week though they think the wage a very low one. The first thing is to get the kitchen garden properly weeded and the new garden completed, and one man will dedockulate. I think the privet hedge must rank after these.

[1] Churchill's brother Jack, and his friend Sir Abe Bailey.

The pig-stys are finished and three Middle White sows have arrived and will enter on occupation tomorrow. A new calf was born this morning. Twenty-five sheep are also busy on nibbling duty in the orchard.

Arnold's idea about the chickens is that we should buy a certain number of live fowls, at a cost of about 2/6d apiece, which he will fatten up for us to eat until the spring. This is much cheaper and far less trouble than using the incubator. In January he will start this up together with broody hens and keep a home supply during the spring and summer. There is a great saving in buying market fowls alive instead of killed chickens from the poulterer.

The dam continues to progress and the water rises a steady inch a day, even when it does not rain. I hope to be really through with it this week. I have only four men now.

The Prime Minister returns tonight and I shall probably go up to see him tomorrow. I will then find out what his plans are for Cabinets, etc and will wire you definitely whether I can come or not. I am enormously attracted by the idea of joining you on the Lido and of painting in Venice by my new method. On the other hand every minute of my day here passes delightfully. There are an enormous amount of things I want to do—and there is of course also the expense to consider. Nevertheless I am poising.

Your telegram has just arrived about Streety. She is still ill though I have no evening report. She has moved into a Nursing Home as her own house has been sold and was being stripped of furniture.

I look forward much to a letter from you telling me all about the Lido and the Schneider Cup. I am so glad we won!

Winston S. Churchill to Clementine Churchill

(*Spencer-Churchill papers*)

26 September 1927   Chartwell Manor

My darling one,

The sun is shining vy brightly here & the valley might almost in its own way rival yr lagoons. I have not yet heard from Baldwin. Perhaps I will come next week; I will wire you later. But do not expect me or alter in any way yr plans. I hope you will stay fixed in Venice as long as possible & not start 'on tour' as soon as you have sat down. Peace comes from staying in one spot. Write me fully of yr intention, & where you will be next week.

I have thought vy tenderly about you my Beloved & our life together. You know how much you mean to me, & what I owe you. I will try & be more of a help to you.

Always your loving husband,

W

[Sketch]

PS. B will perhaps lunch here tomorrow.

Winston S. Churchill to Clementine Churchill

(*Spencer-Churchill papers*)

27 September 1927   Chartwell Manor

My darling,

Yr dear note has just arrived. There is a Cabinet on Wed 5 wh I think I ought to attend. But I will start for Venice on Thursday (or at the latest Friday) arriving 7th or 8th. Meanwhile (you will think it odd of me) I am going up to Bendor for three or four days.

The dam is quiescent & slowly filling up; & he promises unparalleled salmon & stags. So I shall fill the interval by a northern flight. What are you going to do? Will you get tired of Venice by then? I hope not; but if you want to make a tour, why don't you do it now & return to the Lido in time to have the *gondola* ready for me on the 8th? My sweet one I was deeply touched by yr letter. It warmed my heart. Yr love for me is so much more than I deserve.

I beg you take things vy easily, & not to move for the sake of moving. But if you must, I will accompany you—tho I shd prefer the Lido to all other places; & wd like to find you there or back there when I set foot upon Italian soil. Write me all yr plans & send me my sailing directions. In particular shall I not bring Furber? She wd tidy up & pack up for us all. At present I am telling her to prepare, & tickets are being taken. It wd be right for you to be out of England during the Epping week & she wd be a convenience.

Dearest Clemmie take a full six weeks break. All will be well here: but let yr rest be a rest, & recharge yr batteries.

Baldwin came to lunch & was treated with much ceremony by Mary. How women admire power! The PM was most friendly. It was nice of him to come down to me. We talked over the vacancy in the Cabinet. He inclines to Ronnie McNeill. I am all for this. How can you compare CL or VL[1] with

---

[1] CL = Cunliffe-Lister. VL = Victor Lytton (who had just returned from India, where he had been Governor of Bengal).

this rugged[1] old counsellor. This wd mean a new Financial Secretary for me—probably Captain Hacking.[2] Do you know him? He is charming & extremely able—lately a Whip & now an Under Secretary. (All the above is absolutely secret, & quite uncertain).[3]

Good night my sweet Clemmie—I am tired with a long day—(Worthing arrived also—separately) & the dam is vy exacting.

So I send my fondest love to you—& dear Diana—
Ever yr devoted
W

6 more heifers bought to replace those sold.

Winston S. Churchill to Sir Richard Hopkins and Alfred Hurst

(*Churchill papers: 18/64*)

27 September 1927
Secret

1. Ministry of Health's Poor Law proposals have still to run the gauntlet of Cabinet and Treasury opposition, which will be considerable.

2. We must not worry too much about block grants. Agreement will never be reached among Departments except on a basis very injurious to the Treasury. Mr Hurst must accept the insuperable difficulties to his plans.

3. The formation of a 'mass of manoeuvre' of 30 millions for a vast reduction of rates upon Producers constitutes the Budget of 1928.

4. I will see Mr Chamberlain and find out whether he is willing to help. If so, we may aid him in his schemes. If not, we must go on alone. Our plan will then be to take the Producers out of the Mediaeval Rating system. 3 is in no way dependent on 2—I care nothing for Block grants, and would not make any exertions on their behalf.

WSC

[1] Ronald McNeill was six feet six inches tall.

[2] Douglas Hewitt Hacking, 1884–1950. On active service in France, 1914–16 (despatches, OBE). Conservative MP for the Chorley Division of Lancashire, 1918–45. Parliamentary Private Secretary, Ministry of Pensions, 1920; Admiralty, 1920–1; War Office, 1921–2. Conservative Whip, 1922–5. Parliamentary Under-Secretary of State, Home Office, 1925–7. Secretary, Department of Overseas Trade, Parliamentary Secretary, Board of Trade, and Parliamentary Under-Secretary of State for Foreign Affairs, 1927–9. Government Delegate, League of Nations, Geneva, 1933. Parliamentary Under-Secretary, Home Office, 1933–4; Dominion Affairs, 1935–6. Chairman of the Conservative Party Organization, 1936–42. Created Baronet, 1938; Baron, 1945.

[3] Ronald McNeill became Chancellor of the Duchy of Lancaster (in succession to Lord Cecil of Chelwood) and was raised to the peerage as Baron Cushendun on 7 November 1927. Douglas Hacking became Parliamentary Secretary at the Overseas Trade Department of the Board of Trade. Churchill's new Financial Secretary was Arthur Michael Samuel (later Baron Mancroft).

Clementine S. Churchill to Winston S. Churchill
(Spencer-Churchill papers)

28 September 1927   Lido, Venice

. . . I must say that my culte for Mussolini is somewhat diminished by the almost ferocious poster Campaign which goes on everywhere.

You might think there was an Election on, tho' that is the last thing which he would allow. His photograph is everywhere, sometimes in very ludicrous attitudes. That sinister stencilled face appears in the most unexpected places —on the walls of Lavatories & on the porphyry pillars of the most ancient churches. You never hear his name mentioned either by Foreigner or native.

October 1927

Winston S. Churchill to Clementine Churchill
(*Spencer-Chruchill papers*)

1 October 1927   Stack Lodge[1]

My darling,

Here I am at the North Pole! Last night the fishing was unexpectedly vy good. I had connexion with 5 fish in 3 hours, & killed 3 viz 16 14 & 12½ lbs.

'Coco'[2] is here in place of Violet.[3] She fishes from morn till night, & in 2 months has killed 50 salmon. She is vy agreeable—really a gt & strong being fit to rule a man or an Empire. Bennie vy well & I think extremely happy to be mated with an equal—her ability balancing his power. We are only 3 on the river & have all the plums. Today the river was 'in perfect order': & of course after 6 hours grinding toil (wh has nearly broken my back) not a fish wd bite. Curious creatures of caprice, these salmon! If they don't choose to be killed, nothing will persuade them.

Just as I was starting from Chartwell the Prof blew in in his motor, arriving from Aix. I thought it wd be nice for him to come out with us. We shall fly to Parigi, if the weather is practicable.

I am delighted by Maurois' Disraeli.[4] I hope Randolph will not imitate him & lose us £7000 at 20 years of age. More than cd be borne by yr ever devoted loving husband.

                                                                          W

The lion of St Porks

[1] One of the Duke of Westminister's houses, at Lairg, in northern Scotland.

[2] 'Coco' Chanel (see page 928, note 4).

[3] Violet Mary Nelson, youngest daughter of Sir William Nelson, Baronet. She married, as her first husband, George Rowley, Coldstream Guards; in 1920, as her second husband (and his second wife), the 2nd Duke of Westminster, from whom she obtained a divorce in 1926; as her third husband, on 8 October 1927, Frederick Cripps, brother of Stafford Cripps and second son of the 1st Baron Parmoor.

[4] André Maurois' biography, *La Vie de Disraëli*, was published in Paris in the spring of 1927. The English edition, translated by H. Miles, was published in London in October 1927, entitled *Disraeli: A Picture of the Victorian Age*. Maurois himself had been attached as an interpreter to Churchill's battalion on the western front in the spring of 1916.

Victor Cazalet: diary

(*Robert Rhodes James: 'Victor Cazalet, A Portrait'*)

3 October 1927

I dined with Winston and stayed up till 1.30 am. Lindemann, Jack Churchill, and Grigg were there. Winston told a wonderful story of Kitchener at a Ministerial meeting early in the war of 1914. Kitchener was very obstinate and very reticent, never having had anyone to question his authority for years. Lloyd George asked for the recruiting figures. But Kitchener refused to give any, while Asquith sat mute writing letters. The other Ministers bar Winston and Lloyd George accepted the situation. Then Lloyd George protested: they were Ministers, eager to win the War; they must know. Kitchener rose majestically and started towards the door. A tremendous crisis was probable, for Kitchener was a popular figure, and the Liberal Government had become unpopular. But Pease, who had been Whip for ten years in the House of Commons, rushed naturally to the door to stop Kitchener going out, and stood there with arms outstretched across the door, smiling. What could Kitchener do? Eventually he smiled and returned!

Josiah Wedgwood[1] to Lord Irwin

(*Irwin papers*)

4 October 1927

Baldwin seems to be getting very much under the influence of Churchill. Perhaps because C never despairs of the republic. He is as young as ever, and the country and politics are still his game. They say that Baldwin is so tired and, perhaps, ill that he will retire before the election, and advise the King to send for Churchill.

---

[1] Josiah Clement Wedgwood, 1872–1943. Naval architect, 1896–1900. On active service in South Africa, 1900. Liberal MP for Newcastle-under-Lyme, 1906–19. Commanded armoured cars in France, Antwerp, Gallipoli and East Africa, 1914–17 (DSO, wounded, despatches twice). Assistant Director, Trench Warfare Department, Ministry of Munitions, 1917. War Office Mission to Siberia, 1918. Granted the Labour Whip, May 1919. Labour MP, 1919–42. Vice-Chairman of the Labour Party, 1921–4. Chancellor of the Duchy of Lancaster, 1924. Created Baron, 1942.

Neville Chamberlain to Winston S. Churchill

(*Churchill papers: 18/63*)

14 October 1927   Ministry of Health

My dear Winston,

You may remember that on the 15th July I wrote to you upon the subject of Block Grants and Poor Law Reform setting out at some length my latest proposals on the subject. You did not then send me any written reply, as of course the subject required detailed investigation and it was very near the Adjournment. But now we shall soon be considering what we are going to put into the King's Speech next year, and we must also be drawing up some sort of programme for the Election, whenever it comes. Therefore, some decision will have to be taken at an early date upon this difficult subject.

I do not think that any new feature has arisen since my letter which would lead me to modify anything I said then, but if anything, feeling has rather stiffened in the direction I indicated as probable, that is to say, the so-called Necessitous Areas are still more urgently pressing their claims for some relief.

I noticed a recent speech by Lord Gainford in which he stressed very strongly the crushing burden of rates upon his particular industries, and I anticipate that the Unemployment Insurance Bill will bring out this aspect of the case still more emphatically.

The conclusion I draw is that we should be wise to take the earliest opportunity of showing our genuine intention of meeting this cry, and I do not believe it will be possible to find any alternative to the scheme I have proposed which it would be possible to put into operation at short notice.

I know that you have in your mind some much larger plan, possibly involving an alteration in the whole rating system. I am not averse from an investigation into the possibilities of such a plan, but I am very sensible of its difficulties and dangers, and I should be very unwilling to enter upon a scheme of such magnitude until it had been exhaustively examined.

What I should like, therefore, to propose to you is that you should consider sympathetically the scheme that I have put before you for legislation next year, and simultaneously we should set on foot an inquiry into your ideas, which could be worked out by the officials of our two departments.

I am just about to begin my official autumn tour, which will not terminate until the end of this month, but when I have finished it perhaps we could arrange a meeting, at which we could have a full discussion of the situation.

Yours sincerely,
N. Chamberlain

Winston S. Churchill to Neville Chamberlain

(*Churchill papers: 18/44*)

18 October 1927   Treasury Chambers
Most Secret

My dear Neville,

A large relief of the rates upon producers (agric and manuf) constitutes the main objective of the Finance of next year. Whether it can be achieved or not, I do not yet know. If the money were available, it could be achieved as a mere Budget relief. But the opportunity is too good, and the safeguards are too necessary, for a purely departmental solution on my part. I see no reason why your plans and mine should not be interwoven. All progress has been arrested since the beginning of June, when I first wrote to you, by the fact that our officials have been studying separate aspects of the question: none can be made until a whole-heartedly co-operative exploration is undertaken. I shall therefore rejoice to thrash the matter out with you on your return—as you suggest. Joint action is indispensable for success. But you really must not expect me to produce 3 or 4 millions a year for a partial scheme of modest dimensions. That would only hurt the Finances without helping the Government. The agencies which we can command are so limited and overstrained that we must utilize them to the highest advantage.

I think I could deal with your 'necessitous areas' in the most economic way—viz by removing the deterrent of high rates which prevents factories from growing up where there is cheap and abundant labour. I will not however inflict this story on you till we meet.

                                With every good wish,
                                Yours very sincerely,
                                Winston S. Churchill

Winston S. Churchill to Stanley Baldwin

(*Baldwin papers*)

19 October 1927   Treasury Chambers

My dear Prime Minister,

My opening talk with the Admiralty revealed abysmal differences. I am proposing no Cruisers in '27–'28 or '28–'29, & they want 3 B class in each of these years, with possibly a smaller type of B substituted in the second year. I will not burden you with arguments at this stage—not because there are none! We were all agreed that the Committee wd have to be set up at once.

Estimates cannot be framed till it has reported. I shd think it ought to begin to sit in the early days of November. Would you therefore vy kindly decide on its personnel? Presumably you wd reproduce the old Committee wh examined the matter so fully three years ago, & is acquainted with the subject. I wd suggest you shd add AJB, who supported the Admiralty at that time in the Cabinet, though I do not think he would now. If Willie has a fancy for some colleague not hitherto committed to a pronounced opinion, it wd only be fair to meet his wish.

You will remember that it was decided that a Sub-committee of the CID shd examine the basis of the Oil Fuel Reserves; but no action has yet been taken. It wd be convenient I think if the new Committee dwelt with this cognate topic.

Yours vy sincerely
Winston S. Churchill

Winston S. Churchill to Clementine Churchill

(Spencer-Churchill papers)

19 October 1927   Chartwell Manor

Our journey was uneventful and the time passed smoothly and swiftly in the Prof's agreeable and always instructive company. All was well when we reached here. Moppet and Mary in the best of spirits gave a royal welcome.

The Chartwell bulletin of today records a number of important happenings. Twelve medium sized black pigs have been purchased for £24 and are now busily at work rooting up a large wired in patch of blackberry bushes. Diana's late sow has had five piggies and the first of the new pedigree sows six. So you see our porcine population has quadrupled. Three calves have been born, two bulls, and some sales are imminent.

Arnold has achieved wonders with his men during the ten days. It is extraordinary the amount he manages to do. Everything is carried out exactly. I have never seen his like. The lake is slowly filling—$4\frac{1}{2}$ inches rise during my absence. Your pathway across the kitchen garden is completed and the steps have been made. They are quite mild in gradient. The box hedge trough is being prepared round the new kitchen garden and will soon be ready for the plants. All the remains of your devastation have been grubbed and cleared away and a smooth bosom of ground alone marks the site of the rhododendrons. In short, everyone seems to have worked hard.

I have received a delightful letter from Ettie[1] to you inviting us to Pans-

---

[1] Lady Desborough (see page 850, note 1).

hanger for the week-end November 5th. AJB, FE and other friends are going. However, as it was Randolph's long leave I rang him up on the telephone and asked him whether he would prefer to come to Chartwell or go to Oxford where he has been invited by the Prof. He was very keen to go to Oxford and will come up to London on Monday to lunch at Downing Street with us before going back to Eton. In these circumstances I have accepted Ettie's invitation for myself and for you unless you wire to the contrary.

The Iveagh Death Duties[1] amount to £4½ millions and ought to place the Budget in security.

Ronnie McNeill will be appointed tomorrow Chancellor of the Duchy, and I expect I shall be given Arthur Michael Samuel,[2] very able and with the money nose, in his place. This is what I have suggested.

The weather continues mild and dry. But I have developed a most frightful cold in my head and throat. Fancy after all these months of perfect health to have this affliction with an endless crop of speeches and going in and out of hot meetings looming down upon me. I have retired to bed tonight to take the most strenuous measures possible to shake it off, and in this posture after a long and tiring day must now try to whip up a speech for Nottingham on Friday.

Winston S. Churchill to Clementine Churchill

(*Spencer-Churchill papers*)

20 October 1927　　　　　　　　　　　　　　　11 Downing Street

My darling,

I send you enclosed a few local notes.

I am curing my cold gradually; but next week will be an infliction if my throat is affected. What a curse these speeches are! They distort ones mind from serious work—& then there is no report—no standard of national controversy.[3]

[1] As a result of the death on 7 October 1927 of Edward Cecil Guinness, 1st Earl of Iveagh, who left property valued at £11,000,000, on which estate duty of £4,400,000 was paid.

[2] Arthur Michael Samuel, 1872–1942. Lord Mayor of Norwich, 1912–13. Member of Council, Association of British Chambers of Commerce, 1915–24. Staff Assistant, Ministry of Munitions, 1915–16. Conservative MP for Farnham, 1918–37. Parliamentary Under-Secretary, Board of Trade, Foreign Office and Department of Overseas Trade, 1924–7. Financial Secretary to the Treasury, 1927–9. Chairman of the House of Commons Select Committee on Public Accounts, 1930 and 1931. Created Baronet, 1932. Created Baron Mancroft, 1937. Author of a history of the herring.

[3] Speaking at Nottingham on the evening of October 21, Churchill made several comments on the Labour Party's proposal for a new surtax, calling it 'another edition of the capital levy'; and he added: 'It struck at the saving power of the nation just when a marked darken-

I expect you will have been rescued from yr hotel by AK[1] by now. Anyhow I know you will enjoy showing the treasures of Florence to Diana.

> With tender love & a thousand (1,000) kisses
> Your loving husband
> W

Winston S. Churchill to Clementine Churchill

(*Spencer-Churchill papers*)

22 October 1927   Chartwell Manor

CHARTWELL BULLETIN

A minor catastrophe has occurred in the pig world. Our best new sow, irritated by the noise of a pick-axe breaking the ground near the pig sty, killed six of a new litter of eight little pigs. She was condemned to be fattened and to die, but to-day she has received the remaining two and proposes to bring them up in a sensible manner. She is therefore reprieved on probation.

I have been vigorously treating my cold. Dover's powders every night, and every kind of spray, etc. I got through Nottingham all right and my voice held out quite well. The day before the Prince telephoned that he and F[2] would come down by the same train. Bridget Colebrooke[3] came too, so

---

ing of it was causing anxiety in many quarters. It would inflict a crushing blow at the revival of trade, and for what? After all, their old friend the capital levy, was proclaimed by the Socialist Party for the purpose of paying off the national debt, but this new surtax was simply to be used for self-indulgence.' Churchill ended his speech with a survey of the existing state of party politics. 'British freedom,' he declared, 'had been very largely gained. It now remained to preserve it. The Conservative Party was alone strong enough to maintain our freedom against dangers which were arising in the political field. They were the old bulwark against all forms of reaction and revolution.'

[1] Alice Frederica Edmonstone, 1869–1947. Youngest daughter of Admiral Sir William Edmonstone, 4th Bt. In 1891 she married Lieutenant-Colonel the Hon George Keppel, MVO, 3rd son of the 7th Earl of Albemarle. Both she and her husband died in 1947. A close friend of Edward VII, and of Lady Randolph Churchill. Between the wars she lived at the Villa Ombrellino, just outside Florence. On learning of the death of Queen Victoria, Churchill had written to his mother (on 22 January 1901): 'Will the Keppel be appointed 1st Lady of the Bedchamber?' Travelling with her in Egypt two years later, Churchill wrote to his mother (on 19 December 1902): 'Mrs Keppel is vy good company.'

[2] Freda Dudley Ward (see page 970, note 1).

[3] Bridget Colebrooke, 1892–1975. Daughter of the 1st Baron Colebrooke, a permanent lord-in-waiting to King George V, 1924–36. In 1922 she married, as his second wife, Lord Victor Paget, from whom she obtained a divorce in 1932 (he died in 1952).

we all lunched together, and Eddie Marsh too; quite agreeable. The Prince was staying with the other sister, Vera, (who was half a mile away) inspecting his horses before the hunting season. I left as soon as possible this morning as I thought the animation of the Birkin household would not amuse me so much as solitude at Chartwell.

I met there an old friend of my father's, Sir Lancelot Rolleston,[1] 79 but apparently a well preserved 60. He told me that he and my father had been the closest friends at Oxford and all my father's life; they hunted neighbouring packs of harriers, lived in the same College, etc. He had been wanting to meet me for thirty years. I was much interested in all he said. These very old people lose the sense of time. He talked about 'Randolph' as one would speak of someone one had seen a week or ten days ago, and all his memories shone across the intervening gulf of years like lights from another world.

Moppet and Maria have shifted their headquarters to London. I looked in upon them on my way through and was very graciously received. In fact as I took my leave Maria said to Moppet, who was calling her 'I must take my visitor downstairs', which she accordingly did with a great air of ceremony. Yesterday she encountered Mrs B in the garden and was taken by her into the Cabinet room and introduced together with the pug to a number of people. I said to Moppet 'Was she dressed all right? meaning, was she tidy?' to which Mary replied 'Oh, yes, she (Mrs B) was wearing a nice grey *frock*!'

It is pouring with rain to-day and my lake has risen one inch and a quarter in 24 hours.

Hawkey is coming over to lunch tomorrow, Sunday. He was in a great state to see me about the campaign and made a long story about the state of the division. At one end the farmers are furious because they are not given more money, and at the other the women of Wanstead and Woodford are furious because the flappers are to have votes. Generally one would have thought from his manner that the whole place was in rebellion. I am sure it is all nonsense and I am really quite glad to be going among them to inculcate a higher standard of loyalty and discipline.

I will let you know how I get on. It will be a pretty stiff week with two meetings a night, several dinners before them, a farmers' deputation, ceaseless motor trips, heavy Cabinet estimates work beginning and a menacing cold held at arm's length. However I expect I shall crash through somehow or other. I am going to support the Flappers' Vote on the well known principle

---

[1] Lancelot Rolleston, 1847–1941. High Sheriff of Nottinghamshire, 1877. On active service in South Africa, 1899–1901 (severely wounded). Knighted, 1911. Chairman, Nottinghamshire County Council, 1928–32.

of making a virtue of necessity. I think it will turn out all right, but anyhow it has now become inevitable.

Freda was very nice about Diana and praised her greatly.

Mr Lewis[1] the artist is coming to spend Sunday night and Monday here. I expect I shall take him over to dine at Holwood whence they have been sending me almost daily invitations. Solly is going to have his portrait painted by him. It will be interesting to argue out the Sickert method with a younger brush.

Jack and Goonie are coming to lunch also tomorrow and all the arrangements will work out smoothly.

I have opened my new controversy with the Admiralty demanding no cruisers this year or next. The first interview with Bridgeman and the Sea Lords though quite friendly showed no likelihood of agreement. On the other hand I am almost certain that the Cabinet Committee and the Cabinet will endorse my views. There may be a very stiff tension before it is settled, and really I think I am bound to fight this pretty hard. I have been looking deeply into the out-turn of the revenue and expenditure in the first six months and the reports which I called for from the Treasury before I went to Venice are now complete.

It looks as if I am going to get through all right but this must not be proclaimed. I have to talk beggary and bankruptcy for the next few months. I have had some awful blows in expense, now from this quarter, now from that. Luckily however there are windfalls and what we lose on the swings we shall perhaps more than recover on the roundabouts. It is really very like our private affairs though on a larger scale.

Harry Rosslyn[2] insisted on seeing me. He is being made bankrupt by the Inland Revenue for non payment of super tax. They have been trying to get it out of him for a good many years but he pleads trustees, moneylenders, etc and meanwhile lives in a sort of insolvent sumptiousness which has excited the wrath of Somerset House. I had to tell him I could do nothing for him.

[1] Alfred Neville Lewis, 1895–1972. Born in Cape Town, studied art at the Slade School, 1912–14. On active service during the Great War in France, Belgium and Italy. Exhibited frequently at the Royal Academy between the wars. Official war artist with the South African Forces, 1940–3. Among his best known portraits were those of Churchill, King Alfonso XIII of Spain, King George II of Greece and Field-Marshals Smuts, Montgomery and Alexander.

[2] James Francis Harry St Clair-Erskine, 1869–1939. Entered the Army, 1886. Succeeded his father as 5th Earl of Rosslyn, 1890. On active service in South Africa, 1899–1901 (including the relief of Ladysmith). War Correspondent for the *Daily Mail* in South Africa, 1900: he published an account of his experiences, *Twice Captured*, in 1900. (It was this book that first cast aspersions on the manner of Churchill's escape from a Boer prisoner-of-war camp in Pretoria. Churchill described the charges—in a letter to the Prince of Wales on 17 October 1900—as 'a cruel and wicked falsehood'.) Major, King's Royal Rifle Corps, 1915–17.

Do you see that Markham youth who married Muriel Beckett's daughter has also got through the fortune of more than a million he inherited 4 years ago.[1]

Orders have been given to begin yr new Pantry on Monday.

Winston S. Churchill to Clementine Churchill

(*Spencer-Churchill papers*)

22 October 1927   Chartwell Manor

Darling,

No letter yet from you! I wonder whether you are still at the hotel or whether you have been rescued by Alice K. And how are you? Naturally I feel anxious not to receive even a telegram. Perhaps I shall get a letter on Monday. I have a vy hard week in front of me, & I want to know that things are well with you, & that you are improving in spirits & health. So I sent a wire this evening asking for a reply.

What a delightful postcard correspondence you carried on with Mary! She showed them all to me with gt pride. I am sorry she has shifted her Headquarters to London. I shall be here alone next week without the interruptions of her charming prattle & ceremonious entrances.

In my 'Bulletin' I have told you of my journey to Nottingham. It was quite pathetic to see the Prince & F. His love is so obvious & undisguisable. But his manners were of the highest quality. We were 5. I had brought Eddie. The railway car table held 4. So Eddie sat on the opposite side at the 2 table.

F	P	‖	O	
Bridget	me		Eddie	X

Seeing wh the P went and sat opposite to Eddie, separated by a forlorn gulf from his idol. I thought it such a lesson. You have undervalued him I think in some ways.

However luckily after an hour I thought of opening the window at X wh made it necessary for Eddie to move out of the draught, & the P to move back across the gangway into the sunshine.

How odd the Birkins[2] shd have produced this delightful little Sèvres

---

[1] On 8 December 1920 Sir Charles Markham, 2nd Baronet, then aged twenty (the son of Churchill's friend, the Liberal MP Sir Arthur Basil Markham, 1866–1916), had married Gwladys Helen Beckett, eldest daughter of the Hon Rupert Evelyn Beckett, and of Muriel Beckett, both of whom Churchill had known since the beginning of the century.

[2] Charles Wilfrid Birkin, 1865–1932. CMG, 1916. A Justice of the Peace; and his wife Claire Lloyd Howe, daughter of Alexander Howe of New York. Parents of Freda and Vera Birkin.

porcelain shepherdess. The atmosphere of manufacturing prosperity & taste of their mansion are with me still. You wd have hopped in it.

My dearest one I do trust you are aiding yr recovery of poise & strength in every way. Not doing *too* much Art treasures—& trapesing to show Diana galleries—Not fretting about troubles wh will never come to pass—& above all not feeling too dissatisfied with

Your ever loving
W

[Sketch of a lion]

He has been reading Ludwig's[1] Bismarck (sent to us by the author) & he has taken a vow tonight to be Valiant,

Goodnight my darling

Winston S. Churchill to P. J. Grigg

(*Churchill papers: 18/46*)

23 October 1927

I have not had time to read all of the Office Memorandum on naval policy. It is a valuable assembly of facts and will be useful for reference. I do not think it is suited for Cabinet consumption. There is so much of it that the Ministers would not give the time to take it in.

The table of the crusier fleets under the 20 years' limit is not well presented. The case cannot be understood unless three separate classes are used. This alone enables the Effinghams, Emeralds and Yorks to be balanced for what they are worth against the Furutakas.

In connection with my letter to the First Lord I wish to add a table showing the cruiser fleets in the financial years 1930 and in 1931, assuming we build no more cruisers in '27 and '28. I attach a rough draft. I am assuming that the Japanese have four A class now built and have already begun two more—or are they only ordered? They have further declared their intention of constructing another two between now and 1931. I therefore credit them

---

[1] Emil Ludwig, 1881–1948. The son of Hermann Cohn, who changed his surname in order to hide his son's Jewish parentage. Educated in Germany. Dramatist and historian. Lived in Switzerland from 1907 until his death; a Swiss citizen since 1932. Biographer of (among others) Jesus, Goethe, Napoleon, Bismarck, Beethoven and Stalin. In 1932 he published *Talks with Mussolini*; in 1934 *Talks with Masaryk*. He called his biographies 'psychological lives', and referred to himself as a 'portrait painter' in words. His biography of Bismarck was first published in Germany in 1926; the English translation, entitled *Bismarck: The Story of a Fighter*, was published in London in October 1927.

with two more in 1930 than the Office does, but I am quite open to argument on this point.

I assume that the Americans will only build three new ones beyond their two for completion in 1930 and three more ie eight in all for completion in 1931.

It is difficult to decide what basis to take about 'Begun'. Whether it should be announced or authorised by the Parliaments or actually begun or laid down.

I credit the Japanese with six A's, two of which are about to be begun. The last two of the eight will not materialise for the years in question. It is important to know in exact detail the position of each one of these ships. When laid down, when launched, when completed or to be completed. This also applies to American ships. Do not hesitate to write in a short note about each ship. The important thing for the argument is the terminal date 'completed' or 'commissioned'. Someone should study with Admiralty information the life history of each of these Japanese ships. I think they are taking more than three years to construct. The five key dates are—'Announced', 'Money authorised', 'Laid down', 'Launched', 'Commissioned'. No doubt it will not be possible to fix these exhaustively, but every effort should be made to do so.

Winston S. Churchill to Clementine Churchill
(*Spencer-Churchill papers*)

25 October 1927   Chartwell Manor

The opening meeting at Chingford in the big hall was a magnificent success. There must have been more than 2,000 people present, and some offence was given to numbers who had to be turned away. Hawkey had taken immense trouble in organising it, and Mrs Douglas Pennant's disgruntled agriculturists were brought in to the number of 50 in an omnibus. I a little bit tackled her and made her feel that I heard she had been critical. I think she is really perfectly tame, only a bit worried.

I spoke an hour and said I would answer all questions for as long as they liked; but none were asked except by a Socialist who was easily squared off, and a gentleman about the Road Fund. The Community Singing was a great success. Hawkey by his personal influence had got a very good singer down without a fee who sang beautifully and led all the choruses. My view of the situation was entirely confirmed by the friendly and even delighted attitude of the people. I told them that these last three months had been the first three months of Peace, social and political, domestic and foreign, that

England has had since the century began, which is quite true. I look back on no three months so utterly undisturbed by action or faction. Pray God it is not a mocking interlude!

Hawkey was divided between delight at the brilliant success of the meeting and fear lest I should think it all came along quite naturally without any trouble on his part. He is a wonderful man at this political job. Lady Lloyd[1] was on the platform and I am to dine with her on Thursday night. She seemed in good spirits. There were many enquiries about you and all the references extremely sympathetic. I told them really you were only having a rest, and that I had no doubt the beginning of the year would find you quite all right; but lots of women made enquiries as I walked through the hall and there was genuine regret for your absence and still more for its cause. You are completely struck off all duties until the New Year.

To-night I dine with the old General[2] and do Waltham Abbey. There is always more opposition there and I shall have to deal with social topics.

Another calf is born.

Tilden is coming down to inspect the dry rot and have his nose rubbed in it.

Wallace has begun the preliminary work on the pantry.

We were exactly one hour and 25 minutes yesterday from this house to the Hotel at Epping and we never went unduly fast. There is a new road open beyond Bromley which seems to save 10 or 12 minutes. It is really very convenient.

I move to London to-night coming back here on Friday under the Mrs Gibbons régime.

The sales of the book still continue to be very satisfactory and all three volumes are affected. For instance we have sold 100 up to the 22nd of this month of Vol III, and about 60 each of Vol I and Vol II. There will certainly be another thousand or so to come in during the course of the next six months, besides the payment due in October of which I told you. This will help to fill the man of the Inland Revenue.

Winston S. Churchill to Clementine Churchill

(*Spencer-Churchill papers*)

26 October 1927 London

Both Waltham & Epping passed off brilliantly. The friendliness displayed was far in excess of any previous year. No oppositions emerged.

---

[1] Mary Leckie, daughter of George Leckie, of Sterling. She had married General Lloyd in 1881, when he was still a Lieutenant. He had died in February 1926. She died in 1942.

[2] General Colvin (see page 200, note 1).

Winston S. Churchill to William Bridgeman

(Baldwin papers)

27 October 1927
Private & Personal

My dear Willie,

I see the enclosed in this morning's 'Times'. It follows very quickly upon the Treasury-Admiralty conversation of last Wednesday, and having regard to the relationship between the First Lord and Lord Jellicoe you must really not be surprised if I consider it at first sight significant.[1]

I think it is a great pity to open this subject in public controversy at this stage. It is likely to make the concluding stages much more dangerous for all concerned. Not that I shrink in any way from public controversy if that is what the Admiralty wish. Nothing would be easier than for me to reply this evening when I speak in my constituency by announcing the decision of the Cabinet to set up a fresh Inquiry into the cruiser position, and it may be that such an announcement will soon become inevitable.

I am sure that you would not approve of any attempt to work upon public opinion or the Press on one side or the other during a Cabinet Inquiry, and relying on this I shall make no answer to Jellicoe's speech at the present time.

Yours very sincerely,
Winston S. Churchill

Clementine Churchill to Winston S. Churchill

(Spencer-Churchill papers)

28 October 1927   Hotel Grande Bretagne
                                        Florence

My Darling Winston,

Thank you for your fat & delightful budget of personal, domestic & political news.

I am glad to think that by now you are more than halfway through the Epping ordeal. I picture you night by night in the various halls & dining beforehand with the Colvins—kind Lady Lloyd—the Goschens etc.

I am sorry not to be there, as although it is all very fatiguing, I like all the

---

[1] On 27 October 1927 *The Times* reported a speech by Lord Jellicoe at the Cutler's Feast at Sheffield on the previous evening. Jellicoe had warned that the 'necessary desire for economy' in naval spending might threaten the safety of Britain's sea communications. He had also challenged the Admiralty to say whether the three cruisers originally included in the 1927 programme were going to be built.

people & I like to think that as time goes on they will become attached, & less discontented! ...

I see in the Times that Sir Warren Fisher's great friend, Florence, Lady Ebury[1] 'died suddenly in her sleep' the other day. I should think he will be heart broken as I believe he was deeply devoted to her. So if he shews signs of strain be very nice to him. She was a very tall curious rather ugly looking woman (a Christian Scientist) about my age. She was married to Alice Wimborne's[2] brother, Bertie Grosvenor who became Lord Ebury. He died some years ago.

How nice of the Prof to have Randolph for Long Leave. I think you said Randolph would lunch with us on Monday the 7th? I hear now & then from Sarah who seems well & happy.

Your loving
Clemmie

William Bridgeman to Winston S. Churchill

(*Churchill papers: 22/175*)

28 October 1927   Admiralty
Private and Personal

My dear Winston,

Thanks for your letter. As a matter of fact I went off to speak in Shrewsbury & never saw the Times report you sent.

Jellicoe as the N Zealand representative at Geneva, had all the building programmes at his disposal, and naturally has the subject well in his head, and there seems to be nothing very surprising in his wondering why the ships agreed to in the 4 year's programme & voted by Parliament had not yet been ordered.

I am sure, on reflection, you will not entertain the idea that he was primed to start propaganda by anyone here. He puts the cruisers we should have at the end of the period as 65 which is much more than we contemplate, and if we had coached him he would have put them lower—as our policy when once we got our fixed building programme was to scrap old ships at the earliest possible moment.

Still less do we desire to start a public controversy at this stage.

I much prefer to hammer out the subject with you—as we have done

[1] Florence Padelford, daughter of Edward M. Padelford of Savannah, Georgia, USA. In 1908 she married Captain Robert Victor Grosvenor, who succeeded his father as 3rd Baron Ebury in 1918. He died in 1921, she on 20 October 1927.

[2] Alice Katherine Sibell Grosvenor, 1880–1948. Daughter of the 2nd Baron Ebury. In 1902 she married Churchill's cousin Ivor Guest, 1st Viscount Wimborne.

before—and have no desire to go to a Cabinet Cttee which was agreed to at a Cabinet when I was absent.

And I greatly dislike having to 'die in the last ditch'—at the same time while I & my advisers are most anxious to relieve you as much as we can safely do, we feel very strongly that a cessation of building is impossible for many reasons, and would be a breach of faith with the Admiralty. It was in reliance on the fulfilment of the programme that we were able to make the reductions which have saved you so much.

You must admit that we have made prodigious efforts to lighten your burden, and done I think more than any other department—and I fully appreciate the difficulties of your position now—but there are limits to our powers of concession and I greatly hope after your conversation yesterday with the 1st Sea Lord we may arrive at a solution honourable for us both at an early date, but as far as I understand what passed, we are still some way from it.

Yrs v sincerely,
W. C. Bridgeman

Winston S. Churchill to Sir Richard Hopkins

(*Churchill papers: 18/46*)

28 October 1927

1. I do not understand why you have increased the Debt charge next year by £4 millions since the original estimate. Why should you assume a continuance throughout this year of the disastrous rates in regard to Treasury Bills and realisation of Saving Certificates which have been the aftermath of the strike? There are no grounds for making such an increase. It is serious when the National Debt increases each year in spite of the operations of the Sinking Fund. Clearly we ought to be £3½ millions less next year than this, apart from economies of conversion in consequence of the £65 millions fund. How will you get people to pay these enormous sums when apparently it is only pouring water into a sieve? Moreoever I understood that the late conversion threw £500,000 in this year as against next. Please explain all this to me in detail.

2. I am counting on £1½ million reduction Army, half a million Air and £2 millions Navy off £115 millions now shown—total £4 millions.

Let me have a list by departments of the Civil Service estimates. At least £6 millions must come off these.

Mr Hurst should prepare a criticism of the Ministry of Health. We simply cannot contemplate advances of £2½ millions in their expenses year by year.

A case must be made for holding the Board of Education to an increase of £1,250,000, ie our grant in consequences of the Teachers' Pensions contribution.

I will deal with the proposal for cutting down the military department myself; but I rely upon Supplies to cut the sketch estimates of the civil departments by at least £6 millions.

Arm me with the materials for writing to Mr Chamberlain and to the Minister of Education, and let cases be prepared for submission to the Cabinet Committee on Economy.

Sir Francis Floud should furnish full reasons for the falling off in his estimates for next year. I have never expected more than £3 or £4 millions from Betting. We shall certainly get £4 millions next year.

The Inland Revenue have sagged back from the recovery estimate of £405 millions by nearly £7 millions. I do not believe this is justified by what is actually taking place in view of the numbers of persons employed and the amount of business being done. I am inclined to think that £402 millions would be much safer for Inland Revenue generally. Anyhow if it is not so we have got to find methods of acceleration, etc. We shall certainly realise this sum.

Let me have a full list of the items included in the original miscellaneous revenue, ordinary and special, together with the variations now foreseen.

Also let me have a forecast of future years, and the outstanding possibilities under both these heads together with all doubtful cases which may possibly come to hand.

WSC

Winston S. Churchill to William Bridgeman

(*Churchill papers: 22/175*)

28 October 1927

My dear First Lord,

I had yesterday, as you wished, a long conversation with the First Sea Lord and Admiral Field,[1] and the proposal which, after much reflection, I

---

[1] Frederick Laurence Field, 1871–1945. Joined Royal Navy, 1884. On active service in China, 1900 (wounded). Captain, 1907. Served at Jutland (despatches). Director of Torpedoes, Admiralty, 1918–20. Rear-Admiral, 1919. Third Sea Lord and Controller of the Navy, 1920–3. Knighted, 1923. Commanded the Battle Cruiser Squadron, 1923. Vice-Admiral, 1924. Deputy Chief of the Naval Staff, 1925–8. Admiral, 1928. Commander-in-Chief, Mediterranean Fleet, 1928–30. First Sea Lord and Chief of the Naval Staff, 1930–3. Admiral of the Fleet, 1933.

make to you is that the series of cruiser programmes should be postponed till the beginning of the financial year 1929. This involves a delay of not more than 14 months from present intentions. The delay is justified even on Admiralty assumptions by the strength of the cruiser fleets on such a basis in 1930 and 1931. The international advantages are obvious. Financially, it will be easier to find the money in 1929 than earlier because of the progressive diminution in debt and war pension charges and the recovery of the Income Tax from the after effects of the Strike. Also it is wasteful to spend the money before it is absolutely needed. Navally, it is uneconomical to begin ships till the last moment and sacrifice fruitlessly a period of their short lives; and better ships can be built as science advances year by year.

I recognise that on this basis some provision would have to be made to mitigate discharges at the dockyards and to keep the armour and gun mounting plants in being. These, however, are matters of detail which, if the main issues were agreed, could certainly be adjusted between us.

Alternatively I make the following proposal. It is more expensive to the Treasury, but it greatly reduces the stringency in the dockyards. Begin one cruiser of this year's programme at the end of March 1928; begin a second cruiser about January 1929, and begin a third cruiser as soon as you like after the 1st April 1929.

If either of these proposals were acceptable to the Admiralty the policy could be stated in terms which involve no derogation from the contentions advanced at Geneva and should be represented as a temporary delay in executing the series of programmes of fleet replacement which we consider necessary. In either case the revised programmes could be stated to Parliament for a five or six years' period showing the quotas of ships required in 1930, 1931 and 1932, viz either

	1927	1928	1929	1930	1931	1932
a	nil	nil	3	3	3	3
or b	1	1	1	3	3	3

Coming to the types of ships themselves, I cannot feel convinced that the 4 gun cruisers which were mentioned would be a wise or far-sighted investment of our limited means at the present moment. Three of them would cost more both to build and maintain than two A's. They would only mount 12 guns against 16. The loss of gun power in reducing an A to a C seems altogether disproportionate to the saving, one-half of the gun power being sacrificed for less than a quarter of the expense; or put another way, a 4 gun ship costs £1,650,000 and 4 more guns can be added for £500,000 extra. The economies which such changes offer are too dearly purchased: we cannot afford to spend our money except to the best advantage. Moreover, as soon as these weak ships are built, the Admiralty will begin to disparage them and point out how valueless they are compared with the new American and Japanese types. These 7,000 ton vessels are both large and expensive, and the Admiralty will, I have no doubt, be accused in future years of having 'forgotten the guns', as happened both in the case of the Europas and the Scout class before the war.

I am not therefore pressing for a reduction in size or power at this juncture. We have made our proposals at Geneva, and they have been rejected. While neither Japan nor the United States are building any vessels smaller than the A's I do not feel that we should be wise in spending large sums in building inferior types. Of course, the moment they start a smaller type, the situation would be changed.

If however your Board feel that the single cruiser for this year under the second alternative had better be a consort of the 'York', I should not of course argue the point. Admiral Field spoke of the importance of beginning a few sloops of the Flower class at £100,000 apiece in the latter part of 1928, and having regard to the number of these which fall out after 1936 I should not cavil at this if we were able to reach agreement on other points of the new construction programme. Neither am I criticising the minor construction programmes, except to ask that in 1928 and 1929 they shall be thrown as far back in the financial year as possible. You have already agreed to do this for 1927.

In making these proposals I have been actuated by a desire to view the situation not so much from a Treasury as from the general standpoint. Further than this I cannot go in new construction.

There remains the very grave question of expense on the other points of naval administration, especially connected with Vote A, with the maintenance section of Vote 8 (Oil Fuel Reserve), and with Votes 9 and 10. But of course you are going to get to work on these yourself before we come to grips upon them.

I hope you and your naval colleagues will weigh very carefully these suggestions, which I am sure are the best for our finance, for our foreign policy and for our naval power.

I am glad to have reached an understanding with the First Sea Lord that the 4 Hawkins may be counted in our discussions as the equals of 2 Furutakas.

William Bridgeman to Winston S. Churchill

(*Churchill papers: 22/175*)

29 October 1927

My dear Chancellor,

Thanks for your letter received this morning, which crossed one of mine. Of course your second alternative comes nearer to our ideas. But we are sending you the latest figures about the Japanese position and the 1st S Lord & Adm Field would be glad to come and talk to you about them on Monday or Tuesday at any time convenient to you, I have an inspection of Holton Heath on Monday & shall be at Portsmouth all Tuesday—and it would probably save time not to wait for me—but to have a further talk with Madden[1] and Field as soon as you can.

Yrs sincerely,
W. C. Bridgeman

PS. Have you ever thought how much could be saved by having less frequent cleanings & paintings of the public offices? I am sure they are unnecessary especially in new buildings like the Admiralty.

Winston S. Churchill to Richard Sickert

(*Churchill papers: 1/194*)

30 October 1927

How very kind of you to send me your masterpiece. Until Wednesday morning I shall not have an opportunity of viewing it by daylight, but what I have seen of it by artificial light interested me very much.

I shall be moving up to London soon and am looking forward to another talk with you. I shall have a few things to show you when we meet.

The Professor came to Venice with me and we experimented on your system with great energy and application. In Paris we bought for £3 10/- a splendid lantern, apparently a trade product, which throws the positive or

---

[1] Charles Edward Madden, 1862–1935. Entered Navy, 1875. Jellicoe's wife's brother-in-law. Fourth Sea Lord, 1910–11. Rear-Admiral in the Home Fleet, 1911–12. Commanded the 3rd and 2nd Cruiser Squadrons in Home Fleet, 1912–14. Chief of Staff to Sir John Jellicoe, 1914–16. Knighted, 1916. 2nd in Command, Grand Fleet, 1917–19. Commander-in-Chief, Atlantic Fleet, 1919–22. Admiral of the Fleet, 1924. First Sea Lord and Chief of the Naval Staff, 1927–30.

negative on the canvas exactly the size one wishes. This enables the cameo to be constructed with extraordinary rapidity and accuracy in four or five tints of monochrome. Either you can do it for the negative and paint the whites black and the blacks white, or you can have a lantern slide made and follow the values directly. I have not had a chance yet of trying a portrait by this method but I am sure that a very fair likeness can be produced with great certainty.

We were not quite long enough at Venice to yield the full results. For five days the cameos were being constructed and were drying, and unhappily the sun disappeared at the time when I wished to take these cameos to the actual scene and mark in the colours upon them. You will quite understand this was not intended to be the picture but only the local aide memoire.

I am so sorry to hear you have not been well and trust you have made a complete recovery. All November I shall be in London and I shall propose you an early rendezvous.

Clemmie was hot on the trail of your picture when I left.

With all good wishes, believe me,

Winston S. Churchill to Sir Richard Hopkins

(*Churchill papers: 18/46*)

30 October 1927

I am increasingly concerned about the Debt. During the four years 1925-28 inclusive we have paid approximately £175 millions Sinking Fund. This should yield upwards of £8½ millions reduction in the annual charge, in addition to which there have been three or four conversions which yielded effectual reductions. Let me have a list of these. I calculate that the traceable reduction by Sinking Fund and conversions ought to be approximately £11 millions. Nevertheless whereas the cost of the debt in 1925 was £308¼ millions you propose to ask for £307 millions four years later. That is to say for £11 millions reduction in interest which the taxpayer secures through his repayments only £1 million emerges in the accounts. What right have we to face the spending departments when our own figures of Debt administration are in this condition. Nearly £200 millions of debt paid off and the cost of the administration almost exactly equal to what it was four years ago.

Let me have a table showing the history of the last seven years of the National Debt administration, showing estimates and results, the costs of the floating and of the long term debt, the amount of the annual sinking funds, new and old, economies realised by conversion. The floating debt column should show separately the cost, both estimated and realised, of Treasury Bills and Savings Certificates.

WSC

Winston S. Churchill to Sir Warren Fisher and Sir Richard Hopkins
(Churchill papers: 18/46)

30 October 1927

I cannot conceal from you the fact that I was much surprised and shocked at the manner in which our paper of possible War Office economies was overturned by the War Office at the conference last Thursday. We had circulated this paper in print to the Economy Committee and invoked the authority of the Prime Minister to press it upon the War Office. The War Office made a reply showing that we were in error in many important particulars. I called for comments on the War Office reply and Supplies provided a controversial answer. It was arranged that the officers of the two departments should meet together and arrive at agreed figures.

Agreed figures have now been arrived at which show that so far from the War Office having a net reduction of £900,000 there is a minimum net increase of £300,000 which may well be expanded by various uncertain items to upwards of a million.

I do not remember to have seen such a complete repulse of the serious contentions of one great Department of State by another. I should be very much obliged if you would give personal attention to this matter. It is most disquieting. Find out who the officers were who were so much in error and how it was they were so little informed upon the perfectly simple and basic figures of the War Office finance. In case any of the officers concerned in this calculation are affected by the proposed changes which I sanctioned the other day will you kindly speak to me before making the changes?

Perhaps you will remember that several times in the last three years I have suggested that there ought to be a closer liaison between the Treasury and the various departments and that the Supplies branch requires strengthening by aiding one or two selected officers from the other departments—possibly on temporary duty. I was however dissuaded from taking any action of this kind.

WSC

Winston S. Churchill to Clementine Churchill

(*Spencer-Churchill papers*)

30 October 1927   Chartwell Manor

Except for two meetings in the Wanstead district on Monday the Epping week is over. I have done nine meetings this week in addition to Nottingham on the previous Friday, so I have had quite enough. It has not been so bad as I apprehended, in fact I have hardly minded it at all. Punctuality was quite all right throughout though I expect you would have had some uneasy journeys had you been here.

The meetings were without exception the best attended and the most friendly I have ever had since the election. Hawkey had taken enormous pains, spent a good deal of money on advertising and provided Community Singing throughout (I cannot get the 'Land of Hope and Glory' out of my head. I have been trying all day to drive it out by humming 'Pack up your troubles in your old kit bag' and now *that* is taking root).

Hawkey was staggered at the meetings. He had been deeply disturbed by half a dozen resignations of individuals from various committees, mostly on the ground of the Flappers' Vote, but one because he did not think I subscribed enough to the funds of the Association. We booted this fellow out and have replaced him at Chigwell by a Mr Partington who according to Lady Lloyd is worth ten of him though of much humbler extraction.

I dined with the old General and with Lady Lloyd, and supped with Goschen who produced a distinguished company, local, and who put two cock pheasants in the car on which we are subsisting during the weekend. Arnold has also shot one in the demesne so that we are really 'living on the country' and 'making war support war' as the great Napoleon always inculcated. Generally speaking I may say of Epping 'Order reigns in Warsaw'. The very strong support from the general mass of the electorate had an instantaneous effect on individuals. Two of the resigning Committee men at one meeting proposed and seconded the vote of confidence respectively. They had not much choice as having been enticed to the meeting they were suddenly called upon. Nevertheless they acquitted themselves quite creditably.

I have undertaken to reply to Ramsay MacDonald in a debate on Socialism at the Hardwicke Society early in December. It is their 'Ladies Night'. You must certainly come and bring Diana. I am going to handle him severely.[1]

[1] On the evening of 9 December 1927, at the Hardwicke Society's ladies night, Churchill and MacDonald debated the motion that 'the principles of Socialism are sound and should be steadily applied in industry and in government'. MacDonald argued that 'capitalism was not

The battle is joined on the estimates. No more airships, half the cavalry, and only one-third of the cruisers. I think it will be all right as the Admirals are showing signs of far more reasonableness than ever before. I do not miss Beatty as much as I thought I should! Neville is costing £2½ millions more and Lord Useless Percy the same figure and we are opening a heavy battery against them this week. It is really intolerable the way these civil departments browse onwards like a horde of injurious locusts. On the whole we think the finance of this year will hold water, and even perhaps may exactly balance.

Ludwig has sent me his 'Bismarck'. I have nearly finished it. You certainly must read it. He certainly makes you like the 'man of blood and iron' as much as Maurois commends Dizzy.

Chartwell Bulletin this week records very little. The lake is practically finished and is rising a few inches every week carrying the leaks and seepage in its stride.

The remaining new sow has had seven piggies, so all our four are now heads of households. We got rid of three more cows and calves just paying expenses. The twelve apostles (the black pigs) are rooting most industriously and there is no doubt they will eradicate the blackberry bushes in a few months. The lambs are also nibbling but I noticed one or two of them taking their meals on their knees and Arnold has tackled the problem effectively.

Although Tuesday is the 1st November the roses are thrusting out as hopefully as in May, there are just as many buds and I am sure they are far away the best in the new garden and gave us more value than anything else. I must admit however that the Dahlias and Chrysanthemums make a fine show. For more than three months they have been a solid mass of bloom. Hill would like to take them up but they are so beautiful that he has not the heart.

---

a permanent phase of society, neither was individualism', that 'industries were getting more and more into the hands of trusts and combines', and that 'if they were going to put backbone, energy, enthusiasm, and idealism into British industry, they must look for it in a time when agency and not ownership came to bear in all industrial processes and from men who spent their time not on the golf links but in the counting houses'. Churchill replied that 'Socialism had always proved destructive of prosperity and productivity in every way the attempt had been made.' 'We have built up,' he continued, 'in this misty and storm-driven island a better material standard of living than was found anywhere in Europe. We have a greater sense of freedom and enjoyment of personal rights than anywhere in Europe or across the Atlantic. Why were we to regard our island home as a monstrosity to be changed by ideas brought from miserable and unhappy nations of Central Europe and Western Asia? They had nothing to teach us, for they reached by different roads always the same conclusion—an undue aggrandisement of the State, and undue prostration of the individual.' After the debate, a vote was taken. The motion in favour of Socialism was defeated by 147 votes to 290.

I am telegraphing to Ettie definitely that you will not come. Pray let me know what your date of return is likely to be and whether I cannot count on you for the Lord Mayor's feast.

I share your views and Diana's about the exploits of Dr Barnes[1] and Dr Logan.[2] The latter is to be prosecuted for perjury, and I should certainly support an Ecclesiastical suit against the former for blasphemy and for taking church money under false pretences.

J. C. C. Davidson to Winston S. Churchill
(*Churchill papers: 18/42*)

31 October 1927
Private

My dear Winston,

I am a little disturbed at an article in yesterday's 'Observer' by young Boothby. Ever since I was at the Treasury with Bonar Law I have understood that the artificial stabilisation of prices was a chimera, and any attempt in this direction which goes beyond orthodox monetary policy is bound to end in disaster. At the same time, as you know, stabilisation of prices is a cliché of the Socialist policy.

The Chairman of the Party has a difficult enough task in any circumstances, but if the PPS to the Chancellor of the Exchequer is to be allowed to write to the press advocating a policy upon which, as I understand it, it is the business of the Party Organisation to throw as much ridicule as possible, it is simply playing into the hands of the Opposition.

If Boothby has original ideas about price stabilisation which he thinks would work in practice, it is surely his business first of all to test them with the experts in the Treasury, and if they survive that ordeal, he can appropriately submit them to the new Policy Committee of which there are special Sub-Committees dealing on the one hand with Agriculture and on the other

---

[1] Ernest William Barnes, Bishop of Birmingham. An evolutionist, he had given a series of sermons in the autumn of 1927 encouraging the Church to 'honestly welcome new knowledge and admit that some traditional Christian beliefs must be changed'. On 16 October 1927 his sermon in St Paul's was interrupted when a man in the assembly cried out: 'Heretic!' Several letters, some defending and some condemning the Bishop's views, were published in the Press.

[2] Dr Dorothy Cochran Logan, who had just perpetrated a Channel swim hoax. She pretended to swim the Channel in record time, claiming and receiving a £1,000 prize from the *News of the World* for doing so. Later she admitted the hoax and returned the prize. On 8 November 1927 she was fined £100 for perjury. She had done it, she said, to demonstrate the 'necessity of independent umpires to prevent abuses in the Channel swim'.

with Trade and Industry, to either of which such views would, no doubt, be of interest. But I must protest against such independent expression of opinion in the public press, particularly where the Member is Private Secretary to the Chancellor of the Exchequer and is therefore presumed by the public to be speaking with a knowledge of his subject and at least a nodding acquaintance with the views of the Treasury.

Yours sincerely,
J. C. C. Davidson[1]

PS. See also Daily Mail leader today.[2]

[1] Churchill replied to Davidson on 8 November 1927 (see page 1097 of this volume).

[2] The leading article in the *Daily Mail* of 31 October 1923 was primarily an attack on Churchill's so-called 'complacent view' of the Government's record on economy, and protested that he had already added £40,000,000 to the heavy burdens of the taxpayers. The article also complained about a speech by Robert Boothby, Churchill's Parliamentary Private Secretary, in which Boothby had said that no reduction of Government expenditure below £800,000,000 a year would be possible for at least twenty years. The article closed by attacking certain 'Socialistic measures' that the paper claimed Boothby had proposed in a book which he had written in collaboration with four other Conservative MPs.

November 1927

Winston S. Churchill to Clementine Churchill
(*Spencer-Churchill papers*)

2 November 1927

The Epping campaign finished in a blaze of success, with two super-crowded meetings at Woodford and Wanstead. Our people are in the best of fettle, and the Socialist opposition, who appeared in South Woodford, were well trounced. Jack Wodehouse came round with me to all the meetings and made himself very agreeable. We ate cold chicken in the car by the roadside instead of dinner, but also drank a bottle of champagne. I am very glad it is over. All the same, I cannot say that I was either tired or bored. Hawkey, Goschen and other friends were all delighted and relieved, and Lady Goschen, after listening to 11 speeches, said with real pathos: 'I do wish this campaign was going on for another week.' To which I could not help replying 'You sweet!'

I came up here yesterday evening, and have been working all today at Cabinet and office work. I find, however, that I can get back to Chartwell again after dinner tonight, and propose to spend Thursday, Friday and Saturday morning there, proceeding to Panshanger after lunch on Saturday.

Randolph will be up for lunch on Monday the 7th. I am afraid you will not be back. Telegraph to me or write in plenty of time exactly the date. It would be nice if you were able to come to the Lord Mayor's Feast. We have been so often, and I should not like to waddle up the hall alone.

Mr Lewis, the artist, is painting a very fine, large picture of me in my robes for his exhibition. Eddie sits for the robes.

There is a new cook at present single-handed, but I am not having any meals at home on account of invitations.

Winston S. Churchill to Neville Chamberlain
(*Churchill papers: 18/64*)

2 November 1927

My dear Neville,

I was greatly disturbed to learn from my Officials that the sketch forecast of the Ministry of Health estimates for next year indicates a rise of two millions or more. I had made some provision for a certain expansion, but two millions puts me in very great difficulties. Percy also wishes to go up much beyond any of the forecasts. Generally speaking, the outlook on the Estimates at this stage is so discouraging for the finance of 1928 that I have had to put in the background for the present all those larger schemes about which I have written once or twice to you. The foundation of them was a substantial cut in expenditure of at least 10 and possibly 15 millions. The present indications are for a heavy increase, and on this basis no constructive policy which costs money is open to either of us.

In these circumstances I think it would be better for us to postpone our talk about rating reform until the financial outlook is resolved one way or the other. I shall be much obliged if you will let me know what are your own personal views of the figures of your Estimates. Before the end of this month we must have the limits of next year's expenditure fairly well defined. Till this is done I am not able to entertain new schemes for expenditure on a large scale, whether they affect next year or subsequent years; and I should have to beg the Cabinet not to put new prospective burdens on the tax-payer till the necessary financial facts were available.

Yours very sincerely,
Winston S. Churchill

Neville Chamberlain to Winston S. Churchill
(*Churchill papers: 18/64*)

3 November 1927   Ministry of Health

My dear Winston,

Thank you for your letter.

I have not yet had an opportunity of going through my estimates myself, but although an increase must certainly result from the prodigious expansion in housing I do not anticipate that it will reach the figure of 2 millions. I should say it would be nearer $1\frac{1}{4}$ or $1\frac{1}{2}$.

With regard to Poor Law proposals I quite understand your difficulty in considering them in presence of these repeated shocks. But the extra money I wanted would not be required till 1930/1, and the policy involved is so large that it cannot be dismissed as impractical without further discussion.

I am going out of town for the week end but I think perhaps a little talk between us next week might be useful.

I will telephone when I come back.

Yours sincerely,
N. Chamberlain

Winston S. Churchill to Sir Warren Fisher

(*Churchill papers: 18/46*)

3 November 1927

I have marked in red numerals on the papers the various points to which I refer here.

I wish:

(1) to be informed beforehand of the amount of Treasury bills to be offered by tender each week, or borrowing on Ways and Means. But action should not be delayed on this account.

(2) to be informed beforehand of any proposals for borrowing either for the Local Loans or for the development of the Post Office or the Unemployment Insurance Fund. I wish to share with the Division the opportunity of considering 'how this expenditure is to be financed with least possible detriment to our general credit'. But here again, unless I give any directions to the contrary, action should proceed on my assumed agreement.

(3) for the present whenever I am in London, to be furnished with a copy of the daily Exchequer balance sheet which is agreed with the bank by telephone.

(4) to be informed weekly of the amount of the Treasury Chest Fund and the Civil Contingencies Fund.

(5) to receive a weekly statement of the Currency Note Investments, showing the variations which have taken place and the total value of the Fund.

(6) to be informed when these Funds are used to take up longer dated loans or to take Local Loans Stock from the National Debt Commissioners, or to support a new issue—but without delaying action.

(7) to be informed of all purchases of dollars to cover the annual payments to the United States, and to know from week to week what balance we hold of dollar securities.

These requirements need not involve any serious labour. All that is necessary is that small slips of paper with the requisite information shall be placed—if necessary in a locked box—in my private office every day. The actual work will proceed as at present, unless I give any further directions.

In case any other information is available which would enable me to understand and view the actual operation of this part of the work of the Finance Department, I should be glad to have it suggested to me.

Action in accordance with this Minute should be begun in the course of next week.

Winston S. Churchill to William Bridgeman

(*Churchill papers: 22/175*)

4 November 1927

My dear First Lord,

I am very sorry indeed to receive your last communication which of course puts an end to all possibility of agreement between us. Encouraged by the apparently reasonable attitude of your Naval advisers, I had gone to the extreme limit and indeed beyond what I consider is justifiable on grounds of national policy.

In these circumstances, and in view of your arguments, I must withdraw altogether the friendly suggestion which I threw out about the possibility of unostentatiously making a few preparations in 1928 to enable two ships to be laid down at the very beginning of 1929. As you say, this might be used by foreign Powers to diminish the value to international goodwill of the limitation of our cruiser programme in 1927 and 1928 to one cruiser only. Similarly you must not hold me committed to the additional construction of the four sloops, the necessity of constructing which in the present series of programmes was not pressed even by Admiral Beatty. I adhere to my proposal of one-one-two for 1927, 1928 and 1929 respectively, and to the dates of ordering which I specified. This will meet a five-three ratio against Japan in 1930, 1931 and 1932, *in new ships alone*, with almost mathematical accuracy. At some periods indeed the ratio is slightly exceeded. Moreover, in this computation of strengths compared to Japan no allowance is made for our very great superiority during the three terminal years we now have to consider, for cruisers under twenty years of age. In fact if the whole cruiser fleets are examined, we shall be in those three years approximately twice as strong as Japan and four times as strong as the United States.

These issues must be submitted to the Committee which I hope can meet early next week, and ultimately no doubt to the Cabinet. The questions they will have to decide is whether, in face of the facts I have set out and when plainly safety is not endangered, the discharge of a few hundred men from the dockyards or to quote your letter 'the grumblings of the Armament Firms' can outweigh the grave financial and Foreign Office issues involved. For me on these points the decision of the Committee and of the Cabinet will be final.

Believe me
Yours very sincerely,
Winston S. Churchill

PS (*private*). I am indeed sorry that we shd have failed so utterly. I tried my vy best.

Winston S. Churchill: Cabinet memorandum

(*Churchill papers: 22/173*)

6 November 1927
Secret

CRUISER PROGRAMMES, 1927–1928

(1) When the Committee last met in the summer of 1925 the Admiralty and the Treasury had reached an agreement upon the series of programmes of new construction up to the year 1930, and the difference was reduced to whether the series should begin in 1925 or whether, as I contended, there should be a blank year before the series started in 1926. The Committee decided in favour of the Treasury in their final report, and this view was confirmed by the Cabinet. However, after certain events—into which it is not now necessary to enter—it was settled that the Admiralty should have their way in respect of the cruiser programmes starting in 1925, but that they should make the largest possible contributory savings. This they have certainly done to the best of their ability, and even beyond what was at the time thought possible. It was always understood that the cruiser programmes were open to review from time to time, either for increase or retardation, in the light of the buildings of other Powers or of other new circumstances.

(2) At the time the Committee reported, the chief danger appeared to be from Japan, who had constructed and authorised a series of programmes which, if continued without reply on our part, would lead to their overhauling our strength in new ships. We were also informed of the great

anxiety of the late First Sea Lord (Lord Beatty) that the Japanese were getting into a position where they could sweep us from the oceans east of Suez, capture our Naval bases one by one, and separate us from our Indian and Australasian possessions; and also of his plans for an offensive counter to Japan. It is for the Committee to consider whether these dangers have receded in the interval or become more real. On this point we shall no doubt be advised by the Foreign Secretary. Certainly, the finances of Japan have shown and are showing a great strain. Their anxiety at Geneva to avoid large new programmes of Naval construction was evident. Instead of beginning programmes of three or four ships every year, their representatives stated at Geneva that they had 'no intention of laying down any other 8-inch gun cruisers (ie, beyond the twelve already authorised) before the 31st December, 1936'. Thus, the total Japanese 8-inch gun cruiser construction is limited to the later eight As, four of which have not even been begun, and the four smaller *Furutakas* (12 in all). It is against these twelve ships, therefore, that we have to match ourselves, at least up to the year 1932.

The British cruiser position, on the other hand, has been vastly improved by the exertions we have made. We have thirteen A class actually built or building, and one B class (14 in all). In addition we have of ships built since the war the four *Hawkins* (9,000 tons; 7·5-inch guns) and the two *Emeralds* (6-inch guns). The First Sea Lord and the Deputy Chief of the Naval Staff stated that for the purposes of these discussions two *Hawkins* shall count equal to one *Furutaka*. This greatly simplifies the calculations of Naval strength, though I regret that no value as against the *Furutakas* has been assigned to the two quite new *Emeralds*. On this basis therefore our 8-inch gun cruiser strength, built or building, is—if no more ships are built—sixteen compared to the maximum Japanese twelve, of which the last two cannot be ready before 1932 and may be much longer delayed.

(3) In these circumstances it appeared to me that our published programmes of cruiser construction could with safety be interrupted by two years' (1927 and 1928) complete Naval holiday. On this basis we should have sixteen 8-inch gun units to a maximum of ten Japanese during the years 1930 and 1931, for which it is our immediate duty to prepare; and any new ships required to face the eleventh and twelfth Japanese vessels could be begun in the year 1929. I therefore proposed that we should drop the 1927 cruiser programme (which has in fact practically lapsed through continued retardation), and also the programme of 1928; and that we should, subject to periodic review, resume our regular series of replacement programmes—three each year—in 1929. This would have the advantage of committing a new Parliament, and possibly a new Government, to the resumption of cruiser building. I still believe this to be the best policy.

In order, however, to bridge the gap in the work of the dockyards and of the armour and gun plants, I offered, after discussion, as an alternative to provide for one cruiser in each of the three years 1927, 1928 and 1929 to be begun at the following dates: one in this financial year at the end of March 1928; one in January 1929; and one in April 1929, ie, as soon as possible after the beginning of that financial year. The First Sea Lord and Admiral Field, who by the desire of the First Lord visited me on two occasions, said that this alternative was far less unsatisfactory to them than the first. On the second of their visits they produced a graph showing the exact position month by month of British and Japanese 8-inch gun cruiser strength up till 1932. These high Naval authorities pointed out that, if the Japanese did in fact construct their eleventh and twelfth cruisers as soon as the slips were free from those already building, we should on the basis of one–one–one (as above set out) be, until any British programme of 1930 was completed, one ship short of the five to three ratio in this class of vessel, for which the Admiralty had contended at Geneva and to which the Japanese were willing to agree.

I do not believe that the eleventh and twelfth Japanese ships will be begun so early. Moreover, as we can build faster than the Japanese, there would be time to decide after they had acted. It may often happen in the working out of programmes that the ratio is exceeded or fallen short of for a few months in each year by one ship or fraction of a ship. But this is not important. Least of all is it important to us, because we can accelerate the completion of any cruiser we wish by deciding to build in 30 months instead of in the 3 years assumed in all our calculations. Nevertheless, we must contemplate an eventual construction of 4 more ships to raise us to 20 against an eventual Japanese 12. I therefore agreed, for the sake of agreement, and in the belief that it was at hand, to add provisionally another cruiser to be begun in the second quarter of 1929. We should then attain in 1932, even if the Japanese complete their whole 12 ships, the Admiralty ratio of 5 to 3. This superiority in 8-inch gun ships will continue indefinitely—even if we build no new ships after the 2 proposed for 1929—until the Japanese announce a new Programme, which will, of course, be a New Fact.

(4) I was in great hopes, from the attitude of my visitors, that we could settle on the above basis and avoid troubling the Committee with a lengthy controversy. Indeed, believing that agreement had been reached, I threw in 4 sloops at £100,000 apiece, for which Admiral Field made a special request. However, the First Lord has now written saying that the Admiralty cannot agree to anything less than one ship in the current financial year 1927, ie, in March 1928, three in 1928, ie, in March 1929, and that 1929 should be left undetermined for the present, ie, that the present published programme of

three ships in 1929 should provisionally hold the field. For reasons which this paper will explain, I have been unable to agree to this, and am forced to ask the Committee to decide between us.

(5) Hitherto I have dealt only with comparative strength in 8-inch gun ships. On that basis the three programmes I have proposed meet with almost mathematical exactness month by month the Admiralty five to three ratio. But the years whose fortunes we are now deciding are the financial years 1930, 1931 and the earlier part of 1932. During those years our preponderance in other cruisers built during the war, under twenty years of age, is still very important. A table has been prepared by my directions in the Treasury of the position in 1930 and 1931. There is a doubt to the extent of six months about the terminal date of a single Japanese ship, but otherwise I do not think this table is challenged in substance by the Admiralty. I am willing to waive this difference, as it does not affect the annual figures. From this table my colleagues will see that if no new British ships are built in the programmes of 1927 and 1928, we shall have in 1930 and 1931 a minimum of sixty ships (8-inch and other kinds under twenty years of age) to a maximum Japanese thirty and a maximum United States fifteen. In other words, we shall be numerically twice as strong as Japan and four times as strong as the United States. In both years we far exceed the old Two-Power standard, having at least 60 cruisers to at most 45 of Japan and the United States combined. These figures will be altered to our advantage, so far as Japan is concerned, by any vessels constructed by us in the programmes of 1927, 1928 and 1929. I submit for the consideration of my colleagues the suggestion that these margins should be sufficient.

(6) No examination has yet been made in this paper of our position against the United States. They are in fact so hopelessly behind in the periods we are considering that it is hardly necessary to compute their strength. Nevertheless, the facts are as follows. We actually have, built and building, sixteen 8-inch gun units. They have two building. Provision has been taken for three more, and a further three will almost certainly be begun in the near future. They have, in addition, the ten *Omahas*, contemporaries of the *Emeralds*, though slightly larger and armed with 6-inch guns. The Admiralty decline to match these even against the *Furutakas*. The United States have no other cruisers under twenty years of age, or, indeed, any other cruisers which can be classed as modern vessels.

One can understand the irritation of American Navalists at seeing what they consider to be the fruits of the Washington Conference in establishing a parity in battlefleets, being entirely swept away by the large British new construction of the most powerful cruisers intended to be continued indefinitely year after year. The Admiralty are evidently aware that their cruiser superiority to the United States is far more than they would desire; for at Geneva they declared themselves willing, if an agreement were reached, to mark time in 8-inch-gun cruisers, while the United States constructed no fewer than twelve of these vessels. There is, however, no likelihood—and in my judgment no possibility—of any such parity being reached or even approached in the periods with which we are now concerned. On the contrary, by the time the United States have eight A class vessels, we shall have sixteen plus any new ships we may now sanction.

(7) The second important consideration to which I invite the attention of the Committee deals not with the *relative*, but with the *actual* scale of cruiser strength which the Admiralty consider necessary for our security. At our last Committee Lord Beatty declared that seventy cruisers was the minimum with which the sea defence of the Empire could be conducted. The Committee accepted this (I dissenting) as the distant goal towards which we should work. This was the foundation upon which our representatives at Geneva were held to be committed publicly to the 700,000-ton cruiser fleet which was so startling to the world. The Admiralty could justly argue that if the size of the cruisers were reduced as they wished, this tonnage would be substantially reduced. I do not seek to ask the Admiralty to make any declarations of policy which would stultify the contentions they publicly advanced. I should be content if the date at which this ideal is to be achieved were indefinitely retarded. We have discovered since the last Committee that Lord Beatty at Washington held that fifty cruisers would be sufficient. The statement is contained in Lord Balfour's telegram from Washington to Lord Curzon, the 28th November, 1921: 'The grand total of cruisers for fleet purposes and for other purposes was put by Earl Beatty tentatively at fifty, a number which is less than we have now, but it is not intended at the present stage to give this number.' The last Committee ought I think to have been informed of this change of view, adding nearly 50 per cent to our burdens.

I brought this statement to the notice of the new First Sea Lord and Admiral Field, and was glad to hear from them that they never expected to realise a total of seventy cruisers, except by keeping alive a considerable proportion of vessels over the twenty years' limit, and that fifty good ships was probably all they were likely to get. This statement, if it is adhered to, appears to be very reasonable. It sensibly affects the problem of the years after 1936 when our wartime vessels begin to pass rapidly beyond the twenty-year veil. It has an important bearing upon the programmes required for the actual upkeep of the Fleet, apart from its strength relative to other Powers.

(8) At first sight it may seem that the differences between the Admiralty and Treasury proposals are only nominal. Certainly, measured by expense

or resulting cruiser strength, they are very small. Both proposals produce twenty 8-inch-gun ships at the end of 1932. Both begin one ship in March 1928. Both begin three ships in March and April 1929. In fact, however, the issue is of great consequence. We are in a critical period of Naval armaments. A very little may start the United States on an effort to construct a cruiser fleet, in new ships at any rate equal to our own. Many years would elapse before they could achieve parity, and perhaps they would never succeed. But the cost of the rivalry in money alone would be grievous. We saved ourselves with great difficulty at Geneva from agreeing by solemn treaty to the doctrine of parity in cruisers with the United States. The Admiralty were even ready to concede this point, apparently upon the principle that so long as they had plenty of cruisers themselves, they did not mind other Powers having plenty of cruisers too. At any rate, we have cheerfully invited America to build up to parity in new cruisers, and have said repeatedly that we should not add a ship in consequence. Nevertheless, the Government of the United States shows itself markedly disinclined to any such extreme and unnecessary American Naval programme. Two or three ships a year, ie, less than our published series of programmes, are now reported to be the limit of their immediate intentions. I am most anxious they should not build to parity with us; and unless we provoke a highly competitive situation by excessive new building in spite of our enormous strength, we shall continue to enjoy for many years—at any rate for the next six or seven years—a very large superiority over them. That is already a long way to look ahead.

(9) Neither is there the slightest danger from Japan. She has shot her bolt for the time being in cruiser building; and in her apprehensions of the two great English-speaking Naval Powers is embarking upon a large programme of submarines, always the defensive counter-offensive of the weaker State. But if we start up American cruiser building on a large scale, further exertions will be extorted from Japan; and this again will immediately react on our own position. We have already brought ourselves to the verge of great dangers at Geneva by the excessive rate at which in the last few years we have constructed these thin-skinned, lightly-armed ships, costing as much as the Dreadnoughts of pre-war days. For the moment we have escaped from those dangers; and our present strength enables us by self-restraint and walking warily to allow all this embarrassing cruiser problem to subside, leaving us still, for as many years as it is profitable to consider, in our old position of large superiority.

(10) It is our interest to state our cruiser programmes at the extreme minimum compatible with security. Parliament, the public and foreign countries judge naval activity by the annual programmes. The actual dates of laying down ships in any particular year do not usually enter into the dis-

cussion. If we can afford safely to delay a ship for a few months, and if by so doing it falls the other side of the 31st March and into the programme of a later year, we reduce the impression of forcing the pace in cruisers far more than we reduce our actual strength. To insist, as do the Admiralty, on bringing the ships forward by a few days, ie, from April 1929 which I propose, to March of the same calendar year, seems a wanton exaggeration of our effective action. To announce that three ships will be built in the programme of 1928 is the worst possible way of stating the fact that no money will be spent on these ships in 1928 and only a few thousands in the first quarter of 1929, and that they will not, in fact, really be begun till the new financial year opens. It combines the loudest noise with the least strength, and raises the greatest antagonism for the smallest practical result.

(11) I believe that we should have a real lull all over the world in naval competition if we were able to drop two complete cruiser programmes in 1927 and 1928. In fact, this would not mean a hiatus of two years in our new construction, for nothing can be done in any circumstances till March 1928, and it is only 13 months from then till April 1929. Far more important than questions connected with dockyard administration, or the complaints of the armament firms, or the finance of this year or next, this great opportunity should attract our minds. If, however, the Committee think that we ought to mitigate the hardship to the dockyards, I would reluctantly consent to provide for one ship in each of these two years, and (if the Japanese eleventh and twelfth ships have been begun), to provide for two more as early as may be necessary after April 1929. I do not doubt that the announcement that we are only going to build one ship instead of three in each of the programmes of 1927 and 1928, and only two instead of three in 1929, will have a beneficial effect on public opinion here and throughout the world, and will give a good chance of producing a naval *détente* between the three leading Powers. It would be an important contribution to Disarmament, and would put us in a favourable position on that score for the rest of this Parliament. If national safety were involved, these considerations would not count; but when national safety is not in question, as the figures plainly show, they deserve to be seriously striven for by the Government.

WSC

William Bridgeman to Winston S. Churchill

(*Churchill papers: 22/125*)

7 November 1927   Admiralty

My dear Chancellor,

Your letter was a bitter disappointment to me—as my last proposal, from a financial point of view, would merely add about £20,000 to the cost of your last proposal during the period of this Parliament.

But if we cannot agree, there is nothing for it, but to go to the Cabinet Committee.

Yrs v sincerely,
W. C. Bridgeman

Egypt Committee of the Cabinet: minutes[1]

(*Cabinet papers: 27/351*)

7 November 1927

MR CHURCHILL . . . wished to draw serious attention to the remarks of the Secretary of State for War. Cairo was the centre of our position in Egypt, and many efforts had been made in the past to bring about the removal of our troops from it. Under the present draft, the Egyptian army could be increased. Their numbers might in fact be doubled and there seemed to be nothing to prevent them from equipping themselves with all modern weapons. The bulk of these increased forces would doubtless be concentrated in the neighbourhood of Cairo, perhaps in such a way as virtually to surround our own troops. This would alter the balance of power, and would necessitate an increase in our own forces and thus more expense. . . .

He feared that we risked incubating a struggle which would end in blood. Our only safeguard would be the League of Nations, and we should have to rely upon persuading Italy, for instance, to back us at Geneva. Egyptians would quickly realise this, and the League would be discredited in their eyes as an impartial arbiter. Ten years, he pointed out, was no long period. During this time Egypt was free to raise what forces she could, and meanwhile corruption was actually spreading in the Egyptian administration; while a

[1] Sir Austen Chamberlain was in the Chair, the other Ministers present being Churchill, Sir Laming Worthington-Evans (Secretary of State for War), Sir William Joynson-Hicks, Lord Birkenhead and Sir Douglas Hogg. Churchill began by stating that he would prefer to delay the withdrawal of British troops from Egypt for 'a period of at least twelve years' as he was 'opposed to doing anything which might lessen the chances of our securing the present Treaty from Egypt'.

wealthy class of Pashas were intent on their own interests. The result would be that the people would suffer. We should inevitably have to bear a share of the blame, but we should lack the corresponding power to put things right. The position would be a most unfavourable one.

Winston S. Churchill to J. C. C. Davidson

(*Churchill papers: 18/42*)

8 November 1927   Treasury Chambers

My dear Davidson,

I wish you wdn't write me these sort of letters. It is so much easier to talk things over in a friendly way. It is no use being intolerant abt young men, & turning a friend into a lifelong foe. Politics, believe me, is an inclusive & not an exclusive art.

Yours sincerely
WSC

Winston S. Churchill to William Bridgeman: unsent letter[1]

(*Churchill papers: 22/175*)

10 November 1927   Treasury Chambers

My dear First Lord,

While quite ready to authorise the construction of one cruiser in the 1927 programme, I cannot agree that it should be a B-Class until both the Committee &, if necessary, the Cabinet here have had an opportunity of considering the practical issues involved. I cannot get over my objections to ordering a vessel markedly inferior to the latest ships of the USA & Japan for the sake of saving a comparatively small sum of money or of anything arising out of the abortive conference at Geneva.

Although this view of mine may appear out of harmony with traditional Treasury opinion, it is based on certain simple principles of naval policy:—

1. to build no more ships than are necessary,
2. to build them at the last possible moment compatible with security,
3. to get the utmost value for money in the construction of each ship, and
4. not to build weaker vessels than the contemporary productions of rival powers.

[1] A note on this letter by P. J. Grigg, dated November 11, states: 'C of E decided not to send this but to limit it to the 1st sentence.'

How can we be considered pledged by Geneva when Geneva broke down? How can you escape the obligation to do the best for the country in the expenditure of any given sum of money.

Yours vy sincerely,
Winston S. Churchill

Winston S. Churchill: message to the Southend electorate[1]

(Churchill papers: 18/46)

11 November 1927

Mr H. G. Wells has sent a message to Southend in which the following sentence occurs—'The Baldwin Government is heading straight for war.' It is wrong to make an untrue statement like this and to try to create those very alarms which foster armaments and create a dangerous atmosphere. It is indescribably mean to make such an untrue statement for the paltry purpose of cadging votes on behalf of any candidate at a bye-election. I do not believe that any decent Liberal wishes for this kind of help. Certainly, no Conservative like Lady Iveagh,[2] representing in her own person the woman's need for peace abroad and at home, will be harmed by it.

Winston S. Churchill: Cabinet memorandum

(Cabinet papers: 27/355)

12 November 1927
Secret

CRUISER PROGRAMMES

Some of my colleagues on the Committee have asked me to make a few points that arose in our discussion more clear.

1. The programme of the financial year 1927 is agreed at one 'B' ship. For the programme of 1928 the Admiralty ask three ships to be laid down in March 1929 for which only a nominal sum will be taken. The Treasury offer

---

[1] A by-election had been called at Southend, following the elevation to the peerage of the Conservative MP, Viscount Elveden (who had succeeded his father as Earl of Iveagh). The seat was won by his wife on 19 November 1927. The Liberal candidate was the Hon D. Meston, who polled 11,912 votes to Lady Iveagh's 21,221 votes.

[2] Lady Gwendolen Onslow, elder daughter of the 4th Earl of Onslow. She married Lord Elveden in 1903. Conservative MP for Southend from 1927 to 1935.

one ship to be begun, if the Admiralty wish, a little earlier, say, in January. The issue for 1928, ie, for the Estimates we have so soon to present to Parliament, is, therefore, one ship or three.

2. There is no imperative necessity to take any further decision at the present time. The situation will be provided for adequately up till the end of the financial year 1931, and we could, of course, meet again this time next year to decide the programme of 1929, which governs the situation of 1932. By that time we should have more exact information about the rate at which the Japanese will be in fact, if at all, proceeding with their eleventh and twelfth new ships.

3. I must make it clear, however, that as long as Japan is not committed to a total of more than 12 ships we cannot be committed in the programme of 1929 to more than 2 ships. I am willing to agree that these two ships shall be begun as early as possible after the 1st April, 1929, and to provide the largest instalments of money to be spent on their construction in that financial year. These 2 ships, together with the two proposed for the programmes in 1927 and 1928, will complete our total of 20 8-inch-gun units to the Japanese 12. Future programmes can be considered later on in the light of (*a*) the cruiser building by other Powers, and (*b*) the wearing out of our older ships.

4. It should not be supposed that the difference between the First Lord and myself is no more than the difference between commencing 2 ships in March 1929 and commencing 2 ships in April 1929. The real situation is that the Admiralty propose 1 ship in the financial year 1927–28, three ships in the financial year 1928–29, and an uncertain number (probably three) of ships in the financial year 1929–30: my proposal on the other hand is 1 ship, 1 ship and 2 ships in these 3 financial years. Thus the real difference between us is 3 ships in the lifetime of the present Parliament.

5. I wish to emphasise that I am not suggesting to the Admiralty that there is any need to accelerate the 2 ships proposed for the programme of 1929. I believe the Japanese contemporaries will be delayed, and in any case, our being fractions of ships behind for some months in 1932 is of no consequence having regard to our general strength. However, if the Admiralty press the point strongly, I should be ready to facilitate the somewhat more rapid construction of these ships after the 1st April, 1929. There will certainly be no need to make any announcement on this point.

6. With regard to the position in 1930, 1931 and 1932: The First Sea Lord spoke of a Three-Power standard in cruisers as having once been mentioned by Mr Runciman as desirable in 1903. Our strength on the basis proposed by the Treasury in those three years will, however, be rather more than would be required by this hitherto impossible ideal. It will be equal to the strength of Japan, the United States and France (or Italy) combined.

7. It should not be supposed that, comparing the Fleets of Britain and Japan in 1930, 1931 and 1932, our great superiority in numbers is discounted by the tests of tonnage or gun power. On the contrary. In 1930, for instance, the 62 British cruisers have an aggregate tonnage of 376,800, compared to the tonnage of 28 Japanese cruisers of 171,080, and the weight of the British broadside is 58,200 lbs, compared to a Japanese broadside of 25,920 lbs. It will be seen that these proportions are larger even than the 2 to 1 in numbers.

I do not deal with the American position because it is agreed that they must necessarily be hopelessly behind in the period under examination.

8. The Committee should note that the Admiralty feel themselves so superior in numbers in 1930, 1931 and 1932 that they actually propose not only to build the 'B' class of new cruiser, but also to acquiesce in the Australians scrapping the 'Melbourne', which is only 13 years old, and scrapping themselves the 'Weymouth', which is only 14 years old. These 2 ships, which have a six or seven years' life in them on the 20 years' standard proposed, are to be got rid of, and the Admiralty ask that 2 new ships costing £2 millions apiece should be built to replace them five or six years before they are needed. If the 'Melbourne' and the 'Weymouth' could be kept in being for the normal 20 years, five or six more years' effective life would be given *to their replacement ships*, and these ships will, of course, embody many scientific improvements in design and equipment.

9. The keeping alive in material reserve of every vessel which is not inferior to vessels kept alive in rival Navies ought to be resorted to as much as possible so as to avoid the construction of new ships before these are needed either to meet the new construction of other Powers or to maintain our absolute requirements.

10. If the cruiser construction of the three Naval Powers is viewed over a long period of time, it will be seen that it proceeds not evenly but in spurts. Thus, Britain built great numbers of cruisers in the war and then stopped almost entirely for six years. The United States have allowed themselves to fall greatly in arrears in cruiser building, and now no doubt for several years will make a considerable effort. Japan built nothing in the war, but launched four or five programmes successively in the years which followed. Thus, each Power in turn reaches a point where either it is in the strong position of having a lot of new vessels, or in the weaker position of having to face a large run off of cruisers over the 20 years' limit. To a very large extent these periods can be mitigated by each Power in turn keeping alive during the period of stringency a large number of their old vessels. The prime factor in new construction ought for us to be the building of other Powers.

WSC

Winston S. Churchill to Sir Douglas Hogg

(*Churchill papers: 22/175*)

14 November 1927
Private and Personal

My dear Douglas,

I was very distressed at the precipitancy with which you pronounced upon the A or B cruiser question. There really was nothing technical in this.

The Admiralty of course admit that an A cruiser is much better than a B, and but for Geneva they would rather have an A. Bridgeman's statement that unless immediate permission is given to construct a B, there would be no cruiser for the programme of 1927 is not true. It is agreed that one of the three cruisers of the 1927 programme shall now be authorised. For this cruiser £5,000 has been taken in the estimates of this year.

This is of course only a sum to allow all plans and preparations to be made prior to the 31st March 1928 so that construction can proceed during the next financial year. If the Admiralty were to order an A cruiser of the improved pattern they are designing there might be a slight delay in beginning this vessel. There are four and a half months to the end of the financial year and it is said that the new designs will not be ready for six months. Therefore the actual work might be delayed six weeks, but the cruiser when begun would nevertheless be a cruiser of the 1927 programme whose preliminary work had been accomplished slightly more slowly, as is often the case. All that would happen would be that the Admiralty would get a much better cruiser a little later. The delay would be of no consequence as our margins at the terminal date ie at the beginning of 1931, are so good, and it would be folly to argue that six weeks delay even if it occurred could have the slightest significance.

There is therefore no truth in the suggestion that by waiting for the improved design of an A they would have lost a cruiser for this year, still less is there any truth in the statement that the delay of a week in coming to a decision would affect the situation in any way. The 31st of March which matters a great deal from the financial and programme points of view, is of no consequence once the building of a ship is sanctioned. It is not for instance necessary in order for a ship to qualify as a 1927 programme vessel—(were such qualification possessed of any meaning)—that it should be laid down before the 31st of March 1928. As long as it is authorised before that date all is well. I was sorry to see such a very false point taken by Bridgeman and apparently accepted.

Judged by the test of naval strength, it seems a very great pity to order a vessel definitely weaker than the contemporary type of other Powers. It is of course absolutely contrary to all the principles of naval administration as practised invariably by all the great naval authorities before the war. One does not build war ships for fun, but in order to have a necessary weapon of defence. It may be wrong to make weapons of war, but it is certainly stupid deliberately to make weapons which will be out-matched. That is like ordering a sword for one's self only three-quarters as long as the weapon actually being forged by your rival; it is like saying as long as we have a race horse it does not matter much whether it can win races or not. It is painful to me to see our hard-earned money invested so unfruitfully.

You must remember that we are working on a 5–3 ratio to Japan, and at about the same time as Japan has twelve 8″ gun cruisers we ought to have twenty. Now it is quite true that among the twelve Japanese ships are the four Furutakas, which were designed four or even five years ago and are now superseded by all the Japanese later designs. But since the Japanese have sunk their money into these weaker ships we—by starting a little later—have been able to design our vessels of a superior type. It was only our duty to reap this advantage for our country so that our strength in fact would be greater than the mere computation of numbers would show. This is what we have always done in past years. We are able to build war ships faster than anyone else in the world and much faster than the Japanese, consequently it has always paid us to lay back as long as possible and then go one better in design. We have no right to make presents of any legitimate advantage to foreign Powers, and our limited resources do not enable us to indulge in such Quixotic chivalry. In fact the penalty which foreign rivals have always had to pay for forcing the pace in naval shipbuilding has been England's power and invariable practice of overtaking them a year or two later, or if need be at the same terminal date, with a superior type.

There remains the question of whether we should consider our number restricted through anything that happened at Geneva. I say 'No'. The Conference was abortive and we are absolutely free. But I admit that the question of whether the Americans would be more annoyed by our building one A in the 1927 programme instead of a B is arguable. For myself I think that as we are dropping two out of the three ships declared for this year this reduction is so substantial as far to out-weigh the difference between an A or a B. I expect we shall only be thought very silly both in America and Japan to build a 6 gun ship, when with a comparatively small additional cost we could have had an 8 gun ship. However this aspect is certainly not technical, it is a question of psychology and diplomacy of which Admirals are no better judges than the common run of humanity.

The classical principles which have for generations guided the Admiralty were never better expressed than in Fisher's well-known couplet

'Build late, build fast,
Each one better than the last.'

Although no doubt as Chancellor of the Exchequer I am glad to have a saving (which the Admiralty now say would be larger than their recent estimate) nevertheless it pains me intensely to see an unsound and erroneous step taken in naval administration.

Although I scout the possibility of a naval war, I cannot help seeing in imagination this B class cruiser, chosen in such indecent haste by the Cabinet, caught alone in some distant ocean by a foreign ship of which she might have been the equal and after a gallant fight at needlessly unfair odds, sinking beneath the waves with all her crew. It is odd how remorselessly sometimes these mistakes come home to roost! We might have had a ship we could have trusted to go anywhere, sure that she could not be out-matched. We are now to have one which unless in company will almost certainly be out-matched; and for this we are to pay nearly £2 millions. There are quite enough inevitable unfair fights in naval war with ships of different ages, classes and qualities engaging each other, without deliberately adding to the number. Of course the moment America or Japan begins to build a smaller type I should be delighted to see us follow suit—but not till then.

Forgive me inflicting all this upon you, and credit me please with some knowledge and experience of these matters. Ever since 1907 I have studied naval affairs under the highest authorities and with all the secret information, and although I am determined not to become responsible for the building of unnecessary ships, no consideration of finance would prevent me from doing what I conceived to be my duty by the Navy.

I was glad to hear you say that you had not prejudged the larger and far more unpleasant issue which our Committee have now to decide.

Yours vy sincerely
Winston S. Churchill

Winston S. Churchill: draft press statement
(Churchill papers: 18/46)

14 November 1927

Mr Lloyd George apparently believes that this country is worse off than it was three years ago. This is not true. There are more people employed in

Great Britain to-day than there have ever been before. They have lost fewer days in industrial disputes this year than in any other year since the war. The British exchange has gone up and the cost of living has gone down. No doubt there are a good many things to worry about but it is no use making them worse by exaggeration.

The country, whatever Mr Lloyd George may say, is improving and is growing stronger. It is very remarkable that it should be improving consider-ing the troubles and difficulties which have been put in its way, and it is certainly no thanks to Mr Lloyd George. When the General Strike was let loose upon us the Public had uncommonly little help from him! When the Government in the hopes of preserving peace in the coal fields granted a temporary subsidy to the coal mining industry, Mr Lloyd George jeered at them in the House of Commons and taunted them with being 'afraid to face cold steel'. It almost seemed that he was looking for troubled waters to fish in.

He now attacks the Government for having severed diplomatic relations with Russia. He pretends that we are losing a great and valuable trade. If this be so why did he not vote against the decision of the Government to turn out the Bolshevists? Surely a Statesman and a Party Leader should have an opinion of his own on a question of that kind, but Mr Lloyd George when the vote was taken was unable to make up his mind which lobby to vote in, so he solved his difficulties by walking out of the House of Commons and hurrying off to the seaside.

Most people think the Government were quite right to throw out the Bolshevists, and the Trade Union Congress has imitated the Government's action by breaking off relations with them too. Mr Lloyd George who had nothing to say at the time and could not make up his mind, or thought it imprudent to express an opinion, is now very voluble on the subject of Rus-sian trade. He says that we have 'deliberately closed the markets of Russia' and that 'no other country has done it'. These loose statements should be examined. The Russian market even before the war when Russia had a better Government than now was never of great importance to us. It was for instance only a tenth part as valuable to us as Canada or Australia (Check). Moreover Anglo-Russian trade is much more useful to the Russians than to us for they sell here over four times as much as they buy.

But whatever the Russian market be worth the Government have not closed it. There is nothing to prevent any British subject trading with Russia —except the fear that they won't get paid for the goods they send. Our trade relations with Russia are exactly the same as those of the United States. That country has been very wise in its relations with Russia. They have refused to give them any countenance or recognition, but they have done a good deal of trade with them.[1] I have always thought we ought to have followed their example and am very glad we have done so at last.

Cabinet minutes

(*Churchill papers: 23/55*)

16 November 1927

IRAQ

THE CHANCELLOR OF THE EXCHEQUER emphasised the importance of not committing the British Government to the defence of Iraq. In view of possible dangers, for example, from Turkey and Russia, which could not now be foreseen, we should take care not to undertake obligations which we might be quite unable to discharge.

Thomas Jones: diary

(*Jones papers*)

16 November 1927

The Home Secretary (Joynson-Hicks) and some of his colleagues have been overhauling the machinery with regard to a General Strike should it recur. Much discussion as to relation of Police to Special Constables, Territorial Force, etc. The idea is to prepare a Home War Book for defence during industrial trouble on the lines of that prepared by the CID—a paper plan which could be put into operation when the emergency arose.

The Chancellor is for leaving the matter alone. He does not think the General Strike is likely to be repeated for some years, and is opposed to the Home Secretary raising a special force. Much better to adapt the previous plan of allowing the Territorials to volunteer not as Territorials but in plain clothes and steel hats.

---

[1] The United States Government did not recognize the Soviet Government until 17 November 1933 (eight months after the inauguration of President Franklin D. Roosevelt).

Winston S. Churchill: Cabinet memorandum

(Cabinet papers: 27/355)

17 November 1927   Treasury Chambers
Secret

CRUISER STRENGTHS, 1930, 1931 AND 1932

1. The First Lord's paper (NP (27) 5) clarifies the issue in several important aspects. It is admitted by the Admiralty on page 3 that 'under the Chancellor's proposal we shall reach a 5:3 ratio in 8-inch gun cruisers with Japan during the year 1932.'

Attention is directed to the First Lord of the Admiralty's telegram from Geneva to the Prime Minister of the 16th July, 1927 (194 LN), in which the following material passages occur:—

'British and Japanese delegations . . . could, therefore, agree to a total tonnage of surface auxiliary combatant vessels:—

(1) For British Empire, 500,000; for Japan, 325,000.
(2) Retention of an additonal 25 per cent of total tonnage in old vessels.
(3) 10,000-ton cruisers to be limited in number. For British Empire and United States, each twelve; for Japan, eight.
(4) Retention of under-mentioned vessels: For British Empire, 'York', four cruisers of 'Hawkins' class; for United States, ten cruisers of 'Omaha' class; for Japan, four cruisers of 'Furutaka' class.
(5) Other cruisers. *Japan having no intention of laying down any other 8-inch gun cruisers before the 31st December, 1936,*[1] will not object to a clause that no other cruisers shall be constructed in excess of 6,000 tons displacement, and to mount a gun exceeding 6-inch before the 31st December, 1936.
(6) That within total tonnage figure for cruisers and destroyers there shall be a definite agreed percentage allocated to cruisers and destroyers respectively.'

Thus the Admiralty were content with 12 A cruisers to 8 Japanese and were obviously ready to set the 'York' and 4 'Hawkins' off in equipoise to the 4 'Furutakas'. In fact, however, under the Treasury proposals, we shall have in 1932 at least 13 A class to the Japanese 8, and 4 more 8-inch gun

---

[1] Churchill had double-underlined the sentence printed here in italics.

cruisers, over and above the 'York' and 4 'Hawkins'. The position in 1932, therefore, on the Treasury proposals stands as follows:—

'A' class cruisers	13	to 8
'York' and 4 'Hawkins', counting as	4	„ 4 'Furutakas'
Additional British cruisers which may, so far as I am concerned, if the Admiralty desire, be all A's	4	
	— Total	—
Total British 8-inch-gun units	21 Japanese	12

These Treasury proposals therefore yield at least the 5:3 ratio in A class cruisers, more than was asked for by the Admiralty at Geneva in A class vessels, and more than the 5:3 ratio in 8-inch-gun units of all kinds.

However, in view of the Admiralty acceptance of the fact that the 5:3 ratio is met in 1932 in 8-inch-gun cruisers, I will not further elaborate the argument that it is more than met.

2. So far as the United States is concerned, I cannot rest myself on any more decisive statement than that of Lord Beatty at the Cabinet on the 29th July, 1927.

'Questioned as to the effect on our building programme of a breakdown of the Conference, Lord Beatty said: ". . . we should continue to build in accordance with our existing programme. We had so long a lead in cruisers compared with United States of America that we could allow them to build two or three programmes of six cruisers apiece without departing in the least from our own programme." '

The Americans are certainly not proposing at the present time to build 2 or 3 programmes of 6 cruisers apiece. Their intentions, so far as they are disclosed at present, are limited to 2 programmes of half that number.

3. I am therefore justified in saying that so far as relative naval strength is concerned either in respect of Japan or the United States, the Treasury proposals not only meet, but more than meet, the Admiralty requirements; and this condition governs not only the relative strengths of the Fleets in 1930 and in 1931, the two years whose fate we are now settling, but also in 1932. This satisfactory position so far as 8-inch-gun ships are concerned will continue after the year 1932 until either (a) the United States have overtaken us in A class cruisers, or (b) until Japan lays down a new programme. This, according to the First Lord's telegram of the 16th July, will not occur: 'Japan having no intention of laying down any other 8-inch-gun cruisers before the 31st December, 1936. . . .'

4. The issue before the Committee has therefore to be decided not on the question of relative strength in any years which we now have to consider, or of rival shipbuilding, but solely upon the adequacy of the replacement programme. It was thought by the Chairman to be an unreasonable question when I asked the First Sea Lord whether, in the event of Japan building no new cruisers after her 12 were completed, the Admiralty would still propose that we should construct 3 each year after the present year. It is, however, exactly the position which the Admiralty adopt, and adopt in the face of the First Lord's statement about the Japanese intentions. This means that the Admiralty wish to build between now and 1936 9 programmes of 3 new cruisers, presumably with 8-inch guns, total 27, although the Japanese from whom we were to expect so much danger, in the same period build none. Thus, in 1939 the British and Japanese 8-inch-gun cruiser fleets would stand as follows:—

> Great Britain 48
> Japan 12

or at the ratio, in 8-inch gun units, of 4:1 instead of 5:3. It is hardly credible that such proposals should be seriously put forward.

5. I turn to the question of replacement programmes. In this part of the controversy the Admiralty have the great advantage of being able to condemn any number of vessels they may think fit to the scrap heap before the 20 years' age limit is reached. Thus, since this discussion started we learn that the 'Melbourne' will be scrapped at 15 years of age for reasons which 'have not been communicated to the Admiralty by the Government of Australia'; that the 'Weymouth' will be scrapped after 16 years' service by the Admiralty: that the 'Yarmouth' and the 'Conquest' will be scrapped in 1928, four and seven years respectively before they reach the 20 years' limit; and that one or more vessels under the 20 years' limit 'will be disposed of in each of the succeeding three years'. Thus, by a stroke of the pen, seven or eight ships under the 20 years' limit are to be eliminated from our available strength in 1932. Nevertheless, while the Admiralty are thus ruthlessly scrapping vessels under the 20 years' limit, they proposed at Geneva to utilise 25 per cent of cruisers over the 20 years' limit. If the Admiralty decision to scrap any particular vessel or any number of vessels before their time must be accepted as proof positive of the immediate need of constructing a brand new cruiser at a cost of £1,660,000 for replacement purposes, financial control becomes absolutely impossible.

6. Even on the narrow financial aspect there is no saving in scrapping a vessel three or four years before its time in order to avoid a refit of £120,000, as proposed in the case of the 'Weymouth', and building in its place, four

years before its time, a replacement ship costing £1,660,000. The interest on £1,660,000 for 4 years alone aggregates £330,000; and as the new replacement cruiser will have been built four years before its normal time, its useful life during the period for which it is needed will be reduced by four years, and it will not be so good a cruiser. It will be much better for the Treasury to provide the money necessary for the refits of all cruisers under the 20 years' limit. If these seven ships condemned by the First Lord to be prematurely scrapped were kept in being for their normal life instead of being replaced at least four years earlier by seven new £1,660,000 ships, the saving on the Estimates of the next seven or eight years would amount to over £10½ millions, after allowing £1 million for the refit of the existing vessels.

7. Even if we accepted the massacre of cruisers under the 20 years' limit proposed by the Admiralty in the next few years, our strength in 1932 in remaining vessels is given by the Admiralty as 'probably about 53 plus those laid down in 1927 and 1928'. We are agreed that anyhow 4 shall be laid down in time to be ready in 1932. Our strength in 1932, even after the scrapping of 7 vessels under 20 years, will be 57. This figure will approach the hitherto deemed impossible ideal of the Three-Power standard, and our cruiser figures in 1932 will be only a few short of equality with those of Japan, the United States and France (or Italy) combined. If, however, the Admiralty wish still further to strengthen their figures they have only to keep alive some of the seven cruisers proposed to be scrapped though under 20 years of age. By this means they can easily raise their numbers in 1932 to 64 vessels under 20 years of age, or more than the 60 limit at which they now aim.

WSC

Winston S. Churchill to Sir Richard Hopkins and Alfred Hurst
(Churchill papers: 18/46)

18 November 1927
Most Secret

(1) I have arranged with Mr Neville Chamberlain that his officials should consult with you and try to elaborate the best possible plan for reconciling his aims with our larger policy. For this purpose they should assume that £35 millions will be available, and not trouble about that any more in this part of the subject.

(2) Having established intimate and comprehending relations with the Ministry of Health and made them feel that our scheme picks up and looks after the points they are keen about, you should extend your discussions *with them* to cover the whole field of the Barstow Block Grants Committee. Do not

however at this stage complicate the task by bringing in the Board of Education. Shape the plan as far as possible without their aid, and let us have alternative plans either to leave them out or take them in. It is better that they should sit up and beg to come in.

(3) Let the Inland Revenue report upon a Profits Tax not exceeding sixpence. This tax would have to come into operation by the time the Budget of 1928 had passed the House of Commons, say July. It would have to be levied on the profits of the preceding year, ie 1927, and would therefore run over the same ground as the Income Tax. It would in fact be, for those who paid it, very like an additional Income Tax. I do not understand the argument of Sir Richard Hopkins about the inevitable lag in imposing a profits tax. Is it not satisfactorily met as here explained?

(4) The scope and application of this tax will of course be related to the rating relief. Those who assume the new burden, or in so far as they assume it, will have the relief such as it may be. Those who do not have the burden will not have the relief. It cannot follow however that new burden and relief will be equal, or that the advantage will be equal for all. On the contrary we are not seeking to leave things as they are, but to redress an existing injustice in the levying of burdens.

The special cases mentioned by Sir Richard Hopkins do not seem to cause great difficulty. Lipton,[1] for instance, would come within the rating relief by a tax on profits over the same proportion of his business as the rating relief would operate in his case. Whether he would be a loser or a gainer is beside the point. It is a question of passing from one system of taxation into another.

The Co-operative Societies would be outside the scheme altogether. They have no profits to tax, and consequently are not entitled to any relief in the rates on their factories. They would not be any worse off than they are now. But as the relief in the vast number of cases exceeds the new burden, they would stand out of benefit and be to that extent disadvantaged against individual competition. This is an issue of the very greatest interest and of immense political significance. It deserves profound study in view of the strong feeling that these bodies have, under the existing law, a very great advantage over private producers. I am not pronouncing upon this aspect at all. It must be studied very closely. But do not suppose that it is not capable of being handled in a manner politically advantageous. We shd negotiate with them.

[1] Thomas Johnstone Lipton, 1850–1931. Born in a Glasgow tenement, the son of Irish peasants. Opened a provision shop in Glasgow, 1871 (with £100 capital). Within four months he had three such shops in Glasgow, and within eight years they were all over the British Isles. Entered the tea trade, 1889, with the purchase of large tea estates in Ceylon. Extended his grocery business to the United States in the 1890s. Knighted, 1898. Created Baronet, 1902. Britain's leading grocer. A friend of King Edward VII, and a noted yachtsman.

(5) I see nothing in the argument about helping inefficient businesses at the expense of the efficient. The line is not drawn that way. There are efficient businesses which are not paying and inefficient businesses which are paying, both in and out of the sheltered trades. The undue burden of rates, the severity of foreign competition, the need of employing large masses of discontented labour and the lack of credit and capital resulting from the above are factors which operate on the fortunes of businesses as much as efficiency or inefficiency. Nevertheless, the limit of the Profits Tax must be drawn at the point where the vast majority of producers would gain more from the relief of rates than they would lose by the tax on profits. I have tried to make some calculations (in a shaky train) on the paper at the end of this file. I should have thought from these that sixpence on profits in exchange for rates would leave nearly everybody better off. How much more 4d? This however must be thrashed out without delay.

(6) The LF Tax (in future so called) affects mainly the motoring public, and is meant to affect them. They constitute the most buoyant feature of our national life, and are well capable of bearing a comparatively small extra burden which might indeed amount to very little more than the reductions in petrol prices in the last few years have given them. The conditions for this tax will be: (1) no rebates or exemptions of any kind except for home produced fuel; and (2) no higher than will yield £10 millions. Let me have some preliminary calculations worked out to show how this burden of £10 millions would be shared between motorists, commercial vehicles, passenger vehicles, industrial engines, agricultural engines, private engines and the paraffin lamp of the working man.

(7) The timing of this finance is extremely important in view of the greatly increased estimate now given by Mr Hurst of the sum required to relieve the producer. It will not be possible to achieve the figure of £45 millions before the financial year 1929. But that is not a bad year from some points of view. I assume therefore that the LF Tax and the P Tax would both run from the end of July, ie eight months in 1928, yielding two-thirds of £25 millions, or £16 millions. This sum would be carried forward in Suspense Account into the year 1929. In that year the revenue will have broadened sufficiently to enable the bulk of the whole sum to be provided. The accumulated £16 millions would be used—two-thirds in 1929 and one-third in 1930—to taper out the cost of the new scheme on to the normal increase of revenue. It is not even necessary that the scheme should come into operation in the first quarter of the financial year 1929. The second quarter might be time enough for the abolition of rates to begin.

(8) It has occurred to me that Agriculture will not benefit as much as other producers under this proposed scheme, as they already have three-

quarters of their rates let off. In order to bring them along the line between the residential and productive parts of their building must be drawn in such a way as to be especially helpful to farmers.

(9) On the general question of Block Grants I do not consider my part of the scheme is dependent upon the solution of these tangled problems. As it is only possible to carry a vast scheme of this kind forward in sections, and on the assumption that the other sections will be made good each in its turn, I have not been willing to see all progress arrested by the difference of opinion between the Treasury and the Ministry of Health. That difference is now in a fair way of adjustment, and by adjusting this difference and in alliance with the Ministry of Health we may be able to move forward, either partly or wholly, into the Hurst–Barstow field. Similarly do not mix up any of this with the raising of the money problem. Solve me the problem of distribution in a harmonious and businesslike manner, and I will find the money by 1929, before which payments need not begin. Do not imagine however that the support or opposition of the general public is likely to be much affected by the inclusion or exclusion of a Block Grants scheme. They will not understand it at all or trouble themselves on the matter. No doubt they would be glad to know that sounder relations were being established between public and local finance. But the movement of public opinion does not depend on this. It depends on the relief accorded to the producers and the consequent stimulus to industry and employment. On that and that alone the driving power of the whole scheme depends. But do not underrate the immense force of that drive.

On the whole it appears to me this morning that the policy is more necessary and more certain of accomplishment than ever before.

WSC

Winston S. Churchill to the Duke of Westminster

(*Churchill papers: 1/194*)

21 November 1927

My dear Bennie,

I have thought a great deal about your delightful invitation,[1] and all being well I could certainly leave here on the sixth, or a day or two earlier if

---

[1] A proposed holiday in January 1928 on the Duke of Westminster's yacht, to the North African coast. In the end, Churchill was unable to accept it, as his derating plans had begun to take up an increasing amount of his time (see his letter to Stanley Baldwin of 9 December 1927, quoted on page 1126).

desired. Clemmie feels that she must stay with Diana, whom she is chaperoning on various occasions during January. Also she has just been abroad and wants to 'stay put' for a little. But she begs me to thank you for wishing to have her. I wonder whether you would let me bring Randolph? He would enjoy it awfully, and I see so little of him unless we are together in the holidays.

Lewis, the painting instructor, is extremely good company and very presentable. He really paints exceptionally well. But don't let me crowd you up, unless you find at the end you want someone else. The only other suggestion I can make is the Prof, who is always most instructive and amusing and loves playing about with us. Somehow or other I feel that yachting with Hilaire Belloc[1] would be rather a formidable undertaking.

Let me know when you return, and we can talk things over. The guide books and Cooks, whom I have consulted, report the weather on the North African coast uncertain in January and often rainy.

Yours ever
W

Winston S. Churchill to J. C. C. Davidson

(*Churchill papers: 18/42*)

22 November 1927

My dear Davidson,

. . . About Boothby, I will find out from the Prime Minister whether he approves of the campaign you are directing against him. I have no doubt he will be quite ready to give up his present work. Indeed he has already spoken to me about some employment which is open to him in the City. Your attitude, however, constitutes an obstacle in my mind and makes it necessary for me to stand by him. As I told you in my last letter, it would be far better to come and talk this sort of thing over instead of sending me letters which I cannot regard as friendly or suitable.

[1] Joseph Hilaire Pierre Belloc, 1870–1953. Poet, historian and polemicist. Born in France, he became a naturalized British subject in 1902. Liberal MP for South Salford, 1906–10. The eldest of his three sons was killed in action in 1918; his youngest son died on active service in 1941.

Winston S. Churchill to William Bridgeman

(*Baldwin papers*)

28 November 1927   Treasury Chambers

My dear First Lord,

Your letter and the black and red table to which it refers interested me greatly. This is the first time that I have realised that the Admiralty contemplate the possibility of dropping to one cruiser a year from 1931 to 1941. Such a reduction of the programme obviously yields figures far below the minimum of 60 which you claim as indispensable to the war plans and even below the 50 which Admiral Beatty tentatively mentioned at the time of the Washington Conference. It even falls as low as 37.

Let me say straight away that I have never asked for any such diminution. Of course I realise that you contemplate it may be forced upon a future Government by the financial pressure of the simultaneous battleship programme and by the difficulties, domestic and international, of heightened estimates. Nevertheless I am of opinion that what is necessary for safety in any period has got to be provided when the proper time comes. I do not believe Parliament would refuse to make the necessary provision year by year and if a Government fell short for a year or two, the movement of public opinion would grow so strong that the policy would be changed and the arrears made up in good time.

The whole future of the battle fleet is very uncertain. We shall not know what agreement will be reached about it until after 1931. The size and number of battleships may be reduced or their life extended. It may well be that the burden after 1931 on account of battleships will not be so great as you apprehend. It may well be also that smaller types of cruisers will have been agreed upon or have come into fashion and that the whole finance of the decade 1931/41 may look far less formidable when we get to it than it does at present.

Remember that if our estimates are increased after 1931 through having to build battleships, that will only be because the United States and Japan are building them too. The increase of their estimates will justify the increase of ours. It is certain that if there is no war we shall be much better off then than we are now. Therefore the additional financial burden of building 1 or if need be 2 more cruisers a year in years after 1931 cannot be treated as one impossible to be borne.

Everything in your table and everything in our discussions go to show that the period of cruiser shortage is not in the next 10 years, but in the 10 years following. Do please see how very much better your figures would look if, for instance, instead of 3-3-3 followed by 10 years of 1's you ran through after this year on a uniform 2. That would give you 1 more cruiser in 1938,

2 more in 1939, 3 more in 1940, 4 more in 1941, 5 more in 1942, 6 more in 1943 and 7 more in 1944 than in column II of your table. You would in fact never drop to the low level of 37 but would consistently maintain a cruiser force of between 40 and 50.

Consider also the 2 cruisers in dispute this year and the 1 that may be argued about next year (ie the difference between 1–3–3 and 1–1–2). These 3 ships ought clearly to be added to the programmes of 1932, 1933 and 1934 to be ready for 1935, 1936 and 1937. You wish to build these 3 cruisers 4 years before their time. Their useful life is abridged by 4 years. Assume they cost £7 millions. The interest charge alone on account of premature construction would almost build another cruiser free, gratis and for nothing. Therefore you would have 5 at the cost of 4 and all of these 5 would have 20 years' life as against 16 during the period they are needed. In addition there is the ceaseless and rapid march of science to be remembered.

I understand the Admiralty point of view that there may be a Socialist or Liberal–Socialist Government in power, that the Admiralty would be black-guarded for an increase in the estimates, and perhaps beaten for the time being in the resulting political struggle: and that in consequence they wish to make cruisers while the sun shines and keep them handy. But this argument, although it is human and not without its practical side, can never justify the economic absurdity of building cruisers for stock and letting their lives waste away before the period for which they are really wanted begins.

Are we not trying to look too far ahead? Are we not quarrelling about other people's troubles, about issues which lie beyond our own responsibility, about problems for the solution of which the data are highly speculative, which may indeed never present themselves in anything like their present form? Let us in this Parliament make adequate provision for the years whose fate is in our hands and for which we are answerable. Let new Parliaments and new Ministers deal in their turn with other times—as be assured they will. Why should we by doing more than is necessary now, make it easy and popular for our successors to do less than their duty? Let us leave our posts with the consciousness that we have done our own job and with the right, uncompromised by admissions or disputes, to impeach any Government who may hereafter default.

Is it really in the long interest of the Navy to provoke a first class political controversy about cruisers at the present time? Suppose the brutal facts had to be proved in Parliament that the Admiralty is now asking for more cruisers than will meet the 5–3 ratio with Japan in 1932; more than double the total strength of Japan in that year; more than 4 times the strength of the United States; more than the Three-Power Standard! Can you doubt the reaction which would follow?

On the other hand there are all those arguments which the Foreign Secretary has put forward, and which I admit weigh enormously with me at this juncture. If we can announce another cut of 2 ships in our paper programme of 1928 it is bound to have an effect which may well be decisive upon the naval policy of the United States as influenced by the approaching Presidential election. Coolidge and the administration are evidently trying their best to go for a moderate programme in making up their large leeway. This renewed retardation on our part, coming on the heels of what has just been announced, will give them the best possible chance of deflecting American opinion from naval expansion to a sober and economical policy, and this again will confirm Japan in her declared intention not to build any more cruisers (after the 12) until after the 31st of December 1936. The Admiralty have a unique opportunity of helping the general interests of the State and at the same time, in the long run, of helping themselves.

Yours very sincerely,
Winston S. Churchill

Winston S. Churchill to Stanley Baldwin
(*Baldwin papers*)

28 November 1927   Treasury Chambers
Private

My dear PM,
I send you the enclosed in order that you may be *au fait* with the later developments of this discussion; & to show you that I am trying my best to give Reason its chance. I hope indeed it may prevail.

Yours very sincerely,
Winston S. Churchill

Winston S. Churchill to Lord Birkenhead
(*Churchill papers: 22/175*)

28 November 1927

You will find enclosed a copy of the Admiralty black and red table, Willie Bridgeman's answer to my enquiries about it and my reply to him. The significance of the table is the fluid condition of the Admiralty minimum as revealed by their idea of only one cruiser a year during the ten years 1931–41. They are really not working on any scientific basis, but only trying to get as much as they can in case an unsympathetic Government should arise. Nothing in my answer to Bridgeman alters the character of the controversy. A very damaging admission has been made by the Admiralty, and I think you should have it in your mind.

Winston S. Churchill: notes of a conversation with King Feisal

(*Cabinet papers: 24/189*)

28 November 1927
Secret[1]

King Feisal came to see me this afternoon. His mood had been much altered by his conversation with Sir Austen Chamberlain at luncheon.

After compliments, he narrated from his point of view the recent course of events in Iraq and the discussions here. He said that Great Britain's object in sending him to Iraq was to secure a reduction in expense and that this had been largely achieved in the six years that had passed.

I said that the reduction of expense was only one of our objects in Iraq, and that the discharge of our mission under the League of Nations and the maintenance of our permanent interests in Iraq were also part of our policy. On the other hand, although Iraq would certainly become rich enough to be independent of British financial aid, she would not for many years be able to protect herself. If the Turks invaded Kurdistan and Mosul, or if the Russians began a prolonged downward pressure through Persia, nothing that Iraq could do herself would preserve the life of the State. Sir Austen Chamberlain had told him at luncheon that if Iraq ran into danger through following British advice we should feel under an obligation to protect her, but that, of course, if the danger arose through her having rejected our advice we should be entitled to disinterest ourselves. In this connection he must understand that even with the best will in the world it might not be in our power to defend the territory of Iraq. We could not undertake to do so on the spot. The influence of England in Europe and in the Council of the League of Nations was, however, very great, and that influence constituted the main protection for Iraq, supplemented as it would be by such forces of aeroplanes, &c, as we from time to time agreed with the Iraq Government to maintain.

The King accepted very well the statement that in certain circumstances it would be beyond our power to defend his country locally. He said that he

[1] The 'Secret' designation was added to these notes when they were printed by Churchill for the Cabinet, and circulated to the Cabinet on the following day, as Cabinet paper 299 of 1927.

quite understood that we could not put large armies on the frontiers of Mosul. He realised that British influence exerted in Europe would be the best safeguard. For that very reason he urged that we ought to encourage Iraq to do the best she could to defend herself and make the largest preparations.

To this I replied that it would be a mistake for his Government to make itself unpopular by forcing through conscription in order to raise an army certainly more feeble than the armies it might have to meet. Feisal said that there was no idea of general conscription. They proposed to take from a population of $3\frac{1}{2}$ millions six thousand men a year, maintaining altogether twelve thousand men as against nine thousand they had at present. I said that nevertheless this would be no real defence comparable to the protection afforded by the support of England.

The King then came to his immediate troubles. He had been wounded by the memorandum handed to him on his first arrival by the Colonial Office. This memorandum was handed to me by his interpreter, and I read it. He complained that there was a lack of confidence, &c. I told him that it would be a grave error for him to go back to Iraq without signing a Treaty. It might not matter much to us, but a rupture between him and his British friends would be the occasion for every enemy, internal and external, to raise his head. Blood might flow and lives be lost if a needless breakdown were published to the world. Above all, I was most shocked last week to hear that he had permitted the word 'abdication' to fall from his lips. Who would rejoice if this were to occur? The French who had hunted him from Damascus would say 'I told you so'; and Ibn Saud[1] who had chased the Sherifian family from the Holy Places would then feel that his work was complete. Our idea in promoting his candidature for the throne of Iraq had been to establish in the dynastic centre of his family a rallying point for Arab culture throughout the East, and the melancholy events which had occurred since in the Hedjaz left it the sole and last stronghold of the traditions of so many centuries.

Feisal admitted his grief and fear at returning without a Treaty. If he had used the word 'abdication', it had only been because of the hopeless position he would be in in face of an advertised rupture with the British.

I said I understood he had told Sir Austen Chamberlain at luncheon that in view of their conversation he would now remain and continue the negotiations. Was this the case? Could I report to my colleagues that he was determined to stay and reach an agreement? He said decidedly that this was so.

[1] Ibn Saud, c. 1880–1953. Began the reconquest of Saudi lands in Arabia, 1902. Received a subsidy from the British in return for fighting the pro-Turkish forces of Ibn Rashid, 1916. Sultan of Nejd, 1921–2. Invaded the Hejaz and besieged Jedda, 1924. King of the Hejaz, 1926, and King of Nejd, 1927. United the Hejaz and Nejd as 'Saudi Arabia', of which he became both King and Imam, 1932. Granted the first Arab oil concession to an American oil company, 1933. Defeated the army of the Yemen, 1934.

Apparently there are three points in dispute. The first is 'complete independence'. I said it was foolish to quarrel about an adjective when the substantive carries the essential meaning. As a matter of fact, complete independence was not reconcilable either with the facts or with our obligations to the League. He said that he would drop the request for the word 'complete'. Could we not, however, do something for him in regard to the power to dismiss British officials? They mostly had ten-year contracts, and we were only talking of a period of four years. In practice the case would hardly ever arise. Was it necessary to placard in the text of a Treaty conditions which were needlessly humiliating to Iraq and weakening to his position? I did not know how this matter stood, so I said that, if the King of his own motion stayed and negotiated with an earnest desire to reach an agreement, these discussions should be resumed.

Lastly, he raised the question of finance in connection with the payment due by Iraq for the Iraq railways and also for the military expenses. I said that in a few years, when the oil began to flow, Iraq would be very rich and quite able to pay all that was justly due; that it would be easier for me to take a somewhat more generous view on financial matters in the next few years if the sums paid by us or held over from settlement were put into a suspense account, to be paid when Iraq was rich enough to do so. This aspect could also be studied in the renewed conversations. He seemed gratified at this.

Generally speaking, I believe that he has no intention of going back without an agreement, and that the prospects of reaching one fully justify a persevering resumption of the discussions.[1]

WSC

Winston S. Churchill: departmental memorandum
(*Churchill papers: 18/46*)

30 November 1927 [2]

Two years ago I examined the question of the extension of taxation ie Americans temporarily resident in this country. I expressed very strongly the view that it was to our interest to facilitate the use of this country for the temporary residence of wealthy Americans as it brought very substantial

[1] King Feisal did indeed continue with the negotiations, and on 14 December 1927 a Treaty 'of Alliance and Amity' between the United Kingdom and Iraq was signed in London by William Ormsby-Gore (Parliamentary Under-Secretary of State at the Colonial Office) and Jaafar Pasha (Prime Minister of Iraq and Minister of Foreign Affairs). Under article 1, Britain recognized Iraq 'as an independent sovereign State', and under article 8, Britain agreed to support the candidature of Iraq for admission to the League of Nations in 1932, provided the 'present rate of progress' in Iraq was maintained.

[2] Churchill's 53rd birthday.

sums of money into the rural areas, especially in the sporting counties. I was reassured to some extent by the explanation of the actual law, which was more favourable than I had understood; nevertheless my general view remained. It now appears that something was done in this year's Budget, to which my assent was no doubt obtained, which had the effect of inducing a considerable number of wealthy Americans, who used to spend very large sums of money at Melton Mowbray and elsewhere, to sell their horses and quit the country, while no doubt others again are being deterred from coming. What has been done that has caused this effect so contrary to my general policy? Pray also report on the facts as far as you can.

Winston S. Churchill to Lord Birkenhead

(*Churchill papers: 22/175*)

30 November 1927

My dear Fred,

You asked me whether I wished to make any reply to the Admiralty paper about destroyers and sloops. I do not myself see that it affects the general argument. We are in our existing programmes replacing destroyers at the rate of 9 a year, and I see no reason why this process should be discontinued after 1931.

I have already told the Admiralty that if a settlement on the basis of 1, 1, 2 is reached I shall be ready to provide for the 4 sloops at £100,000 apiece which Admiral Field pressed so strongly upon me in the course of our private discussion. This offer still holds good provided a settlement is reached on the Treasury basis. The building of these sloops would be a make-weight in helping the dockyards.

I sent you a copy of the letter I have written to the First Lord on his 'black and red' paper. The central paragraphs of this letter re-stated for the twentieth time our arguments against building cruisers for stock before they are needed in order to lighten the burden during the years when the battleship programme *may* have to be resumed. Parliament will be quite ready to vote the additional money for battleship construction if and when the estimates of the United States and Japan are simultaneously similarly raised from that same cause. No charge of aggressive armaments could be brought against the Admiralty in those days if they could show that their action was consequential on identic action by the other two great naval Powers.

Again for the twentieth time let me repeat that the finances of the country after 1931 will be substantially stronger than they are at present. In spite of the terrible injuries wrought upon them by the coal troubles our finances have steadily improved. The next two or three years are years of great financial stringency owing to the sudden increase in encashments of savings certificates. Whereas my predecessors and I myself in 1925 found £7 millions sufficient to meet this charge, I had to pay last year £12 millions, I expect to have to pay £12 millions this year instead of £9 millions provided, very likely £14 or £15 millions in 1928, and perhaps more in 1929 and 1930. The corner will then be turned and considerable easement may be expected after 1932.[1]

My case is that no immediate need for cruiser construction exists: that 1, 1, 2, is accorded by the Treasury mainly to meet difficulties in the dockyards and at the gun plants: but beyond this there is no justification of any kind or even excuse for building unwanted ships: that to build such unwanted ships and let them waste away, sacrificing their lives and the interest on their construction, is an offence against sound administration of a serious character which the House of Commons would never countenance once the case were made: that we are afflicting ourselves needlessly with problems which lie beyond our responsibility and endeavouring amid the great difficulties ourselves to relieve our successors of the duty which would properly fall to them, which they will be in a better position than we to discharge, and which they will be in every respect able to discharge both through increased financial strength and through the immense elasticity of the British shipbuilding yards. It is now virtually admitted by the Admiralty that no question of national security arises in the years 1930, 1931 and 1932. The naval service will be adequately provided for in those years if the proposals of the Treasury are adopted. The case for building cruisers prematurely is felt by the Admiralty to be so weak on examination that at the last minute they have to drag in the subsidiary programmes of destroyers and sloops about which no difficulties arise at the present time and which in any case it is common ground will have to be provided continuously in future years, no matter what happens to the battleship programme.

Anyhow, I wish to make it perfectly clear that the final position which the Treasury adopt is a refusal to provide beyond the years for which the present Government is responsible, so long always as the country is not without the power to make any necessary provision year by year in the future which our safety may require.

You are at liberty to read this letter or the correspondence with the First Lord which I sent you to the Committee.

Yours vy sincerely,
Winston S. Churchill

[1] P. J. Grigg noted for Churchill, in the margin of this paragraph (whose last sentence he underlined): 'Jesuitry. It won't really be better.'

December 1927

William Bridgeman to Winston S. Churchill

(Churchill papers: 22/175)

1 December 1927   Admiralty

My dear Chancellor,

I am sorry that our 'black and red table' has led to further misunderstanding. I hoped I had made its meaning clear.

It has always been one of the Admiralty's principal arguments for carrying out the Government approved Programme of three Cruisers a year, that we may be forced to reduce Cruiser replacement to the lowest limits, or possibly stop altogether cruiser construction, during the Battleship replacement programme. This must commence in 1931, and the best that can be hoped for in mitigation of it is that the size and cost of Battleships may be reduced to, say, $5\frac{1}{2}$ millions apiece, and the average replacement reduced to one ship per annum. This would necessitate the age of Battleships being increased to an average of 25 years and some of them would have to be made to last 27 years.

I admit that the increase in our Estimates for this purpose will be balanced by a corresponding increase in the United States and Japanese Estimates, but I regard it as entirely fallacious to argue that we can do without the Cruisers allocated in the approved programme of the Government to the next 2 years on the ground that the Admiralty are contemplating (not, I may say, with equanimity) an enforced reduction in the years following 1931 which your optimism refuses to accept as a possibility.

I must remind you of two points which were, I think, clearly brought out at the Naval Programme Committee of 1925; firstly, that 88 of our destroyers will reach the end of their life during the years 1933 and 1934, and it will be necessary to increase the construction of destroyers if our strength in these vessels is to be maintained. Secondly, that practically all the sloops will have to be replaced before 1936.

In fact, the Fleet is wearing out and numerous replacements fall due in 1931 onwards, and I cannot admit the wisdom of a policy of waiting for the replacement years to build battleships, cruisers, destroyers, submarines and sloops simultaneously. The Admiralty policy is one of gradual replacement so that the Fleet may be at reasonable strength in 1936 in accordance with the Government's requirements.

Yours v sincerely,
W. C. Bridgeman

Winston S. Churchill to Lord Birkenhead
(*Churchill papers: 22/175*)

2 December 1927
Secret and Personal

My dear Fred,

Could you not guide your report to an alternative conclusion: (a) 1 in '28 and 3 in '29, implying resumption of normal programmes, and (b) 2 in '28, and the programme of '29 to remain open for unprejudiced discussion next year? This issue might be remitted to the Cabinet. I am very much against (b), as it gives us so much less chance of affecting American opinion on the eve of the Presidential election. Nevertheless I might under protest have to put up with it, and renew the discussion under more favourable conditions next year. It is most important to me that those members of the Committee who think (a) sufficient should so record their opinion. I would far rather the divergence were presented as alternatives, than that there should be an united report on the lines of (b). There really ought to be no ships in either '27 or '28, except for the dockyards.

Yours always,
W

Winston S. Churchill to Adam Curtis Brown
(*Churchill papers: 8/207*)

4 December 1927
Confidential

Dear Mr Curtis Brown,

I have decided to write a fourth volume which will be called THE AFTERMATH OF THE WORLD CRISIS. I shall shortly have the synopsis ready. The book will be between 100,000 and 125,000 words. I am arranging myself direct with 'The Times' and with Butterworths. I shall be glad to discuss with you the disposition of the rights in Canada and in the United States and in foreign countries generally. I have every hope that we shall come to a satisfactory arrangement. Perhaps you will come to see me some time this next week.[1]

---

[1] On 26 January 1928 Churchill wrote to Thornton Butterworth about the possibility of publishing *The Aftermath* in September 1929. 'The General Election,' Churchill wrote, 'will almost certainly be over by then, and if I were out of office, a great deal more freedom could be used in telling the tale' (*Churchill papers: 8/220*).

Winston S. Churchill to Stanley Baldwin

(Churchill papers: 18/67)

5 December 1927   Treasury Chambers

My dear Prime Minister,

At the present time I am repulsed by every Department, except the Air Ministry, in any suggestions I may make. You have seen how flatly the War Office reject the idea of reductions. You know well the personal burdens wh the Admiralty question has put upon me. It is certainly possible to effect reductions, if the Cabinet really wills them. But without such driving power I don't see how one single Minister can succeed. In my belief, if the Cabinet insisted upon the Estimates of the various Departments being marked down by 10 millions according to an apportioned scale from the total of this year, the result wd follow with surprising ease.

Yours sincerely,
Winston S. Churchill

Winston S. Churchill: notes

(Churchill papers: 18/46)

6 December 1927

(1) A Cavalry Division, an anachronism.

(2) Making allowance for the removal of the Air Force from its charge, the Army costs about as much today on the old money values as it did pre-war. The staff of the War Office is far larger, more costly and presumably more highly organised. Why then should it take five months to mobilise five Divisions now, as against one month to mobilise six Divisions pre-war? It would seem as if our Expeditionary Force diminishes in inverse ratio to the growth of Headquarters.

(3) CIGS[1] will have some difficulty in proving that we are really in more danger now than on the sultry eve of the greatest war. We then faced a concentrated peril, whereas now there are dispersed annoyances. It was always the case that our Expeditionary Force was never calculated in relation to any particular emergency or any particular foreign Army.

---

[1] George Francis Milne, 1866–1948. Entered the Royal Artillery, 1885. Commanded a battery at Omdurman, 1898. Served on Kitchener's Intelligence Staff in South Africa, 1900–2. Brigadier-General, commanding the 4th Division artillery, 1913–14. He took part in the battles of Le Cateau, Marne and Aisne, 1914. Lieutenant-General commanding the British forces at Salonica, 1916–18. Knighted, 1918. Commanded the British Forces at Constantinople (Army of the Black Sea), 1919–20. General, 1920. Chief of the Imperial General Staff, 1926–33. Field-Marshal, 1928. Created Baron, 1933. He wrote no account of his military experiences, and destroyed most of his personal diaries.

Winston S. Churchill to Sir Richard Hopkins

(*Churchill papers: 18/65*)

6 December 1927
Private and Personal

It now becomes of the greatest urgency to obtain from the Board of Trade as much information as possible about the burden of rates on industry, and particularly on heavy industry. The President[1] mentioned to me last night that in the case of one firm, according to the calculations which he had made, the burden through the rates amounted to 4/- in the ton on steel. The President is on the whole a strong supporter of the project, and I have no doubt will give all possible information.

I am asking Sir Horace Hamilton to come to see me this afternoon. Has he yet been told about the project? If not, he should be told everything and kept in the closest touch. Could you meanwhile have prepared a short questionnaire for the Board of Trade? It is to be noted that the effects of any remission are cumulative, ie a relief of the rates on railways means cheaper freight; and on coal, cheaper coal; and on ore, cheaper ore. All these inure ultimately to steel, in addition to the specific relief which steel receives in respect of its own rates; and the cheaper steel embodying all these advantages again contributes towards cheaper shipbuilding, in addition to the specific relief of the shipyards. You have a virtuous instead of a vicious circle.

Could you also draw up your idea after our conversation of the reference for Duckham's[2] Committee? Or would you rather I did this?

After reading this, come and talk it over with me this morning.

WSC

[1] Sir Philip Cunliffe-Lister, President of the Board of Trade.
[2] Arthur McDougal Duckham, 1879–1932. Educated at Blackheath School. Engineering apprentice; engineer specializing in furnace work, the carbonization of coal, and chemical engineering. Member of Council, Ministry of Munitions, 1916–17; Member of the Air Council, 1917; Director-General of Aircraft Production, 1917–18. Knighted, 1917. On 20 August 1926 he had been appointed a member of the Standing Committee on Fuel Economy, and on 17 February 1927 he was appointed Chairman of the Standing Committee on Mineral Transport. This latter committee was instructed: 'To review the equipment available in connexion with the transport of coal from the coalfields to the ports and internal markets of the country and the methods of conducting such transport, and, with special reference to the recommendations of the Royal Commission on the Coal Industry (1925) to devise means of promoting such improvements in that equipment and its use as will lead to the greatest economy and efficiency in transport and be of mutual advantage to the coalmining industry and the transport agencies.'

Winston S. Churchill: departmental note
(Churchill papers: 18/65)

7 December 1927

1. In confirmation of our discussion yesterday: Profits Tax will be levied on all businesses as units irrespective of every variety of condition if they are in any respect within the producers area: but in no case will the assessment for profits tax exceed the rates paid in the datum year by the same concern.

2. At the present stage assume that new businesses and extensions of businesses will be immune after zero hour.

3. The question of whether the rates they now pay shall be equalised down for the purpose of the limitation in paragraph 1 to an average standard of so much in the £ for the whole country should be reserved for the present.

4. Work out in outline the following variants

(a) A Profits Tax to produce £10 millions.

(b) A Profits Tax not over 6d in the £.

(c) A declining Profits Tax beginning at a shilling and dropping by 2d a year.

5. Simultaneously with the above but quite apart from it consider how the fact that rates would no longer be deductible from profits under Schedule D would by increasing profits automatically increase the Income Tax. The answer to this might come in separately.

WSC

Winston S. Churchill to Stanley Baldwin
(Churchill papers: 18/67)

9 December 1927

I shall be ready on Tuesday, the 20th, to put before the Cabinet the outlines of the particular plan I have discussed with you. These outlines will cover *policy* and aim, not detailed method. But the main blockings in will be plainly established. The Cabinet discussions on business would, as I have said, be more fruitful if they had these larger possibilities in their minds. Finally our colleagues could think over the scheme during the Christmas holidays; and if the conclusions were generally favourable, we should be able to come to grips with its many difficult details by the middle of January. So definite do I regard the possibilities in this field that I have cancelled the short journey I had hoped to make abroad in January and shall be continually at work.

WSC

Harold Macmillan[1] to Winston S. Churchill

(*Churchill papers: 18/65*)

11 December 1927

My dear Chancellor,

I send you a few rough notes. I have not dealt with the many patent advantages to the scheme.[2] These you know well enough, & they are indeed tremendous. I have tried to think of a few objections and difficulties. Doubtless there are many more, but they will be of a technical character mainly.

I am trying to get some detailed figures from some of the Employers Organisations on the effect of rates on costs. These I will send you if I can obtain them.

I feel it a great honour to be taken into your confidence, and I am quite certain that you have found a really wonderful plan. It has enormous advantages from every point of view. It is original, and yet (like all original ideas) it seems so obvious & simple that it appears self-evident. Everyone will say 'Yes—of course. That's what I've always said the Govt ought to do.'

At the same time the scheme forms part of a daring and imaginative policy, & provides us with what we really want—the foundation of a constructive Conservative policy, full of interesting developments & possibilities.

Unless you get your way, we are done. I'm quite sure that if we merely drift to the election, we shall drift to 1906 again. So I hope you will be bold & triumph.

I am afraid these notes are very rough & may be quite useless. But I hope they are the kind of thing you want.

Yours very sincerely,
Harold Macmillan

[1] Maurice Harold Macmillan, 1894– . Educated at Eton and Balliol College, Oxford. On active service, Grenadier Guards, 1914–18 (wounded three times). Conservative MP for Stockton-on-Tees, 1924–9 and 1931–45. Author of *Reconstruction: A Plea for a National Policy*, 1933; *Planning for Employment*, 1935; *The Next Five Years*, 1935; *The Middle Way*, 1938; and *Economic Aspects of Defence*, 1939. Parliamentary Secretary, Ministry of Supply, 1940–2. Privy Councillor, 1942. Minister Resident, Allied HQ, North-West Africa, 1942–5. Secretary for Air, 1945. Minister of Housing and Local Government, 1951–4. Minister of Defence, 1954–5. Secretary of State for Foreign Affairs, 1955. Chancellor of the Exchequer, 1955–7. Prime Minister, 1957–63. Chancellor of the University of Oxford from 1960.

[2] The derating scheme, which Harold Macmillan had suggested to Churchill in conversation two years before. Churchill had already drafted his own twenty-two-point memorandum on the scheme, the second draft of which was printed for the Cabinet on 12 December 1927 (see pages 1128–37), but not circulated (see P. J. Grigg to Churchill of December 16, quoted on page 1137). Churchill did send a copy, however, to Stanley Baldwin, Neville Chamberlain and Sir Philip Cunliffe-Lister, on December 17 (see page 1138).

Winston S. Churchill: Cabinet memorandum[1]

(Churchill papers: 18/65)

12 December 1927
Most Secret

1. Our system of national finance is revised and refined by Parliament every year and probably the immense sums required by the State are raised on the whole in the least burdensome manner. Our system of local rating, on the other hand, stands substantially on the foundation of the 16th Century, since when all economic facts have changed entirely. Under this old system productive industry of every kind suffers an excessive and injurious oppression. The burden falls most severely upon the heavy producer. The more plant and real property he has to use for his business, and consequently the more labour he employs, the more he is penalised. The ratio of rates to profits in the accompanying table 'A' shows how seriously the irrelevant accident of a man having to use bulky tools and extensive premises to earn a living exposes him to invidious local taxation. Moreover, the rates, unlike the income tax, are levied even when no profit is made. They vary at different times and in different parts of the country, thus handicapping businesses which ought to have an equal chance on economic merits. They are dependent upon the caprice of local elections, and their burden grows heavier with the increasing difficulties of the business and the increasing poverty of the district in which it is carried on. Finally, the heavy basic industries which suffer the most are the very industries which have the greatest responsibilities in the employment of the people, are most directly in contact with labour discontent, are most unsheltered from foreign competition, most markedly charged with our elaborate social services, and principally affected by the high and uneconomic wages which prevail in the sheltered transport trades.

2. At this stage in the life of Parliament we should survey our financial policy as a whole. By resuming the gold standard we have helped the merchant and the banker; by remitting sixpence upon the income tax we have benefited the general taxpayer and especially the rentier; by the Widows' and Old Age Pensions Acts we have given a new and most important security to the wage-earner. But so far we have done nothing for the producer on whose continued vitality the heart-beat of the nation depends.

3. It must be recognised that a further reduction in income tax is not justifiable in the present state of the National Debt, and would, moreover, be regarded in all the circumstances as a class measure. A reduction of the Beer Duty, which would carry far-reaching benefits to the economy of a great

[1] The finally revised version of this memorandum was circulated to the Cabinet on 20 January 1928 (see pages 1187–94).

number of working-class homes, is not attractive to an electorate which for the first time in world history will comprise a majority of women. Accordingly at Whitsuntide I proposed to the Prime Minister that the final effort of our finance in the present Parliament should be devoted to aiding the hard-pressed Producer, manufacturing and agricultural, and especially the basic producer, who is the most hard pressed.

4. The adoption of a general system of protection for home manufactures and home-produced food would divide the country upon lines much less advantageous to the Conservative Party than the present cleavage between Socialism and anti-Socialism. To give protection to the manufacturer while denying it to the farmer vitiates the logic of the argument. Agriculture, which is still the main industry of the island, will never tolerate manufacturing protection without being itself included in the tariff. The vast additions to the consuming vote contemplated in the female franchise seem in themselves conclusive against the policy of protective taxation of food. That has been found electorally impossible in the past; it will be doubly impossible in the future.

5. There is a profound difference between conferring favours upon producers at the expense or alleged expense of the consuming population and relieving producers from undue, exceptional and invidious burdens. The long successes of Liberalism in the 19th century in the political and economic sphere were due to the fact that their policy consisted mainly in striking off out-worn fetters on the enterprise and growing manhood of the nation. The relieving of the producers from their present oppression by antiquated laws constitutes almost the only remaining large task of liberation within the reach of Governments in these days. It is to this task that we should now address ourselves.

6. Out of a total of about £160,000,000 paid in rates, between £40,000,000 and £50,000,000 are paid by producers, manufacturing and agricultural. The definition of 'Producer' can obviously be drawn in various ways. It can be drawn so as to include or exclude railways and other services, such as heat, light and power. In the present calculation we have adopted for the purpose of rating relief the following definition of 'Producer':—

Agricultural land and buildings occupied together with agricultural land or being or forming part of a market garden, and in either case used solely in connection with agricultural operations thereon.

Mills, manufactories, steel and iron works, blast furnace works, chemical works, smelting works, shipbuilding or repairing works, mines and quarries, water, gas and electricity supply undertakings, dyeing and cleaning works (including laundries), workshops, and any other hereditaments used in connection with gainful manual or mechanical productive operations thereon (including any machinery and plant forming part of the hereditament).

Railways, docks, wharves, canals, tramways, and any other hereditaments used in connection with gainful transport undertakings, including, eg, any machinery and plant, and warehouses used in connection therewith.

Provided (1) that all parts of any such hereditament used for the purposes of a dwelling-house, place of refreshment or recreation, office, sale-room, show-room, or any other non-productive and non-transport purpose shall be valued and rated as a separate hereditament, except that in the case of any rateable unit essentially of a productive or transport character, any small portions of a character normally rateable which amount in the aggregate to less than (say) 10 per cent in rateable value of the whole or £20 rateable value whichever is the greater, shall not be rateable.

(2) that rateable units containing less than 10 per cent of property of a character normally non-rateable shall be rateable in full.

The cost of complete relief from rates of these producers may, for the purpose of working out a scheme, be taken as £45,000,000, to which should be added not less than £3,000,000 for the purpose—as will presently be explained—of negotiating on favourable terms with the local authorities, total £48,000,000. How to find such a gigantic sum!

7. The first essential is that the Budget of 1928–9 should balance naturally. It would be regrettable and harmful if in the existing situation we were forced to impose new taxation merely for the purpose of paying our way. We ought at least to live upon our actual income and make both ends meet by economy. This task, though difficult, is by no means impossible provided a resolute effort is made in minor ways by all Departments of State. I assume therefore for the purposes of further argument that this result is substantially achieved by the Cabinet. I assume also that there will be no sudden and utterly unexpected collapse of the Income Tax.

8. The revenue must next be strengthened (not for the purposes of new expenditure but for a transference of burdens) by a new tax on imported Liquid Fuel. It is the only great simple new indirect tax now available. The progressive decline in the revenue from alcohol renders its advent in the next ten years inevitable. This field is fertile. A flat specific duty of 1d per gallon on liquid fuel provides £6,000,000 a year; and such a duty will not lose its force through diminished consumption if raised to 4d. We thus have the power of adding £24,000,000 to the revenue.

I will not at this stage discuss in detail this duty. It falls upon the buoyant pleasure motor vehicles of every class, upon commercial motor transport, upon an innumerable variety of private and trade oil engines, upon the lighting of public places and in a small degree upon the lamp of the cottager. Nevertheless, so wide is the scope and so low the proposed duty that it does not seem that it would prove vexatious or injurious. It is scarcely more than the reduction effected in the last two years by the fall in prices consequent upon the over-production of oil. Moreover, the probabilities are that this fall will continue in the immediate future, and will mask and mitigate the imposition of the tax.

It may be proposed to shift the incidence of a flat specific duty per gallon by a corrector scale device, in harmony with some scientific principle which will throw the onus more upon the buoyant pleasure or convenience traffic and less upon the trade users. Relief can be accorded to commercial and passenger vehicles by a modification of the existing lately raised scale of licence duties, and a superior relief can be afforded to the cottage by a minor concession on Sugar, which incidentally meets the hard case of the sugar refiner. Allowing (say) 4 millions for these and other minor adjustments, the total new revenue would be £20,000,000.

9. The effects of this tax will of course be especially beneficial to two of our greatest industries, viz, Coal and Railways, and it will be viewed with general favour not only by the employers but by the great mass of coal miners and railwaymen. The tax would have a protective effect as, following good precedents, no countervailing excise would be levied on home-produced shale oil or upon oil distilled from coal. Although the rate of tax is so low that it cannot be said to make oil distilled from coal a commercial proposition immediately, the gap would be narrowed, and a stimulus *pro tanto* afforded to all forms of scientific treatment of coal, liquid or pulverised. It is only possible here to mention these reactions.

10. Armed with this new fiscal weapon we can deal with the rates upon producers. They will be invited on the average to exchange their present burden of local rates for a contribution to the Imperial Exchequer of about a quarter the weight. This contribution will be secured by a Profits tax. Where there is no profit there will be no tax, and thus those industries facing the greatest difficulties, working on the smallest margin, bearing the greatest burden of rates, employing the largest numbers of workmen, will throughout gain the greatest advantage. No insuperable technical difficulties in levying this tax are apprehended. Several variants present themselves. The tax would not exceed 1s in the £ on profits, nor seek to gain more than £12,000,000 a year. No one who did not get the relief would pay the tax. A string-halt provision would limit the tax in every individual case to the amount now paid by the same business in rates. Thus even in those trades where the profits are greatest and the rate burden least, no one will be worse off, and the advantage will grow progressively greater as the scale of fortune is descended. We

may estimate at this stage the yield of such a tax at an average of £12,000,000 for the first years: It will grow with industrial prosperity. Total net new taxation, £32,000,000.

11. It is at present contemplated that this tax shall be temporary, and that if trade revives it will be diminished progressively. Therefore there will be no need to lay it upon new businesses or extensions of old businesses which come into existence during the lustrum in which it will operate. This avoids a field of intricate difficulties in valuation and assessment. It gives a marked impetus to new enterprises of all kinds.

12. The timing of the new National income and out-goings is cardinal. The new taxes will, if the Cabinet approve, be imposed in the Budget of 1928. The Liquid Fuel tax will operate for ten months of that year, and should yield £20,000,000, minus (say) 4 millions for relief in licensing duties, or compensation to the cottager; net yield in 1928 £16,000,000. This sum will be carried forward in a suspensory fund. The Profits tax on the basis of the previous year will likewise be imposed in the Budget for 1928. It cannot in any case be collected until the whole scheme comes into force in 1929. Thus no producer will pay the Profits tax until the moment when he receives a far greater relief upon his rates.

It would not anyhow be possible on account of the needed Rating bill to bring the scheme into operation before the first rate payment of the financial year 1929, viz April; and it is probable that the rate payment to October 1929 may be the earliest possible date of relief. In this case the finance of 1929 would be very strong; for in addition to the Suspensory Fund of 1928, it would be armed with a whole year's currency of the two new taxes aggregating £32,000,000 net in 1929 and have only to pay in 1929 a half-year's relief. Moreover the General Revenue of 1929 will have got clear of the Strike period and an increase is to be expected. The passage and bringing into force of the necessary Rating legislation and the life of Parliament are therefore both within our control, and simultaneously affected.

13. Attention is drawn at this stage to the numerous factors of elasticity which guarantee, even in our present knowledge of the revenue out turn for this year and next, the solvency of the scheme.

Firstly. The power to restrict the frontiers of rating relief by excluding, as some hold desirable, railways, or (and) power, light and heat services, saving on each head about £10,000,000 of expense.

Secondly. The accumulation during 1928 of the Suspensory Fund of £16,000,000 to balance 1929 and if necessary 1930.

Thirdly. The possibility that we may be compelled—or even choose—to make the relief effective from the October payment of rates in 1929, thus saving half the relief of £48,000,000, £24,000,000. On these three heads alone margins can be commanded aggregating £50,000,000. This will put us in a sure position having regard to the hazards of affairs and may possibly offer superior solutions at a later stage.

14. It will be seen that under this scheme the Exchequer accepts an ultimate liability of £44 millions a year and provides only £32 millions of revenue, permanent as long as required, to meet it. On the other hand the full reliefs will not begin to be paid till the financial year 1930. The Suspensory Fund at the end of the financial year 1929 would, on the basis of the figures in this Memorandum, be between £35 and £40 millions. This would suffice to cover the expense of the year 1929 and leave between £12 and £15 millions available to bridge the gap in 1930. This would however exhaust the Suspensory Fund. What is to happen to the year 1931, when the new revenue will fall short of the new burden by £10 or £12 millions? This difference could, if necessary, be met by an increase in the Profits Tax or Fuel Tax or, if preferred, by an increase in the Income Tax. All these resources are obviously at our disposal and would meet the case, even if Railways and Heat, Light and Fuel Services were included from the beginning. But I look forward to the normal growth of the revenue through the expansion of population and wealth, to the discovery of new sources of revenue in our general finance, and above all the savings which will be effected in the unemployment sphere and the increased yield of our existing taxation through the revival of trade prosperity which it is the object of these proposals to procure.

15. Subject to the above it is proposed at Zero date to abolish all rates upon 'Producers', agricultural and manufacturing, present and future; and the future Producers will not even have to pay the much smaller profits tax.

16. The case of agriculture is special. Farmers and agriculturists are already by law relieved of the greater part of their rates. Hence they would not stand to gain by the change if they were made to pay the Profits Tax. It will be right therefore to give them the full relief at once without exacting any Profits Tax from them. The relief in their case, as in all others, will, of course, not extend to residential property, which will continue to be rated as now. Thus the farmers and agriculturalists, though fully relieved from all rates as producers, will still have a full incentive to enforce economy in local administration.

17. Although we have estimated the cost of the scheme at £48,000,000, an important diminution of charge can immediately be made. Rates are a legal deduction from the computation of profits for assessment of Income Tax under Schedule D. As Income Tax stands at 4s in the £, one-fifth of the burden is already in fact borne by the State. The charge upon the Exchequer and the boon to the recipients are therefore both lessened in principle by one-

fifth. This equals on the present expense of £45,000,000, £9,000,000. From this however has to be deducted quite a large proportion of businesses which make no profits and pay all their rates, but no Income Tax, and allowance must also be made for the Profits Tax (£12,000,000). Counter to this again are the reactions upon the Super Tax in consequence of the disallowance of rates. We may therefore reduce the total bill from £45,000,000 by £4,000,000 to £41,000,000 and increase it again by (say) £3,000,000 new expenditure for making the scheme attractive or tolerable to the local authorities. The relief through Schedule D assessments will, however, only reach its full in 1931. Final total of new charge upon Exchequer £44,000,000!

18. We may now examine the effects of the rate relief upon the producer.

Tables will be circulated shortly showing the effect upon various basic industries as a whole, and upon a sample of particular firms whose actual affairs have been examined by the Board of Trade or the Inland Revenue. These are the direct and individual effects, but the cumulative results ought to be much greater. We should in the first place bargain with the Railways that if they are allowed into the scheme they should give an immediate and substantial relief to heavy freight traffic on their lines. In the present bad system the railways, finding commercial lorries and buses picking the plums of inland transportation, have little choice but to recoup themselves upon the heavy traffic which cannot escape the railroads. Like many other people in this country they 'take it out of the basics'. The relief which the railways would be required to accord to heavy traffic in return for the quite exceptional advantages they will receive could be settled by an agreement subsequently regulated by the Railway Rates Tribunal. The actual relief in rates to the railways (apart from their satisfaction at the Liquid Fuel Tax) would amount to not less than £7,000,000 a year. They ought to be made to pay the whole of this into relieving freights and particularly heavy freights, agricultural and industrial, and seek their own advantage in the greater traffic of a more prosperous nation.

Cheaper freights would help Coal, Ore, Lime Stone, &c, already helped in themselves. These products when they arrive at the Steel Works will be winged with a proportion at least of the savings due to their own relief and from cheaper transport. Therefore the relief upon the ton of steel is not measured by its direct and total immunity from rating; there is added to it all that has been gathered before. These cumulative effects increase as the qualitative scale of production is mounted. The steel plate arrives at the shipyard potentially cheaper. It finds there the shipyard already relieved of all local charges on its plant and premises; and so on. We shall in fact enter upon a virtuous instead of a vicious circle and the propensity will throughout be beneficial and not injurious.

19. My colleagues who for so many years have been deeply concerned about the state of Industry and Unemployment will see how this treatment of the problem brings into action all those powerful arguments about native industry and employment, about the adverse balance of trade and the so called 'Dole' which are so much in the public mind. These arguments could now be deployed with local illustrations in every part of the country, in every class of business, in every firm and in every constituency. But they would not encounter as in the case of a Protective Tariff the vast traditional organised school of opinion and the perilous political reactions mentioned in a previous paragraph. It may I think be shown that the relief of rates on the Producer would have the effect both upon home industry and export trade of a moderate scientific tariff; but without raising any of its antagonisms. It may be possible later to compute the *ad valorem* equation.

20. We may now consider the effect of these proposals upon what are called the 'necessitous areas'. We must not expect that they will solve the problem of derelict Welsh mining valleys. But taking not only the officially described 'necessitous areas' but also hard-pressed areas like the Tyne, the Clyde and the Thames, it would appear that the reaction would be highly beneficial.

Under our present arrangements when the industries of a district flag, unemployment, distress and pauperism increase and to meet them the rates are raised. These higher rates aggravate the trouble of the failing industries and more unemployment results. The miseries of the working class are the fertile breeding ground of what is called 'Poplarism';[1] and a virulent Socialist and pauperising propaganda arises. What with the ever growing burden of the rates and the poisonous atmosphere created, industry flies from these districts, or dies within them. Who would start a factory in West Ham? On the contrary, everywhere we see industries shifting outside heavily rated areas, starting afresh at needless capital outlay in grass meadows without population or communication. They then demand motor roads to bring at uneconomic expense workmen to the scene and to deliver their products. They demand new houses subsidised by the State for a new community. Frequently we see the factory erected just outside the municipal boundaries to escape from being made a starveling milch cow. The whole impulse is for industry to quit the melancholy areas and leave behind them political agitation, State assistance and a forlorn mass of derelict humanity.

Two things drive industry away from the necessitous or hard-pressed areas. First, the high rates consequent upon poverty; secondly, their child Socialist spite. We can deal with the first and, when we have dealt with the

[1] The paying of high wages, and high relief scales, by the local Board of Guardians (see page 106, note 1).

first the second will gradually cure itself. Man is naturally sensible and friendly if you give him half a chance. And after all, many of these necessitous areas, but for rates, pauperism and their political consequences, would be quite good places for old established businesses to thrive and even for new ones to be founded. Here it is that the working population have their homes, their institutions, their schools, their churches, their recreations, their small shops, their gas and water. How much better to bring industry back to the necessitous areas than to disperse their population at enormous expense and waste as one would from a plague-stricken or malarious region! Enough has been said upon this subject to indicate the outlines of the argument.

21. The method of applying the rating reliefs aforesaid form the concluding chapter of this argument. Here we enter the domain of the Ministry of Health. The Government is deeply committed to a scheme of Poor Law Reform which seeks to sweep away the evils and waste of the present small disjointed, conflicting and overlapping areas. Mr Neville Chamberlain has prepared his plans. To commend these plans to the local authorities Two or Three millions a year from the Exchequer would be needed; but even so it is doubtful whether such a Bill in isolation would be sufficiently above inertia and local jealousies as to be good politics in the immediate Parliamentary situation. The Treasury are anxious that advantage shall be taken of any measure for the improvement of the Poor Law, to come to terms with the local authorities and to effect a reform of the relations between local and national taxation by a large general scheme of Block Grants. Hitherto it has not been found possible to arrive at any satisfactory solution. But on the crest of large changes such as those proposed all the reforms in contemplation, and the finance necessary to sustain them, can be carried through.

Moreover, it is impossible to convey to the Producer the reliefs which are purposed except through a system of Block Grants, reviewable at fixed intervals. Only by this means can the responsibilities of the local authorities for Good Housekeeping, and the due control of the National Exchequer over fluctuating expenditure be effectually established.

It is physically impossible to settle the share of the local authorities in the increased Exchequer grants otherwise than by a general process. We cannot, for instance, calculate what a local authority would have made out of any particular firms, if it had been left to rate them freely in any given period; nor what it would have made out of new enterprises or extensions which arguably might have been undertaken within its jurisdiction. The fact of withdrawing the Producers altogether from the scope of the local rates may be alleged to diminish an element of responsible control. The industries have virtually no voting power except occasionally through their charwoman, but in the last resort they can threaten, in protest against extravagance, to quit the district, and this regardless of expense they frequently do. Some substitute for this albeit despairing check must be devised. It can only take the form of Block Grants for fixed periods. These Block Grants can as has been suggested be settled in the first instance upon lines attractive to the local authorities. We may subscribe to the principle that just as no producer, even the least favoured, will be worse off by the change, so no local authority will suffer curtailment of revenue. I do not attempt to carry this argument through as it passes in many decisive respects beyond the Treasury sphere.

22. Action proposed. To announce the proposed policy in the Budget of 1928. The fact that all producers will know that as from April—or at the latest from October 1929, all their rates will be taken over by the Exchequer, will from that moment enable forward contracts to be made upon a greatly improved basis. This on a rising tide of trade will help business and diminish unemployment and all its deleterious reactions on the health and economy of the State. It will hold the political field. The opposing parties will, out of partisanship, attack it to their disadvantage. This is a controversy from which, pushed in every field, we have nothing to fear.

I do not wish to exaggerate the scale of the operation. The only levers at our disposal are financial. Fifty millions obtained at a certain cost in national life-strength are not overwhelming. I wish the levers were larger. They are, however, serious and potent; and I do not know from what quarter their equals in power and in practicability can be found.

WSC

P. J. Grigg to Winston S. Churchill

(*Churchill papers: 18/65*)

16 December 1927

C of E,

I beseech you not to send these until you have seen the results of the departmental check (which will be completed on Friday). Some of your memo must *clearly* be altered & you don't want to give Neville—who is not over-friendly—a chance of bowling you out at once. Wait at any rate for the first revise please.

PJG

Winston S. Churchill to Stanley Baldwin

(*Baldwin papers*)

17 December 1927   Chartwell
Private

My dear Prime Minister,

This draft plan is only a sketch. A gt deal of work has been & is being done behind it. I am sure the policy is practicable.

Is it sufficiently attractive? That is what you must judge.

Do not I beg you think that I am asking for this plan to be put through as a treat & favour to me. If it is not thought well of by you or by the Cabinet, the only consequence to me will be the saving of an immense amount of toil, worry & responsibility. I offer it as my best contribution to the successful culmination of yr Government in 1929.

But if you decide that it ought to be tried, then I must ask not for ordinary approval or for Cabinet acquiescence, but for active & concerted aid: & for all yr countenance & authority to make it go.

Of course you will see how many things can be said against it. It is a new heavy burden for the Exchequer. The Treasury officials hanker for larger Sinking Funds, & hate to see future margins disposed of. The Ministry of Health while mildly attracted, wd rather have their own compact little scheme for 2 or 3 millions. The Industrialists wd rather have Protection. Rothermere will crab anything yr Administration proposes.

How much easier to slip back into the arm chair, pay our way stolidly, make a few small surpluses for the Sinking Funds, & leave the rest to the effluxion of time & the caprice of the new electorate!

It is because I believe you will repulse such moods that I send you now My Best Endeavour.

Yours very sincerely,
Winston S. Churchill

Winston S. Churchill to Neville Chamberlain

(*Churchill papers: 18/44*)

17 December 1927
Secret and Personal

My dear Neville,

I send you herewith an advance draft of the large project we have discussed together. It is not complete, and will require many alterations. Nevertheless it embodies in outline the whole policy as I see it. May I ask you to keep it in your own possession and only show it to one or two of your most trusted assistants. I shall ask for its return before Christmas, when I will send you the completed draft with the appendices, on which all my departments are now working. I need not say how earnestly I desire your aid. Without that aid I do not believe it will be possible to carry this scheme through. In that case I shall be saved an immense amount of risk and trouble, and shall have to recast my finance on purely negative but highly orthodox lines. 'Think well, think wisely, think not for the moment but for the years that are to come, before you reject this Bill.'[1]

Winston S. Churchill to Sir Philip Cunliffe-Lister

(*Churchill papers: 18/44*)

17 December 1927
Secret and Personal

My dear Philip,

I send you herewith an advance draft of the scheme we have discussed together at intervals during the last few years. It is incomplete, and is being checked, completed and amplified by the various Treasury departments. Nevertheless it gives the true outline of a considerable policy—the only one which I can think of now. I most earnestly beg your active aid, both in the Cabinet and through the powerful agencies of the Board of Trade. Please show it at this stage only to Hamilton, with whom we have kept in touch, and before Christmas I will send you in exchange for it a document finally hammered out with appendices etc.

I shall be bitterly disappointed if this plan is knocked on the head, for I am quite sure it carries with it a great hope for the Party, and still more for the country. It would be quite easy for me to save myself an immense amount of worry by falling back on the traditional negative but highly orthodox Treasury attitude.

---

[1] The quotation is from Gladstone's final speech before the Division on the second reading of the Government of Ireland Bill, on 7 June 1886. Gladstone concluded his speech: 'Think, I beseech you, think well, think wisely, think, not for the moment, but for the years that are to come, before you reject this Bill.' Despite Gladstone's appeal, the Bill was defeated by 340 votes to 311, largely through the co-operation of two powerful critics, Churchill's father, Lord Randolph Churchill, and Neville Chamberlain's father, Joseph Chamberlain.

Winston S. Churchill to Sir Warren Fisher and Sir Richard Hopkins

(*Churchill papers: 18/65*)

17 December 1927
Private and Personal

I am very much obliged to you for the help you are giving me in exploring the finance of my scheme. I attach your Memorandum—minus appendices which I have kept—with its figures brought into harmony with the paper I have prepared, as a first sketch of the plan for working purposes among a few indispensable persons.

Of course I recognise that all these figures can at this stage be little more than tokens. But the margins in hand on the scheme are so considerable that there is no doubt of its practicability in a greater or lesser form. Even on your rather pessimistic figures no deficiency is apparent till 1931–2. That is already a good long way to look ahead. But even so, I see no difficulty in carrying the solvency of the scheme further.

It is important you should realise the premises on which I proceed.

(1) I count on a progressive improvement in the revenue. The Income Tax of 1929 will recover its normal position after the Strike disaster has run off. How much increase that will amount to over the present year (apart from Schedule A) I do not attempt to calculate. Thereafter, although acceleration is exhausted, we may expect at least £2 or £3 millions increase per annum in accordance with wealth and population. But this figure may be very greatly increased if there is a real trade revival, such as I hope to assist. Customs and Excise will advance by £2 or £3 millions a year (apart from Fuel). The shrinkage in Liquor will probably be supplied by additions under Safeguarding. Thus I estimate for a revenue which will grow by £4 or £5 millions a year *after* the Income Tax has regained its norm. I have no doubt whatever that, unless there is some great disaster creating a new situation, the revenue from existing taxes will stand in 1931–2 £20 millions above its present figure. I predict it with the confidence born of everything that has happened in the last three unlucky years.

(2) I conceive myself entitled to proceed on the basis that expenditure will not increase beyond the levels fixed in the forthcoming Budget of 1928–9 until the year 1935. The progressive decline in the War Pensions operating against a fixed payment for our Widows and Old Age Pensions, the progressive growth of surplus on the Post Office and Road Fund accounts, the enforcement of a strict economy—all justify this conclusion. Of course the Government may change, and will change if we do not exert ourselves. Great new schemes of expenditure may be introduced as the result of electioneering rivalries. I exclude such chances from my responsibility. Let

those who incur the new expenditure find means of paying the new bill. That is their affair. The long forecasts of expenditure furnished me in connection with the Colwyn Committee report show a static condition for some years to come. Everything in the new scheme tends to make the Exchequer contributions to Local Rates also static. These £3 or £4 millions we are giving to sweeten a Block Grant system would certainly be taken from us in the absence of such a system in the same period. In fact on a five years' basis I feel entitled to budget for an equation between automatic increases and decreases.

(3) There remains the Debt problem. It is quite unsolved. Do not delude yourselves by supposing that our policy of Sinking Funds, Conversions, etc, have in any effectual way met this formidable difficulty. We are making no impression on the Debt at present: in fact rather the contrary. I do not therefore believe that additions of £10 or £15 or £20 millions a year to the true Sinking Fund constitute a means of escape. Either something very much larger—as Mr Snowden seems inclined to propose—or some novel or fortunate scheme of conversion on a great scale will be required to deal with this problem. The mere adding at great inconvenience to the taxpayer and at undue strain upon industry of a few millions a year to the new Sinking Fund is quite irrelevant to any real solution. I have tried it, and it has failed. It has been thoroughly proper and orthodox, and it was right to try. It is now quite clear either that other plans will have their chance or else that we must be content to wait for a slow improvement in the rent of money.

A scheme must be devised during my tenure, such as Sir Richard Hopkins is hammering out, to keep the provision for Sinking Fund and Savings Certificates together in the neighbourhood of £60 millions. There is something to be said for making that provision £100 or £120 millions. There is nothing to be said for making it £65 or £70 or £75 millions. Such a policy, if prolonged, would only be the prelude of even more drastic remedies. On this matter I have reached definite conclusions which I am prepared to explain most candidly to Parliament.

(4) Looking far ahead we see certain evils: (a) A battleship programme (if the Air cannot kill battleships earlier) after 1931 costing perhaps £4 or £5 millions a year, but not reaching that cost till 1934 or 1935. (b) The rise in the contributions for *our* Widows and Old Age Pensions of over £10 millions in 1935. This will have to be met, I think, by increased pennies above the statutory provision, and may well be justified then by decreased pennies for Unemployment. (c) The rise of the American Debt from £33 to £38 millions. Coupled with this there may be a failure of German reparations. But these two evils have a sphere of their own. Any great failure of Reparations or of the balance of payments to the United States on that account may at any

time have to be met, and could justifiably be met, by an increase of the Income Tax.

(5) But I protest against being forced to go so far afield. If we can see three or four years ahead, as we can in our new plan, without any additions to taxation save those which it comprises, and if the deficiency in question is in the order only of £12 or £15 millions a year, it is certain that the situation will not be nearly so difficult as those which we have ourselves successfully surmounted in the last few years. The best way to prepare for such difficulties is to stimulate and liberate the life energies of British industry, so that a far stronger economic power will be at our disposal in those future emergencies.

I must beg you to inscribe hope and confidence in the growing strength of the country upon all your Memoranda. The attached quotation from a speech by Mr Milner Gibson three-quarters of a century ago shows an outlook which was vindicated by events.[1] Although we have had many disappointments in the last few years, we must not conceive ourselves excluded from such a prospect. A steady Government, a firm hand on new expenditure, the lightening and judicious redistribution of burdens will, as the war years recede, bring us into more easy circumstances. Indeed in spite of the follies of the Strike and of many other national errors, we are far stronger financially and economically today than we were only three years ago. By all means confront me with facts and put the worst complexion on figures, but let this dominant belief subsist between us.

Winston S. Churchill to Sir William Joynson-Hicks
(Churchill papers: 18/59)

19 December 1927

My dear Home Secretary,

I am concerned at the development of greyhound racing. From all accounts a great deal of money is being subscribed for Companies to put up greyhound racing tracks in working class districts all over the country. The growth of this habit has been so rapid that no serious person has yet addressed his mind

---

[1] Speaking at the Albion Hotel, Manchester, on 1 February 1851, in the presence of Cobden and Bright, Milner Gibson MP said: 'I want to see our taxation based upon something like well considered principles; and, even if there should be a deficit at any particular time, I see no reason why a Ministry should not persevere in endeavouring to carry out those financial arrangements which would enable them to remove oppressive taxes without injury to the revenue, and with great benefit to the people. The experiments which Sir Robert Peel made upon taxation are pregnant with valuable lessons to statesmen. I wish them to profit by those lessons, to see that you may reduce a tax without losing revenue.'

to it. However I am pretty sure that the spectacle of these animated roulette boards, where the attraction is betting pure and simple, is one which will arouse the moral and anti-gambling forces in the country. The silly newspapers write as if the fact that there is a betting tax would influence me or any Chancellor of the Exchequer in favour of such a development. Of course you understand that in a Budget of between £800 and £900 millions such profits weigh less than the falling of a leaf in autumn. Nevertheless this new degeneracy affects the whole sphere of the Betting Tax with its child, the totalisator, and also tends to prejudice the cool consideration of the question of premium bonds which in a proper atmosphere might have a part to play in the promotion of working class thrift and the mitigation of the debt problem.

The movement for the totalisator as set on foot by the Jockey Club has behind it a great deal of Parliamentary support. On the merits the case for it is in my opinion clear. The experience of every country which has adopted it has been good. The rowdy rascal element so prominent on our race courses is eliminated. The running of horses to suit the interests of the bookmakers disappears, and an altogether cleaner and healthier condition prevails. The Cabinet have decided that if the House of Commons pronounces in favour of the principle of a totalisator, they will give facilities for a Bill. I am strongly of opinion that this Bill should not apply to dog races. I think it would be a scandal to see the Stadium at Wembley packed with people gambling through the agency of a State-approved machine upon a succession of dog races. On the other hand, illogical as it may be, I see no objection, but positive advantage, in allowing the Jockey Club or other responsible parties to put up totalisators on suitable race courses. It would yield a revenue to the upkeep of *bona fide* racing sport, and the State contributions could be collected in the easiest manner.

Cognate to the above is the general question of the Betting Tax which I shall have to re-examine before the General Election. My present inclination is to let it run exactly as it is. It has diminished betting. Perhaps it has driven some betting underground. It has provided only half the revenue expected. But nevertheless it has provided £3 millions by a tax on the luxury of excitement, and I do not know where or how an equal sum can be obtained with less economic injury. I may have to recast the tax and collect it by Licence Duties, as is proposed by the bookmakers, instead of by a percentage on turnover. I think this is improbable, but still it is an alternative which must now be studied.

You will see how all these matters are connected; and I give you my own view at this early stage in the hopes that we may be able to act in accord. I should like to see dog racing checked effectually in the near future. If it is to be done at all, it must be done soon unless great hardship is to be caused to those who are investing their money in these new courses. I see no reason why Local Authorities of an adequate size should not be given the power to grant, renew or withhold, say, three-year licences for the erection of dog racing courses. Such a power, if taken at once, would put us in an absolutely sound position. Those that are started could have their run; and if the evil should turn out to be permanent and serious, all would wither in quite a short time. That is the first step which I think should be taken.

Coupled with this, if the House of Commons approve—and their opinion should be taken without Party Whips—I think a general permission should be given for the creation of totalisators on horse race courses; and I hope the Home Office will facilitate this. The check to new gambling in the one case would more than cover the sensible reform proposed in the other. I expect that the people who are disturbed about the growth of dog racing gambling would be so well content to see that checked that they would give their confidence to a measure which allowed the totalisator on horse race courses. At any rate that is what I should like to do, provided Parliament approved the principle. I am not asking you for any action at the present moment, but I should be glad to know where you stand in the matter and whether you think a double advance on these lines is possible. We could of course scrap the Betting Tax, refuse the totalisator and impose no obstacle on the spread of dog race tracks. I cannot think such a solution would be a sensible way of handling this rather difficult, highly controversial and moderately important subject.

Yours sincerely,
Winston S. Churchill

Sir William Joynson-Hicks to Winston S. Churchill
(*Churchill papers: 18/59*)

20 December 1927   Home Office

My dear Chancellor of the Exchequer,

I have received and read with much interest your letter of yesterday dealing with the subject of betting, in what—if you will forgive me for saying so—savours more of my rather puritancial views than those of your broadminded self.

In all that you say in regard to the animated Roulette Board, I am entirely in sympathy with you. Information which reaches me from labour sources goes even further and tells me that Greyhound Racing and the consequent betting upon it is leading to petty thefts by the collectors of Friendly Societies and Trade Unions, who place their colleagues' hard-earned payments on the hazard of the dog race.

I am, therefore, delighted that you should be somewhat anxious in your mind in regard to this question; but, on the other hand, may I say to you that it is a very thorny one and that I have deferred bringing the matter before the Cabinet from the moral point of view because I realise that with horse racing permitted to the rich man and the breeding bloodstock equally permitted to him, it would be very difficult to destroy the poor man's sport and even the working man's possibility of making a fortune by breeding bloodstock greyhounds.

So far as the totalisator is concerned, on general grounds you will receive no opposition from myself. I have seen it in action in India[1] and it certainly is much preferable to the raucous yelling of Tattersall's Ring on our Race Courses.

I think, however, I ought to warn you that from a political standpoint such dregs of support as we now receive from the betting fraternity will almost completely disappear if you place the burden of the totalisator upon their shoulders and, in effect, destroy by scorpions what little business your whip of the betting tax has left to them.

I think you will have suggestions that it ought to be included in greyhound race courses but I should certainly be prepared to support you again in declining this.

With regard to the betting tax: you will remember the memorandum which I put before the Cabinet when you first introduced it. I have always regarded it as a bad tax mainly from the political standpoint because it angers both God and Mammon; in other words, the Churches and the betting fraternity, both of whom are supporters of the Tory Party.

I have not, however, differed from the tax in public and am quite prepared to bear my share of the responsibility as a Member of the Cabinet in regard to it.

One definite suggestion you make, however, which I should like you to consider carefully, namely, the grant of local option in regard to dog racing to the local authorities. The grant of local option in this matter by the Party would be for me an evil omen. Local option is being pressed on me as a solution of the licencing question and I do not want you to create a precedent

---

[1] In 1920 Sir William Joynson-Hicks had visited India and the Sudan. While in India he had gone to Amritsar in order to investigate the shooting there, and on his return to London had defended, in the House of Commons, the action of Brigadier Dyer in ordering his troops to open fire. In February 1922 Joynson-Hicks had made a strong attack on the policies of the then Secretary of State for India, E. S. Montagu.

in regard to greyhound racing which might be utilised in an attack upon the present licensing system.

I have tried to put my views quite frankly before you and should be very glad at any time to have a chat with you upon the whole matter.

Yours ever,
W. Joynson Hicks

Winston S. Churchill to Sir William Joynson-Hicks
(*Churchill papers: 18/59*)

21 December 1927

My dear Home Secretary,

Many thanks for your letter. I remember that you did not like the betting tax at the time it was proposed. The main argument in its favour is that one cannot find any other source from which £3 millions may be obtained with less economic injury to the community. The inevitable political reactions must be studied carefully. I am glad to know that you are in principle not opposed to the Totalisator. It is possible that its introduction would be coupled with some alteration in the methods of collecting the betting tax with which the bookmakers would be less discontented. There is much in what you say about Local Option. But I do not see what other authority could issue the suggested licences for Greyhound race tracks. Do you think that you would ever issue any at all if it rested with the Home Office? It seems to me on reflection that, supposing the licensing system were adopted, the grant of the licence would imply a liberty to use the Totalisator if that were legal. There would be no point in imposing the restriction twice over.

Lastly, I do not think there is very much in the Rich and Poor argument. Horse racing is not the sport of the rich but of all classes and there is all the difference in the world in people going in daylight to witness field sports like horse racing and sitting round a mechanical roulette board like a dog race track night after night after working hours. The popular holidays like the Derby and the St Leger, or a local horse race meeting, are on quite a different footing from the development of a gambling craze by mechanical means. Moreover, if there is any subject in the world in which there may be one law for the rich and another for the poor, it is in regard to gambling, since the former gamble with luxuries and the latter with the housekeeping money for food and clothing. This distinction is in fact largely recognised in our existing practice which, though it should be reformed, is not so muddle-headed as it looks.

Yours vy sincerely
Winston S. Churchill

Sir Warren Fisher to Winston S. Churchill

(*Churchill papers: 18/65*)

20 December 1927   Treasury Chambers
Private

Ch of Exchequer,

I do indeed share the confidence expressed in your personal minute of 17th instant about the future of our country. I always feel that the character of a people is its richest & most abiding asset; & our people are of a quality which defies pessimism. So, if from time to time a note of caution is apparent in my view of the situation for the next few years, it is, I can assure you, from no lack of belief in the country's destiny.

Sir Warren Fisher to Winston S. Churchill

(*Churchill papers: 18/65*)

20 December 1927

Ch of Exchequer,

I attach, for what they are worth, such conjectures as we have been able to make in regard to the trend of future Budgets.

The datum line is the present moment (December 1927); and, while full allowance has been made for tendencies which are assured eg the decreasing cost of War pensions and the effect of a Sinking Fund, there are or may be tendencies of an opposite character for which no allowance or insufficient allowance is included.

I hate to appear to you in the role of a Jeremiah; on the other hand I know you expect from me a genuine expression of the views I hold.

As I understand it, the vital question is whether a prospective failure—which I estimate at some £17,000,000 a year—of the new revenue in connection with the Rates scheme to balance the new expenditure involved by that scheme can with certainty be made good by a corresponding annual surplus on the ordinary Budget.

The guess-work figures of the attached tables appear to me to afford a quite insecure foundation on which to build any assurance of the kind.

I will not develop the argument against mortgaging a future surplus of this size, even if guaranteed to occur, when the insistent cry is for a reduction of taxation such as a surplus like that would make possible.

I honestly don't believe that any such surplus will mature.

Guesses made in 1927 will at future dates find themselves subjected to the acid test of such issues as eg

(1) an increase in the bill during the '30's for naval construction when the building of capital ships will synchronise with that of cruisers

(2) an expanding cost of an expanding home air force, little more than half of which is now in being

(3) an addition to social and local expenditure consequent on a growing population and continuing pressure for improved conditions

(4) a strengthening case for more rapid debt redemption, brought home by the growing difficulty of conversion, the depreciation of Government credit, and the increasing malaise on account of the strangle-hold of our huge debt

(5) from December 1932 an increase of the payment to the USA by £5,000,000 a year

(6) after 1935 a rise by £6,500,000 of the Old Age and Widows' Pensions (after taking into account the drop in War pensions) and increasing rapidly.

On the revenue side the guesses in these tables have, I think, underestimated the likelihood of Germany's failing to continue payments to us on the scale of £15,000,000 a year; they have also assumed during the period a net growth in profits.

The cumulative effect on my mind of these considerations amongst others is a disbelief that these guess-work figures will in fact materialise in the form of a £17,000,000 annual surplus, free and available for the sole purpose of making good an equivalent annual deficit under the Rates scheme.

Neville Chamberlain to Winston S. Churchill
(*Churchill papers: 18/65*)

20 December 1927   Ministry of Health
Secret & Personal

My dear Winston,

Thanks for your letter of the 17th and the advance draft which accompanied it. I will keep it in safety until you forward the final document which I presume you intend to circulate to the Cabinet some time in January.

Until I have had time to consider the project more carefully I do not wish to commit myself to a final judgement. But it is only fair to say that in its present form I see grave difficulties, departmental or administrative, financial and political and it is evident that the most careful consideration must be given to the possible reactions of the plan in all directions.

I notice that you have suggested the possibility of including or linking up Poor Law Reform with the plan. I confess I do not see how this is to be done. From my conversations with the PM I gather that he does not see time for Poor Law next session. But if it be postponed till after the General Election it will be too late to pass under cover of your lubricating grant to Local authorities.

I am still trying to find a way out, but I can't see one at the present.

Yours sincerely,
N. Chamberlain

Winston S. Churchill to P. J. Grigg

(*Churchill papers: 18/65*)

21 December 1927

Copies of these papers X, Y and Z should be sent to Lord Weir. I will discuss the question generally with Sir Arthur Duckham to-day. The papers are also to be included in my own file.

Mr Boothby should arrange with Mr Harold Macmillan to read this file through in my office—if possible before Parliament rises. Especially he should see Mr David Allan's[1] paper which constitutes the most damaging and disheartening criticism yet levelled at the scheme.[2] From the beginning I have said that all turns upon whether the attraction of the scheme to Industry would be sufficient to over-bear all other difficulties and objections. Naturally one is not going to take trouble and run risks for people who do not want to be helped, or for people the helping of whom would only cause ill-will among their workmen.

[1] David Howat Allan, 1872–1943. Born in Glasgow. Qualified as a Chartered Accountant, 1902. Subsequently senior partner of Allan, Charlesworth & Co of London, Cambridge and Rangoon. Member of the Advisory Committee on Finance, Ministry of Munitions, 1915–18. Member of the Codification Committee on Income Tax. A Commissioner of the Welsh Church. Among his professional colleagues, he was noted for his remarkable capacity for work, and for his ability to inspire both confidence and affection among those with whom he worked.

[2] On 5 December 1927, P. J. Grigg had written to Duckham, conveying Churchill's permission to take Allan 'into secret consultation' on the derating scheme. Allan had submitted his criticisms on December 17, contending that no rating relief nor profits tax were advisable. They would, he had argued, free local government from local control, favour one section of society overmuch and liberate the desires of Labour, who were only just learning that the country had to live poorer for a time to recoup the losses of the war. In a section which Churchill had underlined in red, Allan had argued that Employers would be frightened of the profits tax, and unwilling to accept a known relief at the cost of a new tax of an unknown amount (*Churchill papers: 18/65*).

It is now very important to get the Board of Trade figures from some specific firms about the weight of rates. I must know where I am about this in the first week of January; by that time also we shall have the reactions of the Duckham-Allan papers on Lord Weir and others. These papers are not to be shown to any persons other than those specified by me, nor are tales of undue despondency or alarm about the scheme to be countenanced by our representatives in inter-departmental discussions. It is only possible to test the practicability of plans like this by pushing them vigorously forward in the teeth of obstacles, being quite sure these obstacles are not likely to give way easily to testing pressure.

Winston S. Churchill to Sir Richard Hopkins

(Churchill papers: 22/175)

22 December 1927

I await the suggestions of the Supply Department in regard to this letter. Apparently Mr Bridgeman contemplates a reduction of about £350,000 on the figure of the present estimates, after allowing for a shadow cut of £2,400,000 and only 100,000 tons for Oil Fuel reserve. This is not sufficient, and proposals must be made to reach the total of £2 millions (ie another £1,700,000) specified by the Cabinet.

The two most hopeful lines of saving which occur to me are: first of all, the laying up of a certain number of cruisers now kept in commission and putting them in material reserve or on a high care and maintenance basis. In this connection Sir Hugh Trenchard has the idea that with flying boats he could take over most of the Naval duties now performed in the Persian Gulf by small cruisers. How many small cruisers are there, and what is their annual cost? You should get into touch with the Air Ministry about this. A further saving could be effected by a similar process of reducing to care and maintenance applied to battleships. Secondly, the oil consumed in the movement of the Fleet might be curtailed to the extent of saving 100,000 tons for reserve, instead of buying this additional quantity. But no doubt the Supply Department will have many other suggestions.

Winston S. Churchill to Sir Warren Fisher

(*Churchill papers: 18/65*)

22 December 1927

If the proposals I have in mind constituted new expenditure of an irrevocable character, the sort of alarmist forecasts you now put out might have validity. But when these proposals aim purely at a relief of burdens and are in fact a remission of taxation (and a peculiarly injurious form of taxation), other considerations apply. The worst that would happen is that the Fuel Tax and the Profits Tax would have to be increased, or alternatively a portion of the Rates restored. Meanwhile the experiment of relieving industry would have had its chance.

Neville Chamberlain to Winston S. Churchill

(*Churchill papers: 18/65*)

24 December 1927   Edgbaston,
Personal   Birmingham

My dear Winston,

It seems a shame to send you the enclosed before you have had time to recover from Christmas but as you asked for it before I went abroad, here it is. I apologise for all the typing errors but I had to do it myself and I am a bit out of practice!

You will see that my attitude, though cautious, is not wholly unfriendly.

Best wishes to you and yours for a Merry Christmas and a Happy and successful New Year.

Yours sincerely
N. Chamberlain

Neville Chamberlain: Memorandum on the Chancellor's Scheme

(*Churchill papers: 18/65*)

24 December 1927
Secret

The main proposition on which the scheme is based, namely that the contributions to local services exacted from the producer are a hindrance to industry and act unfairly upon one producer as compared with another is sound. The present practice of rating industry accords neither with the benefits received nor with ability to pay. A bold and comprehensive plan, which transfers some of this burden to the National Exchequer and places it upon the shoulders of those best able to bear it is undoubtedly attractive.

The scheme proposed for carrying out this transference involves some very large transactions affecting all local authorities as well as the Exchequer and industry generally. It cannot be successfully carried through without careful and perhaps prolonged negotiations, for there are many difficulties to be overcome.

I will not now enter into many details, but I will indicate in outline some of the matters to which it seems to me criticism may be directed, and I will first consider the financial aspect of the scheme.

It is estimated that the rating reliefs proposed will amount to £40 to £50 millions. This is only a guess, as is indicated by the wide margin between these two figures, but I have some doubts whether the limit of £50 millions would be maintained. Under the scheme certain items are specified for exclusion from the relief. Among these are offices. I doubt if offices in a Works can be cut out. A cost office or a manager's office is essential to the functioning of a rolling mill or manufactory, and it would be difficult, if not impossible, to separate them from the office concerned with selling. If all these offices were included, the London offices of provincial firms would also have to come in, and generally, I rather anticipate that the estimate of total relief to be provided for would tend to increase as the definition came to be applied in actual practice.

Taking, however, the figures given in the memorandum a deficit of £12 to £15 millions is expected in 1931, after the suspensory fund is exhausted. It is hoped that increasing prosperity will enable this deficiency to be met without further additions to taxation. But the fact remains that the scheme does definitely impose further burdens on the Exchequer, and it will surely be argued that the effect must be *pro tanto* to injure national credit and render more difficult the conversion of our liabilities on favourable terms. Moreover, the deficiency is likely to grow with each revision of the grants to local authorities, even supposing it possible to get off with the £3 million *douceur* suggested for the first transaction.

Consider next the effect of the scheme on local government. All the producers are to cease to have any further financial interest in good administration. This seems to me a very serious contingency. It is argued that as Directors and Officers of Companies have no votes as such, they are already deprived of any influence in this direction. But that is not so. They can form ratepayers' associations, they can put forward their views through Chambers of Commerce and Trade, they can come forward themselves as candidates or finance others who will represent their interests. Quite recently there was a meeting of business men in one of the London Boroughs who declared that, having appealed to the Government in vain, they must now themselves defend the pockets of the ratepayers, and they decided to run a number of candidates at the next election. It is already difficult to find business men to take part in local government; this proposal would remove one of the most powerful inducements to do so, and it might have the effect of turning local government over entirely to professional men and those representatives of 'Labour' who regard office as a means of advancing Socialist theories and benefiting their own particular supporters at the expense of the community.

A second serious difficulty is undoubtedly the fact that many local authorities would find their rateable value so drastically cut down that they would no longer have any margin from which to meet the cost of new services. To secure themselves against such a danger, they would demand an extra bonus in the block grant, and thus the finances of the scheme would be still further swelled.

Again, when revision took place, it would be difficult to leave out of account changes in the relative position of industry in an area. New factories mean new services, new streets, new drains, new water supplies: these streets have to be cleansed, lighted and policed, and local authorities will require some guarantee that increased charges due to these causes will be reflected in an increase of the Exchequer grant, which is to be fixed for a period of years.

Lastly, in considering administrative difficulties, there is the problem of distribution among the local authorities of the grants to be given. In County Boroughs this would be comparatively simple, but in the County areas distribution would have to be so arranged as to ensure that the minor spending authorities, the non-county boroughs, the Urban and Rural District Councils should be secured against definite loss or the crippling of their activities by reason of the rate exemption. I do not say that these difficulties are insurmountable, but the subject is so complicated that prolonged examination would be necessary and I am doubtful whether it could be completed in time for legislation next year.

There remains for consideration the political aspect of the proposal. No doubt relief from rates would be welcomed by any section of the community, but that relief would be a good deal tarnished, if it were accompanied by further taxation, and I fear the feature that would be seized upon would be the addition to the taxpayer's liabilities. The fuel tax would be resented by every motorist, already irritable on the subject of the road fund, and the motorists are now a formidable body. When the General Election arrived, the benefits would have already have been received, and nothing would be left but to pay for them. Past experience shows that political gratitude is confined to the anticipation of favours to come. The inducement to local authorities to support the scheme would have to be very substantial and definitely secured to allay the apprehensions that would be aroused by so far-reaching a disturbance of the known sources of their income.

Although I have felt it necessary to set out a rather formidable list of doubts and difficulties, I do not wish to be considered hostile to the main idea of the proposal. In particular, if the proposed exemption from rates were partial instead of total, many of my objections would be greatly lessened if not removed.

But I am disposed to think that rather more time should be given to the preparation of a scheme on these lines than is now available to us before the main features of the Budget are finally decided.

N. Chamberlain
Christmas 1927

Neville Chamberlain to Lord Irwin

(Irwin papers)

25 December 1927

. . . I have also been occupied with another surprise which Winston sprang on me some time ago. Looking around for some new thing to ornament and illuminate his next budget and having had his attention drawn to rating by my Poor Law proposals, he conceived the idea of a great transference of burdens from local to national shoulders in such a way as to relieve industry and farming, the two interests at present dissatisfied and rebellious. He could not carry through such a scheme without the Minister of Health, but he might be tempted to throw himself in to it by promising him that the finance should be so arranged as to carry Poor Law on the crest of the wave.

Such was the great idea—characteristic of Winston in its ingenuity, audacity and vagueness. No details were thought out, that was to be done by his officials and mine. He doesn't of course care a rap about Poor Law, but he has a keen political nose and he saw the makings of a first class political sensation in this startling proposal suddenly launched upon an unsuspecting world next April.

It was an awkward situation for me. I was still hoping to get poor law through, but I could not do it without the Chancellor, for I wanted about 2 or 3 millions to even up the changes in rate burdens which would follow a readjustment of areas. On the other hand, I believed Winston's scheme to be

impracticable. It would make such a vast disturbance that prolonged negotiations would be necessary with local authorities, and it required fresh taxation which appeared to me unwise. I suggested that he should finance my
scheme now and then we would see if we could make something of his, but
this did not attract him. He wanted his plan for 1928 so finally I agreed to
let my people look into it with the Treasury officials. They have been doing
so and the result confirms my first impressions. But meanwhile it had become
evident to me that Stanley had made up his mind to exclude Poor Law from
his Parliament. Rightly or wrongly he thinks we have tired our people with
over-legislating, and he is very anxious to cut down the remainder of the
programme. But, characteristically, he would not tell me so. At last I went
to him and had a frank talk with him, as a result of which I agreed to withdraw Poor Law this Parliament, while he agreed to put it in the party
programme for the election.

Winston has been very much excited all summer over his idea which he
seems to have imparted to everyone he met, always binding them to secrecy,
as if no one else knew anything about it. But in the last week or two there has
been a perceptible cooling of the fires. First Warren Fisher warned him that
its finance was unsound then I sent him a very chilly letter and now he tells
me he has had some very 'knobbly criticism' from certain industrialists whom
he had consulted. He doesn't want another Gallipoli, he says, and I am in
good hopes that he will have the wisdom to construct his next budget on
more orthodox lines.

Neville Chamberlain to Sir Philip Cunliffe-Lister

(*Swinton papers*)

27 December 1927

I thought I heard Winston asking for your opinion of his great scheme,
and I concluded that he had sent you a copy of that Secret Print which must
now be known to half London. You may like to know that I have sent him
a very critical study of it setting out a long list of difficulties. The fact is that
I do not believe such a disturbing scheme to be practicable in time for next
Budget. But if he would make his exemption partial (say 50%) instead of
total we might make it into quite an attractive feature of our election programme.

Winston S. Churchill to Neville Chamberlain: not sent

(*Churchill papers: 18/65*)

Secret and Personal   Chartwell Manor
29 December 1927

Many thanks for your memorandum.

I see no insuperable objection to limiting the relief to two-thirds of the rates. This would reduce the expense from £45 millions to £30 millions, plus £3 millions douceur, total £33 millions. The alternative would then be open for consideration of whether to keep the profits tax and show a permanent solvency for the scheme or whether to drop that tax altogether, thus lightening the load but leaving the finance after 1931 somewhat uncertain. Retaining one-third of the rates would meet your point about interesting the manufacturers in local government by rating ('its so bracing'). It would also provide for growth in local resources. If re-casting the scheme in this way would as your memorandum seems to indicate bring us effectively together in the matter, I would agree to the change. I dare say all the arguments about the unsound system of rating industry to which I attach much importance could equally be hung on a remission of two-thirds of the rates as on total remission.

If any action is to be taken however the Budget of this year is the last opportunity. I must pass the Fuel Tax this year if I am to count on its yield in 1929. Anyhow I should need a suspensory fund such as this tax would afford to guard against contingencies. On the other hand I will not propose any new extra tax except in conjunction with a large scheme of alternative relief simultaneously announced. I have made up my mind not to impose any more taxes in the present Parliament except for purposes of making more desirable remissions. Thus a decision to postpone this matter beyond the Budget must be fatal to the scheme.

I do not believe that the Fuel Tax will be very unpopular, or that the motorists will vote against us in consequence. On the whole the enquiries I have made lead me to believe that there will be great support for this tax and no violent opposition. Nevertheless, if it were not imposed this year I should certainly not impose it on the eve of the election in 1929. Under my time table we impose our burdens this year and distribute our favours next. The policy of imposing our burdens next year and promising favours if we are returned at the General Election, which favours will already have been paid for, would I am sure not be wise. So far as I am concerned therefore it is now or never.

Moreover I do not see why more time is needed. There are more than three months, in fact nearly four before the Budget need be introduced—more time in fact than was needed to prepare the infinitely more complicated

Widows' Pension scheme. So far as the Treasury end is concerned I see no difficulty at all in having the scheme ready for the Budget. So far as the block grants part of the scheme is concerned you would have 18 to 20 months before the first rate relief would operate and the new system begins. There would certainly be plenty of time to frame and pass the necessary legislation assuming that the policy was adopted as dominating our affairs.

I gather that you will be abroad when we meet on the 11th. I shall then explain verbally the policy, but of course I shall ask for no decision. Unless however the reception is really favourable I shall not press a policy which for the sake of general interests involves a very great toil and burden for the Exchequer. We shall then have as our culminating feature the agreeable topic of Votes for Flappers supported by an emasculated Factory Bill! And then there is always the House of Lords! Bon voyage.

Yours vy sincerely,
Winston S. Churchill

Winston S. Churchill to Donald Fergusson
(Churchill papers: 18/65)

31 December 1927

(1) I do not think it is necessary to re-type the whole of the Weir papers. The Neville Chamberlain paper should be multiplied as I have said. The Weir papers may be sent in the first instance to Mr Hurst with a duplicate of my Minute of today. He can then send them to Sir Richard Hopkins who meanwhile will be studying the more important Neville Chamberlain Memorandum, of which however Mr Hurst should have a copy. This will save time. I will write a letter to Mr Chamberlain a little later. He will not want to be bothered on his holidays.

(2) Mr Hurst's memorandum on Rating Reform should be printed on a long blue sheet of paper, and twenty copies obtained for my personal use. This should be ready Monday. There is one point at the top of page 2 about fire brigades paying for their services which is not quite clear. Mr Hurst should look at this when he corrects the proof. The preliminary minute to Mr Hurst's memorandum should not be reproduced. The memorandum itself should not at this stage be signed, and Mr Hurst should revise it so as to make it impersonal. Only a very few alterations are needed. I will take full responsibility for the memorandum. I am keeping my copy.

(3) You will realise that I am anxious to revise my own printed paper in

the light of all the subsequent information which has come in. The process should be expedited as much as possible. In particular what has happened to Sir Josiah Stamp?[1] You had better ring up Hamilton himself and ask him about the effect of Rates on particular firms and when that is to be expected. I have not yet decided whether to adumbrate my scheme to the Cabinet on the 11th or to put it off a fortnight.

WSC

[1] Josiah Charles Stamp, 1880–1941. Economist and statistician. Entered the Inland Revenue Department, 1896; Board of Trade, 1898; resigned from the civil service, 1919. Secretary and Director, Nobel Industries Ltd, 1919–26. Knighted, 1920. Joint Secretary, Royal Statistical Society, 1920–30; President, 1930–2. British Representative on the Reparations Commissions Committees of 1924 (Dawes) and 1929 (Young). Member of the Court of Enquiry, Coal Mining Industry Dispute, 1925. Director of Imperial Chemical Industries, 1927–8. Created Baron, 1930.

January 1928

Harold Macmillan to Winston S. Churchill

(Churchill papers: 18/85)

1 January 1928   Chatsworth

My dear Chancellor,

In response to your invitation, I venture to write to you on the high matters which you were good enough to discuss with me just before the prorogation of Parliament. Christmas, with its accompaniment of large numbers of children to be amused and vast quantities of pheasants to be shot, is not conducive to serious thought. But I have done my best, and sent you accordingly the results. I hope you will forgive the loose writing of the letter and the apparent conceit involved in my undertaking to deal with seeming confidence with matters on which I am no expert.

I should also like you to know how deeply I appreciate the favour of your confidence. You have always been most kind to those of us who are ordinarily classed merely as troublesome young men, & if I can be of any assistance to you at any time in this or similar matters, you have only to command me.

A. OBJECTIONS TO THE SCHEME

It seems that the most formidable criticism which is likely to be made of the scheme as a whole, will probably be advanced by the Ministry of Health. These objections, while fundamental, will be of a dual character. First, there is the argument that the exclusion of the producer from liability to local taxation, either in whole or in part, will remove the incentive from the Industrialist to use his influence in the direction of good local government.

Secondly, there may perhaps be discerned a certain reluctance on the part of the Ministry of Health to face the undoubted legislative difficulties and administrative problems which, as a result of the very boldness and comprehensiveness of the scheme, must be grappled with if it is to operate successfully. This line of objection will appear in many different forms. Every puny obstacle will be represented as insurmountable. Every technical problem will be declared insoluble. Every artifice of argumentation will be used to show the impracticable character of any proposals which have not emanated originally from the Ministry itself.

But these are the common symptoms attendant upon the birth-pangs of every great reform. This line of objection cannot be seriously maintained against the force of reasoned argument, such as is brought to bear in your memorandum to the Cabinet. It is so plainly an attitude of timidity that it cannot be maintained beyond a certain point by a Minister who has hitherto appeared in the role of the constructive & progressive politician, only hampered in working out his policy by the force of vested interests & the obscurantist activities of the Tory squirearchy. Every possible means of pressure ought to be brought to bear on the Minister of Health. He ought, in reality, energetically to support this scheme, which provides him incidentally with the only method—the sugared pill—by which he can hope to carry into law his own proposals for the reconstruction of Local Government & the reorganisation of the Poor Law.

The first line of objection, however—the argument that the new scheme involves a certain loss in the sense of responsibility of the employing classes to local government has more substance. It will no doubt be used with great fervour, sometimes simulated and sometimes real, by all the opponents of any readjustment of the burdens of taxation & by all supporters of the policy of negation. These Conservatives are anxious to see a policy of drift erected into a system. They suffer from 'Tranquillity' as men suffer from sleeping sickness. They are the most formidable of those who are making 'Socialism in our time' a possibility, if not a certainty.

It must however have become apparent to these critics that the 'representation' nowadays secured, either in local or imperial affairs, by the liability to 'taxation' per se, is really negligible. 'No taxation without representation' was the reasonable cry of a plutocracy struggling against the perogatives of the Crown, exercised, as they so often were, in defence of the common people. It is not a slogan applicable to modern democracy. Like the Whig historians who gave it such a vogue, it is dead & forgotten.

Nor is it to be supposed that defence of property is the sole object which induces men to enter public life, whether in local or national affairs. Even if, as I understand you contemplate as a possibility, the final stage of your scheme may see the exemption from liability to local taxation of all except residential property, every ordinary person must be to some extent interested in good local government, in so far as he is bound to reside somewhere. Nor is there any reason to suppose that those higher motives of ambition or patriotism will not still, as far as they now do, continue to lead men & women of all kinds into the public service.

Indeed, it is just as easily to be argued that the rescue of the industrialist

Andromeda from the clutches of the socialist dragon will have an excellent effect on the character of the dragon. Bereft of his prey & forced to live on honest work, he may become comparatively innocuous, & live to bless the name of the political Perseus who has been responsible for the happy transformation.

To put the argument more seriously, if by the 'Block Grant' system the power of restraint of the central government is strengthened & its liabilities defused; if by the removing from local authorities of the temptation to prey upon the producer we can to some extent exorcise the spirit of Poplarism; if by the stimulus given to industry we can give it back some of its ability to compete in the markets of the world; if by the security afforded to capital, plant & opportunity for employment can be made available at those very localities with every advantage geographically and geologically, where the population is, where the houses are, where the transport system is ready to hand—places now shunned as plague spots by the capitalist solely because of the unknown liabilities by way of local taxation;—then, if all this can be achieved, surely the benefits will far outweigh the harmful results, if any, of weakening a principle of government which has, in fact, largely ceased to function. . . .

Winston S. Churchill to Sir Richard Hopkins

(*Churchill papers: 18/85*)

2 January 1928   Chartwell Manor[1]
Secret

(1) You should see the enclosed from Lord Weir. In conversation I have reassured him about the effect of the Profits Tax in spite of its string-halt provision. He had not seen the elaborate figures which I have been provided

[1] Churchill had spent the New Year at Chartwell with Professor Lindemann and Edward Marsh. On January 2 Sir Archibald Sinclair came down for two nights, writing to Churchill, on 22 January 1928: 'We enjoyed our visit to Chartwell quite inexpressibly—I have never left anywhere except my own home more sadly' (*Churchill papers: 1/199*). Churchill's Treasury adviser on derating, A. W. Hurst, stayed overnight at Chartwell on February 26, April 16, April 21–23 and September 7–9. Among the other overnight guests during 1928 were Professor Lindemann (January 12–16, March 3–5, April 7–9, April 13–15, April 21–23, September 20–24 and December 30–January 2), Lord Londonderry (January 19–20), Robert Boothby (January 19–20, January 21–23, April 21–23 and October 5–8), Richard Sickert (January 19–20), Venetia Montagu (January 28–29), P. J. Grigg (April 7–9), Lord Hailsham (August 26–27), Lord Riddell (September 1), Lord Lloyd (October 13–14), Parker Gilbert (October 13), Lord Birkenhead (October 13), Owen O'Malley and Edward Marsh (throughout September) working on *The Aftermath*, and James Headlam-Morley (December 27–29).

with by the Inland Revenue. The result of our conversation left him decidedly favourable to the plan on general principles. As will be seen from my Minute of today,[1] I now contemplate discarding the Profits Tax in my first presentment of the scheme.

(2) I have been questioning whether gas, docks, tramways, light, water, etc, should or should not be excluded from the scheme. £12 millions would be saved thereby. These are sheltered trades in which employment cannot be a serious factor, as they have a regular demand. If the railways are included, it will only be on condition that they pay over the whole relief in improved freights. I therefore felt inclined to lighten the scheme by dropping out the services in Category (d) of the Inland Revenue Memorandum. However Mr Hurst showed good reasons to the contrary, which he should record on paper. It seems that water can anyhow be omitted, saving £3 millions.

(3) I should be glad to receive the results of the enquiries made by the Board of Trade into the incidence of rating on various concerns. This matter is most important, and Sir Horace Hamilton should be pressed personally to expedite at least an instalment of the information.

(4) In the Appendix of the Inland Revenue Memorandum figures are given of the effects of Rates and Profits on a great number of firms in different trades. It would be very helpful if some approximation could be given of the number of persons employed in each of the groups and in each of the divisions of the groups. Mr Hurst's paper mentions that 'interesting figures were collected by the Balfour Committee showing both the rates and the contributions to National Insurance'. The contributions to National Insurance are of course an accurate measure of the amount of employment given by particular firms. It ought thus to be possible without much trouble to add the extra information to the table. My idea is that probably quite substantial numbers of employed persons will be found to be maintained by the industries which suffer most from the Rates and will benefit most from the scheme.

(5) You should see Mr Neville Chamberlain's letter and memorandum marked 'B'. This should be multiplied six-fold. There is no doubt—as you will see from the concluding passages of the memorandum—that the Ministry of Health would be very largely reconciled to the scheme if, say, one-third of the Rates were left on industry. This would provide partially for the growth of local needs and would also meet the argument about keeping the business men interested in Local Government through the pressure, albeit reduced, of the Rates ('It's so bracing!') The former argument is serious and must of course be covered in any scheme of distribution. The second argument I regard as illusory. Lord Weir shares this opinion, and I think Sir

---

[1] Churchill's minute to Sir Richard Hopkins, entitled 'Final Notice', printed, as the next document, on pages 1165-7.

Arthur Duckham too. The arguments set out in Mr Hurst's paper on this subject appear to me conclusive. The expense of the scheme is reduced by one-third or £15 millions. The need of a new Profits Tax is avoided. As the whole of the one-third rating relief to the scheme would operate continuously whereas the Profits Tax would lag, the finance of the scheme would be improved even without a Profits Tax, and we could probably see our way up to 1932 or even as far as 1933.

Nevertheless I have been reluctant to agree with Mr Chamberlain on such a solution. I take the view that the whole principle of taxing Plants and Tools, instead of the profit arising from their use, is unsound. All the arguments against our present system which would support a total remission of Rates might of course be hung on a partial remission. But they would have lost a good deal of their force and logic. The relief which we wish to carry to the unfairly rated industries and to those which are struggling most must pro tanto be reduced. All the business of assessment of industry in consequence of improvements and extensions would still continue. Every new machine put down or new workshop erected would be inspected, assessed and rated.

If the rates on industry were only one-third, the tendency of the valuation authorities would be to put up the assessments. These would be continually raised, and the deterrent on new enterprise and up-to-date methods would continue. Mr Hurst's paper uses arguments on this subject which are convincing to me. Moreoever, we have to consider the case of Agriculture which already receives three-quarters remission of Rates. Even under our present scheme Agriculture will say: 'We are not getting as much as the industrials. We have only been let off the last quarter of our Rates, while they have got off the whole lot.' To which I should answer: 'But how would you like to pay the Profits Tax like the industrials have to? You are getting your relief for nothing.' If on the other hand there were no Profits Tax but one-third of the Rates maintained in lieu, comparison between the agriculturists and the industrialists would be the naked one of one-quarter compared to two-thirds.

The proposals for a National Rate dealt with in my Minute of today are the furthest I can go in the direction of meeting Mr Chamberlain. They leave the difference between the two Departments unadjusted. The Ministry of Health would agree to a rate relief which followed simply upon the lines of the Agricultural Rates Relief Act, whereas the National Rate now contemplated is in fact a Profits Tax levied under a different name and on a different basis but preserving the great principles of being unalterable by local caprice or circumstances, being uniform for the whole country and making it unnecessary to maintain—so far as productive industry is concerned—the cumbrous machinery of the rating system.

(6) The Ministry of Health may continue obstructive and may withhold their indispensable aid in the sphere of distribution. It is always possible that the time may not be available this Session for the necessary Bill, and it may be (please advise me) that such a Bill passed only in 1929 could not be brought into operation simultaneously with the granting of the first relief in October of that year. We are therefore forced to consider proceeding in two stages: carrying our own scheme in the present Parliament, announcing that a block grant scheme will be proceeded with in the first Session of the new Parliament, and providing for an interim period of, say, one or at the outside two years till the necessary arrangements with the Local Authorities can be made. There would be many disadvantages in this, especially the one set out in Mr Hurst's paper of missing the opportunity of overriding the small local prejudices at the moment of a great extension of relief to farmers and industrialists. Nevertheless we must explore this alternative, and Mr Hurst should write a separate paper showing the best plan possible for the interim period.

Obviously for one year, and as a temporary expedient in the advent of a large reform, I could simply repay to the interests relieved the amount, or two-thirds of the amount, they have paid in Rates. Pray examine this or suggest some better method. The plan would thus be brought entirely inside our own Budget area. The mere existence of such a paper would, I am sure, act as a disciplinary spur to the Ministry of Health. It is most important they should not feel they have a prevailing power of veto.

(7) It would also be well to work out the finance of the following four variants of the scheme.

(a) £45 millions Rates plus £3 millions *douceur* beginning in October 1929, to be met by LF Tax at 3d—£18 millions—P Tax at 1/-—£12·6 millions—aided by Suspensory Fund accumulated in 1928 and 1929.

(b) As above, but one-third of the Rates, ie £15 millions to remain; no Profits Tax; LF Tax and Suspensory Fund as before.

(c) As in (b), but keeping the Profits Tax as well as one-third of the Rates.

And lastly (d). Reduce the £48 millions charge by £12 millions through excluding gas, water, tramways, etc, leaving £36 millions charge. Meet this by LF Tax at 3d (£18 millions), P Tax at 1/- (£12·6 millions) and Suspensory Fund as before. *Note.* On this basis we might get through with only 9d P Tax producing £10 millions.

Where the figures given in the above examples differ from those set out in my Minute of today, they are to be superseded by the later Minute.

These should all be worked out as far as they will go up till 1932 or 1933, showing deficits which emerge. Credit should be given where appropriate for the rebates under Schedule 'D' in respect of Rates. Sir Warren Fisher's minute to me shows how these schemes could be worked out; and as all the data are available, the task should not be laborious. Each variant should be on a separate sheet of paper this size. The basis taken of the total cost of the scheme is to be £45 plus £3 millions *douceur*, ie £48 and not £50 millions. It will be easy to add an additional margin of safety later on when we choose between the variants. At present all I recognise is £3 millions *douceur*. The LF Tax is to be taken throughout at £18 millions, and no allowance is to be made for any concession to the heavy vehicles or for any compensation to the cottage paraffin. These aspects are not inherent in the scheme. Concessions might well be forced upon us in its discussion. But the cost of such concessions, eg sugar, will be met as part of the general finance of the country. This simplifies the calculations.

(8) How much labour would be involved in the Inland Revenue working out the tables in their Appendix on the basis of a 9d instead of a 1/- Profits Tax, and secondly of a 6d tax? If the labour is not too great, I should like at any rate the 9d rate to be worked out. Is there no means of getting later information than 1923–24?

WSC

Winston S. Churchill to Sir Richard Hopkins

(*Churchill papers: 18/85*)

2 January 1928
Secret

FINAL NOTICE

See all my previous Minutes. I propose to unfold the Rates scheme to the Cabinet on the 11th, and to ask for a Cabinet Committee to hammer it out. After much balancing I have decided provisionally on the following form and data:—

(1) The relief will apply to all properties comprised by the definition in my printed paper, excluding only waterworks at a saving of £3 millions. Total cost of relief: £45 millions minus £3 millions water, plus £3 millions *douceur*. Total: £45 millions.

(2) In lieu of the Rates of which they are relieved, the producers will pay a National Rate to yield to the Exchequer approximately one-third of the total volume of the relief, ie £14 millions minus £1 million to allow for complete exemption of Agriculture from the start equals £13 millions.

The National Rate will be levied on the rateable value of the exempted property as arrived at in the datum year 1928. The amount of the National Rate will be at a standard level for the whole country sufficient to produce the £13 millions above mentioned, and probably at about 5/- in the £. Neither the 5/- rate nor the datum year assessments on which it is based will be alterable from year to year, except on *ad hoc* appeals in respect of property whose rateable value is claimed by the owners to have declined. As however it is intended that the retention in principle of one-third of the Rates is in itself only to be a temporary expedient for the first one or two five-year periods, no new property or extensions of old property will be the subject of new assessments or be required to bear any charge. Thus all complications and deterrents upon industry arising from the uncertainty of local rate increases or of new assessments on extensions or new businesses, will be eliminated. All producers will pay at the same rate in all parts of the country, and the maximum of relief will be afforded to the most heavily rated areas.

(3) On the other papers I have asked for further calculations of variants of the Profits Tax. These should be pursued in order that this alternative may be thoroughly explored. In consequence however of the imposition of the National Rate yielding £13 millions, the Profits Tax will at this stage be omitted from the scheme.

(4) The Liquid Fuel Tax is to be calculated upon the basis of a flat rate charge of 3d per gallon, without exemptions or rebates of any kind. Some compensatory concessions may be forced upon us at a later stage in our discussions. But they need not be brought into the finance of the scheme at this stage. The yield of the LF Tax is estimated for the purposes of this paper at £18 millions for the first year, of which £15 millions will be collected; at £19 millions for the second; at £20 millions for the third; and at £22, 24 and 26 millions for the three succeeding years. This is a lesser increase than the 10% rise which has now been for some time operative. It may be that further study of this tax will yield larger figures.

(5) The Exchequer has therefore to meet a new annual charge of £45 millions. The LF Tax to be imposed by the Budget of 1928 should yield £15 millions in that year, which will be carried to a Suspensory Fund. Payments of relief will not begin until the October rate of 1929.

The receipts of the Suspensory Fund in that year will be: LF Tax £19 millions in a full year, plus £1 million Schedule D, plus £6½ millions National Rate. Total Suspensory Fund: £41½ millions. Out of this the first half-year's rate relief of £22½ millions will be paid, leaving the Suspensory Fund £19 millions in credit.

For the year 1930 the receipts will be: LF Tax £20 millions; Schedule D £2 millions; National Rate £13 millions; add Suspensory Fund £19 millions.

Total £54 millions. From this the full relief of £45 millions can be paid, leaving the Suspensory Fund in credit £9 millions.

1931: LF Tax £22 millions; Schedule D £4 millions; National Rate £13 millions; in Suspensory Fund £9 millions. Total £48 millions. Deduct £45 millions for rate relief, leaving Suspensory Fund plus £3 millions.

1932: LF Tax £24 millions; Schedule D £4 millions; National Rate £13 millions; from Suspensory Fund £3 millions. Total £44 millions. Cost of full rate relief £45 millions. Deficit: minus £1 million.

1933: LF Tax £26 millions; Schedule D £4 millions; National Rate £13 millions. Total £43 millions. Deduct £45 millions rating relief. Total deficiency: minus £3 millions.

(6) It must be remembered that we shall enjoy the use of a Suspensory Fund until it is exhausted. There is a small interest accretion probably amounting to nearly £2½ millions. This should be calculated and the figures amended accordingly. The Finance Department should consider to what extent the temporary possession of the Suspensory Fund in Government hands would facilitate our ordinary borrowings on Ways and Means.

(7) All the figures above should be carefully checked in the light of the latest information, and an amended version presented to me before the end of the week. In particular the National Rate scheme in paragraph 2 should be the subject of immediate study inside the Treasury, and a fuller report in detail supplied at the earliest moment. The idea of a National Rate will not of course meet the views of the Ministry of Health, any more than a national levy on profits. It does not seem worth while therefore at this stage to call them into council, but they should be asked for any information which may be required. It is specially important to make sure that the National Rate will not lead us into some of those complications which the latest form of the Profits Tax was intended to avoid.

WSC

Lord Weir to Winston S. Churchill

(*Churchill papers: 18/85*)

3 January 1928
Secret & Confidential

My dear Chancellor,
    With the Treasury figures you recited, which are destructive of my original assumptions, I have again reviewed the subject. I feel that you should *include* railways, but *exclude* gas, water, electric supply, trams and commercial

road transport, but *include* the Central Electricity Board. This would cut the rates off main transmission, and make the high tension current cheaper to the supply companies, and thereby vastly strengthen the electricity scheme. Moreover, such a course is thoroughly justified, as the full saving is passed on, and it is a new development and would start clear of defective rate. I still feel that there is nothing unfair in the fuel tax, but you will need to look out for the push and drive it would cause on home produced fuel. You will do more for the coal industry by this action than all the coal commission reports put together. I dislike the partial exemption, because it leaves the local authority the power to re-assess industrial property, and possibly to annul the benefits. Leaving out gas, water, you may not need the profits tax, but I hope you will not leave it out as it is fair and wisely corrective in the sense that it does make industry pay rates when industry is profitable enough to stand rate paying. Really this tax sufficiently provides for the point of making industry pay some rates.

I am not sure that the term 'Profits Tax' is good! What about 'Rates Adjustment Tax'? I don't wish to throw laurel wreaths, but this ought to be the wise financial step your Government has taken in the national as well as in the party interests.

With best wishes,
Yours sincerely,
Weir

Winston S. Churchill to Stanley Baldwin
(*Churchill papers: 18/85*)

4 January 1928

My dear Prime Minister,

I have been using the leisure and isolation of the last fortnight to recast and develop my project in the light of the various criticisms it has received. I shall be ready to unfold a scheme at the Cabinet which you thought of holding on the 11th or 12th. The following are the main alterations in the plan set out in my printed paper:—

(1) The scope of relief is unchanged except that waterworks may be omitted, saving £m 3. Total charge £m 45.

(2) The Profits Tax is dropped provisionally. Nearly all opinions were agreed that the extra burden of this new, or rather dug up, tax would affect the popularity of the scheme. People would be afraid that once it had been

established, even on the lowest basis, other Governments might screw it up to meet current needs. Duckham, Stamp, Neville Chamberlain and yourself—all had a prejudice against it. Neville's paper, a copy of which I enclose, will show you that he prefers, for quite different reasons, that a portion at least should be left on the Rates. I therefore propose to give a relief of two-thirds only of the Rates and to omit the Profits Tax. However let me make it clear that I have no doubt that the Profits Tax is the sound method. The idea of rating or taxing the Tools and Plants of production is essentially vicious. The proper course is to tax the profits arising from their use. Therefore in consenting to leave one-third of the Rates upon the producers, I am in no way condoning the bad system, but only bowing to the need of obtaining more general agreement and defacing the classical purity of the conception for the sake of an easier passage.

(3) This change undoubtedly simplifies and reduces the problem. It does not prevent the use of all the arguments against the rating of Tools and Plants which are so important to the case. Nevertheless the course I now propose will not fully meet the objections of the Health Ministry. Their idea is that industry should share local fortunes and local decisions, and they would be content if say one-third of the Rates were left upon Tools and Plants *on the existing rating system*. The relief would be afforded in the same manner as by the present Agricultural Grants Relief Act. My new plan is to substitute for the Profits Tax a National Rate for producers, equivalent in volume to one-third of what they now pay. This National Rate, once struck, would be unalterable except at stated periods of at least five years, would be uniform throughout the country (probably at about 5/-), and would not apply to any new Plants or extensions of existing Plants. Thus productive industry would be completely relieved from the whole vexation and uncertainty of assessment and rating of Plants. No one thinking of improving his Works would have to take such matters into consideration. No one in any one part of the country would be penalised as against a competitor elsewhere. No one would have any temptation to move his Factory on account of heavy or increasing Rates. They would not only get the substantial relief which is offered, but they would know where they were and that they could not be injuriously affected by any local event. In other words, while I drop the Profits Tax in name, I reproduce it under another form called a National Rate. But this of course will be much more popular, though less high class.

(4) The Liquid Fuel Tax will therefore be the only new tax required, and 3d per gallon will yield £m 18 rising by probably 10% a year. It will be flat, universal, without rebates or exemptions of any kind. In so far as it falls on industry, it will be the only burden they will have to bear in exchange for a

relief, not Alas! of the whole but, of two-thirds of the Rates and for the certainty and standardisation of the remaining one-third. None of those I have consulted are at all worried about the Liquid Fuel Tax. Please see the paragraph about it in my printed paper, which I will not here repeat.

(5) The finance of the scheme on the new basis is more satisfactory than on the old. £m 45 total Rates on producers minus £m 3 for leaving out waterworks plus £m 3 for *douceur* for Neville Chamberlain's distribution scheme, involves a charge upon the Exchequer of £m 45 minus £m 13 for the one-third Rates still left on and minus in 1931 £m 4 relief under Schedule D. Final nett total charge £m 28. (See my print.) But this charge will only begin to operate from October 1929 (a pregnant date!) when for the first time the great rate reductions begin. The Fuel Tax should yield £m 15 in the first year, viz 1928, and £m 19 in 1929, against which only one half-year's payments for 1929 will have been made. Thus the payments for the years 1930, 1931 and 1932, during which the Fuel Tax grows year by year, can be defrayed by the new taxation plus the Suspensory Fund of which meanwhile the Treasury has the use. I do not trouble you with the financial details. For the general solvency of the scheme I will accept full responsibility, and I shall be in a position to show a satisfactory out-turn year by year until the year 1932 which, God knows, is far enough for mortal eye to focus.

(6) I must of course explain to the Cabinet that I can only advance into this field if the Budget of 1928 balances naturally without new taxation. I ask your aid in resisting the imposition of any new taxes merely for the purpose of paying our way. Secondly, I am still reckoning without the results of the Income Tax sample, which will come to hand by the beginning of March, being apparent. I do not myself expect any collapse like last year's. Indeed my tendencies are all the other way. Nevertheless this decisive factor remains till March uncertain.

(7) There remains the distribution of the relief (two-thirds of £m 45) to the Local Authorities, and the legislation and valuations, etc, necessary to convey it. And here we enter the Block Grants, rating reform, Neville Chamberlain Health and Poor Law jungle. Up till now I am sure of the path, and it all lies within the picket lines of the Treasury. I have been worrying about the basic producer and the finance necessary to give him what little help we can. But now comes the question of the Local Authorities, to square whom the *douceur* of £m 3 asked for by Neville for his rating scheme has been set aside. Let me at this point state the case in the most comprehensive terms.

(8) We have given tranquillity to the country, we have given stability, and through strife unsought by us we have achieved a breathing space of peace in industry. Better days are coming, and the fruits of three or four years of steady Government will be reaped—by someone.

At the same time we lack for our concluding Sessions any large, constructive and creative policy. The Lords and the Ladies, coupled with an emasculated Factory Act and a small scale but very boring Rating Bill, are no programme on which to end the Parliament. We are carped at for being unprovided with solutions of current social problems, or even with remedial ideas upon them. These problems are ineffectually attacked by each of the Departmental Ministers concerned from his separate point of view. Neville has his rating plans to help the necessitous areas and to improve Local Government. Steel-Maitland has had his run on Unemployment Insurance. We are groping for a policy about Coal Mines. The Ministry of Transport have plans about traffic and for allowing the railways to compete with the roads. All these efforts will fail. They will be quite useful; they will cost money; but they will not be related to any design; and they will not be strong enough to produce any appreciable effect. Two things are wanted in peace or in war for a successful assault: first, unity of command; and secondly, heavy artillery. The latter I am trying to provide in spite of the expense; the former rests with you.

The kind of scheme which I hope you will adopt and press forward covers all these inter-related problems, and provides us with concerted arguments applicable to the whole field of domestic affairs. The heavy burden of the basic industries is to some extent lightened, and lightened in exact proportion to the invidious load they bear: the necessitous areas are helped not by doles, but by the application of healthy, economic means; justice is done to the railways by taxing their competitors fairly, and aid is given to their customers through reducing their freights; some real and deep help is afforded to our vast local possessions through rates, through freights, through protection, however partial, against imported fuel, and through stimulus to distillation and pulverisation; the balance is righted between the treatment which merchants and rentiers have received from the Government and that hitherto meted out to the producer; the rating anomaly, instead of being tackled on a petty scale in isolation, is reformed with all the driving power of an immense financial engine; and the relations between national and local finance are placed partially at least upon a basis, liberal at the outset and thrifty in the outcome.

(9) Please let me know as soon as possible whether I am to open these matters on the 11th or whether you wish them postponed till the beginning of February. Either course is possible, but I recommend that time should be gained wherever possible. All I shall ask in the first instance is that a Cabinet Committee should be appointed to hammer out the main principles of the scheme, so that we may know more or less where we stand when the Session begins.

I must point out finally that it is this year or never. I cannot impose the Fuel Tax without unfolding the scheme of relief; and unless I impose the Fuel Tax in the Budget of 1928, no scheme of relief will be possible within the lifetime of the present Parliament.

> With all good wishes for the New Year,
> Believe me,
> Yours v. sincerely
> Winston S. Churchill

Winston S. Churchill to Stanley Baldwin
(Baldwin papers)

5 January 1928

My dear Prime Minister,

The following notes by Harold Macmillan reached me after my letter to you was drafted. I have in strict confidence told him about my scheme, as it was by a chance remark of his to me two years ago that the seed of this matter was planted in my mind. You will see how extremely sensibly the whole question of the Profits Tax *versus* one-third of the Rates and of a standard rate *versus* the present system is discussed. It is the most clear explanation I have seen.

Please also see the enclosed from Weir. I have had long confabulations with him, but he does not know the latest form of the scheme. Nevertheless his comments, together with my letter and Macmillan's disquisition, are extremely illuminating and really display all the pros and cons.

> Yours vy sincerely,
> Winston S. Churchill

Winston S. Churchill to Harold Macmillan
(Churchill papers: 18/85)

5 January 1928   Chartwell Manor

My dear Macmillan,

It is always pleasant to find someone whose mind grasps the essentials and proportions of a large plan. I made you party to it because I was sure you would enrich its preliminary discussion, and also because—though you may have forgotten it—a chance remark of yours about the rating system, made more than two years ago, first implanted in my mind the seed of what may become a considerable event.

Broadly speaking we are agreed on the lines advocated in your 'Finance of the Scheme'. In fact your statement under this head tallies almost identically with the decisions and arguments which quite separately I have arrived at here. No doubt the original fountain of proposals is mainly Hurst's memorandum. But nevertheless I am glad to think that quite separate cogitations have reached the same conclusion.

If you will call at the Treasury when next you are in London, my private office will show you all my papers on this subject and you can read them there. I hope this will not be inconvenient, but it is on general principles better not to circulate secret papers except in locked pouches or boxes. I am now planning to bring this matter before the Cabinet on the 11th or 12th, and to ask for a Committee of five or six to study it with me. Of course everything in my sphere remains uncertain until the results of the Income Tax this year and of the sample taken to frame the estimates of the next year are to hand. A bad crash therefore would leave me with no strength to spare for other than purely Treasury concerns. I see however no reason to suppose that all will not be well.

We have been for a spell completely isolated here by quite formidable weather. In fact the wireless was our only connection with the outer world; and that can be switched off at will—altogether a most unusual and by no means a disagreeable sensation.

Yours vy sincerely,
Winston S. Churchill

Stanley Baldwin to Winston S. Churchill
(*Churchill papers: 18/85*)

6 January 1928   10 Downing Street

My dear Winston,

Forgive a brief note: I am in labour with my Annual speech to my Association and it always wants thinking out carefully.

I have read your last memorandum and your accompanying letter with keen interest. I shan't get up till Wednesday afternoon but I should like to have a good talk on the Thursday. I will write to you in a day or two pretty fully for I have been meditating at leisure during the holidays.

There are several members of the Cabinet away but we can have a meeting after next week. I couldn't manage the 11th as I originally intended.

The best of everything to you in 1928.

Yours ever,
SB

Winston S. Churchill to Sir Roger Keyes

(*Churchill papers: 22/175*)

6 January 1928
Private

My dear Roger,

It was nice to hear from you again. The year has slipped by horribly fast since we met. Indeed it hardly seems a month ago that we were lolloping out of Malta harbour on your flagship. I do not find it possible to escape from England this January, as I have several saucepans cooking on the fire which require constant watching. But I hope to pop across for a couple of days next week and have a hunt with Westminster for wild boar in the forests near Dieppe.

Naval affairs have bulked rather large this year, and I have had to fight very hard in two apparently different directions: first, to prevent our being bound by solemn treaty to agree to equality in numbers of cruisers with the United States; and secondly, to delay our building programme of cruisers which had got far ahead of any practical requirement.

Beatty's Japanese bogey has completely collapsed. The poor creatures do not intend, as you will see, to build any more cruisers until after the 31st December 1936. However I will not repeat the arguments which I used, as I am sending you herewith (for your personal information and in strict secrecy) the paper which I wrote about Geneva, and three papers which were prepared for the Cabinet Committee on cruiser construction. I should add that of course I would never build any 'B' vessels as long as the contemporary ships of Japan and the United States were all 'A' class. So far as the one cruiser of 1927 is concerned, I failed to carry my point against the Admiralty and she is a 'B'. But I have no doubt the two for this year will be the larger size. I am dead against the policy of 'plenty of weak cruisers'. I am glad to say a satisfactory agreement was reached on numbers with the Admiralty, though we are still engaging in a laborious discussion about the expense.

When are you coming home on leave? Please let me know, as I greatly look forward to seeing you again. Send me back my papers after you have read them.

With all good wishes, believe me
Yours vy sincerely,
Winston S. Churchill

Winston S. Churchill to Sir Austen Chamberlain

(*Austen Chamberlain papers*)

6 January 1928   Chartwell Manor
Private

My dear Austen,

I will have the point mentioned in your letter about the Persian Debt examined in the Treasury, and naturally I will do the very best I can to meet your wishes. I must however first hear what the Department has to say.

I am absolutely counting on the China Indemnity to turn the corner this year, and I do trust you will help to your utmost to get this timely and substantial contribution. I really do not see how I can put on additional taxes for the purpose of paying our way.

I am sorry that I have had to hold up some Foreign Office requests about new Embassies in different parts of the world from sheer lack of means. We might talk about these matters when we meet. You know well the straits to which the occupants of my office are from time to time reduced.

I am relieved to see from your telegram to Lloyd that you do not contemplate any further alteration of the draft treaty, and I am sure before anything of that kind were done you would ask for a Cabinet. I am afraid that Sarwat will not make good, but that the draft treaty will remain on record, or even as you say be published, and will thence forward be held to bind us though not binding Egypt, and will be taken as a starting point for all further negotiations.

My wife tells me what a pleasant dinner and party you were at together last night. I wish I had been there! However I am always well content to be at home in the country.

With all good wishes for the New Year,
Believe me,
Yours vy sincerely
Winston S. Churchill

Winston S. Churchill to Stanley Baldwin

(*Baldwin papers*)

7 January 1928   Chartwell Manor

My dear Prime Minister,

Many thanks for your letter. I am rather glad that the Cabinet is postponed for a week or so as much activity of preparation is still going on and I shall be on surer ground towards the end of the month. Moreover, tomorrow night I am going to hunt the pig with Westminster in Normandy. 'Cras ingens iterabimus aequor.'[1] I shall be back on Wednesday however if all is well, and will go up to London on Thursday to see you. We might lunch at Bucks if you have nothing better to do. I shall be available from 11 o'clock on that day.

I send you a print of a very fine Memorandum by Hurst on this damnable question of the redistribution of rating relief and generally on the evils of the rating system. It is rather long but if you could find the time to read it, it would repay you.

It astounds me that successive Governments have allowed us to drift into this rating muddle, and have produced such forlorn monstrosities as the poverty-stricken suburb which no local authority will include in its boundaries if it can help it, and from which all productive industry is remorselessly driven. Of course I know very little about the rating system. None of my official work has brought me into contact with it. It is almost the only large block of our affairs of which I have had no ministerial experience. It is a mass of compromises, makeshifts and anomalies, and perhaps for this reason I find it very difficult to understand. Nevertheless both the need and the possibility of a great reform loom up through the fog. But never will you get that reform except on the flood tide (topical metaphor)[2] of some big financial scheme, such as I am now proposing, which conciliates farmers and manufacturers by a substantial boon, and which at the same time provides a douceur to the local authorities.

Yours vy sincerely,
Winston S. Churchill

Winston S. Churchill to Sir Richard Hopkins

(*Churchill papers: 18/85*)

7 January 1928

1. Sir Arthur Duckham should be made acquainted with these and other relevant papers.

2. I do not wish the deficit to be shown in a cumulative form. Each year should stand by itself. Obviously no additional assistance for the scheme is required until the year 1932, and then only to the extent of six or seven mil-

---

[1] The quotation, 'To morrow we journey over the boundless sea', is from Horace, *Odes*.

[2] During the first week of January 1928, melting snow had caused serious flooding throughout central and southern England. The river Medway in Kent spilled over its banks for several days, disrupting road and railway traffic, and inspiring a local writer to publish an article in *The Times* comparing the Medway to the Mississippi.

lions a year. This is satisfactory and can be accepted. Nevertheless an alternative should be worked out leaving half the rate burden on industry in the form of a national rate. This will greatly improve the finance. Let me see the tables corrected and amplified accordingly.

3. In all these papers I have dealt with the LF Tax on a basis of a flat 3d. This is a very good foundation on which to calculate the revenue and to test the financial aspect. But obviously very interesting and intricate questions arise as between the flat rate scheme and some of the variants designed to throw a heavier burden on the lighter oils. These must all be thrashed out after the general policy of proceeding with the scheme has been adopted. I have not at present formed any final opinion upon them. Customs and Excise should zealously explore alternatives and be in a position to advise on every point when and if we come to detail.

It will clearly be necessary to consult with the heads of the Oil companies beforehand and find out in what form the tax is least likely to be injurious to them. This follows the precedent of our negotiations with the Tobacco industry last year. As long as we get the important growing revenue you specified in the latest estimates the method of its collection must be most carefully adapted to secure the goodwill of the public and of the trade affected. I think it would probably be best for me to see Sir John Cadman[1] and Sir Robert Waley Cohen as soon as I know that the project is desired by the Prime Minister and the Cabinet. They would not of course be made parties to the whole scheme but only to the fact that we intended to raise a certain revenue by an LF tax and were inviting their suggestions as to the least disagreeable way of doing this.

Meanwhile the point at A (in red ink) requires further elucidation. Explain to me why companies refining crude oil in this country would be specially hit. I have always contemplated that the Refineries would be in bond. But I can see that that does not fully meet the competition of those companies who have no commitments in heavy oils. In this sphere it is important to hold the balance evenly between the two principal groups, the Anglo-Persian and the Shell, and not to favour one at the expense of the other.

I shall be glad to hear more from Customs and Excise about this aspect.

[1] John Cadman, 1877–1941. Manager of the Silverdale Collieries, North Staffordshire, 1900. Government Inspector of Mines, East Scotland, 1902; Stafford District, 1903. Government Mining Engineer, Trinidad, 1904. Professor of Mining and Petroleum Technology, Birmingham University, 1908–20. Knighted, 1918. Adviser to the Coal Mines Department of the Board of Trade. Petroleum Adviser to the Government. President of the Institute of Petroleum Technologists. Member of the Government's Industrial Transference Board, 1928; of the Economic Advisory Council, 1930; of the Television Committee, 1934. Created Baron, 1937. Chairman of the Anglo-Iranian Oil Company Ltd and the Iraq Petroleum Company Ltd.

I do not see why the tax on fuel oil would make it unmarketable. A great many small consumers are committed to its use for private plants, etc. I myself would have to pay double as much for my electric light engine fuel. I cannot however escape this and revert to coal; but I do not think the burden would be very heavy. Let me have a note on the past history of heavy fuel oil prices. Have they fallen by as much as 3d since the war?

I should gravely question the justification of the companies adding an extra 1d to their own expenses for such a small tax as is now proposed. I should have thought ½d would have more than met their extra charges.

On the whole it is very satisfactory that this tax should show so much expansion.

WSC

P. J. Grigg to Winston S. Churchill
(*Churchill papers: 18/85*)

13 January 1928   Treasury Chambers

My dear Chancellor,

Eyres-Monsell came in this morning after seeing the PM & asked me to send you two messages.

He is desperately anxious that you shd do what the PM declared to be impossible, viz separate in point of time *not* the relief & the reform, *but* the taxation and the whole scheme of relief & reform, ie he wants you to impose the taxation next year, indicate in a general way what you want it for & say that the considered scheme will be the first task in the new Parliament. He wants something to talk about in the General Election, not as having been given but as about to be given & he seemed to think that in these circumstances the extra taxation would not make any electoral difference.[1]

Winston S. Churchill to Sir Richard Hopkins and Frederick Leith-Ross
(*Churchill papers: 18/74*)

13 January 1928

PREMIUM BONDS

There is only one justification for the adoption of schemes of premium bonds or bonus shares, ie that it would encourage thrift among a wider

[1] Churchill noted, on Grigg's letter: 'I shall not touch it, except to put it through & I shall not tax for ord[inary] rev[enue] purposes.'

circle of the investing public and would interest the wage-earning masses. A wage earner at present is not attracted to save by the interest he will receive on his money. The prospect of saving enough for the interest to be a substantial contribution to the family livelihood is so remote that it does not enter his head. If by great thrift he can save £20, this will yield him in the Post Office Savings Bank between 10/- and 12/- a year. Not losing a couple of days' work will produce the same result. The whole field of *interest* lies outside the real life of the wage-earning home. Far too little saving is effected by the wage-earning classes. They have a hard struggle to make both ends meet, and every little luxury is highly taxed and very dear. New forms of expenditure—the wireless set, the cinema, the gramophone, above all the motor bicycle—are thrusting themselves seductively upon their attention. To live from hand to mouth, to enjoy what few pleasures may come their way, and to trust increasingly to the working of State Insurance schemes for old age, sickness and unemployment is the mood of the time. If a workman saves, it is not for the sake of interest, but to have a sum of money handy to meet an emergency or provide for a treat. The immense amount of gambling which already takes place, and the dangerous and unhealthy manner in which dog racing threatens to develop, reveal another aspect of the working class mood.

The question we have to consider is whether a form of investment can be offered to the wage-earner which will compete in allurement with the motor bicycle, the glass of beer or betting, but will conduct him to a more advantageous position than any of the above indulgences. If Thrift presents herself continually in a drab garb amid these bright coloured attractions, she will long continue to be ignored. A recognition of these facts forms the foundation of the compulsory thrift enforced by our vast system of National Insurance. This is available as a bulwark and lifebelt in case of the commoner forms of accident or disaster. Insurance however is no enemy to domestic waste or extravagance. For that a counter-attraction must be provided which holds its place in the wage-earner's mind.

I am of opinion that a system of capital accretion like the Savings Certificates, combined with a system of drawings—the two together being the substitute for interest—would make a powerful appeal to the wage-earner and would have the effect of leading to the gradual accumulation of a large amount of capital in working class hands, which otherwise would merely have been consumed. If this were so, it would be a justification in itself for the departure from our present principles, irrespective of any bearing it might have upon conversion of debt or of Savings Certificates. The sole test by which all schemes must be judged is—would they lead over a period of years to an accumulation of capital in working class hands?

As contributions to the Debt problem all such schemes appear to me to be ineffectual and almost inappreciable, and I agree with the various adverse arguments put forward by Mr Phillips[1] and Mr Leith-Ross and others on this point. Moreover the introduction of what would no doubt be called State lotteries into British finance would have a detrimental effect upon our financial prestige. Nothing would prevent it from being represented as a sign of strain and as a resort to laxer Latin methods. I weigh this argument of prestige or *morale* as high in national finance as in actual war.

Nevertheless, difficult as it is to balance the opposite considerations of an increased capital accumulation by the working classes on the one hand and a certain smirching of our financial correctitude on the other, I incline in favour of the former to the extent at any rate of wishing to see the best possible scheme prepared. My general ideas are as follows:—

The scheme should cost the State no more than 3%. The bonds should carry no interest, but like a Bank note be always redeemable at par. The bonds would have a currency of ten years. If held for the full ten years, they would be repayable with compound interest at 1%. The other 2% would be distributed in quarterly drawings upon the principle that one bond in (say) a hundred received the usufruct of the other ninety nine, ie that the hundredth bond received concentrated interest. There would be no large prizes. The bonds would be issued in small series of (say) a thousand, or at the outside ten thousand; and the drawings, quarterly (or biennially as might be decided) would be confined always within the limits of that particular group.

The figures are only token figures, and the intention is that the winners should receive not less than ten to twenty times their holding.

But when the drawing has taken place and the hundredth bondholder has received the interest of the other ninety-nine, we do not want him to take that money and spend it, but on the contrary to re-invest it in the scheme. In consequence he will be offered as an alternative to the concentrated interest a further and still more favourable investment in the shape of a 'Star Bond'. The extra inducements for this can readily be elaborated. The money for them would be found by the savings effected by the State through the fact that many bonds would be held for a certain number of years without interest and then thrown up before they acquired their accumulated 1% compound interest at the end of the tenth year. All the advantage of this, whatever it might be, would go to create further inducements for the owners of winning bonds to re-invest in a special class of security with larger prizes and other additional advantages, including always in every case immediate

[1] Frederick Phillips, 1884–1943. Entered the Treasury in 1908; Principal Assistant Secretary, 1927; Under-Secretary, 1932. Knighted, 1933. Treasury Representative in the United States, 1940–3.

repayment at par. The governing principle would be that the State paid 3%
on all the money invested, and no more; but that the whole yield and profit
went into the scheme which would be self-contained, and inure continually
to the benefit of its participants. Pray have this examined in the Treasury
with a view to giving the most workable expression to the idea and not
simply of pulling it to pieces.

On the general question, this matter will probably be the subject of a
debate in the early part of next Session. I shall encourage its ventilation on
a Private Member's motion. In the meanwhile, apart from the foregoing
paragraph, I should like the subject re-explored by the kind of informal
Committee suggested. Sir Herbert Hambling[1] advocated premium bonds
to me with great insistence a few weeks ago, and I think it would be very
suitable if he were added to the three members mentioned by Mr Leith-Ross
in his minute on 1A.

Before taking action pray let me have your comments upon these ideas of
mine.

Winston S. Churchill to Harold Macmillan

(Churchill papers: 18/85)

15 January 1928
Private

My dear Macmillan,

I considered your statement of the pros and cons for the P Tax *versus* leaving one-third on the Rates so lucid and well balanced that I sent it to the
Prime Minister. I thought it would interest you to know that he spoke to
me about it on Thursday in extremely complimentary terms. Have you yet
had time to read the various papers that are accumulating and which await
you in my private office? I am bringing the whole issue before the Cabinet
on Friday.

Yours vy sincerely,
Winston S. Churchill

[1] Herbert Hambling, 1857–1932. Entered the service of the London and South Western
Bank at the age of 18; General Manager, 1911. Member of the Financial Advisory Committee
of the Ministry of Munitions, 1916–17. Knighted, 1917. Finance Member of the Munitions
Council, 1917–18. Deputy Chairman of Barclays Bank from 1918 until his death. Director
of several marine insurance companies. President of the Institute of Bankers, 1923–5.
Created Baronet, 1924. Government nominated Director of Imperial Airways, 1923–30.

Winston S. Churchill: departmental memorandum[1]

(Churchill papers: 18/71)

15 January 1928
Secret

To make assurance doubly sure I take this opportunity of repeating formally what I have several times said in conversation, ie that the first immediate objective of Treasury policy must be to prevent a deficit in the current year, and that this must have priority over all other considerations, until such time as you are satisfied all danger has passed away. Pray give me timely notice of any unsatisfactory development; and meanwhile consider and explore every possible method of meeting such dangers, should they appear.

WSC

Winston S. Churchill to William Bridgeman

(Churchill papers: 22/175)

16 January 1928   Treasury Chambers

My dear First Lord,

1. I have received with much concern your letter of the 21st December, sending me your proposals for next year's Estimates. I explained to the Cabinet on December 15th that the threatening deficit required that the cost of the Navy in 1928 should be restricted to £56 millions net. Your letter however leaves the net figure no less than £330,000 above the Estimates of the current year (£58 millions). It is impossible to balance the Budget without additional taxation unless economies at least equivalent to those indicated in the scheme outlined by me to the Cabinet and now circulated in my paper CP 323 (27) are put into effect.

The failure of any one Department to achieve its quota of economies throws an equivalent amount upon another Department. When however the quota, as in your case, amounts to £2 millions, no other Department or Departments can make good the difference. I must ask you, therefore, as a matter of decisive financial importance, to revise your figures in accordance with the position disclosed to the Cabinet on December 15th.

2. In your letter to the Prime Minister of August 24th you wrote 'I do urge that when the Cabinet Committee requires figures as to Naval expenditure, it should get authentic figures from me, and that when it has decided

---

[1] Churchill circulated this memorandum to Sir Warren Fisher, Sir Richard Hopkins, Sir Ernest Gowers and Sir Francis Floud.

at what reduction the Admiralty are to aim, it should leave it to me and my advisers to consider under what heads reductions can be made.' I will not therefore at this stage enter into detailed figures, but I venture to suggest that in making your present proposals you have not taken full account of the favourable political situation, especially as regards Japan, now existing or of the decision of the Government that no great war need be anticipated for at least ten years.[1] On this basis I earnestly hope that in your review of the whole matter you will find it possible amongst other things, to reconsider the items mentioned in the following paragraphs.

3. OIL FUEL.

I trust that you will not press your proposal to provide in 1928 Estimates for increasing purchases by 230,000 tons for additions to the reserve, and I would urge you in this exceptional year to find the 100,000 tons which have been added to reserve in each of the past two years by economy in the movement of the Fleet, so as to restrict the total purchases in 1928 to approximately 770,000 tons. Have you made full allowance for the lower prices now current (which may also be expected to obtain as regards coal)?

4. RE-ARMAMENT.

I should be glad to have an opportunity of going more fully at leisure into your large schemes involving expenditure over a series of years in the case of cordite, torpedoes and anti-aircraft guns and ammunition. These schemes may well be desirable or necessary. But the rate at which they require to be executed must be settled in the light of the facts mentioned in paragraph 2. Doubtful cordite, if likely to endanger life and vessels, must of course be removed from ships. The period of replenishing reserves might well however be spread over the next eight years, instead of four. The recent history of the Admiralty cordite policy seems to show extravagance: a rate of production far beyond what the Geddes Committee thought necessary: a very large accumulation in reserve; sudden discovery that the greater part of this reserve is 'doubtful'; demand to scrap it and replace it with equally improvident rapidity.

I suggest also that the scheme of anti-aircraft armament should be post-

---

[1] Just over three years earlier, on 26 November 1924, Baldwin's Cabinet had recorded in its conclusions: 'The desirability and practicability of renewing the decision taken by the Cabinet Committee on Finance on August 11th, 1919, that the Fighting Services should proceed on the assumption that no great war is to be anticipated within the next ten years, although provision should be made for the possible expansion of trained units in case of an emergency arising.' Six months later, in June 1928, the Cabinet approved Churchill's suggestion that this 'Ten Year Rule' should remain in operation, unless specifically altered (see page 1302 of this volume).

poned for this year. In any case, before agreeing to the latter, I should
think it essential to know what is the opinion of the Air Council on the
question whether the large expenditure involved is likely to be justified by
the probable results against aircraft attack.

5. NEW CONSTRUCTION.

It is to be expected that the agreed postponement of the cruisers should be
accompanied by an equivalent reduction in the expense of new construction.
The date of beginning the two 1928 cruisers is already fixed for the end of
March 1929. But what dates are you proposing for the Minor Programme? I
trust that by retarding this and by other means you will be able to secure a
reduction upon 1927 of something like £1,500,000 on new construction
instead of the £400,000 you offer.

For the purpose of further discussion I should be glad if you would let me
have a detailed analysis of your proposed expenditure split up into the
various annual programmes and show me the proposed dates of beginning
each individual vessel. If you can meet me on the total, I should raise no
objection to your proceeding next year with the four new Sloops as you
propose.

6. PERSONNEL.

I beg you to give further consideration, as regards both officers and men,
to the important recommendations made by the Colwyn Committee on the
subject of the manning of the Fleet (paragraphs 33 and 36 IB of their
Report). No action whatever appears to have been taken on these recommendations, and in view of the present urgency of economy, I feel that they
ought now to be seriously considered by the Admiralty. If necessary, I would
ask you to consider the question of laying up to reserve, or putting on a high
care and maintenance basis, a certain number of battleships and cruisers
with corresponding economies in personnel and material. Such a step would
also give an opportunity for adding to the reserves of oil fuel by economy in
fuel consumption.

7. SINGAPORE.

The recent report by Lieut Gen Sir Webb Gillman[1] and the covering
memorandum by the Secretary of State for War (304-C) shows that the

---

[1] Webb Gillman, 1870–1933. Entered the Royal Field Artillery, 1889; Captain, 1899.
On active service in South Africa, 1899–1900, Nigeria, 1902, and the western front, 1914–18.
Lieutenant-Colonel, 1914; Major-General, 1918. Knighted, 1919. Commandant, Royal
Marine Academy, 1920–4. Inspector of Artillery, War Office, 1924–7. Master-General of
the Ordnance, 1927–31. General Officer Commander-in-Chief, Eastern Command, from
1931 until his death.

nature and extent of the Singapore scheme requires careful reconsideration and suggests that considerable economies should be obtained on the original plan of military defence. Clearly there may be reactions on the Naval plans. I hope therefore that you will consult me before any contract for the main work is let, and I suggest that it would be desirable to restrict expenditure in 1928 on the preliminary works programme.

8. Finally I should be grateful if you would specify in somewhat greater detail the reductions which you anticipate in Appropriations in Aid and the reasons for the falling off in each case, and would also let me have particulars of the Reconstruction programme. I notice that in dealing with Dockyard numbers you allude to a falling off in reconstruction, but you do not specify what is the saving on this account.

9. May I beg you to treat the matter as one of great urgency and to let me know at a very early date what is the result of your further review. It will be necessary for me to ask the Cabinet to have another discussion in the course of this month on the whole question of expenditure in 1928 in the light of the responses to my Cabinet Paper CP 323 (27). I should be prepared after this Cabinet—assuming that we have not reached any agreement—to propose a series of reductions which could be submitted seriatim to a Cabinet Committee. But I hope it will be possible for us by agreement to avoid this exhausting procedure.

Yours very sincerely,
WSC

Winston S. Churchill to Lord Burnham
(Churchill papers: 2/157)

16 January 1928

My dear Burnham,

It was with many feelings of regret that I read the momentous announcement of the sale of THE DAILY TELEGRAPH and of its severance from you and your family.[1] I have been a regular reader since those very early days in 1897 when I was its War Correspondent. During all these thirty years its policy has always been fair, and wise and patriotic; and it has been

---

[1] Lord Burnham, the principal proprietor of the *Daily Telegraph*, had sold the newspaper to Sir William Berry (later Lord Camrose), Sir Gomer Berry (later Lord Kemsley) and Sir Edward Iliffe (later Lord Iliffe). In 1937 Lord Camrose acquired the interests of Lord Kemsley and Lord Iliffe. In 1966 Lord Camrose was succeeded as Editor-in-Chief by his son Michael Berry (later Lord Hartwell). From 1924 to 1950 the Managing Editor was Arthur Watson.

a pleasure amid so many changeabilities to see one cool, steady and comprehensive outlook consistently maintained. All this is due to you, and it distresses me that your task is now ended. Let me however take this opportunity of thanking you for the invariable courtesy and kindness with which, even in times of the sharpest political opposition, your paper has always treated me.

With kindest regards, believe me

Winston S. Churchill to Lord Balfour

(*Balfour papers*)

20 January 1928   Treasury Chambers

My dear Arthur,

I unfolded the plan of wh I told you in September to the Cabinet this morning. We only mustered 14—luckily not 13! & the reception, as you will see from the Cabinet papers, was on the whole vy favourable. They seemed a little oppressed with the amount of labour wh wd be involved; but after all, the bulk of this will fall on me,—I am quite ready to undertake it, & pretty sure I can produce a satisfactory result.

I send you herewith the first printed copy of the paper I am circulating to the Cabinet—an egg hot from the hen! There are only two points to add to it, (1) the scheme is self-contained financially,—does not cost me a groat. Therefore anything I can save or find in '28 & '29 is still free for actual concessions to other tax-payers, & a good Dissolution Budget is in no way compromised. Secondly, we cannot dissolve before the young ladies have reached the register in May; but at any time after that, even tho' the longer Rating Bill was only introduced, we cd go to the country, if convenient, on the issue *inter alia* of these large rate-reductions: therefore we are not fettered in any way.

I trust you are regathering strength after those vy severe teething troubles. I heard from Hankey that you were demanding papers, & was encouraged to think that you wd like to have this line from me.

With all good wishes,
Believe me
Yours always,
Winston S.C.

Winston S. Churchill: memorandum[1]

(*Churchill papers: 18/85*)

20 January 1928
Secret
To Be Kept Under Lock and Key

It is requested that special care may be taken to ensure the secrecy of this document

A PLAN

To relieve and encourage Manufacturing Producers by reducing in October 1929 their rate burden on the average by two-thirds, and Agricultural Producers by abolishing their rates entirely, and freeing both of them from the uncertainties and variations of an antiquated rating system, thus helping Trade and Employment: To raise for this purpose a revenue rising from £15 millions in 1928 to £23 millions in 1933 by a Tax on Imported Liquid Fuel with Protective effect upon the British Coal Trade and stimulus to scientific methods of treating Coal: To correct by both processes the present unfair conditions between Road and Rail transport: To remove the deterrents upon successful industry in the necessitous areas: To give assistance to hard-pressed local authorities: To further the projects of the Ministry of Health and the Ministry of Transport for the creation of wider areas for Poor Relief and Road Administration respectively: and To reform the relations of National and Local Finance through the establishment of a scheme of Block Grants to take the place of percentage grants for Health services and the obsolete system of Assigned Revenues.

II. THE SCOPE OF THE RELIEF

6. The primary object of the present plan is to accord to all producers a large and ultimately complete relief from rating in respect of all property used for the manual and mechanical processes of production, starting from the winning of the natural supplies and including the various stages of transport and conversion culminating in the finished article of commerce. It is not suggested that producers should be placed in any preferential position over other ratepayers in regard to property still generally rateable; in so far as they occupy residential accommodation, offices, sale-rooms, garages, &c, they will continue to be assessed as at present. On the other hand, premises

[1] This memorandum is the revised and enlarged version of Churchill's memorandum of 12 December 1927 (printed on pages 1128–37). Only the additional paragraphs are printed here. As revised, this memorandum was circulated to the Cabinet as Cabinet paper 8 of 1928, following the Cabinet meeting of 20 January 1928.

used for gainful productive purposes will enjoy relief even when occupied by public authorities or charitable institutions.

The definition of productive purposes can obviously be drawn in various ways. In the present plan we have adopted a provisional definition, printed in Appendix B, which includes not only agriculture, mines, mills, factories, workshops, &c, but also such public utility services as railways, canals, docks, and the supply of power, light and heat, the cost of which represents a very considerable element in the total cost of production. It is suggested, however, that the mutually complementary services of water supply and drainage should remain rateable and that the transport services operating upon the public highway should continue to contribute directly to its upkeep. Out of a total of over £175 millions now paid in rates, it is estimated that rather more than one-fifth—say £38 millions—is being paid on property comprised within the definition.

Much study has been expended upon a so-called Profits Tax, and no insuperable technical difficulties in levying it need be apprehended. Nevertheless, I have decided to discard the plan of a Profits Tax. It would be a new tax, or rather a dug-up embodiment of the lately repealed Corporation Profits Tax. Manufacturers would be afraid that once reimposed, even on a small scale, it might be used in bad hands as a means of extortion. The process of passing it through the House would constitute an onerous feature of the Finance Bill, and would tend to rivet attention upon the less pleasing aspects of the policy.

Instead of remitting the whole of the Rates in exchange for a Profits Tax equal to one-third of them in the aggregate, the relief might be limited to two-thirds in the first instance. Instead of saying, 'We will let you off all your Rates in exchange for a Profits Tax,' we could say simply, 'We will let you off two-thirds of your Rates.' We should be presenting a somewhat smaller rose, but without a thorn.

But it would be a poor way of working merely to leave upon the producer one-third of his Rates as at present levied. The uncertainty of what the Rates would be, the disparities between districts, the high Rates of the necessitous areas, the uncertainty of new assessments, the penalty of new and higher assessments for every improvement or extention of the business—all in fact of the vices and anomalies, which it is a fundamental part of the policy to denounce and remedy, would be left reduced only in scale. Our arguments would be to a considerable extent stultified, and clear presentation would be confused. I accordingly reject this alternative also in favour of a plan which embodies the advantages of the Profits Tax in its uniformity, certainty and generous relief to the more oppressed areas, while it avoids its complications and political objections.

15. It is proposed that, in lieu of the rates of which they are relieved, the non-agricultural producers shall pay to the Exchequer a National Rate assessed on the reduction in the rateable value of their property granted to them in the datum year 1928, and of an amount sufficient at the outset to produce the required £13 millions—probably about 5/- in the £. Neither the 5/- rate nor the datum year assessments on which it is based will be alterable from year to year, except on *ad hoc* appeals in respect of property whose rateable value is claimed by the owners to have declined. As, however, it is intended that the retention in principle of one-third of the Rates is in itself only to be a temporary expedient for the first one or two five-year periods, no new property or extensions of old property will be the subject of new assessments or be required to bear any charge. Thus all complications and deterrents upon industry arising from the uncertainty of local rate increases or of new assessment on extensions or new businesses, will be eliminated. All non-agricultural producers will pay at the same rate in all parts of the country, and the maximum of relief will be afforded to the most heavily rated areas.

17. On the basis that the Liquid Fuel Tax is imposed this year and its proceeds are accumulated in a Suspensory Fund, and that the first payments of rating relief do not begin till October 1929, the finance of the whole scheme is according to my estimates solvent and self-contained up to the year 1933 inclusive. The following table shows the out-turn year by year for the next six years:—

Year	Receipts					Payments	Surplus + or Deficit − on Year	Suspensory Fund at end of Year
	LF Tax	Nat Rate	Sched D*	Interest	Total			
	£m	£m	£m	£m	£m	£m	£m	£m
1928	15	...	...	0·3	15·3	...	+15·3	15·3
1929	19	6·5	...	0·7	26·2	20·5	+5·7	21·0
1930	20	13	0·5	0·7	34·2	41·0	−6·8	14·2
1931	21	13	2·0	0·5	36·5	41·0	−4·5	9·7
1932	22	13	3·0	0·3	38·3	41·0	−2·7	7·0
1933	23	13	3·0	0·2	39·2	41·0	−1·8	5·2

* Rates are legal deduction from the computation of profits for assessments of Income Tax under Schedule D. A proportion of the burden is therefore already borne by the State and the new charge upon the Exchequer is diminished accordingly.

I think it is right to present such a definite financial forecast for a large new scheme. But even were the forecast less satisfactory, I should look confidently forward to the normal growth of revenue through the expansion of population and wealth, and to the increased yield of our existing taxation through the revival of trade prosperity and the disappearance of the dead weight of unemployment which it is the object of these proposals to promote.

18. Lest it be thought this scheme can be introduced in instalments or dallied with, I now point out that all turns upon the imposing of the Liquid Fuel Tax in the coming Budget. It is only through the Suspensory Fund created in advance by the Liquid Fuel Tax that the finance of the scheme will balance. On the other hand I cannot introduce the Liquid Fuel Tax merely for the purpose of paying our way or increasing the revenue, without announcing at the same time the reliefs which are in prospect. Under the present time table the extra taxation will be imposed and got out of the way this year; and the much larger reliefs will very nearly synchronise with the end of the Parliament, and will either have been actually accorded or be within grasp at the moment of the General Election. Obviously it would be foolish to impose the Liquid Fuel Tax in 1929 and have all that row going on with the certainty that no relief could be given by the authority of the present Parliament, and the uncertainty whether we should be in a position to give it in the next. It is therefore now or never for the plan, and the Budget date is zero hour.

The Ministry of Transport is faced with an ever-growing demand for more aid to hard-pressed rural authorities, while it is anxious to secure greater efficiency and economy in the maintenance of our highway system by concentrating the administration in the hands of the County authorities. Both Departments are faced with almost insuperable obstacles in the parochialism of the existing authorities and the unfortunate financial reactions of either scheme when taken alone. The present scheme incorporates the aims and plans of the two Departments in one indivisible whole; and, as explained in the Treasury memorandum, it provides powerful arguments, both political and financial, which should suffice to overbear the forces which have hitherto obstructed these reforms.

20. These questions of Local Government Reform are of course the peculiar responsibility of the Minister of Health. While I understand that he is in sympathy with a great part of the present scheme, I have not as yet been able to reach complete agreement with him on certain important questions of principle. In the Treasury view a mere proportionate reduction of the

present Rates on Industry, on the lines of that conceded to Agriculture in the past, with an Exchequer grant to make good the loss, could not lead to a satisfactory permanent settlement. The history of agricultural rates is an object lesson. It began in 1896 with a half reduction of the rates on land and a fixed grant of the immediate loss sustained by Local Authorities. The second phase was reached in 1923 with a further relief of a quarter of the full assessment and a new grant to make good the loss, this time a variable grant changing with the actual loss from year to year. The third phase is already appearing in the resolutions passed by the Agricultural Committee of the House of Commons and other bodies interested in agriculture, demanding the complete exemption of agricultural land from all Rates, and of course another grant to make good the loss. All these grants have been sops, and not a vestige of reform has been achieved for the heavy expenditure involved. Even had it been consistent with the underlying principles of the present scheme to leave industrial enterprise still subject, though in a reduced measure, to the uneconomic, uncertain and unequal burden of local rates, a compensatory grant from the Exchequer on the lines of the Agricultural Rates Act of 1923 would be unsound. The Exchequer would find itself paying a percentage of the expenditure in every rating area in the country, the percentage varying between wide limits but on no systematic basis, the highest proportion being given as a rule where the forces making for economical government are least developed. Such a result would be, alike from the national and local Government standpoints, a veritable disaster.

The argument that if industrial property is relieved from all contribution to local rates, the influence which manufacturers, &c, exert in local affairs will *pro tanto* be diminished, would apply for what it is worth even more to a scheme on Agricultural Rates Act lines. The producers indeed would have been removed, wholly or partly, from the zone of uncertainty and extortion. But in their place the Exchequer would be invited to assume the function of milch cow, and of a milch cow of almost unlimited capacity. I would therefore rather see the scheme abandoned than expose the Exchequer to such perils.

Personally I doubt (and such information as I have been able to gather confirms me in my doubts) whether producers, other than farmers, do in fact exercise any considerable influence on local affairs, especially in those areas in which the forces making for extravagant expenditure on social services are most powerful. The industries have virtually no voting power. But in the last resort they can threaten in protest against extravagance to quit the district, costly though such a removal may be. Some substitute for this albeit despairing check must be devised, and a substitute which shall operate at a much earlier point in the progress of local extravagance. The present scheme contemplates that for the Rates hitherto received from industrial property, a new form of revenue in the shape of a Block Grant revised only at five-yearly intervals shall be substituted. At the outset the actual loss in each area would be made good; no Local Authority would be worse off; but any extra revenue given to ease the passage of the new scheme and to provide for further development of social services, in addition to the revenue which is to take the place of the percentage and other discontinued grants, would be fixed according to general considerations and be independent of local expenditure. Thus such spasmodic influence as producers may have been able to exert on local administration would give place to the more powerful, direct and continuing pressure of the local electors, who would experience in greater measure than at present the ill-effects of extravagant administration and on the other hand enjoy in greater degree the fruits of thrifty management.

21. It will be observed, however, from the Treasury memorandum (Appendix D) that, to achieve a satisfactory distribution of new revenue on this basis, wider areas of administration for poor relief and roads are essential; and the whole policy is therefore intermingled with reforms which the Ministry of Health and the Ministry of Transport have long had in mind. There can be no such favourable opportunity for achieving these reforms as is offered by the present proposals.

But if this opportunity is to be used to the best advantage, the temptation to proceed with the measures of relief by themselves, while leaving to a later date the difficult questions of Local Government Reform, must be resisted. Under such conditions we should pay the price and never get the reforms.

22. The following would appear to be the necessary sequence of events: First, the imposition of the Liquid Fuel Tax in the Budget of 1928, so as to begin the accumulation of the Suspensory Fund; secondly, if the relief is to operate from October 1929, a Bill must be passed this summer providing for an apportionment of the rateable value in each area between property which is under the scheme to cease to be rateable locally, and other property. This apportionment of the valuation is estimated to require twelve months to carry through. These are the urgent matters.

It will also be necessary some time before October 1929 for legislation to be passed: (a) altering the basis of rating industrial property and providing for a levy of a national rate to be paid with the proceeds of the Liquid Fuel Tax to the central fund; (b) abolishing the system of Assigned Revenues to clear the way for the Block Grants scheme of the Ministry of Health; (c) providing for the new distribution of the revenue from the central fund to make good the deficiencies in local revenues due to the exemption of industrial property and also to provide the new Block Grant; (d) carrying through the Ministry of Health's scheme of Poor Law Reform, including the adoption of the County and County Borough as the future areas of administration; and (*e*) transferring from the District Councils to the County Councils the responsibility for highways other than residential streets. As long as the legislation adopting the County basis for poor relief and rates is on the Statute Book by October 1929, there is no insuperable objection to the relief provisions of the scheme being allowed to operate as from that date, although a further period may elapse before the actual administration of so complicated a service as the Poor Law can in fact be handed over to the new authorities.

It may, however, be pointed out that after the unfolding of the full programme in the next Budget, the Government would always be in a strong tactical position for dealing with any obstructive measures in the House of Commons or challenge by the Opposition. At any time it could interrupt its legislative programme and appeal to the country on the whole scheme for the relief of rates and for the abolition of agricultural rates, throwing upon the Opposition the responsibility for the postponement of the promised benefits.

VI. UNITED ACTION

23. We all feel in the concluding phase of this Parliament the lack of any constructive and comprehensive plan for dealing with clamant social problems. Five or six Departments of State have been making independently their contributions. The Ministry of Health seek to deal with Poor Law reform, and at the same time to grapple with the problem which confronts them in the necessitous areas. The Ministry of Labour are preoccupied with Unemployment, a remedy for which is from all sides demanded. The Ministry of Transport is faced with an immense programme of Road reconstruction to meet the ever-growing traffic which our system of local taxation is encouraging on to the roads, largely at the expense of the railways. The Ministry of Agriculture pleads the woes of the farmers; and our Conservative Agricultural Committee in the House of Commons has just demanded, apparently as an exceptional largesse, the complete relief of agricultural rates. The Mines Department is daily confronted with the depression on the coal fields and the resulting unemployment and distress. From every side we hear the cry of the basic industries for some relief from rates and social services. Month by month the Board of Trade statistics point to the adverse trade balance and the difficulty in maintaining our indispensable quantum of exports.

But all efforts undertaken independently, however well conceived, will fall by the way. They encounter all the resistances of petty interests and all the eddies and cross-currents of partial solutions, without having the indispensable driving power. That driving power can only be provided by money. The money which can be obtained—and I believe comparatively easily and painlessly obtained—through the Liquid Fuel Tax—will afford not only the necessary impulse, but the medium which unites and at the same time simplifies all these problems in a common solution. All can be dealt with together. None can be handled apart. We have, therefore, to choose, and choose in the next six weeks, between a positive constructive policy in its integrity or just carrying on and hoping that things will grow better—as no doubt they often do—of themselves.

24. There is no need, however, to exaggerate the scale of the operation. There is nothing to prevent it being achieved, or virtually achieved, in the present Parliament. There is nothing in it which, if it were challenged (and it certainly will be), would prevent an earlier appeal to the constituencies, if we thought it opportune. The only levers at our disposal are financial. £40 millions obtained at a certain cost in national life-strength are not overwhelming. But we are not using money as a mere expense, but as a motive and combining power. I wish the levers were larger. They are, however, serious and potent, and I do not know from what quarters their equals in power and practicability can be found.

WSC

Cabinet minutes[1]

(*Churchill papers: 18/85*)

20 January 1928
11 am
Secret

THE CHANCELLOR OF THE EXCHEQUER described a plan he had devised to relieve and encourage manufacturing producers by reducing their rate burden on the average by two-thirds, and agricultural producers by

---

[1] The Ministers who spoke at this meeting were Churchill, Cunliffe-Lister (President of the Board of Trade), Walter Guinness (Minister of Agriculture and Fisheries) and Neville Chamberlain (Minister of Health). The other Ministers mentioned in the Minutes were Sir Laming Worthington-Evans (Secretary of State for War), Sir John Gilmour (Secretary of State for Scotland) and Lord Eustace Percy (President of the Board of Education).

abolishing their rates entirely, and freeing both of them from the uncertainties and variations of an antiquated rating system, thus helping trade and employment: to raise for this purpose a revenue by a tax, of which particulars were given to the Cabinet: to correct by both processes the present unfair conditions between road and rail transport: to remove the deterrents upon successful industry in the necessitous areas: to give assistance to hard-pressed Local Authorities: to further the projects of the Ministry of Health and Ministry of Transport for the creation of wider areas for Poor Relief and Road Administration respectively: and to reform the relations of national and local finance through the establishment of a system of block grants instead of percentage grants in health services.

The Chancellor of the Exchequer undertook to circulate particulars of his plan forthwith. While he had little doubt as to the feasibility of his plan, Mr Churchill particularly desired the advice of his colleagues as to whether the substantial relief which it would give to producers would be sufficiently popular to justify the exertions required to finance the scheme.

A preliminary discussion on these proposals then took place, in the course of which the PRESIDENT OF THE BOARD OF TRADE stated that he had had an examination made of the effects of the scheme on the principal industries of the country, and he was convinced that the benefit to our hard-pressed industries would be so great that the scheme ought to receive the most careful consideration. He gave particulars of the advantages that might be expected to accrue to certain of our staple industries, including steel, shipbuilding, coal, engineering, textiles.

THE MINISTER OF AGRICULTURE AND FISHERIES considered that, from the agricultural point of view, it was impossible to exaggerate the importance of the scheme.

THE MINISTER OF HEALTH, while supporting the principle underlying the scheme, namely, that a larger burden should be borne by the taxpayer and some relief given to the producer, reserved his opinion in regard to certain of the details. He doubted if the revenue to be raised from taxation would be sufficient to compensate the Local Authorities for the loss of rates. He viewed with some anxiety the possibility that, when relieved from rates, manufacturers would withdraw from all active participation in local government. And he apprehended that in some districts the Local Authorities would be deprived of so large a proportion of their rateable area as to make it impossible for them to carry out essential improvement schemes, such as water-supply or drainage.

The views expressed by other members of the Cabinet were favourable to the principle of the scheme, though doubts were raised on various points of detail and as to the time-table for carrying it into effect.

The Cabinet agreed—
(a) That a Cabinet Committee, composed as follows:—

> The Chancellor of the Exchequer (In the Chair),
> The Secretary of State for War (on his return from India),
> The Secretary of State for Scotland,
> The President of the Board of Trade,
> The Minister of Health,
> The Minister of Agriculture and Fisheries,
> The President of the Board of Education

—should meet to consider the Chancellor of the Exchequer's proposal as set forth in his Memorandum (Paper CP 8 (28)) with a view to advising the Cabinet as to whether it would be possible to carry it into effect during the present year:
(b) That, as soon as the Committee has reported, the Cabinet should consider the political aspects of the question with a view to a decision as to the adoption of the scheme:
(c) *THAT EVERY CARE SHOULD BE TAKEN TO KEEP THE SCHEME SECRET AT THE PRESENT STAGE.*

Winston S. Churchill to A. M. Samuel

(Churchill papers: 18/72)

23 January 1928

My dear Financial Secretary,

Many thanks for showing me the speech you propose to deliver shortly. As it will be your first important speech on assuming your new office it is probable that it will attract the particular attention of those who wish to find fault with us. I must say I think it would be a mistake for the Financial Secretary to the Treasury to deliver an argument the whole purpose of which is to show that all is for the best in the best of all possible worlds; that economy ranks supreme in all our affairs; that we should be 'traitors' unless we 'instantly' stopped all 'wastefulness'; that practically nothing more remains to be done and that the country is very lucky to have its expenditure so well controlled. Undoubtedly such a line of argument would be held most inappropriate in the holder of your office; moreover it is not I think justified. I still believe the expenditure of the country is capable of substantial reduction and that a great deal of waste, some of it avoidable, goes on. It is above all things our duty at the Treasury to strive to reduce the expenditure, and even if we find the task very difficult it would be fatal to utter a cry of despair, still more to give a whitewashing certificate to the spending departments.

My political experience makes me sure that such a speech by you would be singled out for censure in important Conservative newspapers, and would weaken your personal position and future usefulness. There is no harm in reciting some of the many difficulties which prevent sensational reductions, but even here I advise you to stick to the figures as presented in the Hurst memorandum of last year and not confuse public discussion by starting a set of personal variants of these very carefully considered figures. In the main however the only note which is appropriate to your office is an earnest, resolute and tireless policy of reducing expenditure and alleviating the crushing burdens which its present excessive height throws upon industry and saving power.

I may add (though this must not be foreshadowed in public in any way) that such a speech as you have drafted would I believe be entirely stultified by the actual facts I hope to present to Parliament in opening the Budget.

I have asked Mr Upcott[1] to put himself at your disposal in case you should wish to re-cast your remarks and bring them into closer accordance with the Treasury position.

> Yours very sincerely,
> Winston S. Churchill

Winston S. Churchill to A. C. Sheepshanks

(*Churchill papers: 1/199*)

24 January 1928
Private and Confidential

Dear Mr Sheepshanks,

Randolph has left us today. He has come on a great deal in the last few months, and his mind is developing fast. I am extremely pleased at his taking his School Certificate with so much time in hand. We think he might well now attempt a History Scholarship at Christchurch. He is going to stay with Professor Lindemann for two days before returning to Eton, and will have his interest turned in that direction by those who actually examine for these scholarships. Pray let me know what you advise and how this matter could be facilitated at Eton. I understand that it is possible for boys to specialise

---

[1] Gilbert Charles Upcott, 1880–1967. Educated at Marlborough and Corpus Christi College, Oxford. Entered the Treasury in 1903; Deputy Controller, 1921–31; Comptroller and Auditor-General, Exchequer and Audit Department, 1931–46. Knighted, 1933.

to a considerable extent on the particular subjects in which they are interested, after they have taken the School Certificate. I trust he will not be
consuming any more time than is absolutely necessary in Latin. Greek, thank
Heaven, is at an end forever. Randolph will, I am sure, do well if he is
encouraged to work for definite objects like passing an examination or gaining a scholarship.

We have managed to get him a little hunting this year. He rides extraordinarily well to hounds, and in spite of his very brief experience gives every
sign of becoming a bold and skilful horseman and a real lover of the chase.

There is just one point I should like to mention to you. He is now half way
to seventeen, and I think it would be a mistake if he were to be caned in the
House without any serious cause. I presume that you are always informed in
these cases beforehand by the Head of the House. As boys begin to grow up
an incident of this kind, without just and good cause, might well have an
embittering effect upon a mind rapidly forming and already in some respects startlingly mature. Randolph of course does not know I am writing in
this way.

With good wishes for a successful and prosperous term, believe me

Winston S. Churchill to Stanley Baldwin
(*Churchill papers: 18/77*)

29 January 1928

My dear Prime Minister,

I send you herewith a report of what has happened as the result of the
efforts to find £11 millions economies. You will see that, in spite of the unexpected saving of over £1 million on the Post Office, we are little more than
half way towards realising the indispensable sum. It will be necessary for me
to obtain the Boxer money to meet the expense of keeping our troops in
China. I am inclined to think from the wording of Austen's letter to me that,
while he will oppose the surrender of the money, he will submit to a Cabinet
decision in its favour. This money is of course absolutely necessary to me.

The second important item is the Navy. Some months ago the Economy
Committee sent some suggestions to the Admiralty, and Bridgeman replied
saying that the Admiralty were willing to work to a specified figure but that
they should be allowed to suggest their own economies. In consequence we
have, apart from a few suggestions, left the initiative to them. In the result
they have nothing to offer, except not to augment their estimates further by
demanding an increase in the Oil Fuel Reserve provision. I assume that the
Birkenhead Committee will at the least say that no increase in the rate of

accumulated reserve is necessary, and that this will be assented to by the Admiralty. Even however with this relief of £350,000, the Navy is nearly £1,700,000 above the sum which I am able to find.

There is a widespread feeling—in my opinion well founded—that the Admiralty give less value for money than either of the other two Services. They are so accustomed to carrying all before them by threats of resignation that they feel able to do themselves sumptuously in every branch and in every establishment. You have perhaps noticed the report on the staffing of the Admiralty presented by the Select Committee of the House of Commons. I am afraid I shall not be able to accept the Navy estimates at their present figure. The procedure which, with your approval, I shall propose to the Cabinet on Thursday will be: first, the detailed discussion of the Navy estimates between the First Lord and his officers on the one hand and myself. Each of the four or five key votes will be carefully gone through. The Treasury have prepared complete analyses of all of them. It may be that some savings will be found on which we can agree. For the rest the differences must be formulated and, I presume, be settled by the Cabinet or by the Economy Committee of the Cabinet. This process may be lengthy and may delay the presentation of the estimates. There are however precedents for this, the latest being, as I well remember, 1913.[1]

Yours vy sincerely,
WSC

Winston S. Churchill to William Bridgeman
(*Churchill papers: 22/175*)

29 January 1928   Treasury Chambers

My dear First Lord,

You will see from the paper I am circulating to the Cabinet that we are still nearly £5 millions short of the minimum savings that will balance the

[1] In November 1913 the increased naval expenditure which Churchill sought (he was then First Lord of the Admiralty) was strongly opposed by the then Chancellor of the Exchequer, David Lloyd George, and by several other Liberal Cabinet Ministers, including Sir John Simon, Reginald McKenna, Walter Runciman and Herbert Samuel. Indeed, on 17 November 1913 Asquith himself wrote to Lloyd George, from 10 Downing Street: 'Don't let Winston have too much money as it will hurt our party in every way—Labour and even Liberals. If we can't be a little economical when all foreign countries are peaceful I don't know *when* we can.' Churchill asked the Cabinet for a total expenditure of £50,694,800 (an increase of £2,985,000 on the previous year). Following a prolonged Cabinet crisis, the total expenditure was fixed at £51,580,000: more than Churchill had asked for originally as, during the crisis, the Canadian Government of Robert Borden had decided *not* to make its contribution of three Dreadnoughts to Imperial defence, and £2½ million was therefore agreed upon as an extra item of expenditure.

Budget. The complete failure of the Admiralty to contribute any reduction (apart from the question of the Oil Fuel Reserve) will make it necessary for me to go through the votes and establishments in detail with you and your officers. This may result, as on previous occasions, in some savings being agreed upon. For the rest we can focus specific points of difference on which the Cabinet will have to pronounce. I am afraid that the delay in presenting the Navy estimates must be faced. I cannot accept them in their present form.

Yours very sincerely,
WSC

Winston S. Churchill to Randolph Churchill
(*Randolph Churchill papers*)

30 January 1928   11 Downing Street

My dear Randolph,

It is always nice to get a letter from you: & I am vy glad that you enjoyed the hunting. I hope things may so unfold that yr undoubted taste for riding & love of the Chase may be indulged.

I wish you wd look at yr letter again & see the various 'caligraphic elucidations'! wh I have ventured to make upon it. In the early years of manhood a really venomous & misleading handwriting will be a serious handicap to you. Yr handwriting is perverse. One can guess what you mean as a rule, but proper names remain undecipherable. It cd so easily be cured by a little care *now*. You certainly have been vilely taught; but there is still time to recover. Do try. Send me yr letter back. There ought not to be doubt about any word. That is the test.

I have filled in the form about Christchurch & return it to you herewith.

I was shocked to learn of Lord Haig's sudden death.[1] Yet it is the best of exits.

Yr loving father
Winston S. Churchill

[1] Haig had died in London that same day, at the age of 66. According to Sir Frederick Maurice, in the *Dictionary of National Biography*, he 'undoubtedly shortened his life by denying himself rest', having, since 1921, both as President of the British Legion and Chairman of the United Services Fund, worked with little respite on behalf of all needy ex-servicemen and their dependents.

February 1928

Winston S. Churchill to Randolph Churchill

(*Randolph Churchill papers*)

5 February 1928   Chartwell Manor

Dearest Randolph,

Many thanks for your letter which is certainly much better written, and very well expressed. The worst of all your characters is the 'o' which is really indistinguishable from an 'a', and strikes the eye and mind with irritating effect every time it so often recurs. I am sure that it will well repay you to resolve that each word you write shall be legible to the ordinary man judging by ordinary standards. Our ancestors used many abbreviations, some of which are quite respectable. I myself use abbreviations for 'very', 'would' and 'should', putting a little half circle over the omitted letters.[1] This really saves time and trouble and causes no inconvenience or offence so long as the context is absolutely clear. To write proper names carelessly, or worse still, misleadingly, is the cause of endless trouble and may well lead to one's correspondence becoming a bore. Some boobies even have illegible signatures. They can often be punished by having their letters put aside until they choose to write again.

I enclose a letter I have had from the Dean of Christ Church[2] with a copy of the form which I had already sent you partly filled in. I expect you will already have sent this on. If not pray ask Mr Sheepshanks to help you fill in this one and send it forward. I have written to the Dean. By the way, are you sure I have filled in the date of your going to Oxford correctly. It is the October term of 1929 that we are aiming at.

I fully approve of your having a thrust at the Scholarship in December. You of course have to ride hard and fast at a fence of this kind. One must do one's best to see the hunt and no one can do more. If you will let me know all

---

[1] Churchill noted in the margin: 'v'y, w'd, sh'd'.

[2] Henry Julian White, 1859–1934. Entered Christ Church College, Oxford, as a commoner, 1878. Domestic Chaplain to the Bishop of Salisbury, 1886–1911. Theological Lecturer and Chaplain of Merton College, Oxford, 1895–1905. Professor of New Testament Exegesis, King's College, London, 1905–20. Dean of Christ Church from 1920 until his death.

the books you are reading I will try to read them too. The 'Prof' said you had to read John Stuart Mill on Economics. Which of his various works is it? I could perhaps be of some help in talking to you about this subject, especially if you could show me a specimen paper on Political Economy. Though quite uneducated on the subject, I have had to argue about it all my life.

I have asked Eddie to get me a copy of the Petition of the Merchants of the City of London of 1828, which in about a page contains more truth and good sense about Economics than has ever been put into a similar compass.

I am trying a new wireless set with 8 valves and the man was nearly three hours showing me how to work it last night. Afterwards I made it go myself. One can get 15 or 20 foreign stations and choose exactly the programme one wants without being interfered with at all by 2 LO or 5 GB. I picked out quite easily Stuttgart, Frankfort, Copenhagen, Vienna, and last of all when all the other stations had stopped, Madrid; but the staple was a splendid concert from Berlin. I do not know whether I shall be able to afford to buy the set but I have got it for a few weeks on approval.

Please do not write any references to my plans as any mention of such topics on paper is dangerous. You will however see from what I said at Birmingham that difficulties are being gradually cleared out of the way and that *design* is taking the place of *chaos*. You should also read the King's Speech, which will be published on Tuesday, with an observant eye.[1]

Your loving father

PS. We have bought a fine new carthorse. Her name is 'Blossom'. She can pull a ton & a half!

---

[1] On the evening of 3 February 1928, in a speech at Birmingham, Churchill had given the first public intimation of the de-rating scheme. Local rates, he said, were 'a harassing burden upon productive industry and agriculture. . . . They vary capriciously between one part of the country and another. They vary with the results of the local elections. They are constantly changing, and usually rising. Unlike the income tax, they are levied whether there are any profits or not. . . . I will go so far as to say that if I had the money, an advance in this direction would round off with singular completeness the Financial policy of the present Parliament. . . . I say there is no direction in which we ought more readily to advance.' The prospect of a de-rating Bill was again hinted at in the King's Speech on February 7, and a week later, during the debate on the Address, Churchill again extolled, and elaborated upon, its merits. All parties, he said, were agreed on 'the burden' of local rates; all sought to relieve that burden; and he, if the money could be found, would favour such relief. 'Money,' he said. 'was the only power in time of peace available at the disposal of Governments to influence administrative reform. It was the one precious and potent agency. To squander it and fritter it away would be at all times a blunder, and at this time a crime.'

Winston S. Churchill to P. J. Grigg

(*Churchill papers: 18/74*)

7 February 1928

So it was not Mr Gladstone who initiated the fixed debt charge, but Sir Stafford Northcote in 1875; and this fixed debt charge lasted till 1914, a period of 39 years, subject to suspension during war scares and five reductions or raises.

Reading this paper with its old time figures shows a staggering growth of wealth in the Twentieth Century, and during and after the war. I remember so vividly the Budgets of 1900–1905, hearing Ritchie[1] for instance stagger the House by taking in successive years 1d, 2d, 3d, 4d off the Income Tax—the petty figures of those days which even I can remember so well. Probably £m840 is a much smaller proportion of the national wealth today than £m150 at the beginning of the century. The contrast loses none of its impressiveness when the necessary reduction for the value of money has been made. The war seems to have flung us all into a gigantic world.

Winston S. Churchill to P. J. Grigg

(*Churchill papers: 18/77*)

9 February 1928

I shall settle with Mr Chamberlain today, which disposes of the first section of the Votes. I do not expect anything more than £m ½ from the Navy and £m ¼ from Works and Air together, with perhaps £150,000 from Health and a few minor scrapings; say, in all, £m 1. So far as the Fighting Services are concerned, the Naval discussions will take a long time. But I trust the Air can be settled today or tomorrow. You should get in touch with them.

WSC

Winston S. Churchill to Lord Beaverbrook

(*Beaverbrook papers*)

9 February 1928   Treasury Chambers
Private

My dear Max,

Of course it wd be frightfully interesting, even thrilling, to go to Russia; & I can sympathize with yr curiosity. It wd not make an irreparable breach in

---

[1] Charles Ritchie, 1838–1906. Conservative MP, 1874–92 and 1895–1905. Home Secretary, 1900–2. Chancellor of the Exchequer, 1902–3. Created Baron Ritchie, 1905.

our friendship. But can you expect me, of all others, to recommend you to go? You wd certainly find yrself in the following dilemma: Either you wd speak up for them on yr return, or you wd run them down. If you did the former, you wd probably (unless they have changed vy much) run counter to prevailing public opinion here.

If the latter, they wd think it rather shabby of you after having lavished, as they no doubt would, their most seductive caresses upon you. Nearly everyone who has had anything to do with the Bolsheviks, in every country, not least in Germany, has come off soiled, or disillusioned, or poorer.

Still, you are a free man: I cannot conceive there wd by any official embarrassment; & the spectacle of yr leading the Red Bruin back to the European Circus wd certainly be impressive. Lastly, as somebody said to somebody (& there are several versions) 'it wd always have been an interesting experience'.[1]

Yours ever
Winston S.C.

Winston S. Churchill to Alfred Hurst
(*Churchill papers: 18/74*)

10 February 1928

Find out from the Ministry of Transport what has happened about a plan on which I spoke to the Minister of compulsory insurance against third party risks. Is there any reason why the driver's licence should not be raised to say £1, and this made to cover third party risks as well? Very cruel hardship arises when people are injured by persons who are much too poor to pay the compensation which the Courts would award. I spoke to Colonel Ashley[2] about this some time ago, and the question must be explored at once.

---

[1] In the autumn of 1928 Beaverbrook went on a cruise to Russia, as well as to Norway and Denmark, accompanied by (among others) Arnold Bennett and Lady Louis Mountbatten. In Russia they visited both Leningrad and Moscow.

[2] Wilfred William Ashley, 1867–1939. Educated at Harrow and Magdalen College, Oxford. Conservative MP for Blackpool, 1906–18; for the Fylde division of Lancashire, 1918–22; for the New Forest and Christchurch division of Hampshire, 1922–32. Honorary Lieutenant-Colonel commanding 20th Battalion King's Liverpool Regiment. Chairman of the Anti-Socialist Union. President of the Anglo-German Fellowship. Under-Secretary of State for War, 1923–4. Minister of Transport, 1924–9. Privy Councillor, 1924. Created Baron Mount Temple, 1932.

Cortlandt MacMahon to Winston S. Churchill

(*Churchill papers: 1/199*)

10 February 1928

Dear Mr Churchill,

On Tuesday last I commenced treatment with HRH the Prince of Wales & directly I saw him he told me that he knew of the successful treatment of yourself & also of Mrs Dudley Ward & others. I did not quite gather whether HRH had heard from you direct but I know that his coming to me is largely due to the kind & generous way in which you have spoken of me & I felt I must write to thank you again very much indeed.

Miss Fisher is so much better that she can now carry on without my help. She will continue her exercises & should, in quite a reasonable time, get quite well. Miss Fisher has been a most conscientious & excellent patient & it has been a very great pleasure to me to have had her here. Again I owe that to your kindness.

With renewed & best thanks, Believe me
Yours sincerely
Cortlandt MacMahon

Winston S. Churchill to Randolph Churchill

(*Randolph Churchill papers*)

13 February 1928   Treasury Chambers

We had a very trying day yesterday.[1] Two separate operations at 2.30 and midnight! Your mother astonished the hardened doctors by her wonderful courage. If you should turn out—as I do not doubt—to be a fearless man, you will know where you got it from.

Today the doctors declare themselves entirely satisfied, and I hope and believe the corner is turned. She still however has a good deal of pain and is a little disappointed at its not stopping as she had been encouraged to expect. The Doctors say that anyhow the cavity is open now, and whatever matter forms can drain harmlessly away. Naturally I have cross-questioned them searchingly. And as a result I do not feel particularly anxious at the moment.

If in a day or two you feel you would like to come up to see her, you should

[1] On 14 February 1928 *The Times* reported that 'Mrs Winston Churchill underwent a successful operation for acute mastoid at 11 Downing Street yesterday'. On February 16 *The Times* reported her condition as 'satisfactory'; and again as 'satisfactory' on February 20. She was said to be 'going on very well' on February 27.

let me know the most convenient occasion from your Eton point of view, and I will ask Dr Alington to let you come. Write on receipt of this accordingly.

With much affection,

Your loving father,

Winston S. Churchill

PS. Both your telegrams and letter were very welcome.

Winston S. Churchill to Consuelo Balsan

(Churchill papers: 1/199)

14 February 1928

It was very kind of you to telegraph about Clemmie. She has had a most trying and painful week—two operations in ten hours—the second one the most severe. It was a very harassing experience. She showed the greatest courage and although since she has had an unusual amount of pain I rejoice that progress is continuous and the Doctors are satisfied. You suggested in your telegram that Clemmie might go out to Lou Sueil to recuperate. That would indeed be delightful for her, and then perhaps you might find room for me, just to bring her out and back. It is quite impossible however to make any plans at the present moment as the Doctors will not say within a fortnight when she will be out of their hands, and even then there will remain some dressings to be done. However, I hope she will get on the sofa this week and be able to get about all right in another week.

If I may I will write to you a little later on when we can see more clearly and then if you have still got room perhaps you will let us propose ourselves.

When do you quit your mountain crag for Northern latitudes?

You remember Voronoff and his cattle pamphlet and our talk last year? I got the Ministry of Agriculture to send out a special Commission to Algiers to investigate the process on sheep, etc. They are far from convinced that the results are what he claims, so that I do not intend personally to make any plunge in his direction at the moment.[1]

With every good wish to you and Jacques,

I remain,

[1] Dr Serge Voronoff, a gland-grafting scientist, resident in Algiers. In November 1927 he had announced the discovery of a method of grafting new glands on to sheep, claiming that this resulted in larger and more productive offspring. On 1 January 1928 His Majesty's Stationery Office had published the Report of a team of scientists sent by the Ministry of Agriculture to review Voronoff's findings. Voronoff himself arrived in Britain on May 22. His visit was controversial, as he advocated gland-grafting experiments on human beings, and had published two short books in the United Kingdom: *The Study of Old Age and My Method of Gland Grafting* (1927) and *The Conquest of Life* (1927). Later, on 14 June 1928, Sir William Joynson-Hicks, the Home Secretary, declared in answer to a question in the House of Commons that Voronoff 'has no license to practise in this country, nor do I propose to grant him one'.

Stanley Baldwin to Winston S. Churchill

(*Churchill papers: 22/190*)

15 February 1928   10 Downing Street

My dear Winston,

I want to thank you warmly for the way in which you met the wish of the Cabinet this morning.

Some of our colleagues have spoken to me already about it and I am sure there is a general feeling that you met them generously and ungrudgingly.

And I felt very sorry that such a worrying matter had to come up at a time when you have burdens enough at home.

Winston S. Churchill to Stanley Baldwin

(*Baldwin papers*)

15 February 1928   Treasury Chambers

My dear PM,

You are always vy kind to me. Some one (& you chose me) has to fight all these points. But you know that I always rank the interests of yr government above any departmental issue, not touching the fundamental interest of The Show.

Unhappily the Treasury has to defend a good many positions wh cannot be reconciled with generosity or gentlemanlike *largesse*. As an ex-Ch of the Exch you know the seamy side; & also what wd happen if it did not receive constant attention.

Of course I shall present the decision *at its best*.

Yours ever,
W

Winston S. Churchill to Edward Marsh

(*Churchill papers: 18/74*)

15 February 1928

I think you might see Beveridge privately and find out from him what other Conservative Ministers are associating themselves with the proposal.

I am personally a great admirer of Webb's[1] work in social matters, but

---

[1] Sidney James Webb, 1859–1947. Social reformer. Author, from 1890, of nearly a hundred works on social problems, many written with his wife, Beatrice. Served on twelve different Royal Commissions, 1903–20. Professor of Public Administration, London, 1912–27. Labour MP, 1922–9. President of the Board of Trade, 1924. Secretary of State for Dominion Affairs, 1929–30, and for Colonies, 1929–31. Created Baron Passfield, 1929. Order of Merit, 1944.

since Sidney Webb went into politics as a Socialist Minister he has invested himself with a partizan complexion. I think Socialism vicious in itself as well as deeply injurious to the community, and I do not want to associate myself with those who spread these dangerous delusions no matter how much I may respect their technical work.

Venetia Montagu to Winston S. Churchill
(Churchill papers: 1/200)

16 February

Darling Winston, a million thanks for letting me see what you have written about Mr Asquith.[1] I think it is quite perfect, and much of it most moving and beautiful. It brings back a very vivid picture of him, far more so than anything else I've read. When I get back to Beccles, where I have kept all the letters he wrote me, there are many allusions (naturally enough) to you, he was extremely fond of you and more than that full of admiration for what he always used to call your ingenuity and resourcefulness, I think it might amuse you to see some of them. The bit about Raymond is particularly beautiful and brings tears to the eyes.[2]

Thank you again so much.

Love
Venetia

[1] Churchill's tribute to Asquith, who had died on 15 February 1928, was eventually published in Nash's magazine in August 1928, and subsequently appeared in book form in Great Contemporaries in September 1937. In his article Churchill wrote: 'Asquith's position of eminence and authority and the air of detachment arising therefrom enabled him to use the potent instrument of Time with frequent advantage in domestic affairs. Repeatedly he prevented the break-up of his Government or the resignation of important Ministers by refusing to allow a decision to be taken. "What we have heard to-day leaves much food for thought: let us all reflect before we meet again how we can bring ourselves together." In time of Peace, dealing with frothy, superficial Party and personal bickerings, this was often successful. War, untamable, remorseless, soon snapped the tackle.'

[2] Raymond Asquith, 1878–1916. Eldest son of H. H. Asquith. Barrister-at-Law. Lieutenant, Grenadier Guards, 1914. Killed in action on the Somme, 15 September 1916. His son Julian, who was born five months before Raymond Asquith's death, succeeded H. H. Asquith as 2nd Earl of Oxford and Asquith in 1928. In his article on Asquith, Churchill wrote: 'It seemed quite easy for Raymond Asquith, when the time came, to face death and to die. When I saw him at the Front in November and December of 1915, he seemed to move through the cold, squalor and peril of the winter trenches as if he were above and immune from the common ills of the flesh, a being clad in polished armour, entirely undisturbed, presumably invulnerable. The War which found the measure of so many never got to the bottom of him, and when the Grenadiers strode into the crash and thunder of the Somme, he went to his fate cool, poised, resolute, matter-of-fact, debonair. And well we know that his father, then bearing the supreme burden of the State, would proudly have marched at his side.'

Thomas Jones: diary

(*Jones papers*)

16 February 1928

When Winston came out,[1] he started addressing me on the importance of his rating policy, and when I said that it really was the application of the policy of minimum standards to local authorities, he retorted that it really was the communist principle, from each authority according to its ability, to each authority according to its need, but that we must not shout that from the housetop.

Cabinet minutes

(*Churchill papers: 18/77*)

17 February 1928
Secret

In view of the large economies already made on the Air Estimates, THE SECRETARY OF STATE FOR AIR found it impossible to give a favourable reply to the further appeal made to him by the Chancellor of the Exchequer for still greater savings, and Mr Churchill felt he could not press this item any further.

In connection with the discussion on Naval Economies THE FIRST LORD OF THE ADMIRALTY drew attention to the reductions in naval expenditure effected during the last few years. In particular he called attention to a Memorandum (Paper CP–360(25)) of July 20, 1925, in which the Chancellor of the Exchequer had contemplated for 1928–29 a naval expenditure of £66,627,791, compared with £57,600,000 now proposed by the Admiralty.

Attention was drawn in particular to an item in the Admiralty Estimates for expenditure on an anti-aircraft weapon which, it was stated, had not yet been tested in concert with the Air Ministry, and the suggestion was made that before serious expenditure is incurred, the merits of this weapon should be discussed by the Committee of Imperial Defence.

THE PRIME MINISTER asked his colleagues at the head of the Departments of the Fighting Services to make enquiries in order to ensure that the activities of their respective Departments in the matter of anti-aircraft artillery are fully co-ordinated.

[1] From a Cabinet meeting at 10 Downing Street, which met following Asquith's death.

Sir Frederick Milner[1] *to Winston S. Churchill*

(*Churchill papers: 1/199*)

19 February 1928   Maidenhead

Dear Winston Churchill,

This is a funny letter to write, but Nancy[2] has asked me to tea to meet you, & for auld lang syne I would like to see you again, & shake you by the hand. But I am now quite stone deaf & cannot hear a sound, which makes things very embarrassing. I go about with a pad of paper in my pocket, in case anybody wants to speak to me, but I don't find that happens often. Anyhow I would like just to shake hands with you again.

The last letter I had from you asked me to come & see you & your children, whom I was anxious to see, but then I had the breakdown which caused this deafness, & since then I have been shut out from the world, from a dread of boring my friends. Nancy is a very old friend & draws me out of my shell sometimes.

I got your wonderful book on the war, & I think I have read all your speeches both in the House and outside. You have had a mighty difficult job, but I think you have come well out of it. I thought I would write you this, & then you will understand, & from what I knew of you, I think you will sympathize, for deafness makes a poor devil's life a Hell. Fortunately I am able to work, & have started a lot of useful centres for our poor disabled men, & these keep me pretty busy, but the work all has to be done in writing, & it gets very wearisome.

Yours ever
Fred Milner

Winston S. Churchill to Edward Marsh

(*Churchill papers: 1/199*)

19 February 1928

See enclosed two letters from poor old Fred Milner. Write for me to sign how sorry I am to have missed him, but I had to go over to Eton to see

[1] Frederick George Milner, 1843–1931. 7th Baronet, 1880. Conservative MP, 1883–85 and 1890–1906. Privy Councillor, 1904. From the age of seventy he devoted much of his energy on behalf of disabled ex-soldiers, and it was largely as a result of his efforts that the Ministry of Pensions was created in 1916. Realizing the need for homes for shell-shock victims, he founded the first recuperative hostel at Hampstead, followed by the Enham Village Centre.

[2] Nancy Astor (see page 962, note 1), whose country house, Cliveden, was only a few miles from Maidenhead.

Randolph and his Master kept me longer than I had expected in conversation, and thank him for the kindness of his letter and say how glad I am he has read my books, etc etc. I have also telegraphed to him.

Winston S. Churchill to William Bridgeman
(*Churchill papers: 2/157*)

20 February 1928

My dear First Lord,

I agreed with you the figure of the Navy Estimates for this year, as I did not wish for the sake of ½ a million in dispute to force you into a Vote on account, and so disclose interdepartmental friction. Nevertheless it is necessary that the various questions at issue between us as to the degree of 'concert pitch readiness' of your equipments and supplies under the 'ten years peace' decision should be thrashed out during the ensuing year. We are accordingly in the first instance preparing an official letter setting out the Treasury view in considerable detail. After you have considered this, I should propose that later on in the summer, long before the Estimates for 1929 are framed, a Cabinet Committee should examine the position.

Our letter should reach you in about a week.

Yours very sincerely,
Winston S. Churchill

Winston S. Churchill: message for the electors of Ilford[1]
(*Churchill papers: 2/157*)

21 February 1928

Mr Lloyd George was very indignant at Lancaster because he thought an unfair attack had been made on him. But this sensitiveness does not at all prevent him from making unfair, unjust, and as he ought to know untrue attacks upon His Majesty's Government. For instance he tells the Ilford electors that 'national expenditure has increased by 40 millions since the Government came into power'. Now this statement is quite wrong and misleading. If you leave out the increased sinking fund for the payment of our debts, which is the highest form of economy, and if you leave out of account

[1] Following the death of the Conservative MP, Sir Frederic Wise, a by-election had been called at Ilford for 23 February 1928. The seat was won by another Conservative, Sir George Hamilton, whose election slogan was: 'Work wins. Apathy is the Friend of Revolution.'

the natural growth of the Post Office and the Road Fund in harmony with the precepts of the new Liberal Yellow Book, the expense of Government has not increased at all since we took office. This has been stated again and again, and never challenged or disputed, in the House of Commons. Nevertheless Mr Lloyd George, in the teeth of facts and of his own Yellow Book, does not hesitate to say that 'the expenditure has increased by 40 millions', hoping, I suppose, that the Ilford electors will be taken in by this gross misstatement, and will not find it out before Thursday.

Mr Lloyd George also said 'There has never been anything like it, His Majesty's Government, and please God there never will be again.' I am sure that any ordinary citizen and voter who studies public affairs will feel that this sort of statement has very little relation to actual facts. It is a heavy brew, made from sour grapes and hot air. We have never pretended to be a Government of supermen or professional cure-alls and know-alls. But we have tried to give England a spell of honest, steady, stable Government in accordance with the wish so strongly expressed by the nation, with the electors of Ilford in the van, at the General Election of 1924. We have preserved peace at home and abroad, and where we could not keep peace, we have kept order. We have promoted the unity of the British Empire, and fostered the fertile trade between its different parts. We have reduced the expenditure upon armaments, but at the same time we have had to say at Geneva that we could not allow the strength of the British Navy to be settled for us, without regard to our island position, by any other Power however great or however friendly. We have passed into law the widest measure of Insurance, giving Pensions to widows and orphans and to old people of 65, which the Statute-book of any country can show. We have other plans for improving our domestic organization at which we are now working, and which in due season will bear fruit. Your late distinguished Member Sir Fredric Wise will be much missed in the House of Commons, and I hope that Ilford will fill his place with a competent and experienced representative like Sir George Hamilton,[1] who will make a real contribution to the hard work and difficult problems which lie ahead.

[1] George Clements Hamilton, 1877–1947. An electrical engineer. Conservative MP for Altrincham, 1913–23. Director of Enrolment, National Service, 1917. Controller of Contract Claims, Ministry of Munitions, 1918. Parliamentary Private Secretary, Ministry of Pensions, 1919–20. Knighted, 1922. Conservative MP for Ilford, 1928–37. Created Baronet, 1937.

Winston S. Churchill to Sir William Tyrrell
(*Churchill papers: 2/157*)

23 February 1928

My dear Beaver,

With some domestic anxieties, now happily clearing, I have only this moment found the opportunity of offering you my warmest congratulations on your great appointment.[1] I never forget your enthusiasm when I went to the Admiralty in 1911, or your letter beginning 'Dear First Lord of the Seas'. Altho' 17 years have passed with all that lay in them, I feel your Embassage at Paris is only another chapter in the same tale. Whereas at the beginning we had at all costs to resist German aggression, now after the victory an equally vital objective is the unity and reconciliation of the three great combatants. In this too England would play the dominant part; and I am sure that she could find no better, more skilful, more experienced or more resolute agent than yourself.

With every good wish,
Believe me,
Yours very sincerely,
Winston S. Churchill

Sir William Tyrrell to Winston S. Churchill
(*Churchill papers: 18/74*)

23 February 1928   Foreign Office

My dear Winston (may I?)

No letter has given me greater pleasure or gratification than the one I received from you today. It is a proof that I still enjoy your confidence and friendship: they will be very powerful props to support me in what I call the 'great adventure'.

The policy you lay down has always appealed to me as the only right & sane one from the day of the armistice. It is a great help to know that I can rely upon your powerful support for its execution. How far we shall succeed in persuading the French to walk that plank remains to be seen, but as far as this country is concerned I have always been & remain an optimist. As regards the French I am also hopeful, because in the long run I back the Frenchman's love of the franc to overcome his hatred of the Boche!

[1] Sir William Tyrrell had been appointed Ambassador to France.

When I hailed you as 'First Lord of the Sea' I had no idea what a prophet I was. You became that in 1914 when *on your own responsibility* you kept the fleet together & thereby made the most material contribution to eventual victory.

Never forget that whenever you feel depressed or discouraged.

I am glad Mrs Winston is making good progress. You were both much in my thoughts during her period of suffering & your period of anxiety. I did not bother you with enquiries, as I kept myself well informed.

Thank you again for your heartening letter & good wishes which I cherish.

Yours always sincerely
W. Tyrrell

Winston S. Churchill to Sir Richard Hopkins and Gilbert Upcott
(*Churchill papers: 18/74*)

24 February 1928
Secret

(1) The bringing of the Pipe Line from Mosul to Haifa must be considered, if the facts alleged are correct, a project of prime public importance. The Mosul oil field is said to be at least as large as the South Persian oil fields. It is even said that it may become one of the greatest in the world. It would thus furnish Great Britain, as the dominant Naval power in the Mediterranean, with a copious and almost unassailable source of fuel supply. The possession of such a supply would relieve the need of the oil fuel reserve which is at present maintained. It would also react in important ways upon the price of oil in this country, which is at present surcharged with Suez Canal dues. I certainly have not heard for a long time of any external scheme of British development comparable to this. Naturally we do not want to engage money or credit if the result can be achieved without it, or to engage more than is needed. But I should be prepared to make very great exertions in order to ensure the arrival of the Pipe Line upon the Mediterranean in Palestinian territory and British control.

(2) A railway from the Mediterranean to Bagdad has also a very definite value; and if in aiding the construction of the railway we can secure a satisfactory route for the Pipe Line, we must be ready to use our financial power. I agree with Mr Upcott and others that the Iraq railways will be prejudiced by this scheme and that we should by no means dissipate our limited resources on assuming liability for them. Still less do we wish to assume liability for the Iraq railways in order to enable the Iraq–Arab Government, always boasting

its independence, to play a leading part in the construction of the far more important line to the Mediterranean.

(3) I agree with what is said in these telegrams as to Sir Albert Stern[1] not being the best or most powerful agency to employ. The Royal Dutch Shell and the Anglo-Persian Companies ought to be encouraged to work hand in hand—as they already seem disposed to do. This extremely powerful combination should enable us to secure satisfactory decisions from the Turkish Petroleum Company. The Iraq Government could no doubt be admitted to a share, and Palestine could do what it can for a matter so greatly affecting its interests. But I am definitely prepared to support this project to a reasonable extent with the power of the Treasury, if such support is found to be indispensable to a right solution.

(4) The fortification of the port of Haifa is not a very important matter. Probably by the time this Pipe Line is completed, the Air Force would be able with a heavy bombing squadron to give the necessary security, having regard to our control of the Mediterranean. I agree however that it would be worth while to thrash the military aspect out in detail at this early stage while the Admiralty are so keen on the main project. They will then take a moderate and sensible view as to the amounts to be sunk in defence. I consider therefore that the matter should be brought before the CID fairly soon and Sir Maurice Hankey should be apprised of my views. Nevertheless I cannot contemplate any Mediterranean Power attacking us in the next twenty years.

L. S. Amery: diary

(*Amery papers*)

26 February 1928

. . . began to tackle Winston's great scheme of rating reform. It is a vote catching scheme and too ingenious, but I see in it a great opportunity for putting in my own tactics for dealing with the fiscal question as an alternative.

---

[1] Albert Gerald Stern, 1878–1966. Lieutenant, Royal Naval Volunteer Reserve (Armoured Car Division), 1914. Secretary to the Landship Committee, Admiralty, 1916. Major, Machine Gun Corps, Heavy Branch, 1916. Head of the Tank Supply Committee, Ministry of Munitions, 1916; Director-General, Mechanical Warfare Department (rank of Lieutenant-Colonel), 1917; Commissioner, Mechanical Warfare, Overseas and Allies, 1917. Knighted, 1918. He published *Tanks 1914–18: The Log Book of a Pioneer*, in 1919. Member of the London Committee of the Ottoman Bank, 1921–64. Director, the Midland Bank, 1933–58, and of the Clydesdale Bank, 1950–8. Chairman, Special Vehicle Development Committee, Ministry of Supply, 1929–43. Member of the Tank Board, 1941.

Winston S. Churchill to Sir Richard Hopkins and Alfred Hurst

(*Churchill papers: 18/41*)

26 February 1928
Secret

I shall probably present the finance of the Rating Scheme in the form of the tables set out on page 9 of CP 8 (28), so as to reassure the country as to the separate solvency of the scheme and to show also that the future is not being mortgaged. But having done this I shall make it clear that no separate fund will in fact be maintained. All will go into the national pool, from which everything will be paid. 'Behind the scheme stands the Exchequer.' There is no question of making an enclave in our finances, or the ear-marking of particular monies to particular purposes. The Exchequer will assume new liabilities and acquire new revenues; and the responsibility for adjusting its resources to its obligations falls each year upon the Government of the day. Pray comment on this.

Winston S. Churchill: Cabinet note

(*Churchill papers: 2/193*)

28 February 1928
Secret

Some statements have appeared in the Daily Mail which inaccurately disclose a portion of certain Government plans. It is a common practice with journalists to float a *ballon d'essai* of this description and then by cross-questioning persons upon its accuracy to unravel the whole matter. It is important that everyone who has become party to the proposals should realise that the strictest secrecy should still be maintained, even though a good deal of guesswork may appear in the Press.

I understand that the papers on this subject have been shown to a certain number of the Parliamentary Private Secretaries, and it is evident that the number of persons who are informed is considerable. It is therefore asked that Ministers will bring this caution to the notice of those concerned.

WSC

March 1928

Winston S. Churchill: Cabinet memorandum[1]

(Churchill papers: 18/87)

1 March 1928
Most Secret
To be Kept Under Lock and Key
It is requested that special care be taken to ensure the secrecy of this document

RATING REFORM

I circulate to my colleagues the chapter in the 'Liberal Yellow Book' on Rating, together with comments upon it made by the Treasury, which I endorse. The Liberal diagnosis of the evils is strikingly similar to that contained in the various Treasury papers on the subject, although both sets of studies have proceeded in absolute isolation. The resources of the Ministry of Health and the Treasury have achieved a more precise, elaborate and refined statement of the evils than was possible to unofficial investigators. Nevertheless, apart from its partisanship, the Rating chapter of the Yellow Book is a creditable and valuable contribution to a most urgent social and administrative problem.

When we leave diagnosis and come to remedies it will, I think, be seen that the proposals now before the Cabinet are immensely superior to those of the Yellow Book. First, they concentrate the relief upon the producers instead of dissipating it over the whole area of the rates. By this means they give a relief of two-thirds instead of one-third to the manufacturers, and they give complete relief to the farmers, instead of a comparatively small modification of the existing burden. Secondly, they avoid the measureless evils which would follow from the Central Government taking upon itself the direct and continuous care of able-bodied unemployed and unemployables and their families. Such a plan of reopening uncovenanted benefit on an unlimited scale, paid for by the Exchequer, would make the House of Commons a continuous cockpit of Poplarism; and the Government of the

---

[1] Circulated to the Cabinet as Cabinet paper 66 of 1928.

day would either spend floods of public money pandering to Socialist sentiment, or else would be abused with many lively instances as harsh towards
suffering. Thirdly, we provide adequate securities for economy in local
administration and inducements to good housekeeping, which protect the
Exchequer from undue demands. Fourthly, we provide a coherent and
progressive scheme for readjusting the rate burden in accordance with the
movements of population and of labour, and ensure an ever closer approximation between the needs and the resources of any given area at any given
time. Fifthly, the Liberal proposal makes no suggestion for finance, except
that £m 40 should be cut from national defence, thus mutilating all three
fighting services and rendering them incapable of discharging their minimum
functions. Or alternatively, or in addition, they propose large increases of
direct taxation on Death Duties and Supertax, which would certainly be
extremely detrimental to the prosperity and saving power of the nation
already flagging under its burdens. We, on the other hand, meet the cost of
our reforms by a proposal which, apart from its justice and comparative
painlessness, claims the powerful support of the Mining and Railway
interests.

WSC

Winston S. Churchill to Thornton Butterworth

(*Godspeed's Bookshop, Boston, USA*)

1 March 1928

My dear Mr Butterworth,

After careful reflection, I am prepared to try to work to the timetable you
suggested in yr long letter. The three solid months, August, September and
October, ought to be sufficient, provided that my reading is focussed in the
interval, & that the collection & arrangement of material proceed. The few
articles, probably four, wh I am going to do for Ray Long in the meanwhile
will not affect the programme. They are only 2,500 words each, & about
personages of whom I have everything already in my mind. The rest of the
series (12 in all) need not be delivered until after the possibility of producing
volume IV this year is settled one way or the other. That issue, as I have
already explained, does not depend upon output, but upon matured
planning & reflection, & upon my wish not to produce an unworthy pendant
to the earlier volumes. We must just see how I get on from the time the
Budget is out of the way in the middle of July onwards. Naturally I am as
keen as you on the earliest possible delivery. I cannot however give any

binding guarantee other than a provision for the return of the advance if publication has to stand over till 1929. But this is a fairly good span, you will have to be content with it. Now let me have the contract.

With many thanks,
Yrs sincerely,
Winston S. Churchill

L. S. Amery: diary

(Amery papers)

4 March 1928

RATING REFORM

It looks as if we may have a real tussle over this as he intends his scheme definitely to bury all questions of safeguarding and preference. I think I have rather riddled his scheme and hope its collapse will pave the way to better things.

Winston S. Churchill to P. J. Grigg

(Grigg papers)

6 March 1928

PG

Always be assured that our friendship is proof agst all minor tiffs. But make allowances for the effect of suddenly pulling me up with a round turn, & forcing me to some measure of self defence—however mild—'Cet animal . . . etc.'[1]

Yours ever
W

P. J. Grigg to Winston S. Churchill

(Churchill papers: 18/72)

6 March 1928

Thank you very much. I don't think I needed the assurance for I have *known* for a long time now that I am permitted a latitude possible only with

[1] The full quotation, from *Le Menagerie* by Théodore P. K., first published in 1828, reads:

Cet animal est très meschant,
Quand on l'attaque il se défend.

This animal is very mischievous;
when it is attacked, it defends itself.

friends. Perhaps I take unfair advantage of this latitude, I know I am often unreasonable. But the real cause of my outburst this morning was far removed from the immediate recession of it.

I really am very worried over the way things are going on the Policy Cte (and I fancy you will find that Hurst also is troubled). The plan can be made a success if all your colleagues do their utmost to make it so, throw all their energies into getting it sufficiently forward by Budget day to be sure that it can survive all attacks on it without loss of any essential part of the structure & without ruin to its finance. But, except in Cunliffe Lister, I find no evidence of any disposition to approach the plan in this spirit. Worthy obviously reads the papers for the first time at the meetings & keeps both eyes on Colchester.[1] Gilmour either does not come or says nothing although the application of the plan to Scotland is a considerable problem. Percy does little but make bright & incomprehensible suggestions.

But it is Neville who frightens me most. He is rather enigmatic but I should say his attitude is something like this:—he is in a great funk about the scheme, does not at all like his part in it. At the same time he wants it for political reasons as well as a measure of reform. Between the two motives he is sulkily negative & you are getting no help from your chief co-adjutor.

Altogether the Dardanelles situation seems to be re-creating itself. Everybody loves the idea, everybody but you is frightened at its boldness & magnitude. Everybody therefore stands looking on idly, perfectly ready to be pleased if it succeeds & equally ready to say 'I told you so' if it doesn't & to kick you downstairs.

Of course it isn't necessary to have everything absolutely cut & dried by April 24 but the Cabinet must realise exactly what the destination is & realise moreover that no material change of route is possible after that date. Or to mix the metaphor—once the decisive start is made retreat is not possible though a rout may be.

And now may I add that all this makes me unhappy not only because I don't want to see a good scheme go wrong but also because I conceive myself to be genuinely attached to its author & his interests. And so I find myself

---

[1] On 23 November 1928 *The Times* reported: 'It is understood that Sir Laming Worthington-Evans desires to represent a seat nearer London. He has no intention of retiring from political life, but, as he is subject to bronchial trouble, he finds the strain of a large country constituency, in addition to his work as a member of the Cabinet, too great. He has been associated with the Colchester Division for over twenty-five years.' On December 3 the Colchester Division Conservative Association adopted Oswald Lewis as their candidate in place of Worthington-Evans. On December 11, at a meeting at which Lewis was formally adopted, Worthington-Evans stated: 'I think it would be fairer to leave you now than after the election, because I am not able to get about on cold nights the way a country division requires.' In the General Election of 1929 he stood for Westminster St George, and was elected. Lewis was returned for the Colchester Division.

wondering whether in the absence of more fervent support he may not find it easier to wait for the plunge until the whole plan has been exhaustively worked out.

Anyhow I beg that author's pardon for adding to his labours the task of pacifying a truculent secretary. But how beautifully he has done it and how heavily have I responded.

PJG

Winston S. Churchill: Cabinet memorandum[1]

(Churchill papers: 18/87)

9 March 1928   Treasury Chambers
Most Secret
To Be Kept Under Lock And Key

It is requested that special care may be taken to ensure the secrecy of this document

RATING REFORM

1. The question at issue, viz, whether the £13 millions national rate should be paid into the Exchequer and repaid thence to the Local Authorities according to the distribution scheme, or whether, on the other hand, the proceeds of the national rate should remain the property of the Local Authorities and be collected by them, does not make much immediate practical difference. The amount received through either channel by the Local Authorities is the same. The variation in distribution between one Local Authority and another is comparatively small. Probably out of the £13 millions in question, say, £11 millions will reach exactly the same destinations in either case. Provided that the basis of assessment remains unchangeable (except through the arrival of extensions and new businesses —a separate question), and provided that the national rate is uniform throughout the country and unalterable by the Local Authority, the producer's position is the same in both cases. It would be extravagant to pretend that a decision on a point so restricted is fatal to the immediate progress of the scheme. It follows also, however, from this, that it is unlikely that a concession, if concession it be, so limited will greatly disarm any opposition to be expected from Local Authorities.

2. Why, then, must I invite the Committee to weigh so carefully and gravely this particular decision? It is because I fear that the proposal to

[1] This memorandum was circulated to the Cabinet's Policy Committee as Policy Committee paper 9 of 1928.

leave the national rate directly in the hands of the Local Authorities represents tendencies dangerous to the Exchequer and subversive of the main
principles which should be our guide.

3. The fundamental principle which has always guided the Treasury in
its policy has been, and is, to withdraw productive industry entirely from
the rateable area and to substitute Grants to the Local Authorities from
the national Exchequer in lieu thereof. This was originally to have been
achieved through a profits tax of about £13 millions. When on tactical
grounds this profits tax was converted into a national rate, I made it clear
that this national tax was in fact the original Profits tax under a new and
less satisfactory form. I fear lest in making this national rate an integral
part of the Local Authorities income, collected directly by them, we shall
open the door to the idea that the Local Authority is to have an interest
however restricted in the developments or fluctuations of the industries in its
midst. Once this principle has re-established itself, the whole future argument
may be, perhaps inevitably will be, deflected into a false channel.

4. For what must be the next stage in the discussion? The Local Authorities where the rates are 20s will say: 'You have let our industries off three-
quarters of what we were getting from them, while across the boundary,
where the rates are at present only 10s, you have only let them off one-half.
This is neither logical nor fair. More especially is it unfair when the area
where the industries are rated at 20s is a much poorer district than that in
which they are rated at 10s. You are therefore making a much larger deduction from the rateable assets of the poorer district than from the rateable
assets of the richer district.' How could we stand on such a line? The demand
would become overwhelming that we should not make an arbitrary, but a
proportionate, deduction from the rateable assets of every area. Compliance
with this demand means variable rates (although reduced to one-third) on
industry, and the whole principle of a uniform and standard treatment of
industry, no matter where it chooses to go, will be destroyed. In fact, we
shall have returned to the position definitely repudiated in the first instance,
of simply letting industry off two-thirds of whatever rates it is now paying in
any particular district.

5. As an alternative to this it would certainly be suggested that the national
Exchequer should make up the difference over the national rate area (ie,
one-third of the remitted rates) between the 5/- national rate and the actual
level of rates in any highly-rated district. Here we enter a field of discussion
most perilous to the Exchequer. In fact, it is the old vicious percentage grant
system. The scale would no doubt have been reduced to one-third, but the
principle would remain unreformed. From this the whole trend of ideas
would move away from the plan of block grants reviewable at five-yearly

intervals, to a policy of compensating the Local Authorities not only for *actual* but *prospective* interest in the growth of local industries. This assails the second fundamental principle of the Treasury conception. We hold that deficiency compensation should be made only in relation to present assets, plus a *douceur* in order that no county authority shall be worse off. In respect of prospective assets arising from industry we deny there should be compensation. In our view the further compensation required by Local Authorities should bear no relation to the growth of industrial assets and should be entirely cut away from them. The further compensation that will be given to Local Authorities will not be based upon their assumed loss of spending power arising from local industries. It will be based on the needs of their population whether the local industries wax or wane. In this part of the field we are not compensating for loss of resources; we are providing for increase of responsibilities; and under this head generous and effectual provision will be made.

6. To recapitulate. The two fundamental principles which are in danger are, first, *Industry entirely out of the local rates*, and, secondly, *Compensation to Local Authorities for expansion to be based on population needs and not upon the potentialities of local assets.* If we once get off these lines we may never get back to them. I would far rather face a larger fixed, not fluctuating, *douceur* than leave these highways of policy for the jungles and swamps which lie on either side.

7. Why should we hesitate to proclaim these principles? Opinions may differ about them, but, at any rate, the nation can understand them and the Local Authorities will not easily break in upon them. Indeed, they will stand in some awe of them, because they conform to what is right and sound, and English people are always influenced by that. Once, however, we are committed to compromise for the sake of an easier journey, we may be driven from pillar to post in complete disorder.

8. The question of whether new businesses and extensions should be immune from the national rate stands on a much lower plane. The argument of the Board of Trade upon the invidious distinction between old and new appears to me massive. As long as the fruits of the national rate on such new businesses and extensions are gathered into the Exchequer, I shall not further contest their view. But this can only apply to industry. The railways are not rated upon extensions, but on a basis of profits, and their extensions are only one of the factors for the computation of profits. The public utility services, like the railways, have got to pass the rate relief on, anyhow, to the public, and do not stand directly to gain from it. This aspect should be further explored by our technical advisers.

WSC

Winston S. Churchill: Cabinet memorandum[1]

(Churchill papers: 18/87)

10 March 1928
Secret

RATING AND FISCAL REFORM

The Secretary of State for the Colonies proposes 'a coherent, constructive scheme of economic regeneration' based upon a Milk Tax; and he suggests that this should be made the issue at the General Election next year.

It seems a pity that this interesting project was not considered before it was decided to extend the franchise to the young women. The large number of young women who will vote for the first time next year have never yet been properly educated on the subject of a Milk Tax, and I really wonder whether there is time enough to do it before the Election takes place. In the absence of proper education upon the subject they might easily be misled by unscrupulous persons.

There is no doubt of course that all women, particularly young women, are brought intimately in contact with the Milk problem, which is also closely related to the Baby problem, milk forming an important part of the dietary of infants. The new voters might in the absence of proper political education be prejudiced against a proposal to tax foreign supplies of milk, so that the British farmer could charge more for his home-produced supply. The unscrupulous and vulgar persons mentioned above would certainly take the fullest advantage of these susceptibilities on the part of the new electorate. They would say a lot of unkind things about 'docking the baby's milk in order to increase the landlord's rent'. They would ask rude questions like, 'Wouldn't it be better to tax site values along all these great motor roads before pinching 5 per cent out of the baby's bottle?' All this might be embarrassing and even distressing to the young ladies in the absence of the fuller political education which there is now perhaps hardly time to impart.

The young ladies would no doubt have 'the satisfaction of having participated in the creation of an Empire Free breakfast table'. But even this might lose some of its attractiveness when the disagreeable persons to whom I have before referred drew attention to the fact that not only milk but butter and eggs—all of which are frequently consumed at the breakfast table—were also for the first time taxed with the definite object of giving the farmer a better price. They might begin to think that in this case the Empire was on one side and the Free breakfast table on the other, and this

---

[1] This memorandum was never circulated. After it had been printed for the Cabinet, Churchill noted on it: 'hold', and kept a copy among his private papers.

apparent antagonism might tend to check instead of help forward the cause which the Colonial Secretary has so much at heart.

These few preliminary difficulties ought, perhaps to be weighed before Mr Amery's scheme is further proceeded with. If by any chance the education of the young women and their conversion to the Milk Tax were not fully achieved before the General Election, they might not make so good a use of their votes as we all hope. Ii we should be beaten, even by a majority of no more than forty, our opponents would not only not pass the Milk Tax, or the Egg Tax, or the Butter Tax, or the Cheese Tax, but on the contrary they would achieve the goal of the 'free breakfast table' by sweeping away the taxes on sugar, tea and the cocoa group. Sugar would destroy the most substantial feature in the existing Imperial Preferences. They would recoup themselves for the loss of revenue by the taxation of site values and by a substantial addition to the Death Duties and Supertax. In further search for revenue they might easily lay their sacrilegious hands upon the Empire Marketing Million. Thus in a very short time they might undo much of the good work which the Colonial Secretary has done, which would be very sad.

My conclusion is that, unless we are quite sure that we can educate the young women into voting for the Milk Tax in time for the next Election, we could not proceed with this particular scheme of 'economic regeneration' without running serious risk of 'political degeneration'.

WSC

Winston S. Churchill to Sir Horace Hamilton and Alfred Hurst

(*Churchill papers: 18/87*)

11 March 1928

I presume that, if the relief which the Railways will obtain on the rates from the new scheme is limited to £m 3 instead of £m $4\frac{1}{2}$, the expense to the Exchequer is also similarly reduced. Is this so? I agree that the lessening of the relief strengthens the argument for concentrating it. On the assumption that there is a saving of £m $1\frac{1}{2}$ to the Exchequer, please recalculate the table of finance in CP 8 (28), noting that the Suspensory Fund will also be slightly increased by this course.

Pray explain to me the bearing of the possible increase of assessment other than Railways by 15%. Would not this provide a margin of growth for the expenditure of local authorities during the next five years, ie if they are

forced to obtain more money for local purposes, the same rate on the
enhanced assessment will afford the necessary margin. All this enhancement
of the assessment constitutes a further argument for removing industry
altogether from the exploitation of the local authorities.

WSC

Winston S. Churchill to Consuelo Balsan

(*Churchill papers: 1/199*)

13 March 1928

My dear Consuelo,

Clemmie had to have another slight operation yesterday, to help the
wound to heal. She got through it all right & is going on quite well. But this
has set her back a week, & she will not now be able to come to you on the
19th. The Drs say there is every reason to believe she can start on the 24th,
& I am hoping [& straining every nerve]¹ very much to come with her to
you on the same date. At the same time however, as I am sure you understand, these critical days before said night on March 31 at the end of the
financial year make it esp hard for me to escape, & you must not count on
me to the extent of putting off other people. Let me take my chance of yr
having a bedroom vacant. [I do hope this change will not be inconvenient,
but we are in the grip of the Fates.] With every good wish to you and Jacques.

Yours affectionately,
W

I shd so like to take C out to yr lovely eyrie & to have a few days sunshine
and trees with you all.

---

¹ Churchill deleted the two passages in square brackets before sending this letter.

Winston S. Churchill to Neville Chamberlain

(*Churchill papers: 18/87*)

13 March 1928
Private and Personal

My dear Neville,

I was not only concerned but startled by the air of antagonism which you seemed to me to show yesterday morning, and I should be very sorry indeed if I have done anything to justify it. I am bound to represent as a colleague not as an opponent the very strong views of my advisers on these important points. I must say that I do not feel completely reassured by the argument which you used. I will await the report of Robinson's[1] Committee in the hope that it may remove my misgivings.

Pray dismiss altogether from your mind the idea that I wish to overbear you in the matter, or that I have any feeling apart from making sure we go on the right lines. Obviously if you impose a veto in the way you did yesterday morning, I must after all arguments have been deployed submit to it. I can make no progress in the face of your opposition. You are therefore the master; and my only remedy, if I find the task too hard or too wearisome will be to withdraw the scheme. It will be quite easy to do this, so far as I am concerned, on financial grounds, and by stating that no satisfactory safeguards for the Exchequer could be devised. Indeed, when I see how very great are the difficulties which you apprehend, and how very hard would be the effort I should have to make, I feel at times not so far from taking such a decision.

Do not, I beg you, suppose that I have set my heart upon the project or that you are doing me a personal kindness by assenting to it. I have been actuated solely by a desire to help the Government in the very critical phase now opening by producing a large constructive plan. Of course the Treasury think it quixotic of me to quit the beaten track of economy and debt-repayment. I am sure however that if we show ourselves incapable of offering solutions of any of the three or four large questions involved in this project, and remain in a rut of blank negation, political disaster awaits us next year. Therefore I have tried, and will continue to persevere.

I have been puzzled from your first rather chilling letter at the outset down to the present moment that this policy did not more appeal to you.

---

[1] William Arthur Robinson, 1874–1950. Educated at Appleby School and Queen's College Oxford. Entered Colonial Office, 1897 (first place in Civil Service Examination). Permanent Secretary, Air Ministry, 1917–20. Knighted, 1919. Secretary to the Ministry of Health, 1920–35. Chairman of the Supply Board, Committee of Imperial Defence, 1935–9. Secretary to the Ministry of Supply, 1939–40.

Without it there could be no poor law reform in this Parliament such as I understood you greatly desired. With it the whole system of Local Government can be the subject of a reform as famous as that of 1834. I always expected that you would be eager for this opportunity, and would supply at least half the driving power. Instead of this, I have felt extremely lonely in the shafts. Without your active aid, not merely acquiescence, I am sure I cannot drag the cart up the hill—nor shall I try.

In view of the line that Worthy is taking I must review the finance of the scheme in hopes of finding resources sufficient to dispense with the national rate entirely. I do not expect to be successful in this quest; but it can go forward *pari passu* with Robinson's study of the distribution formula. Meanwhile I am sure it would be a good thing if we talked the whole position over together. Perhaps you will let me know whether tomorrow morning, now blank, would suit you. I do hope we shall be able to work together at this large plan.

Neville Chamberlain to Winston S. Churchill

(*Churchill papers: 18/87*)

14 March 1928   Ministry of Health

My dear Winston,

I only received your letter this morning just as I was about to change and go to the Guildhall Luncheon, so that it was impossible for me to see you today. But of course I shall gladly meet you whenever we can arrange a time mutually convenient.

Meanwhile your letter needs some reply. The 'air of antagonism' with which you reproach me was forced upon me by your own proceedings. If, instead of firing off a memorandum to the Committee, you had spoken to me personally you would have realised that I felt strongly and perhaps we might have agreed to differ privately if no further compromise could have been found. But in the circumstances I had no alternative but to speak plainly.

As I see the position it is I who am in the shafts in this business while you are the leader in the hansom and if we are to work together there must be give and take on both sides. Up to now I have done all the giving but very little weight had been attached to any views if they have differed from yours.

I had a scheme which I believed would reform the Poor Law and deal with the necessitous areas. I could have carried it with your help but you were not satisfied unless you could have something much bigger and incidentally much more difficult from the point of view of Local Government.

I am trying now to fall in with your views and have gone a long way further than I should have liked to meet them. Yet you are puzzled that I am not as enthusiastic over your scheme as over my own. Is not that natural and only a reflection of your own case?

I have no time to write more now but I will tell my Secretary to arrange for an appointment.

Yours sincerely,
N. Chamberlain

Harold Macmillan to Winston S. Churchill
(*Churchill papers: 18/87*)

14 March 1928

My dear Chancellor,

I have to go North tomorrow and do not return till Saturday. In the greatest hurry I have ventured to scribble the enclosed, after spending a morning with Bob among the papers at the Treasury.

Yours sincerely,
Harold Macmillan

Harold Macmillan: notes for Winston S. Churchill
(*Churchill papers: 18/87*)

14 March 1928

A

Assuming that the Treasury cannot afford a complete de-rating of Industry and Agriculture, there appeared at the beginning of the enquiry to be 3 courses open for raising the amount of money required.

i. *The Profits Tax.* It was agreed that this was logically sound, and theoretically preferable to partial de-rating. But it was also agreed that the political and psychological effects of starting an entirely new form of tax, parallel to the present income tax, would be dangerous and unwise. Indeed, it cannot be denied that the existing income tax is really the best form of profits tax; nor does there seem any justification for the institution of a new tax, which in its effect on industry would be similar to income tax. There is no necessity to forge a new weapon; there is an efficient and powerful engine ready to hand, if it be thought desirable to employ it.

ii. *The remission of ⅔ of the rates, leaving ⅓ to be raised as at present.*

I felt very strongly, and I think you agreed, that this would defeat the real object of the whole scheme. It would not secure uniformity. It would not produce that feeling of security and confidence which we are aiming at. Indeed, on this basis, I think the whole scheme would not be worth while at all.

iii. *The flat-rate of 5/- in the £.*

It appears that this can be raised in 2 forms
(a) as a contribution to be paid to the Treasury, and reissued by the Treasury to local authorities. Presumably in this case the rate would be levied on present assessments, which would be stabilised for at least a period.
(b) as a direct contribution to the local authorities.

I gather that there is a strong objection to (a) on various grounds. But the arguments in your own memorandum in favour of (a) seem to me conclusive. The whole object of the plan is to give the producer not only financial relief but moral relief. We want to free him not only from the present burden of local taxation, but also from the fear of future local oppression. This oppression is making him shun localities which are economically advantageous but politically dangerous. *Nor is there any argument which can be advanced against iii (a) which is not destructive of the whole principle of the plan itself.*
For instance, the Ministry of Health appears to believe, like the Whig historians, in the principle of 'No taxation without representation.' It is true that it inverts the principle into one of 'No representation without taxation.' But has this principle, even if it applied properly to the England of the period before the first Reform Bill, any reality today? Is it not merely the pedant's adherence to an obsolete theory? Does a citizen in fact go into local government, or into public life generally, simply as a ratepayer? It is true that he may vote, as a ratepayer, for the party that keeps down or promises to keep down the rates. But after all the industrialist seldom has a vote in respect of his works. This privilege is more commonly exercised by the charwoman or the night watchman. Actually the citizen goes on the Town Council or on the County Council for the same reasons that he goes on the board of a Hospital—because he is a good citizen; because he has a tradition of service; because it amuses him; because he thinks it the right thing to do. Pride, Tradition, Patriotism—these are quite as powerful motives as Interest. It certainly cannot be alleged that the mere fact of a 5/- flat rate being collected *locally* instead of *nationally* is going to affect the

character or maintain the probity of local government. If the argument has any weight at all, it is equally an argument against any form of remission of the incidence of local taxation.

B

Is there any chance of the Treasury being able to afford complete de-rating?
If there is any possible hope of this, I feel it would be far the best solution.

1. It would be simple—and therefore attractive.
2. It would sweep away all the discussion about flat rate and proportional rates and systems of collection.
3. It avoids the objection to giving special favour to new industries (against which the Board of Trade argument appears powerful) but at the same time it secures the advantages you desire—ie the new enterprises will go to the populated areas instead of settling in the rural areas.

    Politically it makes the whole difference. The partial scheme is good; the complete scheme is overwhelmingly good.
4. It is true that it would probably be a gamble. But it is a gamble that could not produce a deficit till 1930 or 1931. It will therefore either be for the Opposition (if we are defeated in 1929) to carry the baby; or (if we win) it will be up to us to get the thing straight in the five years which we shall have for the purpose.

On all these grounds, therefore, I feel that every effort should be made to go all out for the complete cut.

There are one or two further points, of a purely political character.

1. It seems to me that, owing to its inherent complications and difficulties, you will only carry the *partial* scheme, in one or other of its forms, if you have the whole-hearted and enthusiastic support of your colleagues. It is too difficult a scheme to carry through with only their grudging support.
2. If you stick to the *partial* scheme, you may be driven to accept an unsatisfactory form even of the scheme (eg the controversy about the 5/- flat rate).
3. If, on the other hand, you are in a position to recommend the *complete* scheme, I think it is such good electioneering (as well as so intrinsically sound) that I believe you could carry it in the teeth of your colleagues.
4. I think you can impress the Cabinet with the *complete* scheme; you can smother the objections under a cataract of advantages. With the *partial* scheme you may only be able to worry and alarm them.

5. The *complete* scheme is a really big thing. The partial scheme may go off at half-cock and prove rather a failure (politically) just because it is partial.

Finally, may I say that I regard the whole question as really vital. Its reception and ultimate fate at the hands of the Cabinet, seem to me to mark the turning point in the history of the Party. We have no other constructive policy. If we do not adopt it, a return to extreme Protection is merely a question of time. We cannot go to the country with no policy at all. It is true that we have been able to cover our nakedness up to now by the (providential) General Strike and Coal Stoppage. We have even been able to occupy a year with the Trade Union Bill. But the Strike and the TU Bill are wearing a bit thin. We cannot go on indefinitely without a policy at all. It seems to me that if this plan goes awry, we shall see the eventual, and perhaps early, dissolution of the Party. If it goes right, it will put new life into the Party. It will provide a constructive policy other than Protection. It will rally the waverers. It will consolidate the moderate vote. It will put fresh hope and enthusiasm into the hearts of all those who have supported the Conservative Party because they honestly believed it to be a Party capable of constructive thought and progressive effort.

HM

Winston S. Churchill to Cyril Alington
(*Churchill papers: 18/87*)

14 March 1928

My dear Alington,

Thank you so much for sending me these milestones of the English language. They are deeply interesting, and I am glad to have them by me.

I think your wife[1] will be interested to see the enclosed Foreign Office

---

[1] Hester Margaret Lyttelton, daughter of the 4th Baron Lyttelton. When she died, in 1958, Robert Birley, then headmaster of Eton, wrote of how, at Eton, 'Mrs Alington would throw out the most unexpected remarks in an English style so individual and so apt that an ability to quote them has become a treasured mark of distinction among those who knew her. But this will not disclose the fact that one found himself talking with someone who was not only very penetrating, but was also a saint, someone who lived constantly, one might really say familiarly, in the presence of God.' She lived her last days at Durham. The Bishop of Derby, who came to know her there, wrote to *The Times* on 2 April 1958: 'Mr Birley has written of her life at Eton: to this her life at Durham constituted a no less notable sequel. The Deanery, hitherto the home of a celibate, became, with the advent of the Alingtons, a fascinating and welcoming family home. The open heart and the open door were the same at Durham as they had been at Eton and Shrewsbury.' One of her four sons was killed on active service in 1943.

paper which contains an extract from a German account of what is happening in the Soviet Union. It illustrates the frightful burdens which Governments assume when they try to regulate the entire economic processes of a vast community, and the process of universal self-torture that results. Pray let me have the paper back as soon as you have both read it, as it is an official document though not intrinsically secret.

Diana and I enjoyed our weekend very much indeed, and it was most kind of you to give us and Randolph such a treat.

With good wishes, believe me,

Winston S. Churchill to Lord Beaverbrook

(*Beaverbrook papers*)

18 March 1928   11 Downing Street
Private and Confidential

My dear Max,

I have read the enclosed with great interest, and it certainly errs—if at all—only on the side of being too complimentary to me.

There are two points of substance.

First, if my recollection serves, it was Germany that declared war upon Russia. This you should verify.

Secondly—the actual step I left the room to take was to mobilise the Navy. The First and Second Fleets, as you will remember, had already been sent to Scapa Flow and were in the fullest state of preparation for instant war. The mobilisation meant that the whole Navy and dockyards were put on a war footing and that 30,000 or 40,000 Reserves were called up from civil life; thus enabling all the Third Fleet ships to be manned, and numerous cruiser squadrons and armed auxiliaries to take their place swiftly upon the various trade routes. The Cabinet had that morning over-ruled my request for mobilisation, holding that the First and Second Fleets being in their position this further step was needlessly provocative. When I left the Admiralty at this moment I went to Downing Street and informed Mr Asquith that I intended to give the order to mobilise, in spite of the Cabinet's decision, and would answer for it to them the next morning. The Prime Minister simply sat and looked at me and said no word. No doubt he felt himself bound by the morning's decision of the Cabinet. I certainly however sustained the impression that he would not put out a finger to stop me. I then walked back to the Admiralty across the Parade Ground and gave the order. Legal authority was not obtained until the Sunday. (This was I think the Saturday.) However all the Reserves came up immediately with hardly one hundred exceptions, in spite of there being no Royal Proclamation.

I don't suggest that you should cumber your excellent account with all this stuff; but the actual fact which is of interest for the future is that the mobilisation was actually ordered against the Cabinet decision and without legal authority. However I never got into any trouble over it.

Yours vy sincerely
Winston S. Churchill

Edward Marsh to Mrs F. C. Roberts

(*Churchill papers: 1/199*)

19 March 1928

Dear Madam,

Mr Churchill desires me to say that he has seen with much regret the announcement of the death of your husband, Sergeant Clement Roberts,[1] and that, as he fears you may be in straitened circumstances, he hopes that you will accept the enclosed cheque which he would like to think might be of some assistance to you.

Winston S. Churchill to Sir Roger Keyes

(*Churchill papers: 2/157*)

22 March 1928
Private and Personal

My dear Roger,

I have been distressed about the *Royal Oak* business and the senseless stir it has made.[2] Dewar is, as you know, a personal friend of mine, and a

---

[1] On 22 February 1928 the following article appeared in *The Times*, from their Johannesburg correspondent: 'The death has occurred near Benoni of Mr Clem Roberts, who as a sergeant during the war rescued Mr Winston Churchill from a dangerous situation in the action near Dewetsdorp. During a skirmish Mr Churchill, while under heavy fire from the Boers, was thrown from his horse, which bolted. Mr Roberts rode up to Mr Churchill, who mounted behind him, and Mr Roberts galloped to safety, though his horse was wounded.'

[2] Captain Kenneth Dewar and Commander Henry Daniel were being court-martialled in Gibraltar for certain events that took place on board Dewar's ship, HMS *Royal Oak*, on 7 March 1928. On that day Commander Daniel had given Captain Dewar a letter complaining of an action by Rear-Admiral Bernard St George Collard, flag officer of the First Battle Squadron, Mediterranean, who was flying his flag in the *Royal Oak*. Daniel's letter stated that on 5 March 1928 Rear-Admiral Collard had become furious in front of the crew when arrangements, under the supervision of Commander Daniel, for the Rear-Admiral's dis-

neighbour in the country. He is certainly one of the ablest of the younger Naval officers I have met, and was specially commended to me by Beatty as representing the 'Forward School' in peace and war. On reaching England he asked to see me, and after obtaining the First Lord's permission I had two interviews with him, of course in a purely private and unofficial capacity. What I write to you now is also purely private and personal.

I strongly urged Dewar not to forget, even in the conduct of his own defence, his duty to uphold the dignity and traditions of the Navy, so that it shall not be made a mockery to foreign eyes. I believe he will act in that spirit.

Beaverbrook offered to pay, on behalf of the 'Daily Express', the whole expenses of a King's Counsel. This Dewar has refused, and their only assistance will be from a young cousin of Daniel's [1] who has some legal training. Dewar further told me that all he had expected to happen as the result of his complaint, was that the Vice Admiral would have brought the Flag Captain and the Rear Admiral to a good understanding, and he was equally surprised and shocked at the vast and lamentable consequences which had developed. On the other hand I quite see your difficulty in that the ship might have been imperilled if sent to sea with its senior officers in such bad relations.

My hope now is that the matter may be conducted to a just conclusion with the fewest words and without vindictiveness. Justice must be done whatever happens, but all friends of the Navy will be greatly relieved if that result can be achieved in a dignified and decorous manner. I sympathise very much with you in having had such a vexatious incident in your Command; and you have now, as always, my very best wishes in your difficult and responsible task.

---

embarkation from the ship were not carried out to the Rear-Admiral's satisfaction. His anger and his conduct, according to Commander Daniel, were unfair, and detrimental to the morale of the ship. Daniel was also charged with reading his letter aloud in the wardroom. Dewar forwarded Daniel's letter to Rear-Admiral Collard together with a covering letter of his own. The covering letter referred to an earlier incident where Rear-Admiral Collard had lost his temper, and he agreed with Daniel that the Rear-Admiral's conduct had on each instance been detrimental to the morale of the ship. On March 20 Collard struck his flag from the *Royal Oak*, and was subsequently replaced. On March 30 a Court-Martial was convened on the action of Commander Daniel. He was found guilty of actions prejudicial to order and discipline, both in writing the letter and in reading it aloud. He was dismissed from the ship and severely reprimanded. On April 5 Captain Dewar was found guilty of the same offence for forwarding the letter, and received the same sentence.

[1] Henry Martin Daniel. Entered the Royal Navy in 1903 as a naval cadet. Lieutenant, 1909. Gunnery officer on board the light cruisers *Isis*, *Royalist* and *Dauntless*, 1914–18. Awarded the DSO for services as executive officer of *Dauntless* in the Baltic, 1919. Lieutenant-Commander, 1920. Commander, 1922. Naval Ordnance Department, 1922. Squadron gunnery officer, *Iron Duke*, 1925. Joined the *Royal Oak*, December 1927.

Lord Beaverbrook to Winston S. Churchill

(*Churchill papers: 2/157*)

22 March 1928

My dear Winston,

Herewith copy of letter to Bonar Law dated May 21, 1915.[1]

Will you please send a message by telephone or telegram. I will not be at the Vineyard, but I have a secretary there who will convey your decision to me.

Yours ever,
Max

Winston S. Churchill to Lord Beaverbrook

(*Beaverbrook papers*)

23 March 1928   Treasury Chambers

My dear Max,

You make me tear open old wounds and their sting returns. Certainly publish the letter as you propose, not as a thing thrust into publicity by me but on your own responsibility. I shall never complain: on the contrary, I am very glad it should see the light of day.

Yours ever
W

Winston S. Churchill to Neville Chamberlain

(*Churchill papers: 18/88*)

24 March 1928

My dear Neville,

I told the Treasury to send you over the week-end some figures comparing the profits of basic industries in 1924 and 1927, showing a fall of no less than

---

[1] On 21 May 1915 Churchill, having been told by Asquith that he must leave the Admiralty, had written to the Conservative leader, Andrew Bonar Law, who was about to enter the Government. The letter is published in full in Companion Volume III of this Biography, Part 2, pages 922–4. In it Churchill wrote: 'On the approach of war I had to act far in excess of my authority to make the vital arrangements for the safety of the country. I had to mobilise the Fleet without legal sanction and contrary to a Cabinet decision. I have had to face 9 months of war under conditions no man has known, and which were in the early months infinitely more anxious than those which confront us now.' Churchill added: 'I ask to be judged fairly, deliberately and with knowledge. I do not ask for anything else,' and he told Bonar Law: 'The rule to follow is what is best calculated to beat the enemy, and not what is most likely to please the newspapers.'

£m 40, ie one-third, in those profits in that time, with corresponding loss to the Revenue. It is the urgent need of giving definite and effectual support to these industries, by relieving them from their invidious burden of rates, that has led me into all the labours of this Scheme. But for that object I should not have made the effort. I was from the beginning conscious of the modest character of the help that could in any case be afforded them by such means within the limits which were possible. A relief, for instance, of not more than 4/- a ton upon steel will not be very appreciable. It was for this reason that I considered the cumulative effect of the concentrated railway traffic reliefs so important. They raise the relief to steel to something well over 8/- on the average.

If the railway reliefs are excluded and nothing substituted in their place, it seems to me very doubtful whether it is worth while going on with the Scheme at all. We shall have all the labours, all the oppositions, all the parochialisms, all the additional expense to the Exchequer, all the friction of a new tax without the strong driving power which would be afforded by a genuine relief to depressed industry.

If on the other hand railways and other public utilities are excluded and the money saved on them becomes available for completely de-rating productive industry, then the inducement becomes once again large enough to justify the exertion. Here however, your difficulties arise. As you explained them to me they are two-fold: first, the complete divorce between local industries and local rates; and secondly, the magnitude of the change involved in the sources from which the Local Authorities will draw their funds. The first objection must, I admit, remain valid so far as it goes; but surely it should be weighed against other considerations. I am not sure that the second difficulty is not greatly modified—if not indeed removed—by the total exclusion from the Scheme of railways and public utilities. *Prima facie* this leaves £m 12½ in the hands of the Local Authorities, as against £m 13 involved in the National Rate. It leaves these £m 12½ unmoved, ie in the area of the Known, and consequently reduces Change considerably. Moreover, one would think that the concentration of docks and railways in particular areas, and the improvement of the gas and electric plants in great cities, would tend to minimise the most violent oscillations which the Scheme would cause to local finance. On this point Robinson has kindly promised to give me some example figures. I trust you will examine and consider this aspect very carefully in the few days that are left to us.

The more I think the whole subject over, the more I am attracted by the larger and bolder plan. Its simplicity and thoroughness appeal strongly to me. All the complications of dealing with the railways and the public utilities vanish. There vanishes also the National Rate, with all the explanations required on that account, and also all the thin explanations of how the National Rate is to be related to the new Exchequer grants. All the machinery of the assessment of industry and of new enterprises or extensions disappears. We have the simple clear-cut proposition of taking productive industry entirely out of national rates by means principally of a tax on imported liquid fuel, the support forthcoming for the one to be balanced against the opposition aroused by the other. The proposition becomes brief, big and plain. I think that Worthy's political instinct has not failed him in this matter.

Failing this solution I am willing to adhere to the original scheme and even to agree to the omission of gas and electricity. But if the heavy industries are neither to get total relief from rates nor two-thirds relief from rates plus the railway relief, then I am increasingly inclined to think that we had better leave the handling of these thorny matters to another Parliament, and perhaps to other hands.

WSC

Winston S. Churchill to A. C. Sheepshanks

(*Churchill papers: 1/199*)

26 March 1928

Dear Mr Sheepshanks,

As my wife is not allowed to do any serious business at the present time, I am sure you will not mind my replying to your letter to her.

I am very sorry that trouble has arisen about Randolph's leave. That leave was asked for and granted for the sole purpose of enabling him to see his mother before her departure for her convalescence in the South of France. The fact that she found herself well enough to spend a few hours in taking him to a theatre appears to be irrelevant. He had no idea of this when he asked for leave, nor was it certain that my wife would be well enough to do such a thing. Had she known that you would have felt a difficulty in granting leave if any portion of the time were to be so applied, she would certainly not have transgressed your wishes. We are both very much obliged to you for letting Randolph come. . . .[1]

---

[1] On 30 March 1928 Clementine Churchill reached Consuelo Balsan's villa at Eze, in the South of France, where she convalesced from her illness. Her daughter Diana accompanied her. That night Clementine Churchill wrote to her husband: 'My Darling One—I do not regret my illness, for it has brought you so close to me. I always love you—you are always deep down in my heart and now your tenderness has unlocked it. I hope your two Budgets will prove not too refractory. Tender love to you my Darling, Clemmie' (*Spencer-Churchill papers*).

Neville Chamberlain: diary

(*Neville Chamberlain papers*)

28 March 1928

Last Monday[1] Hogg came to see me in my room at the House in considerable distress of mind. The PM had informed him that the Ld Chancellor[2] had resigned. FE had refused the office. He had looked all round for someone else but could see no one capable except Sumner[3] whom he would not have in the Cabinet. He had therefore asked Hogg to take it.

Douglas said to me, only now that I am face to face with the decision have I fully realised that I don't want to take the Woolsack & he gave various reasons. He didn't like the proposal of listening for long hours in the Lords, his style was not adapted to them &c &c. But of course the real difficulty was that it barred any chance of the premiership. 'I don't know that I have much ambition that way, but I don't want to see W Churchill Prime Minister. I have the greatest respect for his brilliant abilities but none for his judgement.'

He was not quite certain that it was not too late to ask my opinion as he was afraid he had rather committed himself & indeed he could see no one else suitable. I therefore vehemently protested. I pointed out that if he accepted he lost the succession to the Premiership but if he refused he did not bar the Chancellorship hereafter. I said I was quite aware that he & I were both talked of as SB's successors. I was sure (on Austen's authority) that FE & Winston would both serve under him. I was not sure that either would serve under me. In any case I had no wish for it; I wd not shirk it if I felt it my duty to take it, but I would not lift a finger to get it & knew it must be fatal to my peace of mind. On the other hand I would joyfully serve under him. . . .

This morning I asked SB for an interview but as I passed to my seat in Cabinet Douglas said 'It's too late. All's settled.' SB at once announced that Inskip[4] was to be AG + Merriman[5] SG. I passed on a note to say

---

[1] Monday 26 March 1928.

[2] Lord Cave (see page 323, note 1).

[3] John Andrew Hamilton Sumner, 1859–1934. Called to the Bar, 1883. A High Court Judge, 1909–12. A Lord Justice of Appeal, 1912–13. Created Baron, 1913. A Lord of Appeal, 1913–30. Chairman of the Working Classes Cost of Living Committee, 1918. Member of the British Delegation of the Reparations Commission, Paris Peace Conference, 1919. Created Viscount, 1927.

[4] Sir Thomas Inskip (see page 712, note 3), served as Attorney-General from March 1928 until the change of Government in June 1929.

[5] Frank Boyd Merriman, 1880–1962. Barrister, 1904. Deputy Assistant Adjutant-General, 1917. Recorder of Wigan, 1920–8. Conservative MP for Rusholme, 1924–33. Knighted, 1928. Solicitor-General, 1928–9 and 1932–3. President of the Probate, Divorce and Admiralty Division of the High Court of Justice, 1933–62. Created Baron, 1941.

how *deeply* distressed I was & he replied that he was feeling rather miserable this afternoon. I saw the PM who was apologetic but said it was inevitable. FE wd have accepted it if he had been told that it was in the party interest but he was afraid to trust him. He might be seen drunk in the street. I said I would have taken the risk. Afterwards SB said FE had told him in the last 24 hrs that he would not go on a new Govt after the election. He wanted to make money.

Winston S. Churchill: Cabinet memorandum[1]

(Churchill papers: 18/89)

28 March 1928   Treasury Chambers
Most Secret
To Be Kept Under Lock and Key

It is requested that special care may be taken to ensure the secrecy of this document

THE EXEMPTION OF INDUSTRY FROM RATES

The proposal to exempt industry totally from rates is and can only be justified by acceptance of the view that it is economically unsound to tax instruments of production. The profits resulting from the use of such instruments are already taxed under the steeply ascending scales now in force. The imposition of rates upon productive plants is double taxation. It is an invidious impost which falls with increasing weight as the instruments become more bulky and afford employment to larger numbers of manual workers. This discourages the employment of manual workers and is a contributory factor to the disastrous unemployment which has now become chronic. The task set to a British employer of labour on a large scale is exceptionally difficult. Compared to the profits yielded to bankers and merchants or producers who do not require to use large plants or employ many workpeople, the rewards of industry have seriously and rapidly diminished. The temptation to seek easier means of wealth getting than those involved in providing employment for labour is increasing and ought to be diminished. An employer paying wages to a large number of workpeople must at the present time in this country be regarded as rendering a service to the community rather than obtaining a privilege at their hands.

[1] This memorandum was circulated to the Policy Committee of the Cabinet, as Policy Committee paper 21 of 1928.

In strict equity individuals should be taxed according to what they have to spend and enjoy and not according to the class of gainful occupation they pursue. If the balance is to be loaded at all, it should certainly not be against those who are discharging a primary and vital function to the community and who are flagging under the load they bear. The services rendered by the community to a large employer in protecting his works and providing for his workpeople are exactly repaid by the effort which he makes to supply the wages of large numbers of citizens, and no further special payment can be required by the community on account of the extensive nature of his premises.

There is no reason of justice and still less of policy for discriminating in favour of the man who makes £10,000 a year from a small office with half a dozen clerks and the man who makes £10,000 a year by employing 100 men: and the idea of exacting from the latter a heavy special contribution for the protection of his works in a year when he has derived no benefit from it although he has provided much employment is irrational in theory and injurious in practice. Let all get their living how they can on even terms and let the State tax their profits according to the magnitude.

The above deals with the relations in our present social system between the employer of labour and the community or the national state. The requirements of the Local Authorities in whose districts particular factories are situated are a most important but altogether separate question. Under the present scheme the state relieves the producer from the invidious burden, and from its own resources reimburses the Local Authority for the diminution in its rateable assets. That reimbursement is at present to be effected partly by direct compensation for the loss, partly by a variable provision based upon the needs, and partly by an extra grant from the State to prevent hardship to any Local Authority.

If it be desired in addition to make Local Authorities partners to some extent in additions to national prosperity, this aspect can be studied. It is not intended that the Local Authorities should be cut off from all share in the expansion of wealth. Any reasonable scheme for associating them with the rise in the national fortunes is entirely in harmony with the main conceptions of the present policy, provided practical difficulties can be overcome. Any such extension as has hitherto taken place is however reflected far more in the residential property which is still left to the Local Authorities than in the producing plants which it is now proposed to remove from their control.

WSC

Sir Samuel Hoare to Lord Irwin

(*Irwin papers*)

30 March 1928

As you know, we wish to do something with the rates, but the difficulty is to decide how much is practicable and whether if we attempt to do a very big thing, we may not be sunk in a mass of details. Neville is very much alive to this danger and is obviously rather nervous of it all.

Winston S. Churchill: Cabinet note

(*Churchill papers: 18/74*)

31 March 1928

I am in full agreement with the policy adopted by the War Office of using the Cavalry personnel to operate mechanical vehicles. I am content with the step that has been taken in mechanising two cavalry regiments, etc, so far as this financial year is concerned, but I consider that further measures should be taken as rapidly as possible to furnish the British Cavalry with an equipment suitable to modern war. I hold most strongly that further transformations of horse soldiers are required in the interests, primarily of war efficiency, but also for the economies resulting from the elimination of redundant units.

In these circumstances I regret that I find myself unable to sign a report which would associate me either with acquiescence in the present military view, or in any suggestion that progress towards mechanisation should not be as rapid as we can possibly afford.

April 1928

---

1 April 1928   10 Downing Street

My dear Winston,

As you know, I am inclined to be—shall we say phlegmatic when the Press is concerned? but I do congratulate you warmly on the leader in to-day's Sunday Times.[1] It seems to me to be a very true appreciation and I hope it has given you pleasure.

Yours ever,
SB

L. S. Amery: diary
(*Amery papers*)

2 April 1928

I came down very strongly on the side of Neville and Jack Gilmour in favour of local contributions and also against derating of railways, the tide flowing pretty definitely in this direction in spite of Philip and Worthy and a majority on Winston's committee.

---

[1] The *Sunday Times* leader described Churchill as 'a dexterous steward of the national finances' and wrote of his Budget decisions: 'The proof that he chose rightly is in the realised surplus with which the financial year has ended. There were, roughly, two courses open to him. One was to treat the deficit with pedantic purism as an objective for a frontal attack by the big guns of new, heavy and direct taxation. The other was to skirmish round it, and so to speak, sharpshoot it into nothingness. Mr Churchill decided on the more daring and less conventional method. He brought out of the national arsenal a variety of financial weapons, which he fashioned anew and turned one by one upon the enemy.' The article added: 'If one can feel to-day that the outlook for British trade is perceptibly brighter than it was a year ago, Mr Churchill's mercifulness in his last Budget has very largely to be thanked for it. He made better trade possible by refraining from saddling it with a new load of taxation.'

Cabinet minutes

(Cabinet papers: 23/57)

4 April 1928

THE CHANCELLOR OF THE EXCHEQUER informed the Cabinet that the policy committee had met on the previous evening and had agreed unanimously to recommend the Cabinet to adopt his original scheme as modified.

(a) (i) The exclusion from the scheme of Public Utility Undertakings including the Railways,

    (ii) The payment, in respect of the de-rated properties of a uniform rate of one-fourth of the poundage of the particular area.

(b) The Chancellor of the Exchequer was to be careful during the Budget statement not to commit the Government to railway rating relief.

Clementine Churchill to Winston S. Churchill

(Spencer-Churchill papers)

4 April 1928   Eze

My Darling,

Your telegram saying 'finally completed agreement' has just come & I do rejoice with you & congratulate you. It must have been a strenuous week with constant meetings & I fear you must be very tired. But not so tired perhaps as the other people. I expect you were like the Widow with the Unjust Judge!

Today I imagine Randolph & Sarah converging on Chartwell.

Yesterday (except the day of our arrival) was the first warm day. It really has been surprisingly cold & bleak & one needs all one's winter clothes. I do not think you would have been able to paint.

Diana returns home with the Blandfords reaching Dover next Tuesday.

On Wednesday I push on to Florence where my address will be:—Villa Ombrellino, Bellosguardo, Florence.[1]

I was startled to see in the local French newspaper that Sir Arthur Steel-Maitland is 'grievement malade'—The Cabinet will soon (it seems) be decimated.

By the way presently Joan Bull and her Mama will require an explanation

---

[1] Alice Keppel's villa.

of your abstention in the Flappers Vote Division![1] The Continental Daily Mail are making a great 'song & dance' over it & are hinting 'darkly at a 'Cave in the Government' & rejoicing prematurely 'at the beginning of the end'. But really as it was bound to go thro' it was naughty of you not to vote—I fear it may cool off some of the Epping Women young & old.

Tender love from
Clemmie

[Sketch of cat]

Winston S. Churchill to Clementine Churchill

(*Spencer-Churchill papers*)

4 April 1928

My darling one,

I am ashamed not to have written before. These last days have been one continuous strain of Cabinets, Committees & personal discussions. But all is settled now: complete agreement and at any rate ¾ of what I was aiming at. Now I have chucked work—am off to Chartwell for a change. You know all of a sudden you feel you do not want to stay any longer in the same place.

Two of yr letters have reached me—I loved to read what you wrote in yr first. I am always 'there': but I am afraid that vy often my business & my toys have made me a poor companion. Anyhow my darling I care for no one in the world but you—& the kittens; & in spite of the anxiety of yr illness I was glad to feel that you relied on me & that I cd help to comfort you a little. I trust you are taking care of yrself: not getting tired: lying down a gt deal: bed early etc. Don't let external things fret yr mind. Blandford has some quite disagreeable things about him: & I can share yr repulsion abt the remark he made. But I don't expect he meant much by it.

The Gibraltar CM [Court Martial] has interested me greatly: & I am all for the poor Dewar & his Daniel. They are not likely to get much justice from such a Court. It is a grief to me that such good officers shd be sacrificed —to the misbehaviour of a bounder & a bully. Roger has I expect taken serious hurt in his future by the whole affair.

---

[1] The second Reading of the Bill to give votes to women between the ages of 18 and 28 was carried in the House of Commons on 29 March 1928, by 387 votes to 10. On April 3 *The Times* reported that 135 Conservatives had been absent from the Division; of these, 18 had paired with Labour Members, 33 were abroad, 15 were ill, 13 were speaking in the country, and 56 were 'unaccounted for'. Esmond Harmsworth was among the Conservatives voting against the Bill. Churchill, who had opposed the Bill in Cabinet, was among the absent Conservatives.

From Chartwell tonight I will send you a 'Bulletin'. There is much local news: all good—chickens, swans, sheep all bringing forth their offspring to greet a Spring—wh let us hope will bring sunshine to all of us.

Your ever loving devoted

W

Winston S. Churchill to Clementine Churchill

(*Spencer-Churchill papers*)

5 April 1928   Chartwell Manor

CHARTWELL BULLETIN

Beloved Clemmie,

Here we are reunited, so far as our broken circle goes. All are well. Mary is a picture of health and enchanted to get back to the country. Sarah looks very well too. Randolph has grown gigantically. I am sending him to play golf with the Professional tomorrow, and on Saturday Johnny[1] is coming down for the weekend. I am also going to teach him Rubicon bezique.

Forty-eight new chickens, out of 49, have been safely incubated—All Moppet's eggs. Two sittings of turkey's eggs are under hens. One sheep has lambed. But today we had a tragedy, as a sheep had to be killed for having a dead lamb which could not be delivered. We are going to eat her, in order to mitigate our loss. The ram is quite cheeky now, swollen with pride at his fertile harem. We are taking all necessary precautions not to be butted or chased by him.

The swans are very sweet. The white ones have begun their nest and laid three eggs so far. They take it in turns to sit. I found Jupiter doing this work last night. He was most affable and tried to explain to me exactly what he was doing. Juno has been reduced to law and order by the black swans. She is allowed to go on to the upper lake; but the moment she misbehaves or is the least above herself, the new female black swan swims quietly up to her, looks her full in the eye, and without even a hiss or a splash or a peck, orders her off, with which command Juno immediately complies. This morning the news is that the black swans[2] have been seen carrying bull-rushes and reeds in their beaks with the presumed intention of constructing a nest. Every care will be taken to protect them from intrusion.

---

[1] John George Spencer Churchill, 1910–   . Churchill's nephew; son of Jack and Lady Gwendeline Churchill. Educated at Harrow. Artist and designer of murals; he painted the Marlborough pavilion at Chartwell, 1938. Served in the Royal Engineers, 1939–45; Major, 1945. He published his memoirs, *Crowded Canvas*, in 1960.

[2] Churchill noted in the margin of his letter at this point: 'Ils font l'amour chaque matin.'

The garden news is quite satisfactory. Old Snowie has made the children's patch perfectly tidy. Next week he will begin again dedockulating. The lawn is looking very nice, beautifully rolled and smooth and mown. The daffodils are lovely and the tulips are pushing forward. The weather has been pretty fair—quite mild with fitful sunshine—in fact all one could expect for April.

How idiotic the 'Daily Mail' is about the Flapper vote division. Nobody expected there would be a division, as only about ten people were known to have the courage of their convictions. The whole episode shows how completely Rothermere is devoid of even the slightest influence upon the House of Commons. I expect in your Riviera retreat his silly headlines may have given you a wrong sense of proportion. No one has paid the slightest attention, and I think Ministers are ceasing to read his paper. At any rate the subject has not been mentioned at any of the numerous Cabinets in which our days have been passed.

I am becoming a Film fan, and last week I went to see 'The Last Command', a very fine anti-Bolshevik film, and 'Wings' which is all about aeroplane fighting and perfectly marvellous. I was so much impressed by it that I went a second time and took the following party: Ronnie McNeill, Worthy, Jack Gilmour, Randolph, Johnny and Pebbin. Their ages ranged from 16 to 65, and all were equally entertained.

The Cabinets on my big policy were very lengthy and difficult. Neville most obstinate and, I thought, unreasonable. But he made his point a matter of *amour propre* and, as I cared about the scheme much more than he, I had to give way. It was not a very important point, and substantially my plan is intact. The great advantage is that we are completely united and the whole Cabinet is keen. The PM intervened, quite decisively and declared that we must act and that the Party authorities whom he had consulted were all sure that, with really energetic propaganda, they could make the whole thing go. This is a great relief for me, as it lightens my heavy load of responsibility.

I was glad of the surplus. It might have been larger if I had pressed very hard. As it is, I am *all right* for the coming year, subject to one or two adjustments and devices.[1] The success of the last Budget, which so many people thought was fanciful and not solid, gives me a good deal of prestige for the very important steps which lie immediately before us.

AJB is still quite ill, though today the report is better. Steel-Maitland is dangerously ill. After a week of temperature of 104°, pneumonia has supervened upon influenza. We shall not know for 48 hours whether he surmounts

---

[1] Churchill noted in the margin at this point: 'secret'.

the crisis or not.[1] The Ministry of Labour would be a very difficult office to fill. I do trust all will be well with the poor man. We had no sooner returned from Lord Cave's funeral[2] than this bad news was broken to us.

Moppet tells me that you are sending Diana home to arrive Tuesday. She had better travel through to London, as I have to go up that day for a Conference. I will have her met at Victoria and bring her down here on the Wednesday when my work is done. Let me know by telegraph if by any chance she is to go on with you to Italy.

Always yr ever loving & devoted
W

PS. I hope you are not punishing me for my neglect to write, by not writing yrself. Every post I ask for a letter—but for two days—none. This is not fair, because I have really been hunted—& you are basking. If it continues I shall demand a Court Martial like Captain Dewar. How curious all you women must be, by the way, to know what was the missing word that caused the trouble.

Alice Balfour to Winston S. Churchill
(Churchill papers: 1/199)

6 April 1928   4 Carlton Gardens

Dear Mr Churchill,

Arthur is going on well, & will I hope be allowed to get up for an hour or two early next week.[3] He is at present only allowed to see one person a day & I have to arrange these one day after another beforehand. He is not to do any work, & all friends are requested to amuse him (which I am sure

---

[1] Steel-Maitland recovered, and remained Minister of Labour until the Conservative election defeat of 1929. He died in 1935, at the age of 59.

[2] Lord Cave had died on 29 March 1928.

[3] On Sunday, 17 March 1928, Churchill, Balfour and H. A. L. Fisher had been guests of Lady Desborough at Taplow Court. Lady Desborough later recalled how Balfour: 'set out for a short time before luncheon, watching the tennis on the red court. After luncheon we sat on at "coffee" in the library, until four o'clock, and he and Winston and Mr Fisher had an enthralling conversation—starting with Napoleon. Mr Fisher has often reminded me of how brilliant Arthur was that day. Then I went out for a walk with Winston, and AJB started to walk round the tennis court with Venetia Montagu. It was then that he had the sudden difficulty in finding the right words, and he used the wrong ones. He was much troubled, and went up to his room to rest. I went up there on returning, a little after five. His speech was then all right, but he was very agitated, and looked ill. We got our doctor, Gilbert Moore, at once. All adverse symptoms had then vanished. and temperature and pulse were normal; but AJB was insistent on going back to his own house at once, and he motored up before dinner' (Balfour papers).

you would do) and not interest him too much (as I fear you are likely to do!).
He has not been allowed to see Sir Maurice Hankey yet, on the latter ground.
I expect Lord Finlay[1] to see him on Tuesday next, but Wednesday at about
5 I can keep free for you if the Drs will allow you to come. He is as keen as
you—in fact too keen, & after the relapse at Taplow the Drs are specially
anxious to keep him quiet. I will tell them about your proposed visit &
hope that they will approve. Meanwhile I shall keep Wednesday at 5 free
for you. . . .

I am so glad to hear that Mrs Churchill is well enough to have gone to
the South of France.

Yours sincerely,
Alice Balfour

Winston S. Churchill: departmental note
(Churchill papers: 18/75)

6 April 1928

It is always a good thing to say how much concessions are estimated to
cost. Expressions like 'inconsiderable', 'inappreciable', etc, make it difficult
for me to judge what is involved. On the assumption, however, that only a
few thousand a year are involved and that the case is a good one, I see no
reason why a private Member should not be encouraged to an agreed
clause. . . .

I repeat my general warning against overloading the Finance Bill with
all sorts of bright ideas and happy thoughts and righteous impulses.

Winston S. Churchill to William Bridgeman
(Churchill papers: 22/190)

6 April 1928
Private

My dear Willie,

I was distressed to learn by telephone the result of the Court Martial. I
see that you have stated in Parliament that you will make a statement upon
this whole matter when we reassemble and when the Admiralty have fully

---

[1] Robert Bannatyne Finlay, 1842–1929. Conservative MP, 1885–92, 1895–1906 and 1910–
16. Knighted, 1895. Solicitor-General, 1895–1900; Attorney-General, 1900–6; Lord Chancellor, 1916–18. Created Baron, 1916; Viscount, 1919. He died on 9 March 1929 (Balfour himself died on 19 March 1930).

considered the reports of the case. I hope you will take the Cabinet into your confidence before final decisions are reached. The case raises issues of far more than ordinary importance. If officers of this distinction are to be punished with such severity for making a complaint absolutely justified in fact, though irregular in form, what chance has an ordinary rating of having his grievances considered? The moral of these Courts Martial seems most threatening to all ranks and ratings who have cause to complain of harsh or unjust treatment by their superiors. Thus a safety valve indispensable to discipline is in danger of being choked. Several of our colleagues have spoken to me in somewhat the same sense, and I therefore trust and ask that you will bring the matter before the Cabinet in due course. I have not mentioned my wish to discuss it to the Prime Minister as yet, but will do so if you wish.

Since dictating the above the newspapers have come in—showing a very general feeling against these officers being professionally ruined. I hear the same view from every quarter. The Navy cannot afford to lose men like Dewar. No one had more to do with the spade work of getting the Convoy system started in the war than he. Ask Hankey. And it was our salvation!

Yours very sincerely,
Winston S. Churchill

Winston S. Churchill to Stanley Baldwin
(Baldwin papers)

7 April 1928   Chartwell Manor

My dear Prime Minister,

In meditation alone here and in the intervals of building a reinforcement concrete dam, my mood has become robust. I am not content to drop the railways out of the original scheme. I am not afraid of any arguments that can be used against 'subsidies' or 'favoured traffics'. I see the target and the bull's eye in the middle of it quite clearly in this country air. To relieve the basic industries in such a manner and on such a scale as will give them a real galvanic jerk is the only thing worth all this trouble and expense. To act by half-measures with a lack of conviction miscalled 'caution', is to run the greatest risks and lose the prize. No, let us be audacious. One does not want to live forever. We have the power: let us take the best measures.

Accordingly I wish to raise again as soon as we meet a relief on the railways rates. I shall not interfere with Neville or my agreement with him in any way. The railways will continue to pay their rates as at present to the local authorities. I shall reimburse *them* (not the local authorities) whatever sum they have to pay in rates at present. This will not be a moving figure, but a fixed figure under control of the Treasury. In fact it will be a State subsidy in relief of rates, which subsidy must be passed on through the selected traffics to the basic industries. These traffics, as you know, have been selected so as to give 95% advantage to our people and only 5% to the foreigner, although of course there is no invidious adverse discrimination. Oh Dear No!

I am writing to Neville and to Cunliffe-Lister on the above lines. I am drafting a paper for the Cabinet; and if you approve, I will seek a direct decision on this question in isolation. I do not feel we have done justice to it so far; and now that all this Ministry of Health rating stuff is settled, there may be a far better opportunity.

Yours vy sincerely
Winston S. Churchill

Winston S. Churchill to Neville Chamberlain
(*Churchill papers: 18/89*)

7 April 1928   Chartwell Manor
Private

My dear Neville,

As the result of self-communing alone down here I find myself in a robust mood. I am in revolt against the Cabinet decision to exclude the railways. The Prime Minister developed a very definite view in favour of using them. I do not feel afraid of any of the arguments, fair or unfair, that may be used against the plan on the score of subsidy or of favour to selected traffics. I believe we shall have a great deal of support from six hundred thousand railwaymen, and the very numerous railway shareholders will certainly not be displeased. But quite apart from that, I am aiming at a relief of something like 10/- a ton on steel, and I cannot possibly get it unless I use the railway freights. To go half way is to pay the price and miss the prize. I am even contemplating 100% remission. I need scarcely say that this will in no way affect the agreement reached with the Ministry of Health. The railways will not be derated. They will continue to pay all their rates to the local authorities exactly as at present, and their rates will rise or fall with the local follies and fortunes. There will therefore be no further disturbance of the local authorities. As they are now with the railways, so they will be actually and prospectively. Instead of derating the railways and reimbursing the local authorities, I shall propose to reimburse the railways for the rates which they will already have paid to the local authorities.

You may have your own views on this as a Cabinet Minister, but I am sure that you will not feel affected departmentally. I should like, however, to hear from you that this is so and that you will not complain that my raising this question again is any departure from our lately compacted peace. I do not know what the Cabinet will decide, but anyhow I propose to place the responsibility for an 'Aye' or 'No' decision directly upon them when we next meet.

Yours very sincerely,
Winston S. Churchill

Winston S. Churchill to Sir Philip Cunliffe-Lister

(*Churchill papers: 18/89*)

7 April 1928   Chartwell Manor
Private

My dear Philip,

I am increasingly disposed not to accept the railway decision as final. All our labour and expense will be lost if we do not bite deep enough to give the basic industries a real jerk. There is no doubt that including the railways would win us a great deal of goodwill from the railwaymen, and even the railway shareholders would see that their interests were far from harmed. The Prime Minister seemed at the Cabinet disposed to make some personal exertion in favour of this section of the plan. At any rate I have decided to bring it up again and leave the Cabinet the responsibility of turning it down if they choose. I have therefore not communicated with the Railway Companies. They can continue to work at their scheme for a few days longer. Neville will not be affected by the change. The railways will remain rated as at present. Instead of disturbing the local authorities and the Ministry of Health by first depriving them of their railway rates and then reimbursing them afterwards from the Exchequer, I shall let the railways pay their rates as at present and reimburse *them* direct. I am asking Hamilton not only to persevere at the details of the original proposal, ie the equivalent of two-thirds de-rating, but also the equivalent of complete de-ratement which I suppose would cost about £m 5. This ought to give very good results on the selected traffics. I am quite prepared to fight for these selected traffics, and am not in the least afraid of any of the arguments (fair or unfair) which could be used about them.

Such is the result of my cogitations in the intervals of building a concrete wall for my new lake. You will see that my mood is robust; and if you are in similar fettle, we will together deliver a vigorous offensive. I must bite as deep as 10/- a ton on steel.

I hope you are reposing. I am thankful that there is much better news about Steel-Maitland.

Yours ever,
WSC

Winston S. Churchill to Sir John Anderson, Sir Horace Hamilton and Alfred Hurst

(Churchill papers: 18/89)

7 April 1928

Please see the letters I have written to the President of the Board of Trade and the Minister of Health. In these circumstances I do not propose to send any negative news to the Railway Managers. Let them continue at their work until the next Cabinet has decided upon a direct issue. You will see that I now contemplate reimbursement of the railways for the rates they pay in the datum year. Any rise on this they will have to pay themselves. The interests of the local authorities will remain unaffected. The procedure will be by selected traffics, and your list is as good as any other that can be devised to go into Act of Parliament. In such matters one must be ready to defer a little to Parliamentary and public opinion.

Pray have some figures prepared which will show the reliefs to certain basic traffics: (a) on the Scheme as now approved by the Cabinet; (b) with the cumulative railway relief thrown in to the extent of 100%. Am I right in thinking this would cost £m 5?

WSC

Winston S. Churchill to Clementine Churchill

(Spencer-Churchill papers)

8 April 1928   Chartwell Manor

My darling Clemmie,

Very satisfactory reports have arrived about Randolph. I enclose the letters of Sheepshanks, Birley[1] & Routh.[2] There is no doubt he is developing

---

[1] Robert Birley, 1903–   . Assistant Master, Eton College, 1926–35. Headmaster of Charterhouse, 1935–47. Head Master, Eton College, 1949–63. Reith Lecturer, BBC, 1949.

[2] C. R. N. Routh, 1896–1976. Known as Dick; a schoolmaster and historian. History and Classics Master at Eton, 1923–57; House Master, 1933–49; sometime senior History Master. A keen historian of Empire and Commonwealth, and a Vice-President of the Historical Association. His obituary in the *Eton College Chronicle* described him as 'an active Conservative', and praised his 'spontaneous gift of encouragement to the new recruit'.

fast, and in those directions wh will enable him to make his way in the world—by writing & speaking—in politics, at the bar, or in journalism. There are some vy strange & even formidable traits in his character. His mind is free & growing more powerful every day. It is quite startling to hear him argue. His present phase is rabid Agnosticism, & last night in argument with Grigg he more than defended his dismal position. The logical strength of his mind, the courage of his thought, & the brutal & sometimes repulsive character of his rejoinders impressed me vy forcibly. He is far more advanced than I was at his age, & quite out of the common—for good or ill.

Today we all went to the Links & I played 18 holes with Grigg in most delicious spring sunshine. When we came to the big drive over the valley, I did miss you so much. I remembered all the strokes of our game—the one before you got ill—& wished indeed we had been playing together again. I have brought myself a set of clubs & a bag—so that all is ready for you— my darling.

After all I shall not go to London till Wedy—so I can meet Diana at Dover with the car. I am extending my plans in various important directions —now that I am sure of the united support of the Cabinet & of the party machine. Pray God these plans bring back a little more prosperity to Poor old England.

I am fed up with the Court Martial & am determined to do my best to secure the reinstatement of Dewar & Daniel. I am taking the extreme step of calling the turkey cock 'Admiral Collard'.

Everything is vy comfortable in the house & seems to go with the utmost smoothness. Butterworth has sent the extra £1,500 advance on the After- math: & I have sent my first 2 articles (£1,000) to America—so that we can jog along. But August, Sept & Oct will be months of hard work at the book.

The Budget speech is half done. I do hope you will be back to hear it. Jupiter was tonight in charge of 5 eggs. No other news.

But my dearest one I think so often & so tenderly of you & of the glory & comfort you have been to me in my life & of your sweet nature wh I love so much, & your unchanging beauty wh is my delight.

With my fondest love
Your ever devoted
W
x x x x

PS. I wish you were coming nearer & not going further away.

Alice Balfour to Winston S. Churchill

(*Churchill papers: 1/199*)

9 April 1928   4 Carlton Gardens

Dear Mr Churchill,

I hope you will come & see Arthur on Wednesday 11th at about 5 o'clock.
He will I expect be sitting in his armchair in his bedroom. *Please do not let
him talk business.* & please do not stay more than ¾ hour. There will be tea in
my sitting room at 4:30 if you like to have some before going up to Arthur.

Yours very sincerely
Alice Balfour

Brendan Bracken to Frederick Leith-Ross

(*Leith-Ross: 'Money Talks'*)

10 April 1928

Your lord and master Winston is now at Chartwell charging his rating
squib and pouring scorn on the advice of the superman Hoppy.[1] Fisher is
restored to favour and now moralises regularly for the benefit of Baldwin
and Arthur Michael Samuel but Winston speaks no longer to the Jew.

Sir Philip Cunliffe-Lister to Winston S. Churchill

(*Churchill papers: 18/89*)

11 April 1928   Yorkshire
Secret

My dear Winston,

Many thanks for your letter. I have also had a letter from Hamilton, and
I shall receive from him, as soon as they are ready, the detailed figures.

My first impressions of your new proposals are as follows:—

1. I was dissatisfied with the Cabinet decision. I have always held the
view that logically, and on merits, complete de-rating of Industry should be
the objective, and that this objective should be reached as soon as possible.
I therefore favoured Alternative 1. I was prepared to accept Alternative 2.
I was doubtful whether Alternative 3 offered enough advantages to Industry
to counterbalance the opposition to other parts of the plan.

[1] Sir Richard Hopkins, Churchill's Controller of Finance and Supply Services.

2. From this it follows that I am in favour of bringing the railways in, and I am prepared to take my share in defending selected traffics.

3. I see great difficulty in an undisguised subsidy. I need not elaborate the difficulties, but the following criticisms at once present themselves. We have abandoned the policy of subsidies and even of Trade Facilities. If we begin direct subsidies, where are we going to stop? Why not Agriculture, and all the futile schemes which Courthope[1] has proposed? Why not cotton &c &c? Again if you want to give a subsidy to steel and coal, why not give them the money direct so that they may use it as they think best? Or more difficult still to answer, why not promise the subsidy in return for approved amalgamation schemes? If I was going to give a direct subsidy to coal or steel, I should be inclined to say; where a good amalgamation goes through and capital is required, we will use the subsidy in the form of cheap state credit, either guaranteed or advance.

I think there is a real danger of our losing the logical basis of our policy. You see, the truth is that you and Neville are out for two quite different things, and you have reached a compromise which it is difficult for either of you to defend. Neville wants to keep as much in the rating area as he can, and treat your policy as an exception grafted on to that rule. You want the opposite. Must you not then treat any railway relief as flowing logically and naturally from your rating scheme. Merely to graft on to your rating scheme a new, and in fact disconnected, subsidy involves you in two dissimilar policies, the second of which is indefensible.

I am therefore, of opinion that the relief of railway rates must be inseparably connected with the rating scheme. It must be so bound to that scheme that you cannot attack it separately. You will say that this leads you straight back to Alternative 2; and I agree that you have got to get back on to that ground. I am afraid I find it difficult to suggest a compromise for the very reason that, as I have said, you and Neville mean different things. It might be possible to have a temporary compromise based on and justified by the fact that railway assessments and the whole railway rating system is at present under negotiation. You might say: The object is to relieve railways of rates or of X per cent of their rates; the justification of this is that the relief will be passed on to selected traffics. For convenience we must have a certain sum fixed, so that the railways may know how much they are to remit in freight charges. Pending the final adjustment of railway local

[1] George Lloyd Courthope, 1877–1955. Conservative MP for Rye, 1906–45. On active service on the western front, 1914–17 (wounded, Military Cross). Assistant Controller of Timber Supplies, 1917. Delegate to the British Empire Forestry Conference, 1923. Forestry Commissioner, 1923–48. Created Baronet, 1925. President of the Central Landowners' Association, 1929–31. President of the Royal Agricultural Society, 1944–5. Created Baron, 1945. Church Commissioner, 1948–55.

rates, we fix a given sum by which freight charges will be reduced, and by which the railways will be relieved of what they pay in local rates. During the first quinquennium therefore, the railways will receive the agreed sum as a grant in aid from the Exchequer. This might not be displeasing to the railways as it might leave them freer to drive the fairest bargain they can with the local authorities.

I do not know whether this suggestion is at all helpful. I only make it because I do feel sure that unless you can link up the railway proposal as an inseparable part of the whole rating scheme, we shall be involved in difficulties of principle and detail which may sink us.

Yrs ever,
P. Cunliffe-Lister

Winston S. Churchill to Stanley Baldwin

(*Baldwin papers*)

12 April 1928
Secret

My dear PM,

You will think me a vy changeable person; but I regard the enclosed from Philip as extinguishing *pro tem* my railway plans. It wd directly upset my pact with Neville if I did it the way Philip wants. Moreover Anderson, Hamilton & Hopkins are all anti. Therefore I shall not disturb the Cabinet by raising the topic again. Thus 'the Chartwell hue of resolution is sickled o'er by the Downing St cast of thought'! Other important decisions practically reached today are: (1) 4d on Whites. The oil Magnates were quite happy about this, & have behaved extremely well. They said 4d wd be no more trouble than 3d, and I might as well have the money while I was about it. They were horrified at the idea of putting another Petrol 6d on the top of the White 4d to relieve the motorists' licence-duties. The Ministry of Transport rather adverse to the change. Hamilton vy doubtful. An immense amount of trouble thrown on the Customs, & no advantage to the Exchequer or the Rating plan—not good enough. Decision No 2. These mean large simplifications, & leave me also much better off. I think in all the circumstances I shall be able to make you rather an attractive proposal to help the small income-tax payer with his children, & so do something *this year* for the classes not benefited by our larger scheme.

I shd like to find out from the Cabinet whether they are keen about relieving the Publicans' license-duties on electioneering grounds. It costs a million, & naturally I don't want to do it unless it is absolutely necessary to our party interests.

Yours ever,
W

Neville Chamberlain to Winston S. Churchill

(*Churchill papers: 18/89*)

12 April 1928

My dear Winston,

Your letter of the 7th has been forwarded to me here and reached me last night, so that there has been I fear some delay, accounted for no doubt by the week end and the Easter break.

As I understand your present proposal, it is to reimburse the railways to the full extent of the rates paid by them on condition that this money is passed on to certain industries in the shape of freight reductions and you wish to know if I have any departmental objections.

In the form in which I understand you to make your proposal in Cabinet I should have none, though I might have had something to say on other grounds. I thought then that you merely meant to give the railways a sufficient subsidy to enable them to make a substantial reduction on steel freights. But now you are tying up the subsidy to the rates and I cannot see why. There must be some motion and whatever it be it will be argued that the arrangement admits that railways ought to be (totally) released of rates.

I must therefore oppose the connection with rates on departmental grounds but perhaps you will be able to do without this feature which seems quite unnecessary. Moreover from the railway point of view it seems unreasonable to ask them to give a reduction which is unlimited out of a reimbursement which is limited.

Yours sincerely,
N. Chamberlain

Neville Chamberlain to Stanley Baldwin

(*Baldwin papers*)

12 April 1928   Aberdeenshire
Secret

My dear Stanley,

The peace of my riverside soliloquies had been broken by the irrepressible Chancellor who says he is feeling robust and has decided to reopen the question of the railways. He asks whether I have any departmental objection to his plan and I have been obliged to reply that I have.

He proposes to have the railways rated but to reimburse them for the rates they have paid on condition they pass on the benefit to the selected industries.

He does not explain why, if he wants to subsidise the steel industry, he should pay the subsidy to the railways and ask them to pass it on to steel, nor why the amount of the subsidy should be proportionate to the rates instead of to the amount of steel carried on the railways. In fact the connection with the rates is so completely lacking that one naturally looks for some motive for thus tying the two things together. It is difficult to guess exactly but I suspect an intention to get the railways relieved of rates at some future time and I think that would be the interpretation of the Local Authorities. Therefore, I am against.

You will observe that on this plan (1) the amount of the subsidy would vary with the extravagance of the Local Authorities—surely rather an odd idea. (2) the more successful the subsidy in restoring the steel industry the more steel will be carried and the larger therefore the subtraction required from the railways. But the amount *received* by the railways will be fixed by the rates they pay. Who will make up the difference? The answer is not difficult to find!

I know you are in favour of a reduction in railway rates to be effected by a contribution from the taxpayer, on the whole I think I am against it. It seems to me economically unsound & I don't like the possible implications & developments. I might think it politically a good card to play at an election. I doubt its virtue if it is played prematurely. But to tie up a subsidy to rates seems to me mad.

Yours ever,
NC

Stanley Baldwin to Winston S. Churchill

(*Churchill papers: 18/89*)

14 April 1928   10 Downing Street

My dear Winston,

You are probably right to bow to the storm and not run the risk of over-loading. Railways may come, and I should have the problem examined in all its aspects in good time before the election.

For a Tory cabinet they have successfully and pretty contentedly swallowed a large morsel and the inevitable cud-chewing must follow before they are ready for more.

Good luck to your hunting!

Yours ever,
SB

Winston S. Churchill to Clementine Churchill

(*Spencer-Churchill papers*)

15 April 1928   Chartwell Manor

My darling Clemmie,

All day long I am grappling with the Budget Speech. It will be 15,000 or 16,000 words long and at the rate of the articles would be worth a lot. It is about three-quarters done. But the number of difficult questions that have to be settled precisely—Yes or No is very large; one keeps on balancing and hesitating and turning and twisting for a comfortable place in the bed up to the last few days before the event. But I have now reached the stage where final answers have to be given of great importance. This is tiring and anxious although there is some exhilaration about it.

All is arranged for the seats and you have nothing to do but to come back and walk into your pew. At the end of the week I go up to Newcastle for a big public meeting in order to ram home the policy in a great industrial centre.[1] I am taking Randolph with me but we shall arrive back at Chartwell on the Sunday morning.

---

[1] Churchill spoke at Newcastle on April 28 before an audience of 5,000 people. He devoted most of his speech to his derating scheme, declaring: 'Production must be liberated and encouraged.' Derating, he said, was 'not a sop, but a lever', and he concluded: 'The levers at their disposal were potent; he only wished they were more potent. By themselves they were not sufficient to give that galvanising jerk that British industry required. They must rely on psychological reactions. This great relief of industry and agriculture was not enough by it-self—they needed the spirit of hope and enterprise, and the child of hope, the spirit of good-will . . . and the iron resolve to lay aside every impediment that stood in the way of rehabili-tating British production and our basic industries, of reviving our export trade and making our country a home for all its peoples.'

The fields look lovely. The daffodils are all in full bloom, the sheep having carefully avoided nibbling them. A veritable shower of lambs descended upon us last Sunday, no fewer than five being born between lunch and dinner. We have now eight lambs, two were born dead and there are two more sheep still with their message to give. They look very pretty in the orchard and I am sure you will be delighted when you see them. They are now couched in front of my windows among the daffodils. The weather which has been lovely for three or four days has now turned bleak and cold—in fact we had a few flakes of snow this morning.

Jack and Pebbin and the Prof are here and Mr Hurst arrives tonight.

I shall not go up to London until Tuesday as I can work down here much better than in the centre of effervescence and unrest called Westminster.

I shall put the Budget to the Cabinet on Thursday, but everything of consequence is settled. There only remains to fire the gun. Please God it hits the bull's eye.

Give suitable messages to Alice from me. I trust you have some sunshine. Don't get mixed up with the bombing outrages. It is rather hard luck on the poor King[1] that in addition to being relegated to the background he should have to serve as whipping boy for his forceful dictator. Still he has always been noted for his courage among the sovereigns left in Europe.[2]

One of the Entrecote geese went for an adventurous walk and had its leg broken by a dog. The resources of the Vet proving unavailing it was put to death. The white swans have now laid nine eggs. They not only sit on these alternately but together, side by side. I never knew that they did this. It will be indeed sad if their hopes and efforts are mocked again this year.

The garden is coming well forward and May should see it very bright. The pink and crimson rhodies in the water garden are at their best. We have no news except that all are in the pink—and that is the best of all.

Tender love my dearest soul and forgive my dictated bulletin.

Your ever devoted
W

---

[1] Victor Emmanuel, 1869–1947. The first in his line to be born in direct succession to the Italian crown, he became King of Italy in 1900, following the assassination of his father, King Umberto, by anarchists. In 1915 he supported Italy's entry into the war on the side of Britain and France. Accepted the Crown of Albania, April 1939. Following Mussolini's declaration of war on Britain in June 1940 he withdrew from political life. Survived an assassination attempt, 1941. Formally authorized the arrest of Mussolini, 1943, and escaped from German-controlled Rome. Withdrew from public life, 1944. Abdicated, 1946, and lived the last four months of his life in exile in Alexandria.

[2] On 12 April 1928 a bomb had exploded at the Piazza Giulio Cesare in Milan, only a few minutes before King Victor Emmanuel was to have driven through the square on his way to open the International Samples Fair. Seventeen people were killed and more than forty injured.

Winston S. Churchill to Lady Cave[1]

(*David Satinoff collection*)

16 April 1928   Treasury Chambers

My dear Lady Cave,

I venture to write to express to you my profound sympathy in yr grievous loss. My wife & I felt most keenly for you both in those tragic weeks. She is herself recuperating abroad from a dangerous illness, & I do not know whether she has had the strength to write herself, but I know how intensely she will share my sentiments, & as soon as she is strong enough you will hear from her.

In the Cabinet we all felt the shock of a heavy blow, & though the office can be filled the vacancy remains. Everyone was poignantly affected by the letter wh you wrote at yr husband's request, from his deathbed. When the allotted span has been accomplished, it is vain to rebel against the fulfilment of life. It is heroic & enviable to die in harness with careful thought for every interest in one's charge & faithfully carrying on to the very end. This came to young people in the war, but in these times of peace the same qualities of firmness of character & integrity of spirit can sometimes find their expression.

I thought you wd not mind my sending you these few lines.

Yrs vy sincerely
Winston S. Churchill

Victor Cazalet: diary

(*Robert Rhodes James: 'Victor Cazalet, A Portrait'*)

16 April 1928

To Winston's for tea and dinner. He was charming and delightful, but almost overcome by work on the Budget. He is really tired. His speech will take three and a half hours to deliver. Hurst of the Treasury, Lindemann, Bob Boothby, and Diana Churchill, grown lovely and charming, were there. I played bezique with Winston and won 75/-.

[1] Estella Penfold Mathews. She married Lord Cave in 1885. He died on 29 March 1928. She died in 1938. Her husband having died on the day he was to have been made an Earl, the grant of the Earldom was made to her in such a way that, had she remarried, her first son by this second marriage would himself have succeeded to the Earldom. As she did not remarry, the Earldom became extinct on her death.

Neville Chamberlain: diary

(*Neville Chamberlain papers*)

19 April 1928

Just before the Cabinet this morning S. Hoare told me that Winston had been speaking to him of his desire to return to the derating of railways & had said that the PM was going to raise it himself. Thereafter I decided to wait & see. Nothing happened at the Cabinet but in the afternoon I received a message that SB wd like to see me. I went to his room in the H of C & found him looking very worried. He said the Central Office which had been much attracted by what he called the 'original scheme' (meaning the plan whereby railways were included in derating & the 5% flat rate was paid to the Rating Authorities) was now feeling very flat because the scheme was shorn of the points which they had thought would most recommend it. He had therefore asked Gowers & Co to see me. I said they had spoken about railways but only about the flat rate. He replied that the former was not within their province. I then said the 2 things were separate & I wd deal with them separately. The flat rate was not so advantageous to industry as the $\frac{1}{4}$ of the variable rate. Only in those districts where the rate exceeded 20% would the 5% have the advantage & they were a minority. As for the railways—Here SB interrupted to say that he understood that before Worthy started his project for total exemption we were all agreed on the original scheme. I said only in the sense that we could all have agreed that the scheme was practicable but I had always objected to the railway plan on the ground that it was only a camouflage subsidy & I had reserved to myself the power of arguing against it in Cabinet though I had never suggested that I should resign if the Cabinet decided against me. I believed that it was too late to bring in the railways as the time table was already completed & further legislation wd be necessary. Would it not be better to reserve the question of railway freight for the Gen Election when we should have time to go into it exhaustively and see what alternative methods were possible. SB said 'Perhaps it would be wise' but maintained his troubled look.

The conversation drifted into other channels. In the evening however he asked me to dine with him at St Stephens Club & I did so. After dinner he said he had had a terrible day. First Cunliffe-Lister then Guinness & then the Chancellor had all been to him and it was evident that all now wished to revert to the original scheme. The Chancellor had made a regular scene. He had marched about the room shouting and shaking his fist & had launched out on a tremendous tirade against me. I had been always pouring cold water on his scheme and evidently I was jealous of him. If he was held to his bond he would fulfil it but never would he feel the same (? towards me) again.

SB had said that W did not understand me, that jealousy was not in my nature & that it was all his own fault for himself deserting his own scheme & running again after Worthy's hare. W then began cursing himself saying he recognised what a mistake he had made & what a fool he had been. SB hoped it wouldn't worry me too much to know of W's attitude but he thought I ought to know where 1 stood. I thanked him & said I was glad to know but W's behaviour was too childish & contemptible for me to be upset over it.

Then SB went on to say that he did not share my views about the railways. He felt that the scheme was so attractive that the objections would be outweighed & he asked me to turn it over again. I replied that I attached great weight to his views both on account of my personal affection for him & because I believed he had a real flair for the way things would appear to the man in the street. I would certainly turn it over and he might take it that I should endeavour to meet him. But I wanted to see the time table again.

Cabinet minutes

(*Cabinet papers: 23/57*)

19 April 1928
Secret

In connection with his statement on the subject of the Budget, the CHANCELLOR OF THE EXCHEQUER informed the Cabinet that he had interviewed representatives of the Railway Companies on the previous day and had informed them that it was not at present proposed to include the railways among the services for which rates would be remitted in the scheme now under consideration. The representatives of the Railway Companies had expressed the greatest regret. Although it had been contemplated that the Companies should pass on to other industries the advantages they would receive in the remission of rates, nevertheless they desired to be included in the scheme owing to the immense advantage which they believed would accrue to trade and industry and thus indirectly to the railways from their inclusion. In these circumstances the Chancellor of the Exchequer asked if the Cabinet would even now be willing to re-examine the question of the inclusion of the railways. He also appealed for reconsideration of the decision that the payment in respect of de-rated properties should be variable, and expressed a strong preference for a fixed national rate for productive industry.

The Cabinet agreed—

To discuss the question at a Special Meeting to be held on the following day, at 11 am, at the House of Commons.

Cabinet minutes

(*Churchill papers: 18/71*)

20 April 1928

As arranged at their previous Meeting the Cabinet re-examined the scheme of Government Policy to be explained by the Chancellor of the Exchequer in his Budget Statement in the following two respects:—

(i) The desirability of including railways, canals and docks among the services for which rates would be remitted;

(ii) The question of whether payment in respect of de-rated properties should be variable, as approved by the Cabinet on April 4, 1928 (Cabinet 20 (28), Conclusion 7), or at a fixed national rate, as contemplated earlier in the discussions of the Cabinet Committee.

THE PRIME MINISTER informed his colleagues of the reasons which had induced him to ask the Cabinet to re-examine this question. He recalled that at one time the Cabinet Committee had nearly reached an agreement on a proposal for a reduction of rates on productive industry, including railways, by two-thirds, the rate to be collected by the Local Authorities. At that moment a new proposal had been made for a complete de-rating of productive industry, which had commended itself to the Cabinet Committee. From this scheme of complete de-rating it had been necessary to drop the railways. The Cabinet, however, had rejected the proposal for complete de-rating of productive industry and had decided on a scheme of payments varying according to the rates of particular districts. Several of his colleagues had suggested to him that the scheme in its present form was not the best possible, and that, now that the scheme of complete de-rating of productive industry had been dropped, railways might well be reinstated. In these circumstances he had felt that the Cabinet ought to give further consideration to the matter.

In the course of a very long discussion the CHANCELLOR OF THE EXCHEQUER gave the Cabinet the following estimates of the cost of various schemes:—

   (i) A scheme for a variable rate of one-fourth, applying to railways, canals and docks, as well as to industries, would cost to the Exchequer £26·7 millions;
  (ii) A scheme for a variable rate of one-third, including railways, canals and docks, would cost to the Exchequer £24·2 millions;
 (iii) A scheme for a flat payment of 5/- including railways, canals and docks, would cost to the Exchequer £22·8 millions.

As the result of a long discussion the Cabinet agreed (*in each case by a majority*)—

   (a) That railways, canals and docks should be included in the scheme;
   (b) To adhere to the previous decision for the payment, in respect of the de-rated properties, of a uniform rate of one-fourth of the poundage of the particular areas.

THE CHANCELLOR OF THE EXCHEQUER informed his colleagues that it would be necessary for him to go carefully into the finance of this decision and to discuss with the President of the Board of Trade the application of the scheme to railways, canals and docks.

L. S. Amery: diary

(*Amery papers*)

20 April 1928

Further Cabinet to reconsider the rating aspect of Winston's scheme, the PM having been persuaded by Winston to bring the railways in after all. This of course is not really a derating scheme but only an indirect subsidy to certain industries, but on the whole the Cabinet were prepared, in view of the PM's attitude, to reverse their previous decision though I'm glad to say stood to their guns in favour of the rate still left being variable and not a fixed one.

Winston S. Churchill to King George V
(*Churchill papers: 18/71*)

22 April 1928

Mr Churchill with his humble duty to Your Majesty:

The scheme which Your Majesty studied in a Cabinet Paper some months ago has now received, with certain modifications, the united approval of the Cabinet, and with Your Majesty's approval will form the staple of the Budget which the Chancellor of the Exchequer will introduce on Tuesday next.

The year which we have passed has been a difficult one, over £m 25 of adverse factors falling upon the slender margin of £1,400,000 which had been provided. Nevertheless, thanks to the deaths of several of Your Majesty's wealthiest subjects, a few unexpected windfalls like the repayment of the Kenya Loan, and above all an economy of £m 10½ recovered after the Estimates had actually been voted, a surplus of nearly £m 4¼ ultimately came to hand.

For 1928 Mr Churchill estimates for a total expenditure of £m 806¼. This is £m 32 less than what we spent last year. The saving, however, is less than appears because a number of items which used to figure on both sides of the Estimates have been presented net instead of gross, effecting a saving of £m 7 on paper only. The actual diminution is about £m 20.

The accounts are being presented this year in a new form. The Sinking Fund and the Post Office and Road Fund monies are shown separately from the general expenditure. On this basis and excluding also the Savings Certificates in order to compare like with like, it cannot be disputed that Your Majesty's present advisers, so far from having added £m 30 or £m 40 to the expense of the country during their tenure, have in fact saved upwards of £m 12 since the days of the Labour Government. Mr Churchill thinks that this fact will be a surprise to a good many people.

The negotiations between the Treasury and the Bank of England have reached a satisfactory conclusion and the Currency and Bank of England Note issues will be amalgamated and transferred to the Bank. This step was, as Your Majesty will remember, forecasted three years ago when the Gold Standard was resumed. A reserve of over £m 13 had accumulated in the Currency Note account which can now be brought into our annual finance. Mr Churchill proposes to use this to strengthen the new Sinking Fund which once again this year will be presented at the record figure of £m 65.

There are no important changes of taxation required for the national service in 1928. Mr Churchill estimates the revenue on the existing basis, with a few minor Customs alterations, at £m 812½, and this would enable him to forecast provisionally a surplus of about £m 6¼. Here he could easily stop but for the fact that the large policy of relieving productive industries of the rate burden and of paving the way for Local Government reform has now to be undertaken. This policy will proceed in three stages—first, finding the money for the relief; that is the task of the Budget: secondly, defining the scope of the relief, which will involve a Valuation Bill; and thirdly, the re-imbursement of the Local Authorities for their loss of rateable value, which will also be the occasion of the main Local Government Bill to be introduced in the autumn by the Minister of Health.

The scheme has not been greatly changed since the Chancellor of the Exchequer first had the honour to submit it to Your Majesty. An oil duty, not only on petrol but on paraffin, will be proposed at the rate of 4d a gallon. This will yield £m 14 in 1928, and rise by annual stages to £m 23 in 1932. The motorists who had been looking forward to a reduction of their licence duties in exchange for a tax on petrol, will be surprised and possibly irritated by this development. It is, however, the only way by which the money could have been found to afford the relief to the basic industries that is so greatly needed. Mr Churchill hopes that they will remember that they are citizens first and motorists after; but he is not quite sure about this.

The Cabinet, after some very protracted discussions, decided that the relief to industry was to take the form of a ¾ remission of their existing rates, leaving the ¼ to vary with local circumstances and fortunes. Mr Churchill was inclined to think that a fixed rate would have been better, but in view of the very large measure of relief which this decision accords to productive industry he does not grieve at the general opinion. A similar proportion of relief will be accorded to the railways, who will pass it on to certain selected heavy traffics likely to benefit the basic industries. Agriculture will be completely relieved of rates, which ought to be an important service to the farmers.

In view of the fact that paraffin will be taxed a remission will be given upon sugar to compensate the cottage budget for any possible loss. This remission, amounting to ¼d a lb will be effected by a means which incidentally helps the refining industry, deterring the importation of refined sugar from Czecho-Slovakia. It is believed that the Greenock refineries will shortly be re-opened.

The Chancellor of the Exchequer finds himself able to make a small remission, costing about £m 1, on the Publicans' Licence Duties, there having been prolonged complaints that the value of the licence has been sensibly reduced by the shorter hours and the more temperate habits of the people. This proposal is likely to cause some adverse comments from the official Opposition and from Lady Astor. Nevertheless it can be solidly defended on grounds of fair play.

A remission of some consequence can also be given on the Income Tax: not indeed upon the standard rate, for that is far too costly for our present resources. The children's allowances will be practically doubled and will be made applicable from the first year of a child's life. This boon affects 650,000 married Income Taxpayers who have children under 16 and should be very welcome to them. In the case of a man with three children and £500 a year of earned income the relief will be equal to a reduction of 2/9d on the standard rate; and even the man of £1,000 a year with three children receives a reduction equivalent to 8d in the £. The cost of these remissions is surprisingly small, amounting to just over £m 2 in the present year and about £m 4½ in the first full year.

Mr Churchill balances the Budget of 1928 with an expenditure of £m 806¼ and a revenue of £m 839¼, including the £m 13 windfall from the Currency Note Reserve. He takes £m 14 from this to raise the new Sinking Fund to the £m 65, as already mentioned, and uses about £m 5½ to give the reliefs in taxation just described, leaving a prospective surplus of £m 13½. This he proposes to increase by appropriating to the service of this year the £m 4¼ surplus of last year which would otherwise have been devoted to the further payment of the Debt. Having regard, however, to the immense Sinking Funds which are being maintained, he feels that he may prudently and properly keep this money in hand in view of the very important rating relief schemes upon which the Government will shortly embark. Thus the final prospective surplus becomes £m 17¾ available either to meet the ordinary contingencies of the year, or to provide the nest egg for the relief of industry in 1929.

Mr Churchill is not troubling Your Majesty with the somewhat technical description of the arrangements for a fixed debt charge. This is in accordance with the principles and practice both of Mr Disraeli and Mr Gladstone, and the procedure was actually adopted by Sir Stafford Northcote in 1875. An annual payment of £m 355 will pay off the National Debt in fifty years without any need for imposing those Sur-taxes or Capital Levies which appeal so strongly to the Labour Opposition. Effectual provision will also be made for the encashment of Savings Certificates.

Mr Churchill fears that the number of topics to be dealt with, and their complicated character and relationship will force him to make an unusual demand upon the attention of the House of Commons on Tuesday next, and it is even being considered by the Prime Minister whether an interval for repose and refreshment might not be instituted at about half time, in order to mitigate the severities of the ordeal to all parties. Your Majesty will remember that a precedent of this kind was made in the case of Mr Lloyd George's Budget of 1909, but Mr Churchill trusts that the procedure attending the passage of the present Finance Bill will in other respects be different from that of 1909, and with his humble duties

Remains Your Majesty's
Faithful & Devoted Servant
Winston S. Churchill

Lord Stamfordham to Winston S. Churchill

(*Churchill papers: 18/71*)

23 April 1928   Windsor Castle

My dear Churchill,

The King is grateful to you for having found time at this moment of the highest pressure of your work to send him so interesting an outline of your Budget Scheme, which he has carefully studied.

There are of course a few points, such as the reference to a fixed debt charge, which His Majesty does not quite understand and, alas! his Private Secretary is incapable of offering any explanation! We quite realise that an annual payment of 355 million pounds would pay off the National Debt in 50 years: but do not quite see how that 355 million pounds is to be raised! But please do not trouble to answer.

The King is afraid that there will be some moaning and groaning from both 'motorist and citizen' over the additional tax on oil. Tomorrow afternoon, the King thinks, you will have an exhausting task and the idea of an interim for rest and refreshment seems rather wise.

Yours very truly,
Stamfordham

Winston S. Churchill to King George V

(Churchill papers: 18/71)

23 April 1928

Mr Churchill with his humble duty to Your Majesty.

Last year we provided no less than £379,000,000 for the service of the Debt; so that to drop to £355,000,000 will be a much lighter burden. Indeed the Chancellor of the Exchequer could not have consented to fix the figure so low, but for the fact that he has a windfall in the Currency Note Reserve of 13 millions, with the aid of which he raises the provision for this year to £369,000,000. Your Majesty will remember that last year's provision was 15 millions above the normal. On the whole, Mr Churchill thinks that the criticism of the financial pundits will probably be that the fixed debt charge ought to be 360 millions instead of 355. However, he is prepared to withstand them on this point. It is curious to note that Sir Stafford Northcote's fixed debt charge in 1875, which lasted for 39 years until engulfed in the Great War, was $28\frac{1}{2}$ millions, and was then spoken of as a tremendous burden. The difference between $28\frac{1}{2}$ and 355 probably represents fairly accurately the advance in financial and economic strength made by Your Majesty's Budget since those days—although of course allowance must be made for the decrease in the real value of money.

Mr Churchill has made one alteration in the Budget of which he wishes to render immediate information. He thinks that the remission on the Publicans' licence duty fits somewhat incongruously into the general scheme of the Budget, which is *national* and non-party. The publicans have a good case, but Mr Churchill feels they can with more propriety be attended to next year.

The motorists no doubt will be more offended than silent. Nevertheless they are by no means the least fortunate, as a class, of Your Majesty's subjects, and the need of the basic industries is severe and urgent.

All of which, with his humble duty, is submitted by Your Majesty's devoted servant,

Winston S. Churchill

Lord Stamfordham to Winston S. Churchill

(*Churchill papers: 18/71*)

24 April 1928   Windsor Castle

My dear Churchill,

The King is indeed most grateful to you for having answered the point raised in my letter of last night, but to which I begged you not to reply, knowing how overwhelmed you must be by your formidable task of today. His Majesty is much interested in your explanation about the fixed debt charge, which he now quite understands: but what a marvellous increase from Sir Stafford Northcote's figure of 28½ millions in 1875. The King quite sees your point in dropping out the remission on the Publicans' Licence Duty. His Majesty is looking forward to the usual telegraphic news from the House this evening to hear how your statement has been received.

Yours very sincerely,
Stamfordham

Stanley Baldwin to King George V

(*Baldwin papers*)

24 April 1928   House of Commons

By 5 o'clock the Chancellor began to unfold the Government scheme of rating relief upon which will be based all local government legislation for several decades to come. He pointed out that our system of local rating based upon ideas of the sixteenth century is no longer applicable to the modern conditions of the twentieth century. When challenged by the Labour Party with having only just made this discovery, he quickly and effectively retorted that it was impossible to proceed with schemes of this kind while in the throes of a general strike and a coal stoppage.

The House became intensely interested in watching a master in the art !oratory and of tantalizing the imagination unfold his ideas in a speech packed with detail, yet so simple and clear that there could be no possible misunderstanding. Having thoroughly examined the rating position and firmly established a case for its revision he proceeded to apportion the burden upon the shoulders of those best able to bear it. For several years in succession motorists have presented a petition for a petrol tax in substitution for the present horse power tax. They must observe a certain grim humour in the fact that the Chancellor has met them half-way and given them the petrol tax. Even with the imposition of a 4d duty the cost of petrol is much less than it was eighteen months ago. There is no reason to suppose that this duty will check the development of the motor industry in its legitimate form and it may have the very desirable effect of putting back upon the railways certain heavy traffic which normally belongs there and so safeguard a thousand millions of British capital invested in railways, and the employment of 700,000 men.

The Chancellor began to equal the young man in 'Excelsior' who went on from peak to peak. He now showed that he does not wish to increase the burden upon the cottage household which uses kerosene for its lamps and he has therefore reduced the price of sugar, thus adjusting the burden the balance of which it is hoped will be in favour of the consumer. He also promised certain rebates in licence duties particularly where motor vehicles use pneumatic tyres. Having accumulated a large fund with which to finance this great scheme of helping the producers of the country, he proposes to bring it into operation in October 1929. The most basic industry, that of agriculture, will then be entirely relieved of all rates on its land and farm buildings, while the other producers will be relieved of 75 per cent of the rates. Finally, in accordance with the Government's policy of assisting the producer, income tax allowances for children will be considerably raised: so much so in fact that a man earning £400 a year and having three children will be relieved of income tax altogether.

So, having spoken for almost three hours excluding an adjournment for half an hour, the Chancellor completed a reliability and a speed test, perhaps not altogether of the kind most appreciated by motorists, but one which the Prime Minister feels the general public will recognise as being almost the most remarkable oratorical achievement of Mr Churchill's career.

Lord Weir to Winston S. Churchill

(Churchill papers: 18/76)

24 April 1928

My dear Churchill,

Just a line to congratulate you most warmly. The Conservative Party and the community are indeed fortunate. The merits while fundamental are non partisan but it should serve as the best political insurance policy accepted for many years. Viewed as an entertainment LG's face I shall never forget. Don't acknowledge this.

Yours sincerely,
Weir

Lord Derby to Winston S. Churchill

(*Churchill papers: 18/76*)

24 April 1928
Personal

My dear Winston,

I have only heard your budget proposals as broadcasted, but I must write you even on such a meagre report. My most hearty congratulations. It is not the budget of an electioneer but of a statesman.

Yours ever,
Derby

L. S. Amery: diary

(*Amery papers*)

24 April 1928

The whole thing was done with Winston's best literary skill and above all with his power of investing the business with importance. He still lives entirely in the 19th century in his outlook on things. There is no doubt that the first impression was very favourable indeed and our party was delighted and is I think still very happy at the end of the week. . . .

Went to Sammy Samuel's[1] usual Budget dinner. . . . Short speeches afterwards by Winston, Stanley, FE and Horne.

Lord Balfour to Winston S. Churchill

(*Churchill papers: 18/76*)

25 April 1928

My dear Winston,

I am not allowed to write—but, doctors or no doctors, I must send you one line of *warmest* congratulation. It is a great moment in the history of British finance and of the Unionist Party:—of your personal fame I must say nothing.

Yr
AJB

[1] Samuel Samuel, 1855–1934. A banker and merchant. Director of Shell Transport and Trading Company Ltd, and of the Anglo-Saxon Petroleum Company Ltd. A Member of the Executive Council of the Shipping Federation. Conservative MP for Putney, 1913–34.

Lord Tyrrell to Winston S. Churchill

(*Churchill papers: 18/76*)

25 April 1928   Foreign Office
Personal

My dear Winston,

May I with great respect join in the chorus of praise so richly deserved which is going up today to a Chancellor of high courage & vision?

Whatever may be the fate of your budget—& I am convinced of its success, especially in the future—it will be a great landmark in your career & your certificate of statesmanship for the historian of the future.

I know you will not look upon this letter of congratulation as either impertinent or presumptuous, but as an expression of very sincere admiration of

Yours sincerely,
W. Tyrrell

Sir Ian Malcolm[1] to Winston S. Churchill

(*Churchill papers: 18/76*)

25 April 1928
Personal

My dear Winston,

I am not going to deny myself the renewal of my pleasure in once more congratulating you on your Annual Triumph. This year's Budget must have been a most exhausting one to prepare and declare. I hope you aren't too much exhausted by these twin efforts. The Rating Reform looks excellent: a tremendous contribution towards the solutions of our agricultural problems —at any rate in Scotland where we lairds, far past trying to make two ends meet out of income, are endeavouring to continue to live among our 'ain folk' by a lavish expenditure of capital—which can't go on for ever—and then our properties must (but for you) go into 'foreign hands'. So, whether this part of your Budget passes or not, we have a great deal to thank you for in the direction of high Statesmanship and bonne volonté.

Ever yours,
Ian Malcolm

---

[1] Ian Zachary Malcolm, 1868–1944. Educated at Eton and New College, Oxford. Diplomatic Service, 1891–5. Private Secretary to the Prime Minister (Lord Salisbury), 1895–1900. Conservative MP for Stowmarket, 1895–1906, and for Croydon, 1910–19. British Red Cross Officer in France, Russia, Switzerland and North America, 1914–17. Accompanied Balfour to the United States, 1917. Knighted, 1919. Private Secretary to Balfour at the Paris Peace Conference, 1919. British Government Representative on the Suez Canal Company, 1919–39.

Winston S. Churchill to Neville Chamberlain

(*Churchill papers: 18/72*)

26 April 1928   Treasury Chambers
Private

My dear Neville,

Only a line to wish you success this afternoon. The speech cannot fail to be of the vy greatest importance. My part helps the manufacturers & landowners: but its indispensable counterpoise is the modernisation of the LG system wh reconciles gradually but ceaselessly needs & resources.

I hope you will unfold a good deal: for otherwise the worst possibilities will be exploited against us.

And wishing you luck

Yours etc.
WSC

Winston S. Churchill to Lord Balfour

(*Balfour papers*)

26 April 1928   Treasury Chambers

My dear Arthur,

Yr letter gives me the vy greatest pleasure & pride. I value yr approval in public things more than that of anyone else.

The whole policy has gone wonderfully well at the first shock: & as you know, all is long & well prepared behind the line of battle.

I do trust you are making good progress.

Yours always,
W

Sir Herbert Hambling to Winston S. Churchill

(*Treasury papers: T172/1649*)

26 April 1928

I congratulate you on your Budget, and you have the satisfaction of knowing that practically it meets with universal approval.

The weakness of the Rating Scheme is its postponement until October 1929. . . .

Winston S. Churchill to Clementine Churchill

(*Spencer-Churchill papers*)

27 April 1928

My darling Clemmie,

Welcome Home! All is well, & I shall be with you tomorrow early. Hartigan[1] does not want you to see Randolph while he is infectious, so we must discuss where you stay for the next few days—Have you had Mumps?

I am just off to Newcastle—tired bored and at the end of too long a week.

Your ever loving & devoted

W

Lord Beaverbrook to William Mackenzie King

(*Beaverbrook papers*)

28 April 1928

Churchill had a great success with his Budget speech—and a united chorus of press praise next day, excepting from the 'Daily Express'.

I thought it would turn out a success d'estime, rather than a solid achievement. And indeed the grumbling is already beginning now that it is realised that all the taxes are on us and all the benefits postponed until October next.[2]

The supporters of the Budget are already pressing their hero to pay up something on account—and I should not be surprised if a payment on account was doled out to meet this clamour.

Further, when a Local Government and Rating Bill—hitherto only vaguely sketched—is produced, as part of the Budget scheme, in the autumn, there will be ructions with the vested political interests that will be disturbed.

The Government will be destroyed at the next election.

---

[1] Thomas Hartigan. Studied medicine at Dublin and Newcastle-on-Tyne. Qualified as a doctor at Durham, 1907. Fellow of the Royal Society of Medicine. Member of the British Medical Association. He practised medicine in London for over twenty years, at 148 Gloucester Terrace, Hyde Park. He died in 1941.

[2] On the following day Lord Beaverbrook's *Evening Standard* published an article by G. H. Mair entitled 'The Artful Chancellor', in which he wrote: 'He was gay, nearly as gay as to be flippant; he had the response of happy and spontaneous laughter; he smiled with a faintly malicious artfulness over the assembled House.'

Frederick Guest to Winston S. Churchill

(*Churchill papers: 18/76*)

28 April 1928

Dear Winnie

You will have had so many letters of congratulations on your performance yesterday that you will hardly want another—but here are mine.

I think it will rank as a 'classic' budget. It has broken new ground—It will be known as 'Winston's Industrial life buoy' and will become a milestone in the history of Reconstruction.

I think also you have made many thoughtful friends of cross bench mind. (Aberconway[1] is a type.)

The press tributes are sincere and have a non party atmosphere that I like.

It seems to me that you have taken a sure step towards your future premiership. I think the PM welcomes your steady & increasing popularity with the Conservative party—on obvious merits.

Bless you—good luck.

Yrs
Freddie

Will you as a favour read my enclosed monthly message to my Bristol Electors.

[1] Charles Benjamin Bright McLaren, 1850–1934. A nephew of John Bright. Shipbuilder, colliery owner and steel manufacturer. Chairman of the Metropolitan Railway Company. Owner of considerable estates, including the seaside holiday resort of Prestatyn. Liberal MP, 1880, 1885 and 1892–1910. Created Baronet, 1902; Baron Aberconway, 1911.

May 1928

Robert Boothby to Winston S. Churchill

(*Churchill papers: 2/158*)

3 May 1928   Treasury Chambers

Dear Chancellor,

I am so sorry I cannot come and see you, but the doctor is firm.[1]

I reproach myself for not having been on the second bench last night, as I might have been able to dissuade the Financial Secretary from granting the concession. At any rate I could have had a shot at stopping him. But it was the dinner hour, the Chamber was practically empty, and there was no reason to suppose a hitch would occur. . . .[2]

There is great sympathy with you in your illness & I have had innumerable enquiries: indeed the widespread and heartfelt anxiety for your return at the earliest possible moment is rather amusing as an indication of the nakedness of the land, & not without significance. Not one but twenty members have observed, in varying terms, how instructive it has been to see a difficult and almost dangerous parliamentary situation superbly dealt with on Tuesday,[3] and a perfectly straightforward & easy one reduced to a shambles last night.

---

[1] Churchill had been taken suddenly ill with influenza. He did not recover fully for five months (see his letter to Lloyd George of 1 January 1929, quoted on page 1409).

[2] During a Ways and Means debate on 2 May 1928, the Treasury was represented by A. M. Samuel, the Financial Secretary, as Churchill was ill. After strong opposition had been expressed to the proposed excise on imported mechanical lighters, Samuel agreed to accept a cut in the tax from 6 pence to 3 pence per lighter. But Philip Snowden, the former Labour Chancellor of the Exchequer, contended that he 'knew something about the official position of the Financial Secretary. It is a well understood thing that the Financial Secretary has no authority whatever, without the authority of his Chief, the Chancellor of the Exchequer, to accept any amendments on the Budget.' A ninety-minute debate ensued as to the precise nature of Samuel's authority. It was finally agreed that it was within his power to make the concession. Snowden concluded the debate with the remark: 'I will only say that I do not envy the honourable gentleman the Financial Secretary to the Treasury when he next meets the convalescent Chancellor of the Exchequer.'

[3] During the evening debate on Tuesday, 1 May 1928, Philip Snowden was about to move an amendment removing the duty on kerosene, when Churchill himself intervened to announce the removal of the duty. Churchill thus forestalled a Labour Party assault on the

I am afraid poor old Arthur Michael is in great distress, and one is very sorry for him. But he made a sad hash of it.

I do hope you will be better tomorrow, and able to get away next week for a brief holiday.

For there will be nothing on here, and the last ten days must have imposed a strain on you greater than any mortal man can sustain.

Yours ever sincerely
RB

Robert Vansittart[1] *to Winston S. Churchill*

(*Churchill papers: 1/199*)

5 May 1928   10 Downing Street

Dear Chancellor

I would like to thank you very much for your kind message to us in our trouble.[2] I've got back from Lympne and am awfully sorry to hear how unwell you've been. I do hope you'll be quite well again very soon, for apart from the discomfort it must be very galling to be absent when you are so much needed. I had heard a great part of your budget speech before news of my trouble reached me; and I would like to say how fine I thought it was and how glad I was it had its due 'bonne presse'.

Yours sincerely
Robert Vansittart

---

tax as an onerous one, on account of the use of kerosene to heat many homes in rural districts. Churchill stated that he had decided to remove the tax on the grounds that a Treasury study had shown that to do so would not destroy the petrol tax. 'From the moment that the conclusion is reached,' Churchill said, 'that dropping the Kerosene Duty will not be fatal to the Petrol Duty—from that very moment it is, I am sure, my duty to give effect to the general wishes of the House.'

[1] Robert Gilbert Vansittart, 1881–1957. Educated at Eton. Entered the Diplomatic Service, 1902. Assistant Clerk, Foreign Office, 1914; 1st Secretary, 1918; Counsellor, 1920. Secretary to Lord Curzon, 1920–4. Principal Private Secretary to Stanley Baldwin, 1928–9; to Ramsay MacDonald, 1929–30. Knighted, 1929. Permanent Under-Secretary of State for Foreign Affairs, 1930–8. Elected to the Other Club, 1933. Chief Diplomatic Adviser to the Foreign Secretary, 1938–41. Privy Councillor, 1940. Created Baron, 1941. His autobiography, *The Mist Procession*, was published posthumously, in 1958. His brother Arnold was killed in action in 1915.

[2] On Budget Day, while Vansittart was in the Prime Minister's office in the House of Commons, the telephone rang, and he learnt that one of his wife's two sons by her previous marriage was dying, as a result of a lift accident. On 3 July 1928 she herself died, of a broken heart. They had been married for less than seven years.

Winston S. Churchill to Sir Laming Worthington-Evans

(*Churchill papers: 18/72*)

7 May 1928
Confidential

My dear Worthy,

The doctors do not want me to do any serious work for at least a fortnight, and preferably three weeks. I really do not feel equal to tackling the Currency Bill on Monday next, and I should be very grateful to you if you would come to my rescue in the matter. You have a great knowledge of these questions, and no one can state the orthodox case better than you, if you choose to do so. The Prime Minister quite approves of your taking charge of the Bill, if you can find the time.

Under the present arrangements Samuel has prepared a speech which has been duly vetted by the Department; and it had been my intention that he should let this speech off textually in introducing the Bill. I should have lain behind to pick up the pieces. In the present circumstances you must do exactly what you think best. But on the whole I should recommend your letting Samuel open while you kept yourself to wind up and deal with the Debate. The Genoa Resolutions will play a part in this discussion, and you know all about them too much! I do not think there is going to be much trouble about the Bill. Whatever you do, make Samuel show you the text of his speech before he delivers it, so that you know that nothing will be said that puts the Debate on wrong lines.

I shall be at Chartwell recuperating, and can give you lunch any day you happen to be in the neighbourhood.

Yours very sincerely
Winston S. Churchill

Winston S. Churchill to Sir Austen Chamberlain

(*Austen Chamberlain papers*)

8 May 1928

My dear Austen,

As I cannot be at the Cabinet tomorrow, I venture to send you this line about China:—Now is surely the time for us to make the Japanese feel that we are in full sympathy with them on the side of civilisation against barbarism and brutality. Do not let us imitate the Americans, and indeed other Powers, who on every occasion in China show their delight at one particular nationality being singled out for ill-treatment, and hope to gain some ill bought favour for themselves. Let us give our countenance to the Japanese and as far as possible assist them in their task, thus perhaps finding the opportunity of taking the first step to a revival of that friendship unhappily, and alas I fear improvidently, chilled some years ago.

I am almost sure this will be your view, but should it not be so, perhaps you would not mind putting my opinion on record.

I am getting on slowly.

Yours vy sincerely
Winston S. Churchill

Lord Rosebery to Winston S. Churchill
(*Churchill papers: 1/199*)

8 May 1928

My dear Winston,

I am very grateful for your kind thought.

I think it must be very pleasant to feel a whole nation trembling before your footstool.

Yours aff⁷
A R

Austen Chamberlain to Winston S. Churchill
(*Churchill papers: 22/190*)

9 May 1928   Foreign Office

My dear Winston,

I entirely agree with you that our attitude to the Japanese in their present trouble should be sympathetic and that we should not exhibit the slightest *Schadenfreude* because this time the trouble has fallen upon them and not upon us. The limits within which we can hope for their co-operation are narrow, for they include only questions in which Japanese and British interests coincide and therefore in co-operating with us they are defending themselves. It would be a mistake not to recognise this, but it in no way affects the general attitude which, in agreement with you, I think we ought to adopt.

Yours ever
Austen

PS. The PM has kept me supplied with news of you. Don't hurry back to work too soon. A gloom was cast over the first Court by Diana's absence. I was watching for her appearance like a love-sick swain. She may count me as a 'faithful if elderly admirer'.

Winston S. Churchill to Sir Richard Hopkins and others concerned[1]

(*Churchill papers: 18/90*)

10 May 1928
Important

In this interlude it is of great importance that everything should move forward so that any fresh decisions that may be required can be taken in good time before the Second Reading of the Finance Bill.

(1) What has happened to the Profits Tax papers? Let me have a short statement from Gowers showing how high such a tax would have to be put on the basis of a stringhalt provision to produce £6 millions; and secondly, what would be the yield of 6d, 7d, 8d and 9d respectively. Let me also have a note on the shape of the legislation and the procedure necessary for incorporating it in the Budget, should it be decided on as it well may be.

(2) Let me have a report from Sir Horace Hamilton about making the use of kerosene for propulsive purposes illegal under severe penalty and for marking this fluid with a pink colourer.

(3) Let me also have a report from him about bringing the Railway rates into operation as from October this year, at a cost of £4 millions, in anticipation of the general plan. I am determined to do this. The state of productive industry is daily deteriorating.

(4) Sir Horace Hamilton should keep in touch with the Oil people, and should not cease to warn them of the outcry there would be if an increase in the price were made while this Bill is passing through the Committee stage. Every effort should be made to deter and to delay any such step.

(5) I am expecting to hear from Sir Francis Floud shortly about the Customs' answer to Mr Snowden's very serious allegations.[2]

[1] Churchill noted on this minute: 'Mr Grigg to operate.'

[2] In his budget speech of 24 April 1928 Churchill had announced an agreement with the sugar refiners to reduce the duty on sugar by 2s 4d per hundredweight, provided the price of sugar were reduced by 2s 4½d for a period not less than three months. On 2 May 1928, during the debate on the Treasury's Ways and Means resolutions, Philip Snowden charged that leaks of Churchill's intention to make this offer before he actually made it had allowed he sugar refiners to 'buy exceptional amounts of Cuban raw sugar at cheap prices, and that they would make high profits on the bargain with the Treasury'.

(6) I should be glad if Mr Hurst would make out another of those financial tables for the new scheme on the basis that we get £6 millions a year from a Corporation Profits Tax, that we lose the kerosene tax, and that we bring the Railways in at a cost of £4½ millions a year earlier.

(7) Mr Hurst should also find out from the Ministry of Health what is happening about the Rating Ascertainment Bill. It was understood between Mr Chamberlain and me that he was to act as liaison. How is the definition getting on? What is the position of the legislation? When is it going to be introduced? Have any points of principle arisen in its discussions about which I should be informed?

Generally the whole of this field wants careful co-ordination and constant attention. The tendency to lapse into inertia is one of the most dangerous in affairs and the most common.

WSC

Winston S. Churchill to Stanley Baldwin

(*Baldwin papers*)

13 May 1928
Personal and Secret

My dear Prime Minister,

I am much better, and I think in another week I shall be fit for work. I am going to Scotland tonight to stay with Westminster at Loch More. Possibly there will be fishing; but if not, there will be sunshine and a keen air. I am taking full advantage of your generous permission to recuperate thoroughly, and I shall not be attending the Cabinet this week.

I have been thinking a great deal about the Budget position and am very contented with it. The Profits Tax corrector would be altogether logical and just. All the same if we could do without it at any rate for the present, it would be better. I had a message from Rothermere, through Esmond, to say that he had been thinking over the Profits Tax and thought that it might cause a lot of uncertainty and anxiety among Chairmen of Companies and other very influential people who would be afraid that it would be put to bad uses later on. This was very much your view; and anyhow I think we shall gain by chewing the cud on this matter for another fortnight.

But what I feel we must do is to bring the Railway Rates business into operation from about October, costing £2 millions in the present year and £2 millions more next year over and above the present bill. I annexed the old Sinking Fund for this very purpose, and I think it might well be announced on the Second Reading of the Finance Bill, June 5. Otherwise I think everything is quite solid. It is astonishing what a lack of criticism there has been.

There are two names I wish to ask you to consider for the June list. The first is Mr J. M. Gatti[1] who is the late Conservative Chairman of the London County Council and who, I am sure, will be recommended to you from various quarters. You will see why I feel called upon to support his unquestionable claim. He gave up the position of candidate for Westminster and vehemently supported me against Nicholson. But this was the only fault he committed in a long life of orthodox service, and by his ability and character he would be in every respect qualified for what is almost the customary Knighthood. You take so broad a view of these matters that I will not expatiate further.

The second request I make more urgently, and I trust that you will not on any account dismiss it until we have had a talk. Mr Max Pemberton[2] is the President of the London School of Journalism. He was associated with Lord Northcliffe from the very earliest days of the founding of the 'Daily Mail'. He is actually at the moment a Director of the Northcliffe newspapers, but this is only a honorific appointment for the sake of old times. He is ailing and aged, and I am assured that a Knighthood would be worthily bestowed upon and would be well received by Fleet Street generally. It would also give pleasure in quarters about which I am looking forward to having some rather important conversation later.

Believe me
Yours very sincerely,
Winston S. Churchill

[1] John M. Gatti, 1872–1929. Senior partner of the proprietors of the Adelphi and Vaudeville Theatres. Managing Director of the Charing Cross, West End and City Electricity Supply Company, Ltd. Mayor of Westminster, 1911–12. Chairman of the London County Council Finance Committee, 1920–7. Chairman of the London County Council, 1927–8. Knighted, 1928. Chairman, Ministry of Health Committee on Public Cleansing in London, 1928–9.

[2] Max Pemberton, 1863–1950. A prolific novelist, he published his first novel, *The Diary of a Scoundrel*, in 1891. Editor of *Chums*, 1892–3. Editor of *Cassell's Magazine*, 1896–1906. Director of Northcliffe Newspapers, and a biographer of Lord Northcliffe (1922). President of the London School of Journalism. Knighted, 1928.

Winston S. Churchill to Clementine Churchill

(*Spencer-Churchill papers*)

15 May 1928   Rosehall
                                                        Invershin
                                                        Sutherlandshire

My darling—

This is a vy agreeable house in a highland valley well equipped with salmon trout & snipe. Only Benny, Coco & one of his ADC's Ernest Ball.[1] The
air is most exhilarating, keen & yet caressing. It is quite different to England.
I was somewhat tired by the journey wh was longer than I expected; so I did
not fish yesterday but lay about on sofas & read musty books. Today however I must sally forth. But I am vy lazy, & curiously averse from anything
requiring work or exercise physical or mental.

Benny goes S tomorrow for the Ball & returns Friday. I remain here at
least till then. Charles Hunter is coming up to play with me. Coco got 3 fish
yesterday. This place is 45 miles from Loch More, but both rivers are available.

This morning it is raining wh is good for fishing. We all play Bezique so
that the time is not burdensome.

I do hope you will make a point of going to the Ball if only for $\frac{1}{2}$ an hour.
Please do this because I am vy fond of Benny & I know he wd so like to see
you & D there.

                                                   Always yr loving
                                                             W

Don't sit up *too* late.

Stanley Baldwin to Winston S. Churchill

(*Churchill papers: 18/90*)

15 May 1928   10 Downing Street

My dear Winston,

Figure to yourself my feelings! Having still a vivid recollection of that frail
invalid in bed and of the enthusiasm with which he welcomed the prospect
of a call at Chartwell (somewhere about lunchtime). I telephoned yesterday
morning that I would farm out my questions and come down right away.

And then to be told that you had gone to Scotland!

I had not recovered from the shock before your letter was brought to me.

[1] Described by the Duke of Westminster's daughter, Lady Mary Grosvenor, as a 'dedicated
fisherman'. (Letter to the author, 22 June 1978.)

Well, I am delighted that you are better, but I beg you don't hurry back.

I am glad you are very contented with the Budget situation. Keep on with the cud.

And don't worry about Rothermere. He has done you all the service he can for the present, and I think you are a little disposed to overrate his influence in the country.

It is suburban mainly, in a wide sense, but the provincial press is very strong and it is working well for us.

And I want you to consider two points when you think it desirable to bring in some of the benefits at an early date.

A. The carrot side of it. If the carrot is to be served after the election it will be hanging up in sight during the contest and our opponents will have to promise not to interfere with our programme.

   If swallowed before, it may be more in their stomach than in their minds.

B. By giving the carrot in instalments, may you not tend to dissipate the effect of the whole?

I know this is Stamp's view and I need not enlarge on it. It also adds to the difficulties on the financial side.

Enough for one day. I go to Manchester tomorrow to address the cotton people in words of one syllable at lunch.

Yours ever,

SB

What a fool R is allowing his boy to make of himself in Hungary! They haven't a ray of humour between them.[1]

---

[1] Esmond Harmsworth and his father, Lord Rothermere, were both severe critics of the Treaty of Trianon (signed on 4 June 1920) which had established the post-war frontiers of Hungary; both gave their active support to those Hungarians who advocated territorial revision in Hungary's favour, especially in Transylvania (which had become part of Rumania), in the Banat region (which had become part of Yugoslavia) and in southern Slovakia (which had become part of Czechoslovakia). Each of these areas had large Magyar minorities. Only under Hitler's patronage were they later awarded to Hungary: but each was given up again, as under the Trianon scheme, in 1945. On 13 May 1928 Esmond Harmsworth had gone to Hungary to accept an honorary Doctor of Laws degree on behalf of his father from Szeged University. He was received everywhere by large and enthusiastic crowds, including 50,000 people who attended the ceremony in Szeged. In his memoirs, *My Campaign for Hungary* (London, 1939), Lord Rothermere said of his son's visit: 'There has never been anything like Esmond Harmsworth's visit to Hungary. The demonstrations which accompanied it were a measure not only of the burning desire of the whole Magyar race to be united with the brethren it had lost, but also of the generosity of the Hungarian temperament, which thus at the cost of much personal sacrifice and without any hope of benefit, expressed, by welcoming my son in such a noble way, its appreciation of the efforts of one who had done no more than come forward as a public advocate of its cause.'

Winston S. Churchill: Cabinet note

(*Churchill papers: 18/75*)

17 May 1928

BROADCASTING OF CONTROVERSIAL POLITICAL SPEECHES[1]

When arranging with Sir John Reith about broadcasting the Budget proposals I learned from him that it was suggested—though he did not agree with it—that each Party in turn should be allowed at fortnightly intervals to make a controversial speech. I immediately pointed out how unfair this would be to the Government, which has to bear the whole burden of events and is the responsible organ of national life, and yet which would have two hostile attacks made upon it for every speech on its behalf whether in defence or exposition.

I pointed out that there are really only two Parties: the 'Ins' and the 'Outs'; the Government who act and the Opposition who criticise. The mere fact that the Opposition is divided in itself constitutes no claim for additional representation. If that were so, further division among themselves would be a ground for claims for further opportunities of attack, ie the more divided the Opposition becomes, the greater are to be its facilities for pouring abuse upon the Government of the day. Such a principle is absurd; and indeed the contrary proposition, viz that the Opposition should have less opportunities because they are divided, would be far more comfortable to reason.

In these circumstances I trust there will be no question of agreeing to the Liberal proposal, and that we should support the views put forward by Sir John Reith, ie and in particular the principle of 'time for time' with each of the Opposition parties.

Lord Irwin to Sir Samuel Hoare

(*Irwin papers*)

17 May 1928

Meanwhile Winston seems to have succeeded in introducing a new and wider factor into current politics. I am not competent to express an opinion

---

[1] On May 14 Lord Beaverbrook had sent Churchill a cutting from Sir William Berry's paper *London Calling*, in which the journalist Hannen Swaffer had written: 'Churchill is a dreadful speaker to listen to, if you have any ear. They call it a "lisp". It is worse than that: it sounds like a turkey trying to say "cuckoo" without hatching the other bird's eggs.' Edward Marsh noted on Beaverbrook's communication: 'Swaffer is Max's dramatic critic (so-called) a pestilential fellow' (*Churchill papers: 2/158*).

on the far-reaching scheme that he has developed, but it certainly seems to be a bold attempt to bring a somewhat antiquated machinery into touch with the necessities and requirements of our present situation. I hope he and Neville have got it all worked out. I am constitutionally a little bit nervous of Winston's impetuousity, but I have implicit faith in Neville and hope he will have been able to keep him straight on the detailed implications of his scheme. Certainly if you have been able to devise a plan for giving relief at once to the heavy manufacturing industries and to agriculture, you ought to be able to face your electoral test next year with a certain amount of confidence.

Randolph Churchill to Winston S. Churchill

(Churchill papers: 1/199)

19 May 1928   Eton College

Dear Papa,

I hope your stay in Scotland has made you quite fit again, and that you are now restored to your usual state of health.

I have just been elected to the Political Society. We had an address last night from Mr Duff Cooper on the meaning of Conservatism. I thought he spoke extremely well, as it must be very difficult to become really vehement when speaking to an audience of about thirty. He was very forcible and convincing, and I enjoyed his speech enormously.

Yesterday afternoon Miss Catherine Mayo[1] lectured to First Hundred. She was very interesting and amusing.

I am so looking forward to seeing you to-morrow. I shall expect you about 4 o'clock unless I hear to the contrary.

Your loving son
Randolph

PS. I have to attend Chapel at 5 o'clock.

[1] Katherine Mayo. Born in Pennsylvania. Her first book, a history of the Pennsylvania State Police Force, was published in 1917. In 1925 she published *The Isles of Fear*, an examination of United States rule in the Philippines. Her books on India were *Mother India* (1927), *Slave of the Gods* (1928), *Volume Two* (1931) and *The Face of Mother India* (1935). She died in 1940. See also page 1042, note 1.

Lord Grey of Fallodon to Winston S. Churchill

(*Churchill papers: 1/199*)

20 May 1928   Morayshire

My dear Winston,

Thank you very much for your letter. Up to June 7 there may still be other nominations for the Chancellorship of Oxford, but if I am elected unopposed I shall be the first non-political Chancellor for many years. Now that my mental & physical activities are so much curtailed by bad sight my thoughts dwell increasingly on early years when life was all before me, and an honour from my old University would please me more than any other public compliment.[1]

I am glad you have been to Angelsey. For 24 years I fished the Rosehall water for the whole or part of April—a very small part alas! very often when I was in office: but each year as April approached I went to sleep at night thinking of the hauls, after the day's work in London was over.

There are naturally criticisms to be made on so huge & complicated a thing as the Budget & it will be our part in opposition to make them; but you have opened up a big subject, which needed to be tackled & have launched a big thing & it is good that this has been done. Your handling of a great subject is always worthy of its size & stimulating to our public life, & a delight to watch.

The river here has been unfishable from flood since Thursday morning, but I do not go South till the 28th & if the weather settles I may still get a few fish.

Yours ever
E G

I hope you are quite renewed. The Angelsey valley is a better health resort than all the watering places in the world.

Winston S. Churchill to Lord Beaverbrook

(*Beaverbrook papers*)

21 May 1928   Treasury Chambers
Private

My dear Max,

I have now been able to read it all. I think it vy valuable & sincere, recalling the earliest Max I knew—when he still had worlds to conquer, & kings to captivate.

---

[1] Grey was elected Chancellor of the University of Oxford.

As for me you have *testified* in a manner far beyond my deserts—with generosity—indeed it has given me gt pleasure to read it.[1] Candour and faithful keeping of confidences are not easy to combine. But you have succeeded. And in addition you have produced a vital—tho limited—too limited—contribution to the slowly emerging truth. 'What happened & Why!' After all that is history or what history ought to be.

But what a tale! Think of all these people—decent educated, the story of the past laid out before them—What to avoid—what to do etc patriotic, loyal, clean—trying their utmost—What a ghastly muddle they made of it!

Unteachable from infancy to tomb—There is the first & main characteristic of mankind.

Let me see you soon.

Yours ever,
W

No more War.

Winston S. Churchill to Sir Richard Hopkins and others concerned

(Churchill papers: 18/90)

24 May 1928

(1) I do not propose to replace the kerosene tax by a profits tax this year. I will draft shortly an outline of the way in which I will deal with the financial position. In principle I must look to expansion of normal revenue and to further economies as means of effecting the balance of future budgets. Please enable me to compare the figures of the latest forecast with those on which I had been working previously.

(2) I accept the report and advice of Sir Horace Hamilton's Committee, and will take no special steps this year to defend the chemical frontier by penal provisions. The form of words to be used for deterring the use of kero-

---

[1] Beaverbrook was dining with Churchill when news of the German declaration of war on Russia was announced, and Churchill took the decision to call out the Reserves. In *Politicians and the War* Beaverbrook wrote, of Churchill at that moment: 'He was not depressed; he was not elated; he was not surprised. He did not put his head between his hands, as many another eminent man might well have done, and exclaim to high heaven that his world was coming to an end. Certainly he exhibited no fear or uneasiness. Neither did he show any signs of joy. He went straight out like a man going to a well-accustomed job. In fact, he had foreseen everything that was going to happen so far that his temperament was in no way upset by the realisation of his forecast. We have suffered at times from Mr Churchill's bellicosity. But what profit the nation derived at that crucial moment from the capacity of the First Lord of the Admiralty for grasping and dealing with the war situation.'

sene for motor purposes must be very carefully considered. I should be glad of suggestions.

(3) The possible acceleration of the railway relief should be brought before the Cabinet. A paper stating the pros and cons should be prepared.

WSC

Winston S. Churchill to Stanley Baldwin

(*Churchill papers: 18/90*)

24 May 1928

My dear PM,

I have today been exploring the next stage of the Budget debates. On the 5th Snowden will move a reasoned motion to reject the Finance Bill. I should propose to reply immediately. L-G tells me that Simon will speak for them; so I shall have him on my tail, and Worthy is quite willing either to follow him before dinner, or—more probably, and better, to wind up before the division at 11. On the whole I think this is a very good lay-out.

Wed the 6th Neville opens his Apportionment Bill. It is now becoming essential that the general outlines of our Rating scheme should be stated to Parliament, including the principles of the formula grant; and I think that Neville should not limit himself to the direct question of the Apportionment Bill, but should also unfold a coherent and complete explanation of our main plan, of course in general terms, and reserving all details. It may well be that a large part of the criticisms of the Opposition will then be shown to be irrelevant or superfluous. I think also Neville should be ready to give the House a memorandum restating his speech in a precise form.

On top of us is also the Scotch position, never yet disclosed. Jack Gilmour is being severely pressed for further and better particulars. He would like to speak on Thursday the 7th early, and explain the Scotch aspect; and he has a memorandum ready which could be laid immediately after his speech. Both these speeches and memoranda add necessary fuel to the development of the controversy. L-G intends to speak after Neville, or sometime during the afternoon of the Wednesday (6th), and if you and Neville thought well, I should be quite ready to wind up on the whole debate on Thursday before 7.30. On the other hand you might both prefer Kingsley Wood. I am quite indifferent.

I have naturally consulted the Speaker on the scope he would allow to these debates. He takes what I consider is a very sensible view. He says that the whole 2½ days, Tues, Wed and Thurs, whether on the Finance Bill or the Apportionment Bill, will virtually range around the central problem of Rating Relief and Reform. A question could be asked him by the Opposition (I am sure it is agreeable to their wish) whether he would give a wide and general latitude in these debates, which he says are virtually all one. I could get this question asked, I am sure. I am sending a copy of this letter to Neville, as he has already gone away, and it is important to have matters planned out in advance. Will you please let me know whether you approve generally, and whether I should work it out with him on these lines?

I am convinced that a fuller disclosure of our policy, in order to prevent needless misunderstanding, should now be made.

All is quiet on the adjournment,
Yours very sincerely,
Winston S. Churchill

PS. I caught Neville on the telephone after all, and put the points to him.

WSC

Stanley Baldwin to Winston S. Churchill

(*Churchill papers; 18/90*)

25 May 1928   Welbeck Abbey[1]

My dear Winston,

I found your letter of yesterday waiting for me and I have read it over with great care. I don't think I could improve on the proposed arrangement of speeches. Worthy has earned a little limelight and he has well merited the winding up on Tuesday night.

I think it would be kind on your part to leave the rating bill for Kingsley Wood to wind up. He will have a searching part to play both in this bill and in the winter and he should have his bit of sugar now.

I should have written you in any case from here, to thank you for readily relieving me of yesterday but principally to BEG of you to keep quiet for the next ten days.

You look run down and you want building up again, and the finance bill will want all your vitality.

Yours ever,
SB

[1] Baldwin was staying with the Duke and Duchess of Portland at Welbeck Abbey. On 28 May 1928 he spoke to more than 70,000 people in the grounds of the Abbey, praising the Government's Franchise Bill, its progress achieved in Housing with the building of more than ¾ million new structures, and its firmness and fairness in dealing with the problems of the coal industry. At one point in his speech Baldwin defended a new pamphlet issued by the Conservative Party, saying: 'It deals with facts and facts alone!', and emphasizing the point so forcefully that he knocked over the microphone. When he recovered his balance and his microphone he said: 'The mere mention of truth on a public platform has almost knocked the table over!'

Winston S. Churchill to Robert Birley

(*Churchill papers: 1/199*)

25 May 1928

My dear Mr Birley,

I send you by Randolph's hand Paget's 'Examen' as Lord Rosebery calls it. I think several of the essays are fully equal to Macaulay's essays, and apparently backed by an immense amount of literary knowledge and authorities. It is remarkable that they did not make a greater impression. I presume that Macaulay's death prevented his defending himself from the very grave accusations of disingenuousness which are preferred. I have been studying Sabatier,[1] but am disappointed so far as I have gone. There is no doubt that translations are necessarily bald and lack the style of either language.

I think Randolph's essay on the 'Dole' quite sensible. But the handwriting is not merely bad but wrong. A different letter is written from the one he means, and we are left to guess from the context.

I was very glad to see that you are drawing his attention to these most irritating malformations.

Winston S. Churchill to Professor Lindemann

(*Churchill papers: 1/199*)

25 May 1928

My dear Prof,

I have discovered that the lower pool in the water garden is at least ten feet higher than the high water level of the new top lake. The distance is rather under two hundred yards. Am I right in assuming that if a watertight pipe is led from the higher level, the water will flow down one side of the valley and up the other and deliver itself in the top lake by gravity? Theoretically I have always been told that water rises to its own level, so that presumably even an inch command would give a certain flow. But ten feet ought to give a fairly rapid delivery. Could you tell me whether this would be all right? Secondly, ought I to have an inch pipe or an inch and a half pipe? An inch pipe would be cheaper. We may take the flow of water at about $7\frac{1}{2}$ gallons a minute. Assuming these $7\frac{1}{2}$ gallons were poured into the (a) one inch or (b) one and a half inch pipe with a ten feet command at two

---

[1] Paul Sabatier, 1858–1928. A French Protestant theologian. Vicar of Strasbourg until expelled by the Germans in 1889. Biographer of St Francis of Assisi, 1893. Returned to Strasbourg, 1919, as Professor of Theology.

hundred yards distance, what would be the rate of delivery at the out-flow end? I do hope these problems are not beyond the range of Oxford mathematics! It would be so nice of you to let me know the answers as soon as possible, because the decision as to the pipes ought to be taken very soon.

The advantage of this plan is that I very nearly triple the flow into the top lake and override the very minor leaks that have developed and make a quicker change of the water. The cost of the one and a half inch pipe is about £20. Would the flow be greatly retarded if the command was only five feet?

With all good wishes[1]

Neville Chamberlain to Winston S. Churchill

(*Churchill papers: 18/90*)

25 May 1928

My dear Winston,

I have just received the copy of your letter to the PM, but I suppose that, as he has gone away, he will not express any opinion upon the suggestions which you have made until after the recess, and that we must, therefore, settle between ourselves what is to be the procedure.

I do not quite follow why you think it desirable on the Apportionment Bill to go into the questions which will have to be dealt with on the Local Government Bill, and I see considerable danger in attempting to do so before these proposals are worked out with greater precision than we have been able to do at present.

I have announced that my memorandum containing full particulars of the proposals will be made public some time during the next month, and the local authorities appear quite willing to wait until they get that memorandum before making any criticisms or suggestions. Although the Apportionment Bill does not actually give relief to rates itself, it indicates quite clearly how the properties are to be distinguished which are to be the subject of this relief, and, of course, everyone knows what the relief is.

Really two sets of people are involved in the two Bills. Industry and the public are interested to know who is, and who is not, going to be relieved, and that must be dealt with fully on the 6th and 7th. But as to how the Exchequer money is to be distributed, industry and the public are not so

---

[1] On 31 May 1928 Churchill wrote to Lindemann again: 'My dear Prof, I am so grateful to you for the wonderful calculations you have made. There is no doubt about the 10 ft command. As I am using new pipes I expect all will be well. I hope the water will be flowing into the upper lake by the end of the week. Once more thanking you' (*Churchill papers: 1/199*).

much concerned as the local authorities; and I would propose, therefore, not to say more about the distribution than I have already said publicly, although there would be no objection to repeating the broad outlines which I gave to the Association of Municipal Corporations.

As we are having two days, I think it might be a good thing to let Kingsley wind up on Wednesday night, and Jack Gilmour open on Thursday afternoon. If then you would wind up at 7.30 on Thursday night, this would give ample opportunity for our front bench to clear up all the points: and I suppose Kingsley and I could take the financial resolution between us.

I shall not be back until Monday, the 4th, but, if there is anything special you want to write to me about, they would forward on any letter from the Ministry of Health.

Yours sincerely,
N. Chamberlain

It looks to me as if the attack would centre on the alleged unfairness of derating the big man who runs a factory and leaving untouched the small man who works at the same trade in his back premises. But it is important not to get drawn into derating every little cobbler, milliner, jobbing tailor, etc.

Winston S. Churchill to Neville Chamberlain

(Churchill papers: 18/90)

26 May 1928

My dear Neville,

Many thanks for your letter, and I am very glad that you can work Kingsley Wood in for winding up on the 6th. If you have the least preference for his winding up the whole debate, I should not be in the slightest degree offended. I am sure, however, it will keep on pretty wide lines.

When I answer Snowden on the 5th, I shall of course make a general restatement of our policy in the light of the criticisms which have developed; and particularly: (1) that we help the rich industries and not the poor, (2) that we ought to pick and choose between industries, (3) that the Liberal Yellow Book plan is better, and (4) that site values would provide the money. I think it possible to demolish all these contentions. Nor can I say that it is necessary *for my purposes* for me to go beyond what I said at Newcastle in explaining the general articulation of the scheme. But I beg you to consider the following points.

You propose to give a memorandum to the Local Authorities about the middle of June. Obviously this memorandum must be simultaneously given to the House of Commons. It is bound to leak out; and Parliament would, I think, rightly resent not having at least simultaneous information, especially while legislation is actually in progress. Therefore, if I am right, only a week is in question. Parliament will no doubt be told that a memorandum for the Local Authorities is in preparation and that negotiations will begin on this basis almost immediately. The demand will then be made: 'Surely the Government can tell us what their plan of repayment is in broad outline. They must know, because in a week they are going to give it to the Local Authorities.

What is the use of concealing these essential matters from the House and forcing us to take a division on the Apportionment Bill without a clear idea of what the policy is? We shall know in a week, and you know now. Why cannot you tell us now; and if you won't tell, how can you blame us if we misconceive and misrepresent your policy?' I am sure this will be their line, and I want to know what is the answer. What is the part of the main rating scheme that you wish particularly to keep up your sleeve at the present time? Is it, for instance, the proposed apportionment of money under the formula? Or is it the arrangements for creating larger authorities? Or both? To what extent will these be treated in your memorandum for the Local Authorities? Surely when you deal with the Local Authorities the first thing they will say is: Fill in the figures of the formula. And then they will begin haggling about these figures, and the matter will become public property.

I must confess that my opinion is that it would be wise to tell the House in the debate, in different words and in a more general form, the substance of what is to be disclosed to the Local Authorities during June. I am most anxious to conform to your wishes; and it would be a great help to me if, after having considered what I have written here, you would put down the principal points you do *not* wish to give away at this stage.

I had not realised, having been away, that the small bakers, etc, were out of the scheme; and I agree with you that the argument that the small man will be further over-weighted in competition is an awkward one. Of course the line of the Factory Act is a very good one to defend. But is there no way of enabling the small man who thinks it worth while to get the relief—in his case probably very small—to put himself within the Factory Act line by making an application to be treated as such? The great bulk would not do this, as it would not be worth their while. But the principle of 'fair do's' would be achieved.

I should like very much to see the draft memorandum to the Local Authorities, in order to know what to avoid. I am sorry to bother you on your hard-earned holidays. Perhaps it would save you trouble if you took this letter and wrote on it your answers on the different points, instead of writing a full reply.

Forgive this verbose communication. I am still rather woolly.[1]

Winston S. Churchill to Sir Ernest Gowers

(*Churchill papers: 18/75*)

29 May 1928

The Opposition amendments to the Finance Bill allege that 'the bulk of the relief is going to the prosperous industries'. This is quite untrue. Mr Hurst has calculated that 7/8ths of the relief goes to industries heavy and depressed where the rate of unemployment is above the normal 6%. I should like to reinforce this by calculations on profits. Take these same industries where unemployment is over 6% and compare their profits with the other more prosperous industries. Take also the profits of the big trades: agriculture, coal, cotton, iron, steel, shipbuilding, engineering, wool, etc. Show what very small profits they made last year, and what a reduced proportion they are in the sample. Let me have the sample paper with all the trades on one sheet again, so that I may study it. Let me also have the papers about the ratio of rates to profits based, I think, on 1924. Please consult with Mr Hurst so as to get me effective figures. I want to show that the great bulk of the relief is going where the profits are lowest, and only a small proportion where the profits are highest by the latest figures we have.

WSC

Winston S. Churchill to Stanley Baldwin

(*Churchill papers: 18/91*)

31 May 1928

My dear PM,

Many thanks for your letter, and congratulations on your survey of the Government achievements at Welbeck.

I sent Neville a copy of my letter to you. He suggested that Kingsley Wood

---

[1] On May 26 Churchill, his wife and Diana went for four days to Wilton House, for the season known there as 'Winstontide'. Among the other guests were Lord and Lady Desborough.

should speak on the Wednesday evening, when he will have to answer Lloyd George, and that I should wind up before dinner on the Thursday. In my view this is the best arrangement. I am very anxious to keep in touch with the rating side of the policy, and equally to associate Neville with the finance. We do not want to get into water-tight compartments on an issue where the consequences of failure or discord would be so serious. As I shall have to sit and listen to these debates, a good deal will probably occur to me which should be said in winding up. However, if you think otherwise I shall make no complaint.

Yours vy sincerely,
WSC

Robert Birley to Winston S. Churchill

(*Churchill papers: 1/199*)

31 May 1928 Eton College

Dear Mr Churchill,

Thank you for your letter. Randolph has lent me the Paget. It is really excellent. I think Macaulay would have been hard put to it to answer the attack, though I feel he would have made some play with the references to Cockneys and townsmen. Paget was too good a writer not to leave a loophole for a clever attorney here and there. Paget says in the introduction that Macaulay was living when the essays were first published. He does not say when they first appeared, but I suppose it is likely that it was not long before he died, as the first collected edition appeared two years after his death. . . .

We are sending Randolph to a local man who teaches handwriting. He is very well spoken of by one of the housemasters. I do not myself feel very confident that he will work miracles, but at any rate it will force him to spend some time thinking about his hand.

I have baited him with some questions in Divinity, (for written answers) to make him express his religious views. I have not argued with him on the subject, but I have written on his papers the headings of arguments which I should use against them for him to consider. I do not wish to argue with him at all fully until he invites it, in case he thinks I am making a full-dress attack on him. I have been much impressed by his answers—they are very well argued and extremely logical. They are also, I think, absolutely sincere, though there is certainly a touch of a rather natural enjoyment in being cynical for its own sake. I feel rather doubtful about telling him he is passing through a phase, (which is certainly what I feel he is doing.) It is rather insulting if he is sincere, and if it was a successful argument it would lead to rather a self-conscious state of mind. On the other hand it is not a particularly good thing for him to feel too proud of himself as an original discoverer of a truth hidden from Man, and I feel he should have the other point of view presented to him. I am trying the experiment of reading some Shelley, particularly 'Prometheus Unbound', with him and some other boys, to show him that other people have had his ideas before.

Yours very sincerely
Robert Birley

June 1928

Brigadier-General Sir James Edmonds[1] *to Winston S. Churchill*

(*Churchill papers: 1/199*)

7 June 1928

My dear Chancellor

The Old Army has really overwhelmed me with congratulations on the Birthday Honour, but there is no message that I value more than the telegram that you sent.[2] I have got a great deal out of the history, but one thing stands out, and that is the thought that it brought me association with you and contact with your genius.

Yours most gratefully
J. E. Edmonds

Winston S. Churchill to Edward Marsh

(*Churchill papers: 18/75*)

10 June 1928

Has Boothby made any progress in selecting some of these speeches?[3]

Tell Mr Curtis Brown that Cassells suggested that a collection of speeches should be published, and offered £300. I was inclined to accept this, but Mr Butterworth wished to take it on the same terms. Nothing was settled about the royalties, American rights or serials. I do not think there are any serial rights of value in this matter, and I very much doubt any American rights are worth contracting for; but I shall always be glad to hear his views.

[1] James Edward Edmonds, 1861–1956. Educated at King's College School, London. 2nd Lieutenant, Royal Engineers, 1881; Major, 1899. On active service in South Africa, 1901–2, and on the Western Front, 1914–18. Colonel, 1909. Deputy Engineer-in-Chief, BEF, 1918 (despatches six times). Head of the Military Branch of the Historical Section of the Committee of Imperial Defence, 1919–49. Brigadier-General. Author of the multi-volume official history, *Military Operations: France and Belgium*. Knighted, 1928.

[2] Brigadier-General Edmonds had just been created a Knight Bachelor.

[3] Churchill had decided to put together a volume of his principal speeches between 1918 and 1928. But the volume was not published.

L. S. Amery: diary

(*Amery papers*)

12 June 1928

INDUSTRIAL TRANSFERENCE BOARD

. . . Winston who was in a thoroughly naughty mood could only denounce all action and say that the miners had better go out and find some work as things improved.

L. S. Amery: diary

(*Amery papers*)

14 June 1928

Winston pre-occupied in his determination to intervene in the Prayer Book debate in order to justify his voting to his constituents. . . .

Winston who had been bubbling over with excitement all the afternoon got in about 7.30. The actual argument of his speech was good but whether it was the Winstonian diction or the fact that he rather lost his temper with interruptors, or the general feeling that he was not the person to intervene, made the speech ineffective and indeed damaging to his cause.[1]

Winston S. Churchill: memorandum

(*Churchill papers: 22/198*)

15 June 1928

I suggest that it should now be laid down as a standing assumption that at any given date there will be no major war for ten years from that date; and that this should rule unless or until, on the initiative of the Foreign Office or one of the fighting services or otherwise, it is decided to alter it.

---

[1] According to the record of the debate in *Hansard*, Churchill was interrupted five times. In reply to demands for an answer to the interrupters, Churchill replied: 'I am expressing my view, and I have every intention of expressing my view without modifying it in the slightest degree.'

Winston S. Churchill to Sir Roger Keyes

(*Keyes papers*)

19 June 1928   Treasury Chambers

My dear Roger,

Welcome home for what I trust will be a brief interlude in your Herculean labours. I have a men's luncheon party on Thursday: Tom Bridges,[1] whom you know; Napoleon Bonaparte Fuller[2] of the Tanks; Archie Sinclair; and possibly Simon Lovat.[3] It would be very nice if you could join us. I am going down in the afternoon to Aldershot for the Tattoo, so we shall have plenty of time to talk. If you are already engaged for Thursday lunch, come and see me at the Treasury any time after five on Wednesday afternoon. Telephone your wishes and hour.

Winston S. Churchill to P. J. Grigg

(*Churchill papers: 18/75*)

19 June 1928

It will be necessary for Major Walter Elliot[4] to help us on the Committee Stage of the Budget. Has he been properly briefed on the subject? You should let him know I am counting on him to assist. Meanwhile would you very kindly look through the amendments and suggest how they should be distri-

[1] George Tom Molesworth Bridges, 1871–1939. Entered Royal Artillery, 1892. Lieutenant-Colonel, 4th Hussars, 1914. Head of British Military Mission, Belgian Field Army, 1914–16. Major-General commanding the 19th Division, 1916–17. Wounded five times. Lost a leg at Passchendaele. Head of British War Mission, USA, 1918. Head of British Mission, Allied Armies of the Orient, 1918–20. Knighted, 1919. Governor of South Australia, 1922–7. He published his memoirs, *Alarms & Excursions*, in 1938 (with a Foreword by Churchill).

[2] John Frederick Charles Fuller, 1878–1966. On active service in South Africa, 1899–1902, and in the war of 1914–18 (DSO, 1917). A pioneer of tank warfare. Lieutenant-Colonel, 1918. Author of many works on military subjects, including *Tanks in the Great War*, 1920, *The Reformation of War*, 1923, and *The Foundations of the Science of War*, 1926. Major-General, 1930. His thirty-second book, a biography of Julius Caesar, was published in 1965.

[3] Simon Joseph Fraser Lovat, 1871–1933. Landowner. 14th Baron Lovat, 1887. Honorary Major Commanding Lovat's Scouts in South Africa, 1900–2. Served as Lieutenant-Colonel at Gallipoli, 1915. Major-General, Director of Forestry, 1916–18. Chairman of the Forestry Commission, 1919–27. Parliamentary Under-Secretary, Dominions Office, 1927–8.

[4] Walter Elliot, 1888–1958. Educated, Glasgow Academy and University. On active service, 1914–18 (Military Cross and bar). Conservative MP for Lanark, 1918–23; for Glasgow Kelvingrove, 1924–45; for the Scottish Universities, 1946–50; for Kelvingrove, 1950–8. Parliamentary Under-Secretary of State for Scotland, 1926–9. Financial Secretary, Treasury, 1931–2. Minister of Agriculture and Fisheries, 1932–6. Privy Councillor, 1932. Elected to the Other Club, 1932. Secretary of State for Scotland, 1936–8. Minister of Health, 1938–40. Director of Public Relations, War Office, 1941–2.

buted among our forces? If there are any very technical Inland Revenue clauses like those on which Sir Douglas Hogg helped us last year, we ought to requisition the services of the new Attorney-General[1] or at least the Solicitor.[2] Pray make me a suggestion for parcelling out the work.

L. S. Amery: diary

(*Amery papers*)

20 June 1928

CABINET

Balfour brought up the Zionist proposal arguing it very ably and I supported.[3] Austen very definitely opposed chiefly on the line that any international collaboration would strengthen the case for interference by other nations in Palestine and might add to any difficulties with France over the Haifa Baghdad railway, a line of argument which undoubtedly influenced me as well as all the Cabinet. I suggested that we need not guarantee the loan at all but simply ask the League Financial Committee to approve the loan as a good one if the British Grant controlled the expenditure but he did not like that.

Winston, who had apparently been seeing Weizmann,[4] to my surprise backed us up at any rate to the extent of being willing to find the money but the PM and most of the Cabinet were definitely against and it was turned down.

[1] Sir Thomas Inskip (see page 712, note 3).

[2] Sir Frank Merriman (see page 1239, note 5).

[3] On 21 January 1928 the Zionist Organization, headed by Dr Chaim Weizmann, had asked the British Government for a loan to develop 'close settlement by Jews on the land, as contemplated by the Mandate'. This was the first Zionist request for British Government money to help Zionist work in Palestine. The request was supported by Lord Balfour, who told his Cabinet colleagues that he was 'not so sure' that since 1920 the British had in fact carried out their obligations to the Jews 'in a very generous spirit'.

[4] Chaim Weizmann, 1874–1952. Born in Russia. Educated in Germany. Reader in Biochemistry, University of Manchester, 1906. Naturalized as a British subject, 1910. Director Admiralty Laboratories, 1916–19. President of the World Zionist Organization, and of the Jewish Agency for Palestine, 1921–31 and 1935–46. Chairman, Board of Governors, Hebrew University of Jerusalem, 1932–50. Adviser to the Ministry of Supply, London, 1939–45. First President of the State of Israel from 1949 until his death. His eldest son, Flight-Lieutenant Michael Weizmann, RAF, was killed in action in 1942.

Winston S. Churchill to P. J. Grigg

(*Churchill papers: 18/75*)

21 June 1928

I have marked the paper sufficiently to cover the first two days at least of the discussion. I am expecting to take away a full brief which I can study on Sunday and coming back in the train on Monday. The Customs should be told that I must know about Turpentine in good time Monday, and the up-shot of their talks with the FBI representatives. What would be the cost of a concession on turpentine? It is outside the Petrol Duty. I must have the Sugar papers in order to attack Snowden; also a report of his offensive speech. Samuel had better stick to lighters under my supervision.

Winston S. Churchill: draft Parliamentary statement

(*Churchill papers: 18/75*)

28 June 1928

I have to inform the House that I have received as Chancellor of the Exchequer an important gift to the nation. Lord Inchcape desires in memory of his daughter, Miss Elsie Mackay, who perished in attempting the passage of the Atlantic by aeroplane, to place in trust for the nation the sum of £500,000, the residue of her estate which passed to him.[1] Lord Inchcape's wish is that this gift should ultimately be applied in reduction of the national debt. He proposes that it should accumulate for a period of roughly fifty years, unless by some earlier date the proceeds with other funds available should be sufficient to redeem the whole of the liabilities of the State. This fund will accordingly be called the Elsie Mackay Fund.[2]

[1] On 9 March 1928 Elsie Mackay had issued a public statement denying 'rumours' that she would accompany Captain Hinchliffe on his attempt to break the long-distance air flight record. On March 14 Hinchliffe had left Britain in his Stinton-Detroiter monoplane *Endeavour*. Although he flew with a passenger, he would neither say who his passenger was, nor what route he intended to follow. In a message to his agent, he wrote that he was leaving on an 'Atlantic attempt', but the wind at the time of his departure was strong to gale force against him across the entire ocean. On March 15 Lord Inchcape (who was in Cairo) stated that he was 'greatly distressed' to feel that his daughter might be in the monoplane. She was: but neither she nor Captain Hinchliffe, nor the plane, were ever seen again.

[2] Lord Inchcape's gift was invested immediately upon receipt by the Treasury Custodian Trustee. On 31 March 1977 its market price was £4,426,218. During the first week of December 1978 the whole of the Fund, both cash and securities, passed to the National Debt Office, where it was applied in the reduction of the National Debt—then standing at more than £52,780,000,000.

July 1928

Winston S. Churchill to P. J. Grigg

(*Churchill papers: 18/75*)

2 July 1928

. . . This is the first time in my experience we have been able to look forward to an official forecasted surplus in a prospective Budget. Many things will have happened before 1930–31, and the figures are certainly not unmanageable, even if they were not improved. Broadly speaking, either things will get better or some very considerable change will take place. With your happy views about the wisdom of the Norman policy you ought to be an optimist. Tiarks,[1] whom I met over the week-end, thinks the corner has been turned and that the future will be bright.

SAFEGUARDING

No one could possibly have thought as much about this matter as I have done, with a quarter of a century of reflection and action behind me. It is no use speaking of Free Trade as if it were something more important than England. The question is not what will vindicate Free Trade but what would really be a sensible and helpful thing for England to do. I am always focussing this in my mind's eye. I am pretty sure we should be better off by doing what I have talked about to you and putting the proceeds into further relief of freights. I should not challenge the theoretical argument against it but present it as a practical step necessitated by revenue requirements and likely to be beneficial to trade and employment, without involving any fundamental change in the long-established fiscal policy of the island.

THE NATIONAL DEBT

I agree broadly. But the complacency of the Treasury and the Bank and their indifference to all the other aspects of our national problem makes it a

---

[1] Frank Cyril Tiarks, 1874–1952. Served in the Royal Navy, 1887–94. Entered banking, becoming a partner in J. Henry Schroder & Co in 1902. Director of the Bank of England, 1912–45. Director of the Anglo-Iranian Oil Company, 1917–48. High Sheriff of Kent, 1927.

duty to put the opposite case sometimes. They have caused an immense amount of misery and impoverishment by their rough and pedantic handling of the problem, in ruined homes, in demoralised workmen, in discouraged industry, in embarrassed finances, in inflated debt and cruel taxation we have paid the price. As the ship goes through the seas its smoke and smells drift to leeward. One always hopes one will make the port in good time when the discomforts of the voyage will soon be forgotten.

So many thanks for your writing to me.

Cabinet Unemployment Policy Committee: minutes

(Cabinet papers: 23/58)

4 July 1928

UNEMPLOYMENT

The Chancellor of the Exchequer pointed out that the proposals of the Industrial Transference Board, as well as those of the Secretary of State for Dominion Affairs, did not touch the immediate problem confronting the Government, which was, how to provide for some 500,000 persons most of whom were already unemployed and the remainder likely to be unemployed in the near future. He suggested that the Cabinet should examine a proposal for an addition to the scheme of Rating Relief whereby relief would be given to the railways in respect of coal, either for exportation or for use in blast furnaces. This scheme, which might come into operation in the Autumn, should have an immediate effect on those industries which were hardest hit. The cost was estimated at £4,000,000 but some of this might be recoverable by reduced expenditure on unemployed, increased receipts from Income Tax and Super Tax, and in other indirect ways resulting from the stimulation of Industry.

Mr Churchill emphasised the impossibility of financing measures for dealing with unemployment without additional taxation, the nature of which he indicated and which he thought the Cabinet was unlikely to desire before a General Election, or, alternatively, by means of savings, postponements of expenditure on approved policy etc, which he commended to his colleagues.

Winston S. Churchill to Sir Laming Worthington-Evans
(*Churchill papers: 22/218*)

14 July 1928

. . . Personally I believe that if we scrapped the Empire Settlement Board altogether and put the existing money into reduced passage, more people would leave this country every year for the Dominions than now.

Winston S. Churchill to Stanley Baldwin
(*Churchill papers: 22/218*)

14 July 1928
Private

My dear PM,

I made up my mind some time ago to appoint a purely departmental committee to help me to 'diagnose' the present situation in trade, finance and employment. It seems to me most important to find out, as far as is humanly possible, what is happening to us, and why. I mentioned this project to Philip, and in conversation with him suggested that we should enquire jointly. Later it occurred to me that Worthy would be an invaluable associate. My idea in its final form is therefore that a group of officials representing the main phases of the problem should be formed inter-departmentally, and that we three Ministers should direct their studies, asking questions in writing and discussing the result between ourselves. I am sure this is the most practical way of reaching a general conclusion in a short time.

However, the committee which you showed me does not seem at all to follow on these lines. It simply meant that two of the Treasury officials were to be detached and to sit under Philip for the purpose of certain enquiries. Of course any information in the Treasury which is necessary to the Board of Trade can be made available, but it would not at all meet my needs and anxieties to have an enquiry of the kind mentioned by you, from which, I myself, whose whole object is to gain knowledge and form an opinion, was to be excluded.

I hope therefore that my project as now set out may be carried out, and with very little delay, as we are separating so soon. Failing this I would prefer to make my own enquiries in a semi-official manner through a purely departmental enquiry.

Yours vy sincerely,
WSC

Winston S. Churchill: departmental minute

(*Churchill papers: 18/75*)

18 July 1928

I do not think this answer ought to have been submitted to the Foreign Secretary before it was shown to me. Thus Sir Austen Chamberlain is led to believe that I have approved it, whereas I have never seen it at all; and I am confronted with what is virtually his decision. It will, I am sure, save a great deal of trouble and misunderstanding if we make our position plain. I think we should add at the end words to this effect.

It must be remembered that Great Britain does not seek to make any profit or return out of the monies lent by her to Allies during the war and only to receive from those Allies such greatly reduced sums as will, together with the reparations received from Germany, balance the payments which it is our duty to make to the United States. This condition has not yet been achieved, there being still an adverse balance of £125 millions between the payments made by Great Britain to the United States and those received from Europe from Allied debt settlements or German reparations. We could not therefore entertain proposals which would expose us to having actually to pay more than we receive. I think it will be well to make this plain from the outset.

Bernard Baruch to Winston S. Churchill

(*Churchill papers: 2/159*)

20 July 1928   Grand Hotel
                                                     Vittel (Vosges)

My dear Churchill,

If it suits you I will arrive in London on Aug 8th and come to lunch on August 9th—at Chartwell I understand.

I received a rather pressing cable from Gov Smith[1] and will have to sail as soon as possible—I will just have time to finish my cure, see Clemenceau come over to lunch with you and get home. No trip would be complete without seeing you.

I hope all of your family are well and happy.

Sincerely
Baruch

[1] Alfred Emmanuel Smith, 1873–1938. Known as 'Al'. Born in New York City. A Member of the New York Assembly, 1903–15; Democratic Leader of the Assembly, 1911; Speaker, 1913. Governor of New York, 1919–20 and 1923–8. Democratic candidate for the Presidency, 1928. Subsequently Chairman of the Board of the Federal Broadcasting Company, the Meenan Coal Company and the Lawyer's County Trust Fund. A Trustee of Fordham (Catholic) University.

Winston S. Churchill to Sir Richard Hopkins
(*Churchill papers: 18/75*)

22 July 1928

(1) It is inconceivable that this point of view should not have been presented to the President of the Board of Trade. A copy of this letter should be sent to him as early as possible tomorrow morning, and you yourself should be ready to put the argument. I do not myself think that the danger is serious. The Niemeyer attitude of letting everything smash into bankruptcy and unemployment in order that reconstruction can be built up upon the ruins, is neither sound economics nor wise policy. Stated shortly his view, and I presume the orthodox Treasury view, is that no aid whatever should be given to industry which should be left to face its own troubles and stand on its own feet. This comfortable Victorian doctrine may have the consequences of throwing scores of thousands of men out of employment and leading to immense expenditure in other directions. What is airily called 'cutting out dead wood' means transferring vast masses of workmen and their families from productive industry to Poor Law, with the results we see around us. I should think on the whole with 300,000 miners unemployed we have cut out enough dead wood for the moment.

Subject to discussion of the point raised in Sir Richard Hopkins' letter, I approve.

(2) I expect the Committee will approve the extension of Export Credits proposal.

(3) I have sent a separate Minute about forest holdings. I make out that £180,000 in two years to get 250 more miners' families bedded out would mean for those two years at any rate an anticipation of expenditure of £1,440 per family. Really it is not worth doing this for such petty numbers.

(4) It must, I think, be taken as certain that the Cabinet will insist upon the emigration proposals. If there are any Treasury safeguards it is now desired to exert, they must be ready tomorrow morning when the Committee meets.

(5) I take it that the question of super-concentration is settled. It is necessary however that a decision should be come to about harbours, docks and canals. Mr Hurst should advise.

On the question of acceleration the most important point is the danger of the Railway Companies obtaining an increase of rates from the Tribunal in the spring. Mr Hurst should be present to put the point of his paper to the Committee tomorrow when called upon, and it will be for the President to re-assure us. The acceleration should certainly be conditional upon: (a) the Railway Companies passing on to the Steel people the latter's full share;

(b) the Railway Companies and railwaymen carrying through the economy programme on which they are now engaged; and (c) a definite understanding that no part of the relief now given on the super-concentrated traffics will be taken back next year as the result of appeals to the Tribunal. These three conditions will have to be announced at the same time as the acceleration, and the Government will then proceed to negotiate with the parties in the recess.

(6) The Parliamentary procedure should also be explored. I cannot believe that any actual payments will be required from us before the end of November.

I think we should resist the demand to include Agriculture in the anticipation, as there is no unemployment in that industry.

(7) It must be an essential part of the Treasury acceptance of these new heavy charges that all Departments shall undertake: (a) to save money by underspending from the existing estimates through a slowing down of approved services; and (b) to produce further economies for next year.

Note. Since dictating the above I have read the Treasury notes on the emigration scheme which furnish me with the points I requested.

Winston S. Churchill to Lord Birkenhead

(*Churchill papers: 22/69*)

22 July 1928   Treasury Chambers
Private but Official!

My dear Fred,
    You will remember that the question of the Oil Fuel Reserves was specifically referred to yr Ctee, but that we came to no decision upon it, & in the clash of conclusion it played no part. On the other hand all the members of the Ctte, headed by Salisbury, had I think formed the strong opinion that the rate of accumulation of these reserves cd be greatly diminished in future years, having regard to our large existing stock. The Admy on the other hand claim that they are governed by the existing decision of the CID. I suggest that you shd write officially to the PM stating the position, & recommending that the subject shd be referred to an early meeting of the CID, having regard to the recent decision of that body upon the probability of war etc.

Winston S. Churchill to Sidney Herbert[1]

(*Churchill papers: 1/199*)

23 July 1928

My dear Sidney,

I expect to come to visit Philip at Lympne, and am looking forward very much to seeing you then. I do hope you are making progress and will soon be able to take an effective part again. I always remember your letter to me on the day when I became Chancellor.

With all good wishes,
Yours ever
WSC

Sir Archibald Sinclair to Winston S. Churchill

(*Churchill papers: 1/199*)

24 July 1928

My dear Winston,

I called on you this evening pour prendre congé as I leave to-night for Caithness via Aberdeen—but I found you immersed in speech preparation, with Cabinet ministers and officials, rate-reformers and safeguarders, protectionists and free-traders jostling each other in the door-way and your faithful Cerberus shooed me away.

I returned your Washington to Fergusson with many thanks for the loan of a book which is most entertaining even apart from the dissertation on the art of bundling!

Don't forget that Oswald Birley[2] wants to paint you. He is a very nice fellow to deal with and an ardent admirer of yours and the PM's. . . .

---

[1] Sidney Herbert, 1890–1939. Educated at Eton and Balliol College, Oxford. On active service in the Royal Horse Guards, 1915–18 (wounded, despatches). Captain, 1918. Private Secretary to Churchill (then Secretary of State for War), 1919–20. Conservative MP for Scarborough and Whitby, 1922–31; for Westminster, Abbey, 1932–9. Parliamentary Private Secretary to the Prime Minister (Baldwin), 1923–4 and 1924–7. Created Baronet, 1936.

[2] Oswald Hornby Joseph Birley, 1880–1952. Portrait painter. Educated at Harrow, and Trinity College, Cambridge. Studied in Dresden, Florence and Paris. Enlisted as a private, 10th Battalion Royal Fusiliers, September 1914; Captain, Intelligence Corps, France, 1916–18 (Military Cross, 1917). Among his portraits were those of four Viceroys of India—Reading, Irwin, Willingdon and Linlithgow—in Viceroy's House, New Delhi; and a collection of portraits of the Admirals of the War of 1939–45, for the Royal Naval College at Greenwich. Knighted, 1949. His portrait of Churchill is at Chartwell.

Winston S. Churchill to General Lawson[1]

(*Churchill papers: 1/199*)

25 July 1928

My dear Algy,

I am most relieved and delighted to hear that you are so much better. I am afraid you have indeed had a wearisome existence for the last few years, and only your courage and unconquerable spirit will have carried you through. Please let me know when you come through London, as it would give me the greatest pleasure to see you again.

With all good wishes,
Yours ever,

Winston S. Churchill to Sir Henry Page Croft[2]: *not sent*

(*Churchill papers: 2/158*)

25 July 1928

Dear Page Croft,

The Chief Whip tells me of the message which you gave him last night from your meeting, and I have also seen the accounts of it which appear in the newspapers. Perhaps you will allow me to say that I think it would have been better if you had come to me. After all we are all colleagues working together to win the next election, and it is most important that there should be no misunderstanding between us.

One of the causes of misunderstanding is the condensed reports of speeches which now appear in the newspapers. For instance at the Mansion House immediately after discussing the question of the reasons of unemployment I referred to the policy of Safeguarding, saying that we had taken some suc-

[1] Algernon Lawson, 1869–1929. Educated at Harrow. 2nd Lieutenant, Scots Greys, 1892. On active service in South Africa, 1899–1902 (despatches twice), and on the western front (despatches twice, CMG, 1916); commanded the 2nd Dragoon Guards, 1915–18; the 2nd Cavalry Brigade (in France), 1918–19; the Cavalry Brigade in Egypt, 1920–4. On 22 July 1928 he had written to Churchill: 'I need hardly tell you how pleased I am to see your vitality is as forceful as ever. The success of the "Tote" bill pleases me greatly; I have preached its value for 10 years to all and sundry. Good luck to you in all things.' General Lawson died on 1 August 1929.

[2] Henry Page Croft, 1881–1947. Educated at Eton, Shrewsbury and Trinity Hall, Cambridge. Conservative MP for Christchurch, 1910–18; for Bournemouth, 1918–40. Served in the Great War, 1914–16 (despatches); Brigadier-General, 1916. Member of the Speaker's Conference on the Franchise, 1918; Civil List Committee, 1936; Committee of Privileges, 1939. Created Baronet, 1924; Baron, 1940. Parliamentary Under-Secretary of State for War, 1940–5. Privy Councillor, 1945.

cessful measures of safeguarding in the present Parliament and that any alteration of our policy in the future would certainly not be in the direction of narrowing. All reference to this was however omitted from the otherwise fairly full report in THE TIMES. Again speaking on Saturday last at Taunton, after saying that under Free Trade many new industries had come into existence, I went on to say that the condition of our basic industries, which were our great export trades, was deplorable. Many reports altogether omitted this second passage. I may add that in this statement of fact I merely repeated what I had said three weeks ago to the National Union of Conservative Associations' Council, which was reported fully in THE TIMES without provoking any comment from our friends. Mr Hannon[1] was present also at the dinner at the St Stephen's Club three weeks ago when, in the presence of about thirty Members of our Party in the House, I said about safeguarding, 'We are embarked upon the path of successful experiment and we intend to march further along it with confidence,' or words to that effect. No reporters were present on this occasion. But I think Mr Hannon, who loudly cheered this statement, might have mentioned the incident at your meeting. Lastly, there is the statement which I made in the House on the vote of censure last Tuesday. The actual text of this is as follows:—[2]

I need scarcely say that I did not use these words upon my own responsibility. Reading them again side by side with the Prime Minister's election declaration of 1924, I cannot feel that there is any difference in principle or scope between the two statements; nor can I see in what way they conflict with the Resolution which your meeting passed.

[1] Patrick Joseph Henry Hannon, 1874–1963. Educated Royal College of Science and the Royal University of Ireland. Agriculturist. Vice-President, Grand Council of the Tariff Reform League, 1910–14. Member of the General Council of the National Service League, 1911–15. General Secretary of the Navy League, 1911–18. Conservative MP for Birmingham Moseley, 1921–50. President of the Industrial Transport Association, 1927–37; of the Institute of Export, 1939–43. Knighted, 1936. Chairman of the Political Committee of the Carlton Club. Deputy Chairman of the Birmingham Small Arms Group of Companies.

[2] During a debate on the Labour Party's motion of censure on Tuesday, 24 July 1928, Churchill argued that no rigid or doctrinaire commitment either to free trade or to safeguarding would supply the answer to unemployment. Instead, he recommended that experiments should be made in three areas: 'First, there is the application of science and higher organization, not only to coal, but to every form of industrial production. Secondly, there is the removal of the burdens upon industry by the removal of rates, of uneconomic transport charges, and also the reduction in the cost of production. And thirdly, in the fiscal sphere, it seems to me that we ought not to contemplate any fundamental reversal of the fiscal system upon which the whole industrial and economic structure of this country is erected, and with which it is profoundly interwoven. But we are perfectly free, and we ought to be, to study and develop exceptional measures for the special culture of particular trades where advantage can be gained, and where we have shown that advantage can be gained, and we should also carry protective aid, perhaps by temporary measures, in cases where the strain is shown to be the greatest, and where it can also be proved that we can give this aid without bringing greater evil in its train.'

I observe that you have also personally complained in public that I attributed to you a desire to tax *all* imports. I carefully inserted the word 'all' in order to differentiate between the general policy of Protection including food, to which I am opposed, and the Safeguarding policy of which now nearly ten years ago I was one of the original authors. As you had spoken in the Debate shortly before me, I mentioned your name in this connection honestly believing that you were personally in favour of full protection. I am glad to find that I was mistaken in this and that we are not in disagreement on this point. On the other hand I am of course most anxious in our general interest that the next election should not drift into a fight between Protection and Free Trade. Probably a million Free Trade votes were cast in 1924 for Conservative candidates, and it is of the highest importance to the Conservative cause that these should not be given away wholesale. No doubt there is something illogical to the doctrinaire in a man saying, 'I am a Free Trader, but I support Safeguarding.' Yet, believe me, this attitude is sincerely helpful to and was adopted by very large numbers of people whose aid we require.

It is for this reason also that I dwell upon the expression 'no fundamental reversal' of our existing fiscal system, as the Prime Minister did in 1924 upon the words 'no general tariff'. It seems to me vital that some of us at any rate should be able to argue effectively that safeguarding does not imply a violent break with the past or raise an issue which has no relation to the practical steps we intend to take.

The important thing for all of us is to agree, as I have no doubt we can, upon practical steps and to rally to that policy the largest possible measure of support.

This is what I should have said to you if you had visited me or invited me to your meeting, as I think in all the circumstances you might have done.[1]

---

[1] On July 25 Lord Derby wrote to Churchill: 'I was very much disturbed at what you told me today but you may rely entirely on my support for what it is worth in opposing the Amery Page Croft gang. I hate the whole lot of them. They ruined our party once and they will ruin it again if they have their way.' But Derby went on to warn: 'Take care that there is not an attack on Free Trade disguised under a vendetta against you—Temporise, because I feel sure that the power at the back of the intrigue is not very strong & can be scotched unless the flames are fanned' (*Churchill papers: 2/158*). For this reason, perhaps, Churchill decided not to send his letter to Page Croft.

George Lane-Fox to Lord Irwin

(*Irwin papers*)

26 July 1928

We have just had a rather depressing debate on unemployment. Certainly SB made a very unimpressive speech, and Winston who is thoroughly tired and nervy did equally badly, ending up by a rather unnecessary and violent defence of our die-hard safeguarders, who were already indignant at having their proposal for the safeguarding of steel turned down. They are now very angry and a lot is going on. It is the first sign of a real party fissure that I have yet seen and though it may come to nothing it is very apparent now. Personally I agree that to raise a definite protectionist issue now just when the rating scheme is going well would be very bad tactics and I quite approve the Government attitude on the subject.

L. S. Amery: diary

(*Amery papers*)

27 July 1928

[At 7 pm] Lovat came in in despair to say that he had had a telephone message that Winston had turned down his proposals for dealing with harvesters for Canada, substituting conditions which made the thing quite impossible. The only thing was to go and see Winston personally but the Treasury reported that he had left the office and gone to his house to prepare a speech for the following night. So I took Lovat over to No 11 where after some considerable waiting we were taken up to Winston's bedroom where we found him in bed in pink undies, very cross at being collared like this and vowing that he had not sent a message of refusal but had empowered Hopkins and Upcott to settle.

After much telephoning Hopkins was discovered shaving somewhere and dressing for dinner with the Treasury, and Winston, unwilling to give any decision himself, asked us to go down to the Treasury Board Room to deal with them and to come back if we arrived at a deadlock. So we went down and discussed but after a few minutes Winston joined us in a flowered dressing-gown and spent half an hour during which he seemed quite incapable of either accepting our proposals or turning them down flat, which he obviously was afraid of doing in view of the strong feeling in the Cabinet in favour of the great scheme.

Finally he started leaving but spent another five minutes backwards and forwards between the door and the table trying to make up his mind and complaining bitterly of the ill treatment to which he was subjected. Never in years had he known a Chancellor of the Exchequer so ill-used. In the end quite incapable of deciding, he told me I had better do what I pleased and he would then bring his complaint before the Cabinet.

Randolph Churchill to Winston S. Churchill

(*Churchill papers: 1/199*)

30 July 1928   Eton College

. . . I am so glad to see in the Evening Papers that the PM has come down on your side re Free-Trade. This is the second time in ten days that that ass Jix has been reprimanded. I thought your speech admirable.

August 1928

Arthur Michael Samuel to Winston S. Churchill

(Churchill papers: 2/158)

3 August 1928

My dear Churchill,

I shall not go away content to my holiday unless I write you just a little word to say how much I have appreciated your always cordial help & kindly friendship since I was appointed Financial Secretary.

I have enjoyed working with you.

Do compel yourself now to take rest; I hope you will store up health & strength. Your life is not entirely your own private property & if you were to suffer a breakdown from overwork it would be the cause of great grief to yours ever,

Arthur Michael S.

Lord Beaverbrook to William Mackenzie King

(Beaverbrook papers)

4 August 1928

We have had quite a storm here over Protection or Safeguarding this week. After the most obvious contradiction on the public platform between Winston Churchill and Joynson Hicks—Baldwin gets up and produces the usual formula which appeases all and settles nothing.

But the cat is out of the bag. You cannot put it back. The cat will scratch too, as the next General Election will certainly show. The Tory party is fundamentally disunited on Protection and the moment the subject is given any prominence the mischief is done.

Joynson Hicks knows his own strength and the weakness of Churchill. He knows that he is the only possible alternative to or successor to Baldwin. He is one of those curious products you sometimes get in politics—a man who is thought a fool by his colleagues, a fine fellow by the private member—and a romantic hero by the Chairman of the local Conservative Association. In this he rather resembles Lord Derby: but then, Joynson Hicks has a real sense of the House. He appeals there to many hearts if to few heads.

He beat Baldwin on the Prayer Book and probably reflects that he might beat him again on the next issue.

Yet Baldwin always treats him with contempt—and Bonar Law used to do just the same. Baldwin, however, is now in Winston's pocket. When the Safeguarding deputation came to see him the other day the first thing Baldwin did was to deny this. The deputation could not exactly reply 'We do think you are'—but they went away saying 'We do think so—we do.'

Stanley Baldwin to Winston S. Churchill
(*Churchill papers: 1/200*)

5 August 1928

My dear Winston,

I am touched by your remembering my birthday and grateful for your most kind telegram.

I intend going to London on Thursday and shall have all Friday at the office.

Remember my counsel to you and abide by it! Paint, pens, dams and nought else.

Yours ever
SB

Clementine Churchill to Winston S. Churchill
(*Spencer-Churchill papers*)

6 August 1928   Mountstewart
                                                Co Down

My Darling,

2nd Instalment of Irish Tittle Tattle. . . .[1]

. . . Charley & Edie are both amiable but I must say I think they are each in their different way absolutely puerile & futile, & much as I desire (as

[1] Clementine Churchill was staying in Northern Ireland with Lord and Lady Londonderry ('Charlie' and 'Edie'). On August 11 she wrote again: 'You will be relieved to hear that it is not only our humble selves who suffer from the "Servant Problem". At Mount Stewart although there were close on 30 servants in the house and 9 (nine) in the pantry the silver was dirty & it was almost impossible to get a pair of shoes cleaned. . . .' (*Spencer-Churchill papers*).

every Mother should & must!) that her daughter should make a good marriage I must say the prospect of a succession of visits here would fill me with
gloom, not to say consternation.

They are completely wrapped up in themselves & their own importance &
cannot see anything further than the Stewart family & perhaps the Royal
Family.

As you enter the front door you are confronted on the door post with a
large brass label on which is inscribed 'King Edward & Queen Alexandra
stayed at Mount Stewart House on such & such a date'—Opposite the front
door are two trees one planted by King E & the other by Queen Alexandra
and so on & so forth.

Charlie by the way is cross because you (ie your secretary) have not replied
to a letter of his complaining about super tax being charged on some money
which was used by him to diminish un-employment. He says the Treasury
Officials are unjust & extortionate & are loathed not only by him but by
every one up & down the country. He told me he was practically ruined &
really his sorrows almost brought tears to my eyes. I nearly offered to lend
him £100—In a fortnight they leave this place & proceed to a deer forest
which they rent from the Sutherlands. He said he did not know how he
should find the money to pay for it!

The two daughters of the house, Margaret & Helen seem charming girls &
Edie has a Mary too aged 7, but of course not a patch on *our* Mary.[1]

If ever you are made PM, I think you will merit *great* displeasure here if
Charlie is not included in the Cabinet as a Secretary of State *of course*, none of
your Board of Trades or Local Government Boards or Ministry of Healths!

Unless you can put this scrawl under lock & key, perhaps better burn it.

I long for my Pig meanwhile. I am used to him, odious as he sometimes is,
& cannot do with these inbred effete sprigs of the ancien regime!

I hope you are happy & comfy at Chartwell & that your Lake is behaving.

Tender love from your Pussy

(not in her basket).

---

[1] Lord Londonderry had four daughters: Maureen Helen (born, 1900), who had married
Lord Derby's son Oliver Stanley in 1920; Margaret Frances Anne (born, 1910), Helen
Maglona (born, 1911) and Mairi Elizabeth (born. 1921) who married Viscount Bury, eldest
son of the 9th Earl of Albemarle, in 1940.

Winston S. Churchill to Clementine Churchill

(*Spencer-Churchill papers*)

7 August 1928   Chartwell Manor

My darling,

Everything has been progressing here, and the zoo has been full of incidents. The black swans have laid two eggs and are sitting stolidly upon them. The horse and foal and the sow both got second prizes at the Show. There was only one other horse and foal, which makes the event resemble Randolph's boxing feats! Still Arnold brought home £3. Five new cows have arrived. They are as big as elephants, and one immediately had a beautiful white calf. Twelve little pigs have been born, and more are expected. Work has started on the children's house, and I hope to have some results to show you when you come.

The Prof and I motored over to see Randolph in Camp on Sunday, and the General commanding the Division invited us and him to lunch. Alas, when we arrived we were informed with much embarrassment that he was confined to Camp for having gone out with some other boys the night before on to the top of a hill to watch the Tattoo from afar. So we had rather a wild goose chase in every sense of the word. However, we saw Randolph in his camp in a state of considerable indignation against the authorities. I am sure the reason they were down on him was because he, almost alone in his Company, had refused to go to the Tattoo on the Saturday night, it being optional. So I suppose being nettled at thus being disdained, they were on the look out for any slip however slight. He looked very nice in his uniform, and the Prof took a photograph of us both. He arrives home tomorrow with, I expect, only a small amount of military ardour left. He puts himself into opposition with all the prevailing acceptances and heartinesses, and was this time very much disappointed at the result.

I have been working fairly hard, and so has Miss Fisher! The article on Savinkov[1] is finished and has gone off to America, and Chapter 1 of Volume IV is well broken into. Nearly 3,000 words in the last two days! I have to keep this rate up continuously, if we are to finish by October 31; and I do

---

[1] Boris Viktorovitch Savinkov, 1877–1925. Russian nihilist. Exiled to Siberia as a student, for revolutionary activity. Escaped to Switzerland. Returned to Russia, 1905; and took part in the assassination of Archduke Serge. Condemned to death. Escaped to Switzerland for a second time. Political commissar for the Provisional Government, charged with restoring discipline on the eastern front, July 1917. Deputy Minister of War in the Provisional Government, August 1917. An opponent of Bolshevism, he joined General Alexeiev's forces on the Don, November 1917. Accredited Agent in Paris, first of Alexeiev, then of Kolchak and finally of Denikin, 1918–20. Organized an anti-Bolshevik army in Poland, 1920. Returned to the Soviet Union voluntarily, 1924. Tried, condemned to death and given a commuted sentence of ten years in prison, 1924. Died in prison.

not conceal from you that it is a task. But it is not more than I can do. The beginning is the difficult part of a book. Once one's thoughts are flowing in that channel, they gather material as they move. Certainly nothing will suit me better than to be quiet here and have hardly any visitors. I am entirely with you in this.

Ranisford tells me he decides to go. You were pretty stiff with him—I gather. But he seems a taciturn and impenetrable sort of man: & it is no use his staying as a favour. Tender love my dearest.

Your own
W

[sketch of pig]

Lord Reading to Lord Irwin

(*Irwin papers*)

8 August 1928

. . . Political interest has in the main centred around the Winston and Joynson-Hicks speeches and the Prime Minister's skilful steering between Scylla and Charybdis but it is obvious we have not yet heard the last of it. With a General Election looming within the next twelve months the position will probably be forced. However, I expect you will hear more of this from your own political associates.

Winston S. Churchill to Arthur Michael Samuel

(*Churchill papers: 2/158*)

8 August 1928

My dear Samuel,

I am very grateful to you for your most kind letter, and also for the loyal and effective help you have given me during this Session. I am sure taking a leading part in carrying a Budget is a valuable Parliamentary experience; and in this case you had the special responsibility of the Currency Note Bill. I think you have every reason to be satisfied with your performances.

I shall take your advice about a holiday, and I hope you will conform to the principles you preach.

Once more thanking you, believe me
Yours sincerely,
Winston S. Churchill

Clementine Churchill to Winston S. Churchill

(Spencer-Churchill papers)

10 August 1928   Vaynol[1]

My Darling Winston,

I was glad on my arrival here to find your chronicle of Chartwell events—Moppett had meanwhile very kindly written to me twice to keep me 'Au courant'. But it is always nice to get a chit from GHQ.

I enclose a charming letter from Countess Potocka[2] again indefatigably inviting me to Poland and this time (having seen her at Consuelo's in the Spring) including Diana—I fear from what you tell me in your letter of the rate at which you will have to write to complete your Book by October the 31st that it will not be feasible to accept this invitation. Otherwise I think it would have been an agreeable adventure & an opportunity of having a little holiday abroad together. I suppose the Book must be finished by October the 31st? It seems a fearful rush in my case & for so serious and important a task I should have thought a little more space, time & thought were required. However you will tell me what you think when we return. Meanwhile Ivor Wimborne seemed to think you were perhaps going abroad with him for a week on September the 3rd. But he did not seem to be banking on it; especially as a week ago we thought in view of Austen & illness you & AJB were to take the PM's place. Now I see (but not official) in the local rag that the Lord Chancellor is to do it.[3]

[1] Vaynol Park, on the Menai Straits, between Bangor and Caernarvon, the home of Lady Juliet Duff. Born in 1881, the only child of the 4th Earl of Lonsdale, in 1903 she married Sir Robert Duff, who was killed in action in October 1914. In 1919 she married her second husband, Major Keith Trevor, MC, from whom she obtained a divorce in 1926. She died in 1965. In 1935 her son, Sir Michael Duff, married Millicent Joan, daughter of Churchill's cousin, the 3rd Baron Tweedmouth, but the marriage was annulled two years later. His sister's husband, John Tennant. DSO, MC, of the RAFVR, was killed on active service in August 1941.

[2] Wife of Count Joseph Potocki, a member of the Polish Embassy in London from 1929 to 1932; on 7 January 1933 he wrote to Churchill: 'We met last this (1932) spring at lunch at Lady Londonderry's and I often recall your words and your interest concerning my country' (*Churchill papers: 8/335*).

[3] The 'rumour' was correct: in Baldwin's absence at Aix-les-Bains, Viscount Hailsham took charge of all Government business.

Winston S. Churchill to Clementine Churchill

(*Spencer-Churchill papers*)

10 August 1928   Chartwell Manor

My darling Clemmie,

All your delightful letters have reached me. I hope you will have found mine awaiting you at Vaynol.

Everything is very peaceful here. Randolph duly returned and his reports are not bad. He and the Prof play golf and tennis. I have persuaded the Prof to stay on until Monday. He is a great companion both for me and for Randolph.

Baruch lunched yesterday and sent you ceremonious messages. I gave him my slogan for the Democratic Party. 'Al for all, and all for Al.' He was so much struck with it that as he proceeded (very confidential) he told me that the Democratic Party believed that there was in existence a letter by Hoover,[1] when in business in Burma many years ago, offering to take up British citizenship if he could get a certain important contract. This letter if produced at the right moment would of course be fatal to Hoover. Baruch seemed to want me to ferret this out for him, but I became unconscionably vague. These American Presidential Elections are extraordinary games in which with the greatest zest and party bitterness the whole nation takes part, although there is no real difference between the parties except that of 'ins and outs'.

Victor Cazalet dined, bringing with him two young men. He dines again tonight and I play bezique with him.

Hawkey arrived with his Mr Spencer to lunch; otherwise we have had no visitors and needless to say I do not stir off the premises.

Mr Spencer sent down one of his best engineers to go into the whole question of our electric light. I make out it costs about £250 a year and we are in the near future sure to be confronted with the need of purchasing a new battery, costing about £400, with a life of only 10 years. Mr Spencer's engineer went and saw the Westerham Electric Light Company. They would supply us it appears with all that we now consume for only about £80 a year, and we could have power in addition if we required it. We could sell our existing engine and the battery probably for a third of what we paid for them. New space would be available for other purposes in the engine room; half Arnold's time would be liberated; no expense would be incurred when

---

[1] Herbert Clark Hoover, 1874–1964. Born in Iowa. Graduated from Stanford University, 1895. A mining engineer. Head of the Relief Commission for Belgium, and United States Food Commissioner during the First World War. Secretary of Commerce, 1921. 31st President of the United States, 1929–33. An ardent supporter of private enterprise.

the light was not being used; strict meter control could be enforced on cottages and servants; the cost of all electric supply is bound to diminish steadily in the future.

Altogether I think the case for having Company's light as well as Company's water is a very strong one. However the question is on what terms will the Company bring the cable to us. The Company's engineer says that his Board are being taken over by a larger organization—the Kent Electric Supply—and he hopes that a more progressive policy will be shortly instituted. At present they are a mile and a half away, and if they would not pay for the cable it would cost about £1,200. On the other hand their existing programme of extension for next year, apart from new progressive tendencies if any, carries them within half a mile, and even if they insisted upon our paying the whole of this cost ie about £400, it would be no more than we shall now have to pay in the near future for the new battery. In these circumstances Mr Spencer's engineer advises no expense on the existing plant except to keep it running and to aim at a turn over to the Company. I am sure there would be a big saving not only in money but also in worry. We might even only have the Arnold family if we wished to curtail the staff.

I thought you would be interested in all this as it fits in very much with your usual ideas.

I have got eight men clearing the site of the new cottage. The work is proceeding very rapidly and we are to start laying it out on Monday. You will be surprised to see what a fine broad plateau we have made. The oak tree comes down this afternoon. (Since down—a wallop! We are going out to burn it & chop it up.)

Mary's house is growing and I hope to have a treat for you when you come. The new bricklayer impresses me; he works with great rapidity assisted by two sons, and considers himself competent to do everything apart from carpenter's work. Mary has taken the greatest interest in the work and laid the foundation stone with great ceremony. She was presented with a bouquet by the Prof and then manifested a great desire to make a speech. We all had to stand for five minutes while she remained deep in thought, her lips frequently moving over the sentences. In the end she said she regarded it as a great honour to have been called upon to lay this foundation stone and that she hopes she would spend many happy hours in the house when it was finished. (Loud cheers.)

All the live stock continue to thrive and multiply. The old man 'Snowey' works steadily tidying up your orchard.

The days slip by with a fearful rapidity. By the time I have dealt with my pouch, done my exercises, eaten my breakfast, read the newspapers and made my toilet it is 10 o'clock. Lunch comes before one notices and the afternoons flash away. I have averaged about 1,200 words a day on the book as well as finishing the Savinkov article. So you see I have not been idle in providing the sinews of war. I shall have to keep this rate up, as I told you in my last, if we are to publish this year.

Ray Long is coming over here and wants to arrange a meeting between me and Hearst.[1] This is important, as my idea is if we go out of office to take on the kind of Lloyd George Fortnightly Letter to the American Press which he has now abandoned owing to other financial windfalls.

You will see by the papers that the PM did not think it expedient to do what I am sure he wished to do—to leave me in charge, so Hogg has been made to give up his Canadian tour. All this reveals how serious is the handicap I have had to carry in the party by warning them off the protectionist question. I do not at all regret the steps I took which are only for their good; but of course all the powerful interests who would make money out of Protection keep up a steady pressure and half the Tory party are religiously convinced about tariff. I am glad the Election is coming in nine months time. The situation will then be very interesting; but it is quite impossible beforehand to see how it will develop. Such is life!

Tender love my dearest one from yr loving
W

[sketch of pig]

Really I feel vy independent of them all.

Stanley Baldwin to Winston S. Churchill

(*Churchill papers: 1/200*)

11 August 1928   10 Downing Street

My dear Winston,

The car is at the door pawing the ground and I am just leaving. My last words are to you.

Do remember what I said about resting from current problems. Paint, write, play with your dams.

---

[1] William Randolph Hearst, 1863–1951. Born in San Francisco, the son of a US Senator. Editor and Proprietor of the *New York American*, the *New York Evening Journal*, the *Boston American*, the *Boston Advertiser*, the *Chicago Herald and Examiner*, the *Chicago American*, the *San Francisco Examiner* and the *Los Angeles Examiner*. In 1903 he married Millicent Willson: they had five sons. Unsuccessful candidate for Mayor, New York, 1905. Congressman. Resident at his self-designed castle, the Hearst Ranch, San Simeon, a treasure house of medieval and renaissance European art and furniture.

But a big year will soon begin and much depends on our keeping fit. You will have a great deal to do as Chancellor and you need to be at your best, and our combined judgement will have many a test.

I am sure if we keep together and go forward boldly into the New Year we can win a great victory.

Yours ever
SB

Neville Chamberlain to Lord Irwin
(Irwin papers)

12 August 1928

SB did not consider the fortunes of the party to be so dependent on DH as I did and do. I think he has all the qualities of a great leader and with him available there would have been no question of a possibility which he and I both consider very dangerous, viz the acceptance of Winston as leader.

However there it is. Douglas is now out of the running definitely and the future is in the lap of the Gods. Assuming that we come back next year with a diminished majority and stay in the full term, most of us will be a good deal older and a good deal the worse for wear. Probably we should then have several years of Opposition and that would give Winston his chance of establishing himself in the party's favour. In opposition his want of judgement and his furious advocacy of half-baked ideas would not matter, while his wonderful debating and oratorical gifts would have free play. Still, it is of little use to speculate yet. You will be here then, younger men will have come on, I may be dead, LG may be a force again, though I don't believe it.

I must tell you something about the rating proposals which have occupied most of my time for the last six months and are likely to do so from now until the election. Their history has been rather a chequered one. In their original form they emanated from a rather clever but somewhat inexperienced Treasury official named Hurst. Hurst at a very early moment got Winston's ear, so much so that the older Treasury men like Barstow were treated with marked discourtesy and eventually resigned. I did not myself form a very high opinion of the top men while I was at the Treasury and I think it a good thing they have gone, though I am sorry about the way it happened.

To go back to the proposals, in their original form they involved the complete freedom from rates of all industrial concerns (this vague description was never defined), and the imposition instead of a National Rate of 5 per cent in the £. The advantage of this plan from an argumentative point of view was obvious. Rating of industry was vicious, it was to be abolished.

Rates now governed decisions as to whether industry should go to this site or that; in future it would make no difference. Indeed, industry would actually drift to the necessitous areas of Durham, South Wales, West Ham and Poplar, where labour was abundant and where the high rates would in future be paid by other people.

When these proposals came to me I declared my approval of the principle that industry should be relieved of a part of its rates, but I strongly objected on Local Government grounds to any plan which completely severed all connection between industry and industrial interests and local Government. It appeared to me most dangerous if a large part of the community were given to understand that they were unaffected by any inefficiency, extravagance or corruption in Local Government. Moreover seeing that industry required and is provided with certain costly local services, I thought it inequitable that they should pay nothing for them.

Over this point we had numerous battles. I accused Winston of reckless advocacy of schemes the effects of which he himself did not understand. He accused me of pedantry and of personal jealousy of himself. At times feelings became rather acute. But I had one advantage over Winston of which he was painfully conscious. He could not do without me. Therefore in the end I was the sole judge of how far to go because whenever I put my foot down he was helpless. As a matter of fact I only put it down once and he gave way directly. But it was a very harassing time for me and to tell you the truth, Edward, Winston is a very interesting but a d——d uncomfortable bed fellow. You never get a moment's rest and you never know at what point he'll break out.

In spite of all that can be said for it I am doubtful if our Rating-Relief-*cum*-Local-Government-Reform plan is a real election winner. I don't believe it is calculated to rouse enthusiasm. It is too difficult to understand, too remote and uncertain in its effects, too disturbing in its immediate changes to afford election slogans or inspire the man in the street with the feeling that here is really something worth working for. On the other hand, its value must not be under-rated even for election purposes. It provides an answer to the criticism so often brought against an ageing Government, that it has exhausted its vitality and its ideas and no longer has a policy. Neither of the other parties has any new ideas for dealing with unemployment. Here is a plan which we can advocate as meeting one of the most generally admitted industrial grievances.

One doesn't often come across a real man of genius or, perhaps, appreciate him when one does. Winston is such a man and he has *les défauts de ses qualités*. To listen to him on the platform or in the House is sheer delight. The art of the arrangement, the unexpected turn, the mastery of sparkling humour, and the torrent of picturesque adjectives combine to put his speeches in a class by themselves. Then as you know there is no subject on which he is not prepared to propound some novel theory and to sustain and illustrate his theory with cogent and convincing arguments. So quickly does his mind work in building up a case that it frequently carries him off his own feet.

I have often watched him in Cabinet begin with a casual comment on what has been said, then as an image or simile comes into his mind proceed with great animation, when presently you see his whole face suffused with pink, his speech becomes more and more rapid and impetuous till in a few minutes he will not hear of the possibility of opposition to an idea which only occurred to him a few minutes ago.

In the consideration of affairs his decisions are never founded on exact knowledge, nor on careful or prolonged consideration of the pros and cons. He seeks instinctively for the large and preferably the novel idea such as is capable of representation by the broadest brush. Whether the idea is practicable or impracticable, good or bad, provided he can see himself recommending it plausibly and successfully to an enthusiastic audience, it commends itself to him. There is too deep a difference between our natures for me to feel at home with him or to regard him with affection. He is a brilliant wayward child who compels admiration but who wears out his guardians with the constant strain he puts upon them.

Ever yours,
Neville

Winston S. Churchill to Lord Cushendun

(*Churchill papers: 2/158*)

14 August 1928

My dear Ronald,

I must send you a line of sincere congratulation on being called upon to act in this very great post.[1] It gives me lively pleasure to see you reaching, though it is so long overdue, a position of prime responsibility. I am so glad to think that your move to the Exchequer was no injury, indeed it often happens that a rolling stone rolls where it ought.

Yours vy sincerely,
Winston S. Churchill

[1] As a result of Sir Austen Chamberlain's illness, Lord Cushendun (formerly Ronald McNeill) had just been appointed Acting Secretary of State for Foreign Affairs: a post he held for four months.

Lord Cushendun to Winston S. Churchill

(*Churchill papers: 2/158*)

16 August 1928

My dear Winston,

I have received a good many letters, but I can quite truthfully say that none has given me so much pleasure as yours. It was really nice of you to write so kindly, & I can assure you I value *most highly* your words of congratulation.

Yours very sincerely
Cushendun

September 1928

Winston S. Churchill to George Bernard Shaw[1]

(Churchill papers: 2/159)

2 September 1928   Chartwell Manor
Private

My dear Bernard Shaw,

   I was delighted to receive your book and greatly complimented by your
kindness in sending me a signed copy. I have delayed thanking you only
because I wished to read it first; and business pressed out leisure. I admire the
simple-brutal style and treatment. I am sure it will do nothing but good to
the thoughtless complacent propertied person. I am buying a copy for my
son who, though not possessing any of the above qualities, is far too ready to
take the existing system and situation as axiomatic.

   I think I am in agreement with you in condemning not only Capitalism
and Socialism, but every other conceivable intermediate variant—so long as
men—and intelligent women—remain what they have so long been. Everything they try will fail—owing to their deplorable characteristics and their
liking for these very characteristics. The only world fit for them is a Hugger-
Mugger world. Ants or Bees would be worthy of better things—tho' even
they have some bad habits. The real fault lies with the Creator; and there
is no apparent way of bringing it home to him. 'He just keeps rolling
along.'

   About this equalization of income—I was much relieved to find that there
were not going to be any immediate changes. I am writing a book—of enormous value (indirect) to mankind and of very considerable value (direct) to
me; and I should certainly not persist in this labour if I thought the tax collector was going to take the whole instead of 2/5ths of its yield.

   Let me once again tell you how very much honoured I am to have received

---

[1] George Bernard Shaw, 1856–1950. Novelist and playwright. Awarded the Nobel Prize
for Literature in 1925. He had just published *The Intelligent Woman's Guide to Socialism and
Capitalism.*

this great courtesy at your hands, and how highly I shall prize its embodiment, and with all good wishes to you and your wife, believe me.

Yours very sincerely,
Winston S. Churchill

PS. My wife is now about to take the treatment (as an intelligent woman) and begs to be remembered to you.

Winston S. Churchill to Stanley Baldwin

(*Baldwin papers*)

2 September 1928   Chartwell Manor
Most Private

My dear PM

Your vy kind letter is greatly valued by me. You may count upon any help I can give in the tussle that is before us. We cannot I think do better than fight it through on the lines of yr letter to Bobbie.[1] I cannot feel that there is any decisive drift agst us. But Labour will have a heavy class vote; & the Liberals will queer the pitch—(What else *can* they do?) The new Parlt will certainly be vy different from this.

But what about the team? Austen I fear very serious—a stroke! AJB: S: Steel M: Willie B: PC-L: (so he says) all riding at single anchor.[2] FE still resolved to go I understand. On the other side Cushendun a real find—but 66. There are others who will stay—but will they help?

You made some fine references to the wealth of young talent wh the Party had produced. But vy little has been done for them. They have just drummed their heels; & some of them if not preserved by office—will not reappear after the fray.

I am for 'The old cause & the new lot.' I am sure it wd be wise to refresh

---

[1] Baldwin's letter of 3 August 1928, to the Chief Conservative Whip, Commander Robert Eyres-Monsell, in which Baldwin stated that there would be no general reintroduction of Protection. On August 8 Clementine Churchill had written to her husband (from Northern Ireland, where she was staying): 'What an excellent letter of the Prime Minister's to Commander Eyres-Monsell. I should think that ought to reestablish the situation? and make things almost as before?' (*Spencer-Churchill papers*).

[2] Lord Balfour (Lord President of the Council), Lord Salisbury (Lord Privy Seal), Sir Arthur Steel-Maitland (Minister of Labour), William Bridgeman (First Lord of the Admiralty) and Sir Philip Cunliffe-Lister (President of the Board of Trade).

the team *before* the match, & not too long before. Painful, worrying but safer. And you must provide for the future of the party. Without a stream of new talent we cannot hold our ascendency. We don't want to be left alone with Jix & Amery!

There is not much in the second line. Walter Elliot is by far the best. It is in the rank & file that the needful new figures can be found. You know them better than I do: but I cd suggest a few names if the occasion arose. Anyhow meet change with forestalling change.

I have had a delightful month—building a cottage & dictating a book: 200 bricks & 2,000 words per day. Hogg came over for a night & I have just returned from him. He is modestly but deeply gratified by yr selection. I am sure you were right in this. We have had lovely weather. Nothing beats England at her best. It is horrible the days slip by so quickly.

Wd you mind telegraphing to me which day the Cabinet is to be. I am due at Balmoral on the 24th & if we are to meet then or on the 25th I shall have to write a dutiful letter in good time. 24th wd suit me best but please let me know.

Your sincere friend
Winston S.C.

PS. The Budget looks like working out fairly well to date.

Winston S. Churchill to Lord Beaverbrook

(Beaverbrook papers)

3 September 1928
Private

My dear Max,

I return you your proofs with a few scribbled comments upon them.

Of course it is all very kind and complimentary but I still feel a repugnance to the Dinner episode being recounted.[1] However, I know what one feels about a thing when it is written and how hard it is to cut off even a little

---

[1] In his book *Politicians and the War*, Lord Beaverbrook described how, at the height of the political crisis which led to Lloyd George's premiership, he had dined with Churchill and Birkenhead, and had given them the (correct) supposition that Churchill was to be excluded from the new Government. His account continued: 'Something in the very restraint of my language carried conviction to Churchill's mind. He suddenly felt he had been duped by his invitation to the dinner, and he blazed into righteous anger. I have never known him address his great friend Birkenhead in any other way except as "Fred" or "FE". On this occasion he said suddenly: "Smith, this man knows that I am not to be included in the new Government." With that Churchill walked out into the street. . . .'

finger (Kruger cut off his thumb[1]) so if you are still anxious to publish I leave myself in your hands.

What divine weather! I am just setting off on my pilgrimage with much reluctance, but I expect I shall enjoy it very much when it starts. The continuity of life has an independent value.

It costs me about £m 1 a year to keep the same troops at home as we are now keeping on the Rhine; so I am not very keen upon an early scuttle.

Yours ever,

Winston S. Churchill: draft letter[2]

(*Churchill papers: 18/75*)

7 September 1928

Dear Sir,

Mr Churchill desires me to say that he does not feel at all convinced that it is the duty of English people at the present time to send money into Russia for the purpose of relieving distress. He does not know what guarantees there could be that the money will not be used merely to bolster up the existing tyrannical régime, and thus prolong the very miseries it would be hoped to cure.

Moreover Mr Churchill considers that the first and abiding call upon any money English people may be able to find should be for our own war sufferers, ex-service men, and particularly Lord Haig's Fund which goes to the root of the matter. There must be many British Jews who fought bravely in the war and are at the present time in distress, and they have, it would seem, a prior claim upon us than the Jews of Russia, who have not been without influence in bringing about the present lamentable condition of the country. Mr Churchill is not aware that anything in the nature of famine prevails in Eastern Europe outside the confines of the Soviet Union.

---

[1] In 1845 Johannes Paul Kruger, later President of the South African Republic, suffered a wound to his hand when his rifle exploded while he was firing at a charging rhinoceros. Kruger was forced to leap on his horse and flee, leaving behind his exploded rifle and his left thumb. He treated the wound for the next six months with turpentine and sugar, and, whenever it became gangrenous, by thrusting his hand into the stomach of a freshly slaughtered goat. Kruger was twenty years old at the time (Kruger, *The Memoirs of Paul Kruger*, 1902).

[2] In reply to a request from British Jews to support an appeal for British funds to relieve famine distress in Soviet Russia. Churchill, who dictated this letter, noted on it: 'To be signed by Mr Fergusson.'

Winston S. Churchill to Donald Fergusson

(*Churchill papers: 18/75*)

9 September 1928

You should call on the Foreign Office, and also on Sir Maurice Hankey, and say that I have not made any comments to the Cabinet on the Anglo-French Naval Agreement. I presume that there is no truth in the suggestion that it will be abandoned in deference to the pressure from America or from British newspapers. If there is any question of this I must ask that the matter should be discussed first in Cabinet. The Cabinet decided on the policy and they are fully entitled to be consulted if any change is contemplated.

We always seem to be getting into trouble over these stupid disarmament manoeuvres and personally I deprecate all these premature attempts to force agreements on disarmament; but having taken up our position before the world it would be a most grave matter to withdraw from it, and the Cabinet alone could take the responsibility for that. I gather however from the latest reports in the newspapers there is to be no change. Pray see that I am kept informed.

Winston S. Churchill to Sir Horace Wilson

(*Churchill papers: 1/201*)

11 September 1928

My dear Wilson,

Please see the enclosed correspondence which has resulted from the publicity of my building operations.[1]

I should be very glad if you will advise me whether the letter I now propose to send marked 'B' (not yet sent) is advisable on the whole. I thought it was nice of them to wish me to belong to their Union, but should I be letting myself in for wrangles; for instance what about the political levy which I certainly could not conscientiously pay? None of my men are trade unionists and about here they rather mock at Trade Unions. Personally, as you know, I am always strongly in favour of organizing workmen for trade purposes.

[1] Following Press publicity about his brick-building activities at Chartwell during the summer, Churchill had been invited, on 4 September 1928, to join the Amalgamated Union of Building Trade Workers.

Who is the Mayor of Battersea?[1] Is he a respectable person, and does he speak with any authority as Secretary of the Building Trade?

Please let me have your personal opinion on this, which is all quite trivial. I am much inclined to join.

Yours,
Winston S. Churchill

Sir Horace Wilson to Winston S. Churchill
(*Churchill papers: 1/201*)

14 September 1928

My dear Chancellor of the Exchequer,

Your letter about the Bricklayers Union has been sent on to me here. It would be pleasing to know that you had joined. The trade is well paid and you would always earn a living at it. You could decline to 'contract-in' for the Political Levy. What you should do if your Board nominated you for the TUC can perhaps be left over till the time comes!

As to your draft B, would it not be better simply to deal with the invitation to yourself (and accept it) without raising the question of any men whom you may employ? If that is raised later, the line you suggest in 'B' is the right one to take.

I do not know Lane personally but I am told he is quite a straight forward person. He is within his rights as a District Secy in organising the local craftsmen. I shall look with interest to see how Hicks,[2] the General Secretary, views the latest recruit.

Yours very truly,
H. J. Wilson

[1] James F. Lane, Divisional Secretary and Organiser of the Amalgamated Union of Building Trade Workers, and in 1928 Mayor of Battersea.

[2] Ernest George Hicks, 1879–1954. Began work as a general builder at the age of 11; later became a bricklayer. National Organizer for the Bricklayer's Society, 1912. President of the National Federation of Building Trade Operatives, 1919 (and 1936–7); first General Secretary of the Amalgamated Union of Building Trade Workers, 1921–41. President of the Trades Union Congress, 1926–7. Labour MP for East Woolwich, 1931–50. Member of the Central Housing Advisory Committee (which led to the Housing Act, 1935), and the Holidays with Pay Committee. Member of the Anglo-Russian Parliamentary Committee, and of the Empire Parliamentary Association. Parliamentary Secretary, Ministry of Works, throughout Churchill's war-time premiership, 1940–5. CBE, 1946.

Winston S. Churchill to Sir Warren Fisher and others concerned
(*Churchill papers: 18/75*)

14 September 1928

As stated on other papers I am opposed to this question being raised until the American elections are over. We shall then know what the Government of the United States will be, and they will be in any case a Government freed for the moment from the electioneering atmosphere.

I agree, of course, that it would be well to abridge the last few years of the occupation of Germany if the Germans are prepared to make improved arrangements about the payment of reparations. There is, however, obviously no hurry for a few months or possibly for a year. It is a good thing to have the Germans asking for something which we can give and are going to give. The moment this is granted they will ask for something else which it may not be so easy to give, as, for instance, the return of their colonies, or some alternative in the Danzig corridor. I am sure it would be wise to hold out favourable expectations but to make it clear that considerable time will be required.

It must be remembered that the return of the British troops from Germany, unaccompanied by disbandment, imposes a charge of nearly £m1 a year additional on British Army estimates. We should at any rate have to make sure that we get this back through the medium of improved reparations, apart from any general improvement in reparations.

Another matter which should be cleared up in one respect is the question of Disarmament. We are frequently told that Germany would disarm on the understanding that other nations would disarm too, and that further France in particular is bound morally to disarm. However I do not admit that any moral obligation exists. The Germans were prostrate and yielded themselves virtually at discretion. Any undertakings about Allied disarmament were not a matter of bargaining but a voluntary declaration on the part of the Allies. Since then important changes have taken place in the position of France. She gave up the Rhine frontier in return for a promise by the United States together with Great Britain to come to her aid in the event of German aggression. This American promise has been withdrawn and France has not now the security on which she was induced to abandon the Rhine. The only securities for the defence of France are the French Army and the Locarno Treaties. But the Locarno Treaties depend for their efficiency upon the French army. As long as that army is strong enough to overpower a German invasion no German invasion will be attempted.

On the other hand, the British undertaking to protect Germany from the misuse of the French Army affords Germany full security, and it is unthinkable that France would attack Germany in defiance of England and Germany together. Thus the strength of the French Army protects us against the most probable danger of our being forced to intervene in Europe, and it is not in our interest at all to press for the whittling down of this force below the point of security. Moreover France will never consent to such a whittling down and all expectations that she will are futile. No doubt the expense and burden of maintaining so large an army will gradually lead to its diminution if a sense of security grows, and this is the best thing that could happen.

It seems to me that if the Germans wish for an earlier evacuation of the Rhineland they should waive finally or for a number of years any paper claim they may have for the reduction of the French Army in consequence of their having been forcibly disarmed under the Versailles Treaty. Any reduction should be a matter of fresh agreement and not of past obligations.

There is the question of reparations. I have on other papers expressed my views on this. But I repeat it is not for us to formulate any new plan. We have suffered unequalled ill-usage having been committed to paying the American debt irrespective of reparations, having had to scale down to a fourth or a fifth of their values the debts due to us from France and Italy, and being now confronted with the repudiation by the French of the foundation of this scaling down, namely that the reduced payments would be made 'on the sole credit of France'. Further, Mr Parker Gilbert[1] is anxious to make a success of his work, and generally to show American generosity at British expense and would naturally like to have the whole question of the Dawes annuities put on a more favourable basis to Germany. In this matter, however, the initiative must come from the United States; they are the sole cause of the pressure upon England and France which England and France pass on to Germany. Our position should therefore be that the initiative in such a matter must come from them. When any scheme is put forward we should meet it by pointing out our position under the Balfour Note and the injustices we have already suffered, and we should ask what remedies will be applied to these under the scheme.

There can be no question whatever of our giving up any claims against Germany or France, or accepting the French repudiation of 'sole liability', except as part of an arrangement to which the United States is a party, whereby undoubtedly our burdens are diminished. We should not be frightened by statements that we may not continue to get what we at present enjoy. I have been told every year that the Germans and the French would be unable to pay the sums agreed; in fact, however, the wealth of these

[1] S. Parker Gilbert, 1892–1938. A New York banker. Counsel to the US Treasury in War Loan matters, 1918–20. Assistant Secretary of the Treasury, in charge of fiscal affairs, 1920–1; Under-Secretary, 1921–3. United States Agent-General for Reparation Payments, Berlin, 1924–30. A partner in the firm of J. P. Morgan & Co from 1931 until his death.

countries is rapidly increasing and the importance to them of maintaining their credit grows with every improvement in their finances.

The attitude which I enjoin upon the Treasury is:—

1. Complaint at the existing situation.
2. No initiative in proposing schemes of mitigation.
3. Critical attitude in regard to all such schemes as are proposed.
4. Rigorous adherence as the last line of defence to the Balfour Note principles.
5. Placing the onus of the situation where it truly lies—upon the United States—for European difficulties.

The Treasury attitude will therefore be one of extreme reserve and vigilant criticism of all proposals made. It is only by such an attitude that we shall obtain the slightest consideration. If it is even thought that we are open-minded and favourable to a review of the position everyone will be benefited as usual at our expense. The French would be quite ready to take full advantage of us.

A paper should now be prepared on this financial side on the lines which I have prescribed for communication to the Foreign Office.

We have given everything, and submitted to everything, and paid everything, and we cannot make any new sacrifice. If we adopt this attitude undoubtedly in the course of the next year we shall be more and more pressed and offered continually improving inducements.

This minute is to be a guide of Treasury policy.

Treasury representatives are not to express opinions inconsistent with it except on purely office files.

Let Germany continue to press for a rapid evacuation. Let France continue to insist upon improved reparation. Let England recite her financial grievances and reiterate the Balfour Note and the Caillaux Agreement, and let us all await the issue of the American elections.

Pinsent[1] had no right to state that I did not regard evacuation and reparation as linked together. I am not aware that I have ever expressed any opinion for or against that idea. It is possible that evacuation may be the means of forcing a reconsideration of reparation.

---

[1] Gerald Hume Saverie Pinsent, 1888–1976. Educated at King's School, Canterbury, and Trinity College, Cambridge. Entered the Treasury, 1911; Principal, 1928; Assistant Secretary, 1931. Financial Adviser, British Embassy, Berlin, 1932–9; Washington, 1939–41. British Food Mission, Ottawa, 1942–3. Principal Assistant Secretary, Board of Trade, 1943; Treasury, 1944. Comptroller-General, National Debt Office, 1946–51.

James Scrymgeour-Wedderburn:[1] *diary*

(*Dundee papers*)

21 September 1928   Chartwell Manor
Friday

I came yesterday to Westerham to stay with Winston till Monday. I have never met him before except at an Oxford Canning Club dinner the year before last, a year after I had gone down. I was delighted to meet Lindemann who came by the same train, as I haven't seen him for a year. The only other guest at Chartwell is O'Malley,[2] whom Austen Chamberlain has temporarily suspended from the Foreign Office because he was involved in some speculation in French currency. He returns to the FO next year but loses four years' seniority. I find him remarkably charming, with a very brilliant mind, and I am sorry for his misfortune, which I think must have been caused by some trifling piece of carelessness. He keeps on making bitter remarks about Austen to Winston and Mrs Churchill, who both try good-humouredly to calm him down.

Winston is building with his own hands a house for his butler, and also a new garden wall. He works at bricklaying four hours a day, and lays 90 bricks an hour, which is a very high output. He also spends a considerable time on a history of post-war Europe which he is writing. His ministerial work comes down from the Treasury every day, and he has to give some more hours to that. It is a marvel how much time he gives to his guests, talking sometimes for an hour after lunch and much longer after dinner. He is an exceedingly kind and generous host, providing unlimited champagne, cigars and brandy. Even poor old Prof who is really a teetotaller, is compelled to drink ten cubic centimetres of brandy at a time, because he was once rash enough to tell Winston that the average human being could

---

[1] Henry James Scrymgeour-Wedderburn, 1902–   . Educated at Winchester and Balliol College, Oxford. President of the Oxford Union, 1924. Succeeded his father as 11th Earl of Dundee, 1924 (claim only admitted by the Committee of Privileges of the House of Lords in 1953). Conservative MP for Renfrew, 1931–45. Parliamentary Under-Secretary of State for Scotland, 1936–9. On active service with the 7th Black Watch, 1939–41. Additional Parliamentary Under-Secretary of State, Scottish Office, 1941–2. Minister without Portfolio, 1958–61. Privy Councillor. Minister of State for Foreign Affairs, 1961–4. Deputy Conservative Leader in the House of Lords, 1962–4.

[2] Owen St Clair O'Malley, 1887–1974. Educated at Radley and Magdalen College, Oxford. Entered the Foreign Office, 1911. Counsellor in Peking, 1925. Suspended from duties on account of a currency speculation, 1926. Worked as Churchill's research assistant, 1926–7. Reinstated in the Foreign Office, with the rank of Counsellor, 1927. Minister to Mexico, 1937–8. In charge of the British Embassy to Spain (at St Jean de Luz, France), 1938–9. Minister to Hungary, 1939–41; to Poland, 1942–5. Knighted, 1943. Ambassador to Portugal, 1945–7. He published his memoirs, *The Phantom Caravan*, in 1954. Married to the novelist Ann Bridge.

imbibe ten cc of brandy without causing any detectable change in his metabolism.

Mrs Churchill, who is a third cousin of my father through the Ogilvies, is a very charming lady. Winston is devoted to her and I think he leans on her a great deal, in all matters.

Diana very kindly took me out riding this morning. I didn't know there would be any riding, and had nothing to ride in except an old pair of very thin flannel trousers, but I enjoyed it.

Winston got a pair of black Australian swans this summer for his lake. They are magnificent birds. In August they proceeded to nest, and three days ago they hatched out eight cygnets, which of course is the wrong time of year in this hemisphere. There is great anxiety as to whether they will survive the winter. So far they look well.

At lunch Winston asked me all about the 'Dr Emil Busch' lecture, which George Edinger[1] gave $6\frac{1}{2}$ years ago in March 1922 at Oxford, a practical joke which was even more successful than its author had hoped. I think Lindemann had told Winston about it. Edinger hired the Grand Jury Room in the Town Hall and advertised with placards and sandwichmen[2] all over the town that Dr Emil Busch, of Frankfurt University, was going to lecture there on 'Freud and the New Psychology'. He then wrote out a lecture which was a brilliant parody of modern psychological jargon. On the evening advertised he disguised himself as a middle-aged untidy German professor with very long thin moustaches[3] and a huge floppy bow tie. I was then a freshman at Balliol and I helped Edinger by disguising myself as the imaginary 'Dr Heythrop, President of the Home Counties Psychological Association', who was to take the chair for our distinguished German visitor. Edinger's lecture was so nonsensical, and so candid in its references to the sexual results of psychological abnormality, that we were sure the audience (which contained some very learned men and women) would quickly see through it, and we had arranged with an accomplice at the door that when Edinger gave the signal we should slip out, locking the door on the outside,

[1] George Edinger, 1899– . Educated at Wellington and Balliol College, Oxford. Co-founder and first editor of the *Cherwell*, 1921. Called to the Bar, 1924. Assistant editor, the *Graphic*, 1928–31. Unsuccessful Liberal candidate, 1929. Leader writer for Express newspapers, 1933–9. Special correspondent with the Nationalists in Spain, 1937. War Correspondent, Royal Navy, Normandy, Scheldt and Rhine crossing, 1944–5; re-occupation of Singapore, 1945. Leader writer, *Straits Times*, 1953–6. Co-biographer of Nelson (1930); biographer of Prince Rupert (1936).

[2] In a letter to the author on 12 August 1978, George Edinger recalled: 'I don't remember any sandwichmen. It would have been too expensive but we did invite all Heads of Colleges.'

[3] George Edinger writes: 'It was a short toothbrush moustache and ordinary black bow tie. But there was a turn down collar and black waistcoat with tails. It was a deliberate solecism. Dr Heythrop by contrast wore impeccable evening dress. I was a German Professor not a Latin quarter artist.'

and escape leaving our audience locked in.[1] To our surprise, the lecture was heard to the end with great approval, and we then had to allow questions, which Edinger answered with great confidence and vigour. It was not until I noticed his left-hand moustache was about to fall off that I announced Dr Busch had a train to catch, and asked for a vote of thanks, which was enthusiastically given. We left as quickly as we could, but were pursued[2] down the Town Hall steps by eager questioners inquiring about the facilities for psychological instruction in Germany, to which Dr Busch replied volubly, gesticulating with one hand and holding his moustache on with the other.

Winston was immensely amused by Edinger's stories, and gems of derisory nonsense in this lecture, especially by one pronouncement which he made me repeat until he had got it by heart—'Mind is a chunk of space-time happenings which forms the basic fundamentum of everything.'

This evening Winston talked very freely about the USA. He thinks they are arrogant, fundamentally hostile to us, and that they wish to dominate world politics. He thinks their 'Big Navy' talk is a bluff which we ought to call. He considers we ought to say firmly that we must decide for ourselves how large a navy we require, and that America must do the same.

I was interested to hear that under the new international financial agreement that Winston had secured, we shall in future actually receive more from Europe than we pay to America. I had thought it was the other way about. I knew that in the Balfour note we had declared that we would not take more from Europe, in Reparations and war debts together, than we pay to America. What I did not realise was that we had actually paid £100,000,000 to America before we began to receive anything from Europe, and what Winston has secured is that we shall now be credited with these payments so that the future annual balance will be in our favour. This is good news and it was very interesting to hear it from the Chancellor of the Exchequer himself.[3]

---

[1] George Edinger writes: 'actually we had arranged that an accomplice in the audience rise to ask "But Dr Koenigsberger says" . . . as soon as things looked precarious. Then a second accomplice by the switch would turn out the lights.'

[2] George Edinger writes: 'We weren't actually pursued. It was a very leisurely walk from the Town Hall to the Carfax answering questions. Arrived at Carfax, Scrymgeour suddenly remembered that I had to catch a train and we went off hurriedly down Queen Street in the direction of the Station. At Carfax all our questioners left us, turning right down the High. We then turned out of Queen Street down Bulwarks Lane to Gloucester Green and so to Beaumont Street and the friend's room where we shed our disguises and walked back to Balliol as ourselves. A note was in the Porters Lodge for Scrymgeour Wedderburn "Well done, you had them all right". It was from a Winchester contemporary called Lenanton who was one of the group that walked with us from the Town Hall and NOT clearly out of interest in psychology, so we were not completely undetected.'

[3] On 26 September 1928 Churchill wrote to P. J. Grigg: 'The whole policy of the Balfour Note is an implied appeal to the United States to release us from being their debt collector in Europe. I should like this recorded.'

I was sorry to hear that Prof is not staying on over the week-end, as he has to get back tomorrow. Today he told us what I think is the most interesting thing I have heard about modern physical science. He says that experiments in the behaviour of the smallest particles (electrons, protons and neutrons) which compose material objects, may possibly lead him to abandon the doctrine of causality altogether. He says that in the behaviour of these particles, of which all matter is composed, similar causes do not produce similar results, although the units of matter large enough to be visible to us do obey the same laws. If this is true (and Prof is one of the greatest living authorities on the subject) it would seem to destroy entirely the basis of materialist or determinist philosophy.

James Scrymgeour-Wedderburn: diary

(*Dundee papers*)

23 September 1928   Chartwell Manor
Sunday

Last night I had the great privilege of two hours' conversation with Winston alone, as Lindemann and O'Malley had both left and the ladies had gone to bed. He began by asking how old I was. When I said twenty-six, he replied 'Ah! The age at which Napoleon was given command of the French Army of Italy,' and he then discoursed for some time on the changes in military tactics and strategy since 1795, and stressed the importance of the revolution brought about by the invention of tanks and armoured cars, which were incomparably superior to cavalry for all purposes. He asked me if I thought anything could be said for the retention of cavalry in a modern army. Without much conviction, I replied that if the new anti-tank gun could do what was claimed for it, the tanks might not reach their objective, and that in the recent Army manoeuvres, the cavalry were reported to have done very well. 'Certainly,' said Winston. 'The cavalry did remarkably well in the manoeuvres. But they had one great advantage—there were no bullets. It is wonderful to see what impressive feats can be performed by cavalry if there are no bullets to stop them.'

Winston then questioned me about the history of my office of Hereditary Standard-bearer, and in particular asked who had carried the Royal Standard at Bannockburn, and at Flodden. I told him it had been carried at Bannockburn by Sir Nicholas Scrymgeour, the Constable of Dundee, and at Flodden by John Scrymgeour of Glassary, who died of wounds six weeks later, and whose nephew and ward, the hereditary standard-bearer, was a boy at that time. Winston said that Flodden was a great and disastrous defeat for the Scots. I agreed and said that their defeat was caused by the chivalrous folly of James IV, who had abandoned an impregnable defensive position in response to an old-fashioned challenge from the English commander. This had a remarkable effect on Winston, who immediately burst into a long recitation of Sir Walter Scott's 'Marmion', which he knows by heart, and which he continued to recite for about a quarter of an hour, with the greatest animation. He seemed particularly to enjoy the passage—

> 'And if thou saidst I am not peer
> To any Lord in Scotland here
> Lowland or Highland, far or near,
> Lord Angus, thou hast lied!'

which he repeated several times with fierce emotion, and with tears starting from his eyes.

But he says he has a great admiration for the Scots, and that he wishes they would increase in numbers.

When he had finished Marmion, Winston suddenly asked me to give him my opinion of Lloyd George. The only description of Ll G which I could remember at once was the old rhyme which I had been brought up on as a child before the War:—

> 'Lloyd George without doubt, when his life ebbs out
> Will be borne in a fiery chariot
> To sit in state on a red-hot plate
> Between Satan and Judas Iscariot.
> Ananias that day to the Devil will say
> My precedence here now fails
> Pray put me up higher, away from the fire
> To make room for this liar from Wales.'

But Winston said he wanted to hear a first-hand opinion of Ll G from some-one in the youngest generation of politics, so I replied that I thought no one ought to disparage a man who had done so much to win victory in the war, raising the public spirit of the people and calming industrial unrest. Winston said 'A very proper answer, and one that is only too seldom heard.' He then defended Ll G's war-time foreign policy, claiming that he had succeeded in bringing America into the war on our side, which no one had thought would ever happen. He asked me if I could give any reason why Ll G made so little impression in Scotland. I said I thought his type of popular appeal, suitable to the tastes of an English or Welsh crowd, did not often impress the more critical audiences in Scotland, who sometimes feel they are entitled to a rational sequence of argument.

Winston is speaking in Cheltenham tomorrow in reply to a recent attack by Ll G on the present Government,[1] and this led him to the subject of their pre-war association as colleagues in the Liberal Government. He gave a brilliantly expressed sketch of British party politics from 1902–1914. The rapid rise of Socialism, he said, had been in any event inevitable, but the pre-war Radical government had delayed it by attaching to themselves a great part of the revolutionary vote.

He went on to point out that both the constitutional struggle, and the long period of Liberal success, was entirely owing to the folly of the Conservatives. At the beginning of the century, they had been in a tremendously strong position, laboriously won by Lord Salisbury and Lord Randolph Churchill. They had wantonly thrown it all away, first by their method of trying to introduce Protection, and next by using the Lords to reject every Liberal measure. They had given the Liberals the unique advantage of being a Government and an Opposition at the same time. If only they had allowed the Education Act and the 1909 Budget to pass, the country would soon have got tired of the Radicals.

Winston then went on—'You will see a repetition of all this within the next ten years. The Socialists must one day succeed in obtaining a Parliamentary majority. They will then introduce some measure affecting property which, in reality, will be comparatively mild, but which will be hailed

---

[1] Cheltenham was in the midst of a by-election, and Lloyd George had visited the town on Saturday, September 22. Upon hearing that Churchill was to visit the constituency on the following Monday, Lloyd George said: 'I should have thought the Conservative choice was a little unfortunate. They are sending their great tax gatherer, the man who has imposed more fresh taxes than any Chancellor for over a century in time of peace.' Speaking at Cheltenham two days later, Churchill replied: 'It is all very well for Mr Lloyd George and others to come along and criticize the Chancellor of the Exchequer because, in the face of a blow like the general strike, he had to reach out in this direction or the other to secure revenues for public services. I take to myself the credit for having been able to get through this difficult time, admittedly by using one shift and another, without having reimposed any of the remissions of taxation which were made by my predecessor on tea or sugar, or having reimposed the 6d which I took off the income tax in 1925, without having in any way impaired the proper upkeep of the defensive forces of the Empire, without having failed to make an ever increasing provision for the repayment of the National Debt, and without having imposed any new direct taxation upon the mass of the income taxpayers or any burden upon the vital necessaries of popular consumption.' Later in his speech Churchill said of Lloyd George: 'Mr Lloyd George's conduct in the general strike was unworthy of one who had held the position of First Minister of the Crown. There was no doubt whatever that he thought the general strikers had a very fair chance of succeeding, and instead of choosing which side he was on and standing by with firmness, he took up an attitude which if they had succeeded and the constitutional government of this country broken down, would have enabled him to come forward as the necessary man and pour oil on the troubled waters and restore the situation.'

by the Tory press as a revolution which must be resisted by every means. There will be a great agitation among the Die-Hards, and strong pressure will be brought on the Lords to reject the measure.' If the Die-Hards were to prevail, he said, the country would support the Socialists, and much greater harm would result. But if wiser counsels were heard, and the measure allowed to pass, the country would become disgusted with Socialist policy, and the Conservatives would be returned again stronger than ever. I asked him how he would regard a measure which actually confiscated property without compensation. 'Ah' he said 'then I would be prepared to draw the sword in defence of property, which is one of the most fundamental of British rights.'

He went on to say 'I can claim for myself complete consistency in supporting the law against unconstitutional action. I defended it against the riots at the time of the great railway strike in 1911, I supported it against the Ulster rebels in 1914, and I upheld it against the General Strike in 1926.' When I asked whether he had supported it against De Valera in 1921 he replied, yes, that he and Lloyd George were the last to agree to negotiation, and that negotiation had been pressed on them for some time by the military commanders in Ireland, and by all the Unionist members of the Cabinet. He also said that the King himself had insisted on negotiation.

He defended the Irish treaty of 1921 because Britain was now rid of the Irish trouble, and the Conservative party permanently relieved of eighty hostile seats in the House of Commons.

I think Winston is right in blaming the Conservatives for the success of their opponents before the war, and his prediction about the Socialists ought to be remembered.

I believe Winston may be the greatest conversationalist who has ever lived. I would say he is superior to Dr Johnson in the depth of his understanding, and the wealth of his vocabulary, and the variety of his interests. I wish there could be some modern Boswell who could write down, or perhaps make gramophone records of most of his conversation. And he is exceptionally easy to talk and listen to, for he has the rare quality of understanding precisely your meaning, whatever you say on whatever subject, and of giving exactly the kind of answer which is appropriate, without any irrelevance or misconstruction of your ideas. He is always eager to hear what everyone else has to say, and he never monopolises the conversation, although he always dominates it.

When he becomes engrossed in his subject, he strides up and down the room with his head thrust forward and his thumbs in the armholes of his waistcoat, as if he were trying to keep pace with his own eloquence. If he shows signs of slowing down, all you have to do is to make some moderately intelligent observation, and off he goes again.

Lord Wimborne arrived this evening. He looks a sorry old roué. Although he is a first cousin of Winston, he appears to be completely brainless. I remembered Belloc's couplet:—

> We must suppose God knew best
> When he created Ivor Guest.

What a sad contrast!

Winston has lately been invited to join the Bricklayers' Union, which I think he will do, but he is first inquiring whether there is any restriction on the number of bricks which he would be allowed to lay in a given time, and whether he may do his bricklaying work with the assistance of non-union labour.

I leave tomorrow morning and must be in Scotland Tuesday morning.

Winston S. Churchill to Alderman Lane

(*Robert Hastings collection*)

23 September 1928   Chartwell Manor
Private

Dear Sir,

I have been looking through your Rules, and should be glad to know whether I can assume that those set out on Page 79 are complete so far as the conduct of individual members is concerned. Would you mind, however, letting me know whether for instance there is any rule regulating the number of bricks which a man may lay in a day? Also is there any rule that a trade unionist may not work with one who is not a trade unionist, and what are the restrictions on overtime?

I have marked this letter 'Private' as I am only writing for information. If you are able to assure me that I should not be undertaking anything I could not perform in your answer to my questions, I will send you a fresh letter accepting the invitation which you tendered me in your first, and this can be published if you wish.

I may say that I should be very pleased to join the Union, if you are of opinion that it would not be unwelcome to your members. I take a high view of the dignity both of craftsmanship and manual labour.[1]

Yours faithfully,
Winston S. Churchill

Winston S. Churchill to Frederick Leith-Ross
(*Churchill papers: 18/75*)

23 September 1928

I am of course strongly in favour of disarmament, provided that it does not mean that France will not be strong enough to defend herself against German aggression or England capable of feeding herself in the face of American naval power. So far as France is concerned political and financial pressures will undoubtedly lead to a continual diminution of the burden of military service. Danger will arise when Germany feels herself strong enough to put pressure upon France and we are reminded by France of our guarantee. I trust this day will be distant. At the present time the naval danger is the greatest. There is no doubt that the United States will seek at Washington in 1931 so to limit the British Navy as to make it quite certain that the Americans will be strategically superior. Once that condition has been established, the centre of the British Empire will have been undermined. I shall do my utmost to resist such a development.

I had hoped that after the naval fiasco at Geneva last year the Armaments question would have been permitted to subside. All was in fact going well: the Americans were reducing their Navy Bill, and the election was passing off without naval issues being prominent. The fussy Disarmament policy at Geneva led to the Anglo-French compromise, not because anybody wanted it or because there was any plan behind it, but because 'our representative must have something to say about disarmament at Geneva or we shall be blamed'. The results have been greatly to stimulate the Big Navy party in America. It is my firm conviction that if no naval agreements are made and

[1] On 18 October 1928 *The Times* reported that the Manchester No 2 branch of the Amalgamated Building Trade Workers had forwarded a protest resolution to the Executive Council, demanding the return to Churchill of his membership fee, and calling on George Hicks, the General Secretary of the Union, to resign, 'for bringing upon the organisation public contempt and ridicule'. Two weeks later, on 2 November 1928, *The Times* reported that the Executive Council had just announced that Churchill was not to become a member of the union, as there had been protests 'from a number of branches', and the Council had ruled that Churchill's admission had not been completed because his cheque for 5s had not been cashed by Alderman Lane, while his admission form had not been filled out correctly.

no further discussions on disarmament take place for five years, very large reductions will in fact occur through the pressure of finance and the increasing sense of world security. Nothing but harm has been done by the disarmament discussions. They constitute the main cause of friction between nations at the present time. They have markedly impaired our relations with the United States.

In fact it seems that the next great war will be fought on the question of how to prevent war.

Winston S. Churchill to Clementine Churchill
(Spencer-Churchill papers)

25 September 1928   Balmoral Castle

My darling one,

Here I am—not at all tired by a racketting journey. The meeting went off well, there was gt enthusiasm and the prospects of the poll seemed healthy. I caught the Scottish Express at 12.45 am at Rugby, & motored on here this morning from Perth—a beautiful drive. There is no one here at all except the family, the Household & Princess Elizabeth[1]—aged 2. The last is a character. She has an air of authority & reflectiveness astonishing in an infant. Princess Cecilie of Greece[2] (Prince Louis' grand daughter) is also here. A beautiful face & complexion but indifferent carriage.

The King is well—but ageing. He no longer stalks but goes out on the hill where the deer are 'moved about for him', & it may be that some loyal stag will do his duty. He & the Q asked much after you.

Miss F does not arrive till late this evening with the heavy luggage. I am much looking forward to my release on Saturday from this honourable & luxurious captivity.

Mind you rest & do not worry about household matters. Let them crash if they will. All will be well. Servants exist to save one trouble, & shd never be allowed to disturb one's inner peace. There will always be food to eat, & sleep will come even if the beds are not made. Nothing is worse than worrying about trifles. The big things do not chafe as much: & if they are rightly settled the rest will fall in its place.

[1] Elizabeth Alexandra Mary, elder daughter of the Duke of York (later King George VI). Born on 21 April 1926, she succeeded her father, as Queen Elizabeth II, on 6 February 1952.

[2] Cecilia, granddaughter of Prince Louis of Battenberg and daughter of Alice of Battenberg (1885–1967) and Prince Andrew of Greece (1882–1944). Born in 1911, a sister of Prince Philip, she married Grand Duke George of Hesse and the Rhine in 1931. Both she and her husband were killed in an air accident near Ostend in 1937.

I trust all is well with the cygnets. The cold will try them hard. However God is responsible both for the cygnets & the change in the weather, & He must settle the problem. Our contribution must be to keep the Fox away by finishing the wire fence. The rest falls in a sphere with wh it wd be impious to meddle too much.

The Prof declares that the Hereditary Standard Bearer[1] enjoyed himself & was favourably impressed by our outfit.

With tender love
Your devoted
W

Alderman Lane to Winston S. Churchill

(*Churchill papers: 1/201*)

26 September 1928

Right Honourable Sir,

I thank you for your letter of the 23rd instant, the contents of which I have noted.

In regard to the question of restriction of output, on many occasions statements have been made by irresponsible persons to the effect that there is some restriction, but I am unable to term the statements anything but terminological inexactitudes.[2] There is no restriction whatsoever as to how many bricks a member of this Union may lay. It would be absolutely impossible to try to enforce such a restriction, because, whilst a member employed on say glazed brickwork would lay comparatively few bricks in a given time, the same man in the same time working on other work might quite conceivably lay many more bricks.

There is nothing to prevent any member from working with non-unionists, as it is only by allowing this that we can expect to get the non-unionists to join this Union. Our members carry on propaganda on jobs in the same manner as is carried on in all trades and professions. It is only by the mutual contact between the trade unionists and the non-unionist that we can con-

---

[1] James Scrymgeour-Wedderburn.

[2] On 22 February 1906 Churchill, as Under-Secretary of State for the Colonies (his first government post) had answered a Conservative Opposition amendment criticizing the Liberals for doing nothing to change the system of Chinese indentured labour in South Africa —a system which, in the General Election two months earlier, the Liberals had denounced as 'slavery'. During his speech Churchill had stated that the condition of the Chinese labourers in South Africa 'cannot in the opinion of His Majesty's Government be classified as slavery in the extreme acceptance of the word without some risk of terminological inexactitude'. This phrase provoked an immediate and derisory protest from Joseph Chamberlain, and was to be used against Churchill by the Conservatives for many years to come.

vince the latter of the value of trade organisation. There are quite a number of jobs throughout the country, where members of this Union are working with non-unionists.

So far as overtime is concerned, this is governed by the National Agreement between the National Federation of Building Trades Employers and the Building Operatives, which provides for Joint Overtime Committees to be set up in the various towns throughout the country. It is the practice for all good employers to apply to the local Committee for an overtime permit, and in urgent and necessary cases, or where it is proved that the Employer is unable to obtain the necessary labour, then there is very little difficulty in obtaining the necessary permission. It will be seen that through this channel we are able to safeguard any members who may be out of employment.

I trust that now I have explained these points to you, you will write me further in regard to the question of membership.

If there are any further points upon which I can enlighten you, I shall be only too happy to do so.

> Believe me to be,
> Yours very truly,
> James G. Lane

Winston S. Churchill to Clementine Churchill

(*Spencer-Churchill papers*)

27 September 1928   Balmoral

My darling,

Yr second letter has just come. I am glad the bricklayer has reformed. I am still more glad you will let me invite the PG's. It is of real public importance as the enclosed from Grigg will show you. I had meant to broach the subject to yr Catship again on my return, but yr letter settles the point. By all means ask Ivor. We cannot fix the day till Monday when I shall go to London for a Cabinet. But provisionally I think Oct 13 week end wd be best. I have little to give him but civility. *She*[1] is vy nice & Ivor will play with her.

I am just back from a vy hardworking day's stalking 10 till 5.30 always on the move. I killed a good stag—10 pointers—but missed another thro being out of breath.

---

[1] Gertrude Charlotte Hough, daughter of the Reverend G. F. Hough. She married P. J. Grigg in 1919. They had no children. She died in 1968.

Tomorrow we are to shoot grouse. Luckily I brought my guns & cartridges. The K is really vy kind to me & gives me every day the best of his sport. Yesterday we had a most interesting talk after picnic lunch about Baldwin's dissolution in 1925, Curzon's chagrin at not being PM etc. The King is a strong advocate of his Government and highly approves of my criticism of LG. I defended him a certain amount. HM also shares my views about the Yankees & expressed the same in picturesque language.

Cheltenham is splendid. I enclose a vy nice telegram from the new member.[1]

I am healthily tired out. With tender love my darling one

from yr ever devoted

W

Winston S. Churchill to Stanley Baldwin

(*Churchill papers: 22/222*)

30 September 1928

My dear Prime Minister,

I put down these rough notes as my contribution towards the answer we should make to the American rebuke. I am most anxious that we should avoid a long barking justification of our Geneva foolishness. It is the worst blunder we have committed, and we did it with our eyes open just for the sake of having something to say. The Americans now take up the main naval issue, which is much better ground for us to make a simple statement upon.

It seems to me this is a turning point in our history. Of course it would be so much easier to 'give in' and follow along meekly in the wake of the new English-speaking authority. But I hope we shall try to keep the flag flying.

---

[1] Walter Reuben Preston, 1875–1946. A civil engineer. President, the Textile Machinery Makers Ltd. A Director of the Midland Bank Ltd. Unsuccessful Conservative candidate in the two elections of 1910. Master of the Avon Vale Foxhounds, 1914–18. Conservative MP for Mile End, 1918–23. Knighted, 1921. Following the death of the Conservative MP for Cheltenham, Preston won Cheltenham, on 26 September 1928, with an increased majority (3,760 as against 2,763 in 1924), holding the seat until his retirement from politics in 1937.

Winston S. Churchill: notes

(*Churchill papers: 22/222*)

30 September 1928

SYNOPSIS OF SUGGESTED REPLY

It gave HMG great satisfaction to reach, at Washington in 1921, an accord with the US upon the basis of parity in capital ships and certain other specified units. HMG made it clear at the time that the extension of the principle of parity to cruisers would not be acceptable to them for the reason that it would not take into account the special circumstances of Great Britain and of the British Empire. Their point of view was set forth by Lord Balfour in terms which still command the assent of HMG. (Here quote the celebrated Balfour passage.)

HMG were not aware from anything that passed at Washington, either in political or naval circles, that the US took exception to this statement of the British position. The Washington Naval Agreement was therefore concluded on a basis which regulated agreeably to all concerned the main offensive power of the respective Navies, and which left the smaller classes of vessels unregulated by agreements but admittedly open to further hopeful and friendly study. When therefore in 1927 the Government of the US proposed a fresh Naval Conference at Geneva, HMG suggested as their contribution that an attempt should be made to limit by agreement the construction of the next largest class of vessels, viz the cruisers carrying 8-inch guns. This type of cruiser is by its offensive power specially associated with the battle fleets, and a lack of parity in this offensive type of cruiser might well be held to derange the parity already established for capital ships.

As HMG had at this time a considerable preponderance in this class of vessels, they felt entitled to hope that this new further extension of the principle of parity would be agreeable to the US and would certainly constitute a marked and important advance towards a comprehensive naval agreement. There would of course remain the still smaller classes of vessels which all Powers would be free to build according to their needs, as they viewed them, or to their choice. But it seemed to HMG that later on other classes of cruisers, even in this quasi-defensive sphere, might gradually be the subject of agreement; and at any rate no door was closed upon the further progress of naval agreement and of economy.

However the Government of the US, for reasons which HMG are bound to respect, preferred either to have a total limitation of tonnage for all cruiser forces, or that all countries should remain free in the sphere of cruiser construction. HMG bowed to this view while adhering to their own.

They felt that an equal tonnage limit translated by the US into cruisers of the highest offensive power, while British needs would require to be translated into a larger number of smaller vessels, would undoubtedly not realise the principle of parity in main naval strength to which HMG have subscribed, and would in fact leave the British Navy in a position of definite and final inferiority to the United States. This was not what the British Government believed the US to desire, nor is it a situation to which they themselves would wish to be committed by treaty.

HMG would have been well content not to stir the subject of naval limitations at the present time. The exigencies however of the discussions of the Preparatory Commission for Disarmament at Geneva have rendered this course impossible. The differences of opinion between France and Great Britain on military and naval questions were not at all serious, and in general the two countries have been in harmony. Nevertheless such differences as existed, if tenaciously held to on both sides, would have imposed a bar on the further preparatory work of the Disarmament Commission. HMG were reluctant to become in any way responsible for such an arrest of an absolutely necessary world effort to reduce armaments. They have therefore sought a common basis with France for the purposes of the discussions of the Disarmament Commission, and they are glad that such a basis has been reached. They have furnished the US with full and immediate information upon the subject, which is intended only to carry the preparatory study of disarmament a stage nearer to a general discussion.

In the presence of the Note which they have just received from the US, HMG now feel that probably the general cause of disarmament, and especially naval disarmament, will be better served by a period of silence and goodwill than by a process of active and detailed negotiation. The sustained and prolonged discussion by technical experts of the problems of relative naval power would only at the present time tend to concentrate attention upon an aspect of international relationships which HMG hope will steadily recede in importance. Such a discussion upon the details of ships and guns, upon the [absurd]¹ hypothesis that such instrumentalities will be again invoked, would be entirely out of harmony with the increasing confidence and intimacy now existing between the Great Powers, and particularly between Great Britain and the United States. More especially is this true upon the morrow of the signature of the Pact of Peace framed upon the initiative and by the wisdom of the United States, and to which almost every country in the world has now adhered, by which the idea of war is solemnly banished from international affairs. HMG have since the war allowed their naval strength to fall continually, and have watched with composure born of

¹ Churchill deleted this word after having dictated it.

[unshakeable]¹ confidence the rise and expansion of the American Navy. They believe that the increasing sense of world security which must follow from the recent Pact, coupled with the constant financial inducements to a reduction of non-productive expenditure, may well be left for a while to play their part in policy. They will endeavour, as they have done in the past, to set an example in restraint and moderation. Their aim is identical with that of the United States, namely that the two nations who have so much in common may be represented upon the waters of the world by what is truly and actually an equal naval strength and status; and they confide themselves with hope and sincerity to a continuance of freedom in naval matters on which agreement has not yet been reached, and to neighbourly goodwill in all.

¹ Churchill deleted this word after having dictated it.

October 1928

Thomas Jones: diary

(*Jones papers*)

1 October 1928

Long discussion this afternoon on course of Government business in relation to date of next year's General Election. Arguments for and against a summer and an autumn election. Present decision depended mainly on Budget and on Local Government Bills. Important that rating reform should come into operation on the advertised date, said the PM, and he was against a dissolution at end of September. 'We would be campaigning all through the holidays after a hard session. . . .

The Conservative Central Office favoured early in June. Should avoid cutting across Scottish holidays. People on holiday are annoyed to have politics thrust on them, though rural constituencies might prefer a summer election. Great increase in use of charabancs. State of register made election before May 11th impossible.

Winston did not see why the Relief Bills need be passed before the Election. Why not have a sudden election and come back and finish off the Bills? The PM could announce policy and give no pledges. Why not have election on May 11th? To which the PM retorted that the Budget could not then be got through and Kingsley Wood said the Bills could not be split as the jam was in Part I and the other parts unpopular. Must take them in one jump. Many of the Guardians were secretly in favour of the reforms.

Lord Birkenhead to Winston S. Churchill

(*Churchill papers: 1/200*)

2 October 1928

My dearest W

At the Cabinet[1] I had not received your charming letter or I should have spoken of it.

It was a great comfort. Lunch next Wednesday.

As always
F

Winston S. Churchill to Alderman Lane

(*Robert Hastings collection*)

3 October 1928   Chartwell Manor

Dear Sir,

I have now carefully considered your letter of the 4th September; and I am obliged to you for having sent me the Rules of the Amalgamated Union of Building Trade Workers, and also for your courtesy in furnishing me with other information for which I asked.

Although I cannot pretend to be fully qualified, I shall be glad to accept your invitation to become a member of the Union. I enclose herewith my entrance fee.

With many thanks for the trouble you have taken, believe me

Yours very faithfully,
Winston S. Churchill

Cabinet minutes

(*Churchill papers: 22/212*)

10 October 1928   10 Downing Street
11.30 am

The Cabinet had before them a Memorandum by the Chancellor of the Exchequer (Paper CP 282 (28)) covering a draft Note to be sent to the French Government on the subject of their failure to secure ratification of the French War Debt Agreement signed by M Caillaux in July, 1926. M Caillaux fell from office shortly after signing the Agreement, but the Chancellor

[1] Lord Birkenhead's last Cabinet. He had decided to resign as Secretary of State for India, and was succeeded by Viscount Peel.

of the Exchequer had received an assurance from M Poincaré in August, 1926, that he would ask the Chamber to ratify the Agreement in the autumn of that year at the latest. In July, 1928, representations had been made to the French Government, and their reply confirmed the assurances given by M Poincaré, but, in effect, took up the position that French debt payments were conditional upon her reparation receipts, whereas it was an essential part of the settlement that the Annuities were on the sole credit of France.

Suggestions were offered for modifying some expressions in the text of the Memorandum which were thought to be unnecessarily provocative. The Chancellor of the Exchequer explained, however, that the Memorandum was only a draft, which would in any case be discussed with the Foreign Office.[1]

Cabinet meeting: minutes

(*Churchill papers: 22/212*)

17 October 1928   10 Downing Street
11.30 am

THE CHANCELLOR OF THE EXCHEQUER informed his colleagues that since the above Memoranda had been circulated he had had the opportunity of long conversations with Mr Parker Gilbert, the Agent-General for Reparation Payments, who had shed some new light on the question. Mr Parker Gilbert was convinced that Germany would be able to pay £100,000,000 a year for a sufficient number of years to enable the Allies to discharge their debts to America. In the coming year the Germans would not only pay but transfer across the Exchange the full amount due under the Dawes Settlement, which would reach its maximum of £25,000,000. It was uncertain if this could continue year after year, since Germany was at present borrowing large sums, partly on short loans at a high rate of interest. Hence, though the position was satisfactory for next year, there was not absolute security for subsequent years. If the German Exchange, for any reason, were upset, it might be impossible for the Agent-General for Reparation Payments to secure the necessary exchange to effect the transfer, and under the Dawes Settlement in these circumstances he would merely keep the Marks in Germany.

---

[1] Thomas Jones noted in his diary, of Churchill's remarks during this Cabinet: 'Winston: Anglo-French agreement not dead—immortal, unkillable. Were we going to object on Preparatory Commission to French military reserves and drop our points on Navy? Sham process should come to an end. Anglo-French agreement a tremendous reality: France, England, and Japan thinking along same lines' (*Jones papers*).

MR PARKER GILBERT'S idea was that Germany should pay £100,000,000 a year and that the transfer clause of the Dawes Settlement should be dropped. The question arose as to how this plan would affect the policy of the Balfour Note. In the present year we should be receiving from Reparation and from Allied Debts as much as we had to pay to America. There was no reason for our losing that position. Under the Parker Gilbert proposal we should receive enough from Reparation payments, combined with payments on account of Allied Debts, to enable us to discharge our debt to the United States of America. We should not, however, recover the arrears resulting from payments already made to America. But in any event the whole of these arrears would not be received even under the payments provided for in the Dawes Settlement.

Before proceeding with this proposal it would be necessary to ascertain definitely the attitude of France. Mr Parker Gilbert believed that M Poincaré was far more reasonable than would appear from the summary of the statement in the French Press referred to in Paper CP 297 (28). If this proved to be the case, and Germany, as anticipated by Mr Parker Gilbert, was willing to pay £100,000,000, there would be no objection to the setting up of an Expert Commission, similar to the Dawes Committee, to work out the details of the plan, though it would be dangerous to embark on such a Committee until there was some hope of a settlement.

In these circumstances MR CHURCHILL suggested that the first step was for him to see M Poincaré at once and ask him (i) if the £100,000,000 payment by Germany would be acceptable to France; (ii) if he was prepared to recognize the British position under the policy of the Balfour Note; and (iii) if France was prepared to ratify the agreement made for the payment of the French Debt. If the answer were satisfactory, then Mr Parker Gilbert, who would be going straight to Berlin *via* Paris, would be able to ascertain how matters stood in Berlin. What Germany stood to gain in this arrangement was, first, the liberation of German soil from Allied troops; second, the liberation of German finance from foreign control; and, third, a reduction of her annual payments from £125,000,000 to £100,000,000.

In the course of a discussion on the above proposals the suggestion was made that it might be better for someone less conspicuous than the Chancellor of the Exchequer to see M Poincaré, but it was pointed out that the Chancellor of the Exchequer was the responsible Minister and could hardly delegate this important duty. Moreover, all the world knew that a Conference of Experts had been proposed, and it could be announced that Mr Churchill was visiting Paris in order to consult with M Poincaré in connection with the setting up of the Expert Commission. Seeing that the British Empire and France, between them, received about 75 per cent of Reparation from Germany, the meeting of the two Ministers ought not to occasion surprise.

The question was raised as to what answer the Chancellor of the Exchequer should give if M Poincaré wished to capitalise a part of the German payments in advance of the other Allies,—a proposal which France had often made before but which we had been obliged to reject. There was general agreement that any capitalisation must be on the basis of the Spa Percentages. There was general agreement also that it would be inadvisable for the Expert Commission to meet in London.

Winston S. Churchill: Cabinet memorandum[1]

(*Churchill papers: 22/206*)

19 October 1928   British Embassy
Secret   Paris

M Poincaré received me cordially this morning and immediately spoke frankly about the French position on the forthcoming Reparations Conference. France was content with the present situation, provided it would continue indefinitely, and she would not have sought the present occasion for altering it. He, M Poincaré, had been led to believe that there was a chance of getting an arrangement of a more durable character. The initiative should come from Germany and if the Germans put forward reasonable proposals the French would consider them in a favourable spirit. The French would require first of all that the German proposals should relieve them of all anxiety about their war debts to England and the United States, and that over and above this there should be 'something important' for them on account of their devastated regions. I said that our general attitude towards the existing arrangement was the same as his. We were content with it, but, like him, would be glad of a greater security for its continuance. Our position was the Balfour note, which meant that the taxpayers of the United Kingdom, apart from the British Empire, should receive from Europe enough to pay America. There was also the question of arrears, which amounted to £180 millions, involving £9 millions a year interest. This, I said, however stood in a somewhat different position from the rest of the Balfour note and might be the subject of further study. I pointed out that, in any mobilisation of German capital as a part of or supplement to German reparation annuities, we should expect that the Spa percentages would rule and that France would not have priority of mobilisation in her favour.

[1] Circulated to the Cabinet as Cabinet paper 311 of 1928.

He made no objection to this. I then referred to the ratification of the Caillaux–Churchill Agreement. He gave his opinion that no French Parliament would ratify it, but that the French Government had the power to ratify without formal Parliamentary endorsement. This was what we (the British) had done, and the French constitution only required the formal assent of Parliament in cases where an increased charge was imposed upon France. In the Caillaux–Churchill Agreement the charges on France were not increased, but, on the contrary, diminished. Once he felt that there was a real security for the continuance of the German payments during the currency of the debt obligation, he would be ready to consider ratification on the responsibility of the executive Government, which the French Parliament would probably allow. I said I had heard rumours, which I did not believe, that there was an idea of ratifying the Mellon–Bérenger Agreement before dealing with ours; that this would cause a most deplorable impression in England, and would upset us all very much indeed. He assured me that both the agreements would be treated exactly the same by him.

He then followed up his remark that the initiative about new reparation proposals rested with the Germans by suggesting that Berlin might be the best place for the Conference. If Paris were chosen France might have to pay for the privilege of holding the Conference. I said I had felt exactly the same about London and that the British Cabinet rather liked the idea of Berlin. As to Geneva, we had had a good deal of that lately. Brussels was another alternative.

M Poincaré then proceeded that the most difficult part of the subject was the composition of the experts committee. He knew that Mr Parker Gilbert wanted a committee of independent experts in order to commend to the German people and the American investors in the most favourable way any scheme which emerged, and that the Germans might be reconciled to giving more on this basis. He himself apparently had been much influenced by Gilbert, but the French Cabinet took the other view and held strongly that they could not part with executive responsibility in a matter which affected the Budget and the whole future of France. The French Cabinet thought that they would be placed in an invidious position if they had to reject the recommendations of an independent expert committee. He was therefore bound to reserve this matter at any rate until the French Cabinet met again on the 30th.

My colleagues will recognise how very similar these misgivings of M Poincaré are to those which I have expressed. I told him that I had felt the same apprehensions and that was why it was so important before we committed ourselves to an independent expert conference, to establish off the stage the main bases on which we could agree. If these were satisfactory, the independent experts might deal with the technical aspects and present the results in the most impressive and favourable form; but that if there was no prospect of agreement disclosed beforehand the Governments had better be represented by persons under their control and thus avoid an open public breakdown. Here again we were altogether in agreement.

All this led me to come into a little closer detail. I said we should expect that France would not in any conference challenge our position on the Balfour note, and he said that he entirely agreed with me. I then said that we thought our requirements might be met on a basis of £100 millions. This would give us the £38 millions which we require from 1932 onwards in order to pay the United States, and it would give the French 'something important' over and above their war debt obligations. He did not noticeably dissent from this figure, so I went on that, if England was to have her £38 millions in 1932 out of a total annuity of £100 millions, that could only be realised if all the military charges for the occupation of the Rhine were terminated and the whole of the £100 millions became available for the creditor Powers. This would mean that the evacuation of both the military zones would have to be faced as a part of such an agreement.

I did not want to press unduly for any statement from him upon this point, but we must go forward together with a clear knowledge of what lay in our path; and I added that nothing would be more likely to induce the Germans to make a really satisfactory offer than the certainty of the early evacuation of their soil from foreign troops. For this part of the conversation I used the interpreter, M Camerlynck, in order that M Poincaré might not interrupt me till I had got it all out. I was very much pleased with the way in which he took it. His face became graver while I was telling the interpreter what to say, but when it was all translated, all he said was that this was a more delicate question and a grave one of general politics. He did not scout it in any way. And when I said that of course alternatively if there was not complete evacuation the £100 million figure would have to be raised in order to cover the creditor requirements, and that anything over £100 millions seemed to be leaving the regions of reality, he assented, or at any rate acquiesced quite amicably.

We then invited Mr Parker Gilbert, who by arrangement had now arrived, to join us, and we explained to him briefly the course of our conversation. Gilbert as usual was helpful and hopeful. He thought we were all in agreement in the main and that our positions were reasonable. He urged the importance of an independent committee whose work was not too much prejudged beforehand, but he recognised the uneasiness which executive Governments and Finance Ministers might feel upon the subject, and he applauded the efforts we were making to explore the ground beforehand. He agreed with us that the next move lay with the Germans and he would himself go to Berlin in a few days and use all his influence to bring them forward to the necessary point. Poincaré suggested and I agreed that he and I should exchange brief and precise notes stating our main requirements, and the Germans could then be made aware of these positions in whatever was thought to be the best diplomatic method. We all agreed it was most important to tell the Italians at the earliest moment to prevent their becoming suspicious. I therefore sent the telegram, which I have reported separately to the Foreign Office.

I am bound to say that M Poincaré's whole attitude fully bore out the accounts which Mr Parker Gilbert had given me. I think he wants a settlement and is prepared to run risks for it. I do not think there is any danger of the French trying to manoeuvre us into an awkward corner. If the Italians will send Pirelli[1] over to London I expect we can reach a satisfactory understanding with them. Everything then will rest with the Germans. It is for them to say what price in prolonged national effort they will pay to secure the liberation of their soil and their finances from foreign control, and a definite reduction in the total of their annuities, a vast scaling down of the capital charge and the end of uncertainty for their financial future. There are great inducements. They have not been promised to them yet, but it is clearly open for Germany to ask and to make an offer proportionate to such prizes.

WSC

Winston S. Churchill: draft note to Raymond Poincaré

(*Churchill papers: 22/206*)

24 October 1928
Secret
To Be Kept Under Lock and Key

It is requested that special care may be taken to ensure the secrecy of this document.[2]

---

[1] Alberto Pirelli, 1882–1971. One of the two sons of Giovanni Battistà Pirelli (who opened his first Milan factory in 1872). Entered his father's business, 1904; Managing Partner, 1904–32; Managing Director, 1932–51; Chairman, 1956–65. Italian Representative on economic affairs and trade at the League of Nations, Geneva, 1920–2; at the Economic Committee of the League, 1923–7. Minister Plenipotentiary, in charge of settling Italy's war debts with Britain and the United States, 1925–30. Founder and President of the Italian Institute of Foreign Trade, 1926–9. President of the International Chamber of Commerce, 1927–9. Founder of the Italian Institute for the Study of International Politics, 1937.

[2] Churchill printed this note for the Cabinet as Cabinet paper 317 of 1928. In his covering note, entitled 'Reparations and War Debts', he wrote: 'I circulate herewith a draft of the note which I propose to send to M Poincaré in accordance with the arrangement made in Paris on the 19th instant and a diagram showing how our proposals would work out on the basis of a German annuity of £100 millions.'

1. The policy of His Majesty's Government in respect of debts and reparations is based as heretofore on the Balfour Note, under which (not as a matter of bargaining, but as a voluntary act of renunciation) His Majesty's Government undertook to limit their claims upon their Allies to such amount as, with the receipts of Great Britain from reparations, would suffice to meet the liabilities they had incurred to the United States in respect of War Debts.

As was made clear in the Anglo-French and Anglo-Italian Agreements, the share of Reparations payable to the British Dominions and Colonies cannot be taken in account in the calculation of British receipts for this purpose, as these payments in no way benefit the taxpayer in the United Kingdom.

2. Up to the present time, the payments of Great Britain to the United States have substantially exceeded the receipts from German reparations and Allied debts together and there is an accumulated deficiency which amounts with interest to upwards of £180 millions. During the present financial year for the first time, the receipts and payments should approximately balance, and it is essential that in any new settlement with Germany His Majesty's Government should be assured that this balance between the receipts and payments of Great Britain should be maintained.

His Majesty's Government conceive that it is the common aim of all the Creditor Governments that any new settlement with Germany must, in the first place, fully cover the liabilities they have each to meet in respect of War Debts. Their aggregate liabilities under this head amount to very considerably less than the normal annuity of £125 millions under the Dawes Plan, and His Majesty's Government therefore see every reason to hope that a settlement could be reached with Germany which would cover not only these liabilities and the comparatively small share of reparations due to the United States and to the other Powers (including the British Dominions) which are not indebted to America, but would provide a balance available towards the costs of reconstructing the devastated regions.

In this connexion, His Majesty's Government are bound to point out that, under the terms of the Balfour Note, they should recover, not only their future payments to the United States of America, but the accumulated deficiency of £180 millions referred to above. His Majesty's Government would however not regard the recovery, in full, of this deficiency as an essential condition of any new settlement provided that the other creditor Powers are willing to agree that the Allied debt liabilities should in future be the first charge on the German annuities and that any supplementary payments towards the costs of reconstructing the devastated regions should be kept within such limits as would not endanger the security of the debt payments.

On this understanding, His Majesty's Government for their part would be willing to refer the question of the total annuities to be paid by Germany to an expert Committee for examination and they would be prepared to accept the conclusions of such a Committee even though it involved some sacrifice of their full claim in respect of the accumulated deficiency due to Great Britain up to date.

It is necessary to observe that, at present, the costs of the Armies of Occupation in the Rhineland substantially diminish the receipts available for Reparations, and in order to make the largest possible amount available for Reparations, these costs should be brought to an end as soon as possible.[1]

3. The question of mobilising the capital Reparation Debt by the marketing of German bonds appears to His Majesty's Government to be a question of expediency rather than of principle. Unless the German Government are prepared to undertake the service of reparation loans *over and above* the current annuity, the service of any Bonds marketed must, *pro tanto*, diminish the German annuities available for distribution to the Allied Governments in future and the extent to which such mobilisation will be in the interests of the Allied Governments will depend on the terms and conditions upon which the Bonds can be placed, *eg*, the rate of discount at which the Bonds could be marketed as compared with the rate of discount at which the proceeds could be utilised by the Allied Governments to meet their liabilities. So long as (in accordance with the provisions of the Treaty) no marketing operation is undertaken except with the unanimous consent of the Creditor Powers, His Majesty's Government do not see any objection of principle to the study of the question. They feel that, on this matter, the advice of an Expert Financial Committee might be most valuable, and they would be glad to invite such a Committee to examine the steps that can be taken to prepare the way for a market operation, without prejudice to the rights of the Allied Governments thereafter to decide whether such an operation is expedient.

4. Finally His Majesty's Government, when concluding the Debt Agreement of July 1926, consented to large diminutions of the total French indebtedness to Great Britain on the assumption that the Agreement would be speedily ratified and that the resulting payments would be upon the sole credit of France. While they must adhere to this position and press for early ratification on this basis in any event, such ratification would, in particular, be an indispensable part of any new settlement that may be reached.

---

[1] British troops evacuated the Rhineland immediately following the Hague Agreements of August 1929. Administered by German civilians, the Rhineland remained demilitarized until March 1936, when it was entered by German troops, and its military fortifications restored.

Stanley Baldwin to Winston S. Churchill

(*Churchill papers: 2/159*)

27 October 1928   10 Downing Street

My dear Winston,

I have been green with envy for two days because I never thought of the Zoo Allegory.[1] It is just perfect and there is no more to be said.

It ought to give food for thought to any one capable of thinking.

What a whoop you must have given when it came into your head!

Yours
SB

Cabinet minutes

(*Churchill papers: 22/213*)

29 October 1928   10 Downing Street
12 noon

THE CHANCELLOR OF THE EXCHEQUER informed the Cabinet that after his meeting in Paris with M Poincaré he had sent a telegram to Signor Mussolini and had suggested that he should send Signor Alberto Pirelli to London to discuss the question. In reply he had received a telegram, which he read to the Cabinet and which was couched in very cordial terms, conveying Signor Mussolini's acquiescence in the proposal as regards Signor Pirelli, who was due in London on Thursday.

The Chancellor of the Exchequer pointed out that the British policy was founded on the Balfour Note. There was one point, however, on which he had a slight reservation to make, namely, in regard to the arrears of £180,000,000 required to carry out in full the policy of the Note. Hitherto we had stood for the whole of these arrears, but it must now be realised that there was not the smallest chance of our recovering them in full, although we might obtain a part. He was anxious, in the Note to M Poincaré, not to reverse the policy, but to indicate that there was room for a little 'give' on this question. He asked the views of his colleagues on this point. MR CHURCHILL stated that there were certain points of detail upon which in any event he would want to alter the Note.

[1] In a speech to his constituents on 25 October 1928, Churchill had told what he called a 'disarmament fable'. set among the animals in the Zoo, to warn against what he saw as premature disarmament. It is published in full in main Volume V of this biography on page 305.

In the course of the discussion it was suggested to Mr Churchill that the reference to the question of arrears should be made at the end of the second sub-paragraph on page 2 of Paper CP 317 (28), where it would be linked up with the cost of repairing the devastated regions. It was suggested that the addition, after the words 'devastated regions', might be in some such terms as the following:—

'and of extinguishing the accumulated deficiency of £180,000,000 referred to above'.

The first four lines of the following paragraph might then be omitted.

Another suggestion was that the fourth sub-paragraph, on page 2, should be amended by referring to the Expert Committee as an 'independent' Expert Committee. In this connection the Cabinet were reminded that Lord Cushendun had committed the country unconditionally to an expert investigation.

Mr Churchill wished at this stage to avoid the word 'Independent', but undertook instead to alter the words 'would be', in the second line, to 'have been', so as to read:—

'On this understanding His Majesty's Government, for their part, *have been* willing to refer the question of the total annuities to be paid by Germany to an Expert Committee for examination,' etc.

Another suggestion made in the course of the discussion was that it was important that any division of capital mobilised by the marketing of German Bonds should not be on different proportions from the arrangements agreed to at Spa as regards the division of the interest. It was suggested that at the end of paragraph 3 the following words might be added:

'and, if thought expedient, the right of the Government to receive the annuities in accordance with the Spa percentages'.

Some discussion took place as to the best procedure to be adopted in order to communicate to other interested Governments the present position in regard to the proposed expert inquiry. On the one hand it was recognised as desirable to avoid presenting the German Government with a formal Note based on the draft Note to M Poincaré and demanding their adherence thereto. On the other hand, the Governments of Berlin, Brussels and Rome had all been made aware that Mr Churchill and M Poincaré were about to exchange precise Notes and consequently would expect some full communication. It was recognised to be necessary to acquaint them fairly and fully with the position, lest otherwise the same sort of suspicions might be aroused as in the case of the Anglo-French Agreement on Naval Disarmament, the gist of which had been communicated to certain foreign Governments, but without the text.

The Cabinet agreed—

(a) That the Chancellor of the Exchequer should circulate a re-draft of the Note to M Poincaré attached to Paper CP–317 (28), and that in the absence of any criticism from any of his colleagues he should have authority to despatch the Note without further discussion at the Cabinet:

(b) That the form and method of the communications to be made to the various foreign Governments concerned should be left for arrangement between the Acting Secretary of State for Foreign Affairs and the Chancellor of the Exchequer.

Winston S. Churchill: Cabinet memorandum[1]

(Churchill papers: 22/207)

31 October 1928   Treasury Chambers
Secret
To Be Kept Under Lock and Key

REPARATIONS AND WAR DEBTS

I was on the point on the 30th October of circulating to the Cabinet a revised draft of the Note to M Poincaré on the subject of the proposed Reparation Enquiry, when the corresponding document from the French Government was delivered at the Treasury. At about the same time the German Chargé d' Affaires[2] called upon the Acting Foreign Secretary and left a statement of the views of his Government on the same question. Translations of these documents are annexed. After considering them I have come to the conclusion that it is advisable to make certain slight modifications in our draft. These modifications are embodied in the attached document which I propose now to send to the British Ambassador in Paris with instructions to him to deliver it personally to M Poincaré on Friday. The modifications made are as follows:—

(a) In view of the emphasis laid by M Poincaré upon the maintenance of the Spa percentages, it has been thought advisable to omit anything

---

[1] Circulated to the Cabinet as Cabinet paper 326 of 1928.

[2] In the absence of the Ambassador, Friedrich Sthamer, the German Chargé d'Affaires was the Counsellor of Embassy, Hans Heinrich Dieckhoff.

which might be construed as a direct challenge to the agreements now in force for regulating the distribution of German payments.

(*b*) In order that the British memorandum may be in a form in which it can be shown textually to the other Allies, the final paragraph of the original draft (relating to the ratification of the Churchill–Caillaux Agreement) has been deleted, but Sir W. Tyrrell will be instructed to hand this to M Poincaré separately but simultaneously.

WSC

November 1928

Winston S. Churchill to Clementine Churchill

(Spencer-Churchill papers)

7 November 1928

My darling one,

I sent you a telegram this morning & hope you have found comfortable quarters.[1] I expect to hear from you tomorrow about it all. I am sure the dullness & tiresome treatment will be a vy small price to pay for a reasonable share of health.

I am to take the main Amendnt on Unemp't tomorrow & have a heavy speech to prepare. So I am dining alone with D, as I did last night & sitting up to work.

The session opens super-tame. The PM almost mute—a sort of Coolidge or Hoover. It is astonishing what goes down in these days of mass politics. One thing is as good as another. All the old Parliamentary drama & personal clashes are gone—perhaps for ever.

So Hoover has swept the board—I feel this is not good for us. Poor old England—she is being slowly but surely forced into the shade. I have a fairly good speech for tomorrow. Perhaps you will read it.[2]

I am taking no end of pains.

Your ever loving
W

[1] Clementine Churchill was at a nursing home at Northampton.

[2] On 8 November 1928 Churchill was the first speaker to speak against a Labour Party amendment to the motion accepting the King's speech. The amendment described the Government's proposals as 'utterly inadequate to meet the existing industrial situation'. For Churchill's speech, see page 1374, note 1.

Cabinet Meeting: minutes

(Churchill papers: 22/213)

7 November 1928   10 Downing Street
11.30 am

THE CHANCELLOR OF THE EXCHEQUER gave a favourable account of his interview with the Italian representative on Reparations, and at his request the Acting Secretary of State for Foreign Affairs read a message he had received from M Poincaré which included a statement to the effect that Mr Parker Gilbert did not now desire to be used as the channel of communication for informing the German Government of the views of the British and French Governments, and that in these circumstances M Poincaré thought it would be advisable for the British and French Governments to communicate to the German Government the messages they had interchanged.

The Chancellor of the Exchequer said he would like to have a few days to think over this question, which appeared feasible, owing to the Government crisis in France,[1] and he would advise the Cabinet on the subject at an early date.

Committee of Imperial Defence: minutes

(Churchill papers: 22/207)

8 November 1928
Secret

THE COMMITTEE had under consideration—

(*a*) An Annual Review of Imperial Defence by the Chiefs of Staff Sub-Committee (CID Paper No 900-B).
(*b*) Papers prepared for the use of the Chiefs of Staff Sub-Committee in drawing up their Annual Review (CID Paper No 899-B).

---

[1] Poincaré had himself resigned on 6 November 1928, following a crisis in which he had secured the resignation of the four Radical Party members of his Cabinet. After five days of crisis, he agreed to form a Government, and did so, without a single Radical Minister. The Government formed on November 11 was the first in thirty years not to contain a Radical Minister. Briand remained Foreign Minister, Painlevé Minister of War, Barthou Minister of Justice and Loucheur Minister of Labour. The new Ministers included André Maginot, Minister of Colonies, and Henri Chéron, Minister of Finance (a post he held until February 1930).

SIR HUGH TRENCHARD said that the Review took the form of a comparison between policy and obligations on the one hand and defensive resources on the other. This method had been adopted not in any critical spirit, but because it was thought advisable to bring together in one paper the various assumptions on which defence preparations were based, and the state of readiness of the various measures which had been approved. Having reviewed the situation, a list of items was included in the Report which, in the view of the Chiefs of Staff, required development gradually, and were therefore shown as of the first category of importance, and also a further list of items which might be defined as falling in the second category of importance.

MR CHURCHILL considered the Report, being a review by the highest military authorities available on the subject of Imperial Defence, was a document of considerable importance, which had obviously been prepared with the greatest care. He did not wish to pass any comment on any of the details contained in this Report, but would confine his remarks to one general observation. He urged that, having regard to all the developments in the international sphere with the object of ensuring peace between nations, there was every reason to secure a reduction in the total amount of the Service Estimates, and that, unless some such reduction was effected in the Estimates for next year, there would be a feeling of disappointment among large classes of the people of this country. In his view, the total sum for all three Services should not exceed £110,000,000, which only involved a reduction of £4½ million on the present Estimates.

After the Ministers at the head of the three Service Departments had entered a *caveat* regarding the difficulties of any large reduction of their estimates following the notable cuts of recent years—

THE PRIME MINISTER observed that, though, in his view, it was proper for the Chancellor of the Exchequer to point out the need for a reduction in the total Estimates of the Fighting Services, yet a meeting of the Committee of Imperial Defence was not the proper occasion for a discussion on this matter. He suggested, therefore, that the Committee should approve the Report of the Chiefs of Staff Sub-Committee, and that the consideration of the point raised by the Chancellor of the Exchequer should take place at the next convenient meeting of the Cabinet.

Winston S. Churchill to Commander Spenser Grey[1]

(*Churchill papers: 1/200*)

9 November 1928

My dear Grey,

I send you a written receipt for the £218 which you have paid me in cash.

It was a pleasure to me five years ago to be of service to you, and I am deeply touched by the punctilious manner in which in spite of all your misfortunes you have insisted upon discharging this debt to a friend who would certainly have never reclaimed it.

I do hope you will keep in touch with me, and let me know if there is anything I can do.

With every good wish,
Believe me,
Yours very sincerely,
Winston S. Churchill

Winston S. Churchill to Clementine Churchill

(*Spencer-Churchill papers*)

9 November 1928

My poor darling Starving Powser,

What a tantalus picture you draw of yr exiguous dietary & the suave odours of luncheon coming thro the door![2] I hope you will not let it depress you. I am sure the eradication of poison must be all to the good, & well worth achieving.

I am writing from the Bench, while Steel-Maitland is speaking. You will

[1] Spenser Douglas Adair Grey, 1889–1937. A descendant of Earl Grey (of the 1832 Reform Bill). Entered the Royal Navy, 1907. Sub-Lieutenant, 1909, by which time he was one of the very few officers of any rank to possess his own aeroplane. An aviator in one of the first sea plane experiments, 1911. In 1912 he took Churchill on his first flight, and later gave Churchill flying lessons. Seriously injured after his plane crashed, following a spin, 1913. Wing-Commander, Royal Naval Air Service, 1914. Awarded the DSO in October 1914, when he commanded a flight of aeroplanes which flew over Cologne (8 October 1914), circling the city while under anti-aircraft fire, and discharging his bombs on a military railway station. Sent on an Admiralty mission to purchase six flying boats in the United States, December 1914. Commander, flying boat experimental tests, Hendon, March 1916. Liaison Officer with the United States Air Force, Paris, 1917. Invalided out of the Royal Air Force, with the rank of Lieutenant-Colonel, 1919. He died, at the age of 48, after falling nine stories while fixing a wireless aerial on the roof of his flat.

[2] Clementine Churchill was still at a nursing home at Northampton (see Churchill's letter to A. C. Sheepshanks of 17 November 1928, quoted on page 1379 of this volume).

perhaps have seen what I said yesterday. It went off all right. It is meant to cover the whole of this depressing ground.[1]

You remember Spenser Grey. Six years ago I guaranteed him a loan at his bank for £200. He failed to repay & the bank came down on me. Yesterday he arrived at the Treasury & left £218 in notes wh he had saved up in 4 years out of an income of less than £250 a year—on wh he has to keep himself & wife. I was deeply moved. It was tragic to see him crippled, ill, poor, sunk in failure, & remember the brilliant daring young figure of our Admiralty days. But his pride was still unconquerable. It wd have been an insult to refuse to accept this hard saved money. That was clear from his manner.

I will send you his letter. Last night Boothby & I went to 'Young Woodley'.[2] I thought it awfully good. Unlike so many plays it maintains its poise to the vy end. The Schoolmaster reminded us both of Sir Robert Horne!

Tonight I take Diana to the Guildhall—& have to make a short speech.[3]

[1] Churchill was the second speaker in the Unemployment debate on 8 November 1928, following J. L. Clynes, who moved the Labour amendment to the Address (see page 1370, note 2). Churchill began by saying that the Socialists, who took the easy course of blaming the government of the day for unemployment, were at fault for a 'large part of the misfortunes of the present day', and he asked Clynes: 'Has the right hon Gentleman forgotten the disaster of 1926—the general strike and the coal stoppage?' These were, Churchill continued, 'The one, supreme, definite, obvious, recent cause of the delay in the general trade revival.' Churchill went on, however, to appeal for an end to party bickering on this 'sorrowful problem', pointing out that serious unemployment plagued both the United States, a purely capitalist country, and the Soviet Union, where the 'most ruthless example of socialism' had come to power. Unemployment was the 'legacy' of the Great War. In Britain, 'the aggravation of the problem of unemployment is summed up in the black word coal'. In the coal industry, the numbers of unemployed 'will not be diminished but may be increased by every improvement in the efficiency of the industry'. Many miners would have to move to new industries. The fortunes of these and other unemployed could 'only be relieved by a general improvement in British trade and by a revival of world trade and prosperity'. 'The first and main contribution,' he continued, 'of the Government is assist trade and employment generally by a comprehensive rating relief scheme to agriculture and to industry,' which would 'relieve industry of ¾, and agriculture of all, of its rates at a cost of £22,000,000 to the Exchequer.'

[2] The longest running play of 1928, 'Young Woodley', by John van Druten, achieved notoriety by having first been banned by the Censor, who then decided to allow it to be shown on account of van Druten's sensitive handling of the otherwise difficult theme, the story of a boy who fell in love with his schoolmaster's wife. The boy was played by Frank Lawton, the schoolmaster by David Horne.

[3] Speaking at the Lord Mayor's Banquet on 9 November 1928, Churchill (who was accompanied by his daughter Diana) said, in the presence of the Turkish Ambassador: 'It is no disparagement of our abiding comradeship and affection for our old friends and former Allies that we should say that there is a pleasure of its own in welcoming at these banquets of peace and good will the representatives of the brave nations from whom we were so terribly sundered in the War.' Commenting on the art of diplomacy, Churchill said: 'There is a tendency nowadays to represent diplomacy as if it was the art of saying polite, agreeable, and highly commendable things. But this is a dangerous error. Diplomacy is a means of telling plain truths without giving offence, and nothing could be worse than that the public relations of great countries should be covered with a veneer of admirable sentiment and impeccable

I have accepted for us both to dine with Sarah W[1] on the 27th Nov.

Chartwell items are 1) the bricklayer Pattenden who went on piece work at 38/- per 1,000 bricks he finding the labour—has nearly finished the wall this week. He has laid about 3 times what he used to; 2) The Cygnets have been ordered a meat diet by the Zoo experts. They say they ought to live all right now.

Your ever devoted & loving
W

Lord Beaverbrook to L. S. Amery

(*Beaverbrook papers*)

12 November 1928

I dined with Churchill last night. He put forward the argument that unemployment will not do the Government any widespread damage at the polls. Bad unemployment, he maintained, was confined to certain areas, which would go against the Government anyhow, but it was not sufficiently spread to have a universal damaging influence all over the country. I cannot say that I agree with him. I think unemployment will be the one and only issue which counts.

Winston S. Churchill to Clementine Churchill

(*Spencer-Churchill papers*)

12 November 1928

My darling one,

Max's show last night was vy good: a little too theatrical this time; but still I enjoyed it vy much. We sat up late talking. He declares the Soc & Libs are coming in. He will not give us any real help. My time wd come he said the moment we got into Opposition. I rather agree.

The other guests were McKenna, Dean Inge[2] & his Deaness—an amiable

---

civility, and that, underneath, all sorts of feelings and all sorts of aspirations should not find their effective personal expression through the representatives who meet together in the different States.'

[1] Lady Sarah Wilson (see page 9, note 2).

[2] William Ralph Inge, 1860–1954. Dean of St Paul's, 1911–34. Author of more than thirty books on religious themes. His wife Mary, whom he married in 1905, was the daughter of H. M. Spooner, Archdeacon of Maidstone, and a granddaughter of Bishop Harvey Godwin.

woman—& a vy delightful Presbyterian minister Canon Fleming[1]—& Arnold Bennett.[2] A veritable odour of sanctity & moral elevation. They all want to hang Montagu Norman (except the Clerics).

I have just come back from the Law Courts. My fifth ceremony! The time flashes away. Next year is in the unknown. Tender love my darling—I was so glad to see you so cheery & brave. It is a trial—but perhaps the result will make amends.

Diana comes to see you tomorrow

Yr ever devoted
W

PS. A harsh speech of Coolidge.[3]

Winston S. Churchill to Lord Rothermere

(*Churchill papers: 2/159*)

14 November 1928
Private

Your letter, though sent by special messenger, was a long time on the road and it is only now that I have an opportunity of answering it.

I do not think you are right about the women. On the whole they are slightly more conservative than men. The Berlin elections showed very clearly that their bias is anti-extremist, either Right or Left. Only a very small proportion of the new voters are industrial, and quite a large proportion are of classes or in situations predominantly Conservative. No doubt

[1] John Robert Fleming, 1858–1937. General Secretary of the Alliance of Presbyterian and Reformed Churches, 1919–27. A leading advocate of 'International Christianity'. One of the founders of the Hymn Society, 1936. A member of the National Liberal Club.

[2] Enoch Arnold Bennett, 1867–1931. Author, playwright and man of letters. Editor of *Woman*, 1896–1900. He published his first novel in 1898, two of his most famous, *The Old Wives' Tale* and *Clayhanger*, in 1908 and 1910. In charge of propaganda in France for the Ministry of Information (under Lord Beaverbrook), 1917–18; acting head of the Ministry of Information, October 1918. He satirized social and political power in two of his novels, *The Pretty Lady* (1918) and *Lord Raingo* (1926).

[3] President Coolidge, in an Armistice Day speech in Washington on 11 November 1928, had paid tribute to the two million American men and women who went to France for combat, and to the thousands who were killed and wounded. 'It is sometimes represented,' he said, 'that we made a profit out of the war. Nothing could be further from the truth.' The cost of the war to the United States had been 'perfectly enormous', amounting to half the national wealth, and she had sought no territories in return. 'No citizen of the United States needs to make any apology to anybody anywhere for not having done our duty to the cause of world liberty.' The US attitude to Europe after the war had been one of 'patience, consideration, restraint, and assistance'. 'We have accepted settlements of obligations, not in accordance with what was due, but in accordance with the merciful principle of what the debtors could pay.'

existing large Socialist majorities in many seats will become much larger. But the country is divided by its constituencies into more or less watertight compartments and each has to be flooded separately. I do not therefore think that this new factor will be adverse. It is quite surprising how many Conservative Members think it is going to be favourable. An MP has a feeling about these things which is instinctive. However, admittedly, much is unknowable.

I think also that you are unduly pessimistic about the general movement of opinion in the country. A great many people will not want to put the Socialists in power. For England to weaken herself in this way when other great Democracies are voting for strong Conservative Governments or supporting stable regimes in other forms would, I am sure, be thought unduly weakening to our national interest. I doubt very much whether the mind of Britain is unconscious of what is taking place in the world, or that it seeks a period of political agitation. I am sure that all Conservative forces will present a solid front on the issue of Tory or Socialist.

Of course, if you and Max rock the boat it will do a good deal of harm and I am sure you will be very sorry after the Socialists are returned. Certainly everything you have stood for, friendship with France, breach with Russia, economy in expenditure, reduction of taxation, will be violently overthrown. The addition of 40 or 50 millions to direct taxation would not particularly hurt the rich individuals affected, but I am sure it would be a great injury to the saving power of the nation. Our capital accumulations are horribly depleted by the war and the strikes, and to draw upon that heavily for further social easements would be injurious to all classes. It is not for the sake of the rich people but for the economic strength of the country that I should deprecate this new assault on capital.

However, this is a free country and everyone may try to make his own bed so long as he is ready to lie in it afterwards.

I am sorry that you have gone off the deep end over de-rating. An enormous amount of labour and thought has been put into this over the last three years and, although the bills have unpopular features, there is no doubt that they are greatly for the good of the country.

I am very sorry we did not have a talk before you went away, but perhaps when you return from Egypt Esmond will fix up some rendez-vous.

The times in which we live are very difficult and might easily become critical, and everyone has a great responsibility, few more than you.

Don't fall foul of Tut-ankh-amen, he is spiteful.[1]

---

[1] The tomb of Tutankhamen was discovered in the Valley of the Tomb of the Kings outside Luxor, in Egypt, on 28 November 1922, by Howard Carter, a British archaeologist who had been searching for the tomb for ten years. Carter entered the section of the tomb housing

Winston S. Churchill to Clementine Churchill

(*Spencer-Churchill papers*)

14 November 1928

My darling one,

My blood boiled too at Coolidge's proclamation. Why can't they let us alone? They have exacted every penny owing from Europe; they say they are not going to help; surely they might leave us to manage our own affairs. I absolutely agree with what you write.

I have had very busy days, trying to push the book forward and at the same time with heaps of engagements and politics. I spent yesterday afternoon preparing a speech on the Safeguarding amendment to the Address but after going through it all with Worthy decided it was better for him to do it, not me. So I handed him over my notes. He is very trustworthy, sound on fiscal matters, and a friend.

Tonight I have to preside at the Munitions Dinner and propose Lloyd George's health. Tomorrow there is Lord Dawson's[1] Medical Dinner—what I am to say God only knows. A. P. Watt, my first literary agent, before the Curtis Brown people, came yesterday with a proposal for a Life of the Duke of Marlborough, for which £8,000 was guaranteed on account of royalties in England and America. He indicated that a better offer would probably be forthcoming. This would be a long job but it certainly lies in the future, and no doubt better terms can be obtained.

Rothermere, having ordered his organs to smash up the De-rating Bill, has gone off to luxuriate in Egypt. The wretched papers loathe doing this sort of work which is against their convictions and sympathies but to which they are forced by an imperious, ill-informed, restless and sore proprietor.

It is a good thing that this stunt should be got over now instead of being kept to work up slowly as the difficulties of the Bill increase. It is like letting off fireworks in the middle of the afternoon. We shall drive the Bill through. It is a great piece of social reform and well worth fighting for amid the shallow chatter of these days.

---

the sarcophagus on 17 February 1923. Among the first five to enter this innermost chamber of the tomb were Carter, Lord Carnarvon (patron of the expedition) and his daughter, Lady Evelyn Herbert (later Lady Beauchamp). On 5 April 1923 Lord Carnarvon, then aged 57, died of pneumonia, which set in after an infected insect bite had given him a fever. This gave new vigour to a legend extending back 3,000 years, to Tutankhamen's time, that anyone who defiled a tomb was cursed, and would suffer an untimely death. In fact, of the original five to enter the tomb, only Lord Carnarvon died before 1939 (when Carter died, aged 66).

[1] Bertrand Dawson, 1864–1945. Physician, 1906. Physician-in-ordinary to King Edward VII, 1906–10; to King George V, 1910–36; to the Prince of Wales (later Edward VIII), 1929–36. Knighted, 1911; Created Baron, 1920; Viscount, 1936. Chairman, Army Medical Advisory Board, 1936–45.

I have thought of two bachelors for the Birthday Dinner, namely, Philip Sassoon and the Prof. This makes exactly eight of each kind. I am sending out invitations accordingly today.

You saw no doubt about Diana Mitford.[1] I suitably congratulated Walter.

Dearest I grieve to think of yr austerities: & what you tell me of yr weight and strength distresses me. However it is half over now—& you are in vy skilled hands. They know I suppose every inch of the barren road along wh they are leading you. Please God there is at the end of it a comfortable inn.

With my fondst love

Yr ever devoted

W

Don't worry about anything: but send for me if you feel the need.

Winston S. Churchill to A. C. Sheepshanks

(*Churchill papers: 1/200*)

17 November 1928

Dear Mr Sheepshanks,

I am much obliged to you for allowing Randolph to come with me tomorrow to see his mother. She is passing through a very trying ordeal in a Nursing Home at Northampton. One feature of her treatment is virtual starvation; and for ten days she had nothing but orange juice, which left an increasing weakness culminating in a fainting fit. The objects of the treatment are now believed to have been achieved. The system has been freed from poison, and it is hoped we shall avoid an operation for tonsils which have been a cause of much anxiety for us. All this, however, is unsettled as yet.

I am most anxious to cheer her in every way, and I am sure a visit from Randolph for a few hours will be a great pleasure and encouragement. I am glad to say that her case is not dangerous, but it is certainly one to which the word 'serious' could properly be applied.

I have told Randolph he must be in London by eleven, as we have a hundred and thirty-five miles of motoring there and back. It will be a long day for him, especially as he feels the motion of a car.

Believe me

Yours sincerely,

[1] Diana Freeman-Mitford. Sister of Nancy, Jessica, Unity and Tom Mitford. Clementine Churchill's cousin. In 1929 she married Bryan Walter Guinness, elder son of Churchill's friend Walter Guinness (later Lord Moyne). The marriage was dissolved in 1934. In 1936 she married Sir Oswald Mosley.

Winston S. Churchill: Cabinet memorandum[1]

(*Churchill papers: 22/208*)

19 November 1928　　　　　　　　　　　　　　　Treasury Chambers
Secret

ANGLO-AMERICAN RELATIONS

If the essay by Mr Craigie[2] on Anglo-American relations, which Lord Cushendun has circulated (CP 344 (28)), has no other object than to inculcate meekness and caution, it need not be dealt with in detail. But if it is intended as a prelude to renewed Naval negotiations with the United States during Mr Coolidge's tenure, I am decidedly of opinion that this would be a great mistake. We shall never agree among ourselves either to abandon our belligerent rights at sea or to cut the British Navy down by treaty to the limits which the United States considers suitable for herself. Any attempt to enforce such an agreement would divide the Conservative Party from end to end on the eve of the Election. There would be a stand-up fight in all the Constituencies on the question of whether British interests had been betrayed to the United States; and there would certainly be enough Conservatives who would sustain that view to destroy us as a political force.

But apart from these domestic aspects, surely it would be most unwise to renew negotiations with Mr Coolidge. He has just explained to the world the view-point of a New England backwoodsman. The crudity and amateurish character of this utterance is likely to offer his successor an opportunity for doing something different. It is very noticeable that Mr Hoover has let it be known that he did not see the Coolidge speech beforehand. Mr Coolidge will soon sink back into the obscurity from which only accident extracted him. His successor has the advantage of starting with the American attitude to Europe at its very worst, and it is hardly in human nature that he should not try to strike a different note and achieve solutions beyond his predecessor's scope. We ought not to make up our minds precipitately that no fair or decent treatment can be got from Mr Hoover, or that it would not pay him as an American President somewhat to improve the Coolidge Armistice Day position.

Therefore there is every reason, before plunging again into the dangerous waters of Disarmament, to wait for (*a*) our own General Election and (*b*) Mr Hoover's installation. Whatever British Government is in power in the

---

[1] Circulated to the Cabinet as Cabinet paper 358 of 1928.

[2] Robert Leslie Craigie, 1883–1959. Entered the Foreign Office, 1907. British Representative, Inter-Allied Blockade Committee, 1916–18. First Secretary, Washington, 1920–3; transferred to the Foreign Office, 1923; Counsellor, 1928; Assistant Under-Secretary of State, 1934–7. Knighted, 1936. Privy Councillor, 1937. Ambassador to Japan, 1937–41. UK Representative to the United Nations War Crimes Commission, 1945–8.

summer of 1929 cannot have a worse, and may conceivably have a better, chance of reopening the Naval controversy.

Above all things I deprecate a panic mood in our relations with the United States. A very sensible article in the 'New Statesman', of all papers, is reprinted herewith as a corrective to undue pessimism. After all, the only bad thing that has happened in Anglo-American relations is our not being able to agree about cutting our Navy down. We are told that this has wiped out all, or most of, the effects of such great events as the abrogation of the Anglo-Japanese Alliance, the settlement of the Irish question, the Washington Treaty and the Anglo-American debt settlement. If so, it only shows how little advantage is to be gained by making such efforts to conciliate American opinion. Whatever may have been done at enormous cost and sacrifice to keep up friendship is apparently swept away by the smallest little tiff or misunderstanding, and you have to start again and placate the Americans by another batch of substantial or even vital concessions.

All our present troubles are admittedly due to Geneva. Our well-meant endeavours to further the work of the Disarmament Commission have led us into an unfortunate and humiliating position both at home and abroad. But this is all passing away. The great mass of the British public do not desire to see England obsequious to the United States, and would be deeply anxious if it were thought the Government were ready to palter with our Naval security. I do not think that the Geneva discussions have cut very deep in England, or that they will play an important part in the forthcoming Election. Anyhow, the least said, the soonest mended.

So far as America is concerned, she is going to build her fifteen cruisers in three years. Why shouldn't she? We have built or are building nineteen at the present time, and in the next three years I suppose we shall build six or seven more. I cannot see how anyone could complain of the United States equipping her costly battle fleet with an adequate modern cruiser force. They have done nothing so far; and nothing they have even talked about seriously up to the present goes beyond the normal balance of a well equipped American fleet equal in aggressive units to our own. And three or four years must pass before they even reach parity in 10,000-ton 8-inch gun vessels.

Obviously our policy is to sit quite quiet, to be independent and cool and polite, to let them build their fifteen ships and to build ourselves as little as we possibly can in the interval. Deeds count much more than words in disarmament. The mere slowing down of our programme last year eased the whole rupture of the Geneva Conference. If the Americans feel they are building a great many more ships in the next three years than anybody else, and we remain quite content and do nothing hurriedly or excitedly, the 1931

Conference at Washington may open under conditions far more favourable than any hitherto experienced.

I cannot see that we shall lose anything or run any great risk by jogging along quietly on our path—which is an honourable and peaceful path—and holding firmly to our rightful Naval position so admirably explained by Sir Austen Chamberlain at Ottawa. In this way the Naval question will drop into the background for the time being. America will be building much more than anybody else, so presumably she will be happy. We shall have kept controversial references to the United States our of our General Election, and the present ill-temper will gradually subside. It is most important, however, to realise that Great Britain and her Empire are a strong force in the world, that her day is not yet over, that we have a right to live as well as other countries, and that we have come through a series of perils and seen the end of many giants in the past. I do not believe that such a policy of wise and deliberate inactivity, and even lethargy, at this juncture will get us into any trouble, or that the United States will either set about us in berserk fury or markedly reduce the volume of her tourist traffic as Mr Craigie so variously suggests.

WSC

Cabinet minutes

(*Churchill papers: 22/213*)

21 November 1928   10 Downing Street
11.30 am

... The Cabinet had before them a Memorandum by the First Lord of the Admiralty (Paper CP 349 (28)) to the effect that the Board of Admiralty consider that the risk involved in the supply of motor-boats and mines to Soviet Russia can be accepted.

THE CHANCELLOR OF THE EXCHEQUER asked to place on record that, while he accepted the views of the Cabinet on this question, he would personally have preferred not to grant permission for the supply of war material to Soviet Russia which might, in certain circumstances, be used against us.

The Cabinet agreed—

That the Acting Secretary of State for Foreign Affairs should be authorised to inform Messrs Vickers that permission would be granted them to carry out an order for the supply of motor-boats and submarine mines to the Soviet Government.

Winston S. Churchill to Clementine Churchill

(Spencer-Churchill papers)

21 November 1928   House of Commons

My darling one,

Baldwin has gone to Scotland & I am in charge. I have been dictating Book for 2 hours after Cabinet & much other business, & am tired. Poor Grey how he is dogged by ill fortune—the 1st Lady G—his brother eaten by a lion. The war wh broke him—blindness—another brother killed by wild beasts: political isolation—no children—& now this. All these vy various trials of different magnitude but all severe have singled him out. Just as he had built for himself a new home—a little island of happiness & charm to end his days—it is destroyed & he is a wanderer. I am grieved for him & have been trying to write a few lines of comfort.[1]

The enclosed correspondence with Rothermere will amuse you. Send it back.

The big debate is next week. It is quite all right & the premature & excessive attack will only strengthen the Govt case.

Tonight I dine with Venetia. No doubt Bezique.

I am in the toils of my book. Only 5 weeks more & such a lot to do & polish. But it will be all right. We have reached the stage where 'le mieux est l'ennemi du bien'.

My precious in 6 days you will be home. How joyous that will be! How I hope the cure will have been effective & will (after a while) restore you to health.

Tender love my dearest Clemmie from
Your devoted
W

[1] The death of Grey's second wife was one of a series of personal blows which had affected his life. His first wife, Dorothy Widrington, whom he had married in 1885, had died in 1906 as a result of a carriage accident only a few months before Grey had become Foreign Secretary. His elder brother had been killed by a lion in 1911. In 1917 his house in Scotland, Fallodon, was burnt down. In 1923 his cottage on the River Itchen in Hampshire was destroyed by fire. By 1925 increasing blindness made work and writing almost impossible. In the summer of 1928 his younger brother had been killed by a buffalo; then, on 18 November 1928, his second wife, Pamela Wyndham (the widow of the 1st Baron Glenconner), whom Grey had married in 1922, died. Grey himself died on 7 September 1933.

Winston S. Churchill to Clementine Churchill

(*Spencer-Churchill papers*)

22 November 1928

My dearest

This is indeed good news.

Find out from the Dr whether it wd be too much for you to be met at Euston by the big motor & brought *straight* down to Chartwell. I do not think it wd tire you if you did not get out of the car but simply ran through. If however you wish to stay in London, kiss Maria, & recuperate on Saturday night, try to come to Ch on Sunday & sleep. Let me know what you will do. I hope to be able to stay at C on Saty night, but if you need me I will come up.

I am to see the doctor this evening. But it is for you to decide.

I enclose you Rothermere's latest.

My fondest love
Yr devoted
W

Here are the new bank notes. They cost 300,000 a year more than the others, & are generally abused.[1] It is said that they are forger-proof.

bring them back
they are No 5

Winston S. Churchill to Sir Warren Fisher

(*Churchill papers: 18/75*)

23 November 1928

The less we talk about Disarmament at Geneva and the more we do in Disarmament on our own estimates, the better. Almost the sole cause of ill-feeling, suspicion and advertisement to military matters has been the Geneva Disarmament discussions. I should very much like to see them broken off for a while. The parity with America forces a jealous scrutiny of every ship and gun undreamed of before. It is far better for nations to be free. All the naval and military agreements now being discussed are designed to preserve armaments at very high levels.

I agree about the Admiralty anti-Japanese agitation having woken up America on cruisers. Let me see what I circulated to the Cabinet about this in 1925–26.

[1] On 22 November 1928 the Bank of England issued new £1 and 10 shilling notes, to replace the Treasury notes then in circulation. (On the same day an anonymous donor sent Churchill £1,000 towards the reduction of the National Debt.)

Stanley Baldwin to Winston S. Churchill

(*Churchill papers: 1/200*)

St Andrew's Day 1928   10 Downing Street

My dear Winston,

I woke this morning to find that it is your birthday.

To communicate with No 11 was the work of a moment and I learned that you had already fled overnight to keep the sacred day in your own home.

A brief reference to Dod[1] shews me that you are still a child, so I may say 'Many Happy Returns' and a happy birthday to you to-day.

Yours ever
SB

[1] *Dod's Parliamentary Companion*, published annually, an indispensable source of information about all Members of Parliament and Peers. On 30 November 1928 Churchill reached his fifty-fourth birthday.

December 1928

Winston S. Churchill to Lord Rothermere: telegram[1]

(*Churchill papers: 18/72*)

2 December 1928

Prolonged debate now beginning will make all clear and enable you to judge. You know my feelings on the private aspects. I have never forgotten our relations in the war.

Winston

Winston S. Churchill to Lord Rothermere: telegram

(*Churchill papers: 18/72*)

2 December 1928

Your papers are being forced into astonishing untruths easily, certainly and swiftly disprovable. Am providing from Exchequer entire cost relief to industry and agriculture and eight and a half millions more for general rate relief. Distribution of this money such that in ninety seven per cent of parishes, new Government grant will always exceed money now lost on derating industry and agriculture and three persons out of four throughout whole country will permanently enjoy lower rates notwithstanding the levelling of the rates for poor relief and highways. Whole scheme of course independent of revaluation now proceeding under Act 1925 which cannot increase total burden of rates or adversely affect proportion of those who gain. All this will be proved to Parliament in next few weeks and ratepayers will know before election. Cannot understand how you have been so misinformed or why you should discredit your organs by driving them up against a wall of utter stultification. No question of dropping or serious modification Bill. No one here at all rattled but deeply regret you should darken counsel. Socialists will not come in but if they do you will have a great responsibility. Do come back and attend to these matters yourself.

Winston

[1] Lord Rothermere was at Shepherd's Hotel, Cairo. He had declared, through the *Daily Mail*, his complete opposition to Churchill's derating proposals, which the *Daily Mail* had described as 'The Higher Rates Bill'.

Winston S. Churchill to Lord Rothermere: telegram

(*Churchill papers: 18/72*)

2 December 1928

Whole thirty five millions will be found by Exchequer. Calculate Petrol Duty and Suspensory Fund will provide all money needed up till April 1931. If more is needed in later years Exchequer must provide. This pays for Colman's mustard relief and for reduction rates Yarmouth landlady amounting to ninepence in pound. Cheltenham comes out all square at the moment and will gain later permanently. Scheme provides new system assisting local authorities according to needs without inciting to fresh extravagance as well as smoothing out disparities poor law and highway rates. Elaboration largely result of care to meet every reasonable claim. LCC have accepted for London and good prospects amicable agreement with principle Associations local authorities to-morrow. Glad you are slowing down papers. Arranging no hostile Ministerial references in debate.

Winston

J. C. C. Davidson to Lord Irwin

(*Irwin papers*)

3 December 1928

Winston as usual is full of vitality and thinks of nothing but 'Der Tag' next year. I hear that even in the contemplation of the Monarch's demise, he has expressed the view that 'the bands will all be playing "God save the King", and that a wave of patriotism will sweep over the country which will be very good for our Party'.

He has already had a telegraphic correspondence with Rothermere who is staying at Shepherd's Hotel, signed Winston and Harold, which has had the effect of damping down the Daily Mail's attack on what they call the 'Higher Rates Bill'.

Esmond Harmsworth to Winston S. Churchill

(*Churchill papers: 2/159*)

3 December 1928   Northcliffe House
                                            London EC4

Dear Winston,

At the dinner to Philip the other night in the House, we really had no opportunity to discuss the cables that had been exchanged between you and my father.

It gave me great pleasure to know that sympathy at any rate had been established between you. The moment my father returns I will discuss the whole matter with him and then come and see you.

Apart from the fact of the friendship that exists and I hope will always exist between us—you have been apparently the only one to fully realise the seriousness of the position that was rapidly being created.

Although my ambitions and interests now are centred firmly in another sphere, that does not prevent keen regret when I see those whom I like having their chances deliberately thrown away through sheer stupidity or carelessness.

Your action must be made successful and if I can do anything to help I am only too willing to do so.

Yrs ever
Esmond

Winston S. Churchill: Cabinet memorandum[1]

(Churchill papers: 22/208)

3 December 1928   Treasury Chambers
Secret

THE ESTIMATES FOR THE FIGHTING SERVICES, 1929

Following upon the preliminary discussion which took place at the last meeting of the Committee of Imperial Defence, I desire to draw the attention of my colleagues to the question of the Estimates for the Fighting Services for 1929. I append a table showing the expenditure for the last five years, from which it will be seen that the expenditure estimated to be incurred in the current year is higher than the expenditure of the year in which we took office. I recognise that during this period substantial economies have been made in the cost of Middle East Defence. On the other hand, the general level of wholesale prices has fallen since the autumn of 1924 by no less than $17\frac{1}{2}$ per cent, and this fact, together with the reduced rates of pay for new recruits introduced in 1925, has afforded considerable relief to the Estimates.

In my opinion, it is necessary for us to effect a marked reduction in these Estimates in 1929 as compared with the current year. In July last the Cabinet decided, on the recommendation of the Committee of Imperial Defence, that it should be assumed, for the purposes of framing the Estimates of the Fighting Services, that at any given date there will be no major war for ten years. In his speech at the Guildhall on the 9th November, the Prime Minister,

---

[1] Circulated to the Cabinet as Cabinet paper 379 of 1928.

referring to the Kellogg Pact, said: 'In spirit, every nation that signs that Pact has got to keep it before its mind whenever it examines its own armaments; wherever it prepares estimates of its own armaments, it must realise what the implications of that Pact are.'[1]

I hold strongly that present political circumstances require us to give substantial effect to these considerations, and to the expectations of economies in the Estimates generally which the public will base upon the language used in the King's Speech, and I do not think that the situation will be adequately met by anything less than a reduction of the total provision for the Fighting Services in 1929 to £110 millions as a maximum, that is, a reduction of at least £4½ millions on this year's estimates. Moreover such provisional indications of next year's revenue and expenditure as are now available make it plain that, in view of the commitments involved by the derating scheme and the unemployment situation, I shall require to secure savings of at least double that amount on the total Estimates in order to balance the Budget. Civil Estimates, excluding the cost of Middle East Defence, have been kept down to practically the same figure as in 1924, in spite of large increases of expenditure under statute on Housing, Widows' and Old Age Pensions, and the Beet Sugar Subsidy, and in view of the reductions effected last year I cannot look for further appreciable savings on this head.

I therefore ask the Cabinet, on urgent grounds of policy as well as of financial necessity, to request the Defence Ministers to arrange in consultation that the total of the Fighting Services Estimates for 1929 do not exceed £110 millions. I suggest, as a rough guide, that the reduction might be divided as to £2,750,000 on Navy Estimates, £1,000,000 on Army and £750,000 on Air Estimates. I shall also be prepared, if desired, to offer suggestions as to the manner in which this might be done, but I should naturally prefer that the necessary reductions should be made in the ways in which the responsible Ministers may themselves think best.

WSC

---

[1] On 28 December 1927 Frank Kellogg, the United States Secretary of State, had proposed a multinational pact outlawing war (based on a scheme put forward by a private American citizen, Salmon Oliver Levinson, a Chicago lawyer). The pact, entitled 'The General Pact for the Renunciation of War', was signed in Paris on 27 August 1928. Known as the 'Briand–Kellogg Pact', it was signed by (among others), Briand for France, Streseman for Germany, Cushendun for Britain and for India, Mackenzie King for Canada and Beneš for Czechoslovakia. At the same time, the British and the French Governments also endorsed Kellogg's statement that sovereign States alone were competent to decide when they were justified to resort to war in self-defence; this upset many supporters of the League of Nations, under whose Covenant the League States specifically undertook in no case to resort to war before submitting the dispute to some form of procedure for its peaceful solution.

Winston S. Churchill: Cabinet memorandum[1]

(*Churchill papers: 22/208*)

3 December 1928   Treasury Chambers
Secret

COMPENSATION FOR IRISH LOYALISTS

1. The Dominions Office now estimate that it will probably require from £50,000 to £70,000 in addition to the £1 million already provided to pay the awards of the Irish Grants Committee on the scale announced in February last (up to £1,000 in full, and 60 per cent over £1,000). I am bound reluctantly to acquiesce in the additional amount required to pay claims on this scale, but I cannot recommend the Cabinet to agree that all awards should be paid in full. The Dominions Office estimate that payment in full may cost £1,400,000, but that it is by no means impossible that this sum may be exceeded. In fact, it appears that no reliable estimate can even yet be made, and that the Cabinet, in agreeing to pay awards in full, would be committing the Exchequer to expenditure of an unknown and possibly much larger amount.

2. The question whether the Committee's recommendations should be paid in full was exhaustively considered by the Cabinet in February, and the view then prevailed that a definite limit must be fixed to the liabilities of the Exchequer. In other words, it was decided to provide against the contingency of the total awards exceeding £1 million by deciding that in that event a reduced payment must be made on the larger claims. This is exactly the contingency which has now arisen. There can be no justification in these circumstances for departing from that decision which was reached after full consideration, and announced to Parliament as the final decision of the Government.

3. I feel bound to point out that the Exchequer has been treated very badly in regard to this whole matter. In July 1926 the Cabinet decided that the maximum which could be provided to meet the Irish Grants Committee's recommendations was £400,000, and while I agreed that this limit should not be formally inserted in the Terms of Reference, it was communicated privately to the Committee. The Secretary of State for Dominion Affairs at that time himself suggested that, if the total awards seriously exceeded that sum, it would be necessary to make a percentage reduction so as to bring them within the amount. In May 1927 he told the House of Commons that, while not prepared to pledge themselves, the Government hoped to be able to pay the Committee's recommendations in full. After the Committee had

---

[1] Circulated to the Cabinet as Cabinet paper 376 of 1928.

proceeded further with its work, it became apparent that a far larger sum would be required to pay the recommendations in full, and when the matter was before the Cabinet in December 1927, it was estimated that the total awards would amount to about £1,160,000. The Dominions Office, however, subsequently expressed the view that the amount would be under £1 million, and on the basis of this estimate the House of Commons was informed on the 20th February, 1928, that the total compensation recommended by the Committee might be approximately £1 million, and on the 23rd February, that it was believed that the total provision of £1 million would enable the awards to be paid in full. It now appears, however, that in reaching this estimate in February the Dominions Office had made no allowance, or a very insufficient allowance, for the additional claims which resulted from the decision which had already been reached to extend the time limit for making claims from the 31st January, 1927, to the 28th February, 1928. This has resulted in 1,096 fresh claims on which the Committee are expected to make 540 additional as a sign of weakness rather than of generosity; and they are much more likely to appreciate an arrangement by which we undertake to waive *future* instalments of the Boxer Indemnity on condition that the existing balance (which now amounts to £2,604,781) is retained by the Exchequer.

THE BOXER INDEMNITY[1]

4. His Majesty's Government are being frequently attacked on the ground that they are too readily disposed to abandon the claims of this country on foreign nations, and I must urge the Cabinet to reject the proposal made by the Foreign Office. Instead, I suggest that Sir M. Lampson should be instructed to negotiate an agreement with the Chinese Government by which His Majesty's Government should surrender all *future* instalments of the Indemnity on condition that, firstly, the existing Fund is paid to the British Exchequer on account of the expenditure incurred over Shanghai; and secondly, satisfactory arrangements are reached about the Commercial Treaty and the settlement of private British claims. As regards procedure, the existing Fund could be taken into the Exchequer by a single clause in

[1] Following the Boxer rebellion of 1900, the Powers reached an agreement with China in 1901 that an indemnity of £67½ million would be paid, in thirty-nine instalments, at 4% interest, mostly to come from a 5% tariff on China's exports. The British share of the annual payment was £400,000. In December 1922 the British Cabinet decided that the annual indemnity would be accumulated, and applied 'to purposes beneficial to the mutual interests of England and China'. In June 1925 the China Indemnity Act was passed, providing a procedure for dispensing from the fund and describing the specific purposes to which it should be applied. In 1928 negotiations were begun with the Chinese government on economic issues, two among which were the termination of the annual instalments and the disposal of the fund. No agreement was reached on either of these points during the Conservative government of 1924–9, or during the Labour government which followed.

the next Finance Bill, and future instalments could be renounced by executive action, a Treasury Minute being laid before Parliament at the time of, or shortly after, the announcement of the decision.

WSC

Winston S. Churchill to George Lambert
(*Churchill papers: 2/159*)

4 December 1928   Eaton Hall[1]

Private

My dear George,

Cogent reasons are clearly set out in the report of my speech in Hansard, advocating the return of Lord Fisher to the Admiralty.[2] These should be read. The motive power was my apprehension and foreboding of the sudden development of a new German submarine campaign, which actually occurred a year later, and my desire to see the utmost energy used in preparing against it. This seemed so important that the differences between Lord Fisher and myself, which had ended with the Dardanelles and lay in the past, ought not to have obstructed his return to usefulness. I do not wish to be quoted however directly in this. Since those days Lord Oxford has published Lord Fisher's ultimatum to the Cabinet when he resigned from the Admiralty. I had never seen this before. It undoubtedly reflects upon the *bona fides* of his action, and shows that it did not arise from worry or lack of nerve as I had supposed but was part of a definite bid for un-Constitutional power. You should read it, if you have not already done so.

Yours sincerely,
Winston S. Churchill

Philippi!

Robert Boothby to Winston S. Churchill
(*Churchill papers: 18/72*)

7 December 1928   Treasury Chambers

Dear Chancellor,

I am bound to make my position clear in my constituency with regard to Russia, and whilst I have no reason to suppose that my views conflict with

[1] The Duke of Westminster's country house, near Chester.
[2] For Churchill's speech of 7 March 1916, see Volume III of this Biography, Chapter 23. On that occasion Churchill was answered, and severely criticized, by Balfour, his successor as First Lord of the Admiralty.

those of many Conservative back-benchers, I do not think it is fair to you to ask you to allow me to advance them in the capacity of your Parliamentary Private Secretary.

Our talk last night convinced me that we are not likely to agree in the near future about our policy towards Russia, both economic and political. And it would certainly be fatal to me personally to fight the next election on an anti-Bolshevik ticket.

If I thought that the interests of my constituents were contrary to the national interests, it would be a very different matter. But I do not. So far as I know we have never had a disagreement of any kind. And I want to avoid one now at all costs.

I must therefore ask you to allow me to resign my position as Parliamentary Private Secretary at the earliest moment convenient to yourself.

I hope on some occasion to be able adequately to express my gratitude for all you have done for me. I have now been with you for over two years, & I have not the slightest doubt that I shall look back on them as by far the happiest years of my political life—and the most interesting. We are now entering troubled waters, and it is due to you as well as to myself that, holding a curious constituency and perhaps curious opinions on some subjects, I should be able to speak with freedom & without official responsibility.

Yours sincerely,
Robert Boothby

Desmond Morton[1] to Owen O'Malley

(*Churchill papers: 8/218*)

7 December 1928

Dear O'Malley,

As Winston is kind enough to ask for more of my impertinent comments on his work, I send them.

---

[1] Desmond Morton, 1891–1971. Second Lieutenant, Royal Artillery, 1911. Converted to Roman Catholicism shortly before the First World War. Shot through the heart while commanding a Field Battery at the Battle of Arras, April 1917, but survived the wound. Later awarded the Military Cross. ADC to Sir Douglas Haig, 1917–18. Seconded to the Foreign Office, 1919. Head of the Committee of Imperial Defence's Industrial Intelligence Centre, January 1929–September 1939; its terms of reference were 'To discover and report the plans for manufacture of armaments and war stores in foreign countries.' A member of the Committee of Imperial Defence sub-committee on Economic Warfare, 1930–9. Principal Assistant Secretary, Ministry of Economic Warfare, 1939. Personal Assistant to Churchill throughout the second world war. Knighted, 1945. Economic Survey Mission, Middle East, 1949. Seconded to the Ministry of Civil Aviation, 1950–3.

By the way, could you get his secretary to note down for use, if any further chapters are coming, that during the week my address is 3 Beaufort Gardens, SW3 London: at weekends Earlylands, Crockham Hill, Edenbridge, Kent.

If a packet goes, as this one did, to Edenbridge during the week, they have to forward it back to London and delay ensues.

For the present, unless you want anything to reach me urgently, on a Saturday say, it would be perhaps better to use the London address always.

Yours sincerely,
D. Morton

Desmond Morton to Owen O'Malley

(*Churchill papers: 8/218*)

10 December 1928

My dear O'Malley,

You ask me if I think Winston's statements in enclosed about Janin[1] are unfair, untrue, unwise or libellous.

I have read the pages concerned very carefully several times. In my opinion, for what it is worth, they are certainly not unfair or untrue. I do not see that they are unwise. Though I am not a lawyer, I cannot see how they can be libellous. Here are more reasoned arguments:—

UNFAIR

On page 132 it is especially noted that 'every allowance must be made' for the difficulty of Janin's position and admitted that 'a more detailed analysis' would reveal these difficulties more clearly. Personally I think a more detailed analysis would brand Janin as a crook and possibly a coward. You could however have nothing fairer than the statement as it appears. Again, I can see no suggestion that Janin made away with any of the gold, or did or said anything which is not based on first hand evidence. In view of the commentaries on Janin's actions, character and efficiency made at the time and since, I think the indictment moderate.

---

[1] Pierre Thiébaut Charles Maurice Janin, 1862–1946. Born in Paris. Entered the French Army, 1882. Lieutenant-Colonel, 1907. Liaison officer to the Russian Staff College, 1910. Général de Brigade, 1915. On active service in North-East France, 1915–16. Head of the French Military Mission to Russia, 1916. Général de Division, 1916. Head of the Franco-Czechoslovak Mission in Siberia, 1918. Commander of the Czech Army in Siberia, 1918–19. Commander in Chief of all the Allied forces in Siberia, August 1918–19. Returned to Paris, May 1920. Commanded the French 8th Army Corps, 1921–4.

UNTRUE

The majority of the statements regarding Janin when analysed are either supported by telegrams from Knox[1] at the time, or consist of quotations which appear to come from the pens of first hand witnesses. So far as I know the facts are absolutely correct.

UNWISE

One point I have never been able to clear up is how far Janin was acting under the orders of the French Government. Incidentally, that Janin was French High Commissioner in Siberia in point of prestige before he was Commander in Chief of the Czechs, does not appear in the story as written. Surely I am right about that? Whether therefore, as regards fairness to Janin, this should be indicated, I am not certain. I feel however that any suggestion that his curious standpoint was taken up by reason of secret orders received from the Quai d'Orsay, might be *very* unwise. There is no hint of that. It must not be forgotten that after apparently making a thorough hash of the Siberian affair, Janin was *promoted* in France and had command of a Corps d'Armée in peace time. I am highly suspicious, but I have no evidence. Anyway, Janin's character as it appears from his recorded acts and sayings, was in itself reprehensible, and such moderation of opinion as might occur if an attempt were made to lessen his personal responsibility would, at best, be no nearer the truth than to leave the burden on his shoulders entirely.

I note the phrase on Page 131 'Janin's first duty was the extrication of the Czechs': though I doubt if this is strictly correct, I would leave it. His first duty was presumably to obey the orders of the French Government as their High Commissioner. Have we any final proof that they gave him orders to regard the safety of the Czechs as absolutely his first care?

LIBELLOUS

I have always understood that any person holding a public position is open to criticism on the score of efficiency, so long as the criticism cannot be shown as likely to cause him unjust financial loss which he would otherwise not have suffered, and so long as his private character is not assailed. Janin, though alive, has long since retired and cannot suffer any loss from non-promotion. There is no accusation of cowardice or an attempt to steal money so far as I can see. The only time the word 'traitor' is suggested is on

[1] Alfred William Fortescue Knox, 1870–1964. 2nd Lieutenant, 1891. ADC to the Viceroy of India (Lord Curzon), 1899–1900 and 1902–3. Lieutenant-Colonel, 1911. Military Attaché, Petrograd, 1911–18. Major-General, 1918. Chief of the British Military Mission to Siberia, 1918–20. Knighted, 1919. Conservative MP for Wycombe, 1924–45.

Page 132, second paragraph. But here it is the words of Kolchak,[1] quoted by Malinovsky and repeated by Winston. Moreover, the adjective 'international' alters the idea altogether.

Winston accuses him of insolence in Paragraph 3. I should not think that actionable in any way. Again, higher on Page 132 he says 'the *atmosphere* was loaded with panic and intrigue'. It would, I suppose, require a very clever lawyer to bring home the accusation—for 'atmosphere' read 'Janin'.

I repeat that I am no lawyer and therefore, if Winston still feels unhappy, he might prefer to show these pages to one who has 'eaten his dinners'. I can only say I think they are admirable, as is the whole of this chapter, though I do notice one thing, namely, that on page 129 he still sticks to the phrase 'pre-*war* casualties'. What are they? Railway accidents?!

Yours sincerely,
DM

Winston S. Churchill to Major-General Sir Alfred Knox
(Churchill papers: 8/218)

10 December 1928

My dear General,

I wonder whether you would be so kind as to skim through for me a chapter I have written on the end of Kolchak's affairs? No one knows more about this than you. Janin seems to have behaved so badly that the telling of the tale gives me a little concern. I trust you will not mind my trespassing upon your good nature, and will allow me to send you the chapter. It is in print and therefore not tiring to read.

L. S. Amery: diary
(Amery papers)

12 December 1928

Possibly the best thing would be that we should be beaten. I confess I cannot at this moment see any other way of getting that 'old man of the sea' Winston off my shoulder.

---

[1] Alexander Vasilievich Kolchak, 1870–1920. A Crimean Tartar by birth. Served in the Russian Imperial Navy. Played a leading part in the siege of Port Arthur, 1905. Vice-Admiral, 1916. Commander-in-Chief of the Black Sea Fleet, 1916–17. Minister of War in the Siberian 'All Russian Government' (anti-Bolshevik), 1918. Declared himself 'Supreme Ruler', November 1918. Resigned the leadership of the anti-Bolshevik forces in favour of General Denikin, December 1919. Shot by the Bolsheviks at Irkutsk, 7 February 1920.

Winston S. Churchill to James Headlam-Morley[1]

(*Churchill papers: 8/218*)

13 December 1928

My dear Mr Headlam-Morley,

I am most grateful to you for the trouble you have taken in reading these proofs, and still more for the very remarkable assistance you have given me in my sketch—it is no more—of the Peace Conference. I will send you as fast as I can the other remaining chapters. Considerable alterations and additions have been made in the second revise and these you should perhaps skim over. There is nothing in them which affects the Foreign Office position, but nevertheless I should like you to see what is in all essentials a complete text.

The Peace Conference presents great difficulties both in selection and compression. I have now reached a point where one more chapter will suffice. This I hope to complete in outline during the week-end.

It would give me and my wife great pleasure if you could come and lunch on Friday. We could have a talk afterwards on a few outstanding points.

Robert Birley to A. C. Sheepshanks

(*Churchill papers: 1/200*)

17 December 1928   Eton College

Dear Sheepshanks,

While there has certainly been an improvement in Churchill's work at the end of the half, I do not think that he has done as well as he might. A long essay which he wrote to me a short time ago was quite up to his best standard, and if he did as well at Christchurch I think he will have made an impression. But it was an almost isolated performance.

I need hardly say again that I feel he is a boy of great ability, with an extraordinarily quick mind and with wide interests. The trouble is that he will not keep up the sustained pressure to master his subjects. He finds it much too easy to write fluently on most questions and he is too readily satisfied.

[1] James Wycliffe Headlam-Morley, 1863–1929. Educated at Eton, King's College, Cambridge, and Berlin University (his mother was German). Professor of Greek and Ancient History, London, 1894–1900. Staff Inspector of Secondary Schools, Board of Education, 1902–20. Assistant Director, Political Intelligence Bureau, Department of Information, 1917–18. Assistant Director of Political Intelligence, Foreign Office, 1918–20. Member of the Political Section, Paris Peace Conference, 1919. Historical Adviser to the Foreign Office, 1920. Diplomatic historian. Knighted, 1929.

The result is that some of his essays have been frankly bad, carelessly written and superficial. He has treated essays on political subjects which ought to interest him in the most perfunctory way.

I think he is beginning to realise this, as his work in the last month has been better. I should not myself regard the good work he did in his long essay, which was the result of working for a week in School Library, as encouraging in itself, as I know quite well that he can do far better if he feels there is occasion for it. But he has done better in his ordinary work as well.

This readiness to do well when he feels there is something at stake is characteristic. One might well think that it merely meant that he recognised a big occasion, and felt he must then do especially well, which is an excellent trait. But I feel it shows in his case more than this. He is lacking in a sense of duty, the normal belief that he ought to do his best. This is rather a serious business. If he lets things slide until the big moments he will never really get on.

He is at a difficult period. I believe myself that he is disappointed at his position in the school and that he consoles himself by taking up a generally critical attitude towards the world in general. I hope he will not take up an entirely negative attitude next half. He should make an effort to do well in the Rosebery prize. I am glad, at any rate, to see that he is getting on better with my other pupils, and having more of the normal heated arguments with boys of his own mental equipment.

Just because his mind moves quickly and because he thinks more critically and deeply about the world in general than most boys, (this I feel is really to his credit,) his mental growing pains will be severe. What troubles me is that there seems so little stability at the back of it all. Worrying about the world is an excellent thing, but it should have a moral backing to it, (if one can use the word.) I wish he were more genuinely convinced that things were not right in the world and less troubled about the whole world itself as an intellectual problem. Some of his essays on political questions have (candidly) shocked me. He finds it far too easy to sweep away most modern problems with rather glib references to Communism or Russia. I realise that this is partly a pose, partly a fairly skilful effort to pull my leg, but I am quite sure it is not all that.

Yours sincerely
R. Birley

Winston S. Churchill to James Headlam-Morley

(*Churchill papers: 8/218*)

17 December 1928
Private

Dear Mr Headlam-Morley,

I send you a copy of the sketch I have made of Chapter XI on the Peace Treaties. Some of it perhaps will be appropriate to the final chapter of the book. (I will also send a copy of the passage relating to the safety of France, which is partial and tentative, later.)

I should be extremely grateful for any help you can give me in clothing this skeleton or straightening any deformities in its bones. You know the whole field so well. What I should really like would be if you would take my skeleton as a text and run through the points verbally with me; give me in fact a sort of lecture. You would find me very apt to learn. After all I have got to compress it into perhaps six or seven thousand words at the outside.

Winston S. Churchill to Lionel Curtis

(*Churchill papers: 8/218*)

18 December 1928
Private and Confidential

My dear Lionel,

Many thanks for the trouble you have taken. I think you must be unaware of the enormous literature already published on this subject, and the extent to which disclosures have been made. I skimmed through more than thirty books myself, selected from a far longer list. Macready[1] of course discloses everything about the Four Courts in the most ill tempered and unhelpful manner, and throws the blame as much as possible on to me.[2] I sent these proofs to Craig who read them all, made few comments and corrections and seemed to like them very much. I asked him particularly to consider them not only from the convenience of the Ulster Government, but from that of

[1] Cecil Frederick Nevil Macready, 1862–1946. Entered Army, 1881. Major-General, 1910. Knighted, 1912. General Officer Commanding, Belfast, 1914. Adjutant-General, British Expeditionary Force, 1914–16. Member of the Army Council, 1916. Lieutenant-General, 1916. Adjutant-General to the Forces, 1916–18. General, 1918. Commissioner of the Metropolitan Police, 1918–19. Commanded the Forces in Ireland, 1919–22. Created Baronet, 1923.

[2] For a fully documented account of the bombardment of the Four Courts, Dublin, in June 1922, and of Churchill's policy towards Ireland at that time, see Volume IV of this biography, pages 740–2.

Cosgrave. Nevertheless I have had some misgivings myself from the point of view of the Free State. It was for that reason that I asked you to read them for me, knowing that your eye would be specially sensitive on their account. I will carefully consider all the points you have noted. I told Craig not to hesitate to cut out three or four thousand words if he thought they were embarrassing; and I will now, in view of your apprehensions, make a further pruning myself. It is very probable that I shall ask Cosgrave to look through a final proof.

I was under the impression that the ultimatum about the Treaty had already been made public; and all such points were of course being checked separately. It is immaterial to the story. The point can easily be made in a few harmless sentences. I will send you a revised proof in a few days, and perhaps you will let me have your further reactions upon it.

I have been astonished myself to find the ignorance which prevailed among younger Members of Parliament about the Irish difficulties of these times, and their utter failure to realise what was the justification or at any rate the compulsion under which we acted. I am sure that it is in the public interest that a true view should prevail, and I have always hitherto found that the accounts I have given of such events have been held to be beneficial and to tread the narrow path between improper disclosure and frank and necessary explanations. I do not think any serious Irish crisis is impending over the Privy Council.

Cabinet minutes

(*Cabinet papers: 23/59*)

19 December 1928   10 Downing Street
11.30 am

THE CHANCELLOR OF THE EXCHEQUER gave the Cabinet an account of the difficulties of the financial situation and asked them to enjoin upon the Ministers at the head of the three Service Departments, individually and collectively, to reduce their Estimates to a total of £110,000,000.

THE FIRST LORD OF THE ADMIRALTY stated that he was doing his utmost, and hoped to achieve a total economy of £1,000,000, but he could not see his way beyond that.

THE SECRETARY OF STATE FOR AIR explained his own difficulties, and produced some remarkable figures regarding the extent to which foreign nations are expanding their Air Forces and the amount of their air expenditure in relation to (a) their total defence expenditure and (b) their national expenditure as a whole.

The Cabinet, in inviting the attention of the Service Ministers to the Chancellor of the Exchequer's appeal, asked the Secretary of State for Air to prepare a Memorandum regarding the figures he had quoted, and requested him in doing so, if possible, to obtain the agreement of the other Services to that part of his figures which concerned them. Sir Samuel Hoare was asked also to include figures for Civil Aviation. He was further asked to bear in mind the desirability of the publication of these figures in Parliament at the appropriate moment.

A. C. Sheepshanks to Winston S. Churchill

(Churchill papers: 1/200)

20 December 1928   Eton College

Dear Mr Churchill,

Mr Birley has written very fully about Randolph's work this Half. I am sorry he is only fairly satisfied.

I am not altogether happy about him myself in some ways, though I have nothing very definite on which to base my impressions. I think he might easily be rather a subversive influence in the House. He cannot be with other boys without airing his views, and his views on many subjects are so very strange, that there is always the danger that some boy may be taken in by them. I cannot prevent him holding unorthodox views on religion. But I do not want him to try and infect other boys younger than himself. Of course, he likes to be thought clever and modern, and also I cannot stop him talking. So there is a slight danger.[1]

One of his present complaints is that there is no-one in the house of any intelligence, except, of course, Churchill. I do not mind him thinking this, though it is fearful conceit, but I do think it objectionable or, rather, bad taste when he airs this grievance in public. It seems to show that he has not much feeling of loyalty to the House. This is, I think, the root of the matter. At present he is too self-centred, and is not capable of having any real feeling for house or school or anything or anyone except himself. The idea of getting himself fit by taking exercise every day, so as to have a better chance of success in the House Football Cup—well, he thought it absurd. Why put oneself to trouble simply for the sake of the House?

[1] Randolph Churchill published his own recollections of his years at Eton, and of the Eton masters, in his book of memoirs, Twenty-One Years, published in 1965. Among his principal friends while he was at Eton were Lord Birkenhead's son, 'Freddie' Furneaux; Sir William Berry's son, Seymour Berry (later Lord Camrose); and George Lewis (son of the famous Edwardian solicitor, Sir George Lewis).

I have tried to talk to him about all this, but it is almost impossible. He gets so angry and talks so fast and interrupts so much that one cannot get anywhere. Nor does he pay any attention to what one says, when he is angry. He is merely preparing some crushing answer to something said long before.

In a way perhaps it is a pity that he is not leaving now. He is so mature in many ways, and seems to dislike being treated with discipline. But I am quite satisfied as long as he confines his conversation to boys of his own age and standing, who are capable of thinking for themselves and who are not deceived by the glamour of his talk.

When not angry, he can be very attractive, and would be nicer still if he could learn to take advice now & then.

Yrs sincerely
A. C. Sheepshanks

Winston S. Churchill to Lord Balfour
(*Churchill papers: 2/159*)

21 December 1928

I was delighted to see from a note you wrote to Austen that you are on the mend. From the accounts I have been given by Evan,[1] Ettie and Maurice Hankey one may hope that you would soon be able to come South and I do trust this may be possible after Christmas. You have been greatly missed here in the Cabinet, and by no one more than me.

I was so glad to hear from Hankey that you approved of my suggested reply to the American Naval Note. I think there is real danger in following with America a policy that cannot be stated openly. We go on repeating that on no account will we ever rival them, or pay any attention to what they build, and yet all the time we adhere to the one-power standard and are bound by treaty to measure ourselves accurately with them in some respects. We subscribe to the doctrine of Parity as we interpret it, but we are at present far ahead of them and we all hope we shall remain so. When the Admiralty wish to draft a note they fall back upon an immensely interesting rigmarole which was recited at Geneva and which is quite unintelligible to ordinary people. I am sure it is of utmost consequence to be able to state our policy in terms which will be understood both by their public and ours.

Side by side with this and indeed in preparation for such a declaration I

[1] Evan Charteris, 1864–1940. 6th son of the 10th Earl of Wemyss. Educated at Eton. Staff Captain, Royal Flying Corps, 1916; General Staff Officer, Grade 3, Tank Corps, 1916–18. King's Counsel, 1919. Knighted, 1932. A Trustee of the National Gallery, 1932–9. Chairman of the Tate Gallery, 1934–40. His nephew Hugo was killed in action in 1916.

have been anxious to profit by our great lead by dropping or postponing the two cruisers of this year's programme. After five hours' discussion we settled last Wednesday to leave the matter open till the end of January, by which time it is hoped we shall know the fate of the Peace Pact and Cruiser Bill. It looks as if Coolidge will cut out the time limit on construction, which would mean that the President need only build as he feels inclined. If this happens my programme would be to drop the two cruisers of this year, to state as the Admiralty wish to do that they are going to develop 6-inch cruisers in next year's programme and on the wing of this detour to state with the utmost goodwill our case against their strategic parity instead of numerical. Thus we should have freedom soberly used and plain language combined with pacifical action. I do not at all despair this will result.

Perhaps you remember my sending you nearly a year ago a note I wrote on belligerents' rights, together with Hankey's rejoinder. I have not shown it to anyone else, but there is no doubt that opinion in the Cabinet has moved a great deal in this direction; the PM and Austen and also Worthy have all independently moved a long way down this road. This really is the largest issue we have to face. We agreed at Washington to equal strength and status upon the sea with the United States. This did not mean that the Fleets should be replicas of one another or that the different circumstances of the two countries should not be considered; still less did it mean that a meticulous parity should be jealously and spitefully enforced. But still I consider we are bound to equal strength and status on the sea. Does it not follow that the two equal Powers ought to have a common law of the sea; and may not the achievement of this common law of the sea reduce the naval parity argument to a far easier and more elastic position? Ahead of us all lies 1931, which will be a very critical year for the British Empire.

I have been working very hard at my new volume which goes to press in three weeks. I really thought the Peace Conference would crush me. I tried to compress it into two or three chapters, but the more one writes about it the more there is to do.[1]

I read with great interest Hankey's admirable memorandum in House's last volume, vindicating you, and incidentally me, from the calumnies of the indescribable Stannard Baker.[2] I thought it might amuse you to see how I

[1] In *The World Crisis: The Aftermath* there were four chapters on the origins, course and conclusions of the Peace Conference, entitled 'The Fourteen Points', 'The Peace Conference', 'The League of Nations', and 'The Peace Treaties'.

[2] Ray Stannard Baker, 1870–1946. Sub-editor of the *Chicago Record*, 1892–7. Associate Editor, *McClure's Magazine*, 1899–1905. One of the editors of the *American Magazine*, 1906–15. Special Commissioner of the Department of State in Great Britain, France and Italy, 1918. Director of the Press Bureau, American Commission to negotiate Peace at Paris, 1919. Author of several historical works, including *What Wilson did at Paris* (1919), a three-volume

have dealt with him up to the present, so I enclose a chapter in case you care to skim over it. It also deals with your speeding up the Paris negotiations.

Would you also very kindly look at the passage from one of your Cabinet papers, which I should like to print if you approve. It states our Russian policy at the close of the war more clearly than any other document. If you have any doubt I can omit it.

Let me in conclusion send you and your sister all my very best wishes for Christmas and the New Year, and tell you with what joy every one of us will welcome your return to London.

Winston S. Churchill to James Headlam-Morley
(Churchill papers: 8/218)

24 December 1928

We are looking forward very much to your coming here on Thursday afternoon and hope you will stay for the night and, if possible, Friday night. Meanwhile I send you the draft of this obstinate chapter. Will you bring it down with you and we can then talk it over. It has been terribly difficult to avoid drifting out into the ocean of the general account. However there are perhaps one or two omissions which must be rectified.

I shall of course send this chapter to Austen after we have licked it into shape.

Believe me,
Yours sincerely,

Lord Beaverbrook to Sir Robert Borden
(Beaverbrook papers)

26 December 1928

Churchill is plunged in despair. He accepts electoral defeat in advance, but then his judgment on such matters is worse than that of any prominent man I know. . . .

---

history of the Paris Peace Conference, entitled *Woodrow Wilson and World Settlement* (1922), and an eight-volume biography of Woodrow Wilson (for which he was awarded the Pulitzer Prize for best biography in 1940).

Winston S. Churchill to Lord Cecil of Chelwood

(*Cecil of Chelwood papers*)

27 December 1928 Chartwell Manor

My dear Bob,

I have a chapter in my new book dealing with the Covenant of the League of Nations, in which I find you played a most important part. I wonder whether you would care to read it through and let me know whether I have done justice to the topic. If so, I should be very much obliged. I presume I am right in attributing to you the first written conception of Articles XIV and XV, and that Phillimore[1] followed on this and Wilson built on both.

Yours vy sincerely,
Winston S. Churchill

Winston S. Churchill to David Lloyd George

(*Churchill papers: 8/218*)

27 December 1928

I am so pressed in finishing my book that I shall not have a complete copy for you to read before the Closure. I therefore send you those passages—not very numerous—in which I have either quoted or described opinions you expressed to me verbally, or which contain extracts from letters or telegrams sent by you to me. They do not contain anything very important, but they fit into the story.

First, 'Make Them Pay' and the Cunliffe–Sumner episode. Second, your telegrams to me when you sent me to Paris about Russia. Most people will agree with you about these, and perhaps I am unwise to publish them. But *magna est veritas*. I am reprinting a lot of your famous Memorandum at Fontainebleau, but this has already been published by Nowak and others. Lastly, I have given an explanation of your Greek policy, with which I did not agree as you gave it to me at the time. I do not think it will take you long to look through these.

On the book as a whole Hankey, who has read it through, says it is scrupulously fair; and, as you know, he is no fair weather friend of yours. Pray let me know as soon as possible what you think of these extracts.

---

[1] Walter George Frank Phillimore, 1845–1929. Barrister, 1883. A Judge of the High Court, 1897–1913. President of the International Law Association, 1905–8. Mayor of Kensington, 1909–10 and 1910–11. Lord Justice of Appeal, 1913–16. President of the Committee which produced the Draft Statutes of the League of Nations, 1917–18 (providing among other safeguards for an International Court). Created Baron, 1918.

Winston S. Churchill to William Cosgrave
(Churchill papers: 8/218)

27 December 1928
Private and Personal

My dear Mr Cosgrave,

In my new volume of THE WORLD CRISIS I am dealing at length with the story of the Irish Free State; and I thought of publishing several letters written by me to Mr Michael Collins. I also have to refer to some of the well known incidents of this unhappy time, when it was my task to try to keep the confidence and goodwill both of Mr Collins and Sir James Craig. Most of this has already been made public property in the voluminous literature which exists upon the subject. I am, however, particularly anxious not to say anything which would make your task more difficult or hamper Irish government in the South or in the North. I have shown all the relevant passages affecting him to Sir James Craig, and I wonder whether you would let me in a purely private capacity send you a few extracts affecting the Treaty. I have of course written always with my eye on the common interest, and I do not think that there is anything to hurt. But your burden is so heavy that I should not like to run the slightest risk of adding to it. Pray let me know whether I may send you the proofs. They will not take you half an hour to read.

Winston S. Churchill to William Lints Smith
(Archive of 'The Times')

27 December 1928   Chartwell Manor

Dear Mr Lints Smith,

In the course of a week I hope to be able to send you advanced revises of twenty out of twenty-two chapters. I will follow these up a week later by what is virtually the final text. At any rate there will be quite enough for your Extractor to get to work upon; and I could then consult with him, as we did before, upon the best presentation to make. The book will amount to 150,000 words. I could not get it into less, and even now there is an extra chapter panting to be born. I presume you will want between thirty and forty thousand words.

There are some passages about the United States which are rather critical. If your selection should fall on these, I should have to ask that the counter-balancing passages of a complimentary and soothing nature should have publicity at the same time. But it will be quite easy to make a good story as we did before.

All these advanced proofs are of course subject to final revise. I must show some of them to the Foreign Secretary, and his word would have to be my law. However certainly not more than a couple of thousand words or so are in doubt, and it is quite probable you will not want to use these.

Yours very truly,
Winston S. Churchill

January 1929

Lord Balfour to Winston S. Churchill: draft[1]

(Balfour papers)

1 January 1929

I must begin my answer to your very interesting letter of December 21st by thanking you and Clemmie for your kind message. I most heartily wish you both every happiness for the twelve months which begin to-day.

I turn now to your observations on the American situation—a most difficult subject. Friendly co-operation with America has always taken the first place in my scale of international values. But it is not easy to attain, and it is not always best attained by too obviously striving for it. Nevertheless, I need hardly say that, holding these views, the tone and temper of your letter greatly appeal to me.

As regards parity and the Treaty of Washington, it really is a matter to remember that the parity attained never professed to be other than the parity between battle-fleets, including in the term battle-fleets the cruisers and other auxiliary craft without which a battle-fleet is blind and helpless. If the Americans sometimes ignore this, it is because they forget the quite explicit statements which I more than once had occasion to make.

Then it would be said that the parity between battle-fleets is not a parity of naval strength; and this is true. The position of a naval combatant must depend in part upon cruisers, submarines and aircraft acting independently and not as parts of an organised fleet. How is parity (by which I mean equality of naval strength) to be reckoned when you are dealing with these portions of a nation's naval force?

The answer is that it cannot be reckoned in any precise numerical fashion; and I am not sure that the way in which the problem was left at Washington, unsatisfactory though it may seem, is not the best at present within sight.

But this statement requires development. The actual facts of international naval construction in the matter of cruisers has left us, as we all know, in a

---

[1] The typescript of this letter, in the Balfour papers at the Scottish Record Office in Edinburgh, is marked: 'neither completed nor sent'.

position of great superiority to the Americans; and it is not surprising that the Big Navy party in the USA, who think of naval problems in terms of war between the two branches of the English-speaking peoples, regard it as unsatisfactory. Are we sure that were we in their place we should not take the same view?

I am sometimes disposed to think that a quite illogical solution of this problem is the right one. Let me explain what I mean. Supposing we laid it down that we propose to adhere to the Washington doctrine of parity in battle-fleets; but that this simple method of determining naval force was not applicable to the far more complicated problem of dealing with lines of communication on which the unity of the Empire, as well as the sustenance of our population, essentially depended.

But as regards battle-fleets, the parity which we require did not depend on geographical or political reasons.

Winston S. Churchill to David Lloyd George

(*Churchill papers: 8/222*)

1 January 1929   Chartwell Manor[1]

I send you herewith the passages from my book where I quote your letters or private expressions of opinion. They are not numerous nor indeed of the first importance to my account. I have ventured to send the whole three chapters about the Irish story as I think they may interest you. As you are going away and I am at the point of giving birth to the new volume I do not trouble you with the whole account. Hankey, who is no fair weather friend of yours, has read it all and thinks it is scrupulously fair. Of course I bulk very largely in it all, but then it is I who am telling the tale. I hope you will tell yours when the time comes.[2]

I fear you have had a very bad time and I recommend the very greatest care. I myself was completely knocked out for two months and no good for three after the dose of influenza I had last year. You are absolutely right to go away and will miss nothing in the opening of the session. It will be very dull—rating not perorating.

---

[1] Churchill was still working at Chartwell on the last volume of his war memoirs, *The Aftermath*. During the first five months of 1929 his overnight guests at Chartwell included Sir Archibald Sinclair (January 5–7), P. J. Grigg (April 4–6), Sir Philip Cunliffe-Lister (April 5–6) and Robert Boothby (April 10–11). Professor Lindemann spent the first five months of 1929 in India.

[2] Lloyd George published *The Truth About Reparations and War Debts* in 1932. His two-volume *The Truth About the Peace Treaties* was published in 1938.

Winston S. Churchill to James Headlam-Morley

(*Churchill papers: 8/222*)

1 January 1929

My dear Mr Headlam-Morley,

This piece has very nearly been the death of me. Here is the eleventh chapter.[1] You will see how much it owes to your guidance. It is, I think, greatly improved and fairly complete. I shall be so much obliged if you will check it for me and make any comments which occur to you. It is being printed meanwhile. I am of course going to submit it textually to Chamberlain.

Having regard to the great complaints which the Germans make of our cruelty to them in maintaining the blockade so long, I ought to have a paragraph somewhere—though not in No XI—on this point. Twenty lines would be enough. What is the truth about it?[2]

Winston S. Churchill to Lord Cecil of Chelwood

(*Cecil of Chelwood papers*)

5 January 1929   Chartwell Manor

My dear Bob,

It is very good of you to let me send you my League of Nations chapter, and I shall look forward greatly to receiving your comments and advice upon it.

I thought you might be interested in a suggestion I have thrown out in the opening chapter. It is so speculative, and many will think so fanciful, that I deliberately put it in the form of a dream. You will find it on page 7.

Up till the end of this next week I can make considerable alterations in the League of Nations chapter, but after that it will be difficult. If you have anything which you think it really helpful to say, please try to let me have it before then.

Yours vy sincerely,
Winston S. Churchill

[1] Entitled 'The Peace Treaties'.

[2] The naval blockade of Germany had remained in force for eight months after the armistice, from November 1918 to July 1919. At the time, Churchill had been strongly opposed to continuing the blockade. On 3 March 1919 Churchill told the House of Commons: 'We are enforcing the blockade with rigour, and Germany is very near starvation. All the evidence I have received from officers sent by the War Office all over Germany shows: first, the great privations which the German people are suffering; and secondly, the danger of a collapse of the entire structure of German social and national life under the stress of hunger and malnutrition.' Churchill quoted these words in *The Aftermath* (pages 66–7), where he devoted forty-five lines to the post-armistice blockade. His account ended: 'These bitter experiences stripped their conquerors in their eyes of all credentials except those of force.'

Winston S. Churchill to Brigadier-General Sir James Edmonds

(*Churchill papers: 8/222*)

6 January 1929

My dear General

I wonder if I might ask you to have a little map drawn for me, illustrating the Archangel–Murmansk campaign and showing the places mentioned in the text enclosed? It need only be quite simple and on a small scale, so as to fit in a single page. I should be so much obliged if you could do this, as my map making aptitudes have fallen into prolonged desuetude since Sandhurst.

Stanley Baldwin to Winston S. Churchill

(*Churchill papers: 1/205*)

Twelfth Night 1929

My dear Winston,

Your Christmas telegram was most kind and welcome.

Accept this belated line to wish you all good in the New Year.

Your proofs never came: but I am greedy for them and hope yet that possibly you can let me have them for an early week end.

I always stick my roots deep into my native soil when I get home, but I am going to pull them up on Wednesday and transplant myself to the cold London clay.

Yours ever,
SB

Winston S. Churchill to Stanley Baldwin

(*Baldwin papers*)

7 January 1929   11 Downing Street

My dear Prime Minister,

I was delighted to get your letter. I have been in the throes of book birth and have only just got reasonably clean proofs. I send you the first eight chapters in a tolerably advanced condition, and will let you have the rest when you arrive in London on Wednesday. There is a further revise of these eight chapters now with the printers, which contains a good many corrections, improvements and additions; so that if you notice mistakes in these, it is probable they have already been repaired. I have sent the two chapters about America to Austen. I am afraid he may wish me to tone them down. Mr Headlam-Morley, the Foreign Office historian, who has read the whole book, is very reluctant to see anything sacrificed. However . . . . .! I shall be quit of the Book by the 15th, and my decks will be clear for the Budget and the Election.

I am probably going over to Normandy on Thursday for a few days' boar hunting, but shall be back on Wednesday week in case you want me. I gather you intend to have a Cabinet on the morning of the 21st to deal with the Naval programme. It may well be that we shall congratulate ourselves on having kept a move in hand. I have to speak at Manchester that night, so I hope the Cabinet may be fixed in the morning.

P. J. Grigg and the Customs are very worried about Wool, and I shall shortly have to send you some serious papers on the subject. It is an issue upon which I shall accept the directions of the Cabinet. But how you can fit a wool tax into the time allotted to the Budget before a May dissolution, is a problem at present unsolved. It must be carefully studied before any decision is taken to extract a report from the Committee before the dissolution.

I liked your Saturday[1] speech. It was solid and calm. I am sure that everything should be done to confront the electors with the direct choice between Socialism and modern Conservatism. The more blunt and simple the issue, the better for our cause. The world tides are favourable. They set in every country towards Conservatism, co-operation and continuity of national policy. Women can feel these tide movements by instinct. I should very much like to use the two cruisers as a noticeable sign of peace consolidation, and as the means of a *détente* in Anglo-American relations.

Mitchell-Thomson[2] has written you a letter about the penny post. It is idle to consider such matters till we see the outturn of this financial year and the outlook of the next. At present I do not feel that there is any chance of our sparing the revenue. The Rating elephant eats all our buns. I hope

---

[1] Speaking at Worcester on Saturday, 5 January 1929, Baldwin declared that Socialism was still the principle aim of the Labour Party, and he defined Socialism as 'some form of national control as opposed to private enterprise'. The Conservatives, on the other hand, stood, he said, for a moderate policy of avoiding shocks to the trade and credit of the country, and this policy would bear fruit in the years to come. The Electricity Bill, the Local Government Bill, and now the Derating Bill were all measures, he said, that would 'aid industry itself to overhaul the trade of the country'.

[2] William Mitchell-Thomson, 1877–1938. Educated at Winchester and Balliol College, Oxford. 2nd Baronet, 1900. Engaged in West India business. Conservative MP, 1906–32. Director of the Restriction of Enemy Supplies Committee, 1916–19. Parliamentary Secretary, Ministry of Food, 1920–1; Board of Trade, 1921–2. Privy Councillor, 1924. Postmaster-General and Chief Civil Commissioner, 1924–9. Created Baron Selsdon, 1932. Chairman of the Television Advisory Committee, 1934–8.

and believe the Budget will work out accurately, but I do not know at present where to turn for new revenue. I have not asked for the Parliamentary time for a taxing Budget.

With all good wishes and all my aid in the critical period now opening, believe me

Yours vy sincerely,
Winston S. Churchill

Winston S. Churchill to William Bridgeman: not sent
(*Churchill papers: 18/102*)

7 January 1929

My dear First Lord,

I have been again considering the subject of reserves of armaments and other stores for the Fleet which is dealt with in your letter of the 29th November 1928, and I have no doubt that you have been doing the same in connection with your efforts to show a substantial reduction on Navy Estimates for 1929.

Although I am grateful for what you are doing to meet me (for example by extending the period of notice for sea for ships in reserve from 14 or 21 days to 3 months) I am by no means in a position to express complete satisfaction.

I still feel that, in view of the new formula as regards preparation for war, really large reductions can and should be made in the standard of reserve outfits of guns, projectiles, cordite, torpedoes and naval stores, at least for the older ships; and I am also sorry that, despite my appeal of the 27th August 1928, you are still maintaining a greatly increased output of cordite. But time has passed and it would be fruitless to isolate these discussions from those soon to take place in regard to your 1929 Estimates.

I should be glad if for this purpose you will let me have at the same time as you send me your Estimate proposals an up-to-date statement, in terms both of money and stores, of the provision contemplated in 1929 as compared with 1928 for:—

Heavy Guns
Medium „
Light „
Shells for each class
Cordite
Torpedoes

On all these items, and as regards naval stores, I still find insufficient reflection in your letter of the Government's decision. Stocks still seem to be based, even for the reserve ships, on the theory that the whole of the Fleet, with all its guns, must be ready to go into action at an early date. I want to see our newest ships fully equipped but I do not see that the same high standard, or anything like it, need apply to the reserve ships. As a small example, why should the guns of all ships be replaced immediately they go for relining?

It is on general grounds, and not in any attempt to dispute with your Naval experts as to the ideal 'requirement', that I question your cordite replacement programme; and I am not in the least impressed by the argument from the annual certificate which the Controller has to render to Parliament. The object of that certificate is not to tie the Government to any particular standard of reserves, irrespective of political and financial exigencies. Rather it is to secure that money intended for maintenance of reserves is not diverted to other purposes. The certificate is a substitute for a valuation statement, devised for reasons of secrecy alone. There is nothing to prevent the Government authorising reserves, at any given period, lower than the ideal which is stated as a general guide. The position is precisely similar to that of the oil reserve. The argument really begs the question 'what should the reserve be?'. I am asking for the reserve to be temporarily fixed at a figure lower than, and without prejudice to, the figure which might be desirable if you assumed the obligation to be ready for a general fleet action immediately. But it is precisely this assumption which you have not to make.

As I have said, we shall now have to thrash out all these questions in relation to the Navy Estimates for 1929 and I need only add here that, even if the Comptroller and Auditor General's figure of £9,384,804 for Naval Stores is whittled down as you propose and reduced to pre-war values, a figure for 1929 which is 80% of the 1914 figure is excessive, having regard to the entirely changed circumstances of the two years.

Yours sincerely,

Winston S. Churchill to P. J. Grigg

(*Churchill papers: 8/222*)

12 January 1929   Château de St Saëns[1]

My dear Grigg,

I am so much obliged to you both for the checkings you have sent me, and surprised at the speed at which you have been able to do them.

[1] The Duke of Westminster's château at St Saëns, Seine Inférieure: seventy-two miles north-west of Paris, and twenty miles inland from Dieppe.

LG comments on the Irish chapters:—'You omit altogether the reference to the Gairloch correspondence and the Inverness meeting of the Cabinet. There were discussions with De Valera. Neither is there any reference to the lengthy negotiations which ensued and which extended from September up till December.' Could you get me something about this? Hankey could probably supply it. Not much is wanted, but we ought to see the principal letters and moves in the negotiations. A page, or two at the outside, would be all I could spare. If these await me on my return, it will be time enough.

Yours vy sincerely,
Winston S. Churchill

Winston S. Churchill to Sir Archibald Sinclair
(*Churchill papers: 8/222*)

14 January 1929

Thank you so much for your letter. Your comments are always so pregnant and instructive, and also appreciative that I venture to send you a few more chapters. If they reach me in the next five or six days there will still be time to incorporate your wisdom in the common stock.

Did you see Lloyd George before he went away, and did you talk to him about the book? I hope so.

Desmond Morton to P. J. Grigg
(*Churchill papers: 8/222*)

14 January 1929

Dear Mr Grigg,

As regards Mr Churchill's first point for me: Kerensky signed what is known as the 'Soldier's Charter'. Is that the Order No 1 referred to? He issued the 'Soldier's Charter' as an Army Order. To see that we are all referring to the same thing I attach an English translation of the 'Soldier's Charter' in question.

It appears to have been the 'Soldier's Charter' which legally abolished the obligatory salute (see Item 12) while the Death Penalty is obviously precluded by Item 15.

On the other hand the Death Penalty was directly abolished by a special Army Order also issued by Kerensky and dated March 20th 1917. I rather think that this last which preceded the issue of the 'Soldier's Charter' is the one referred to by Mr Churchill. Anyhow both were issued by Kerensky, the Soldier's Charter as Minister for War, the Death Penalty abolition order as Minister for Justice.

As regards the other point on page 07 line 16 'The All Russian Congress of Soviets' is still the nominal holder of power as witness the Bolsheviks' own description of their organisation in their Ejegodnik (Annuaire Diplomatique) 1928 where they say:—

L'organe suprême du pouvoir de l'Union des Républiques Soviétistes et Socialistes est le Congrès des Soviets. . . .'

Admittedly the above statement is drivel but one would be in a technical error in including the 'All Russian Congress of Soviets' where Mr Churchill has so done. The Duma & the Democratic Congress all went in title as well as actuality, but the existing Congress of Soviets was replaced by another body bearing the same name but 'elected' by force & not by free voting or anything approaching it. The 'All Russian Congress of Soviets' changed its title later to the 'Congress of Soviets of the USSR' but not until the separate republics forming the USSR were defined and established.

Otherwise I can spot no technical mistake on page 07.

Yours very truly,
Desmond Morton

Winston S. Churchill to Cyril Alington
(*Churchill papers: 2/572*)

17 January 1929

Your very kind letter reached me almost at the moment when I was writing to Mr Sheepshanks to tell him that Randolph will not go back to Eton this term. We have both reached the conclusion that in the present development of his mind he will do better by going earlier to Oxford than by remaining only an additional term at school. I have only just been able to find a last minute vacancy at Christ Church through the kindness of Professor Lindemann and Randolph will actually go there as an undergraduate on Saturday next. This is a considerable event in our circle. I hope, however, you will nevertheless permit me to come down for a night during this term and that you will allow Randolph to come with me at the same time.

This is the moment when I must thank you and Mrs Alington for all your kindness to my son. His four years at Eton have certainly made him a most agreeable, well-mannered though very argumentative member of society. Although his views on religion are at present far from orthodox, I am delighted to find his moral outlook high and honourable. I am sure he has greatly benefited by his education at Eton and I am sure he will always look back with pleasure and with pride to his associations there.

Believe me,

Winston S. Churchill to Lord Beaverbrook

(Beaverbrook papers)

18 January 1929   Chartwell Manor

My dear Max,

This is the best set I can put together. Some of the chapters have undergone very marked improvement. There are a few chapters missing, namely—The Irish Settlement and 'The Rise of the Irish Free State' and the final chapter, 'The End of The World Crisis'. But you will be able to gain the general impression from these. Please guard them very strictly for me—they are for your eye alone.

I trust the voyage will give you the means of regathering & repoising yr nervous forces. Time & peace are the vital things. All good wishes,

Yours sincerely
Winston S.C.

Cabinet minutes

(Cabinet papers: 23/60)

23 January 1929

AIR EXPANSION

THE CHANCELLOR OF THE EXCHEQUER drew attention to those parts of the memorandum which indicated a possibility that it might be necessary before long to increase the Air Estimates. If this were done, MR CHURCHILL pointed out, there would be an end to any peace policy.[1]

[1] In its conclusion, the Cabinet agreed with a proposal made by Austen Chamberlain, that when the preparatory Commission on the reduction and limitation of armaments met at Geneva, 'no opportunity should be lost in urging a reduction in air forces'.

Sir John Shuckburgh[1] to Winston S. Churchill

(*Churchill papers: 8/222*)

23 January 1929   Colonial Office

Dear Mr Churchill,

Herewith the memorandum that you asked me to prepare for you. I have done my best to compress, but in spite of that it works out a little longer than I intended.[2] If there are any other points on which you would like further particulars, I need not say that I shall be very glad to furnish them to the best of my ability.

I mentioned to Mr Amery this afternoon that you had asked me to prepare this memorandum and that I was complying with your request.

Yours sincerely,
E. J. Shuckburgh

Randolph Churchill to Winston S. Churchill

(*Churchill papers: 1/205*)

28 January 1928   Christ Church
                                                            Oxford

Dear Papa,

I am so enjoying being here, and I cannot tell you how glad I am that I did not have to return to Eton. There are so many interesting and enjoyable things to be done each day that the time passes very rapidly.

My tutor is a very brilliant man called Feiling.[3] He wrote the 'History of the Tory Party', which I believe you have read.

---

[1] John Evelyn Shuckburgh, 1877–1953. Entered the India Office, 1900. Secretary, Political Department, India Office, 1917–21. Appointed by Churchill to be Assistant Under-Secretary of State, Colonial Office, 1921. Knighted, 1922. Remained Assistant Under-Secretary of State until 1931; Deputy Under-Secretary of State, 1931–42. Appointed Governor of Nigeria, 1939, but did not assume office owing to the outbreak of war. Worked in the historical section of the Cabinet office, 1942–8.

[2] Sir John Shuckburgh's memorandum, written in the first person as if by Churchill, appears as the only Appendix to *The Aftermath*, entitled 'A Memorandum upon the Pacification of the Middle East'. It is unsigned, and unindexed, and takes up just over five printed pages.

[3] Keith Grahame Feiling, 1884–1977. Lecturer and historian. Fellow of All Souls, Oxford, 1906–11; tutor at Christ Church, 1911–46. 2nd Lieutenant, Black Watch, 1915. Secretary to the Central Recruiting Board, India, 1917–19. OBE, 1918. University Lecturer in Modern History, Oxford, 1928–36; Chichele Professor of Modern History, 1946–50. Knighted, 1958. His first book, *The History of the Tory Party, 1640–1714*, was published in 1924. In 1946 he published a biography of Neville Chamberlain.

I do hope that your hunting was successful and that Mummie enjoyed herself.

I am so looking forward to seeing you and telling you all about Oxford. I shall be in London on Wednesday for Diana's wedding.[1]

Your very loving son,
Randolph

[1] The wedding on 30 January 1929 of his cousin Diana Mitford to the Hon Bryan Walter Guinness.

February 1929

Edward Marsh to R. C. Sherriff[1]

(*R. C. Sherriff papers*)

1 February 1929   Treasury Chambers

With the Compliments of
Mr Winston Churchill,
Chancellor of the Exchequer.

Mr Churchill was deeply interested in the brilliant play and presentation of *Journey's End*. He ventures to note three points in the last scene, which were not quite clear to him.

(1) With what purpose did Captain Stanhope write a note and send it down the line? Was it mere routine? A harmonious explanation would be that he was sending Captain Osborne's ring and letters back to Battalion Headquarters, knowing well what the Company's position was.

(2) Why did the Sergeant-Major think it odd that Mr Raleigh when wounded should be brought into the Company's dugout? Surely in all the circumstances it was almost obviously the place. There would be nothing unusual in bringing a wounded or dying officer into Company Headquarters, especially if the communications to the rear were under heavy fire.

(3) Why did Captain Stanhope ask for Raleigh almost immediately afterwards? Surely he was not going to send him down the line while the firing lasted, even had he lived a few hours longer.

Mr Churchill wishes once more to express his admiration for this remarkable production.

---

[1] Robert Cedric Sherriff, 1896– . Playwright and novelist. Worked in an insurance office, 1914–16. Captain, East Surrey Regiment, 1917. *Journey's End* was his first play to be performed on the London stage. His motion picture screen plays included *Goodbye Mr Chips*, 1936, *Lady Hamilton*, 1941 (one of Churchill's favourite films), and *The Dam Busters*, 1955. He published his autobiography, *No Leading Lady*, in 1968.

Winston S. Churchill to James Headlam-Morley

(*Churchill papers: 8/223*)

6 February 1929

My dear Mr Headlam-Morley,

This is only the very rough assembly of the last chapter and I should greatly welcome your comments—destructive and constructive.

Cabinet minutes

(*Cabinet papers: 23/60*)

7 February 1929

THE PRIME MINISTER explained that he had summoned this emergency Meeting of the Cabinet at the request of the Chancellor of the Exchequer.

He recalled that on December 19, 1928, the Cabinet had decided to adhere to the programme of naval construction for the financial year 1928–29, but that tenders in connection therewith should not be sent out until after the first meeting of the Cabinet after the Recess, and it had been understood that members of the Cabinet would be entitled to reopen the question of the construction of the Cruisers at that Meeting in the event of some new factor affecting the situation arising out of events in America in connection with the passage of their Cruiser Bill; but that in the absence of some such new factor the question should not be raised. The subject had been discussed at the first Meeting of the Cabinet after the Recess, but the American Cruiser Bill was at that time still under consideration in the Senate and the Cabinet's discussion had been adjourned. The American Cruiser Bill had now been passed, without any alteration in the time-limit, but the Chancellor of the Exchequer had brought to his notice a new factor of another kind affecting the situation, and he had acceded to Mr Churchill's request that the matter should be considered by the Cabinet. It was essential that the Cabinet should reach their decision that morning as a Question was being asked in the House of Commons by the Member for Devonport[1] in regard to the carrying out of the 1928–29 programme.

[1] Leslie Hore-Belisha, 1893–1957. His father, an Army officer, died when Hore-Belisha was nine months old. Known, on account of his Jewish origins, as 'Horeb Elisha'. Educated at Clifton and St John's College, Oxford. On active service in France, 1915–16, and at Salonica, 1916–18. President of the Oxford Union, 1919. Liberal MP for Plymouth Devonport, 1923–42 (National Liberal from 1929; Independent from 1942 to 1945). Parliamentary Secretary, Board of Trade, 1931–2. Financial Secretary, Treasury, 1932–4. Minister of Transport, 1934–7 (with a seat in the Cabinet from October 1936). Privy Councillor, 1935. Secretary of State for War, 1937–40 (Member of the War Cabinet, 1939–40). Minister of National Insurance, 1945. Created Baron, 1954.

THE CHANCELLOR OF THE EXCHEQUER brought to the notice
of the Cabinet that the Germans were building a new 10,000-ton vessel embodying novel features. By lightening weights and developing a very high
horse-power per ton they had been able to design a very remarkable ship,
particulars of which were contained in a secret memorandum prepared by
General Gröner,[1] which had somehow been obtained and published by 'The
Review of Reviews'. The new ship was to be armed with 11-inch guns; it
would have a greater radius of action than our Battle Cruisers, and would fire a
heavier weight of shell per minute than they. The speed would be 26 knots.
He gave other particulars to show that the appearance of this new class of
ship would tend to discredit the older types. France, for example, was said
to be contemplating a 15,000 to 16,000-ton ship in reply, for which purpose
she could employ her unused Battleship tonnage under the Washington
Treaty. All this indicated that Cruiser design was passing into a phase that
would render obsolete our existing Cruisers. No doubt the effect on America
would be to induce an attempt to incorporate in the new design lighter
engines and a greater radius of action. Mr Churchill then gave a number
of particulars, taken from 'The Times', of the speeds and radius of action
of Cruisers of various foreign Powers, which did not flatter the comparative figures for British Cruisers. He recalled the greater speed of the German
Cruisers over corresponding British vessels during the War.

The important point which Mr Churchill impressed upon the Cabinet
was that the 18 vessels that we now had on our hands would almost certainly
be out-classed by the new American Cruisers. This illustrated the mistake
of building prematurely. He suggested that the two 8-inch gun 10,000-ton
Cruisers approved for the present year should be postponed in order that
they might be introduced in later years so as to incorporate all the most
recent technical improvements. By postponement we should get the advantage not only of better ships but also we should show to the world a more
pacific policy. As it was, we were not making the best use of the limited
funds available for naval construction, and we were casting away a great
opportunity for easing the pressure for armaments all over the world. What
he desired was a sounder policy and better ships.

---

[1] Wilhelm Groener, 1867–1939. Entered the German Army, 1885. Chief of Field-Railway
Transport, 1914–16. In charge of the economic intensification of war production, 1916–17.
First Quarter-Master General to the Kaiser, October 1918. The leading military supporter
of the Weimar Republic. Minister of Transport, November 1918. Minister of Defence,
January 1928–May 1932; in October 1931 he was also appointed Minister of the Interior.

Sir Austen Chamberlain to his wife

(*Austen Chamberlain papers*)

11 February 1929

I dined at the Speaker's, my 37th such dinner. What a veteran I am! Setting aside AJB only Winston has a comparable Cabinet experience. He & I run nearly neck & neck I believe. AJB actually attended the *Cabinet* yesterday for the first time since his illness. It was a great pleasure to see him but in discussion he was not up to the mark, tho' he has written a paper which shows all his deadly skill in controversy. . . .

Thomas Jones: diary

(*Jones papers*)

12 February 1929

I talked[1] about Winston's 'Aftermath' which is appearing in the *Times*. Winston had sent the chapter on the League to RC who thought it rather poor stuff. I said I thought the Irish chapter brilliant. 'Oh! of course he is brilliant,' replied RC, 'but if you were to take a list of Winston's political prophecies for a period of years you would find 90% of them had been falsified.' Turning to Winston's dream of the Armistice, RC said: 'Not one of the Big Three at the Peace Conference knew anything about finance.'

Winston S. Churchill to William Bridgeman

(*Churchill papers: 18/102*)

13 February 1929

My dear First Lord,

I do not wish to continue our disputes about the Navy Estimates as I know how anxious you are and how urgent it is to have them settled. I should, therefore, be ready to agree to the presentation of the Navy Estimates of 1929–30 at the figure of £55,865,000. This figure would include a repetition of last year's shadow cut of £2,400,000; but the shadow cut must be upon a somewhat different basis from previous years. There is some danger that your economies have, in part at any rate, discounted the shadow cut, and I cannot therefore agree that the Admiralty must regard themselves as

---

[1] At a private dinner party, where Jones was sitting next to Lord Cecil of Chelwood.

entitled without question to present a Supplementary up to the total of £2,400,000 if the progress made with the approved services warrants it. On the contrary, the Treasury must be free during the year to press the Admiralty to effect further economies so as to make sure that the expense is in fact kept within the total vote.

I propose also that your programmes for the Fleet Air Arm and for cordite manufacture shall be referred to a Cabinet Committee for particular examination in the light of the Cabinet ruling about the ten years' improbability of a major war. I do not suggest that these enquiries should begin until after the immediate political crisis has been settled in one sense or the other, but I would ask that meanwhile you should defer the placing of orders for the air craft necessary to form the new flights contemplated by your programme. A decision by the Cabinet Committee could, if we remain responsible, easily be procured by the end of June.

I trust that you will be able to confirm these arrangements.

Winston S. Churchill to William Bridgeman
(*Churchill papers: 18/102*)

14 February 1929

My dear First Lord,

Provided, as your letter agrees, that the Treasury shall be free to press for further economies in expenditure during the currency of the year, and that the Admiralty will on their part do their utmost to keep it at a minimum, the figure £55,865,000 can be accepted in spite of the fact that you apprehend this year as in previous years that some Supplementary Estimate may be involved.

I have no objection to the Cabinet enquiries into the Fleet Air Arm and the Cordite Reserve proceeding without delay. The only urgent matter is the programme of the Fleet Air Arm as we are not asking you to hold up your Cordite pending an enquiry. In view of the burdens upon Ministers at the present time I suggest therefore that the Fleet Air Arm should be the only one which it is necessary to carry through before the end of the financial year.

I take this opportunity of putting on record what I told the First Sea Lord last week, namely, that I shall make no objection to the inclusion in the three cruisers of next year of one of the largest type, and that as a Cabinet colleague I deprecate the closing down of this particular type on account of the possible objection that will be raised should it be necessary to re-open the construction of this type later.

R. C. Sherriff to Winston S. Churchill

(Churchill papers: 1/205)

15 February 1929

The Author and Producer[1] of 'Journey's End' greatly appreciate the interest taken by Mr Winston Churchill in their production, and very much regret the lateness of their reply owing to delay in the letter coming into their hands.

To his questions they would reply as follows:—

(1) It was their intention that Stanhope's message to Battalion Head-quarters should be a routine one to indicate that whatever the stress, the routine must continue uninterrupted.

(2) The Sergeant Major's apparent doubt about bringing Raleigh into the dugout is due rather to his slowness in taking in a quick, un-expected order than to any reluctance or surprise. The dialogue reads as follows:—

Stanhope: Bring him down here.

SM: Down 'ere, sir?

Stanhope: (shouting) Yes! Down here—quickly!

(3) When Raleigh is brought down, Stanhope asks for Stretcher Bearers immediately because he realises the German attack will almost in-evitably sweep over the dugout. He prefers the great risk of having him carried through the shelling, with the possibility of getting him to safety to the chances of such a badly wounded man remaining where he is.

Once again the Producer and Author would like to thank Mr Winston Churchill for the compliment he has paid to 'Journey's End'.[2]

---

[1] James Whale, 1896– . Began his career as a cartoonist for the *Bystander*. Taken prisoner-of-war by the Germans, 1917; began his acting career while a prisoner-of-war. First appeared on the stage in Britain in 1918. Stage Manager at the Savoy Theatre, 1923. Designer of stage scenery. Producer of *Journey's End*, London, 1928; New York, 1929. Film director, including *Journey's End*, *Waterloo Bridge*, *Frankenstein*, *Bride of Frankenstein*, *The Man in the Iron Mask*, and many other films, 1930–9.

[2] In the first production of *Journey's End* the part of Captain Stanhope was played by the 22-year-old Laurence Olivier, with David Horne as Captain Hardy and George Zucco as Lieutenant Osborne.

W. P. Crozier:[1] *'Note of an Interview with Mr Winston Churchill'*

(*Crozier papers*)

18 February 1929   Chancellor of the Exchequer's Room
Very Secret   House of Commons

Discussing the probable results of the coming General Election and what might happen afterwards, I warned him that he must not be too optimistic about the prospects of his Party; that I had caused careful investigation to be made into the chances and that although the agents were never the best judges as to the prospects of their own party, they very often were able to form a more impartial view as to the prospects of another party, and when they took a roseate view of another party's prospects, then it might be assumed there was a good deal of ground for it.

I told him that according to these reports, it was quite on the cards that the Conservative Party might be the second party in the State instead of being the first. I then urged him to persuade the Prime Minister in a case of that kind not to resign in a hurry before giving an opportunity for consultation with the Liberal Leaders; that we were just as anti-socialist as they were and had no anxiety to see a socialist government in control of the affairs of this country.

He said that they had no thought of such a contingency; they had no intention to resign if they were the first party in the State but they had not contemplated the possibility of being the second, but he was glad I had invited his attention as to what would happen at such a chance. I told him that there were several things which the Liberal Party would insist upon before they could support any government—

First, that their electoral grievance should be redressed. Here, Mr Churchill admitted quite fully that we had a grievance and that in common justice it ought to be set right.

The second point was that we could not possibly agree to any tariff being imposed upon either iron, steel or wool or any other commodity. That if anything of that kind were attempted our supporters in the House of Commons would all vote against it whatever the consequences might be in the way of putting in a socialist administration.

Mr Churchill said that they were bound to institute some sort of enquiry, that they had given definite pledges on that subject but we both agreed that the result of that enquiry depended very largely upon the character of the tribunal set up.

---

[1] William Percival Crozier, 1879–1944. Director of the *Manchester Guardian*, 1921–32. Editor of the *Manchester Guardian* from 1932 until his death. A life-long Liberal.

The third point discussed was the reconstruction of the Ministry. I made it quite clear that under no conditions could any support be given to the existing administration. Some of the most important offices were held by men who were quite incompetent to discharge their duties. Mr Churchill told me there was some discussion going on between himself and the Prime Minister as to whether reconstruction should come before or after the election, but that the Prime Minister was contemplating recasting his Ministry. I then made it quite clear that we could support no Ministry which would not tackle the problems of Unemployment—more or less on the lines of our programme—Agriculture, Roads, etc. I told him that this would involve raising a very considerable sum of money by a loan.

There was some discussion as to the method of procedure at the first meeting of the new Parliament. I told Mr Churchill that I had no doubt at all that Ramsay MacDonald would move a vote of 'want of confidence' in the government and that all the members of our Party would be anxious to vote for such a resolution but that an addendum might also be moved humbly to present to the King that the House of Commons had no confidence in an administration drawn from a party which was not committed to the nationalisation of all the means of production, distribution and exchange. In that case, if the first motion were carried and the second, Baldwin would be absolved from an obligation to advise the King to send for Ramsay MacDonald, as that would be in direct defiance of the vote of the Commons. The leaders of the three parties might then be sent for by the King; Baldwin might undertake to form a new Ministry upon the conditions which I have indicated.

Churchill said that if those terms were accepted the government would have to be kept in power for two years and I told him if there were an arrangement, naturally no one in this country wanted another election in twelve months and that two years seemed to be reasonable.

He was very anxious for an electoral understanding that would draw candidates from seats where the only result would be to split the anti-socialist vote and give the Socialist Party a number of seats which otherwise they had no hope of capturing, but I told him that any arrangement of that kind was quite impossible; that we were pledged to our 500 candidates and must run them.

He asked me if I had any objection to his reporting the conversation to the Prime Minister. I told him that I had none; that I had consulted the whole of my colleagues who represented fairly fully the views of the Liberal Leaders but that it would be quite impossible to enter into any arrangement at this stage—so much depended upon the result of the election and the attitude of our supporters.

Sir Austen Chamberlain to his wife

(Austen Chamberlain papers)

20 February 1929

We discussed today the course we should take in reference to the vote for the Irish loyalists which caused yesterday's parliamentary crisis. We did not take a definite decision but I think we are pretty well agreed. It was very hard on Amery & still more on Winston on whom a bitter personal attack was made by Hugh Cecil.[1] The fact is that Hugh cannot forgive Winston his position or his share in the Irish treaty. In this case both ministers were defending a decision taken by the Cabinet for which we all had equal responsibility, but in truth we have bungled this case all through & yesterday no one had anticipated a serious or difficult debate & the ministers were not prepared for the very full & detailed recital which alone could have altered the mind of the House.

Neville Chamberlain to Winston S. Churchill: note passed in Cabinet

(Churchill papers: 18/101)

20 February 1929   10 Downing Street

I did not hear what had happened yesterday till it was all over.

We had to face a possible defeat & I think the PM took the only possible course. But I feel great sympathy for you. You made a gallant attempt to hold a position for which we are all responsible & though we shall all have our share in the discredit, it falls with unfair weight on you.[2]

[1] Lord Hugh Cecil had spoken after Churchill during the debate on a supplementary estimate for the Irish Free State. The sum of money under debate was to relieve the Free State of previous obligations to pay for property damage, land purchase and benefits to ex-servicemen. Churchill having opposed the grant, Lord Hugh Cecil accused him of violating a debt of honour, and called for the defeat of the Government. They would deserve defeat, he said, 'for the transaction is a last disgraceful item in an inheritance of shame, and my right honourable Friend is one of those who have brought it on the Government and the country'. No vote was taken, but on 22 February 1929, Baldwin told the House of Commons that 'the Cabinet are collectively responsible for the various decisions taken in this matter during the present Parliament, and that the statements made from time to time on their behalf by various Ministers have at every stage carried with them our united assent and approval. The Cabinet have never taken the view that these payments are debts of honour.' Baldwin went on to explain that the Cabinet had subsequently decided to pay those charges recommended by the Wood Renton Advisory Committee, which was then sitting, and would from time to time introduce new supplementary estimates.

[2] On 24 February 1929 Randolph Churchill wrote to his father: 'I was very disappointed with the Prime Minister's behaviour about the Irish Loyalists. After all we have heard about his honesty, it is surprising to find him abandoning his subordinates. However it all seems to have passed over satisfactorily' (*Churchill papers: 1/205*).

Lord Irwin to Winston S. Churchill
(Churchill papers: 2/164)

25 February 1929   Viceregal Lodge, Delhi

My dear Winston,

Our correspondence has been too slender to permit me to delay in writing one line to tell you that your friend Professor Lindemann came to see me with your letter this morning. I had a long talk to him and found him everything that you had said as regards interest and entertainment. I have asked him to let us know if and when he comes back to Delhi so that we might be able to put him up.

I watch your approach to the Election with absorbing interest, and you can guess how anxiously I shall await the result. Most people seem to think that you will succeed in securing a reduced but adequate majority. I hope these prophets will be right. It will be a curious sensation to me to be watching the contest from so safe and remote a distance.

I have just this moment heard that Humphrys[1] has got safely out of Kabul. It is an intense relief, for, although I think there are great disadvantages about his coming away, the risks of sitting on the edge of a volcano always seem to me almost prohibitive. And as he leaves Nadir Khan[2] enters. I wonder whether he will do the trick. Unless Humphrys is entirely wrong, he is the only man who has got a chance of doing it and the brigand usurper seems to have as poor a prospect of retaining his precarious throne as Amanulla[3] has of regaining it. It is sad to think how much hospitality, to say nothing of Oxford DCL degrees and royal presents of stallions, has been thrown away on that headstrong reformer.

[1] Francis Henry Humphrys, 1879–1972. 2nd Lieutenant, 1900. On active service in South Africa, 1900–1. Served as a Pilot with the RAF, 1918. Political Agent, Khyber, 1919. Deputy Foreign Secretary to the Government of India, 1921. British Minister to Kabul, 1922–9. Knighted, 1924. British High Commissioner and Commander-in-Chief, Iraq, 1929–32; Ambassador in Baghdad, 1932–5. Chairman of the British Sugar Corporation, 1936–49. Chairman, Air Training Corps, Central Council of Welfare, 1940–7.

[2] Nadir Khan Shah, who succeeded to the throne of Afghanistan after the dethronement of Amanulla. In 1931 he introduced a new constitution, and in 1932 he founded Kabul University. In August 1933 the British bombed several frontier villages whose inhabitants had attacked across the Indian border. Nadir Khan was assassinated in November 1933, when he was succeeded by his son Nadir Khan Shah.

[3] Amanullah Khan. Became Amir of Afghanistan following the assassination of his father, Habibullah, in February 1919. Declared his country's total independence from British control April 1919. When the peace was signed at Rawalpindi on 8 August 1919 Afghanistan was released from British control of its foreign policy, and quickly sent representatives to Moscow, Berlin, Paris, Rome, Teheran and Angora. Many foreign legations were also set up in Kabul. A Russo-Afghan Treaty was signed on 28 February 1921. On 22 November 1921 Britain and Afghanistan signed a Treaty of good relations, and an Afghan Legation was established in London. In the 1920s Amanullah introduced European style reforms. This provoked widespread discontent, and eventual civil war; he was forced to abdicate in January 1929.

We are living in rather stormy times here, and I am sure that our principal purpose ought to be, in the next few months, to try to dissipate the somewhat artificial unity that the appointment of the Parliamentary Commission[1] has evoked. Believe me always that at the present moment the Indian political problem is 90 per cent psychological and 10 per cent rational.

I must stop. All good luck to you. If by any unhappy hazard you are relieved of responsibilities after the Election why not come and pay us a visit? But meanwhile I shall hope to see you if I get home in the late summer.

Please remember me to Mrs Churchill.

Yours ever,
Irwin

Thomas Jones: diary

(Jones papers)

25 February 1929

I outlined a vague agricultural policy which I discussed with Sir Howell Thomas[2] last week and the PM said he had urged Winston quite recently to use some Post Office profits for the spread of rural telephones. The PM went on: 'What do you think about Winston at the India Office?' I said it was a splendid notion, as Winston at the Irish job had shown that the bigger the post the better he is, and that he would stand for the double duty in India as he had in Ireland to the Indians and the Empire. The important thing was to see that he had around him officials who were not afraid to stand up to him at critical moments when he was going off the deep end, eg the Battle of Belleek.[3] I did not know what the India Office officials were

[1] The Simon Commission, headed by Sir John Simon (see Churchill's recollections quoted on pages 1431–2).

[2] Charles John Howell Thomas, 1874–1943. Member of the Treasury Committee on Post Office buildings, 1911. On active service in France and Egypt, 1914–18. Member of the International Valuation Board of the Reparations Commission, 1919. Member of the Irish Compensation Commission, 1922–5. Chief Valuer, Board of Inland Revenue, 1925. Permanent Secretary, Ministry of Agriculture and Fisheries, 1927–36. Knighted, 1928. Member of the United Kingdom Delegation to the Imperial Economic Conference, Ottawa, 1932, and to the World Monetary and Economic Conference, London, 1934.

[3] Following the occupation of the Ulster border villages of Belleek and Pettigo by Republican forces on 30 May 1922, Churchill, as Secretary of State for the Colonies, had been actively involved in the British decision to regain the villages by force. Lloyd George had criticized Churchill's action, and done so to Thomas Jones himself, but by June 8 both villages had been occupied by the British without loss of life on either side. For a full account of the incident, and of the controversy which it aroused, see Main Volume IV of this biography, pages 723–31 and 736.

like, but they could be reinforced before the Commission reports. The PM continued: 'I could make Peel[1] Lord President of the Council and give him an earldom, which his grandfather refused because he did not want it, and if Salisbury goes I could make Peel Leader of the Lords. I assume Neville will go to the Treasury, though he would prefer to go to the Colonies.' 'That is just filial piety,' I interpolated.

Winston S. Churchill: recollections[2]

(Churchill papers: 4/113)

Before the election Mr Baldwin had sounded me about my taking the India Office if we were successful. The problem of British relations with India had weighed upon our Cabinet. A Royal Commission, headed by Sir John Simon, comprising all parties, and including Mr Attlee,[3] had gone out to India in the autumn of 1928. They made an exhaustive tour and study. Their report was impending. Mr Baldwin seemed to feel that as I had carried the Transvaal Constitution through the House in 1906, and the Irish Free State Constitution in 1920, it would be in general harmony with my sentiments and my record to preside over a third great measure of self-government for another part of the Empire. I was not attracted by this plan.

[1] William Robert Wellesly Peel, 1867–1937. Educated at Harrow and Balliol College, Oxford. Conservative MP, 1900–6 and 1909–12. Succeeded his father as Viscount Peel, 1912. Chairman of the London County Council, 1914. Chairman of the Committee on the Detention of Neutral Vessels, 1916. Under-Secretary of State for War, 1919–21. Chancellor of the Duchy of Lancaster and Minister of Transport, 1921–2. Secretary of State for India, 1922–4 and 1928–9. Created Earl, 1929. Lord Privy Seal, 1931. Member of the Indian Round-Table Conference, 1930–1 and of the Joint Select Committee on the Indian Constitution, 1933–4. Chairman of the Burma Round-Table Conference, 1931–2; and of the Palestine Royal Commission, 1936–7.

[2] Written by Churchill immediately after the Second World War, in an early draft of his war memoirs, but never published.

[3] Clement Richard Attlee, 1883–1967. Educated at Haileybury and University College, Oxford. Called to the Bar, 1906. Tutor and lecturer, London School of Economics, 1913–23. On active service at Gallipoli. Mesopotamia (wounded) and France, 1914–19; Major, 1917. First Labour Mayor of Stepney, 1919, 1920; Alderman, 1920–7. Labour MP for Limehouse, 1922–50; for West Walthamstow, 1950–5. Parliamentary Private Secretary to Ramsay MacDonald, 1922–4. Under-Secretary of State for War, 1924. Chancellor of the Duchy of Lancaster, 1930–1. Postmaster-General, 1931. Deputy Leader of the Labour Party in the House of Commons, 1931–5. Leader of the Opposition, 1935–40. Lord Privy Seal, 1940–2; Deputy Prime Minister, 1942–5. Lord President of the Council, 1943–5. Prime Minister, 1945–51 (Minister of Defence, 1945–6). Leader of the Opposition, 1951–5. Created Earl, 1955.

My friendship with Lord Birkenhead, then at the India Office, had kept me in close touch with the movement of Indian affairs, and I shared his deep misgivings about that vast sub-continent.[1]

Winston S. Churchill to Lord Derby

(*Churchill papers: 2/164*)

27 February 1929
Confidential

My dear Eddie,

You may well imagine that I am thinking a great deal about the betting tax at the present time, and I am grateful to you for your letter and advice which tallies with much I have received from many less friendly quarters.

I think the Labour Party are making themselves ridiculous by the eagerness with which they are welcoming the Bookmakers' support, and that there is no harm in this phase continuing for the present. If later on I were able to propose some effective change in the direction desired the Bookmakers would return to their Conservative allegiance and the Socialists would be left compromised and deserted. On the other hand we ourselves must be very careful not to appear to be so pliable that we cannot stand up against any pressure. There are then dangers in each direction, but I can assure you that I am searching for a satisfactory exit between them.

If you are free tomorrow (Thursday) will you not come to lunch with me here? We should be alone and can talk.

Yours ever
WSC

L. S. Amery: diary

(*Amery papers*)

27 February 1929

DISCUSSION WITH NEVILLE CHAMBERLAIN

The cardinal point of course was Winston. We both agreed that nothing would help the situation more than if he could be moved.

I suggested the Presidency of the Council with a direct mission to co-ordinate the policy of the fighting services; Winston has hankered after this

---

[1] Churchill added: 'Owing to our failure to gain a working majority at the polls, the personal question vanished.'

all his life, regarding it as a filial inheritance, and would be kept happy and busy planning wars in Afghanistan and elsewhere.

[As to the suggestion of sending Churchill to the Foreign Office] Neville thought the PM would not run such a risk and would dread to find himself waking up at nights with a cold sweat at the thought of Winston's indiscretions. I suggested that Winston was not really so rash as picturesque, that there were no really critical situations in foreign policy just now, and that a little colour and vivacity would do no harm and that my experience of Winston as a negotiator with his equals was that he was both skilful and reasonable.

March 1929

Neville Chamberlain to Winston S. Churchill

(*Churchill papers: 8/224*)

3 March 1929

My dear Winston,

It is very generous of you to send me your new volume[1] and I thank you most warmly for it.

I have purposely restrained from reading the extracts in the Times as I prefer to take my pleasures in a lump. But I look forward to reading the Aftermath at the earliest opportunity and I have no doubt that I shall find it as enthralling as I did its predecessors.

Yours very sincerely,
N. Chamberlain

Sir Samuel Hoare to Winston S. Churchill

(*Churchill papers: 8/224*)

3 March 1929

Dear Winston,

I greatly value your friendship in sending me a signed copy of the 'Aftermath'. There is no volume of contemporary history that I have read with keener interest, or with greater pleasure for you have not only a wonder-

[1] *The World Crisis: The Aftermath*, of which 7,500 copies were published on 7 March 1929. Churchill inscribed more than eighty copies as personal gifts. Among those who received these advance copies were many Cabinet colleagues (including Sir Laming Worthington-Evans, Sir Philip Cunliffe-Lister, Eustace Percy, Sir Arthur Steel-Maitland, Lord Peel, Sir William Joynson-Hicks, Lord Cushendun, Sir John Gilmour, L. S. Amery and Lord Salisbury); several Treasury officials (including Sir Warren Fisher and Sir Richard Hopkins); all those who had helped him with the book (including General Edmonds, James Headlam-Morley, Owen O'Malley, Lionel Curtis and Sir John Shuckburgh); and many personal friends and former colleagues (including Lord Cecil of Chelwood, Sir Ian Hamilton, Sir Bolton Eyres-Monsell, Lady Desborough, Lady Oxford and Asquith, and General Sir 'Tim' Harington).

ful power of narrative but, what is very rare among public men, an equal skill with the written as with the spoken word.

Again, many thanks, and though the volume may end your history of the war, may it by no means end your literary output!

Yours,
Samuel Hoare

Lord Rosebery to Winston S. Churchill

(*Churchill papers: 8/224*)

4 March 1929   The Durdans
Epsom

My dear Winston,

Many thanks. I love these tokens of recollection.

Yours ever,
AR[1]

Lord Hailsham to Winston S. Churchill

(*Churchill papers: 8/224*)

4 March 1929   House of Lords

My dear Winston,

Ever so many thanks to you for sending me your book, and for writing my name in it. I do appreciate receiving it from you very much; I have been following the excerpts in 'The Times', but it is quite another thing to have the complete volume, together with those which you were good enough to send me last time. I am very proud to know that I can claim you as a colleague and (I hope) a friend.

Yours ever,
Douglas

[1] Signed by Lord Rosebery in his own hand. Rosebery died on 21 May 1929.

Sir Maurice Hankey to Winston S. Churchill

(*Churchill papers: 8/224*)

4 March 1929

My dear Churchill,

Very many thanks indeed for the valuable addition to my library which your autographed copy of the new section of the World Crisis forms.

I have heard nothing but praise of the Times extracts—not a single word of criticism.

Yours ever,
M. P. A. Hankey

William Bridgeman to Winston S. Churchill

(*Churchill papers: 8/224*)

4 March 1929

My dear Winston,

I am indeed grateful to you for your very kind thought in sending me so acceptable & handsome a present as your Aftermath.

I have abstained from reading the Times extracts, because I like to imbibe anything you write in long and deep draughts rather than in mouthfuls—I look forward to indulging in this pleasure forthwith and return you my warmest thanks.

I hope you will get some holiday and sunshine before the Budget.

Yrs ever,
W. C. Bridgeman

Desmond Morton to Winston S. Churchill

(*Churchill papers: 8/224*)

4 March 1929

Dear Mr Churchill,

It is really most kind of you to send me a copy of 'The Aftermath' and above all to write on the flyleaf that it was a present from yourself.

This volume will join the other four of the 'World Crisis' on my bookshelf but I shall always regard it with special veneration.

I hope the few rough notes I was able to send you on one or two chapters were not quite valueless. At any rate I am more than proud you should have sought my humble opinions on any matter.

With renewed thanks,

Yours sincerely,
Desmond Morton

Philip Snowden to Winston S. Churchill

(*Churchill papers: 8/224*)

4 March 1929

My dear Mr Churchill,

I do so much appreciate your kindness in sending me this autographed copy of the new volume of your great work 'The World Crisis'.

I shall treasure it not only for its own worth but as a memento of the friendly personal relations which can and do exist between keen political opponents.

With renewed thanks, I remain

Yrs v sincerely,
Philip Snowden

James Ramsay MacDonald to Winston S. Churchill

(*Churchill papers: 8/224*)

5 March 1929   House of Commons

My dear Churchill,

It is so good of you to send me your book. I am sure it will be lively and also important, and I shall take it with me to read at Easter. I suppose you are going to give us a few days holiday!

With kind regards,
Yours very sincerely,
J. Ramsay MacDonald

Thomas Jones to Winston S. Churchill

(*Churchill papers: 8/224*)

5 March 1929

My dear Chancellor,

I am delighted to have the inscribed copy of 'The Aftermath' to add to the family possessions, & shall look forward with keen interest to its successor!

Yours

TJ

Lord Balfour to Winston S. Churchill

(*Churchill papers: 8/224*)

6 March 1929

My dear Winston,

The last volume of your great work has safely arrived, and I must send you a line of thanks and admiration. It is a most remarkable performance, and I count myself as fortunate in living long enough to see its accomplishment.

Nobody is better qualified than I to speak of its merits;—not merely on the general grounds that in my own way, and in a very different fashion, I have spent much time in mixing up politics with writing and writing with politics, but that I have had unique opportunities of seeing you at work in both these exacting spheres of activity.

Do you remember my visits to the Admiralty at the beginning of the war when you were good enough to explain all the difficulties and anxieties of a First Lord in a great Naval War dealing with wholly novel problems both of tactics and strategy? That was little more than fourteen years ago. Into those fourteen years you have not only compressed unique experiences in war by sea and land, in diplomacy, in House of Commons' work, and in constructive legislation; but you have contrived to write a book which, both as an original authority and as a most admirable literary performance, will hold a permanent place in the history of our country.

During all those years I have been a friend and admirer, and, unless my memory fails me, an occasional opponent. It amuses me to think of this period as beginning with discussions on the defence of our trade routes in the Pacific, and opening its final act with your explanations to me at

Whittinghame of your ideas of de-rating,—now in process of being happily embodied in a great legislative effort.

Five volumes of immortal history is a wonderful addition to this great period of administrative activity.

With warmest congratulations,
Believe me
Yours affectionately
AJB

Robert Vansittart to Winston S. Churchill
(*Churchill papers: 8/224*)

6 March 1929

My dear Chancellor,

Very many thanks for sending me a copy of your book which I shall always value. It was a great interest to me to be allowed to read it in advance like that, and I *really* looked forward to each fresh slice as it came. I have to thank you for some very absorbing days and evenings.

Yours very sincerely,
Robert Vansittart

Sir Warren Fisher to Winston S. Churchill
(*Churchill papers: 8/224*)

6 March 1929

Dear Churchill,

Your thought in giving me a copy of your book, & the kindness of feeling that it signifies, are a true joy to me. And the book itself will be full of interest & stimulation.

Thank you so much.

Yours v sincerely,
N. K. Warren Fisher

Thomas Jones: diary

(Jones papers)

6 March 1929

Much speculation[1] about the Election, and general agreement that 'we must get our people properly frightened at the prospect of a Socialist Government'. Winston (more and more voluble as the luncheon proceeded) inclined on the whole to wish Labour could be in for a short spell to allow him to display his powers in Opposition. He had never had the experience except during the War. What was the Labour Government like? he asked his colleagues. 'Awful,' replied Cunliffe-Lister. 'It was like hammering a pillow. Clynes, who was Leader of the House, didn't know the rules, and often had to consult Bobby (Monsell).' Ramsay impotent, vain, weak, agreeing with you privately, denouncing you publicly. Snowden an exception. Cunliffe-Lister did not like the prospect of Labour coming in because all the Board of Trade evidence indicated that trade was improving, and for this the Labour Government would take full credit if they came into office. 'We should not try to compete with LG,' urged Winston, 'but take our stand on sound finance. I remember in Gairloch[2] when the unemployed figures were tremendous, we toyed with these big national schemes of artificial employment, but LG came down after a few days' reflection solidly against them.' There were congratulations for the Lord Chancellor on his son's[3] election as President of the Union at Oxford. 'Randolph,' said

---

[1] At a lunch given by Sir Philip Sassoon. In London, Baldwin was also discussing his future Cabinet in the event of a Conservative victory. On March 5 Baldwin discussed Cabinet placing with Thomas Jones, who noted in his diary Baldwin's question: 'What did I think of Winston for India? I said I was all for it, that he would rise to the height of a great opportunity, that there was nothing petty about him, that we officials might quarrel and denounce him to his face, but he was not vindictive' (*Jones papers*).

[2] On 21 September 1921 Lloyd George had held a Cabinet meeting at Gairloch, on the west coast of Scotland. The main problem discussed had been that of Ireland, but Churchill had also raised with Lloyd George the urgent need, as Churchill saw it, for a comprehensive social policy. A week later, on 28 September 1921, Churchill had circulated to the Cabinet a memorandum entitled 'The Unemployment Situation' in which he declared: 'It is not possible for a civilized State with a large portion of its members living in luxury and the great bulk of its members living in comfort to leave a proportion of its citizens with neither work nor maintenance.' The memorandum is published in full in Companion Volume IV of this biography, pages 1630–4.

[3] Quintin McGarel Hogg, 1907– . An undergraduate at Christ Church, Oxford, 1926–30: President of the Oxford Union Society, 1929. Fellow of All Souls College, Oxford, 1931–8. Barrister, Lincoln's Inn, 1932. Conservative MP for Oxford City, 1938–50; for St Marylebone, 1963–70. Parliamentary Under-Secretary of State for Air in Churchill's 'Caretaker Government', May–July 1945. Succeeded his father as 2nd Viscount Hailsham, 1950, but disclaimed his peerage for life. First Lord of the Admiralty, 1956–7. Minister of Education, 1957. Lord President of the Council, 1957–9 and 1960–4. Lord Privy Seal, 1959–60. Minister of Science and Technology, 1959–64. Secretary of State for Science, 1964. Lord Chancellor, 1970–4. Created Baron (Life Peer), as Lord Hailsham of Saint Marylebone, 1970. Companion of Honour, 1974.

Winston of his boy, 'is a bitter Tory. He tells me (to Hailsham) your son will give him a chance at the Union.'

J. C. C. Davidson: diary

(*Davidson papers*)

6 March 1929

I lunched with Sir William Berry. He is very anti-Lloyd George and I also suspect very anti-Winston, and is pinning his faith on Neville as the first lieutenant to the Prime Minister. He feels that Jix ought to go and also Winston from the Exchequer and he thinks that Neville would make an admirable Chancellor.

In a little monologue about Winston he put the position exactly as I understand it myself, the main point being that he is not trusted in the party because he is always out for office and never prepared for opposition, and therefore people suspect he is already in negotiation with Lloyd George to secure a post as second man on the new ship if it is ever launched.

Robert Boothby to Winston S. Churchill

(*Churchill papers: 8/224*)

8 March 1929

Dear Chancellor,
    Very many thanks for the book. It will be one of my most treasured possessions.

Yours ever,
RB

PS. I have just got a copy of the 'Spectator'. They have massacred my review. Cut it wildly and idiotically so that frequently it doesn't make sense, and never let me know. I am so angry I have told them I will never write for their beastly paper again![1] I hope your weather will continue as it has begun. My regards to Mrs Churchill & Diana, and again many thanks.

[1] On 7 March 1929 Thorton Butterworth wrote to Churchill: 'I would like to offer you my most sincere congratulations upon the wonderful reception "THE AFTERMATH" has had in the Press. So far as I have seen there has not been one discordant note,—expressions of opinion have been in the superlative! I cannot but feel that it is a great honour that I should be connected with the publication of such an important work.' On that day, subscription sales amounted to 6,745 copies, out of a first edition printing of 7,500 copies.

Lord Eustace Percy to Winston S. Churchill

(*Churchill papers: 8/224*)

10 March 1929

My dear Winston,

Thank you very much for sending me your book. The first book of yours that I ever read gave me a quotation from Ruskin which I have never verified, to the effect that what matters most in one's judgements of men is whether they are kind or unkind. There are very few people whose work in 1929 can claim to live up to the maxims they quoted in 1900! There's another remark somewhere in Ruskin about 'magnanimity, the great measuring virtue'. I think that's true and it explains why your book is the first which gives a real measurement of the unmeasurable experiences of this generation.

That sounds fulsome, but at least it's sincere!

Yours sincerely,
Eustace Percy

Neville Chamberlain: diary

(*Neville Chamberlain papers*)

11 March 1929

Last Tuesday[1] I dined alone with the PM at his invitation. He said he wanted to have a talk and it presently appeared that the subject was reconstruction of the Cabinet. A little while ago Amery suggested to me that it would be a good tactical move to make changes before the Election instead of waiting till afterwards. He said he was going to speak to the PM about it and asked for my support. Thinking about it afterwards I was disposed to agree with him but I doubted whether SB would care to undertake it. I was agreeably surprised therefore to find that he was considering it seriously. He had some thoughts of putting Winston at the India Office provided that were agreeable to him and he was sounding Austen and Edward Wood to see how they would view such a change. E. Percy was doing very well at Education and he wished to keep him there for the present. Ultimately he might make a very useful ambassador to the USA. He enquired whether I would prefer the CO to the Exchequer. I said I would but that if it suited better that I should go to the Treasury I would

[1] Tuesday, 5 March 1929.

not refuse to consider it. His comment was that it would be an extra-ordinarily popular appointment in the Party. For one thing they liked to have the next man to the PM in that office and they did not want Winston in that position.

Arthur Ponsonby[1] *to Edward Marsh*

(*Marsh papers*)

11 March 1929

That a war atmosphere gives him opportunities for exercising his great talents and that he naturally enjoys such opportunities is generally admitted. That he would miss something in the absolute elimination of all such possibilities of threatened or possible conflict is obvious enough. . . .[2]

I referred to his 'eloquent indictment' of modern warfare, and I quite admit that with his literary talent and imagination he has done this better than it has been done before. Sam Hoare has not done it badly in the House before now, Baldwin's platitudes on the subject pass muster and even Austen Chamberlain occasionally squeezes out a phrase on the subject. But quite frankly all this makes me rather impatient. Denunciations of war, however eloquent, coming from the leaders of one of the most powerful Governments of modern times speaking for a nation which still has a leading position in the world, ring false and appear as pure hypocrisy. . . .

I have been criticized for having buttered up Churchill too much. I have a great admiration for him. He is so far and away the most talented man in

[1] Arthur Augustus William Harry Ponsonby, 1871–1946. A great-grandson of Lord Grey, Prime Minister at the time of the 1832 Reform Bill. Educated at Eton and Balliol College, Oxford. Page of Honour to Queen Victoria, 1882–7. Served in the Diplomatic Service, 1894–1903. Principal Private Secretary to the Prime Minister (Sir Henry Campbell-Bannerman), 1905–8. Liberal MP for Stirling Burghs, 1908–18. Labour MP for Sheffield Brightside, 1922–30. Under-Secretary of State for Foreign Affairs in the first Labour Government, 1924. Parliamentary Under-Secretary for Dominions in the second Labour Government, June–December 1929. Parliamentary Secretary, Ministry of Transport, 1929–31. Created Baron, 1930. Chancellor of the Duchy of Lancaster, 1931. Leader of the Opposition in the House of Lords, 1931–5.

[2] In a review article published in the *Daily Herald* on 7 March 1929, Arthur Ponsonby had written, to Edward Marsh's distress: 'If war were abolished it is difficult to imagine anyone who would be more put out than Mr Winston Churchill. The excitement, the strategy, the manoeuvres, the intrigues and the whole vast field of crisis and upheaval provide him with an atmosphere in which his talents thrive and stimulate him like a lively intoxicant. Life for him would indeed be drab if all possibility for the use of the war weapon were removed.' Ponsonby ended his review by asking, of Churchill: 'Will this man, matchless as a parliamentarian, with few rivals as an orator, unsurpassed in careful industry, brilliant as a writer, whose paintings even show that in that sphere, too, he might have excelled, will this man ever be given *his* chance by Destiny? On bended knees we devoutly hope not.'

political life besides being charming and a 'gentleman' (a rarish bird in these days). But this does not prevent me from feeling politically that he is a great danger, largely because of his love of crises and faulty judgement. He once said to me years ago, 'I like things to happen, and if they don't happen I like to make them happen.'

L. S. Amery to Stanley Baldwin

(*Baldwin papers*)

11 March 1929   Dominions Office
Very Personal

. . . The essential thing is to move Winston. I say this not only because he is fundamentally opposed to all ideas of Empire development and Empire preference, as well as to safeguarding, but because, in spite of all his brilliancy and verbal originality, he is entirely lacking in constructive thought and imagination in the economic field. His recent interview with the motorists, and his whole treatment of the motor question, show that he simply does not realise that he is dealing with an industry which, properly encouraged, might mean as much to us as the railway industry did eighty years ago. He has been, in every direction, a paralysing negative influence, and the Party knows it and would breathe a profound sigh of relief if he were shifted.

I suggested to you two alternative places where his qualities would have much better scope. One would be to let him, as Lord President of the Council or Privy Seal, be entrusted with his long cherished dream of coordinating the fighting services. I don't mean a Ministry of Defence, but giving him a pretty free hand at the CID and in particular making him chairman of a small Committee consisting of the Defence Ministers and Chiefs of Staff to coordinate not only strategy but expenditure. The Air debate the other day showed how much that idea is in the mind of the House, and both your decision and your choice of the man to carry it out would be applauded by all (except, perhaps, the defence ministers immediately affected!).

The alternative would be the FO. To this Winston would bring great gifts. He has a fine sense of the historic sweep and diversified drama of the world's affairs, and would make foreign policy much more interesting without, I believe, making it dangerous. For one thing there are no real dangers in foreign policy just now—our dangers are much more in the economic and Imperial field—and for another he is, occasional fits of temper apart, fundamentally cautious and a good negotiator. He possesses the further great advantage of speaking French very badly, and is not likely to get too fond of Geneva! Here, too, to speak quite frankly, the public, especially our party, would be relieved by a change. I do not know, of course, what Austen thinks, but I should have doubted if he had the physique to go on with so heavy a department, and he is the obvious successor to Balfour as principal Elder Statesman in a non-administrative office. Failing Winston, Sam would be safe at the FO.

The obvious successor to Winston at the Treasury is Neville. I need not expatiate to you on his qualities. All I know is that the change would be acclaimed with enthusiasm by our Party. As for myself I should be perfectly happy—if that is your wish—to stay where I am, if I had Neville to deal with. There is, however, a possible alternative. If, as I have some reason to believe, Neville would really like to succeed his father more than anything else,[1] I would be equally happy at the Treasury: either way we could work hand in glove and do big things, even within the limits which political exigencies set to the development of Imperial Preference. And either way I believe the combination would appeal to the public imagination.

Winston S. Churchill to Lord Stamfordham

(*Churchill papers: 18/101*)

15 March 1929

My dear Stamfordham,

Very many thanks for both your letters. I have no doubt that the announcement about Prince George[2] will be well received. I think modern opinion will welcome the idea of a Royal Prince studying peaceful administration, instead of only being trained in the armed forces. Indeed I think it would be a very good thing if a tour of the Treasury were included in his experiences. After all no one has ever doubted that British finance is upon the highest level.[3]

---

[1] Joseph Chamberlain had been Colonial Secretary from 1895 to 1903, when he resigned in order to devote himself to a campaign for Imperial Preference.

[2] George Edward Alexander Edmund, 1902–42. Third son of King George V. Entered the Royal Navy as a Midshipman, 1921. Duke of Kent, 1934. Rear-Admiral, Major-General and Air Vice-Marshal, 1939. Governor-General Designate of Australia. Killed while on active service.

[3] In March 1929 Prince George had retired from active service in the Royal Navy on medical grounds, and was attached to the Foreign Office. The announcement giving this information was issued from Buckingham Palace on the evening of March 18, and appeared in *The Times* on the following day: 'Acting upon the advice of medical authority, the King has approved that Prince George shall now retire from active participation in the work of the Royal Navy. His Majesty had decided, with the concurrence of the Prime Minister, that His Royal Highness shall be attached to the Foreign Office in order to gain knowledge of the

I am so thankful to find from your letter practical evidences of the King's recovery. But it must not be disturbed. His Majesty's case is that of England after the Great War. We have never had the chance to get well and *grow* strong again. I trust that those who have charge of the King's convalescence will make sure he has better fortune. I am quite sure things are going to work out all right in politics, and that ten years hence we shall have much more to rejoice in.

With all good wishes, believe me

Lord Grey of Fallodon to Winston S. Churchill
(*Churchill papers: 8/224*)

18 March 1929

My dear Winston,

'The Aftermath' has come, made doubly valuable by being your gift & inscribed to me by you. I can read only very slowly, but look forward to much pleasure in reading it gradually.

You have a wonderful gift and it is great and rare to be able to write books that are not only a record of great contemporary events, but are also a permanent contribution to literature.

Yours ever,
EG

T. E. Shaw to Winston S. Churchill
(*Churchill papers: 8/224*)

18 March 1929

338171 A/c Shaw
RAF Cattewater
Plymouth

Dear Winston,

I've now read it all, with very great care. I like it best of them all. It is riper, and your sense of decaying comes uppermost—though the first note I made at the end of it was vigour. The buoyancy of the writing, and the confidence with which you swim across these broken waters are both wise and encouraging. Yet it comes back to the moderation & the generosity of

---

administration and work of a Department of State.' Later in the year Prince George transferred to the Home Office where he worked as a supernumerary Inspector in the Factory Department, and continued to inspect factories on behalf of the Home Office until his death.

your presentations of everybody—nearly. (except De Robeck!)[1] I particularly like your fairness toward Ll George. The future is going to flay our generation for its unfairness to him. He's ever so much bigger than the statesman of the Napoleonic times. He's said magnificent things, & his own performances, with that team, were marvellous. You give him, not full marks, but more than's the fashion: and so you do yourself great credit. It made me glad, all through 1920 and 1921, to find him and you so close together. Of course your later advantages over him are partly due to your being young enough to try again: and partly to your greater strength. But Ll G has been a very grand figure. He was a big man in Paris.

Of course the Greek business was awful. Venizelos[2] stole the wits of Harold Nicolson,[3] & so cajoled the Foreign Office: and Ll George's nasty little Nonconformist upbringing fell for him. It was the ruin of a Middle East situation that was a clear gift to us. I wonder if we will ever get much of it back? Not, I suppose, till Turkey fights Russia and badly wants a friend.

You do President Wilson full justice. A fish-like, clammy hand, he had: and conceit, and terror of giving himself away. Yet he had the fanatic scholar's power of holding firmly to an idea or two: partly because he was so afraid of practicalities. House I liked, but couldn't respect, as a brain. Old Clemenceau was wise, and broad-minded (off his hobby) and laughter-loving. He comes out of your story with honour. I am glad you say a decent word for Mustapha Kemal.[4]

It is a very fine effort, this book, and it does you more honour—in all

[1] John Michael de Robeck, 1862–1928. Entered Navy, 1875. Rear-Admiral, 1911. Commanded the 9th Cruiser Squadron, charged with protecting British merchant ships in the mid-Atlantic, 1914–15. Second in command of the Allied naval forces at the Dardanelles, February–March 1916. Vice-Admiral commanding the Allied naval forces at the Dardanelles, March 1915–January 1916. Knighted, 1916. Commanded the 2nd Battle Squadron in the North Sea, 1916–18. Created Baronet, 1919. Commander-in-Chief of the Mediterranean Fleet, and High Commissioner at Constantinople, 1919–21. Admiral, 1920. Commander-in-Chief of the Atlantic Fleet, 1922–4. Admiral of the Fleet, 1925.

[2] Eleutherios Venizelos, 1864–1936. Prime Minister of Greece, 1910–15. Forced to resign by King Constantine, May 1915. Prime Minister for the second time, August to October 1915. Subsequently Prime Minister, 1917–20, 1928–32 and 1933.

[3] Harold George Nicolson, 1886–1968. Son of Sir Arthur Nicolson (1st Baron Carnock). Entered Foreign Office, 1909; Counsellor, 1925. Served at Teheran, 1925–7, and Berlin, 1927–9. On editorial staff of Evening Standard, 1930. National Labour MP, 1935–45. A Governor of the BBC, 1941–6. Joined the Labour Party, 1947. Knighted, 1953. Among his many publications were Some People, a satire in which the Foreign Office was prominent (1927), a biography of his father, Lord Carnock (1930); Curzon: the Last Phase (1934) and King George V: his Life and Reign (1952). His book Peacemaking 1919 was published in 1933.

[4] Mustafa Kemal, 1881–1938. Served in the Libyan and Balkan campaigns, 1911–13. Turkish Military Attaché in Sofia, 1913–14. Served at Gallipoli, 1915, in the Caucasus, 1916, and in Syria, 1917–18. Assumed command of the Turkish National Movement, 1919. First President of the Turkish Republic from 1922 until his death. Known as Atatürk.

except writing—than the others. I still feel that the first was the finest writing: but there are patches of delirious humour, here: and the 'Armistice dream' is the real stuff.

Your 'Memo' at the end does more than it deserves in favour of my particular garden-plot. Yet I will maintain that it was, in its tiny way, a very good little plot: pitiably small, it looks, doesn't it, in its proper place beside the great events?

I marked a misprint on page 111: 'Stated that' misplaced: on page 150, line 13, the 'has' should be 'had', I fancy: on page 300, the fresh invitation, of the 19th, is sent before the Committee met on the 21st. I suspect the sentence has got twisted. I'm no good at seeing misprints in a book though. You have EM who's a champion at that.

The book, as I say, has delighted me. It is not the end of the story either. There is room for more, when the slowness of post-war policy has at length produced something worth writing about. Three years of today make about a month of war-time.

If the gods give you a rest, some day, won't you write a life of the great Duke of Marlborough? About our only international general . . . and so few people seem to see it. He hasn't had a *practical* book written about him: and you are deep enough into affairs to see all round him.

Ever so many thanks for the Aftermath.

Yours,
T. E. Shaw

Excuse the rotten letter. There is a sort of dog-fight going on all over and round me in the hut, and I'm listening to two of its arguments with half an ear each. They affect me, you see!

John Buchan[1] to Winston S. Churchill

(*Churchill papers: 8/224*)

19 March 1929

My dear Churchill,

I have just finished your last volume, and I cannot resist writing to tell you the admiration with which it fills one who has himself tried the same kind of work.

---

[1] John Buchan, 1875–1940. Author, historian and novelist. Private Secretary to Lord Milner in South Africa, 1901–3. Lieutenant-Colonel, GHQ, France, 1916–17. Director, Department of Information, 1917–18. Conservative MP, 1927–35. Created Baron Tweedsmuir, 1935. Governor-General of Canada, 1937–40. His brother Alastair served in Churchill's battalion on the western front in 1916, and died of wounds received in action in 1917.

I think that your subject is the most difficult conceivable. There is not the unity which you find in a war, even in a war of many scattered campaigns. The field is terribly encumbered with prejudice, and it looks at first sight as if the most one could hope for would be a book of annals with comments.

But out of this welter you have made a real, artistic whole. The architectural power of the book leaves me gasping. I always put architecture first among the qualities of the historian, and your proportions are perfect.

Almost more remarkable is your superhuman detachment. Few writers could attain this and at the same time provide brilliant and exciting narrative. More than in any of the other volumes I feel the justice and sagacity of your outlook, and this is not attained by any flattening out of salient features, or monotonous charitableness. Your character drawing is as acute as it is just, and all your people live fiercely.

I am very grateful for the book, for it has given me a point of view which I had never had before. For one thing, it has made me realise the remarkable act of courage involved in the Irish settlement. That is a subject on which my mind has become cumbered with violent prejudices—the eternal dislike of the Lowland Scot for the Celtic Irish. That people who share all my prejudice could sink them in the public interest, makes me think better of human nature. It is another illustration of Minto's[1] saying that no man is so strong as he who does not mind being called weak.

The writing is pure delight. I think the book much the best of the volumes, and, indeed, the best thing anyone has done in contemporary history since Clarendon.[2] I cannot imagine how, after a heavy session, you had the vitality to produce such a book in a short autumn holiday.

I offer you my most admiring congratulations.

This letter must on no account be answered. You must be up to your neck in the Budget.

Yours ever,
John Buchan

---

[1] Gilbert John, 4th Earl of Minto (1845–1914), Governor-General of Canada and Viceroy of India, of whom John Buchan had written a biography, *Lord Minto: A Memoir*, published in October 1924.

[2] Edward Hyde, Earl of Clarendon (1609–74), whose 'History', entitled *The True Historical Narrative of the Rebellion and Civil Wars in England*, was first published thirty years after his death, in 1702–4. Clarendon had himself been Lord Chancellor and Chief Minister to Charles II from 1658, but in 1667, following the ill-success of the Dutch war, he was impeached, and fled to France.

20 March 1929

My dear Winston,

It seems almost absurd of me to want to bring a pebble to put on your cairn—& I am sure it must be very high by now—but I have wondered if you could know of the great wave of admiration & gratitude that *every* one feels on reading the last vol of your marvellous book. I couldn't put it down but read it from cover to cover as one does an enthralling novel—I feel really grateful that anyone shd have put down for us the story of the great events we have lived thro' so that she who runs may read (whatever that means!) & in so fascinating a way. The only wonder to us all is how did he find time to do it all. It is a *very* great achievement.

I was deeply interested in the Russian part, as there was so much one did not *realise* of the *inner* side of it all.

Wherever I go it's always the same thing, 'Have you read Winston's book? Isn't it a wonderful masterpiece'—and it's so delightful to really feel proud of a friend.

So I am sending you this for *my* gratification, not for yours, & if you send me a message thro' Clemmy that it has caused you pleasure I shall feel all the more content at having taken up a feeble & halting pen to express myself.

Your affectionate
Francis Horner

20 March 1929

THE CHANCELLOR OF THE EXCHEQUER reported to the Cabinet that while passing through Paris he had learnt that the deliberations of the Expert Commission of Reparations was proceeding comparatively favourably and were not unlikely to proceed to some acceptable agreement.

Lord Beaverbrook to Sir Robert Borden

(Beaverbrook papers)

26 March 1929

Churchill himself appears to be more defeatist than ever. I dined with him last night and I judge he is certain the Government is going out. The Conservative faith in Baldwin as a leader has evaporated.

Churchill has no intention whatever of allying himself with Lloyd George, although rumours to this effect in Conservative circles are doing him a great deal of harm.

Cabinet minutes

(Cabinet papers: 23/60)

26 March 1929

THE CHANCELLOR OF THE EXCHEQUER reminded the Cabinet that he had already informed them that he had travelled with Herr von Kuhlmann[1] from Paris. On that occasion Herr von Kuhlmann had referred to the former German Colonies. He had replied that he himself would not have prolonged the War for five minutes for the sake of the colonies, but that he was absolutely convinced that no British Government could possibly discuss handing them back, and that not a single member of the Cabinet would be ready to consider such surrender. The conversation had been purely private and he had not thought it worth while to record it.

SIR AUSTEN CHAMBERLAIN recalled that he had made our position clear as far back as the Locarno Conference, namely, that if a Mandate became available Germany would have the same right to apply for it as any other country. He mentioned, however, that the Mandates were allocated by the Powers represented at the Versailles Conference and not by the League of Nations.

---

[1] Richard von Kühlmann, 1873–1949. Entered the Berlin Foreign Office, 1893. Counsellor of the German Embassy in London, 1908–14. On missions to Turkey and Scandinavia, 1915–17. Secretary of State for Foreign Affairs, 1917–18. An advocate of a negotiated peace, he tried to arrange for negotiations with Sir William Tyrrell in Holland in the summer of 1918, and was dismissed by the Kaiser.

Lord Irwin to Stanley Baldwin

(*Baldwin papers*)

28 March 1929   Viceregal Lodge
Secret   Delhi

My dear Stanley,

You have put rather a poser to me about Winston and the IO.

I can very well guess that there might be advantages in substituting Neville for him at the Treasury. And I can also see a great hand for him to play over India with his capacity for seeing the big thing & presenting a broad case. But I think my doubts tend to outweigh my confidence that it would be a good appointment. Let me try to put some of my feelings—which are more instinctive—than rational—on paper.

India today seems to be vy much at a cross ways—and on whether she turns the right road or the wrong, much will depend. She needs the guidance of somebody with courage; and with vision—but with both the courage and the vision of a real desire to help India, and making themselves felt through sympathy with all her difficulties. The 'inferiority complex' is just now very inferior & very complex: & India is very sore. And I am sure that more than half her problems are psychological & of that order of difficulty. How would WSC fit with these necessities? FE did an incredible amount of harm here—not by policy, for that on the whole was good—but by the impression he produced upon sensitive self important Indians visiting England, whom either he would not see & so mortified: or saw and produced the impression of one out of sympathy & rather disposed to despise.

Frankly I should fear that Winston at bottom would have rather the same point of view & would never be able—as one never can—to conceal it. I remember his attitude of mind vis à vis Indians in Kenya & I doubt.[1] And he has become—or perhaps it is more true to say—has always been, a much more vigorous Imperialist in the 1890–1900 sense of the word than you & me.[2]

---

[1] In 1921 Churchill (then Colonial Secretary) had clashed with Edwin Montagu (then Secretary of State for India) over the status of the Kenyan Indians. 'The Indians in East Africa,' Churchill wrote to Montagu on 8 October 1921, 'are mainly of a very low class of coolies, and the idea that they should be put on an equality with the Europeans is revolting to every white man throughout British Africa' (*Churchill papers: 17/10*).

[2] On 22 March 1929 Lord Irwin had written to Churchill, in thanking him for a copy of *The Aftermath*: 'I look forward to seeing you & your lady if I get home in July. May you still be in No 11,' and he added: 'what a nice fellow Lindemann is. Thank you for putting us on to him.'

Lady Wimborne to Winston S. Churchill

(*Churchill papers: 8/224*)

29 March 1929

Dearest Winston,

Sent here by a select committee of the medical faculty after a severe attack of this year's uncompromising influenza bacillus, I am consoled in exile by your book. I have read & reread it in solitary evenings, mastering information & detail often longed for in the past. How masterly it is! A child could follow the most abstruse & difficult & involved problems as you put them—how stirring is the narrative so that one can not put it down—perfect in style, consummate in language. I am indeed enthralled by the latest child of your generosity.

And so, inspired by you, must write and tell you so, hoping you will not object to so humble a tribute!

My fondest love & unbounded admiration—have you seen Ivor, returned from hunting the Boar, in the Forêt de Fontainbleau?! I have just left him in Paris on the way home.

An affectionate
Alice

Winston S. Churchill to Stanley Baldwin

(*Baldwin papers*)

29 March 1929   Chartwell Manor

My dear PM,

It is most urgent to settle how our share of the Broadcasting is to be disposed of, and the dates. I have to-day provisionally approved my programme of constituency meetings. Alas! they are very numerous. I have told Davidson that I will do Edinburgh and Glasgow for him in Scotland, and three or four large meetings, not yet fixed, in England. If, as I assume, you will want me to speak once or perhaps twice on the Broadcast, I ought to know these dates in the course of the next ten days, as otherwise other arrangements will be disturbed after they are made. Will you, therefore, settle how you wish to play your team and, having done so, tell Davidson to work out the roster with us as quickly as possible. My advice is that yourself, Neville, Austen and I are likely to be able to state the Government case between us as well as anyone else, and that we are all sufficiently well known to command very large audiences. The opportunity is of immense importance and, having regard to the unwieldy character of the electorate, no personal consideration should stand in the way of using it to the best advantage. I did not think Davidson's suggestion of the working-man Chairman of the Unionist Association was a good one. This new instrument is effective at this critical juncture only with people who are, for good or ill, well known.

I may add that I am trying to get in addition the same facility for a non-controversial statement of the Budget policy as was accorded to me last year, and I have written both to the BBC and to Davidson about this. Last year it helped enormously.

You will be glad to know that the Surplus will certainly be £21 m. I cannot tell you how thankful I am at the end of this long and difficult voyage that all the figures come out better than I had hoped or promised.

Yours vy sincerely,
Winston S. Churchill

April 1929

3 April 1929   Chartwell Manor

My dear PM,

I think we ought to meet on Monday. I shall then be ready to tell you what I should like to propose, and also to read the actual text of certain statements of financial policy which require your approval and Cabinet sanction. Could we meet in London on that morning? We shall need some time, as a number of decisions have to be taken.

I should like very much, if you think well, that Neville should be present as he is so long headed and sagacious in counsel. Philip CL is staying with me here Friday night, and I shall have thrashed out with him matters affecting the Board of Trade. In case we are at variance, he ought to come too; but I do not expect this, and I know he is planning to be in Yorkshire.

I hope you will be able to come to London on Monday, and if you can, I will take the necessary steps to warn the numerous officials concerned to be available.

Time is short, for we have promised the Cabinet to acquaint them with the Budget on the Wednesday: indeed we are already in the—always exhilarating—realm of action.

Yours vy sincerely
Winston S. Churchill

5 April 1929

My dear Alice,

How charming of you to write me such a delightful letter. I am so glad you enjoyed the book. I expect your being in solitude and exile gave it the opportunity it required to make its appeal effectually.

No one can tell what is going on at the moment. As soon as it is over it is all forgotten, and the future is a mystery. Such is life!

Let me know when you return.

Yours affectionately,

Winston S. Churchill to Lady Horner

(*Churchill papers: 8/224*)

5 April 1929

My dear Frances,

I really was delighted by the kindness of your letter and by the fact that my book had given you pleasure.

How strange it is that the past is so little understood and so quickly forgotten. We live in the most thoughtless of ages. Every day headlines and short views. I have tried to drag history up a little nearer to our own times in case it should be helpful as a guide in present difficulties.

I showed your letter to Clemmie who was delighted with it.

L. S. Amery: diary

(*Amery papers*)

10 April 1929

Cabinet at which Winston unfolded his Budget proposals. Nothing very sensational on the positive side, except the total remission of the tea duty which I protested against but found no support. I don't suppose it helped win a single seat, and I know it will upset many good Empire Preference men & give away our case.

Lord Salisbury to Winston S. Churchill

(*Churchill papers: 18/97*)

10 April 1929   Hatfield House

My dear Winston,

As I reflect over our discussions today I have become more hardened against the remission of the tea duty. The three points which have influenced me are:

1. Austen's observation and your own that you would not have dreamed of allowing it except for Electoral reasons. This of course confirmed an uneasiness I had expressed to you that the thing was risky from the point of view of good administration.

2. Eustace's reminder that in the face of the unemployment crisis and the Lord Mayor's fund such a financial sacrifice could not be justified to public opinion.

3. My own thought late in the day that the proposal was not merely a sacrifice of revenue but the complete elimination for ever of tea as a source of revenue.

These last two considerations had not occurred to me till this afternoon.

As regards the first, if you would shrink from it as Chancellor of the Exchequer, whatever you are inclined to do as a party politician, that is by itself almost conclusive. After all unless we stand for stability and sobriety and responsibility as compared to the other people we stand nowhere.

I hope upon reflection you will reject what Jix indiscreetly calls an electoral bribe.

Yours ever,
Salisbury

Winston S. Churchill to Lord Salisbury

(*Salisbury papers*)

12 April 1929   Chartwell Manor

My dear Salisbury,

I think it will be all right now the Manufacturers forestalment is excluded.

I am all for a restrained and sober policy; but sobriety ought not to exclude sympathy; and a proof of the sympathy which the Conservative Administration has for the mass of the people, and the poorest among them, may be found to be an important factor in maintaining the stability of the State.

Yours ever,
Winston S. Churchill

Winston S. Churchill to Stanley Baldwin

(*Baldwin papers*)

12 April 1929

> Secret
> but for Cabinet
> if you think well

My dear PM,

La nuit porte conseil. Since it is physically impossible to give rating relief to the manufacturers before October I think it will be better to leave them as they are. The nine millions rent in the Suspensory Fund which their extra help will entail might have been worth while making for the sake of bringing the whole scheme into action at once; but it is not worth while simply for the sake of making them a double payment in October. Therefore I propose only to relieve the April payments in the case of the agricultural producer and explain why it is impossible technically to do the other part. The cost of this will be about 2 millions, which can either be taken from the Suspensory Fund of 22½ millions or charged against the Budget surplus as the Treasury may find most convenient. This leaves me in a strong position on the finance of de-rating.

I also propose to remit the whole of the Tea duty but to leave Coffee, Cocoa and Chicory untouched. Cost 6·2 millions, leaving a final prospective surplus of 4·1 or 2·1 according as whether the 2 millions of agricultural relief is taken from the Budget or the Suspensory Fund.

I hope the Cabinet will like this arrangement and that nothing more will be put upon me now. My last few millions of surplus are not quite so robust as the earlier ones and I do not wish to place a real load on their shoulders.

So far as your declarations on Thursday are concerned, I should promise definitely *if we are returned* to provide a fund for Imperial development either by direct use or capitalisation: to deal with maternity and to clear or re-condition the slum areas. There is no objection to mentioning figures even, but it should also be said that 'if responsible we shall in due course make any proposals that may be necessary to supply additional revenue'. I really cannot take any more on the Budget as now constituted.

Yours very sincerely,
Winston S. Churchill

Winston S. Churchill to King George V

(*Churchill papers: 18/97*)

13 April 1929

Mr Churchill with his humble duty to Your Majesty.

The surplus of £18 m realised last year was at least £8 m better than our expectations.

Beer fell short by £7¼ m but the Death Duties came to the rescue with an increase of £8½ m.

Nearly £6 m were saved out of the estimates during the year by economical administration.

Adding this surplus of £18 m to the £4½ m from the surplus of 1927-8, we have £22½ m in the Suspensory Fund as a nest egg for the finance of the Rating Relief scheme. This is £4½ m more than what Mr Churchill originally proposed last year before Kerosene was left out of the Oil Duties.

Although trade and revenue improve very slowly there is a steady progress.

The expenditure of 1929 apart from rating relief is £13¼ m less and the revenue apart from the Currency Note transfer in 1929 is £10 m more. After providing for the new grants to Local Authorities Mr Churchill looks forward to a prospective surplus of £11,976,000. This he will propose to distribute in the following way.

First. Certain minor concessions upon the Publicans' Licence Duties; upon improved telephone facilities in the rural districts; upon relief of stamp duty on the amalgamations of companies; upon Scottish herring fishery harbours, will all together cost about £1,100,000 a year together with a certain amount of capital expenditure.

Secondly. He will repeal the turn-over tax on Betting which has proved a failure, and will substitute for it an increased licence duty of £40 per each telephone used for betting purposes, in addition to the £10 personal licence duty on Bookmakers. These new duties will yield about £500,000, to which must be added the fruits of ½% upon the Totalisator when it comes into action. The Bookmakers are contented with the changes which in all cost Mr Churchill £850,000 this year.

Thirdly. He proposes to remit the Railway Passenger Duty which has lasted since 1832 and brings in nearly £400,000 a year. The railway companies have pressed continually for this relief and Mr Churchill has now decided to accord it to them on condition that they spend nearly the whole of its capitalised value ie £6½ m upon new works designed to make their railways more efficient and more capable of carrying heavier modern waggons. They have agreed to this and considerable activity involving useful employment will shortly follow.

Fourthly. Mr Churchill feels that as the Suspensory Fund is now £4½ m more than he had expected, he may prudently use £2½ m of it to bring the rating relief for Agriculture into immediate operation. The farmers will not therefore have to pay any of the April rates, and this may possibly lead them to cease, at any rate for a few weeks, their perpetual chorus of complaints and demands for assistance.

There is no doubt that bringing the rating relief for the producer into earlier operation is sound and right, and the Chancellor of the Exchequer is only sorry that technical difficulties have prevented him equally ante-dating the relief to industry. This however must wait its prescribed time in October.

As the £2½ m for earlier rating relief will be taken from the Suspensory Fund, Mr Churchill still has in hand a surplus of £10,300,000. He proposes to spend £6·2 m of this in the total, immediate and he trusts final abolition of the duty on Tea. No tax will be retained even against foreign Tea, as this is the tea drunk by the poorest people who otherwise would be the only ones left out of the benefit. Tea will go down by 4d a pound. There has been a tea duty in existence ever since the reign of Queen Elizabeth, and Mr Churchill is glad to think that your Gracious Majesty's reign should witness its removal.

The ladies who are to take so important a part in our political affairs may recognise that it is right to raise £6 m as we are doing from the taxes on Silk and thus be able to remit the tax on Tea.

These various concessions and reliefs leave the Chancellor of the Exchequer in possession of a prospective surplus of £4,100,000. This he will keep for contingencies during the year.

The provision for Debt Service, as governed by the legislation of last year, is a fixed annual charge of £355 m which if adhered to perseveringly will extinguish the whole debt in fifty years.

Mr Churchill cannot close this report without expressing the very keen pleasure that he feels in being able to write to Your Majesty again upon affairs of State, and his most heartfelt wishes for the steady continuance of Your Majesty's progress to complete recovery.[1]

All of which with his humble duty is submitted by

Your Majesty's faithful and devoted

Servant and Subject,

---

[1] On 21 November 1928 King George V had been taken ill with acute septicaemia at the base of his right lung, and at one moment it was thought that he was dying. On 9 February 1929 he had gone to Bognor to convalesce, and had remained at Bognor throughout March and April. On 20 May 1929, five days after his return from Bognor, he had suffered a short relapse, but on 7 July 1929 he was well enough to attend a Thanksgiving Service at Westminster Abbey for his recovery. But his health remained poor until his death six years later.

Thomas Jones: diary

(Jones papers)

13 April 1929

Breakfast alone with the PM. We turned to Cabinet making. He had written to Lord Irwin to ask him what he thought of the plan of sending Winston to the India Office, and was expecting a reply any moment. Did I think Winston would be courageous in a crisis, right to the end of it? I said, No, he would not be, unless there were more determined and courageous Ministers at his side.

Thomas Jones: diary

(Jones papers)

14 April 1929

At 5.30 to the study again. All through the weekend I have been trying to pin the PM down to some definite lines for his Thursday speech, but he has immense powers of resistance to anything definite. 'I can't do like Winston,' he protested, 'put it all down for days in advance, and commit it to memory.'

Lord Stamfordham to Winston S. Churchill

(Churchill papers: 18/97)

14 April 1929   Bognor

My dear Churchill,

I have come here to see the King whom I found in possession of your deeply interesting letter of the 12th inst and I am desired to thank you sincerely for this full explanation of your Budget which His Majesty has read with the utmost satisfaction and offers you his hearty congratulations upon what you will be able to put before the people in your speech in Parliament tomorrow.

Yours sincerely,
Stamfordham

Private

PS. The King was touched and gratified by your kind allusions to his health which really is wonderfully improved. I see hardly any change in look & ways from those of the pre-illness period—and he is taking keen interest in public affairs & thinks your Budget & especially the abolition of tea duty & the immediate relief of farmers from all rates ought to help the Govt materially at the Genl Election!

S

Lord Irwin to the Archbishop of Canterbury[1]

(Irwin papers)

15 April 1929

I wonder whether you have yet had time to read Winston's book. He sent it to me about a fortnight ago, but I have not yet been able to give myself the pleasure of reading it. What an astounding thing it is that any man should be able to combine authorship on that scale with being Chancellor of the Exchequer. I suppose his critics would say that, having dissipated all our finance and mortgaged every service, there was nothing more for him to do from the financial side. I cannot help feeling that it would be well for him and for national finance if he found other ministerial activity.

Lord Irwin to Neville Chamberlain

(Irwin papers)

15 April 1929

I was greatly amused in reading your judgement of Winston formed at close quarters after all the work you had been doing together. I can quite

---

[1] Cosmo Gordon Lang, 1864–1945. Educated at Glasgow University and Balliol College, Oxford; Fellow of All Souls, 1889–93. Dean of Divinity, Magdalen College, Oxford, 1893–6. Honorary Chaplain to Queen Victoria. Bishop of Stepney, 1901–8. Archbishop of York, 1908–28. Privy Councillor, 1909. Archbishop of Canterbury, 1928–42. Knighted, 1937. Created Baron, 1942. In a broadcast on Sunday 13 December 1936 he criticized Edward VIII for having 'sought his happiness in a manner inconsistent with the Christian principles of marriage, and within a social circle whose standard and way of life are alien to all the best instincts and traditions of his people. Let those who belong to this circle know that today they stand rebuked by the judgment of the nation which had loved King Edward.'

believe I should have felt exactly the same. Francis Floud, who used to be with me at the Board of Agriculture and is now with Winston on the Board of Customs, writes to me periodically with complete freedom and indiscretion and evidently regards Winston as a public danger at the Treasury, and according to him Winston has left a very *Damnosa Hereditas* for his successors for many years to come. He must have had a pretty good bang over the Irish debate in the House of Commons some weeks ago. It is a curious thing how Linky always seems to fall most foul of Winston on matters where Linky can introduce conscience. I suppose it must be some kind of subtle complex arising from the closeness of an earlier friendship. I suspect Winston feels it a good deal. . . .

It is astounding to me that anyone should be able to combine authorship on such a scale with the charge of national finance. But I suppose the first comes easily to him and the second no doubt sits lightly on his shoulders.

Stanley Baldwin to King George V

(Baldwin papers)

16 April 1929

The Chancellor of the Exchequer rose at 3.15[1] to introduce his fifth consecutive Budget. By common consent, his exposition of two and a half hours was one of his most masterly performances. The revenue having come in better than was expected, the word 'repeal' was used on several occasions, in cheerful contrast to the makeshift devices which have had to be employed in the last year or two in order to make good the ravages in the national finances caused by the troubles and follies of 1925. . . .

When he had made his arrangements so far, the Chancellor found himself in possession of a surplus of over £10,000,000. The great moment had arrived. Mr Churchill asked, 'What shall we do with it?' and, having thus tantalised the House, he remarked that he would first of all make a preliminary digression into the burning question of whether national prosperity can be restored or enhanced by the Government's borrowing money and spending it on providing more work. When he had satisfied himself that on the whole such is not the case, he proceeded to deal out his surplus. The first duty to be repealed is the Railway Passenger Duty, which has been levied upon the railway companies for nearly a hundred years and which yields £400,000 per annum. This is being done in order to assist the com-

[1] On 15 April 1929.

panies to evolve a system for dealing with heavier rolling stock. Agriculture then received Mr Churchill's attention, and, in consequence, farmers will have the satisfaction of being able to tear up the demand notes for rates in the current quarter which they will have received; for that part of the Local Government Act which relieves agriculture of all rates is to be brought into force as from the first of this month. Although farmers will doubtless continue to grumble, they may at least display a little gratitude for the time being.

Having shown that considerable relief has already been granted to the smaller class of income tax payer, the Chancellor announced the total repeal of the tea duty, a form of tax which has been in existence since the reign of Queen Elizabeth. So great was the dismay of the Labour Party at learning of this relief from a burden which weighs most heavily on the poorer sections of the community, that not a cheer was raised from their benches.

Balancing the Budget finally, Mr Churchill estimated for a total expenditure of £822,584,000 and a revenue of £826,680,000, leaving a final prospective surplus of £4,096,000.

Stanley Baldwin to Winston S. Churchill

(*Churchill papers: 18/101*)

16 April 1929   10 Downing Street

THE MORNING AFTER

My dear Winston,

Just before I leave for Worcestershire I must send you a line to tell you how it all strikes me after thinking it over in the early morning, the hour (provided it be the beginning and not the end of the day!) in which the eternal verities are stark naked.

I have never heard you speak better, and that's saying a great deal. I hate the word brilliant: it has been [used] to death and is too suggestive of brilliantine: but if I may use it in its pristine virginity, so to speak, it is the right one.

I congratulate you with both hands.

SB

Sir Harcourt Butler[1] to Lord Irwin

(*Irwin papers*)

17 April 1929

Winston is said to be very pleased over his budget. It has been very well received. Opinions differ as to whether it will catch many votes. A good many people think that his sanguine estimate of the future suggests that he has no intention or expectation of being Chancellor again. There has been much plain talking about him, Austen Chamberlain, Jix and Lord Balfour. . . .

Some criticise the total abolition of the tea duty as making it impossible to tax tea in the future. I hear there was much discussion on this point in the Cabinet. It is difficult to do these things by halves. The city seems to like the budget on the whole.

Cabinet minutes

(*Cabinet papers: 23/60*)

24 April 1929

1. THE CHANCELLOR OF THE EXCHEQUER informed the Cabinet that he was not yet in a position to say whether the Expert Conference on German Reparation now proceeding in Paris was going to break down or not. He wished to warn his colleagues, however, that if agreement was reached there was little doubt that we should be asked to surrender at any rate a portion of the arrears of approximately £200,000,000 due to us under the policy of the Balfour Note. Future payments would no doubt be satisfied, but the arrears would not be wholly covered even by annual payments by Germany of £125,000,000 unless the index of prosperity of Germany was brought into the scheme and applied. MR CHURCHILL recalled that at the outset he had thought the summoning of the Expert Conference premature. However, we had accepted it and had agreed that the Experts should be independent. In the circumstances he himself had not interfered in any way with the negotiations, in which Sir Josiah Stamp had become perhaps the leading figure on the Allied side. He thought that, broadly speaking, Sir Josiah Stamp was

---

[1] Spencer Harcourt Butler, 1869–1938. Entered the Indian Civil Service, 1890; Deputy Commissioner, Lucknow, 1906; knighted, 1911. Foreign Secretary to the Government of India; Lieutenant-Governor of Burma, 1915–17; of the United Provinces, 1918. Governor of the United Provinces, 1921–3; of Burma, 1923–7. Chairman of the Indian States Committee, 1928. Author of *India Insistent*, 1931. Uncle of R. A. Butler (later Lord Butler of Saffron Walden, Under-Secretary of State for Foreign Affairs, 1938–41; Secretary of State for Foreign Affairs, 1963–4).

in agreement with the Treasury, although in some respects perhaps the Treasury took a stiffer line. Mr Churchill himself had from the beginning taken the view that the Balfour Note was our *ne plus ultra*, but had pointed out that arrears of payments occupied a slightly different position from future payments. When, in conversation, Treasury officials had criticised the Experts' plan from the point of view of the recovery of arrears, Sir Josiah had replied rather sharply to the effect that while everyone was prepared to criticise, nobody gave him any constructive help.

Mr Churchill himself had replied that the Government were committed to no decision that went back in the least degree on the Balfour Note, including the collection of arrears of payment. It was possible that the Conference might break down in the early future. If, on the other hand, agreement was reached, the Cabinet would have a difficult decision to take. They would be in the dilemma of having to choose between wrecking at a very inconvenient moment the results of the Expert Meetings for the sake of claims that were at the best of a somewhat speculative character, or making further concessions which might be represented as rather greater than the concessions to be made by other countries concerned. Mr Churchill said that his own policy had been not in any way to hamper the negotiators by instructions of any kind, while reserving the final decision to the Government.

THE SECRETARY OF STATE FOR FOREIGN AFFAIRS thought the attitude of the Chancellor of the Exchequer had been strictly correct. Once the principle of independent Experts had been decided on it was necessary to respect their independence, while reserving the position of the Government towards the Report, for the production of which they were not in any way responsible. The German Government had stated that they themselves had respected the independence of their own Experts, and this, no doubt, was true. Nevertheless, Sir Austen Chamberlain had the impression that in Berlin at the beginning of the week the German Government had probably taken their Expert to task, for he believed that the German Government desired the Conference to succeed. Sir Austen doubted whether the Cabinet would have to take a definite decision before the Election. He did not think this point was likely to be reached until the General Election had reached a stage when Ministers would find it impossible to proceed to Paris for the interchange of views which would probably follow the Conference. For his part he thought it unlikely that the people of this country would expect from the Government, or support them in, insistence on arrears of payment if that would jeopardise a settlement.

THE CHANCELLOR OF THE EXCHEQUER said that he had been considering what action he could take to assist the Cabinet in reaching a decision when the moment arrived. The weakness of the Balfour Note was that, in undertaking that we should receive no more on account of Reparation and Allied Debts than we had to pay to the United States, it opened the possibility of an awkward situation if one day Russia should agree to pay some part of her debts. In these circumstances, if the Government did agree to accept the recommendations of the Expert Conference, he thought it should be made clear that its acceptance applied only to the countries represented at the Conference and that an indication should be given that, in the event of payments being received from Russia, we should hold ourselves free not to include those payments within the scope of the Balfour Note.[1] Mr Churchill said that he had asked the Treasury to study this aspect of the question with a view to keeping our hands free. Any statement of our interpretation of the Balfour Note in this respect should follow directly out of the changes of the situation introduced by the Experts' Report.

Mr Churchill then adverted to the curious attitude of the French Government in regard to the Debt Agreement both with Great Britain and the United States of America. After describing the position in some detail he informed his colleagues of his intention to circulate Papers before the end of the week and to ask for a decision at the next Meeting of the Cabinet.

In taking note of the statement summarised above the Cabinet approved the attitude which the Chancellor of the Exchequer had adopted towards the British Experts on the Reparation Conference sitting in Paris.

Winston S. Churchill to Sir Samuel Hoare

(*Churchill papers: 18/102*)

26 April 1929   Treasury Chambers

My dear Sam,

I read with astonishment the tale of your airship construction. £1,250,000 in March, 1924 has now been extended to no less than £2,051,000. Even since April, 1926 £450,000 have been added to the cost of these ships. I think this is a very melancholy episode in the relations of the Air Ministry and the Treasury.

Yours vy sincerely,
Winston S. Churchill

[1] Since the spring of 1918, when Russia withdrew from the war, she owed Britain £757 million for munitions and war materials, and was Britain's largest debtor (France owed Britain £638 million and Italy owed Britain £592 million). For its part, Britain owed the United States more than £900 million. The Soviet Union having declared in 1918 that it would honour neither the Tsarist debts of 1914–17, nor the Kerensky debts of 1917, the sum owed by Russia was considered irrecoverable; nor was it ever recovered.

Neville Chamberlain to his sister

(*Neville Chamberlain papers*)

27 April 1929

Winston's speech which took $2\frac{1}{2}$ hours was one of the best he has made and kept the House fascinated and enthralled by its wit, audacity, adroitness and power. I think the general public were a little disposed to complain that it was a humdrum Budget; if so, it was because W has taught them to expect something startling each year, and their anticipations had been aroused accordingly. But frankly it is constructed with both eyes on the election and from that point of view there is no doubt that it is a very serviceable affair. Indeed it has contributed materially to the marked reaction from the depression in our ranks which was so apparent a few weeks ago but has now largely disappeared.

The press, the clubs and the lobbies, have been full of gossip about reconstruction of the Cabinet. I think it is generally accepted that there will be none before the election but it seems almost as universally believed that W will not return to the Exchequer but will be succeeded by the present Minister of Health. There is where the molasses jug is likely to get broken. W himself keeps silence even to the PM but I suspect that he would be glad to leave the Treasury if he could find a new sphere sufficiently in the light. It is certain that India must be very much in the foreground during the next Parliament.

During the Budget week I myself made an Election Gramophone Record and gave a half hour's broadcast from 2LO. It is a very curious sensation, sitting alone in a room and talking to the microphone, knowing that you are being heard by listeners who may number millions but unable to obtain the faintest indication of the impression you are making. It was a great relief when it was over to find the BBC people quite enthusiastic. They said every syllable was clear and distinct, pace and tone excellent, matter and manner the best they had had yet. Since then I have had many most gratifying testimonials. The London correspt of the Post who is a Liberal said he had heard from 10 other Liberals in different parts of the country and they were without exception 'fascinated' being equally impressed by the force of my argument and the moderation of my tone.[1]

[1] Churchill also broadcast during the election campaign. In addition, he recorded a short film speech, or 'phonofilm', for use by constituency parties. 'The Central Office would like you to do this very much,' Edward Marsh wrote to him on April 29, '& the van can come round to Downing St any time at 24 hours notice. The speech should be *not more than 600 words*.' But on May 6 the Central Office wrote to Marsh: 'Nothing could have excelled the Chancellor's delivery, but after the first few sentences the voice dies almost completely away and the film is quite useless for exhibition. The failure is entirely due to British Talking Pictures. The loss of this speech is a catastrophe . . .' (*Churchill papers: 2/165*).

L. S. Amery to Stanley Baldwin

(*Baldwin papers*)

27 April 1929   Dominions Office

. . . I am sure for instance that an announcement that Neville was going to the Exchequer would be worth twenty or thirty seats at least. I don't want to be disloyal or unfriendly to Winston but the fact remains that he is a handicap rather than an asset to us in the eyes of the public. Since I spoke to you last on this subject I have wondered whether he might possibly do at the India Office. If the situation in India were really out of hand and in open rebellion or if there were war on the North West Frontier, he would do it admirably. But I am not so sure whether he might not precipitate the former even if it were not otherwise coming about.

Winston S. Churchill to Major J. J. Astor

(*Churchill papers: 18/102*)

28 April 1929

I wish you would look again at the enclosed article from the Times of April 1.[1] It has I think done a lot of harm. Especially such expressions as 'clandestine burglary' and 'open robbery', although intended in a spirit of facetious illustration, have been wrested from their context, and form part of the considerable abuse which Socialist and Liberal partisans apply to the financial record of the Government. Again and again in the next few weeks we shall hear—'Even the Times newspaper, a Conservative organ, describes the finance of the Conservative Party as "clandestine burglary" and "open robbery" '.

Generally speaking I thought the article an unfair one, for after all, it would have been at any time quite easy for me to escape from the difficulties I have faced since the General Strike by the simple expedient of replacing the 6d remitted from the income tax of 1925. Perhaps I ought to have done so; but is that really the view of the Times?

[1] On 1 April 1929 a leading article in *The Times* congratulated Churchill on the largest budget surplus of his Chancellorship But it said he had achieved this surplus by a 'series of covert raids on the Sinking Fund', which constituted a 'clandestine burglary'. *The Times* went on to accuse Churchill of 'open robbery' 'through the appropriation of the "surpluses" of the last two years, totalling over £22,000,000' for the derating scheme. The article also complained that 'economy was not Churchill's strong point', but admitted that he had faced formidable problems, such as the general strike, which he had solved with what it described as 'courage and ingenuity'.

May 1929

Sir Francis Floud to Lord Irwin

(*Irwin papers*)

1 May 1929

Winston's budget is on the whole a good one. As usual he has inflated the estimates of revenue to produce a surplus, but it might have been worse and we are indeed thankful to have got rid of the betting tax. . . .

I am rather sorry he has abolished the Tea Duty. It brought in £6m without hurting anyone and once the machinery of the Duty has gone it would be a difficult business to set it up again if the time comes when additional revenue is necessary. But Winston couldn't resist the opportunity of dishing Snowden, who would certainly have done it at the first opportunity. . . .

When we come back I may find a new master, but, though I think Winston is bored with the Treasury, I expect he will stay here. He is credited with ambitions for the Foreign Office, but that would be too dangerous to the peace of the world and moreover Austen wants to carry on. Any other post would be regarded as a move down except possibly India and I don't suppose you want him there. In addition there seems to be no other candidate for the Treasury. Neville doesn't want it and it is said that he will take the Dominions.

Winston at one time was excessively tiresome, but lately he has been particularly friendly and he can be extraordinarily nice and likeable when he wishes.

Clementine Churchill to Winston S. Churchill

(*Spencer-Churchill papers*)

6 May 1929

The Wood House
Epping

My Darling Winston,

I think you will find this house a snug retreat from which to sally forth upon the Constituency. Sarah, Mary, Moppett & I have been here 36 hours & we have already been active. . . .

Today your talking film is being shewn at Epping at 2.30 it being Market Day. We are all going to see it & I will report to you if it is good. . . .

Tonight at 8 o'clock Sarah & I visit all the ladies at the Central Office who are toiling addressing envelopes & filling up canvas cards.

At luncheon yesterday Sir Harry Goschen asked me ('if it is not indiscreet') what office you were going to after the G Election, if the Tories are returned again. I said you would remain where you are & I told him confidentially about your writing to the PM about the newspaper rumours & his assuring you that as long as *he* was PM *you* would be Chancellor—I thought it best to do this as he seemed quite certain you were going to the War Office of all places!

Darling I do hope you enjoy your Scotch Meetings—I wish I were coming with you. But I think it is wise for me to be here & to start the ball rolling.

Your loving & devoted
Clemmie

Thomas Jones: diary

(*Jones papers*)

9 May 1929

Lunch at Philip Sassoon's. Austen, Hailsham, Winston, Worthy, Cunliffe-Lister, Sam Hoare, Londonderry. Winston had travelled through the night from two meetings in Scotland, and was very proud to have heard his son address an audience of about 2,000 for 20 minutes without a note, just over 17 years of age. So we all stood up and drank the health of Randolph II, and passed compliments to Londonderry's young son[1] who is likely to win a seat at Darlington, and Quintin Hogg, who is not in the Cabinet yet as he has his Greats to do.

[1] Edward Charles Stewart Robert Vane-Tempest-Stewart, Viscount Castlereagh, 1902–55. Only son of the 7th Marquis of Londonderry. Educated at Eton and Christ Church, Oxford. Unionist MP for County Down, 1931–5. Assistant Managing Director of Londonderry Collieries Ltd. Served in the Royal Artillery, 1939–45 (Middle East, 1941–2). Succeeded his father as 8th Marquis of Londonderry, 1949. Member of the Church Assembly.

Walter Runciman to Winston S. Churchill

(*Churchill papers: 1/205*)

16 May 1929

My Dear Mr Churchill,

It was a real pleasure to see that your bonny son had made his first speech last night and that you and Mrs Churchill had the joy of hearing him.[1]

Your reference to him is fine.

I trust he will go far in anything he has the aptitude for which I trust will be politics. No matter what side he is on.

Yours sincerely,
Walter Runciman

Winston S. Churchill to Robert Boothby

(*Churchill papers: 2/164*)

21 May 1929

My dear Bob,

I send you these few lines of good wishes in the spirited fight you are making. I know of no one more fitted to represent a Scottish County seat than you. As an advanced Tory-Democrat you are largely akin in sentiment to those soberly patriotic Liberals who though they approach political problems from a different angle, would on all the largest issues of social reform and of Imperial safety think and feel as we do. Like them you are separated by an impassable gulf from the barbaric fallacies of Socialism. Like them you are repelled by the moral and intellectual bankruptcy of its adherents. Your warm sympathy with the causes of social justice, and your indefatigable efforts on behalf of your constituents should entitle you to their good will. If they are as true to you as you have been to them, the representation of East Aberdeen in the new Parliament will not be without effectiveness or distinction.[2]

[1] On 16 May 1929 the *Evening Standard* reported that Randolph Churchill's oratory had won 'parental commendation'. The newspaper added: 'He is a frequent visitor to the House of Commons and has not missed one of his father's speeches.'

[2] Robert Boothby was re-elected for Aberdeenshire and Eastern Kincardineshire by an increased majority (of 3,244, as against 2,683 in the 1924 election). He continued to hold the seat in 1931 (10,097 majority), 1935 (3,121 majority) and 1945 (2,372 majority).

Thomas Jones: diary

(*Jones papers*)

30 May 1929

. . . at Vansittart's desk sat the PM with narrow slips of paper on which he inscribed the three lists as they arrived. At Duff's[1] desk sat Winston doing similar lists in red ink, sipping whisky and soda, getting redder and redder, rising and going out often to glare at the machine himself, hunching his shoulders, bowing his head like a bull about to charge.

As Labour gain after Labour gain was announced, Winston became more and more flushed with anger, left his seat and confronted the machine in the passage; with his shoulders hunched he glared at the figures, tore the sheets and behaved as though if any more Labour gains came along he would smash the whole apparatus. His ejaculations to the surrounding staff were quite unprintable.

THE GENERAL ELECTION was held on Thursday, 30 May 1929. The Labour party won 288 seats (with 8,389,512 votes). The Conservative Party won 260 seats (with 8,656,473 votes). The Liberal Party won 59 seats (with 5,308,510 votes). On 5 June 1929 Ramsay MacDonald took office as Prime Minister, at the head of Britain's second Labour Government. Philip Snowden succeeded Churchill as Chancellor of the Exchequer.

[1] Patrick Duff (see page 810, note 1).

June 1929

T. E. Lawrence to Edward Marsh[1]

(Lawrence papers)

3 June 1929

The General election means that Winston goes out, I suppose. For himself I'm glad. He's a good fighter, and will do better out than in, and will come back in a stronger position than before. I want him to be PM somehow.

Winston S. Churchill to Stanley Baldwin

(Churchill papers: 2/164)

4 June 1929
Private & Personal

My dear PM,

I have a few requests to make to you for the resignation list, which I sincerely hope you will grant me. First of all Freddy Guest and Jack Seely. These two life long friends of mine are in every way qualified for the House of Lords. They have both given 20 years service in the House of Commons, they have both held Secretaryships of State as well as other Ministerial offices, and they served throughout both the British wars of this century with credit, and in Seely's case with high distinction. Freddy has supported us in every possible way, and has, as you know, been execrably treated by Lloyd George. Jack Seely through his honorary work as Chairman of the National Savings Committee has kept clear of politics, but you know all about him. I cannot think of two cases of men who would more reach the sort of requirement which would be set out to qualify for membership of a

---

[1] Following the General Election of 1929, Edward Marsh, who had served as Churchill's Private Secretary at the Treasury since 1924, returned to the Colonial Office, where he was Private Secretary to successive Secretaries of State for the Colonies until his retirement in 1936. Churchill frequently enlisted his help after 1929 as a proof-reader and stylistic adviser for his books and essays.

reformed Second Chamber. I hope and trust that you will put them forward, and that if difficulty is made by Stamfordham on grounds of numbers, you will allow me to plead with him and point out the non-party character of these qualifications.[1]

I have always tried very hard to see that justice is done to friends of mine who have borne the battle and the breeze, and I should be deeply grateful if you could help me in this.

There are one or two minor points which I would like to mention to you when we meet.

I am so glad you are going to take steps to secure the return of the able young men who have been unhorsed in the fight.

---

[1] Frederick Guest (who died in 1937) received no Peerage, but remained an MP until his death. J. E. B. Seely was created Baron Mottistone in 1933 (by the National Government).

Biographical Index

Compiled by the Author

For subject headings, see under the index
entry for Churchill, Winston S.